SOFTWARE ENGINEERING PRODUCTIVITY

CHAPMAN & HALL COMPUTING SERIES

Computer Operating Series
For micros, minis and mainframes
2nd edition
David Barron

Microcomputer Graphics
Michael Batty

ACCESS
The Pick enquiry language
Malcolm Bull

The Pick Operating System
Malcolm Bull

A Course of Programming in FORTRAN
3rd edition
V.J. Calderbank

Formal Methods for Concurrency
C. Fencott

Expert Systems
Principles and case studies
2nd edition
Edited by Richard Forsyth

Machine Learning
Principles and techniques
Edited by Richard Forsyth

Software Quality
Theory and management
Alan C. Gillies

Expert Systems
Knowledge, uncertainty and decision
Ian Graham and Peter Llewelyn Jones

Computer Graphics and Applications
Dennis Harris

Usability Testing and Systems Evaluation
A guide for designing useful computer systems
G. Lindgaard

Software Metrics
A practitioner's guide to improved product development
K.-H. Möller and D.J. Paulish

Artificial Intelligence and Human Learning
Intelligent computer-aided instruction
Edited by John Self

Formal Concepts in Artificial Intelligence
Fundamentals

Rajjan Shinghal
Software Engineering Productivity
A practical guide
C. Stevenson

Techniques in Computational Learning
An introduction
C.J. Thornton

Artificial Intelligence
Principles and applications
Edited by Masoud Yazdani

To the memory of my sister, Margaret, who died so suddenly just weeks before this book was published and so never had the joy of seeing the completed work.

SOFTWARE ENGINEERING PRODUCTIVITY

A practical guide

C. Stevenson

Cape Town
South Africa

CHAPMAN & HALL

London · Glasgow · Weinheim · New York · Tokyo · Melbourne · Madras

Published by Chapman & Hall, 2–6 Boundary Row, London SE1 8HN, UK

Chapman & Hall, 2–6 Boundary Row, London SE1 8HN, UK

Blackie Academic & Professional, Wester Cleddens Road, Bishopbriggs, Glasgow G64 2NZ, UK

Chapman & Hall GmbH, Pappelallee 3, 69469 Weinham, Germany

Chapman & Hall, USA, One Penn Plaza, 41st Floor, New York NY 10119, USA

Chapman & Hall Japan, ITP-Japan, Kyowa Building, 3F, 2–2–1, Hirakawacho, Chiyoda-ku, Tokyo 102, Japan

Chapman & Hall Australia, Thomas Nelson Australia, 102 Dodds Street, South Melbourne, Victoria 3205, Australia

Chapman & Hall India, R. Seshadri, 32 Second Main Road, CIT East, Madras 600 035, India

First edition 1995

© 1995 Chapman & Hall

Typeset in 10/12pt Palatino by Photoprint, Torquay, Devon
Printed in England by Clays Ltd, St Ives plc

ISBN 0 412 37840 X

A catalogue record for this book is available from the British Library

Library of Congress Catalog Card Number: 93–74447

∞ Printed on permanent acid-free text paper, manufactured in accordance with ANSI/NISO Z39.48–1922 and ANSI/NISO Z39.48–1984 (Permanence of Paper).

CONTENTS

PREFACE

Productivity is a subject which has long interested me. Over the past few years I have made an in-depth study of the productivity of software engineers by reading extensively in books, magazines, academic journals and newspapers. This book is the distillation of the knowledge of all those experts, combined with my own extensive experience. It is an almost encyclopaedic repository of facts and figures about software engineering, and is worth buying for that reason alone.

This book is therefore basically a literature survey. I was tempted to give it the subtitle 'a literature survey', but decided against this. With the vast body of literature available (see Appendix C), making it impractical to read *every* book and article, I was bound to upset someone because I had left out *their* favorite.

Because this book is largely a literature survey, it relies heavily on the work done by many hundreds of other people. Without their efforts, this book would not have been possible. I recommend that readers purchase at least some of the books and magazines referenced here. This recommendation is partly a token of my gratitude, but is also because my book is a summary, and it is necessary to consult the original sources for more detailed information.

When I first began this study, I gained the strong impression that very little was really known about the subject, that there was very little solid scientific evidence to back up the claims made for the many ideas for improving productivity. After digging more deeply, however, I discovered that there is far more factual evidence than is at first apparent, but it is not widely known, at least not amongst ordinary practising software engineers and their managers, and is even not widely available to them, so the computer industry is not deriving the potential benefits.

This book also had another, and earlier, origin. During my long career in Data Processing, I had often been asked questions such as: what is a typical productivity rate? what is the average size of a program? It was embarrassing not to know the answers, so I started a notebook, in which I jotted down all such figures I came across. When, later, I began the present work, these statistics proved a valuable source of information.

This study is aimed at software engineers and their managers. It shows them how productivity can be improved. It is also therefore of value to people who teach software engineering, and their students. The latter might not be familiar with all the topics discussed, but productivity should be included in Computer Science and Management Information Systems curricula. Other categories of Data Processing staff will also find valuable information in this book.

Because it is intended for practitioners rather than researchers, I – like Macro and Buxton (1987) – have concentrated on known tools and techniques rather than those which are still in the research realm.

This is a study, not a 'cookery-book'. It provokes thought, and provides guidelines, rather than crystal-clear recommendations of what to do in different circumstances. It is a study, not a 'pep-talk'. However, although I have tried to make it as authoritative as possible, I have also tried to make it readable and not too academic-looking. It is therefore non-mathematical and non-statistical.

Because of the importance of productivity, and the major benefits that improving it can provide, this book is a 'must' for everyone involved in software engineering.

C. Stevenson

ACKNOWLEDGEMENTS

Material from 'Programmer Productivity: Myths, Methods, and Murphy's Law' by Lowell Jay Arthur, copyright © 1983 by John Wiley & Sons, Inc., reprinted by permission of John Wiley and Sons, Inc.

Material from Datamation Magazine excerpted with permission of Datamation Magazine, © by Cahners Publishing Co.

PART ONE
INTRODUCTION

INTRODUCTION

1

Software engineering productivity is a critical problem. The demand for new software is increasing faster than our ability to supply and maintain it (Boehm, 1981; Fairley, 1985). This increased demand stems largely from pressures throughout the economy to improve commercial, industrial, and service productivity through automation. Inability to meet the demand has already led to serious delays in responding to user requests for work to be done, and a large backlog of work has built up (Chapter 8). As a result, the users have become very dissatisfied, and their work has been adversely affected, which is particularly serious as programming systems have become vital in all types of organization, and especially in the design and development of many high-technology products (Jones, 1986b). This is possibly the most serious and urgent problem in data processing (DP), especially as the situation is likely to worsen due to the decreasing price of computer hardware (Chapter 5), the resultant proliferation of microcomputers in particular, and the consequent rapid growth in demand for DP services (Chapter 12). (Data processing is also known as information systems (IS) and information technology (IT). Although not identical in meaning – see, for example, Collin (1989) – I have not attempted to distinguish between these terms.)

One way to meet the demand is to increase the number of staff, and in fact the severe shortage of staff (Chapter 9) can be attributed to the high demand. To alleviate the shortage, much attention has been given to increasing recruitment into the industry,

with a fair amount of success. Attention is also being devoted to improving the productivity of existing staff, and a variety of ideas and methods to achieve this end have been advanced. This is an inherently superior solution because:

- the software engineers can complete their assignments sooner;
- they can complete more assignments than before;
- the employer gets better value for money from his staff;
- the staff are happier, more confident, and derive greater job satisfaction (which in turn provides additional motivation, which further increases productivity – see Chapter 11), as they know they are being more professional and will be recognized as such (Beware of the future. *Systems Stelsels*, April 1980, p. 3; Parikh, 1984);
- they can devote more time to producing better products, ones that have fewer errors, are more efficient in their use of system resources, and are easier to use and maintain; and
- the user is given better systems sooner.

The net result is that the organization as a whole becomes more efficient, it in turn can provide its customers with a better service or better products sooner, so it becomes more competitive and more profitable (Johnson, 1980b; Jones, 1986b).

Improving software productivity also has major direct financial benefits. DP is a multi-billion dollar industry, and software comprises much of this amount.

- 120 of the top US companies intended

spending over $50 billion on IS in 1989, of which about $8 billion would be for software, $18 billion for hardware, and $21 billion for personnel (Davis, 1989a).

- It was estimated that the total amount spent on all aspects of computing in the US in 1980 was about $130 billion, or approximately 5% of GNP (compared to only 2.3% for the automobile industry), and that this would rise to 12.5% by 1990 (Fairley, 1985).
- The top 100 vendors in the world sold $243 billion worth of information technology in 1988, of which $20 billion was software (Kelly, 1989).
- IBM's OS/360 operating system is estimated to have cost $200 million, while the software costs of the USA's manned space program were $1 billion between 1960 and 1970 (Bell *et al.*, 1987).
- DP people seem to believe that the split between hardware cost and software cost is about 50:50, but it is actually 9:91 (De-Marco, 1982).
- In the military applications area, the cost of software was expected to reach about 80% of the total computer systems budget by 1985 (Boehm, 1973; Boehm and Standish, 1983).
- The value of existing software (in the US alone?) may have exceeded $250 billion by 1981 (Charette, 1986).
- Large organizations such as ITT (International Telephone and Telegraph Corporation) and IBM may have more than 30 000 separate programs, which can approach 100 million source code statements, while the Department of Defense and the combined US military may have over 100 000 programs, and a total of 250 million source code statements (Jones, 1986b).
- The worldwide number of professional programmers is in excess of 3 million (Chapter 8), the number of current applications probably exceeds a million, and the number of lines of source code in the world is in the billions (Chapter 6) (Jones, 1986b).

1.1 OBJECTIVES

This book is concerned with the productivity of software engineers.

- Why is it inadequate, and how can it be improved?
- By how much is it inadequate, and by how much can it be improved?

Various authorities have identified inadequacies and inefficiencies in the existing situation. They have advanced ideas and methods, and developed a variety of tools to improve productivity. The book examines the alleged problem areas, and especially the proposed cures, to establish how effective they are, including the sometimes contradictory evidence and opinions relating to these factors. The ultimate aim is to find a way to increase productivity sufficiently to eliminate the shortage of staff (see Chapter 9), clear the backlog of work (Chapter 8), and provide a fast service to users, for at least the next few years, to cope with the predicted rapid growth in demand for software (Chapter 12).

Because of the considerable benefits it can bring, increasing software productivity is an extremely important subject. Concerted efforts to date include:

- the STARS (software technology for adaptable, reliable systems) program to improve software technologies and create more powerful tools (Chapter 13);
- the EEC's ESPRIT (European program for research and development in information technology) programmes, the major components of which are the development of a fully integrated project support environment (and specifically the portable common tools environment, PCTE); the development of a life-cycle process which supports rapid prototyping; and the specification, development, and support of reusable software components; and these programmes have had a sizeable software

measurement component (Charette, 1986; Macro and Buxton, 1987; Fenton, 1991; Sommerville, 1989);

- the Japanese fifth-generation project, which aims to develop hardware and software systems to support 'knowledge information processing' in a wide range of applications, including expert systems and natural-language understanding by machines (Schach, 1988; Chorafas, 1986);
- and the Software Productivity Consortium, which was set up to develop new and improved software development methods, and more powerful and advanced tools, for US defense contractors (Hughes, 1989).

However, these projects are mostly neither directly nor exclusively aimed at improving productivity. Similarly, although there is a vast amount of DP-related literature, only about 1% of it is directly concerned with productivity (Appendix C). (Likewise, COBOL (Common Business-Oriented Language) is the most widely-used language (Chapter 6), yet few articles are published about it (Goodwin, 1986).) In particular, most books on software engineering have little to say about productivity – the sooner this situation is remedied, the better: productivity is probably inadequate *because* too little attention is paid to it.

This book offers the most comprehensive investigation yet to be published. It contains a large number and variety of facts and opinions relating to software productivity; the author has compared them, attempted to 'separate the wheat from the chaff', drawn conclusions, and made recommendations. Furthermore, it is hoped this book will stimulate further interest and research.

1.2 SCOPE

The factors discussed are generally applicable – though not necessarily to the same extent – to a wide range of circumstances, e.g.:

- small organizations as well as large ones;
- organizations which are new to DP, as well

as to those with long-established DP departments;
- organizations which make extensive use of modern technology (database management systems, fourth-generation languages, structured methodologies, etc.), as well as to less sophisticated ones;
- centralized as well as decentralized organizations;
- commercial, industrial, scientific and government organizations;
- the production of application software (including application 'packages') as well as system software (e.g. compilers);
- all stages of the software life-cycle (from feasibility study to maintenance);
- all sizes of computer (some of the factors discussed even apply to Data Capture machines and Word Processors).

The factors discussed are relevant to commercial, industrial, scientific and government organizations, but the emphasis is on commercial data processing, because 'the vast majority of computer purchases are made by business' (Baron, 1988) and 'the immense majority of analysts and programmers work in commercial environments' (Babilonia, 1988). According to Couger *et al.* (1982) over 70% of all computer use is for business information processing. The preponderance of COBOL, a business-oriented language, relative to other languages (Chapter 6), confirms this.

1.3 OVERVIEW

This study describes the existing situation:

- the software engineering *process* (particularly its subdivision into various functions, the tools and methods used, and the productivity rates currently being achieved);
- the *context* in which software engineering takes place (particularly the people who perform the process, the organizational structures, the physical environment, the

hardware available, and the rapid increase in demand for software); and

- the resultant *product* (particularly its size, complexity, and quality).

Factors affecting productivity are examined, with extra attention being paid to those thought to have the greatest effect.

Current trends are included, as are known problem areas (to which the inadequate productivity of software engineers has been attributed) and new technologies which promise to yield major improvements in productivity.

Software engineering is labour-intensive (Humphrey, 1985; Fairley, 1985), and yet has *resisted* automation (Conte *et al.*, 1986). Much of the discussion therefore revolves around people and people-problems, such as people-structures (Chapter 3), ergonomics (Chapter 4), the shortage of staff, their high turnover and low level of expertise (Chapter 9).

Conclusions are drawn, and recommendations are made on how organizations can improve their productivity.

Note

DP is a specialized field, and uses many technical terms. The reader is assumed to have a knowledge of DP in general, and of software engineering in particular. Nevertheless, many definitions are included at the relevant places within the text. In addition, general definitions have been listed as Appendix B. Similarly, the meanings of abbreviations are given when they are first used, but are also listed in Appendix A. People with several years' DP experience will be familiar with most of the terms, techniques, etc. used in this work, and those with less experience will need to refer to more detailed works from time to time, to supplement the brief explanations given here.

The use of ostensibly sex-identifying terms is a sensitive issue nowadays. Masculine pronouns have been used here for simplicity and improved readability, and 'no offence is intended to the many ladies among us' (Patrick, 1980a; Heller, 1981; Martin, 1982a). Similarly, 'man' e.g. as in man-hours has been used as a generic term: 'We are well aware that much of the manpower and man-hours in software development are being expended by female analysts and programmers' (Conte *et al.*, 1986).

The noun 'data' has no singular (Puterbaugh, 1986; Sproul, 1990); here we write 'data is', rather than 'data are', although many other writers use it differently.

1.4   CAUTIONS

The results of many surveys and experiments are quoted, but these have their limitations. For example, it is exorbitantly expensive to write actual production programs using several teams of professional programmers, with each team using a different method to see which method is best. (As Conte *et al.* (1986) put it, 'How many times does one company assign three programming teams to work from the same software specifications simultaneously?') Most experiments therefore involve students individually writing very small ('toy') programs, and what is true for this small-scale experiment is not necessarily also true for a team of professional programmers working on a large-scale production system. Furthermore, some information was obtained from vendors, who are unlikely to be impartial in their claims!

Some studies have revealed wide productivity ranges due to a small number of extreme performances (Chapter 9). Bell *et al.* (1987) when discussing on-line programming, stated that 'any differences between the two modes of working [batch and on-line] are grossly overwhelmed by the enormous differences between individuals' (Chapter 6). The same is probably true of many other factors examined here; also, a disproportionately large proportion of the figures may have been quoted from large projects, and are probably therefore not typical. Measurement is particularly important in large projects, so in all probability, more figures are available from them. For example, Kemerer (1987) deliberately chose medium- to large-sized projects, as this was an explicit requirement of the cost estimation models he was evaluating.

The quoted productivity ranges found by Walston and Felix (1977) for many factors affecting productivity may include the effects of correlated factors (Boehm, 1981; Conte *et al.*, 1986). Also, the productivity ranges (effort multipliers) used by various effort-estimation models are quoted, although they produce estimates which are sometimes very inaccurate (Chapter 8). Worse still, the evaluation by Kemerer (1987) of the COCOMO model found that the advanced versions, which include productivity ranges for many factors believed to affect productivity, did not do as well as the Basic version, which does not. This surely casts doubt not only on the accuracy of the model's productivity ranges, but even on which factors influence productivity. Some studies have produced widely differing results, as can readily be seen from the various sets of values tabulated later, such as the productivity rates listed in Chapter 2. This may be due to the reasons just given, but whatever the reason, one cannot confidently draw any conclusions from them – and in fact, 'much of the literature on software engineering productivity cannot be used for serious research' (Jones, 1986b). Nevertheless, highlighting such differences draws attention to the unsatisfactory situation, serves as a warning to anyone who wants to use the information, and hopefully will encourage an improvement.

Another potential pitfall is exemplified by Halstead's *Software Science* (Halstead, 1977).

Martin and McClure (1985) describe it as 'amazingly accurate', and it has led to new insights about programming (Boehm, 1981; Jones, 1986b), but the supporting evidence has been challenged, and even the theoretical basis of this method has been questioned (Conte *et al.*, 1986; Kearney *et al.*, 1986), while (Jones, 1986b) believes it has 'major limitations' that will eventually cause it to become 'a technological dead end'.

This book includes whatever evidence and opinions were found, not excluding extreme valus or minority opinions.

Authorities such as Bell *et al.* (1987) discuss some of these problems, while Conte devotes a whole chapter to the subject. Some problems in gathering data are given in Chapter 13, while some problems in comparing data from different sources are discussed in Chapter 2.

Organizations must therefore critically examine the findings of surveys and experiments, the claims made by vendors in particular, and even the advice given here, and convince themselves that the findings etc. will be applicable in their own environment, before adopting new tools or methods.

Chapter 10 points out that much computer software is sold without any guarantees. Some authors are similarly cautious, so I will end this list of cautions with the disclaimer in Bourdon (1987): 'Whilst every effort has been made to ensure the accuracy of this book, the author cannot guarantee that the book is error-free or accurate, nor can he accept responsibility for any problems associated with its use'. Nevertheless, I would appreciate being notified of any errors that may have slipped through. In fact, I would welcome any feedback, particularly more facts and figures, that could be used to improve this book.

The productivity currently being achieved is discussed: most relates to development productivity, with maintenance productivity being discussed at the end.

This study is concerned with DP productivity, and specifically software development and maintenance productivity. However, Gilb (1988) argues that productivity 'should be measured in terms of net real effects on high-level management goals' of the organization. Measures to improve software productivity must be relevant to management objectives, and the side-effects – such as the costs, and the effect on user productivity – must be taken into account. Poor quality software may adversely affect user productivity, e.g. if a program is difficult to enhance, then users will have to wait longer before receiving the benefits of the enhancements.

Productivity measurement has important benefits (Parikh, 1984; Conte *et al.*, 1986; Kemerer, 1987). It shows which tools and techniques are the best, by how much they are better, and under what circumstances. This, in turn, aids the development and spread of improved tools and techniques, permits more appropriate choice of tools and techniques, and so leads to productivity improvements. The knowledge gained from productivity measurement enables realistic project deadlines to be set, and resources to be scheduled, thereby avoiding rushed, incomplete, and second-rate jobs.

Productivity measurement also shows management which members of staff are good, and so should be paid more or promoted; and which ones are weak, and so should be given extra training or transferred to a different type of work (Parikh, 1984; De-Marco, 1982). The weaker ones will themselves see that they must strive to improve. According to Arthur (1983), people perform better when they know they are being measured. This is particularly true if they can earn more by producing more (Chapter 11). There are, however, dangers involved. They might resent being measured (Short, 1977), though it might be more accurate to say they resent being *mis*measured (DeMarco, 1982): as will become apparent later, the methods used can be very inaccurate and misleading. The weakest ones often *avoid* being measured (Martin, 1985). The staff might, consciously or unconsciously, distort the measurements. If, for example, total lines of code is used as the unit of measurement, then the programmers might 'pad' their programs with additional, non-essential lines, such as reams of comments, in order to appear more productive (Shneiderman, 1980; Schach, 1990). If they are responsible for recording how they spend their time, then they might *under*estimate their time in order to appear more productive, or *over*estimate it in order to appear overworked (Conte *et al.*, 1986). Incentive payments can eliminate resentment, but they can also aggravate this situation, and have other dangers, e.g. they can harm the team spirit (Chapter 11).

The staff must therefore be persuaded of the benefits of productivity measurement, and be encouraged to co-operate, and methods of measurement must be as non-obtrusive as possible, so as not to interfere with or modify whatever is being measured. Because of these dangers, Conte recommends that productivity measurements should *not* be used to evaluate performance.

2.1   UNIT OF MEASURE

2.1.1   CHOSEN UNIT OF MEASURE

Productivity is defined as the rate of output, or production per unit of effort (Sykes, 1977), i.e. the output achieved with regard for the time taken but not for the cost incurred. There are thus two aspects to be considered when deciding on a unit of measurement: quantity of output and period of time.

Period of time

The most common periods of measurement are one day and one month: as a standard, rates given by other authorities for different periods have been converted to daily rates.

Quantity of output

The most widely used measure of output, and therefore of productivity, is lines of source code, usually abbreviated to LOC, probably because it is so easy to use. However, it suffers from several disadvantages.

- It does not allow adequately for re-used code ('copying code involves almost no time or effort'), for quality and complexity, or for software produced under very high reliability requirements or under time and storage constraints ('it assumes every source instruction is equally easy to produce') – for example, a small program with many conditional statements and loops can take much longer to develop than a large program with mainly sequential code (Conte *et al.*, 1986; Boehm, 1981).
- Some authorities (Walston and Felix, 1977; DeMarco, 1981b; Yourdon 1978–80; Conte *et al.*, 1986) include comments (or even blank lines) in the line count – this is the most convenient method if the counts are obtained from automatic librarian counts (Johnson, 1980b), or if the lines are counted manually (Jones, 1986b); others, such as

Boehm (1981), Wingfield (1982), and Jones (1986b), exclude them, making comparisons difficult and potentially misleading.

- Similarly, some authorities, such as Conte and Jones (1986b), include data declarations in the line count, while others such as Arthur (1983) count only executable statements; some, such as Johnson (1980b) and Boehm (1981), include JCL (job control language) statements, while others, such as Jones (1986b), exclude them; and generally (Jones 1986b) non-delivered source code (development support code such as test drivers), on which less effort was expended – less documentation, fewer reviews, no user training, etc. – is excluded, but it should be included if it was developed with the same care as the delivered software (Boehm, 1981).
- It can only be used after a program has been written, so it cannot predict how long it should take to write a particular program (and over-optimistic predictions lead to rushed, second-rate jobs, with consequent adverse effect on long-term productivity (Chapter 11)).
- It may encourage programmers to produce lengthy rather than lucid programs (Shneiderman, 1980).
- Purchased software (such as application packages (Chapter 7)) sells better if it is more efficient. In the eyes of the vendor, therefore, programmers who write more efficient code are more productive (Conte *et al.*, 1986). Also, the development costs are spread over more customers. However, extra effort is required to achieve the greater efficiency, yet more efficient code is often more compact. In these circumstances therefore, *fewer* LOC means *higher* productivity.
- Studies have shown that experienced programmers use about 20% fewer lines than novices (Chapter 9).
- Some programmers write more than one statement on a line, while others spread a statement out over several lines. Struc-

tured Programming convention (discussed in Chapter 8) for the IF-THEN-ELSE statement, has each clause coded on a separate line (Arthur, 1983) and can therefore give misleadingly high productivity rates (but see comments below).

- Some authorities, such as Boehm (1981), count the *physical* statements ('card images'), while others, such as Jones (1986b) and Arthur (1983), count the *logical* statements (terminated by programming delimiters), e.g. just the verbs. This method is therefore not influenced by whether the programmer spreads a statement over several lines, or not. (In an example in Johnson (1980b), the total number of source records was over three times the number of verbs.)
- Some authorities use more than one method, e.g. Johnson (1980b) counts the number of verbs for some of his rates, and the total lines of code for others.
- The number of LOC is affected by the type and degree of modularization. In an experiment by Woodfield *et al.* (1981a), the 'functionally modularized' (subdivided into different functions) version of a small FORTRAN program was 25% longer than the unmodularized version; the version modularized by data type was 53% longer; and the 'super' modularized version (where modularization was carried to extremes), was 73% longer.
- LOC usually gives lower productivity rates for high-level languages than for Assembler (or Assembly) language, even though high-level languages actually give higher productivity (see example below).
- According to Conte *et al.* (1986), strongly-typed languages like PASCAL result in more LOC than say FORTRAN. NB A data type is a category of acceptable values that a variable can take (Baron, 1988): numeric, alphanumeric, date, pointer, integer, Boolean, etc. Some languages have more data types than others, and some enforce the typing more stringently (Chapter 6).
- LOC is not suitable for technological aids

such as utilities (file reformats, prints, etc.), and many fourth-generation software products (such as screen painters).
- It does not apply to the non-programming portions of a project, such as requirements analysis, user training, and installation planning, or even to the secretarial, librarian, clerical, administrative, and supervisory duties which are an integral part of any programming project (Schach, 1990; Jones, 1986b). In spite of this, some authorities, such as Boehm (1981), include some or even all of these functions, in project effort estimation models based on LOC.

Non-delivered source code complicates the situation. If productivity is measured by *total* LOC (delivered plus non-delivered), then because of the higher productivity for non-delivered code, productivity increases as the proportion of non-delivered code on the project increases. If, instead, productivity is measured by just the number of delivered LOC, but the *time* taken to produce the non-delivered code is still included, then this reduces the productivity (or, rather, reduces the numerical value expressing productivity). The Walston and Felix (1977) figures show a productivity rate of 8 LOC per day where 0–90% of the code was delivered, 16 for 91–99%, and 13 for 100%, i.e. there was not a steady change in productivity as the delivered code formed an increasingly larger proportion of the total. Typically, non-delivered code only includes things like test drivers and so does not make a big difference – temporary programs probably only comprise about 5% of the total software effort (Walston and Felix, 1977) – but on a very large project it could involve developing tools, utilities and even compilers, and could then amount to as much as four times the delivered (operational or mission-oriented) code (Boehm, 1981). Non-delivered code is sometimes referred to as 'throwaway' code, as it may never be used again in another project. To eliminate such a waste of effort,

Bell *et al.* (1987) advocates top-down development to avoid the construction of test drivers; and, more generally, the standardization of tools, so that suitable ones will more often be available 'off the shelf'.

On a small project, the non-programming portions of a project may be performed by the programmers, whereas on a large project they are performed by specialist staff. Further, on a microcomputer (PC), the programmer even does his own operating. This further increases the unreliability of LOC as a measure, by potentially distorting comparisons between small and large projects, and PC- and mainframe-developed projects, especially as most commentators do not state which functions have been included in their time measurements.

Because it spreads IF-THEN-ELSE statements over several lines, structured ('GOTO-less') programming can give misleadingly high LOC counts. This is consistent with the experience of Rubin (1987a) that 'GOTO-full' programming reduces the number of LOC by around 20 to 25%. Conte *et al.* (1986), however, express the opposite opinion: they believe that structured programming results in more *succinct* programs. However, the evidence they advanced – the average size of programs developed by a group of programmers was 30% smaller after they had been taught structured programming (Elshoff, 1977) – is weak because it refers to *different* programs, which might have been 30% smaller than the previous programs anyway, even without structured programming! Conte recognizes, but dismisses, this possibility. In an example in Jones (1986b), the structured and unstructured versions of a system had identical numbers of lines of code. However, this may just have been an intentional simplification on his part. An additional complication is that the structured version was written in a slightly more powerful language, and so should have had correspondingly fewer statements. Jones also reported that programs are typically 10–15% larger after they have been restructured.

It is not clear what effect the inclusion or exclusion of comment lines has on productivity figures. As programmers do not like writing documentation (Chapter 8), one would have thought that comments formed only a small proportion of the total LOC in the average program, and therefore the discrepancies would usually be small. However, this is not consistent with the productivity rates quoted later from Conte – an average of 36 LOC/day for projects in which comments were counted, compared to only 6 LOC/day for those in which comments were omitted. However, the projects which included comments were much smaller, on average, than those which excluded comments (they were only about one-third the size), and they may also have included a large amount of re-used code. It is interesting to note that Walston and Felix (1977) who *included* comments, obtained a rate of only 14 LOC/day, which is closer to the Conte rate with*out* comments; while Kemerer (1987), who *excluded* comments, obtained a rate of 56 LOC/day, which is closer to the Conte rate *with* comments. Boehm (1981) claimed that comments often comprise over half the source; Bailey (1982) reported that they comprised 30–50% of the total source code for the projects in the Bailey and Basili (1981) set; and Conte stated that they comprised up to 50% in the Walston and Felix set of projects.

Comments are usually either counted in full, or are left completely out of the count. As a first approximation, the latter method is adequate, as it normally takes much less effort to create a comment line. However, there is the danger that programmers will be reluctant to spend time on 'non-productive' commenting (Schach, 1990). Furthermore, creating comments does require *some* effort, so *some* allowance should be made for this, particularly for programs with a high proportion of comments. Perhaps an adjustment factor could be applied to the number of

Table 2.1 Effect of different goals on LOC productivity (Weinberg and Schulman, 1974)

Team	Size (LOC)	Time (man-hours)	Development productivity Apparent (LOC/man-hour)	True (Time ratio)
Fewest LOC	33	30	1.1	1 (base)
Highest LOC productivity	166	30	5.5	1
Quickest	126	28	4.5	1.1:1

comment lines, in the same way as Bailey and Basili (1981) applied a factor of 20% to the number of lines of re-used code, to arrive at an *equivalent* number of lines of new code, as less effort is required to re-use code than to write new code.

Lines of code has been criticized as being 'like trying to estimate the cost of an automobile by its gross weight, or by the total number of parts in it' (Boehm, 1981). Wirth (1987), during a panel discussion, described using LOC as 'utter nonsense', but the example given – a maintenance change which reduced the size of a program would give an apparent *negative* productivity – was not a good one. He also stated that 'the art is to write a *small* program', which is consistent with the comment above regarding lengthy rather than lucid programs, but this must not be carried too far, as attempts to make a program small may make it less lucid.

An added complication is revealed by the experiment performed by Weinberg and Schulman (1974). Six teams were each given the same programming assignment, but were set different goals:

- to complete the task with the least effort;
- to minimize the number of statements in the program;
- to minimize the amount of memory required;
- to minimize execution time;
- to produce the clearest program; and
- to produce the clearest output.

The team which was instructed to use as few statements as possible produced the program with the least clear output, and was only average in program clarity (with consequent impact on user productivity and maintenance productivity). By contrast, the team that wrote the program quickest (and therefore had the highest *true* development productivity), had the second highest number of statements, and only the second highest productivity, if measured by LOC. The team with the highest *apparent* productivity, when measured by LOC, used 166 statements and took 30 man-hours, giving a productivity rate of 5.5 LOC per man-hour. These figures are given in Table 2.1.

When measured by LOC, therefore, there was an *apparent* productivity difference of (5.5/1.1=) 5:1 between the teams, whereas the *true* productivity difference was only (30/28=) 1.1:1, or just 10%.

Yet another complication is revealed by an experiment by Wang (1984), involving 44 students, of approximately equal experience and training, who each wrote the same program using the same language (PASCAL), and the same methodology (top-down design and data-structure-first development). Unlike the Weinberg and Schulman experiment above, they were *not* asked to optimize anything, yet there was nevertheless a 3:1 range in the number of lines of code of their programs, which Conte *et al.* (1986) attribute to differences in individual ability.

The following example, which is derived from Jones (1981, 1986b), provides another graphical illustration of how misleading LOC can be as a measure of productivity, in this case due to its inability to adequately cater

Table 2.2   Effect of language level on LOC productivity (Jones, 1981, 1986b)

Function	Effort (man-months)	
	Low-level language	*High-level language*
Design	1 (10%)	1 (20%)
Coding	5 (50%)	1 (20%)
Testing	2 (20%)	1 (20%)
Documentation, etc.	2 (20%)	2 (40%)
TOTAL	10	5
Cost (@ $5000/man-month	$50 000	$25 000
LOC	1000	250
Cost/LOC	$50	$100
Productivity (LOC/man-month)	100	50

for differences between programming languages. Suppose that a program is written twice, once in a low-level language, and once in a high-level language. The high-level language requires fewer source statements, and takes less coding and testing time, but there are certain overheads such as design and documentation time, which are independent of the language. The comparison is shown in Table 2.2.

The low-level language appears to give double the productivity of the high-level language, whereas in fact the reverse is the case: the high-level language version was completed in half the time, and therefore *it* gave the doubling in productivity. Similarly, the low-level language appears to be cheaper, as it only costs half as much per line of code, whereas in fact the reverse is the case: the *total* cost of using the high-level language was *half* that of the low-level language, so *it* gave the halving of costs. Jones (1986b) therefore describes this as a 'mathematical paradox'. However, the productivity rates quoted later, and specifically those from Macro and Buxton (1987) and Boehm (1981), do not seem to confirm the existence of this paradox: their productivity rates for higher-level languages are higher than those for lower-level languages; and even the remaining rates in Jones (1986b) – he gave over 50 sets of rates, for a variety of situations – although on the whole they confirm the paradox, do not show such a marked discrepancy as that in Table 2.2. Presumably, in practice, low-level languages are only used for difficult programs, such as operating systems or real-time programs, where the coding rate is low, and this masks the effect of the paradox.

Productivity was previously defined as the quantity of output divided by the effort. Apparent variations in productivity of over 5:1 can be caused just by different organizations or researchers using different line-counting methods to measure the quantity of output (Jones, 1986b). In fact, by varying definitions of either the numerator (the quantity of output) or the denominator (the quantity of effort), we can obtain productivity measures for the same product that differ by an order of magnitude or more! (Conte *et al.*, 1986). The example from Boehm (1981) given in Table 2.3 illustrates this point.

The productivity, if calculated as the non-commented applications software divided by the total development effort (including management and clerical effort), is only (100 000/(1200*1.2)=) 69 LOC per man-month; whereas if it is calculated as all developed software (including comments), divided by the code and unit test effort (excluding management and clerical effort), it is (560 000/250=) 2240 LOC per man-month, i.e. more than 30 times as high.

Table 2.3 Effect of line- and effort-counting methods on measured productivity (Boehm, 1981)

Applications software	100 000 delivered source instructions
Support software	250 000 "
Test drivers	50 000 "
Additional comment cards	40%
Total development effort	1200 man-months
Code and unit test effort	250 "
Management, clerical effort	20%

Counting lines of code is therefore not as straightforward as it seems (Schach, 1990), and in fact, 'an entire subarea of research has developed to determine the best method of counting source lines' (Kemerer, 1987).

Notwithstanding these shortcomings, I have used LOC almost exclusively, because:

- it is the most widely-used measure – e.g. according to Conte *et al.* (1986), most of the effort models currently in use rely on LOC as a primary factor;
- it is used in five of the nine cost-estimation models surveyed by Boehm (1981);
- it is so widespread, so it permits comparison with many projects, including historical ones for which productivity rates have been published (Conte *et al.*, 1986);
- the alternatives also have problems (Conte *et al.*, 1986) – examples are given later;
- it is simple, and easy to compute (Conte *et al.*, 1986);
- though it may be unreliable for individual programs, it is much more reliable for averages of many programs (Johnson, 1980b), especially where only large differences are being examined – and I am much more interested in factors which have a large impact on productivity than those which have only a small impact;
- even in the case of individual programs, it is much more reliable provided it is qualified, i.e. if the rate specifies what language the program was written in, the size and complexity of the program, whether comment lines were included, and so on;
- the discrepancies caused by including or excluding JCL are usually small;

- similarly, the discrepancies caused by including or excluding clerical work, supervisory duties, etc., would also usually be small (clerical and managerial time together typically comprise only about 16% of the system development effort, according to Table 8.28);
- if we consider only the coding function in Table 2.2, then there was, in fact, a small increase in LOC productivity with the high-level language, from (1000/5=) 200 LOC/month to (250/1=) 250;
- pressure of work and peer code review or inspection (Chapter 10), should minimize any intentional padding of code with extra instructions in order to appear more productive (Boehm, 1981), and an adjustment factor could be calculated for any individual programmers who were particularly verbose;
- cost-estimation models like COCOMO (Boehm, 1981) which use LOC, frequently show a close agreement between predicted and actual effort – see Chapter 8 – and these models often include non-programming functions, to which LOC might appear irrelevant (in fact, it is the non-programming functions that cause the mathematical paradox referred to earlier);
- a survey by Ingham (1976) of 11 installations, and the Nelson (1978) examination of the RADC database of over 400 project data points, both showed a strong correlation between effort and LOC;
- van der Poel (1982) found a close correlation between LOC and his alternative unit of measure (which used the number of master files, record types, etc.).

In addition, according to Matos and Jalics (1989), Hogan (1986), and Boehm (1981), studies such as those of Walston and Felix (1977) and Nelson (1978) have shown that a programmer can write a certain number of lines of code per day, regardless of the programming language, i.e. it takes about the same amount of time to code (and test?) a line of source code, no matter which language is used. (Though Martin (1985), in comparing fourth-generation languages with COBOL, stated that a programmer writes more lines of code per day with languages that are relatively easy to use.) Therefore, a language which requires say 30% fewer statements, delivers a 30% higher productivity for the coding (and testing?) function(s). This can be seen even from Table 2.2 – the higher-level language version of the program, with only one-quarter as many statements, took only one-fifth as much time to code (and only two-sevenths as much time to code and test). The relevant sets of rates in Jones (1986b) exhibit the same phenomenon.

I would draw an analogy with athletics. One could argue that time is not a reliable measure of a runner's performance, as some races are won in less than ten seconds, while other races take over two hours. However, as soon as the *distance* of the race is taken into account, the major discrepancies are explained; and when the ages of the runners, their sex, any wind, the height above sea level, and so on, are included, the smaller anomalies are also explained. Lines of Code is similar – by itself, it is not reliable, but once qualified or seen in context, it becomes reliable. The factors needed to qualify it are discussed in this study.

Arthur (1983) put it rather well: 'LOC is not a good productivity measure because it penalizes high-level languages: Assembler programmers produce five statements to a COBOL programmer's one. But you should not compare COBOL to Assembler: they are as different as night and day. If you compare COBOL programs only to other COBOL

programs, and PL/1 to PL/1, then LOC provides a stable comparison tool'. In similar vein, Conte *et al.* (1986) concluded that LOC can easily be misinterpreted or misused, and the range of productivity values is too large for it to be a universally valid measure, but as long as appropriate caution is exercised, productivity rates derived from it can still yield valuable information about the effect of various factors on productivity, and it is still used for lack of a better measure.

Quality of output

Quantity can be misleading if quality is not taken into account: one programmer may code quickly but inaccurately, and then spend much time debugging; whereas another may code more slowly but more accurately, and so spend little time debugging. Testing and debugging time must therefore be included for a true comparison, i.e. we must compare the number of *fully debugged* statements per day. It is likely that most (if not all) of the productivity rates quoted later take this into account, but this is not the only aspect of quality. Ease of maintenance is another, but this is more difficult to allow for, and it is not usually taken into account when measuring or comparing development productivity. Similarly, there are many other aspects of quality, such as ease of use and portability, but they too are not usually taken into account. In fact, as can readily be seen from the many productivity rates quoted later, references to quality are conspicuous by their absence. The various aspects of quality, and the trade-offs between them and between development productivity and maintenance productivity, are discussed in Chapter 10.

Documentation

Just as a program is not completed until it has been fully debugged, so it is not completed until it has been fully documented. Documentation time must therefore also be included.

Summary

The unit of productivity measurement used here is therefore the number of fully debugged and documented source statements per person per day.

2.1.2   ALTERNATIVE UNITS OF MEASURE

Because of the inadequacies of LOC, authorities such as Aron (1974) have proposed alternative methods, and some organizations have also developed their own, more complex formulas – though many, including leading ones, do not have an effective measure of productivity (Carlyle, 1987c). These alternative methods typically use (Boehm, 1981; Parikh, 1984):

- combinations of parameters such as the number of routines, operators (arithmetic symbols, keywords, etc.), operands (variables, constants and labels), files or master files, inputs and outputs;
- the number of variables in the program (e.g. as shown by the cross-reference list);
- the amount of documentation;
- the number of paragraphs in the requirements specifications;
- the number of structure-chart (Chapter 8) or HIPO-chart elements in the software design specifications;
- the number of lines of Program Design Language; and
- a subjective estimate of difficulty.

The nine cost-estimation models reviewed by Boehm (1981) use some of these parameters; the Doty (Herd *et al.*, 1977) and the Walston and Felix (1977) models use the amount of documentation as one of their parameters; and the SDC (Nelson, 1966) and RCA (Freiman and Park, 1979) models use the number of routines. Such models not only give the factors which affect productivity, but also the *magnitude* of their effect, which is typically a complex, and often non-linear, relationship.

Boehm (1973) and Brooks (1975) used the number of machine instructions as a unit of measure; Brooks (1975) also used the number of words (presumably in the object program); while Murray (1983) would like to use 'how happy the user is with us', if only this could be measured. The number of machine instructions can also aid productivity comparisons between different programming languages. FORTRAN, for example, has an expansion ratio of about 6.5 to 1 (the number of machine instructions generated is about 6.5 times the number of source instructions), while PL/1 has a ratio of about 4 to 1 (Conte *et al.*, 1986). However, these ratios are averages, and the actual figures can vary widely between different programs, as shown by three studies quoted by Boehm (1981) which gave expansion ratios of 4:1 to 8:1 for FORTRAN, and 5:1 to 13:1 for PL/1 (Chapter 6). Boehm later rejected using the number of machine instructions, as LOC correlated more closely with total effort – a fact confirmed by Nelson (1978) and Walston and Felix (1977) – which is not surprising as the number of machine instructions does not account for the relative effort required for data declarations, format statements, and other non-executable portions of the program: 'it does not distinguish between programs with large, simple data regions, and programs with more complex data and instruction regions' (Boehm, 1981).

Some of these suggestions, such as the amount of documentation, are more relevant to the non-coding functions than is LOC. Jones (1986b) listed possible units of measurement for the non-coding activities:

- the number of pages for the functional design, internal design, documentation, and design review functions;
- the number of tests for the testing function; and
- the number of repairs for the defect repairs function.

His list did not include suggested measures

for the management, initial proposal, planning, requirements, education, budgeting, quality assurance, travel, and installation functions.

In general, these alternatives have not been successful, primarily because of definition and normalization problems, e.g. in distinguishing between a small and a large routine, or between a simple and a complex report; and one programmer may use two routines to code a particular function, while another may use only one (Boehm, 1981). As Jones (1986b) put it, 'the same practical counting difficulties which hamper use of lines of code also hamper taking measures of operators and operands'. These alternatives have therefore not proved to be better than LOC. In fact, the range of variability in how operators and operands can be counted, can actually exceed the variability in lines-of-code counts.

Some other possible measures of productivity are described below. Some are variations on the preceding methods so they cannot be any more reliable than the methods already described. Further alternatives may have to be found, e.g. the number of enquiries or transactions processed by a program, or the number of screens (for on-line systems), though these probably suffer from the same problems outlined above.

Cost

Cost has been suggested as a productivity measure by authorities such as Jones (1978) and Conte *et al.* (1986), but does not seem to be widely used (Parikh, 1984).

Cost, as Conte points out, is ultimately the best measure of productivity. This is what interests the employer or customer the most. It takes into account not just the amount of time taken to write a program, but also the salary of the programmer, thereby distinguishing between low- and high-paid programmers. It also takes into account the computer time consumed, thereby distin-

guishing between programmers who make many mistakes and those who are accurate, between those who consume additional computer time in testing in order to save their own time, and even between those who write inefficient programs. However, it is difficult to compare costs from projects several years apart, and particularly between projects from different regions or even different countries, because of inflation, the reduction in hardware costs (Chapter 5), variations in programmers' salaries e.g. due to differences in supply and demand (Chapter 9), and international money fluctuations (Boehm, 1981).

Number of personnel

This factor is used in the Boeing model (Black *et al.*, 1977), and indirectly in the Walston and Felix (1977) model.

If two organizations, particularly if they are in the same sector of industry, are of the same size (measured, for example, by the total number of User Department staff or the total annual sales), but have different numbers of DP staff, then the one with fewer DP staff may have a higher DP productivity, i.e. the number of DP staff can be used as a measure of DP productivity. Conversely, if the organizations have the same number of DP staff, but one charges lower prices for the same goods, then that organization may have a higher DP productivity.

This unit of measure may be even less reliable than the others, as many non-DP factors affect the comparison; there are practical difficulties, e.g. in comparing organizations of different sizes; and the Boeing model (which has large effort multipliers for many-programmer projects) overestimated the costs of some projects by factors of five or six (Boehm, 1981). On the other hand, van der Poel (1982) found that different sectors of industry had the same DP productivity when measured in a more conventional way, so the comparison might be easier than is at first apparent.

Number of systems

LOC is not a suitable unit of measure for utilities (file reformats, prints, etc.) or for fourth-generation languages (4GLs), making it more difficult to compare the overall productivity of two different organizations. They may have the same productivity for programs developed in the conventional way, but one may complete each system much faster, either because it makes more extensive use of utilities and 4GLs, or because the available utilities and 4GLs are more powerful: IBM (1976), for example, claimed that 70–80% of the programming on their S/32 computer could be done with the utilities. You could therefore count the number of systems in use at each installation as a measure of its productivity. However, because of large variations in system size (Chapter 8), and the difficulty in defining a system – e.g. in distinguishing between a system and a subsystem – it would be difficult to make this a reliable measure.

As a by-product, and provided figures were obtained from enough organizations, this method would also give data on the relative merits of the software for different makes and models of computer. It would also confirm if the reported 'user friendliness' of smaller computers does in fact result in higher productivity.

Number of programs

A variation on counting the number of systems is to count the number of programs (Blum, 1990; Jones, 1986b). Two comparisons could be made: one counting utilities as if they were programs, the other excluding them. Better, an adjustment factor could be applied to the number of utilities, in the same way as Bailey and Basili (1981) applied a factor of 20% to the number of lines of re-used code, to allow for the smaller amount of effort required to use utilities.

Number of modules

Instead of counting the number of programs, one could count the number of modules or routines (Conte *et al.*, 1986; Boehm, 1981). However, there are difficulties here as well. A study by Smith (1980) showed that modules ranged in size from less than 10 LOC to nearly 10 000. By contrast, some installations specify that modules should be a certain length, say about 100 LOC (Chapter 8). The programs may then be arbitrarily subdivided, and the resultant number of modules does not tell us more than the number of LOC. If, instead, the programs are subdivided by functions, then the number of modules correlates with the number of functions, and that could be used instead.

Number of functions

This metric has been proposed by authorities such as Conte *et al.* (1986) and Parikh (1984). A 'function' is a task performed by a program, or the group of statements in the program which performs the task. This unit of measure is similar to, and follows on from, the number of modules. There may be disagreements about definitions, e.g. whether a particular group of lines in a program is one function or several. Nevertheless, Basili and Reiter (1979) showed that programmers use a similar number of functions to solve a problem, but a different number of modules, so number of functions is a more *stable*, and therefore preferable, unit of measurement. Furthermore, Crossman (1979a) assumes that the time to develop a function is independent of the LOC required, though Johnson (1980b) seems skeptical of this. Counting functions is more appropriate than LOC where existing software – packages, re-used code, and even program generators – is used (Boehm, 1981). In the case of software packages, only *required* functions should be counted, as packages typically contain many functions which are not required by specific individual user organizations. This is relevant to 'make or buy' decisions. LOC cannot be used where the DP staff spend time in finding non-software solutions to users' requirements, though it may still be possible to count functions in these circumstances. However, an even more difficult problem is to measure productivity where the DP staff spend time establishing that some proposed functions are not needed, and so need not be developed.

Number of function points

This method of measurement was developed by Allan Albrecht at IBM (Albrecht, 1979; Albrecht and Gaffney, 1983) and is widely used in the USA and UK (Fenton, 1991). Productivity is defined in terms of a weighted sum of delivered functional units – the number of inputs, outputs, enquiries, master files and interfaces. (This definition does not coincide with the more common meaning of the word 'function', a task performed by a program.) This method has major advantages over LOC: things like the number of input transaction types and the number of unique reports can be estimated early in the life-cycle, at about the time of the requirements definition document, so they can be used for early development effort estimates; they can be estimated by a relatively non-technical project member; and they avoid the effects of language and other implementation differences (Kemerer, 1987) – in fact, the motivation for developing the method was to avoid the mathematical paradox which arises when dealing with programs written in high-level languages, and examples in Jones (1986b) show that it succeeds.

Kemerer's results seem to validate Albrecht's claim that function points correlate well with eventual LOC. However, caution should be exercised when the method is used for early development effort estimates. Fen-

ton (1991) stated that, if function points are counted from a specification, and then from the implemented system, there can be an under-estimate in the former value of 400 to 2000% due to the introduction of non-specified functionality, and especially because there is less detail in a specification than in the actual implementation. (Effort estimation is discussed in Chapter 8.)

Albrecht found good agreement between his model and the costs for a set of commercial programs. However, according to Conte *et al.* (1986), the 'function units' in these programs were homogeneous and clearly defined. For other types of programs such as compilers, they are more difficult to define, and may differ significantly in size and scope, and in fact function points cannot be used effectively to compare dissimilar applications, or to measure the productivity of real-time software (Carlyle, 1987c). Conte also pointed out that this unit of measurement is highly correlated with program size. One could therefore conclude that it is not a better measure of productivity than LOC. However, according to Schach (1990), Capers Jones has observed errors in excess of 800% counting delivered source instructions, but 'only' 200% in counting function points (though this was apparently when programs in different languages were being compared, and LOC, as previously explained, should not be used in such circumstances, or at least not without an adjustment factor). Jones (1986b) claims that this method has been 'exceptionally fruitful' in triggering new concepts and fresh research, but warns that it has gaps and sources of ambiguities of its own. In particular, it is 'substantially incomplete', since it lacks any effective quantification for the structural aspects of software, such as branching, loops, and recursive calls. This is an area covered by McCabe's cyclomatic complexity measure (discussed in Chapter 8), and attempts are being made to develop a hybrid measure. More generally, the function point method has been extended to include complexity adjustments (e.g. batch versus on-line, and ease of use), and environmental factors (e.g. project management techniques and people skills) (Schach, 1988).

Jones (1986b) states that this method can be used to estimate lines-of-code sizes, and gives a conversion table (Table 2.4). He warns that these figures have a high margin of error (possibly ±50%), but nevertheless, the fact that such a table can even be considered does support the belief that there is a correlation between function points and lines of code.

Martin (1985) reported a study of 21 systems developed in six corporations, ranging in size from about 10K to 200K LOC, in which one function point was equivalent to 114 lines of COBOL, on average. This is very close to the Jones value of 106.

By contrast, Kemerer (1987) found that an average of 4.6 function points, or 1113 LOC, were coded per man-month, giving an average of 242 LOC per function point (the range was 58–430), for mainly COBOL programs, which is more than double the Jones and Martin values. However, it will be seen from

Table 2.4 Function point conversion table (Jones, 1986b)

Language	No. of statements required per function point
Assembler	320
C	150
COBOL, FORTRAN, and ALGOL	106
PASCAL	91
RPG and PL/1	80
MODULA-2 and ADA	71
BASIC, PROLOG, and LISP	64
Fourth-generation database	40
APL	32
Query languages	16
Spreadsheet languages	6

the productivity rates tabulated later, that the development rates based on LOC in Kemerer's projects were quite high, which may explain the discrepancy.

Halstead's (1977) software science

Seven years after this method was developed, Parikh (1984) stated that it was being experimented with at universities and large companies, but was not widely used.

The numbers of unique operators and unique operands, and the total occurrences of operators and of operands, are counted in different combinations. This method has the effect of weighting each line of code according to its difficulty, and thereby avoids problems which occur in the LOC method, such as whether or not to count comment lines. However, definition problems occur with this method as well (Conte *et al.*, 1986):

- Should data declarations be included?
- How should statement labels be counted?

It can be used to measure productivity across languages (Parikh, 1984), but the rules depend on which language the program was written in. Also, Halstead's volume metric is insensitive to such factors as personnel experience, hardware constraints, and the use of tools and modern programming practices, all of which can have a significant effect upon software development effort (Boehm, 1981). Operators and operands are features of written code, so Halstead's method, like LOC itself, can have little or no real value as a predictive estimating method (Macro and Buxton, 1987).

Nevertheless, experiments by Curtis *et al.* (1979b) showed that Halstead's effort metric is well correlated with the observed effort required to debug and modify small programs (Fairley, 1985). Woodfield (1979) found that a 25% increase in the number of distinct operands in a program doubled the programming effort. Still other experiments show that his time equation gives a good estimate of the implementation time actually observed, e.g. a difference of only 12% for some machine language experiments (Gordon and Halstead, 1976). Various authorities such as Halstead (1978), Curtis *et al.* (1978, 1979a, 1979b), Elshoff (1978), Milliman and Curtis (1980), and Sunohara *et al.* (1981), have shown a reasonable correlation between both Halstead's size (volume) metric and McCabe's (1976) cyclomatic complexity measure (Chapter 8), and both the amount of programming effort and the number of instructions in a program. Effort is therefore related to both LOC and complexity. However, no results have shown either measure to be a significantly better predictor of software development effort for large programs (over 1000 delivered source instructions) than is the number of instructions (Boehm, 1981). It is not surprising that current measures based on complexity do not give better results than measures based on size, as the most popular complexity measures are themselves all related to size (Conte *et al.*, 1986). Complexity is discussed in Chapter 8. I must also repeat the warning given in Chapter 1 about Halstead's software science, that the supporting evidence has been challenged, and even the theoretical basis of this method has been questioned.

Number of characters in source code

This measure was used by Matos and Jalics (1989) to compare the power of various languages, which is one factor affecting productivity, but it could also be used directly, i.e. you could measure the rate at which the characters were produced, in which case it would be a refinement of the LOC measure. (Matos and Jalics wrote the same program in a variety of languages – one third-generation and seven fourth-generation – and used the number of characters in the source code of the completed programs as a measure of the power of the languages, and in particular, the power of the fourth-

eneration compared to the third: the fewer characters required, the more powerful the language.)

2.1.3 PRODUCTIVITY IMPROVEMENT

Different authorities express a productivity improvement in different ways. Supposing a job which previously took five hours, can now be done in four. In a period of say 40 hours, ten of these jobs can now be done, compared to eight previously. Then:

- productivity has increased by ((10 – 8)/8=) 25%
- the time taken to do the job has decreased by ((5 – 4)/5=) 20%
- it now takes (4/5=) 80% as long to do the job

These three different numbers express the same improvement, so to aid comparison between different claims, a standard basis has been chosen,

time taken previously : time taken now

and the figures contained in the literature have been converted to this basis, where relevant. The productivity improvement ratio in the above example is (5/4=) 1.25 : 1.

Using LOC, a productivity improvement can be expressed as:

- a *difference* in LOC (LOC now – LOC previously); or
- a *ratio* of LOC (LOC now / LOC previously).

It may be debatable whether an improvement from:

1 to 3 statements per day (a ratio of 3:1 but a difference of only 2)

is superior to an improvement from:

20 to 40 (a ratio of only 2:1 but a difference of 20)

but I have used ratios because they conform to my general definition, they are a more common method, and they are more generally useful, e.g. ratios obtained from different languages can be compared directly against each other, whereas differences cannot. Also, as Conte *et al.* (1986) pointed out, many statistical tools can be applied to ratios. In any event, the top ten factors in the Walston and Felix (1977) survey when measured by differences, are also the top ten when measured by ratios (though not in the same sequence).

Because of the lack of a good predictive capability, estimates of how long a job would take have proved unreliable. In several cases recorded in the literature (McClure, 1969; Weinberg, 1971; Van Zijl and Evans, 1978; Yourdon, 1975) jobs took *twice* as long as had been estimated (though in some cases, the technical staff knew beforehand that the estimates were unrealistic), while others took only a *quarter* of the time, or even less (Boehm, 1973; Yourdon, 1975). (Estimation methods, and their lack of accuracy, are discussed in Chapter 8.) This places a question mark over claimed improvements: unless a program was developed in full using the two methods being compared, the magnitude of the claimed improvement is suspect.

2.2 PRODUCTIVE TIME

Staff can only spend part of their time on productive work, the rest of their time being taken up by meetings, paperwork, sick-leave, personal time, coffee breaks, machine downtime, supervision, and so on. Some of these activities, although strictly speaking non-productive, are part of a project – e.g. building security and recovery procedures into a system, progress meetings, co-ordination, rewriting code due to errors in specifications, and learning time if one is not familiar with the type of problem or special techniques which may be necessary – so the time spent on them should be included i.e. from the point of view of productivity measurement, these activities will be treated as productive. Nevertheless, they can be very time-consuming – in two projects quoted in

Boehm (1981), 'incidental' activities (reading, reviewing, meeting and fixing) consumed about 40% of the development effort – so their effect on productivity is significant and is discussed later.

Some non-productive activities consume time on a daily basis, e.g. time-recording and personal time; others are at irregular intervals, e.g. sick-leave, waiting time between jobs, and training. Furthermore, staff often work on more than one job at a time, so productivity measurements for each job must carefully exclude time spent on the other jobs.

For any comparison of productivity rates from different sources to be meaningful, all the rates should have been calculated on the same basis, i.e. should include and exclude the same activities, and should cover the same period of time. Where different authorities use different bases, their figures must be converted to a standard basis before they can be compared. The standard chosen here is LOC per day, with all activities connected with the project – whether strictly speaking productive or not – being included in the time. The purpose of this section is to estimate how much time is spent on the various non-productive activities, so that the necessary conversion factors can be derived.

Different authorities give different figures for the amount of time staff spend on productive and non-productive activities (Table 2.5). A time and motion study of 70 programmers at Bell Laboratories found that roughly 30% of their workday was devoted to non-project activities (Bairdain, 1964). Booz and Allen found that 25% of knowledge workers' time is spent on 'less productive' activities: seeking information, waiting, travel, copying, and transcribing (Martin, 1982b) – a 'knowledge worker' is someone who works with information and makes decisions, such as managers and professionals. McDonough (1981) claims that improvements in productivity of 10–25% are consistently being realized where supervisors are helped to make

Table 2.5 Percentage time spent on productive
activities

Source	%
Aron (1974)	91–95
McDonough (1981)	75–90
Common belief (Hayman, 1982)	80
McCue (1978)*	70–80
Booz and Allen (Martin, 1982b)	75
Maudlin (1983b)	70
Bairdain (1964)	70
McKenzie (1982)	55
Johnson (1980b)	50–80
Portman (Brooks, 1975)	50
Hayman (1982)	40
Average (approximate)	70

* excluding holidays and illness from non-productive
time

an environment more orderly, e.g. so that
staff do not have to wait for the necessary
data or documentation to do a rush job.
Similarly, Maudlin (1983b) estimated that
office productivity was only 60% of what it
should be, but could be improved to 90%
through better management alone (see
Chapter 4). Hayman (1982) rejects the
'common assumption' that a systems analyst
can be productive for 80% of a working year,
as this overlooks training time 'and all the
other things a systems analyst needs'. He
believes that a company is doing very well if
it gets 40% productive operation out of a
systems analyst.

There is a large discrepancy between these
figures, probably reflecting the differing activities that the various authorities included, so
it is necessary to examine the question in
more detail. How much of a person's time is
spent on each of these activities?

- The project being measured
- Other, unrelated jobs
- Non-productive activities
  - daily
  - irregular.

If staff work on more than one job at a time,
the amount of time spent on 'other, unrelated

jobs' may be considerable, but any good time-
recording system would apportion time
accurately between the various jobs. In the
present context therefore, this factor is only
relevant where productivity rates were based
on rough estimates rather than on facts, and
therefore may have included time spent on
unrelated tasks: it is of more relevance in the
context of predicting project completion
dates.

There are about (365/7*5=) 261 weekdays
in a year. Johnson (1980b) uses a figure of 240
man-days in a man-year, presumably excluding just vacations. McKenzie (1982) estimated
that the equivalent of 16 weeks per annum
(=31% of 52) is lost through irregular non-
productive activities, but his allowances for
training, sick-leave, and waiting time
between projects, seem rather high – for
example, staff are more likely to receive two
weeks training per annum than the four
weeks he quotes (see Chapter 9). Boehm
(1981) uses a figure of 228 productive days a
year (=87% of 261), but this only allows for
different types of leave, and not for training,
attending conferences, etc. On balance therefore, a figure of 10 weeks (about 20%) non-
productive time may be more typical and has
been used here, i.e. software engineers probably do productive work on about 80% or
210 of the weekdays in the year.

A normal working week is 40 hours, which
implies 8 hours a day for five days, though
the average programmer or analyst in the US,
because of overtime, tends to work 46–50
hours (Conte *et al.*, 1986; Jones, 1986b).
However, much of this time is lost through
daily non-productive activities. One manager
stated that 'typically only 4 or 5 hours of an 8-
hour day are applied to the project' (Putnam,
1978). At the other extreme, Conte *et al.*
(1986) use a figure of 8 productive hours a
day. Boehm (1981) also appears to use a
figure of 8 hours a day. Even allowing for his
assumption that slack time is kept to a
minimum by good management, this seems
too high. Presumably these authorities are

including overtime, or are not allowing for time-recording, lunch-time, personal time, etc. Johnson (1980b) for example, also uses a figure of 8 hours a day, but he explicitly includes non-productive time, and he also gives a figure of 6 hours a day for the actual time reported on a task, and 2 hours for 'general and administrative' activities. On balance therefore, software engineers are probably productive for 6 hours of each working day – 75% of the official working day.

Combining the figures from the preceding two paragraphs implies that software engineers are probably productive for (80% * 75% =) 60% of the working year.

In the literature some productivity rates are monthly and so some of the irregular non-productive activities, such as sick-leave and public ('bank') holidays, are relevant to a typical month, while others such as annual holidays and long training courses, are not. Of the 10 weeks worth of non-productive days per annum estimated above, perhaps half are relevant, i.e. 25 days per year, or about 2 days per month. Of the potential (365/7*5/12=) 22 working days in each month, therefore, perhaps 20 are spent on productive activities. This figure is used by Johnson (1980b), it was applied on the New York Times (NYT) project (Baker, 1972), and is also implied by Yourdon (1975) and Conte *et al.* (1986), though Chorafas (1986) uses the higher value of (18/0.8=) 22.5 (based on his statement that 18 worker-days is 80% of a worker-month). It means that people are productive for (20*6=) 120 hours per month. By comparison, Boehm (1981) and Kemerer (1987) use 152 hours, and Conte *et al.* (1986) 160 hours, but they appear to make no allowance for non-productive activities; while the SLIM (Software Life-cycle Methodology) model (Putnam, 1978; Putnam and Fitzsimmons, 1979) uses 168; and Inmon (1976) gives a figure of 200 hours per month – but his project was urgent, so the team probably worked a considerable amount of overtime.

Over periods longer than a month, the remaining irregular non-productive activities become relevant, but their effect is small (not more than 10%), so I have not adjusted the published rates quoted below in order to allow for it.

To sum up, a person does, on average:

6 hours productive work per day;
20 days productive work per month; and
210 days productive work per year;

and so is productive for ((6/8)*(210/261)=) 60% of the working year. These are the basic adjustment factors which have been applied to the published figures, where relevant, to arrive at the productivity rates listed.

Can the amount of productive time be increased? Better organization reduces waiting time; increased motivation reduces time spent on personal telephone calls; and so on. However, there are limits. Less time could be spent on training or attending conferences, but long-term productivity and morale might suffer.

2.3 PRODUCTIVITY RATES

The rates given in Tables 2.6–2.15 are the number of fully debugged and documented statements per person per day, unless otherwise stated (though many of my sources did not state if debugging and documentation time were included). Brief information – e.g. size and type of program, and language used – is given with the rates to assist comparison. Global averages are given first (Tables 2.6–2.12), then figures for individual projects or programs (Table 2.13). Better still would be figures for individual modules, as large programs might have been written by several programmers of varying ability and experience and therefore of varying productivity, and even different portions of a program vary in complexity with corresponding variations in productivity. Combined productivity figures are averages which obscure these effects. Conversely, the tools available affect

Table 2.6 Global averages

Source	Program type/detail	Statements/person/day
Sommerville (1989)	Complex real-time	2
	Straightforward business, if well understood	30
Van Tassel (1978)	Large systems	5– 10
Johnson (1980b)		6–180
Johnson (1980b)	Commercial, 1970–78, including comments, total project time	
	Large (> 2 man-years); 11 projects	23 (range 9–44)
	Small (< 2 man-years); 5 projects	69 (range 54–100)
Johnson (1980b)	Difficult programs	19 verbs per day
	Medium	25 verbs per day
	Easy	33 verbs per day
Pomberger (1984)	350 real-time programs, 150 000 LOC	10 (Assembler)
	174 applications programs, 17 882 LOC	12 (various languages)
Pomberger (1984)	Extremely difficult	about 2[a]
	Very difficult	about 4[a]
	Difficult	about 8[a]
	Medium	about 10[a]
	Easy	about 40[a]
	Very easy	about 90[a]
Albrecht and Gaffney (1983)	Business applications	17
Boeing (1979)	Difficult programs	5
	Medium programs	13
	Easy programs	25
Black *et al.* (1977): (Boeing)	Real-time	1
	Signal processing	3
	Logical	4
	Report/commercial	6
	Mathematical	8
Pirow (1981)	900 LOC	12
Ingham (1976)	11 installations, typically 30–50 programmers, COBOL	mode[b] 13 (50% in range 7–22)
Bell *et al.* (1987)	Average programmer	10–20
Macro and Buxton (1987)	Assembler	5–10[c]
	High-level language	20–30[c]
Martin (1985)	COBOL	20
	4GL	40[d]
Walston and Felix (1977)	60 projects, 28 languages, 4–467K LOC (average 20K), including comments	median[e] 14 (range 1–50)
Brooks (1981) – (subset of (Walston/Felix))	Small – < 100 man-months	
	Unstructured	15
	Structured	20
	Large – > 100 man-months	
	Unstructured	15
	Structured	14
Kemerer (1987)	15 projects, average 187 000 LOC, excluding comments, business applications, mainly COBOL	56 (range 20–125)

Table 2.6   *continued*

Source	Program type/detail	Statements/person/day
Brustman (1978)	Real-time, interactive command and control (6 samples, average 143K LOC)	3
	Special-purpose operating system (13 samples, average 58K)	5
	Process control (6 samples, average 9K)	10
	Interactive information retrieval (13 samples, average 78K)	17
	Models and simulators (9 samples, average 77K)	18
	Batch (13 samples, average 27K)	20
Howden (1982)	Large projects (1000K LOC)	17
	Medium size projects (100K LOC)	34
Chorafas (1986)	Mature programmers, COBOL	50–60[f]
Yourdon (1975)	Operating systems	1–3
	Systems programs – compilers	5–10
	Application programs	10–15
	Structured programs	35–65
	Super-programmers	50–200
Brooks (1975)	Large programs (>300K LOC)	
	many interactions	4
	few interactions	24
Jones (1979): Assembler	Superlarge (>512K LOC)	4 (range 2–13)
	Large (64–512K LOC)	8 (range 3–25)
	Medium (16–64K LOC)	13 (range 6–50)
	Low-Medium (2–16K LOC)	20 (range 10–63)
	Small (<2K LOC)	33 (range 17–100)
Jones (1986b)	Excluding re-used code ('development' productivity)	up to about 15
	Including re-used code ('delivery' productivity)	> 150 possible
	No re-use	8
	25% re-use	13
	50% re-use	19
	75% re-use	42
Boehm (1973)	Machine instructions: 10–90 percentile	
	1955; machine language	3–45
	1970; FORTRAN, JOVIAL	8–170
	1985; Structured Programming	30–500 (predicted)
Conte *et al.* (1986)		1–75

[a] Including analysis and documentation.
[b] The mode of a set of numbers is that value which occurs with the greatest frequency, i.e. it is the most common value (Spiegel).
[c] All life-cycle activities.
[d] 100 not uncommon.
[e] The median of a set of numbers arranged in order of magnitude is the middle value, or the arithmetic mean of the two middle values (Sykes, 1977; Spiegel, 1972). Half of the numbers are therefore greater than the median, and half are less. The median is also called the 50th percentile.
[f] Documented and tested.

the productivity of every program they are used for; and the ability and experience of the systems analyst affects the productivity of every program he analyses and specifies.

Some of the rates include programming time only, while others include all project activities, depending on the information source.

Caution should be observed when comparing productivity rates from different sources. For example, different organizations and researchers use different line-counting methods and, as previously discussed, this alone can cause variations of over 10:1. Similarly, variations of a further 10:1 or more can be caused by counting or not counting the effort spent on requirements analysis, testing, management, non-delivered support software, and so on. Where sources specified which lines were counted, and which activities, these are stated, but many do not, as a result of which 'much of the literature on software engineering productivity cannot be used for serious research' (Jones, 1986b).

The Jones (1986b) values were synthesized from actual projects, or were produced by an effort-estimation model. Although the model was calibrated against actual systems, caution should be observed when using the values because of the possibility of distortions due to any inaccuracies in either the model or the data it was calibrated against, or simplifications in either the model or the synthesized data.

The Boehm (1981) figures include the total project effort. If programmer time only (detailed design, code and unit test) is taken into account, then the figures should roughly be doubled. The Conte *et al.* (1986) figures are based on the effort to design, code, unit test, and system test, and presumably therefore include non-programming effort.

I have used unweighted averages, i.e. I have taken the productivity rates for the individual projects, and averaged them, rather than adding the lines of code and the man-months for the projects, and then dividing the totals. This method avoids the rates from many small projects being dominated by those from a few large projects – i.e. it is biased in favour of small projects – and therefore generally resulted in higher average productivity rates. As small projects are probably in the majority, this seems an advantage rather than a disadvantage.

It is notable that there are vast differences in productivity between projects of similar size, or the same language, application area, etc. This could mean, for example, that none of these factors has a major impact on productivity; or that an additional, possibly unsuspected, factor has the major impact; or, more likely, that several factors have a significant impact.

2.3.1 HIGHEST RATES

- 1st (Table 2.6): the range of 30–500 given by Boehm (1973) for structured programs, but this was only a prediction and anyway is the number of machine instructions.
- 2nd (Table 2.13): the 240 of Halstead (1977), achieved on very small programs which only took about half an hour each to write – it would be dangerous to generalize from it, as one cannot expect the intensity achieved during a short experiment to be maintained over the months required to complete more typical projects. Conte *et al.* (1986) illustrated this graphically with an athletics analogy: 'Someone who could run each 100 meters of a marathon in 10.2 seconds would be considered superhuman'. Also, the rate presumably excludes systems analysis time.
- 3rd (also in Table 2.13): range of 96–214 given by Brooks (1975) which was also for small programs.
- joint 4th: range of 50–200 given by Yourdon (1975) for super-programmers (Table 2.6), and by Wang (1984) for 44 students on a small (463 LOC), structured program – one of the students may have been a super-programmer (Table 2.13).

Table 2.7 Source: Jones (1986b)

		Lines of code per day	
		All time (range)	Coding time only (range)
SIZE (TOTAL LOC)			
0–4K	11 systems	10 (5–17)	37 (20–67)
4–16K	19 systems	8 (4–13)	33 (17–50)
16–64K	7 systems	7 (3–15)	29 (15–50)
64–256K	20 systems	5 (2–25)	29 (21–43)
>256K	2 systems	7 (6–8)	34 (31–38)
Combined	59 systems, average 67K	7 (2–25)	32 (15–67)
AVERAGE TEAM SIZE			
0–4	11 systems, average 1K LOC	10 (5–17)	37 (20–67)
4–8	16 systems, average 8K	9 (4–13)	34 (28–46)
8–50	8 systems, average 46K	6 (3–15)	25 (15–38)
50–80	11 systems, average 168K	5 (4–8)	30 (23–38)
>80	8 systems, average 175K	3 (2–5)	27 (21–32)
Combined	(54 systems, average 70K)	7 (2–17)	31 (15–67)
DURATION IN MONTHS			
0–4	12 systems, average 2K LOC	11 (6–17)	40 (25–67)
4–8	12 systems, average 9K	9 (5–15)	32 (20–38)
8–16	11 systems, average 41K	5 (3–8)	26 (17–32)
16–24	11 systems, average 94K	4 (2–5)	28 (15–34)
>24	8 systems, average 268K	4 (2–8)	29 (21–38)
Combined	54 systems, average 70K	7 (2–17)	31 (15–67)
LANGUAGE			
ASSEMBLER	3 systems, average 50K	15 (5–25)	32 (15–43)
C	5 systems, average 62K	6 (3–10)	31 (21–46)
COBOL	38 systems, average 81K	7 (2–17)	30 (17–50)
PASCAL	2 systems, average 10K	10 (9–11)	38 (38–38)
PL/1	3 systems, average 75K	7 (3–13)	37 (30–50)
ADA	2 systems, average 100K	3 (2–4)	32 (30–34)
BASIC	2 systems, average 2K	10 (6–14)	38 (25–50)
4GL	1 system, size 50 LOC	6	25
APL	2 systems, average 6K	7 (6–8)	45 (40–50)
Spreadsheet	1 system, size 400 LOC	9	67
Combined	59 systems, average 67K	7 (2–25)	32 (15–67)

- 6th (Table 2.6): 6–180 by Johnson (1980b). No further details were given, and the top of the range may have been a rare exception.
- 7th (Table 2.6): 8–170 given by Boehm (1973) – unlike his highest rate, this was not a prediction, but it was also for machine instructions.
- 8th (Table 2.10): 165 for the best of the Yourdon 78–80 projects (Conte *et al.*, 1986). Comments were included, and possibly a large amount of re-used code.
- 9th (Table 2.13): 155 given by Matsumoto (1989) which was equivalent assembler source lines, and included re-used code.
- 10th (Table 2.6): Jones (1986b) gave a rate

Table 2.8 Basic COCOMO model

Mode	Small 2K LOC	Interm. 8K LOC	Medium 32K LOC	Large 128K LOC	Very large 512K LOC
Organic[1]	20	19	18	16	–
Semi-detached[2]	15	13	11	9	8
Embedded[3]	12	9	7	5	4

Source: Boehm (1981).

[1] In organic mode projects the teams are small and the development staff are familiar with the application and the environment (thus minimizing learning and communication); the constraints are flexible (i.e. the specifications can be negotiated to reduce development effort, e.g. 'what you really want is what I have written'); and early completion is not a priority.

[2] Semi-detached mode projects are in between extremes 1 and 3, e.g. contain a mixture of experienced and inexperienced people.

[3] In embedded mode projects the staff are working in areas unknown to them, reliability is very important, and the project must operate within tight and inflexible constraints of hardware, software, regulations and operational procedures. An example is an air traffic control system – the environment in which it will be run cannot be changed.

of more than 150 as possible if re-used code is included. This figure is much higher than the other rates he gives for re-used code (up to only 42), which implies that the 150 is rarely achieved.

To sum up, the factors that accompanied – and may have been responsible for – the highest productivity rates quoted above, are: small size, high ability, structured programming, and re-used code. If comments are included in the line count, or if the count is based on machine instructions instead of source instructions, then a very high productivity figure is obtained, but this is misleading.

2.3.2 VARIATIONS BETWEEN ORGANIZATIONS

The efficiency rates quoted in Table 2.14 are not LOC, so they cannot be directly compared with the other figures. They are based on one project per organization.

The figures given by Jones (1986b) indicate that 'leading-edge' organizations are twice as productive as 'trailing-edge' organizations for development, and four times as productive for maintenance. (Leading-edge organizations use automated estimating and project planning and tracking, whereas trailing-edge organizations use manual methods; leading-edge organizations use joint workshops and prototypes to determine users' requirements, whereas trailing-edge organizations use text requests and responses; leading-edge organizations use standard designs and re-usable code, whereas trailing-edge organizations hand code nearly all modules; and so on. (A prototype is an *initial* and *partial* version of a system. This technique is discussed in Chapter 8.))

The productivity rates quoted in Table 2.15 are from three of the five data sets comprising the Conte data used earlier in Table 2.10. Each set was from a single organization.

These figures indicate that some organizations have similar productivity, but some – e.g. Bailey and Basili – appear to have a much higher productivity than others – perhaps five times as high. However, it is appropriate to repeat here the caution about comparing productivity rates from different sources: variations of well over 5:1 can be caused, for example, just by different organizations or researchers using different line-counting methods, and it may be significant that Bailey and Basili (1981) include comment lines, whereas Wingfield (1982) does not. Wide variations in reported productivity therefore

Table 2.9   Source: Boehm (1981)

		LOC per day (mean and range)	
	No of projects	*Total*	*Equivalent[1]*
Language			
Assembler	20	9 (1–33)	8 (1–33)
JOVIAL	5	10 (2–29)	10 (2–29)
Other High-level	3	10 (6–16)	9 (6–15)
COBOL	5	14 (3–43)	13 (3–43)
FORTRAN	24	20 (1–64)	17 (1–44)
PASCAL	2	22 (17–28)	22 (17–28)
PL/1	4	25 (5–63)	25 (5–63)
Combined (63 projects, average 80K)		15 (1–64)	14 (1–63)
Size (Total LOC)			
0–4K	6	13 (2–20)	10 (2–17)
4–16K	18	19 (4–63)	19 (4–63)
16–64K	25	15 (1–64)	12 (1–36)
64–256K	8	15 (3–29)	14 (3–29)
>256K	6	11 (1–28)	8 (1–19)
Combined	63	15 (1–64)	14 (1–63)
Application type			
Process control; 10 projects, 3–37K LOC		7 (1–20)	6 (1–15)
Man/machine interaction; 13 projects, 2–1,150K		7 (1–17)	7 (1–17)
Operating systems, compilers; 8 projects, 6–27K		14 (1–33)	14 (1–33)
Support (tools, utilities); 8 projects, 4–464K		14 (4–29)	14 (4–29)
Business; 7 projects, 4–293K		18 (3–43)	17 (3–43)
Scientific; 17 projects, 3–390K		27 (3–64)	22 (2–63)
Combined (63 projects)		15 (1–64)	14 (1–63)

[1] The 'equivalent' line count is obtained by reducing the total line count by a factor which depends, amongst other things, on the number of lines of re-used code in the program. This is done in order to allow for the smaller amount of effort required to re-use code than to write new code. Productivity rates based on total LOC should therefore be higher than those based on equivalent LOC, and this is confirmed by the actual figures. Only about half of the projects included re-used code, so the effect on those which did is greater than is apparent from the above figures. The average productivity rate for just those projects was 16 lines of code per day based on total LOC, compared to only 11 based on the equivalent line count.

do not necessarily reflect true differences in productivity.

2.3.3   TRENDS

In 1973, Boehm stated that productivity was increasing by 9% p.a. (based on the number of machine instructions), and he predicted that the rate of increase would remain constant until beyond 1985. Eight years later, he stated that this had not happened (Boehm, 1981), and it is apparent from the figures quoted in Table 2.16, most of which are less than 9%, that many authorities share his newer and more pessimistic view. Similarly, the figures given by Jones (1986b) and Hodges (1987b) show a decline in the rate of increase (Table 2.17).

Jones (1986b) also used a constant figure of 2000 LOC per programmer per year from 1950 through to 2000, in a table of estimated worldwide annual code production, which implies a *zero* rate of growth, but this may have been an intentional simplification, or

Table 2.10   5 data sets[1] – Source: Conte *et al.* (1986)

Data set	LOC per day (mean and range)[2]
Wingfield (1982): 15 projects, average 180K LOC	9 (range 3–22)
Belady and Lehman (1979): 33 projects, average 90K	11 (range 1–25)
Boehm (1981): 63 projects, average 80K	15 (range 1–64)
Bailey and Basili (1981): 19 projects, average 38K	39 (range 19–103)
Yourdon 1978–80 (DeMarco 1981b): 17 projects, average 34K	53 (range 13–165)
Combined: 147 projects, average 80K	21 (range 1–165)
Comments	
without (Boehm; Wingfield):	
78 projects, average 100K LOC	6 (range 1–64)
with (Bailey/Basili), Yourdon 78–80:	
36 projects, average 36K LOC	36 (range 13–165)
Average team size (all 5 data sets):	
0–3 (36 projects, average 16 000 LOC)	43 (range 10–165)
3–5 (20 projects, average 23 000 LOC)	23 (range 3–103)
5–10 (36 projects, average 36 000 LOC)	19 (range 2–51)
10–30 (29 projects, average 92 000 LOC)	10 (range 1–28)
>30 (26 projects, average 265 000 LOC)	6 (range 1–20)
Duration in months (all 5 data sets):	
0–10 (29 projects, average 12 000 LOC)	27 (range 2–103)
10–13 (27 projects, average 32 000 LOC)	17 (range 2–73)
13–19 (36 projects, average 43 000 LOC)	29 (range 3–119)
19–30 (28 projects, average 116 000 LOC)	20 (range 1–165)
>30 (27 projects, average 218 000 LOC)	10 (range 1–57)
Total LOC[2] (all 5 data sets):	
0–4K (7 projects)	14 (range 2–20)
4–16K (42 projects)	22 (range 2–64)
16–64K (52 projects)	26 (range 1–165)
64–256K (34 projects)	19 (range 3–103)
>256K (12 projects)	12 (range 1–28)

[1] There were a total of 147 projects with 12 million LOC (and an average of about 80 000 per project). The five data sets were: Boehm (1981): 63 projects, 5 million LOC (average about 80 000 LOC per project), comments excluded; Belady and Lehman (1979): 33 projects, 3 million LOC (average about 90 000 per project); Bailey and Basili (1981): 19 projects, 700 000 LOC (average about 38 000), since 1976, mainly FORTRAN, comments included; Yourdon 78–80 (DeMarco, 1981b), 17 projects, 600 000 LOC (average about 34 000), COBOL, comments included, mainly business, high productivity rates, suggesting a large amount of re-used code; and Wingfield (1982): 15 projects, nearly 3 million LOC (average about 180 000), COBOL, comments excluded, mainly business. Conte also had a sixth data set, comprising 40 projects, but the data was proprietary and so was not published, and therefore has not been included here. The Belady and Lehman data is apparently a subset of the Walston and Felix (1977) data. There are actually 19 projects in the Yourdon 1978–80 data set, but two were eliminated by Conte; one because it was not completed, and the other because it was an 'outlier' on productivity.

[2] Productivity rates based on Total LOC, i.e. they included re-used code, thereby giving a misleadingly high productivity.

may reflect the decreasing amount of time available for development, due to the increasing number of systems which have to be maintained (Chapter 8).

The global productivity rates (Tables 2.6–2.21) vary widely, so it is difficult to draw any conclusions from them, but they do not appear to show any significant trend, and in fact it could be concluded from them that productivity remained roughly constant, at about 20 LOC per day, over the fifteen or so years covered. However, the figures may cover too short a period for a trend to be discernible: 'There is no guarantee that as many as eight years are adequate to establish a trend' (Flaherty, 1985).

Worse, Nies (1983) and Cohen (1983) claimed that productivity was *decreasing*.

Table 2.11 Effect of re-used code (Boehm, 1981; Bailey/Basili, 1981)

Size (Total LOC)[2]	LOC per day[1] (mean and range)	
	Total	*Equivalent*
0–4K (7 projects)	14 (2–20)	12 (2–19)
4–16K (26 projects)	25 (4–64)	23 (4–63)
16–64K (29 projects)	17 (1–64)	14 (1–36)
64–256K (14 projects)	28 (3–103)	21 (3–42)
>256K (6 projects)	11 (1–28)	8 (1–19)
Combined (82 projects)	21 (1–103)	17 (1–63)

[1] Only about half of the projects in the data sets actually included re-used code, so the effect on those which did is greater than is apparent from the figures. The productivity rate for just those projects was 26 LOC per day based on total LOC, compared to only 19 based on the equivalent line count.

[2] The size categories are based on Total LOC for both columns, to ensure that the same projects are being compared. For example, a project with 5K Total LOC, but only 3K Equivalent LOC, would be shown under 4–16K: *both* productivity rates for it would be shown under 4–16K.

Table 2.12 New LOC[1] (Bailey and Basili, 1981)

Size (Total LOC)	LOC per day (mean and range)	
	New	*Equivalent*
0–4K (1 project)	19	19
4–16K (8 projects)	29 (16–46)	31 (20–49)
16–64K (4 projects)	24 (16–30)	26 (18–35)
64–256K (6 projects)	26 (16–36)	30 (18–42)
Combined (19 projects)	26 (16–46)	29 (18–49)

[1] This set of rates, for only that data set from Conte which gave the number of lines of new code, compares the productivity rates for new code with the corresponding adjusted rates. If the adjustment factor is accurate, then the adjusted rates should be very similar to the corresponding new rates. The close agreement between the 'new' and 'equivalent' productivity rates shows that the adjustment factor used is quite accurate.

This may be true of *conventionally*-developed software – the rate of increase in the past has been so low that just one factor (such as the easier work being done by end users with fourth-generation software, or lower quality staff, as discussed in Chapters 6 and 9) could reverse the trend – but seems unlikely to be true of the *overall* productivity, i.e. if the use of fourth-generation software and application packages are taken into account.

Furthermore, apart from the anomalously low productivity for 1972–1975, the projects in Boehm's (1981) own data set *do* seem to show a steady increase in productivity over the years, in apparent contradiction to his newer and more pessimistic view (Table 2.18) – and, in fact, one *could* infer that productivity approximately doubled in about ten years, which is equal to a consistent increase of around 7% every year, and is only slightly lower than his 1973 prediction of 9% p.a.

On balance, therefore, I would conclude that productivity is increasing steadily at about 5% p.a. Nevertheless, whether the true figure is 1% or 10% (or −10%) caution must be observed when comparing productivity rates from different years, to allow for this effect.

However, *all* of these figures seem too *low*. They may be true for *conventionally*-developed systems, but if fourth-generation software and the use of application packages are taken into account, the *effective* increase should be much higher. This is confirmed by Martin (1981, 1988) who, quoting an unnamed IBM survey, stated that the number of installed applications was increasing by 45% p.a., which suggests that productivity is increasing rapidly (Chapter 12). Similarly, the number of deployed systems at the Department of Defense in 1960–1978 increased by 32% p.a. compound, from 3 systems to 450 (Charette, 1986); while the table of estimated worldwide annual code production in Jones (1986b) implies a 26% p.a. compound increase in the cumulative total lines of active installed code in 1950–

Table 2.13 Individual projects

Source	Project details	Statements/person/day
Johnson (1980b)	Commercial, 1970–78, including comments, total project time	
	large project (140K LOC),	
	limited innovation/new technology	41
	small project (6K LOC),	
	high motivation, known technology	100
Prentiss (1977)	Viking: 278 575 LOC	8
Brooks (1975)	operating system; Assembler	3–4
	MULTICS: Operating System; PL/1	6
	compilers; Assembler	10–14
Brooks (1975)	800 000 (words?); operating system; batch	2–5
	120 000 ("); compilers; batch	10–16
	8 300 ("); " ; "	19
	32 000 ("); " ; on-line	38
Weinberg and Schulman (1974)	Small (33–166 LOC)	4–33
	Quick completion not required	14
	Quick completion required	27
Wang (1984)	(average of 44 students)	110[a]
	PASCAL, 463 LOC, structured	2[b]
Harr (1969)	Operational/Control, 83 programmers, 52K words	3
	Maintenance/Control, 60 programmers, 51K words	11
	Compiler, 9 programmers, 38K words	11
	Translator, 13 programmers, 25K words	
Pomberger (1984)	(Assembler)	
	Control program, real time system, 77 000 LOC	6
	Operating system, 26 000 LOC	11
	File catalog system, 7000 LOC	14
	SPOOL system, 24 000 LOC	17
	Database compiler, 7000 LOC	39
Van Zijl and Evans (1978)	Batch: junior staff	19
	experienced staff	32
	Interactive	51
Matsumoto (1989)	Excluding re-used code	80[c]
	Including re-used code	155
Halstead (1977)	FORTRAN, 11 very small programs (7–59 LOC)	240
Baker (1972)	New York Times; 83 324 LOC; COBOL, PL/1, Assembler	
	all time	32
	programming time only	65
McClure (1978)	SAMI: COBOL, Assembler; 10 000 LOC	17
	Australian Payroll: COBOL: 30 329 LOC	27
	McAuto: COBOL – IMS	31&49
	– Application	36&58
	PAMUSE: operating system; 32 700 LOC	40
	FORTRAN Engine: PL/1; 27 600 LOC	65
Inmon (1976)	COBOL; 31 000 LOC; programming time; CPT: Structured Programming; Walkthroughs	66[d]
Orkins and Weiss (1975)	Small programs (191 LOC)	105
Brooks (1975)	Small programs	96–214

[a] Range 50–200.
[b] Words/day.
[c] Equivalent assembler source lines.
[d] Excluding overtime.

Table 2.14 Efficiency variations between organizations (van der Poel, 1982)

Lines of Code	Sample size	Efficiency Range	Efficiency Average	Efficiency Ratio
0– 9999	10	17–90	40	5.3 : 1
10 000–19 999	3	16–28	21	1.8 : 1
20 000–39 999	2	19–25	22	1.3 : 1
40 000–59 999	2	23–25	24	1.1 : 1
60 000–79 999	1		23	
COMBINED	18	16–90	32	5.6 : 1

Table 2.15 Productivity variations between organizations (Conte *et al.*, 1986)

	No. of Projects	Bailey/ Basili	Belady/ Lehman	Wingfield	Range	Ratio
Total LOC						
0–3999	1	19	–	–	19	–
4000–15 999	20	39	11	–	11–39	4:1
16 000–63 999	16	34	12	3	3–34	11:1
64 000–255 999	24	46	8	11	8–46	6:1
256 000–	6	–	13	6	6–13	2:1
Combined	67	39	11	9	9–39	4:1
Duration (months)						
0–10	15	46	13	–	13–46	4:1
10–13	8	38	13	14	13–38	3:1
13–19	17	40	7	5	5–40	8:1
19–30	12	25	16	7	7–25	4:1
>30	15	–	6	10	6–10	2:1
Combined	67	39	11	9	9–39	4:1
Team Size						
0–3	10	38	–	–	38	–
3–5	6	66	20	–	20–66	3:1
5–10	20	33	12	–	12–33	3:1
10–30	16	–	6	14	6–14	2:1
>30	15	–	10	5	5–10	2:1

2000 (41% p.a. in 1960–1980). However, these rates of increase seem very *high* – i.e. they go to the other extreme. In the case of Jones, this is surprising, as the figures he gives for the total lines of active code in the world (e.g. 5 billion in 1980), are much lower than the estimates given for individual languages in Chapter 6, and the Martin (1985) estimate of 116 billion lines of code in mainframe instal-lations alone. It may be significant that his figures show a large drop from 1980 onwards: a predicted increase of only 13% p.a. in 1980–1990, and just 4% p.a. in 1990–2000. The reason for this is not clear. It is partly due to the increasingly larger base the increases are measured against, but is not due to a change in development productivity, as this was assumed to remain constant. Presumably, an

Table 2.16 Quoted productivity increases: various sources

Source	Dates applicable	Rate of increase (% p.a.)
Bell *et al.* (1987)	previous 10 years	< 1 (in Britain)
Ever (1980)		3
Tanaka (1977)		3
Martin (1983a)	previous 10 years	4
Dolotta *et al.* (1976)	1955–1985	4
Schach (1987)		4
Boehm/Standish (1983)	next decade	4 (prediction)
Morrisey and Wu (1979)		5–6
Matsumoto[1] (1989)	1977–1985	6 (equivalent assembler source lines)
Charette[2] (1986)	1960–1978	6
Liquor[3] (1986)	previous 10 years	7
Flaherty (1985)	1977–1984	7
Ohno (1989)		9
Martin (1982b)	1955–1985	9
Boehm (1973)	1955–1985	9 (based on machine instructions)
Flaherty (1985)	1977–1984	15 (equivalent assembler)
Average (approximate)		5% p.a. (excluding equivalent assembler/ machine instructions)

[1] Rate applies to both with and without re-used code, and is from projects developed at the Toshiba Fuchu Software Factory.
[2] Refers only to the Department of Defense.
[3] Refers to the doubling of productivity in ten years at one organization, the Liquor Control Board of Ontario.

increasing proportion of the systems being developed have only a short life, or many older systems are being retired.

2.3.4 FACTORS INFLUENCING PRODUCTIVITY

Several factors appear to influence productivity and are readily identified from the above rates:

- productivity depends on the type of application;
- productivity decreases as program size increases;
- productivity decreases as team size increases;
- productivity decreases as project duration increases;
- productivity decreases as complexity increases;
- productivity increases with high-level languages;
- advanced techniques increase productivity;
- productivity increases with ability;
- on-line programming increases productivity;
- productivity increases with experience;
- productivity increases if it is set as a goal.

What is less certain is *how much* effect these factors have. This is discussed later, e.g. high-level languages in Chapter 6, and ability in Chapter 9, but it is interesting to try to assign provisional values based on the preceding information. The scarcity of additional information about the above productivity rates, the different units of measure, the many different factors affecting productivity and the interrelationships between them, make it dangerous to assign even provisional values to the magnitude of their effect. In addition, there may be other factors, such as user/machine interface requirements, which influence productivity but which are not

Table 2.17 Quoted productivity increases: Jones and Hodges

Source	Dates applicable	Rate of increase, % p.a. compound
Jones (1986b)	1964–1974	9
	1974–1984	3
	1964–1984	6
Hodges (1987b)	1955–1965	7
	1965–1975	3
	1975–1985	3
	1955–1985	4

Table 2.18 Boehm's data

Date	No. of projects	LOC per day (mean and range) Total	Equivalent
1964–1971	7	13 (1–39)	13 (1–39)
1972–1975	13	8 (1–28)	7 (1–19)
1976	10	14 (3–44)	13 (3–44)
1977	10	17 (2–63)	15 (2–63)
1978	16	21 (4–64)	16 (4–36)
1979	7	21 (10–43)	20 (10–43)
Combined	63	15 (1–64)	14 (1–63)

revealed by the rates – the attributes recorded for each rate really just tell us what the researcher *thought* might influence productivity. There are also some apparent contradictions between the rates, the most serious of which is possibly the effect which size has. Some of the rates indicate that productivity decreases rapidly with increasing program or system size, while other rates show no such effect. In particular, the Conte data shows little, if any, decrease in productivity with increasing product size (or rather, shows an increase in productivity with size for projects up to 16–64K, and a decrease for larger projects), but shows a large decrease in productivity with increasing *team* size, and partly shows a decrease in productivity with increasing project duration, even though product size increased with increasing team size and duration (Table 2.10). An examin-

ation of the data shows that some small projects were developed by relatively large teams with low productivity, while some large projects were developed by relatively small teams with high productivity. The Jones (1986b) figures also mostly show a decrease in productivity with increasing team size and project duration (Table 2.7). The effect of size on productivity is discussed in Chapter 8.

Despite these difficulties, some tentative values are assigned (Table 2.19) which show, e.g., a complex program may take up to eight times as long to write as a simple one, and a program may take up to four times longer to write in a low-level language than in a high-level language.

These figures can be viewed as the maximum ranges which will normally be encountered; higher values are possible in exceptional circumstances and the differences will be much smaller in the average installation.

Taken together, these factors indicate that productivity differences of well over 10 000:1 can occur. (By comparison, the SOFTCOST cost estimation model (Tausworthe, 1981) assumes a productivity range of 50:1 for projects of the same size. The Basic version of the COCOMO model (Boehm, 1981) gives a range of only 1.5:1 (excluding the effect of size), and the intermediate version of this

Table 2.19 Factors affecting productivity

Factor	Effect ratio
Program complexity	8:1
Program size	8:1
Team size	8:1
Application type	8:1
Re-used code	5:1
High-level languages	4:1
Advanced programming techniques	4:1
Project duration	3:1
Ability	3:1
Organic versus embedded mode	3:1
On-line programming	2:1
Experience	2:1
Productivity as a goal	2:1

model a range of around 1000:1 (also excluding the effect of size). Adding the effect of size typically increases the ranges by a factor of about three – see Chapter 8.) However, the above factors are not independent, e.g.:

- large programs are generally also more complex (but see comment below), so the 8:1 range for program size includes some allowance for complexity, and therefore the productivity on a small, simple program would seldom be as high as $(8 * 8 =)$ 64 times the productivity on a large, complex program;
- the productivity of large teams may be low because of the increased communication between the members of the team, or because the programs are larger and more complex; and
- the relationship between on-line programming, experience and productivity is not a simple one (Chapter 6).

For this reason, when deciding which factors to include in the intermediate version of his COCOMO model, Boehm (1981) made a point of eliminating those factors which were closely correlated.

For the same reason, Boehm (1981), Conte *et al.* (1986) and Brooks (1981) are critical of the findings of the Walston and Felix (1977) survey, as no attempt was made to factor out the interactions among the attributes or variables, many of which are strongly related. For example, Walston and Felix found a large productivity effect due to Chief Programmer Teams, but that may merely have been because this technique was used more often on smaller projects, so the high productivity observed was actually due to the small size of the projects and not to the team organization; or because the technique was used with other modern programming practices such as structured programming, so the high productivity was actually due to that.

There is a difference of opinion on the relationship between size and complexity. According to Aron (1974), complexity is proportional to the square of the size, whereas Boehm (1981) maintains that complexity is an inherent property of the code which is independent of size: large programs, for example, may contain a large amount of simple housekeeping code. There is truth in both points of view. Complexity is discussed in Chapter 8.

Effect of type of application on productivity

Some of the productivity rates quoted earlier indicate that productivity depends heavily on the type of application, and this factor is used in seven of the nine cost-estimation models surveyed by Boehm (1981), but Boehm does not believe this to be the case. For example, productivity is very low for the development of operating systems, but that may just be because operating systems are large and complex, and not because they are operating systems.

2.4 MAINTENANCE PRODUCTIVITY

This chapter concentrated on development productivity. Little information is available on maintenance productivity. Figures by Jones (1986b) indicate that enhancement productivity is 20–60% lower than development productivity (Chapter 13); while according to DeMarco (1982), it is one or two orders of magnitude lower. Maintenance productivity is more difficult to measure than development productivity. Some methods count the total number of systems, programs, or LOC a programmer is maintaining, or the number of change requests he handles or modules he modifies, and divide by the amount of time he spends on maintenance (Parikh, 1984; Conte *et al.*, 1986). Function points may be one of the better methods for measuring development productivity, but it suffers from a serious disadvantage for measuring maintenance productivity: major changes can be made to a product without changing the number of function points (Schach, 1990).

Walston and Felix (1977) found that one person could maintain between 5000 and 24 000 LOC (the median value was 15 000).

Studies quoted by Boehm ((1981), which included Griffin (1980), Graver (1977), and Lientz and Swanson *et al.* (1980) show an even wider range, from 3000 to 132 000 LOC, with most values being in the 10 000–40 000 range (the median was 20 000 – quite close to the Walston and Felix value). Boehm himself gives the much lower figure of 8000.

Although the number of lines of code maintained by a programmer indicates his productivity, it varies to a considerable extent, depending on the structure of the system, programs, and documentation, the reliability of the software, the programmer's experience and application knowledge, and the adequacy of vendor support (Parikh, 1984).

The 2 million lines of code studied by Johnson (1980b) were maintained by 40 programmers, giving an average of 50 000 LOC per programmer, but he warned that this ratio varies from one organization to another, as it depends on definitions, and the nature or type of support activities. For example, his lines of code counts include comments and job control statements.

Gilb (1988) stated that, depending on its quality, 0.1–0.5 minutes are spent per year maintaining each line of non-commentary source code. If we assume 6 hours productive work per day, and 210 days per year, this means each programmer can maintain between $(6*210*60/0.5 =)$ 151 200 and $(6*210*60/0.1 =)$ 756 000 non-commentary source lines. This is much higher than the other estimates, which therefore suggests that much more than 0.1–0.5 minutes are spent per year maintaining each line of code.

The studies quoted by Boehm (1981) indicate that maintenance productivity depends mainly on the type of application: programmers can maintain fewer LOC for aerospace and real-time applications than for business applications. The studies also show that, as is the case for development, maintenance effort per source instruction is independent of language level. Programs written in Assembler language are perhaps four times as long as they would have been had they been written in a high-level language (Chapter 6), so they take perhaps four times as much effort to maintain.

The COCOMO model (Boehm, 1981) takes into account not just the total LOC to be maintained, but also the number of lines which are likely to be changed or added each year, the 'annual change traffic', and the original development effort, which should therefore be a more accurate measure. As an example, if the original development effort comprised 32 000 LOC and took 91 man-months, and the annual change traffic is (2400 modified plus 4000 new =) 6400 LOC, then the annual maintenance effort should be $(6400/32\ 000 =)$ one-fifth the development effort, i.e. 18 man-months.

According to Boehm (1981), the factors affecting maintenance productivity are the same as those affecting development productivity, and by and large, the magnitude of the effect is the same, e.g. if some programmers are twice as productive as others during development, then they will be twice as productive during maintenance as well; and if high reliability was a requirement during development, then it must also be a requirement during maintenance. However, if a system was developed by highly capable staff, this does not necessarily mean it will be maintained by equally capable staff; and if a program had a low reliability requirement during development, then it will be disproportionately more difficult to maintain due to the lower quality of both code and documentation. Conversely, if modern programming practices are used during development, then they reduce the maintenance effort. (They also make it easier to maintain large programs with the same efficiency as small ones, i.e. they reduce the large productivity difference between large and small programs.)

These and other factors are quantified in his COCOMO model. They are used to estimate how long a job should take, and individual productivity, productivity in particular instances, and productivity variations, can be measured using that as the base.

Arthur (1983) lists twelve factors (summarized below) affecting maintenance productivity, but does not quantify them.

- The number of executable LOC, i.e. the size of the program. Maintenance effort for non-trivial tasks increases dramatically as the number of executable LOC increases, so an upper limit of about 100 executable lines per module should be observed.
- The total number of decisions (e.g. IF, UNTIL and WHEN, statements), and the decision 'density' (the number of decisions per hundred executable LOC). This is a measure of the complexity of the program, as each decision adds another path through the code which the programmer must remember when trying to maintain it. Normally a module should not have more than seven decisions (at most, 15), and the decision density should also be under 15. (CASE statements count as only one decision.)
- The number of pre-programmed functions (such as COBOL's CALL, SEARCH, and PERFORM, and PL/l's built-in functions), and the function 'density', as such functions are pre-tested and error-free, and they make it easier to understand and modify the program. The function density should be greater than 20%.
- The number of GOTOs, and the GOTO 'density', which can make programs unmaintainable.
- The number of entries and exits of a module – normally, there should only be one of each.
- The number of NOT conditions, as these are often misread.
- The number of comments, and the comment density. The comment density (which is calculated on the *total* LOC), should normally be about 10%.
- The number of EJECTs and SKIPs in the program source code, which improve readability.
- How well structured the code is, e.g. indented IF-THEN-ELSEs, and one statement per line.

In short, the size and complexity of the program, and how well it was written, are the main factors. (Guidelines for well-written programs are given in Chapter 8.) Other factors could be added to this list, e.g. programs are easier to maintain if they, and their accompanying documentation, were subjected to walkthroughs or inspections during development.

2.4.1 RE-USED CODE

Sometimes an existing program or subroutine is adapted for use in a new system. In one application area, NASA (1977) re-used 70–95% of its existing software (Charette, 1986). (Other figures quoted below are much lower. In fact, Tracz (1988) claimed that well under half of any system can be formed from re-used components.) Intuitively, one would expect this to require far less effort than writing new code, and Conte *et al.* (1986) believe that the very high productivity rate achieved on one of the projects in their database was due to this factor, which is plausible as some of the projects had an 'equivalent' line count which was only half the size of the total line count. Similarly, the figures from Matsumoto (1989) in Table 2.13 show that the productivity rate is almost doubled if re-used code is included in the line count. Bailey and Basili (1981) use a factor of 5:1, but this applies only to the re-used lines. Only 30% of the lines in their set of 19 projects were re-used, so the effect on overall productivity was correspondingly limited (only 1.3:1). Similarly, the figures given in Table 2.11 show very little difference in overall productivity due to re-used code. The figures given by Jones (1986b) show up to a 5:1 or even 10:1 gain from re-used code, depending on how many re-used lines are contained in the delivered product (Table 2.6).

One would expect the effort required to re-use code to lie somewhere between no effort, and the effort required to write new code to perform the required functions. (The effort *could* exceed that required to write it from scratch, but in such circumstances writing it from scratch would be preferable!) Bailey and Basili's (1981) proposed figure of 20%, i.e. that re-using code requires only one-fifth as much effort as writing it from scratch, gives reasonable agreement with the actual effort for the projects they studied, as shown by the close agreement between the 'new' and 'equivalent' productivity rates (Table 2.12). Thebaut (1983) proposed a non-linear (exponential) relationship. Conte *et al.* (1986) compared the two formulas, and found good agreement between them: they gave answers which differed by less than 10% for most of the values he tried. (The discrepancy was 50% for the most extreme case, in which *all* the code in the program was re-used code.)

These formulae are based on averages, and so give incorrect values in instances where significantly less or more effort than average is required. Boehm (1981) therefore adopted a different approach. Adapting code for re-use is like a maintenance task, but according to him, standard productivity measures for maintenance do not apply in such cases. Instead, the amount of effort involved depends on the number of lines in the adapted code, how extensively the design of the program or sub-routine is modified (which is a subjective estimate), how extensively the code is modified, and the relative effort (compared to what it would have been had the software been developed from scratch) required to integrate the adapted software into the new product and test the combination. This method is more sophisticated, and so should give even better results, and the figures for the projects in his data-base suggest that it does: effort estimates based on adjusted LOC for those projects having re-used code were on average at least as accurate as estimates based on total LOC for those projects not having re-used code.

Boehm (1981) warns it is easy to underestimate, because of unexpected side-effects and complicating factors. To counteract this tendency, he recommends taking a small, representative portion of the program or sub-routine, and working out in detail what will have to be done to adapt it, and from that, obtain a conversion productivity rate. He warns that frequently one expends more effort adapting a piece of existing software to meet one's needs, than it would have taken to develop a new piece of software.

2.4.2 CONVERTED (PORTED) CODE

During the life of a program, it sometimes happens that it must be converted or *ported* to another computer, e.g. if the organization replaces its computer with a different and incompatible model (Chapter 5). What are the productivity rates for a conversion?

A conversion is a project in its own right, and is similar in many ways to a system development project. A feasibility study is necessary, and so is planning, testing, and so on. However, files will need to be converted, which may not be the case with a development project. On the other hand, a development project comprises a large amount of coding, which a conversion project probably does not.

Boehm (1981) treats conversion as a special case of re-used code, so the factors affecting conversion effort and therefore productivity, are the same as those affecting the re-use of code, namely the number of LOC converted, how extensively the design of the program is modified to adapt it to the new environment (e.g. for improved efficiency), how extensively the code is modified, and the relative effort required to integrate the converted software. To this must be added a factor to

Table 2.20 Conversion Productivity (LOC per day)

Source	Average	Range	Manually converted	Sample size	Type of application	Programmer experience
Dittman (1980)	30	18–41[a]			compilers	senior
Boehm (1981)	38[c]		25–50%			
Dittman (1980)	47	33–63[a]			operating systems	senior
Oliver (1979)	50		25–50%	9		
Oliver (1979)	55		10–25%	15		
Dittman (1980)	57	44–70[a]			application programs	junior
Boehm (1981)	75[c]		10–25%			
Dittman (1980)	76	60–92[a]			application programs	senior
Oliver (1979)	91		<10%	30		
Boehm (1981)	110[b]	21–1538		9		
Boehm (1981)	188[c]		<10%			
Average	74[d]					

[a] 90% confidence limits, i.e. 90% of the rates lie within these ranges.
[b] Actual rate achieved on 9 projects.
[c] Rates calculated by the formula Boehm derived from the results of these 9 projects.
[d] The overall average of 74 is the unweighted. If the majority of systems have only a small percentage of code that must be manually converted, as implied by the Oliver data, then the typical conversion rate will be higher.

allow for the additional costs of a feasibility study and conversion planning. Boehm also uses the higher, maintenance, values for the reliability and modern programming practices cost drivers, to better reflect the difficulty of converting unreliable, poorly-structured, and poorly-documented code. The availability of automated conversion tools has a major impact on the conversion effort. The better they are, the fewer the lines of code which have to be manually converted. Other factors affecting the amount of effort required are the type of program, with more effort being required to convert system software than application software; and the seniority of the programmer, with senior programmers being more productive than juniors, as would be expected. These factors are quantified in Table 2.20.

The figures in Table 2.20 show that conversion productivity is much higher than development productivity, as would be expected. There are wide variations between the figures, but they indicate that conversion productivity is often (or even generally) more than five times higher than development productivity (the average productivity on the 63 projects in the Boehm (1981) data set was only 15 LOC/day), which is consistent with my own, more limited experience in this area. Conversions are discussed further in Chapters 5 and 6, and more quantitative information given in Chapter 8.

2.5 SUMMARY AND CONCLUSIONS

Productivity measurement has a number of benefits, including showing how productivity can be improved. However, there are also dangers involved: it might arouse resentment, or cause distortions in the values being measured, so the staff must be persuaded of the benefits.

There are a number of ways of measuring productivity, none of which is completely satisfactory. The method used here is to count the number of lines of fully debugged and documented source statements per person per day.

The number of lines of code in a program does not depend only on the tasks the program must perform. It is also affected by many factors, some expected, others surprising. These factors include: the ability and experience of the programmer, the language and methodology used, and so on. In other words, two versions of the same program, written to the same specifications, can have widely varying sizes. Worse, some authorities count some types of lines which others do not, such as comments and data declarations. LOC is therefore not a very stable unit, and so must be used with caution.

Apparent variations in productivity of an order of magnitude or more can be caused just by using different line-counting or effort-counting methods. Considerable caution must therefore be observed when comparing productivity rates from different sources.

Programmers can only spend about two-thirds of their time on productive activities, and this must be allowed for when measuring productivity and when drawing up project schedules. The amount of non-productive time can be reduced, particularly by better management, but cutting down on activities such as training may prove a false economy in the long-term.

Productivity rates for software development vary widely according to the size of the product, the level of language used, the ability of the programmer, etc. For traditional programming languages such as COBOL (i.e. not the fourth-generation), they can range from as little as one fully debugged and documented statement per person per day, to over 200. More typical values are 15 statements per day in prosaic circumstances, and 50 for small programs, where advanced techniques are used, or where the staff are of high ability or are highly motivated.

There are indications that some organizations may be five times more productive than others. Investigating the reasons for this could prove highly fruitful.

Most authorities believe that productivity is only improving very slowly, by perhaps just 5% p.a., but this probably excludes the effect of fourth-generation languages and application packages.

One major way to improve productivity is to re-use code. This probably requires only one-fifth the effort of writing new code.

One person can maintain around 10 000–20 000 LOC, but here again there is a wide variation, depending for example on whether modern programming practices were used during development, and on how much attention was paid to reliability: 'increased investment in software reliability and use of modern programming practices have a strong payoff during maintenance' (Boehm, 1981).

Converting programs, e.g. to run under a different operating system, may require as little as one-tenth the effort it took to write them.

The purpose of this chapter was merely to discuss current productivity, but in doing so, it has already revealed many factors affecting productivity, and ways in which productivity can be improved. These topics are discussed in more detail in the succeeding chapters.

PART TWO

FACTORS AFFECTING PRODUCTIVITY

Programming, which comprises a major portion of software engineering, is generally thought of as an individual activity (Weinberg, 1971). It tends to attract people who have low social needs and who like to work alone (Couger and Zawacki, 1980). However Data Processing as a whole is a social activity, and even the loner programmer has to interact with at least the systems analyst – in fact, Weinberg stated that the average programmer spends two-thirds of his time working with other people rather than working alone. (This figure seems rather high to me, but Bell *et al.* (1987) gave the figure of 50%, which is not much lower.) This social aspect of DP is more obvious with larger systems, where many people are grouped together into a project team to develop the system.

Groupings of people are thus an integral part of DP, and this aspect should be examined in any discussion of DP productivity. Our aim must be to design, and then implement, 'optimal organizational structures'. These terms are defined below.

Optimal

The efficiency and productivity of the organization must be maximized. To achieve this end, conflict within and between each group comprising the organization must be minimized (Bebbington, 1980; Weinberg, 1971).

Organization

The title of this study might give the impression that the 'organization' in our context is the DP Department (even just the analysis and programming section) and while most of this study refers only to DP, the DP Department is recognized as an integral part of the company (firm, corporation, etc.), and the productivity of the company, etc. as a whole is more important than that of the DP Department alone. So 'organization' here refers to the entire company (and to avoid confusion, it is not used in the sense of the structure of the company). Generally, there is no conflict: measures which improve the productivity of the DP Department do not adversely affect the productivity of the other departments. Nevertheless, the possibility of such adverse effects must always be borne in mind, and where such a conflict does arise, the productivity of the DP Department must be allowed to suffer for the greater good.

Structure

This means the 'configuration of functions and people' within the organization (Bebbington, 1980).

Team

The Concise Oxford Dictionary (Sykes, 1977) defines a team as a 'set of persons working together' – this implies interaction between the persons. Weinberg (1971) identifies 3 types of assemblages: the group, the team, and the project team.

- An example of a **group** is a collection of programmers working in the same place but independently and on separate programs, such as occurs in a university computing center;

- an example of a **team** is a collection of programmers working together in a co-ordinated, coherent effort to produce a single program;
- and an example of a **project team** is a collection of analysts, programmers and supporting staff working together in a co-ordinated, coherent effort to develop a new system.

Teams are formed in response to a work requirement, e.g. to write a program that is too big to be produced by one person in a reasonable time-scale. Co-ordination problems arise with consequent loss of productivity. To minimize them, teams which would number more than about seven persons – 'the magic number seven, plus or minus two' (Miller, 1956) – are split into multiple, smaller teams, a solution which suffers from its own co-ordination problems. Aron (1974) explains why there is a limit on team size: a manager's limited 'span of attention' or 'span of control' leads to a loss of control if he has, on average, more than seven people reporting to him. Applying this to programming teams implies that a first-level manager can supervise only up to four to eight programmers (plus some non-programmers). The average span of control was five in the early 1970s, and has now increased to seven (Chorafas, 1985). Jones (1986b) gives a slightly higher figure: about eight direct reports appears to be the norm in the US. Jones, however, believes that individual managerial skill is a very significant factor. The function split (work breakdown) percentages given in Table 8.28, imply a typical span of control of 9 for software engineering departments.

Teams differ from groups in that, in a team, the members interact with each other. Teams may exist within a group. Similarly, a project team may comprise several smaller teams, plus a manager and a bureaucratic organization. Teams correspond to the Type

1 to Type 4 DP structures discussed in the next section, while project teams correspond to Types 5 and 6.

3.1 STRUCTURE OF THE DP DEPARTMENT

3.1.1 SOME TYPICAL STRUCTURES

Groupings of people form an integral part of DP, and of the many different groupings possible, some typical ones (based on a study by Bebbington (1980)), are described below. These are the basic groupings: alternatives can be classified as variations or hybrids thereof. Some of these are mentioned in the descriptions, and some specific examples – chief programmer teams (CPTs), information centers (ICs), development centers, and family teams – are discussed later.

Advantages and disadvantages of each structure, particularly those having a bearing on productivity, are discussed. The information flows have been included in the descriptions – this is relevant to quality assurance (QA), to management, and to other organizational aspects such as communication and co-ordination.

The charts illustrating the structures are simplified, e.g. they do not include clerks whereas, in my experience, the Operations section of DP Departments normally includes some control clerks, and perhaps some coding clerks as well. There are other categories of staff which have also been omitted: secretarial staff, testers, quality assurers, network administrators, work study officers, operations researchers, business analysts, and so on. Also, large DP departments may have extra levels of management, such as the project manager discussed under Type 5. The organization charts given by other authorities generally include more of these additional categories, e.g.:

- Sommerville (1989) shows extra levels of management.
- Lee (1978) gives a 'Management Services Department Organisation Chart', which

includes the functions of training, database administrator, planning, O&M (Organization and Methods), operations research, etc.

- Gunther (1978) gives a detailed chart of a 'Publications Department' (his book is aimed at 'heavy-duty' software such as Applications Packages, for which documentation is of even greater than usual importance).
- Brandon's (1978) chart of the Type 3 structure includes:
  - a database administrator;
  - Project control (not defined: it appears to be a low-level Steering Committee, rather than a QA function such as the separate testing groups discussed in Chapter 8);
  - research (also not defined, but presumably includes the Development Center concept referred to under Type 4);
  - Data control.
- Lee (1978) and Martin (1982b) show additional job categories existing in the operations section: librarian, job reception, output dispatch, systems programming, communications, etc.

Other examples are referred to below. These additional job functions are generally independent of the department structure: the fact that a particular function is mentioned under only one structure does not mean that it can exist only with that structure. For example, project managers are not restricted to the Type 5 Structure under which I have mentioned them; the separate group to handle the 'staff' functions (such as personnel development), is not restricted to Type 2; and the Development Center and Information Center are not restricted to Type 4.

Although the charts are incomplete without these categories, it is justifiable to omit them because:

- they generally number few people;

- many organizations, particularly the smaller ones (which form the majority), do not have separate staff to perform these functions;
- they may not be situated in the DP Department;
- they are generally less directly involved in the day to day programming process, and so have less effect on productivity in this area;
- truly comprehensive charts would be large and complex, so those aspects of greatest relevance to this study would be buried in detail.

Boehm (1981) gives a generalized chart, corresponding to my Type 3, plus guidelines for tailoring it. It was designed so that functions shown next to each other, such as Configuration Management (Chapter 11) and QA (Chapter 10), are ones which can more easily be merged with each other, because of the greater similarity in the objectives, tasks and skills required. (They would generally be merged for small projects, where the number of staff performing the functions was insufficient to justify separate groups. One supervisor fewer is therefore required – an economy measure discussed later.) Boehm also gives a *series* of charts, one for each phase of the software life-cycle, showing how the organizational structure can be changed to meet the differing requirements of each phase.

Some of the alternative organization charts – e.g. some of Gunther's charts, and those which include functions related to DP such as O&M – show how DP fits into the remainder of the organization. This is relevant to section 3.2.

DP staff need to understand organizational principles, and the functioning of the organization and its management, so they can make the maximum contribution to the department and the organization (Lucas, 1985).

Notes

Singulars and plurals have been used loosely, e.g.:

- an installation with a basic structure, which is shown here as having more than one operator (Fig. 3.1), may have only one;
- one with a matrix structure may have more than the two project teams shown in Fig. 3.9.

The term 'systems analyst' is a misleading one, since people classified as systems analysts are generally also systems designers (Jackson, 1975). Throughout this study therefore, unless the context indicates otherwise, the term 'systems analyst' refers to people who both analyse and design systems. (This, and other usages which might cause confusion, are repeated in Appendix B.)

The term 'programming' is sometimes used to refer to the program design and coding stages only, i.e. excluding testing and debugging, or even just to coding, but in my experience these are less common uses of the term. Therefore, unless otherwise indicated, the term programming here includes the program (detailed) design, testing and debugging functions.

Type 1: basic DP structure

This structure occurs in small departments, e.g. first time users. Staff report directly to the DP manager (DPM). There may be an overlap of roles, particularly in the smallest departments, e.g. the DPM may also be the systems analyst, and/or the systems analyst may also be a programmer (Garber, 1976; Bebbington, 1980), although this is not shown on Fig. 3.1. The DPM acts as the interface between the DP department and the users, establishing their requirements and passing on these requirements to the DP staff. The limited career paths mentioned in Chapter 9 as one cause of high staff turnover, refers specifically to this structure because of the small number of staff.

The structure is essentially permanent, i.e. it will only change because of a change in conditions such as growth in the size of the department. It is also hierarchical, and flow of information follows the lines of authority. Figure 3.2 shows a two-way flow within the DP Department, although relatively little information passes from the members of the department to the DPM. If the user department is small, the flow of information within it is likely to also be largely one-way, but a small DP Department does not necessarily imply that the average user department will also be small.

Information must travel the length of the hierarchy to be conveyed: rather than involving just two people, it may take four. This is a disadvantage inherent in any hierarchical structure.

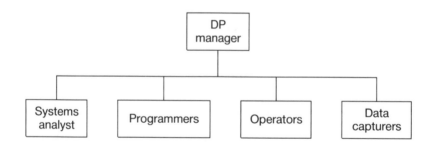

Figure 3.1 Type 1: Basic DP structure (after Bebbington, 1980).

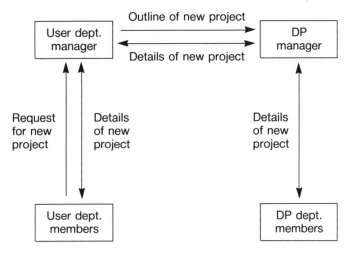

Figure 3.2 Information flow in a basic DP structure (after Bebbington, 1980).

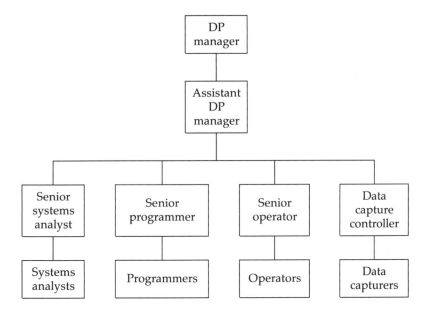

Figure 3.3 Type 2: Simple DP structure (after Bebbington, 1980).

Type 2: simple DP structure

The structure shown in Fig. 3.3 occurs in larger departments than those which have Type 1. Each function is headed by a senior specialist, who may spend part of his time performing some lower-level managerial functions such as job scheduling. He may also be responsible for some of the 'staff functions': personnel training/development; contract change control; development and enforcement of standards; and research into equipment and techniques (Metzger, 1981; Gildersleeve, 1974b). Some of the personnel development functions might be handled by

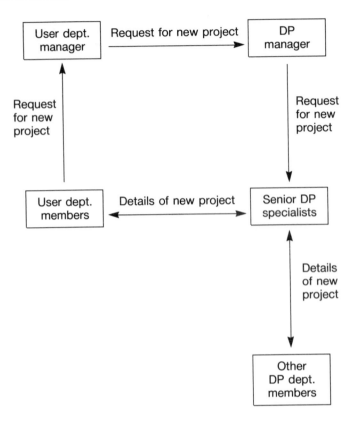

Figure 3.4 Information flow in a simple DP structure (after Bebbington, 1980).

the DPM (or an assistant, if any), i.e. they would be split between two supervisors, which may not be desirable. As Lucas (1985) put it: it is comforting to have just one manager responsible for evaluation, raises, and promotions. Large organizations may have a separate team to handle the staff functions.

The overall supervision of each project is performed by the DPM (or assistant DPM) but he is not the immediate supervisor of the work during any of the functions, and so might be too far removed from the day to day work to have adequate control.

The initial interfacing with the users is done by the DPM (or assistant DPM). Most of the subsequent interfacing during the development phase is done by the senior

analyst. After installation, most interfacing is done by whoever performs the function of the senior control clerk, but where system modifications are required, the same procedure as for development would be followed.

As for Type 1, this structure is essentially permanent and hierarchical, though much of the information can bypass the DPM, as shown in Fig. 3.4, and so does not follow the lines of authority.

Type 3: functional supervision DP structure

The structure in Fig. 3.5 is likely to be found in larger organizations than those which have Type 2. Operations and data capture are combined. Senior specialists function mainly

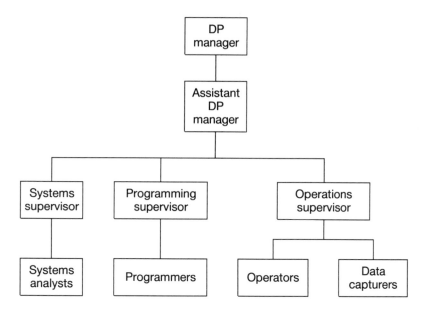

Figure 3.5 Type 3: Functional supervision DP structure (after Bebbington, 1980).

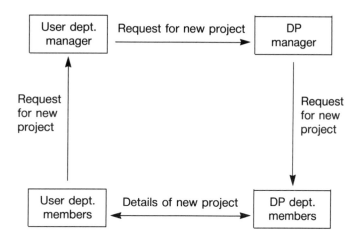

Figure 3.6 Information flow in a functional supervision DP structure (after Bebbington, 1980).

as supervisors, and hence are shown as such. (The advantages and disadvantages of this are discussed in Chapter 9.) The interface with the users is the same as that for Type 2, with the supervisors filling the senior specialists' roles, but other specialists may also deal directly with users.

Like the previous types, this structure is essentially permanent and hierarchical. Since non-supervisory specialists also interact directly with the users, the information-flow is as given in Fig. 3.6.

There are several variations on this structure. Gildersleeve (1974b) shows design and installation as two separate and additional functions. Where this is the case, a basic weakness in the structure is accentuated: as a system passes through its life-cycle, so it is passed from one group of functional specialists to another, making overall control of the work more difficult, and the more groups there are the more difficult it is. On the other hand, the functional supervision structure should ensure that the quality of each function is of a high standard: having a separate installation team, for example, should minimize some problems (such as the slow, difficult to use airline reservations system discussed in Chapter 8).

Type 4: hardware/software split DP structure

The structure shown in Fig. 3.7 is likely to be found in larger organizations than those having Type 2. A change to this type may also occur because of a technical change, such as providing the programmers with interactive facilities. Systems analysts and pro-

grammers are combined, and are physically separated from, and may be denied entry to, the Operations section. The functional separation between systems analysts and programmers begins to blur, as can happen under a Type 1 structure, resulting in greater flexibility. (The advantages and disadvantages of this are discussed in Chapter 9.) Supervisors are chosen for their supervisory skills, but must still be familiar with the work they are supervising. A systems analyst is more likely to be chosen as the systems/programming supervisor (see Appendix D), thereby depriving senior programmers of the career path available with Type 2 and 3 structures.

The interface with the users is the same as that for Type 3, with the systems and programming supervisor filling the roles of the systems supervisor and the programming supervisor. This structure is also essentially permanent and hierarchical, and the information flow is as for Type 3 (Fig. 3.6).

Gildersleeve (1974b) and Brandon (1978)

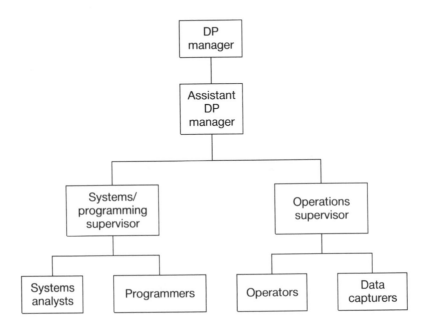

Figure 3.7 Type 4: Hardware/software split DP structure (after Bebbington, 1980).

would probably view this structure not as a fundamentally different type, but as a variation of Type 3.

Some variations of this structure are:

- having a development machine, i.e. a separate computer for the exclusive use of the analysts and programmers, to provide them with a faster and more consistent response;
- creating a 'development center', a group of specialists whose purpose is to improve the productivity of the software engineers (section 3.5);
- setting up an 'information center', to help users do their own computing (section 3.4).

Type 5: project team DP structure

The type of structure shown in Fig. 3.8 is fundamentally different from the preceding ones, as the staff are grouped together according to the project they are working on, not the specialist function they perform. An organization would install it as a result of a new management theory rather than an increase in size (Bebbington, 1980). In fact, it can be used with organizations of the size required by Types 2, 3 and 4. Each project leader has total responsibility for his project, possibly including maintenance after the system has been installed, so he is approximately equivalent to a DPM (although his authority might not extend to, say, the power to hire and fire). However, a large project may be split between several teams, with an overall project manager. Each project manager may therefore have several project leaders reporting to him. Similarly, in a large organization, with many project teams, an extra level of management is required.

Lucas (1985) stated that this structure, by grouping people together, satisfies the programmers' need for social interaction, but caution should be observed in view of their low social needs (Couger and Zawacki, 1980). Another danger is that the subdivision into teams introduces a degree of rigidity: it is

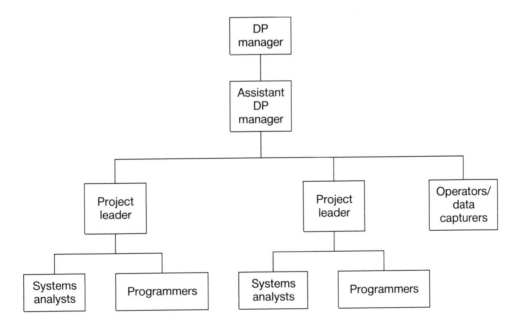

Figure 3.8 Type 5: Project team DP structure (after Bebbington, 1980).

unlikely, for example, that a programmer without work in one team (e.g. while waiting for an analyst to finish a design), would be allocated to another team, to relieve a shortage there (Arthur, 1983). (This rigidity is discussed further in Chapter 9.) Teams must be *balanced*, i.e. they must be staffed with people whose technical skills complement each other, and who can work harmoniously together (Boehm, 1981).

Operators and data capture staff are sometimes included in the project teams, e.g. in distributed DP environments, or when project teams are temporarily located at remote sites – the data capturers are then on hand to key in the programs (Bebbington, 1980).

The interface with the users is the same as that for Type 4, with the project leader filling the role of the systems and programming supervisor. One fundamental difference between this type and the preceding ones is that, whereas the first four types are all essentially permanent structures, the project team is not necessarily so, as a team may be created for each new project and then disbanded on termination of the project. The information flow will be as for Types 3 and 4 (Fig. 3.6).

One particular variation of this structure is the 'application organization' (Gildersleeve, 1974b; Lee, 1978; Lucas, 1985; Martin, 1982b) in which the project teams are permanent, though some members may be temporary, e.g.:

- users may be temporarily assigned to the teams (as members, not as leaders);
- some of the programmers may be temporarily recruited from a pool of programmers according to the numbers required by the current projects.

Each team specializes in a particular application area, so the (permanent) members thereof come to know their applications very well. This structure is, in fact, user-oriented, and can develop in the team members a

loyalty toward the organization which can reduce staff turnover. (Loyalty and turnover are discussed in Chapter 9.) However, it is more suited to an organization new to computing. As the organization becomes more mature from a DP point of view, so the systems become more integrated, necessitating corresponding changes to the boundaries between the teams.

In another variation on this structure, systems analysts are apparently the immediate supervisors of the programmers (Arthur, 1983), which may not lead to high quality programming.

By contrast, in yet another variation, there is a programming supervisor who is not himself a member of any of the project teams, but who supervises programmers in the project teams (Lee, 1978), i.e. he is a functional supervisor as in Type 3. The project programmers therefore report to him in addition to their project leader. In other words, a functional supervision structure is superimposed on the project team structure. The separate reporting lines should ensure objectivity of information, thereby rectifying a weakness of hierarchical structures (Weinberg, 1971). In hierarchical structures there is a lack of separation between doing the work, and evaluating it. For example, people would prefer their manager not to know about the silly mistakes they make, and the ensuing delay in project completion. They are therefore tempted to conceal information from the very people who need to know it.

The Pomberger (1984) version is similar, but the functional supervisors are members of the teams, and there is a project manager rather than a project leader, to whom the functional supervisors report, i.e. there is an extra tier in the hierarchy. This structure is suitable for larger projects. The supervisor of the project is therefore one step further removed from the actual work, and so is less involved in detailed planning and control. This extra tier hinders communications and control. It also exacerbates a weakness of the hierarchical structure: people tend to rise to their level of incompetence – the Peter Principle (Peter and Hull, 1969).

The 'chief programmer team' (section 3.3), is an example of the project team structure, and it is designed to address the above problems.

Type 6: matrix DP structure

According to Arthur (1983), the structure of Fig. 3.9 mimics Japanese management philosophies that provide for enhanced lateral and vertical communications. The objective is to maximize personnel productivity by allowing flexible resource management.

Lucas (1985) uses a tabular rather than a graphic format to illustrate this structure. The rows in the table represent the staff members, and the columns the projects.

This structure can be implemented by organizations meeting the same requirements as for Type 5. As in Type 5, the department is divided into project teams. Where it differs from Type 5 is that firstly, project teams under a matrix structure are invariably temporary; and secondly, and more fundamentally, there is overlap between the teams, i.e. each person may be a member of several different teams at the same time, and therefore may report to several different project leaders simultaneously (Fairley, 1985). (Under Types 1 to 4, a person may also work on several different projects at once, but reports to just one supervisor for all of them.) Reporting relationships are therefore complex. Each programmer may also work with several analysts, thereby encouraging the interchange of design and development philosophies ('cross-fertilization').

The situation is, in fact, more complex than shown in Fig. 3.9, as the leader of one team may be an ordinary member of another. Furthermore, the project leader may report to (i.e. be responsible to) the user department. Extensions of this idea are that the leader may be a senior member of the user department; the entire team may be loaned to the user department for the duration of the project, or may even be permanent members of the user department – the DP department would thus consist solely of operations staff (Bebbington, 1980; Zimner, 1978a). With these structures, the team members gain more knowledge of the application area,

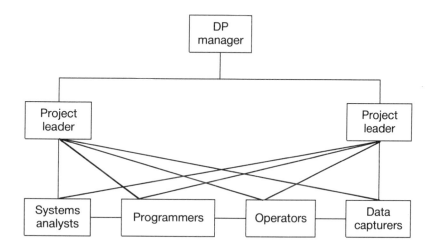

Figure 3.9 Type 6: Matrix DP Structure (after Bebbington, 1980).

which is good. However, if the project leader is a user, then the most experienced DP staff occupy less important and central positions, so there is the danger that maximum use would not be made of their knowledge, and they may even be overruled. Dissatisfaction would result, and harm may be done. (This is discussed further in Chapter 9.) Further, if the DP staff are situated in the user department, they would be cut off from their DP colleagues, which would restrict the interchange of DP knowledge, particularly recent advances – and DP is a rapidly changing industry. Extra attention would therefore have to be paid to these aspects, to ensure that the benefits of these structures were not negated by their disadvantages. With the spread of distributed DP, microcomputers, and fourth-generation software, these considerations have a wider application and importance than is at first apparent.

The matrix structure, at least as shown here, retains a hierarchical component, but it is less hierarchical than Type 5, both because of the overlap of teams, and because of the informal nature of authority (Bebbington, 1980). Democratic teams are a related concept (section 3.1.2), but go one step beyond the structure described above. In democratic teams, there is no fixed leader (Weinberg, 1971). Instead, leadership is constantly changing, devolving on whoever is best able to lead the team at the time, e.g. the best debugger might be the leader for the duration of the debugging phase.

The interface with the users is the same as for Type 5. The information flow is also as for Type 5, i.e. both of them have the information flow shown in Fig. 3.6, though there will be more lines of communication *within* the DP department.

One version of this structure – the 'project-functional organization' (Gildersleeve, 1974b) – seems to be mentioned more often in the literature. It can be viewed as a cross between the matrix and functional supervision structures, as it has a functional supervision structure superimposed on the matrix structure (just as it can be superimposed on the project team structure). There is a systems analysis supervisor, a programming supervisor, and so on, to whom the project staff report in addition to their project leaders: the analysts report to the analysis supervisor, the programmers to the programming supervisor, and so on. The separate reporting lines should ensure objectivity of information, thereby rectifying a weakness of hierarchical structures (Weinberg, 1971). Reporting relationships in this version are more formal.

3.1.2 PRODUCTIVITY CONSIDERATIONS

Span of control

Jones (1986b) believes that the average span of control should be increased from 8 to 16. This would make organizations much more effective, as there would be 12% more people doing technical work; eight-person departments almost never include trained support personnel for documentation, quality assurance, planning, etc.; there may not be enough capable individuals to manage so many small teams; and so on. If, for example, an organization changed from a Type 3 (functional supervision) to a Type 4 (hardware/software split) structure, it would require one supervisor fewer. This process should, however, not be carried too far, as it means more work for the remaining supervisors, and results in larger groups, with consequent disadvantages such as the staff feeling like small cogs in a large wheel.

In the mid-1970s, Citibank had 50 000 employees and a span of control of 6, resulting in 8000 managers (Chorafas, 1985). It was estimated that, if using computer technology could help managers work more effectively, and thereby increase their span of control by 12%, 1000 fewer managers would be needed, and savings would amount to nearly $50 million per year, and in fact a span of control of 7 was achieved in 1984.

Flat structures

IBM was criticized for its policy of having as few people as possible reporting to each manager (Yang, 1986). This should result in better control, but it also has the disadvantage of more levels of management, resulting in a 'taller' organization structure, which acts as a buffer against change.

Modern organization theory generally recommends a relatively flat organizational structure, i.e. few levels of subordinates and superiors (Lucas, 1985). Increasing the span of control results in a flatter organizational structure. There is a tendency for organizations to become top-heavy. Where this has occurred, costs can be reduced without impairing the work of the organization. Once again, this process should not be carried too far, as it means more work for the remaining supervisors, and results in larger groups, with the usual consequent disadvantages.

Democratic teams

Schach (1988) claims that democratic teams are 'enormously' productive, work best when the problem is difficult, and should function well in a research environment. However, he also describes them as 'impractical to implement'. They have to spring up spontaneously, are difficult to introduce into an undemocratic environment, and management may have difficulty working with a group working for a common cause with no single leader. Furthermore, once a solution to a difficult problem has been arrived at, the team should be reorganized in a more hierarchical fashion to implement the solution (Schach, 1990).

Weinberg (1971) is an enthusiastic supporter of democratic teams. He acknowledges that they have disadvantages:

- it is more difficult for them to accept a new member; and
- their efficiency is more impaired by the presence of an anti-social member – and

programmers, having low social needs (Couger and Zawacki, 1980), are probably more anti-social than the general population;

but their adaptability to changing circumstances makes them especially suited to handle unexpected difficulties such as the loss of a team member – and programmers do have a high turnover (Chapter 9).

His support for democratic teams derives in part from a common disadvantage of hierarchical structures: the lack of separation between doing the work, and evaluating it, as explained earlier. One way to achieve this separation is to set up a separate testing group – a deviation from a simple hierarchical structure. Another way is to retain functional supervision under project team and matrix structures, as was discussed earlier under those types.

Matrix structure

The matrix structure's fluid nature fits in well with the rapidly changing technological environment and suits the innovative personalities of DP staff (Bebbington, 1980). (This is discussed in Chapter 9.) It should also better meet the participatory, employee-centered leadership style preferred by DP staff (Mumford, 1972). (Participative management is discussed in Chapter 11.) These advantages must be set against the problems caused by the complexities of the reporting structure, and the potential conflict caused by the dual responsibilities and the amorphous nature of authority (Bebbington, 1980). Furthermore, its informality is incompatible with a rigid, hierarchical, bureaucratic organization, such as a government body. For a DP department in such an environment, it may be advisable to have an alternative, more compatible structure, even if this is inherently less efficient, to reduce conflict between the DP department and the rest of the organization.

Arthur (1983) stated that the matrix structure may seem chaotic, but the improvement in dialogue, employee skills, and productivity, override the problems.

Weinberg (1971) discusses the difficult situations which can arise because of a conflict of goals, e.g. when a team has two distinct programs to produce. This conflict is likely to be heightened in a matrix structure where the programs are being produced for different project leaders. Time and energy are expended before such conflicts are resolved, with consequent loss of production.

Macro and Buxton (1987) seem to have a strong preference for the hierarchical structure; they warn that authority and accountability in a matrix structure may be unclear or fragmented for a particular product or project; that temporary migration of staff from their department(s) to the team(s) can cause problems of reporting; and that too democratic a style may lead to 'paralysis by analysis', where no decisions are ever taken without full team consensus, and no leadership is given either for that consensus or in the event of its absence. However, they believe the more flexible matrix structure is appropriate early in the software life-cycle, particularly if prototyping is used. The two types can therefore co-exist.

Jones (1986b) conducted a review of software management literature, and discovered that matrix management is usually cited as a source of trouble and confusion, or as a potentially useful method that needs a great deal of extra care for successful use, and is not often regarded by experienced software managers as a useful method for large systems. Specific criticisms, which apply more to the 'project-functional organization' version, are that 'no man can serve two masters', there is no single person responsible for the success of each project, and there is apparent conflict between the authority of the project manager and that of the functional manager. Matrix managed projects have a much higher rate of schedule delays and cost overruns (figures are given in Chapter 11).

Gunther (1978) does not seem to approve of the matrix structure, and has some harsh words to say about it: it causes friction and confusion; it is tough on the staff, as everyone has two bosses; and there is continual ambiguity and conflict. Nevertheless, he acknowledged that it was becoming more popular. His concept of the matrix structure, however, seems to be very different from the informality and loose authority described above. Instead, he emphasized managerial control and accountability, and the need for organized planning, perhaps to overcome the weaknesses in the structure.

Scott (1986), writing about organizations in general and not specifically DP departments, stated that, although many organizations had adopted formal matrix management systems, almost all used matrix management for only a part of their operations. Furthermore, two management information systems (MIS) are needed in these organizations, one for the functional organization and another for the product lines. Each MIS must provide information to, and receive information from, the other. Because of all this complexity, a matrix structure could not work without the processing power of computers.

Lucas (1985) advocates a hierarchical structure for the operations section. It is not clear if he has any preferences in the case of other categories of DP staff.

To sum up, the matrix structure has disadvantages as well as advantages, so it is to be viewed with caution, especially as significant productivity gains have been claimed for chief programmer teams and family teams, neither of which is a matrix structure. Some authorities are strongly in favour of it, while others are against. Perhaps their standpoints are influenced by philosophical preferences and by whether their background is technical or in management: technical staff may prefer the matrix structure, and management a hierarchical structure. The first description I saw of it made it sound as though it was more suited to intellectual high-flyers than ordinary programmers, and this may have colored my thinking. I have elaborated on this aspect in my discussion of family teams (section 3.6). Organizations should probably use a mixture of matrix and hierarchical structures.

Centralization

All eight of the large, multidivisional organizations in a survey quoted by Withington (1969) initially had decentralized computing. However, nearly all of them subsequently either centralized their systems analysis and programming functions, or at least had brought these functions under centralized control. This contrasts with the more recent statements that few organizations have recentralized (Lucas, 1985) – though he may have had wider considerations than just computerization in mind – and that decentralization is a trend seen throughout the DP world (Winkler, 1986).

Centralization takes advantage of economies of scale. It

- aids standardization;
- eliminates duplication of effort and data;
- optimizes the use of resources, especially scarce skills (particularly important in view of the shortage of staff (Chapter 9), the increasing demand for software (Chapter 12), and the growth in application complexity (Chapter 8)); and
- eliminates disputes between separate DP groups (Withington, 1969).

Centralization is one of Brandon's suggestions for reducing costs, and he quoted an organization which reduced its DP budget by 25% by centralizing its hardware and partly centralizing its DP staff (Brandon, 1978). By contrast, a more recent study by Mendelson (1987) of the price and performance of computer systems found that, although there were economies of scale in the 1960s and

early 1970s, there were neither economies nor diseconomies of scale in the 1980s, except for microcomputers, which have a much lower cost in relation to their performance. However, he did not take into account the cost of linking multiple computers together, which might change the picture. Centralization does not have to be total, as is shown by Brandon's example and by Withington's survey. In fact, Alfred Sloan of General Motors stated as long ago as 1920 that the production operations of the corporation should be fully decentralized, while the financial functions should be centralized (Wright, 1979). In addition, Gurbaxani and Whang (1991) quote several instances of centralization, e.g. Chevrolet built an efficient information system to take control of business functions that previously were dispersed in thirteen plant sites. They concluded that an organization may use IT to centralize some decisions while decentralizing others. Centralization does have disadvantages as well. If, for example, there is only a centralized programming group, then they are at the center of a 'tug-of-war' between the different parts of the organization for their services.

Decentralization or distributed DP (DDP) also has advantages. From a general point of view, it provides more autonomy for lower-level managers (Lucas, 1985). From a DP point of view, it is more user-oriented, and a DDP structure is more likely to match the processing needs of the organization. There will always be a need for data and computers to be located where the work is, e.g. because of the relatively high cost and low speed of long-distance communications (Withington, 1969). On the other hand, DDP can make it more difficult to manage the data. For example, data may be duplicated, with the danger that inconsistencies will be introduced if the different copies are not updated simultaneously. (This can be avoided with a suitably networked or distributed database.) DDP also adds complexity, and it is more difficult to control system development. For example, standards may not be observed at each site. Organizations can become so highly decentralized that they 'have a real problem' in obtaining a unified view of their data (Carlyle, 1987c). All in all, the situation can get out of control, necessitating the imposition of more centralized management control (Davis, 1991a).

A large measure of centralization can co-exist with DDP, e.g. the kind of equipment used in a decentralized organization, the way it is used, and the programs run on it, can be under central control. However, problems can arise here as well. Where some programmers are in a central group, and others are distributed throughout the organization, then the dispersed ones have to try to meet the requirements of the division they are situated in, and at the same time must comply with the standards laid down by the central group (Withington, 1969). A spirit of co-operation is needed by all parties.

With the proliferation of PCs, a large amount of *de facto* decentralization of computing has taken place, and this has even been encouraged by information centers (Brzezinski, 1987). This also represents a significant shift in the balance of power from DP departments to users, with the result that end users get more involved, e.g. with purchasing decisions for both software and hardware, which in turn means that DP staff must keep more up to date with PC trends in order to maintain organization-wide standards, but with so many PC products available, this is difficult (Wiener, 1986).

Gary Biddle, Vice President of MIS at American Standard, stated that, in manufacturing organizations, 80% of the transactions should never leave the functional area where they are used (Carlyle, 1987b); a study by the Massachusetts Institute of Technology found that the scope of most of the new applications that were being demanded had been reduced from organization-wide, to personal, i.e. they would be used by only one person or one

department (Grulke, 1983); 85% of the respondents in a 1986 survey rated departmental systems as critical to corporate systems architecture (though they still had a long way to go to achieve this) (Mayfield, 1986). These opinions point to a departmental, or DDP, solution.

The structure of the DP facilities should match the structure of the organization, e.g. if the organization's management structure is decentralized, then DP should not be centralized (Donaldson, 1975; Etheridge *et al.*, 1987).

Having mixed teams of users and DP staff – which may be more common in a DDP environment – or mixed progress meetings, assists in the interchange of knowledge and encourages greater user involvement, which is important to DP success. Greater user involvement, even to the extent of making the user responsible for the system from start to finish, can be particularly beneficial where the user is suspicious of computers, or the DP staff know very little about the application area (Zimner, 1978a). In these circumstances, the benefits might outweigh the disadvantages discussed earlier, such as the DP staff's expert advice being overruled.

Other DP structures

One of Brandon's suggestions for reducing costs which is related to the structure of the DP Department, is eliminating excess functions (Brandon, 1978). An example which has already been quoted is that an organization would require one supervisor fewer by changing from a Type 3 (functional supervision) to a Type 4 (hardware/software split) structure.

Interactive facilities, which can increase productivity (Chapter 6), might lead to a change in the department structure. The organization could use the opportunity to separate the hardware and software functions, i.e. it may introduce a Type 4 (hardware/software split) structure.

Introduction of information centers (section 3.4) and development centers (section 3.5) represent changes to the department structure, and both can result in improved productivity: the development center is claimed to be able to double productivity (Abbott, 1983a).

3.1.3 CONCLUSION

There is little evidence as to which kind of team organization is best (Bell *et al.*, 1987). In particular, I have not seen a direct comparison of the productivity of the different structures. To some extent, this is understandable: e.g. a large DP department would reject a Type 1 structure, as it would instinctively believe that having so many people reporting directly to the DPM would prevent the department from operating effectively. However, the choice is not always as clear cut, and there is insufficient guidance available on which structure would best fit a particular organization's circumstances.

3.2 OTHER ORGANIZATIONAL STRUCTURES

DP is not an isolated function, but an integral part of the organization, and an integral factor in achieving corporate objectives (Knox, 1978). The DP department interacts with both other departments and top management, so the structure of the rest of the organization must be taken into account when discussing DP productivity. To function effectively, DP staff must understand the functioning of the organization and its management (Lucas, 1985). This is too big a subject to be examined fully here, but some of the considerations are listed below, giving an indication of the factors involved.

Structure of the organization

An organization is made up of a number of decision levels. The organization can itself be viewed as a system, housing permanent sub-systems (the major functions of the business), and temporary sub-systems (such as projects). It is much influenced by strong personalities, and becomes unstable in times of change. Information flows through the organization, and must conform to the structure thereof. Organizations must have open internal communications to transfer information effectively.

There may be conflict between departments, but they are mutually dependent so conflict must make way for a spirit of co-operation to achieve mutually beneficial solutions (MacMillan, 1975). Such conflict may be caused by (MacMillan, 1975; Leibhammer, 1980):-

- competition for limited resources;
- a narrow, departmental outlook;
- differing priorities between departments, due to their differing functions;
- an incompatibility between types of structures, as can occur with a matrix DP structure as discussed above; or
- even by resentment of the high salaries paid to computer staff, and of the jargon they use, which is meaningless to others.

Lucas (1985) stated that other departments may resent their dependence on the computer department, and that, as a result, they may stop using a system, or not seek more computer help even when it could be of great assistance to them. Conversely, the computer staff are heavily dependent on the users to supply them with the information and understanding they require to develop computerized systems. If the computer staff are not sensitive to any resentment which may exist, or to the danger of it arising, then they will not get the information they need for the systems to be a success.

Gary Biddle, Vice President of MIS at American Standard, believes that organizations 'have little understanding of their cost structure' (Carlyle, 1987b). They have been unable to relate their MIS spending to the organization's earnings, and so have spent millions on information technology without knowing if they were getting value for their money. This can result in the DP department being allocated too much money (to the detriment of the other departments) or too little (to its own detriment, and therefore, indirectly, to the detriment of the other departments as well). Biddle devised a 3-dimensional model of an organization showing spending level objectives by machine size (micro, mini, mainframe), type of user (e.g. factory automation and end user computing), and so on, which should help to rectify this.

According to Lucas (1976, 1985), there is a tendency amongst DP staff to concentrate on the technical aspects of systems and to overlook organizational behavior considerations, resulting in inadequate user participation and clumsy implementation, and this has caused many systems, including technically elegant ones, to fail, with consequent waste of the effort already expended and the costs incurred. Emotional problems within an organization should be faced, as they will not disappear of their own accord. Instead, they will remain to continually obstruct the implementation of rational plans (Argyris, 1976).

The structure of the organization is not necessarily permanent: it may change in response to changes in its environment (Lawrence and Lorsch, 1969), or even to accommodate new DP systems (see below).

Informal structures

In addition to the formal structures shown on organization charts, there exist within all organizations extensive informal structures. These structures are a more realistic portrayal of the organization, as they reflect how people actually interact (e.g. how they cut red tape and bypass standard procedures) yet there is no formal documentation describing them (Lucas, 1985; Mittra, 1988). They reflect social interaction, and depend on the personalities of specific individuals, and on patterns of behavior that have developed over time. These structures therefore also

have an important role to play in the performance of the organization, and are a vital source of information for management: their disruption can have a serious impact (Weinberg, 1971). One DP director even claimed he probably achieved more through informal conversations than in an entire formal status meeting (Winkler, 1986). The structure of the DP function, and the design of DP systems, must therefore take into account the informal structures.

Top management

There is a communication gap between top management and DP – they are 'alien cultures' (Carlyle, 1987b). DP is more in tune with the computing industry than the business it is supporting, while the situation is reversed in the case of top management. Biddle believes that his 3-dimensional spending-level model of an organization, referred to above, helps to bridge this gap.

The attitude of top management to DP is vital: with its support, virtually all problems can be overcome (Zimner, 1978a; Expert, 1980). The needs of the computer, and the contribution it can make, should always be taken into account. Often, top management tells the DPM what is wanted, but lays restrictions making it almost impossible for it to be done. On the other hand, there may be an abdication of responsibility by top management: they may delegate systems planning and development to the DPM, with the result that the computer ends up running the organization.

Ideally, the DPM (or an equivalent person such as the information systems manager) will be involved at top management level, and will report directly to the President or chief executive officer (CEO), so that he will be aware, on an ongoing basis, of new demands on the organization and the direction being taken by top management. In return, because DPMs have a greater opportunity than most to obtain a broad under-standing of how the organization works, what management's problems and opportu-nities are, and how to implement change, they can and should contribute more at an organizational and managerial level.

In the vast majority of organizations, the DP department was originally organized under accounting (Lucas, 1985). This was logi-cal, as the initial applications were account-ing ones. However, as non-accounting appli-cations were added, the other departments, often with good cause, felt they were being ignored. The problem was complicated by applications which transcended functional lines. With DP separated from accounting, and seen as a separate, service-oriented entity, reporting directly to the President or CEO, this problem is solved.

A Diebold survey showed that 26% of senior MIS executives reported directly to the CEO or at board level (up from 5% five years earlier) (Carlyle, 1987b), and so complied with the ideal described above.

Winkler (1986) recommended that MIS chiefs move their offices away from the DP department and near the CEO or senior executive to whom they report, so they are not absorbed in day to day fire-fighting, and to indicate to everyone that they are focusing on broader issues.

Top management should have clear corporate business objectives which are com-municated and understood throughout the organization. Besides minimizing the inter-departmental conflict referred to earlier, this enables the staff to co-ordinate their activi-ties, encourages a concern for the organiza-tion as a whole, and helps engender a loyalty to the organization rather than to individual technical professions. (Loyalty is discussed in Chapter 9.)

Steering committees

Top management, possibly acting through senior inter-departmental committees ('steer-ing committees'), can (Lucas, 1978; Winfield, 1986; Boehm, 1981; Gildersleeve, 1974b):

- set objectives for the DP department, approve its budget, evaluate its perform-ance, and decide strategy;
- veto requests for uneconomical DP projects, and establish (fair) priorities for economical ones (thereby overcoming the favoritism discussed above);
- veto marginally useful features ('gold-plating');
- ensure sufficient resources are available;
- enable the DP department to identify the officially recognized and responsible user of a proposed new system;
- ensure that corporate standards are com-plied with in all DP systems; and
- ensure that action taken is consistent with long-term plans and corporate goals – in particular, that these plans and goals are not undermined by emergencies or the sudden introduction of new procedures.

In addition, steering committees help to:

- ensure user participation;
- provide some DP education to users;
- make users feel part of the system develop-ment process; and
- make the DP staff feel part of the organiza-tion, thereby fostering loyalty toward the organization.

Because all affected parties work closely together, communication is improved. In particular, users know *why* a particular alter-native was selected.

However, there are dangers:

- DP is controlled by a committee (as the modern proverb warns, 'a camel is a horse designed by a committee');
- the users on the committee may not have sufficient DP knowledge to be able to make informed choices; and
- priorities may be decided according to a 'decibel auction' (whoever shouts loudest and longest – see Chapter 8), or according

to whoever is the most articulate (see Chapter 10), rather than on merit.

Steering committees constitute part of the bureaucracy which often stifles DP, and so are often counter-productive (Davies, 1988).

When asked to make a decision, the steering committees must be provided with alternatives from which to choose (Lucas, 1978).

Changes to an organization

Organizations are not static – according to Brzezinski (1987), major organizational changes occur in three to five year waves.

Implementation of DP systems can result in changes in an organization, both to the structure thereof and to its staff, and even to outsiders (Dickson and Simmons, 1976):

- management information systems (MIS) often change departmental and organizational boundaries, and the formal subdivision of responsibilities;
- the organization may have to change some of its management approaches, to make systems viable and fully utilized;
- staff may be affected by redundancies, changed job requirements, less freedom of action, or transfers to different jobs, and they may resist these changes;
- auditors, customers, suppliers and the Receiver of Revenue, may be affected.

Sometimes, both the DP department and the rest of the organization are affected. An example of this is end user computing (section 3.4).

On the other hand, nearly half of over 500 installations in the GUIDE (1979) survey found that the introduction of modern programming practices improved the organizational stability. (GUIDE is the commercial IBM users group.)

Computerization requires an organizational discipline (e.g. procedures and controls for input documentation) that small businesses often lack: it is probably advisable for them to develop this discipline before attempting to computerize (Nel, 1978).

Attempting too many changes at once can lead to resistance: a step by step, modular 'building-block' approach may be preferable. Changes are more readily accepted in an organization with clear and open lines of communication: employees have avenues for expressing opinions or airing grievances. Resistance is often due to the *way* the change is introduced, rather than to the change itself.

3.3   CHIEF PROGRAMMER TEAMS

A number of common structures for the DP department have already been discussed, and various disadvantages they suffer from were pointed out. This section examines an alternative structure, one which was designed to overcome some of these disadvantages.

Experimental evidence on DP teams is lacking, and in fact many generally accepted principles are based on research on group dynamics in general and not on software development teams (Schach, 1988), but one particular team project was comparatively well documented, and has subsequently been well publicized and discussed in the literature. This was a conversational database information retrieval/maintenance system developed by IBM for the New York Times (NYT) around 1970 (Baker, 1972). Several known techniques, including a method of team organization, were brought together under the name 'chief programmer team' (CPT), and used consistently throughout the project to improve productivity.

Because hard facts are available for this project, I have referred to it a number of times during this study, and particularly in this section. It would be dangerous to place too much reliance on the results of just one project, but the NYT project is not an isolated case:

- it was preceded by the similarly organized

and equally successful 'super-programmer' project (Van Tassel, 1978);

- Inmon (1976) describes a more recent project which also used the CPT concept, and which achieved an almost identically high productivity;
- according to Schach (1988) many successful projects have used CPTs (or variants thereof), and the figures reported were good (though not as good as those obtained for the NYT project);
- Walston and Felix (1977) surveyed 60 projects, and found that the CPT concept significantly improves productivity (though their figures have been challenged – Chapter 2);
- Holton's (1977) survey, of 40 organizations, included too few (only 7) CPT projects to be able to draw any conclusions, but it did show that some of the components of the concept – structured programming, top-down design, etc. – improve productivity.

History and aims

The CPT concept is a refinement of the super-programmer project, which was also developed by IBM. The name is an apt one, as it correctly implies that, as in the case of the CPT, the project is organized around a highly-skilled programmer. The super-programmer project was also highly success-ful, producing a 50 000 instruction program in one-fifth the normal time, and with almost no errors (Van Tassel, 1978).

According to Baker (1972), the objective of the CPT was to increase programmer produc-tivity. Yourdon (1975) expands on this. According to him, IBM's intention was prob-ably to find a technique which would permit a program to be developed with a small number of people, because morale is better in a small group, communications are better, and less management is required. However, Yourdon (1975, 1979b) also implies that the motivation was to remove bugs by scrutiniz-ing coding before it was fed into the machine.

This goal goes hand in hand with the productivity goal: the earlier an error is detected, the cheaper it is to fix (Chapter 8).

3.3.1 DESCRIPTION

Definition

A CPT is a small, highly disciplined group of personnel, organized to work effectively as a programming production unit (Baker and Mills, 1973). It normally comprises a senior programmer who is the leader of the team and who designs the system; his assistant who is also a senior programmer; about three other programmers; a systems analyst; a secretary/librarian; and other specialists, as required. Each person's role is clear, and communication requirements are minimized (van Wyk and Kamfer 1976; Bell *et al.*, 1987).

This organization contrasts sharply with that of conventional programming groups, which frequently lack functional separation, discipline, and teamwork (Baker and Mills, 1973).

CPTs change programming from private art to public practice, thereby substantially improving the manageability, quality, and productivity of programming.

The concept combines technical advances in programming with a fundamental change in managerial framework, including:

- restructuring the work into specialized jobs;
- defining relationships among specialists;
- developing new tools to permit these specialists to interface effectively with a developing, always visible, project; and
- providing for training and career develop-ment of personnel within these specialties.

(A chief programmer must not be confused with a super-programmer. A chief program-mer is the project leader in a CPT, while a super-programmer is a programmer of out-standing ability and achievement. A chief programmer may or may not be a super-programmer; conversely, a super-programmer may or may not hold the position of chief programmer.)

Note

From this definition, it can be seen that the CPT is a Type 5 DP structure, and a 'project team' assemblage (section 3.1), but it has certain distinguishing characteristics, many of which can be used in the other five DP structure types.

Moving programming 'from private art to public practice' is a move toward 'ego-less programming'. (Ego-less programming means that all programs are public property, and are reviewed by the programmer's colleagues, so they are actually joint efforts. It is the basic concept underlying the democratic team (Schach, 1990), and is discussed further in Chapter 10.)

'Visibility' refers to the top-down programming, structured programming, and program production library (PPL) components. The latter is a set of procedures for carrying out the clerical-type duties of a programming project: filing all documentation (source code listings, job control language (JCL) listings, test data listings, etc.), maintaining documentation, backups, libraries of common modules, etc. (Baker, 1972; Schach, 1988; Bell *et al.*, 1987). The objective is to take away from programmers the least skilled parts of their work, thereby enhancing their productivity by allowing them to spend more time doing what they are good at, namely programming.

The 'new tools' for interfacing with the project is another reference to the PPL.

The 'technical advances in programming' are top-down programming and structured programming.

The name 'chief programmer team' is really a misnomer. Macro and Buxton (1987) would like to rename it a 'small software engineering peer group'. As will become apparent later, the chief programmer (CP) performs some of the analysis and design functions normally done by a systems analyst, and so is really a programmer/analyst rather than just a programmer. In addition, as has already been implied, it is not just a new personnel configuration, but includes other concepts (top-down programming, structured programming and clerical/secretarial assistance), and part at least of its success must be attributed to these other factors (Yourdon, 1975).

In an environment where project teams are temporary (such as a matrix DP structure), Gunther (1978) recommends that the title 'chief programmer' be an informal one. Thus a relatively junior programmer can be a CP on a small project, with consequent boost to his ego; and an experienced programmer can be a support programmer on a large project, without hurting his ego.

Components of the CPT concept

The CPT concept is a combination of several factors. Officially, it comprises (Baker, 1972):

- clerical assistance and procedures;
- structured programming;
- top-down programming;
- high experience; and
- an organizational structure.

Also included are:

- small teams;
- a programming emphasis;
- specialization; and
- good technical people remaining in a technical capacity,

which can be considered part of the 'organizational structure' aspect. In practice, it may also include:-

- high ability; and
- high motivation.

It is not clear if structured walkthroughs (Chapter 10) were intended to be part of the concept. Yourdon (1975) implies that walkthroughs were employed during the NYT project; Macro and Buxton (1987) describe peer-group based design review and code reading as methods 'associated' with the concept of CPTs; and Lucas (1985) appears to view CPTs as a vehicle for implementing egoless programming; whereas Weinberg (1971) looks upon CPTs as the very antithesis of egoless programming. Van Tassel (1978) and Baker and Mills (1973) describe in more detail the code reviews which took place on the NYT team, and these seem to bear more resemblance to traditional inspection of code by the lead programmer than to walk-throughs. Baker and Mills claim that this provides the benefits of egoless program-ming. Schach (1988) recommends using CPTs in conjunction with code walkthroughs or inspection. As the CP is personally respons-ible for every line of code, he must be present at the walkthroughs or inspections. How-ever, he is also the manager responsible for the primary evaluation of the programmers in the team, and therefore must *not* be present (Chapter 10). The way out of this dilemma is to remove much of the managerial role from the CP. He should be responsible for technical issues only, not budgetary and legal issues, or performance appraisal.

The programming secretary's duties include compilation and running of test cases (Schach, 1988). However, although clerical assistance was one of the original compo-nents of the concept, none of the 40 organiza-tions surveyed by Holton (1977) had program secretaries (though the survey included too few (only 7) CPT projects to be able to draw any conclusions). In the much larger GUIDE (1979) survey, 38% (of over 600 installations) were using a librarian function, 45% were considering it, and only 17% had rejected it. According to Johnson (1980b), 95% of the administrative and clerical tasks initially pro-posed for the librarian can now be performed by the programming personnel using auto-mated software such as TSO (time sharing option) and ROSCOE. Furthermore, pro-grammers do not program for eight consecu-tive hours all the time: they take breaks, during which they can perform the necessary administrative and clerical tasks. The post of librarian is therefore now an unnecessary overhead.

The CPT is hierarchical in nature, and so are two of its components, structured pro-gramming and top-down programming, so they fit together very neatly (Bell *et al.*, 1987).

3.3.2 BENEFITS

A number of benefits have been claimed for the CPT concept. These are discussed below.

Productivity

For a number of reasons – the separation of clerical work, clear interfaces, reduced com-munication requirements, modern program-ming practices, etc. – the CPT concept should result in higher productivity (Bell *et al.*, 1987). Results, however, have been 'highly mixed' (Boehm, 1981).

The NYT project team achieved a *program-mer* productivity rate of 65 debugged instruc-tions per programmer per day (taking into account only the time spent directly on programming work: program design, coding, debugging and testing); and a *team* produc-tivity rate of 32 (taking into account the remaining functions: requirements analysis, systems analysis, managerial, secretarial, librarian and documentation) (Baker, 1972). The latter figure is the productivity of the entire team on the completed system.

In theory, it should be a simple matter to determine the productivity gain achieved on this project: the productivity rate obtained there need only be compared against the rates listed in Chapter 2. In practice, how-ever, it is not so easy, as it is difficult to determine which of the many listed rates, covering a wide range, it should be compared against.

For example, the NYT rate of 65 statements

per day is five times higher than the 13 statements per day given by Ingham (1976), and the 14 by Walston and Felix (1977). However the average project in their surveys was probably somewhat smaller than the NYT project – the projects in the Walston and Felix survey contained, on average, only 20K LOC, compared to 83K for the NYT – in which case, bearing in mind that the larger the system, the lower is the expected productivity, the true productivity gain was greater than 5:1. On the other hand, the figures from these surveys probably mostly include non-programming time, in which case the comparison should not be with 65 statements per day on the NYT project, but with 32, so the productivity gain was less than 3:1 (32 divided by 13 or 14).

Because of this uncertainty, it may be better to examine the productivity gains claimed for the NYT project by other authorities.

According to Yourdon (1975), the rate of 65 instructions per day is four to six times better than the average programmer. This agrees with the similarly organized super-programmer project, which was completed in one-fifth the normal time (Van Tassel, 1978).

Martin and McClure (1985) claim a similar order of improvement, namely that the productivity achieved was four or five times higher than the norm.

McClure (1978) also claims a similar order of improvement, namely five to six times, but her figures are not directly comparable to those of the other authorities for several reasons.

- She is not referring specifically to the NYT project, or even to CPTs in general, but to several projects the common factor of which was not CPTs but structured programming. As the other projects produced productivity figures comparable to the NYT team, one could deduce that structured programming was the major, if not the sole, factor responsible for the latter's

success. In other words, the organizational and other aspects of the CPT concept may have a negligible effect on productivity.
- Similarly, some of her projects used walkthroughs, and may owe some (most?) of their success to that.
- Her base rate is 5–10 debugged instructions per programmer per day, compared to Yourdon's 10–15.
- Further, her base rate is for 'traditional non-structured programs', while Yourdon's is for the 'average programmer'.
- She gives a productivity rate of 35 for the NYT project. This figure includes analytical, managerial, and clerical time. While this is a more important figure than for the programming time alone, any reference to productivity figures should at least state that non-programming time has been included, especially when the reference appears in a book which is specifically about programming. It is not clear if non-programming time is included in the figures for the other projects she quotes.

Baker (1972) is more modest, claiming only a doubling of productivity for the NYT project, while Basili and Baker (1975) claim even less for it: 11–25%.

The Walston and Felix (1977) study of 60 projects found that productivity was 1.9 times higher when CPTs were used for more than 66% of the code, than when they were used for 33% or less. However, as pointed out in Chapter 2, that may merely have been because this technique was used more often on smaller projects, so the high productivity observed was actually due to the small size of the projects and not to the team organization; or because the technique was used with other modern programming practices such as structured programming, so the high productivity was actually due to that.

The Albrecht (1979) study of 22 projects found a productivity gain of about 3:1, which he attributed mainly to the use of structured programming, a programming development

Table 3.1 Claimed productivity gain of CPTs

Source	Ratio
Super-programmer project	
Van Tassel (1978)	5:1
NYT	
McClure (1978)	5–6:1
Yourdon (1975)	4–6:1
Martin and McClure (1985)	4 or 5:1
Baker (1972)	2:1
Basili and Baker (1975)	1.11 to 1.25:1
Inmon (1976)	same productivity as NYT
Albrecht (1979) (4 components of CPT)	3:1
Walston and Felix (1977)	1.9:1
Boehm (1981)	mixed

library, high-level languages, and on-line programming, which are four of the factors applicable to the NYT project, so these rather than the organizational aspects may be responsible for the observed gain on that project.

(Other, similar claims, for the combined effect of several modern programming practices are given in Table 8.71. These are mostly slightly lower than Albrecht's 3:1.)

Some of these claimed improvements (summarized in Table 3.1) are so large as to warrant caution in accepting them, and it is not clear why there are such big differences between the claims.

- Are the claimants comparing like with like?
- Is the base (standard) against which they are comparing, an average or a worst case?

Baker's estimate appears to be an attempt to avoid such pitfalls. He is comparing the NYT results against 'comparable projects that were organized more conventionally', and he may also be allowing for the greater than average level of experience of the members of the NYT team. Thus his estimate is probably of the improvement which is due to the organizational aspects alone.

In contrast, Yourdon and McClure are probably using as their base projects which use none of the CPT concepts.

Schach (1988) believes that the high pro-

ductivity on the NYT project was due to the high ability of the staff – 'IBM, with superb software experts, sent in their very best people' – and the team had strong technical backup, including language and JCL experts. Furthermore, this was a prestige project, the first real trial for PL/1.

Boehm (1981) similarly believes that the high gains attributed to CPTs were due to the high ability of the staff on those individual projects, and to the fact that the method is generally used on smaller projects, where productivity is in any case higher. Both he and Conte *et al.* (1986) appear to credit structured programming with the gains which Walston and Felix (1977) implicitly attributed to CPTs. There are two reservations I have here. Firstly, structured programming and CPTs were usually used together, and where two factors are closely correlated, how can you be sure that any observed effect is due to one factor rather than the other?; secondly, Boehm (1981) uses, with apparent approval, a CPT structure in one of his examples – would he do this if he believed they are of no benefit?

Errors

For a number of reasons – the team organized around a highly-skilled programmer, clearer module interfaces, reduced communication

Table 3.2   Effect of error reduction in production programs on overall productivity

	Conventional Time and %	CPT Time	%
Development	50.0	50.0	55.1
Maintenance: errors	10.0	0.7	0.8
other	40.0	40.0	44.1
Total	100.0	90.7	100.0

requirements, etc. – the CPT concept should result in fewer errors (Bell *et al.*, 1987).

According to McClure (1978), the number of errors detected during production running of the NYT project was only one-fifteenth as many as normal: 0.3 per 1000 lines of code, compared to 5 (which is in good agreement with the average of about 8 in Table 8.41). This represents, as a first approximation, a reduction of fifteen times in the time spent correcting errors in production programs. However, bearing in mind that maintenance comprises about 50% of the total software time, while error correction accounts for only about 20% of maintenance activity (Chapter 8), and therefore only about 10% of the total time, the effect of this improvement on overall productivity is less dramatic. Thus the reduction of fifteen times in the number of errors produces a reduction in the total time spent on the system of only (10.0 − 0.7 =) 9.3, which is an improvement in productivity of just 100.0:90.7 or 10% (Table 3.2).

To this improvement, however, must be added other factors, such as (Weinberg, 1971; Boehm, 1973):

- the disruptive effects of the errors and their correction: 'auditing the files for the effects of the restart was a gargantuan labor which stretched out over several months';
- the hardware costs;
- the adverse effect on the image of DP and the organization;
- direct losses to the organization due to the errors, e.g. loss of business;

- the effect on customers, e.g. undelivered welfare cheques, bad credit reports, and even loss of life in cases such as an air traffic control system.

These losses depend heavily on the specific application, so it is meaningless to try to estimate an average, but it must be borne in mind that they do exist and may be considerable. They are alleviated by any method which reduces the number of errors, and not just by CPTs. Errors and their consequences are discussed later, particularly in Chapters 5 and 10.

Other

Several other benefits are claimed for CPTs (Baker, 1972; Hanata, 1989; Bell *et al.*, 1987):

- the small size of the teams reduces communications problems significantly, and makes the teams highly responsive to changes;
- team members concentrate on those functions they do best;
- projects are more visible and therefore more manageable, which in turn means that deadlines are more reliably met;
- an improved career path for the best programmers; and
- an improvement in workers' ability.

The productivity effects of these factors are automatically included in the rates already quoted.

In addition, Baker (1972) claims ease of maintenance. This claim is plausible because of the use of structured programming, a technique which is claimed to give this benefit (Chapter 8), and because of the emphasis on documentation (e.g. the use of the PPL), but is difficult to quantify, and was not quantified. Because of the large amount of time spent on maintenance, any improvement in this field would have a significant effect on overall software productivity.

Because of the concentration of the design function on one person, a CPT-developed system should have 'conceptual integrity', which Brooks (1975) identified as the most important design consideration.

Another benefit, which applies not just to CPTs but to any factor which improves quality, is the 'ripple effect'. If CPTs are used to develop system software, such as operating systems, it should result in better products: ones which are easier to use and have fewer bugs. This will benefit everyone who uses the products, including software engineers, so their productivity will rise. Even if the magnitude of the effect is small, the number of people affected will be large, so the total impact will be large.

3.3.3 PROGRAMMING EMPHASIS

Various aspects of the CPT concept are examined individually in this study, thereby identifying those factors which were responsible for the concept's success on the NYT and other projects, and determining how widely it can be used and what further improvements can be made. The programming emphasis is specific to CPTs and so is discussed in this section. Other factors, such as experience, ability, structured programming, and top-down programming, are more general in nature, and so are discussed elsewhere. Perhaps the most striking aspect of CPTs is the apparent shift of emphasis away from the conventional systems analyst, to the programmer.

Programmer as project leader

This shift of emphasis is exemplified firstly by having a programmer, instead of the more customary systems analyst, as the project leader (Appendix D). The systems analyst is subordinate to the chief programmer, and one organization even transferred to the O&M department those analysts who had neither the programming experience nor the potential to become CPs (van Wyk and Kamfer, 1976). The rationale behind this

move is that a systems analyst cannot adequately control the quality of the programming. This is particularly true if the analyst has had no programming experience, but even where he has had such experience, he will probably be out of date (Yourdon, 1975). In any event, he is no longer a programmer, and may have no desire to revert – even on a part-time basis and in a supervisory capacity – to programming. In practice, therefore, his supervision is limited to the externals of the programs: deficiencies in the internals, e.g. the structure of the programs, will go unnoticed until it is too late (e.g. when difficulties are experienced while debugging).

Time-dominance of programming

Programming is a vital part of any software system: if it fails, so does the system. Besides, it forms a large portion – perhaps as much as 60% – of the total system development time (Chapter 8). (The figure varies according to circumstances, e.g. it is lower where fourth-generation languages are used.) By contrast, perhaps as little as 30% of the time is consumed by systems analysis (including system design). Programming time thus dominates analysis time by a ratio of perhaps two to one. From this viewpoint, therefore, it is logical to have an organizational structure which places its main emphasis on programming. The CPT concept does just this.

Another way to achieve this objective is to virtually abandon the project team idea and revert to the Type 2 or Type 3 DP structure. Within the group of programmers, there would be a team which handled all the programming for that project. The team could be organized around a senior, highly-skilled programmer, thereby retaining one of the central concepts of the CPT. However, the analytical and programming functions would be separate, causing a weakening of the centralized control of the CPT and probably leading to an increase in communications, so a lowering of productivity might result.

This idea is similar to an unsuccessful experiment tried by one organization, a large life assurance company, in which a programmer and an analyst were joint CP, but does not suffer from the same disadvantages (the large amount of coding for the programmer, and the analyst's lack of programming knowledge preventing him from controlling the programming effectively) (van Wyk and Kamfer, 1976).

No full-time specialist analyst

Other aspects in the shift of emphasis from analysis to programming are that (Baker, 1972):

- the project team may not include an analyst at all – on small, simple projects, the CP does all the analytical work himself;
- where there is an analyst, he might not be a member of the team for the full duration of the project;
- on the NYT project, the analyst was also a programmer and did some of the programming, a practice which Macro and Buxton (1987) encourage.

Earlier in this chapter, I referred to the opposite situation, namely a greater emphasis on the user. Thus we find users in the position of project leader, and an increasing use being made of business analysts. There is much to be said for this approach too. The system is being developed, not to give enjoyment to programmers, but to satisfy a requirement of the users. If the completed system does not meet the users' needs then, no matter how high the quality of the programming, documentation, etc., no matter how elegant and original the programming, nor how quickly it was completed, that system will represent time wasted, as it will have to be at least partially re-written to make it comply with the users' needs. In the extreme case, it must be totally discarded: 'a brilliant solution to the wrong problem' (Yourdon, 1979b).

The CPT concept is not necessarily inconsistent with this opposite trend. In a CPT (the analyst/programmer on the NYT team notwithstanding), the systems analyst concentrates largely on the externals of the system, i.e. what the user sees (Baker, 1972). The internal design of the system, e.g. its subdivision into programs and utilities, and the specification of the programs, is done by the CP (assisted by the back-up programmer (BUP) and the systems analyst). A case can be made out for this, as such functions require someone who is close to the machine. This arrangement reduces the amount of work the systems analyst has to do, and can be used to free him to concentrate on the user aspects, so his functions could be performed by a business analyst.

Conclusion

There is thus a need for both a programming, and simultaneously, a user orientation. Having a programmer/analyst as the project leader, which is what happens in a CPT, may well provide the ideal balance between the two, and therefore the highest productivity. It is significant that Walston and Felix (1977) found that productivity was greatly improved – by 2.6:1 – if programmers participated in the design of the functional specifications. While this figure seems rather high – and Walston and Felix's figures have been challenged (see Chapter 2) – an even higher improvement of 20:1 has been claimed for the joint application design (JAD) methodology, which operates on a similar principle (Chapter 8). However, part of the improvement may be apparent rather than real, as it may derive from a simplification in the specifications, i.e. the developers may have taken advantage of their closer initial contact with the users to negotiate changes in their requirements in order to reduce development effort.

Does this change of emphasis work? The NYT system went through *six* revisions, which included 'major changes' (Baker, 1972). The literature I surveyed did not contain the corresponding information for other, similar, projects, so I do not know if this is better or worse than normal. If the team had been less programming-oriented, e.g. if it had been led by a specialist analyst, would they have determined the user's real requirements sooner, thereby saving much reprogramming? It should be borne in mind that the high productivity on the NYT project was achieved in spite of all these revisions. Would a shift of emphasis part of the way back to systems analysis, but still retaining the basic CPT concepts (perhaps merely by having a specialist analyst instead of the analyst/programmer used on the NYT team), result in an even higher productivity?

3.3.4 DISADVANTAGES

The CPT concept has a number of disadvantages. Some of these disadvantages, and some ways of overcoming them, are considered below.

- The emphasis is on high experience – Macro and Buxton (1987) recommend at least seven years relevant experience for the CP, and three to six for his deputy – so there is less scope for trainees. Various possible solutions, such as a training section, are proposed in section 9.4.
- It focuses all design and implementation on one person – without this characteristic, the structure becomes a standard pyramid – which places an upper limit on the size of the problem the team can undertake. To overcome this, Baker (1972) suggests using a hierarchy of CPTs.
- It requires a paragon as the CP. This problem is discussed later, particularly in Appendix F.
- The BUP must be in every way as good as the CP, but must take a back seat (and lower salary) while waiting for something to happen to the CP, and neither top programmers nor top managers are prepared to do that (Schach, 1988). However, it is probably relatively uncommon for

something to happen to the CP, so I think it is acceptable for the BUP to be less experienced than the CP, as recommended by Macro and Buxton.
- The secretary/librarian position is a responsible one which is central to success, yet it could become a bottleneck (Pomberger, 1984). Further, the work is largely routine, and so is performed by a junior who might become dissatisfied and even leave, especially as software professionals are notorious for their aversion to paperwork (Schach, 1988). However, in the Macro and Buxton (1987) version of the CPT, the librarian monitors and expedites the tasks rather than doing all the work himself. It is therefore not a full-time job, and they suggest that the role be rotated between the different members of the team. The Johnson (1980b) opinion quoted earlier was that nearly all the administrative and clerical tasks can now be performed by the programming personnel themselves using automated software; and in any case, the programmers could perform the tasks during the breaks they take from programming. The post of librarian is therefore now unnecessary.
- The accusation that it tends to de-skill the work is only partly true, and is discussed in Appendix F.
- It is thought to adversely affect workers' morale (Hanata, 1989). This problem, and ways of addressing it, are also discussed in Appendix F.

3.3.5 RESISTANCE TO CPTs

Only a minority of organizations have implemented CPTs – 18% in the Holton (1977) survey of 40 organizations, 34% (of over 600 installations) in the GUIDE (1979) survey (though a further 46% were considering it), and 30% of the operational systems in the Lientz *et al.* (1978) survey (of 69 organizations) – even though the concept had been publicized for several years. The question therefore arises: why has it not been more widely used? The concept does have disadvantages, as listed above, but it may also be attributable to resistance to change. General reasons for resistance to change are given in Chapter 9. Some general reasons relevant to CPTs, and some specific reasons applying to CPTs, are listed below.

Ignorance

Many software engineers are rather insular and are pre-occupied with their own immediate tasks – possibly because they are overworked – and so are ignorant of developments outside their own immediate world. The average programmer, for example, has only 0.4 books, reads only 0.2 journals, and never attends a technical meeting (DeMarco, 1981a, 1992; Dunn and Ullman, 1982): 'Many programmers go through their complete working life without reading a book or an article on programming or without ever discussing techniques with a colleague' (Bell *et al.*, 1987). It is possible, therefore, that many programmers know little about the concept and its benefits.

Amateur programming

The rapid increase in amateur programming from about 1968 onwards obscured the CPT and many other good practices (Macro and Buxton, 1987).

Conservatism

Software engineers, no less than the population in general, tend to stick to methods with which they are familiar.

Morale

Because it is thought to adversely affect workers' morale, it has largely been avoided in Japan (Hanata, 1989).

Skepticism

Software engineers have a healthy skepticism, which is justified in this instance to the extent that the productivity on the NYT Project *was* atypical: the CP was exceptionally able (Appendix F), and everything 'jelled' together. Also, there was initially a high failure rate (20–30%) of CPTs, but this has now been reduced to less than 10% (Macro and Buxton, 1987).

Too few potential CPs

The CP needs to be a paragon of many abilities: for example, he needs to be both a highly skilled programmer and a successful manager, but there is a shortage of both (Schach, 1988). It is therefore understandable that organizations are reluctant to implement the concept. If the CP is poor, productivity can be very low (Boehm, 1981). Nevertheless, I think the seriousness of this disadvantage is generally overrated. The topic is discussed in Appendix F, and the conclusion reached that productivity gains can generally still be expected even if the CP falls short of the ideal.

Too few skilled programmers

Similarly, the CPT concept has connotations of skilled people and elite teams – the principle of top talent: use better and fewer people (Boehm, 1981) – but the shortage of skills is such that there simply are not enough skilled people to go around (Glass, 1979). Elite teams will therefore not solve the shortfall in productivity. This objection to CPTs is only partly valid. Although the well-publicized CPT projects in the past may have used elite teams, this is not an essential requirement. In fact, the CPT concept, by concentrating the most complex work onto the CP, tends to *de-skill* the tasks of some of the remaining members of the team. (This is discussed in Appendix F.)

Opposition

There may be opposition to CPTs for a variety of reasons. Systems analysts stand to lose by a switch to CPTs, and so are likely to oppose such a move. In an egalitarian society, there is opposition to even the suggestion of elite teams (Macro and Buxton, 1987). Matrix organizations will resist the introduction of the hierarchical CPT. Programmers may resent the constraints, and the increased visibility of the work can induce stress in them (Bell *et al.*, 1987).

3.3.6 CONCLUSION

Expert opinion is divided on the merits of the CPT concept. At the one extreme, authorities like Boehm (1981) and possibly Conte *et al.* (1986) as well, appear to reject it. Their opinions are based on a rigorous analysis of the evidence, and so must be respected. Schach (1988) expressed the view that classical CPTs are as impractical to implement as democratic teams (but for different reasons). At the other extreme, IBM continues using CPTs, and claims they are effective (Bell *et al.*, 1987); and Macro and Buxton (1987) claim they are the best way of achieving high levels of quality and adherence to time-scale and budgets, and that, in modified form, they will become the norm in many organizations.

Faced with this difference of opinion, it is difficult to reach a conclusion. The well-publicized, highly successful CPT projects probably owe much of their success to the high experience, ability and motivation of the team members, rather than to the organizational structure, clerical assistance, and maybe even the structured programming and top-down programming components of CPTs. In other words, in more prosaic situations, the concept will be less successful. Worse, if the CP is poor, the concept may even do more harm than good. Nevertheless, I believe that CPTs *can* increase productivity in many instances, even where circumstances do not quite measure up to the ideal.

3.4 INFORMATION CENTERS

An information center (IC) is a section within the DP department. It is staffed by people who are experts in end user software (such as spreadsheets and fourth-generation languages), or in the application areas. They act as consultants to the users, advising and helping them to use these tools; set up prototypes; etc. Programmers may also make use of the facilities in an IC, as they also use fourth-generation languages, or they may use the word processing facilities to create program documentation.

There is a second type of IC, one whose purpose is to supply users with data, especially statistics about the organization's business operations, and which would probably be staffed by user department clerks (Gildersleeve, 1978). This type will not be discussed here.

Medium-sized software organizations (50–200 staff) are exploring the use of ICs, while large organizations have formal ICs (Jones, 1986b). In one organization, only 20% of the capabilities of the IC machines were being used (McKee, 1986). Similarly, 65% of the organizations in one survey had implemented an IC in the previous two years, but these centers had not been extensively used (FTP, 1983). Few of the organizations were therefore able to pinpoint specific benefits, but the situation was expected to improve. In fact, the concept is not a new one, but has been around since the late 1970s (Mittra, 1988; Etheridge *et al.*, 1987). Many organizations have successfully implemented it (Grulke, 1983), and the number of ICs has been growing by 15% p.a. (Mittra, 1988). According to Mittra, the key to success is finding the right manager.

End user computing

End user computing is the use of computers directly by end users. Typically, the end users do *ad hoc* enquiries on corporate data; produce *ad hoc* reports from the data; display the data in graphical form; and work with spreadsheets or financial modelling packages, e.g. to do 'what if' calculations. They may even write their own programs using fourth-generation languages: according to a Price Waterhouse survey in Britain, in 31% of installations, users did more than three-quarters of the systems development work (Etheridge *et al.*, 1987); and in one large organization, users wrote 'several hundred imaginative business solutions', and supported the systems themselves (Brzezinski, 1987). *Bank Systems & Equipment* predicted that user applications would at least double in the next two to three years (PC users equipped – but undertrained. *Bank Systems & Equipment*, January 1986, p. 62). Jones (1983c, 1986b) estimated that there were over 2800 000 end users in the US in 1984 who could perform at least some programming, and they outnumbered professional programmers by nearly 3 to 1. However, he also estimated that they developed only 10% of very small applications (less than the equivalent of 500 LOC), and did not develop any applications larger than the equivalent of 16k LOC. According to Shneiderman (1980), for every professional programmer, there are probably ten occasional programmers who write programs for scientific research, engineering development, marketing research, business applications, etc., and there is also a rapidly growing number of hobbyist programmers working on small business, personal, and home computing applications.

The hardware used was originally mainly terminals linked to the mainframe (or mini), but PCs are increasingly being employed (Martin, 1985). The software tools are mostly spreadsheets, financial modelling packages, graphics, database management systems, word processing, and fourth-generation languages. The data users work with maybe either their own data which they type themselves, or corporate data. In the latter case, they would probably work with extracts from the corporate data which had been downloaded onto the PCs, rather than directly with the data on the mainframe.

End user computing can occur with any of the DP department structures described earlier, but it may lead to a change in the structure of the department. Traditionally, DP provides a 'help desk' to assist users, but a survey showed that in 70% of organizations, the 'help desk' was only staffed part-time; many of the staff had not been trained; it was not situated in a separate office; and it was frequently ignored (Etheridge *et al.*, 1987). With the large amount of computing now being done by users, and the increased interaction between them and DP staff, there is a need for a better method of assisting them. The IC does just this. Help is necessary because end users 'can make all sorts of mistakes', and sometimes expensive mistakes, when they create their own systems (Martin, 1985). In fact, much of the Santa Fe railroad system, although it was eventually spectacularly successful, had to be completely rebuilt before it became successful.

Setting up an information center

Reasons for setting up an IC include (Martin, 1982b, 1983b; Etheridge *et al.*, 1987; Brzezinski, 1987; Duffy, 1983):

- to provide technical support to user staff and management in acquiring and using PCs;
- to manage the orderly introduction of PCs, train users in the concepts of desktop computing, and install software;
- to control the demand for PCs: usage of PCs in the IC is monitored, and a PC is only given on a permanent basis to those users who spend enough time on the machines to warrant having one of their own;
- to aid decentralization and the distributed development of systems;
- to make data available to users, while keeping databases intact;
- to give the DP department more visibility and credibility.

Estimates of the number of staff required to man an IC range from one per 20 users, to one per 100 users (Grulke, 1983).

In one organization, setting up the IC with terminals, PCs and software, took six months (McKee, 1986). Training the users in sound computer practices took another year. The training also weeded out those users who were attracted merely by the novelty. The IC users in this organization were nearly all senior clerical staff and middle managers.

Because it is a fundamental change, problems can arise, e.g. (Swidler, 1986; Mittra, 1988; Etheridge *et al.*, 1987):

- starting with vague or minimal management support;
- initial resistance from DP staff;
- end user fear of computers;
- inadequate needs assessment;
- inadequate resources;
- inadequate consideration of training needs;
- inappropriate staff selection;
- trying an immediate, large-scale implementation;
- inadequate communication with MIS;
- lack of standardization on product selection;
- duplication of data and effort; and
- lack of a chargeback structure.

Benefits

Apart from facilitating assistance to users, several other benefits are claimed for the concept, e.g. (Grulke, 1983; Etheridge *et al.*, 1987; Mittra, 1988):

- by working away from their offices, users avoid interruptions and can concentrate on the task at hand;
- it trains users, making them more computer-literate and giving them a better appreciation of DP, resulting in more realistic requests for mainframe services;
- it makes the 'IS ivory tower' more accessible;

- it leads to a better understanding of users' needs;
- it has a beneficial effect on DP staff, who produce more user-friendly mainframe programs;
- the programmers also document their programs better because of the availability of word processing facilities in the IC;
- it opens a new career path; and
- it ensures orderly growth.

In short, it allows maximum benefit to be derived from the software tools, and ensures that maximum use is made of scarce DP resources.

Martin (1985) reported one IC which gave a 100% return on investment compared to only 37% for DP-developed applications, and another IC which gave a 300% return. The returns are so high because users are tackling problems that have a direct impact on cost or revenue, e.g. making better financial decisions, optimal purchases of bulk chemicals, or maximizing the goods that can be handled with given resources.

Phasing out

Some organizations manage without an IC – the Banque Nationale de Paris, for example, has adopted many IC concepts without actually setting one up – while other organizations are dismantling theirs (Etheridge *et al.*, 1987). An IC may be phased out because (Brzezinski, 1987):

- it runs counter to attempts to build an integrated data, communications and technology infrastructure;
- it propagates fragmented solutions;
- it duplicates existing DP chargeback procedures;
- it evolves into 'maintenance mode', which does not make the most effective use of the staff's skills;
- users find it easier to ask the IC than read their manuals, and this overloads the IC staff; and at the other extreme,

- many users have become experts, and train and support themselves.

ICs should not be dismantled suddenly, but should be phased out. Users must be prepared beforehand so that they rely less on IC staff; the IC functions, including a more limited hot-line support, must be transferred to another DP department; new career opportunities must be created for the IC staff, so that their skills are not wasted; etc.

3.5 DEVELOPMENT CENTERS

A development center is typically a section within the DP department, reporting directly to the highest level manager responsible for software development (Boehm, 1981). It consists of a group of specialists who are usually experienced DP professionals, and its aim is to improve the productivity of other DP professionals. According to Jones (1986b), low-medium-sized software organizations (10–50 staff) have impromptu development centers by virtue of their 'seasoning' of programmers who specialize, and are therefore expert in, selected topics such as networks and database products; large software organizations (200–1000 staff) have formal development centers; and very large ones (more than 1000 staff) have departments whose full-time work is to screen potentially interesting software packages, and arrange corporate licences for suitable ones.

A development center actively explores, and then transfers, technology (Jones, 1986b). It is responsible for research and standardization. It investigates, and then selects, implements, promotes, and measures the effectiveness of hardware, software tools, and techniques – anything which will improve productivity. It provides education, advice, and support to DP professionals working in all stages of the software life-cycle, and to DP management. It makes available libraries of common modules (reusable code), updates the standards manual, and provides management with an analysis of productivity improvements (Abbott, 1983b). A development center might, for example, recommend that a separate computer be purchased for the sole use of the programmers.

There is an overlap between the goals and functions of the development center and the IC, as both aim to maximize use of resources, and analysts and programmers also use end user tools such as fourth-generation languages. However, the development center is technically oriented, and the IC is end user oriented, so the functions might be too dissimilar for them to be performed by the same people. The development center seems to have received far less attention than the IC. The few I have known have tended to have a narrow technical orientation, i.e. they concentrated on software utilities such as for optimizing hardware performance, rather than covering the full range of factors affecting productivity.

The development center ensures that productivity is given the attention it deserves. It is claimed to be able to double productivity (Abbott, 1983a).

3.6 FAMILY TEAMS

A family team is a permanent team in which special emphasis is given to the training and development of the team members. It could be a project team, i.e. contain a mixture of job functions, or consist solely of specialists in one function, e.g. programmers. Thorpe (1976) described the concept in an article, though Weinberg (1971) also likens a programming team to a family, and discusses the implications this has for leadership of the team.

Training of juniors is frequently neglected, and a number of them flounder as a result, so Thorpe's analogy with the upbringing of underprivileged orphans is impressive. Thorpe claims that his ideas lead to a probable quadrupling in productivity.

Family teams are claimed to provide the following benefits:

- consistent methods, so that staff do not continually have to unlearn one set of methods and learn a new set in its place;
- the members help each other, which assists the spread of experience, and they also compensate for each other;
- greater commitment to training;
- more knowledgeable, factually-based allocation of work to promote personal (career) development;
- clear responsibility and authority;
- acknowledged leaders;
- established succession; and
- the systems for planning, directing, controlling and motivating, can only work effectively with this type of organization.

Many of these benefits are because a family team is a permanent team.

Comparison of matrix and family team structures

These two structures appear to be diametrically opposed, with the former being transient, and the latter permanent, yet persuasive arguments can be advanced in support of each of them. Thorpe estimated that the family team can produce a quadrupling in productivity, but this claim was not supported by experimental or observational evidence, and is so optimistic that it should be treated with caution. I have not seen such an optimistic prediction for the matrix structure.

The main difference between the two structures may lie in the training aspect, which is emphasized in the family team. According to Sommerville (1989), informal teams can be very successful, particularly where the majority of team members are experienced and competent. The matrix structure may therefore be the better where all the staff are highly experienced, whereas family teams may be superior where trainees are present. If so, as the latter situation is the

more common (DP is an expanding industry, and senior staff are promoted or retire), family teams would be of more general use. Alternatively, a training section or a training supervisor could be incorporated into the matrix structure, to strengthen it in this area.

Another difference between the two structures may lie in the ability of the staff. As indicated earlier, my first impression of the matrix structure was that it was more suited to high-ability staff – people who can work very well independently – whereas family teams may suit average staff, who need more assistance. Once again, the expanding nature of the DP industry, the consequent lower level of skills and the fact that most staff are average, means that family teams would be more generally useful.

A third difference may lie in the low social needs of programmers: they 'are not actively seeking a team experience' (Couger and Zawacki, 1980). This should favor the looser matrix structure, but its greater number of contacts (i.e. with a greater number of people) is a disadvantage.

We are not necessarily in an 'either-or' situation. On an industry-wide basis, there should be room for both structures, and even within an organization it may be possible for the two types to coexist, with staff being allocated to one type or the other depending on their individual circumstances. The organization would thereby gain the best of both worlds.

3.7 COMMUNICATION AND CO-ORDINATION

Members of a team have to communicate with each other, and their work must be co-ordinated. These activities are essentially non-productive, and are one reason for the exceptionally low productivity – perhaps only one program source statement per person per day – achieved on projects on which very large numbers of people are working. As Glass (1979) put it, communication (between people and between modules) is often the bane of the large project.

Time is required to communicate with other team members about updating common information, handling errors, resolving the use of shared resources, module interfaces (module names, number and type of parameters), etc. (Boehm, 1981; Bell *et al.*, 1987). Also, the more people on the team, the more opportunities there are for personality conflicts, differences in programming philosophy, and conflicts in work habits between individuals, to retard the overall productivity of the team – and the greater the chance of illness or staff turnover, entailing job handover and training of new members in standards and procedures, etc.

3.7.1 MAGNITUDE OF PRODUCTIVITY LOSS

When people work together, the time spent communicating with each other and co-ordinating their activities, is essentially non-productive. The question arises: *how much* time is thus spent? A variety of estimates and observations have been made, and these are discussed below.

Weinberg (1971) states that, as a rough rule, a team of three programmers working together can only do twice as much productive work as a single programmer of the same ability, because of the time spent on co-ordination. Similarly, three teams of three programmers each, working together, can only do twice as much productive work as a single team, i.e. nine programmers working together can only do four times as much productive work as a single programmer of the same ability working alone. If this progression can be extrapolated (which is by no means certain: Weinberg did not claim that it can), then:

- 27 programmers working together can only do as much productive work as 8 programmers of the same ability working alone;
- 81 as much as 16;
- 243 as much as 32, and so on.

This is an example of diseconomies of scale.

Conte *et al.* (1986) give a more rigorous analysis of the subject, and does so from both a practical and a theoretical point of view. He looked at the underlying reason for the decrease in productivity with increasing team size, namely the number of communication paths between the team members. For example, with only two people in the team, there is only one communication path, but with 48 people, there are no fewer than (48* (48 – 1)/2=) 1128 (Boehm, 1981). However, the number of communication paths depends not only on the number of team members, but also on the organizational structure or style: in a hierarchy, each person might be restricted to communicating with their supervisor only (i.e. very few paths); while in a matrix structure, they might communicate directly with every other member of the team (i.e. very many paths). Intermediate options are also possible. The number of communication paths, and therefore productivity, are thus under our control. Conte also applied this theory to one of the sets of projects comprising his database. He assumed that the amount of team interaction was midway between the minimum and maximum values, and obtained a figure of 10% as the amount of productivity lost for each communication path. He also examined the relationship between team size (*N*) and productivity (in LOC per man-month) on the 187 projects in his database, and derived a formula (LOC/MM=777/(*N***0.5)) which best fitted the actual productivity figures. The figures attributed to him in Table 3.3 were obtained using this formula.

Using Weinberg's figures, if there are three programmers in the team, they can only do as much work as two people, a ratio of 3:2 (or 1.5:1). Put another way, for every two hours productive work, one hour is spent on non-productive co-ordination, so the staff are only productive for (2/3 =) 67% of the time, and co-ordination consumes (1/2 =) 50% as much time as productive work, i.e. there is a productivity loss of 50%.

Table 3.3 Productivity loss through communication and co-ordination

Source	Team size	Amount of work LOC/MM	Amount of work People	Ratio	Productivity loss (%)	Productive time (%)
Weinberg (1971)	3		2	1.5	50	67
	9		4	2.25	125	44
(Extrapolate)	27		8	3.4	240	30
	81		16	5.1	410	20
	243		32	7.6	660	13
	729		64	11.4	1040	9
	2187		128	17.1	1610	6
Conte *et al.* (1986)	3	449	1.7	1.7	70	57
	9	259	3	3	200	33
	27	150	5.2	5.2	420	19
	81	86	9	9	800	11
	243	50	16	16	1500	7
	729	29	27	27	2600	4
	2187	17	47	47	4600	2
Brooks (1975)	1000			21	2000	5
Yourdon (1975)				5–50	400–4900	20–2
Aron (1974)				1.05–1.10	5–10	95–91

By comparison, a time and motion study of 70 programmers at Bell Laboratories found that roughly 30% of their workday was devoted to job communication (Bairdain, 1964). Separate figures for the time spent at meetings and on the telephone, which are specific forms of communication, are given later. The figures quoted vary widely, but it would appear that professional staff spend 20% – and possibly much more – of their time on these activities.

The figures attributed to Brooks were based on his factor of seven difference in productivity between small teams (10 members) and very large teams (1000 members). This has been increased by a factor of three – the approximate difference in productivity between small teams (with about half a dozen members) and individual programmers – to put his figures onto the same basis as Weinberg's.

The figures attributed to Yourdon were based on his productivity rates quoted in Chapter 2. The productivity assumed for small programs is 50 (the average of the figures of 35 and 65 for 'structured programs'),

and that for very large programs ranges from one to ten. Furthermore, it is assumed that the small programs were written by individual programmers (i.e. working alone), therefore the adjustment factor of three used for Brooks does not apply.

It is not clear how Aron's figures can be reconciled with the others, especially as he is including time lost due to other factors such as sickness and rest periods. Perhaps he is referring to co-ordination *problems* as distinct from co-ordination *work* (analogous to the difference between debugging a program and writing it).

The factors given by Weinberg (for small teams) and Brooks (for very large teams), seem rather high. They were not directly supported by experimental evidence, but – as can be seen from Table 3.3 – are in approximate agreement:

- with each other (via the extrapolated figures);
- with Conte's figures (which are based on the observed productivity of 187 projects);
- with Yourdon's figures (which are based on the observed productivity differences

between small and very large programs); and particularly

- with the very low productivity on very large projects.

However, there are too many other factors at work – rewriting code, testing and debugging, etc. – to be able to ascribe the very low productivity on very large projects wholly, or even largely, to communication and co-ordination requirements. In fact, Van Tassel (1978) implies that communication is *not* the major factor. Nevertheless, even if it is not, the productivity is so low that Weinberg's and Brooks's factors can still be true.

Supposing more programmers are added to a team, as often happens when a project is late. The new programmers will not be very productive initially while they familiarize themselves with the project, and with the standards and procedures. However, even after this initial period, the work they produce is offset by a lowering in the output of the original programmers, because of the extra communications paths introduced by adding the new programmers. Taking both aspects into account, adding more programmers might even *reduce* the total output of the team. This is the basis of Brooks' Law: men and months (effort and schedule) are not interchangeable – adding manpower to a late project makes it later (Brooks, 1975; Dunn and Ullman, 1982). (A study by Abdel-Hamid (1989) indicates that Brooks' Law should be revised to: 'adding more people to a late project always causes it to become more costly, but does not always cause it to complete later', which seems more reasonable.)

3.7.2   CAUTIONS

Communication is an integral part of any DP project. It comprises many facets: progress reporting, informing programmers of the interface requirements for modules, etc., much of which is documented. If a program is written entirely by one person, he can do away not only with much of the communication, but also with much of this documentation, with consequent increase in his productivity. However, the lack of documentation will prove a handicap when the program is subsequently maintained, i.e. the productivity of the maintenance programmers will be lowered. Care should therefore be taken when trying to economize in this area.

Similarly, co-ordination is an integral part of any DP project. If it is neglected, then there might be duplication of effort, or someone might be left idle because he needs something which is not yet ready. Singer (1982) claimed that the time spent in group communication is quickly repaid by the increase in morale and co-ordination, and the subsequent rise in productivity.

3.7.3   MINIMIZING PRODUCTIVITY LOSS

How can the significant amount of time spent on non-productive communication and co-ordination be reduced? Several possibilities are discussed below. Generally speaking, these factors are independent of the structure of the DP department, but there are exceptions:

- The amount of communication and co-ordination required depends on the size of the project: the larger the project, the larger the number of people required to complete it. Usually, small departments only handle small projects, so there is an indirect relationship between the factors discussed here, and the size of the DP department. Similarly, the potential productivity improvements are generally greater for large departments than for small ones (though Jones (1986b) reported that some very large software organizations have high productivity – see Chapter 13).
- Reporting relationships in a matrix structure are complex, and this structure also has more communication paths. This

lowers productivity, and also makes the success of each project more dependent on the *quality* of the communication – another productivity influencer. To minimize the problem, the team can be subdivided into smaller teams, with communication *within* each subdivision being unrestricted, but communication *between* each subdivision being limited (Conte *et al.*, 1986).

- On the other hand, in the matrix structure in particular, people communicate directly with each other, rather than via intermediaries, which should speed up communication and reduce misunderstandings and misinterpretations, leading to an improvement in productivity.
- The style of the department (formal or informal) might affect the quantity and quality of communication. For example, in an informal department, documentation might be neglected, resulting in a lowering of productivity over the longer term.
- Where teams are transient (whether because of the organization's management philosophy, or because of a high staff turnover), communication and especially documentation become more critical, not just to productivity, but even to the success of the project.

Clerical standards

One source of inefficiency is the lack of standards for the clerical tasks associated with programming. The use of standards (under the collective name of Program Production Library) on the NYT project, may be one reason for the high productivity achieved on that project (Baker, 1972). Furthermore, the standards were so well defined that non-programming staff were used to perform these functions, thereby further increasing the programming output – and therefore the productivity – of the programmers. (An additional cost saving is that clerks are paid less than programmers.) Yourdon (1975) pointed out that similar standards were

already being used by some maintenance sections and also on large projects.

Streamlining documentation

Various suggestions have been made for reducing the amount of documentation, thereby improving the productivity of the people who produce it. For example, some experiments have indicated that program flow-charts are of no value, while other studies have indicated that program source listings should not contain comments (Chapter 8).

Small teams

The amount of communication and co-ordination required depends on the number of members of the team. By keeping the team small, communication and co-ordination are reduced, and productivity increased.

There are several ways to keep a team small.

- It can be staffed with only the best and most experienced people available. However, this method suffers from the disadvantage that the other teams in the organization are deprived of the best people (Mumford and Henshall, 1979), so they need more members, to compensate – i.e. they are increased in size, with consequent adverse effect on their productivity, and the productivity loss on these other teams may more than offset the gain on the first team, in which case this solution should only be chosen for urgent projects.
- If the productivity of the staff is increased, e.g. by using technological aids (Chapter 6), improved methodologies (Chapter 8), and training (Chapter 9), then fewer staff will be required to perform a given task.
- If a project is too large to be handled by a small number of people, it can be subdivided by the system architect. The subdivision must not be artificial, i.e. it must follow the natural division of the product into functions, so that the sections have

clear and simple interfaces, with each section being handled by a (virtually) self-contained team. (In more technical language, the most important consideration is to organize the teams along clear lines of the software product functions using the principles of cohesion, coupling and information hiding (Boehm, 1981).) Each of these teams, being small, would suffer from minimal internal co-ordination losses, and so would operate at maximum efficiency. (The high productivity rates reported by Orkins and Weiss (1975) support the view that subdividing systems into many small programs significantly increases productivity.) However, there would still be some interaction between the teams, plus a higher-level management structure to which the teams reported, and the time consumed by these activities must be taken into account.

- The amount of clerical work can be reduced, as discussed above. Alternatively, it can be performed by non-programming staff – the studies quoted by Aron (1974) indicate that a programming manager can control more people if some of them are non-programmers. Thus, although the team would not have been reduced in size (it may even be bigger), it should be able to handle larger projects without being split up into smaller teams, with that solution's attendant problems.
- The size of the project can be reduced by eliminating unnecessary or only marginally-useful functions ('gold-plating'). As Boehm (1981) so succinctly expressed it: 'On a software project, there are an unlimited number of temptations to make the product, and the job, bigger and more grandiose. Avoid them'. Included in this are unnecessarily stringent performance requirements, e.g. a fast response may only be necessary for a few transaction types. Further, some tasks – such as a one-off job with a small volume of data – may be done more easily manually. Each feature

requested should be evaluated for both its contribution to the effectiveness of the product, and its contribution to the cost. Following this guideline leads in turn to simpler, and more reliable programs, with the additional benefits of a higher development productivity, and lower maintenance.

- The completion date for the project can be extended, thereby enabling a smaller team to handle it.

Subdividing a project into small teams must not be carried to extremes. Whether developing a large system or implementing a system-wide change, a small number of large teams is easier to manage than a large number of small teams, as there may be dozens of teams that need to co-ordinate their work (Boehm, 1981; Jones, 1986b). Furthermore, very small teams, of only one or two people, tend to lack the perspective that comes from alternative views of a problem, which is particularly crucial in design (Macro and Buxton, 1987).

Disadvantages such as these, and those discussed below under Duration, indicate that the team should not be made too small, i.e. there is an *optimum* size. Conte *et al.* (1986) examined this topic from one point of view, the number of communication paths, and found an optimum team size of 5.5 where there is maximum interaction between the team members. (The optimum size is higher if there is less interaction.) This was just an example, but the figures he fed into his calculations are reasonable: a productivity of 15 LOC per day is quite common, and a 10% productivity loss for each communication path is the value he obtained when he applied his theory to one of the sets of projects in his database. It is interesting to note that this team size, 5.5, is very similar to the maximum number of staff one manager can control (seven plus or minus two, as discussed earlier). What Conte actually produced is a *productivity model*, showing the relationship between team size and individual and team productivity. The model has to be calibrated by each organization to fit their own circumstances (e.g. the average complexity of their applications), after which they can use it for crude preliminary estimates of project effort and duration. Of more relevance here, they can also use it to choose an optimum size for each team, or even to *change* their organizational style. However, the productivity rates listed in Chapter 2, from five of the six sets of projects in his database, do not show an optimum size, and in fact productivity decreased steadily as team size increased. Possibly this is because the projects came from several different organizations, but the Jones (1986b) data also shows a steady decrease in productivity as team size increased (Chapter 2). However, the team sizes shown in Chapter 2 are the *total* number of people working on the systems: information on how they were subdivided into smaller teams was not published.

Chief programmer teams

One of the objectives of the CPT concept was to keep the team small, possibly with a view to reducing communication and co-ordination losses (Baker, 1972). The NYT team was not large. Even including the project manager and secretary, it comprised only eleven members, most of whom were not on the team for the full duration of the project, as is inherent in the CPT concept. Four of the task programmers spent very little time on the project. In fact, the five task programmers together spent only 32.5 man-months on the project, compared to the individual figures of 24, 23 and 27 for the CP, BUP, and systems analyst, respectively. The average staffing level over the duration of the project was about 5.5: a total of eleven man-years of effort in about two years. (The duration was 22 months according to Baker and Mills (1973) and Van Tassel (1978), but this is not consistent with the 27 months the

systems analyst spent on it, or the 24 and 23 months of the CP and BUP. Perhaps the 22 months excludes the requirements analysis time? As a compromise, I have assumed that the duration was 24 months.) By comparison, the average staffing level of the projects surveyed by Walston and Felix (1977) – which were on average only one-quarter the size of the NYT project – was six, which is almost the same as the NYT project. At the other extreme, the average staffing levels of the Jones (1986b), Boehm (1981) and Conte *et al.* (1986) projects – which were on average almost as large as the NYT project – were 3–7 times as high (and these projects had a much lower productivity than the NYT). By contrast, the projects in the Kemerer (1987) database were, on average, much larger than the NYT project, and the teams were, on average, also much larger, but the productivity was nevertheless much higher. A comparison of the NYT with these and other projects is shown in Table 3.4.

The Brustman figures are for a subset of the Walston and Felix projects, containing only those projects which were similar in type (interactive information retrieval) to the NYT, thus providing a better comparison. A second subset, containing projects similar in size to the NYT, and having stringent timing constraints, gave virtually identical figures to the first subset.

Inmon's productivity rate was reduced to allow for the large amount of daily overtime worked on the project.

The Jones figures are the average of 54 projects; the Boehm figures are the average of 63 projects; the Conte figures are the average of 147 of his set of 187 projects, and include the Boehm projects; and the Kemerer figures the average of 15 projects.

These examples support the view that the NYT project team was comparatively small, and therefore that communication and co-ordination losses were kept to a minimum.

Table 3.4   Comparison of NYT with other projects

Source	No. of projects	Average LOC (K)	Team size (average)	Duration (yrs)	Productivity (LOC/day)	Av. staff/ duration (mths)
Walston and Felix (1977)	60	20	6	0.9	15	0.6
Inmon (1976)	1	31	3.6	0.3	66	1.0
Jones (1986b)	54	69	37	1.2	7	2.7
Boehm (1981)	63	77	19	1.6	15	1.0
Brustman (1978)	13	78	19	1.1	17	1.4
Conte *et al.* (1986)	147	81	20	1.6	21	1.0
NYT (Baker, 1972)	1	83	5.5	2	32	0.2
Kemerer (1987)	15	187	16	1.2	56	1.1
IJCS[1] (1973)	1	200	20?	3	16	0.6
Viking (Prentiss, 1977)	1	279	?	4	9	?

[1] IJCS: International Job Costing System, developed in Britain by IBM between about 1971 and 1973, for world-wide use.

Duration of project

There is one way to use this 'communication and co-ordination loss' phenomenon without incurring the disadvantages of the above trade-offs, and that is by extending the deadline/completion date.

There is a trade-off between the number of members of the team, their ability and experience, and the duration of the project. If the ability and experience are kept constant (which is what happens in practice because of the fixed pool of staff in the organization), then the shorter the duration, the more people are needed on the team, resulting in much time being spent on non-productive communication and co-ordination, with corresponding large losses in productivity. The converse should also be true. Simply by extending the deadline for the project, the size of the team required is reduced, thereby reducing, perhaps considerably, the large amount of time lost through non-productive communication and co-ordination. This is a very simple way which is open to any organization to increase its productivity, and which requires no extra ability or experience, and no extra expense on hardware, software or training.

How big an impact on productivity does

this factor have? Taking into account the large amount of time consumed by communication and co-ordination, one would expect the impact to be very large.

If a schedule is compressed, productivity will be degraded by an amount which depends on the complexity of the task, the adequacy of its specification, and the adequacy of resources (software engineers, development tools and methods) (Macro and Buxton, 1987). According to Boehm (1981), imposition of impossibly short schedules has often been responsible for *doubling* software development costs. Boehm (1981) and Conte *et al.* (1986) analysed several effort-estimation models. These models calculate a nominal or recommended project duration. Compressing the schedule results in a rapid increase in the predicted effort – a 25% compression increases the predicted effort by around 25% – and a 25% compression is the maximum practical or even possible, i.e. you cannot compress a schedule to less than 75% of the nominal value. (Schedule compression can be achieved not only by adding extra people to a project, but also by acquiring additional hardware or software, or adopting improved methodologies, and training the staff in their use, provided advance notice of the requirement is given and sufficient funds are available. This avoids the heavy productivity penalty of adding extra staff.)

However, *extending* the schedule does not necessarily produce the opposite effect, as one might have anticipated. With the Air Force (1974), RCA(1978) and COCOMO (Boehm, 1981) models, extending the schedule surprisingly results in an *increase* in the predicted effort – a 25% extension increases the predicted effort by around 10% – i.e. the nominal value is the optimum value. (Possible reasons for this are suggested later.) Perhaps more reasonably, the Putnam (1978) model predicts a decrease in effort, but its prediction – extending the schedule by only 60%, reduces the effort required by around 85% – seems unrealistically high, and is not borne out by evidence from actual projects. Similarly, Walston and Felix (1977) found that, for example, it would take 20 people 20 months to develop a 70 000 statement program, but if only 10 people were used – a reduction of 50% – then their productivity would be so high that the schedule would only have to be extended to 23 months – an increase of just 15%. A 15% increase in schedule would therefore produce a $(((20*20) - (10*23))/(20*20)=)$ 40% reduction in effort. In between these extremes is the COPMO model (Thebaut, 1983). In an example given by Conte *et al.* (1986) for a 200k LOC program, this model gave a minimum schedule of 33 months, and predicted that a 3% increase in the length of the schedule (to 34 months) would reduce the total effort required by 10%, while a further 3% increase would result in a further 7% reduction. Overall, a 12% increase in the length of the schedule resulted in a 24% decrease in the predicted effort. This model gave better agreement with actual productivity values for a range of projects than the other models studied by Conte, but he nevertheless cautioned that further validation must be done on it.

The NYT system was developed over a two year period (Baker, 1972). As can be seen from Table 3.4, this is a comparatively long schedule, and this may have contributed to the high productivity on that project.

The obvious disadvantage of extending the duration is that the user has to wait longer for a system to be completed, and therefore for its benefits. In many cases this should be more than offset by the overall higher productivity of the DP department (Appendix E). However, there may be other, hidden disadvantages: e.g. if the project stretches out over too long a time, then (Weinberg, 1971; Brooks, 1975; Boehm, 1981; Orkins and Weiss, 1975):

- the system may be overtaken by advances in technology;
- it may be overtaken by changes in the user's requirements – a program that is late is often worthless – so to prevent that happening, the specifications would have to be continually revised while the program was being written, which lowers productivity and makes it more difficult to maintain high quality (the impact on productivity of requirements volatility is discussed in Chapter 8);
- the benefits of some systems are so great that the losses caused by late installation can never be recovered – put the other way round, the value to the organization of getting the system into operation earlier may be much more than the effort that would be saved by using a smaller team;
- the team members may lose interest in the project, so their motivation and productivity may decrease accordingly (see Chapter 11); and the team members are likely to lose the overall picture (in their minds) of the system, and to forget important details, resulting in errors and general inefficiency.

It is therefore reasonable to conclude that there is an optimum length of schedule, that this is one of the factors which determines the optimum size of the team, and that sometimes the disadvantages of extending the schedule are so serious that this technique cannot be used. A compromise solution is 'incremental delivery' – phase in the system, e.g. by deferring the non-essential ('nice-to-have' or 'wish-list') features (Yourdon, 1975; Boehm, 1981). Instead of blindly extending the schedule, an intelligent, selective extension is made. This will not alter the pessimistic picture painted by some of the effort-estimation models – in fact, it introduces an additional effort overhead – but it will alter, perhaps significantly, the disadvantages of extending the schedule, making this a much more viable option.

Staff size/duration

Walston and Felix (1977) defined the ratio:

average staff size : duration in months

and found that projects with a low ratio (less than 0.5:1) had a productivity 1.8 times higher than those with a high ratio (greater than 0.9:1). This ratio combines the previous two aspects discussed, and might be expected to accentuate their effects.

For the NYT project this ratio was 0.2:1, which is very low on Walston and Felix's scale. The high productivity on that project is therefore consistent with Walston and Felix's finding. At first glance, it would appear that the other ratios in Table 3.4 are not consistent with their finding, as the (unweighted) average productivity of those (groups of) projects with a ratio greater than 0.9 is 30, which is only marginally lower than that of the NYT. However, this average is distorted by two high productivities (Inmon, 1976 and Kemerer, 1987), which together come from only 16 projects, whereas the other figures come from 277 projects. If we allow for this factor, and also exclude the Boehm and Brustman figures, because they are from subsets of the Conte and Walston and Felix groups of projects, respectively, then the (unweighted) average productivity of those (groups of) projects with a ratio greater than 0.9 is 20. This means that the only project or project group with a ratio less than 0.5:1 had a productivity of 32, while the four with a ratio greater than 0.9:1 had an average productivity of 20. The former value is (32/20=) 1.6 times higher than the latter, which is in very good agreement with the 1.8 found by Walston and Felix.

Other benefits

This communication and co-ordination loss factor depends on the number of staff involved. Therefore any factor, be it an increase in experience, or new hardware, software or management tools, which increases the productivity of individual members of staff can produce a ripple effect: it can be employed to decrease the number of staff used to complete the project, thereby reducing the amount of communication and co-ordination required, and so further increasing productivity. Thus the total increase in productivity will be greater than that due directly to the new factor alone. The NYT project is probably an example of this, as several factors (the combination comprising the CPT concept) were involved, a small team produced the system, and the team had a high productivity.

Other benefits are likely to follow (Yourdon, 1975): one level less of management, and an improvement in communications and in morale, as each person would no longer feel like a small cog in a large wheel, and so may work harder and may learn more about software engineering, thereby further increasing productivity both short- and long-term.

Meetings

Communication and co-ordination generally require periodic meetings. According to Stefik *et al.* (1987), office workers spend 30–70% of their time at meetings, but this seems very high. By comparison, according to Chorafas (1985), meetings comprise 7% of professionals' daily job-oriented activities,

13% of middle managers', and 28% of senior managers', though he also gave a figure of 36% for executives. Martin (1982b) gave a figure of 46% for knowledge workers. This figure includes telephone as well as face to face meetings.

The time spent at meetings is, in a sense, non-productive, and so should be kept to a minimum, while maximum benefit must be obtained from the meetings. As Wait (1986) so pointedly remarked: 'Meetings are places where the boastful can find listeners, the aggressive can find victims, and the indolent and slothful can find repose. The amount of time consumed by meetings will, if allowed, approach the total work time'. Potential problems include the 'decibel auction', inarticulateness, and the low social needs of programmers; one already quoted DP director suspects that he gets more done through informal conversations than in an entire formal status meeting. One study found that (Chorafas, 1985):

- only 52% of management meetings are scheduled;
- only 19% of scheduled meetings are conducted with agendas;
- 35% of all meetings are too long; and
- 34% of meetings are non-productive.

To prevent such problems, Wait (1986) and Parikh (1984) proposed a number of guidelines:

- meetings held too often (e.g. more than once a week) degenerate into social affairs;
- resolve all issues within, at the most, three meetings;
- participants must be notified in writing three days beforehand;
- the notification must include the objective of the meeting and an itemized agenda;
- coming to a meeting unprepared is less than half as productive as coming prepared;
- if there is no agenda, there can be no preparation by anyone;
- any departure from the agenda is cause for

an immediate adjournment, e.g. because people affected by the new topic may not be present;

- try to be frank and honest, but diplomatic;
- no meeting may continue for more than an hour, as concentration wavers and productivity starts to decrease;
- if a meeting is worth holding, the minutes are worth taking;
- good minutes reveal if there was any purpose to the meeting;
- schedule the next meeting, if one is needed, before ending the meeting; and
- after a few meetings, make a master summary of previous meetings.

Meetings can be made more effective by technological advances such as electronic copyboards, while the travel time to meetings can be eliminated by teleconference facilities (Chapter 4).

A structured walkthrough is a particular form of meeting, discussed in Chapter 10.

3.7.4 WIDER CONSIDERATIONS

The tables in Appendix E although hypothetical and simplified, contain important lessons which have a wider validity than the current topic.

- The cost of running a DP department is basically the same whether the department is efficient or not, but the financial benefits to the organization (from savings or increased sales), depend heavily on the department's efficiency.
- These benefits can far outweigh the cost of developing the computer systems.
- The increase in net profit (it trebled after a few years in Table E.1) was greater than the increase in productivity (which was double throughout), and at no extra cost.
- Furthermore, the method which produced the higher benefits in the short-term, did not produce the higher benefits in the long-term. This point requires emphasizing in an industry where stress is placed on

immediate results (Chapter 11). (The obvious analogy is maintenance. By looking at only the user's immediate needs, or by economizing on documentation, a higher productivity can be achieved when a system is first developed, but this increases the amount of time subsequently spent on maintenance – see Chapters 8 and 10.)

3.7.5   SUMMARY AND CONCLUSIONS

A large proportion of time is spent on non-productive communication and co-ordination, so this factor can justifiably be classified as having a large negative effect on productivity. However, much of this work is unavoidable, so the question is: how much of this time can be saved?

The savings from standardizing and streamlining procedures, from reducing the amount of documentation, and from clerical assistance, are probably small in most cases.

Much larger savings may be possible by reducing the amount of interaction between staff, through reducing the number of communication paths. This can be attained by having smaller teams (which can be achieved by improving productivity, by having elite teams, or by subdividing large teams, provided this is not carried too far), and also by changing the structure or style of the organization from matrix to hierarchical.

Large savings are sometimes possible by eliminating unnecessary or only marginally-useful functions, thereby reducing the size of the product to be developed (which leads in turn to both smaller teams and to simpler and more reliable programs, with the additional benefits of a higher development productivity, and lower maintenance).

One attractive method is extending the duration of projects (particularly by phasing them in), so that smaller teams can be used. However, although some of the evidence indicates that this results in a large productivity improvement, other evidence indicates that it gives little if any improvement, and may even result in a *decrease* in productivity.

All of these methods have dangers, so caution must be observed when choosing and implementing them.

There is frequently a ripple effect: an improvement in one area leads to other improvements.

To sum up, there are many ways that the large amount of time spent on communication and co-ordination can be reduced, with consequent large improvement in productivity.

Software is usually developed and maintained in offices. To obtain a complete picture of it therefore, it is necessary to examine the office: the environment in it, its layout and equipment. Much of the following discussion relates to ergonomics: the study of the efficiency of people in their working environment, particularly in relation to the equipment they use (Sykes, 1977; Ringo, 1980). Such a study requires a knowledge of the principles of human engineering, and of time and motion study (Leibhammer, 1980).

The justification for the study of ergonomics is simple: efficiency (and therefore profitability) depends on worker comfort (Ringo, 1980; Mulder, 1981). If workers are uncomfortable, or are even merely dissatisfied with their surroundings, they are not motivated to work to capacity, they make more (costly) errors, and they may resign. Management is often not aware that workers are uncomfortable, and also does not realize that attention to human needs is repaid with increased productivity and job satisfaction ('VDUS: are they really a health hazard?' *Systems for information management*, May 1981, pp. 2–3; Marcus, 1986). If you have to look at, or attend to, two things at once, then you make more errors; if you are exhausted, then you take longer to complete a task (Winfield, 1986). Worse, poor ergonomic design can lead to health problems: fatigue, headache, eyestrain and nervous conditions (Ringo, 1980). Strain, tiredness, and musculoskeletal problems such as low-back pain, can result simply from remaining in the same position and concentrating on a specific task for long periods without rest (Rosenthal and Grundy, 1980; Schatz, 1988).

Many workers have to adapt their lives to bad equipment: 'few computers treat operators as human beings . . . there is a big gap between what we know and what we do' (Stewart, 1981). It is thus understandable that workers, while appreciating technical aids to ease their daily work, consider ergonomic factors more important. These considerations are all the more important because people spend so much time at their offices – some spend more time there than at their homes (Ringo, 1980).

What is good enough for general office workers is not necessarily good enough for programmers, who require a private, personal work area that permits intense concentration, screens distractions, and discourages interruptions (Bell *et al.*, 1987). Boehm (1981) put it rather well: 'Anyone who has attempted to develop good software efficiently in a hot, noisy, overcrowded programming bullpen, with poor clerical and telephone support, awkward work procedures and computer access, inadequate supplies and conference facilities, and frequent moves, will certify that these have a strong negative effect on both motivation and productivity'. These aspects are covered in this chapter.

4.1 OFFICE ENVIRONMENT

There are several factors in the office environment which are relevant:

- lighting
- temperature
- humidity
- ventilation
- noise

Workers should have individual control over their environment.

DP departments are generally situated in modern, air-conditioned buildings, so these aspects of the environment are of a high standard, and extreme conditions – which lead to health problems – are rare (Ringo, 1980). This is consistent with the Fitz-Enz (1978) survey of programmer analysts, which found that working conditions were rated the least important of the 16 motivational factors surveyed. This does not, however, mean that there is no room for improvement. One particular DP department is an 'open plan' office situated in a very large square room – the lighting is therefore almost entirely artificial, but worse, the partitions separating the workers are dark in color, giving the area a gloomy appearance, and making it look more like a warehouse. Other DP departments are noisy, mostly because several people are situated in the same small room.

Specific areas of interest or concern are: temperature, lighting, humidity, noise and sick building syndome.

Temperature

If the air temperature is greater than 27°C, then reading speed and comprehension decrease, probably because of discomfort; if it is less than 13°C, then manual dexterity decreases, probably because cold hands are clumsy (Winfield, 1986).

Lighting

If the light level is less than 7–10 footcandles, then reading speed decreases, probably because small details are not sufficiently visible (Winfield, 1986) – a footcandle is the illumination given by a source of one candela at a distance of one foot (Sykes, 1977).

The recommended level of lighting is about 300–500 lux, but when working with VDUs, a lower level of 100–300 lux is recommended, except for older operators (Rosenthal and Grundy, 1980) – lux is a measurement of the intensity of light, where a lux is one lumen per square meter, and a lumen is the flux per unit solid angle from a uniform source of one candela (Sykes, 1977).

Incorrect room lighting levels (too much or too little), or reflections (of room lights and windows) from a VDU screen, can cause health problems and fatigue, and increase error rates.

Improvements in the room lighting can lead to improved productivity; but paradoxically, productivity can improve even if the lighting has worsened (as happened during the Hawthorne experiments discussed in Chapter 11), if the workers believe that management is showing an interest in them – it raises their morale, and this can outweigh the adverse effects of the poorer lighting.

There must be a balance between indirect (ambient) lighting, and high-density task lighting, so that there is not a high contrast between the primary work surfaces and the immediate surroundings (Kessler, 1986).

Humidity

A dry atmosphere results in static electricity, which can cause electric shocks and possibly contact dermatitis (Tjonn and Rycroft, 1981).

Noise

If there is a continuous noise at a volume of 100 dB, or a random intermittent noise of 65–95 dB, then workers make more errors, probably because of distraction caused by the noise (Winfield, 1986).

If there is a noise at a volume of 70 dB, at a frequency of 600–4800 Hz, then there is reduced comprehension of speech, probably because it is masked by the noise (Winfield, 1986).

Noise can be medically harmful, causing strain, fatigue, and even ill health. It can also increase frustration, decrease efficiency, and cause loss of perspective ability.

High noise levels interfere with auditory cues from the terminal or PC. Conversely, terminal or PC noise may disrupt nearby workers.

The noise problem is accentuated in 'open plan' offices (discussed later).

The noisiest item in many offices is the computer printer.

Noise can be blocked out by wearing earplugs.

Noise should be absorbed at its point of origin, e.g. by placing a special cover (an 'acoustic enclosure') over a printer (but this must not interfere with the operation of the equipment).

Fabric-covered chairs absorb noise, while hard surfaces (e.g. of computer equipment) do not.

Carpets prevent footsteps from making a noise, and also absorb other noises.

Walls and ceilings should be sound-absorbent.

Speech disturbs more by the distraction it causes than by its volume (Crabtree, 1979). Injecting a random noise signal, at the same volume as nearby speech, 'drowns' the speech, thereby eliminating the distraction – this is a *controlled* noise and a form of 'white' noise which contains many frequencies with about equal energies (Sykes, 1977).

The noise of air-conditioning units is not controlled, as it varies in volume and frequency spectrum, and can cause resonances at particular frequencies, which are most disturbing (Crabtree, 1979).

Some people *prefer* a noisy environment (Weinberg, 1971), e.g. they like to have the radio on when studying.

Sick building syndrome

The sick building syndrome has enjoyed increasing publicity recently. Occupants of some buildings report a wide range of symptoms, ranging from coughing, sneezing and muscle aches, to nausea, depression and irritability (Truter, 1991).

Occupants of air conditioned buildings generally report more symptoms than those in naturally ventilated buildings. This is because these buildings are frequently in polluted inner city environments; neglected air conditioning systems become sources of pollution; man-made fibres in the machines may be released into the air; and negatively charged atmospheric ions tend to be removed within earthed air handling ductwork, as well as by steel framed buildings and VDU screens.

Carpets, soft furnishings and even books are repositories for pollutants. Additional factors may be high temperatures and humidity, low frequency fluorescent lighting, low ventilation rates, and airborne allergens such as fungal spores.

4.2 OFFICE LAYOUT

Suppliers of office equipment and office planning consultants will advise on office layout and equipment to (Koffler, 1986)

- achieve the most efficient flow of work and overcome bottlenecks;
- increase productivity;
- reduce complaints of physical discomfort;
- enhance employee satisfaction and well-being;
- control stress; and
- minimize health and safety risks.

The Business Design Group in Britain has a software program for space analysis and planning which is centered around a database, and takes into account the number of employees, how much space is required for them to work efficiently, and how much floor space can be afforded (Redgrave, 1986). Some organizations have a 'facilities manager' who supervises the layout, lighting, heating, ventilation, security, safety, furniture, and equipment (PCs, network, etc.), and how these integrate with each other (Tilley, 1986).

An IBM study indicated that programmers

require an area of ten feet square, and IBM's Santa Teresa Laboratory was custom-designed and built to meet the needs of software people (Bell *et al.*, 1987; McCue, 1978). This was claimed to provide an 11% productivity gain compared to the same personnel's old facility (Jones, 1986b). In stark contrast, DeMarco (1982) quoted a bank which spends just 3.5% of its programming payroll on space and amenities for programmers. The result is that the workers are crowded together in an environment that inhibits any form of concentration. Jones speculated that overcrowded, physically poor surroundings, would cause about a 10% productivity loss compared to a normal environment of two persons sharing an office of reasonable size and a terminal.

Communications requirements must be taken into account. This refers to both the provision of conference rooms for meetings, and the availability of telephones and data communications equipment, and all of these should be close by. Computer printers should also be near by, and so should support equipment such as photocopiers and word processors. There must therefore be adequate power points. Library facilities, and refreshment and rest areas, should be provided, and once again should be close by. Finally, the design should be flexible, so that it can accommodate future advances.

According to one manufacturer, it has been scientifically proven that correctly planned offices more than justify the capital cost of the equipment (Ringo, 1980). Planned workflow systems and working environments can increase office efficiency by as much as 100%, and save up to 50% on costly floor space (Leibhammer, 1980; Infra-Structures, 1986). The decreasing size of computer equipment aids in this respect.

One organization saved some $1500 per month simply by relocating its photocopying machines (Haigh, 1980).

The manufacturers of the DISPO (1982) filing system claim it improves productivity by 50%. The VRE (1986) filing system is based on color coding of folders. One customer who used this system in conjunction with a PC, achieved an increase in filing and retrieval efficiency of 100% after only 40% of their files had been converted.

Documents are an integral and important part of office work, so offices should be planned as part of the document flow. The mere existence of document distribution lists can help accelerate the paperwork 'explosion' (Grossman, 1978). A thorough review can reduce the number of documents spectacularly. This would not only save on paper costs, but also on the time staff spend reading documents which are not relevant to them.

The 51 million white-collar workers in the US generate 91 billion documents per year, from which a total of 149 billion copies are made, amounting to 482 billion pages per year, weighing over 2 million tons of paper (Chorafas, 1985). (This works out at an average of nearly 10 documents per person per day, comprising nearly 20 pages, which seems unrealistically high.) According to Diamond (1986), the number of new documents produced in 1985 comprised about 2 billion pages, and this figure was expected to grow to more than one trillion in 1995. This represents almost a doubling every year, which seems unrealistically high. According to Chorafas (1985), the number of new documents is growing at 20–22% per year, which is a doubling every four years.

As would be expected from the large number of documents, document collection and distribution may comprise as much as 12% of an organization's total overhead. More than half of this can be saved by installing an automated distribution system (de Jager, 1980). Part of these figures is made up of the salaries of senior staff, who may spend 35–40% of their time doing work they were not employed for, such as photocopying, filing and errand-running (Pritchard, 1978; McCormick, 1980), while Booz and Allen found that knowledge workers may spend 30% of their time creating, analysing, and reading documents (Martin, 1982b). According to Holton (1987), clerical and non-technical tasks comprise 10–15% of the programmer/analyst workload, a claim which is supported by the 11% secretary/librarian time on the NYT project (Baker, 1972). Other figures – some higher, others lower – are given in Chapter 8.

Staff also spend time socializing and on personal telephone calls. Access control not only improves security, but by stopping people wandering around in areas where they have no need to be, can improve productivity by 10–30% (Wibier, 1980). Similarly, telephone management systems (such as the Ansafone Telecost), by recording the source and destination of all calls, can lead to a reduction of 50% in non-business related calls during peak times, and a saving of up to 48% in telephone bills (Manta, 1983; Brandon, 1978). Telephones may even be entirely removed from programmers. Staff, however, are likely to resent such restrictions and react negatively to them (Weinberg, 1971), and they *do* need access to telephones from time to time for their work, e.g. to resolve problems with their programs, and people must also have a break 'to recharge their batteries', so productivity will suffer if extreme measures are taken.

Some of the high savings listed above are possible because, although every second worker is employed in an office, conditions there are not in line with the high standards made possible by existing techniques: 'every conceivable piece of equipment is bought, but the people to operate the machines are given secondary consideration' (Haigh, 1980). This attitude is a short-sighted one: 'If they throw good equipment at you, it's useless if you don't know how to use it' (Schatz, 1988). Furthermore, organizations spend, over a 40-year period, more than a million dollars per employee on salary, office space, furniture and pension, and an increase in output of only 5% could pay for the

upgrading of the office situation in just 18 months (Haigh, 1980). The upgrading could also decrease staff turnover.

The changes here envisaged are not merely cosmetic or interior decoration (Haigh, 1980), but are designed to (Ringo, 1980):

- improve methods of storage, handling and transportation;
- give rapid access to files and stationery;
- arrange the office and its equipment to meet the office workers' needs and habits;
- enable them to communicate with other people with the minimum waste of time;
- provide unobtrusive supervision, which can increase productivity.

New equipment should be judged by its contribution to this approach.

Open plan offices

One controversial practice is 'open plan' offices: large offices with many people, separated by movable partitions, instead of small permanent offices. This is very flexible, but it is also disliked, as the partitions may provide insufficient noise absorption and inadequate privacy (Crabtree, 1979; Rubinstein, 1982; Ringo, 1980), while restricting useful communication and personal contact – there are situations where people need both visual and speaking contact with each other (Hinomoto, 1980). According to Bomberg (1986), the fault does not lie with the original concept, but rather with the fact that it has been carried too far.

The Ohio Bureau of Motor Vehicles, which installed open plan offices, new carpeting, and improved lighting, reports increased space efficiency, and improved productivity and employee morale (Fernberg, 1986); and there are no private offices anywhere in the Tokos Medical Corp. ('Open-plan solves private office dilemma' *The Office*, October 1986, p. 136). Nevertheless, the concept may not be suitable for software people with their need for intense concentration and freedom from distractions. It is significant that, when IBM custom-designed and built the Santa Teresa Laboratory to meet the needs of software people, individual offices were provided (McCue, 1978).

4.3 FURNITURE

There is a wide choice of furniture available. It should be selected by the people most affected, namely those who will use it, and they may also have more time to conduct the investigation than their busy managers.

Office furniture is being integrated with DP tools. Modularization of furniture and equipment allows for greater compatibility.

The chair

Most office workers spend more than 70% of their time seated at their desks, so seating is very important. The chair should be at the correct height (420–550 mm) (Mulder, 1981). It should be scientifically designed to ensure correct posture and maximum comfort: people of any shape or size should be able to sit at the desk with a minimum of physical strain ('VDUs: are they really a health hazard?' *Systems for information in management*, May 1981, pp. 2–3). Cloth upholstery is well-suited to a variable hot and cold climate. Wheels, and a tilt and swivel capability, aid comfort and mobility.

The desk

The desk surface should be at a height of 580–730 mm (Mulder, 1981), and should be large enough to accommodate computer listings, the computer terminal or PC, and other equipment. The desk must also have adequate storage compartments. It should permit direct access to files and stationery, i.e. the worker – left- or right-handed – should be able to reach the perimeters of the work area without excessive stretching, bumping or bending, especially for those items with a high retrieval rate (Ringo, 1980; Low cost computer can grow with your

business. *Systems for Information Management*, April 1981, p. 45). This can be achieved by:

- desks with optional attachments and extensions, enabling the work area to be individualized;
- trapezoidal tables, giving endlessly adjustable table/desk arrangements, thereby maximizing the use of limited floor space;
- swivel-arms attached to the desks, to hold, for example, the telephone and filing trays; and
- L-shaped desks, or desks and tables with left- or right-hand configurations.

There are also safety aspects to be considered:

- power cables should be carried inside hollow legs;
- materials used should be fire-resistant; and
- corners should be curved.

As an example, the Fleximetric desk from Flexiform, designed to comply with ergonomic principles, is claimed to meet all current British and DIN (German) standards on cable management, strength and stability (Turner, 1986). It should therefore be safe and comfortable. The Fleximetric range features linking sections, provision for PCs, side storage units, and bookcases.

Instead of a conventional desk, work surfaces may be panel mounted and have vertical storage ('Work station systems: their importance grows.' *The Office*, October 1986, pp. 95–97). The Infra-Structures' 'Command Center Technology' is an example of this approach (Infra-Structures, 1986).

4.4 WORKSTATIONS

In common usage, the word 'workstation' generally refers to both the furniture and the equipment used by an individual. In the computer world, it refers to just the computer terminal or PC (or even to a small but high-powered scientific or engineering computer), and this is the meaning used here. The discussion is, however, also relevant to other devices, such as dedicated word processors and data entry machines, having a keyboard through which the operator enters information and commands into the machine; and a visual display unit (usually a cathode ray tube), through which the machine displays information and instructions.

Some terminals have a typewriter instead of a VDU. These provide a permanent record of the work session (useful for tracing problems), and experiments have shown that users make fewer typing errors (Walther and O'Neil, 1974; Carlisle, 1970). However, paper is more costly and polluting; printers are less reliable and noisier (except non-impact thermal printers, which are quiet), they have limited character sets, and are slow and inconvenient (Shneiderman, 1980). Typewriter terminals are therefore only used in special circumstances, such as when programmers temporarily work from their homes.

Because of increased miniaturization, the 'footprints' of computer terminals and PCs – the area they take up on a desk (Collin, 1989) – are becoming progressively smaller, thereby increasing the amount of usable desk space.

4.4.1 THE KEYBOARD

There are several desirable attributes for the keyboard. According to 'what to do, how to do it', an article in *Computer Systems in Southern Africa* (July 1982, pp. 41–7), Mulder (1981), and Rosenthal and Grundy (1980), it should be:

- movable, but not so light that it moves when unintentionally knocked;
- at the right height – the maximum recommended height is 750 mm (Mulder, 1981);
- tilted, or with the keys stepped like a typewriter's, for ease of use;
- non-reflective;
- have adequate spacing between the keys;
- have a numeric pad for fast keying of numeric data;

- and should indicate if keys such as the capitals-lock key, are on (unless the screen shows this).

The distance the keys have to be depressed should not be excessive, and they should not require excessive pressure. Too little pressure can also cause problems. With a PC keyboard which has a reset key among the ordinary keys, all too often, a stray finger causes the system to reboot! In later versions of this keyboard, the reset key was in the same place, but required more than the normal pressure, and the number of unintentional reboots decreased.

The keyboard should be easy to use whether the operator is left- or right-handed.

The function keys should be clearly marked, possibly even being successively illuminated from beneath to guide the operator step by step through control sequences (Lyne, 1980).

The keyboard should be in the operator's home language. Acorn's COMPACT computer, for example, supports foreign-language keyboards, and there are cartridges available which allow IBM's ASCII terminals to be operated in several foreign languages (Acorn, 1986; IBM, 1986).

The traditional QWERTY keyboard was reportedly designed to *prevent* fast typing, so that the mechanism would not jam (Montgomery, 1982; Winfield, 1986; Shneiderman, 1980). For example, for 68% of keystrokes, the user has to reach from the 'home' row to another row (Winfield, 1986). With the faster mechanisms currently available, this precaution is no longer necessary, so the sequence can be improved (Russell, 1983). Resequenced keyboards have been built, and have proved their worth in experimental studies (Shneiderman, 1980). The Dvorak keyboard, for example, makes greater use of alternate hand sequences, and minimizes awkward fingering sequences. Various claims have been made for it (Winfield, 1986; Yamaha, 1980; Pfaffenberger, 1990):

- reduced fatigue;

- beginners take only one-third as long to reach expert standards;
- it generates only half as many errors;
- more than two-thirds of the words typed only require the home row keys (compared to only 32% for QWERTY keyboards);
- 15–20% higher speeds are achieved; and
- the world's typing speed record of 170 words per minute was set on a Dvorak keyboard.

US Navy experiments during the 1940s showed that the increased efficiency obtained with the Dvorak simplified keyboard would amortize the cost of retraining a group of typists within the first *ten days* of their subsequent full-time employment (David, 1991). Furthermore, keyboards are available which allow the user to rearrange the keys to suit himself, e.g. IBM's 3163 and 3164 ASCII terminals have redefinable and recappable keys (IBM, 1986). However, the traditional QWERTY sequence is so widely accepted that it is unlikely to be replaced, except perhaps for occasional users such as programmers, who might prefer an alphabetic sequence, yet the potential gains are so great that it is a pity not to take advantage of them.

Touch-sensitive keys – such as on the Sinclair ZX81 computer, and some Bang & Olufsen audio equipment (B & O, 1977) and bank cash terminals (ATMs) – have the potential to improve typing speed. In particular, they can be used with a resequenced keyboard to permit a faster and more natural 'wiping' action with the fingers (Montgomery, 1982). However, they may not be suitable for all applications, and may require improvement – the ZX81's is not easy to use (possibly just because it is too small) ('Home Computers', *Which?*, August 1981, pp. 435–40) – and there was once a rumor that B & O had technical difficulties with their touch-sensitive controls.

An audible confirmation signal could be emitted when a key is successfully pressed, giving the operator confidence to type faster,

but this could disturb nearby workers. (Similarly, audible error warnings are effective, but can be embarrassing when workstations are situated in public places.)

Training can result in a significant improvement in typing speed – 25%, or even over 100% in exceptional circumstances – and a 75% increase in accuracy (Wybrow, 1977; Burnstein, 1982). (These figures are for professional typists. Software engineers, who frequently use a one-finger 'hunt and peck' technique, stand to gain much more, though for a smaller proportion of their working day.) Such large improvements are credible, as training is often neglected, and in one organization only 15% of the available features were in regular use (Matthews, 1982). Even part-time users such as managers, programmers, and other professional staff, may spend as much as 80% of their time at workstations, so their productivity should improve noticeably if they are taught typing skills, even though they do not type continuously during this time (Erickson, 1982; Gill, 1982; Spencer, 1982). In fact, the major productivity gains promised by the new types of equipment may only be realized if the originators of the work are taught typing skills and type their own programs and documents (Computer Services Association, 1980a, 1980b). However, a survey of information systems professionals and managers at various corporations, pointed out that computer applications can prove 'phenomenally expensive' if you have a $150-an-hour executive doing typing or data entry (Hayes, 1992).

Training has another benefit. By being taught how to position arms and hands, muscle strain is avoided (Schatz, 1988).

Productivity Software International's PRD+ program for IBM PCs allows the user to type abbreviations instead of the full words, thus permitting faster typing (O'Malley, 1986). It can cut the number of keystrokes by half, but the user must first memorize the list of abbreviations: if he pauses at each abbreviation, or types the wrong one, then there will be little if any improvement.

4.4.2 THE VISUAL DISPLAY UNIT (VDU)

Health problems

The VDU is one piece of equipment which has been widely discussed, probably because it has been blamed (unjustly?) for many health problems: eyestrain, headaches, tiredness, muscular aches and pains, and even stress, depression, irritability, facial rash, contact dermatitis and miscarriages (Rosenthal and Grundy, 1980; van den Nieuwenhof, 1983). For example, a study commissioned by the British Trade Union, NALGO, found that VDU operators had more health problems and took more sick leave than other employees; and a California study found that women in early pregnancy who spend more than 20 hours per week on VDUs are about twice as likely to have miscarriages (Schatz, 1988).

However, according to Schatz (1988), for each report that links VDUs and adverse health effects, there is another that says the two 'are not in the same universe'. According to Batson (1983), the reports of higher levels of miscarriages among VDU operators were based on small samples, and so may be due to localized viral infections or even to statistical chance alone. Large-scale studies will generally show pockets of high incidence of whatever is being studied, but they will also show pockets of low incidence. The former does not prove there is a health risk, any more than the latter proves that the suspect factor reduces the risk. According to Blair (1986), many surveys on VDUs and health have been conducted on an *ad hoc* basis, without even paying lip service to elementary scientific rules or rules of correct statistical procedure. Therefore, while they may have correctly identified that there is a problem, they may not have correctly identified the cause.

VDUs emit a piercing high-pitched 'shriek' that is inaudible to most people (it is usually at a frequency of 15.75 kHz), but which causes serious discomfort and headaches to those people who can hear such high frequencies (Braner, 1986).

Although programmers and analysts are only part-time users, it is justifiable to discuss the factors in some detail, because:

- they may spend as much as 80% of their time using VDUs;
- VDUs are becoming widespread among the remaining categories of DP staff, among user departments and executives, and even in schools and homes – i.e. among amateur and part-time programmers;
- the health and safety problems are potentially serious;
- sick people have a low productivity (zero if they are seriously ill); and
- apprehensive people are unlikely to give of their best – they may avoid using the suspect equipment, go on strike, or even induce the illnesses in themselves by auto-suggestion 'VDUs: are they really a health hazard?' *System for information management*, May 1981, pp. 2–3) (Rosenthal and Grundy, 1980).

Causes of health problems

The problems which have been observed may not be due to the VDU as such, but to (Rosenthal and Grundy, 1980; TASS, 1979; Schatz, 1988; Neill, 1980c):

- existing eye defects, which are more common among older operators;
- psychological problems;
- low humidity, static electricity or airborne dust particles;
- adjustment to a new and unfamiliar type of equipment (and so will disappear with time);
- poor siting of the equipment with respect to the room lighting, air-conditioning, or other equipment;

- inadequate engineering maintenance; or
- remaining in the same position and concentrating on the same task for long periods without a rest.

Cures

The cure, in most of the above cases, is obvious. For example, operators should have their eyesight tested regularly, and remedial action (such as spectacles) should be taken where necessary. Suffolk County in the USA has enacted legislation enforcing a minimum 15-minute break every three hours (Schatz, 1988). (As a general rule, productivity can sometimes be increased by spending less time at work, and more time in rest breaks (Lucas, 1985).)

Even where the VDU is a contributory cause of the problem, the operator may be able to cure it himself (Mulder, 1981; Rosenthal and Grundy, 1980; TASS, 1979):

- angle the screen to reduce reflections;
- adjust the height of the unit, or of his chair, to suit himself;
- adjust the brightness of the display to suit his preference and the room lighting;
- keep the equipment clean (the characters may be difficult to read if the screen is dirty); and
- look away from the work from time to time to rest his eyes.

See also 'What to do, how to do it' in *Computer Systems in Southern Africa*, July 1982, pp. 41–7.

In other cases, where the problem is caused by design limitations of the equipment, the solution lies in the hands of the manufacturer (Rosenthal and Grundy, 1980; Mulder, 1981).

- The VDU should be light in weight so that it can be moved easily to the desired position (e.g. to eliminate reflections) or out of the way.
- It should have a swivel base so that it can be angled to reduce reflections, or if it has to be shared by more than one operator at a common workstation.
- Controls should be at the front for easy access.
- The screen should be recessed or have a special anti-glare coating to reduce reflections.
- It should be large so that the characters can be large, or to display more information at once, or it could have a 'zooming' feature.
- The characters should be sharp, distortion-free, large and easy to read – screen resolution is typically only around 5000 dots per square inch, which compares unfavorably with the nearly 100 000 of the average desktop laser printer (Townsend, 1986).
- They should be bright, highly-contrasted, non-flicker, and of a pleasant color.

Furthermore, the high-pitched 'shriek' emitted by VDUs is not a problem with higher-resolution screens having higher scanning rates. With these screens, the 'shriek' is at such a high frequency that nobody can hear it (Braner, 1986).

Plasma displays are non-flicker, their orange and soft black color is 'gentle on the eye', and they are claimed to show clearer detail, so they cause less user fatigue (Jensen, 1987). They are also flat and very compact, and it was claimed that they would replace conventional VDUs within ten years. LCDs (liquid-crystal displays) share some of these advantages. They also have disadvantages, such as a narrow viewing angle, but improved versions – supertwisted and backlit displays – are becoming more common. LCDs are commonly used in lap-top computers.

Some VDUs, such as the Multitech MDM-14, can display black characters against an 'easy-to-look-at' soft white phosphor background, in a way which resembles paper documents.

Highlighting of information

Information on screens can be highlighted by using:

- different colors (which can also be used as a step by step guide to the operator);
- higher intensity;
- background reversal;
- flashing (possibly at more than one frequency);
- a mixture of large and small characters.

Studies indicate that the use of color increases productivity, decreases errors, and promotes user satisfaction (IBM, 1986). It can also aid decision making, e.g. when combined with graphics or when a decision must be made quickly (Benbasat *et al.*, 1986). Information can be retrieved more quickly and more efficiently from tabular information if the rows or columns are presented in alternate colors (Winfield, 1986). However some colors, or combinations of colors, are difficult to read, so care must be exercised when designing multi-color screens.

Graphics are an alternative way to highlight information – they make it more interesting and easier to assimilate, provided they are not crammed with too much information (Swain, 1986; Winfield, 1986; Chapter 8). Even ordinary VDUs can display (crude) graphics, but special high-resolution displays are also available, such as IBM's 8514 Color Display for their PS/2 PCs.

Carrying this one step further, even more dramatic highlighting is achieved by integrating laser disks with PCs and terminals to provide sound and 'live' images. This has been used for teaching purposes and in ATMs ('Australian bank sets the pace for automated branches', *World of Banking*, Sept–Oct 1986, pp. 31–2).

Software design

The display is software driven. Software designers are often unaware they are designing the workstation operator's job and not just a piece of equipment, so the working life of the operator – who may be a programmer or an analyst – is made unnecessarily difficult and boring (Stewart, 1981). Use of workstations is facilitated by:

- prompts in the operator's home language;
- placing information which needs a response at the bottom of the screen, i.e. as near as possible to the keyboard, to minimize eye movement (Winfield, 1986);
- function keys, which may be user-programmable, and which can increase keyboard productivity by 25% or even 50%, (*Computing S.A.*, Nov 19, 1982, p. 9; Low cost computer can grow with your business. *Systems for Information Management*, April 1981, p. 45; Church, 1980);
- full-screen editors – which studies show are twice as fast as line editors (Shneiderman, 1980);
- periodic messages giving the state of the system and explaining any delays (e.g. 'System busy sorting . . . please wait'), or prior warnings about laborious or dangerous commands (such as deleting a file: 'Are you sure (Y/N)?').

Other, similar, requirements for interactive programs are given in Chapter 10.

As an example of a function key, after making program changes with the CLARION editor, a single keystroke terminates the editor, loads the compiler, compiles the program, loads the processor, and executes the program (Barrington Systems, 1986).

4.4.3 IMPROVED INPUT METHODS

The use of workstations can be simplified and speeded up by:

- touch-sensitive screens;
- light pens;
- sonic pens;
- touch-sensitive plates used as a writing surface;
- joysticks;
- a 'mouse' cursor control;
- trackballs;
- voice (speech) recognition.

Voice recognition (Myers, 1983) is still in an early stage of development and so is limited in its usefulness, but it has considerable promise (Chorafas, 1986), particularly for software engineers, most of whom are slow and inaccurate typists. It has the advantage that it leaves the hands free, which is of particular benefit to some categories of user, and to physically handicapped people. It may be able to double the productivity of some workers, such as design engineers. Current voice recognition systems have limited vocabularies, of only a few hundred words (Yourdon, 1989; Pfaffenberger, 1990) which is a serious disadvantage in programming because of the many different names (of fields, paragraphs and sub-routines) in the average program: 'the freedom in inventing identifiers is generally very wide' (Sakkinen, 1989). They are affected by room noise, and are sensitive to variations in voice, so they have to be 'trained' to recognize each individual, and may temporarily stop recognizing a person while he has a cold (Ciarcia, 1986b).

Cheap systems therefore have relatively high error rates of up to five per hundred words, though even that is probably much better than the typing of the average programmer.

Card (1978) found clear evidence that a 'mouse' is faster and more accurate than a joystick or keys for selecting text. In fact, once a user has had a few days practice, it is typically twice as fast, while the error rate is only half as large (Martin, 1985). Use of a mouse enabled one executive at Silicon Valley Bank to process financial statements 50% faster, 'and with far less aggravation', than with his PC keyboard ('Optical mouse eases transition to working with PC programs', *Bank Systems & Equipment*, February 1986, pp. 63–4). This bank also found that using mice overcame difficulties they had experienced from having a variety of different keyboards. Another organization evaluated mice and touch-sensitive screens, and chose the mouse because it allows more

precise positioning, does not need to be calibrated periodically, and obviates the fatigue caused in some users by having to reach up frequently to touch the screen (Hawkridge *et al.*, 1988). It is also good for editing text, though not for typing it (Daley, 1991): 'Writing with a mouse is like writing with a potato' (Levine, 1988). Furthermore, Pournelle (1988) complained that he can never find his mouse, as it is always buried under a pile of papers on his desk! This highlights another disadvantage of a mouse, namely that an area must be kept clear to move it back and forth. Trackballs do not suffer from this disadvantage, and Seymour (1991) also finds them more comfortable, more accurate, and having a more natural motion.

4.4.4   SAFETY

Productivity also depends on safety. Where there is danger or threat of injury, then more errors are made in remembering and following complicated tasks, and difficult tasks take longer (Winfield, 1986). If workstations are situated in a building in a dangerous district, or if the users thereof live in a dangerous district, then they may be reluctant to work late. They may therefore work harder during the day in an attempt to avoid overtime, but when they do work late, they may have difficulty concentrating on their work because of worry.

Of more direct relevance, if a VDU implodes – a rare occurrence – or if the operator spills liquid on the unit causing a minor explosion or a fire, productive time may be lost:

- at least one VDU fewer is available for use, so queues are likely to form or be longer;
- staff may have been injured and so take sick-leave; and
- they may refuse to work with that make of VDU again.

See also: 'What to do, how to do it', *Computer Systems in Southern Africa*, July 1982, pp. 41–7.

Several health risks have already been mentioned. The most worrying is probably the radiation emitted by VDUs, which is a special source of concern to pregnant women, as higher levels of miscarriages have been reported among VDU operators. However, as has already been pointed out, these reports are suspect because they were based on small samples (Batson, 1983), but even if they are confirmed, it seems unlikely that the VDUs can be responsible, because the amount of radiation they emit is 'negligible' ('VDUs are cleared', *Computer Week*, 10 October 1983, p.4; Ward, 1983). One experiment showed that a television set emitted less than the background (natural) radiation, and that its radiation decreased rapidly with distance from the set (Mims, 1986). (Interestingly, the set emitted almost as much radiation when it was switched off as when it was on.) This does not mean that the VDUs cannot cause any problems at all, but it does mean that they can cause very little. Operators who are worried in spite of these reassurances, can wear protective lead-lined aprons or trousers if they so wish (Ward, 1983; Hammond, 1986). This might not be comfortable or convenient, but it should alleviate the worry.

Ward (1983) stated that the radiation from conventional VDUs could be reduced but not eliminated, but this may now be out of date, as the Multitech CVM-14 VDU is claimed to have full X-ray shielding. VDUs based on plasma technology or LCDs do not emit dangerous radiation ('What to do, how to do it,' *Computer Systems in Southern Africa*, July 1982, pp. 41–7; 'Workstation is radiation-free', *Computer Week*, 24 January 1983, p. 7).

There are a number of screen filters available which are attached to the front of the VDU screen, and which reduce glare. The Softwave screen filter is claimed, in addition, to provide protection against the electromagnetic radiation emitted by VDUs, and to have anti-static properties which eliminate the build-up of electromagnetic charge

(Greyling, 1987). One person who used it, found that it cured the constant headaches and sore eyes that he previously suffered.

4.4.5 NUMBER OF WORKSTATIONS

Aron (1974) recommended that, where terminals are provided for common use, to minimize non-productive waiting-time, one terminal should be provided for every four programmers, with a minimum of three terminals. Terminals are used much more now than previously, and prices have dropped – a dumb terminal can now be acquired for less than $500 (compared to $3000 ten years previously) (Yourdon, 1989), or can be rented for between $50 and $100 per month, depending on the type and rental agreement (Sanders, 1985), while according to Grulke (1983), the cost of an IBM 3178 display terminal was already under a dollar a day. Aron's ratio is therefore now out of date.

IBM expected to have one terminal for every two employees by 1986, with a one-to-one ratio in some departments (Grulke, 1983). A report by British Telecom and the UK Department of Industry ('Information technology threatens to swamp contemporary offices,' *Computer Week*, 9 May 1983, p. 17) predicted that, in ten years' time, one in three office workers was likely to have an electronic workstation which would give access to computers, word processors, satellite communications, and video conference links. It was predicted that three out of four office workers would use PCs by the end of the decade (Future Computing, 1985). (This does not necessarily mean that each person would have their own PC, as each PC in this survey was used, on average, by 2.3 people.) Another prediction was that 26 million USA workers would be using computers by 1990 ('Work station systems: their importance grows,' *The Office*, October 1986, pp. 95–7). A survey conducted in 1986 showed there was one terminal for every six potential users, while a ratio of one in two was predicted by

1991 (Mayfield, 1986). According to Jones (1986b), organizations with more than 200 software employees generally already had about one workstation for each of these employees, while smaller organizations had fewer than this and would benefit by having more. These figures may differ, but they agree that the number of workstations is already very high. There is, however, the danger that some workstations will not be used, but will just be status symbols (Weinberg, 1971; FTP, 1983).

When calculating the number of workstations required, allowance must be made for the type of work and the total number of people who will use them. Workstation usage will probably be higher for maintenance or for a conversion project than for development. When counting the number of users, allowance must be made for:

- freelancers (independent contractors) and part-time staff;
- operations staff (if their terminals or PCs are down, they will want to use those allocated to the software engineering staff);
- non-DP staff
  - user departments (who may not have their full quota of workstations);
  - outside organizations (who may, for example, have a reciprocal agreement for the use of facilities, e.g. in the case of hardware failure);
  - the computer manufacturer (who may also have an agreement, or who may need to do some systems programming from time to time);

and not just the DP department's own full-time programmers and analysts.

At one organization, back in 1980, there were only three terminals in the software department, with 16 users (if all the above categories are included). This impaired the efficiency of the organization's software engineers not merely because of the bottlenecks at the terminals, but also because they had the lowest priority for use thereof.

4.5 OFFICE AUTOMATION AND THE OFFICE OF THE FUTURE

Office equipment is used during software development and maintenance – word processors, for example, lighten the documentation workload – so office automation has a bearing on software productivity. Another example is telephones, because programmers and analysts also use the telephone. According to Chorafas (1985), professional staff spend 11% of their time on the telephone, compared to 12% for middle managers, and 17% for senior managers. Booz and Allen (1980) found that telephone calls successfully reached the intended person less than half the time. An unsuccessful call wastes someone else's time (a secretary or colleague of the person being called), and when the call is returned, that too has only a 50% chance of success. An unsuccessful call consumes an average of 45 seconds. A successful call consumes up to five minutes in 'shadow functions' (identifying and greeting each other, restarting your previous activity after you have finished the call, etc.), over and above the time spent on the purpose of the call. In total, a manager typically wastes 30 minutes (about 5%) a day due to these factors. This wastage can be reduced by facilities such as call forwarding, electronic mail, and cellular radio.

'Office automation' is difficult to define (Finlayson, 1979). It does not consist solely of electronics-based office equipment, nor is it just the convergence of computer, word processing and communications technologies. In fact, it incorporates streamlined administrative processes and MIS as well. It has therefore been defined as 'a new approach to management communication and control' in 'Encounters of four kinds', *Systems for information management*, (November 1980, pp. 16–18). It is the first phase in 'the office of the future' (Davis and Blackmarr, 1983).

According to Kleinschrod (1986), progress does not happen because of technological breakthroughs, but because of a series of managerial mind-openings, each one seeing office operations in a larger context, each one leading to wider use of the technology for a greater business benefit. Management initially perceived office technology as a cost-cutter, and then successively as a value-adder, and a competitive tool, and is now beginning to view the information held and generated by advanced office systems as a corporate asset.

The aim of office automation should not be to replace workers but to stimulate their minds, and to enable managers to communicate instructions (Shinn, 1983).

The above definitions are very wide; perhaps when the average man in the street thinks of office automation, he thinks more in terms of electronic equipment such as word processors and facsimile.

Some of the electronics-based facilities which will be commonplace in 'the office of the future' are listed below. Most of the required technology already exists. In fact, the 1983 report by British Telecom and the UK Department of Industry mentioned before stated that most of the technology that would have the greatest impact on office design over the following 10 years already existed and was in use by leading organizations. Furthermore, some of these facilities are already in widespread use, as office automation is not new.

Electronic typewriters These have many of the ergonomic and productivity-improving features found in word processors, and have advantages over the latter in lower price, simpler servicing, and being easier to learn and to use.

Word processors Studies have shown these can double typists' productivity, but even so they have not always proved cost-effective (Central Computer and Telecommunications Agency, 1980; Hennecke, 1981; Marais, 1980; 'Civil service trial attacks WP costs', *Computer Systems in Southern Africa*, Sept 1981, pp. 21–22). The better word processors have spelling

checkers, which can improve the writer's productivity by 5% by decreasing the time required for proofreading (Arthur, 1983). Most programmers are careless about spelling, yet correct spelling improves the productivity of the reader. When a misspelled word is noticed, it causes the reader to pause, mentally correct the word, and then start reading again.

Electronic calendars, diaries, appointment scheduling, clocks, alarms, reminders, calculators, notepads, list managers (e.g. for address lists and telephone lists), and file managers, all prove useful.

Desk top publishing DTP typically links special software packages (which are like enhanced word processing packages) to laser printers, enabling organizations to do their own in-house publishing: authors can compose, print and publish near typesetting quality documents, which can merge text and graphics (Gell, 1986). Inter Consult estimates that corporate expenditures on printing and publishing services consume 6–10% of gross revenues, and that electronic publishing could reduce these outlays by 25–60% (Lallande, 1987).

Personal computers with word processing, spreadsheets, statistical facilities, graphics, etc., are now essential.

Computerized telephones, and advanced telephone calling features: call forwarding, call waiting, etc. – although computerized telephones only save a few seconds each time they are used, they were surprisingly nominated among high technology products which had become necessities (McCartney, 1986).

Electronic mail reduces disruptive telephone calls, avoids busy signals or no-answers, and allows staff to carefully prepare outgoing, and read incoming, messages when convenient. (There is now a terminal, the TEXT LITE PX1000, shaped like a telephone handset, which is so small it can fit into a suit pocket, and so permits electronic communication to and from virtually anywhere.)

Another major advantage of electronic mail is speed – instead of taking several days to cross a country, a written note can be received within minutes of being sent – and it also ensures that important documents are not lost in the post. Electronic mail should give the ability to send an editable document of unlimited length to anyone (or any group of people on a distribution list), on the electronic mail system; it should notify the recipient that there is a message waiting, and the sender that the message has been received; it should have priority levels so that non-urgent messages are sent when system usage is low; and it should also have a reminder feature that a letter is due for a reply (Doyle, 1986). An interesting discussion of the advantages of electronic mail is given in Arthur (1983).

Voice mail is a form of electronic mail in which spoken messages are used rather than written ones (Fordham, 1988). It does not require a computer terminal. Voice and data are being integrated, and Plant (1988) reports on the introduction of software and hardware which converts computer text into voice, and sends it over the telephone.

Cellular radio According to 'Goodbye telephone tag' (*Office Equipment and Methods*, Jan–Feb 1986, pp. 53–6) telephone tag, in which one party leaves message after message for the other before finally establishing contact, is probably the greatest single contributor to lost time in an average workday. Cellular radio reduces this. It enables you to get much more done by allowing you to make or receive telephone calls virtually anywhere – in your car (though that can be a traffic hazard), in a cafe, in a meeting (though that can be disruptive), in someone else's office, and even in the street. Some of the portable cellular telephones available today weigh less than a pound, and literally fit into a pocket.

Microfilm and microfiche eliminate much paper, save on document storage space, and provide quick retrieval (Manuel, 1986).

Photocopiers, some of which can enlarge or reduce, make multiple copies, and may have facilities such as duplex (copying onto both sides of the page), editing, and full color copying ('Copiers '88', *Mind Your own Business*, May 1988, pp. 19–39).

Facsimile or fax (telephone copiers) combine photocopying technology and telephone communications to deliver paper copies remotely (Mortensen, 1986; Kreitzman, 1986). They can transmit an A4 size page in half a minute or less. Documents can consist of text, diagrams and even photographs.

Optical Character Readers (OCRs), including handheld scanners and even bar code readers (Yourdon, 1989) allow text and graphics to be scanned and stored in a computer for subsequent processing.

Teleconference facilities save on travel time and costs, avoid the resultant jet lag on long journeys, allow organizations to make decisions faster, increase productivity, eliminate duplicated or needless effort, and raise morale ('Teleconferencing: efficiency exemplified,' *Dun's Business Month*, February 1986, pp. 68–70; Chess and Cowlishaw, 1987; Hall, 1986). They are also claimed to lead to greater and more equal participation (Martin, 1982b), with the participants measuring their words more carefully, but feeling less threatened in making controversial remarks, behaving more democratically, and being able to vote quickly and in privacy. Teleconferencing can be subdivided into:

- video teleconferencing, which allows the parties to see as well as hear each other;
- direct broadcast satellite technology, which offers one-way video but two-way audio; and
- audiographic, which provides audio supplemented by freezeframe video.

Interpersonal computing (also known as work-group computing, computer-supported groups, and group decision support systems): much of the work in offices is done by small groups of people who interact with each other. With appropriate software linking them together, such as multiuser database management systems (DBMSs), electronic mail, co-authoring systems and real-time conferencing running on networked PCs, their productivity can be improved (Markoff, 1986). An advanced example of this is Xerox's 'Colab' (Stefik *et al.*, 1987).

Bulletin boards: such as the one operated by ITC to notify customers of bugs in its products (Bridger, 1986).

Electronic copyboards are used typically in meetings, and enable copies of the material written on the board to be made and distributed to the participants, thereby reducing the need to take notes ('Electronic copyboards add to visual graphics,' *The Office*, October 1986, pp. 100–101). Images on the board can also be transferred into a PC, so this facility can also be used for teleconferencing.

Several functions may be integrated into a single apparatus, such as terminals handling text, data, voice, and images; laser printer/copiers; fax/copiers; and fax boards for PCs that double as modems. Because of the lack of office space, multi-function equipment should have become widespread (Shinn, 1983), but has not done so for a variety of reasons, such as its high cost, because it does not meet the real needs of users, and because of technical difficulties, e.g. if a laser printer were used as heavily as a copier, it would burn out (Butler Cox, 1983a; Blankenhorn, 1988).

Similarly, some software products can perform several of the above functions (such as electronic mail and electronic calendars), e.g. DEC's All-in-1 and IBM's OfficeVision. There are also integrated software packages which typically include a spreadsheet; a DBMS with query language, screen painter and report writer; a word processing program; and graphics. Examples are Software Products International's Open Access II, Intuitive Systems' Intuitive Solution (Jones, 1986a), Ashton Tate's Framework II, and Microsoft's WORKS for the Apple Macintosh.

From the large number and variety of facilities listed above, it is clear that there are many tools available which together provide a comprehensive office support environment, with a correspondingly high potential for improving the productivity of all office workers, including programmers and analysts.

Extent of use

Although some of these facilities are widely used, only 4% of the organizations in a 1986 survey by Arthur D. Little, Inc., reported widespread use of video teleconferencing; and only 12% expected to have widespread use of voice mail, and only 4% audio teleconferencing, by the end of 1987 (Mayfield, 1986). Such figures, and some of those quoted later, lend credibility to the claim that many organizations are getting little or no support for automation from top management (Hart, 1986).

Furthermore, although fully integrated systems (with similar user interfaces and easy data transfer) are the ideal, only 2% of the organizations in the Arthur D. Little survey had achieved it, while 20% had implemented only word processing (Mayfield, 1986). The lack of integration was caused by the limited ability of terminals and personal computers to communicate effectively with each other, even with other equipment from the same vendor; the difficulty in networking personal computers (the easiest way was through an existing mainframe or departmental computer); and the difficulty in connecting office systems to the mainframe. However, these areas have since been improved.

The above limitations explain Datamation's 1986 mini/micro survey, which showed that organizations planning to implement an integrated office made the following choices (Verity, 1986b):

- Departmental mini   55% of all sites
- Mainframe-based system 22
- Networked PCs   15
- Stand-alone PC   9

Purchase of equipment is often recommended as a relatively easy way to boost productivity (Bain, 1982). Sometimes, the purchases are made or approved by people who understand neither the equipment nor the need for it. It is therefore not surprising that sometimes equipment is purchased which is not suited for its intended use. This is not a satisfactory situation, but it would appear from the limited usage discussed above that many organizations have not yet reached even this stage.

Nevertheless, it was predicted that equipment sales would increase by 50% over the next five years (Information technology threatens to swamp contemporary offices. *ComputerWeek*, 9 May 1983, p. 17). Chorafas (1985) reported estimates that capital investment per office worker would rise from about $2000 in 1984, to $10 000–12 000 in 1990. Worldwide expenditures for office automation equipment might have reached $80 billion by then. In fact, the PC market might become oversold (Chapter 5).

Effect on productivity

In Chapter 2, I quoted the claim by McDonough (1981) that improvements in productivity of 10–25% are consistently being realized where supervisors are helped to make an environment more orderly, and the estimate by Maudlin (1983b) that office productivity was only 60% of what it should be, but could be improved to 90% through better management alone. (Presumably, these figures do not take technological advances into account.)

Productivity figures for different industry sectors since the 1950s are given in Table 4.1; the highest increase (185%) represents an improvement of only about 2 or 3% p.a., compound. By contrast, software engineering productivity is increasing by perhaps 5% p.a. (see Chapter 2).

The figures in Table 4.1 imply a close relationship between capital investment and productivity increase. The solution to low office productivity would therefore appear

Table 4.1 Productivity return on capital investment

Industry sector	Amount invested per worker ($US)	Productivity increase (%)	Ratio
Office	2 000	4	500:1
Factory	20 000	45	444:1
Agriculture	100 000	185	541:1

Source: Hennecke (1981); Erickson (1982); Finlayson (1979); Edwards and Loveday (1982).

obvious. However, some authorities claim that productivity in all sectors is at a standstill, or is even decreasing.

- For all practical purposes, US productivity has shown no growth since 1977 (Bain, 1982);
- From the end of the Second World War to the early 1970s, productivity showed significant gains, then it suddenly slowed down, reached its peak in 1978, and has been falling since (Chorafas, 1985);
- The 1986 Peat Marwick cost performance study showed that data capture productivity was down by 5% (Stone, 1986).

In view of the increased availability of technologically advanced office equipment, it is difficult to understand how office productivity can be allowed to decrease.

Office costs are high – Chorafas (1985) reported estimates that equipment, compensation, and support costs for white-collar workers would reach $1.5 trillion by 1990 in the US alone – and they can comprise up to 70% of an organization's total expenditure (Davis and Blackmarr, 1983), so there exists the potential for large savings. According to Black (1989), studies have shown that, by implementing general purpose office applications (word processing, electronic mail, electronic diary, etc.) productivity can improve by 15–30%. Chorafas reported claims by a leading office automation manufacturer that its equipment makes possible savings of 16% in executive time, through reductions in the time spent in meetings, on the telephone, reading and analysing documents, creating documents, travelling, filing, searching files, seeking information, and telephone tag. Similarly, Booz and Allen (1980) believe that the effective use of office automation can improve productivity by 15%, and can save $300 billion p.a. in office worker costs in the US alone. Further, it can save more by improving the productivity of managers and professional staff than that of clerks and secretaries, so software engineers will benefit substantially from these advances.

This aspect is expanded on by Hossack (1986). An intelligent workstation is a multifunction tool that can provide word processing, message delivery, data storage and management, etc. The justification for these workstations is to enhance the effectiveness of 'knowledge workers' – people who work with information and make decisions, such as managers and professionals. Improving their productivity is a complex and ambitious goal that contrasts sharply with the early target group of office automation, clerical workers, but the potential payoff is greater since the benefits of their improved decisions are substantial.

4.6 SUMMARY AND CONCLUSIONS

In this chapter, a large number and variety of factors relating to the office were discussed.

To work at maximum capacity, staff need a well-designed and equipped environment. Lighting, heating, noise, and so on, must all be carefully controlled. Meeting rooms, and library and other facilities, must be provided. The office must be well laid out to ensure smooth work flow, and convenient access to equipment and facilities. Adequate space must be provided. Professional advice is available, and organizations can appoint a facilities manager to oversee these arrangements.

This is true of office workers in general, but software engineers have more stringent requirements. In particular, they must be free of distractions and interruptions, so they can concentrate intensely on the difficult problems they have to solve.

There are stringent ergonomic requirements for the furniture and the equipment (particularly terminals and PCs). Failure to meet these requirements affects not only productivity, but also health and safety. Fears over the safety of VDUs, however, seem to be exaggerated and misplaced. There are problems, but informed opinion attributes them to other causes, such as ergonomic failings in the design of the equipment and the workplace, and not to radiation from the VDU. The staff can solve some of the problems themselves, often with simple measures.

Software engineers should be taught typing skills, and the sequence of the keys on the keyboard can and should be improved. Both these measures could have a significant impact on productivity.

Many advances have been made in office equipment, but the evidence indicates that the equipment is not as widely used as it could be.

Some requirements conflict with each other, e.g. absence of a telephone eliminates one source of distraction, but makes it more difficult to resolve one's own problems.

To provide the ideal environment is expensive, but there is evidence that the investment is repaid in improved productivity. One trial example brings together several of the aspects discussed in the chapter.

One organization, a telephone plant in Norway, had serious sick leave and staff turnover problems. To cure these, it improved the lighting and ventilation, and redesigned the work area to give the operators greater flexibility to vary their working posture. The workstations were previously at a fixed height, resulting in awkward posture leading to muscle strain and excessive sick leave. After the redesign: musculoskeletal sick leave was reduced from 5% of total production time to 3%; long-term sick leave was also reduced; and staff turnover was reduced from 30% to 8% (Corlett *et al.*, 1986). The total investment in ergonomics, and in installation and running costs of ventilation and lighting, was $46 000; but the reduction in recruitment costs, training costs, instructors' salary costs, and sick payments, came to $437 000, which is a return on investment of nearly 10:1.

Computer hardware is used during software development and maintenance, and the finished systems run on hardware. Hardware considerations can therefore affect software productivity, and so must be included in this investigation.

Computer hardware consists of a variety of different types of equipment:

- the Central Processing Unit (CPU);
- read-only memory (ROM);
- random-access memory (RAM);
- permanent storage devices (such as tapes and disks);
- input and output devices (such as terminals and printers);
- communications equipment (such as modems and telephone lines).

There are numerous different makes and models of each of these items, having different speeds and capacities, but the design, construction and internal working of the equipment are outside the scope of this study, except insofar as they affect observable factors such as reliability, response time and expandability.

The situation is complicated by the close connection between hardware and software.

- The interactive programming capability, for which large productivity improvements have been claimed (Chapter 6), requires not just a terminal network but also the software to drive it.
- Micro- and mini-computers may be chosen in preference to mainframes, not because of hardware considerations – though they may give faster response than an overloaded mainframe, or better price/performance (Mendelson, 1987) – but because

the software is more 'user friendly', they are claimed to be faster and more economical to program, and 'a PC has the flexibility to do some very fancy things with a mouse, pull-down menus and dynamic scrolling, which cannot be done with a mainframe' (Pienaar, 1987).

- Mainframes may be chosen because: higher-level languages may be inferior or not available on smaller machines (Chapter 6); a 16-bit machine is easier to program than an 8-bit machine; and the available tools are more sophisticated on larger machines (Anderson, 1982; Dieperink, 1977).
- Software complexity can be built into the hardware, thereby speeding up programming (Zachmann, 1981).
- Software may be inefficient, thereby slowing down powerful hardware.
- Software may be unreliable, and it is not always immediately apparent whether a particular fault was caused by a hardware or a software failure – Weinberg (1971) quoted an instance in which an apparent bug in the operating system, after six months of investigation, was actually determined to be a faulty circuit card.
- More pre-written software is available for some computers than others (Chapter 7).

Software therefore should be, and has been, a major factor in the choice of hardware (Blakeney, 1983). In fact, the success of an installation usually depends more on software and the peripherals than on the performance of the central processing unit (Wingfield, 1976).

Despite these difficulties, some aspects of hardware will be examined: the reductions in price and improvements in performance, the proliferation of computers, their reliability, their diversity (lack of standardization), and finally their power and capacity.

5.1 PRICE/PERFORMANCE IMPROVEMENTS

Perhaps the most striking aspects of the DP industry have been the spectacular hardware price reductions and the performance improvements. These aspects are relevant to software productivity because, as discussed later, price and performance improvements increase the demand for software, thereby making productivity improvement an urgent necessity; but they also make productivity improvements possible, e.g. because of the faster turnaround or machine response, and the more powerful tools which become possible.

5.1.1 PRICE REDUCTIONS

The average purchase price of comparable computers decreased by a factor of eight between 1953 and 1975 (a reduction of 9% p.a., compound) (Wright, 1978).

The price of a PDP-8 computer decreased by a factor of six from 1965 to 1975 (16% p.a.) (le Roux, 1976).

There has been a 100-fold reduction in ten years in the cost of executing a COBOL instruction (37% p.a.) (Huskisson, 1977).

There has been a fourfold reduction in ten years in the cost of storing a byte of information in main memory (13% p.a.) (Huskisson, 1977).

Hardware costs are decreasing by an average of 15% annually (Johnson, 1980a).

The cost of primary memory has been dropping at a rate of about 30% a year (Ever, 1980).

A graph in Martin (1982a) shows that the cost of computer time, for executing 300 000 instructions per second, was $10 000 in about 1956, that this decreased to $100 in 1970, and that it further decreased to nearly $10 in 1980.

This represents an overall reduction of about 33% p.a., compound.

Microprocessor prices have dropped by about 28% a year, and the prices of computer memories have come down by a compound yearly rate of 42% (de Benedetti, 1982).

The cost of externally storing (on a lease basis) one megabyte decreased from $2.61 per month in 1978, to $0.94 in 1984 (16% p.a.) (Gelb, 1989).

The average cost per MIPS (million instructions per second) of the systems in *Computerworld*'s 'Hardware Roundup' in 1985 was $169 670, which is just under half the 1981 average (this equals a reduction of 17% p.a., or about 21% if inflation is taken into account) (Mendelson, 1987).

The cost of data processing power fell by a factor of ten over the ten years to 1986 (21% p.a.) ('Main street blues', *Computer Mail*, 27 February 1987, pp. 32–40).

The average yearly decline in the cost of various system elements over the past three decades ranged from 11% (for card readers and punchers), to 27% (for internal memory) (Hodges, 1987b).

The average cost of a general purpose mainframe CPU is now about a third of what it was 30 years ago, which is a reduction of about 4% p.a., compound (if inflation is not taken into account) (Hodges, 1987b). However, the cost of an average system, without terminals, was only slightly lower in 1986 than it was in 1955.

Conclusion

There are large differences in the above figures, but that is only to be expected in view of the wide range of different hardware covered, and the different time periods. The increase in power and capability makes it still more difficult to compare the various figures and draw any conclusions. The difficulty is compounded by the effect of inflation: 'inflation in the late 1970s played havoc with prices; for almost a decade, prices rose instead of fell' (Hodges, 1987b). Nevertheless, the figures indicate that hardware prices have decreased significantly – probably by about 20% p.a., compound.

5.1.2 PERFORMANCE IMPROVEMENTS

Faster computers are required to provide software engineers with faster turnaround and response. Extra speed is also generally required in scientific and engineering computation, and more recently for artificial intelligence (AI), but there are commercial uses as well: 'some econometric models can dim the lights on even the largest Sierra mainframe' (Verity, 1987a).

Past performance improvements

The processing power of high-end IBM processors doubled between 1974 and 1978 (an increase of 19% p.a., compound), and doubled again between 1978 and 1981 (an increase of 26% p.a., compound) (Clark, 1989).

The processing power of the median IBM customer site increased from 0.2 MIPS in 1966, to 29 MIPS in 1984 (= 32% p.a. compound) (Gelb, 1989). (This figure may, however, refer to the aggregate power of all the computers installed at the site.)

The MIPS rating of the average system in *Computerworld*'s 'Hardware Roundup', increased by a factor of 2.24 over the 4-year period 1981–1985 (an increase of 22% p.a., compound) (Mendelson, 1987).

The improvement in the performance of conventional computers has been limited to about 10–15% per year (Fisher, 1986).

Machine performance has recently been growing by a factor of 100 per 10 years (an increase of 58% p.a., compound) (Ohno, 1989).

Predictions

In the next ten years, computers will increase in speed by a factor of at least ten (= 26% p.a.) (Martin, 1981).

The average computer will perform 20–100 million instructions per second by 1990 (Blakeney, 1983). (If we combine this prediction with the 6.25 average MIPS rating of the systems in the 1985 *Computerworld*'s 'Hardware Roundup' (Mendelson, 1987), it implies an annual compound increase of at least 26%, and possibly more than 50%.)

The processing power of the median IBM customer site will increase from 29 MIPS in 1984, to over 300 MIPS by 1990 (an increase of more than 47% p.a. compound) (Gelb, 1989). (This figure may, however, refer to the aggregate power of all the computers installed at the site.)

The processing power of high-end processors was expected to more than double between 1981 and 1983 (an increase of over 41% p.a., compound) (Clark, 1989).

Conclusion

Once again, there are large differences in the above figures, and difficulties in comparing them and drawing conclusions, but they indicate that hardware performance is increasing significantly – probably by over 20% p.a., compound.

5.1.3 PRICE/PERFORMANCE IMPROVEMENTS

The cost/performance ratio of processing hardware has improved by a factor of 100 each decade since 1955 (an increase of 58% p.a. compound) (Tanaka, 1977; Hodges, 1987b).

The IBM PC represents an improvement in price/performance over the IBM 702 of 17 000 times (= 37% p.a.) (Austrian, 1983).

The performance/price factor (the time to perform one million additions times the cost of CPU and main memory) has decreased by an order of magnitude with each succeeding generation of computers, i.e. by an order of magnitude six times over the past 30 years (= 15% p.a.) (Schach, 1990).

Conclusion

Once again, there are large differences in the above figures, and difficulties in comparing them and drawing conclusions, but taking into account both the figures in this subsection and those in the previous ones, it appears that hardware price/performance has improved significantly – possibly by as much as 40% p.a., compound.

5.1.4   FUTURE DEVELOPMENTS

According to some authorities, price reductions have shown a levelling off (Dieperink, 1977; Wright, 1978), and the average system in *Computerworld*'s 'Hardware Roundup' in 1985 did cost about the same as in 1981 (though it was more powerful) (Mendelson, 1987).

Most authorities predicted that performance, and price/performance ratios, would continue improving: 'the end is nowhere in sight' (Norman, 1978; Ever, 1980); but other authorities disagreed: 'the heady days are over . . . it is much more difficult to introduce each advance in technology' (Mazor, 1982; Uttal, 1980). Their pessimism is understandable: 64% of the area of IBM's 512K-bit memory chip is occupied by storage cells, and the smallest images on them are just 1.5 micron (millionths of a metre) wide, which is only about three times the wavelength of light, the etching tool (US, 1983; Woolcock, 1983). With existing technologies therefore, only another two or three doublings of circuit density are possible. Reducing the packaging area might give an additional tenfold improvement ('Spare space on wafers', *Computer Week*, 23 April 1984, p. 13). Making the chips bigger is equivalent to reducing the packaging area, but it increases the chances of flaws.

However, a Belgian company, UCB, has invented a process that permits far denser packing of information on chips using conventional equipment. This has already permitted pathways only 0.4 micron wide, and has brought into reach pathways only 0.1 micron wide, making 64 megabit chips possible ('Chemical breakthrough', *Computer Mail*, 31 October 1986, p. 7). Similarly, using electron beams as the etching tool instead of light, TRW, Inc. have produced circuitry features only half a micron wide ('Battle to produce the next superchip', *Computer Mail*, 31 October 1986, p. 7). Using semiconductors which are faster than silicon would improve performance, e.g. gallium arsenide is five times faster than the fastest silicon currently available (though it is more expensive, and there are still technical problems to be overcome) (Fisher, 1986).

Further improvement would require new technologies, such as using molecules instead of silicon-based circuits, or radiation with wavelength shorter than that of light, e.g. X-rays. Such technologies would make possible storage densities 100 000 to 10 million times greater than now available, but this could take ten or more years ('Spare space on wafers', *Computer Week*, 23 April 1984, p. 13). The DARPA (Defense Advanced Research Projects Agency) goal is to 'achieve a factor of 1000 improvement every three years' (Fisher, 1986). This latter figure includes the effect of software as well as hardware, but even so, these goals and predictions seem too optimistic, especially as most observers predict that the state of the art will advance in incremental rather than bounding steps over the next decade (Fisher, 1986); and the number of components per chip has only been doubling every year ('Information technology trends: the next five years', *Computer Week*, 19 March 1984, p. 10) – and this slowed to a doubling every two years (Davis, 1987b).

However, there are alternative approaches to achieving improved performance or price/performance: parallel processors, vector processors, VLIW (very long instruction word), RISC (reduced instruction set computers), light, electronic neurons, and super-conductivity.

Parallel processors

The traditional uniprocessor (single CPU) seems to be reaching a power plateau as its pacing component, the logic gate, runs into the upper limit of its switching speed (Verity, 1987a). Two or more slower processors, operating in parallel, may therefore be faster. This is a proven technique, used in multi-processor mainframes (such as IBM's 3090–400) and co-processing PCs (with maths or graphics co-processors), and the principle is now being extended. Thousands of micro-processors can be linked together, with powerful software keeping them aligned and synchronized. Parallel processors are there-fore a class of system offering performance that can rival that of conventional super-computers, but at a fraction of the cost.

Parallel processors use multiple processors or CPUs linked together so that they appear to the user to be a single, extremely powerful unit. They are fast because, instead of execut-ing the application program serially, one step at a time, they execute different portions of the program at the same time. If, for exam-ple, the machine contains 64 processors, then it can execute 64 parts of the program simultaneously, and thereby complete the program in a fraction of the time.

The disadvantage is that the program must be designed – broken-down – into parallel parts. Not all applications can be so divided – even technical programs vary widely in the amount of code that can be processed in parallel (Verity, 1987a) – and only 10% of the respondents in the Datamation/Cowen & Co. 1986–87 mini/micro survey said their appli-cations warranted parallel or multi-processing minis (Verity, 1986b). (Appli-cations which can be subdivided include searching textual databases, processing images, and speech recognition.) Further-more, to subdivide an application is difficult and time-consuming, and adds significantly to the complexity. If it is not done properly, bottlenecks arise, as one part of the program has to wait for another to complete (Fisher, 1986) – in the extreme case, the machine is slowed to the speed of an ordinary computer. The compiler may also be complex, putting the program through many transformations, any of which might introduce unknown bugs (Verity, 1987a).

Examples of large parallel processors are Bolt, Beranak and Newman's Butterfly machine, which has up to 256 processors; Fifth Generation Corporation's DADO machine, which links up to 8192 microproces-sors; and Thinking Machines Corporation's Connection Machine, which has 64 000 one-bit processors, and can process data at an aggregate rate of one billion instructions per second (Fisher, 1986; Verity, 1987a; Thinking Machines Corp., 1986).

Vector processors

These are usually added to large mainframe computers to give them supercomputer per-formance, e.g. the Sperry (Unisys) 1100/91 ISP runs six to nine times faster than the ordinary 1100/91 (Gullo, 1986).

VLIW

A wide instruction word can do more work during each clock cycle, e.g. simultaneously load, add and store (Verity, 1987a). This has been described as 'fine-grain parallelism'. It requires a sophisticated compiler, and a major problem is how to handle conditional jumps – branches whose direction depends on run-time conditions. The compiler for Fisher's Multiflow machine handles this problem by making an 'educated guess' as to the most likely destination of the jump.

RISC

Computer architectures have become increas-ingly complex with the gradual introduction of more and more instructions to match application areas, yet most of the instructions are seldom used – in a frequency count on the IBM 360 computer, it was found that only 10 of the 200 available instructions made up two-thirds of all the instructions executed (Hopkins, 1987). RISC reverses this trend. With fewer instructions, the machine's data-flow is simplified, with the result that the basic instructions run faster. Speed is further increased if the instructions are simple ones, which can be executed in one machine cycle. One would therefore expect RISC computers (e.g. IBM's RS/6000 series) to be several times faster (Meredith, 1986a). However, according to Mallach (1990), the saving in processor time is typically only about 25%. Furthermore, it is not sufficient to merely reduce the instruction set: 'The skill in this exercise is the combination of reduced instruction set, better register utilisation and the design of capable optimising compilers' (Meredith, 1986a). Part of the performance improvement is therefore not due to the reduction in the instruction set as such, or – put the other way round – the potential performance improvement is greater than one would expect from the reduction in the instruction set alone ('Enormous power locked in IBM's RT – like Prometheus bound?' *Computing SA*, 22 September 1986, p. 34).

Light

An optical computer driven by light instead of electrical signals could be 1000 times faster than conventional electronic machines (Huang, 1986) – light travels at four times the speed of electricity in copper (Davis, 1987b), and the switching speed would also be much higher. Some authorities believed that optical computers might be available in as little as three to five years (Leopold, 1986; Huang, 1986), but Davis (1987b) thought they were still a 'remote dream'.

Electronic neurons

An electronic neuron (so-called because they emulate biological neurons or brain cells) has a response time of only 400 nanoseconds, which is much faster than a biological neuron (Jackel, 1986). An electronic neuron network has an inherently parallel structure, making it 100–1000 times faster than a conventional computer for pattern-recognition type tasks, and 10–30 times faster than special-purpose hardware. The small size of resistors on these chips makes possible a very high chip density.

Superconductivity

This refers to the transmission of electricity without any resistance being offered by the medium through which it is being transmitted. Because there is no resistance, there is no heat generation, so electronic components can be placed closer together without over-heating, leading to smaller and faster computers (Davis, 1987b). Switching speeds are also much higher – Josephson junctions (superconductor-based switching devices) operate 50 times faster than the fastest silicon transistors. The disadvantage was that, in the past, superconducting could only be achieved at very low temperatures, and very expensive cooling systems were required to maintain these temperatures. Previous attempts to exploit this phenomenon were not very successful – IBM abandoned their Josephson Junction project in 1983 – but the discovery of 'high-temperature' super-conducting (at liquid nitrogen temperatures of −196°C or maybe even room temperature, instead of liquid helium temperatures of −269°C), holds promise – the optimistic view was that an all-superconducting computer might be available in ten years (Davis, 1987b).

At a more fundamental level, there are certain physical limits, namely the speed of light and the non-zero width of an atom, which place an ultimate limit on hardware size and speed (Schach, 1990). However, we are nowhere near these limits yet. Computers can easily become at least two orders of magnitude faster and smaller without impinging on them.

Conclusion

Although there are still technical difficulties to be overcome, and some of the above possibilities will be expensive, these developments are promising, and indicate that major improvements are in the offing. To the extent that demand for software is fuelled by hardware capabilities and by lower hardware prices and improved price/performance, this in turn indicates that the demand for software will continue to escalate, so productivity improvement will continue to be a pressing need.

5.2 PROLIFERATION

5.2.1 INDUSTRY GROWTH

The price reductions and price/performance improvements have led to the wider application of computers. They can now be used for new kinds of jobs, ones which previously would not have been economically viable because of the high hardware costs. In particular, the reductions have brought computers within the financial reach of smaller organizations. (The availability of good software, such as the VisiCalc spreadsheet and subsequently Lotus 1–2–3, has also contributed to the rapid industry growth.) In addition, the lower prices permit trade-offs of computer time against programmer time; the automation of activities in the computer room, even to the extent of unmanned operation (Ever, 1980); and so on.

The net result has been to cause the industry to grow rapidly.

- The market for minicomputers multiplied 15 times over the 10 years to 1976, a growth rate of 30% a year, compound (Gillin, 1983).

- There were 2 million personal computers in the USA in 1982, and 16 million were forecast for 1986 (an increase of 68% p.a. compound) (Gilchrist *et al.*, 1983).
- Federal government workers in the USA had an estimated 200 000 micros in 1986, and this number was expected to grow to 500 000 by 1990 (26% p.a. compound) (Kirchner, 1986).
- The graphics market was predicted to grow at 30% a year (Crutchfield, 1986a).
- The desk top publishing (DTP) industry was expected to grow by 40% in 1987 ('Huge DTP Market', *Office Product News*, May 1987, p. 24).
- The total electronic publishing market in 1985 was $503 million: it was predicted to reach $4.03 billion in 1990 (52% p.a. compound) (Lallande, 1987).
- Facsimile was growing by 30% a year (Kreitzman, 1986).
- The database business was predicted to grow at around 28% annually over the next five years (Tate and Runyan, 1986).
- The market for project management software was predicted to grow from $1.8 million in 1985, to $4.2 million by 1990 (18% p.a. compound) (Barry, 1986b).
- The data networking market was growing at 15% a year (Verity, 1987b).
- Parallel processing for technical computing was growing at 35% a year (Verity, 1987a).
- Fortune 1000 firms were predicted to increase their usage of departmental software products by 32% annually over the next 5 years (compared to 19% for the overall software market) (Barry, 1987).
- Some IBM personnel said that customer demand for processing power was growing between 30% and 100% a year ('The King is dead; long live the King,' *Computer Mail*, 27 February 1987, pp. 21–31).
- The number of employees in the computer industry increased by a factor of five (from 101 000 to 501 000) between 1960 and 1987 (an increase of 6% p.a., compound), compared to a factor of under two (from 70

million to 120 million) for the total civilian labor force (an increase of only 2% p.a., compound) (Hodges, 1987b).

Conclusion

There are large differences in the above figures. That is only to be expected in view of the wide range of different aspects covered, and the different time periods, but it makes it difficult to compare the various figures and draw any conclusions. Nevertheless, the average of the figures is around 30% p.a., compound.

5.2.2   TRENDS

About a decade ago, the number of computers was reported to be growing by:

- International Data
  Corp. (1980)   23% p.a.
- Phister (1979)   24% p.a.
- Martin (1981)   more than 25% p.a.
- Gilchrist *et al.* (1983)   52% p.a.

and the value of the market by (Martin, 1982b):

- small computers   29–49% p.a.
- mainframes   8–10% p.a.
- total industry   11–15% p.a.

Most authorities at that time saw no sign of the market becoming saturated, or even of a slowdown because of the recession (Kessel, 1976). According to Dolotta *et al.* (1976), the industry grew by a factor of 20 each decade since 1955 (an increase of 21% p.a. compound), and he predicted that this would continue in the next decade.

Nevertheless, there were some dissenting voices:

- 'The micro market will become very oversold' (Tireford, 1976; Duffy, 1983; Anderson, 1982).
- In most cases, the functionality of personal computers 'will be much greater than the average user will need' (Blakeney, 1983), so

their owners were unlikely to replace them with more advanced machines.

- A study by IBM showed that central computers were only being utilized at 23% of their efficiency (Shinn, 1983), so there was spare capacity which might have caused postponement of upgrades.

Also, many microcomputer staff were out of jobs (Steyn, 1982). That may have been largely because of the recession and therefore temporary, but more recent figures confirm the pessimistic forecasts.

- The Datamation/Cowen & Co. 1986–87 mini/micro survey showed that PCs were only used for 5.1 hours a day, thus confirming there was spare capacity (Verity, 1986b).
- The same survey showed significant reductions in shipments compared to the previous year for both minis and micros: 'for minicomputers, the boom times are over and show no signs of returning' (Verity, 1986b).
- The market is getting saturated: 73% of the responding sites in the 1986 Datamation/Cowen & Co. Computer/Telecommunications Industry Survey already had Lotus 1–2–3 installed, less than 4% of the sites planned to acquire additional copies, and initial acquisitions of the package were contemplated in only 6% of the sites during the following year (Verity, 1986a). The Datamation/Cowen & Co. 1986–87 mini/micro survey showed that upwards of 90% of sites in the banking, education and government sectors had PCs installed (Verity, 1986b).
- Offices in Silicon Valley were only about 50% full (Appun, 1987).
- The income of the top twelve computer manufacturers in 1985, was only 13% higher than in 1984 ('The King in dead; long live the King,' *Computer Mail*, 27 February 1987, pp. 21–31).

The IS revenues of the top 100 companies in the business showed total sales in 1988 of

Table 5.1 Growth figures (% p.a., compound) (Hodges, 1987b)

	Mainframe	*Mini*	*Micro*	*Total*
Increase in number of machines shipped				
1957/70	18			21
1970/80	6	32		43
1980/87	1	13	48	45
1957/87	10	24	48	33
Increase in value (based on 1986 dollars)				
1957/70	23			23
1970/80	10	27		13
1980/87	3	12	26	10
1957/87	13	20	26	17

$243 billion, which is an increase of only 16% over the previous year, compared to a 19% increase the previous year (Kelly, 1989). Worse, the increase was only 5% in 1989, 9% in 1990, and 4% in 1991 (Marion, 1992).

In 1986, Datamation/Cowen & Co. gave the following growth figures (Verity, 1986b):

- PCs 15% (user base)
- corporate PCs 10–20% (shipments)
- mini < 8% (shipments)
- hardware budgets 9%

The more recent figures are roughly half the older figures, indicating that there has been a significant slowdown in the growth of the industry. This is confirmed by the more detailed figures given in Table 5.1. (There were a couple of discrepancies in the published figures from which I calculated these percentages, but they were not large enough to distort the overall picture.)

Future trends

It seems reasonable to suppose that, at some date, the hardware price/performance ratio will level off, and/or the market will become saturated, causing sales to drop. The increase in the number of computers in the past, and the accompanying increase in demand for software, have been fuelled by the hardware price and performance improvements. In fact, the market for computers has increased

so much that this, rather than staff inefficiency, appears to be the main reason for the shortfall in software output.

Provided the factories can meet the demand, a drop in hardware sales in the future may be caused by:

- no further applications to be computerized;
- insufficient programmers to create enough software to use additional hardware;
- people-costs too high, making it uneconomical to computerize further applications;
- low productivity (which has the same effect as the previous two points);
- computerization of more applications uneconomical because of high hardware costs.

Therefore, even if there is not a causal relationship, the demand for software can be expected to decrease as hardware sales fall, and this appears to have already begun: 'just as the corporate PC market is showing signs of saturation, so is PC software' (Verity, 1986a). It is important to know how rapidly and to what extent this will happen, as it places an upper limit on the amount of software required and therefore determines how big a productivity increase is needed.

5.2.3 CONCLUSION

As in the case of price and performance, there are large differences between the various figures quoted. Nevertheless, they show that the industry grew very rapidly in the past; that it is still growing, though not as rapidly as before; and that it may slow down still further in the future. Nevertheless, it *is* still growing, so the demand for software staff, and for an improvement in their productivity, will continue.

5.3 RELIABILITY

Hardware failures and malfunctions disrupt software development and maintenance, lowering productivity. Furthermore, the possibility of hardware problems during development, maintenance, and use, makes preventative action necessary. Such action is essentially non-productive and so also lowers productivity. The topic of hardware reliability is therefore relevant in a discussion of software engineering productivity.

This study is not concerned with hardware reliability as such, but with the *effect* it has on software productivity. Because other factors such as natural disasters, software failures, and even computer crime, can have the same effect as, or in some cases even cause, a hardware failure, and because some of the precautions taken against hardware failure (and the consequences thereof) also protect against these other factors (and their consequences), and vice versa, mention is made of these other topics as well.

According to Bell *et al.* (1987), studies show that, where both the hardware and software are at comparable levels of development, hardware fails three times as often as software.

5.3.1   CAUSES OF BREAKDOWNS

Hardware failures may be internal (design error; production error; or life expiry) or external (environmental disturbance, including overload).

Preference should be given to equipment which is rugged and has broad environmen-

tal requirements (Wingfield, 1976). Environmental disturbance may be caused by (Sims, 1977; Anning, 1986; Marcus, 1986):

- malicious damage, sabotage, civil unrest and terrorist attacks;
- negligent handling
- dust; humidity; air-conditioning failure
- fire; leaks or floods; static electricity; lightning; earthquakes; tornadoes;
- voltage fluctuations and power cuts
- radar; radio frequency interference (RFI); powerful external magnets.

It is not only the organization's own equipment which is at risk. A fire in one town 'took out telephones, telexes and data communications facilities. Many computer users were left with no recovery plan, and were unable to contact anyone to find out what to do' ('Heading for disaster,' *Computer Mail*, 31 October 1986, pp. 9–10).

Computers are inherently sensitive, so they cannot tolerate imperfect power and must be protected against irregularities, yet they are found in places like machine shops and factories which have inherently 'dirty' power (Leaf, 1986).

The most common problem with power supply is not a total power failure, but deviations such as spikes, surges, dips, transients, electrical noise, 'brown-outs', and frequency shifts. These can be caused by, for example, something as mundane as all the elevators in the building suddenly having large loads, or by natural phenomena such as lightning and wind ('Powering computers', *Computer Mail*, 27 February 1987, pp. 56–9; Leaf, 1986). Even a dip or surge in electricity lasting only a few milliseconds can cause a computer to 'forget' important data or give out misinformation, or cause damage to its hardware (AT&T, 1986). It is not just data in RAM that is wiped out: even ROM can be destroyed (Leaf, 1986). Further, even if the equipment does not fail immediately, its life may be shortened. Surveys by AT&T and IBM show that these disturbances occur on average 135 times a year – Leaf (1986) gives the much higher figure of two to four 'significant glitches' a day – and can account for as much as 50% of all computer downtime (AT&T, 1986).

Fire has been cited as the greatest single hazard in the operations department (Rickerby *et al.*, 1975).

One PC I worked on had a tape unit for backups placed next to the VDU. We were getting parity errors when using the tape unit, and were advised that this was caused by magnetism from the VDU. We removed the tape unit, placing it just a short distance away, and the parity errors were cured. Another PC I worked on was initially installed near a Magnetic Resonance Imaging machine. This is used for medical diagnosis, and produces a powerful magnetic field. There was a noticeable distortion of the display on the VDU, so the PC had to be resited.

Radio frequency interference can be caused by nearby ships. Low to moderate levels can cause read/write errors, while high levels can be hazardous to both personnel and equipment (Marcus, 1986).

A survey by Deloitte Haskins & Sells (1986) of the computer systems of financial organizations, showed that up to one-fifth of the organizations surveyed were so risky that they were likely to suffer losses within a year. Even more likely than fraud were losses arising from interruptions of business due to systems breaking down.

Another survey gave an even higher figure, showing that 65% of businesses with medium and large computer installations were unprepared for a disaster, even though any major interruption of their operations would threaten their existence ('Heading for disaster', *Computer Mail*, 31 October 1986, pp. 9–10). A further 24% had made some preparations which would ensure recovery 'at some cost and public embarrassment', while only 11% could survive a disaster with little disruption to day to day operations.

Poor quality diskettes can cause not only loss of data through diskette failure, but also costly damage to diskette drive heads (Kuflik, 1986). Diskettes should therefore be checked visually before purchase and use – they should have a shiny, smooth surface, and their jackets should be flat. 3.5 inch diskettes are more rugged than 5.25 inch ones.

Cut-rate PC clones are reportedly less reliable than IBM's own PCs (ben-Aaron, 1986).

5.3.2 PREVENTION OF BREAKDOWNS

Organizations must take steps to prevent hardware failures, and to minimize the losses if they should materialize (Rickerby *et al.*, 1976; Parkin, 1980; Marcus, 1986; Anning, 1986; Dieperink, 1977).

access control	staff training
preventative maintenance	insurance
adequate air conditioners	humidifiers
anti-static mats	shielding against radio frequency interference
tamperproof modems	voltage regulators
uninterruptible power supplies (UPS)	lightning protection devices
fireproof safes	smoke detectors
water detection system	waterproof ceiling
recovery utilities	recovery and restart procedures

backup hardware   standby site
fire extinguishing system
security copies of data/programs/job control/ documentation (on and off site).

It is 'warranty suicide' to take liberties when it comes to air-conditioning, temperature, humidity, and electrical specifications, as computer manufacturers 'are going to point to every piece of support equipment and every engineer in the room, before taking a look at their computers' (Marcus, 1986).

Organizations should not try to save money by running computers off power circuits that have other equipment on them (Marcus, 1986).

A UPS is the only type of power conditioning system that can provide total protection against power irregularities and failure. They have been used mostly for large mainframe systems, but are advisable even for PCs where these are used for business, though they may cost as much as the PC itself ('Powering computers', *Computer Mail*, 27 February 1987, pp. 56–9). As an example of their effectiveness, in the first six months after installing a UPS, the Midlantic National Bank enjoyed 100% uptime in spite of about 30 power outage problems (Iovacchini, 1986). However, some systems advertised as UPS only provide backup power in the case of total power failure, and so should be called 'standby' power supplies, not UPS.

Water fire extinguishers can be used on electrical equipment without damaging it, provided power to the equipment is switched off beforehand (Marcus, 1986). Afterwards, however, the equipment must be disassembled and dried out, which could take *days* or even *weeks*. Halon gas does not suffer from these disadvantages, but a halon system costs ten times as much, and the pipes used must be thoroughly cleaned before installation, otherwise metal filings from them will get into and damage the computer equipment.

A smoke detection system should be programmed to shut down the computer equipment and air conditioners, and charge the sprinkler system or set off halon gas.

There are three ways of instituting a disaster recovery plan: organizations can develop one themselves; they can call in a consultant; or they can use a generic model, such as EDP Security's DPlan 80 ('Heading for disaster', *Computer Mail*, 31 October 1986, pp. 9–10). Each of these alternatives has

disadvantages. The organization's own staff may have neither the time nor the requisite specialized knowledge; a consultant may not be given enough time; and generic models are nevertheless quite expensive and time-consuming, and require customizing (though the benefits outweigh the disadvantages).

The computer room should be isolated for environmental control, security, and fire protection. For example, walls should not go only as high as the dropped ceiling (Marcus, 1986).

The computer room should be designed so that traffic through it is minimized (Marcus, 1986). For example, paper should be stored near the printer, so that it is not constantly being dragged across the floor. Similarly, if tapes are sent off-site, and the storage area for them is at the far side of the computer room, then someone has to walk through the room every time a tape is sent away, with consequent possibility of the person bumping into and damaging a sensitive piece of equipment. There is also a security risk if people walk through the computer room to fetch tapes, though storing tapes near the entrance in itself poses a security risk.

Computer rooms should be carefully designed before being built, and future expansion should be catered for, as building work, installing additional power cables, and so on, can lead to equipment damage, either directly or from dust, water leaks, exposure to the elements, interruptions to the air-conditioning, etc. (Sharon, 1986).

Access control can be physical or logical. Physical access control restricts access to the computer room, terminals and communication equipment, by using keys, magnetic cards, voice recognition, fingerprints or palmprints, and locks on terminals and PCs. Logical access control restricts access to programs and data, by using passwords, encryption, and file protection software such as IBM's RACF (Resource Access Control Facility) and Computer Associates' CA-TOP

SECRET. Audit trails supplement access control, by providing information on what was done, by whom, from where, and when. Passwords, audit trails, etc., are generally built into file protection software.

Japanese DP managers believe that the foundation of trust, lifetime employment contracts, racial homogeneity, and sense of company and family unity, protect them from computer crime (Poe, 1986).

Making security copies of disks is speeded up if only altered files are backed up. This facility is provided, for example, by the BACKUP command on IBM PCs.

Tandem's Encompass DBMS can continuously update a duplicate database at a remote site, which can become the primary site if the original primary site is damaged or becomes inaccessible (Tandem, 1987).

PCs are often bought by first time users who do not fully appreciate the importance of frequent and regular backups. Even if they do, the problem is compounded if the PC has a hard disk: as many as 32 360K floppies might be needed to back up a 10MB disk. (Higher capacity diskettes, particularly 1.2 MB and 1.44MB, are now widely used, but hard disks also have much higher capacities than before, with up to hundreds or even thousands of megabytes.) However, tape units are available to simplify and speed up this task. Four such units, manufactured by Tecmar Inc., Sysgen Inc., Alloy Computer Products Inc. and Tallgrass Technologies, were reviewed by Rubel (1986).

Recovery utilities are programs which either undelete files which have just been deleted, and restore them in full provided nothing has been written to the disk since the erase command was issued; or enable the programmer to examine and change the information on disk byte by byte, thus repairing damaged files; or both. Examples are SODU (Screen Oriented Disk Utility), UNERA, The Norton Utilities, PC Tools, and Super Utility (Meeks, 1986; Rabinovitz, 1986).

Software staff are not involved in all the preventative measures listed above, but they do have to:

- participate in fire drills;
- build security and recovery features into systems;
- build audit trails into systems;
- build access control into systems; and
- help to ensure that the systems will run at standby sites.

Such activities are important, and they provide protection not only against losses caused by hardware failure, but also against losses due to operator errors, program bugs, user errors, sabotage, hackers, etc., which together are probably much more frequent than hardware failures. In fact, 70% of all database violations are caused unintentionally by end users ('Reliability – a critical factor', *Systems Stelsels*, August 1978, p. 37; Infotech, 1978), while other statistics indicate that 80% of all DP disasters are caused by human errors and omissions, 9% by fraud and embezzlement, 9% by malicious damage, and only 2% by natural or non-human factors ('Heading for disaster', *Computer Mail*, 31 October 1986, pp. 9–10).

Nevertheless, preventative measures are time-consuming and are essentially non-productive, so they can lower the productivity of software engineers significantly. However, Operating Systems and Data Base Management Systems may have built-in security and recovery features (such as the passwords, and the checkpoints, transaction logging, roll-back, roll-forward, and restart procedures in many DBMSs), thereby minimizing the amount of effort required, and thus the productivity loss. Add-on products such as VMBACKUP, RACF and CA-TOP SECRET, also help to automate security and/or recovery.

A balance must be struck between the cost of building security and recovery into a system, and the potential benefits to be gained, which depend on both the likely extent of the losses in the event of hardware failure (or operator error, program bug, etc.), and on the likely frequency of failure (Parkin, 1980). When a hardware failure etc. occurs, the duration of down time, and therefore the degree of disruption and extent of the losses, depends on such factors as (Wingfield, 1976; Doepel, 1977; Pountain, 1986b; Mallinick, 1977):

- the nature of the cause;
- the extent of the damage;
- which piece of equipment is affected;
- the diagnostic and self-rectification features built into the equipment (e.g. does it isolate a faulty portion of memory, or lock out bad sectors on a floppy disk?);
- how easy it is to repair (e.g. replaceable modules);
- the availability of technicians and engineers, and their familiarity with the equipment;
- the availability of spares;
- the supplier's backup capability;
- the remoteness of the site.

The standard of service provided by different manufacturers varies. One Japanese user, for example, stated that IBM's service is much better than Fujitsu's (Tamaki, 1987). Some manufacturers provide advanced maintenance capabilities. Nixdorf, for example, have their 'Remote Support' system whereby both hardware and software faults are diagnosed, and may even be corrected, over the telephone. They claim that nearly 100% of software faults can be diagnosed and corrected immediately, and at least 50% of hardware faults can be diagnosed instantly and accurately, thus enabling their engineers to correct them more quickly (Nixdorf, 1987). By diagnosing the trouble beforehand, service technicians know which replacement parts to take with them, and the 'Remote Support' system can even inform the operator of 'pseudo faults', such as no paper in the printer. Stratus Computer has a similar system, and the savings from it have enabled them to charge their customers one-third less

for annual maintenance than the industry average (Brady, 1987). The supplier must therefore be a factor in the choice of hardware ('Big business for minicomputers,' *Computronics*, 13th February 1980, p.8; Norman, 1978).

The independent maintenance company, Sorbus, has a 230 000 part-number inventory (Sorbus, 1987). They claim a 2-hour average response time, and a 1.5 hour average repair time.

Fault-tolerance of computers

A certain amount of error checking and fault tolerance has long been built into computers, their peripherals, and their software.

- PCs test their memories when they are switched on – the power-on self test (POST).
- PC operating systems bypass sectors on a disk which were marked as bad by the FORMAT program.
- BATRAM, the RAM-based external storage system from Santa Clara Systems, has error detection and correction capabilities (Santa Clara, 1986).
- Text editors and word processing packages may automatically make a backup copy of the file when they are invoked (as with EDLIN on IBM PCs), or may provide an automatic save facility while they are being used (as with IBM's XEDIT on mainframes running the VM operating system, or WordPerfect on PCs).
- The BRU backup utility for UNIX verifies backup files (Root Computers, 1986).
- The Irwin Magnetics 400 series tape backup subsystem for IBM PCs has an error correction feature which enables it to recover data even from a damaged tape (Barry, 1986c).
- Softguard's VM/386 operating system for PCs will be able to run 'ill-behaved' programs, i.e. ones which bypass DOS input/output (Thompson and Allen, 1986).
- By contrast, Informix claim fault-tolerance

for their UNIX-based DBMS *because* it bypasses UNIX for input/output (Barry, 1987).

- The OKITEL 1200 PC modem contains self-diagnostic loopback and automatic error detection (Okidata, 1987).
- The Adds Mentor 6000 series computer has error checking and correction in RAM, and automatic relocation of faulty sectors on the disk during processing which allows the system to correct itself without affecting operations (Scott-Rodger, 1986).

By contrast, the 8088 microprocessor chip does not have many features to protect the monitor, debugging facilities, and interrupt vectors from damage done by a runaway program (Ciarcia, 1986a).

However, there are now specialized fault-tolerant computers which take this further. They contain redundant hardware and special software to protect against system failure (Connell, 1986). Fault-tolerance should be incorporated into computers at the fundamental architectural level, rather than having it added as an afterthought. The capability is particularly valuable for organizations with on-line transaction processing (OLTP). According to Connell, the market was growing rapidly, but only 4% of the respondents in the Datamation/Cowen & Co. 1986–87 mini/micro survey had this capability; 41% said they wanted it, but only at no extra charge; and only 15% were prepared to pay extra for it (Verity, 1986b). Fault-tolerance carries a performance penalty of only 10% on Nixdorf's TARGON system (Borg *et al.*, 1989).

5.3.3 EFFECTS OF BREAKDOWNS

Hardware problems can cause large losses to an organization for a variety of reasons.

- They may result in staff overtime and lost business (due to loss of repeat customers, goodwill, and the organization's image of reliability).

- Computer down time can cost around $5 a minute depending on the size of the computer (Boehm, 1981) – in fact, people who lease time on supercomputers can currently be charged as much as $10 000 per CPU hour (Abbott, 1991).
- Data may be lost or corrupted (Arthur, 1983).
- Lightning transmitted through to a mainframe computer with say 100 remote users, could cause damage to the hardware alone to the value of 5% of the cost of the installation ('Powering computers', *Computer Mail*, 27 February 1987, pp.56–9).
- A single hour's downtime at a large steel works could cost more than the total value of the computer equipment ('Five "very large" 7800s as Burroughs land Iscor deal', *Computer Week*, 3 December 1979, p.1).
- Laboratory processes being controlled by the computer will cease.
- On-line data capture ceases (Church, 1980; Doepel, 1977).
- Users who cannot do their work without access to information on the computer come to a standstill, and there may be hundreds of them (Arthur, 1983).
- In most cases, it is not downtime but *recovery* time that is the 'killer': a computer may only be without power for a few milliseconds, but it may take hours or even days to repair the *results* of the failure, e.g. if the database was completely wiped out, and recover to the pre-downtime state (Leaf, 1986; Schach, 1990).
- A one-hour (or even a one-minute) delay in its overnight transfers, can cause a bank to miss the daily deadline, thereby losing a day's worth of interest, which can cost it a million dollars (Vincent, 1983).
- A programmer may spend considerable time establishing that a failure was caused by a hardware and not a software fault, or in circumventing the problem (Weinberg, 1971).
- Even if the fault is clearly due to a

hardware failure, programming, especially if on-line, is disrupted and time is wasted.

The total cost of all this can come to thousands of dollars a minute (Boehm, 1981; Arthur, 1983).

Breakdowns can have even more serious consequences than these, e.g. if the computer is running an air-traffic control system or an emergency vehicle despatching system, or is controlling the X-ray dosage being administered to a patient. In such cases, loss of life can result (Joyce, 1987).

5.3.4 EFFECT ON PRODUCTIVITY

There appear to have been few attempts to quantify the effect of these factors on software productivity.

- In organizations with a high level of security, access to the computer is restricted, so turnaround may be degraded. Boehm (1981) therefore incorporated this effect in the computer turnaround time factor in his COCOMO cost-estimation model. This factor has a 1.3:1 effect on the amount of effort required, but the contribution of restricted computer access to this figure may be slight. However, he warns that, where security and privacy requirements are particularly stringent, e.g. even access to documentation is restricted, an additional 5–10% should be added to the total estimated project costs.
- The Doty cost-estimation model (Herd *et al.*, 1977) includes three factors (such as the developer using a computer at another facility) which are related to computer accessibility. These factors affect the amount of effort required by about 1.4:1 each.
- Similarly, Walston and Felix (1977) included three factors related to security and restricted computer access, and found that they affected productivity by 1.6 to 1.9:1, but these figures may include the effect of correlated factors.

- Security is used in only one of the nine cost-estimation models surveyed by Boehm (1981); computer access is used in five of them.

These figures, however, embrace only a small proportion of the factors covered here, so the combined effect of all the factors may be high.

In an extreme case of hardware failure, because the computer is the nerve center of many organizations, the organization may even go out of business, resulting in a loss of the software effort expended. One Australian survey showed that 43% of organizations suffering a serious fire involving their records *do* go out of business (Sims, 1977), while USA insurance industry statistics show that more than 60% of all businesses which suffer a major DP disaster for which they are unprepared, fail. Barbara Foster stated in the *Washington Post* that 70% of businesses that sustain a 'significant interruption', go under ('Heading for disaster', *Computer Mail*, 31 October 1986, pp. 9–10). Furthermore, research in Britain shows that, without its computer facilities, a business tends to lose momentum, and some cannot function at all: after 4.5 days of downtime, the average organization is operating at only 52% of capacity; after 10 days, this figure declines to about 9% ('Heading for disaster', *Computer Mail*, 31 October 1986, pp. 9–10). Less serious disasters may result in the software engineers re-creating programs and documentation which were destroyed and for which inadequate backup existed. Such activities are essentially non-productive.

In the event of a disaster, problems are compounded: there is less time to make decisions, fewer options are available, staff are more likely to miscalculate while under pressure, and stress and shock may cause even level-headed and responsible people to lose the ability to make decisions ('Heading for disaster', *Computer Mail*, 31 October 1986, pp. 9–10). Plans should therefore be drawn up beforehand.

However, external disasters, both major and minor, are probably too infrequent for the losses to affect the productivity of software engineers significantly on a total, industry-wide basis, even when all the many possible causes are taken into account. Also, modern equipment is intrinsically very reliable – it is capable of giving uptimes of 99% or better (Doepel, 1977).

- A typical Winchester disk drive has a mean time between failures (MTBF) of 25 000 hours (equivalent to nearly three years of non-stop running) (Pountain, 1986b).
- Control Data (1986) claim a 30 000 hour (3 year) MTBF for the head disk assembly on some of their disk drives.
- A solid-state RAM disk is even more robust, with a MTBF of 100 000 hours (11 years), and it is suitable for portable PCs and hostile environments (Pountain, 1986b).
- Fujitsu (1986) claim an average of 70 000 hours (8 years) before their modems need a service.
- Even some PC printers are claimed to have a MTBF of 6000 power-on hours (Micro & Peripheral Distributors), and a mean time to repair (MTTR) of only 20 minutes (Dataproducts, 1985).
- Equatorial Communications' satellite network has a claimed uptime of more than 99.5% (Equatorial Communications Co., 1986).
- Reliability improved 'tremendously' over the preceding 10 years – the Hughes Aircraft Co. has an IBM 3090 processor 'that goes 2000 to 4000 hours between failures' (Pantages, 1987).

These figures are impressive, but it should be borne in mind that some components are intrinsically more reliable than others (e.g. electronic components are more reliable than mechanical ones), and a chain is only as strong as its weakest link: when one component fails, the entire system may also fail.

It is therefore the worst figures which are the most important. The aggregate failure rate is also more important than the failure rate of specific individual components. Nevertheless, productivity losses resulting from internal hardware failures, like those from external causes, are probably relatively small.

The most significant productivity loss may therefore be due to the time spent on preventative measures, especially building security and recovery features into systems, but these are justifiable as they provide protection against many problems other than hardware failure, and are insurance against *consequential* losses caused by both hardware failure and the other problems.

5.3.5 SUMMARY AND CONCLUSIONS

Hardware failures have a multitude of causes, both internal and external. Most problems are preventable – many are easily preventable – yet few organizations are well prepared for them.

Hardware failures result in many problems, from disrupting programming up to loss of human life. The combined cost of these effects can be very high.

There is little information available on the impact that hardware failures and preventative measures have on software productivity. Most of the problems are rare, and so can have little impact overall, but other factors may have a significant impact.

Many other factors, such as software failures, user or operator error, and even computer crime, can have the same effect as hardware failures. Preventative measures also overlap.

5.4 DIVERSITY

Because of the close relationship between hardware and system software – some hardware runs only certain system software – and because the system software is more visible to the computer user than the hardware it runs on, this discussion on hardware diversity also mentions system software.

5.4.1 REASONS FOR DIVERSITY

There are many different makes and models of computer, and a lack of standardization between them which extends to their software – programs written for one computer will generally not run on a different one. Even different models from the same manufacturer may not be fully compatible, even if they are in the same range (Wright, 1978; DeLamarter, 1986b). This is understandable as standardization, by depriving them of a captive market, may cause manufacturers to lose revenue (Small, 1983).

Each manufacturer provides his own features, which he believes the users need and which may be unique to his equipment; and he provides a variety of models to meet the differing needs of different customers. Manufacturers also patent and copyright their inventions – and even the 'look and feel' thereof – and take legal action against anyone violating their rights. Diversity therefore does have advantages, and can result from innovation, which should be encouraged. Apple Macintosh software is ahead of hardware, because Apple's position as the single source of hardware had inhibited overall development (Lu, 1986).

However, diversity also has adverse effects on productivity. The most obvious of these is probably that a program written for one computer will generally not run on a different one, i.e. it is not 'portable', and so has to be modified – converted – to enable it to do so. When an organization changes its computer, therefore, it may have to convert all its programs (and Job Control Language, and even some documentation). In particular, once it has begun using any special features in the software, it is locked in: not only is it even more difficult and expensive to change, but it will lose the special features.

5.4.2 CONSEQUENCES OF DIVERSITY

Usually, the workload on a computer increases with time, until it is being used at its maximum capacity, and additional capacity is required. Sometimes, the computer can be easily upgraded to provide the additional capacity with minimal disruption:

- by adding to or replacing the processor, storage or peripherals (Wright, 1978); or
- by changing to a 'plug compatible' computer, where one is available with greater power or capacity.
- Some manufacturers have a high degree of compatibility between their models – DEC has a good reputation in this regard, while IBM does not (Carlyle, 1987b): it has even been accused of deliberately introducing unnecessary incompatibility, such as changing interfaces to peripherals, to 'foil its competitors' and protect its profits, and it has resisted outside standards such as ASCII (DeLamarter, 1986a, 1986b).

If the computer is already at the top of its range, the organization will have to change to a different range or even to a different manufacturer. This is particularly true for smaller computers.

The organization may face the same choice if it requires not additional power or capacity, but better price/performance, or additional capabilities (Wright, 1978). Some computers support more than one operating system – e.g. IBM's larger computers can run their MVS, VM, and DOS/VSE operating systems – and a change from one operating system to another, even with no change of hardware, may require a conversion of the organization's programs. Even a new release of the same operating system may necessitate some modifications to the programs (Weinberg, 1971).

Conversely, both the old and the new computers may support the same operating system – MS-DOS, OS/2, CP/M, PICK and UNIX are industry standards, or the new computer may be in the same range, or be a plug compatible – but a program conversion may still be necessary because of hardware differences (STAX, 1983), because there are different versions of the operating system for the different computers, or because the new computer supports a different version of the language the programs are written in (e.g. FORTRAN 77 instead of FORTRAN 5 (Gullo, 1986)). Even if a change of operating system is not necessary, it may be desirable for improved machine efficiency: one user, when changing from an IBM 370 to a 4341, estimated that they would suffer a 10% loss of performance if they retained their OS/VS1 operating system instead of changing to DOS/VSE. A similar situation exists if the new computer emulates the old one (McWilliams, 1987b).

The situation may be worse than just requiring a conversion. IBM-compatible PCs run the MS-DOS or PC-DOS operating systems, but may not be able to run some graphics or data communications programs, because of differences in their BIOS (Basic Input/Output System) (Blankenhorn, 1987), and it is beyond the capability of most PC users to convert such programs or modify the BIOS. According to ben-Aaron (1986), Compaq was the only clone maker that claimed 100% compatibility, and the AT&T PC 6300 was probably only 95% compatible.

IBM's VM operating system sometimes eliminates the need for a program conversion. It can, for example, run programs under both DOS/VSE and MVS simultaneously, so an organization which upgraded from DOS/VSE to MVS could continue running its old DOS/VSE programs, but do all new production work under MVS. Amdahl has an equivalent capability, the 'multiple domain feature' (Verity, 1987c); and in the PC world, Softguard's VM/386 operating system will provide an equivalent capability: different versions of MS-DOS and PC-DOS, XENIX, and perhaps even proprietary operating systems, will all be able to run at the same time (Thompson and Allen, 1986). Similar, but more limited capabilities, are provided by CA-DUO, which gives DOS/VSE emulation under MVS; and the 'open architecture'

version of PICK (now Advanced PICK), which will permit several different releases of the operating system on the same machine (Wilcox, 1988).

Concurrent hardware development

Concurrent hardware development, i.e. where the hardware is being developed while the software is being written, is similar to hardware diversity, as the hardware changes, and the software must be changed accordingly to accommodate these changes. Boehm (1981) groups this factor with changes to the basic system software (operating system, DBMS, compilers, etc.), under the title 'virtual machine volatility'. (A virtual machine is therefore the operational computer's hardware and system software.) Concurrent hardware development is used in five of the nine cost-estimation models he surveyed.

5.4.3 EFFECT ON PRODUCTIVITY

If the new computer is not compatible with the old one, then the organization may have to convert not just its programs, but also its files, job control and documentation, and retrain its staff: 'you're changing the work environment of your users' (Gullo, 1986). The conversion may be long, difficult and expensive, depending on (Oliver, 1982; Wright, 1978; Waller, 1979):

- which language the programs were written in – high-level languages are generally more portable than low-level languages (though BASIC is very non-standard) – see Chapter 6;
- which Data Base Management System was used, as some run on a variety of different computers (Chapter 6);
- the availability of automated conversion tools – vendors such as Computer Associates have developed tools which convert DOS/VSE programs to run under MVS, or non-IBM to IBM, while MS Associates

market CGEN, which translates Microsoft BASIC programs into C (Pountain, 1986a);

- which new manufacturer was chosen, as some provide better education, documentation, and conversion tools, than others – some, such as Prime, even had conversion centers (McWilliams, 1987b);
- which software packages the organization uses, as some run on a variety of equipment;
- which computer the organization currently has, especially the uniqueness of its features, and what size it is (according to McWilliams (1987b) mainframe conversion tools are rare).

A conversion can thus cause a major disruption to an organization: 'the day DP managers fear most'; 'one of the most monumental tasks any data center will face' (Davis, 1983a; UCCEL, 1986; Oliver, 1982). It can be a major waste of resources (Wright, 1978; Oliver, 1982).

- The organization may discard part of its investment in developed systems: one organization I know discarded its custom-built interactive capability because this facility was built into the new computer's operating system.
- It is costly and essentially non-productive.
- It temporarily diverts resources away from providing new and better solutions for end users.

The possibility of future conversions must therefore always be considered when choosing new hardware (Martin, 1982b).

Nevertheless, conversions are a relatively infrequent occurrence. Out of 10 000 DOS/VSE sites in the USA, only about 300 (3%) convert each year to MVS (Crutchfield, 1986b). A further 150 non-IBM sites also convert to MVS each year. Only 16% of the largest user organizations in the British Isles said they would be downsizing to a mid-range system (Martin, 1992). The overall, industry-wide effect on productivity is therefore relatively small.

A university planned to spend 12% of their resources for ten years converting to 4GLs (Chapter 6). In one case quoted by Gilb (1988), it was specified that the software be convertible to any major manufacturer's equipment also having COBOL, for less than 5% additional cost to the original development cost. One organization I know purchased a different computer, from the same manufacturer but a different range, and spent three man-years converting their mainly COBOL systems, which had taken about 30 man-years to produce. (This includes both the development effort, and the maintenance effort up to the time of the conversion.) The conversion effort was therefore about 10% of the total effort to date. However, the figures given in Chapter 2 suggest that a higher value may be more usual: if conversion productivity is typically only five times higher than development productivity, then conversion effort is typically 20% of the original development effort.

These figures cover a wide range. Figures given in Chapter 8, for conversion as a percentage of maintenance effort, cover a similar range. Nevertheless, combining even the highest of these rates with the previous figure of 3%, for the proportion of DOS/VSE sites in the USA converting each year to MVS, even though that is only one of the many possible conversions, indicates that only a small proportion of the total software effort each year goes into conversions. This is confirmed by figures for the US Government. In 1977, it was estimated that the annual cost of software conversion activities in the US Government was about $450 million (Boehm, 1981). By comparison, the total annual US Federal Government spending on information resources (admittedly nearly 10 years later) was $15 billion (Schatz, 1986a).

There are, however, other disadvantages arising from non-standardization which are more common, and may have a much greater detrimental effect on productivity than conversions:

Table 5.2 Effect of concurrent hardware development on productivity

Source	Effect
RCA model (Freiman and Park, 1979)	1.4:1
COCOMO[1] (Boehm, 1981)	1.5:1
Walston and Felix[2] (1977)	1.6:1
Doty model[3] (Herd *et al.*, 1977)	1.8:1
Average	1.6:1

[1] The COCOMO figure is for virtual machine volatility, and therefore includes the effects of factors other than concurrent hardware development.
[2] The Walston and Felix figure, in common with their other figures, may include the effects of correlated factors (Boehm, 1981; Conte *et al.*, 1986).
[3] The Doty figure is for the first software developed on the CPU, and is therefore not strictly comparable to the others.

- retraining staff who change jobs;
- thinly-spread expertise among staff who work on a variety of equipment, e.g. employees of some software houses, freelance programmers (independent contractors), and employees of firms having a variety of equipment; and
- the diversity restricts the portability of application packages and technological aids, limiting their market and therefore their benefits, or necessitating multiple versions.

Concurrent hardware development

The effect which concurrent hardware development can have on productivity is given in Table 5.2.

The modularization and information hiding techniques given in Parnas (1979), provide ways to minimize the adverse effects of virtual machine volatility – and therefore concurrent hardware development as well – by identifying in advance those virtual machine characteristics most likely to change, and 'hiding' (i.e. concentrating) all the information about them in a single module. Then, when they do change, only this module needs to be changed.

5.4.4 STANDARDIZATION

Years ago, it was predicted that standardization would come about (Withington, 1975), and this prediction is being fulfilled, as IBM has become the *de facto* standard, at least for commercial work, for both mainframes (the 370 architecture) and micros (PC- or MS-DOS, and now OS/2 as well) (Bowen, 1987; Verity, 1987c). Programs written for one mainframe will therefore run on many others with little or no conversion, and programs written for one micro will run on many others. However, a program written for a mainframe will normally not run on a micro, and vice versa. Similarly, UNIX is the *de facto* standard for technical workstations (Moad, 1987) – it held an estimated 56% share of existing and planned technical workstations (McWilliams, 1987c). However, although UNIX is often claimed to be the *de facto* standard for minis, and while use of it is growing rapidly, only 13% of the organizations in the Datamation/Cowen & Co. 1986–87 mini/micro survey were using it (Verity, 1986b). There are also several different versions of it. (More figures are given and this is discussed further in Chapter 6.) Programs written for one mini will therefore not run on most others, or at least not without a significant amount of modification, nor will they run on most mainframes and micros. As one example of non-standardization (Wiener, 1986) pointed out, IBM's graphics programs work in all-IBM networks, but do not run on DEC or other non-IBM minicomputers.

Linking different machines together is a growing problem due to the proliferation of PCs, and in organizations which are geographically dispersed and have multiple sites. This problem has been described as one of the toughest in computing today, but it is being addressed. Also, there are products currently available, e.g. from REALIA (1986), which permit programs to be developed on a PC and then run on a mainframe. In the longer term, IBM's Systems Application Architecture (SAA) will permit portability of applications across the whole spectrum of IBM computers.

An alternative way to link different equipment together is by means of protocol converters. This allows, for example, the direct linking of PCs to mainframe computers, or ASCII terminals to link into IBM's System Network Architecture (SNA), or an ASCII printer to look like an IBM 3287 printer ('Trend to protocol conversion', *Computer Mail*, 31 October 1986, pp. 13–14). Even apparently incompatible computers can readily be linked together. One benefit is that, if an organization has several different computers, then instead of staff requiring several terminals on their desks, one for each computer, they need only one.

The discussion in this section referred specifically to a change of CPU, but the problem is wider than that, e.g. there is a lack of standards and consequent incompatibility among tape units for PCs. 'Probably the only thing that can be said about standards and compatibility is that they do not exist' (Rubel, 1986). Ample justification is required before choosing a terminal with unusual features, as that limits the portability of the programs written for it, and acquiring a new printer for a personal computer means that a corresponding printer driver may have to be obtained, and one may not be available.

There are many standards in existence, covering a variety of different areas. Some are official, some *de facto*, some widely observed, others not. Examples are the Hayes AT command set for dial modems; LU 6.2 for communications management; High Sierra for formatting data stored on CD-ROM disks (Sehr, 1986); SNA, OSI (Open Systems Interconnection), X.25 and X.400 for data communications; and so on. (X.25 is a major international networking standard which has already been adopted by more than 50 countries (Moskovitz, 1987).)

A plethora of standards complicates, and even hinders, development (Clark and Oppe, 1986). The goal of a standard should, ultimately, be to benefit the user. When defining a standard, the element of flexibility must not be lost, and the standard must not be too narrowly defined, otherwise software and hardware designers will not be able to respond to the user's best advantage: 'standards which are too rigid can be counterproductive by inhibiting development'.

5.5   POWER AND CAPACITY

The power and capacity of the computer influence software productivity in several ways.

- If the computer is not powerful enough, response during on-line development and maintenance is slow and turnaround in batch mode poor, and production programs may have to be 'tuned' at considerable effort to speed them up.
- If the capacity of its main memory is too small, considerable additional effort may be required to 'shoehorn' programs so they will fit into it.
- If the speed or capacity of its peripherals is inadequate, bottlenecks will result, degrading response and necessitating time-consuming corrective action.

These aspects are discussed below. The factors are however interrelated, e.g. attempts to make a program faster may make it larger. Bell *et al.* (1987) gives the example of a program to calculate tax. The program could either carry out a calculation, which would involve using fairly slow machine instructions; or it could use a look-up table, which would involve a fairly fast indexing instruction. The former option is slow, but small; the latter is fast but big.

5.5.1   RESPONSE TIME

The power of the computer affects the turnaround time in batch-mode processing, and the system response time in interactive mode. The latter mode is more time-critical and is becoming increasingly widespread (Chapters 6 and 8), so the following discussion concentrates on it, though some of the considerations are also relevant to batch processing. The difference in productivity between the two modes is discussed in Chapter 6.

Intuitively, it would seem desirable to provide a fast response to all users at all times.

- They complain if response is slow (Vincent, 1983). A study by Rushinek and Rushinek (1986) showed that good response is the major factor contributing toward user satisfaction; Williams (1973) and Youmans (1981) showed that some users have a much lower tolerance level than others, and users who are accustomed to a fast response, are more intolerant of a slow response.
- Guynes (1988) showed that poor response increases 'state anxiety' (feelings of tension, nervousness, and apprehension which fluctuate over time), which leads to increased heart rate, respirations, and blood pressure. This is worrying in view of the large amount of time staff spend at terminals. High anxiety also interferes with short-term memory (Leherissey *et al.*, 1971; Sieber, *et al.* 1970), thereby lowering productivity.
- Users may be unwilling to work during periods of peak load, and instead cram their work into off-peak periods, but then work so quickly, and become so anxious – after all, they are measured by their output, and naturally become upset if the machine slows them down – that they make errors (Vincent, 1983).
- Subsecond response times can give double or triple the productivity of an application developer (Martin, 1985).
- In an experiment by Goodman and Spence

(1978), halving the response time increased productivity by two-thirds.
- Thadhani (1981, 1984) showed that user productivity drops rapidly as response time increases beyond half a second. For example, it took twice as long to complete a given task with a response time per interaction of two seconds, compared with one of 0.25 seconds. People have a sequence of transactions in mind. If response is slow, continuity of thought is disrupted, and the sequence may have to be worked out again.
- By contrast, according to Conte *et al.* (1986), other studies suggest gains of only 20% in productivity due to rapid response times.
- Johnson (1980b) estimated that a fast response during on-line editing (one second instead of an average of three), can produce cost savings equal to 10% of the savings from on-line programming.
- If response is longer than 3–4 seconds, 'psychological closure' occurs, with the result that the terminal user becomes bored or starts daydreaming (Grilz, 1981), or may even think that something has gone seriously wrong, and panic. Then, when the computer eventually does respond, he first finishes his daydream, and must then refresh his memory as to what he was doing, interpret the computer's response, and compose a new command (Arthur, 1983). The time between the computer's response and the programmer's next command, is the 'think time' or *user* response time. According to Arthur, think time increases twice as fast as computer response time, and can amount to as much as 25–50% of the duration of a terminal work session. As programmers spend 20–50% of their day at terminals, 'think time' can amount to (25–50% * 20–50% =) 5–25% of their working day.

However, a universally fast response is not necessarily desirable.

- An experiment by Grossberg *et al.* (1976), in contrast to the others quoted, showed no correlation between response and productivity. Similarly, a study by Carbonell *et al.* (1968) found little performance difference when subjects used two systems, one of which was twice as fast as the other.
- Users may find a fast response disconcerting, especially if they are not yet ready to enter the next command.
- Some users report surprise and disruption if the response is too prompt (Shneiderman, 1980).
- Turner (1984) found an increase in mental strain, and a decrease in job satisfaction, among workers who had almost immediate response (though this may have been due in part to their output being higher).
- A fast response may induce users to work so quickly that they become careless and make expensive errors, e.g. due to not seeing information displayed on the screen (Vincent, 1983). Similarly, the experiment by Grossberg *et al.* (1976) found that the error rate decreased as response became longer, presumably because the users became more cautious in order to avoid the long delays; while Barber and Lucas (1983) found that errors increased for response times both above *and* below 12 seconds. Card *et al.* (1983) found that about 26% of the time spent performing experimental text editing tasks was due to errors, so reducing the number of errors can improve productivity by up to that amount.
- A slower response may be adequate, especially if the users have some thinking or preparation to do before they can enter the next command. The terminal can even be locked out for a few seconds or even minutes to try to force them to do the necessary thinking, and the Boehm *et al.* (1971) experiment showed that, while this caused dissatisfaction, it *halved* the amount of machine time.
- Users are more prepared to accept a slow response if they know their commands are making the computer do a considerable amount of work, e.g. they will accept a delay of several seconds to load a file (though the computer should provide a running commentary of what it is doing, to reassure the user), whereas they expect immediate response to, say, editing commands or emergency requests (Winfield, 1986). (Winfield gives a list of acceptable response times, e.g. two seconds for a simple request, and five seconds for a complex one.)
- A slower but *consistent* response was shown experimentally by Miller (1977) not only to be more acceptable than a highly variable response, even if the average response is slightly slower, but also to increase productivity by around 25% – where the users know they have time available, they make use of it. As Arthur (1983) put it, 'Human work habits adapt easily to consistent response times'. Winfield (1986) even recommends forcing a longer response in some circumstances, e.g. when the interactive system is new and lightly used, or during slack periods during the day, in order to avoid dissatisfaction later when usage increases and response becomes slower.
- Although the study by Carbonell *et al.* (1968) found little performance difference when subjects used two systems, one of which was twice as fast as the other, he also found that performance was much worse on a system with the same mean response time, but with large variability in individual response times.
- By contrast, Guynes (1988) quoted three studies which showed no significant relationship between response time variability and user performance and satisfaction, but the tasks involved were relatively complex (implying that long think times were necessary), or all the response times were relatively short (implying that the range of variability was limited).

In addition, a more powerful and expensive computer is generally required (Vincent, 1983), i.e. the benefits of a faster response must be weighed against the cost of providing it. Further, there is evidence that the effect of adding more users is out of proportion to the number of users added. For example, when the number of users at the National Institutes of Health in the USA increased by 33%, the time needed to complete an average terminal work session increased not by 33%, but by 50% ('Time is money – rapid response shows why,' *IBM Inform*, August 1983, p. vii). The time thus wasted cost 15 times as much as a new processor powerful enough to rectify the situation. This can be a reason for providing a separate computer for software staff only.

It is not necessarily a bad thing for users to have to wait longer for response to complex, and therefore expensive, commands. This should encourage them to use faster, and therefore cheaper, commands wherever possible, (Winfield, 1986).

The ideal response time thus varies between different types of work, and even between different types of transactions, depending on their complexity and priority (Vincent, 1983; Holtshousen *et al.*, 1979). Developers are usually allocated a low priority with correspondingly slow response, as testing is considered less important than production, yet according to Abbott (1983a), 80% of their transactions are 'trivial', i.e. consume minimal resources (an example is editing program source code). It is therefore not excessively expensive to provide the sub-second response times they need for maximum productivity, especially if the operating system or DBMS examines the transactions, and allocates a higher priority to trivial ones.

Response can be improved by sharing the load of the CPU:

- by having microprocessors to control disk input/output;
- by providing users with personal com-

puters, onto which they can download data from the mainframe, and process it; and

- by having special-purpose hardware, such as maths or graphics co-processors.

Response time is the combined effect of the power of the hardware, the efficiency of the system software, and factors relating to the application program. The latter is largely the responsibility of the programmers, so they do have some control over the response time:

- by making their programs more efficient, they will not have to wait so long per interaction while testing interactive programs.
- if they subdivide their programs into modules, then, when an error is found and fixed, they need only wait for one module to be compiled, instead of the whole program.

Response is degraded by such factors as:

- checkpoints taken as part of the security backup procedure with DBMSs (Chapter 6);
- locking of records to ensure integrity of data during concurrent processing;
- access (security and privacy) checks to ensure the user is permitted to perform the function requested;
- validation of data as it is entered;
- bottlenecks – these are discussed below.

However, these factors are more relevant to users running production jobs than software engineers doing development or even maintenance.

5.5.2 BOTTLENECKS

Turnaround and response time are degraded by 'bottlenecks'. These can be caused by:

- too few, or too small, storage devices: disks, for example, should not be more than 70% full (Patrick, 1980a);

- fragmentation of files, which occurs if a PC disk is too full: it slows down all operations on the files – loading, sorting, retrieving and backing up (it also results in excessive disk head movement causing extra wear and tear, which can shorten the life of the drive) (SoftLogic, 1986a, 1986b);
- poor allocation of files or records, also resulting in excessive disk head movement: heavily used files, for example, should be centrally situated;
- too few input/output channels, or ones which are too slow;
- programs with large main memory requirements, which restricts multiprogramming, or can cause excessive paging in virtual storage (virtual memory) systems (Van Tassel, 1978; Pfaffenberger, 1990);
- printers or card-readers allocated directly to a job (instead of via the spooler), but not used, thereby preventing others from using them (Dolphin, 1978).

Some of these points do not apply to computers which have virtual storage, or whose operating system allocates files dynamically.

An inefficient sort/merge utility could be added to the above list. According to Hymers (1987), the most frequently executed program is the sort/merge: in fact, about 65% of program activity in the machine is sorting. (Singer (1982) gives the much lower figure of 25%.) SYNCSORT, which is reported to hold 85% of the IBM MVS sort market in the USA, is claimed to be up to 100% faster than its competitors (Hymers, 1987).

The width of the data bus (e.g. 8-bit or 16-bit) could also be included here as it affects input/output speed, but the bus is a fundamental property of the hardware which is outside the user's control (though it is possible to replace PC mother boards, e.g. upgrading an XT to an AT, thereby replacing the bus as well).

Similarly, the computer's single- or multi-tasking capability could be included – on a single-tasking machine, the user must wait for one job to finish before the next one can begin – but that is a fundamental property of the operating system which is outside the user's control. (Though there are products, such as Microsoft's Windows (Bartimo, 1986) and SoftLogic's DoubleDOS (SoftLogic, 1986a), which permit a single-tasking machine to do multi-tasking; while the batch processing facility with IBM's VM operating system has a similar effect.)

Software aids

Detection

Sometimes, a bottleneck will be apparent to the computer operators. In other cases, it can be detected by software products such as IMPROVE, PLAN IV, LOOK, and, more recently, X-VIEW 86 (Osborne/McGraw-Hill, 1986) and Disk Optimizer (SoftLogic, 1986a, 1986b) for PCs. Corrective action – which may involve programmer time – can then be taken.

Cure

There are software products which can relieve some of the problems.

- SQZ! reduces the amount of disk space needed for Lotus 1–2–3 spreadsheets by 80–95% (Turner Hall, 1986). It also cuts file retrieve/save time and, since the files when sent over electronic mail are sent in compressed form, saves 80–90% in transmission time as well.
- Products such as VM Software's VM-ARCHIVE (for CMS files on IBM VM mainframes), and Cubit (for PC files), compress disk files into perhaps half their original space (SoftLogic, 1986a; Ideal Software, 1986).
- 'Disk Optimizer' rearranges fragmented files on IBM PCs to occupy contiguous blocks – 'it puts all the separate pieces of the files back together' – reducing access

time by up to a factor of five (SoftLogic, 1986a, 1986b).

Sneddon (1986) put forward an interesting idea whereby double ASCII bytes would represent whole words instead of individual characters. He estimated that this would compress textual databases to one-quarter of their original size, and would also considerably speed up data transmission. (Though he did not comment on the effect this would have on data retrieve/write time.)

Hardware aids

Input/output bottlenecks can be alleviated by having solid-state devices which act as a high-speed buffer, bridging the gap between RAM storage (fast but expensive), and disk storage (slower but cheaper). Examples and variations on this concept include the following.

- RAM-disks: a RAM-disk is a solid-state mass memory system which allows the most frequently used files to be kept in immediate access semiconductor storage. The First City National Bank in Austin experienced a 20% improvement in overall performance, and a reliability improvement as well, after installing three REACT RAM-disks ('First City National Bank enhances Burroughs hardware with high-speed REACT RAM-disk,' *Magazine of Bank Administration*, October 1986, p. 93).
- Santa Clara Systems manufacture a non-volatile RAM-based external storage system called BATRAM for use with IBM PCs, which is functionally the same as a hard disk drive but which has no internal moving or mechanical parts, and which can transfer data up to seven times faster than a hard drive (Santa Clara, 1986). It can also be treated as external memory.
- Sir Clive Sinclair produced a solid-state Winchester disk drive which is basically a wafer full of RAM chips connected by a serial path. To the computer, it looks like a serial disk drive, but it has no moving parts and so is potentially more reliable. It is slower than ordinary RAM because of the serial access, but data transfer is 17 times faster than a Winchester disk, and access time is 1000 times faster (Pountain, 1986b).

Similarly, part of main memory may be designated as a virtual disk drive. Data and programs needed often are loaded into this memory, which behaves like a very fast disk drive. This saves time in processing disk-intensive applications such as database searches. This facility has long been available on PCs, but was only made available by IBM on its mainframes in 1986 ('The King is dead; longlive the King', *Computer Mail*, 27 February 1987, pp. 21–31).

5.5.3 PROGRAM SIZE

If the computer's main memory is too small, additional effort is required to 'shoehorn' programs so they will fit into it (Kessel, 1975; Yourdon, 1975). This applies not only to the machine a program is developed *on*, but also to the machine it is developed *for*. If an application package, for example, requires a large amount of memory, its market potential is limited.

Reductions in the size of a program are usually achieved by many small savings scattered throughout the program (Van Tassel, 1978), and are therefore time-consuming to achieve, and are essentially non-productive. They also make the program 'trickier' to code and debug, and therefore lower productivity.

It is not only programmers whose productivity is affected: system designers would have to expend extra effort to subdivide the system into smaller units.

The loss of time does not occur only with system development, and may be even greater for maintenance. Many of the programs being run on a small microcomputer may occupy nearly all its memory. When such a program is modified, it may increase

Table 5.3 Effect of storage constraints on productivity

| Source | Extent of saturation | | | |
	85%	90%	95%	Not specified
GTE (Daly, 1979)				1.3:1
Doty (Herd *et al.*, 1977)				1.4:1
COCOMO (Boehm, 1981)	1.2:1		1.6:1	
Walston and Felix (1977)				2:1
RCA model (Freiman and Park, 1979)[1]	1.7:1	2.3:1	3.8:1	
Rockwell-Autonetics (Williman, 1971)[1]		2:1	3:1	
Boehm (1973)[2]	2:1	3:1		
GRC (Carriere and Thibodeau, 1979)				7:1

[1] Includes timing constraint effect.
[2] Programmers.

in size and no longer fit into memory, so considerable additional effort – perhaps much more than was expended on the actual modification – may be required to reduce its size sufficiently.

It can thus be readily understood that program cost per instruction increases rapidly as the computer becomes saturated. According to Boehm (1973), programming costs twice as much on a computer which is 85% saturated, and three times as much if it is 90% saturated. However, he subsequently gave a reduced estimate in his COCOMO model: only 1.2 times as much development effort (including non-programming effort) is required if 85% of the available main storage is expected to be used, than if not more than 50% is to be used; and only 1.6 times as much if 95% is to be used (Boehm, 1981).

The Rockwell-Autonetics figures show that software cost per instruction is about twice as high if 90% of the available speed and memory capacity is being utilized, than if only 50% is being utilized, and about three times as high if the utilization is 95% (Williman, 1971; Williman and O'Donnell, 1970). For 50% utilization, there is virtually no penalty compared to 0%. It is only at about 80% utilization that there is a rapid increase in effort. The RCA model (Freiman and Park, 1979) has very similar figures.

Walston and Felix (1977) found that productivity was twice as high where main storage constraints were minimal compared to where they were severe, but, as indicated before, this figure may include the effects of correlated factors.

In the experiment by Weinberg and Schulman (1974) described in Chapter 2, the team which was required to write the program using the least amount of memory, expended more effort than any of the other teams, and both program and output clarity also suffered, with consequent impact on both maintenance and user productivity.

These, and other figures, are given in Table 5.3.

Storage constraints are used in six of the nine cost-estimation models surveyed by Boehm (1981).

Elimination of marginally-useful features ('gold-plating') keeps program size down, thereby helping avoid the heavy productivity penalty from storage constraints.

Past

Boehm (1973) stated that it was common to obtain hardware having a capacity only 15% greater than sizing prescribed, so the computer was 85% saturated to begin with. Worse, sizing estimates are often too low.

Thus programming productivity could frequently be doubled simply by acquiring additional hardware. The cost thereof has to be set against the improved productivity, but generally speaking, total system costs could be minimized by obtaining double the absolute minimum hardware. (He later reduced this estimate to 30–50% (Boehm, 1981).) Furthermore, it is far more risky to err by obtaining too small a computer than one too big. As software becomes progressively more expensive than hardware, so increasingly more excess hardware is required to minimize overall costs. There is the danger, though, that where excess capacity is available, staff will be extravagant in their use of it, thus negating the reason for which it was bought.

Present

It is about twenty years since Boehm expressed the above views, and ten years since he repeated them in only slightly modified form. The principles are still valid, but are less relevant today because of the wider use of virtual storage, and the much lower price of hardware. Virtual memory systems 'allow a software developer to act as if there was no main storage constraint, but often at a cost of hardware efficiency', 'provision of a virtual machine costs both storage and speed of execution' (Lemmons, 1986; Van Tassel, 1978; Pfaffenberger, 1990); and today's computers generally have an abundant supply of memory – even microcomputers have large memories, e.g. 640K is common on IBM PCs, and in fact is probably the minimum nowadays. By comparison, the first mainframe I programmed commercially had only 128K, and a minicomputer I was using ten years ago had only 16K.

Future

However, this idyllic situation may not last forever: 'the size of programming problems increases to fill the machine storage available for use' (Van Tassel, 1978) – for example:

- ten years ago, the Visi-On integrated software package required 512K RAM even though it was intended for microcomputers at a time when 512K was a large amount (Edwards, 1984);
- nowadays, Microsoft's Windows and IBM's OS/2 require a *minimum* of *several megabytes* of RAM; and
- 'artificial intelligence' will need very large amounts of memory.

A levelling-off in the price/performance improvement, or an increase in the size of programs, would bring about the return of the situation described by Boehm (1973). Productivity would once again be seriously degraded.

5.5.4 PROGRAM EFFICIENCY

Time constraints are used in eight of the nine cost-estimation models surveyed by Boehm (1981).

Effect on productivity

Fast program execution can be achieved not only by having a powerful computer, but also by efficient programming techniques. This reduces execution costs and, if it is an interactive program, gives a faster response to users (and to programmers during testing), but it can consume much programmer time to achieve it (Van Tassel, 1978; Weinberg, 1971). In an experiment by Weinberg, those programmers who were explicitly instructed to produce an efficient program, took *three* times as long as the programmers who were told to write it as quickly as possible. They also used more than twice as much machine time during the development stage, but they achieved their objective: their programs *did* execute more quickly. One of the test programs was *twice* as fast, and the other *ten* times.

Table 5.4 Effect of timing constraints on productivity

Source	Productivity impact	
Brooks (1980)[3]	not significant	(structured projects)
"	not significant	(small projects)
"	1.4:1	(unstructured projects)
"	2.4:1	(large projects)
Kraft and Weinberg (1975)	1.1:1	
COCOMO (Boehm, 1981)	1.1:1	(70% utilized)
"	1.3:1	(85% utilized)
"	1.7:1	(95% utilized)
GTE (Daly, 1979)	1.3:1	
Doty (Herd *et al.*, 1977)	1.3 to 1.8:1	
Walston and Felix (1977)[1]	1.4 and 1.8:1	
GRC (Carriere and Thibodeau, 1979)	1.6:1	
RCA model (Freiman and Park, 1979)	1.1:1	(60% utilized)
"	1.2:1	(70% utilized)
"	1.5:1	(80% utilized) includes
"	1.7:1	(85% utilized) storage
"	2.3:1	(90% utilized) constraint
"	3.8:1	(95% utilized) effect
Rockwell-Autonetics (Williman, 1971)	2:1	(90% utilized)
"	3:1	(95% utilized)
TRW (Wolverton, 1974)	3:1	
Weinberg (1971)	3:1	
Boeing (Black *et al.*, 1977)	3.3 to 6.7:1	
Brustman (1978)[2]	9:1	

[1] Walston and Felix found that productivity was 1.8 times higher where timing constraints were minimal than where they were severe. They also found that productivity was 1.4 times higher if less than 10% of the code was for real-time or interactive operation or executing under severe timing constraint, than when more than 40% of it fell in these categories. However, as stated before, their figures may include the effects of correlated factors.
[2] Brustman analysed the Walston and Felix data, and found that small projects with minimal timing constraints had a productivity *nine* times higher than large projects with severe constraints, but it is possible that much of this difference is due to the effect of project size.
[3] /Brooks also analysed the Walston and Felix data, and found execution time constraint productivity ranges of 2.4:1 for large projects, and 1.4:1 for unstructured projects, and nonsignificant ranges for small projects and structured projects. This shows that the use of modern programming practices reduced the negative effects of hardware constraints.

This experiment, however, was not representative of the typical programming situation. While programmers are often required to write programs as quickly as possible, they are much less often required to make them as efficient as possible. The figures obtained in the experiment are therefore maximum values rather than typical ones, so the potential for productivity improvement is rather less than a factor of three in most cases, as is confirmed by the other figures quoted in Tables 5.4 and 5.5.

Weinberg also quoted a case in which a program (for reading matrices) took an inordinate amount of time to develop, simply because the programmer was using a more complicated method in an attempt to make it more efficient.

Return on effort (Table 5.5) is the ratio of the improvement in machine efficiency to the corresponding increase in programmer effort – the higher the ratio, the better.

Programmer time can thus be traded against machine time, i.e. program efficiency

Table 5.5 Relationship between programmer effort and program efficiency

Source	Programmer effort	Machine efficiency	Return on effort
Lim (1980) – COBOL[b]	?	<1.25:1 to > 5:1	?
Aron (1974) – PL/1[c]	?	9:1	?
Kraft and Weinberg (1975)	1.1:1	1.45:1[a]	1.3:1
Weinberg (1971)	3:1	2:1 and 10:1	0.7 to 3:1

[a] Nine production programs: the effort involved probably represented about 10% of the original development effort. This is lower than the other figures given here, but Kraft and Weinberg only spent a small amount of time on the exercise, and so would only have found the most obvious inefficiencies, as evidenced by the smaller improvement they achieved.

[b] Lim gives several techniques for improving the execution speed of COBOL programs, such as using indices instead of subscripts, or binary operands instead of decimal. These techniques do not consume much programmer time. Some of them give improvements of 5:1 and more, but others give only 25% or less. Furthermore, these figures apply only to small portions of the average program, so the overall improvement would be much smaller.

[c] Aron (1974) refers to features in PL/1 which can improve execution speed by up to 9:1, but it is not clear if he is referring to the total run time of the program, or just the execution time of isolated individual instructions (as in the case of Lim). It is also not clear if any additional effort is required to achieve the improvements.

can be maximized at the expense of programmer productivity, and conversely, programmer productivity can be maximized at the expense of program efficiency. The factors which must be taken into account if programmer productivity is maximized, are:

- savings in programmer time during development;
- the effect on machine time during development – test runs will execute more slowly, but fewer tests should be necessary;
- the additional benefits derived from having the system operational sooner;
- additional machine time during production (and consequent impact on user productivity), which depends heavily on the volume of data, the type of program, and how often it will be run, though this should be partially offset by fewer reruns due to program errors;
- savings in programmer time during maintenance, as the more efficient program may be difficult to read and maintain (Chapter 2);
- the effect on machine time during maintenace – test runs will execute more slowly, but fewer tests should be necessary, especially as there should be fewer errors to correct.

Whitfield (1989) described an interesting case history which dramatically illustrates the trade-off of the benefits from faster completion against slower execution. A client complained that an application system for administering a new range of business products was very inefficient. On investigation, it was discovered that the system had been badly written due to haste. However, the new products 'were selling quicker than real lemonade in summer, and cash was rolling in' – in fact, the funds realized were more than a hundred times the cost of any upgrade necessary to contain the inefficiency of the code.

It is therefore not simple to determine in any particular case if it would be economical to encourage faster programming at the expense of execution speed, and to make up for the lower efficiency of the programs by obtaining more powerful hardware, and so take advantage of the lower hardware prices prevailing today. Cost-estimation models are of help, but do not include all these aspects.

Minimizing productivity loss

Performance requirements, such as average transaction processing times, are often arbitrarily determined, so they can often be relaxed. Boehm (1981) gives an example of how relaxing the required response time from two to three seconds, transformed a 95% execution time constraint with its corresponding 66% productivity penalty, to a 63% execution time constraint with only a 7% productivity penalty. Furthermore, programs which have not received any special efficiency attention are usually acceptably efficient (Yourdon, 1975; Van Tassel, 1978). This means that, if more emphasis is placed on programmer productivity, and therefore fast completion, the resulting degradation in program run times may also be acceptable. It also means – and this is true whether more emphasis is placed on programmer productivity or not – that usually a program should not be given special efficiency attention while it is being developed. If, after it has been written, a program is found to be unacceptably slow, it can be 'tuned'. This can be very time-consuming, and may involve systems programmers or a partial redesign of the system, and it usually gives little return for the effort (Yourdon, 1975, 1979a; Van Tassel, 1978; Brandon, 1978). For these reasons, and because the modified program may be less readable, and the modifications may introduce errors, only programs which consume a large amount of machine time (say 30% of the total monthly availability and these would usually be programs which process high volumes of data) or programs which are time-critical (e.g. air traffic control), should be considered for tuning. Van Tassel gives further guidelines for estimating if the return will be worth the effort. Cost-estimation models are also of help – the example at the

beginning of this paragraph was based on figures from the COCOMO model.

Usually, it will be found that much of the execution time is being consumed by only a small portion of the program, such as a loop which is repeatedly executed (Van Tassel, 1978). Typically, 50% of the CPU time is consumed by only 5% of the code (Knuth, 1971). This portion can be determined by various techniques, such as inserting counters into the program, or using monitor packages or 'profilers' such as the Manx Aztec C Profiler, and it is sufficient to optimize just this portion, e.g. by rewriting it in a lower-level language such as Assembler (Van Tassel, 1978; Yourdon, 1975, 1979a; Brooks, 1975; Brandon, 1978; Manx, 1986). The portion which consumes the most CPU time may depend on the input data (Yourdon, 1975) – it might, for example, be the routine which processes the most common transaction type – which is an added reason for postponing major efficiency considerations until after the program has been written. (While good systems analysis will tell you beforehand which transaction types are the most common, it may not be as easy to predict if the program will take much longer to process them.)

An alternative method which also minimizes the amount of effort required, is to use an optimizing compiler where this is available, e.g. for PL/1, or CA-OPTIMIZER for COBOL. This can decrease program run time by 10–25% (Brooks, 1975; Arthur, 1983, 1988; Van Tassel, 1978). Structured programming techniques help an optimizing compiler (Van Tassel, 1978).

Similarly, some languages such as BASIC are commonly run in interpretive mode, but may have a compiler available, and the compiled versions execute much faster (Chapter 6). Screens created by Atech's SYSTEM BUILDER, an application generator for the PICK operating system, can also be compiled, with similar improvement in execution speed. (This product must not be confused with the Walker financial packages of the same name.)

Some compilers are faster than others:

- They *compile* faster, e.g. the LOGITECH MODULA-2/86 PLUS compiler is claimed to increase compilation speed by 50%, while FoxBASE+ is claimed to compile dBASE III programs up to 60 times faster than other compilers (Logitech, 1986; Fox, 1986).
- Programs compiled by them *execute* faster, e.g. C86PLUS is claimed to give 20% faster program execution than Microsoft C (Computer Innovations, 1986), while Fox-BASE+ is claimed to run programs more than twice as fast as Clipper (Fox, 1986).

Both of these aspects should increase programmer productivity, as programmers would not have to wait as long for their compilations and tests to complete.

New releases of products are sometimes faster than the previous release, e.g. Release 1.3 of ADR's IDEAL language is claimed to be 30–50% faster (see section 6.6).

5.5.5 SUMMARY AND CONCLUSIONS

For maximum productivity, on-line users require a fast response, especially for 'trivial' requests, but it must also be consistent. Paradoxically, response can also be *too* fast. The optimal response depends on, for example, the type of transaction.

If a computer is too small or too slow, then software productivity, and particularly programmer productivity, can be seriously affected, as additional effort is required to counter the limitations, by making the program smaller or more efficient. Also, response during interactive sessions (e.g. when testing) is slower.

Because the programming solutions to these problems can be very time-consuming, caution must be observed before embarking on such action, especially as most programs are acceptably fast. With the lower price of hardware nowadays, it is generally more cost-effective to acquire additional or faster hardware to cure the problem. Sometimes, an even better solution is to leave out marginally-useful functions ('gold-plating'). Switching to a faster compiler, where one is available, may be the most cost-effective solution to efficiency problems.

Sometimes, low speed is caused by bottlenecks. There are hardware and software aids which detect or even cure such situations.

The software engineering process uses many software tools; to create a program, other (pre-written) programs are used – operating systems, compilers, text editors, test data generators, etc. Some of these tools, like the operating system, are essential; others, like test data generators, are optional.

6.1 OPERATING SYSTEMS

The basic software tool is the operating system: it controls the others. While there are benefits in modifying or enhancing operating systems, e.g. to take advantage of new hardware, it is nevertheless risky to modify such complex system software, and it might also mean that the user organization has to forego the benefit of remote maintenance by the supplier (Carlyle and Moad, 1988; Martin, 1982b).

Differences between operating systems

There are many different operating systems, from a variety of different vendors, causing the portability and conversion problems discussed in Chapter 5. Their internal working is outside the scope of this study, except insofar as it affects factors such as reliability, efficiency and extendability.

- **Reliability** IBM's OS/360 operating system, for example, reportedly contained 1000 or even 11 000 errors (Chapter 8), while ICL's VME (Virtual Machine Environment) system for its Series 39 mainframes had between 2000 and 10 000 errors (Sayers, 1986).
- **Efficiency** This also depends on the goal of its designers. Microsoft's new operating system to succeed MS-DOS (presumably a reference to OS/2), is based on algorithms which optimize response time, whereas UNIX optimizes throughput (Lemmons, 1986).
- **Extendability** (or lack thereof) e.g. the 640K memory limit of MS-DOS; the upward compatibility of the PC XT version of the PICK operating system; the ability of IBM's new PC operating system, OS/2, to run the older PC-DOS programs; and even the ability of IBM's System/36 computer to link into their Token Ring PC network (Moad, 1986a).

Different operating systems also have different external features which affect productivity:

- built-in security and recovery (Chapter 5);
- good diagnostics and a remote maintenance capability for the resolution of software errors, thereby decreasing downtime (Chapter 5);
- logging facilities, e.g.
  - job accounting information, which can be used to record the amount of machine time each programmer has used, the amount of machine time consumed by re-runs of production programs (categorized by the cause of the re-run: programmer error, operator error, etc.), or to terminate a run if it exceeds a predetermined amount of time;
  - the number of key depressions and errors on data entry machines, which can be used to measure keypunch operator efficiency (and thus help determine their salaries), though some staff would object to being monitored so closely (Wingfield, 1976; Short, 1977);

- multi-tasking, which permits the user to run more than one job at a time, may be built into the operating system such as in UNIX, or may be provided by an add-on program running under the operating system, such as Microsoft's Windows under MS-DOS (Bartimo, 1986);
- a multi-user capability, which permits more than one person to use the computer at the same time, may be built into the operating system such as with mini and mainframe computers, or may be provided by an add-on program for microcomputers;
- error messages and memory dumps may be printed by the operating system following some types of program error, such as division by zero (Lim, 1980);
- some operating systems are more 'user friendly' than others – e.g. the Apple Macintosh, or PCs compared to mainframes (Chapter 5) – or have a user-friendly add-on program available, such as Microsoft's Windows for MS-DOS (but see below).

Operating systems also differ in complexity, so some need more support staff than others. One organization was running an IBM 4341 computer (presumably with the DOS/VSE operating system), with three support staff. They calculated that, if they upgraded to the MVS operating system, they would have to increase their support staff to seven or eight. Instead, they changed to an IBM System/38 computer, and were able to *reduce* their support staff to one (Moad, 1986b). Similarly, one organization replaced its IBM 4341 mainframe with a PICK-based Prime 2755, and reduced its DP staff complement from 24 to 2 (Stefanski, 1987). Unisys claimed that independent tests have shown that their mainframes require 29% fewer operators, systems programmers, and systems analysts, than other comparable mainframes, and that this is due to the sophistication of their system software (Unisys, 1988a). Bill Gates of the Microsoft Corporation claimed that appli-

cations on Apple Macintosh computers typically require only 50% of the support of an MS-DOS-based competitor, due largely to the quality of the Macintosh's graphical interface (Woock, 1988). One MIS manager went further: 'Our Mac people produce more than the DOS/Windows/OS/2 people because the technology seems to aid, rather than get in the way of, the work' (Corley, 1991). Similarly, a survey of information systems professionals and managers at various corporations, found that PCs are *not* easy to use, and that graphical user interfaces are *not* intuitive (Hayes, 1992). Perhaps worse, easy-to-use features do not guarantee that the job will be done faster, e.g. DTP features in a word processing package can encourage users to spend an hour 'tweaking' a memo that should take ten minutes. Worse still, easy-to-use advanced features may make it far easier to make a mistake, with 'horrendous, enterprise-damaging consequences', due to users lacking a clear understanding of what they are doing.

Extent of use

The number of installations (or users) reportedly running some popular operating systems is given in Table 6.1. In the case of multi-user operating systems, the number of users may be more significant than the number of installations. For some systems I found widely differing figures, and have listed more than one of the claims because of the resulting uncertainty as to which is correct.

In addition, there were more than 300 000 installed IBM System/3x systems (Pine, 1989).

Of the UNIX installations, 450 were mainframes, and 100 000 were commercial (Moad, 1987; Nel, 1986). The Cunningham figures are for the number of UNIX licences issued. Licences are often bought in bulk by manufacturers and then never used. The actual number of installations may therefore have been much lower than the figures he gave.

Table 6.1 Extent of use of various operating systems

Op. system	Source	No. of installations/users
MS-DOS	McMullen (1990)	40 000 000
MS-DOS	von Oppell (1988)	10–20 000 000 users
UNIX	Woock (1988)	1 000 000 (5 000 000 users (Kelly, 1988))
UNIX	Cunningham (1990)	1 000 000 licences (2 million in 18 months)
DEC VMS	Sivula (1990)	300 000 (8 000 000 users)
UNIX	Verity (1987b)	250 000
OS/2	McMullen (1990)	214 000
PICK	Figueroa (1990)	200 000 (1 300 000 users (Hohmann, 1988))
PC-MOS	Software (1989)	100 000 users
QNX	Quantum (1989)	80 000
PICK	Bourdon (1987)	70 000 (650 000 users)
MultiLink	Software (1986b)	30 000 (250 000 users)
IBM DOS/VSE	Carlyle (1989b)	30 000 (10 000 in USA (Crutchfield, 1986b))
IBM VM	McCusker (1987b)	10 000

The UNIX and the PICK figures include the different versions/derivatives of these products. (The Bourdon figures for PICK, but apparently not the Figueroa and Hohmann figures, include those versions which consist only of the Data Base Management System (DBMS) portion of PICK, running on top of another operating system.)

The various figures were obtained from different years, so caution must be observed when comparing them. In particular, some operating systems are increasing more rapidly in popularity than others.

An alternative way of looking at the extent of use of different operating systems is provided by a number of surveys, detailed in Tables 6.2–6.5.

Utilities

Utilities – e.g. to monitor hardware usage, or to do file sorts, copies, reformats and prints – are associated with operating systems. They can provide functions missing from an operating system, e.g. control of cursor movement and repeat keys (Shapiro, 1986b), or automation of the operations function (such as file backup). Some operating systems have better utilities than others, e.g. the software

Table 6.2 Datamation/Cowen & Co surveys – estimated PC operating system usage for 1991 and beyond (Pinella, 1990b)

Op. system	Year of survey		
	1988	1989	1990
MS-DOS	73%	71%	59%
MS-DOS/Windows[1]	–	–	23
OS/2	10	9	4
OS/2-Extended	8	8	4
UNIX	9	12	9

[1] MS-DOS/Windows was not included in the 1988 and 1989 surveys.

Table 6.3 The market share figures for multi-user microcomputer and minicomputer operating systems, with predictions for 1992 (Unix, 1988)

Op. system	Year of survey		
	1982	1987	1992
Proprietary	78%	59%	40%
CP/M and MP/M[1]	11	6	–
UNIX	10	27	39
DOS, OS/2 (networked)	–	4	16
PICK	–	3	5
Other	3	1	2

[1] MP/M is a multi-user version of CP/M.

Table 6.4 The distribution of IBM mainframe computers in a 1983 survey of nearly 200 sites (Harding, 1986)

Op. system	%
DOS/VSE	60
MVS	25
OS/VS	15

Table 6.5 The distribution of supercomputer operating systems in a survey of over 100 respondents (users, designers, and supercomputer managers) (Crawford, 1989)

Op. system	%
UNIX	50
Cray's COS	50
Cray's CTSS	50
DEC's VMS	25

Many of the respondents evidently used more than one supercomputer.

utilities available on ICL's VME operating system 'far surpassed' those in its older DME operating system (Doepel, 1984). (Similarly, some operating systems have better application packages than others – see Chapter 7.) This can therefore be a factor in the choice of computer: if a utility is available, then the organization does not have to write a program to perform that particular task. For example, the utilities on IBM's System/32 computer could be used for 70–80% of the programming (IBM, 1976).

Utilities can therefore improve programmer productivity in a variety of different ways:

- as fourth-generation languages;
- by drawing attention to hardware bottlenecks so they can be eliminated and response improved; and
- by making operations more efficient, and reducing operator errors such as overwriting tapes, so programmers will not have to

waste time recreating lost programs or data.

6.1.1   UNIX

UNIX is a multi-user operating system which runs on all sizes of computer from micros through to minis, mainframes and even supercomputers (Verity, 1987b). It runs on more than 100 makes of computer, which is more than any other operating system, and 'has the potential of a truly portable operating system' (Main, 1987; Meyer, 1986; Tate, 1986). It therefore alleviates the portability and conversion problems discussed earlier, and so can affect productivity, particularly in those organizations which have a variety of equipment. As an example, it took one software house less than a day to convert (port) a general accounting and manufacturing package from one UNIX machine to run on the UNIX-based IBM RT ('A counter to DP sanctions?' *Computer Mail*, October 31, 1986, pp. 49–53).

UNIX was developed about 20 years ago by AT&T, and is currently the center of a considerable amount of attention: 'the crusade gathers momentum' (Tate, 1986). It has long been used for academic, scientific and engineering applications, but has not been used as much for commercial work, particularly large-scale, critical applications (Verity, 1987b; Meyer, 1986). (In fact, even among scientific sites, it is not as extensively used as one might have expected – in the Datamation/Cowen & Co. 1986–87 mini/micro survey, only 13% of scientific and factory sites said it was their primary choice (Verity, 1986b); and four years later, only 34% of technical sites were using it as their primary minicomputer/workstation operating system (Pinella, 1990b).

Many benefits are claimed for UNIX.

- Because it runs on a variety of hardware, organizations are not locked into one supplier – they can shop around for lower prices, higher quality or better support (Meyer, 1986).

- For the same reason, it protects the organization's investment in software.
- Also for the same reason, and because it is good at communications, it is good for distributed decision support systems in organizations having a variety of computers (Meyer, 1986). A decision support system is a MIS designed to assist in the decision-making process (Chandor *et al.*, 1988; Avison and Fitzgerald, 1988).
- There are standards for it (AT&T's System V, the IEEE's POSIX, and the Open Software Foundation's OSF/1), and there is a European vendors' group, X/OPEN, devoted to furthering UNIX as an open standard. Their goal is to create a free and open market where software writers need produce only one version of their programs, portable at source code level onto many vendors' machines, and where users' software investment is protected (Tate, 1986).
- UNIX systems are cheaper than mainframes.
- More and more governments and big users are insisting on it, e.g. the US and Swedish governments, and General Motors (Main, 1987; McWilliams, 1987a).
- It supports many languages – COBOL, FORTRAN, etc.
- It is good at data communications, e.g. it works hand in hand with Xerox's Ethernet, and there is a network link between XENIX (Microsoft's version of UNIX) and MS-DOS (Meyer, 1986).
- It permits rapid software development, by connecting many small modules together (Meyer, 1986).
- It allows applications to be device independent, as it typically contains a database of features of hundreds of output devices, and it is relatively easy to move an application to new devices (Meyer, 1986).
- It has flexibility to adapt to new computing environments (Meyer, 1986).

- It is good at sharing data between programs (Meyer, 1986).
- There are catalogs available nowadays that are 'bulging' with the amount of software available under UNIX, and these packages cover a wide variety of applications from business accounting through to spreadsheets and word processing.
- More and more developers are writing or converting software to run under UNIX, thus the user has a rapidly growing pool of applications.
- It gives small machines the capability of large machines.
- MS-DOS is becoming more like UNIX, and is therefore serving as a training ground (Meyer, 1986).
- Training in the UNIX environment is easier and cheaper than on mainframes, so expertise in it will grow faster.
- The software tools that have become available, e.g. menus and help screens, have made UNIX easy to use.
- It was originally given to many universities, so thousands of students gained experience in the UNIX environment before graduating.

For most of the above points refer also to 'A counter to DP sanctions?' *Computer Mail*, October 31, 1986, pp. 49–53. However, many criticisms have also been levelled at UNIX.

- There are *two* (rival) 'standard' versions (AT&T's System V, and the Open Software Foundation's OSF/1), and many non-standard versions. The University of California at Berkeley added many extra functions, thereby creating a second 'camp' (Meyer, 1986). Microsoft's version of it (XENIX) was proliferating faster than the standard versions (Verity, 1986b), XENIX had 90% of the market for desktop UNIX (Moad, 1986a), and IBM introduced no fewer than four versions (for the PC, RT, 370, and Series/1 computers) (Verity, 1987b).
- IBM's support has been lukewarm ('under-

whelming'), they have yet to market any in-house developed programs running under XENIX, and they have even been accused of deliberately introducing multiple versions in an attempt to prevent UNIX from becoming too popular and therefore a threat to their proprietary systems (Moad, 1986a, 1987; Verity, 1987b).

- It is 'notoriously unfriendly' (Meredith, 1986b).
- Programmers have had to write their own user interfaces, which is not easy, giving UNIX a bad reputation (Meyer, 1986).
- It needs improved facilities for transaction processing, record locking and error recovery (Moad, 1987; Meyer, 1986).
- It is rigid and monolithic, and therefore difficult to adapt (Quantum, 1986).
- Students exposed to UNIX are likely to be computer science and engineering graduates. Not all of them will enter the DP world, and the expertise they gained from the academic environment will not be of much use unless they stay in that environment ('A counter to DP sanctions?' *Computer Mail*, October 31, 1986, pp. 49–53).
- Its main proponent is AT&T, and there are doubts about their long-term commitment to the computer industry. For example 'they have failed to become a major player in the PC race', and they have no long-term relationship with DP managers, unlike IBM (Meyer, 1986; Appun, 1987; DeLamarter, 1986a).
- It is not being used in AI (Meyer, 1986).
- There is a relative dearth of good, well-supported commercial applications software – insufficient to make it worthwhile for IBM to totally support UNIX (Main, 1987; Verity, 1987b).
- It has a high overhead: 'Some estimate that it is at least 3 times as high as DEC's VMS, which is not an optimal system' (St. John Bate and Vadhia, 1987).
- Similarly, Hewlett-Packard think their proprietary operating system, MPE-XL, gives

up to 50% better performance than UNIX (Etheridge, 1990).

In short, UNIX has been accused of 'promising much but delivering less than had been wished' (Barna, 1987).

Furthermore, it is not the only way to lessen dependence on a single hardware vendor: products like the ORACLE database management system also provide a high degree of portability – 'I would pick ORACLE over the UNIX operating system if I were looking for vendor independence' (McWilliams, 1987a). In fact, COBOL also provides a measure of independence – I gave an example in Chapter 5 in which the effort to port one organization's systems onto a different computer amounted to only about 10% of the total effort which they had previously expended in developing and maintaining those systems. Similarly, FORTRAN is claimed to now be 99% transportable ('The technology is there', *Computer Week*, 19 September 1988, pp. 22–23).

Some of the above claims are contradictory, or are out-of-date, or the disadvantages are being addressed. For example, record locking is addressed in the System V version of UNIX (Meyer, 1986); the Triple X PC (from Torch Computers) provides a graphics-based addition to UNIX which is claimed to make it as easy to use as any other operating system (Meredith, 1986b); and IBM's new version of UNIX, AIX, runs on PS/2 microcomputers, RISC workstations, and mainframes ('AIX operating system Version 3 announced', ISM inform, March, 1990, p. 9). Nevertheless, some users and vendors 'have their doubts whether UNIX will ever make it into the MIS department': it is particularly good in some fields, but if it were modified to cover every application, it would lose its strengths (Moad, 1987).

Non-UNIX users have too large an investment in applications software for other operating systems such as MVS to want to convert, while UNIX users may prefer their vendors to improve UNIX in other areas rather than make it compete against MVS (Moad, 1987). Etheridge (1990) reported that most European users of midrange systems are remaining faithful to their existing proprietary operating systems; and a North American survey found that 72% of IBM mainframe sites had 'absolutely no interest whatsoever' in UNIX (Kerr, 1989).

In a survey in Britain, less than 5% of users said they had a multi-user PC (Bis, 1986). A multi-user capability is a major reason for choosing UNIX on a PC, so perhaps somewhat less than 5% (1 in 20) of the PCs in this survey ran UNIX. This figure is roughly consistent with the relative sales figures for MS-DOS and UNIX: 250 000–1 000 000 UNIX, to 10–40 million MS-DOS (which suggest a ratio of around 1 to 40).

Vendors such as Amdahl and Hitachi have versions of UNIX running on their mainframes, but still market it primarily to technical and government users (Moad, 1987). It would be expensive for them to add the extra features which UNIX lacks, and they are unwilling to do so because they have higher priorities; because they would be competing against their own, proprietary operating systems if they did; and because that would make it easier for their customers to change to a competitor's computer. IBM is therefore not the only vendor with an understandably lukewarm attitude towards UNIX.

Andrew Schroter of AT&T sees UNIX 'infiltrating' MIS through the back door (Moad, 1987). Organizations will have an application running on a UNIX minicomputer. When more power is required, they will upgrade to a UNIX mainframe. He predicted that UNIX would soon be able to do everything MVS can do, and that in 5–7 years, UNIX would be the dominant operating system for mainframes. This seems rather optimistic. Although the number of UNIX mainframe installations was expected to double (from 450 to 900) in the next three years – which is much higher than the growth expected for MVS – nevertheless the number of mainframe UNIX installations would still be only 3% of the number of DOS/VSE installations (see Table 6.1).

An even higher growth rate has been predicted for the total number of UNIX installations: Jack Scanlon of AT&T predicted that it would quadruple in only two years (Verity, 1987b). However, while the growth rate will be high, his prediction seems far too optimistic, especially as previous high forecasts were not fulfilled (Verity, 1986b). According to the figures from the 1986 Datamation mini/micro survey, the proportion of organizations using UNIX would only double in the next 18 months (from 13% to 28%); while Yates Venture predicted that the UNIX market would grow from 8% or $3.9 billion in 1985, to 19% or $10.8 billion in 1990 (an increase of only 23% p.a. compound) ('A counter to DP sanctions?' *Computer Mail*, October 31, 1986, pp. 49–53). This latter prediction was apparently fulfilled, as Judge (1990) estimated that the European UNIX market was worth $3.7 billion in 1989, and that this represented roughly one-third of the total worldwide market. Robert Kavener of AT&T predicted that the proportion of installed machines using UNIX would increase from only 3% in 1988, to 23% by 1992 (Woock, 1988). (The 23% is in line with the other predictions, but the 3% is lower than other claims.)

6.1.2   PICK

PICK is an operating system which shares some of UNIX's fundamental characteristics. It is a multi-user system, and runs on a wide variety of different makes and sizes of computer, e.g. on IBM and compatible PCs, on DEC minis, and on IBM mainframes (Sandler, 1989). There are also several different versions of it, which are marketed under different proprietary names (such as Prime Computer Incorporated's 'Information'), so few people realize how widely used it is. The US market was valued at between $2 and $3 billion (Shandel, 1988); an Info-Corp. survey found that the PICK market had a 41% compound annual growth rate in total value between 1982 and 1987 (Hohmann, 1988); and more than 80% of the Fortune 100 companies (i.e. the largest organizations in the US), have at least one PICK application running (Pick User Group, 1989). PICK has captured 50% of the operating system market in Australia (putting it ahead of UNIX in that country), 40% of the market in France, and 20 to 30% in the UK (Shandel, 1988). According to Figueroa (1990), in the multi-user business applications market, only IBM, with its combination of S/3x, 370, 43xx and 30xx computers, has sold more than the estimated 200 000 PICK-based 'business solutions' sites.

Unlike UNIX, PICK has a built-in data base management system (DBMS), and this must be one of the most widely-used DBMSs: 'PICK has more customers and applications than all its mainframe relational database competitors added together' (Sandler, 1989) (Table 6.6). PICK is especially intended for commercial data processing, where it is well-liked by users for its ease-of-use, the rapidity with which it can build applications, and its flexibility: it models real-life situations extremely well (Wood, 1986). It only supports one third-generation language, a highly extended version of BASIC (though COBOL and RPG-II implementations have been developed), but it does have a built-in fourth-generation query/retrieval language, ACCESS (St. John Bate and Wyatt, 1986; Sandler, 1989). It is claimed to be highly efficient: a computer running PICK typically supports 3 to 6 times as many terminals as the same computer running UNIX, and provides 4 or 5 times the throughput when compared with the same computer running the same application written using UNIX (Sandler, 1989).

PICK shares UNIX's potential for becoming a universal operating system, and so eliminating the compatibility and conversion problems previously discussed, with their adverse effect on productivity. PICK, how-

ever, has not been marketed as vigorously as UNIX; it lacks a backer of world status, and in fact has little support among the major hardware vendors – one of its major suppliers, McDonnell Douglas, 'does not use the word Pick in its sales pitch' (Wood, 1986). All this is reflected in the fact that there are probably only a quarter as many PICK sites as UNIX sites (Table 6.1). However, one derivative of PICK, VMark Corporation's UniVerse, can run on top of UNIX, which could give organizations the best of both worlds. (UniVerse is just a DBMS, not an operating system, and it must not be confused with the CA-UNIVERSE DBMS.) Merged versions of PICK and UNIX have also been developed, such as ADDS Mentor's M/ix operating system (Yulke, 1990). Another derivative of PICK, Cosmos's REVELATION, runs on top of MS-DOS. (REVELATION, like UniVerse, is just a DBMS, not an operating system.) One could argue, therefore, that PICK is even more portable than UNIX (Sandler, 1989; Bourdon, 1987).

6.2 JOB CONTROL LANGUAGES

Job control language (JCL) is an informal term describing the instructions a programmer uses to tell the operating system how the program should be executed – how much memory it requires, what priority it should have, what names have been given to the physical files, and so on (Yourdon *et al.*, 1979a). The JCL is part of the operating system, and differs from one operating system to another (Baron, 1988; Weinberg, 1971).

JCLs are like programming languages, and can be difficult to learn. Redesign, e.g. bringing them closer to spoken languages, should make them quicker and easier to learn, and reduce the amount of programmer and machine time lost through re-runs to correct mistakes (Weinberg, 1971).

One experiment showed that positional parameters in JCL gave a 30% increase in coding speed compared to keyword parameters, but had an error rate 2–4 times higher; while two-thirds of the implementation phase errors in another study were JCL errors (Weinberg, 1971; Hecht *et al.*, 1977). An experiment by Shneiderman (1980) using database query languages, suggested that verbal people (left-brained) preferred keywords, and visual people (right-brained) preferred positional methods. According to Ruete (1991), recent studies have indicated that as many as 95% of computer professionals are left-brain dominant. The great majority of computer professionals should therefore prefer keywords. (The same, however, may not be true of say end users using database query languages. In a study of 600 children aged 11–16, only one-third of the boys, and one-quarter of the girls, were found to be left-brain dominant (Lewis, 1987) – about half of each sex were right-brain dominant, and the remainder used both hemispheres equally. It is likely, therefore, that amongst the general population, those who prefer positional methods outnumber those who prefer keywords.)

With device independence, the linking of a program to specific input or output devices is done in the JCL and not the program. This means that the device can be changed without having to recompile the program.

The set of job control statements for a program can normally be stored so it does not have to be re-typed every time it is needed. A set of stored statements is also known as a 'canned' procedure. Some operating systems, e.g. IBM's OS/VS1, allow temporary changes to such procedures to be fed in as separate overrides, so that the procedure itself is not changed, and the possibility of errors is reduced.

Some programming languages, such as REXX (Restructured Extended Executor, a language for IBM's VM operating system), and the statistical language SAS, allow job control commands to be embedded in the source code.

6.3 DATABASE MANAGEMENT SYSTEMS

A database management system (DBMS) is a computer program which manages data – stores it, structures it, links it together, and retrieves it. The data managed by it is called the database. A database can be viewed as a model of part of the real world, and as such must be dynamic and flexible (Curtice, 1986).

DBMSs are similar in function to operating systems. Like operating systems, they have built-in security and recovery features, and there is a variety of different DBMSs in existence, each with its own advantages and disadvantages (Ross, 1978). Also like operating systems, DBMSs are large and complex. When something goes wrong, the consequences can be serious. Schroeder (1986) describes how a DBMS failure at the Amsterdam air cargo terminal caused all data to be lost. It took several days to solve the problem, during which time several giraffe in transit died.

Unlike operating systems, there is a standard for DBMSs – the CODASYL recommendations – but many, including widely-used ones like TOTAL and IMS, are not based on this standard (Ross, 1978). In fact, only around 15% of users had a CODASYL-type system (Schussel, 1983). Among the newer, 'relational' DBMSs, SQL (structured query language) has become the *de facto* standard language. There is now an official ANSI (American National Standards Institute) standard for it, though vendors tend to have their own, enhanced versions of the language (St. John Bate and Vadhia, 1987; Schroeder, 1986). However, SQL is not a DBMS as such, but rather just a language for manipulating the data, particularly for querying it, as the name implies. All in all, there are currently few standards, and wide differences among the DBMS packages (Lucas, 1985). The result of all this diversity is that the incompatibility and portability problems already discussed apply to database systems as well.

There are fundamental differences between an application computerized using a DBMS, and a traditional computerized system. In traditional systems, the data is intended for a narrow, specific application, and is used by a narrow, homogeneous group of people who are familiar with it and the associated terminology. By contrast, a database is intended for general use, by a variety of different people, for a variety of different applications. The data is therefore *shared*. Several difficulties arise. Sharing of data needs different management from that of separate files (Martin, 1982a). There may be human problems caused by users losing control of data they previously 'owned'. It is not known in advance what use will be made of the data, so it is difficult to know what data should be included and what left out. As Curtice (1986) so graphically put it: 'How do we decide that the number of parts going through a heat-treat oven is worth including, but the color of the socks worn by the oven operator is not?' Data which could be useful might nevertheless be left out if it is not technically feasible or economically justifiable to include it.

Furthermore, different users must understand and interpret the data in the same way. For example, if the maintenance engineers in a factory want a list of machines in the factory, they want the list to include machines waiting to be scrapped, whereas the manufacturing engineers in the same factory want such machines left out of a list intended for them (Curtice, 1986). The two groups must therefore agree on what is to be stored in the database, and must know how to extract only the data of interest to themselves. In theory, the database administrator (this position is discussed in section 6.3.3) takes charge and resolves the issue, but according to Johnson (1980b), there has not been much success with this. The entire organization must therefore develop a *shared* understanding of the concepts and terminology, and how they relate to the business (Curtice, 1986).

The above examples show that, for a database system, greater initial effort is required, and this must be set against the later productivity gains.

DBMSs require more fundamental changes to an organization than do ordinary systems – they 'cut across the entire organization' (Webster, 1976). This has several consequences: systems need to be designed by someone with a broader view of the organization; more support from top management is needed, as there may be political problems to be overcome; and the long-term view is even more important than usual (Webster, 1976; Martin, 1982b). DBMSs are bought to last for 10–15 years (Mill, 1986). It is more difficult to plan over the longer term, and management may be unwilling to invest in longer-term payoffs (Curtice, 1986).

A DBMS is not a solitary product. It normally comprises, or is supplemented by, an entire group of tools (from both the DBMS vendor and independent software houses), such as a data dictionary, query language, and screen painter. These products are integrated with each other, and together form a total *environment*. When selecting a DBMS, therefore, an organization should compare the capabilities of the rival environments (Mill, 1986). Evaluations, comparisons, and benchmarks of different DBMSs are published from time to time, e.g. Matos and Jalics (1989) and 'Spotlight on software – DBMS review', *Bank Systems & Equipment*, November 1986, pp. 77–80; by the Datapro Research Corporation (e.g. Datapro, 1986, 1987); and in *InfoWorld* (e.g. Petreley, 1988).

6.3.1   EXTENT OF USE

DBMSs are not a new concept. They first came onto the market in about 1968 (Schroeder, 1986; Curtice, 1986), and they are widely used. Of the operational systems in the Lientz *et al.* (1978) survey (of 69 organizations), 22% used DBMSs, and over ten years ago, nearly 50% of installations in an International Data Corporation survey (of over 1000 MIS managers, programmers, analysts, academics, and other industry experts) were using them (Hoard, 1981). According to Hymers (1987), the high-end DBMS market was showing signs of saturation, as only 20% of these organizations had no DBMS or had an outdated one. In apparent contrast, only 54% of the sites in the Computer Intelligence Corp. survey of IBM and compatible mainframe sites had a DBMS (Wiener, 1986), indicating that there was still substantial room for growth in that market, particularly as many sites had more than one DBMS. (On average, they had 1.3.) In the PC market, purchasing figures for the Microcomputer Managers Association indicate that only 30% of PCs run a DBMS (Kerr, 1987). Similarly, Barnett (1985) estimated that most 'office systems' (the context indicates that he was referring to PCs) are bought with a 30% need for data manipulation. There is therefore even more room for growth in that market. Chorafas (1986) predicted that, by 1987, no PC would be sold without a DBMS, though that prediction seems to have been rather optimistic.

The total worldwide DBMS market was estimated by a US survey at $1.32 billion in 1986, and was predicted to grow to $1.75 billion in 1987 (an increase of 33%), with 67% of the latter amount being for mainframes, 21% for minis, and 12% for micros (Mill, 1986). Frost and Sullivan's figures were much higher – a worldwide income of $4–5 billion in 1985 (apparently from public on-line databases alone) – but their predicted growth rate was similar: 28% annually over the next 5 years (from both on-line and off-line databases) (Tate and Runyan, 1986). (Public on-line databases consist of information such as bibliographic data which is made available on-line to the public; see section 6.3.6). The usage of DBMSs on PCs is also growing rapidly. According to a Datamation survey,

in 1986 database packages were used for 13% of the total elapse time on PCs, compared to under 6% the previous year (Verity, 1986b).

Of the DBMSs used at IBM and compatible sites in the Computer Intelligence Corp. survey, 46% were IBM-supplied DBMSs (Wiener, 1986). Among non-IBM sites, usage of the vendor-supplied DBMS, where one was available, was much higher. According to Wiener, it was 68% in the case of DEC VAX computers, and 88% for Sperry mainframes. By contrast, Honeywell and NCR, instead of developing their own DBMSs, co-operated with Cincom to have a version of TOTAL developed for their machines. This arrangement had benefits for all parties: the hardware vendors were spared the costs and risks of developing their own packages; the DBMS vendor was assured of a captive and profitable user base; and the user gained because the pool of TOTAL programmers is far larger than a pool of Honeywell- or NCR-specific programmers would have been.

The number of installations (or users) reportedly using some of the more popular DBMSs is given in Table 6.6. In the case of multi-user operating systems, the number of users may be more significant than the number of installations.

Since licences are often bought in bulk by manufacturers and then never used, the actual number of installations may therefore be much lower than the figures Moad gave. However, according to Appleton *et al.* (1991), there were 15 000 installed Rdb sites, which matches that given by Moad for the number of licences.

The CI Survey figures refer to the Computer Intelligence Corp. survey of 11 000 IBM and compatible mainframe sites (Wiener, 1986), so these figures are from a smaller sample than the others, and must be adjusted upwards to permit comparisons. (If there are more than 40 000 MVS and DOS sites (Baxter, 1988b), and 10 000 VM sites (McCusker, 1987b), giving a total of over 50 000 IBM and compatible mainframe sites, then the adjust-

Table 6.6　Extent of use of various DBMSs

DBMS	Source	No. of installations (users)
dBASE[1]		(over 2 million users)
PICK	Figueroa (1990)	200 000 (1 300 000 users[2])
UNIFY	Stratus (1990)	(over 650 000 users)
PICK (or derivative)	Bourdon (1987)	70 000 (650 000 users)
PC/FOCUS	Myers (1987)	60 000
PROGRESS	Realtime (1989)	15 000
DEC Rdb	Moad (1990c)	15 000 licences
ORACLE	Datapro (1986)	14 000 (10 000 on PCs)
SQL/DS	IBM (1990b)	7500 (400 in CI Survey)
DB2	Garcia-Rose and Fosdick (1990)	5000 (100 in CI Survey)
DEC DBMS	Moad (1990c)	5000 licences
ADABAS	Software AG (1986a)	2200 (500 in CI Survey)
FOCUS	Myers (1987)	2600 (700 in CI Survey)
DATACOM/DB	Computer Associates (1988)	1800 (400 in CI Survey)
DL/1	Wiener (1986)	1500 (CI Survey)
IMS	Wiener (1986)	1500 (CI Survey)
RAMIS	Schatz (1986b)	1200 (300 in CI Survey)
IDMS & IDMS/R	Wiener (1986)	1100 (CI Survey)
SIR	Datapro (1987)	450
CA-UNIVERSE	Computer Associates (1988)	200
SUPRA	Cincom (1987)	150 (600 000 users[3])
System 2000	Wiener (1986)	100 (CI Survey)

[1] From 'Punch line "GO IV IT!"' *Computing S.A.*, 13 February 1989, p. 22.
[2] Hohmann (1988).
[3] Cincom (1992).

ment factor is about five. This estimate is in good agreement with the value obtained directly from those DBMSs for which two values (CI Survey and total) are tabulated, e.g. (2200/500 =) 4.4:1 for ADABAS.)

The various figures in Table 6.6 were obtained from different years, so caution must be observed when comparing them. In particular, relational DBMSs have grown rapidly in popularity in recent years, as can be seen from the figures for DB2 and SQL/DS: instead of being about five times higher than the CI Survey figures obtained four years earlier, they are 20 or 50 times higher. The SUPRA figures also show that a dramatic increase occurred, over a period of just five years.

FOCUS and PC/FOCUS together have a total of 350 000 users (Myers, 1987), though some may use FOCUS as a fourth-generation language only, i.e. with a DBMS other than the FOCUS DBMS.

The PICK figures include the different versions of it. However, it is possible that the Figueroa and Hohmann figures do not include those versions which consist only of the DBMS portion of PICK, running on top of another operating system.

A database is 'important, if not vital' in CIM (computer integrated manufacturing) applications, while industrial networks, transaction-oriented business systems, and CAD (computer-aided design) hosting applications 'all beckon' databases, so increased growth can be expected (Wiener, 1986).

6.3.2　TYPES OF DBMS

There are different types of DBMS. Currently, the three most popular ones are:

hierarchical, network, and relational models (Shneiderman, 1980).

The **hierarchical** model has a tree structure, and is excellent if the data is simple and tree-structured (Shneiderman, 1980). Provided information access follows the structure of the data, access is fast, especially as vendors have had years in which to fine-tune their products (Schroeder, 1986). Hierarchical DBMSs are therefore suitable for applications which handle large volumes of data, but knowledge of the data structure is nevertheless necessary to achieve efficiency. IBM's IMS, and SAS Institute's System 2000, are examples of the hierarchical model. According to Mill (1986), IMS had 50% of the total DBMS market.

The **network** model is based on the CODA-SYL (Conference on Data Systems Languages) recommendations. TOTAL and SIR (Scientific Information Retrieval) are examples. It is an extension of the hierarchical model: instead of just one-to-many relationships, it can readily handle many-to-many (Date, 1977). Data is linked together by pointers, and complex relationships can be handled, but it is difficult to use: 'Trying to teach end users how you go through a network database from Point A to Point B is not conducive to what end users would really appreciate' ('ADR/IDEAL a big hit at Canadian Broadcasting Co.', *ADRWARE News*, **3**(2) pp. 1, 10, 11, 15). Like the hierarchical model, information access is fast provided it follows the structure of the data.

The **relational** model is the newest of the three. First proposed by Codd (1970), it is based on mathematical principles (Shneiderman, 1980). Data is arranged in tables, and so is easy to visualize, though joining of tables is less easy to visualize. Data is linked together by its *values* rather than by physical pointers. The advantage of this model is its flexibility and power in querying data, making it ideal for *ad hoc* queries, and providing a better environment for end users (Schroeder, 1986). However it is heavy on machine resources

(Mill, 1986); see section 6.3.5. Relational databases have also been criticized as being 'vastly more complicated' to design (Artz, 1989). Furthermore, their increased power and flexibility 'brings the danger of making design errors in places where, previously, design decisions simply did not exist'. Older DBMSs such as IDMS and DATACOM/DB, have had relational features added to them – leading to the description 'born again' (Mill, 1986). According to Mill, the proportion of users with relational-type products was only about 10% for large systems, and 20% for micros. By contrast, Schroeder (1986) stated that microcomputer-based DBMSs tend to be almost exclusively relational 'or at least billed as such'. Furthermore, an International Data Corporation report forecast that relational database systems would grow from 30% of the market in 1986, to 70% in 1990 ('Sybase of US reckons on impact in crowded UK market', *Computing SA*, 17 August 1987, p. 25).

Different types of data have different natural organization patterns. For example, a tree structure would be natural for the terms 'occupations', 'professional', 'laborer', 'doctor', etc., and it is difficult to use structures which do not match the natural pattern (Shneiderman, 1980). Shneiderman therefore concluded that no one data model is universally superior, and different problems require different models. It may therefore be advisable for organizations to have more than one DBMS, each one being of a different type.

Some PC-based DBMSs are much simpler than others. They are intended for end users, to do simple data storage and retrieval. Others are intended for application development by programmers. Dissatisfaction arises if the wrong type is used (Schroeder, 1986).

The above types all belong to the same class (sometimes described as 'numerical' or 'fixed field-length' databases), but there is another class: 'text' or 'textual' databases which are more specialized. They are used for semi-structured or even unstructured data, e.g. bibliographic work such as storing abstracts of scientific research papers (Tate and Runyan, 1986). Examples are IBM's STAIRS, Harwell Computer Power's STATUS, and Information Dimensions' BASIS. Many of the 'numerical' DBMSs, such as ADABAS, FOCUS, PICK, askSam, and dBASE, also provide a textual capability, e.g. note or memo fields, but this is usually limited, i.e. it may not be possible to index on, or to perform searches on, individual words, portions of words, or combinations thereof, in these fields.

6.3.3   EFFECT ON PRODUCTIVITY

Nies (1983) stated that 'It is "bunk" that applications programming is more efficient in a database environment'. This surprising statement, coming as it does from a DBMS vendor, should be seen in the context of his belief that productivity in general, both DP and non-DP, is decreasing (Chapter 2). A major motivation for installing a DBMS has been the expectation of productivity improvements for both development and maintenance – over 90% of the approximately 1000 respondents in an International Data Corporation survey agreed that using the right kind of DBMS 'can save you a lot of programming time' (Hoard, 1981) – but there is no unanimity on the magnitude of the productivity gains. Various claims are given in Table 6.7.

The higher claims refer to the use of relational databases, active data dictionaries (discussed below), and query languages. With less powerful software, the productivity gains are more modest. Part of the claimed improvement is therefore attributable to fourth-generation languages (4GLs) rather than to the DBMS as such. One organization saw a 30–40% drop in both development and maintenance costs when it converted from a hierarchical DBMS, IMS, to a relational DBMS, DB2; while another organization cut development time in half, and in some places by as much as 80%, when it migrated from a

Table 6.7 Productivity gain from database management systems

Source	Gain
Nies (1983)	–
Johnson (1980b)	–
Wulf (1976)	1.3:1 (maintenance)
Mill (1987)	2:1
Maguire (1976)	2:1–10:1 and above
[1](1976)	4:1 (maintenance)
van Breemen (Development, 1983)	5:1
Martin (1982b)	5:1 (maintenance)
Average (approximate)	3:1

[1] 'Adabas performs better than any other DBMS', *Systems Stelsels*, November 1976, p. 30.

network DBMS, IDMS, and IBM's VSAM (Virtual Storage Access Method), to DB2 (Davis, 1991b).

DBMSs lend themselves to use with 4GLs – query languages operate off the database – and to the use of prototyping. DBMSs can therefore also play a significant role in improving the productivity of systems analysts (Martin, 1981).

The Q & A DBMS goes one step further. It has a query language, the Intelligent Assistant, which incorporates the beginnings of artificial intelligence. The Intelligent Assistant gives Q & A the capability to create a synonym list for preprocessing users' requests, so they can query a database file in ordinary English ('Symantec's Q & A', *Modern Office*, September 1986, pp. 47–8). It can therefore be taught to understand such requests as 'Where is John Smith's home?', and 'Who are the big spenders?' (Badgett, 1986; Reed, 1986). This makes it more flexible and easier to use, with resultant increase in user productivity, though setting up the synonym list can be time-consuming.

Data dictionary

A data dictionary is a computerized repository of information about the data defined within a system – it contains 'data about data'

(Schach, 1988; Date, 1977). It contains information such as a description of the data structures (e.g. the name of each field, the length of the field, and whether it is alpha or numeric), where-located and where-used information, and so on (Avison and Fitzgerald, 1988; Ross, 1978; Lucas, 1985). Dictionaries may be 'active' or 'passive'. Different authorities use different definitions of these terms, but generally, the information in a *passive* dictionary serves purely as human-readable documentation of the application system (Gillenson, 1985). An *active* dictionary goes further; the information in it is used by the computer to control or drive the application system. This is done in one or more ways. The information may be utilized by screen and report generators to provide the headings for fields on screens and reports. It may control access to the data. It may include validation checks which are actioned when data is entered or updated, or processing or business rules, i.e. a change to the data can automatically trigger other actions. For example, if the value of one field is changed, then the system automatically recalculates the values of any dependent fields, as specified in the rules. The logic is therefore associated with the database rather than with independent applications. Martin (1982a) terms this an 'intelligent' database.

Programmers therefore do not have to repeatedly hard code this information into each application, and systems analysts and database administrators do not have to repeatedly design the data (Schroeder 1986, Martin, 1982a). Systems can thus be developed more quickly. Furthermore, most of the errors in this common code would be detected when the first program to use it was tested. Subsequent programs can therefore be tested more quickly, and there are fewer errors to escape detection and find their way into production programs.

The dictionary for IDMS/R can include information about non-IDMS/R files (Culli-

net, 1985); definitions of graphs can be stored in the INGRES dictionary (Barry, 1986a); and where-used information is stored in the ADABAS dictionary (Software AG, 1986d). The PICK dictionary includes the headings to be used for fields on reports, the widths of the fields, and formatting information such as for sums of money; while SYSTEM BUILDER, an application generator for the PICK operating system/DBMS, adds a validation capability. By contrast, the dictionary for IBM's relational DBMS, DB2, is not active: 'DB2, like many relational DBMSs, does not have a full-featured data dictionary' (Schroeder, 1986; Schussel, 1986).

Of the operational systems in the Lientz *et al.* (1978) survey, 26% used data dictionaries, while 70% of the installations in the Lee (1986) survey were using text processing and/or an automated data dictionary.

To sum up, an active data dictionary integrates and controls the entire software environment, and plays a major role in giving DBMSs their power and flexibility, and therefore in improving productivity (Schussel, 1986).

Data independence

The data independence provided by DBMSs has been cited as a major factor in improving productivity, especially maintenance productivity (Wulf, 1976; Ross, 1978; Date, 1977). The relational model provides the greatest degree of data independence – according to (Ferg, 1986), this is arguably the most important feature of a relational DBMS.

In older DBMS models (hierarchical or network), application programs are 'cluttered' with information about how the data is physically stored, e.g. sort order and pointer chains – this is how the data is presented to the programs (Ferg, 1986). The programs are therefore *dependent* on this representation: if the way the data is stored is changed, the programs will no longer work, so they will have to be converted or rewritten, often at substantial cost.

If the way the data is stored is *in*dependent of the way it is presented to the application programs – and this is the goal of the relational model (Schroeder, 1986; Ferg, 1986) – then changes can be made to the way it is stored without affecting the programs. Thus the 'physical' issues – the way the data is stored – are separated from the 'logical' issues – the way it is presented to the application programs (Shneiderman, 1980). The relational model provides a way of describing the data with its natural structure only, without imposing any additional structure for machine representation purposes (Codd, 1970). There are therefore considerable savings in maintenance effort. The data might still be stored in a specific order, or might still contain pointer chains, but if so, this is invisible to the user (Ferg, 1986).

Organizations with existing, non-relational DBMSs would naturally like to have the benefits provided by the relational model, but to convert their existing applications would be prohibitively expensive (Ferg, 1986). Next best is for the vendors of their existing DBMSs to add a relational interface. This would be used for all new applications, while existing applications continue to work undisturbed through the old, non-relational interface (though with the benefit of a query facility). Their existing applications would not have data independence, and so these organizations would still have a maintenance problem.

However, this solution is difficult, and therefore expensive, for the vendors. They are more likely, at least initially, to add only a semi-relational interface. The user will then be able to *retrieve* data (from both old and new applications) by relational means, but will have to revert to non-relational means to *update* it (even data from new applications). Such systems are likely to be advertised as relational, which is misleading, and this solution is also claimed by its critics to be slow, but nevertheless, for existing users, it is an advance over their previous completely non-relational systems (Ferg, 1986).

Other productivity considerations

Other facilities contributing to higher productivity, which are not available with every DBMS, include automatic reorganization of the data to improve efficiency, and built-in security and recovery (Ross, 1978; Date, 1977). Security and recovery encompass:

- access control (through password protection and read-only restrictions);
- protection against major failures such as disk crashes (through checkpoints, logging of transactions, restart, and restore);
- protection against minor failures such as application program crashes (by backing out all 'uncommitted' (incomplete) data changes); and
- record locking (to prevent harmful interactions between tasks).

Against all these improvements must be set the greater initial effort, and the need for an administration function, to manage the database. Johnson (1980b) expressed concern that the effort is not reduced, but is merely shifted to a separate group of individuals: no study had quantitatively demonstrated a productivity increase for the total design and programming effort. (Hence his zero productivity gain in Table 6.7.) The database administrator (DBA) needs a variety of different skills, as he is both machine and user oriented (Wulf, 1976). Together with the system analyst, he must analyse information requirements and design the database (Ross, 1978; Martin, 1982a). He must co-ordinate user requests, ensure security, protect integrity, and create a system which runs effectively for the entire user community (Shneiderman, 1980) i.e., the DBA must co-ordinate and direct all DBMS-related activity in the organization (Ross, 1978).

DBMSs can be complicated and difficult to learn and to use. Some DBMSs therefore need more technical support staff than others. E.I. Du Pont de Nemours and Company, for example, found that IMS needed four times as many as ADABAS (Webster, 1976). This is equivalent to a lower productivity, but the complexity may in some cases be a reflection of additional or more powerful features in the software, which would in turn provide a higher productivity to users. On the other hand, relational DBMSs, which are the most powerful type, are claimed to need less support because the complexity is handled by the software. (This is reminiscent of the claim by Unisys that their mainframes require fewer DP staff because of the sophistication of their system software.) It may be more accurate, though, to say that the simplicity and flexibility of the relational model *avoid* complexity.

6.3.4 OTHER BENEFITS

Data resident in a database is typically accessible by many users concurrently. Communications monitors such as DATACOM/DC and ENVIRON support the online network (Ross, 1978).

In conventional computerized systems, data is repeated wherever it is needed, resulting in considerable duplication. An IBM study of 100 organizations in Europe showed that 18% of the computerized data was duplicated up to 20 times (Grulke, 1983). This wastes disk space, but worse, when data is updated, it must be updated in all of the duplicated places at once, otherwise they get out of step with each other, causing confusion and errors. DBMSs reduce this problem, as it is generally only necessary to store each piece of data in one place, from where it can be accessed by every program. In particular, an organization should aim at having one combined database – a 'corporate' database – which is shared by all application systems in the organization, rather than a separate database for each application (Martin, 1982a). This helps to reduce the duplication of data.

Sometimes, however, redundant data is desirable, to speed up data access (Edwards, 1990) – in technical terms, the data is not fully normalized – though Martin and McClure (1985) believe this is rarely necessary. Also, if an organization has more than one DBMS, then because of incompatible data structures, the data may be repeated in each system – Schroeder (1986) quoted one organization which had *five* copies of each employee's name, for this reason. Tools such as FOCUS and MANTIS, which can read a variety of different structures, minimize this problem (Hymers, 1987; Cincom, 1986).

6.3.5 DISADVANTAGES

There are disadvantages associated with DBMSs. Some have already been referred to, such as incompatibility between different DBMSs, the requirement for a DBA, sharing and ownership of data, the greater initial effort, and the long-term considerations. Other problems are mentioned below.

In the early phases of implementing a data-centered approach, there is pressure to take quick alternate solutions, or to maintain the status quo (Martin, 1982a). (The data-centered approach treats data as the foundation stone on which applications are built. The processes must employ data in the database, and the whole of data processing could be regarded as a succession of changes to data.)

Although not inherently difficult, the technology of good database design is often not understood (Martin, 1982a).

Information is centralized, so the failure of the DBMS, through either hardware or software failures, can cause major losses (St. John Bate and Vadhia, 1987).

Minicomputer and mainframe DBMSs are often criticized for their inflexible user interfaces (Schroeder, 1986).

Those DBMSs which run on PCs are – as might be expected – slow, inflexible, and unable to handle sophisticated programming tasks, and there are additional problems with data integrity and security if the PCs are linked together in a network (Schroeder, 1986). Things change in the real world – as evidenced by the US post office's sudden decision to make zip codes longer – and DP must be able to respond quickly, yet to change a field size using a DOS-based DBMS with fixed-length record formats requires some kind of reprogramming, and can be very expensive.

Because of the cost of the DBMS, the large initial effort, and so on, DBMSs may require a substantial investment in capital and labor (Lucas, 1985). Furthermore, because they are very complex programs, they can be very difficult to learn to use and install. For the same reason, they tend to be inefficient in computer time and costly in storage. Relational DBMSs in particular are criticized as being too slow to handle high transaction volumes or large numbers of users: 'all those great features cost you additional processing' (Schroeder, 1986; Stamps, 1990). One organization which converted from a hierarchical DBMS, IMS, to a relational DBMS, DB2, found the latter to be about 20% more costly in operations (Davis, 1991b). These factors make plausible the claim that database users can find themselves paying two or three times more for data processing than non-database users (Webster, 1976). On the other hand, Schroeder reported 40–50% performance increases each year for relational systems; and DB2, which was originally advertised as being suitable only for IC and decision support work, was subsequently marketed for all applications that did not require high-performance, and now even for high-performance work (Living up to the hype', *Computer Week*, 11 July 1988, pp. 16–17).

6.3.6 SPECIAL HARDWARE AND SOFTWARE

The concept of a specialized database machine has been around since 1972, but has not been adequately exploited (Leopold, 1986), even though these machines give a far better price/performance than DBMSs in software (Cashmore, 1988). Examples of such machines are those from Teradata Corp. and Britton Lee, Inc., and ICL's Content Addressable File Store (CAFS). CAFS allows users to store data in unstructured files, but nevertheless access it very quickly ('Providing fast access to database management systems', *Retail & Distribution Management*, Sept–Oct, 1986, pp. 20–22). One clear application for these machines is artificial intelligence (AI).

IBM's System/38 computer, and its successor the AS/400, have an integrated DBMS, and so does the PICK operating system.

CD-ROM (Compact Disk, Read Only Memory) technology has been introduced. A compact disk is like a floppy disk. Physically, it is about the same size and shape, but it has a considerably higher storage capacity, being able to store some 550MB (equivalent to about 1500 floppies) (Schindler, 1987). Generally, the data on it (which is burned on by a laser) cannot be erased, and the average access time is as long as one second, which is much slower than the equivalent magnetic disks, and so can frustrate and impair the work of users who are accustomed to quicker retrieval (Sehr, 1986). However, erasable versions (especially magneto-optical) are becoming available, and performance is improving: 'Magneto-optical technology is fast approaching the point where its access and transfer times will be equivalent to those of current conventional magnetic media' (Harvey, 1990).

One use of CD-ROM is for public databases. At present, many databases containing airline schedules, news, commercial, credit, financial, marketing, bibliographic, technical, biomedical, and scientific information, are stored on-line (Tate and Runyan, 1986). (Examples are MEDLINE and Datasolve's World Reporter, while Dialog Information Services is the biggest worldwide data provider.) These databases are available on a bureau basis, and are typically accessed over telephone lines, with customers being charged according to their connect time, so users must learn efficient search techniques (Sehr, 1986). Alternatively, copies of the database can be made onto compact disks and sold to the customers, who then access the data on their own equipment and at leisure, without a meter running. The cost of a blank disk may be as low as $2, and a new European replication process could bring down the cost of disk duplication (i.e. of the data on it) to as little as 25¢ each (Sehr, 1986). The copying and distribution process have to be repeated periodically as the database is updated, so this method is not practical for databases which are updated frequently, but it is suitable for those which are not, such as industrial credit ratings, legal code revisions, and even the Yellow Pages.

Any electronic manuscript could be stored on this medium as a searchable database and, from the above prices, it can be seen that the cost of doing this is much less than that of printing a book. This method could be used for computer manuals and textbooks, thereby making information more readily available to software engineers.

6.4 TECHNOLOGICAL AIDS

This section discusses software products which aid the software engineering process, but which are generally more limited in scope than the tools already discussed. High-level languages, fourth-generation languages, interactive programming, and CASE (Computer-Aided Software Engineering) tools are also technological aids, but they are claimed to give large gains in productivity, and so are discussed separately later. However, because of the lack of a generally-accepted definition of fourth-generation languages, some of the tools in this section could be classified as fourth-generation.

Perrella (1986) and Carlyle (1987c) have pointed out that, in certain fundamental respects, programming has not changed much in 27 years: we are still using 27-year old technology. Programs are still designed with, perhaps, pencil-drawn flowcharts, they are entered by hand, and use simple documentation methods (e.g. comments): 'Can you imagine an electrical engineer spreading out a large sheet of paper on the kitchen table to design even a very simple microprocessor?'. At one time, the only aids were the compiler and the linking loader (Howden, 1982). Today, however, there are a large number and variety of aids available, covering every stage of the software life-cycle from requirements analysis to maintenance. It is therefore no longer necessary to use 27-year old technology, and productivity can increase accordingly. The tools listed in this chapter give an idea of what is now available.

Availability of specific tools is adversely affected by the diversity of hardware and basic system software: a different version of a tool may be required for each language and each make of computer (Glass, 1979; Boehm, 1973). Sometimes, therefore, organizations would have to build their own tools. Very large organizations tend to develop their own tools, and many have developed superior ones (Chapter 13).

Each organization normally acquires several tools: as many as it can afford and justify. Small organizations thus have only a small number of tools, and large organizations, a large number. The tools recommended by Jones (1986b) for different sized organizations are listed in Chapter 13. The combination of tools is the *software environment* (Howden, 1982).

Costs

Building a tool can be very expensive. Typical costs would be perhaps $50 000 per tool, but of course vary considerably both from one tool to another and according to the degree of sophistication. A simple Test Coverage Analyser, for example, might cost only $20 000 to develop; a sophisticated one, over $250 000 (Glass, 1979). (These estimates were made in 1979, and should be adjusted to allow for subsequent inflation.)

The larger or more critical the project, the greater the need for technological aids. Small projects might require tools having a total capital cost of $35 000 (to cover purchase price, training and documentation); large projects (having perhaps about 70 programmers and a budget of $20 million), might require tools costing $3 million (Howden, 1982). The comprehensive set of tools envisaged by Stone (1978) – interactive debug, DBMS, test data generator, simulators, etc. – would have cost $20 million. (Once again, these figures should be adjusted for inflation.)

Benefits

Technological aids improve productivity. Glass (1979) believes that they may be the only solution for large projects, though he does add a cautionary note: software development is a thought-intensive process – *can it be automated?* Another benefit is that appropriate tools, specifically 4GLs such as spreadsheets and query languages, enable many end users to meet some of their own data processing needs (Jones, 1986b). Tools can also improve communication, e.g. between systems analysts and the users for whom the system is being developed. Yet another benefit is that tools can improve quality (Chapter 10). Automated tools also help programmers and systems analysts concentrate on the creative parts of the job, and spend less time worrying about the mundane parts (Yourdon, 1989).

Extent of use

Despite the supposed benefits, most computer scientists have taken no interest in the new tools (Martin and McClure, 1985) and programmers generally make little use of

tools (Parikh, 1984). Usage of the five automated tools surveyed by Lientz *et al.* (1978) ranged from only 36% (for test data generators) down to just 4% (for the ISDOS automated design aid), and the average was only 20% – this survey, however, was limited to operational systems, and the figures might have been somewhat higher for systems being developed at the time the survey was made. Worse, an interactive debug system which was available in one experiment was rarely used, even though the participants were familiar with it (Gould, 1975).

To ensure that tools which are acquired are used, organizations should involve the programmers in their selection. Organizations should also keep track of the usage of each tool, and any increase or decrease in usage, and establish the reason. Appropriate action can then be taken, e.g. to promote use of a particular tool, or to replace an inferior one.

Toolkits

Some vendors provide a set of tools, known as toolkits or workbenches. (Different authorities (Loh and Nelson, 1989; Baron, 1988; Collin, 1989) give different definitions of these terms. Here we use the terms loosely, to mean a group of associated tools.) Each set of tools provides a software environment. The tools may be integrated with each other, and may provide a *uniform* environment which further increases productivity: once you have learnt one tool, it is easy to learn the others, and users can easily switch from one tool to another, e.g. between the editor and the debugger (Baron, 1988). This also helps novices understand that programming is an integrated network of tasks.

Examples of sets of tools are:

- Jaybe Software's **Cdb**, a C DBMS toolkit with 25 programs, for developing UNIX applications (Jaybe, 1986);
- Computer Software's **Clisp**, a LISP library and a programming environment for C

that runs on IBM PCs, which contains over 100 functions (Drasch, 1986);

- Borland's **TurboBasic** (and TurboPascal and TurboProlog), a language development environment for IBM PCs, consisting of a compiler, full-screen editor, run-time library, spreadsheet, etc. (Borland, 1987);
- Texas Instruments' **Explorer** environment, the built-in development and implementation tools of the TI Explorer AI workstation (Barry, 1986a); and
- Microsoft's **Windows Software Development Kit** for PCs, which provides a 'rich graphical environment' and device independence. It includes editors, a debugger, a program maintenance utility, and so on (Microsoft, 1986b).

Furthermore, UNIX is a programming environment as well as an operating system; the FORTH language consists of an interpreter, an editor, and an operating system; and the BASIC language is embedded within an environment containing an editor and debugger (Baron, 1988). According to Martin and McClure (1985), UNIX is the most widely available programming environment. Boehm (1981) described the UNIX Programmers' Workbench (Dolotta *et al.*, 1978), the Xerox Alto system (Thacker *et al.*, 1979), and the ETH Lilith system (Wirth, 1981), as particularly good examples of well-integrated tool environments. (ETH is the Swiss Federal Institute of Technology, Professor Wirth's institution in Zurich.)

List of tools

The following list, comprising the remainder of this section, is largely based on that given by Glass (1979). Howden (1982) gave a similar list, but placed more emphasis on project management. Myers (1979) also gave a similar list, but it was limited to checkout tools. Jones (1986b) devoted several pages to a list of dozens of kinds of tools he envisaged, which would form a full and integrated life-cycle support environment, from planning and estimating, through requirements, documentation, etc., to maintenance, and he anticipated that such an environment would be available by the 1990s. Computer Associates lists the tools they supply in their magazine, *CA-Insight*. Lists of tools are published from time to time (see the sources of packages given in Chapter 7), and news items about individual tools appear frequently in the computer press. Information from these sources has been included in the list below, to supplement the information given by Glass, and to bring it up to date.

Some of the information in this section – the specific tools which are available and their features – tends to change rather rapidly. Even the vendors of particular tools change, due to mergers and takeovers. Furthermore, like Vincent *et al.* (1988), my purpose is not to recommend any specific vendor's product. The information given here should therefore be treated purely as a guide to the type of facilities which are available.

The list provides a general overview. Additional information about some types of tool is given later, e.g. tools that restructure source code are discussed further under structured programming (Chapter 8), and the names of individual tools which automate some of the diagramming methods discussed in Chapter 8 are included in the discussions of those methods. Where a particular type of tool is closely related to a specific software engineering methodology, it seemed more logical to discuss it with the methodology rather than here.

The tools are grouped by function in the software life-cycle. Some tools may be used in more than one function – e.g. an automatic flowcharter can serve as both a debugging aid and a documentation tool; librarian programs can be used for managing code, documentation, and test cases (Myers, 1979); while most development tools can be used for maintenance as well – but for simplicity each tool is only shown under one function.

6.4.1   PROJECT MANAGEMENT

Howden's 1982 list of technological aids emphasized project management, including items such as milestone charts and Gantt charts. He described a database containing information which would aid project management: test plans, design documents, relationships between tasks, etc. Small projects would not use the database; large projects would make extensive use of it. Ideally, the tools would interact with the database and not with each other. When a tool was used, it would – as a by-product – automatically update the database, which would thus always be up to date. The 'Stoneman' ADA Programming Support Environment (APSE) is based on the concept of a unified database which acts as the repository for all information associated with a software project (Boehm, 1981).

Of the large organizations (1000–10 000 employees) in a Datamation/Price Waterhouse survey, 40% were using automated project management tools (Statland, 1989). Project management software is a growth area. Many products have become available, running on all sizes of machine. However, few of these products are suitable for the management of software projects (McCusker, 1989), and Frank (1990) recommends using MRP-II (Manufacturing Resource Planning) software packages instead.

One example of a project management package is Nastec's (1986) **LifeCycle Manager**, which supports project managers with planning, estimating and control features. It integrates with Nastec's tool for systems analysts, DesignAid. Another example is Microsoft's **Project** program, which includes PERT charts and Gantt charts, and is in color (Simenon, 1986). Also, some 4GLs (such as Pacbase from CGI Systems, Telon from Pansophic Systems, and APS from Sage Systems assist project management, and may even be complete life-cycle management tools, with modules for project planning and

control, librarian functions, and documentation (Schussel, 1986). Furthermore, some of the tools listed below for systems analysts also assist project management, e.g. in organizations using the CASE tool Excelerator, even large projects have been delivered on time and under budget (Index Technology Corp., 1986).

6.4.2   REQUIREMENTS/SPECIFICATIONS

There are various tools which aid the requirements analysis and specifications functions. Requirements/specification languages may be subsets of actual programming languages (Glass, 1979). They make possible automated consistency checking. Specific products which aid the requirements/specifications functions are the University of Michigan's Problem Statement Language, PSL, and Problem Statement Analyzer, PSA (Teichroew and Hershey, 1977). They are the first two components of ISDOS (Information System Design and Optimization System) (Teichroew and Sayani, 1971). PSL enables the analyst to state the requirements in a formal, machine-readable form which are then analysed by PSA, e.g. for consistency. However, PSL and PSA assist documentation rather than genuinely automating analysis and design (Avison and Fitzgerald, 1988). ISDOS goes further, as it generates code, which may be either machine code, statements in a higher-level language (such as COBOL), or parameters to a software package (Couger *et al.*, 1982). Similarly, Hoskyns System generates COBOL programs from the specifications (Duffy, 1976). The systems and programs are described in terms of matrices, which are then automatically translated by a preprocessor into COBOL programs (Couger *et al.*, 1982). Couger classifies Hoskyns System and PSL/PSA as third-generation system development techniques, PSL/PSA II as fourth-generation, and ISDOS as a fifth-generation technique.

Problem definition packages have been

criticized as cumbersome because they try to do too much. ('What does the future hold?', *Computer Systems S.A.*, June 1982, pp. 19–27).

According to Glass (1979), requirements and specification languages were still in the research phase, and 'few, if any, industrial computing installations use the technique', but according to Couger *et al.* (1982), PSL/PSA were being used in a number of organizations, including AT&T, Boeing, British Railways, IBM, and TRW.

This topic overlaps with CASE tools (section 6.8), while Structured English, which is a specifications language, is discussed in Chapter 8.

Screen generators

Screen generators or painters should meet a number of requirements. They should:

- be able to 'paint' the user's screen designs interactively (Martin, 1985);
- have an on-line HELP facility, supply default responses wherever possible, and be operated by means of function keys (Birkholtz, 1983);
- be able, possibly by means of a menu, to create highlighting, lines and boxes, color blocks, reverse video, fields for user entry of data, fields to display variables, and so on;
- permit the creation of 'fast paths' for use by expert users (Radice and Phillips, 1988);
- permit not only rapid design of screen layouts, but also rapid changes to these layouts, as software development is an iterative process (Avison and Fitzgerald, 1988) – this also makes them suitable for prototyping; and
- produce the code to generate the screen as required, once the required design has been drawn on the screen.

This tool is very common. Most, if not all, DBMSs have a screen generation or painting facility. Also, Martin (1985) lists screen painters as one of the tools needed for a 4GL.

One example is Data General's Screen Generator Utility, SGU (Birkholtz, 1983), while a screen painting and generation capability is included in SYSTEM BUILDER, an application generator which has already been mentioned.

System modelling and simulation

Glass (1979) gave the following example to illustrate the difference between modelling and simulation. Building a scaled-down replica of an aircraft is modelling; placing it in a wind tunnel to determine flight characteristics is simulation.

These techniques are powerful but expensive. A simulation language is used to build a model of the system to be developed, and to simulate the model's interaction with its environment, which may itself be simulated (Glass, 1979; Enos and Van Tilburg, 1979). This gives a better understanding of the required system, and so can lead to improvements to the specifications. According to Jones (1986b), of the common methods for detecting requirements and design errors, evidence indicates that formal group inspections (Chapter 10) and design simulation or modelling (where users are able to work with running examples of the program's functions), have the highest overall efficiencies, and alone may remove over 65% of the problems. The techniques can be used during the feasibility study as well. IBM's GPSS (General-Purpose System Simulator), SIMSCRIPT, and SIMULA, are languages designed for simulation. Other software products, such as a data postprocessor, may also be needed. In one case, Kosy obtained a 3.5:1 productivity improvement by using Rand Corporation's ECSS (Extendable Computer System Simulator), a special-purpose language for simulating computer systems (Boehm, 1973; Nielsen, 1970; Kosy, 1974, 1975).

This is a well-established concept, and in fact simulation languages 'are decades old', but because of problems such as cost, their use has been largely restricted to professional systems analysts running large computers (Glass, 1979; Baron, 1988). However, with the growing interest in simulation in education, along with the expanding memory capabilities of microcomputers, the situation is likely to change.

These techniques overlap with prototyping (Chapter 8), but the terms modelling and particularly simulation are generally used for more specialized areas, as illustrated by Glass's aircraft example, and special languages are used, whereas prototyping generally refers to commercial computing (such as accounting), and 4GLs are used.

6.4.3 DESIGN

There has been little automation of the design process, because of the difficulty of doing so. For example, 'it is difficult to automate the support necessary to stimulate and capture creativity, which is unique to each individual designer' (Charette, 1986). This function will probably therefore be the last to be automated. The automation that has occurred has been largely limited to documentation support tools (Avison and Fitzgerald, 1988), such as for the graphical design methods (Chapter 8). However, products which generate code from the specifications, such as ISDOS and Hoskyns System (discussed earlier), and even 4GLs (section 6.6), may eliminate, or nearly eliminate, at least the detailed, internal design function. In addition, text editors can be used with program design languages, though there are specialized tools as well. (Program design languages are members of the same family as structured english, and are also discussed in Chapter 8.)

Although the automation that has occurred has been largely limited to graphics, the value of this should not be underrated. Tools which can graphically represent design documents are of great value to software engineers (Pomberger, 1984; Martin and McClure,

1985). Requirements methods, such as structured analysis and SADT (Structured Analysis and Design Technique), use graphics extensively, whereas design methods such as structured design and Jackson's, do not (Charette, 1986). (Methods like HIPO diagrams and Nassi-Shneiderman structured flowcharts are highly graphical detailed design methods, but their usefulness is limited.) For automation to be useful in design, some type of graphics must be supported by the methods. Furthermore, without these tools, designers are reluctant to make changes to their designs because of the effort involved in changing the diagrams, and the danger of introducing errors in redrawing; but with them, it is easy and much safer to make changes.

These tools can also contribute to the accuracy and consistency of diagrams, e.g they can cross-check that levels of data flow diagrams (Chapter 8) are accurate, that terminology is consistent, and documentation standards are adhered to. It is valuable for a design to be automatically checked. For this to be possible, the design must be machine-readable, and only a limited range of checks can be performed, but it is a cost-effective method – acquisition costs are moderate (perhaps $50 000 in 1979), and usage costs are relatively minor (Glass, 1979). However, Glass stated that this concept was less than half a dozen years old, and little used.

Tools which can graphically represent design documents are of great value; better still are tools which permit diagrammatic designing, so that the design can be accomplished entirely on the computer, without pencil or paper (Pomberger, 1984).

There has been little automation of design in the past – and only 4% of the operational systems in the Lienz *et al.* (1978) survey used the ISDOS automated design aid – but the situation is improving. Structured design makes higher levels of automation possible (Martin and McClure, 1985). Some systems analysis tools also include design aids. For example, the CASE tool Excelerator enables designers to create and modify a design (Index Technology, 1987). In addition, there are specific design tools such as Teamwork/SD (from Cadre Technologies), an interactive software package which helps system designers create and analyse their designs (Barry, 1986a). As its name implies, it is intended for a team of designers. It enables them to decompose interrelated system components into manageable tasks, while minimizing interfaces between the components. It runs on Apollo, Sun Microsystems, and IBM workstations. Higher Order Software (HOS) (Chapter 8) includes automated aids. Other examples of automated design tools are given below.

- M. Bryce and Associates' PRIDE, which is an automated systems design methodology (Bryce *et al.*, 1978). With it, designers and analysts interact with the computer throughout the development process. As they design, specifications are input to PRIDE, which validates the completeness and accuracy of these designs.
- DDI's 'Data Designer', which is a tool for data modelling. User views and functional dependencies are fed into it. It synthesizes them into a non-redundant data model, plots the result, and produces various reports for the data administrator (Martin and McClure, 1985).
- Meta Systems' DESIGN software package, which is not a full-fledged CASE toolkit, but is more sophisticated than most simple graphics packages (Yourdon, 1989).
- TRW's DACC (Design Assertion Consistency Checker), which was developed to process assertions made of the inputs and outputs of the various parts of the design, in order to find inconsistencies of range, number of data items, data type, and other interface definitions (Boehm *et al.*, 1975c; Dunn and Ullman, 1982).
- Boeing's DECA (Design Expression and Confirmation Aid), which uses design trees

and transition diagrams as input. Users have found it to be highly cost-effective (Carpenter and Tripp, 1975; Glass, 1979).

6.4.4 CODING

Some tools which aid program writing are listed below.

- High-level languages, and the time-saving features built into them, such as powerful verbs and the COBOL COPY library (section 6.5).
- Preprocessors: program generators like EZICOBOL and SpeedCobol use preprocessors, and can halve coding time by using abbreviations, etc. to reduce the amount of writing (Goodman, 1978; Parikh, 1984). For example, Parikh saved 25–50% in coding time alone on small, simple programs, by using the SCORE package which permitted abbreviations for 17 COBOL reserved words, such as F for FILLER and P for PIC. Preprocessors also reduce the number of coding errors, thereby reducing checkout time as well. They are also used for decision tables (Chapter 8).
- Programs which indent or restructure code to make it easier to read or to comply with structured programming rules, and which therefore also reduce the maintenance effort (Chapter 8).
- 'Librarian' programs such as CA-LIBRARIAN, which make it easier to maintain libraries, including libraries of source code. These libraries would contain any common modules. As much as 60% of the coding in a program may be a repetition of code in other, existing programs (Lee, 1981). Use of common modules can drastically reduce this figure, and significantly speed up testing and debugging as well as coding, so any tool which facilitates the use of common modules is valuable.

Standardization, such as that imposed by

structured programming, may lead to auto-mation of the coding process, and in fact structured techniques have an important part to play in the automation of programming (Martin and McClure, 1985).

6.4.5 CHECKOUT (STATIC CHECKING, TESTING AND DEBUGGING)

Automated testing is necessary because manual error-checking is itself an error-prone process (Yourdon, 1975). Automation:

- relieves testing personnel of time-consuming, routine chores, and may permit the use of less expensive technical personnel (Miller, 1975; Miller and Wise-hart, 1974);
- permits a higher volume of testing for the same cost, or the same volume at a lower cost (Deutsch, 1979);
- brings more rigor to the testing process, is more likely to be widely used, and may result in cost and time savings (Hetzel, 1973).

Brown *et al.* (1973) reported that the re-testing of a very large program, aided by automated tools, was accomplished with a 30% reduc-tion in computer time and human effort, but with an increase in thoroughness. Martin and McClure (1985) quoted one organization, the Hughes Aircraft Co., which found 400 errors in a software project, saving 4400 man-days, due to the use of a formalized test plan supported by automated test tools (Deutsch, 1981).

However (Deutsch, 1979; Yourdon, 1975),

- automated tools are not always cost-effective, e.g. for simple programs with small volumes of test data, the cost can outweigh the benefits, especially if modifi-cations to the tools are required;
- tools such as an automated output checker may only be useful when working with fairly large volumes of test data; and
- program measurement tools increase execution time and storage utilization –

figures are given below for test coverage analysers – which can limit their useful-ness, e.g. when testing real-time systems.

(A real-time program is one that controls or responds to stimuli in the real world, such as a heart-monitoring device that detects heart rate and sends appropriate signals to a central nursing station in case of dramatic changes (Baron, 1988).) Martin and McClure (1985) stressed the importance of tools that check for completeness by providing a link to system requirements.

Lists of checkout tools are given in Myers (1979), Glass (1979), and Martin and McClure (1985).

Static analysers

Static analysers (also known as program, static-flow, and structural analysers) are pro-grams which (Glass, 1979; Fairley, 1985; Parikh, 1984; Pomberger, 1984):

- examine other programs without executing them, looking for
  - errors (such as variables being used before they are initialized, variables de-clared but not used, and code which cannot be reached),
  - violation of an installation's coding standards (such as naming conventions), or
  - inefficiencies; or
- calculate complexity and other metrics (such as those of Halstead (1977) and McCabe (1976), or the nesting level of loops and the number of GOTO state-ments).

(Complexity measures, and potential dangers of using them, are discussed in Chapter 8.) Such features can also be built into compilers (Shneiderman, 1980), and in fact, static ana-lysers are particularly valuable in the case of languages such as FORTRAN which do not allow much compile time checking (Sommerville, 1989). Source code auditors are analysers which concentrate on coding standards, though Parikh (1984) uses this term to refer to a specialized file comparator (section 6.4.7) which lists the changes made to a program.

This tool is particularly valuable in a training environment, as it detects poor technique and permits corrective action, before the bad practices become entrenched. It can also be used to measure the work of contract programmers, and the quality of software packages where the source code is available – and thereby warn prospective customers against unwise purchases.

The cost of an analyser can range from trivial (because some are in the public domain), to over $100 000 for an elaborate one, while a project-oriented code auditor might cost $20 000–40 000 (Glass, 1979). However, neither computer time nor the time spent manually analysing the results should be significant, so they are not expensive to use, and the errors detected should more than pay for their usage. Static analysis was responsible for detecting 16% of the errors 'seeded' in one large program (Gannon, 1979). (Seeding is also known as 'bebugging', and is discussed in Chapter 8.) By comparison, path testing caught 25% of the errors. Static analysers were responsible for error-detection rates of 1 per 200 statements in one case, and 13 per 200 in another (NASA, 1977). (The higher figure probably includes coding-standard violations – see Chapter 8.) However, static analysers do have limitations, as there are many types of error which they cannot detect, e.g. they can detect uninitialized variables, but not incorrect initializations (Sommerville, 1989; Fairley, 1985).

There are a number of analysers in existence, but few were in common use (Glass, 1979). For FORTRAN programs, there are DAVE, RXVP, and FACES (FORTRAN Automatic Code Evaluation System). (RXVP was used in the Hughes Aircraft Co. example quoted earlier, and FACES in the NASA

example.) For COBOL there is Meta COBOL. C programs can be passed through 'lint', a filter program which checks for many errors or potential errors, or features which are likely to be non-portable or wasteful, such as unreachable statements, loops not entered at the top, variables declared but not used, and illegal function definition and usage (Ritchie *et al.*, 1978; Baron, 1988; Bell *et al.*, 1987).

Test coverage analysers

This tool monitors a program while it is running, counting the number of times each segment of the program is executed (Myers, 1979). It is a simple tool; it is not sophisticated enough to count the number of times each *combination* of segments is executed, so it is limited in its usefulness. Nevertheless, it shows which parts of the program have not been tested. It also shows which parts are most frequently used and so may need optimization, so it can also be used when tuning inefficient programs. One study, at the Boeing Aerospace Company, showed that a simple analyser could help find 25% of program errors; a sophisticated one, which would check all sequences of segments (not yet technologically feasible because of the astronomical number of possible combinations), 65% (Glass, 1979). Glass (1979) stated that the concept was new and was not commonly used (Glass, 1979). Examples are the McDonnell Douglas Astronautics' Program Evaluator and Tester (PET), and the JOVIAL Language Automated Verification System (JAVS), for FORTRAN and JOVIAL programs respectively (Myers, 1979). The capability is also built into the ALGOL W compiler, and the CAPEX Optimizer III compiler for COBOL (Glass, 1979; Arthur, 1983).

This tool is expensive to use. It may add as much as 45% to the memory requirements of the program, and cause its execution time to increase by a factor of up to 8.5 (Glass, 1979). A postprocessor program is required to print out the accumulated totals. These must be manually analysed, which requires a considerable amount of time.

A computer hardware analyser is a special form of test coverage analyser.

Test data generators

Test data generators are not new but are mostly not very powerful – they are little more than random-number generators (Glass, 1979). They can result in a reduction of 50% in machine time, and 30% manpower savings during the testing and debugging phases, due to the use of smaller test files, less time coding test data, and so on, but Johnson (1980b) warned that such high savings can only be achieved in about 5% of situations. Nevertheless, they are not expensive – the one he discussed had an installation charge of only $8500 – and he estimated that they typically had a payback period of 6–12 months. He recommended that they be used in addition to, not instead of, live files and user-generated data. According to Glass (1979), because of their limitations they were seldom used, but they were used for 36% of the operational systems surveyed by Lientz *et al.* (1978), making them the most widely used automated tool in that survey. Research is being conducted to develop more useful ones, which would, for example, analyse the structure and logic flow of the program being tested, or the expected input (Myers, 1979; Martin and McClure, 1985).

Examples of advanced test data generators are TRW's ATDG, General Research Corporation's RXVP, and the General Electric Corporation Research and Development Center's TPL (Martin and McClure, 1985; Dunn and Ullman, 1982).

Test drivers

The concept of test drivers is an old one, and has been heavily used (Glass, 1979).

Large programs are built in blocks (or modules). As each block is coded, so it must be tested. However, as it is only part of a program, some 'scaffolding' code is necessary to allow it to be tested. This scaffolding is the test driver (or test 'harness'). (With top-down testing, the top-level routines can serve as the driver, but it may be very expensive to use a large evolving program as a test driver for new routines (Fairley, 1985).) The driver passes input to the block of code being tested, executes it, and collects or prints the output (Van Tassel, 1978).

A test driver is a program, and therefore has to be written and debugged. Furthermore, once all the blocks have been written, the driver is no longer required and so is thrown away. According to Glass (1979), the cost of such throwaway code is only a minor part of the overall development costs on a program of any magnitude, but according to Fairley (1985), test harness preparation can amount to 50% or more of the coding and debugging effort. ('Throwaway' code was discussed in more detail in Chapter 2.)

A new driver has to be built for each program, as generalized drivers are still being developed. However, test data generators have been 'somewhat successful' in generalizing test drivers (Glass, 1979). In addition, there are products such as IBM's AUT (Automated Unit Test), TESTMASTER, and the General Electric Corporation Research and Development Center's TPL (Test Procedure Language), which automate related aspects (Myers, 1979; Dunn and Ullman, 1982; Fairley, 1985). AUT, for example, permits programmers to encode test cases (input and expected output), and feed these into the driver, which then compares the actual output against the expected output, and reports any discrepancies (Myers, 1979). These tools may provide a language in which the test cases can be expressed, which reduces the effort required. The capabilities of test driver and test data generator may be combined into the same tool (TPL is an example).

One experiment found that the use of a

module driver tool reduced working time by 11% during the module-test phase (Itoh and Izutani, 1973).

Environment simulators

Environment simulators simulate the environment surrounding the system. They are like very sophisticated test drivers, and can repeatedly reproduce an exact sequence of events (i.e. inputs to the system), including the timings of the events (which is important in real-time and interactive systems) (Glass, 1979; Sommerville, 1989; Deutsch, 1979). They are a testing aid, and are particularly valuable when testing in a live environment is impractical, e.g. harmful, dangerous, or too costly, such as in medical applications and air traffic control (Myers, 1979; Baron, 1988).

Mathematical checkers

Compilers may have built-in features which can detect arithmetic errors – e.g. the ON SIZE ERROR clause in COBOL detects if a computed number is too large to fit into its receiving field (Yourdon *et al.* 1979a). As Glass (1979) put it, because of such computing artifices as word length, even a correctly coded algorithm may behave improperly. A graphic example of the impact of rounding errors was provided by Kelso (1987), who used a program (the Savage benchmark from *Byte* magazine), which he wrote in several languages (BASIC, FORTRAN, and PASCAL), and ran on a variety of computers (from a Z80A processor using the CP/M operating system, through 8086 and 80286 processors using MS-DOS, to a Cray supercomputer), with and without maths co-processors, with single and double precision, and different interpreters and compilers (including BASICA, QuickBASIC, and TurboPascal), and obtained answers ranging from 2304.86 to 2716.961, where the correct answer was 2500.

However, the compiler's built-in features can only detect a limited range of errors. Mathematical checkers extend this range. They can, for example, show the magnitude of rounding errors. They also provide an independent check on the calculations performed in the program, but a large amount of manual effort may be necessary to use this facility, as the programmer may have to calculate the anticipated results manually, feed them into the computer, and then manually check a parallel printout of the manual and computed results.

This tool was not in common use (Glass, 1979). Acquisition costs are high, because additional, supporting software may be required. Running costs may also be high, as the tool can significantly affect program execution speed, especially if it necessitates use of an interpreter instead of a compiler, so the cost of each test run may be increased by a factor of 20 to 30 (Glass, 1979).

Source language debug

Source language debuggers permit a program to be debugged in the language it was written in, rather than in the more customary but more difficult machine language. For example, audit trails are printed, or human-readable memory dumps. Source language debug was previously not common, and the requirements definition for the ADA language only dealt with it in passing (Glass, 1979) – possibly because the payoff is not obvious and measurable – so programmers often resorted to manually inserting diagnostic statements in problem programs (Chapter 8). However, more attention is now being paid to the concept, perhaps because of the proliferation of PCs and the wider use of UNIX, so that Stevens (1989) was able to state that source level debuggers are quite common.

The IBM PL/1 Checkout compiler has some source language debug capabilities, and so do most JOVIAL compilers (Glass, 1979). Static analysers such as the filter program 'lint', mentioned earlier, provide information in source language rather than machine language (Sommerville, 1989). The capabilities are widely available for PCs, with products such as: Logitech's Run Time Debugger for MODULA-2 (Logitech, 1986); Microsoft's CodeView for C, and their QuickBASIC (Microsoft, 1986a, 1986c); Mark Williams' csd for C (Williams, 1986b); and Atron's PC and AT PROBEs (which work in conjunction with a 1-megabyte memory board which must be added to the PC) (Atron, 1986). System Designers Software's ADA Debug System runs on a PC while controlled remotely from a DEC VAX mini (System Designers Software, Inc., 1986). With many of these products, you can set conditional breakpoints, or step through the program a line at a time as it executes, watching the values of variables, registers and flags. csd is claimed to cut development time in half.

Assertion checkers

Assertion checkers (or program state monitors) are similar to test coverage analysers (but are primarily a debugging rather than a testing aid), and one often sees both functions in a single tool (Myers, 1979), e.g. McDonnell Douglas Astronautics' Program Evaluator and Tester (PET). The programmer inserts 'assertions' into the program (Glass, 1979), which may consist of the legitimate values of the variables in the program (e.g. that a sex code may only be 'M' or 'F'), or that a particular table must be in ascending order, and so on. As the program executes, these assertions are checked for validity. If an assertion is violated, e.g. if a variable becomes out of range, then the error is reported or the program may even be terminated. This tool therefore provides an early warning of errors, thereby shortening testing time. Glass (1979) stated that it was a new concept which was little used. PET (mentioned above), and ALADDIN (Assembly Language Assertion-Driven Debugging Interpreter) (Fairley,

1985), are examples of the tool, and assertion checking capabilities are built into the ALGOL W compiler (Glass, 1979). Building the necessary assertions into the program is time-consuming, so this tool is expensive to use.

6.4.6 DOCUMENTATION

Jones (1986b) complained that documentation requirements have been largely ignored, there are few tools available, and it was even left out of the ADA Programming Support Environment (APSE). Nevertheless, some of the tools already mentioned also aid documentation. Excelerator for example, is claimed to simplify, and therefore encourage, documentation, and it also ensures that documentation is done uniformly (Index Technology, 1987).

Word processing

Dedicated word processing machines such as IBM's old Displaywriter, and word processing packages such as WordPerfect, AmiPro and DisplayWrite IV (on personal computers), and DisplayWrite/370 (on IBM mainframes), are invaluable when creating program specifications, operating instructions, etc. In the absence of specialist packages, ordinary text editors such as IBM's XEDIT with their VM/CMS mainframe operating system (preferably combined with the SCRIPT text formatter), can be used. In the UNIX environment are text formatting programs such as troff (Kernighan *et al.*, 1978), and the Writer's Workbench toolkit, a comprehensive set of proof-reading and document checking tools (Cherry and MacDonald, 1983). For mathematical/scientific work, there is Donald Knuth's TeX (Knuth, 1984).

Graphics

It was pointed out earlier that requirements methods use graphics extensively, and that tools which can graphically represent design documents are of great value to software engineers. Design diagrams may be flow-charts or their more modern equivalents such as Nassi–Shneiderman diagrams (Chapter 8), and the software tools may be general graphics editors or more specialized tools for specific types of diagram (Chapter 8). Graphics screens should be used for the creation, display, and updating of the diagrams.

Flowcharts

Graphics programs can be used to draw flowcharts. The resulting flowcharts are neater than those drawn by hand. In addition to general packages such as Software Publishing Corp.'s Harvard Graphics, there are specialized flowcharting programs such as Clear Software Inc.'s DOS-based allCLEAR, and RoyKore Inc.'s Windows-based ABC Flowcharter, which are easier to use, particularly for updating (McMullen, 1991b). Alternatively, there are a number of tools – such as AUTOFLOW and FLOWGEN – which examine a program, and automatically produce a flowchart from it (Weinberg, 1971; Dunn and Ullman, 1982). The idea is good – correct and up to date flowcharts can be produced cheaply and painlessly after every change to the program – but it has limitations. For example, a flowcharter cannot improve the symbols (names) and comments created by the programmer: if the symbols were poorly chosen, or the comments misleading, they remain poor or misleading on the generated flowchart (Weinberg, 1971). As a result, Weinberg looks on it more as a debugging aid than a documentation tool. One would therefore expect few organizations to use such a tool, and only 10% of the operational systems in the Lientz *et al.* (1978) survey used it (compared to the average tool usage in that survey of 20%). However, according to Dunn and Ullman (1982), it was one of the most widely used tools.

6.4.7 MAINTENANCE

Maintenance is a microcosm of development, so the tools already described should also prove useful during maintenance (Fairley, 1985). The tools listed below are considered particularly valuable during maintenance, but they should also be useful during other functions, especially testing and debugging. Furthermore, tools such as relational DBMSs and fourth-generation languages are generally believed to reduce the maintenance workload. (The impact of these tools on maintenance is included in the discussion of the tools.)

Fastbol (from The Analytic Sciences Corporation) is claimed to be the fastest way to maintain COBOL code (Analytic Sciences Corp., 1986). It 'provides intelligence about the program from the program itself'. Information which otherwise would take hours to extract is available in seconds. Fastbol is an on-line product running under IBM's VM and MVS operating systems.

File comparators

A file comparator compares two files and reports the differences (Fairley, 1985). For example, after a program modification, it can compare the new output file against the old (or against a file which is known to be correct), and can thereby provide rapid confirmation that the modification achieved the desired result and did not introduce an error into the output file (Glass, 1979). However, it may not be powerful enough to distinguish between differences due to errors, and those caused by the change in the user's requirements. Similarly, by comparing the new version of the source code (or JCL, test data, or documentation) against the old, it can show the maintenance programmer exactly what changes were made to the program (or JCL, etc.) (Parikh, 1984). Examples of this tool are IBM's IEBCOMPR and the UNIX Source Code Control System, SCCS. According to

Arthur (1983), a file comparator can often halve bug-finding time.

Cross-reference listings

These listings show the name of each variable, paragraph, etc. in the program or module, where it is defined, and where it is used or modified. They are commonly produced by compilers for individual modules or programs, and less commonly by linkage editors, showing the same information for large systems of programs (Glass, 1979). They can improve testing and maintenance productivity, particularly with large programs, and in fact are extremely valuable in maintenance (Arthur, 1983). They simplify the search for fields whose contents have been modified incorrectly. They help the programmer spot potential errors, such as unreferenced fields. When a change is requested, they help gauge the magnitude of the change (the number of references to a name in itself provides a rough idea of the amount of work which might be necessary); and when the change is implemented, they help ensure that, if one reference to a name is changed, all the other references are analogously changed.

The CASE tool Excelerator has a where-used reporting capability (Index Technology, 1987). The Integrated Data Dictionary for IDMS/R documents the source and use of all data, whether in the IDMS/R database or not, making it 'a valuable reference tool and central index to a company's total information source' (Cullinet, 1985). The ADABAS dictionary has a similar facility (Software AG, 1986d).

6.5   HIGH-LEVEL (THIRD-GENERATION) LANGUAGES

Languages are the prime means of communication with the computer, used to instruct it how to perform the required tasks. Languages have become increasingly powerful since the invention of computers:

- machine languages;
- assembly languages;
- high-level or third-generation languages (FORTRAN, COBOL, PL/1 and BASIC etc.);
- very high-level languages – the fourth-generation.

According to Chorafas (1986), COBOL, FORTRAN, and so on, were called high-level languages in the 1950s and 1960s, but are now referred to as third-generation languages (3GLs). However, the term high-level languages still seems to be widely used, e.g. it appears in many of my references, such as Jones (1986b) and Baron (1988), and some of these sources use both terms.

As a general rule, low-level languages are economical on machine time – for example, the US Internal Revenue Service's programs required 4–5 times as much CPU time after being converted from Assembler to COBOL (Kirchner, 1986) – and high-level languages are economical on programmer time. For improved productivity, therefore, the highest-level language possible should be used (Van Tassel, 1978). The greater power and lower price of hardware nowadays makes this the cheaper option in most cases (Tireford, 1976).

The evidence presented in Chapter 2 indicates a slow but steady increase in the productivity of the software industry. This has coincided with, and can be at least partly attributed to, the increasing power of the languages used. However, according to Kessel (1976), the cost of software development remained constant over the preceding ten years, which implies that the increase in productivity due to the introduction of high-level languages was only enough to balance the increase in costs such as salaries. The figures given by Jones (1986b) are similar. They show a decrease of 33% in overall development costs in ten years due to the change to 3GLs. (By contrast, the figures for the next ten years, during which there was a change to structured methods but no improvement in language level, show an *increase* in overall development costs, albeit by only 1%.) However, the cost per program instruction doubled (from $19 for Assembler in 1964, to $37 for unstructured COBOL in 1974). (Part – most? – of this increase, though, is because fewer statements are required with higher-level languages, i.e. it is due to the mathematical paradox discussed in Chapter 2.) Similarly, Wright (1978) pointed out that total EDP budgets are rising in spite of the 'enormous erosion' in hardware price levels. In fact, over the preceding two dozen years, the cost per program instruction doubled due to the ever increasing cost of people. (Once again, though, part of this rise may be due to the mathematical paradox.) A graph published by Martin (1982a) shows that people costs increased by about a factor of ten in the preceding 25 years (an increase of about 10% p.a., compound).

Because of their lower productivity, machine and assembly languages are no longer widely used for development work. They are mostly restricted to specialist applications like writing operating systems, compilers or input/output routines, where large volumes of data are being processed or time is critical, and even this is changing (Yourdon, 1975). Nevertheless, they might be revived and be used for writing fourth-generation software products, packages and video games. For example, the ESS (Electronic Spread Sheet) package from Trax Softworks, Inc., is written in Assembler for fast execution and low memory requirements (Trax, 1986); while large production runs, which require efficient implementation, 'will probably always be written in lower-level languages' (Shneiderman, 1980). At the other extreme, 4GLs are relatively new, but are becoming increasingly widespread. However, they give large gains in productivity, and so are discussed separately later (section 6.6). The present discussion therefore con-centrates on the widely-used high-level languages or 3GLs.

There are many different high-level languages. This is because each one was intended for a different purpose, and has appropriate pre-programmed functions or macros to speed up programming of applications in that area (Jones, 1986b). For example, FORTRAN has convenient statements for mathematical operations, and COBOL has convenient statements for business applications.

6.5.1 PRODUCTIVITY GAIN

High-level languages give improved productivity because of their greater power: the pre-programmed functions mean fewer statements need be coded. For example, Hogan (1986) stated that it typically takes three lines of Assembler code to generate the equivalent of one line of C. Similarly, Jones (1986b) gave the approximate conversion ratios – the number of machine instructions a given source statement will typically be expanded to – for a number of languages, while Boehm (1981) quoted the ratio of deliverable, executable machine instructions to delivered source instructions from three different organizations, also for a number of languages. These ratios for some of the more popular languages, and including some fourth-generation languages, to give a broader view, are given in Table 6.8. (Jones gave FOCUS, IDEAL, and RAMIS (Rapid Access Management Information System), as examples of database languages, but did not give any examples of query languages. Database languages, including these three, do typically include a powerful query capability.)

Basic Assembler language programs contain the same number of statements as the corresponding program written in machine language (Avison and Fitzgerald, 1988; Baron, 1988), so Table 6.8 also allows comparison between Assembler and high-level languages.

Table 6.8 The number of machine instructions a given source statement will expand to

	Jones (1986b)	Climis (1979)	TRW	RCA (1978)
C	2.5			3
ALGOL	3			
COBOL	3	5	4–6	2.5–3.5
FORTRAN	3	6–7	4–6	4–8
PASCAL	3.5	8	5–7	3–5
PL/1	4	5		7.5–13
RPG	4			
MODULA-2	4.5			
ADA	4.5			
BASIC	5			
Fourth-generation database languages	8			
APL	10	12		15
Query languages	20			
Spreadsheet languages	50			

These ratios show differences of 30% and more between different high-level languages. For example, using the figures given by Jones, PL/1 is (4/3=) 33% more powerful than COBOL; and BASIC, in turn, is (5/4=) 25% more powerful than PL/1. Together, this means that BASIC is no less than (5/3=) 66% more powerful than COBOL!

An interesting aspect here is that it is the functional side more than the data definition side which has experienced these improvements. For example, a typical Assembler program might consist of 70% executable statements, and 30% data definition statements. In COBOL, the corresponding proportions might be 60% and 40%, because COBOL has a more powerful set of executable functions, but the data definition method is not that different from Assembler (Jones, 1986b). However, the data area is addressed by, for example, the COPY statement in COBOL, and Data Dictionaries. (Dictionaries are external to the languages.)

Because fewer statements are required for high-level languages, coding time is reduced, but probably more important is that fewer errors are made (Weinberg, 1971; Brooks,

1975), which in turn reduces testing and debugging time, and maintenance time as well. Also, source listings are easier to understand (Jones, 1986b), thereby further reducing maintenance effort. High-level languages allow programmers to concentrate more on the problem to be solved, rather than on the hardware on which the solution will be run, or on language syntax (Glass, 1979; Weinberg, 1971; Baron, 1988).

Halstead (1977) defined a 'language level' metric, a formula for determining the power of a language, and therefore if one language is more powerful than another. He obtained the average values of

1.53 for PL/1
1.21 for ALGOL
1.14 for FORTRAN
0.88 for CDC assembly language

but there were large variances in these values (as there are in the machine instructions/source statement ratios of Table 6.8). For example, the values derived from some programs were over 50% higher than the average for that language, and for other programs over 50% lower (Conte *et al.*, 1986). Nevertheless, if we compare them with the machine instructions/source statement ratios in Table 6.8, then we find they are about half of Jones's values (which in turn are mostly lower than the figures given by the other authorities). For example, the Halstead ratio for PL/1 is (1.53:0.88 or) 1.7:1, compared to the corresponding Jones ratio of 4:1. (It is interesting, though, to note that an example in Jones (1986b) gives a 2:1 ratio for PL/1 for *total* effort, which agrees quite closely with the Halstead language level ratio for this language, and his examples for other languages suggest that this might be true for them as well.) However, other studies have failed to confirm that there is a 'language level' constant for any language; this is not surprising since the values depend not only on the language, but also on the nature of the problem being programmed, on the size of

Table 6.9 Productivity gain from high-level languages

Source	
Jones (1986b)[a, d]	–[c]
Martin (1979)[d]	1.3 to 1.6:1
Aron (1974)	2:1
Jones (1986b)[a, d]	2.4:1
Boehm (1973)[e]	about 3:1
Brooks (1975)	3:1 and 5:1
Graver *et al.* (1977)	4:1[c]
Arthur (1983)[e]	5:1[c]
Arthur (1983)[a]	> 5:1
Davis (1987a)[b, e]	up to 10:1
Average (approximate)	3:1

[a] COBOL.
[b] FORTRAN.
[c] maintenance.
[d] total development effort.
[e] programming effort only.

the program, and on the proficiency and style of the programmer (Conte *et al.*, 1986). Halstead's language level metric therefore suffers from similar problems to those of using LOC as a productivity measure.

High-level languages have various powerful time-saving features. COBOL, for example, has powerful verbs, like SEARCH and VALIDATE, a COPY library facility, and a REPORT WRITER (Yourdon *et al.*, 1979a).

The productivity gain of high-level languages over low-level languages is shown in Table 6.9. (Some authorities did not say what their ratios referred to, but most of the figures were explicitly stated to be for development, or this was implied by the context. The ratios for programming effort are only perhaps three times higher, on average, than those for total effort (about 5:1 compared to about 1:6:1) which indicates that, not surprisingly, languages have a much greater impact on programming productivity than on non-programming productivity.)

A zero maintenance (defect repair) gain is attributed to Jones, because the example he gave showed no reduction in the amount of time spent repairing defects during the maintenance phase. However, this is surprising,

as he stated that high-level languages lower the probability of making coding errors, and that they reduce the maintenance effort, as maintenance personnel 'can usually make more sense out of the listings' than they can with Assembler. Perhaps he believes that the quality assurance process during development is so effective that very few errors find their way into production programs irrespective of the language used, making differences in defect repair time much smaller and so more difficult to detect. In his example, the amount of time involved *was* small – the total defect repair time was only 2 man-months (in five years), and with only integers being shown, almost a halving of this amount would have been necessary to make a visible difference. Furthermore, this example emphasized development and the danger of using LOC as a productivity metric, so perhaps we should not pay too much attention to the maintenance effort figures in the example.

Albrecht (1979) found that PL/1 gave a 25% better programming productivity than COBOL. Similarly, Rubey *et al.*'s (1968) PL/1 study for the US Air Force showed differences of up to 2:1 in development time for the same program written in two different languages. (The combinations he tested were COBOL:PL/1, FORTRAN:PL/1, and JOVIAL:PL/1. The 3.5:1 productivity improvement obtained by Kosy using ECSS, a special-purpose language for simulating computer systems, mentioned earlier was obtained over one of Rubey's examples.) Similarly, the machine instructions/source statement expansion ratios in Table 6.8 show differences of 30% and more between different high-level languages. (These ratios refer to the number of statements required to write a program in a particular language, and do not necessarily convert directly into productivity differences. For example, even if a language which requires 30% fewer statements delivers a 30% higher productivity for the coding function – and evidence presented in Chapter 2 indicates that it does – it would not necessarily

Table 6.10 Comparison of full language with a subset thereof (Weinberg, 1971)

	Subset	Full language	Ratio
Average number of lines of code	319	243	1.3:1
Average number of test runs	41	32	1.3:1

also deliver a 30% higher productivity for the design function, and in fact may have little impact on this function. An example which illustrates this point was given in Table 2.2.) Nevertheless, it is interesting to note that the average productivity gain claimed in Table 6.9 (about 3:1) is similar to the average of the expansion ratios given by Jones (1986b) for 3GLs (about 4:1). The corresponding average of the figures given by the other three authorities quoted is about 6:1, which is similar to the average productivity gain of about 5:1 in Table 6.9 for the programming effort only. It should also be pointed out that different languages are optimized for different kinds of applications (Jones, 1986b), so it is not necessarily meaningful to compare productivity between them. When writing a program in a particular application area, you would use a language which was well suited to that type of application. If you used a different language, then – if it could do the job at all – it would deliver a much lower productivity than it was capable of in its own application area.

More than one version of a language may be provided by the same manufacturer, e.g. a powerful version for large computers, and a subset thereof for small computers. In an experiment by Weinberg (1971), the full version of a language (the OS/360 version of PL/1) delivered a productivity that was perhaps 30% higher than that delivered by the subset of the language (the DOS/360 version of PL/1) – Table 6.10. Such facts help explain the lack of unanimity in the productivity gains claimed for high-level languages which were tabulated earlier. Other reasons

are the advantages and disadvantages of specific languages, some of which are mentioned later.

6.5.2 COMPILERS

Before it can be run, a program written in a high-level language may have to be compiled. Programs written in traditional high-level languages such as COBOL, PL/1 and FORTRAN, generally require this extra step. Programs in BASIC are more likely to be interpreted at execution time, depending on the computer: some do not have a BASIC compiler.

Interpreters provide faster program development because (Dunn and Ullman, 1982; Cole *et al.*, 1979; Jones, 1986b):

- you do not have to compile the program before running it;
- they simplify debugging because
  - you are working with the original source code and not the machine language equivalent, so
  - the program being executed and displayed is identical to that coded and entered, so
  - you can see what is happening as the program runs, and
  - you may even be able to interrogate it and change it (interactive source language debugging – see section 6.7.2), and
  - it is possible to present the programmer with diagnostic messages relating to program errors that are much more pertinent to the debugging process; and
- they allow immediate prototyping of many functions (and therefore reduce the design effort and paperwork).

However, the program executes much more slowly than would a compiled one, e.g. PASCAL, which is usually compiled, runs perhaps ten times faster than interpreted BASIC (Varley and Graham, 1983). In one benchmark comparison, BetterBASIC, which is compiled, ran five times faster than interpreted BASIC (Summit, 1986). Similarly, Fox-BASE is claimed to run six times faster than dBASE III Plus (Fox, 1986). BASICA programs are claimed to run up to ten times faster once they have been compiled by Microsoft's QuickBASIC (Microsoft, 1986a) and dBASE III programs compiled by Clipper are claimed to run 2–20 times faster (Nantucket, 1986).

Despite the disadvantages of interpreters, BASIC and APL are often implemented as interpreters because they are typically used by students or mathematicians to solve a specific problem, and the program is then discarded, so development efficiency is more important than production efficiency (Dunn and Ullman, 1982).

More than one compiler may be provided for a language. PL/1 has a checkout compiler giving good error diagnostics, for use when debugging, and an optimizer compiler giving faster program execution, for use in production. Provision of interactive debugging (an extension of interactive programming), may require creating interpretive versions of languages which are usually compiled.

Some compilers include a few features considered to be technological aids (section 6.4) (Glass, 1979):

- the PL/1 checkout compiler provides additional information which speeds up debugging; and
- the ALGOL W compiler includes a test coverage analyser and an assertion checker.

More such features should be provided.

Van Tassel (1978) believes that a good debugging (checkout) compiler can often reduce debugging time by half. According to him, 70% of the programmer's time, and a high percentage of machine time, are spent debugging, so a good debugging compiler will soon pay for itself. However, his 70% is high compared to the other figures in Chapter 8.

6.5.3 ADVANTAGES AND DISADVANTAGES OF SOME 3GLs

Each language has its advantages and disad-vantages. Some, such as productivity differences, have already been mentioned; others are listed below.

High-level languages are usually 'typed', i.e. the definition of a field specifies if it is numeric, alphanumeric, etc. Almost all languages support the concept of data typing to some extent, but some, being stricter than others are said to be 'strongly typed'. Fairley (1985) defined no fewer than five levels of typing. A 'typeless' language would try to add a numeric field to a character field, whereas a strongly typed language only permits those functions that are appropriate to the field's type (Jones, 1986b). This forces the programmer to consider more carefully how data is to be defined and used within a program (Bell *et al.*, 1987). Studies have shown that programs written in strongly typed languages are clearer, more reliable, and more portable, but less flexible. For example, in an experiment by Gannon (1977), programs written in typed languages had only about half as many errors.

Some languages lend themselves more easily to the use of structured programming: ALGOL and PL/1 are more suitable than COBOL, which in turn is better than FORTRAN; Microsoft's new version of BASIC, QuickBASIC, is more structured than the older BASICA (Chapter 8).

BASIC is easy to learn – 'it seems to accord with the way a beginner sees things inside a computer' – and is often taught to beginners: 'For years, BASIC has been everyone's first language'; 'hobbyists, occasional computer users and the overwhelming population of schoolchildren often begin – and end – their programming experiences with BASIC' (Pountain, 1986a; Microsoft, 1986a; Baron, 1988). It does some things very well: its string-handling features 'are immeasurably superior to those in C or extended PASCAL'; and the error handling in Microsoft's version is easy to use, making it suitable for commercial applications (Pountain, 1986a). It is provided free with most micros, and although it was developed as long ago as

1964, a considerable amount of business software is still written in it on both mini-computers and micros – 'the language's popularity has generated vast amounts of software written in BASIC' (Baron, 1988).

Golding (1986) pointed out that the vast majority of people who use PCs for business applications use proprietary packages for spreadsheets, DBMSs, etc., and 'have probably never used BASIC nor ever will'. Furthermore, most of the language usage surveys I have seen either do not mention it at all, or give a low figure for it. For example, it is not mentioned in the Lientz *et al.* (1978) survey (of 69 organizations) and the Johnson (1980b) study (of nearly 3000 programs), while only 6% of the programmers in the Computer Services Association (1980b) survey (of nearly 400 organizations), and only 6% of the companies in the Comcon/FSA (1985) survey (of more than 200 companies), were using it. However, this may just be because those surveys are several years old, and the usage has probably increased in recent years with the growing number of PCs; or it may be because small organizations (which probably use it to a greater extent) are under-represented in some surveys, and few end users are included (Adams, 1981; Philippakis, 1977). The true usage of BASIC may therefore be much higher than indicated, and in fact, other and mostly more recent surveys *have* given higher figures for it: 34% of the over 400 companies in the 1985 CPL/P-E Corporate Services survey used it ('4GL is becoming a strong voice in SA industry – Steyn', *Computer Week*, 2 September 1985, p.17), and 40% of the respondents in the 1988 P-E Corporate Services survey were familiar with it (P-E Corporate Services, 1988).

Languages such as PL/1, which permit for example nested parentheses, are difficult to read and understand quickly (Jones, 1986b). This is because the large amount of information – and the complexity thereof – permitted in each statement, far exceeds the capacity of the average human temporary memory. This is one of the reasons programming can be so difficult.

FORTRAN gives access to hundreds of existing programs, and uses established skills (Prospero, 1986). The same is true of other established languages like COBOL.

There is a lack of standardization. Quite apart from there being many different languages, there are even differences within the same language:

- BASIC is very non-standard, e.g. the vendors of ZBasic claim it 'retains the old commands', but SORT does not work (Tottle, 1986), while PICK BASIC has extensions to enable it to deal with PICK's more powerful but more complex data structure (St. John Bate and Wyatt, 1986).
- Some of the extensions to the FORTRAN 5 compiler for the Sperry 1100/80 computer are not compatible with FORTRAN 77 (Gullo, 1986).
- There is an ANSI standard for COBOL, but many compilers have their own modifications and extensions (Ashley, 1980).

Improvements can be made to the languages:

- Compilers are designed to minimize coding time; they should rather be designed to speed up debugging (Boehm, 1973; Fong, 1973).
- Compilers could compute and print metrics such as Halstead's metrics and McCabe's complexity measures (Chapters 8 and 10), to give programmers direct feedback on how well written their programs are (Shneiderman, 1980).
- Programs can become 'smothered' in brackets, making them difficult to read, whereas different brackets – curly, round or square – would simplify them considerably (Winfield, 1986).
- Computer languages should be more natural, more like spoken languages: the right-to-left rule in APL is an example of an unnatural feature. However, it may be years before this can be achieved, as there are difficulties and pitfalls to be avoided.

For instance, natural languages lack power – an average of 7–20 English words are needed to specify the meaning of a single line of Assembler language source code – precision of meaning must not be lost, and ambiguity (which is common in speech) must be avoided (e.g. undefined adverbs and adjectives such as 'user-friendly') (Weinberg, 1971; Shneiderman, 1980; Jones, 1986b).

- When we read natural language text, we often pass over misspellings without noticing them, even when they make nonsense words, whereas similar errors usually cause compilers to produce error diagnostics – where what was meant may have been perfectly clear (Weinberg, 1971). Compilers should therefore attempt to correct errors (Chapter 8).

- Uniformity: 'The same things should be done in the same way wherever they occur' (Weinberg, 1971). For example, the operator '=' should not serve as both the assignment operator and the equality operator (Bell *et al.*, 1987) otherwise uncertainty results which leads to loss of time while the uncertainty is being resolved, and to errors, which can have more serious consequences than just lost time. (The Weinberg experiment quoted earlier, in which the full version of a language delivered a productivity that was perhaps 30% higher than that delivered by the subset of the language, was actually devised to test the effect of uniformity (or, rather, the lack thereof), and the lower productivity delivered by the subset of the language can be attributed, at least in part, to the lack of uniformity.)

In an experiment by Gannon and Horning (1975) comparing the TOPPS language with TOPPS II (an improved version of TOPPS, with a CASE statement added, with expressions evaluated from left to right instead of right to left, and so on), the improved version led to fewer programming errors, and the

errors were more easily corrected, though the differences were not spectacular.

6.5.4 NEWER HIGH-LEVEL LANGUAGES

In the last 20 years or so, a number of new high-level languages have been developed e.g. PASCAL, C, ADA and MODULA-2. The basic difference between them and the traditional languages is that they have been designed from the outset with software engineering principles in mind, so they should make it more difficult (though not impossible!) for programmers to write badly structured programs (Goodwin, 1986). The programs should therefore have the advantages of structured programming, such as fewer errors and easier maintenance (Chapter 8).

PASCAL

PASCAL, developed by Professor Niklaus Wirth, is used mainly as a teaching language (i.e. to teach programming), but also as an easier and faster alternative to Assembler for writing real-time programs and system software (Goodwin, 1986). For example, Cray Research's FORTRAN compiler, CFT 77, was written in PASCAL (Davis, 1987a). It is claimed to be excellent for education and for long-term projects, and to be useful for building large, complicated programs from many modules (Prospero, 1986; Bridger, 1986), and PASCAL programs are generally easy to maintain (Butgereit, 1983). There is a standard for it, but because it is weak at data handling and lacks enough features to handle really large applications, a number of extended and therefore non-standard versions have appeared (Goodwin, 1986). It has been criticized as being over-structured – 'an overly formal language that stifles creativity'; also because it can be used in 'tricky' ways, and is not portable (Bridger, 1986).

C

C is a small language (Marshall, 1987), more difficult to learn, but less restrictive, than PASCAL (Goodwin, 1986). It is powerful and flexible, combining features from both high- and low-level languages. It is easier to handle than Assembler, and is used for system software and software tools, e.g. UNIX, the CA-UNIVERSE DBMS, and the SAS statistical analysis system, are written in it. It provides fast execution: one software house tested their C-based accounting package on a 100-user system against similar systems written in COBOL, and found that their system was up to three times faster (van Tonder, 1988). C can run on microcomputers. It is becoming increasingly popular because of its portability and its association with UNIX, but if COBOL is declining (section 6.6.8) due to competition from 4GLs, it is difficult to see how an even lower-level language can reverse the trend.

C allows the programmer to get very close to the machine, e.g. for bit manipulation and input/output control, but has come in for some strong criticism (Goodwin, 1986; Baron, 1988; Prospero, 1986; Pountain, 1986a).

- It has been described as a language written by a professional programmer for professional programmers.
- It is structured, while at the same time violating some of the cardinal rules of structured programming.
- It is a 'dirty tricks' language which 'appeals to the hacker mentality'.
- It is very easy to write obscure programs, and to make a mistake.
- It is high on performance but low on safety, structure, portability and maintainability'.
- The cost of retraining programmers to become expert in it is considerable.

(The claim that it is low on portability is surprising, as portability is generally claimed to be one of C's strengths, and can probably be explained by the fact that it appeared in an advertisement for rival languages.) The work of Kernighan and Ritchie (1972) constituted a *de facto* standard, and there is now an ANSI standard.

Computer Innovations' (1986) C compiler, C86PLUS, incorporates AI.

ADA

This language was developed for the US Department of Defense. They were using a multitude of different languages, which created a severe problem, particularly for maintenance, so their objective was to standardize on a single, portable language, and thereby reduce their vast bill for software maintenance (Baron, 1988; Goodwin, 1986). However, none of the existing languages met all their requirements, so a new language was created. An additional goal was to produce a support environment for the language, and the ADA Programming Support Environment, APSE, has accordingly been developed. It contains debugging aids and project management support facilities, but has gaps, the most serious of which is that it surprisingly omits documentation support – surprising, because documentation is usually the largest cost element in the military projects for which it was intended (Jones, 1986b). The US Department of Defense has set a standard for it, and holds a trademark on it, and legally no one else can produce a subset, superset, or variant of any kind – and there is an ANSI standard as well (Baron, 1988).

ADA was intended for one specific type of system, embedded real-time, but it is an all-purpose language which is in use all over the world for all sorts of programs (Jones, 1986b) – an embedded system is one in which the computer is embedded within a larger mechanical system, such as a robot or a pilotless plane (Baron, 1988). ADA is a block-structured language, and it forces programmers to use top-down design (Goodwin,

1986) – a block-structured language permits individual statements to be grouped together and treated as a compound statement (Yourdon, 1975). In some languages, blocks are delimited with explicit words such as BEGIN and END (Yourdon *et al.*, 1979a). ADA is similar to PASCAL, but is five times bigger, so only (non-authorized) subsets were initially available on microcomputers (Goodwin, 1986; Baron, 1988). It supports concurrent programming and reusability, and has many other features, but this has led to criticism that it is too big, unwieldy, and inefficient (Jones, 1986b; Goodwin, 1986). It takes 3–13 months to train someone to be a competent ADA programmer: 'programmers must absorb an incredible amount of information. They must remember not only the keywords of the ADA language, but also a very sophisticated syntax. They are easily overwhelmed' (Schach, 1987; Perrella, 1986). Because of the type of system it was intended for, ADA was designed to produce highly reliable programs, e.g. it has strong data typing, but because of its size, programmers may unwittingly introduce errors into their programs.

Many experienced programmers believe that ADA is greatly superior to FORTRAN or COBOL (Zachmann, 1981). Cho (1987) compared ADA with five other languages: FORTRAN, COBOL, PL/1, PASCAL and LISP. Based on 12 criteria, reflecting support of software engineering principles (abstract data typing, information hiding, etc.), and type of application (scientific, commercial, etc.), ADA emerged the clear winner. Schach (1987, 1988) quoted a survey which revealed an average productivity improvement of 500%, and gave individual instances of 700% and above. By contrast, Martin (1982c) stated that, for ordinary commercial applications, COBOL gives a much higher productivity than ADA. Jones (1986b) stated that no productivity data was yet available, as no large projects had yet been completed, but he did give some estimated figures. These figures show a 30% *lower* productivity than

PL/1 initially, but that this will change to a 30% *higher* productivity when the full ADA support environment is available. However, his figures for ADA, but not those for PL/1, were based on a military system, for which the requirements are typically more stringent, with correspondingly lower productivity. Had he instead compared like with like, ADA would probably have fared better.

MODULA-2

This language, like PASCAL, was developed by Professor Wirth, and is an improved version of PASCAL: it has a wider set of functions and is better at handling data (Goodwin, 1986). It has features of both low- and high-level languages, and has been claimed to be able to do everything ADA can do: 'You could use it for anything' (Goodwin, 1986), but Baron (1988) disagrees – 'ADA is an exceptionally large language and able to do many things in programming that Modula-2, a much smaller language, cannot'. If Goodwin were correct, then MODULA-2 could replace all of the preceding languages. However, Baron's opinion is more plausible, as ADA compilers have hundreds of thousands of lines of code, whereas MODULA-2 compilers have only about 5000. MODULA-2 is therefore compact enough to run on a microcomputer.

MODULA-2 has been criticized for requiring too much care and attention to detail – e.g. correct capitalization, and tracing out of library genealogy – though Bridger (1986) believes this type of care and attention may be an advantage on very large programs, where dozens or hundreds of programmers are working on projects involving tens of thousands of lines of code, and the code must be modular and portable. MODULA-2 is easy to learn, and its modular structure is claimed to prevent inexperienced programmers from making potentially disastrous mistakes (Goodwin, 1986). For these reasons, it is used as a teaching language, and because it is new, this is its main use at present. A standard for it is being developed.

Comments

None of these languages has been widely accepted in commercial programming (Goodwin, 1986). It is not just a question of inertia, or because they are new, or even because of having to convert all an organization's existing programs – tools to do that automatically could be developed – but also a case of programmers not having enough time to undergo the necessary training. College-leavers know the new languages, but they lack commercial experience.

Use of these languages has been largely restricted to teaching, or to specific areas such as systems programming where Assembler was used previously. One fundamental criticism which has been levelled at them is that, while they may be elegant and aesthetically beautiful, they were designed by academics and do not reflect real commercial problems (Goodwin, 1986). This provides an interesting contrast with non-procedural languages (4GLs), which were mostly created by pragmatic craftsmen-programmers with no knowledge of computer science theory (Martin and McClure, 1985).

6.6   FOURTH-GENERATION LANGUAGES

One of the most exciting and talked-about developments in the DP world in recent years has been fourth-generation languages (4GLs). They have been described as 'the most significant direction that computers (hardware or software) are moving in at present, because the benefits are so enormous', and have been claimed to provide 'productivity beyond our wildest dreams' – 'this is the single greatest way of increasing people productivity,' 'you can prototype, refine, test, and release an application for production in a single interactive session'

(Winer, 1978; Thomson, 1983; Cincom, 1986). Productivity improvements of 10:1 are often claimed, and some of the claims are higher than 100:1 (Table 6.13).

On the other hand:

- 4GLs have also been described as a 'marketing gimmick', for which 'exaggerated claims' are being made by suppliers (Cullum, 1983; Davis, 1983a; Campbell, 1978);
- they cannot be used for all types of program;
- there are plenty of reports of bad experiences (Schach, 1988);
- one organization, Playtex, obtained an 80:1 productivity increase over COBOL by using IBM's ADF (Application Development Facility), but it has used COBOL for subsequent applications because ADF did not fit them well (Schach, 1988; Martin, 1985), and other organizations have abandoned ADF because of its poor human factoring (analysts find it difficult to learn), and because it is limited in the screen dialogues it can generate (Martin, 1982a);
- substantial training is needed to use some generators (Martin, 1982a);
- to achieve the high productivity, changes in DP management and methodology are needed (Martin, 1982a);
- and a comparison of the ratio (value of sales / number of DP staff) for two organizations quoted by Martin (1981), gave a 3:1 advantage to *conventional* programming methods.

4GLs – including the above criticisms – will therefore be examined here, to see if they are as good as they are claimed to be.

6.6.1   DESCRIPTION

Definition

What are 4GLs? Jones (1986b) says the term is ambiguous and lacking in true meaning. Any very high-level language, file utility (such as reformats and prints), program generator, etc., can be classified as a 4GL. For example, with a file utility, a program can be quickly and easily generated with just a few parameters. However, it may be difficult to draw a dividing line, e.g. between a preprocessor and a program generator. (The former would typically be third-generation, and the latter fourth-generation.) For the purposes of this study, any product which gives a large gain in productivity compared to the high-level languages like COBOL, will be treated as a 4GL. Martin (1982a) is more specific: a language must give productivity at least ten times higher than COBOL to qualify as a 4GL.

Other authorities specify requirements such as ease of learning, security, interface to other systems, and providing users with a total solution (Jones, 1983a; Dean, 1983).

None of the products currently available meets all of these criteria. For example, there is as yet no single language that can meet the needs of a query-type end-user facility and the 'nuts and bolts' application development (Hymers, 1983). Organizations are therefore likely to use a mixture of fourth-generation products, and probably a mixture of fourth-generation and conventional products, for some time to come. Furthermore, if we look at the 10:1 productivity criterion alone, then only query languages and spreadsheets can supply such a large decrease in the total effort i.e. including requirements analysis and other non-programming functions (Jones, 1986b).

Classification

Many different software products come under the classification 'fourth-generation'. Martin (1982c) counted 300 of them, and the number has probably increased considerably since then with the rapid growth in their popularity: 'We will see new fourth generation languages popping up every month or two' (van der Meer, 1985). Jones (1986b)

Table 6.11 Classification of fourth-generation languages (Martin 1982b)

Type	Approximate proportion (%)
Query language	80
Report generator	70
Graphics generator	10
Application generator	20
High level programming	30

counted 50 program and application generators alone.

Table 6.11 shows the different types of products (Martin, 1982b). An alternative classification is (Schussel, 1986):

- products usable by end users (mainly query and report languages), e.g. FOCUS, RAMIS II, and NOMAD2;
- products for use by DP staff, e.g. NATURAL, MANTIS, ADS/OnLine, and IBM's CSP (Cross System Product), for building more complex applications.

As can be seen from Table 6.11, most 4GLs are query languages or report generators. Some of the products, e.g. EASYTRIEVE and FOCUS, belong to more than one category, which is why the total is greater than 100%. Apart from products such as MAPPER and NATURAL, Martin's list also includes less obvious items such as APL, RPG, EASYTRIEVE, and utilities for one of IBM's minicomputers, the S/34. Other authorities have also classified such products as 4GLs (van der Poel, 1982; Macaskill, 1983). Their inclusion can be justified since they do possess fourth-generation characteristics: they can create significant programs with a minimum of effort, e.g. very large productivity improvements (up to 20:1) claimed for APL are given in Table 6.13 below.

It is apparent from the variety of different types of product, that the fourth-generation is not merely a number of high-level languages, but a total environment, like the software environments described earlier.

History

Although the fourth-generation was heralded as if it were new, the inclusion of RPG, etc. shows that it was not:

- RPG was originally developed in 1964 (Baron, 1988);
- very high-level languages, which enabled an analyst to generate a 10 000 word program in about 10 minutes, existed in the mid-1950s (Boehm, 1973);
- IBM's AS (Application System) was first released in about 1975 (IBM, 1983);
- EASYTRIEVE was being used long before the term 'fourth-generation' was widely used, and 4000 organizations were using it in 1983 (Software Catalogue, *The 1983 S.A. Computer Users Handbook*, Johannesburg: Systems Publishers (Pty) Ltd, pI1–94).

Extent of use

McCracken (1978) predicted that more than 50% of all application programs processed by computers in the mid-1980s would be developed using non-procedural languages. ('Non-procedural' means that the programmer need specify only *what* is to be done, *not how* to do it. Many 4GLs are non-procedural.) However, his time-scale may have been a little optimistic. According to Scott (1986), non-procedural languages currently utilized only about 10% of all CPU time. (By comparison, knowledgeable observers have estimated that as much as 25% of the world's available machine cycles run with code generated by some form of FORTRAN (Davis, 1987a).) However, Scott added that current predictions were that, within five years, this would increase to approximately 50%, and that probably 70–80% of all programs processed would be written in non-procedural languages. (The proportion of programs is higher than the proportion of CPU time because programs written in non-procedural languages are typically smaller and are run less frequently, and these factors more than offset the lower efficiency of the

languages; see sections 6.6.2, 6.6.3 and 6.6.5.)

Of the respondents in the 1988 P-E Corporate Services survey, 73% were familiar with a 4GL (P-E Corporate Services, 1988).

Of the more than 200 companies in the Comcon/FSA (1985) survey, 37% were using a 4GL: 18% of the companies did more than 50% of their programming in a 4GL; 7% did more than 75%; and 2% used a 4GL for all their programming. These figures are not sufficient to determine the overall usage of 4GLs, but at a rough guess, it may have been around one-third of all programming.

According to many surveys (Lientz *et al.*, 1978; Computer staff become scarcer, *Computronics*, 6 February 1980, pp. 1, 8; Hoard, 1981; Comcon/FSA, 1985), the early 4GL RPG was the second or third most widely-used language, with perhaps 10–15% of the market. Furthermore, according to Adams (1981), small organizations are under-represented in some surveys. As RPG is probably used much more extensively in small organizations than in large ones, the true usage may be much higher, and some other surveys *have* given a much higher figure for it, e.g. 34% of the 439 respondent companies in the 1985 CPL/P-E Corporate Services survey used it (4GL is becoming a strong voice in SA industry – Steyn, *Computer Week*, 2 September 1985, p. 17), while 45% of the DP managers in the Dick (1980) survey used it as their main language. This is plausible, as there were reportedly more than 30 billion lines of RPG application code, apparently for IBM System/3x applications alone (Pine, 1989). By comparison, it was estimated that there were 70 billion lines of COBOL code in use worldwide (Gullo, 1987). Martin (1985) stated there were about 75 000 mainframe installations worldwide, and about 80% of them used COBOL. An average mainframe installation had about 1.5 million lines of code, giving a total of about 116 billion LOC, of which about 77 billion were COBOL. (By contrast, Jones (1986b) estimated that there

Table 6.12   Extent of use of various 4GLs

4GL	Source	Sales	Users
Lotus 1-2-3	Appunn (1988)		>3 000 000
PC/FOCUS	Myers (1987)	60 000	
AS	IBM (1983)	20 000	
SYSTEM BUILDER	(1990)[1]	9000	
SAS	(1986a)[2]	8500	2 000 000 (Pinella, 1990a)
MANTIS	Macfie (1988)	8000 (sites)	
EASYTRIEVE PLUS	McCusker (1991)	7500 (sites)	
FOCUS	Myers (1987)	2600	
NATURAL	Software AG (1986c)	2200 (organizations)	
RAMIS	Schatz (1987)	1200	
IDEAL	Applied Data Research (1986)	750 (companies)	
NOMAD	Schatz (1987)	300–400	>100 000 (D & B, 1987)

[1] System builder sales top 9000, *Computer Week*, 9 April 1990, p. 8.
[2] The software buyers' guide, *Computer Mail*, 31 October 1986, pp. 3–53.

would only be 25 billion LOC in the world in the year 2000 – see Chapter 2.)

However, APL, and more modern 4GLs, have not fared as well in these surveys. For example, none of them was mentioned in the Lientz *et al.* (1978), Dick (1980), Adams (1981), Hoard (1981) and Garcia-Rose and Fosdick (1990) surveys; while APL was only used by 1% of the companies in the above-mentioned 1985 CPL/P-E Corporate Services survey; and MARK IV, the only 4GL mentioned, was used for just 2% of the programs in the Johnson (1980b) study of nearly 3000 commercial programs comprising nearly 2 million lines of code. However, few end users are included in some surveys, so the true usage of APL and other similar languages, may also be much higher than indicated (Philippakis, 1977). Broader surveys, containing a more representative cross-section of the DP industry, or more recent surveys, may therefore paint a different picture.

The managing director of one training organization reported that 40% of his students never write a COBOL program after they leave, because more and more organizations are moving to 4GL/DBMS environments (van der Meer, 1985). I recently conducted a survey of job advertisements (section 6.6.8),

which showed a slightly higher demand for 4GL skills than high-level language skills.

The number of installed copies of some of the better-known 4GLs, or the number of organizations or users reportedly using them, is given in Table 6.12. In the case of products running on multi-user operating systems, the number of users may be more significant than the number of installations; while the number of copies that have been installed will generally be higher than the number of organizations using them, as some organizations purchase multiple copies.

The AS figure includes bureau users. The number of SAS installations does not include PCs, but the number of SAS users does.

In addition, between 70 000 and 200 000 installations, and between 650 000 and 1 300 000 people, used PICK's ACCESS 4GL (Table 6.6). FOCUS and PC/FOCUS together had a total of 350 000 users (Myers, 1987). Over three-quarters of a million people were using a Unisys 4GL (LINC and MAPPER) (Unisys, 1988b).

Benefits

Several benefits are claimed for 4GLs, the major one being improved productivity, which is examined in detail later in this chapter. Another major benefit is 'user programming'. The fourth-generation has been described as 'application development without programmers' and 'end-user-driven computing' (Martin, 1982a), because, in an increasing number of cases, programmers are not needed – systems are created either by the users working alone, or by users and systems analysts working together. Non-programmers can develop simple, quality software for themselves (Sandler, 1989). With high-level languages (3GLs), only a small proportion of end users could do their own programming. It is 4GLs, particularly spreadsheets and query languages, which allow many end users to carry out some of their own DP needs (Jones, 1986b; Martin, 1982a). Arthur (1983) predicted that non-procedural languages would someday make everyone into a computer programmer or analyst.

An analogy has been drawn with the automobile industry: 50 years ago, the widespread use of chauffeurs was replaced by users driving their own motor cars (Henkel, 1983). The analogy illustrates one reason cost savings may be expected. It has been calculated that a user can write his own programs for one-third the cost of having a programming department do it for him (Microprocessors – choosing wisely! *Computronics*, 14 May 1980, p. 3).

Various other benefits, some of which contribute to the improved productivity, are claimed for 4GLs (Duffy, 1983; Murray, 1983; Wetherbe and Berrisford, 1979):

- fewer errors (see below);
- peace of mind because of the reduction in errors;
- greater user involvement;
- a marked improvement in relations between DP and users;
- better staff motivation (because of the better relationship);
- prototyping is quicker and easier if a 4GL is used to create the prototype;

- improved requirements definition (because of the better relationship and prototyping), provided sloppiness (see disadvantages, below) does not ensue;
- fewer modifications (because of the improved requirements definition), provided sloppiness does not ensue;
- data is more accessible – one organization claimed that accessible data had tripled (Software AG, 1986b).

The programs which are generated are largely error-free, thereby reducing the amount of time-consuming testing and debugging. This is especially true where the program consists of non-procedural code operating off a DBMS with a data dictionary. Martin and McClure (1985) gave an example of a one-line program written in NOMAD:

List by customer average (invoice total)

which requires no testing. The 4GL decides the report layout and page skips. You can see if the program is correct by just looking at the output. This is an extreme example, but Martin and McClure gave a table showing what tests are necessary under what circumstances.

Easier maintenance is another frequently claimed benefit, but some authorities disagree; see section 6.6.3.

Department structure

4GLs can be used with any of the DP department structures discussed in Chapter 3, but may lead to a change in the structure, namely the creation of a new section, the IC, to help end users generate applications using 4GLs.

6.6.2 PRODUCTIVITY IMPROVEMENT

The basic reason for the productivity gains achievable with 4GLs, is that much of the work is performed by the computer, i.e. it is automated. For example, many of the

Table 6.13 Global averages: claimed productivity improvements from 4GLs

Source	Language	Ratio	
Forage (1986)		1.3:1	specifications
Duffy (1983)		1.4:1–1.7:1	productivity
Forage (1986)		2:1	implementation
Winer (1978)		2:1–10:1	programming/debugging
Arthur (1983)		2:1–10:1	productivity
Jones (1986b)	APL	3:1	total development effort
[1] (1983)	Speed II	5:1	labor costs
Jones (1986b)		8:1	total development effort
van der Poel (1981)		up to 10:1	programmer productivity
ICL (1983)	Application Master	10:1	development time-scale
Parikh (1984)		10:1	productivity
Martin (1982a)	database user languages	10:1	programmer productivity
Software AG (1986c)	NATURAL	at least 10:1	development time
Applied Data Research (1986)	IDEAL	10:1–15:1	development time
Martin (1982b)	query languages	10:1–50:1	productivity
Matos and Jalics (1989)		17:1	(source code characters)
Unisys (1988a)		up to 20:1	productivity
Macaskill (1983)	APL	20:1	programmer productivity
IBM (1983)	AS	20:1–100:1	productivity
Martin (1983b)	Application Builder	50:1	development time-scale

[1] Software packages, *Computer Systems in Southern Africa*, April 1983, pp. 37–44.

languages are 'non-procedural', i.e. the programmer (whether a professional programmer or an end user) need specify only *what* is to be done, *not how* to do it. They represent a move toward natural languages (An answer to software crisis, *Computing S.A.*, 11 September 1981, pp. 1–2).

Additional reasons (which do not apply in all circumstances) are:

• bug-free code, prototyping, etc., as discussed earlier;
• there is a synergistic effect – 4GLs generally work with a DBMS, and so benefit from the productivity gains delivered by DBMSs, just as DBMSs benefit from the productivity gains delivered by 4GLs: 'most of the products for application development without programmers give greater productivity if they are linked to a data base' (Martin, 1982a); 'only NOMAD2 can unleash the full power of SQL' (D & B Computing Services Inc., 1986);

• transparency: the user need not know how the data is structured, whether the job will be run in batch mode or on-line, nor which operating system will be used (Davis, 1983a).

Claimed productivity improvements from 4GLs are given in Table 6.13. Additional information is included to make the figures more useful. In particular, if the claim refers to a specific 4GL, then the name of that 4GL is given. Most of the claims are the productivity gain compared to COBOL, and a few are the gain compared to FORTRAN or BASIC, but some of the authorities did not specify which language they were comparing against, though they were probably comparing against third-generation languages in general. In any case, the productivity differences between the various third-generation languages are generally much smaller than the differences between 3GLs and 4GLs, so which 3GLs were used in the comparisons

Table 6.14 Individual cases: claimed productivity improvements from 4GLs

Source	Language	Ratio	
Canadian Broadcasting Corp. (ADR/IDEAL, 1986)	IDEAL	1.3:1 and 5:1	experienced programmers
Krupp MaK Engineering (Software AG, 1986b)	NATURAL	2:1	development time
AT&T[2]		3:1	
Unicorn[1]	Speed II	6:1	productivity
(Boehm, 1973)	AED	8:1	man-months
Canadian Broadcasting Corp. (ADR/IDEAL, 1986)	IDEAL	10:1–20:1	inexperienced programmers
Chorafas (1986)	INGRES and RBF	18:1 and 26:1	excluding systems analysis
Martin (1982b)	FOCUS	>26:1	for a complete system
ASEA (Cowpar, 1983)	AS	30:1 and 120:1	excluding systems analysis

[1] Software packages, *Computer Systems in Southern Africa*, April 1983, pp. 37–44.
[2] The quest for zero defect software, *Computer Week*, 13 February 1989, p. 21.

has not been indicated. Most of the claims are the productivity gain for program development, but many of the authorities did not specify which functions they were comparing. In particular, it is generally not clear if systems analysis time was included in the development effort. Maintenance productivity is discussed separately later.

Some of the organizations in the Forage survey obtained more than 10-fold increases in development productivity.

Martin (1982a) claimed his improvement of 10:1 was 'not uncommon', which implies that in many (most?) cases, the improvement was lower.

In a PC-based experiment by Matos and Jalics (1989), comparing seven 4GLs (with their associated DBMSs) against COBOL (with ISAM files), the COBOL source code was about 17 times as large as the average 4GL code. It takes about the same amount of time to write a line of source code, no matter which language you use (see Chapter 2), so it is likely that the average productivity of the seven 4GLs in this experiment was around 17 times higher than that of COBOL, at least for the coding function. Similarly, the size range among the 4GLs was 2:1, indicating that some are twice as powerful as others. How-ever, these ratios may reflect differences in the power of the DBMSs, as well as differences in the power of the 4GLs. (The 4GLs in this experiment were CONDOR, FOCUS, INFORMIX, ORACLE, PARADOX, RBASE, and dBASE.)

Table 6.14 lists individual cases: Speed II is supplied by Seattle-based TOM (The Office Manager); AED is the Automated Engineering Design programming system; RBF is the INGRES Report by Form language; and AS is IBM's Application System.

The Speed II claims appear to refer to the total development effort. The Chorafas figures apply to an unskilled novice, and include training time. The 18:1 ratio is for output functions, and the 26:1 for table and file management. Martin's FOCUS ratio was obtained from a large bank holding corporation. It appears to refer to the programming functions only.

Program and application generators

A generator is a program which accepts parameters and converts them into program source code, but there are no agreed definitions of the terms 'program generator' and 'application generator' (Jones, 1986b), and

Table 6.15 Rate at which source statements are generated

Source	Generator	Statements per day
Jones (1986b)		30
Chiswell (1986)	CA-Promacs	1000
Black (1979)		2000
[2] (1975)	COBOL AUTO-PROGRAMMER	2400
Mullin (1978)[1]	System 2170	5000

[1] System 2170 is an audit retrieval package.
[2] Generative software – a local development, *System Stelsels*, November, 1975, p. 32.

most authorities seem to use only one or other of them, i.e. they do not distinguish between them, or even between them and ordinary 4GLs. Here we do not attempt to distinguish between them, but, in this section, only those products which were described as generators are included, whereas the other sections cover both generators and ordinary 4GLs.

What productivity gain is provided by generators? One way to determine this is to consider the reduction in the amount of code required, and another is to consider the rate at which source statements are generated.

Applications developed with American Management Systems' Generation Five application generator require 50–75% less code than applications written in COBOL (because much of the typical 'housekeeping' code is provided automatically by the generator) (Grochow, 1981). Figures given by Jones (1986b) indicate that only one-fifth as many source lines need to be coded when using a generator. These figures suggest a gain in coding productivity of 2:1 to 5:1. However, the impact of generators on other functions in the software life-cycle is likely to be different. The impact on testing and debugging may be higher, because fewer errors will probably be made, but the impact on functions such as requirements analysis may be much smaller.

Alternatively, we can consider the rate at which source statements are generated (Table 6.15). In each case, COBOL code was produced. Where the claim referred to a particular generator, its name is given.

The Jones figure is considerably lower than any of the others. It was based on the total effort, i.e. the number of generated statements was divided by the total development time (including requirements analysis, management, etc.). However, even if only coding time is used, his figure is raised to just 200 statements per day, which is still well short of the others. The opposite adjustment should be made to at least some of the other figures, as the COBOL AUTOPROGRAMMER figure includes only programmer time, and the Mullin (1978) figure apparently does not even include testing and debugging (which explains why it is the highest of all the figures). However, these adjustments are smaller in magnitude, and therefore cannot explain such a large discrepancy. (The percentages in Table 8.28 indicate that testing and debugging typically consume about as much time as detailed design and coding. Therefore, if testing and debugging time were incorporated into those statements-per-day ratios which do not already include it, it would only halve them.)

The higher tabulated figures (1000–5000 statements per day) represent apparent productivity gains of around 20–400:1 over the more typical rate of 15–50 (see Chapter 2). This is the apparent productivity improvement provided by generators. However, there is a flaw in this method of calculation, as program generators tend to be verbose: they 'create reams of computer code' (Wright, 1983). In the example given by Jones (1986b), each coded statement generated, on average, seven statements (and the corresponding figures derived from other authorities are even higher: 20:1 (Chiswell, 1986), 25:1 (Mullin, 1978), and 40:1 (COBOL AUTOPROGRAMMER)). However, we cannot use these ratios by themselves, as fewer source lines need to be coded when using a generator, i.e. the generated code was not seven times

Table 6.16 Claimed true productivity gains

Source	Generator	Ratio	
Johnson (1980b)		1.1:1	report generators
Johnson (1980b)		1.3:1	application generators
Kapur (1980)		1.5–1.8:1	program generators
Arthur (1983)		1.5–3:1	program/application generators
Jones (1986b)		2.4:1	program generators
Chiswell (1986)	CA-Promacs	up to 4:1	program generator
Grochow (1981)	Generation Five	8 or 9:1	application generator
Appleton (1983)		9:1	program generator
Edwards (1983b)	ALL[1]	10:1	application generator
Parikh (1984)		10:1	program generators
Martin (1982a)	ADF and DMS[2]	10:1	application generators
Martin (1982a)	ADF[2]	10–50:1	application generator
Martin (1982b)		10–50:1	report/application generators
John Deere Inc. (Holtz, 1979)	ADF[2]	13:1	application generator
Playtex (Martin, 1982b)	ADF[2]	80:1	application generator

[1] ALL is McDonnell Douglas Corporation's Application Language Liberator.
[2] ADF and DMS are IBM's Application Development Facility and Development Management System.

longer than the program would have been if it had been written in COBOL: in fact, it was only 1.4 times longer. (This is very similar to the expansion ratio in an example in Martin (1985). The COBOL code generated by MIMER/PG was (428/368 =) 1.2 times longer than the version coded directly in COBOL.) This suggests that the apparent productivity gains of around 20–400:1 should be reduced by a factor of 1.4, giving a true gain of around (20/1.4 =) 14:1 to (400/1.4 =) 286:1. This is still a very large gain, and it was derived by applying the 1.4 expansion ratio from Jones to productivity ratios derived from the statements-per-day rates given by Chiswell and Mullin. If the generators referred to by the latter authorities were more verbose than the one Jones had in mind, then a (much?) larger factor than 1.4 should have been applied, and the calculated productivity gain would have been correspondingly lower. Furthermore, this method, like the first, refers primarily to the gain in coding productivity: the gain (if any) for the other functions in the software life-cycle may be very different.

The two methods used above produced vastly different answers (2:1–5:1, and 14:1–286:1, respectively), and both applied particularly to the coding function. What, therefore, is the true coding productivity gain, and what is the overall gain?

Various authorities have made claims (Table 6.16). The Johnson ratios are the improvement in total LOC per man-day of programming personnel during the implementation phase. However he also pointed out that application generators can be used for prototyping, which implies that they can increase systems analysts' productivity as well. The Arthur ratio may apply to analysts as well as programmers. The Jones ratio is for the total development effort. The Chiswell ratio refers to programmer time. The Grochow ratio is for programmers only: systems analyst effort was also reduced, but the amount was not specified. The Edwards ratio is for the development effort, and includes prototyping time, i.e. some requirements analysis and even system design time. Martin (1982a) stated that his claimed improvement of 10:1 was 'not uncommon', which implies that in many (most?) cases, the improvement was lower. His higher improvement, of 10–

50:1, can only be achieved by experts ('acrobats'). The 13:1 quoted for John Deere was the average value. The gains obtained ranged from 2:1 to 46:1. They probably refer to programmer productivity only. The Playtex ratio was derived from the increase in the number of programs installed per man-month, which implies a significant increase in systems analyst productivity as well as in programmer productivity.

Another consideration is that the quality of the generated code 'can be pretty rough' (Pountain, 1986a), making it difficult to maintain. Pountain complained that he once inspected the BASIC output from a 'much-touted' program generator, and found that the code was not only unreadable but barely recognizable as BASIC.

General comments

The following comments apply to all three sets of productivity ratios given above, namely the global averages (Table 6.13), individual cases (Table 6.14), and program and application generators (Table 6.16).

Average

The average of the figures is about 10 or 20:1.

Discrepancies

The figures cover a wide range – 1.1:1 to 120:1. Several factors could account for this, such as variations in power between different 4GLs, and 'sloppy' work; see section 6.6.5.

No adequate standard of comparison

Short of doing a job twice, possibly using different teams, there is no adequate standard of comparison for measuring productivity, either among 4GLs, or between them and conventional methods (though some possibilities were suggested in Chapter 2, and function points in particular make it easier to compare productivity using both

conventional languages and 4GLs (Garnham, 1988)). Most of the given ratios are probably therefore just estimates – for example, some of the data making up the Holtz (1979), Cowpar (1983) and Chorafas (1986) figures, were based on estimates – and estimation methods, as discussed in Chapter 8, tend to be unreliable.

Variations between different fourth-generation products

It is probable that some 4GLs are better and more powerful than others, especially as some are old and others are new, but there are hundreds of different products, so a detailed comparison is outside the scope of this study. In any event, the products are of different types.

- Some are just query languages; others are fully-fledged programming languages.
- Some are just screen design aids; others are prototyping aids.
- Some are intended for use by professional programmers, others for use by end users.

This makes comparison difficult, but the given figures indicate that the gains from end user languages such as FOCUS and AS are much higher than those provided by professional programmer languages such as NATURAL and IDEAL, though this could just mean that they were used on simpler programs.

Machine size

Most computers are small, yet many 4GLs (64% in the Duffy (1983) survey, and 82% in the Forage (1986) survey) run only on larger machines. None of the early 4GLs used PCs (Martin, 1985). Just as Weinberg (1971), in an experiment referred to earlier, found a 30% lower productivity from the subset of a language – a subset intended for smaller mainframe computers – so the 4GLs on small computers are probably less powerful – and therefore give lower productivity – than those on larger machines. (Similarly, the COCOMO model uses a productivity difference of 10% between maxicomputer tools and minicomputer tools, and 24% between maxicomputer tools and microprocessor tools (Boehm, 1981).) This would significantly reduce the productivity gains from 4GLs for the industry as a whole.

Although the products available for small machines will become more powerful (Myers, 1982), so will those for larger machines, therefore a differential will remain.

Other functions in software development

The tabulated values refer mostly to programming. However, Brooks (1987) believes that the difficult part of building software is the requirements, specification, and design functions. Translating them into code, and testing the code, is much easier. What therefore is the effect of 4GLs on these other functions? Opinion is divided.

- Requirements analysis should be speeded up because of prototyping, and because users will generate many systems themselves and they already know their own requirements: 'end users know the subtleties of what they want to accomplish' (Martin, 1981).
- Chorafas (1986) estimated that the productivity of systems analysis is increased by nearly 40:1, which is double his estimate for the gain in programming productivity.
- Martin (1982b) believes there is a significant effect on documentation, because formal specifications are not usually created, and the systems may be self-documenting.
- By contrast, according to Johnson (1980b), documentation is only about 25% as detailed as that provided for by COBOL, FORTRAN, or PL/1.
- Jones (1986b) stated that program and application generators were most effective for internal design and coding, and had

little impact elsewhere, e.g. on external user documentation and external design.
- Similarly, Jones stated that 4GLs produce a dramatic reduction in design time – often, very little flowcharting or internal design is required other than defining the data, and new 4GLs such as database query languages and application generators, come very close to eliminating the design phase: the design proceeds by simply doing the program, or at least a prototype thereof – but other activities, such as requirements analysis, 'remain significant'.

Even with the most optimistic view, non-programming tasks do not fall away completely, not even when users generate the systems themselves, so there is a limit to the overall productivity improvement attainable. Furthermore, the reduction in time spent on tasks such as documentation can aggravate the chaos and maintenance problems (see sections 6.6.3 and 6.6.5), which emphasizes the need for control.

Different types of program

A 4GL can have a significant impact on productivity 'if the application is suited for such a method' (Jones, 1986b; Parikh, 1984). Martin and McClure (1985) warned that some 4GLs can only generate certain well-defined classes of application. Johnson (1980b) warned that 4GLs 'can be a disaster for systems that are not simplistic in nature'. Programmers are then 'forced to play tricks' with the language to accomplish the objective. Also, with a non-procedural language, you are confined to the built-in structure of the language, which may not be appropriate for some of the programs in the system (Williams, 1986a).

The preponderance of query languages and report generators amongst 4GLs, and the emphasis on prototyping, suggest that the productivity gains differ from one type of program to another, e.g. it seems likely that 4GLs give higher productivity gains on report-type programs than on, say, programs with complex logic and edit programs. Most 4GLs exhibit an impressive COBOL-to-4GL ratio (e.g. a program needing 1000 lines of COBOL might be written in only 50 lines with the 4GL) for certain activities such as report generation, but a low ratio for other activities, such as complex logic, and vendors tend to select applications that demonstrate the highest ratio (Martin, 1985). Edit programs are frequently very large and complicated because of the many validation checks and exception conditions built into them (Lim, 1980; Jackson, 1975). Programmable data-entry machines can relieve some of this burden (especially if the keypunch operators do the programming), and screen format generators may incorporate validation checks for input data (e.g. if they operate from an active data dictionary), thereby also relieving part of the burden, but nevertheless, this factor may significantly reduce the overall productivity gains achievable.

Similarly, the use of the terms 'complete' (Martin, 1982b) and 'fully implemented' systems (Davis, 1983a) by some when claiming gains suggests that other claims may refer to only portions of systems, e.g. to some types of program such as report programs, or to simple programs – 'you would not program the moonshot in RPG or ADF'; 'the problem with most 4GLs is they're finished before you are' – or to some functions in the software life-cycle, such as coding (Martin, 1981; Holtz, 1979; Cullum, 1983; Relational Database Systems Inc., 1986). Even the claim for a 'complete' system appears to refer to the programming functions only.

As an illustration, in one case, an oil exploration firm implemented a relational-type DBMS, with on-line capabilities and query facilities, to process a geophysical database (Wetherbe and Berrisford, 1979). It took them two days to develop the initial prototype, several days to enhance it into an effective output (information retrieval) system, and one-and-a-half *months* to deve-

lop the input system, to edit amendments and update the database. Even if this is an atypical case – it occurred some years ago, and subsequent improvements in 4GLs may have rendered the figures out of date – it does serve as a caution when interpreting the claimed improvements.

In some cases, the 4GL would be able to handle the task, but the finished program would execute too slowly. For example, 'programs performing complex calculations would be more efficient if they were structured in COBOL' (Ford, 1983). (Execution speed is discussed later in section 6.6.5.) In other cases, the 4GL would not be able to handle the task at all (e.g. if it was just a screen design aid, or a query language without an updating capability). Either way, you would have to change to a different, and probably lower-level, language (Relational Database Systems Inc., 1986).

However, there is evidence – though some of it is not impartial – that this limitation is not severe; most of the work in ordinary commercial installations can probably be done using 4GLs.

- Most users of IBM's System/32 computer should be able to achieve 70–80% of their programming runs by simply using the powerful Source Entry and Data File Utilities (IBM, 1976).
- The GENASYS system generator was able to generate eight out of the ten programs in a system described by Lite (1975).
- Bearley (1980) quotes a case in which 4GLs were able to handle all of an installation's requirements.
- INFORMIX (from Relational Database Systems) is claimed to be able to handle every programming task, and in their advertisements they acknowledge that even competing products can handle about 90% (Relational Database Systems Inc., 1986).
- Some users of MANTIS report that they

use it for all new on-line development work (Cincom, 1986).

The average of these figures is about 90%, but they may not be typical. Vendors in particular are likely to publicize the highest figures available in an attempt to sell more of their products. It is therefore useful to compare the above figures with those from the Comcon/FSA (1985) survey, in which only 2% of the organizations used a 4GL for all their programming, only 7% did more than 75% of their programming in a 4GL, and so on (section 6.6.1). The estimate based on this survey was that 4GLs may have been used for around one-third of all the programming in the surveyed organizations at the time of the survey. However, this does not necessarily mean that one-third is the maximum possible for the average organization. In fact, it is possible that usage will increase at most of the surveyed organizations.

4GLs which have procedural features, such as NATURAL and IDEAL, offer enough detail control to solve almost any problem that can be handled by COBOL (Schussel, 1986). These languages usually also have performance features which allow them to be used in applications supporting hundreds of simultaneous terminal users and high volumes, whereas, from a performance point of view, FOCUS, RAMIS II and NOMAD2 are more suitable for departmental systems.

Design restrictions

Limitations of a 4GL's design may restrict its use. Some examples have already been given, i.e. it may be just a screen design aid or a query language, or it may not have procedural features. Others are (Holtz, 1979; Martin, 1982a; Schussel, 1986; An answer to software crisis, *Computing S.A.*, 11 September 1981, pp. 1–2):

- it may not be able to access multiple files;
- it may not be able to access data stored in a Data Base Management System;

- it may be tightly coupled to a single DBMS (e.g. IDEAL to DATACOM/DB, and ADS/ OnLine to IDMS/R);
- conversely, loosely-coupled languages, like FOCUS and NOMAD2, which offer interfaces to a number of DBMS packages from different vendors, are sometimes only able to retrieve information, and not update it;
- it may not support an active data dictionary (e.g. IBM's CSP);
- the building of batch logic may require a separate system (e.g. with Cullinet's ADS/ OnLine).

However, future enhancements can be expected to reduce the limitations, making the products – and their benefits – available in a larger proportion of circumstances. For example, IBM's AS language now has an interface with their SQL/DS DBMS, thereby broadening the scope of applications available to end users, and enabling them to read from and write to a corporate database (IBM, 1985, 1987); and interfaces between the SAS statistical language and various DBMSs, including SQL/DS and ADABAS, have now been released, thereby similarly extending the usefulness of SAS (DB2, 1987; Interface Products announced for DATACOM/DB and ADABAS, *SAS Communications* 1st qtr. 1989, pp. 6–7).

Improvements

Improvements to the products, e.g. the addition of new functions and features, may increase the productivity achieved. For example, NATURAL 2, an improved version of NATURAL, has windowing techniques, integrated help facilities, automatic validation and rule processing, and complex array processing, and one organization claimed that it improved their productivity by a factor of at least three over NATURAL (Felton, 1988).

Meeting user requirements

Although there is evidence of 4GLs meeting user requirements better than conventional methods, this may not always be the case. For example, Martin (1982b) quoted a case in which a 4GL achieved all the specifications whereas conventional methods did not, but this may just have been because the conventional methods were too slow. The improved results may also be attributable to the greater user participation – and especially the end user programming – which tends to occur with the use of 4GLs: 'end users know the subtleties of what they want to accomplish' (Martin, 1981). Program generators are typically inflexible, 'so they cannot bend to the needs of a corporation', and 'don't produce the perfectly polished programs' that the user wants, and they also concentrate on only a subset of all program designs, such as reports or simple sequential programs (Arthur, 1983). They can therefore only meet some subset of the users' real needs.

However, the fourth-generation represents an advance, supplying users with requirements they would otherwise not get or would have to wait a long time for. In particular, conventional methods are not very good at providing one-off reports – the reports would not be ready until after they were required, and they would not be economical to produce (Duffy, 1983) – so 4GLs will be used to a large extent to produce these reports. Because the reports are only used once, their layout need not conform exactly to the ideal.

Therefore, even if 4GLs do not provide exactly what users want, it is unlikely that they would complain; it is more likely that they will be so grateful for getting the reports at all, that they will regard the DP staff as 'heroes' (Dean, 1983). By contrast, users expect perfection in systems developed conventionally (especially as DP staff have to create conventionally-developed systems, whereas users might have to create 4GL systems themselves). This may account for part of the apparent productivity advantage of 4GLs: an imperfect 4GL report is being compared with a perfect 3GL report, so like is not being compared with like.

In some 4GLs, special processing is available to accommodate special requirements – and therefore give users exactly what they want – but the productivity gains in such cases are smaller or may even be lost, and the programs may be difficult to maintain (Holtz, 1979). Perfection, even in the layout of a report, can thus be very difficult (if not impossible) to achieve, thereby adding significantly to the development cost. (An analogy can be drawn with program efficiency. Making a program more efficient can add significantly to the development time – see Chapter 5.)

As users become more sophisticated in working with computers, so they become more demanding. They discover how much more computers can do for them, and start asking for it (Wright, 1978). Systems developed in future – including those developed using 4GLs – will therefore take increasingly longer to develop to meet the extra and more complex requirements, so the productivity gains will be lower.

Non-productive time

Staff spend perhaps only two-thirds of their time on directly productive work, the rest being taken up by meetings, holidays, etc. (Chapter 2). Because systems are developed quickly using 4GLs, the amount of time recorded as having been spent on their development probably excludes the non-productive time, whereas longer-term time recording – on which productivity rates for conventional systems development are based – may include non-productive time, giving a comparison which is unfair to conventional methods. Where appropriate, therefore, the productivity gains claimed for 4GLs have been reduced.

Similarly, staff may have many interruptions while they are working, and this wastes time, not just the duration of the interruption (which may be relevant to the task), but also the remembering ('warm-up') time afterwards, as they pick up where they left off (Chapter 11). Because 4GL systems are developed more quickly, there are fewer interruptions and so less time wasted. However, this is an intrinsic benefit of any method which boosts productivity. It is therefore not unfair to credit 4GLs with it, so no adjustment has been made for it.

Motivation

Some of the quoted productivity gains refer to specific, important projects, so higher motivation may have temporarily inflated staff productivity (Chapter 11).

Experience

The staff in the Duffy (1983) survey, which produced one of the lowest of the productivity gains tabulated above, were inexperienced in their use of 4GLs. Their productivity can therefore be expected to rise as they gain experience. How big a rise can be expected? Walston and Felix (1977) found a productivity gain of over 3:1 for previous experience with the programming languages. However, this figure may include the effect of other, correlated factors (Chapter 2), and in any case, the figure for 4GLs should be lower than this, as ease of learning is one of the requirements for a 4GL. Based on his experience with the IDEAL language, Rick Dancer of the Canada Systems Group stated that 'there is a learning curve associated with IDEAL, but compared to command level COBOL, it is trivial' (ADR/IDEAL, 1986). Collin (1989) defines a program generator as software that allows users to write complex programs using a few simple instructions. The Generation Five application generator ensures that the generated applications are efficient, even if less experienced programming personnel are used

Grochow, 1981). (It also produces similarly-structured applications, thereby ensuring that programmers can move from one application to another with a relatively short training period.)

On the other hand, Holtz (1979) quoted a case (in which ADF was used) where productivity increased by a factor of 23 with increased experience. (A new employee, inexperienced in programming, achieved a productivity twice that of the COBOL team on the first application he wrote in ADF, 32 times that of the COBOL team on the second, and 46 times on the third.) This indicates that some 4GLs are not so easy to learn. Worse, Jones (1986b) stated that experts (professional programmers or very sophisticated end users) were currently needed to use even program and application generators, while specialists in a particular generator may be needed to write sizable programs with it. This is reminiscent of the claims by Martin (1982a) that substantial training is needed to use some generators, and that thorough learning and practice are required to produce rapid results with them. (He uses the term 'acrobat' to describe someone who possesses such expertise, and who can therefore achieve a very high productivity.)

4GLs can be classified as either procedural or non-procedural. The latter are easier to learn: MANTIS, for example, can be installed and used productively very quickly (Schussel, 1986). Conversely, 4GLs which offer additional functionality are, as would be expected, also more difficult to learn. For instance, it normally takes more education and investment to make a complete life-cycle support system productive; Pacbase, for example, provides a great deal of support for development, but requires a major initial commitment.

Staff overheads

4GLs may incur additional, overhead, staff – a co-ordination function equivalent to the

DBA function, and an IC – which are probably not allowed for in the claimed productivity gains.

Rewrites

In some cases (e.g. three of the programs making up the Holtz (1979) figures), part of the apparent increase in productivity may be attributable to the fact that they were re-writes: 'writing a program for the second time is far easier than writing it the first' (Weinberg, 1971). For a start, little if any requirements analysis, or even system design and data structure design, is necessary (Jones, 1986b). Even if only programming functions are taken into account, there can be a significant reduction in development time. Few, if any, specification or system design errors will be discovered during the rewrite, so re-programming to rectify the consequent coding errors is greatly reduced or totally eliminated. Depending on which language is used in the rewrite, the second programmer can see which techniques in the original program were good and may be able to copy them, and which were bad and avoid them; and it may even be possible to re-use parts of the original program, though this may not apply if a 3GL program is being rewritten using a 4GL.

In an example given by Weinberg, the rewrite took only one-twentieth of the original development time, even without using a more powerful language. However, this was not a typical case, as the original programmer 'made a mountain out of a molehill', and the program was 'a confusing mess'. (A different programmer – apparently a much better one – wrote it the second time, so much of the reduction in effort can be attributed to differences in ability.) In another example, given by McClure (1969), a 5:1 improvement was obtained in writing three successive FOR-TRAN compilers (the third compiler took only one-fifth as long to write as the first). Figures derived from Holtz (1979) show a reduction in the region of 33%. (The average productivity increase on the three rewritten programs was 17:1, and only 11:1 on the remaining five programs.)

Management techniques and system design methodology

According to Schach (1988), where the expected productivity increase has not been observed, this has generally been due to poor management techniques and/or poor system design methodology. James Martin suggests the use of prototyping, iterative design, computerized data management, and computer-aided structuring.

6.6.3 MAINTENANCE

This section discusses the impact 4GLs have on maintenance productivity, and conversely, the impact that the maintenance mill-stone has on the overall productivity gain delivered by 4GLs.

Maintenance productivity gain

The productivity gains in Tables 6.13, 6.14 and 6.16 refer specifically to development, whereas maintenance comprises a large proportion of the total effort: 50% is a fairly typical figure, and many of the estimates are 80% or more (Chapter 8). How much effect will 4GLs have on the maintenance effort?

Maintenance consists of the maintenance of systems which were developed using conventional languages, and the maintenance of systems developed using 4GLs. The general opinion is that maintenance of convention-ally-developed systems will remain a problem (Vaughan, 1982; Martin, 1983b; National Productivity Institute, 1983).

- 'Existing applications will not be readily rewritten or replaced, and will have to be maintained for many years' (Vaughan, 1982).
- 'The cost of reprogramming this amount of COBOL [about 77 billion lines] would be over $1 trillion' (Martin, 1985).

- 'You can't throw away all of the old stuff' (Martin, 1983b).
- 'Existing systems will need to be maintained in the foreseeable future, and maintained in COBOL.'

(The Martin (1985) figures work out at $13 per LOC, which is in reasonable agreement with the figure of $9 (for 1984) given by Baron (1988). Other rates, for development and maintenance, are listed in Chapter 13.)

By contrast, the general opinion is that little effort is required to maintain 4GL-developed systems.

- With non-procedural languages, maintenance effort is reduced by at least as large a margin as development effort (Winer, 1978).
- 'Subsequent modification is equally simple' (Thomson, 1983).
- Forage (1986) gives a productivity gain of 2:1 for maintenance, which is the same as the figure he gives for implementation.
- Grochow (1981) found that the productivity gain delivered by his organization's application generator, Generation Five, was the same for maintenance and development (8 or 9:1).
- MANTIS applications are claimed to be easy to maintain (Cincom, 1986).
- One organization which now uses 4GLs exclusively, reduced its maintenance from 80% of the total effort when it was using low-level languages (Autocoder and Assembler), to 10% (Bearley, 1980).
- Maintenance programmers benefit greatly from program generators, but not as directly as development personnel, e.g. program generators enable them to rewrite error-prone programs in the same time it would take to correct or enhance the programs. The generators use only tested, error-free program logic, so there are fewer errors to be corrected in the delivered product, and the generators ensure that programs of the same type have the same structure, so the maintenance programmers can easily move from say an update

program in one application to an update program in another (Arthur, 1983).

However, there are some dissenting opinions over the amount of effort required to maintain 4GL systems.

- It is not always easy to follow the logic of generated programs – just as it is not always easy to follow someone else's program – so subsequent changes cannot be handled as easily as with 'pure' fourth-generation development (Avison and Fitzgerald, 1988).
- Martin (1982a) stated that APL is difficult to understand unless the programmer followed structuring rules designed for ease of maintenance, and he 'could find almost no APL writers who *do* follow such rules'.
- Baron (1988) stated that APL is sometimes termed a 'write-only' language because, while it is reasonably straightforward to write programs in it, it is often difficult – even for the original programmer – later to make sense of what has been written. APL programs are tightly written, and so are difficult to decipher: the symbols used tend to be very short, and bear few clues to their meaning, so a line of code 'can easily begin to look like hieroglyphics'. (Though Blum (1990) believes that compactness 'is not a problem when that language provides a natural representation for the designer's intent'.)

The difficulty in understanding APL programs may not be such a serious disadvantage: as was pointed out earlier in this chapter, this language is typically used to solve a specific problem, and the program is then discarded.

Jones (1986b) discussed the question in more detail. According to him, the impact of 4GLs on maintenance is 'ambiguous'. Some 4GLs may actually be harder to maintain than earlier languages, as the lack of procedural logic makes the programs difficult to grasp. In one example he gave, comparing APL and a spreadsheet against COBOL, there was no reduction in maintenance as a result of using a 4GL. There was therefore no improvement in productivity. However, as pointed out earlier (Table 6.9), this example emphasized development and the danger of using LOC as a productivity metric, so perhaps we should not pay too much attention to the maintenance effort figures in the example. Alternatively, bearing in mind that his maintenance figures include only defect repair time, perhaps he believes that the quality assurance process is so effective that very few errors find their way into production programs irrespective of the language used, making differences in defect repair time much smaller and so more difficult to detect. The figures in this specific example (a small system), may therefore have been too low to show the impact of 4GLs on maintenance productivity – the total defect repair time was only 2 man-months, and with only integers being shown, almost a halving of this amount would have been necessary to make a visible difference.

A second example also showed no reduction in defect repair time – in fact there was no maintenance to be reduced – though this may have had more to do with the even smaller size of this specific system, or with its short life, than with the impact of 4GLs on maintenance productivity, or the effectiveness of the quality assurance process. (The life expectancy of the application was only a few months, so the amount of maintenance would in any event have been minimal. This would not be true in every case, but relatively short life is a characteristic of many 4GL applications, e.g. one-off reports.) However, there is a discrepancy in the figures for conventional development in this example – the project total (3.3 man-months) is greater than the sum of the development effort (3.0) and the maintenance effort (0). If the maintenance effort for conventional development was actually 0.3 man-months, then there was in fact a small reduction through the use of a 4GL.

Jones (1986b) also stated that maintenance may be difficult with generated programs and applications, unless the generator merely produces COBOL source code. In an example he gave in which it did, there was a substantial reduction in maintenance effort (2.6:1) through the use of a generator, and this was in fact slightly higher than the corresponding gain for development (2.4:1). This, however, seems to conflict with the statement by Avison and Fitzgerald (1988) quoted above, that it is not always easy to follow the logic of generated programs.

Overall productivity gain

The important role played by maintenance in the overall productivity gain delivered by 4GLs can be seen from the following example. Suppose:

- 4GLs give productivity gains of 10:1 on development (a typical value, as discussed earlier);
- maintenance comprises 50% of the total effort – a fairly typical value (Chapter 8);
- only half of the current systems will be rewritten using 4GLs, so only half of the current maintenance effort will be replaced – as discussed later in this section and in section 6.6.5, it is not advisable to rewrite all existing systems, e.g. because it would not be cost-effective to do so, or because some programs might execute too slowly;
- subsequent maintenance of the replaced portions shows the same productivity gain as development – in the absence of quantitative evidence, this seems a reasonable, middle-of-the-road, assumption; and
- the replacement cost (rewriting using 4GLs) is spread over several years, and more important, is small enough to ignore. One organization, a university, planned to phase in 4GLs over ten years and estimated this would take 60 man-years effort (Old software dumped, *SA Software News*, February 1984, pp. 1–2). They had a

Table 6.17 Effect of maintenance on fourth-generation productivity gains

| Function | Time spent | | Ratio |
	Conven-tional	Fourth-generation	
Development	50	5	10:1
Maintenance:			
replaced	25	3	10:1
not replaced	25	25	–
Total	100	33	3:1

staff complement of 52, which works out at about 12% of their resources during this period (Installations, *The 1983 SA Computer users Handbook*, Johannesburg: Systems-Publishers (Pty) Ltd, M1–179).

The overall productivity gain is then given in Table 6.17 and two conclusions may be drawn from these figures.

*   The time spent maintaining conventionally-developed systems significantly reduces the overall productivity gain from 4GLs – with these figures, from 10:1 to 3:1, i.e. by a factor of three.
*   The gain for maintenance alone is ((25 + 25) : (3 + 25) =) 50:28, i.e. about 2:1. It is interesting to note that this figure agrees with the halving of maintenance costs reported by the Pic 'N Pay shoe chain, which uses IDMS/R with ADS/OnLine (Cullinet, 1986). The assumptions here were made independently, and were chosen to be realistic.

Table 6.17 represents the position after all the programs which should be rewritten using 4GLs have been rewritten. This will take several years. The overall productivity gain will be lower initially, but will gradually improve as more and more programs are replaced.

In practice, the situation is even more complex than this. The productivity gain for report programs, for example, is probably higher than that for edit programs. The overall productivity gain achieved therefore depends on the job mix – including, for example, the report:edit program ratio, the batch:on-line ratio, and the development: maintenance ratio. The job mix will not necessarily remain constant when the productivity gain is as high as 3:1. The staff will be able to complete their current assignments in a fraction of the previous time. This will enable them to take on many new assignments, particularly from the backlog of work, and the job mix of the new work may differ markedly from the present mix.

How can overall productivity be improved?

It was shown above that maintenance significantly reduces the overall productivity gain from 4GLs. How can organizations minimize this loss? James Martin's (1982b) advice is: 'Convert systems with high maintenance costs to software which is easily maintainable'. The argument below is an extension of this view.

As stated earlier, maintenance consists of the maintenance of systems which were developed using conventional languages, and the maintenance of systems developed using 4GLs. The latter should not have high maintenance costs because, as already discussed, the majority opinion is that these systems are easy to maintain, because many 4GL programs have a short life, and because they probably still form only a minority of the total at present (though their proportion is increasing). The remainder of this discussion therefore concentrates on the maintenance of conventionally-developed systems, and especially on how this can be reduced by rewriting these systems using 4GLs.

The rewrite effort depends on the intrinsic power of 4GLs, and on the maintenance 'profile', of which two aspects will be considered: the concentration of changes, and the type of program.

The intrinsic power of 4GLs

As was shown above, there is considerable doubt over this factor, with claims ranging from under 2:1 to over 100:1.

Concentration of changes

Figures quoted in sections 8.3.2 and 8.3.3 show that maintenance changes, and particularly errors, are not evenly spread, but are concentrated in specific modules. An accepted maintenance-reduction technique is therefore to rewrite the most frequently maintained portions of a system (Van Tassel, 1978; Martin, 1982b; Aron, 1974). 4GLs make this technique cost-effective in a higher proportion of cases. However, although it is likely to be effective for error-filled modules – or for poorly-designed ones which therefore take longer to modify – it may not be as effective for modules which are modified frequently because the change-prone information is concentrated in them. In fact, good design attempts to achieve just that. The portions of the program which are most likely to change are identified in advance, and are concentrated together in a single module, as far as possible. Then, when they do change, only this module needs to be changed. (This is known as 'information hiding', and was described in Chapter 5.)

Type of program

The situation here is rather complex. 4GLs may, as previously discussed, be more effective for some types of program – specifically enquiry and report programs – than others. The distribution of the different types of program may not be the same for maintenance as for development. For example, maintenance may comprise a higher proportion of enquiry and report programs, in which case rewriting frequently maintained programs may be an even more cost-effective option. Furthermore, if the productivity gain for *developing* enquiry and report programs is

higher than for other types of program, then the gain for *maintaining* them may also be higher. If so, maintenance costs of the rewritten programs will be low, which will make the rewriting option even more attractive.

What will the effect be on overall productivity, if the productivity gain from 4GLs is higher for maintenance than for development? If, for example, the productivity gain for maintaining 4GL systems is 20:1 instead of 10:1, then applying this ratio to Table 6.17 implies that the overall productivity gain will be 100:31 instead of 100:33, a difference of only 6%. The effect of this factor is therefore small, as it is swamped by the time spent maintaining conventionally-developed systems which it would not be advisable to rewrite. However, the picture would change, and change radically, if 4GLs make rewriting cost-effective in a much higher proportion of cases.

Another complication is that some maintenance tasks consist of *modifying* existing programs, while other tasks consist of *developing* additional programs. The former case has already been discussed. With the latter situation, the option of rewriting obviously does not exist. However, there is an interesting aspect. If maintenance does consist of a higher proportion of query and report programs, and if 4GLs are more effective for them, then the average productivity gain for developing new programs within the maintenance phase will be higher than the average gain for developing new programs within the development phase.

Cost-effectiveness

The overriding consideration is cost-effectiveness. Consider the following example. Suppose a program originally took 100 hours to develop conventionally. The user requests a modification to it which would take 10 hours (or an error is discovered in the program which would take 10 hours to fix). Would it be cheaper to rewrite the program

Table 6.18 Comparative costs

Activity	Time taken
Original development	100
Conventional modification	10
Fourth-generation rewrite:	
If productivity gain is 100:1	1
If gain is 1.4:1	71

using a 4GL? Table 6.18 shows the comparative costs (100:1 is one of the highest claims I quoted, and 1.4:1 is one of the lowest).

Therefore, if the productivity gain from the 4GL is 100:1 (for that type of program), a rewrite would be the cheaper solution; but if the gain is only 1.4:1, then a rewrite would not be economical (unless there were many subsequent modifications, or many fixes to an error-prone module).

Programmer time is not the only factor. The running costs, for example, might increase, so that would also have to be taken into account.

6.6.4 EFFECT ON BACKLOG

The general opinion is that 4GLs will result in a substantial reduction in the backlog of work, even eliminating it altogether, but the experts do not predict how long this will take (Macaskill, 1983; Murray, 1983). The backlog is large (Chapter 8), so the time-scale may be long. Bearley (1980) reported that one organization which now uses 4GLs exclusively had eliminated its backlog of six months' work, but it is not straightforward to extend this experience to other organizations which cannot use 4GLs exclusively, or which have larger backlogs. For example, would a backlog of 18 months also be eliminated, or merely reduced to 12 months?

4GLs can affect the backlog both directly and indirectly: directly, because they can be used to do the work comprising the backlog; and indirectly, because by improving produc-

tivity, current tasks will be completed more quickly, so resources will be freed and can be diverted to the backlog.

Like maintenance, the backlog of work also has a 'profile'. It consists of a mixture of development and maintenance, and much of it is short-lived, end-user type applications (Chapter 8), which are particularly suitable for 4GLs, i.e. the backlog should be rapidly reduced. However, because the applications are short-lived, it is more difficult to cost-justify them: each time they are run, they must provide considerable benefit, otherwise the development cost will not be recouped.

6.6.5 DISADVANTAGES

4GLs have a number of disadvantages: some have already been given (e.g. they cannot be used for all types of program); others are efficiency, cost, sloppiness, chaos and non-standardization, as discussed below.

Efficiency

4GLs (including generated programs) are generally heavy in their use of hardware (Jones, 1986b), although this can at least partly be ascribed to the fact that many use an interpreter instead of a compiler (Martin, 1985). One example, programs performing complex calculations, has already been given. Johnson (1980b) implies that, where complex processing is required, and programmers are 'forced to play tricks' with the language to accomplish the objective, processing times are two to three times longer than necessary. In a case quoted by Holtz (1979), the ADF application generator used twice as much CPU time as COBOL. In the PC-based experiment by Matos and Jalics (1989), comparing seven 4GLs (with their associated DBMSs) against COBOL (with ISAM files), the average 4GL took *five* times as long to run as COBOL on small files (containing a couple of hundred records), and no less than *seventy-*

five times as long on large files (containing several thousand records). (The 4GLs in this experiment were CONDOR, FOCUS, INFORMIX, ORACLE, PARADOX, RBASE, and dBASE.) 4GLs are therefore generally not suitable for applications with high volumes of data, or which are run frequently, or where extremely quick response times are needed (Jones, 1986b).

However, there is also evidence to the contrary. According to Thomson (1983), ADS/OnLine gives 10% *better* performance than COBOL or PL/1. One of the 4GLs tested by Matos and Jalics (1989), PARADOX, gave about 30% better performance than COBOL, even on large files. MANTIS is claimed to offer execution speeds equivalent to that of COBOL (Macfie, 1988), and almost equivalent to that of PL/1 (Pryce-Williams, 1988). Some application generators create object code which is better than that from the same applications programmed in COBOL or PL/1, because they use blocks of code which have been written in assembler language and tightly optimized, better so than the object code which is compiled from COBOL or PL/1 (Martin, 1982a). Furthermore, the products are continually being improved: Release 1.3 of ADR's IDEAL, for example, was claimed to be 30–50% faster than Release 1.2 (Goetz, 1986). In any event, even if a 4GL program is less efficient than the same program written by a *good* programmer using conventional methods, it may be more efficient than if it were written by a *poor* programmer using conventional methods. 'Tuning' of 4GL programs can also make a big difference. In one case, a batch program written using DATACOM/DB and IDEAL, took more than 24 hours to run. After some fine-tuning to it over a 3-month period, this was reduced to 75 minutes – a reduction of 95% or 20:1 (McMahon, 1987). Furthermore, many programs are not run very often, and many 4GL programs have a short life, so execution efficiency is of correspondingly less importance (Martin, 1982a).

Cost

The costs of introducing and using 4GLs may be significant.

- The software itself is expensive (van der Poel, 1981).
- If, as some of the evidence above indicates, 4GLs are less efficient, then they will require more powerful, and therefore more expensive, hardware. According to Thomson (1983), it is quite common to encounter systems that are 'devouring' 20% more computer capacity than would be the case with programs written in COBOL. Generated programs may take more memory according to Jones (1986b). For example, in the Holtz (1979) case quoted earlier, the applications coded in ADF used 'substantially more main memory' than the COBOL versions. All in all, it may therefore be necessary to obtain a larger computer. (The first user of Sperry's MAPPER upgraded their hardware extensively within a short time of acquiring it – they even bought additional machines (An answer to software crisis, *Computing S.A.*, 11 September 1981, pp 1–2) – though that may have been because of increased usage rather than less efficient usage.)
- If the wrong type of 4GL is used on the wrong type of program, e.g. if a user-friendly query language is used to code a large corporate system, the result is a 'huge impact' on machine resources (Hymers, 1983).
- Parkinson's Law (1957) applies: end users, when given access to these facilities, may make excessive use of them.
- End users do not restrict themselves to short and simple enquiries. They generate complex enquiries which use considerable amounts of machine time, and the runs may take even longer than necessary because of their ignorance of the structure of the data and consequent inefficient use of the resources (Thomson, 1980).

For software engineers, these costs must be

set against the productivity gains achieved, as the total cost to the organization must be taken into account and not just software engineering productivity. For end users, higher hardware costs may be justified on the grounds that the time they spend on programming is time spent away from their areas of expertise, so it must be kept to a minimum (Van Tassel, 1978).

One commentator estimated that a productivity improvement of 5:1 was needed just to justify the extra machine resources (IBM, 1988a).

Sloppiness

The speed of development and ease of change encourage 'sloppy' initial design: 'Just throw it together and produce something that works, we can always change it later' (Thomson, 1983). For the same reason, there is probably sloppiness in analysing the user's requirements. As a result, more changes to the 'completed' system are needed. This problem is surely aggravated by the lack of documentation referred to earlier – formal specifications are not usually written, and documentation is only about 25% as detailed as that provided for by COBOL, FORTRAN, or PL/1 – which in turn makes debugging and modifications more difficult (Johnson, 1980b). Users can be equally guilty, so this sloppiness can occur even where prototyping is used, and even where users develop their own systems.

If, for example, every job had to be redone because the first version did not meet the user's needs, then the productivity actually achieved would be only half the potential and apparent productivity. (This is a simplified view. On the one hand, to avoid such rewrites, additional time must be spent initially in establishing the user's needs; and on the other hand, rewriting a program does not take as long as writing it the first time. The net productivity loss is therefore not as great as this factor of two.)

Furthermore, 4GLs do not guarantee against 'spaghetti code'. ADR claimed that their IDEAL language was the only fully structured 4GL (Applied Data Research, 1986).

Chaos

4GLs make programming possible by a much larger number of end users. However, if many users write programs independently in an undisciplined environment, there is the danger they will create inflexible systems, and will duplicate effort and data (Coetzer, 1983a; Martin, 1982b). (These problems can occur even when only DP staff use 4GLs, but are likely to be far more common when large numbers of end users are using them.) The ability to implement easily uncontrolled changes to data structures will actually create a demand for such changes, and Thomson (1983) quoted one organization using fourth-generation facilities which had *four* versions of their active, current, database, with more changes planned. An IBM study of 100 organizations in Europe showed that 18% of the computerized data was duplicated up to 20 times (Grulke, 1983). This is expensive, as it wastes disk space, and can result in chaos: when data is updated, it must be updated in each of the duplicated places at once, otherwise the different copies get out of step, causing confusion and errors.

The situation can be contained by strategic entity charting and top-down planning of data and procedures; a co-ordinator (equivalent to the DBA); and copy files, as provided for by e.g. the COBOL COPY library, or better, a DBMS and active data dictionary; though there are time and cost factors associated with these measures (Martin, 1981, 1982b; Jones, 1983a; Thomson, 1983; Software packages, *Computer Systems SA.*, April 1983, pp. 37–44). Also, some 4GLs, such as Pacbase, Telon, and APS, include tools for project management (e.g. planning and control, library functions and documentation), which should help contain the chaos (Schussel, 1986).

Non-standardization

There are many different 4GLs, and there is a serious lack of standardization among them – far more than that which previously existed (Thomson, 1983). The semantic and syntactical differences among them are far greater than the differences between, say, FORTRAN and COBOL (Schussel, 1986). Portability and conversion problems apply here as well.

However, some 4GLs are highly portable. Applications written in MANTIS, for example, can be run without change (Cincom, 1986):

- under different operating systems, e.g DOS/VSE and MVS;
- with different DBMSs, e.g. DL/1 and SQL/DS; and
- on machines from different manufacturers, e.g. IBM, DEC and WANG.

6.6.6 RESISTANCE

Introduction of 4GLs may cause resistance from the DP department and users alike – more so than for most of the other factors examined in this study, because it represents a more fundamental change.

DP staff may resist the changes for a variety of reasons, e.g. (Martin, 1982b; Murray, 1983; Abbey, 1984):

- inefficient use of hardware; the possibility of chaos; and other disadvantages already discussed;
- skepticism of the claimed benefits; technical people are often very conservative; they fear losing their jobs; the DPM's authority may be eroded; and other general reasons (Chapter 9).

Users may also have a variety of reasons for resistance, e.g. (Martin, 1981; Duffy, 1983):

- they may believe they have something

more important to do, as the time they spend programming solutions to their requirements is time spent away from their areas of expertise;
- they may think that using a terminal is beneath them;
- they may be frightened of displaying their ignorance of computers;
- if their DP department provides an adequate service, the users may prefer this to continue.

The degree of resistance also depends on how 'user friendly' the products are. As would be expected, people learn more quickly, and give less resistance, if the products are straightforward (Lowrie, 1983).

Martin (1982b) pointed out that the objections are insignificant in comparison with the benefits provided by 4GLs; not surprisingly, therefore, the changes may be welcomed.

- In nearly every case in one survey, the DP department *asked* for the software, and they took to it 'like ducks to water' (Duffy, 1983).
- There is a 'high level of acceptance' from both DP and end users.
- Some of the greatest enthusiasts are professional programmers who showed great initial skepticism (Murray, 1983).
- The anticipated productivity gains are a major motivator, and some organizations have bought a particular make of computer specifically because of its 4GL capabilities.

(Reduced lead times produce more, sooner, *Computer Week*, 25 October 1982, p. 12; An answer to software crisis, *Computing S.A.*, 11 September 1981, pp. 1–2.)

6.6.7 NET PRODUCTIVITY IMPROVEMENT

Several factors have been discussed which reduce the productivity gains delivered by 4GLs. How great is their effect? The following example shows that the reduction may be large. The reasoning is an extension of that used earlier for Table 6.17.

The following assumptions will be made.

1. 4GLs give a productivity gain of 10:1. (This is a typical value, and was one of the assumptions for Table 6.17.)
2. Of programming done, 80% is on small machines, and the products available on them give a 30% lower productivity gain – see section 6.5.1 (Weinberg, 1971) and section 6.6.2 (Boehm, 1981).
3. 4GLs will be used for 80% of development work. (Figures quoted earlier ranged from 70% to 100%.)
4. Maintenance comprises 50% of all programming, and 50% of the current maintenance effort will be replaced by 4GL systems. (These were two of the assumptions for Table 6.17.)
5. The productivity gains on some types of program are only half the above figures, and these programs comprise one-quarter of the total. (Earlier it was noted that productivity gains are lower, and may even be lost, when special processing features are used in order to accommodate special requirements.)
6. The 'sloppiness' in design, etc., and the decreased amount of documentation, reduce the productivity gains by 30%; see section 6.6.5. In practice, the sloppiness would not be so severe that it was necessary to completely redo every job – though some might have to be redone more than once – so the loss of productivity would probably be somewhat less than 50%.
7. Duplication of effort reduces the gains by a further 30%. (This figure was derived by analogy with the loss due to sloppiness.)
8. Plus the other assumptions for Table 6.17 i.e. the gain for maintenance is the same as for development, and the rewrite cost is small enough to ignore.

(Assumptions 3 and 4 mean that 4GLs will be used for ((50%*80%) + (50%*50%) = (40%+25%) =) 65% of all programming. This is roughly midway between the McCracken (1978) prediction that more than 50% of all application programs processed by computers in the mid-1980s would be developed using non-procedural languages, and the Scott (1986) prediction, that within five years, probably 70–80% of all programs processed would be written in non-procedural languages.)

The net productivity gain with these assumptions is given in Table 6.19 using the intermediate calculations as follows.

By assumption 1:	Theoretical gain	→ 10:1
By assumption 6:	less 30% sloppiness	→ 7:1
By assumption 7:	less 30% duplication	→ 4.9:1

gives the base figure for large machines.

less 30% for small machines (assumption 2)   → 3.4:1

gives the base figure for small machines.

Thus the productivity improvement of 10:1 only raises the productivity of the industry as a whole by 1.7:1 or 70%.

Based on these figures therefore, the overall productivity improvement from 4GLs will be:

Development	50:24.5	=	2:1
Maintenance	50:35.3	=	1.4:1
Total	100:59.8	=	1.7:1

This prediction reflects the situation in a few years' time, when 4GLs are used as much as possible.

6.6.8   THE DEMISE OF COBOL

The productivity gain predicted above will only be achieved when COBOL and other third-generation languages have been replaced (as far as practical) by 4GLs. Because of the large amount of COBOL code in use, and the high cost of rewriting it (Martin, 1985), this could take many years. Some

Table 6.19 Effect of the fourth-generation on overall productivity

	Time spent		
Function	*Conventional*	*Fourth-generation*	*Ratio*
Small machines			
Development:			
suitable – low gain	10.0	5.9	1.7:1
high gain	22.0	6.5	3.4:1
not suitable	8.0	8.0	–
Maintenance:			
suitable – low gain	10.0	5.9	1.7:1
high gain	10.0	2.9	3.4:1
not suitable	20.0	20.0	–
Large machines			
Development:			
suitable – low gain	2.5	1.0	2.5:1
high gain	5.5	1.1	4.9:1
not suitable	2.0	2.0	–
Maintenance:			
suitable – low gain	2.5	1.0	2.5:1
high gain	2.5	0.5	4.9:1
not suitable	5.0	5.0	–
Total	100.0	59.8	1.7:1

authorities predicted that, in 10 years, only a minority of programmers would be using conventional languages, and they would be doing maintenance only (Crossman, 1983; Frater, 1983). Other authorities were more cautious: 'the DP shop will still use COBOL' (Duffy, 1983); 'we will see investments in COBOL-structured programs for many years to come' (van Rensburg, 1988). Cullum (1983) maintained that, because 4GLs were not appropriate in all circumstances, there would continue to be a need for a *variety* of different languages. He did not forecast to what extent conventional languages would continue to be used, or for how long, but criticized advocates of 4GLs for giving far too optimistic an impression of the time-scale involved.

The more cautious views are indicated by the fact that COBOL is still extensively used, several years after some of the more extreme COBOL-demise predictions were made. 4GLs will be used increasingly, especially by end users, but traditional languages (including COBOL) will continue to be used for development and especially for maintenance, for years to come. In particular, traditional languages (though not necessarily COBOL) will be used to develop packages and more 4GLs, and wherever there are high volumes of data, where processing speed is critical, or where running costs must be kept low (van Rijswijck, 1983; Jones, 1983b).

Furthermore, there are ways to improve COBOL, e.g. by introducing high-level pre-processors, which will extend its life (Parikh, 1984; Thompson, 1982). In fact, improvements have already been made: 'COBOL hasn't stood still over the past 20 years' (Easirun International, 1988). For example, the latest version, COBOL 85, included 'desperately needed' structured programming features. Furthermore, one organization reported that, when its accounting package was upgraded from RM/COBOL 74 to RM/

COBOL 85, the system's speed was increased, and the organization saved up to 50% in disk space (Blij, 1988). This solution also raises COBOL productivity, and has the added benefit of preserving organizations' investment in the language, which is an important factor when its large share of the market is taken into account. According to most surveys and authorities, it has 50%, or even more, of the market (Holton, 1977; Lientz *et al.*, 1978; Johnson, 1980b; Nies, 1983; Parikh, 1984; Easirun International, 1988; Garcia-Rose and Fosdick, 1990; etc.). (By comparison, knowledgeable observers have estimated that as much as 25% of the world's available machine cycles run with code generated by some form of FORTRAN (Davis, 1987a).) It was estimated that there are 70 *billion* lines of COBOL code in use worldwide (Gullo, 1987). (By comparison, there are reportedly more than 30 billion lines of RPG application code, apparently for IBM System/3x applications alone (Pine, 1989).)

The historical evidence is inconclusive. Not only does COBOL, despite its inadequacies, have such a large share of the market, but usage of it apparently *increased* during the 1970s despite the availability of early 4GLs (Philippakis, 1977). However, the following points should be noted.

- According to some surveys (quoted earlier), the early 4GL RPG was firmly established in second or third place, with perhaps 10–15% of the market, so more powerful languages should do better.
- Some surveys do not contain a representative cross-section of the DP industry.
  - Small organizations are under-represented (Adams, 1981), so the true usage of RPG may be much higher than shown (the very large number of lines of RPG code quoted above makes this suggestion plausible, and some other surveys *have* given a much higher figure for it, e.g. 45% of the DP managers in

the Dick (1980) survey used it as their main language).
  - Few end users are included, so the true usage of APL and other similar languages may also be much higher than indicated (Philippakis, 1977).

The true usage of COBOL may therefore be much lower than is generally believed.

- The situation may now be changing rapidly, and so is not adequately reflected by these surveys.
- According to a survey (Computer staff become scarcer, *Computronics*, 10 February 1980, pp. 1, 8) the usage of Assembler dropped off just as dramatically as the usage of COBOL is predicted to drop (64% of programmers used Assembler in 1970, but only 16% used it in 1979).

Many years ago, Philippakis (1977) concluded that 'The established momentum of currently popular languages will prove difficult to arrest. The merits of newly designed languages may remain academic subjects for some time to come, at least as far as administrative data processing users go'. Subsequent developments indicate that his conclusion was correct (Goodwin, 1986). However, there is evidence that the situation is changing. Hoard (1981) reported that there seemed to be a clear, though not overwhelming preference shift to the newer and more powerful programming languages: over one in five of the approximately 1000 respondents in an International Data Corporation survey 'would prefer to use PL/1 or PASCAL'. It seems reasonable to suppose that there is a similar trend towards 4GLs. The managing director of one training organization reported that 40% of his students never write a COBOL program after they leave, because more and more organizations are moving to 4GL/DBMS environments (van der Meer, 1985). According to Scott (1986), non-procedural languages would increase their share of all CPU time from 10% to approximately 50% within five years, and probably

70–80% of all programs processed would be written in non-procedural languages. In 1991 I conducted a small survey of job advertisements, which showed a slightly higher (by about 25%) demand for 4GL than high-level language skills. (The survey used two issues each of *ComputerWeek* and *Computing S.A.* for 1991, and the total number of advertisements was about 1000.) By comparison, a similar survey about five years earlier showed a roughly equal demand for high-level and 4GL skills, whereas in another similar survey about five years before that, demand for high-level skills was three times as high as for 4GL skills. These figures are in broad agreement with the earlier estimate in this chapter that 4GLs may have been used for around one-third of all the programming in the Comcon/FSA (1985) survey.

6.6.9 THE FUTURE

The following developments are anticipated.

- A study by the Massachusetts Institute of Technology found that the scope of most new applications had been reduced from organization-wide, to personal, i.e. they would be used by only one person or one department (Grulke, 1983). Personal systems can be developed by the people needing them, if they have the requisite DP knowledge and the tools. The wider availability of microcomputers assists this trend.
- 4GLs will thus be widely used by end users for small, simple, personal systems, and particularly for one-off reports which would not be obtained in time and at reasonable cost using conventional methods (Jones, 1986b; Duffy, 1983). This will take much of the pressure off DP departments.
- More sophisticated end users, e.g. those with technical backgrounds such as engineers, will use 4GLs for more complex tasks.
- DP staff will also use 4GLs, but not to the same extent as end users, as they will spend a significant portion of their time using conventional methods to create systems for which 4GLs are not appropriate, and to maintain systems developed by conventional methods.
- The overall productivity gains achieved by DP departments will therefore be much smaller than the gains obtainable from 4GLs, and the productivity of DP staff, like that of manual telephone operators, may only go up slightly (McCracken, 1978). In fact, if most of the easy (and therefore high productivity) work is done by end users in future, leaving only the most difficult (i.e. low productivity) work for the DP department, the productivity of DP departments may even go *down* (or at least *appear* to go down).

However, the comparison is misleading. Much of the programming will be done by non-DP staff. They will use 4GLs almost exclusively, so – provided their activities are controlled and the situation does not degenerate into chaos – their productivity will be high. This may be termed 'invisible productivity' – by analogy with James Martin's (1981) 'invisible backlog' – as it will not be obvious, nor will it be easy to measure. Combining the productivity of DP and non-DP staff will give the overall (and therefore true) productivity, which will be high.

- The improved productivity will make economical many tasks which at present are not cost-justifiable. This will be of benefit to the users, but it will add to the work-load of DP departments, offsetting the decrease in work-load caused by end user programming.
- Martin (1981) expressed concern over the future of the industry as, at the then rate of hardware growth (the increasing power of computers as well as their increasing number), 28 million programmers would have been needed by 1990 in the USA alone, if productivity did not improve.

(This prediction is discussed in Chapter 12.) This represents an increase of 100:1 over the number at the beginning of the decade, and is an impractically large number. However, 4GLs do not merely increase programmer productivity: they also permit non-programmers to do programming. Jones (1986b) estimated that there were over 2 800 000 end users in the USA writing programs in 1984, compared to only 1 000 000 professional programmers; while according to Shneiderman (1980), for every professional programmer, there are probably ten occasional programmers who write programs for scientific research, engineering development, marketing research, business applications, etc.; and there is also a rapidly growing number of hobbyist programmers working on small business, personal, and home computing applications. With scientists, engineers, market researchers, and hobbyists, as well as systems analysts, clerks, managers, and keypunch operators (Chapter 9), all writing programs (albeit on a part-time basis), the total number of 'programmers' may now *exceed* 28 million. This may be as big a benefit as the improvement in productivity.

6.6.10   SUMMARY AND CONCLUSIONS

4GL-type software products have been in existence for many years. Initially, they were not as widespread as might have been expected, but this is changing, probably because they are more powerful now, i.e. give a higher productivity gain to the increasingly more expensive staff; and because hardware, which they generally make heavy use of, has decreased in price (Murray, 1983; IBM, 1983). They are therefore much more cost-effective now than in the past.

The improvement in 4GLs may be partly attributable to marketing and to psychological reasons. According to Grosch (1978), IBM had started to release the technological products it has created in recent years, and it was doing so because of competition, boredom with the old, established products, and because the developers want to see their new products used.

The greater acceptance now of 4GLs may also be attributable to psychological reasons: the climate may not have been ripe in the past; the idea may have been ahead of its time; or perhaps they have become a 'fad'.

There will be resistance to 4GLs in some quarters, but on the whole they will be welcomed by DP and users alike – they are gathering momentum, and their growth will be 'dramatic' (Crossman, 1983).

4GLs will give significant productivity improvements for both development and maintenance, so their use should be encouraged, but these improvements will not be as large as many people anticipate. Furthermore, the overall productivity gains in the area of maintenance will probably be much lower than for development, because of the large number of conventionally-developed programs that still have to be maintained. Thus, although the maintenance millstone will be lightened, it will continue to impede progress for years to come. Similarly, although 4GLs will have a noticeable impact on the backlog of work, the backlog is so large that it will take years to clear.

6.7   INTERACTIVE PROGRAMMING

It has been claimed that the main obstacle to high programming productivity is the poor turnaround of testing run in batch mode (Van Zijl and Evans, 1978). (The terms 'interactive', 'on-line' and 'time-sharing' will be treated as synonymous with each other, as will the terms 'batch' and 'off-line' with each other.)

In a short session at a terminal, a programmer can run several successive jobs which, had they been run in batch mode, would have taken several days because of the long delays between each run (Glass, 1979). There is thus a dramatic reduction in the time it takes to debug a program, so systems can be installed much sooner – one study showed a one-third reduction in elapsed time (Schatzoff *et al.*, 1967), while another yielded a fourfold improvement (Van Zijl and Evans, 1978).

Programming can be subdivided according to the degree of interaction between the programmer and the computer, ranging from batch mode where he has no direct interaction, through remote job entry and interactive programming, to 'hands-on' where he is working from the operator's console, and is in sole control of the machine (Glass, 1979). (The term 'hands-on' usually has the wider meaning of interactive programming in general.) All the methods require an appropriate operating system to provide the capability. Other software tools may also be required, e.g. an interactive, full-screen text editor helps to derive the full benefit of interactive facilities.

Remote job entry (RJE) probably gives little advantage over batch, and is not very common any more. 'Hands-on' is also not common, except on PCs where it is the standard method of programming.

Interactive programming takes place under different circumstances:

- on a microcomputer, the programmer normally has the machine to himself;
- with IBM's VM (Virtual Machine) operating system (on a mainframe), it appears to the programmer as if he has the machine to himself, even though he does not; whereas
- on most other machines, he has to be aware that he is sharing the files and libraries with others.

These aspects provide an alternative classification of interactive programming, and they are relevant to productivity – e.g. on a micro, response is normally not degraded by other users, and fewer security measures (to ensure confidentiality and integrity) are required. Some attempts have been made to quantify these aspects. For example, evidence presented in Chapter 5 indicates that restricted access to the computer may degrade software productivity by 50% or more, while some of the other evidence in that chapter indicates that a slow or variable response can sometimes have an equally large impact on productivity.

Interactive programming can be used with any of the DP department structures (Chapter 3), but may lead to a change in the structure to Type 4: Hardware/Software Split. Similarly, systems run interactively by end users 'have a powerful organizational impact' – communication patterns are restructured and responsibilities are reassigned (Shneiderman, 1980).

Shneiderman reported a decrease in literature comparing interactive and batch programming, and an increase in articles on interactive systems. Furthermore, program development systems are now overwhelmingly interactive in nature (Bell *et al.*, 1987). (Evidence of a similar trend in production applications is presented in Chapter 8.) This suggests that interactive programming is now generally accepted as being superior. However, Shneiderman believed the question was still open because of the bad habits which interactive programming encourages, and because hardware speeds and software capabilities have changed substantially since the debate began. (These aspects are discussed later in sections 6.7.1–6.6.3.) Therefore, even if batch programming were no longer used, it would still be worthwhile to discuss interactive programming and its effect on productivity.

How extensively is interactive programming used? Only 30% of the systems in the Lientz *et al.* (1978) survey were developed using on-line programming, and only 30% of the organizations in the van der Poel (1982) survey used on-line programming, but the proportion must have increased significantly since then, especially as systems developed on the millions of microcomputers must be included in the count, and it is probable that the vast majority of these are developed interactively. Furthermore, the number of interactive systems (ones which are run interactively), has increased rapidly (Chapter 8), and they need to be developed, or at least tested, interactively. Nevertheless, it seems unlikely that all the systems currently being developed are being developed using interactive programming. In particular, a Datamation/Cowen & Co. survey found that 45% of new applications would be developed on mainframes (Appleton *et al.*, 1991), and it seems unlikely that all of them will be developed interactively. This gives an added reason for discussing the topic: some organizations are not yet deriving whatever benefits interactive programming provides.

6.7.1   EFFECT ON PRODUCTIVITY

Productivity improvements are possible because interruptions – and therefore 'warm-up' time and remembering when restarting after each interruption – are minimized (Sackman *et al.*, 1968; Applied Data Research, 1986). (The adverse effects of interruptions are discussed in Chapter 11.) In spite of this advantage, Martin and McClure (1985) quoted one installation where productivity was *lowered* because the programmers made more mistakes – 'they seemed less able to contemplate their code carefully when entering it on a screen than when using off-line coding sheets'. This is consistent with Gayle (1971), who reported a negative correlation between productivity and the distance between the programmer and computer, measured in feet. Also, some evidence was given in Chapter 5 that response could be *too* fast, and this might even degrade productivity. Furthermore, Bell *et al.* (1987) stated that a number of experiments had been carried out, but their results were inconclusive. (Bell did not provide details of these experiments.) Nevertheless, most authorities claim significant improvements in productivity due to

interactive programming. These claims are given in Table 6.20, together with the life-cycle functions to which the claims apply. In this table, Unilever used ICL's MAXIMOP package; Sanlam used IBM's TSO (Time Sharing Option); and Anmercosa used ADR's ROSCOE and LIBRARIAN.

Johnson's 1.15:1 is the improvement in total LOC output of programming personnel per implementation man-day due to on-line compile and debug. The Jones and Nelson figure is the average of four studies. Two figures are given for the Boeing model, and two pairs of figures for the COCOMO model. In each case, one figure or pair of figures represents the productivity gain for system development as a whole (including e.g. systems analysis), and the other the gain for the code and unit test functions only. The ranges given for the COCOMO, Daly (GTE), and NARDAC models reflect the fact that interactive programming has a greater benefit over batch when batch turnaround is slow than when it is fast. For example, according to the COCOMO model, on-line has a 15% productivity advantage over batch (for system development as a whole) if the average batch turnaround time is less than 4 hours, compared to a 32% advantage if it is 12 hours or more. Productivity using batch mode is therefore (1.32/1.15 =) 15% higher when turnaround is fast than when it is slow. By comparison, the NARDAC model has an effort multiplier of 0.8 for more than one batch run per day, compared to 1.2 for less than one. Productivity is therefore (1.2/0.8 =) 50% higher when batch turnaround is fast than when it is slow. The Griffin figure is the productivity range between instant turnaround and a turnaround of 12–24 hours. It is not clear if the Anmercosa figure includes all development activities, or just programming.

In addition to the figures in Table 6.20, Reaser *et al.* (1974) described an evaluation by the US Army using COBOL programs and the IBM Time Sharing Option, TSO, in which

Table 6.20 Productivity claims

Source	Ratio	
Global Averages		
Boeing model (Black *et al.*, 1977)	1.1:1	overall project
NARDAC model (Williamson, 1979)	1.1 to 1.6:1	overall project
Johnson (1980b)	1.15:1	implementation
COCOMO model (Boehm, 1981)	1.15 to 1.32:1	overall project
Doty model (Herd *et al.*, 1977)	1.2:1	overall project
GTE (Daly, 1979) model	1.3 to 1.4:1	overall project
van der Poel (1981)	up to 1.4:1	labor productivity
COCOMO model (Boehm, 1981)	1.4 to 1.7:1	code and unit test
Griffin (1980)	1.5:1	
Boeing model (Black *et al.*, 1977)	1.9:1	code and unit test
Jones and Nelson (1976)	2:1	code and unit test
Individual Cases		
Johnson (1980b)	1.2:1	programming and testing
Sackman (1970)	1.2:1	code and unit test
Unilever (Van Zijl and Evans, 1978)	1.3 to 1.6:1	compile and test
Johnson (1980b)	1.5:1	testing
Sackman *et al.* (1968): experienced staff	1.5 to 3:1	debug
Sackman *et al.* (1968): trainees	1.5 to 7:1	debug
Sanlam (van Wyk, 1978)	2:1	code, test, debug
Harr (1969)	> 2:1	programmer productivity
Anmercosa (Winer, 1978)	4:1	

programmer productivity and development cost were found to be significantly improved using time-sharing.

Comments

Discrepancies

The average of the figures in Table 6.20 is about 2:1, but they cover a wide range – 1.1:1 to 7:1 – and the higher ratios seem unrealistic in view of the reason for the improvement (the saving in 'warm-up'/remembering time). The average is, in fact, distorted by two or three values that are much higher than the others. The true impact of interactive programming on productivity is probably therefore somewhat less than 2:1. Particularly noteworthy is the fact that the highest ratio came from Sackman, who also provided one of the lowest.

Doubt has been cast on the findings of some experiments because of their 'labora-

tory nature' – they were small and involved no group activity – or because they were mathematically oriented, and therefore not typical, as the great majority of programs are commercial in nature (Chapter 1) (van der Poel, 1981; Aron, 1974). This may account for some of the discrepancies. Other possible explanations are contained in the following discussions.

Sackman

Sackman *et al.*'s (1968) experiments are referred to several times in this discussion. The figures he obtained were, for experienced staff:

50.2 man-hours against 34.5
= 1.5:1 (algebra problem);

and

12.3 man-hours against 4.0
= 3:1 (maze problem)

and for trainees:

4.7 man-hours against 0.71
= 7:1 (sort problem);

and

13.6 man-hours against 9.2
= 1.5:1 (cube problem).

where the first figure for each problem is the time taken using batch programming, the second figure is the time taken using interactive programming instead, and the third figure is the corresponding ratio.

The programmers in these experiments apparently used different languages. In view of the large productivity differences between different languages, and the effect of language-level on interactive programming, caution should be observed when interpreting the results. Weinberg (1971) also pointed out some limitations of the experiments, e.g. they did not allow for co-operation between the programmers.

Elapsed (calendar) time versus man-hours

Two of the highest figures tabulated are the 3:1 and 7:1 given by Sackman *et al.* (1968), who appears to include all the time between tests run in batch mode, i.e. he assumed that all the waiting time was either spent working on the program (e.g. on documentation, or on other portions of the code), or was wasted. While time-wasting may occur in some cases, especially with junior programmers who have not yet learned how to plan their work and who are accustomed to having access to a terminal at all times (Weinberg, 1971), it is not generally true: programmers *do* work on other programs while waiting for testing, and this time must be excluded from the comparison (Glass, 1979; Yourdon, 1979b). Productivity therefore does not increase as dramatically as calendar/elapse time drops.

How large is this effect? Reaser and Carrow (1975) found that only about 16% of programmer time was spent waiting for batch results, which indicates that only a small adjustment need be made to Sackman's figures. This factor therefore appears to be insufficient to account for the large difference between his figures and most of the others. However, Sackman's figures were obtained in small laboratory experiments; such findings should be treated with caution. In particular, the idle waiting time in these specific experiments might have been much higher than 16%, as there was probably little documentation to work on while waiting for test results, and the programs were small so it is unlikely that there were other parts of them that could have been worked on while waiting.

Turnaround

Sackman *et al.* (1968) found that, for experienced programmers, the advantage of on-line testing disappeared as the turnaround time for off-line testing decreased, implying that the productivity advantage of on-line does not lie in the interactive nature as such. However, as he treats part of the waiting time as idle (wasted) time, this finding is not surprising.

Productivity is lowered if batch turnaround is very short, or very long (Weinberg, 1971; Brandon, 1978).

- If it is very short, the programmer does not value the run, and so is careless in preparing it, with the result that he makes errors and the run is wasted.
- If it is very long, he puts 'everything he can think of' into the run, thereby increasing the possibility of errors, and he may also make mistakes out of sheer anxiety caused by knowing how long he will have to wait for another attempt.

Weinberg therefore recommended two to five tests per day, and Brandon a turnaround of less than three hours.

Similar considerations apply to on-line testing.

- Because turnaround (the response time) is fast compared to batch mode, programmers value the runs less (Weinberg, 1971).

(This is not necessarily a bad thing: programmers may deliberately use extra machine time with trial-and-error runs to reduce their own time and effort (Sackman *et al.*, 1968). Provided this is not carried to excess, it can result in overall savings.)

- Unless the response time is very short, it becomes difficult to maintain continuity of thought, and the terminal user may even start daydreaming, so efficiency drops; this was discussed in Chapter 5.

Personality differences

Weinberg (1971) identified two types of programmer personality: humble and assertive. 'Humble' programmers carefully check their work before running it; 'assertive' ones make hasty changes, resulting in many errors and consequent reruns. On the other hand, assertive people ask for help when they need it, which aids the learning process, whereas non-assertive people avoid equipment or methods which entail them having to ask for help.

Experiments conducted by Weinberg show that 'humble' programmers perform much better than 'assertive' ones in batch environments, while 'assertive' ones perform much better with on-line. Programmers should therefore attempt to adjust their style to suit their circumstances, or to change their circumstances to suit their personality (Aron, 1974).

Weinberg's finding is consistent with that of Lee and Shneiderman (1978) who found that assertive programmers who have an *internal* 'locus of control' (i.e. who believe that they control their environment) have a much stronger preference for on-line programming than non-assertive programmers having an *external* 'locus of control' (i.e. who believe that their environment controls them).

Other differences between people

Bell *et al.* (1987) speculated that some people can think quickly and clearly, while others need peace for contemplation (like the 'intellectual thinkers' mentioned in Chapter 9). The former can be expected to perform better with on-line programming, and the latter with batch.

In addition, there are differences in performance between individuals which can be so large that they exceed the effect of the factor being tested (Bell *et al.*, 1987). In some studies by Sackman, the wide productivity ranges were due to a small number of extreme performances. This means that even more care is required when interpreting experimental results. Knowledge and experience also affect an individual's performance, which highlights the need for training; see Chapter 9.

Beginners

Weinberg (1971) indicates that on-line programming gives greater productivity benefits to beginners and part-time users, because they make a larger number of trivial errors. This claim is supported by Sackman's figures, which showed productivity gains of up to 7:1 for trainees, and up to only 3:1 for experienced programmers (Sackman *et al.*, 1968).

(Similarly, any technique or technological aid which reduced the number of errors, such as structured walkthroughs, would reduce the advantage of on-line.)

Complexity

Comparisons of batch and on-line have usually been carried out with small, simple programs (Weinberg, 1971). If simple errors form a larger proportion of the total in such programs, then the productivity advantage of on-line in typical situations will be lower than that indicated by the experiments.

The Sackman *et al.* (1968) experiments support this view, as on-line gave greater productivity gains on the smaller programs:

3:1 and 7:1 for the smaller programs; and
1.5:1 for the larger ones.

Language level

Programs written in low-level languages contain more statements and more errors (Weinberg, 1971; Brooks, 1975). On-line programming should thus be of greater benefit with low-level languages, and therefore for systems programming. This theory is consistent with the fact that Brooks, who was the manager of the team which developed IBM's OS/360 operating system, quoted the relatively high (>2:1) (Harr, 1969) figure. However, there is a trend to write system software in higher-level languages, e.g. the UNIX operating system is written in C, so this particular advantage of on-line programming must be decreasing in importance.

Different functions in the software life-cycle

The productivity improvement ratios (Table 6.20) indicate that the gain for some of the functions comprising software development, namely code, test, and debug (an average of about 2:1), is higher than the overall gain for development (about 1.2:1). The gain for code, test, and debug must therefore be significantly higher than that for the remaining functions. In fact, one organization found that systems analysis took about the same amount of time as before (van Wyk, 1978), and the COCOMO model uses, at most, a 4% gain during the requirements and product design functions (Boehm, 1981). This is not surprising, as use of interactive facilities has in the past been largely restricted to only some of the software life-cycle functions. However, this is changing as more interactive systems integrate programming support and word processing support, allowing more efficient performance of requirements and design documentation, and also with the increased use of prototyping and CASE tools, so the productivity of the other functions can also be expected to increase.

The figures in Table 6.20 refer specifically to development. If on-line benefited only development, then the ratios should be adjusted

Table 6.21 Adjusted productivity improvement

Function	Batch	Interactive	Ratio
Development	50	42	1.2:1
Maintenance	50	50	1:1
Total	100	92	1.1:1

downwards to take maintenance into account and give the overall improvement. For example, if maintenance comprises 50% of the total effort (a fairly typical figure – see Chapter 8), and interactive programming improves development productivity by 1.2:1, i.e. 20%, as stated above, then the overall productivity improvement is only 10% (Table 6.21).

However, on-line facilities do *not* apply solely to development. In fact, they may be even more useful during maintenance (if testing and debugging comprise a larger proportion of the time, as some of the evidence in Chapter 8 indicates), but estimating productivity improvement there is more difficult (Van Zijl and Evans, 1978). Nevertheless, Johnson (1980b) estimated a 30% reduction in the cost of resolving production problems, which is double the 15% productivity improvement he claimed during the implementation phase.

In addition, I have seen large gains reported for end users, i.e. during the production or operational phase. For example, one life assurance company was able to provide a faster service to its customers, at reduced administration costs, with only half the previous number of clerks (van Wyk, 1978), while facilities engineers in a manufacturing installation obtained a 3 or 4:1 productivity improvement using interactive graphics terminals instead of drafting boards for building design, and layout of electrical conduits and pipes (Ever, 1980).

Feedback

An experiment by Hansen (1976) into the quality of management decision making, showed that interactive facilities led to better decisions where feedback was required, i.e. in an iterative situation where a succession of decisions is made, with each decision depending on the result of the previous interaction.

Improvements

Interactive products are continually being improved – they are made faster and are given more powerful features (Boehm, 1981; Shneiderman, 1980). More recent studies should therefore show higher productivity rates, and a higher gain compared to batch programming, than those conducted several years ago.

6.7.2   TECHNOLOGICAL AIDS

Two software tools, valuable in interactive programming, are text editors and interactive debug.

Text editors

Text editors can be very powerful. Apart from the usual simple insertion, replacement, and deletion of text, they can provide 'the magic of full-screen editing' (Arthur, 1983), and have features such as multiple 'windows', replacement of multiple occurrences of character strings, and so on, which contribute to the productivity gain provided by interactive programming. A study of text editors by Walther and O'Neil (1974) found that people who were experienced in the use of on-line systems worked faster with the flexible version of an editor (which permitted abbreviations, default values, etc.), whereas inexperienced users were overwhelmed by its many features. (This also indicates that productivity is improved if full use is made of the available features.)

Editors can have 'intelligence' built into them, e.g. syntax checking of program source code: for instance, ADR's IDEAL 4GL uses intelligent editors to generate syntactically correct code (Applied Data Research, 1986). ('Point-and-shoot' or 'point-and-select' user interfaces can produce the same result, e.g. the TABLETALK front-end for FOCUS produces error-free report requests (Information Builders, 1987).) The muLISP-86 editor (from Soft Warehouse) causes matching parentheses to blink (Schalkoff, 1986). In the edit mode, moving the cursor to a left parenthesis causes the corresponding right parenthesis (if one exists) to blink, and vice versa. This enables the programmer to identify errors and omissions quickly. Word processing packages usually also have 'intelligence' built into them, e.g. spelling checks (particularly if they suggest alternatives for misspelled words), grammar checks, usage checks, and checks for repeated words; or if they measure the readability level or clarity of the text (the 'fog index' (Gunning, 1962; Arthur, 1983)). Examples of such programs are: IBM's office automation system, PROFS; DecisionWare's RightWriter (DecisionWare, 1986); and Writing Consultant's WordFinder (Pournelle, 1986).

Text editors are particularly valuable with interactive programming. Boehm (1981) assigns a 'nominal' rating to interactive source editors, and only a 'low' rating to batch editors. The group of tools with the nominal rating together provide a 10% higher productivity than the group with the low rating. However, the prices given by Stone (1978) show a 30% higher cost for interactive editors than for batch ones.

Text editors are useful throughout most of the software life-cycle. For example, they can be used to enter and make corrections to the program design (e.g. where a program design language is being used), the program source code, the JCL, test data, and documentation. They are therefore useful during design, coding, testing, debugging, etc.

Of a programmer's time, 80–90% is spent in some editor, so enhancements to the editor to provide more efficient interfacing could significantly improve productivity (Thadhani, 1984). Editor usage is characterized by numerous simple commands, and the need for short response time (Shneiderman, 1980).

Interactive debug

Some of the debugging tools discussed earlier are interactive: you can step through a program a line at a time as it executes, watching the values of variables, registers and flags. However, some tools go even further – they allow the programmer virtually to step backwards through the program, or even to make corrections while it is running.

Not all organizations with on-line programming facilities have interactive debug. It requires either a special debug support package working with a compiler (an example of which is the Computer Sciences Corporation's Program Checkout Facility, PCF, which operates with FORTRAN), or an interpreter (many BASIC and APL language systems have this facility) (Glass, 1979). RealDBUG is an interactive source-level debugger on PCs (REALIA, 1986). So is Orion's Unilab II. With it, the programmer can scroll back through previous displays (Orion, 1986). Other examples are Prospero's PRO PASCAL and PRO FORTRAN-77 (Prospero, 1986), and Morgan Computing's Advanced Trace86 (Webster, 1986), all of which permit both backtracking and corrections.

The acquisition cost of the software may be high, but ongoing costs are probably low (Glass, 1979). Together with interactive testing, interactive debug gives large reductions in program development calendar time, but it is not clear how much of the reduction is due to interactive debug as such, and how much to interactive testing. Furthermore, as is the case with interactive programming in general, the increase in productivity is normally somewhat less than the reduction in calendar time. Nevertheless, where interactive debug is used with a 'high-technology'

workstation, comprising a graphics screen with more than 24 lines and 80 columns; with multiple windows enabling the programmer to simultaneously see his source code, results, and debugging information; and with forward and reverse tracers; then productivity improvements of 2 or 3 to 1 are claimed (Schach, 1987). (There is though, the danger that such tools will be used as a substitute for thinking, which could result instead in a lowering of productivity. This is discussed in Chapter 8.) These workstations are much more expensive than the average terminal or PC, so it could cost around $20 000 to provide a programmer with these capabilities (Schach, 1987). However, some of the other products mentioned here provide some of these capabilities, at a lower price.

6.7.3 DISADVANTAGES

As has already been indicated, interactive programming has disadvantages: costs, bad habits, reliability, number of workstations, interchange of knowledge, and security.

Costs

Interactive programming incurs a capital cost – additional hardware (such as terminals) and software are required – and it consumes more machine resources, so a bigger and more powerful computer may be necessary. In one comparison, disk usage increased by 50% (Huskisson, 1977); a study by Schatzoff *et al.* (1967) showed a 50% higher total cost for time-sharing; and Brandon (1978) even argued that the cost outweighs the benefits. Furthermore, with interactive facilities, the processor is idle for much of the time, as the terminal operator spends a large amount of time just thinking. Worse, with on-line you have twin peaks of use, at mid-morning and mid-afternoon, when 'everybody gets down to work', and mainframe (and other centralized) computers need spare capacity to cope with this (Butlein, 1985). The amount of spare capacity required is growing due to the steady swing to on-line. The idle time on big mainframes amounted to only 15% in 1978, but rose to 25% by 1983, and Butlein predicted that mainframe sites would have to allow for 39% idle time by 1988. (These figures presumably cover both production work and programming.)

On the other hand, Sackman (1970) found that neither method had a cost advantage: time-sharing used 40% more machine time, but this was balanced by the 20% saving in man-hours; while Johnson (1980b) believes that on-line programming incurs minimal extra cost, and there may even be savings, e.g. because there is less printed output. Johnson did, in fact, quote one system which was developed on-line, and which used only one-quarter as much CPU time per person per month as a batch-developed system of about the same size, which was developed using otherwise identical tools and methods, but a large volume of production data was used to test the latter, so the comparison is not a fair one.

As hardware becomes relatively less expensive, so efficient use of it becomes less important than efficient use of people – the one is traded against the other, and the net result is that the overall development cost is reduced (Reaser *et al.*, 1974). Aron (1974) was more specific: the experiments he reported found that on-line was cost-effective for staff with above-average salaries. That was several years ago. At present, with lower hardware prices and higher salaries, on-line should be cost-effective for lower-paid staff as well. A terminal by itself now only costs a couple of dollars a day (Chapter 4). To this must be added some $10 per hour of actual use (Sanders, 1985). The latter figure, taken in conjunction with a salary of around $20 per hour (Chapter 13), is in good agreement with the claim by Grulke (1983) that even if 'all the processing power a typical user can consume' is taken into account, the cost is only about half the user's salary, and he predicted that

this would decrease to less than 15% by 1986 or 1987.

In apparent contrast, REALIA (1986) claimed that mainframe development costs thousands of dollars per programmer per month. However, a large amount of programming nowadays is done on microcomputers, which are cheap. Furthermore, vendors such as REALIA supply products which enable mainframe programs to be developed on a PC. If, therefore, mainframe development really is as expensive as REALIA claim, this would reduce development costs significantly. In addition, Yourdon (1989) believes that the higher cost of a PC compared to a dumb terminal ($3000 against $500), is justified, because most mainframes cannot provide a sufficiently consistent, fast response. One Fortune 1000 company which now does 70% of its program development with PC COBOL, has netted cost savings of 20–30% (McMullen, 1991c). It must also be borne in mind that many of the above figures are merely the cost of on-line programming. Costs would also have been incurred using batch mode. What we are really interested in here is the *difference* in cost between batch and on-line. The latter is intrinsically more expensive, and probably encourages higher usage as well, but the above figures only place an upper limit on what the difference might be.

Bad habits

With the machine doing much of the work, it is easy to grow lazy, to make snap judgements, and to adopt careless and inefficient work habits (Sackman *et al.*, 1968; Van Zijl and Evans, 1978; Glass, 1979). (This corresponds to the 'sloppiness' which 4GLs can result in.) Schatzoff *et al.* (1967) found that more compilations were made with on-line programming; while the on-line (Johnson, 1980b) system quoted above required 8 tests per 10 verbs, and 13 jobs per person per day, compared to only 5 tests per 10 verbs, and 9 jobs per person per day, for the batch system, which suggests that less time is spent in preparation and desk checking with on-line. As Bell *et al.* (1987) put it, it is tempting to try to fix bugs by inserting experimental pieces of code. Furthermore, 'it is uncomfortable to sit at a terminal without using it' (Aron, 1974). To keep the terminal busy, the programmer may recompile the program for each bug solved, instead of solving several bugs and doing one compile for all of them (Weinberg, 1971). (Though some programmers do a separate compile for every bug even in batch mode (Yourdon *et al.*, 1979a).) It therefore needs a very disciplined programmer not to waste more money than he saves.

The consequences may be more serious than just wasted machine time. Evidence, e.g. from Martin and McClure (1985), suggests that productivity may be lowered instead of raised. Some managers and researchers believe that time-sharing encourages hasty program development, and increases the number of errors, whereas the slower turnaround of batch processing produces more careful program design and thorough desk debugging (Shneiderman, 1980). Furthermore, the presence of numerous ill-thought out corrections in a program may seriously degrade its clarity and structure, and therefore its readability and quality (Bell *et al.*, 1987). Shneiderman concluded that time-sharing was beneficial for correcting minor errors quickly, but for more fundamental work was abused by some programmers.

These bad habits can grow worse with time. Adequate control must therefore be exercised. For example, interactive programming should be accompanied by other 'modern programming practices', such as structured walkthroughs. The computer's system software may help to provide this control. For example, some operating systems and database management systems can record the amount of time used by each programmer or by a particular query, or can even terminate a programmer's runs if their execution time exceeds a pre-determined limit. IBM's SQL/DS DBMS estimates the cost of a query (IBM, 1988b). This warns users which queries are heavy on machine resources, thereby enabling them to police themselves, and e.g. use alternative, cheaper, queries where possible. IBM's VM operating system can allocate a lower priority to heavy CPU users, thereby slowing down their processing, which in turn encourages them to be more economical in their use of machine resources (IBM, 1988c).

Reliability

Reliability (of hardware and system software) is even more important in an on-line environment. Breakdowns have a more immediate and obvious impact, and some people have a low tolerance to problems (Shneiderman, 1980).

Number of workstations

Sufficient workstations (terminals or PCs) must be provided to minimize queueing time at common workstations. However, as discussed earlier, it should nowadays be cost-justifiable to provide all programmers with their own terminals, or even their own PCs.

Interchange of knowledge

Unless the workstations are in a common area, on-line facilities tend to isolate programmers from their colleagues (Weinberg, 1971). Each programmer works alone at his workstation, and the social interaction between them, with its consequent interchange of knowledge, is minimized.

Security

On-line facilities carry a security risk (Brandon, 1978). On-line users – programmers, end users, etc. – may gain access – perhaps unintentionally – to unauthorized and possibly confidential information, including personal and financial data, and operational programs. They may use this information to their own benefit or to someone else's detriment, or may corrupt it, either by accident, for fun, or to commit sabotage or fraud. They need not even be in the same building as the computer, but could be linked via a telephone line or data communications network from another town or even another country or continent. Installations with on-line facilities therefore have to expend additional effort on security measures.

6.7.4 RESISTANCE

Resistance in general is discussed in Chapter 9, but some aspects related specifically to interactive programming are discussed below.

There may be some initial resistance to the introduction of interactive programming because of the disadvantages discussed above (such as cost), or for a variety of other reasons, e.g. fear of losing the work done during an editing session, and poor quality terminals (Van Zijl and Evans, 1978; Shneiderman, 1980). However, the benefits soon emerge, transforming opponents into staunch supporters. Beginners, in particular, are enthusiastic from the outset (Weinberg, 1971).

Programmers like the fast turnaround, the ease of amending and compiling programs, the ease of amending test data and JCL, and the ability to concentrate their efforts – in short, the sheer convenience (Van Zijl and Evans, 1978; Sackman *et al.*, 1968). Disadvantages, such as disruptions because of breakdowns, are disliked but tolerated. Overall, therefore, programmers *prefer* interactive programming – it is a *motivator*.

6.7.5 SUMMARY AND CONCLUSIONS

Interactive programming can increase productivity. The magnitude of the increase depends on various factors, e.g. it is particularly beneficial for correcting minor errors quickly, or where a high-technology workstation is used with interactive debug. Estimates of the magnitude differ widely, and the lower ones are probably the more accurate. According to Bell *et al.* (1987) 'any differences between the two modes of working are grossly overwhelmed by the enormous differences between individuals' (see Chapter 9).

In general, interactive programming is welcomed by programmers, and it is widely used.

Interactive programming increases hardware costs, but this is generally more than offset by the increased productivity.

Programmers can get into bad habits. If this happens, the anticipated productivity improvements will not be realized, and quality will suffer. Control is therefore necessary, and interactive programming should be accompanied by other 'modern programming practices', such as structured walkthroughs.

Interactive facilities can improve the productivity of many categories of staff, both DP and non-DP, such as programmers, systems analysts, and end users.

6.8 CASE TOOLS

Recently, a number of toolkits that provide a software environment for systems analysts have appeared on the market. These are known as CASE (computer-aided software engineering) tools. In fact, CASE tools can help all phases of the software life-cycle, from requirements analysis through to maintenance (Schach, 1988). They can be subdivided into *upper* CASE or front-end tools, and *lower* CASE or back-end. The former consists of planning, analysis and design tools, and the latter of code generators and data dictionaries (Moad, 1990a, 1990b).

CASE tools are claimed to be the most important advance in software development since the database management system (Bergen, 1989). They are the culmination of 15 years' evolution of structured analysis, design, and programming techniques, and are fundamentally changing the way application systems are developed (Howard, 1989).

6.8.1   PRODUCTS

Some examples of these tools are given below.

- **Excelerator** (from Index Technology) automates systems analysis and design, and is claimed to be the most comprehensive productivity tool for systems analysts (Index Technology, 1986). In a survey, users reported an average productivity increase of 35%, while one user reported a 4:1 increase (Index Technology, 1986, 1987). However part of these increases may be attributed to the increased involvement of end users, and prototyping. Excelerator also increased programmer productivity in this survey, including maintenance productivity, because the specifications were more complete and consistent, and it helped project management as well.
- **DesignAid** (from Nastec Corp.) automates structured analysis and design (Nastec, 1986). It validates and balances data flow diagrams (Chapter 8), and supports multiple design techniques. It can be integrated with the same vendor's project management tool, LifeCycle Manager.
- **Teamwork/SA** (from Cadre Technologies) is a structured analysis tool which integrates with the same supplier's design tool, Teamwork/SD, with which it shares a data dictionary (Barry, 1986a). Windows from both products can be displayed simultaneously. According to Charette (1986), Teamwork/SA increases productivity by 200–300%.
- The **Yourdon Analyst/Designer Toolkit** for PCs incorporates graphics, error and consistency checking, an integrated data dictionary, and an easy to use menu

system (Yourdon, 1987). Purchasers also get technical support 'from the people who wrote the book' on structured analysis and design. It is claimed to raise productivity by 30%.
- IBM's **AD/Cycle** contains an 'arsenal' of tools for planning, analysis and design, as well as application generators, knowledge-based systems, a repository for sharing information, and cross life-cycle tools that tie everything together (IBM, 1990a). These tools will be able to produce code for multiple IBM operating systems. Key elements in AD/Cycle will be produced by other organizations, such as Index Technology Corporation.

Arthur Andersen's Method 1 can be included in this category, as it is not just a methodology but is supported by technological aids ('Methodology for productivity', *Computer Mail*, 31 Oct 1986, pp. 55–58.) Furthermore, future development of it will include the generation of code directly from the design.

25 products are described in Gane (1988).

CASE products are usually PC-based (Yourdon, 1989).

6.8.2   PRODUCTIVITY GAIN

Productivity gains claimed for individual products were quoted above. These indicate that gains of about 30% can typically be expected, but much higher gains, of about 300%, can sometimes be achieved. Other claims are quoted below.

The highest gain in a survey by Don Reifer of 45 companies in ten industries was 25%, and the average gain was only about 10% (Schach, 1992). Loh and Nelson (1989) report a reduction of 20% in the average number of hours spent per project, for projects of up to two years' duration, but no significant reduction for longer projects. Moad (1990a) stated that, in isolated cases, users have reported fivefold productivity gains in new product development. He also quoted one organization which believes that gains of five or ten times can probably be achieved, if sufficient training and support are provided. (The amount of training required can be significant, and this is discussed later.) Texas Instruments set itself the goal of improving its own internal DP productivity by a factor of five by 1990 (i.e. in only three years) through using its own CASE tools (Carlyle, 1987c). One organization, First Boston Corporation, estimated that they have received 100-fold (i.e. 10 000%) increases in application programmer productivity from the CASE tools they developed themselves (Clemons, 1991).

The Hartford Insurance Group reduced maintenance costs by 20%, and achieved an improvement of almost 30% in their overall productivity (Carlyle, 1987c). Respondents in a survey by the University of Houston reported a 35% increase in maintenance productivity, because applications required less rework (Loh and Nelson, 1989). Moad (1990a) quoted one organization which calculated that, by automating much of the analysis and design phases, they had achieved a 97% improvement in system quality, as measured by the number of user change requests. Moad also quoted one organization which achieved a 70–90% reduction in maintenance through the use of iterative development, heavy user involvement, and CASE tools. He also quoted a third organization, which rewrote an IMS-based application in DB2 using CASE tools. (IMS is an old, hierarchical DBMS, and DB2 is a new, relational DBMS.) New functions, that used to take up to eight weeks to add to the original system, can be added to the rewritten version in four to eight hours. (This represents a productivity improvement of perhaps 30:1. It is not easy to say how much of this can be ascribed to the CASE tools, and how much to the improved DBMS environment.) Most of the organizations in a Datamation/Price Waterhouse opinion survey believed that CASE tools had little impact on productivity in the short term, but half of them predicted

gains of up to 100% – and some predicted up to 200% – over the next five years because of decreased maintenance in particular, but presumably also because of anticipated improvements to the tools: 'Users forecast that CASE's prototyping muscle will be even stronger by 1993, when screen painters and end-user reporting tools are incorporated within the CASE environment' (Statland, 1989). (Excelerator is already claimed to have easy-to-use screen and report prototyping, and analysis facilities including 'where used' reporting and extensive *ad hoc* reporting capabilities (Index Technology, 1986, 1987).)

Conclusion

The additional information in this section confirms the figures given in the introduction to the section. Productivity gains of about 30% are frequently achieved, for both development and maintenance, while much higher gains, of 300% and above, are sometimes possible. Furthermore, future gains will be higher than those obtainable today. However, the productivity gains which have been observed may be due, at least in part, to associated factors, such as greater user involvement.

6.8.3 EXTENT OF USE

Only one-quarter of the organizations in the Datamation/Price Waterhouse survey referred to above were using CASE tools (Statland, 1989). (Large organizations were making much greater use of the tools than small ones.) Worse, only 2% of the systems analysts in the US had CASE tools available to them in 1987, and it was estimated that only 10% would have them in 1990 (Yourdon, 1989). Carlyle (1990) reported that only 4% of programs were coded using CASE technology, while Hughes and Clark (1990) reported that, in one large firm, 80–90% of the CASE toolkits purchased remained unused.

6.8.4   DISADVANTAGES

The widespread introduction of CASE technology may be premature and even dangerous at present, as organizations are not yet ready for it because of a lack of software development standards, incompatible data structures, and the uncontrolled proliferation of incompatible data: 'Companies with expanding populations of personal computers also have a widening pool of corrupt data that is more of a liability than an asset, and those with CASE tools write programs that utilize bad data even faster than before' (Carlyle, 1987c, 1990). The low usage of CASE tools reported above may therefore may be a good thing, at least at present.

The amount of training required can be significant. Loh and Nelson (1989) reported an average of 155 hours per person (made up of 69 hours learning on their own and 86 hours in group training sessions and private instruction), after which it might still take a few months to become proficient in the tools: 'The learning curve was much more difficult than we thought it would be'. Furthermore, to take full advantage of CASE tools, existing software staff will have to be more extensively trained in the use of structured analysis and design (Statland, 1989).

The Reifer survey found that the average cost of introducing CASE was $125 000 per seat (Schach, 1992).

CASE may also lead to resistance from the staff. Programmers will, in future, spend most of their time analysing and designing applications, and working with users, and may see CASE 'as a threat to the creativity they enjoy and to the control they exercise in their jobs' (Moad, 1990a).

A major gap in current CASE tools is that they are of limited use for the maintenance of existing systems: they generally have little or no ability to 'reverse engineer' existing applications to enable them to take advantage of the CASE tools' capabilities for design, analysis, etc., and one authority predicted that it would be five years before usable reverse engineering tools were available (Moad, 1990b). McMullen (1991a) stated that Index Technology's Excelerator for Design Recovery 'may be one of the more far-reaching solutions' to this problem. (Reverse engineering here means analysing existing code to reconstruct the original source information, design documentation, and specifications 'that have long since been lost or forgotten' (Moad, 1990b; Radice and Phillips, 1988).)

Other limitations are that 'upper' and 'lower' CASE tools are not adequately linked together, and the tools are weak at coordinating the multiple activities involved in software development (Moad, 1990a). Current tools have difficulty sharing data, making them particularly inadequate for complex projects; and they lack, or have inadequate interfaces to, other tools (Loh and Nelson, 1989). (The lack of 'prototyping muscle' – screen painters and end-user reporting tools – was referred to earlier.) CASE tools are inflexible, making it difficult to tailor them to particular methodologies or organizational standards (Statland, 1989). This is presumably why more than 80% of the organizations in the University of Houston survey 'altered their chosen methodology' as a result of using CASE tools (Loh and Nelson, 1989). (It is not clear from the wording whether these organizations made changes to their existing methodology, or switched to a different one, but some – and perhaps all – of them, did switch to a different one.) Furthermore, a problem affecting the productivity gain achievable with 'upper' CASE tools (which are used for requirements analysis), is that users do not know their current or future needs, 'so the solution of using a PC drawing package isn't going to solve the problem' (Moad, 1990a).

6.8.5   BENEFITS

Benefits claimed (or anticipated) for CASE tools, in addition to improved productivity, include (Statland, 1989; Loh and Nelson, 1989; Schach, 1992):

- shorter development time;
- higher quality;
- improved documentation;
- better enforcement of standards;
- consistency (e.g. standardized design formats, and similar screens and menus), which in turn permits easier movement of people from one job to another;
- enhanced user participation (e.g. because of prototyping and joint analysis and design workshops, which are often used in conjunction with CASE tools);
- better communication between users and designers (e.g. because of the enhanced user participation, and the graphic depiction of complex systems provided by the CASE tools), resulting in better understanding;
- improved fitness for use of the resulting product;
- better project control; and
- longer program life (because of the level of decomposition that can be achieved in the analysis and design stages).

6.8.6 CONCLUSION

CASE can be expensive. It is not just the cost of the tools, but also the extensive training and experience required. CASE also leads to a change in the programmers' duties, and to changes in the organization's standards and methodologies. Most organizations are not yet ready for CASE.

Current tools have limitations, but high gains in productivity can nevertheless often be achieved. The magnitude of the gains depends on such factors as the size and complexity of the project, staff proficiency in the tools, and their acceptance of the tools. Part of the observed gains may be due to associated factors, such as greater user involvement. The reduction provided by the tools in maintenance effort is likely to be greater than that in development effort, but

at present only for systems which were developed using CASE tools.

6.9 PRODUCTIVITY GAIN

Many software tools have been discussed in this chapter. What productivity gain can be expected from them? Figures were given for the most important tools discussed, and these are summarized below, but what gain is delivered by the many other tools discussed, for which quantitative claims were not made? What gain is delivered by using a comprehensive *combination* of tools?

As one might expect, the gain varies greatly from one software tool to another. The figures given earlier indicate, for example, that data base management systems can improve productivity by 3:1, high-level languages by the same amount, fourth-generation languages by 10:1 or more, on-line programming by 2:1 (and by a further 2 or 3:1 if used with a 'high-technology' workstation and interactive debug), and CASE tools by typically 1.3:1, while a file comparator can often halve bug-finding time. (These figures apply specifically to development. Quantitative information about the impact of tools on maintenance productivity was much scarcer, but suggests that the productivity gains there are often higher than for development.) However, these figures should be viewed with caution. For example, DBMSs may only give such a high gain in productivity if used in conjunction with 4GLs; the overall productivity gain from 4GLs is much lower than 10:1 – probably only 2:1 – if we take into account the fact that they are of limited use for maintaining systems written in lower level languages; the figure of 2:1 for on-line programming applies to only the code, test, and debug functions, the overall gain being only about 1.2:1; the gain delivered by CASE tools will be higher in future; and the claims for file comparators and a 'high-technology' workstation with interactive debug, were isolated ones.

Furthermore, authorities like Gilb (1988) and Jones (1986b) believe that tools have failed to deliver substantial and scientifically proven improvements in productivity. The large gains (10:1) attributed to them are based on isolated cases, small projects, ambiguous data, or coding only. The gains may therefore have been due, for example, to super-programmers on particular projects. In addition, the claims are narrow in scope, e.g. they do not address quality, cost, and user benefits, and they do not take into account undesirable side-effects, such as performance destruction or portability reduction. Tools may, in fact, do more harm than good: they may, for example, just help us produce the wrong product faster. However, with the wider use of prototyping and CASE tools, it is surely less likely that the wrong product will be produced. (These aspects are discussed further in Chapter 13.)

What productivity gain, therefore, does Jones (1986b) think that tools can deliver? He has observed that the most productive organizations are those which are well equipped with software tools. He calculated that organizations which spent $50 000 per programmer/analyst had a development productivity 2.5 times higher than those which spent only $2500. (The additional expenditure of $47 500 increased productivity from 51 to 126 lines of code per month, and reduced the cost from $103 to $40 per line of code. If the value of the code to the organization is at least equal to its development cost, i.e. at least $103 per line (to cover the worst case), then programmers in the worst environment were generating at least (51 * $103 =) $5253 of value for their organizations each month, while those in the best environment were generating at least (126 * $103 =) $12 978, i.e. $7725 extra per month. The cost of the extra tools was therefore recovered in only (47 500/7725 =) 6 months.) Jones also calculated that the effect on maintenance was even greater: productivity there was six times higher. Furthermore, although he described the

organization with the higher productivity as a 'best case', DBMSs and 4GLs were not included amongst their tools. Even higher productivity gains are therefore possible.

Yourdon (1989) estimated that the cost of a sophisticated workstation, including project-level minicomputer support and an automated workbench, was about $25 000. (This is very similar to the Schach (1987) figure, quoted earlier, of around $20 000 per programmer for a 'high-technology' workstation with powerful interactive debug capabilities.) Yourdon pointed out that this was only about the annual salary, in 1987, of a typical computer programmer with one or two year's experience. If staff overheads of insurance and pension are included, and the cost of the hardware and software are amortized over three years, then the equipment cost is roughly equal to 15% of a programmer's annual cost. If, therefore, the equipment increases programmer productivity by just 15%, it pays for itself. Yourdon also pointedly commented on the irony of investing $50 000 to $75 000 per worker in capital equipment for farm and factory workers (see Table 4.1), while begrudging a much smaller amount for information workers. However, he warned that an automated software development workbench does not guarantee that productivity will improve by a factor of ten: 'Stupidity, arrogance, laziness, and other human frailties will always make it possible to fail despite the best of tools and support'.

Parikh (1984) stated that tools generally increase staff effectiveness dramatically, and that productivity gains of 1000% are sometimes claimed for 4GLs. However, he emphasized that such high gains will only be achieved if the tools fit your work. Almost identical comments are contained in Martin (1982a).

According to Boehm (1981), there has been relatively little assessment of the impact of tools on software cost and productivity, but he nevertheless quoted the following results.

- According to his COCOMO model, productivity is 1.5 times higher if a comprehensive set of tools is used, than if the only tools are the assembler, basic linker, basic (language dependent) monitor, and batch debug aids. (The comprehensive set of tools consists of a full programming support library with configuration management aids, a full, integrated documentation system, a project control system, a database management system, and so on. It therefore corresponds to the ADA Programming Support Environment (APSE).) The COCOMO figures also show that tool use produces a larger reduction in effort in the later phases of software development than in the early phases. This is due partly to the earlier elimination of errors through the use of tools, and partly to the greater number and maturity of tools to aid in the later phases. (CASE tools are rectifying this situation.) The figures also show that maxicomputer tools give a 10% higher productivity than minicomputer tools, and a 24% higher productivity than microprocessor tools. (Similarly, in an experiment referred to earlier, Weinberg (1971) found a 30% higher productivity from the full version of a language (intended for larger mainframe computers), than from the subset of the language (intended for smaller mainframes).)
- A Delphi survey by Scott and Simmons (1974) gave a high rating (+5 on a scale of −7 to +7) to the impact of tools on software cost and productivity. (A Delphi survey is a technique for anonymously obtaining consensus between a group of people (Helmer, 1966).)
- Another Delphi analysis, by Boehm *et al.* (1974), estimated potential cost savings of about 20%, for both development and maintenance, by using the National Software Works tool capability (Millstein *et al.*, 1976) on a very large business data processing project.
- Various software development teams recently coming from well-tooled environments onto poorly-tooled projects, have estimated typical productivity losses of 33%.
- A study by the System Development Corporation found a productivity range of 2 or 3:1 (Stone, 1978; Stone and Coleman, 1979). (They defined a set of capabilities corresponding roughly to the capabilities provided by the comprehensive set of COCOMO tools and the ADA Programming Support Environment (APSE) described above. Software tools which together provided 70% of these capabilities delivered a productivity 1.9 times higher than those which provided only 30%; and tools which provided 80% of these capabilities delivered a productivity 2.7 times higher than those which provided only 20%. The full set of tools, providing 100% of the capabilities, would have cost $20 million in 1978.)

6.10 CONCLUSION

There are numerous tools available to aid software engineers, and some of them form comprehensive and integrated environments.

Very large gains in productivity have been attributed to the use of tools. Some authorities have criticized these claims, but the criticisms seem to apply only to the highest claims, i.e. there is general agreement that significant gains are possible.

Application packages, also known as pre-programmed or pre-planned applications, and generic software, should have a significant impact on the computer industry and its productivity. Claims made for them rival in enthusiasm those made for fourth-generation languages.

- 'In the long term with more packages becoming available, the programmer will be virtually redundant and packages will become the main outlet for computer software.' (Ramsey, 1980)
- 'Most of the programs used in micros will be bought as complete and ready-to-run packages.' (Martin, 1981)
- 'This method should accelerate the proliferation of computers in all industry segments.' (Norman, 1978)
- 'The abundance of packages has become the driving force for unlocking the great potential of the personal computer as a business tool.' (Schechter, 1986)
- 'There is an overwhelming demand from customers for packaged software that will allow them to apply computer power to an exploding variety of new tasks.' (Schechter, 1986)
- 'The smaller business will be able to obtain total business application packages catering for all their needs.' (Knox, 1978)

However, not all authorities share these views.

- 'Application packages will not meet the needs of most applications that will be computerized.' (Vaughan, 1982)
- 'The buyer of a minicomputer prefers to have software customized for his own particular, and sometimes peculiar, way of doing things.' (Dieperink, 1977)

- 'No package can satisfy all the needs of a package user.' (Garber, 1976)
- 'They do not cater for all the idiosyncrasies of individual businesses.' (Big business for minicomputers, *Computronics*, 13th Feb. 1980, p. 8)
- 'The chances are remote that such a package would exactly fit a user's needs.' (Campbell, 1978)
- 'Application packages were designed to meet approximately 80% of any user's requirements.' (Holgate, 1983)
- 'Purchased software may meet only 30–50% of your needs.' (Arthur, 1983)

Packages will therefore be examined here, to determine which of these opposing viewpoints is correct.

7.1 INTRODUCTION

Definition

Packages are simply *generalized* computer systems. Instead of being usable by only one organization, they can be used by many (Lucas, 1985). This is possible because different organizations have similar needs: 'What you want to do has almost certainly been done before' (Expert warns of pitfalls for new computer users, *Computronics*, 13th Feb. 1980, p. 5). So instead of each organization re-inventing the wheel at great cost to each of them, the generalized system is developed just once, is used by many organizations, and the development cost is spread over all the many user organizations.

Generally, the term 'package' refers to the software only, but some authorities, such as

Arthur (1983) and Boehm (1981), include 'turnkey' packages, i.e. both the software and the associated hardware, in their definitions. Both these authorities include re-used code as well: 'with minor modifications, your existing systems may meet your needs'. This is especially true in large organizations with little communication between departments about the software each uses.

Productivity improvement and cost reduction

Application packages have great potential for cost reduction, and this is equivalent to a productivity improvement. Taking a simplistic view, if a particular package is used by 100 organizations, then in effect, 100 systems have been developed in the time it would have taken to develop just one, and at the cost of just one – a productivity improvement and cost reduction of 100:1. If 1000 organizations use the package, then the improvement is 1000:1. (This view is simplistic because good packages take longer to develop than ordinary systems, e.g. because they must be more general (Lucas, 1985), and because many user organizations require their packages to be customized. Both of these factors reduce the gains, and so are discussed further later.)

In practice, the cost reductions are so great that, frequently, for the price of one person's salary, a package can provide information an organization could only otherwise produce by employing several extra staff (Moir, 1980).

Choice of computer

Packages may also be a factor in the choice of computer. It has been recommended that organizations should first find a suitable package, and then find a machine on which it can run (Lucas, 1985; Big business for mini-computers, *Computronics*, 13th Feb 1980, p. 8), and a number of organizations have taken this advice (Business systems range gives more for less, *Computer Systems in Southern Africa*, Aug. 1983, p. 47). Some, for example, have bought a Sperry (Unisys) 1100 computer so they could run its MAPPER 4GL (Martin, 1985), while one organization bought an IBM S/38 in preference to a DEC VAX 'because DEC lacked adequate payroll, general ledger, and costing software' (Moad, 1986b). Arthur (1983) stated that the availability of software is one of the reasons IBM dominates the mainframe market, and DEC the mini market.

However, this advice might mean acquiring a second, or even more, incompatible computers (Arthur, 1983). Furthermore, some packages – such as the Millenium financial packages – run only on large computers, so this advice might entail acquiring a bigger and more expensive computer than would otherwise be necessary. On the other hand, packages for PCs were rated better in surveys than those available for minis (Verity, 1986b).

Sources

Packages are produced by

- computer manufacturers
- specialist firms (software houses and bureaux)
- individuals, and
- (even) user organizations.

A user organization may develop a system for its own, internal use, and then realize that it has marketing potential; this is reportedly how the SAS statistical analysis system originated. Alternatively, a user organization requiring a particular system may approach other organizations which are similar, or are even direct competitors, and buy from them the corresponding system they had already written for themselves (Arthur, 1983; Carlyle, 1989a).

In the case of re-used code, the organization requiring the system is itself the source.

Some packages are the result of a joint effort, e.g. the MEDICL health care package was written by the St James Hospital in Leeds in Britain, but the ICL implementation thereof was by the University of Leeds (Heath, 1986).

Packages are obtainable from the developers or their agents (particularly independent stores). Some packages are run on bureau machines. Cheap or free packages are obtainable from computer users groups, computer club libraries, electronic bulletin board systems, or magazines.

Lists of available packages, and details of individual packages, are published from time to time in the computer literature, or the literature for specific industries. For example, the 1987 *Radio Shack Software Reference Guide* lists over 600 software programs (Radio Shack, 1986). Similar information is provided by International Computer Programs, Inc., Auerbach Publishers, Inc., and Datapro Research Corporation, while vendors such as IBM produce catalogues of their software – Computer Associates, for example, list their products in their quarterly magazine, *CA-Insight*.

Classification

Packages are generally classified according to their use, with different authorities using different classification systems, e.g. Kessel (1976) suggests

- **system software packages** e.g. programs for improving hardware throughput;
- **software development aids** i.e. tools such as preprocessors and fourth-generation software, for improving programmer productivity;
- **application packages** i.e. systems generally developed by ordinary organizations for their own user departments, including general ledger, debtors, creditors, and payroll.

Lucas (1985) gives a similar classification:

- **systems software**, such as DBMSs (e.g. TOTAL and ADABAS);

- **higher-order languages/applications generators**, such as NATURAL and FOCUS;
- **problem-oriented languages**, which includes statistical packages like SAS and SPSS (Statistical Package for the Social Sciences), graphics packages such as CA-TELLAGRAPH, and spreadsheets such as VisiCalc and Lotus 1–2–3;
- **dedicated**, such as accounts receivable, or a garment system.

Arthur (1983) uses just two categories:

- **systems software**, which helps people use the computer; and
- **application software**, which helps people run the business.

An alternative and far more detailed classification system (more detailed than required here), is that by International Computer Programs, Inc. (Software Catalogue, *The 1983 SA Computer Users Handbook*, Johannesburg: Systems Publishers (Pty) Ltd., 1983, pp. 11–94). It has three main categories:

- **data processing management**;
- **general industry applications**; and
- **industry specific applications**.

Each of these categories is further subdivided, to a depth of up to five levels, giving a total of over 300 categories.

Data processing management includes the system software packages and software development aids of the Kessel (1976) classification, while general industry applications and industry specific applications both come under the application packages classification.

Boehm (1981) also classifies packages according to their use. His subdivision is:

- **management information systems** e.g. payroll and general ledger;
- **industrial support systems** e.g. process control;
- **office automation** e.g. word processing and electronic mail;
- **utilities** e.g. sorting and report generation; and

- **software tools**.

However, he also gives two alternative views of packages:

- **forms** i.e. whether the package consists of a small, single-purpose module (e.g. for sorting), an integrated software subsystem (e.g. DBMSs and Programmers' Workbenches), or integrated hardware/software turnkey systems (e.g. word processing and process control);
- **arrangements** e.g. whether the source code is provided, whether the vendor provides customizing, and the method of payment.

The discussion in this chapter concentrates on application packages, using the Kessel (1976) definition, but the principles involved do have wider validity. The other types of packages were discussed in Chapter 6.

7.2 ADVANTAGES AND DISADVANTAGES

7.2.1 ADVANTAGES

There are various reasons for using packages.

Cost

Because the development costs are spread over many user organizations, packages cost much less than custom-built systems. Various estimates are given in Table 7.1.

The usage figures (Table 7.3) show wide variations between packages, indicating that we can expect similarly high variations in the ratio of purchase to development cost.

Table 7.1 Cost of packages compared to custom-built systems

Gunther (1978)	2%
Boehm (1981)	10% (0.4% to 33% in extreme cases)
Arthur (1983)	10–20%
Computer Sciences (1978)	20%
Merrick (1976)	20%

Even greater savings are possible in some cases.

- Some packages are obtainable from computer user groups for a nominal fee, or from computer club libraries.
- Similarly, 'public domain' packages for PCs can be had for as little as $3 per diskette, and 'shareware' packages are not much more expensive; see, for example, the advertisements in *PC Magazine*.
- The source listings of other packages appear in the computer literature, such as in *PC Magazine*, and even in non-computer magazines, such as *Sky & Telescope*, and so can be obtained for the price of the magazine or book. (These are mostly very small programs, though the 'COBOL Software Metric Program' listed in Arthur (1983) extends to 32 pages.) Alternatively, the magazine might include a diskette containing the source code, or the publishers of the magazine might provide an electronic downloading service, such as *PC MagNet*.
- Yet other packages may be used at bureaux without having to be purchased.

Furthermore, both the acquisition cost and the running costs are known in advance, which is not generally the case for custom-built systems.

Time-scale

Software development is a very time-consuming process. By opting for a package, the organization acquires a ready-made system, and can start deriving the benefits from it much sooner, i.e. there is earlier payback. Boehm (1981) gives one example where a custom-built system would have taken six times as long – the package would have been installed within two months, compared to eleven for the custom-built system; while Arthur (1983) believes a custom-built system may take 10–100 times as long. If the facilities are required urgently therefore, a package may be the only solution. Furthermore, it is difficult to estimate how long it will take to develop a custom-built system. Provided a package has been wisely chosen (e.g. minimal customizing required), the organization will know much more reliably when the system will be installed and ready for use.

Manpower

By purchasing a package, the staff who would otherwise have had to custom-build the system remain available for other tasks, such as ones for which no suitable packages are available. With a shortage of staff, this is a major benefit (Boehm, 1981).

Expertise (development)

Building a system generally requires a much higher level of expertise than choosing a package to perform the same functions. If the organization has only limited expertise, or if the application area is highly specialized, then a package is the better – and safer – solution. A custom-built system in such circumstances carries a high risk of failure, whereas the package would usually have been developed by people with the requisite specialist skills (Boehm, 1981). Nevertheless, if the organization elects to build its own system anyway, the packages on the market can be a source of ideas (Parkin, 1980).

Expertise (operational)

If the organization is embarking on a new application area, the package vendor should be able to provide training in this area. If the package is a specialized one, there may be a user group from whom the organization can learn additional uses of the package.

Error-free

Packages are generally well tested before they are released onto the market. They are

subsequently used by many organizations, so most remaining bugs are soon uncovered and corrected. Packages are therefore essentially bug-free, unlike many custom-built systems. This results in further time and cost savings to user organizations.

Low-risk

Because of the known costs, reliable installation date, freedom from errors, etc., packages are a low-risk option, and therefore also have a lower *emotional* cost (Theron, 1977). The supplier might also allow a free trial period. Packages can be likened to prototyping (Chapter 8): the output can be produced with very little effort, so the user can see if it meets his needs, and it can help him to define his requirements.

User involvement

Some custom-built systems have 'failed completely' to involve users (Lucas, 1985). While the same danger exists when a package is chosen for individual organizations, the dangers should be less serious because users generally participate in the development of packages, and after they are released onto the market, customers provide feedback. The multiplicity of options in many packages further reduces the danger of their not meeting individual organizations' needs.

Error checking

Packages generally have comprehensive editing of input data, and provide helpful error messages e.g. for operator errors, whereas these features may be skimped on in custom-built systems, because they are time-consuming and costly to provide. It is easier to justify the cost of building them into a system if the system will be used by many organizations.

Documentation and user interface

Similarly, packages generally have better documentation, built-in on-line help facilities, and so on, than custom-built systems, again because of the time and cost factors, and because existing customers have asked for it.

Features

Packages often have extra features that would not be cost-justifiable to include in a custom-built system (Lucas, 1985).

Changing requirements

Changing tax and reporting requirements, shifting economic conditions, and 'the insatiable curiosity' of end users, make it difficult and expensive for DP departments to keep up (Wiener, 1986). The only way to satisfy these changing needs may be with increasingly sophisticated and flexible software packages, rather than custom-built systems. (On the other hand, the same article which expressed this opinion, also admitted that 'Lotus still hasn't upgraded most 1–2–3 version 1A users to 2.0, let alone gotten them to learn to use an even more complicated tool kit' (Wiener, 1986).)

7.2.2 DISADVANTAGES

Packages have a number of disadvantages as well.

Meeting users needs

Packages generally do not meet all the user's needs: according to van der Merwe (1988), they only satisfy about 80–90% of requirements, while according to Holgate (1983), application packages are designed to meet only about 80% of any user's requirements. The user must therefore change his procedures to fit in with the package, or just live with the inadequacies, or the package must be modified or added to (which reduces the time and cost benefits, and may also introduce errors and invalidate the guarantee).

Furthermore, a user organization can only modify a package if it has the source code; otherwise it is dependent on the supplier to do so, and he may not be willing (section 7.5).

Changing requirements

Even if the package initially meets the user organization's requirements, over a period of time users' needs change. If the user organization does not have the source code, it is unable to make the corresponding alterations to the package itself, and it may be difficult to negotiate an acceptable cost and schedule for the vendor to make them (Boehm, 1981).

User involvement

Packages, by their very nature, impose a predetermined system on users (Lucas, 1985).

Unwanted functions

Because a package is generalized, it contains many functions that individual users do not require, but must still pay for. These unwanted functions have other disadvantages, such as consuming additional hardware resources and causing additional operational complexity (see below).

Cost

Brandon (1978) maintains that, because a package will not meet an organization's needs as well as a custom-built system, in the long run the latter will prove cheaper. Boehm (1981) appears to agree with this view. In an example, he uses a figure of $15 000 as the monthly payback from one particular custom-built system, and only $10 000 from the package alternative. Furthermore, because packages are more general, they are larger, more complex, and often less efficient, thereby increasing hardware and other running costs (Lucas, 1985).

Time-scale

There may be procurement delays. Many organizations have 'long, cumbersome authorization and acquisition procedures which may take longer to surmount than it would take to develop a small product in-house' (Boehm, 1981).

Expertise (development)

If an organization which lacks expertise in a particular area chooses a package because of this, then it loses the opportunity to gain this expertise, which will prove detrimental in the long term if this knowledge is required on subsequent projects (Boehm, 1981).

Expertise (operational)

Because a package is generalized, it has more options and so may be more difficult to install and run than a custom-built system (Lucas, 1985).

Hardware

The best package might not run on your computer, so either you have to buy another computer, or you have to buy a second-best package.

Incompatibilities

Similarly, the best package might not be compatible with your system software, or your other application software (Boehm, 1981).

Support

With a package, you are dependent on the vendor for support and subsequent enhancements. With a cheap package, support is non-existent.

7.2.3 CONCLUSION

Packages have disadvantages as well as advantages, but the disadvantages are often outweighed by the advantages.

For example, the additional functions *can* increase running costs, but normally this is small in comparison with the savings from the lower cost of the package compared to a custom-built system. Furthermore, the package might have been written with better efficiency techniques than the typical custom-built system – it may even have been written in Assembler, which few user organizations are able to do nowadays. (An example of such a package, the ESS spreadsheet, was given in Chapter 6.) Similarly, the extra functions *can* make the package more complicated to use, but more attention might have been devoted to its user interface, thereby offsetting this disadvantage. In addition, in the longer term, the organization might find that these extra functions are useful.

It therefore seems likely that there are many cases where packages provide the better solution, and this is confirmed by the high sales figures given below.

7.3 EXTENT OF USE

7.3.1 NUMBER OF PACKAGES AVAILABLE

There is a great deal of commercial software available, from many different organizations around the world; there were reportedly 14 000 organizations marketing 27 000 different products in the USA alone (Schechter, 1986). A few years ago, over 700 software products were available for the Victor Sirius computer, and 12 000 for the Apple IIE, while there were 800 free programs for the COMMODORE (A profile of the Victor Sirius, *Computer Systems in Southern Africa*, Aug. 1983, pp. 48–49; Vaughan, 1984; Harris, 1983). There were 22 000 educational programs for the BBC micro, and 20–30 000 application programs for MS-DOS; while more than 1000 applications were announced with IBM's Application System/400, and over 2500 by the time it became generally available (Pine, 1989).

7.3.2 SALES FIGURES

The usage figures given here were obtained from a variety of sources, but mostly from the vendors, so they should be treated with caution, e.g. they may be the number of licences sold, which is generally higher than the number of organizations actually using the products; some organizations may merely be using the products on a trial basis, or may only be using them to a limited extent, or may even have discontinued using them. The objective in giving these figures is firstly to show that there is a considerable amount of packaged software in use, and secondly to give a rough idea of the impact this has had on productivity (and the impact it will have in future), so precise figures are not necessary. In any case, these figures are changing all the time.

Several catalogues show the number of organizations using each of the packages listed. The number varies widely from one package to another, ranging from 'new product' (so there may not be any users yet), to 'plenty'. The average number of user organizations for the packages in one of these catalogues is given in Table 7.2.

Table 7.2 Average number of user organizations per package (Rodney, 1986)

Type of package	No. of packages	Total users	Average
Data processing management	3	3 866	1 289
General applications	35	29 993	857
Industry specific	15	1 365	91
Total	53	35 224	665

According to Price (1987), packages for niche markets have generally had greater success than more generalized packages. This statement appears to contradict the above figures. Presumably, specialized packages enjoy greater success within their niche than generalized packages; but outside the niche the generalized packages have high sales, while the specialized packages may have none. Alternatively, perhaps he is referring to how well they meet the users' needs, rather than the number sold.

Sales figures for some individual packages, of all three Kessel (1976) types, are given in Table 7.3. As would be expected, the packages with the highest sales are PC packages. However, these are, to a large extent, used by only one person each, whereas packages on minis and mainframes are generally used by many people, so caution should be observed when interpreting the figures.

Similarly, the sales figures for system software packages and software development aids are generally higher than those for application packages. This is consistent with the 1986 Datamation/Cowen & Co. Computer/Telecommunications Industry Survey finding that approximately 61% of users' spending for unbundled mainframe software goes on systems packages, and only 39% on applications packages (Verity, 1986a).

7.3.3 PROPORTION OF SOFTWARE MARKET

Packages also form an increasing proportion of the total software in use: in 1978, it was estimated that purchased software would increase its share of the total from 10–15% of the executed instructions, to 75–80% in ten years (Norman, 1978). With tens of millions of copies of MS-DOS in existence, perhaps 1 million copies of UNIX, and so on (Chapter 6), and with the figures in Chapter 8 indicating that there are currently probably less than one million professional programmers in the USA, the number of computers must exceed the number of professional programmers by

Table 7.3 Sales figures

Package and type	Source	Sales
Lotus 1-2-3 (spreadsheet)	Appunn (1988)	over 3 000 000 users
VisiCalc (spreadsheet)	VisiCorp‡ (1984)	700 000
WordStar (word processing)	Kerr (1987)	500 000–1 000 000
TurboPascal (compiler)	Borland (1986)	500 000
DAC EASY ACCOUNTING (accounting)	Software§ (1986a)	95 000*
TYPEQUICK (keyboard training)	Software§ (1986a)	50 000
DATA ENTRY EMULATOR (bulk data capture)	Software§ (1986a)	40 000*
COMET (accounting)	Software§ (1986a)	40 000
POP-UP DESK SET (desk top utilities)	Software§ (1986a)	35 000*
AI: TYPIST (word processing)	Software§ (1986a)	30 000*
DAC EASY WORD (word processing)	Software§ (1986a)	30 000
C86 (C compiler)	Computer Innovations (1986)	20 000
SOLUTIONS (accounting)	Software§ (1986a)	12 000
IBM's MAPICS (manufacturing)	McCusker (1987a)	10 000
SYNCSORT (sort utility)	Software** (1984)	8500
LIBRARIAN (utility)	Software†† (1983a)	6000
UFO (User Files Online)	Schatz (1986b)	2000
SAS Graph (graphics)	Wiener (1986)	1100
IBM's GDDM (graphics)	Wiener (1986)	1100
SAP R/2 System (multiple)†		1000
Conserv's Amaps (manufacturing)	McCusker (1987a)	850
FCS-EPS (decision support)		700
MSA's Arista (manufacturing)	McCusker (1987a)	575
IBM's COPICS (manufacturing)	McCusker (1987a)	500
OPEN PLAN (critical path)	Software§ (1986a)	500
Cullinet's Applications System Manufacturing	McCusker (1987a)	250‡‡
MANCOS (manufacturing and inventory control)	Software§ (1986a)	140

* In USA.
† SAP's R/2 System contains a data base interface, word processing, inventory control, invoicing, a personnel planning and control system, cost accounting, and many other modules.
‡ VisiCorp, hot a year ago, is now under siege, *Computing S.A.*, 13 Apr 1984, p. 23.
§ The Software Buyers Guide, *Computer Mail*, 31 Oct 1986, pp. 3–53.
** *The 1984 Software Catalogue*, Supplement to *SA Software News* Feb 1984.
†† Software Catalogue, *The 1983 S.A. Computer Users Handbook*, Johannesburg Systems Publishers (Pty) Ltd. pp. I1–94.
‡‡ Mainframe.

at least a factor of ten, making this prediction plausible. (As James Collins of Johnson & Johnson put it, 'Depending on your definition of a computer, there are roughly six or more computers to every programmer. You can't have a $30 000 programmer for every $10 000 machine, and your users can't do everything by themselves' (Pantages, 1987).)

On the other hand, among the sites in the 1986 Datamation/Cowen & Co. Computer/Telecommunications Industry Survey, packaged software consumed only 10% of the average mainframe DP budget (Verity, 1986a). Similarly, the Datamation/Cowen & Co. 1986–87 mini/micro survey found that spending on PC packages accounted for only

20% of the cost of the PC systems (Verity, 1986b). Although higher, this still casts doubt on the 75–80% prediction.

Perhaps the discrepancy is apparent rather than real, and is caused by the lower cost of packages compared to custom-built software. In apparent confirmation of this theory, Wiener (1986) stated that surveys by the Computer Intelligence Corp. showed that more than 55% of the accounting software running on IBM mainframes was 'home-grown', implying that up to 45% was packages.

7.3.4 PENETRATION OF MARKET

Yet another way of looking at the extent of package usage is given by surveys conducted by the Computer Intelligence Corp. of over 13 000 business sites, and of 11 000 IBM and compatible mainframe sites (Barry, 1986b; Wiener, 1986). Their figures, in Table 7.4, show the extent of package penetration. Included are the purchasing figures for PCs for the Microcomputer Managers Association (MMA), given by Alan Gross (Kerr, 1987).

These figures show that nearly every PC runs a spreadsheet, so further sales of spreadsheet packages depend heavily on more computers being sold. By contrast, project management and graphics packages

could still enjoy high sales even if few new computers were sold. Among mainframe sites, there might appear to be scope for high sales of all types of package, but in fact most sites already have custom-built accounting systems, so further sales of accounting packages depend on continued mobility within the user base (Wiener, 1986).

The preceding figures do not include word processing packages, yet Barnett (1985) estimated that most office systems were bought with a 60% need for word processing. (He also estimated a 30% need for data manipulation (which agrees with Gross's figures), and a 10% need for mainframe communications.)

7.3.5 AMOUNT OF USE

The Datamation/Cowen & Co. 1986–87 mini/micro survey (Table 7.5) looked at package usage on PCs from a different angle, namely the amount of time, as a percentage of the total elapsed time, each type of package was used (Verity, 1986b).

A survey by the International Data Corporation found that users spend as much as 90% of their work day using word processing, spreadsheet, and database software, and less than 10% using presentation graphics programs (McMullen, 1991b).

Table 7.4 Penetration of market (Barry, 1986b; Wiener, 1986)

	Gross MMA (PCs) (%)	Computer intelligence	
		business (%)	mainframe (%)
Project management		4	
Graphics	1–2	8	20
DBMS	30		54
Spreadsheets	100	92	7
Accounts receivable			7
Fixed asset			10
Personnel			11
Accounts payable			14
Payroll			17
General ledger			24

Table 7.5 Package usage (percentage of total elapsed time) (Verity, 1986b)

	Average package usage	
	1985 (%)	1986 (%)
Database packages	6	13
Spreadsheets	33	31

Table 7.6   Intentions to purchase software

	PC (%)	Mainframe (%)
CAD/CAM	8	
Graphics	7	2
Project management	7	
DBMS	4	
Accounts payable		4
General ledger		3
Office automation	3	4
Micro/mainframe	2	3
Personnel		2
Spreadsheet	1	2

Source: Computer Intelligence Corp. (Weiner, 1986)

7.3.6   RATE OF GROWTH

Sales of packages may have lagged in the past, but they are now being more actively promoted, with the result that there has been a rapid growth in their use (Norman, 1978; Merrick, 1976; Douglas, 1979). A few years ago, growth figures of 30–50% p.a. were being quoted, e.g. by Douglas (1979). More recently, with the current industry slowdown, a lower figure of 19% has been quoted (Barry, 1987) – about double the current growth rate for hardware (Chapter 5).

Parikh (1984) predicted that annual sales of all standard applications software packages would 'skyrocket' from $2 billion to $25 billion during the 1980s, an increase of nearly 30% p.a., compound.

The Computer Intelligence Corp. figures for IBM and compatible mainframe sites show that package penetration nearly doubled between 1982 and 1985, from an average of 8% for nine product groups, to 15%, an increase of around 20% p.a., compound (Wiener, 1986).

Lucas (1985) attributes the increase to the rising cost of programming (so non-essential features are often left out of custom-built systems); improvements in the packages (many have been through several generations of improvements); and the declining cost of hardware (making it more cost-justifiable to run an inefficient package rather than custom-build a more efficient system).

Computer Intelligence Corp. figures (Table 7.6) revealed intentions to purchase software. Most mainframe sites already have account-ing systems, so the figures given for accounts payable and general ledger show there is great mobility within the user base (Wiener, 1986).

Piracy and inadequate copyright protection affect the spread of packages. They increase the number of copies in use, but without financial reward to the developer, which might dissuade others from developing packages. The USA information processing business may have lost as much as $20 billion over the preceding five years because of copyright rip-offs and software piracy (Davis, 1986). There are signs of a hardening in attitude against these practices. For example, the granting of copyright status to microcode (software embedded in a microchip) should help create an environment which encourages innovation. Attempts by Apple to protect the 'look and feel' of their graphical user interface may have the same effect, but this gave rise to concern that it would deprive users of IBM PCs of a better interface (or at least delay improvements).

7.3.7   PORTABILITY

The increased use of packages is limited by lack of portability due to the diversity of hardware and system software.

• Different versions of a package may have

to be created for different models of computer – 'the leading vendors in the IBM and compatible market frequently migrate their established products to other machines' (Wiener, 1986) – thereby adding to the initial development cost.

- Compatibility over a range of different computers can be built into a package (Mullin, 1978). For example, both SAS Institute and ISSCO (Integrated Software Systems Corporation) are trying to keep their graphics software as machine independent as possible by offering user-compatible and data-compatible versions for many operating environments (Wiener, 1986). However, there may be performance or storage capacity penalties.
- If the package is integrated with a DBMS, then its portability is linked to that of the DBMS. To avoid this, the developer might choose not to integrate the package with a DBMS, but by so doing, deprives the package of the power and flexibility provided by a DBMS. (This is an example of the 'lowest common denominator' effect.)
- A package may not run on small computers, e.g. the Millenium financial packages which do not run on PCs, or the package may be too expensive for users of small computers, unless the supplier has a variable pricing policy. (With the introduction of its small 9370 mainframe computers, IBM introduced sliding charges for some 90 system software packages depending on CPU size, and other vendors followed suit (Benchmarks, *Datamation*, 1 Nov 1986, p. 50).)
- Subsequent enhancements by a computer manufacturer may make the equipment (hardware or software) incompatible with some packages, thereby restricting the packages' market potential.

Since IBM has become the *de facto* standard for both mainframes and micros (Chapter 5), some of these disadvantages have dimi-

nished. IBM's announcement of Systems Application Architecture (SAA) will, once implemented, increase portability across the full range of their machines. UNIX already provides a high degree of portability, and will provide even more in the future if it becomes as popular as its enthusiasts predict. PICK is also very portable. High-level languages and some DBMSs also provide a high degree of portability. (These products were discussed in Chapter 6.)

7.4 RESISTANCE

Resistance in general is discussed in Chapter 9, but some aspects related specifically to packages are discussed below.

Despite their considerable advantages, packages meet with prejudice and resistance: 'computer users have for many years had a marked reluctance to purchase prepackaged computer programs' (Big business for mini computers, *Computronics*, 13th Feb 1980, p. 8). However, this is changing, as evidenced by the sales penetration and growth figures in Tables 7.2–7.4 and 7.6, and by the fact that 47% of the respondents in the 1986 Datamation/Cowen & Co. Computer/ Telecommunications Industry Survey said they were increasing expenditures on packaged software by more than anything else in their budgets for application software (Verity, 1986a).

Sometimes, the resistance is valid. Application needs are very diverse, so it is more difficult to create a generalized application package than a system software package, as evidenced by the sales figures in Table 7.2. Packages, therefore, may not meet all of a user's needs. It is probably also more difficult to satisfy the needs of large organizations than small ones (Martin, 1981). Many packages, for example, cannot handle very high volumes (Doepel, 1977). However, even large organizations like American Standard and the USA Federal Government use packages (Carlyle, 1987b; Schatz, 1986a), and some packages such as airline reservation systems have to be designed for large volumes.

The organization may have investigated the available packages, and found that none met its requirements.

- Packages may not meet an organization's needs at all, e.g. the manufacturing industry is extremely diversified and its needs change (Zimner, 1978a).
- A particular organization may have some very specific requirements which are an important aspect of its business, e.g. there are considerable differences between the way different railway companies operate because of their differing environments (van der Veer, 1976).
- The uniqueness may give the organization a competitive edge.
- The packages might have built-in assumptions about the end users (such as their level of computer expertise), or the user organization (such as centralized or decentralized, matrix or project-oriented). Modifying such assumptions is generally a big job, and is not always successful (Boehm, 1981).

On the other hand, the organization may reject the use of packages without an investigation. This may be due to:

- a general feeling that its needs are 'quite different' (Oakley, 1975);
- an arbitrary rejection of anything 'not invented here' (Arthur, 1983); or even to
- a liking for re-inventing the wheel: people 'prefer to develop their own solutions to interesting problems' (Aron, 1974).

While some users spend considerable time defining their needs, others just 'jump in' without defining their needs at all (Wingfield, 1976; Big business for mini computers, *Computronics*, 13th Feb. 1980, p. 8).

The question also arises: if an organization's mode of operation differs from that of comparable organizations, is that organization using the best methods?

Lucas (1985) believes that often an organization need only make a small change to its procedures to suit the package.

According to Grandison (1986), in the preceding two years, the emphasis was on integrated packages, but this met with user resistance, so many software manufacturers began breaking up the modules in their packages.

7.5 CUSTOMIZING

To satisfy the needs (both immediate and future) of as many users as possible, a package may contain many options, which effectively allow the user to tailor the package for his environment (Lucas, 1985). These options may be in the form of parameters or tables. However, too many options can make a package overly large, complicated and inefficient. Packages can be made flexible, and their usefulness extended, in several other ways.

Some of these methods involve modifications to the package. Modifications can be done by either the vendor or the user. As a general rule, users should not modify packages (and if they are not supplied with the source code, then they *cannot* modify them), as this may invalidate the guarantee. It may also introduce errors, and the modifications will have to be reapplied to every subsequent release of the package (Seddon, 1983), so every attempt should be made to confine them to as few modules as possible, and they must be carefully documented. These modifications reduce the cost and time advantages of packages. However, the cheapest packages do not have guarantees and are not updated by the suppliers; and some types of packages are intended to be modified or added to by user organizations (they are described below). Walker Interactive Products even offered 'personalizers' with their financial applications packages, which enabled users to modify the packages without having to do any programming (Myers,

1986). The number of packages which are modifiable has increased (Folb, 1984).

The process of modifying or adding to a package for a particular customer, or even just selecting certain of the options or feeding in certain values for a customer, is known as customizing. The different options are discussed below.

Additional reports

Provided the package's master files or database contain all the necessary information (i.e. the input portion of the system must be adequate to capture, edit, store and update it), additional reports can be created to supply information not produced by the basic package. The package may include a report writer for this purpose, or suitable high-level languages can be used to write these report programs, provided file and record layout information is available, and the files are in an industry standard format. If the package is built around a DBMS, then it will be more flexible, facilitating the creation of additional reports (Zimner, 1978b). However, if the package operates off another system's database, e.g. an audit retrieval package, then the package itself may require extra modification (Mullin, 1978).

Modular

The package may contain different modules for different situations. For example, a registration package for universities may have separate modules for different types of grading systems (A to F, 100 to 0, etc.), and the user organization simply selects those modules applicable to it (Lucas, 1985). Alternatively, the user may even incorporate the package's modules in user-written programs.

Skeleton

The package may consist of a skeleton, around which the user can build a system to meet his specific requirements, using either functions which are part of the package, or user-written modules. UNIS (Univac Industrial System) is an example of this approach (UNIS launch in S.A., *Systems Stelsels*, Apr. 1978, p. 43). Similarly, investment packages are being developed as templates that incorporate Lotus 1–2–3 features (Campbell, 1986).

Source code

Purchasers may be given the source code of the package (Zimner, 1978a), or it may have been published in a magazine or book. They can then use whatever portions of the coding they need, add their own coding to provide additional functions, and generally modify it to suit their own requirements. Customizing in this way is simplified if modern programming practices had been used when the package was developed, and if it is well documented, and it should already contain most of the required functions. Ease of customizing also depends on the language in which the package is written. However, there is always the danger that errors will be introduced if the source code is modified.

Custom-built

Where several organizations each need the same application computerized, they could create a team to write a set of similar, custom-built systems, one for each organization. Strictly speaking, these will not form a package, but the concept can be viewed as an extension of the above ideas. As all the development will be done by the same team, the 'learning curve' (Chapter 9) will be particularly in evidence, and large savings are possible. Boehm (1973) quotes a case in which a team took 72, 36 and 14 man-months respectively, to write three successive FORTRAN compilers (McClure, 1969).

Comments

According to de Raay (1975), it is generally not difficult to determine in advance if a package caters adequately for a particular user organization's needs. End users should be closely involved in the selection procedure, and outside experts can be called in. Lucas (1985) recommends doing a preliminary analysis of the requirements, followed by a high-level logical design (including output requirements, file contents, and input needed). This will give a good idea of the required functions, and should be used as the basis for evaluating packages. This method helps ensure that the evaluation will be objective, and that the prospective user will not be 'swayed by a convincing sales presentation'.

Apart from having the functions the user requires, packages should integrate with the user organization's existing manual and DP procedures (de Raay, 1975). Furthermore, care should be taken if it is proposed to use several different packages, one for each individual application, as they may not integrate with each other (Zimner, 1978a). Production and inventory control, for example, are no longer a collection of loosely-related techniques, so the computerization thereof must now be similarly integrated.

Application packages only satisfy about 80–90% of the requirements, and this leads to 90% of the effort in implementing the package being spent on providing the 10–20% that are not satisfied (van der Merwe, 1988).

In some cases, the basic package could be installed first so that its benefits were immediately available, and customizing done later. This is a type of phasing in or incremental delivery (Brandon, 1978).

If a large amount of customizing would be required, then that particular package may not be suitable, so a more appropriate one should be found. If one is not available, it might even be cheaper, and better, to develop a custom-built system.

Customizing, whether done by the vendor or the user, can be expensive. As an alternative, the user could adapt his mode of operation to the package's capabilities –

sometimes, all that is required are 'a few inessential compromises' (Boehm, 1981). Lucas (1985) quoted one large services company which only sells its packages 'as is'; but in spite of this, many organizations have bought them, and adjusted to them. However, this may not always be possible. The organization might have been using a particular method for years, e.g. a warehouse might have a specific procedure for allocating orders to preferred customers (Lucas, 1985), and both the organization and its customers are used to it; or a change might cause the organization to lose its competitive edge.

Customizing, however, is not always time-consuming. According to Lucas (1985), it often merely entails selecting different modules or options already available within the package, or using a report writer supplied with the package, so little or no programming is required.

An intermediate solution which is sometimes possible is to create an interface between the package and the existing system(s), so that neither need be changed. For example, if the package is to process data from an existing system, then the files from the existing system can be converted so that they are compatible with the package's requirements. The conversion would have to be repeated every time the package is to be run afresh, so that it processes the latest data.

7.6 QUALITY

The quality of a package is very important. As Varley and Graham (1983) put it: 'A poor entertainment program for the home may cause disappointment and frustration when it does not meet with expectations; however, bad business software costs not only the purchase price but also the time spent retraining operators, waiting for bugs to be eliminated and, possibly, lost business'.

The quality of a package, using a broad meaning of the term, comprises many aspects (James, 1980; Mullin, 1978; Merrick,

1976; Arthur, 1983; Lucas, 1985; Brickman, 1986; Varley and Graham, 1983; Schechter, 1986; Boehm, 1981; Theron, 1977):

- How well was the system researched and designed?
- Is it free of known bugs?
- Does it have comprehensive validation of input data?
- Does it include audit trails, control totals, and security and recovery features?
- How well were the programs written? (Were modern programming practices used?)
- Will the source code be available if the supplier defaults?
- Were the programs efficiently written (i.e. does the package meet the user's storage capacity and performance requirements)?
- Is the package flexible? (Has it many options? Is it based on a DBMS?)
- Does it have all the functions it claims? ('The programs were called MRP programs, but in fact they were nothing more than order launchers' (Barry, 1982).)
- Is it easy to modify (both to meet immediate requirements and possible changed requirements in the future)?
- Will it have future upgrades?
- Is it easy to learn? Is it easy to use (i.e. does it have a good user interface)? Is it easy to install? (Is it menu driven? How much installation effort is required?)
- Does it have helpful error messages?
- Does it crash if you do something silly?
- How good is the documentation? (Is it easy to understand? Does it summarize the package's capabilities? Does it list all the commands in one place? Has the manual got an index? Is there a fault-finding section?)
- Are the warranty and legal contract fair to the user? (Do they specify what is delivered, such as how many copies of the documentation? Do they cover training, installation, and maintenance? Is payment linked to acceptance testing? Is there a penalty if the vendor does not meet his obligations?)
- Is it reasonably priced and does it give good value for money?
- Are the training and after-sales service adequate? (Is a 'hot-line' provided? Are error fixes provided periodically?)
- Is it well-liked by its present users?
- Is it one of a family of integrated packages?
- How portable is it? (Does it run on a portable operating system, or a portable DBMS, or was it written in a popular high-level language? Are different versions available for different operating systems?)
- Does it allow for growth? (Can it handle higher volumes or extra terminals? Can it run on a larger computer? Is the language in which it was written available on larger computers (and the DBMS, if any)?)

Interviewing existing users will throw much light on many of the above questions. The relative remoteness of the developers makes quality especially important in a package, but even more so if it was developed in another country.

The cheapest packages are shareware, public domain software, and those whose program source listings appear in the press. They are usually written by only one or two people, and so should have 'conceptual integrity' (Brooks, 1975), and the developers can generally also respond more quickly to user-requested enhancements than a large organization (Shapiro, 1986a). However, they may otherwise be of lower quality, especially as they may not have had the extensive testing and so on which is possible in large organizations. Furthermore, even if they are of high quality, installation and use are on a do-it-yourself basis.

Some packages were originally written just for one particular user, and then made available to a wider market. Others were developed over a long period and at great cost, after extensive market research, and with much more testing and documentation than normal – these systems merit the 'heavy-duty software product' classification (Gunther, 1978). The former will require far more customizing, unless they were heavily extended before being put on the market, but in that case further modifications may be difficult, as the programs will probably be messy. (The impact of maintenance on maintainability is discussed in Chapter 8.) The latter may take nine times as long to develop as an ordinary system (Brooks, 1975) – in fact, a good package may cost millions to develop (Schechter, 1986), and may cost ten times as much as cheap packages (Microprocessors – choosing wisely, *Computronics*, 14th May 1980, p. 3). (The development time should normally be much less than nine times as long, as the Brooks ratio quoted was actually a comparison with amateur programming. Figures given by Jones (1986b), for a commercially marketed system compared to an internal system, imply that less than 30% extra development effort is required.)

Because of the variability in quality, it has been suggested that packages should be subjected to official inspection and approval, as is done by MSS (Manufacturing Software Systems) in America for manufacturing software (Barry, 1982), and which AT & T intend doing for versions of UNIX. From time to time, evaluations and comparisons of various packages are published in both the computer press and in trade journals, e.g.:

- a list of the benefits of 35 retail systems, compiled by Touche Ross, was published in *Chain Store Age Executive* (Touche Ross, 1986);
- 23 database products were reviewed in 'Spotlight on software-DBMS review' *Bank Systems & Equipment* (Nov. 1986, pp. 77–80).

In addition, the Datapro Research Corporation compiles information on application software, including descriptions of the various systems and surveys of user satisfaction.

7.7 EFFECT ON MAINTENANCE AND BACKLOG

Maintenance

There are two aspects to be considered: maintenance of custom-built systems, and maintenance of packages.

If an organization already uses a custom-built system for a particular application, it is unlikely to replace it with a package, unless the system had a high maintenance rate, or major changes were required (Seddon, 1983). Packages will therefore have little effect on the existing maintenance workload.

Maintenance of packages is cheaper for each user organization, and for the same reason as development: the costs are spread over many organizations. Sometimes, an organization will discover that the new features it desires are already built into the package, or are available as an extra, optional module, because the developers foresaw the need or because existing customers asked for them; but even if not, packages may be designed with future change in mind, making them quick and easy to change. This advantage would be partially offset by the custom-built portions of the system: maintenance of them would not be reduced. Nevertheless, if packages become more widespread in the future, we can expect the overall maintenance workload to decrease.

Backlog

Packages can be used to do some of the jobs comprising the backlog of work, thereby directly reducing it. However, much of the backlog consists of *ad hoc* reports (Chapter 8), and probably maintenance as well, and so is not suitable for application packages, so the reduction may be small. However, by relieving staff of some new development work, thereby freeing them for other tasks – such as those comprising the backlog – packages might have a larger *indirect* impact on the backlog.

Table 7.7 Productivity gain of individual packages

Assumption	Additional time	Total time	Total benefit	Productivity gain
1. 300 sold	1	1	300	300:1
2. Longer development time	8	9	300	33:1
3. Several versions	2	11	300	27:1
4. Customizing	30	41	300	7:1

7.8 NET PRODUCTIVITY IMPROVEMENT

Packages give very large gains in productivity but some inherent factors reduce these gains. How big an increase can therefore be expected? The following two examples give an indication.

7.8.1 INDIVIDUAL PACKAGES

The first example estimates the productivity gain delivered by individual packages.

1. A particular package is sold to 300 organizations. (This places it among the low-selling packages; see Table 7.3. It is therefore a conservative estimate which understates the benefits that packages can and do provide.)
2. It took nine times as long to develop as an ordinary system. (As discussed earlier, this is probably an over-estimate, so once again, it understates the benefits of packages.)
3. Several versions were created for different makes and models of computer, thereby adding about 20% to the total system development time. (Figures given in Chapter 5 indicate that a conversion to a different computer typically consumes about 10% as much time as the original development effort. If we allow for the effects of the 'learning curve', and specifically the 72:36:14 effort ratios quoted earlier, then probably an extra four or so versions can be created for an additional 20% of effort: the first extra version would consume 10% of the original effort; the second extra version would consume (36/72) times as much effort as the first extra version, i.e (36/72*10=) 5% of the original effort; and so on.)
4. Half the purchasers required some customizing – say the equivalent in each case of 20% of the time it would have taken them to develop their own systems. (From Table 7.1 a package typically costs about 20% as much as a custom-built system. This provides perhaps only 80% of the required features. To build the remaining 20% of features should thus cost about 20% as much as a full custom-built system. Customizing would therefore cost about the same as the package, and so represents a premium of 100% on the package price. By comparison, Lucas (1985) quoted one organization which will normally not consider a package if customization of it would amount to 50% of the cost of the package; and another organization which spent only 20–25% on customizing one package. In practice, therefore, the assumption of a 100% premium is probably unfair to the package, even if all the purchasers require customizing rather than just half of them as assumed.)

These assumptions lead to the productivity gain shown in Table 7.7. (The productivity gain is the ratio of the total benefit to the corresponding amount of total time.)

Thus the apparent productivity gain of 300:1, in practice is only 7:1. This ratio is not over-sensitive to the number of sales. For example, if three times as many copies were sold (900), then the ratio would only increase to 9:1, not 21:1; while if 3000 were sold, then the ratio would only become 10:1. The ratio is similarly not very sensitive to the amount of additional effort required to develop a commercially marketed product, e.g. if only twice as much effort is required instead of the nine times I assumed, then the productivity gain increases from 7:1 to only 9:1. The ratio is much more sensitive to the amount of customizing. For example, in the case of Systems Software such as sorts and spreadsheets – which are the biggest-selling packages, and which usually need little if any customizing – the gains will be 27:1, 82:1 and 273:1 respectively, in this example, depending on whether 300, 900, or 3000 were sold.

7.8.2 INDUSTRY PRODUCTIVITY

The second example estimates the combined effect of all packages on the productivity of the software industry.

The preceding calculation refers to individual packages taken in isolation. Because packages are used for only some of the users' requirements, their effect on the total industry productivity is smaller. The following five assumptions produce the productivity gain shown in Table 7.8.

1. The productivity gain for individual packages is 7:1 (Table 7.7).
2. Only 50% of all organizations use packages. For simplicity, assume also that these organizations use packages for all their work, and that the remaining ones use no packages at all.

   (As most organizations are small, and small organizations make relatively greater use of packages (Knox, 1978; Martin, 1981, 1982a), these assumptions are not unreasonable. The comparison earlier in this chapter of the number of computers with the number of programmers indicates that perhaps as many as 90% of organizations use only packages; and the USA Federal Government, which

is a very large user, spends nine times more on custom software than on commercial software (Schatz, 1986a). Using 50% instead of 90% is conservative, but also takes into account the fact that small organizations spend less on software than do large ones.)
3. Maintenance occupies 50% of all software engineering time (Chapter 8).
4. The productivity gain for the maintenance of packages is the same as for development. (The greater generality and flexibility of packages might in fact reduce the amount of maintenance required, so the productivity gain may be higher than for development. On the other hand, it can be very expensive for vendor personnel to install the packages on the customer computers, and make on-site visits to resolve problems. However, even in this case, figures given by Jones (1986b) show that the per customer cost of maintenance is considerably lower for many customers than for just one, even though the decrease is not as impressive as for development.)
5. The maintenance of the basic packages will be done by the suppliers, but they are part of the industry, so their time is incorporated into the comparison (through the 7:1 ratio taken from Table 7.7).

Based on these figures, therefore, the productivity of the industry will be increased by 1.75:1, which is only one-quarter the gain provided by individual packages. This ratio is relatively insensitive to the proportion of organizations using packages, e.g. if only 10% use packages instead of 50%, then the ratio is reduced to 1.1:1; while if 90% use packages, then it is only increased to 4.4:1. In the individual packages example, the amount of customizing had a large impact on the overall productivity gain. The amount of customizing is incorporated in the current example by virtue of the 7:1 ratio from Table

Table 7.8 Effect of packages on software industry productivity

Function	Time spent		
	Before packages	After packages	Ratio
Development			
Organizations using packages	25	3.6	7:1
Not using packages	25	25	–
Maintenance			
Organizations using packages	25	3.6	7:1
Not using packages	25	25	–
Total	100	57.2	1.75:1

7.7. However, even a large change in this ratio would not have much effect on the final answer. Similarly, even if the productivity gain for maintenance is very different from that for development, e.g. if it is much less because of field delivery and field maintenance, it will not have much effect on the final answer. The conclusion to be drawn, therefore, is that only a large change in at least *two* assumptions simultaneously – e.g. much less customizing and many more organizations using packages – would have a large effect on the overall productivity gain for the whole computer industry.

7.9 THE FUTURE

Can packages be made still more valuable?

- If resistance to them can be further reduced, more organizations would install them and derive their benefits.
- Greater standardization among computer manufacturers would extend the potential market for individual packages, and reduce the number of versions required.
- The increasing cost of software might encourage:
  - more co-operation between similar organizations (or ones with similar needs), to pool their resources and to develop packages for their own mutual use;
  - more organizations to standardize their

mode of operation, to enable them to use packages;
  - the development of packages for applications for which there are none at present.

For these reasons, and because of the increasing number of small organizations using packages extensively, they will become more widespread in the future, and so have an even greater influence on the productivity of the industry. Also, new application areas, such as expert systems and artificial intelligence, will lead to more packages.

On the other hand, once the 'bread-and-butter' applications (payrolls, stock control, etc.) have been computerized, organizations turn their attention to management information systems, which are less amenable to the use of packages, so packages may have a *smaller* influence on productivity in the longer term.

Furthermore, while packages may have played a considerable role in the growth of the industry and in improving productivity, if they really do comprise 75% of the total software currently in use as Norman (1978) predicted, then their capacity for making further improvements is limited.

Fourth-generation software may reduce the need for packages because it will be much easier for organizations to develop their own custom-built systems; but on the other hand, by simplifying customizing, they may actually encourage more organizations to acquire packages. Furthermore, the packages can themselves be written in fourth-generation languages, thereby reducing their cost and encouraging their wider use.

7.10 CONCLUSION

Application packages, even allowing for a large amount of time spent on market research, development and customizing, represent a significant gain in productivity for each package individually, and are a particularly valuable tool for the many small organizations which are computerizing for the first time (Martin, 1982a).

Their combined effect on the productivity of the industry as a whole is less easy to calculate. It is much smaller because of their limited use, but is still significant.

There is resistance to them, but this is decreasing, and the number used is increasing rapidly, especially on smaller computers.

It therefore seems likely that packages are already responsible for a significant improvement in the productivity of the industry, but that this is occurring 'on the quiet' (i.e. it is an 'invisible' increase) and without the software industry being given full credit for it.

It also seems likely that packages will continue to enjoy high sales for some time to come, and so will continue to play a major role in productivity improvement. However, there may come a time when the market becomes saturated, so their productivity-improvement role will decrease, and be limited mainly to new application areas.

Computers have no intelligence of their own: without software, the hardware is 'expensive scrap', 'useless lumps of sand, metal and plastic' (Philips Data Systems, 1982; Gunther, 1978). Software is therefore indispensable. It also forms a large proportion of the total costs (Chapter 1).

This chapter examines the process of creating and maintaining software: the various functions in the process, the techniques used, and so on. The discussion is oriented toward conventional methods: some technological aids, such as application generators, do not merely automate individual functions in the process, but eliminate some of them.

8.1 BACKLOG

Size of backlog

The shortage of staff (Chapter 9), and the shortfall in productivity, have resulted in a large backlog of work. A few years ago, backlogs of three or four years were commonly quoted, with some organizations reporting a backlog of 30 years and more, and users having to wait 6–12 months for even a simple change (Martin, 1981; Grulke, 1983; Mallinick, 1977). Hall (1987) gave a figure of four years as typical, and Yourdon (1989) claimed that the typical large organization had a backlog of between four and seven years of new work, and that most organizations had a backlog of seven years. However, other evidence indicates that the situation has improved. Of the respondents in the 1986 Datamation/Cowen & Co. Computer/Telecommunications Industry Survey, 24% had a backlog of less than one year, while only 34% had a backlog of more than two years (Verity, 1986a). This was the second year in a row that the backlog had decreased, but it is still too long.

In addition, Martin (1981) stated that there is an 'invisible' backlog: work which users need but have not bothered to ask for because they know they would have to wait so long for it to be done. This backlog may be even greater than the documented backlog.

These claims should be viewed with caution. Although organizations have been prepared to pay high salaries to attract staff, they have in the past shown a reluctance to train would-be entrants to the profession, provide advanced training for their staff, contract out work to freelancers, use packages, conduct research into productivity, implement advances, and so on. There has been evidence of some change in the situation (Sivers, 1978), but there still does not appear to be the crisis atmosphere and emergency corrective action that such a large backlog should warrant. It therefore seems likely that the backlog consists largely of low-priority work: work which is not needed quickly, which has high costs or low benefits (particularly one-off jobs), or which can be done manually. The long backlog thus acts as a sieve, ensuring that only the most needed and cost-effective jobs are done. (The argument being advanced here is not just a statement of the obvious. The backlog, almost by definition, consists of the least urgent and cost-effective jobs, but the argument goes one step further: it expresses the view that many of the jobs are not cost-justifiable with conventional technologies (Jones, 1983a).)

Composition of backlog

van Rijswijck (1983) stated that 80% of the backlog consists of short-lived, end-user type applications. This means that, from a DP view, they are low-payoff jobs, because they are not run many times. It also confirms that they are more suitable for fourth-generation languages; in Chapter 6, one organization eliminated its backlog after switching to 4GLs. Other aspects of the composition of the backlog – the proportion of maintenance, the proportion of edit programs, etc. – are not known, but they affect, for example, the productivity gain obtainable from the fourth-generation.

8.2   SIZE AND COMPLEXITY

According to the provisional list in section 2.3, size and complexity are two of the factors which have the greatest effect on productivity. They are discussed further below.

8.2.1   SOFTWARE SIZE

One of the highest productivity rates quoted in Chapter 2 was that of Orkins and Weiss (1975), where a major design goal was to have small programs. Large programs are also more complex, more difficult to write and understand, contain more errors, and are more difficult to debug (Conte *et al.*, 1986; Charette, 1986).

Unit of measurement

How should size be measured? As was the case with productivity in Chapter 2, there are several possible units of measure, such as the 'volume' metric (Halstead, 1977), but once

again, the one chosen here is the number of lines of source code. The definition problems discussed in Chapter 2 – e.g. whether comment and blank lines should be counted and how re-used code should be treated – apply here as well.

Typical sizes

What is a typical program or system size? As would be expected, there are large variations: P-STAT's statistical package for the AT & T PC consists of a single source file of 300 000 lines of code (P-STAT, 1986); IBM's mainframe teleprocessing package, CICS (Customer Information Control System), has 750 000 (Formal attraction, *Computer Week*, 27 June 1988, pp. 18–19); MSA's Arista manufacturing package contains one million lines of code (McCusker, 1987a); and IBM's Operating System/400 has more than seven million (Pine, 1989). Different versions of the same program can also vary widely in size: the UNIX operating system reportedly contains only 11 000 lines of code (Arthur, 1983), but Amdahl's version of it contains 1.55 million (Amdahl, 1988). Different languages can also vary widely in size: MODULA-2 contains only 5000 lines of code, whereas ADA has hundreds of thousands (Baron, 1988). Various authorities have given values for average program and module sizes, as shown in Table 8.1.

The (unweighted) average of these figures is about 900 LOC, but this is largely due to a few very high values, most of which are for very large organizations or are for Assembler. The median is about 500 LOC, and this is a more typical value. Also, two of the high values are from Jones (1986b), and do not appear to be consistent with his figures of one million applications worldwide, comprising perhaps 10 billion LOC (based on an estimated 5 billion in 1980 and 17.5 billion in 1990), giving an average of only 10 000 LOC per application, and therefore only three or four programs per system. (On the other

Table 8.1 Average program and module sizes (LOC)

Source	Basis	LOC
Pomberger (1984)	174 programs	103
AT & T (Quest, 1989)	1986; single-function modules	186 (executable LOC)
Orkins and Weiss (1975)		191
IBM (Shen *et al.*, 1985)	1980–1983; 25 modules; 7000 LOC	280 (PASCAL)
Marsh (1983)		340
Pine (1989)	200 000 programs and procedures	350 (70 million LOC COBOL/RPG)
IBM (Shen *et al.*, 1985)	1980–1983; 764 modules; 269 000 LOC	352 (PL/S)
Johnson (1980b)	256 programs; 93 000 LOC	363 (on-line)
Kendall and Lamb (1977)		400 (median)
Pomberger (1984)	350 programs	429 (Assembler)
AT & T (Quest*, 1989)	1981; multi-function modules	433 (executable LOC)
Bearley (1980)		500
IBM (Shen *et al.*, 1985):	1980–1983; 639 modules; 326 000 LOC	510 (Assembly)
Bell Canada (Clemons, 1991)	5000 modules	540 (2.7 million LOC)
Knuth (1971)	440 programs	568 (FORTRAN)
Johnson (1980b)	2719 programs; 1 864 000 LOC	686 (batch)
Kraft and Weinberg (1975)		700
Johnson (1980b)	100 programs; 75 000 LOC	750
Pirow (1981)		900
Yourdon (1975)		<1000
US IRS (Kirchner, 1986)		2125 (Assembler)
Parikh (1984)		2000–3000
Jones (1986b)	US Military	2500
Akiyama (1971)	9 modules; 24 955 LOC	2772 (Assembler)
Jones (1986b)	large corporations approaching	3333

* The quest for zero defect software. *Computer Week*, 13 Feb. 1989, p. 21.

hand, his figures for the number of lines of code in the world may be too low – see Chapter 6.)

The average and median values given above refer to the programs and modules combined. Separately, the average values are about 1000 LOC for programs, and 700 for modules, with median (more typical) values of about 500 and 400, respectively. It would therefore appear that the modules in these projects were, on average, about 75% of the size of the programs, i.e. only slightly smaller. Presumably, however, those projects which had large modules had correspondingly larger programs. Furthermore, none of the authorities gave both module and program sizes, so perhaps the term 'module' was sometimes used for what other people would call a program.

In addition to the tabulated values, Gilb (1988) gave a figure of 5000 LOC as an average program size, but this is much higher than the other tabulated values. It appeared in a similar context to his statement that from 0.1 to 0.5 minutes are spent per year maintaining each line of non-commentary source code, queried in Chapter 2 as it seems to be far too low.

Various authorities have given values for average system sizes, as shown in Tables 8.2

Table 8.2 Average system sizes (LOC)

Source	Average	Range	Comments	Re-used code
Yourdon (1975)	<10 000			
Jones (1986b)	10 000			
van der Poel (1982)	18 000			
IBM (Walston and Felix, 1977)	20 000	4000–467 000	included	
Pirow (1981)	26 000			
Bailey and Basili (1981)	27 000	2000–85 000	included	new LOC
Bailey and Basili (1981)	29 000	2000–90 000	included	adjusted LOC
Yourdon 78–80 (Conte *et al.*, 1986)	34 000	7000–132 000	included	
Bailey and Basili (1981)	38 000	2000–112 000		total LOC
Jones (1986b)	61 000	50–495 000	excluded	
IBM (Brustman, 1978)	62 000	4000–467 000	included	
Albrecht and Gaffney (1983)	66 000			
Boehm (1981)	67 000	2000–966 000	excluded	adjusted LOC
Boehm (1981)	77 000	2000–1 150 000	excluded	total LOC
Belady and Lehman (1979)	92 000	5000–712 000		
Johnson (1980b)	100 000			
Wingfield (1982)	180 000	50 000–450 000	excluded	
Kemerer (1987)	187 000	39 000–450 000	excluded	

and 8.3. The (unweighted) average of these figures (Table 8.2) is about 60 000 LOC, though the median value of about 50 000 would be more typical.

In addition to the tabulated figures, Matsumoto (1989) reports an average size of 1 million source lines, or 4 million equivalent assembler source lines (with a range a 1 to 21 million), at the Toshiba Fuchu Software Factory.

By type of application

If the figures given in Tables 8.1–8.3 are typical – only medium to large projects were chosen for the Kemerer database – then the typical program contains about 500 lines of code, and the typical system about 50 000, so there are about 100 programs in the typical system, which is in reasonable agreement with the statement by Johnson (1980b) that, in a typical large organization, a major application system may contain 100 programs. However, caution should be observed when comparing sizes, as the number of lines of code can vary for a number of reasons:

Table 8.3 Average system size (LOC)

Application type	Number of samples	LOC
Process control	6	9000
Batch	13	27 000
Special-purpose operating system	13	58 000
Models and simulators	9	77 000
Interactive information retrieval	13	78 000
Real-time interactive command and control	6	143 000

Source: Brustman (1978)

- Programs written in a low-level language contain perhaps four times as many statements as they would have had if they had been written in a high-level language (Chapter 6).
- Boehm (1981) found that his COCOMO model achieved better predictions with COBOL programs by weighting non-executable source statements by a factor of one-third, because COBOL programs have large numbers of non-executable source statements.

- Studies have shown that experienced programmers use about 20% fewer statements than novices (Chapter 9).
- The Weinberg and Schulman (1974) experiment showed that:
  - if programmers are instructed to keep LOC to the minimum, they will do so – in this experiment, the program written by the team given this objective was only *one-third* the average size of the same program written by the teams set different goals (33 LOC compared to 107);
  - even where minimizing LOC was not an objective, programs varied considerably in length. The program whose goal was output clarity, was *three* times as long as the program whose goal was minimum memory usage (166 LOC compared to 52).
- Other factors, some of which can *double* the number of statements, include re-used code, the inclusion or exclusion of comment and blank lines in the count, the impact of structured programming and modularization, the padding by programmers to make themselves appear more productive, and individual differences (Chapter 2).

Sizing (predicting the size) is discussed further by Boehm (1981). His COCOMO cost-estimation model is based on size, but he admits that sizing is not reliable (and he criticizes the PERT sizing technique for making the task appear too easy). This can be counteracted by examining the requirements in more detail, and by doing separate sizing estimates for each component. Size gives economies of scale – large projects can afford technological aids which increase productivity – but it also gives diseconomies – relatively more time is required on large projects for design, testing, integration, management, communications, etc., and this drop-off in productivity is more pronounced with 'embedded mode' projects (as defined in Chapter 2). According to Boehm, most studies indicate that the diseconomies outweigh the economies. Boehm also warns that on products with less than 2000 LOC, personal differences tend to dominate any other effects.

Accurate sizing is important, as incorrect sizing usually means underestimates (due to some factors having been overlooked), which in turn results in rushed and low-quality work, with consequent impact on maintenance productivity. Under-estimates can be caused by a desire to please the user or manager, and by attempts to avoid confrontation with them (Chapter 11), making objective sizing measures necessary.

Trends

There seems to be a general belief that software written today is, on average, bigger than software written in the past (Yourdon, 1975). According to Hawkridge *et al.* (1988), for example, there is a 'general drift' towards larger systems, while according to Bell *et al.* (1987) 'the sheer size of projects has mushroomed'. As an example, NASA's space shuttle system has about four times as many lines of code as their earlier Apollo system (Charette, 1986). (Based on the dates on a graph in Boehm (1981), 1970 to 1977, this is an increase in size of about 20% p.a., compound.) In fact, according to Boehm (1981), it has 40 times as many object instructions as the earlier Project Mercury, which is an increase in size of nearly 30% p.a., compound, based on a date (1962) from the same graph. This is due to the automation of many functions, which was necessary to reduce the large numbers of people required to support each manned launch – for other applications, the growth rate is probably lower. This is confirmed by the fourfold increase in ten years (only 15% p.a., compound) at the Liquor Control Board of Ontario (Liquor Control Board moves to national DBMS with DL1 TRANSPARENCY,

Table 8.4 System size classifications (LOC)

Size	Brooks (1975)	Jones (1979)	Boehm (1981)	Howden (1982)	Fairley (1985)	Charette (1986)
Small		<2K	2K		1–2K	1–2K
Low–medium		2–16K				
Intermediate			8K			5K
Medium		16–64K	32K	100K	10–50K	100K
Large	>300K	64–512K	128K	1000K	50–100K	100K–1M
Very large			512K		1000K	1–10M
Superlarge		>512K				
Extremely large					1–10M	10–25M

ADRWARE News, 1986, **3** (2), 12–14). Similarly, Humphrey (1985) reported that, in the previous eight years, the overall size of large IBM operating systems had nearly doubled (an increase of only about 9% p.a., compound). However, he also stated that the scale of large systems had grown by three orders of magnitude in the past 30 years (which is the much higher increase of 26% p.a., compound), and predicted that this rate of growth was likely to continue or even increase in the future.

However, the program and system sizes (Tables 8.1 and 8.2), and even the 63 projects comprising the Boehm (1981) dataset, do not show any obvious trend. Perhaps the figures cover too short a period for a trend to be discernible, though 20 years should be long enough.

Another way of looking at the question is to compare the size classifications of different authorities, arranged in chronological sequence in Table 8.4 (K is one thousand LOC; M is one million LOC). These figures indicate that sizes within a category are increasing, and that larger categories are being created, thereby supporting the view that projects are getting bigger.

What is the effect of maintenance on software size? Conte *et al.* (1986) stated unequivocally: 'Systems grow in size over their useful life'. One of the facts on which he based this conclusion is that the number of modules comprising OS/360 grew by a factor of five in eight years (Belady and Lehman, 1979) – an

increase of about 20% p.a., compound. Another example is given by Charette (1986) of a Navy system which grew from 100 000 LOC to one million, in less than ten years – an increase of about 25% p.a., compound. (It is interesting to note that these growth rates are similar in magnitude to those for new systems.)

The trend is thus towards increasing size, and probably therefore, lower productivity.

Size reduction

One might have thought that program size was outside our control, but in fact, the number of LOC written can be considerably reduced by: using higher level languages and program generators; re-using code; buying packages; and by not including functions which would only be marginally useful (gold-plating), or at least deferring such functions – putting them on a formal 'wish list' – until there is stronger justification for including them. As Boehm (1981) so graphically expressed it, one of the primary controllable factors for improving productivity is the number of instructions we choose *not* to develop. According to Boehm (1973, 1981), in many cases a significant amount of effort has gone into developing software that was never used. In a review of a small number of government projects (Comptroller General, 1979; Charette, 1986), some of which were admittedly examined precisely because they

Table 8.5 Effect of product size on productivity

Authority	Magnitude	Range
IBM (Flaherty, 1985)	0.5:1	<10K vs >50K LOC
IBM (Walston and Felix, 1977)	0.7:1	1K vs 100K LOC
Doty model (Herd *et al.*, 1977)	1.2:1	10K vs 512K LOC
COCOMO model (Boehm, 1981)	1.3–2.5:1	1K vs 100K LOC
IBM (Brooks, 1981)	1.4–3:1	<100 man-months vs >100
Howden (1982)	2:1	1K vs 100K LOC
Jones (1986b): development	2:1	1K vs 100K LOC
IBM (Brustman, 1978)	2–4:1	15K vs 30K; 80K vs 165K
Johnson (1980b)	3:1	7K vs 165K LOC
Doty model (Herd *et al.*, 1977)	3:1	1K vs 10–512K LOC
Willett *et al.* (1973): Assembler	4:1	<2K vs 512K LOC
Jones (1986b): maintenance	4:1	10K vs 100K LOC
Jones (1979): Assembler	8:1	<2K vs >512K LOC
Willett (1973): Assembler	9:1	<2K vs >512K LOC
Average (approximate)	3:1	

were in trouble, it was found that only about 2% of the software contracted for could work on delivery, 3% more could work after some reworking, over 45% was delivered but never successfully used, 20% was used but either extensively reworked or abandoned, and 30% was paid for but not delivered! This can usually be avoided by involving the users, and making sure they fully understand in their own terms what the software will do for them.

Effect on productivity

Most of the productivity rates quoted in Chapter 2 indicate that productivity decreases – perhaps rapidly – with increasing program or system size. However, some of the rates show little, if any, decrease. This, however, may just be because some small projects were developed by relatively large teams with low productivity, and vice versa: the majority opinion is that size adversely affects productivity (Table 8.5).

According to the Doty model, productivity drops suddenly for products of 10 000 LOC, after which there is only a slow and steady decline with increasing size. (This is actually a simplified view, as there are two models, one for programs with less than 10 000 LOC, and one for programs with more. In any given case, the change in productivity at 10 000 LOC would depend not only on the size, but also on the specific values of the effort multipliers for that project.)

According to the COCOMO model (and many others), size has an exponential, and potentially unlimited effect, on productivity. A complication here is that the model allows for three modes of development (organic, semi-detached, and embedded – see Chapter 2), and the different modes use different values for the magnitude of the effect. For example, for an organic mode product, productivity on a 1000 source statement product is 1.1 times higher than on a 10 000 statement product; 1.3 times higher than on a 100 000 statement product; and so on. For an embedded mode product, productivity on a 1000 source statement product is 1.6 times higher than on a 10 000 statement product; 2.5 times higher than on a 100 000 statement product; and so on. For a semi-detached mode product, productivity is in between these values.

According to the Walston and Felix (1977)

model, product size has an exponential effect on productivity, but the effect is *opposite* to that predicted by most other models and authorities, i.e. productivity *increases* with increasing size. In other words, the economies of scale outweigh the diseconomies. (This is consistent with the high productivity reported by Jones (1986b) for very large organizations, and with Flaherty's findings in Table 8.5.) According to this model, the productivity on programs with 10 000 LOC is 1.2 times higher than on programs with 1000 LOC; the productivity on programs with 100 000 LOC is 1.5 times higher than on programs with 1000 LOC; and so on.

Brustman, using the same projects as Walston and Felix, gave productivity rates for several combinations of product size and timing constraint – e.g. productivity is 576 delivered source lines per man-month for small projects with less stringent timing requirements, 256 lines for medium-sized projects with more stringent requirements, and so on. His rates show that these two factors together affect productivity by up to 9:1. It is not clear what the effect of each factor separately is, but by choosing pairs of rates for which the timing constraint was roughly the same, we can almost eliminate its effect. The figures in Table 8.5 given for Brustman are therefore an approximation, and may be a little too high.

There is an inconsistency in the figures from which the Jones ratio for maintenance is derived. According to his figures, 2.5 man-months of effort are required to maintain a program of 1000 LOC over a period of 5 years; 13 man-months are required for a 10 000 LOC program (only 1.3 man-months per 1000 LOC); and 480 man-months for a 100 000 LOC program (4.8 man-months per 1000 LOC), i.e. there is no consistent increase in effort with increasing size. There is actually an error in the figures, as the 13 man-months is the sum of three amounts, 5, 10, and 0, and it is not clear if the 13 should be 15, or if the 5 should be 3 or the 10 should be 8. It is

assumed that the 5 or 10 is wrong, but if instead it is the 13 which is in error, then the tabulated ratio should read 3:1 (4.8/1.5) not 4:1 (4.8/1.3), but this does not resolve the inconsistency.

Conclusions

As was the case with productivity, LOC is not an ideal measure of software size, but is probably the best currently in widespread use.

The typical program probably contains about 500 LOC, and the typical system about 50 000.

The majority opinion is that productivity decreases with increasing program/system size.

New systems are probably bigger, on average, than those written in the past, and maintenance increases the size of production systems. This must be having an adverse effect on productivity.

By using higher-level languages, re-using code, including only cost-justifiable features, and so on, the number of lines of code that have to be developed can be kept to a minimum, with corresponding improvement in productivity.

8.2.2 DATABASE SIZE

In a typical large organization, a major application system may include 300–1000 data fields (Johnson, 1980b).

Various authorities (Table 8.6) believe that the size of the database affects productivity. According to Boehm (1981), it takes 20% longer to develop a program for which the

Table 8.6 Effect of database size on productivity

Authority	Magnitude
Herd *et al.* (1977)	minor
Boehm (1981)	1.2:1
Walston and Felix (1977)	1.7:1
Air Force (1974)	important

ratio of database size in bytes (characters) divided by the program size in delivered source instructions is very high (greater than or equal to 1000), than when it is low (less than 10). According to Walston and Felix (1977), it takes 70% longer to develop a program when there are more than 80 classes of items in the database per 1000 LOC, than when there are not more than 15. This figure may, however, include the effect of other, correlated factors (Chapter 2). Nevertheless, these opinions are consistent with the claim by Martin and McClure (1985) that, in most cases, control flow is simple while data structures are complex, and data structure errors are more common than procedural logic errors.

On the surface, productivity may appear to be unrelated to the amount of data, but there are several reasons why this is not the case.

- The lower productivity with larger size may be a reflection of greater variety in the data, i.e. the more data there is, the more likelihood there is of extra conditions which have to be catered for in the programs, e.g. extra record types.
- The larger size may be a reflection of a larger number of files, or of more fields in each record. This increases the amount of coding, and the effort to create test data, etc., and extra design work is likely, e.g. to avoid redundant (duplicated) data.
- Where volumes are high, the system developers may consider it justifiable or even essential to devote more time to improved user interfaces, additional documentation, error messages, validation checks, and special efficiency techniques to ensure that execution speed is adequate.
- The lower productivity might be attributable to problems due to limited storage capacities being exceeded (e.g. files too large to store on disk); slower response times when testing; longer test runs; extra, volume testing; or extra test planning.

The impact of this factor can be minimized, for example by cutting out unnecessary extras, but the possible causes indicate that it is generally unwise to counteract the lowering of productivity, e.g. if the user interface is not improved then *user* productivity will suffer. Fortunately, however, this factor has only a small impact on DP productivity: reducing the database size by a factor of ten, for example, would only improve DP productivity by around 6–8% (Boehm, 1981).

8.2.3 SOFTWARE COMPLEXITY

One factor which intuitively has a large effect on productivity is complexity: the more complex a program is, the more difficult it is to develop and, once developed, the more difficult it is to maintain it, or even to understand it. Schedules are therefore longer. In addition, complex programs contain more errors (Troy and Zweben, 1981).

Studies have shown a high correlation between the complexity of a program on the one hand, and the number of bugs it contains and the ease of maintaining it, on the other (Fitzsimmons and Love, 1978; Walsh, 1979; Feuer and Fowlkes, 1979). For example, TRW's reliability metric, which is based on the assumption that complex programs are less reliable, was applied to two versions of the same program. The straightforward version of the program not only scored higher on the metric than the version with clever loops and tricks, but also proved to be the more reliable in testing (Gilb, 1977).

It is not surprising, therefore, that complexity is used in four of the nine cost-estimation models (Boehm, 1981) surveyed. However, if we understand what makes a program complex, then we can try to avoid it.

Definition

Complexity is anything which increases the difficulty, and therefore the effort required by a programmer, to develop or maintain software (Conte *et al.*, 1986).

Types of complexity

Shneiderman (1980) divided complexity into logical, structural, and psychological. **Logical complexity** refers to characteristics which make it difficult to prove a program correct, e.g. the number of distinct paths in it. Logical complexity has been found to be a good predictor of program cost. **Structural complexity** refers to the number of modules in a program, and the number of linkages between them. **Psychological complexity** refers to characteristics which affect the ease a person has in understanding a program, such as the use of comments and mnemonics.

Causes of complexity

There are several reasons why a programmer may find a program difficult to write or maintain: the problem may be intrinsically complex; the solution to the problem may be poor; the tools may be inadequate; or the programmer may have limited expertise. (A systems analyst may find a system difficult to analyse or design for similar reasons.)

Intrinsic complexity

Generally, there is nothing the computer staff can do about this. Sometimes, however, the complexity is due to the presence of many features to meet the users' *wants*, as distinct from their *needs* (Schach, 1988), or to internal sophistication, to make a program more compact or efficient. Some of the complexity may therefore be unnecessary, e.g. some of the user-requested features may be 'gold-plating', and the efficiency requirements may be more stringent than necessary. In the past, when hardware was more expensive, programmers had to be economical in their use of machine resources, even if this resulted in more complex ('contorted') programs (Bell *et al.*, 1987). Nowadays, with people being more expensive, the emphasis is on pro-

grams which are quick and easy to understand and modify. Programs must therefore be kept simple. Programmers might resent this, fearing that the skills they accumulated will no longer be used, and in a sense their programs will be inferior, but Bell provides a number of answers to these objections.

- Finding a simple solution to a problem is not always easy, so creativity is still needed.
- Simple programs are usually completed sooner, and are more reliable, which is good for the programmer's self-esteem.
- Maintenance programmers will have more respect for the development programmer, and thank him, if they can understand his programs.

Similarly, Boehm (1981) argues that software is so complex that attempts to organize parts of it still leave more than enough challenging jobs.

Managerial decisions (e.g. which features to include) thus affect technical complexity, and conversely, technical feasibility guides management goals.

Poor solution

This refers to poor programming, which can turn even a simple problem into a complicated program. In an example given by Weinberg, a programmer 'made a mountain out of a molehill', and the program was 'a confusing mess' (Chapter 6). It was then rewritten by a different programmer in only one-twentieth of the original development time.

How well a program is written depends on a number of factors, such as coding conventions, comments, mnemonics, 'impurities', modularization, structured programming and the avoidance of GOTO statements, and standard (generic) designs. A study by Brooks (1980) showed that the use of modern programming practices reduced the negative effects of complexity.

Table 8.7 Effect of complexity on productivity

Source	Ratio
Daly (1979)	1.2:1 (inter-module complexity)
Daly (1979)	1.5:1 (intra-module complexity)
Wolverton (1974)	1.4–1.5:1 (uniform sample)
Griffin (1980)	1.5:1
COCOMO model (Boehm, 1981)	2.4:1
Weinberg (1971)	3:1
Walston and Felix (1977)	up to 4:1*
Aron (1974)	2–4:1 (Assembly language)
Aron (1974)	4–6:1 (higher-order languages)
Aron (1969)	4–6.7:1
Boeing (1979)	5:1
Pomberger (1984)	5:1 (easy vs difficult)
RCA model (Freiman and Park, 1979)	6–7:1
Brooks (1975)	6:1
SDC model (Nelson, 1966)	6:1 (20–80% complexity level)
NARDAC model (Williamson, 1979)	12:1 (individual modules)
Average (approximate)	4:1

* The Walston and Felix figure may include the effect of other, correlated factors (Chapter 2).

Inadequate tools

The tools available are becoming more powerful (Aron, 1974), but they are also becoming more complex. The level of the programming language used affects the ease of program development and maintenance. In general, the higher the level, the easier it is, so a low-level language should only be chosen if there is good reason to do so. Languages without a GOTO statement help to enforce structured programming. Relational data base management systems also simplify program development and maintenance, compared to older DBMS models.

Programmer expertise

The degree of difficulty which a programmer has in understanding a program depends not only on the above factors, but also on his level of skill and relevant experience (Christensen, 1980). Programmers build up a body of knowledge and expectations which enable them to understand typical programs quickly. However, if a program violates normal structure or conventions, then experienced programmers become confused, whereas novice programmers, without such expectations, do not (Soloway and Ehrlich, 1984). Experienced programmers therefore have more difficulty understanding some programs than do novices.

Magnitude of effect on productivity

Various authorities (Table 8.7) have quantified the impact which complexity has on productivity. In addition, a Delphi survey by Scott and Simmons (1974) concluded that productivity is *higher* with increased complexity, but this seems implausible, and is contradicted by the tabulated values. (A Delphi survey is a technique for anonymously obtaining consensus between a group of people (Helmer, 1966).)

There are wide differences between the tabulated figures. The Williamson ratio would be lower, and therefore more in keeping with the other values, if applied to whole programs instead of individual modules: different modules in the same program can differ considerably in com-

Software development and maintenance

plexity, so there would be an averaging-out effect (Boehm, 1981). In general, the wide variations might be due to different authorities choosing different cut-off points for extreme values. For example, if the difference between the 10% and 90% complexity levels for the SDC model had been used, instead of the 20% and 80% levels, then the productivity range would have been 10:1 not 6:1. (A program at the 20% level is more complex than 20% of the programs in the SDC database of 169 projects; a program at the 80% level is more complex than 80% of the programs in the database; and so on.) Similarly, if the 'very easy' versus the 'extremely difficult' ratio for Pomberger had been used, instead of the 'easy' versus the 'difficult', then the productivity range for him would have been 40:1 not 5:1. Operating systems, which are very large and complex, and have exceptionally low productivity rates, are examples of these extreme cases.

Walston and Felix subdivided complexity into several factors (Table 8.8); their ratios reflect the productivity where complexity was less than average, compared to the productivity where it was greater than average. Each figure may, however, include the effect of other, correlated factors, as previously stated; and in particular, these four factors may be correlated with each other.

Wolverton subdivided software into different types (Table 8.9), and found the effect of

Table 8.8 Effect of type of complexity on productivity

Type of complexity	Productivity ratio
Customer interface complexity	4.0:1
Overall complexity of code developed	1.7:1
Complexity of application processing	2.1:1
Complexity of program flow	1.4:1

Source: Walston and Felix (1977)

Table 8.9 Effect of complexity on productivity for different types of software (Wolverton, 1974)

Type of software	Productivity ratio
Control	2.3:1
Input/output	2.5:1
Pre/post processor	2.6:1
Algorithm	2.3:1
Data management	2.4:1
Time critical	1.0:1

complexity on cost (and therefore productivity) for each type. For most types of software, therefore, complexity can double the effort required, and the magnitude of the effect is virtually independent of the software type. Time critical software, however, has only one complexity rating – *very high* (on average, it requires twice as much effort as any of the other types).

Some of the productivity rates quoted in Chapter 2 indicate that productivity depends heavily on the type of application (a range of 8:1), but that may be largely because some types of application, such as operating systems, are large and complex, i.e. the observed differences in productivity may be due to size and complexity rather than type of application.

Wolverton found that, except for time critical software, for products of the same level of difficulty, application type only affected productivity by 50 or 60% (Table 8.10).

Walston and Felix found that productivity was 1.4 times higher when more than 66% of the code was classified as non-mathematical application and I/O formatting programs, than when 33% or less fell into these categories. By contrast, the Boeing rates quoted in Chapter 2 show a higher productivity for mathematical software than any of the other types (real time, signal processing, logical and report/commercial) (Black *et al.*, 1977). In fact, the productivity for mathematical software was about double the average for the other types.

Table 8.10 Effect of application type on productivity for different levels of difficulty

Level of difficulty	Productivity range	
	Excl. time critical	Incl. time critical
Old-easy	1.6:1	5.0:1
Old-medium	1.6:1	3.8:1
Old-hard	1.6:1	3.4:1
New-easy	1.5:1	3.0:1
New-medium	1.5:1	2.5:1
New-hard	1.6:1	2.1:1

Source: Wolverton (1974)

Trends

Is the average program written today more complex than the average program written a few years ago? There is a general belief that programs are becoming more complex (Weinberg, 1971; Yourdon, 1975; Van Tassel, 1978; Wright, 1978; Hawkridge *et al.*, 1988). As Bell *et al.* (1987) put it, 'the sophistication of today's software far outstrips that of the past. For example, complex user interfaces are now seen as essential'. The Liquor Control Board of Ontario claim a fourfold increase in complexity in ten years (15% p.a., compound), but they apparently equated complexity solely to size (Liquor Control Board moves to relational DBMS with DL1 TRANSPARENCY, *ADRWARE News*, 1986, **3** (2), 12–14).

The effect of maintenance is not clear. According to Lehman (1978), as a large program is continually changed, its complexity increases unless extra work is done to prevent this. As an example, Belady and Lehman (1979) showed how successive releases of OS/360 had to modify more and more modules each time to accommodate more and more side effects. However, a study by Lawrence (1982), in which complexity was measured by the proportion of modules changed, produced mixed results: the fraction of modules handled increased with system age in only two of the five systems studied. The effect of maintenance on maintainability is discussed further later.

Measurement of complexity

There are many complexity metrics – possibly more than the number of computer scientists (Conte *et al.*, 1986). Quantitative measures are more useful if they are easily automated (Shneiderman, 1980), e.g. counting the number of IF and GOTO statements, or the number of lines of code, or computing the more complex measures discussed below, can be done by compilers or programs like the static analysers (Chapter 6).

McCabe (1976) developed a graphical ('cyclomatic') complexity measure which assumes that complexity depends on the decision structure (the number of paths) in a program, and not its size. It therefore depends on the number of IFs, WHILEs, etc. – and thus on the number of ANDs, ORs and NOTs as well, as these are actually disguised IFs (Arthur, 1985). McCabe's method provides a quantitative basis for modularizing a program, which may be better than the usual more arbitrary restriction to one or two pages of source code (about 50–100 LOC). (Arthur (1988) recommended that 95% of all modules be under 100 executable lines of code or 10 decisions.) His method also identifies modules that will be difficult to test or maintain. Use of his measure on production programs has confirmed its validity, e.g. modules in one study with a complexity count of less than ten were free of errors (Arthur, 1985). According to DeMarco (1982), there is evidence that the McCabe metric is correlated with development effort, and several references were given in Chapter 2 indicating that it is correlated with lines of code (which in turn is correlated with development effort). According to Schach (1988), *most* complexity measures show a high correlation with the number of lines of code, which is not surprising, as the most popular complexity measures are themselves all related to size (Conte *et al.*,

1986). Therefore, when you think you are measuring the complexity of a product, you are actually just measuring its lines of code. When applied to structured and unstructured programs, McCabe's metric gives a higher count for unstructured programs, as would be expected (Vincent *et al.*, 1988). However, Bell *et al.* (1987) are critical of this measure because it denies that size affects complexity, and because it 'ignores references to data' (presumably the number of fields or variables), which can vary widely between different programs. As Conte put it, 'A reasonable hypothesis is the more data items that a programmer must keep track of when constructing a statement, the more difficult it is to construct'. Vincent *et al.* (1988) are also critical of the measure, because it does not take into account the ordering of the statements, particularly nested loops.

Woodward *et al.* (1979) counts the number of 'knots' in a program. If lines are drawn on a program source listing showing the flow of control – for example, a line would be drawn from a GOTO statement to the label it goes to – then a knot is the point at which two lines intersect. Use of GOTOs does not necessarily produce a knot, but knots are produced by GOTOs (Vincent *et al.*, 1988). Unlike McCabe's cyclomatic complexity measure, Woodward's does take the ordering of the statements into account. If, therefore, a portion of coding appears complex, it should be rearranged to a functionally equivalent version, and the number of knots counted for both, to see if there has been an improvement: the one with the lower knot count is believed to be better designed (Conte *et al.*, 1986). However, this metric does have disadvantages, e.g. it depends on the programming language, and it cannot measure the complexity of straight line (sequential) coding (Baker and Zweben, 1980).

Halstead's (1977) volume metric, a formula based on the number of operands and operators in a program, is a measure of the size of the program, which is one cause of complexity: the more operands and operators there are in a program, the more difficult it is to develop and maintain. Evidence presented in Chapter 2 indicated that this metric is correlated with both development effort and lines of code, but, as stated in Chapter 1, his methods have been questioned, and the supporting evidence has been challenged.

McClure's 'control variable complexity' and 'module complexity' measures are almost a combination of Halstead's and McCabe's methods, as she counts both the number of compares in a module and the number of unique variables referenced in the compares (McClure, 1978; Martin and McClure, 1985). She believes that complexity should be evenly distributed throughout the program. Any module which is more complex than the average for that program should be examined. This conclusion is hardly surprising. What is less expected though, is that modules with a *lower* than average complexity should also be examined, as this indicates that the program was subdivided into too many modules, which also makes the program difficult to understand. This method should therefore be used after a program has been designed, but before it has been coded: it *evaluates* the design.

Nesting of statements increases complexity, so Zolnowski and Simmons (1981) defined a 'depth of nesting' or 'nesting level' metric, and Dunsmore and Gannon (1980) an 'average nesting level'. Briefly, each executable statement is assigned a number – 1, 2, etc. – corresponding to the depth to which it is nested. The numbers are added, and the total divided by the number of executable statements, giving the average nesting level.

Potier *et al.* (1982) used a combination of metrics (Halstead, 1977; McCabe, 1976; etc.), and 'normalized' them for program length (by dividing them by the number of operators and operands). They found that procedures which were error-free had a much lower complexity value, on average, than those containing errors.

Schneidewind and Hoffman (1979) defined metrics for the logic structure of a program (the minimum number of paths in a program, and the 'reachability' of any node), and found high correlations between them and e.g. the number of errors found and the time to find errors.

Boehm (1981) provided a set of guidelines for determining objectively the complexity of a program. In contrast to the above methods, it is in the form of a checklist rather than a mathematical formula. For example, straight-line code with a few non-nested structured programming operators is of 'very low' complexity, while multiple resource scheduling with dynamically changing priorities is 'extra high'. Similarly, simple read and write statements are of 'very low' complexity, while device-timing dependent coding is 'extra high'.

There are many other possible ways to measure the complexity of a program, e.g. the amount of time taken to write or modify the program, the number of errors found in it, the number of debugging runs, and the ability of a programmer to recall, reconstruct, and answer questions about the program.

Use of complexity measures

Some complexity measures can be used before a program is coded, others only after. If, for example, there are two algorithms that solve the same problem, then a complexity measure such as that of McCabe can be applied to both of them to determine which is the simpler: it therefore helps us choose which one to use. Complexity measures can also provide a guide to the development effort, though they are not very satisfactory for two reasons. Firstly, they are not very accurate (Conte *et al.*, 1986); secondly, they can only be applied after a significant amount of effort has already been expended – even those used at the design stage are used at a time when perhaps 35% of the ultimate effort

has already been expended (Macro and Buxton, 1987).

After a program has been coded, a complexity measure identifies which portions are the most complex and error-prone. According to Schach (1988), complexity metrics and lines of code are equally good for predicting fault rates. A complexity measure therefore identifies which portions should either be rewritten or be subjected to earlier testing or extra testing (Martin and McClure, 1985; Conte *et al.*, 1986). This extra testing is known as 'complexity-based' testing, as opposed to the more common 'coverage-based' testing which attempts to test every statement, decision branch, etc. Complexity-based testing should therefore make the testing effort more effective. Because complexity measures are related to the difficulty programmers experience in locating errors in programs, they provide a guide to the amount of resources which will be required to maintain a program (Conte *et al.*, 1986).

Validity of complexity measures

I gave above some evidence supporting the validity of complexity measures, but I also mentioned some weaknesses and criticism of them. The erratic performance of the various metrics, including Halstead's Software Science and McCabe's metrics, indicates that there are other variables which must be taken into account (Shneiderman, 1980). Kearney *et al.* (1986) condemns the complexity measures. He stated that early claims for their validity have not been supported, and that the methodology of the experiments that provided the earlier supporting evidence is suspect. Complexity measures must be based on a theory of programming behavior to be valid, yet programming behavior is not well understood. Current measures are usually based on program code, which in itself is too narrow a view, but nevertheless ignore comments, indentation, and naming conventions, all of which affect the degree of difficulty a programmer has when debugging or maintaining a program.

If complexity measures are used to evaluate programmers, then the programmers will write programs that minimize the measure. It is important therefore for the measure to be valid, otherwise lower quality programs will result – the measure would in effect be *penalizing* quality. However, Kearney *et al.* quote several studies, e.g. Baker and Zweben (1980), which show that there is not good agreement between complexity measures and commonly accepted axioms for good programming. There is thus the danger that good programs – and therefore the good programmers who wrote them – may be unjustly condemned by poor complexity measures.

Current complexity measures therefore provide only a crude indication of complexity, and anyone who uses them must be aware of their limitations.

Conclusions

There is general agreement that complexity has a major impact on productivity, though there are wide differences of opinion on the magnitude of the effect.

Complexity has several aspects: the intrinsic complexity of the problem to be solved; the quality of the methods used in the solution; the power and suitability of the tools used; and the capability of the programmer.

These components suggest ways to reduce complexity, and thereby improve productivity, for example: the problem should be reduced in size by eliminating marginally-useful features where possible; additional training should be given, to teach good methods; standard (generic) designs should be used; and more powerful tools should be provided.

Programs written today are more complex, on average, than those written in the past, but it is not clear if maintenance increases the complexity of production programs, as the evidence is mixed.

There are many different complexity metrics, and there is some evidence supporting them, but there is still a question mark over their validity. They have a number of (potential) uses: estimating the effort that will be required to develop, test, or maintain a program; choosing between different solutions to a problem; and pointing out which modules are complex and so should either be re-written, or subjected to additional or earlier testing.

8.3 FUNCTION SPLIT (WORK BREAKDOWN)

The functions in the software life-cycle correspond roughly to different stages, but documentation is, or should be, a continuing activity throughout all the stages; and testing, particularly if the extreme form of top-down testing is used, overlaps with program design and coding (Yourdon, 1975). In any event, software development is an iterative process. It does not follow a linear progression from one stage to the next, but reverts occasionally to earlier stages. It is therefore better to think of the different portions of the process as functions rather than stages.

Each function should culminate in a formal verification ('are we building the product right?') and validation ('are we building the right product?') activity, to minimize the number of problems created in that function from being carried forward to the next (Boehm, 1981), after which the product created in that function (specifications, etc.) is temporarily 'frozen': no changes are permitted to it without the formal agreement of all affected parties. This is known as **baselining** (Vincent *et al.*, 1988).

There are many different models of the software life-cycle. The most common seems to be the 'cascade' or 'waterfall' model. This is a diagrammatic representation of the different functions. It shows the functions in a stepped fashion, with the function steps linked together by arrows, in a way which resembles a waterfall. However, it has limitations: it has difficulty coping with the iterative nature of software development – an error discovered during one function may necessitate reverting to a much earlier function – and it does not realistically integrate activities which span several functions e.g. resource management and quality assurance (Charette, 1986). Various refinements and alternatives have therefore been proposed: the 'incremental development' and 'advance-manship' models are described by Boehm (1981); and the 'rapid-prototyping', 'operational', and 'knowledge-based' models by Charette (1986). In view of the large amount of time spent enhancing software after it has been developed, some authors have suggested that the most appropriate life-cycle model is: development, maintenance, maintenance, . . . (Fairley, 1985). A more extreme view is that the life-cycle concept is harmful – apparently because system development is too complex, varied, and dynamic to be represented in this way – and so should not be used (Gilb, 1988).

Cho (1987) identified three steps which are missing from the conventional software life-cycle – product (i.e. output) concept formulation, product quality characteristics specification, and product design – without which it is difficult to apply statistical quality control to software development, and in fact he cites this as the root of the technical problems in software engineering management, such as incomplete requirement specifications, poor project planning, poor cost and schedule estimates, etc. (Cho defines the product of a software development process – the product desired by the software user – as *not* the software itself, but the *output* of the software. The software is merely the means to an end.)

Quantitative information about the different functions is contained in this section. The methods used during each function are then discussed later.

8.3.1 DEVELOPMENT

This section examines what proportion of the time and cost is commonly spent on each function in the software development process. However, there is no generally accepted classification scheme for the functions comprising the software life-cycle: different authorities use different schemes, as can be seen from the information listed below. Worse, few authorities list the activities they include in their categories. (Boehm (1981) is a notable exception.) In this study, a distinction is drawn between testing and debugging, but in common usage, the term 'testing' usually includes debugging, so the testing figures shown below include debugging except where otherwise indicated. Similarly, the term 'programming' generally includes testing and debugging, but it is sometimes used to refer to just the design and coding, or even just the coding, of programs, and authors do not always state which usage they are employing.

The subdivision (work breakdown) percentages differ in different circumstances. In particular, where fourth-generation languages are used, some functions may even be eliminated – hence the phrase 'application development without programmers' (Martin, 1982a). Also, technological aids reduce the amount of time spent on a function, thereby altering the ratios. Furthermore, the early functions are often skimped – not always successfully – on small, simple systems (Boehm, 1981).

Factors affecting productivity may affect it to a different extent for each function. For example, if the project staff are not familiar with the application area, then initially their productivity will be low as they learn and make mistakes; but as the project progresses, and passes from one function to another, e.g. from design to coding, so this effect dimi-

Table 8.11   Composition of development activity

Source and activity	% breakdown
Glass (1979)	
Requirements/specifications	20% of costs
Design	20%
Implementation	20%
Checkout	40%
Boeing model (Black *et al.*, 1977)	
Requirements definition	5% of total cost
Design and specification	25%
Code preparation	10%
Code checkout	25%
Integration and test	25%
System test	10%
Bell *et al.* (1987)	
Requirements	9% of time
Specifications	9%
Design	15%
Coding	21%
Unit test	24%
System test	21% (33–50% of time scale)
Conte *et al.* (1986)	
Product design	15% of effort
Detailed design	25%
Programming/coding	40%
System integration	20%
Couger (1973)	
Systems analysis	5–20% of costs
Systems design	20–25%
Programming	40–55%
Conversion	15–20%
Gunther (1978)	
a) Development	55% of effort
Test	28%
Publication	17%
b) Analysis, feasibility, design	50% of calendar time
Programming	25%
Evaluation	25%
Van Tassel (1978)	
a) Planning	14% of programming time
Writing	14%
Debugging	57%
Testing	14%
b) Debugging	50–90% of programming time
Parkin (1980)	
Feasibility study	10–20% of costs
Requirements, specifications	40%
Program development, testing	40–50%
Charette (1986)	
Concept development/requirements analysis	5% of effort
Design	35%
Implementation	20%
Testing	40%

Table 8.12 Global averages (hours per 100 verbs)

	Program complexity		
	Easy	*Medium*	*Difficult*
Structure diagram	2 (11%)	4 (17%)	8 (25%)
Coding/compile	12 (67%)	12 (50%)	12 (38%)
Unit test	4 (22%)	8 (33%)	12 (38%)
Total	18	24	32

Source: Johnson (1980b)

Table 8.13 Global averages (% of cost)

	1970s	*1980s*
Documenting existing system	5%	10%
Logical system design	10	20
Physical system design	20	25
Programming the new system	45	35
Testing and implementing the new system	20	10

Source: Couger *et al.* (1982)

Table 8.14 Global averages (% of effort)

	Mode	
	Organic	*Embedded*
Requirements analysis	6%	4%
Product design	14	12
Programming	45–48	42–45
Test planning	4	4–7
Verification and validation	10–13	12–14
Project office	7	6–10
Configuration management/ QA	5	6–8
Manuals	6	6–8

Source: Boehm (1981)

nishes. Similarly, a slow computer response time has little or no effect on the requirements analysis function (unless prototyping is being used), but can have a considerable effect during testing. Some authorities and effort-estimation models, such as Boehm (1981), give separate figures ('effort multi-

pliers') for each function for each factor affecting productivity.

The figures (Tables 8.11–8.27) are important, as they indicate which functions are the largest, and therefore have the greatest potential for time (and therefore productivity) savings, and so deserve the most attention. (Strictly speaking, the function deserving the most attention is whichever one gives the biggest saving for the least effort. The size of the function only gives an indication as to which one this might be. The impact of any reductions on other functions, specifically subsequent ones, and on user productivity, must also be considered.) In addition, organizations can compare their profile against these figures, for projects of similar size and type, and see, for example, if they spend enough time on QA, documentation, installation and training. Most books give just one set of figures, whereas here figures are given from many different authorities. This was done to obtain a broader, more comprehensive, and detailed picture, and to derive more authoritative conclusions, but the differences between the various sets of figures do serve to show that it is risky to rely on just one author's figures.

In this section the figures apply to development only. (Maintenance is discussed in the next section.) Where authors included maintenance, it has been omitted, and their figures adjusted accordingly. For example, the function split figures given by Glass (1979) were doubled and those given by Bell *et al.* (1987) trebled. Boehm (1981) excluded the 'plans and requirements' function, so his figures have been reduced to include it.

Comments

Gunther's figures (Table 8.11) refer to 'heavy-duty' software, e.g. systems which will be used by people not known to the developers, so higher standards of planning, documentation, testing, etc. are necessary. Similarly, Boehm's splits for embedded mode projects

Table 8.15 Global averages (% of effort)

	Small (2K LOC)		Medium (32K LOC)		Large (128K LOC)	
	Organic	*Embedded*	*Organic*	*Embedded*	*Organic*	*Embedded*
Plans and requirements	6	7	6	7	6	7
Product design	15	17	15	17	15	17
Detailed design	25	26	23	24	22	23
Code and unit test	40	30	36	26	34	24
Integration and test	15	20	21	26	24	29

Source: Boehm (1981)

Table 8.16 Global averages (% of schedule)

	Small (2K LOC)		Medium (32K LOC)		Large (128K LOC)	
	Organic	*Embedded*	*Organic*	*Embedded*	*Organic*	*Embedded*
Plans and requirements	9	19	11	24	11	26
Product design	17	24	17	26	17	26
Programming	57	39	49	30	45	27
Integration and test	17	18	23	20	27	21

Source: Boehm (1981)

(Table 8.15) show slightly higher figures for all functions except code and unit test than in the corresponding organic mode projects. (It is interesting to note that the schedule splits he gives show a similar trend: the 'plans and requirements', and the 'product design' functions comprise a considerably larger portion of the project schedule in embedded mode projects than in organic mode (Table 8.16).)

If a high level of reliability is required in the finished product, or there are hardware constraints, then testing costs are considerably increased (Boehm, 1981).

Aron's 'utilities' figures (Table 8.18) show the subdivision for systems which make extensive use of utilities.

Couger's figures (Table 8.13) show that, for more recent projects (1980s versus 1970s), more time is spent on the initial functions (systems analysis and design) – 55% com-

pared to only 35% – and less on the later ones (programming and testing) – only 45% compared to 65%.

Jones (1986b) (Table 8.17) warns that several factors cause the percentages to be different in otherwise similar projects: the language the programs are written in; whether they were written at one or several sites; and staff familiarity with the application area and the tools used. However, it is difficult to determine any significant trends from his figures. In particular, most of his figures are for COBOL programs, so it is difficult to conclude what the effect of language is on the percentages, though the proportion of time spent on coding does decrease with increasing language level. It also appears that the proportion of time spent on requirements, design, and coding decreases with increasing product size, team size, and project duration, while the propor-

Table 8.17 Global averages (% of effort)

	No. of projects	Require-ments	Design	Coding	Testing	Documen-tation	Repair	Manage-ment	Other
Language									
Assembler	2	3	7	38	14	12	16	10	0
C	5	5	7	19	10	34	15	11	0
COBOL	38	6	8	22	11	15	25	10	3
PASCAL	2	7	10	26	13	8	24	11	0
PL/1	2	4	6	13	8	24	33	11	0
ADA	2	4	5	9	6	43	23	11	0
BASIC	2	6	9	26	13	9	17	19	0
4GL	1	0	0	25	25	0	25	25	0
APL	1	11	11	21	11	16	21	11	0
Spreadsheet*	1	9	9	14	9	23	36	9	0
Combined	56	5	8	22	11	17	24	11	2
Lines of code									
0–4K	11	9	10	27	12	9	20	12	0
4–16K	18	6	8	26	13	8	28	11	0
16–64K	6	4	6	23	11	23	21	10	0
64–256K	19	4	6	14	9	28	24	11	5
>256K	2	4	11	19	16	16	18	11	6
Combined	56	5	8	22	11	17	24	11	2
Team size									
0–4	13	8	9	25	12	13	21	12	0
4–8	16	6	9	26	13	7	28	11	0
8–50	8	4	7	24	12	17	26	10	1
50–80	10	5	7	18	12	18	25	11	5
>80	9	3	5	11	7	40	19	11	5
Combined	56	5	8	22	11	17	24	11	2
Duration (months)									
0–4	14	7	9	26	13	14	20	11	0
4–8	12	6	9	27	13	6	27	11	0
8–16	11	5	7	20	10	23	25	11	0
16–24	11	4	6	16	10	24	26	10	4
>24	8	4	7	15	11	22	22	11	7
Combined	56	5	8	22	11	17	24	11	2

Source: Jones (1986b)
* The percentages for the spreadsheet do not add up to 100, as there is a discrepancy in the figures from which they were derived.

tion of time spent on documentation increases. As warned in Chapter 2, his values were synthesized from actual projects, or were produced by an effort-estimation model, so there is the possibility of distortions due to any inaccuracies in either the model or the data it was calibrated against, or simplifications in either the model or the synthesized data.

The Boehm (1981) estimate (Table 8.25) that about one man-month of effort is required for documentation per 1000 delivered

Table 8.18　Global averages

	Aron	*Polanyi*	*Utilities*
Designing program	35	30	60
Coding, test data, documentation	30	40	10
Debugging	35	30	30

Source: Aron (1974)

Table 8.19　Global averages (% of costs)

	Pomberger	*Kopetz*	*Gewald*
Requirements analysis/definition	25	20	} 39
Design	25	19	
Implementation/ coding	15	22	20
Test	35	28	42
Documentation		11	

Source: Pomberger (1984)

LOC, works out at about 25% of the total development effort. (Based on an average productivity of 12 LOC per day, including documentation effort, and 20 working days per month – see Chapter 2 – it would take (1000/12/20 =) 4 months to develop 1000 LOC.) This seems very high, bearing in mind that his figures exclude the creative design and planning time, which one would have thought was the major component. Nevertheless, a large amount of time *is* spent on documentation, emphasizing the need for word processing facilities.

By comparison, the Jones (1986b) figures (Table 8.25) for documentation of a large telecommunications system – more than 60 000 pages, in excess of 30 million words, and an average of 120 words per line of source code – imply the system contained (30 000 000/120 =) 250 000 LOC, and therefore had (60 000/250 =) 240 pages of documentation per thousand lines, which is much higher than any of the other estimates, which

range from 10 to 157 pages. It is even higher than his own figures for an internal program and a commercially marketed version thereof, each comprising 50 000 lines of COBOL code. The former had approximately (1400 /50 =) 28 pages per thousand lines of code, and the latter approximately (3300/50 =) 66. In the former, documentation consumed (108/537 =) 20% of the development effort, while in the latter it consumed (247/715 =) 35%, and these figures include most, if not all, the directly relevant effort. In both cases, the documentation required about 9 hours per page, assuming 120 hours work per month (Chapter 2). (108*120/1400 and 247*120/3300, respectively.) This is in good agreement with Boehm's 2–4 hours, bearing in mind that Jones's figures include most, if not all, the directly relevant effort, whereas Boehm's do not.

In Table 8.27, the SAGE project is probably the Semi-Automatic Ground Environment air defense system.

Other subdivisions

One set of figures not contained in the literature surveyed, is the split by type of program:

- edit
- update
- report.

These ratios would be useful in calculating the productivity gain obtainable from fourth-generation languages.

Another figure which is relevant to productivity, is the split:

- batch
- on-line

for which a number of figures are available. In a study quoted by Johnson (1980b), there were 11 times as many batch programs as on-line programs (2719 compared to only 256), for a group of projects totalling 1975K LOC.

Table 8.20 Global averages (% of costs)

	Maths (Kopetz)	Scientific (Gewald)	Command/ control (Gewald)	Commercial		System software	
				(Kopetz)	(Gewald)	(Gewald)	(Gewald)
Analysis	20			20			
Design	20	44	46	20	55	30	33
Coding	24	26	20	25	10	20	17
Testing	28	30	30	25	35	50	50
Documentation	8		*	10			

Source: Pomberger (1984)
* It is not clear why the percentages for Command and Control Systems do not add up to 100.

In a further 17 projects, also totalling nearly 2 million lines of code, batch programs comprised eight times as many lines of code as on-line programs, but lines of code is a less reliable measure, as the on-line version of a batch program may not contain the same number of lines (see below). However, the ratio may be much lower now as batch processing 'has faded' (Wiener, 1986): 'The last ten years have seen a dramatic increase in the number of on-line interactive data processing applications, at the expense of traditional batch production systems' (Maurer, 1983). Butlein (1985) expanded on this. According to him, on-line work will have grown to take up an average 20% of the mainframe's capacity by 1988, while batch processing will have dropped from a 1983 level of 25% to just 7% by 1988. (The remaining capacity is either consumed by 'environmental' software, i.e. operating systems, or is idle time, to cope with the peaks in usage experienced with on-line processing.) Martin (1981) reported the following planned changes in the batch:non-batch ratio in a giant petroleum company: 3:1

in 1978; 2.1:1 in 1980; and 0.7:1 in 1983. Martin (1982a) quoted two organizations in which the ratios were 9:1 and 1.2:1. The first ratio was for a medium-sized corporation with a 20-year old DP department, and the second for a small organization new to DP. Of the 500 or so organizations in an International Data Corporation survey (of about 1000 DP professionals, etc.) which used a DBMS, 86% reported on-line use 'in some fashion': 61% used it for query language access, and 36% for on-line query language update (Hoard, 1981).

This ratio is relevant to productivity. Until recently, it might have been believed that developing an interactive system was far more time-consuming than developing an equivalent batch system, as designing a good interactive system is difficult and time-consuming, and error checking and handling consume a considerable amount of effort (Shneiderman, 1980). Furthermore, nearly every application creates its own user interface (Gould *et al.*, 1991). All in all, an enormous amount of work – often over half the code – is required, and it is usually not possible to re-use such code. The average batch system studied by Brustman (1978) had only one-third as many lines of code as the average interactive information retrieval system (27 000 vs 78 000). However, things have now changed: a recently conducted brief evaluation of a financial system (admittedly a very small and simple one), concluded that an interactive version would

Table 8.21 Global averages

TRW survey	Analysis/design	46% of costs
	Code/test	20
	System test	34

Source: Boehm (1973)

Table 8.22   Installation

	Installation		Training	
	Average	*Range*	*Average*	*Range*
% of development effort				
Boehm (1981)				
Application program on existing general-purpose computer	0.2	0–0.6	3.6	0–10
Application program on different general-purpose computer	0.8	0.2–1.8	1.6	0–2.7
Process control, new computer	3.3	3–4	1.5	1.3–1.9
Human–machine systems	13	6–20	6	3–8
% of development costs				
Gehring (1976)	2.3			
Carriere and Thibodeau (1979)		2.5–7.5		

require less development effort because an application generator was available which did much of the work. (The application generator was SYSTEM BUILDER, which runs on the PICK operating system. This product won the first British 4GL Grand Prix in 1987 (Miller, 1987), and one can see why.) In addition, the average batch program in the Johnson (1980b) study quoted above, had nearly twice as many lines of code as the average on-line program (686 compared to only 363).

Conclusions

There are several obstacles in the way of obtaining useful information from Tables 8.11 onwards.

- Different authorities use different units, e.g. cost, time and calendar time. (To compound the difficulty, for Table 8.11, the pie-chart from which Bell's figures were obtained stated that they referred to cost, whereas the accompanying text said they were time. A similar discrepancy exists (Table 8.27) in the case of the figures listed for Boehm (1973) as cost percentages; they are described in Boehm (1981) as referring to effort.)

- They also use different groupings: in Table 8.11 Van Tassel (1978) gives separate figures for coding and testing, while in Table 8.27 Boehm (1973) includes part of testing with coding; Martin and McClure (1985) consider unit testing to be part of the coding function, and in Table 8.26 Baker (1972) gives just one combined figure covering nearly all programming activities.

- Those based on cost do not specify *which* costs are included: machine costs and salaries, or just salaries? (One would expect that, as systems analysts are generally more highly paid than programmers – by about 20% (What are you worth in 88, *Datamation*, 1 Oct 1988, pp. 53–66) – the percentages for costs would be higher than the corresponding percentages for effort for the analytical functions, and lower for the programming functions, if only salaries are included. Similarly, if machine costs are included, then one would expect the percentages for costs for the testing functions to be higher – by about 20% (Boehm, 1981) – than the corresponding percentages for effort. However there is no clear and consistent trend in the figures, though this may just mean that these differences are swamped by the general discrepancies.)

Table 8.23   Quality assurance

Source	Details
Myers (1979)	Approximately 50% of the development elapsed time, and over 50% of the total development cost, are spent testing.
Boehm (1981)	Unit testing can be performed at the rate of around 16 LOC per man-hour, with error detection rates of around 58%.
Johnson (1980b)	On one system, individuals submitted 9–13 jobs per day; the number of tests required per ten verbs ranged from five to eight; and the (CPU?) charge per person per day ranged from $20 to nearly $50.
Martin and McClure (1985)	Testing is disproportionately time-consuming with very large programs. The number of combinations that need to be tested tends to increase roughly as the square of the program size.
Pomberger (1984)	A given extra effort during system specification yields more than double the savings in effort during implementation and testing.
Yourdon (1975)	Testing – small project <30% of total project time large project >50% Testing and debugging = ⅓ to ½ of total project time.

DeMarco (1982)	Yourdon 1978–80 Project Survey
	   Projects delivering above median quality: testing = 21% of total effort.
	   Projects delivering below median quality: testing = 28% of total effort.

Cho (1987)	The majority of commercial programmers use as much as 50% of project time on debugging.

Glass (1979)	Software reliability activities as a proportion of the total software development budget:
	   small project 25%
	   average project 35–50%
	   large project >50%

Hartwick (1977)	Composition of independent verification and validation (excludes fixing errors):
	   management and reporting 24%
	   tool enhancement and maintenance 11%
	   requirements analysis 15%
	   equations analysis 12%
	   code analysis 18%
	   testing 20%

Table 8.24   Defect removal

Source	Product size (delivered LOC)	Effort Man-months/1000 LOC	Effort % of total
Boehm (1980a)	2K	0.6	17–22%
Jones (1977)	2K	1	50%
Jones (1977)	2048K	22	73%
Arthur (1983)	For programs larger than 100 executable LOC, repair times increase exponentially with the executable LOC and decision density.		

Table 8.25   Clerical/documentation

Source	Details
Lallande (1987)	The documentation of technologically advanced products may consume anywhere from 10–30% of the design process.
Holton (1977)	Clerical and non-technical tasks comprise 10–15% of the programmer/analyst workload.
Boehm (1981)	Clerical work 7–10% of total effort 3–4% of total costs About 60% of a project's activity results in a document as its immediate end product, and only 40% results in code. Depending on project size, about 2–4 man-hours are required to produce each page of documentation (excluding the creative design and planning time). At a rough estimate of typically about 50 pages per thousand delivered source instructions, about one man-month of effort is required for documentation per 1000 delivered LOC.
Martin (1981)	In typical installations that are well controlled with a development standards manual, there are about ten pages of program documentation for each 1000 lines of code.
Jones (1986b)	An analysis of the documentation of a large telecommunications system revealed a total of more than 100 different kinds of documents produced and more than 60 000 pages, with an overall total in excess of 30 million words, giving an average of 120 English words per line of source code. At IBM in about 1977, 6.6 hours were required to produce the requirements, functional design, and logic design for a program of 1000 lines of Assembler; while nearly 22 000 hours were required for a program of 1024K lines (about 21 hours per 1000 lines). These figures cover only the mechanical tasks of longhand drafts, text entry and graphics, and not the mental effort, dialogs with users, and any travel. In two examples quoted by him, an internal program and a commercially marketed version thereof, each comprising 50 000 lines of COBOL code, the former totaled approximately (400+1000=) 1400 pages of documentation, which consumed (30+78=) 108 man-months out of a total of 537 man-months of development effort, while the latter totaled approximately (1300+2000=) 3300 pages, which consumed (99+148=) 247 man-months out of a total of 715 man-months: IBM internal business program (50 KDSI) 28 pages per KDSI Marketed version (also 50 KDSI) 66 pages per KDSI IMS/360 Version 2.3 (about 166 KDSI) 157 pages per KDSI

- Some authorities do not give individual figures for system design and program design, while others do not include the analytical functions at all.
- Some functions, e.g. publication, appear in only one of the alternative subdivisions. ('Conversion' also appears in only one subdivision, but the context indicates that this may be just another name for acceptance testing.)
- Books on systems analysis and design generally give high percentages for systems analysis and design; books on reliability generally give high percentages for testing and debugging.
- There are differences between the different sets of figures. (One would expect considerable differences between individual projects, e.g. because of a high reliability requirement in some projects, or because

Table 8.26 Individual projects

Price Waterhouse/New York City (original quote) (Hodges, 1987a)

Workflow analysis and user requirements definition	17% of cost
Functional and technical design	34%
Detailed design implementation, code and test	49%

NYT (Baker, 1972)

Requirements analysis	9% of staff time
System design	10%
Unit design/programming/testing/debugging	49%
Documentation	8%
Secretarial	5%
Librarian	6%
Managerial	13%

NASA Apollo (Yourdon, 1975): Nearly 80% of the cost was spent on testing.

Table 8.27 Individual projects (% of costs)

	Analysis/ design	Code/test	System test
SAGE	39	14	47
NTDS	30	20	50
GEMINI	36	17	47
SATURN V	32	24	44
OS/360	33	17	50
Average	34	18	48

Source: Boehm (1973)

the staff lack knowledge of the particular application in others, but these should be averaged-out in global figures.)

Nevertheless, some conclusions can be drawn:

- There is broad agreement between the authorities, i.e. most figures are within about 50% of the typical values for system development given in Table 8.28.
- Larger projects require relatively more time to perform integration and test activities.
- High-level languages require relatively less coding time than Assembler.
- Large projects (in terms of LOC, team size, or duration) require relatively less requirements, design and coding, and relatively more documentation.
- Although embedded mode projects require more effort in every function, the increase is greater in the initial functions to ensure the specifications are correct, and in integration, to ensure the product meets the specifications.

- The Yourdon 1978–80 figures (Table 8.23) show that products with many errors require more testing time.
- Aron's 'utilities' figures (Table 8.18) show how technological aids can reduce the proportion of time spent coding and debugging.
- Boehm's 'TRW Survey' figures (Table 8.21), compared to his figures for individual projects (Table 8.27), suggest that more thorough analysis and design (46% versus an average of only 34%) pays for itself in reduced system testing costs (only 34% versus an average of 48%) (Boehm, 1973).

Approximate typical work breakdown values for system development are given in Table 8.28. Debugging time is included in the testing figures, because very few references gave separate debugging figures, and the average of those figures is about 40% (of the development activity), which is out of proportion to the combined testing/debugging figures given by the other authorities (an average of only (11+15 =) 26%). Jones (1986b) gave over 50 sets of effort estimates, for a variety of situations, depending on some 20 factors, such as the level of language

Table 8.28 Breakdown of development activity

Feasibility	9% of effort
Requirements	5
Specifications/product design	8
Detailed design	13
Coding	11
Unit test	11
System test	15
Installation	3
Training	3
Documentation	6
Clerical	6
Managerial	10

used, the amount of experience of the programmers, the complexity of the program, and so on. For these situations, testing (excluding debugging) consumed an average of about 11% of the development effort, and debugging an average of about 24% (Table 8.17). The two combined therefore consumed an average of about 35% of the development effort, and debugging consumed, on average, about twice as much effort as testing. By comparison, the other references which gave separate debugging figures suggest that debugging consumes perhaps four times as much effort as testing. Taking all these facts into account, as a round number, debugging probably consumes about 20% of the development effort.

The programming functions (detailed design, coding, and unit test) and system test are the biggest functions, but there is little difference in their sizes, so one cannot say from these figures alone that any one function should receive much more attention than any of the others.

The figures in Table 8.28 indicate that the design:coding:test ratio is about (8+13):11:(11+15), or 36:19:45 if the other functions are excluded, which is in good agreement with the '40–20–40' rule (40% design, 20% coding, 40% test) (Pomberger, 1984).

There is one way to provide an independent check on these figures, and that is to determine the programmer/systems analyst time ratio from them, and compare it with the

actual number of people employed in these categories. However, this is not as easy as it might seem:

- Some of the above functions – such as system test and documentation – would usually be shared between these two categories of staff. The programming and systems analysis percentages could therefore be 60% and 30% respectively (a ratio of 2:1), but it seems more likely that programming time comprises only about 48% of the total, and analytical time about 42% (the remaining 10% being managerial), so programming time only exceeds analytical time by around 1.1:1 (Table 8.29).
- There is no general agreement on the ratio of programmers to analysts (Table 8.30). In my experience, project teams typically consisted of about three programmers led by a systems analyst giving a 3:1 ratio, but the ratios in the literature, which are listed in Table 8.30 in chronological order, are mostly much lower than this.
- There is even a lack of agreement as to the number of people employed in each category in the USA (Table 8.31). Jones (1986b) estimated that there were more than 3 250 000 professional programmers worldwide.
- The proportion of programmers is likely to be much lower in organizations making extensive use of 4GLs and application packages. Therefore, as these tools become more widely used, so the ratio will change.
- A further complication is maintenance: the breakdown of maintenance activity might be very different from that of development. However, figures (in section 8.3.2) indicate that this is not the case.

These figures vary too widely to be able to confirm the breakdown of development activity, and the difficulty is compounded by the apparent steady decrease in the programmer:analyst ratio (presumably because of the increasing use of 4GLs and application packages), but nevertheless they seem to point

Table 8.29 Work shared between categories of staff

	Program-ming	Systems analysis	Managerial
Feasibility		9%	
Requirements		5	
Specifications/ product design		8	
Detailed design	13%		
Coding	11		
Unit test	11		
System test	5	10	
Installation	2	1	
Training		3	
Documentation	3	3	
Clerical	3	3	
Managerial			10%
Total	48	42	10

Table 8.30 The ratio of programmers to analysts

Source	Date	Ratio
Hodges (1987b)	1972	2.5:1
	1973	2.2:1
	1974	2.1:1
	1975	1.8:1
Brandon (1978)	1975	0.9:1
Hodges (1987b)	1976	1.7:1
	1977	1.7:1
	1978	1.6:1
	1979	1.8:1
	1980	1.7:1
Data[†] (1980)		2:1
Brandon (1978)	1980 (predicted)	0.5:1
Hodges (1987b)	1981	1.7:1
Martin (1981)		1:1*
van der Poel (1982)		3:1
Hodges (1987b)	1982	1.8:1
	1983	1.6:1
	1984	1.5:1
	1985	1.4:1
Chorafas (1986)		2–2.2:1
Hodges (1987b)	1987 (estimated)	1.4:1

* For two organizations.
† Data processing expenditure profiles, in *The 1979/80 S.A. Computer Guide*, Johannesburg: Thomson Publications (Pty) Ltd, 149–152.

to a programmer:analyst ratio of probably a little under 2:1 in the mid-1980s. This suggests that the programming vs analysis function split was nearer 60:30 than 48:42 at that time.

The position regarding the ratio of managers is also confused. Brandon (1978) gives a ratio of 1 manager to 3 programmers and analysts, while Martin (1981) gives ratios of 1 to 4 and 1 to 10, for two organizations. At present, the number of people typically reporting to each manager is about 7 or 8, and this is also about the maximum number that theoretically a manager can adequately control (Chapter 3). The low ratios (1:3 or 4) presumably refer to part-time supervisors, and the high ratios (1:7 to 1:10) to full-time managers.

The lack of standardized groupings of activities and standardized units of measure has been noted. Standardization would be particularly beneficial when collecting more data to help refine and update the above figures. It would also help individual organizations to 'customize' global figures to their own circumstances, so they could obtain more meaningful comparisons with their own performance.

8.3.2 MAINTENANCE

Maintenance is generally defined as any work done on a software system after it becomes operational (Parikh, 1984). Boehm (1981) gives a narrower definition: changes which leave the primary functions of the system intact. He provides guidelines to determine whether a particular change should be classified as maintenance or not. For example, major redesign and redevelopment, involving more than 50% new code, is not maintenance. Jones (1986b) includes only defect repair time in his maintenance figures.

The US Department of Defense spent $2 billion on maintenance of software in 1983, and estimated that this would rise to $16 billion by the end of the 1980s, while the US

Table 8.31   Employment data (USA)

Source	Year	Programmers	Analysts	Total
Gilchrist and Weber (1972)				360 000
Hodges (1987b)	1972	188 000	75 000	263 000
	1973	190 000	87 000	277 000
	1974	203 000	99 000	302 000
	1975	228 000	124 000	352 000
Brandon (1978)	1975	240 000	260 000	500 000
Hodges (1987b)	1976	235 000	139 000	374 000
	1977	228 000	132 000	360 000
Brandon (1978)	1977 (excl. vendors)			600 000
Hodges (1987b)	1978	255 000	155 000	410 000
	1979	330 000	181 000	511 000
	1980	351 000	205 000	556 000
Brandon (1978)	1980 (predicted)	350 000	750 000	1 100 000
Martin (1981)		300 000		
Boehm (1981)		500,000		
Hodges (1987b)	1981	367 000	213 000	580 000
	1982	434 000	242 000	676 000
	1983	443 000	276 000	719 000
	1984	455 000	300 000	755 000
Parikh (1984)		500 000		
Jones (1986b)	1984	1 020 000		
Hodges (1987b)	1985	485 000	335 000	820 000
Mittra (1988)	1986			600 000
Davis (1989b)	1986			600 000
Hodges (1987b)	1987 (estimated)	563 000	408 000	971 000
Missing* (1980)	1990 (predicted)	1 500 000		
Davis (1989b)	2000 (predicted)			1 200 000

* Missing computer software *Business Week* 1 Sept. 1980, pp. 46–53.

as a whole spent about $30 billion per year on maintenance (Martin, 1985).

Maintenance therefore consumes much of the total time and cost – hence the terms 'buried in maintenance' and 'maintenance iceberg' (Canning, 1972).

Tables 8.32 onwards show that it is the largest single function. Suppose it comprises 50% (a typical value): if it can be halved, then the amount of time available for development will increase from 50% of the total, to 75%, which is a $((75 - 50) / 50 =)$ 50% improvement, so the number of new programs and systems produced will rise by 50% – a substantial increase. Furthermore, maintenance is the function most often underestimated when resources are allocated (Simpson, 1987). This is liable to result in hasty, and therefore low quality work, which in turn causes more maintenance to rectify the problems.

Because of its importance, additional information is given below about this function.

Development/maintenance split

Global averages

Figures for maintenance are given in Table 8.32.

Table 8.32 Global averages, maintenance

Source	%
Purvis (1979): per vendors	25–30 of total cost
Brooks (1975) (per McClure, 1978)	up to 29 of the total cost
Brandon (1978)	35 of systems resources
Brooks (1975) (per Boehm, 1981)	40 of the total time
Lientz *et al.* (1978)	48 of personnel hours
Hall (1987)	up to 50 of total cost
Van Tassel (1978)	50 of programming time
Glass (1979)	50 of costs
Shooman (1983)	50 of costs
Parikh (1984)	50 of budget
Yourdon (1975): average organization	50 of DP budget
Parikh (1984)	50–80 of programmer time
Lientz and Swanson (1980)	53 of costs
Conte *et al.* (1986)	up to 60 of software budget
Putnam and Fitzsimmons (1979)	60 of effort
Canning (1972)	60 of software expense
DeRose and Nyman (1978) (in 1976)	60–70 of software expense
Dunn and Ullman (1982)	60–70 of overall costs
Winer (1978)	60–80 of all programming effort
Charette (1986)	60–80 of all software costs
Cashman and Holt (1980) (in 1979)	60–80 of software expense
Fairley (1985)	60–90 of effort
Parikh (1984)	67 of software life-cycle
Purvis (1979): survey	67 of total cost
Zelkowitz (1979)	67 of software expense
Hall (1987)	up to 75 of software cost
Curtis *et al.* (1979a)	75 of costs
Shneiderman (1980)	75 of programming work
Mills (1976)	75 of software expense
Yourdon (1975): large organization	80 of DP budget
Martin (1978)	80 of computer effort, and DDP could push it much higher
Wulf (1975)	80 of total programming cost
Stone and Coleman (1979)	82 of effort

Individual cases

In addition to the data given in Table 8.33, large corporations often have some systems or application areas where 100% of the programmer effort is spent on maintenance (Martin, 1985).

The New York City figure, which at 9% is by far the lowest tabulated, presumably refers to only part of the total maintenance, e.g. just the initial maintenance.

It is interesting to note the large difference between the US Federal Government (40%) and the Department of Defense (60–70%).

Trends

The figures in Tables 8.32 and 8.33 do not show any discernible trend. By contrast, according to Boehm (1981), the proportion of time devoted to maintenance was 23% in 1955, and 36% in 1970, and he predicted it would be 58% in 1985. This is an increase of only 3% p.a. compound, which is low, and –

Table 8.33 Individual cases

Case	Source	%	
New York City	Hodges (1987a)	9	of cost
US Federal Government	Schatz (1986a)	40	of software costs
US DoD	Arthur (1988)	60–70	of software costs
Krupp MaK Engineering	Software AG (1986b)	67	of programmer time
OS/360	Van Tassel (1978)	80	of total costs

coupled with the relatively short time span of the above figures – may partly explain the lack of any discernible trend in them. It is reasonable to expect the proportion of maintenance to increase as more and more new systems, of increasing size and complexity, are developed, all of which must subsequently be maintained (Fairley, 1985). Furthermore, Warnier (1978) warned that the large number of children being taught by people who were more interested in the technical aspects of computers than in logical reasoning, would lead in the long run to a major increase in maintenance. However, the increase may be slowed by:

- an increasing backlog of urgent new development work;
- the increasing use of modern techniques, resulting in software that is easier to maintain;
- the increasing use of fourth-generation languages, relational DBMSs (with their data independence, flexible data structures and report generation capabilities), application packages, and so on.

Furthermore, unless new application areas arise, and continue to arise, the number of applications remaining to be computerized will decrease.

Other statistics

Details are given in Table 8.34.

Conclusions

It is difficult to compare the above figures.

- Some refer to time, others to cost – and Boehm (1981) treats the two as interchangeable.
- Some refer to programming only, others to the total.
- Van Tassel (1978) and Yourdon (1975) obtained their development/maintenance split figures from the same source. They use different units of measure but nevertheless still arrive at the same value.
- Parikh's 67% of the software life-cycle probably refers to cost, and not duration as implied (Chapter 13).
- If a particular line of code is changed more than once in the same year, in different modifications, is it counted more than once?

In spite of these difficulties, some conclusions may be drawn:

- Estimates of the proportion of time spent on maintenance vary widely, ranging from under 30% to 90%.
- Most estimates are about 50 to 70%.
- About 10% of the coding in a program is changed each year, and this takes about 25% of the original programming time.
- The development/maintenance ratio for a given system is therefore not static, but depends on how long the system has been in use, with maintenance forming an increasingly larger proportion of the total effort: after 4 years, maintenance has consumed about 50% of the total, and after 10 years, about 70%.
- The maintenance proportion of the *overall* total effort, i.e. for all systems combined, is also increasing, possibly by about 3% p.a.

Table 8.34 Other statistics

Source	Details
Van Tassel (1978)	For each year a system is in production, the programming time spent maintaining it amounts to 17–33% of the original programming time. The average production program will be maintained by 10 different people before being rewritten or discarded (Canning, 1972).
Yourdon (1975)	An informal survey by a major computer manufacturer indicated that, after a program was written by one person, it was typically maintained by ten generations of subsequent programmers before it was redesigned.
Fairley (1985)	The typical lifespan for a software product is 1–3 years in development, and 5–15 years in use (maintenance).
Charette (1986)	A software product currently spends over 80% of its life in maintenance.
Lientz and Swanson (1980)	For every 1000 delivered source instructions, on average 92 (9.2%) are changed every year.
Boeing (1979)	On average, 15% of the LOC in an easy program are changed each year, 5% in medium programs, and 1% in hard programs.
Boehm (1981)	For each dollar spent on software development, another dollar needs to be budgeted just to keep the software viable over its life-cycle. After that, another optional dollar can be spent on desirable enhancements.
DeMarco (1982)	When a system costing $1 million over its lifetime is retired, less than 5% of it will have changed, yet the cost of changing that 5% was at least as great as the cost of building the 95% that did not need to be changed.

It is not clear what effect organization size has on the ratio. According to Yourdon (1975), the proportion of maintenance is much higher in large organizations (Table 8.32), yet this is contradicted by the low figure for the US Federal Government (Table 8.33), which is a very large organization.

The effect of program size is also not clear. The figure for OS/360 (Table 8.33) implies that large programs have a higher proportion of maintenance, but this may just be a consequence of its long life.

Composition of maintenance activity

Details are given in Tables 8.35–8.37.

Composition of conversion activity

Details are given in Table 8.38.

Concentration of changes

Details are given in Table 8.39.

Comments

Smith (1981) implied that the functional composition of maintenance – the requirements/design etc. split – is the same for maintenance as for development. This is consistent with the figures in Table 8.40 (Martin and McClure, 1985).

Similarly, according to Arthur (1988), testing may take up to 50% of the development budget and a similar amount of the maintenance budget to ensure a high-quality product. However, this seems unlikely. d'Agapeyeff's example (Table 8.37) is admittedly an extreme case, but it does draw attention to the possibility that more testing, and probably therefore more programming time, is required for maintenance than for development. This is borne out by Walston and Felix (1977), who found that programming consumed 72% of maintenance effort, and only 60% of development effort. By contrast, the figures given by Boehm (1981) imply that 4 or 5% *less* time is spent on programming during maintenance. To sum up, these figures differ, but

Table 8.35   Composition of maintenance activity

Source and activity		% breakdown
Glass (1979)		
Perfective (improvements)		60% of activity
Adaptive (to external changes)		18%
Corrective (fixes)		17%
Other		5%
Charette (1986)		
Perfective		55% of effort
Adaptive		25%
Corrective		20%
Dunn and Ullman (1982)		
Performance enhancement		60% of effort
Adaptation (conversion)		>20% (mainly testing)
Defect correction		<20%
Lientz and Swanson (1979)		
Emergency program fixes		12% of effort
Routine debugging		9%
Accommodate changes to input data, files		17%
Accommodate changes to hardware, operating system		6%
Enhancements for users:		42%
New reports	17%	
Added data for existing reports	11%	
Reformatting existing reports	4%	
Condensing existing reports	2%	
Consolidating existing reports	3%	
Other	4%	
Improve documentation		6%
Improve code efficiency		4%
Other		3%
Brooks (1975) Rule of thumb for allocating maintenance work		
Planning and design		33%
Coding		17%
Component and early system test		25%
System test with all components in hand		25%

they agree that there is very little difference between the composition of development and that of maintenance.

Further evidence that changes tend to be concentrated, i.e. that some programs or modules are modified much more frequently than others, is given later: evidence is presented that errors, which are one type of change, tend to be concentrated. The literature surveyed did not specify how much maintenance effort is consumed by the different types of program (edit/update/report). These aspects would be useful in calculating how big an increase in productivity can be provided by the fourth-generation.

Conclusions

Maintenance consumes a large and increasing portion of the total software effort.

Table 8.36 Composition of maintenance activity (% of effort)

	Mode	
	Organic	*Embedded*
Requirements analysis	7%	5–6%
Product design	13	11
Programming	42–45	38–41
Test planning	3	3–6
Verification and validation	10–13	12–14
Project office	7	6–10
Configuration management/ QA	5	6–8
Manuals	10	11–12

Source: Boehm (1981)

Software maintenance is not optional (Boehm, 1981). Maintaining a system is an ongoing activity: maintenance does not die away as the years pass. A large program that is used undergoes continuing change or becomes progressively less useful (Lehman, 1978). The same is probably true for smaller programs as well, though perhaps to a lesser extent.

Most maintenance is really development in disguise (Glass, 1979) – only about 20% is the correction of errors – so Martin (1978) overstated the case when describing it as 'a waste of intellect'.

The functional composition of maintenance – the proportion of time consumed by the requirements, design, etc. functions – is approximately the same for maintenance as for development.

8.3.3 ERRORS

A large amount of time and money is spent on errors:

- trying to avoid making them;
- looking for them;
- correcting them; and
- correcting errors in the corrections.

In addition, program errors, like hardware breakdowns (Chapter 5), can have serious and expensive consequences. This topic therefore deserves closer attention:

- How many errors are made?
- Where are they made (in which function)?
- What types of error are made?
- Where are they discovered (in which function)?
- How much do they cost to fix?
- How can they be prevented?

This section deals with quantitative information regarding errors. Methods for avoiding and detecting them are dealt with later.

Number of errors

It is not possible to know with certainty the total number of errors in a program – only the number which have been found. This depends not only on how many there are, but also on how thoroughly the program was tested or inspected, how often it is run in production, and how random the input data is. Counting methods vary, e.g. you can count the number of problem reports for production programs, the number of 'action items' from walkthroughs, or the number of lines of code or modules changed. The count can be incorrect for a number of reasons: an error report may be invalid (i.e. it is not an error at all); the same error may be reported more than once; or there may be consequential errors (i.e. one error causes others). Definition problems can also occur. For example, if changed lines of code are being counted, should blank and comment lines be included in the count? Should deleted lines be counted? Should a group of contiguous lines be counted as one? How should non-delivered (development support) source code be treated? Most of these aspects are discussed by Conte *et al.* (1986). The net result is that comparing error counts from different authorities is subject to the same type of difficulties as comparing productivity rates (Chapter 2).

Table 8.37   Composition of maintenance activities

Source	Details
d'Agapeyeff (1969)	It might cost nearly 100 times as much to test a change to a large on-line system as to make the change.
Parikh (1984)	Maintainers spend at least half of their time trying to understand – the request, the existing system, and its documentation.
DeMarco (1982)	As much as half of the lifetime maintenance cost of a typical system is due to requirements that were not properly elicited by the initial specification process, i.e. *analysis failure*.

Table 8.38   Composition of conversion activity

Activity	% breakdown	
a) Management	7%	of effort
Technical	76%	
Support	7%	
Clerical	10%	
b) Preparation	25%	of effort
Translation	15%	
Testing	50%	
Installation	10%	
c) Labor	60%	of costs
Computer	25%	
Miscellaneous	15%	

Source: Oliver (1979)

Errors in production programs

Despite perhaps extensive testing, inspection, etc., some errors evade detection until the program is being run in production. *How many* such errors are there? Various error rates (also known as defect densities) obtained from different authorities are shown in Table 8.41.

Most of these figures are averages from many programs. The rates for OS/360 are based on claimed errors of 11 000 and 1000 (Yourdon, 1975; Bell *et al.*, 1987), and a reported size of one million LOC (Charette, 1986). The Dunn and Ullman (1982) figures show that a quality assurance program halves the number of defects (from 5 down to 2 per 1000 LOC), but the figures are apparently hypothetical. The MPPs (Modern Programming Practices) referred to by Carpenter and Hallman (1985) are the methodology taught at IBM's Software Engineering Institute – modularity, stepwise refinement, structured programming, defect prevention, etc.

The average of these figures is about 8, but the rates differ too widely for their average to be meaningful. In fact, the rates could almost be subdivided into two categories: low quality and high quality. One of the very low rates was just a target: the value actually being achieved was not stated, and might have been somewhat higher. Another very low rate was stated to be 'not uncommon', which implies that it was (much?) lower than average. Yet another very low rate was on high-profile, life-critical software, for which exceptionally high quality is mandatory. Nevertheless, this average of about 8 is consistent with the statement by Jones (1986b) that, for operational systems, organizations should do a formal code inspection on any module that has accumulated more than 10 defects per 1000 source statements in the last year or 18 months.

The highest of the tabulated figures is Yourdon's 30–50. This figure refers to the number of errors detected during the 5–10 year lifetime of a system, and probably includes errors caused by modifications, whereas some of the other rates were obtained from systems which had been in production for two years or less, but these factors are probably too small to account for such a large discrepancy. Yourdon's figure is therefore suspect. It appeared in a book advocating walkthroughs, and the higher the

Table 8.39 Concentration of changes

Source	Details
Blum (1990)	Over an eight-year period, half the programs in a 7000-program product were edited 10 or fewer times; only 10% were edited more than 33 times. These edits included all changes for development, debugging, and product evolution.
Arthur (1988)	20% of the programs consume 80% of the costs or resources. Only 5–10% of all code suffers continuous change.

Table 8.40 Functional composition of maintenance

	Percentage of costs	
	Initial development	Maintenance
Development effort		
Specification and design	20%	18%
Programming	20	18
Finding and fixing errors		
Specification and design	20	18
Programming		
Verification and testing	40	36
Residual errors		10

Source: Martin and McClure (1985)

error rate in programs not subjected to walkthroughs, the more impressive are the claims made for walkthroughs, so he may have selected an atypically high value to emphasize his point. Nevertheless, the figures *do* reveal an improvement accompanying the use of improved methods.

Another fairly high rate is that of Kraft and Weinberg. Their figure does not refer solely to errors, but includes coding which was merely inefficient or which caused operational difficulties.

An alternative point of view is provided by Johnson (1980b). For a system of 50 000 lines of code (this is a typical system size, according to Table 8.2), there is typically about one abnormal ending per month due to all causes: hardware errors, disk space, operating system failures, data entry, JCL and program bugs. (This figure presumably excludes those runs which go to normal end of job, but which nevertheless produce incorrect results. These cases would probably outnumber – perhaps greatly – the abnormal endings. Normally, errors are corrected as soon as possible after they are detected, but sometimes the conditions resulting in the error recur before the error has been fixed. It is not clear if such recurrences are included in the stated rate, but they are probably relatively few in number.) By comparison, Boehm (1973) quoted one large real-time system containing 2 700 000 instructions, in which one error per day was discovered, i.e. about 20 per month, which is (50 000/2 700 000*20 =) about one-third the rate quoted by Johnson. Factors such as system age, run frequency, and rate of modification, all contribute to a variance from the average. Error rates during operation of a system, such as the MTBF (mean time between failures), are discussed further in Chapter 10.

Intuitively, one would expect error densities to be higher for large modules because of their greater complexity, and according to Jones (1986b), modules larger than 500 source lines tend to become error-prone more or less in correlation to their sizes, because they exceed the capacity of most human minds in terms of the internal structures and data interactions, but other studies have shown the opposite (Motley and Brooks, 1977; Basili and Perricone, 1984). This could mean that programmers are aware of the dangers of large modules, and code, or at least test, them more carefully to compensate, or that a

Table 8.41 Error rate in production programs

Source	Details	Errors/1000 LOC
Yourdon (1979b)	No walkthroughs	30–50
DeMarco (1982)	American average	10–50
Thayer *et al.* (1978)		10–20
OS/360 (per Gilb) (Yourdon, 1975)		11
Joyce (1989)	Industry average	8–10
Jones (1983d)	Large Assembler systems	8
McGonagle (1971)		7 (range 2–11)
Kraft and Weinberg (1975)		7
Bauer (1973)	Non-structured programs	5
Yourdon (1979b)	Walkthroughs	3–5
Dunn and Ullman (1982)		2–5
Walston and Felix (1977)		1
OS/360 (per Hopkins) (Yourdon, 1975)		1
Misra (1983)		0.5
DeMarco (1982)	Major manufacturer	0.4 internal target
Yourdon (1979b)	Diligent walkthroughs	0.3–0.5 not uncommon
McClure (1978)	Structured programs	0.3
DeMarco (1982)	Japanese average	0.2
Matsumoto (1989)	Toshiba Fuchu	0.1–0.3
Joyce (1989)	Space shuttle	0.1
Fagan (1977)		0
Carpenter and Hallman (1985)	MPPs	0

large number of interface errors are distributed evenly across all modules, thereby having a disproportionately large effect on the smaller modules. It is therefore unwise to use error density alone as a measure of program quality; complexity and size must also be taken into account (Conte *et al.*, 1986).

Trends

Does the average program written today contain more errors than the average program written a few years ago? According to Ohno (1989), system reliability had recently been growing by a factor of five every 10 years – an improvement of 17% p.a., compound. Similarly, since 1983, AT&T had reduced the number of failures per job steps executed from 1 per 159 to 1 per 555 (The quest for zero defect software, *Computer Week*, 13 Feb. 1989, p. 21). On a defects-per-line-of-code basis, the quality of large IBM systems improved by a factor of approximately two in the preceding eight years – an improvement of about 9% p.a., compound – and in programs then completing development, quality was three to five times better than it was only eight years previously – an improvement of 15–22% p.a., compound (Humphrey, 1985). By contrast, the figures in Table 8.41 do not show any discernible trend. One might have expected a steady decrease in error rate due to increasing use of improved methods and tools. Perhaps the methods and tools are not as good as claimed, are not being widely used, or their benefits are being offset by the increase in the size and complexity of programs. Alternatively, the figures may cover too short a period for a trend to be discernible – though 18 years should be sufficient – or, more likely, the trend may be swamped by these other factors.

Do programs currently in use contain more errors on average now than when they were written? Software, unlike hardware, does not wear out – errors which are detected were present from the beginning. The number of

Table 8.42 Error rate during development

Source	Detail	Errors per 1000 LOC
Gannon and Horning (1975)		100 ?
Boehm (1980a)		65–85
Boehm (1981)		60
Carpenter and Hallman (1985)	historical average	60
NASA (1977)		5 and 65 ?
Jones (1983d)	large Assembler systems	> 50
Dunn and Ullman (1982)		50
Sommerville (1989)		50
Fagan (1977)		46
Thayer *et al.* (1978)		40–80
Jones (1977)	512K program	35
Jones (1978)		30–35
Jones (1977)	64K program	21
Gilb (1988)	Project Omega (part of)	21
Akiyama (1971)	Assembler	20 (range 13–35)
Jones (1977)	8K program	15
Carpenter and Hallman (1985)	MPPs	6
Walston and Felix (1977)		3 (range 1–8)
Yourdon (1975)	THE system	2

errors in a program therefore does not increase with time. On the contrary, as errors are found and fixed, the number remaining decreases. The exception to this rule is maintenance: changes to a program often introduce new errors – see Table 8.52.

A distinction must be drawn here between the number of errors in the product, and the rate at which they are found. The number of errors continually decreases, but the rate at which they are found may show an initial rise shortly after the product is released, as more and more use is made of it. Errors in frequently executed portions of the system are soon found, but not those errors in portions which are only executed under unusual conditions. Conte *et al.* (1986) provided a graphical illustration of these trends, by plotting a graph of the number of defects detected in three versions of a popular commercial compiler, against date detected. These three superimposed graphs show dramatically how the number of defects detected first rose as more and more customers started using the product, but then dropped off as

the errors were detected and corrected, only to be followed by another rise as the current version of the product was superseded by the next, and its errors started to dominate the picture. The number of errors detected therefore alternately rose and declined.

Errors during development

It is informative to compare the number of errors detected during production with the number detected during development (Table 8.42).

- The Gannon and Horning figure is an estimate based on 1248 errors in 50 programs which ranged in size from 123 to 306 lines.

- The Akiyama figure is also an approximation, based on about 500 errors in nine modules comprising nearly 25 000 lines of Assembler. It includes errors found in the first two months after the product was released.

- The MPPs (Modern Programming Practices) referred to by Carpenter and Hallman are the methodology taught at IBM's Software Engineering Institute – modularity, stepwise refinement, structured programming, defect prevention, etc. The quoted rate was from a large system consisting of an operating system, real-time control, data management plus specific application-type control, and was for a new version of the system which contained significant modifications to the existing system, plus large amounts (more than 100K lines) of new code.

- The NASA figures are the number of errors detected by static analysers. This tool is intended to be used on a program before testing begins, i.e. when the number of errors is normally at its maximum. The NASA figures should therefore be amongst the highest.

The lower NASA rate is much lower than many of the values in Table 8.41, of errors in production programs, which reinforces reservations about the highest rates in that table, unless the Analyser was used, in this case, on a production program. However, the lower NASA rate is not the lowest development rate tabulated, so further investigation is required to explain the high production error rates.

The higher of the NASA rates is higher than any of the production error rates. At first glance, this renders even Yourdon's high production error rate plausible. However, the higher of the NASA rates refers to the number of 'problems' detected, which suggests that it is not only errors which were being counted but also violations of the installation's coding standards and even inefficiencies: the actual number of errors might thus have been much lower. However, the higher NASA rate is not the highest development rate tabulated, so the high production error rates cannot be dismissed on this evidence.

There is a large discrepancy between the two NASA error rates. This may have been due to one of the above suggestions, or to differences in the difficulty of the programs, or in the quality of the programmers, though it seems unlikely that two teams in the same organization would differ so markedly in ability.

Programs that were inadequately tested (or walked through or inspected) will have misleadingly low development error rates (Conte *et al.*, 1986). A low count of defects discovered during testing may therefore be the result of either good design and coding, or bad testing.

The average of the tabulated figures is about 40, but the rates differ too widely for their average to be meaningful. Nevertheless, when compared with the average number of errors found in production programs (about 8 from Table 8.41), they suggest that around 48 errors per 1000 LOC are introduced during development, of which around 80% are detected before the program is released to the users, and therefore around 20% are detected during production.

Source of errors

By function

If we know where the most errors are made, then we know which aspects of development are the most troublesome, and can concentrate our attention on finding ways of improving them (Dunn and Ullman, 1982). Tables 8.43–8.45 show the proportion of the total errors which are made in each function.

An informal study by Jones in 1975 at IBM, indicated that the error density in the test materials (test plans and test cases) for a program exceeded the error density in the program itself (Jones, 1986b). Test materials should therefore also be subjected to walkthroughs (or equivalent measures).

The distribution of serious software errors is not the same as that of minor errors (Rubey *et al.*, 1975).

Table 8.43 Source of errors, by function

Source	Function	%
Fries (1977)	Design	50% of errors in one study
Glass (1979)	Design	61–64%
	Implementation	36–39%
Infotech (1979)	Design	up to 74% of total software errors
Martin (1982b)	Design and analysis	64% of all bugs
Bell *et al.* (1987)	Design	50%
	Programming and logic	33%
	Syntax	17%
Charette (1986)	Requirements specification/	
	design	64%
	Implementation	36%
Herndon and Keenan (1978)	Specification	19%
	Programming	58%
	External	13%
	Testing	10%
Jones (1977)	8K Functional spec	40%
	Logic spec	27%
	Code	33%
	64K Functional spec	38%
	Logic spec	33%
	Code	29%
	512K Functional spec	34%
	Logic spec	37%
	Code	29%
Baker (1977)	Requirements	16%
	Design	24%
	Code	60%

Table 8.44 Source of errors, by function

Function	Jones (1978)	Thayer et al. (1978)	Boehm (1980a)	Boehm (1981)
Requirements	15%	10%	8–10%	8%
Functional design	20	} 55	15–20	} 42
Logical design	30		25–35	
Coding	35	35	25	25
Documentation			17–20	25

Source: Boehm (1981)

Requirements volatility

Details are given in Table 8.46.

Comments

Most of the figures shown indicate that the majority of errors are requirements/design errors. The only exceptions were Herndon and Keenan (1978) and Baker (1977), but their results are consistent with those of Schneidewind and Hoffman (1979), who found that the type of error that occurred most frequently was clerical, followed by coding, design, and finally, testing. Also, Martin and

Table 8.45   Source of errors, by function

Source	Detail
Thayer *et al.* (1978)	Without consistency checking, about 34–74% of operational software errors are the result of design documentation inconsistency. Of all errors found in four large systems, 62% were later found to have originated before the program code was ever written.
Yourdon (1989)	Of the errors in a typical systems development project today, 50% are due to misunderstandings between the end user and the systems analyst.
Gilb (1988)	Over 60% of the bugs which will occur in your operational software will be there before the code is ever written.

Table 8.46   Requirements volatility

Source	Detail
Climis (1979)	The average project experiences a 25% change in requirements during the period of its development.
Boehm (1981)	If there are frequent major redirections in the requirements for a project, 1.8 times as much effort is required. Requirements volatility is used in six of the nine cost-estimation models he surveyed.
Walston and Felix (1977)	If a customer requires many changes to a design, then productivity is 34% lower than if there are few changes.
Schluter (1977)	Software costs on one highly ambitious radar application escalated by a factor of four because of changes in requirements.

McClure (1985) believe that the majority of bugs in programs today are caused by the mechanics of programming, inconsistent data, sequence errors, and the like.

This minority view is appealing, because many syntax and spelling errors are usually made when coding a program, and two-thirds of the implementation phase errors occurring in one study were due to JCL (Weinberg, 1971). Such errors are usually not recorded, as there are so many of them and they are easy to detect and fix. In a TRW study (of errors detected during or after acceptance testing), coding errors took, on average, only 2.2 hours to diagnose and 0.8 hours to correct (a total of 3 hours), compared to 3.1 plus 4 hours (total 7.1) for design errors; while only 9% of the coding errors were detected after implementation, compared to 45% of the design errors (Boehm *et al.*, 1975c). As Dunn and Ullman (1982) put it: 'surely one does not want to include defects found by the compiler?'; 'the first few hours of unit testing generally reap a bountiful harvest of bugs'. Taking both this and programmer resistance into account, they recommend that error recording begin four hours after the start of unit testing. According to Jones (1986b), organizations typically only start measuring quality at the testing stage. The recording of errors may even only begin after the system has been released to the user (Glass, 1979). According to Conte *et al.* (1986), defect measures during the design and coding phases have not been thoroughly investigated. The figures given are probably therefore incomplete. One could argue that these additional types of error consume so little time that it might be misleading rather than helpful to include them in the count, but Martin and McClure (1985) would apparently not share such a view. They believe that the total effort expended on these errors may even exceed that expended on requirements

Table 8.47 Detailed analysis (Boehm, 1973)

	Batch		Real-time	
	PL/1	Other	Benchmark	On-board
Computation and assignment	9%	25%	28%	20%
Sequencing and control	20	17	27	51
Input/output	8	8	7	6
Declarations	32	35	38	16
Punctuation	31	15	n.a.	n.a.
Corrections to errors	n.a.	n.a.	n.a.	7

and design errors, and add that some coding errors (such as uninitialized variables, out-of-range subscripts, and non-termination of loops) are not detectable by ordinary compilers.

It is not clear what Bell *et al.*'s (1987) position is here. He apparently shares the common belief that most errors are design errors (as can be seen from the above figures); but he also stated that JCL is commonly a major source of errors and time-wasting.

Detailed analysis

A more detailed analysis is given in Table 8.47. (The fourth column refers only to errors detected in the final validation phase. The other columns refer to all errors. The batch programs were subdivided according to the language they were written in, with 'other' being other high-level languages, namely COBOL, JOVIAL and FORTRAN. Both the real-time columns refer to space booster control programs.)

The figures in Table 8.47 indicate that:

- the causes of errors differ from one language to another;
- the causes of errors differ between batch and real-time;
- only a minority of errors are sequencing and control errors – the type which can be reduced by GOTO-less programming – but, although few in number, they are the most persistent.

Shneiderman (1980) reported the results of several studies.

1. A study by Moulton and Muller (1967), of programs submitted by computer science students, showed that 36% of them had compilation errors and 33% had execution errors which caused termination. The breakdown of the errors is shown in Table 8.48.
2. A study of professional programmers at IBM's Yorktown Heights Research Center showed the following proportion of syntactic errors (Boies and Gould, 1974):

FORTRAN	16%
Assembler	12%
PL/1	17%

3. An experiment by Gould and Drongowski (1974), in which one-line bugs were added to small FORTRAN programs, produced

Table 8.48 Types of errors made

Error type	
Compilation errors	
arithmetic assignment	26%
statement format and sequence	22%
identifiers	15%
DO statements	7%
Execution errors	
input/output operations	64%
reference and definition	31%
arithmetic faults	4%

Source: Moulton and Muller (1967)

Table 8.49 Performance of novice and advanced programmers

	Proportion of total errors	
General cause of error	Novices	Advanced
Syntax	12%	17%
Semantic	41	21
Logic	35	51
Clerical	5	4
Other and unknown	7	7

Source: Youngs (1974)

Table 8.50 Sources of errors

	Lloyd/ Lipow	Mendis/ Gollis	Craig et al.
Computational	9%	24%	19%
Logic	26	38	16
Input/output	14	4	19
Data handling	18	10	16
Interface	16	20	16
Database and data definition	10	–	10
Other	7	4	4

Source: Dunn and Ullman (1982)

Table 8.51 Analysis of errors

	Missing	Wrong	Extra
IBM			
Design	61%	34%	5%
Code	26	62	12
ICL (Project Omega)			
Requirements	63%	34%	3%
Development plans	61	33	6
Product specifications	56	40	4
Design specifications	53	39	8
Alpha test plans	71	26	3
Beta test plans	51	39	10
Code listings	26	45	29
Average	56	37	9

Source: Gilb (1988)

median debugging times of 6 or 7 minutes, and showed that bugs in assignment statements were substantially harder to identify than iteration or array bugs – in fact, they took about four times as long to find, and the number not found at all was more than four times as high (Conte *et al.*, 1986).

4. A study by Youngs (1974) of programs written in ALGOL, BASIC, COBOL, FORTRAN and PL/1, showed that both novice and advanced programmers averaged six errors on the first run of a program, but that the novices averaged 19 errors in total, compared to 15 by the advanced programmers, indicating that the advanced programmers were more competent at removing the bugs. The breakdown of their errors is given in Table 8.49.

5. Studies quoted in Chapter 6 showed that the improved version of a language led to improved programmer performance, and that statically-typed languages, such as COBOL, FORTRAN and PL/1, had half as many errors.

Dunn and Ullman (1982) also reported the results of several studies (Table 8.50).

Of the 2000 programming errors in machine language programs in one study, 65% were attributable to such housekeeping matters as incorrect operation codes, or incorrectly calculating a displacement (Weinberg, 1971). Weinberg commented that, by using an assembly language of even the most primitive design, these programmers could have eliminated two-thirds of their coding errors.

Gilb (1988) analysed errors into missing (something was left out), wrong, or extra (e.g. programmers added their own ideas). His figures (Table 8.51) show that the majority of defects in high-level documents are omissions, while the majority in low-level documents are 'wrong'. The alpha test plans were produced by the developers, who had generally not been formally trained in the art of testing, and so did not always know what was required in a test plan, so it is not surprising that most of their errors were omissions. By contrast, the beta plans were written by professional validators, who should know better – and their lower percentage for omissions shows that they did – but who were not as familiar as the developers with the product specifications, so it is not surprising that the beta plans contained a higher proportion of 'wrong' errors.

Errors in modifications

When a program is modified, there is always the possibility that there will be an error in the modification, and the bigger the modification, the greater the possibility of an error (Boehm, 1973):

- if about five statements are changed, there is only about a 50% chance of the modification being correct; but
- if about 50 statements are changed, then the possibility of the modification being correct decreases to about 10%.

Similarly, according to McClure (1978), correcting an error has a 20–50% chance of introducing another error. This is consistent with the finding by Levendel (1990) that new defects are introduced at repair time with a probability of more than 30%. This finding also indicates that there has been no significant improvement over the intervening decade.

These high figures are consistent with the statement by Myers (1979) that experience shows that modifying an existing program is a more error-prone process (in terms of errors per statement written) than writing a new program.

The proportion of errors caused by corrections of prior problems is variously given as shown in Table 8.52. These figures indicate that the error rate is higher in a maintenance environment, which is only to be expected as maintenance programmers often have to maintain programs they do not know well,

with the result that there are unexpected side effects to changes.

The figures in Table 8.52 emphasize the need for regression testing – a well-defined set of tests is applied to the changed version (Glass, 1979).

Where discovered

Many errors are not discovered until long after they were made – often only in a much later function. Boehm (1975a) states that 54% are found during or after acceptance test. Crossman (1978) analysed the number of errors at various stages (Table 8.53) and Boehm (1981) reports on findings of Jones, Thayer and his own earlier studies (Table 8.54). (In Table 8.54 the Thayer data excludes most of those categories of error which were not recorded by the other authorities; and his percentages are calculated accordingly.)

Table 8.52 Proportion of errors caused by prior corrections

Source	% breakdown	
Fries (1977)	6%	
Boehm (1973)	7%	in development environment
Myers (1979)	17%	large program
McGonagle (1971)	19%	in maintenance environment (range 5–25%)
Yu (1985)	20%	

Table 8.53 Discovery of errors

Function	No. of errors found	%
Inspection	10	25
Unit test	5	12.5
System test	10	25
User test	5	12.5
10 Executions	10	25
Total	40	100

Source: Crossman (1978)

Table 8.54   Error analysis

How discovered	Jones (1978)	Thayer et al. (1978)	Boehm (1980a)
Functional specifications review	18%		22–29%
Logic specifications review	14–18		24–29
Module logic inspection	21–25	19%	
Module code inspection	23–27	21	
Code standards auditor		7	
Unit test and function test	11–26	24	
Component test and subsystem test	11–39	15	24
System test	4–13	15	24

Source: Boehm (1981)

Table 8.55   Discovery of errors during Project Omega

Function	%
Project Omega (ICL)	
Requirements specifications	5
Development plans	12
Product specifications	43
Design specifications	13
Alpha (unit) test plans	13
Beta (system) test plans	7
Code listings	6

Source: Gilb (1988)

Table 8.55 gives details of the findings of Gilb (1988).

Concentration of errors

Details are given in Table 8.56.

Comments

A study of IBM products by Shen *et al.* (1985) showed that most modules were free of defects, which supports the above figures (Table 8.56). Furthermore, Shen's study showed that those modules that had defects after release typically had only one or two. Taken together, this indicates that only a small proportion of errors escape detection during the development process. This agrees with the earlier estimate that only around 20% of known errors are detected during

production, but contrasts with the 54% detected during or after acceptance test given above by Boehm (1975a), and the (12.5 + 25 =) 37.5% during user test and production, by Crossman (1978).

Cost to find and fix

According to DeMarco (1982), the effort dedicated to the diagnosis and removal of the faults that were introduced during the development process represents about 55% of the total lifetime cost of the average system. Martin and McClure (1985) gave the very similar figure of 63%.

Where made

Correction costs depend on the function in which the error was made (Table 8.57).

Comments

The statements quoted above (Table 8.57), that analysis and design errors are expensive to correct, require qualification. If these errors are detected soon after they are made, then they are cheap to correct (Boehm, 1981), but if they are not detected then, they will probably only be detected much later in the software life-cycle – perhaps even after the system test – and so will be very expensive to correct. Analysis and design errors detected early in the software life-cycle are often not formally

Table 8.56 Concentration of errors

Source	Details
Myers (1979)	Of the errors found by users in OS/370, 47% were associated with only 4% of the modules.
	Of the corrections to a 120 000 statement avionics control program, 85% involved the alteration of only a single module.
Potier *et al.* (1982)	No defects were found in 606 (55%) of the 1106 procedures in a compiler written in the LTR language, even after 10 years of maintenance.
Blum (1990)	Over an eight-year period, half the programs in a 7000-program product were edited 10 or fewer times; only 10% were edited more than 33 times. These edits included all changes for development, debugging, and product evolution.
Endres (1975)	No errors were found in 220 (52%) of the 422 modules in a large system.
Schach (1988)	Almost half the subprograms in the NYT system were correct at first compilation.
Gilb (1988)	Inspections of the test plans for the Omega project found no defects in 52% of the planned tests.

Table 8.57 Correction costs

Source	Details	
Infotech (1979)	Design errors are far more difficult and expensive to correct than implementation errors.	
Martin (1982b)	Analysis and design bugs are expensive to correct. The distribution of effort to fix bugs is:	
	requirements	82%
	design	13%
	code	1%
	other	4%
Bell *et al.* (1987)	Design	80%
	Programming, logic and	
	syntax	20%

recorded, so those which are recorded are mostly the ones which are expensive to correct.

Where detected

The later an error is discovered, the more it costs to fix. For example, if a specification error is only discovered during production running, then specifications, code, test plans, user manuals, and training material must all be updated, and operational costs were also incurred. As Boehm (1981) put it, 'we accumulate a larger inventory of items to fix', which in turn necessitates a more formal change procedure. The approximate ratios of correction costs per error, as a function of where the error is detected, are given in Tables 8.58–8.61.

Comments

In the requirements function, it is expensive to find an error, but cheap to fix it. During the maintenance (operational) phase the position is reversed, as errors reveal themselves through incorrect output picked up by routine controls.

Caution

Jones (1986b) warns that statements such as 'it costs up to 100 times as much to fix a bug

Table 8.58 Ratio of correction costs per error

Source	Function	Ratio
Glass (1979)	Requirements/	
	specifications	2
	Design	2
	Implementation	3
	Checkout	3
	Maintenance	30
Rudolph (1979)	Specification function	1
	Coding	4
	Testing	8–20
	Usage	40
Remus (1980a)	Design and coding	1
	Testing	20
	Maintenance	80
Gilb (1988)	During design	1.5
	Before code	1
	Before test	10
	During test	60
	In production	100
Van Tassel (1978)	Design	1
	System test	10
	Maintenance	100

Table 8.59 Ratio of correction costs per error

Function	Smaller projects	Larger projects
Requirements	5	1.5
Design	7.5	4
Code	10	10
Development test	15	21
Acceptance test	19	60
Operation	21	150

Source: Boehm (1981)

during maintenance as it does during development' are incorrect. There is a mathematical paradox associated with the common method of calculating cost per defect by simply dividing the total defect removal expenses by the total number of defects removed. There are fixed costs associated with removing defects, such as writing test cases and running them, which are independent of the number of defects removed. Since the number of defects found during development is usually much greater than the number found during production, the cost per defect will always be higher during production. Similarly, high-quality software, with few defects, has a higher cost per defect than low-quality software. This metric therefore penalizes high quality, just as the LOC productivity metric penalizes high-level languages (Chapter 2).

It is not clear if, or to what extent, the above figures suffer from this problem, and therefore if and by how much they should be adjusted.

Conclusion

Once again, the different categories used by the various authorities make it difficult to obtain useful information from the figures. There are also wide variations between the various ratios, which diminishes confidence in any averages derived from them. Nevertheless, the above figures indicate that typical correction costs, as a function of where the error was detected, are in approximately the ratios given in Table 8.62.

The figures depend on project size, being lower for smaller projects (a range of perhaps only 4:1), and higher for larger ones (a range of perhaps 100:1). This is because, if a fix will be very time-consuming, it is easier to negotiate a simpler fix with small, informal projects; and because with larger projects, more extensive activity is required to validate the correction, update code and user manuals, etc., which in turn necessitates a more formal change procedure (Boehm, 1981).

To sum up, it pays to spend extra time on verification and validation procedures early in the development process, and to test or

Table 8.60 Ratio of correction costs per error

Function	No. of errors	Total cost	Average cost	Ratio
Inspection	10	200	20	1
Unit test	5	150	30	1.5
System test	10	500	50	2.5
User test	5	700	140	7
10 executions	10	2000	200	10
Total	40	3550	89	

Source: Crossman (1978)

Table 8.61 Correction costs

Source	Detail
Gilb (1988)	IBM's Santa Teresa Laboratories have reported that errors caught at test were 67 or 82 times more costly to fix than at inspection time. Repairs to poor design at the testing and delivery stages cost 10–100 times as much as if we identify the design errors early.
Shooman and Bolsky (1975)	Correcting a design error during the coding phase requires twice the effort of correcting it during design, and requires ten times the effort if not found and corrected until testing.
Yourdon (1989)	Of the cost of error removal in an operational system 75% is associated with errors that originated in the systems analysis phase.

Table 8.62 Ratio of typical error correction costs

Requirements/specifications	1
Design	2
Coding	3
Unit test	6
System test	12
Acceptance test	40
Maintenance	60

inspect programs more extensively and more intelligently (Conte *et al.*, 1986).

Miscellaneous

Terminal typing errors

A study by Segal (1975) showed about a 25% improvement in terminal user performance if an error warning was issued immediately a wrong key was depressed, rather than waiting until the user reached the end of the line.

Programmer performance

In a debugging experiment described by Gilb (1977), some programmers were ten times faster than others.

Remaining errors

It takes increasingly longer (and therefore costs increasingly more), to find the remaining errors in a program. Van Tassel (1978) stated that, if you had already found 95% of the errors, it might take twice as long to find the next 1 or 2%. Bell Laboratories took *eight years* to raise the availability of their computerized telephone switching system from 99.9 to 99.98%, an improvement of *only 0.08%* (Gilb, 1988). The relative effort depends on the defect detection method used: if inspections are used, then 60% of the errors are detected with 10% of the effort, but it takes three times as much effort to detect the next 20%, and the remaining 20% are only found during production running; by contrast, if unit testing is used, then 75% of the errors are detected with 50% of the effort, but it takes an equivalent amount of effort to detect the next 15%, and the remaining 10% are only found during production running (Boehm, 1981).

Severity of errors

Up till now, all errors have been treated equally, yet some have much more serious consequences than others. Documentation errors, for example, are much less serious, on average, than other errors, as might be expected (Rubey *et al.*, 1975). The European Space Agency classifies errors according to the severity of their effect, and applies a weighting factor to each category, e.g. failures affecting all spacecraft have a weighting of 10 000; those affecting only one spacecraft, a factor of 1000; and at the other extreme, a trivial failure such as a typographic error, carries a weighting of only 1 (Formica, 1978). Conte *et al.* (1986) suggested a similar method. For a payroll program for example, the severity metric would be the percentage of erroneous paychecks produced. If the run crashed, producing no paychecks, then the severity would be 100%. (This suggestion could be extended by weighting the figures by the *size* of the errors in the paycheck amounts.) Conte also suggested counting the number of lines of source code which had to be changed: the more lines, the more serious the error. The amount of time taken to correct the error – the MTTR (mean time to repair) – can also be used.

Prevention of errors

Some of the information already given indicates how errors can be prevented, e.g. by the use of GOTO-less programming. In addition, Hamilton and Zeldin (1976) reached the conclusions shown in Table 8.63 from a study of the post-delivery error statistics for NASA's Apollo system.

Table 8.63 Prevention of errors in NASA's Apollo system

Would have been prevented by:	%
Design techniques	23
Improved programming style	30
Techniques of building software	34
Other	13

Source: Hamilton and Zeldin (1976)

Error predictions

Error statistics can be used to develop and to validate reliability models, which can point to programs or modules which probably contain a disproportionate number of errors, and so should be rewritten or subjected to earlier or extra testing or inspection.

Various attempts have been made in this direction, with some success. It has already been indicated that program size gives an idea of the number of defects. In addition, Motley and Brooks (1977) found that the number of variables referenced but not defined, the number of data handling statements, and the number of unconditional jumps, were good predictors of defects (Conte *et al.*, 1986). However, considerable variation from program to program suggests that functional differences among the programs, programming languages, the test environment, and the overall personnel-management environment, influence the effect of the structural elements (Dunn and Ullman, 1982). Potier *et al.* (1982) found that the number of unique operators and operands (Halstead, 1977), were good predictors. Shen *et al.* (1985) found that the number of unique operators was the best single predictor overall, but also found that the decision count (the number of IFs, DOs, etc.) was a good predictor. The metrics found to be the best single predictors at the end of the design phase remained the best at the end of the coding phase, even though many more metrics are available. A study by Takahashi and Kamayachi (1989), using data from 30 projects, found that the three factors with the greatest influence on error rates, were:

1. the amount of change to the program specifications (measured by the number of pages of problem reports generated to change the design specifications);
2. programmer skill (defined as the average number of years of programming experience); and
3. the amount of program documentation (defined as the number of pages of new and modified program design documents).

A regression model using these factors is a better predictor of error density than one based on program size (LOC) alone.

There are therefore several measures which are useful in pointing to the most error-prone modules, though none is the best predictor in every case.

Error rates during operation of the system, such as the MTBF (mean time between failures), can be used to predict future error rates. These are discussed further in Chapter 10.

Uses

The information and figures in this section can be put to a number of uses.

- They show where, in global terms, there are problems, what the problems are, and how serious they are. For example, the rapid escalation in correction costs if an error is not discovered soon after it is made points to the importance of additional testing, etc.
- They show where there may be weaknesses in languages: for example, the high punctuation error rate for PL/1.
- They can be used for predictive purposes, to point to coding which probably contains a disproportionate number of errors, and so should be tested more thoroughly, which could mean delaying the release of the product.

- Individual organizations can compare their performance against the figures, and see if, and where, they are worse than average: for example, if their production programs have a higher error rate than the industry average.
- Similarly, they show where more training is necessary.
- The effect of new tools and methods can be judged more reliably if there are comprehensive figures against which to compare.

Main conclusions

Most authorities believe that the majority of errors are requirements and design errors. However, there is some evidence to the contrary, though they may well consume most of the cost.

Most errors (over 80% ?) are detected during development. Nevertheless, on average, perhaps 8 errors per 1000 LOC are detected during production running.

Improved methods, such as structured programming and structured walkthroughs, reduce the number of errors in production programs significantly. Improved languages also result in fewer errors.

The later an error is detected, the more it costs to correct. An error detected after a program has gone into production may cost much more than ten times as much to correct as it would have cost had it been detected soon after it was made.

Quality assurance should therefore be improved, particularly of the analysis and design functions. In addition, more testing (inspection, reviews, etc.) should be performed, or at least should be concentrated on those modules most likely to contain errors.

8.4 METHODS

Many techniques are used during software development and maintenance, so this is a large subject; Price Waterhouse's methodology fills no fewer than five volumes (Hodges, 1987a). It is not possible to reproduce all this vast body of information here, nor would there be any point in doing so. This book therefore does not contain 'everything you always wanted to know about software engineering but were afraid to ask', nor does it teach you 'how to become an expert programmer in one easy lesson'. The goal instead is to show that there *are* methods; that there are, in fact, *many* methods; that these methods have advantages and disadvantages; that more information on these methods is readily available; and finally to give some idea of how effective these methods are. Nevertheless, brief descriptions of many of the methods, and their advantages and disadvantages, are given. According to Cerveny *et al.* (1987), the process of software development is not well understood, and there is no one best approach. A word of warning is therefore in order: 'be careful of claims made by their authors (and other enthusiasts) for these methodologies. All of them are of some use in some circumstances' (Macro and Buxton, 1987). This implies they may not be of much use in many circumstances.

Some methods may have a large effect on productivity, and so are discussed separately and in more detail, namely prototyping and structured programming, and structured walkthroughs and inspections (in a subsequent chapter). The chief programmer team concept can be included in this list, as part of its success is attributable to the methods it uses – structured programming, top-down programming, etc. Many of the methods are commonly grouped together under such titles as 'modern programming practices', so a section is included in which they are discussed as a group, in addition to the individual discussions.

The methods discussed here are manual ones. They can be aided or maybe even replaced by technological aids (Chapter 6). In particular, some software tools eliminate the need for some life-cycle functions and therefore some of the methods, e.g. program generators eliminate the need for program design (Bell *et al.*, 1987). (Hence the term 'application development without programmers' (Martin, 1982a). The programmers at one organization which bought an application generator, for example, 'will begin to focus their skills and company knowledge on a creative role of systems and information needs of the company as opposed to the emphasis on technology' (Cox, 1989a).) Some of these manual methods are therefore becoming less important than in the past.

The methods are grouped by the function in which they are used. However, software development is an iterative process, and so does not strictly follow the order listed here. During the design function, for instance, an error in the specifications may be revealed, necessitating a reversion to the requirements/specifications function to rectify it.

Some methods apply to more than one function. For example, HIPO (hierarchical input processing output) was intended for use from logical design through program construction, and can also be used for maintenance (to document and evaluate existing systems); and, though SADT (structured analysis and design technique) is intended for the analysis of a problem, its principles can be extended to the design of the solution (Couger *et al.*, 1982). Couger gives a diagram showing, for a number of different methodologies, which functions the methodology covers; whether it is oriented towards, or can merely be applied to, the functions; and how strongly it supports the functions.

A methodology must produce reliable, high-quality systems which are implemented on time and within budget, and which are easily maintainable. It must also help establish communications between users and DP. It must permit management control, and eliminate surprises, which affect cost, quality and schedules. It must therefore also reduce the number of maintenance changes.

8.4.1 FEASIBILITY STUDY

The system life-cycle begins, typically, with a request from a user. Before the request can be met, it must go through a selection process, where it competes for attention against other requests. The first decision is merely whether it is sufficiently promising to warrant the time and cost of a formal feasibility study. Ideally, the selection will be on the basis of the anticipated costs and benefits of the proposed system, but in practice, the importance of the user, and the vigor with which he fights for his request (the 'decibel auction'), generally also play a major role in priority setting.

The next step towards meeting the request is, or should be, a feasibility study. The objective of a feasibility study is to determine (Boehm, 1981; Lee, 1978):

- if the proposed system is technically feasible – 'due to the advanced nature of the hardware and software technology in the mid-1980s, practically any business or standard scientific application system can be implemented' (Mittra, 1988);
- if it is economically desirable (which includes development and running costs, determining the volume of data, the development time-scale, and so on);
- if it will fit in with the structure (e.g. centralized or de-centralized) and long-range plans of the organization;
- if key personnel will be available; and
- if it will be acceptable to the people who will be affected by it (both directly and indirectly).

A feasibility study therefore evaluates the impact (both positive and negative) of the proposed system, including the effect on staff morale.

This process therefore involves the requirements definition and other functions described later. It also involves studying alternative methods of meeting the user's request (including packages and use of a bureau), so that the best solution is found, and the 'go, no-go' decision based on that.

However, at this stage, only a preliminary investigation is performed, which does not go into as much depth as is necessary later – you merely 'develop the design to a point where a reliable prediction can be made of the costs and benefits, and reliable assurances can be given that there will not be unacceptable economic, technical, organizational, social or time-scale side-effects' (Parkin, 1980). The investigation therefore merely has to be in enough detail to arrive at approximate figures; but if it is not done, serious mistakes can be made, e.g. in estimating how long the job will take. Furthermore, this lays the foundation for the subsequent steps, if a decision is made to go ahead with the project.

A feasibility study should take anything from a couple of days (for a minor modification to an existing system), to several weeks (for a totally new problem costing several million dollars) (Mittra, 1988).

Software cost/effort estimation methods

Chapter 2 referred to the lack of a good predictive capability, and gave examples of jobs which took much more, or much less time, than had been estimated. Many of the estimated sizes (in LOC) in the Yourdon 1978–80 Project Survey were out by more than 100% (DeMarco, 1982). (Most of these were under-estimates. Some reasons for under-estimates in estimates based on specifications have already been given – over-optimism, unexpected side-effects, the introduction of non-specified functionality, and especially because there is less detail in a specification than in the actual implementation (Chapter 2). More reasons for under-estimates are given later.) Accurate estimates can be used to resist management pressure for unrealistic deadlines (Chapter 11). Estimation methods will therefore be examined here.

There are various methods for estimating the duration and cost of developing a computerized system, including (Boehm, 1981; Macro and Buxton, 1987): algorithmic models, expert judgement, analogy, top-down, and bottom-up. Each is considered, below.

Algorithmic models

This method uses mathematical formulae. Examples are COCOMO (Boehm, 1981; Walston and Felix, 1977). The method has a number of advantages, e.g. it is objective and can be used for sensitivity analyses, but it does not handle extreme conditions (such as exceptionally capable staff), or changed circumstances (such as the introduction of new methods and tools) – the model has to be recalibrated, and this can only be done after sufficient data based on the new circumstances has been obtained. Another disadvantage is that the data required by the models is not available sufficiently early in the life-cycle, e.g. only at the functional specifications stage or later. Also, many of these models are based on the number of LOC, which is not known at the beginning of a project, and so must estimated, thereby introducing a further inaccuracy. (Conte *et al.* (1986) gave an example of how a 50% size error leads to a 63% error in the effort estimated by one model.) The accuracy of the method is discussed further below. According to Macro and Buxton, this method consumes 10–15% of the total software engineering development effort.

Expert judgement

One or more experts give their considered opinion. This method can cater for new or exceptional conditions, but it is not objective, being influenced by the biases of the experts, and its accuracy also depends on their competence. The experts are likely to use analogy (discussed below) in making their estimates. This method runs the risk of overlooking some especially difficult subtasks, which may be unique to the current project (Conte *et al.*, 1986).

The cost can vary greatly, depending on whether one expert makes a quick estimate (according to Macro and Buxton (1987), a true expert would not do this), or a group of experts makes a thorough, well-documented, group-consensus estimate. In one experiment, Yourdon, Incorporated took 16 completed projects, the average size of which was 35 000 LOC, and asked several experienced managers to estimate their sizes, based solely on the project specifications. (Size is related to effort and, as stated above, many algorithmic models are based on it.) Their average error was 60% (Conte *et al.*, 1986). Of the 16 projects, 12 (75%) were *under*-estimated. In another experiment, at Purdue University, 44 senior students were given two 400-line PASCAL programs to write. After they had designed the programs, but before they had begun coding them, they were asked to estimate the sizes of the completed programs, and the amount of effort that would be required. The average error in their size estimates was about 20–40%, and in their effort estimates, about 40–90% (Conte *et al.*, 1986). Another experiment, at the Rand Corporation, compared the Delphi (anonymous group-consensus) technique (Helmer, 1966) with a standard group meeting. The specifications for a project which had taken 489 man-months to develop were given to four groups, with two groups being assigned to each method. All four groups were instructed to arrive at an effort-estimate for the system, based solely on the specifications (though the project team size was known, and this information was used by one group). Their average error was over 50% (Farquhar, 1970). (Their errors ranged from under 1% to well over 100%, with the Delphi technique proving the less accurate.)

Analogy

The proposed project is compared against past projects. This method therefore has the advantage of being based on actual experience. However, the accuracy of the estimate depends not only on how similar the comparison project is to the proposed project, but also on the similarity of external factors, such as the tools and techniques used, and the quality of the personnel. The error can therefore be high, and can even exceed 400%, but the method is quick, and so might add less than 1% to the development cost (Macro and Buxton, 1987). It should therefore only be used as a quick and cheap way of doing crude, order of magnitude estimates for first budgetary approximations.

Top-down

An overall estimate is produced (e.g. by analogy) from the global properties of the product, and then split between the components. This method is not very detailed, so it is quick (and adds less than 5% to the development costs), but by the same token low-level components or feasibility problems may be overlooked, leading to underestimates. The result is that it is not very accurate, giving errors of 200–300% (Macro and Buxton, 1987). It should therefore also only be used as a quick and cheap way of doing crude, order of magnitude estimates.

Bottom-up

A separate estimate is calculated for each component, and the figures are added up. This is a more detailed method than top-down, and it lessens the danger of low-level components or feasibility problems being overlooked, but has the opposite danger that *system*-level components (such as documentation, quality assurance, configuration management, integration and project management) may be overlooked. According to Macro and Buxton (1987), an accuracy of

plus–minus 10% can be achieved. (If this is true, then it is the most accurate method.) It takes much longer than top-down. (According to Macro and Buxton, it can comprise as much as 30–40% of the development cost, but this seems rather high, even allowing for the drawing up of a detailed activities plan. Elsewhere, however, they imply that this is not the proportion of the total development cost, but of the development cost up to the time the estimate is made, in which case it might comprise only 10–15% of the total eventual cost, which seems more reasonable.) Other benefits are that it results in a better understanding of the job; and, if the component estimates are made by the people who will program the components, it results in greater commitment and motivation on their part: people work hard to meet deadlines they themselves have set (Metzger, 1981).

Other methods include **Parkinsonian** (assume the job will consume all the available resources, but no more) (Parkinson, 1957), and **price-to-win** (assume that external constraints of budget and deadline can be met with the available resources, even if these seem inadequate, in order to win a contract). As is obvious from their descriptions, these methods are unscientific and highly inaccurate – they are *wishes* rather than estimates. One Parkinsonian estimate gave a figure of 180 man-months for a job which eventually took 550 man-months, i.e. *three* times as long (an error of 200%); and, although the price-to-win technique has won a large number of software contracts for a large number of software companies, 'almost all of them are out of business today' (Boehm, 1981). Macro and Buxton (1987), however, pointed out that sometimes it is a commercial necessity to make a price-to-win estimate, e.g. to keep a client or market base, to prevent a competitor getting a toehold, or to keep a work-force occupied over a temporary slack period. Where this is done, though, the organization

Table 8.64 Accuracy of estimation

Phase	Accuracy
Feasibility study	0.25:1 to 4:1
Requirements specifications	0.5:1 to 2:1
Product design specifications	0.7:1 to 1.5:1
Detailed design specifications	0.8:1 to 1.25:1

Source: Boehm (1981)

should also make an accurate 'cost-to-do' estimate, so that adequate resources can be scheduled. Even though the organization may make a heavy financial loss on the project, at least it should be completed on time. (Alternatively, the organization may have two schedules: the optimistic one in the proposal which everyone knows is unlikely to be kept, and the true internal schedule which the customer discovers after the contract is started (Jones, 1986b).)

The accuracy of an estimate also depends heavily on *when* the estimate is made, i.e. on how early in the life-cycle: the earlier the estimate is made, the less accurate it is. As our knowledge of the product increases, so the uncertainties are removed, e.g. vagueness or ambiguities in the requirements are resolved; costing and timing for portions of the product which have already been completed are known with certainty; and there is less time before the final deadline, so there is less time in which surprises can occur, e.g. a sudden increase in staff turnover. In particular, specifications may grow in scope, and complexity is often under-estimated, so early estimates are likely to be much too low. Boehm (1981) provided the guidelines given in Table 8.64, i.e. an estimate made at the feasibility stage will only be accurate to within a factor of four, on either side of the final, actual cost, and then only 80% of the time – the remaining 20% of the time, it will be even less accurate.

In most cases, therefore, the eventual cost of a system will be anything from a quarter to four times the estimate made during the feasibility study; between half and double

the estimate made during the requirements/ specifications; and so on.

Cost estimation is a project in its own right. If treated as such, there is less danger that it will be rushed. It takes 1–4 weeks to estimate a project of 9000 statements (Londeix, 1987). Once completed, the results of the study must be presented to the decision makers.

The GUIDE (1979) survey found that modern programming practices improved project estimating.

Accuracy of algorithmic models

Macro and Buxton (1987) claim an accuracy of plus–minus 20% for algorithmic models. However, they quoted one user of two models who complained: 'if I can get within 50% to 100% of cost I'm doing well'.

Boehm (1981) claimed that the basic version of his COCOMO model was accurate to within a factor of two, 60% of the time, which is not very good. He claimed a much higher accuracy for the more detailed versions, e.g. the intermediate version is claimed to be accurate to within 20%, 68% of the time.

None of the models studied by Kemerer (1987) fared very well. This study was of four algorithmic models – COCOMO, SLIM (Software Life-cycle Methodology) (Putnam, 1978; Putnam and Fitzsimmons, 1979), Function Points (Albrecht, 1979; Albrecht and Gaffney, 1983) and ESTIMACS (Rubin, 1983, 1984) – in a business environment, and gave average error rates ranging from roughly 100% to 800%, mostly over-estimates, which is very poor. However, most of this was due to the models having been derived from environments such as real-time, where productivity is low. Had they been calibrated for the new environment – as should have been done, and as would normally have been done in a real-life situation (Agresti, 1989) – their accuracy would have been much better. The study was therefore of limited value. (The numerical constants and effort-multipliers in the equations are tuned to a particular environment. Calibration means that they are modified for the new environment. According to Macro and Buxton (1987), calibration can take as long as one or two years, so it is understandable why it was not done in this study.)

There are three versions of the COCOMO model: basic, intermediate, and detailed. The basic version is the simplest, and estimates software development effort and cost solely as a function of the number of program source instructions. The intermediate version includes other factors which have a major influence on effort and cost, such as complexity, required reliability, execution time and storage constraints, ability and experience of the staff, length of schedule, and available software tools. The detailed version looks at each function in the software life-cycle separately. Kemerer found that the more advanced versions did not do as well as the basic version, which is surprising and implies that the cost drivers 'are not adding any additional explanation of the phenomenon'. Conte *et al.* (1986) criticized the large amount of work required to perform an intermediate COCOMO estimate (16 parameters, with up to 6 ratings for each). Because such detailed information is not generally available for other projects, he was only able to evaluate the basic version of COCOMO, which requires far less information. He evaluated it on six sets of projects (the original set plus five others), and found that it performed reasonably well on only two of them. (Surprisingly, the original set was not one of them.) This may have been due to such factors as comment lines being counted for some sets of projects but not for others, but it is consistent with the poor performance found by Kemerer. Conte also studied a number of other models, including SDC (System Development Corporation) (Nelson, 1966); Walston and Felix, 1977), SLIM (Software Life-cycle Methodology) (Putnam, 1978; Putnam and Fitzsimmons, 1979; Jensen, 1984), Software Science (Halstead, 1977), and

SOFTCOST (Tausworthe, 1981), but was critical of them as well, e.g. serious overestimates of effort on small- or medium-size systems, or accurate to within 25% only 20% of the time. He was, however, enthusiastic about the generalized version of the COPMO model (cooperative programming model) (Thebaut, 1983), which proved accurate on all the projects it was evaluated on. It appeared capable of achieving an accuracy of within 25%, 75% of the time, and even outperformed intermediate COCOMO on that model's own database. This, however, was on historical projects for which the productivity was known and was used to calibrate the model: its predictive capability may not be as good. More research is therefore required.

The Bailey and Basili (1981) model was accurate to within 25% for 78% of the projects in their database. This is good, but needs to be confirmed on different data (Conte *et al.*, 1986).

When calibrated against historical data from a broad spectrum of programs and systems, the SPQR (software productivity, quality, and reliability) model has generally come within 15% of the observed results, except at the extreme ends of the model's range, but this does not take into account errors in the historical data itself, which are often more than 25% (Jones, 1986b).

Mohanty (1981) viewed the question from a different angle. He compared 13 cost models, using a hypothetical software system comprising some 36 000 executable machine-language instructions. The models produced estimates ranging from about $360 000 to nearly $2 800 000, a difference of nearly 8:1. This is consistent with the high inaccuracy discussed earlier.

Conclusion

Pressman (1982) concluded that no one algorithmic model convincingly represented all types of task and all environmental factors.

Macro and Buxton (1987) concluded that

none of the many models had yet proved conclusively to be the most consistently accurate predictor of effort and time-scale in all circumstances. They therefore designated the topic a research area. However, they did say that research in this area had already produced many insights into the software engineering process. They singled out COCOMO and Jensen (1984) as currently the best.

Conte *et al.* (1986) stated that a number of organizations had found that existing models had generally proved unsatisfactory. Some seemed to lack adaptability to different environments, or to a broad range of application areas, while others emphasized particular productivity factors while neglecting the effect of others. Different models therefore had different strengths and weaknesses. As stated previously, Conte singled out the generalized version of the COPMO model, and the Bailey and Basili (1981) model.

Boehm (1981) concluded that none of the cost-estimation methods was better than the others in all respects. However, they complemented each other, particularly the algorithmic model and expert judgement, and top-down and bottom-up. He therefore recommended the following combination:

- top-down, using expert judgement and analogy;
- bottom-up, using an algorithmic model;
- followed by comparison and iteration of both estimates.

Humphrey (1985) was more optimistic than the above authorities. He stated that initial program LOC estimates were often optimistic by 20% or more, but manpower estimates were within 10%, and costs were typically in error by less than 5% over the full development life-cycle, and added that this was a dramatic improvement. However, he was probably referring specifically to large IBM systems: estimates by other organizations were probably generally less accurate.

Cost-benefit analysis

The anticipated costs and benefits of the proposed system must be estimated, and compared against the existing system, if any. The entire life-cycle costs must be included: hardware, software and personnel (including staff overheads such as insurance and pension); training; development and maintenance; consumables (such as stationery); overheads (such as electricity); capital outlay or rental, loss of interest, depreciation, etc. (Lee, 1978). (The time value of money, and the lost use of money, which are relevant to cost-benefit analyses, are discussed in Appendix E; and another example, involving a choice between rental and purchase, is given in Chapter 13.) Generally, a contingency allowance is included, though Couger *et al.* (1982) describes this practice as 'laziness'. The benefits must include not only how much the proposed system will *save* the organization, but also how much it will *do*, including 'intangibles' such as improved quality and service and the resulting increase in sales, and the opportunities presented by the information. For example, a POS (point of sale) system permits more cost-effective inventory management (Boehm, 1981). These benefits vary greatly from one system to another, and are difficult to quantify. (When quantified, they are expressed in money terms – the dollar equivalent – so that all costs and benefits are in the same units for easy comparison.) The problem is compounded by the fact that one must take into account not only 'how much?', but also 'how soon?' (Lee, 1978).

The investigation should include a sensitivity analysis, so that major potential problem areas can be identified and investigated more thoroughly. (The example used by Boehm (1981) was of a transaction processing system running on multiple microprocessors, in which the multi-processor overhead increased from the anticipated value of 80 000 operations per second, to

160 000.) If the best solution is very sensitive to a change in any assumption, then it is safer to choose an alternative solution. The cost of the investigation should be kept in proportion, i.e. one should not spend more on the investigation than one can hope to save by getting a better solution.

If the proposed system will replace a manual system rather than an existing computerized system, then the development costs are likely to be high, but so will the benefits.

Product size has a major impact on the amount of development effort required. It is important therefore that only those requirements which can be fully justified be included in the system. The remaining, low payoff, requirements ('gold-plating') should be identified at this stage, and placed on a 'wish-list', for possible later implementation (Boehm, 1981).

When a manual system is computerized, the computerized version should contain all the functions in the manual system, otherwise the users will complain. They will ignore all the new functions provided, and concentrate only on the missing ones.

Presentation methods

To aid in the choice between alternatives, all the facts – cost, development time, response time, reliability, security, etc. (Lee, 1978) – must be presented to the decision makers. This can be done in a variety of ways (Boehm, 1981).

- **Criterion summaries** These are prose discussions – a brief discussion of how well each alternative satisfies each criterion. This method is suitable for a small number of alternatives (2 to 3) and criteria (2 to 10).
- **Preference table** This is a table of pros and cons. It contains one column for each alternative, in which are listed that choice's strengths – which are therefore by implication the other choices' weaknesses. It is more concise than a criterion summary,

but nevertheless becomes cumbersome with a large number of alternatives and criteria. It is therefore suitable for a moderate number of alternatives (2 to 5) and criteria (2 to 20).

- **Screening matrix** This is a rating table having the alternatives as columns, and the criteria as rows. Each entry in the table consists of one or more stars (or blobs, etc.), with the number of stars indicating how well that alternative meets that criterion. The matrix should have an extra column, with the stars in it showing how important each criterion is. This method provides a strong visual impression of which criteria are the most important, and of how well the different alternatives meet the criteria. It is suitable for relatively large numbers of alternatives (2 to 10) and criteria (5 to 30). It is less precise, and so is suitable where the factors are not quantifiable. (This is one example of a general rule: the precision of the display should match the precision of our knowledge.)
- **Graphical methods** An example of this is the bar chart or histogram. Graphical methods can be used where the data is quantifiable, and they provide a strong visual impact, but the scale must be carefully chosen to avoid misleading impressions.

All these methods are inadequate where there are large differences between the alternatives. All have weaknesses, but they have *different* weaknesses. It is therefore best to use a *combination* of techniques, such as a table containing a mixture of stars, numbers, and prose, so that they complement each other.

8.4.2 REQUIREMENTS/SPECIFICATIONS

The end product of this function is a detailed and validated specification of the required functions, interfaces, and performance for the software product. Pomberger (1984) gives a list of nine sections which should be contained in the specifications, ranging from a description of the initial situation and goals, through to a glossary and index. The specifications must, of course, be consistent, and must be complete, e.g. they must specify how the product will behave under all conditions, including unusual, extreme and error conditions (Boehm, 1981; Charette, 1986). Legal requirements for the finished system must also be taken into account. A general rule is that specifications should concentrate on the business procedures: systems analysts should not try to solve the programming problem in the program specifications (Parkin, 1980).

The specifications are the 'contract' between the programmer and the customer, and so must be understandable to both sides e.g. they should be free of computer jargon (Pomberger, 1984). ('Contract' is an appropriate term, as it emphasizes the legal-like precision which is necessary; but it is also an unfortunate term, as many legal documents are difficult for laymen to understand.)

Of the respondents in an International Data Corporation study of about 1000 DP professionals, 75% reported that the programmers and analysts do not typically work from clear, well-defined specifications, and the performance of these organizations was apparently inferior to that of their counterparts (Hoard, 1981).

The questions to be resolved in this function include the following (Boehm, 1981).

- What are the objectives of the proposed system? This includes both the obvious objectives, e.g. it must produce paychecks, as well as less obvious or more detailed objectives, such as speed, reliability, accuracy, user friendliness, and even providing challenging jobs for the staff.
- How can we balance and reconcile opposing objectives?
- What are the constraints we have to work under? This includes organizational policy, government regulations, system availabi-

lity, staff availability, and interface requirements with other systems.
- Which of these constraints do we control?

Information must be gathered, recorded, analysed, and presented, both verbally and in writing. Various possible solutions must be devised and evaluated, and the best one chosen. A decision must be made, based on the more detailed information now available, whether or not to proceed with the system. If the decision is favorable, then the chosen solution must be specified in detail.

Gathering of information

This is the fact-finding stage. Information can be gathered by a variety of different methods, including (Lee, 1978):

- collecting a set of completed documents;
- observation;
- sampling;
- questionnaires;
- interviews.

Skills needed to perform these tasks include (Lee, 1978; Gildersleeve, 1978; Batt, 1981; Fast, 1981):

- reading skills;
- specialist knowledge of questionnaire design;
- communications skills;
- interviewing skills;
- listening skills;
- interpersonal skills;
- knowledge of body language.

However, knowing *which* facts to find is more important than skill in the techniques used to find the facts – but, unless the analyst already has knowledge of the application area, it is difficult for him to know what questions to ask, and the alternative possibilities (Parkin, 1980). Knowledge of the application area is thus of great help to the systems analyst in quickly and accurately determining the user's requirements. The application organization (Chapter 3) is one way of ensuring the analyst acquires this knowledge. Morgan Stanley & Co., a major investment bank, recruits liberal arts students rather than computer science graduates: 'They are more like investment bankers than programmers. They attack problems from a business perspective rather than from a technical one. They look, talk, and act like our users because they have similar academic and intellectual backgrounds' (Dight, 1986). If the analyst does not have the requisite knowledge, he should study equivalent external systems (such as packages), to obtain it. He should also acquire a good understanding of the business, so that he has a framework into which he can fit the facts of the particular application.

Recording of facts

The facts gathered during the requirements investigation need to be recorded. There are various standard methods for doing this. The National Computing Centre (NCC) in Britain, for example, has a comprehensive set of standard documents for this purpose (NCC, 1977). There are documents for recording the terms of reference, discussions, clerical procedure flowcharts, and so on. In spite of claims made for the various methods, successful system development is not particularly sensitive to the method of documentation, so it is not important which standard is adopted (Parkin, 1980).

Processing of facts

Top-down and structured techniques exist for the requirements and specifications function, thus we have for example structured analysis, while specifications can be produced in a top-down fashion and can be written in structured English (Rudkin and Shere, 1979; Gane and Sarson, 1979). These, and other methods, are discussed below.

Methods

Structured analysis

Structured analysis is a general method for analysing the activities, typically the clerical activities, in an organization (Bell *et al.*, 1987). It views the world from the viewpoint of the flow of data in the organization, and the operations (transformations) performed on the data. The output of structured analysis is a DFD (data flow diagram), appropriate parts of which are then selected for computerization. Structured analysis has been used mainly in traditional business data processing, where data flow is the dominant aspect (Charette, 1986). Couger *et al.* (1982) classify it as a fourth-generation system development technique. There are, in fact, two similar versions of structured analysis: DeMarco (1978), Yourdon (1976), and Gane and Sarson (1979). The latter version incorporates database concepts (Fairley, 1985).

Structured analysis is a top-down, hierarchical technique. It provides a systematic, step-by-step approach (Martin and McClure, 1985). It makes extensive use of graphics as well as text, and comprises (Charette, 1986):

- Data flow diagrams;
- Data dictionary;
- Structured English;
- Decision tables;
- Decision trees.

It is a requirements analysis rather than a specifications technique, and is mainly used for business applications, where the distinction is less critical (Charette, 1986). It does not address performance issues. The specification it produces is a graphical model that is concise and easy to understand, so the user can become familiar with the system long before it is implemented (Martin and

McClure, 1985). This permits the user to review the system, and discover any errors or misconceptions early. In addition, because it partitions the specifications into small, manageable pieces, it is easier to implement changes.

The benefits of structured systems analysis are hard to quantify. The analysis itself takes longer, but the reduced number of subsequent problems should more than compensate for this (Martin, 1981; Gane and Sarson, 1979). However, Martin and McClure (1985) describe structured analysis as an improvement over previous methods, but say it is only the 'beginnings' of an analysis method, not a fully-fledged methodology. The data flow diagram, for example, is neither a complete nor a rigorous representation of the system, and as a result, many diagrams contain mistakes and omissions. Data analysis receives only secondary attention. The analyst is not given sufficient guidelines on how to subdivide a problem, or how to check for completeness and correctness of specifications, or when to stop the subdivision process. Martin and McClure (1985) therefore recommended that this technique only be used for small, simple systems.

SADT (Structured analysis and design technique)

SADT (Ross, 1977) is very similar to structured analysis, and so is also a top-down technique, and Couger *et al.* (1982) classify it too as a fourth-generation system development technique. It incorporates (Fairley, 1985; Charette, 1986):

- a set of modelling principles;
- graphics (activity and data diagrams);
- proprietary interviewing techniques;
- a set of review procedures (and an emphasis on reviews).

Its purpose is to force structure on the systems analysis task, and to aid understanding of the functions of complicated systems

(Lucas, 1985; Charette, 1986). It can be used for all types of problem, including non-software problems, but would probably only be used on large, complex projects, with 4–6 analysts, and of 6–9 months duration (Fairley, 1985; Lucas, 1985). It is used primarily for requirements analysis. It is not rigorous enough by itself to yield a specification, but the techniques have been applied successfully to system design (Lucas, 1985). It produces models of the system. It does not address the performance of a system, but can be extended to do so (Charette, 1986). This is called 'behavioral diagramming'. Structured analysis emphasizes the data viewpoint of a system, whereas SADT emphasizes both a data and a function viewpoint. Structured analysis provides more guidance, and is easier to use, whereas SADT contains more information on the diagrams, and is more powerful. Activity diagrams are used more often than data diagrams, but the latter assist in checking the completeness and consistency of an SADT model (Fairley, 1985). The diagrams are reviewed, which has led to the term 'egoless analysis' (Charette, 1986). SADT has been credited with reducing costs and development time, and improving the quality of the final system (Lucas, 1985).

Program definition and design languages

PDLs are a family which includes structured English and pseudocode, both of which are discussed separately later. Program definition languages are a specification method, and program design languages are a design method, but for convenience we discuss them together. A precise definition or distinction is not attempted here, and we treat structured English as a specification method, and pseudocode as a design method; different people use different definitions of these terms, e.g. they might refer to pseudocode as structured English. The following comments should therefore be taken as general statements which apply to the family as a whole, and supplement the individual comments about structured English and pseudocode.

PDLs are intended to aid communication between designers, and to capture the design decisions in a machine-processable form (Enos and Van Tilburg, 1979). They are a stylized version of English, with well-defined grammatical structure and rules (Parkin, 1980). Various conventions can be observed, e.g. use capitals for reserved words. Only structured programming constructs are permitted, so it forces programs coded from it to be structured (Dunn and Ullman, 1982). In fact, this technique ensures that the implementation closely matches the design, though there is the danger that designers will concentrate on the implementation rather than on the design (Charette, 1986). It is a non-graphic technique, but indentation lends it a graphic 'flavor' (Glass, 1979). PDLs are a substitute for flowcharts, and are easier to maintain than flowcharts. Charette implies that it is difficult to build large systems using this technique. Programmers might resent it because it restricts their flexibility: 'using this methodology slows down and warps my thought processes' (Glass, 1979); 'the expressive power of the language used may severely limit the design capability' (Charette, 1986).

PDLs can be extended, e.g. by additional syntax rules, to produce machine-processable text, which can then be subjected to consistency checks (such as for unused data items or unreachable code) by an automated consistency checker (Glass, 1979); or be used to produce design aids such as cross-reference listings – an example of which is the Program Design Language System, PDL, of Caine, Farber, and Gordon, Inc. (Caine and Gordon, 1978) – or even executable code, e.g. the PASCAL-based PDL2 language (Davis and Vick, 1977), and the Urban Mass Transportation Administration's USL, which produces FORTRAN statements (Cheng, 1978) (Dunn and Ullman, 1982). The Program Design Language System improves specification read-

ability, helps designers to find and cross-reference items in the specifications, makes updating much easier, and provides a number of useful formatted summaries of the design information, but does no consistency or ambiguity checking, and lacks features to support terminology control and version control (Couger *et al.*, 1982; Martin and McClure, 1985).

Glass (1979) stated that PDLs were a new concept, and were not heavily used, probably because of inertia. Few are available, so organizations may need to define their own.

The cost of PDLs is low, but increases with increasing formality, and an automated consistency checker will entail a substantial acquisition cost. Initial results with the Program Design Language System have been 'quite favorable' (Couger *et al.*, 1982).

Structured English

As defined above, this is a specification method. Traditional, narrative specifications suffer from the imprecision and ambiguities which are inherent in natural (spoken) languages. Structured English is an attempt to overcome this. It is a programming-type language, i.e. specifications written in structured English look very much like a program, particularly a program written in a fourth-generation language. Structured English is actually a concept, not a standard language. Organizations are free to create their own versions, with their own rules, keywords, etc., but it is advisable for them to model their choices on the corresponding rules etc. in whatever 4GL they use (Martin and McClure, 1985).

The use of structured English and diagrams has been claimed to improve 'vastly' the analyst's productivity (Atkins, 1982). By contrast, Parkin (1980) warned that analysts who were not familiar with structured programming might require a considerable amount of practice in structured English. Gildersleeve (1978) warned that it is so 'loose' that you cannot determine if specifications written in it are complete and consistent (i.e. it does not achieve its goal of overcoming the imprecision and ambiguities in traditional, narrative specifications). Martin and McClure (1985) concluded that structured English has been a useful tool for describing program logic, but there are now other diagrammatic tools which are better, specifically Nassi–Shneiderman diagrams, action diagrams, and decision trees and tables. (Their definition of structured English is therefore closer to a program design language than to a program definition language.)

Pseudocode

Pseudocode is very similar to structured English, but whereas structured English is intended to be understood by end users, pseudocode is intended for DP professionals. It is therefore more formal, though it avoids details such as opening and closing files, initializing counters, and setting up flags (Mittra, 1988). (The amount of detail required is dictated by the degree of knowledge and the initiative expected from the programmers in the particular working environment (Parkin, 1986).) Pseudocode is intended as an intermediate step between structure charts, HIPO diagrams, etc., and actual code, but because it is close to actual code, why waste time on it: why not just write the actual code? (Mittra, 1988). This is especially true if the processing logic is available in the form of either a diagram or structured English. Furthermore, some 4GLs are so powerful that they provide *executable* code that 'is simpler and easier to read than some of the more cryptic breeds of pseudocode' (Martin and McClure, 1985). As implied by this quotation, there is no universal standard for it. Gildersleeve (1978) was also critical: 'it may be all right for ACM Journal articles, but it will repel the bulk of users'.

Other methods

There are many requirements and specifications methods in addition to those described above. For example, Charette (1986) described two specification methods, SCRS (software cost reduction specification) (Heninger, 1980; Hester *et al.*, 1981), and TRW's SREM (software requirements engineering methodology) (Alford, 1977). In one case, SCRS gave a 5000% reduction in the amount of documentation needed to specify a change to a system (Redwine *et al.*, 1984). Couger *et al.* (1982) classify SREM as a fourth-generation system development technique. Both IBM's Vienna Development Method (VDM), and Oxford University's specification language, Z, provide a mathematically-based mechanism for writing mathematically unambiguous system specifications (Formal attraction, *Computer Week*, 27 Jan. 1988, pp. 18–19; Sommerville, 1989; Schech, 1990). (This is similar to higher-order software, discussed later.) One user of Z claims that, at the high-level design stage, they are 'pulling out' twice as many defects as with traditional methods, and at subsequent stages, they are finding fewer errors.

Conclusion

Pomberger (1984) compared three methods for describing requirements – SADT, PSL/PSA, and HIPO – and concluded that all of them emphasize only certain facets of specification. They are inflexible, and are tailored only to particular types of problem. Similarly, Townsend (1980) compared some of the different approaches to systems analysis, and concluded that all of them have weaknesses: they do not, for example, give adequate guidance for dealing with large and complex systems.

Pomberger concluded that there was no generally acceptable method; that this shows that specification technique was an under-developed area; and in fact that specification is a creative task which cannot be replaced by rules and methodology.

Shafer (1989) stated that PSL/PSA, SREM, and SADT date from the early 1970s, and have often given way to newer techniques. She did not name these techniques, and it is unlikely she was referring to the system planning model (Verrijn-Stuart, 1975) and ISDOS (Information System Design and Optimization System) (Teichroew and Sayani, 1971), which Couger *et al.* (1982) classify as fifth-generation techniques, as these are also from the early 1970s.

User involvement

The purpose of this study is to determine how to produce software faster, but there is little point in producing it faster if it is the wrong product, or if it will still not be cost-effective. Close user involvement helps avoid these dangers: 'for internal projects, close relationships between the users and the development staff can head off painful changes late in development' (Jones, 1986b).

Users want to improve their working environment themselves, so they should be made to feel part of the development process and not just pawns in the hands of technical, computer experts (Shneiderman, 1980). They should regard the system as *theirs*, rather than as one imposed on them (Mittra, 1988). They will then voluntarily use the system, and will use and act on the information it provides. Close user involvement is therefore important to success (Stockton, 1981). This can be achieved by prototyping, by appropriate organizational structures, e.g. by having users on DP project teams, or by having regular meetings. There is generally closer user involvement in small organizations or with distributed data processing (de Raay, 1975). Close user involvement is particularly important when interactive systems are being developed.

The JAD (joint application design) concept is a combination of a structured design methodology and an intensive workshop in which users and DP staff together define user requirements and systems specifications, and produce the design. (Despite the name, the emphasis is on analysis rather than design (Moore, 1990).) It has been claimed to improve productivity by 20:1 (JAD earns hurrahs in Canada, *IBM Inform*, Aug. 1983, p. vii), but this seems very high, even though it is the combined effect of a structured methodology and user participation. Wood and Silver (1989) give a figure of only 40%, which is more plausible. An intermediate figure is the 2.4:1 improvement found by Walston and Felix (1977) where users participated in defining the requirements, though this may include the effect of correlated factors (Chapter 2). (Development productivity was 2.4 times higher where there was much user participation than where there was none.) (Walston and Felix also found that productivity was 2.6 times higher where up to 50% of the development programmers participated in the design of the functional specifications, than where only up to 25% participated.) Where users participate, there should be fewer subsequent changes, and this is probably the reason for the increased productivity.

Lucas (1985) quoted two cases in which the users played the leading role in designing their own systems. Both systems were successful. However, Mittra (1988) believes that this can only work in small organizations, and not in large ones with a complex array of activities, as users are not knowledgeable in the intricacies of information systems theory.

Fairley (1985) warned that user involvement is a 'sensitive and difficult' issue. While it does have benefits, there is also the danger that users will continually change their requirements. He therefore concluded that 'experience indicates that too much customer involvement can hinder progress'. However, he was referring to involvement later in the development process. If the requirements are not stable – e.g. if the user changes his requirements while the system is being developed – then quality and productivity are degraded. Figures given in section 8.3.3, on errors, indicate that at least 50% more effort is required if there are frequent changes in the requirements. It was also shown in that section that a change to the specifications after a system has been installed may cost 60 times as much to implement as it would have cost had it been made during the original requirements analysis.

The GUIDE (1979) survey found that modern programming practices improved communication with users.

Close management involvement is also necessary, not only to ensure co-operation from the users, but also 'so that surprises may be avoided', e.g. so that the system being developed does not conflict with management's plans for the future (Shneiderman, 1980).

8.4.3   DESIGN

Design consists of several aspects, such as the design of:

- computer logic and procedures (of both systems and programs);
- manual procedures;
- documents;
- reports;
- files and databases;
- screen dialogues;
- codes.

Fairley (1985) subdivided design into internal and external, and further subdivided internal design into architectural and detailed. External design consists of the design of report layouts, record layouts, etc.

Human skills

According to Glass (1979), design is the most thought-intensive function, which is probably why often too little time is spent on it. Charette (1986) described it as 'wicked': solving one aspect of a problem uncovers other aspects that may be even more difficult to solve. It is the function most in need of

automation, but is also the function least amenable to it. It is difficult to develop methodologies: 'designers produce designs, methods do not'; 'it is not possible to offer an algorithm for optimal or even satisfactory design'; 'some aspects of designing will remain an art' (Peters and Tripp, 1977; Shneiderman, 1980).

Designers need (Glass, 1979; Lee, 1978; Shneiderman, 1980; Fairley, 1985):-

- experience in the application area;
- experience with the tools and techniques;
- thinking skills;
- a high tolerance level;
- flexibility;
- creative insight; and
- 'some gift of prophecy';

and it is difficult to develop tools or methods to enhance (or replace) such traits. Nevertheless, some technological aids are available, e.g.:

- RPG, which contains a built-in program logic (Garber, 1976);
- program generators, which eliminate programming in some cases, and therefore eliminate program design, though system design is still necessary (Bell *et al.*, 1987);
- the CASE tools (Chapter 6) e.g. DesignAid, which automates structured analysis and design, validates and balances data flow diagrams, and supports multiple design techniques (Nastec, 1986), and Teamwork/SD, which helps system designers create and analyse their designs, and enables them to decompose interrelated system components into manageable tasks, while minimizing interfaces between the components (Barry, 1986a).

Constraints

Designers seek a workable compromise between multiple, complex, and conflicting constraints. Systems should be powerful, with many facilities, they should have extensive help features and be well documented, and should be fault-tolerant, yet at the same time they should be simple, easy to maintain, and efficient, while development costs and time must be kept to a minimum (Boehm, 1981). Design of interactive systems is particularly difficult.

Software should be designed so that it is *adaptable*: it should be easy to modify; it should be device independent; it should be easy to port to a different computer configuration; and it should be easy to incorporate it (or its components) into another system (i.e. re-used code) (Boehm, 1981). The information hiding techniques (Chapter 5) mentioned in connection with virtual machine volatility, help to make software adaptable. (A virtual machine is the operational computer's hardware and system software – operating system, DBMS, etc.)

Walston and Felix (1977) found that productivity was 1.8 times higher where there were minimal constraints on design than where the constraints were severe.

The design must be 'adequate', i.e. it must meet the specifications (Charette, 1986).

General considerations

Brooks (1975) cited conceptual integrity as the most important consideration in system design. Systems which have been designed by just one person – as happens in a CPT – should possess conceptual integrity.

Designers should avoid unnecessary duplication of program logic. They should also create and use a library of pre-written, pre-tested, error-free subroutines for common functions, i.e. re-used code (Van Tassel, 1978; Glass, 1979). Re-used code is a topic referred to several times. The majority opinion is that it is a major productivity booster, and Arthur (1988) reported that up to 80% of any system can be re-used, though in one centre at AT&T, only 15% of the production modules were re-used (The quest for zero defect software, *Computer Week*, 13 Feb. 1989, p. 21). However, a word of caution: one organ-

ization which subdivides its systems into many small, simple programs, rather than into a few large, complex, generalized ones, reported very high productivity (over 100 LOC per day compared to the more usual 15–50), including high maintenance productivity (Orkins and Weiss, 1975). Additional effort is required initially to develop generalized modules, and this may not always be recovered by subsequent savings (Jones, 1986b).

Zachmann (1981) reported that it was 'still common for the individual who must finally sit down to write code for a module, to find he must resolve remaining design questions'.

Designers with a background of batch processing may continue using the same techniques when designing interactive systems, and so not make full use of the available facilities, e.g. for validation of input data (Dieperink, 1977).

Traditional wisdom in system design is to strive for the minimum of change to existing systems (de Raay, 1975). The opposite view is that existing procedures should be changed to obtain maximum benefit from the new system (Expert warns of pit falls for new computer users, *Computronics*, 13 Feb. 1980, p. 5). The costs, benefits and risks of these alternatives should be weighed in each case, and a compromise reached.

The design should be verified before being implemented, e.g. by desk checking, or by presenting it to managers and users (Shneiderman, 1980).

Methods

Charette (1986) listed four basic design methods:

- functional decomposition (e.g. stepwise refinement);
- data flow (transform driven) design (e.g. structured design);
- data structure design (e.g. Jackson); and

- procedural design (axiomatic mathematics or PDLs).

To these methods can be added the general principle, KISS: *keep it simple, stupid* (Van Tassel, 1978).

Individual design methods are discussed below. Some of the methods are mutually exclusive, but others can be used together. The modular and structured programming design techniques, for example, can be used with the top-down and data structure methodologies. Couger *et al.* (1982) expand on this. Hierarchical design methods could be combined with a preliminary evaluation of data flow, and a follow-up evaluation of coupling, cohesion (both discussed below) and control, to produce a result much like data flow design; and HIPO designs can be similarly evaluated. The designer can therefore 'mix and match' portions of these methodologies to alternatively stress data flows or general structure.

The GUIDE (1979) survey of about 600 installations found that modern programming practices improved design accuracy.

Modular

There is a limit on the mental capacity of human beings to manipulate information (Woodfield *et al.*, 1981b). A person cannot manipulate information efficiently if its amount exceeds that limit. A programmer therefore breaks down a complex program into several smaller modules. The modular approach thus makes the software easier to design, build, understand, test and modify, though it also 'creates a complexity of interfaces' between the modules (Dunn and Ullman, 1982). In fact, the objective of the various design methods is to subdivide the job into smaller, more manageable tasks. The top-down methodology subdivides the job into different functions (the traditional approach), whereas the data structure subdivision is based on the structure and flow of data (Glass, 1979). Systems using a database are based on data structure.

Coupling and **cohesion** are two concepts associated with modularity. Software should be divided into modules in such a way that there is *minimum* interaction *between* modules (low or loose coupling), and a *high* degree of interaction *within* a module (high cohesion) (Bell *et al.*, 1987). Cohesion therefore measures how strongly the elements within a module are related to each other – the stronger, the better (Martin and McClure, 1985). Modules performing only one function have high cohesion. Modules should therefore only perform one function each. Products composed of single-function modules are easier to test and enhance; and changes are less likely to affect the performance, maintainability and stability of the system (The quest for zero defect software, *Computer Week*, 13 Feb. 1989, p. 21). Single-function modules also contribute to re-usability: in one centre at AT&T, 15% of the production modules were re-used. Modules with loose coupling are largely self-contained and independent. They can therefore be designed, coded, tested, and modified, without complications caused by what is happening in other modules. Another benefit is that the damage due to errors is restricted to the module in error. To ensure independence, one module should not be permitted to modify another, and temporary storage should not be shared between modules (Yourdon, 1975). The number of data items shared by modules is one indication of how independent or self-contained the modules are (Shneiderman, 1980; Bell *et al.*, 1987).

(Similarly, programs should initialize main memory prior to use, otherwise erratic and unpredictable results may occur, and should likewise position input and output devices prior to use (Shneiderman, 1980). These techniques therefore also make programs and modules independent.)

Modules should have only one entry and one exit (Yourdon, 1975). They should also be short. Typical guidelines are (Law and Long-worth, 1987):

- up to 100 statements, for limits of comprehension;
- up to 60 statements, to fit on one sheet of program listing.

Arthur (1988) recommended that 95% of modules should contain less than 100 lines of executable code, or 10 decisions. (By contrast, the typical module in Table 8.1 was about 400 lines long; and a study by Smith (1980) showed that modules ranged in size from less than 10 LOC to nearly 10 000!)

These limits are fairly arbitrary. A better guideline is that a module should be large enough to contain one function, but that it should contain only one function.

Halstead's Software Science has been challenged, but nevertheless programs modularized according to his ideas (e.g. size measurement) should be easy to write, debug, understand, and maintain (Shneiderman, 1980).

Modular programming is one aspect of structured programming, and so is discussed further under that topic.

Stepwise refinement

Stepwise refinement (Wirth, 1971) was one of the first methods which changed programming from a craft to a structured discipline (Martin and McClure, 1985). The problem is solved several times, at first in general outline only, and then in successively greater detail, with each solution being more complete than its predecessor (Peters and Tripp, 1977). Each solution is a refinement of the preceding solution, with both the tasks and the corresponding data structures being refined at each step (Martin and McClure, 1985). Put another way, the primary function of the system is identified first, and then successive subfunctions (Couger *et al.*, 1982).

The steps in this process correspond to Dijkstra's 'levels of abstraction' (Dahl *et al.*,

1972). The first step in the refinement hierarchy is the highest level of abstraction, and represents the program in its most abstract, i.e. general, form. The lowest level components can easily be coded in a programming language (Martin and McClure, 1985).

Guidelines to help direct the refinement process include (Martin and McClure, 1985):

- separate aspects that are not related;
- take into account efficiency, storage economy, clarity, etc.;
- attempt to make the easiest decisions first;
- decide as little as possible at each step; and
- do not address implementation details until late in the design process.

According to Pomberger (1984), practical experience shows that, even for simple tasks, a systematic, stepwise design strategy reduces the number of design errors, and leads to better program structures.

Pomberger believes that task oriented stepwise refinement is the most general and reasonable design concept, because it is a production as well as a design technique. It also seems to be – from both a practical and theoretical point of view – the most promising concept for the future. It is equally suitable for all types of application, it is practically self-explanatory, and it does not require a great degree of formalism.

A comparison of this method with the bottom-up method is contained in Schulz (1982).

Top-down

Top-down design is a general, informal strategy for dividing ('decomposing') a large or complex problem into its components, i.e. into several smaller problems (Martin and McClure, 1985). Use of top-down analysis and design is central to all of the structured methodologies (Couger *et al.*, 1982). Top-down design can be applied to the design of a module, program, system, or data structure. It is used in conjunction with 'stepwise refinement'. The highest level in the hier-archical structure is designed first. Its compo-nents are then defined in successively more and more detail. The decomposition process need not be carried to its limit, but can be stopped earlier if the person who will code the program is experienced.

Top-down design provides some general principles and guidelines, such as (Martin and McClure, 1985):

- separate the problem into parts, such that the components of each part are related to each other;
- attempt to make the easiest decisions first;
- decide as little as possible at each step;
- specify the input, function, and output of each module as it is designed;
- do not address implementation details until late in the design process; and
- pay as much attention to data as to processing, because the interfaces between modules must be carefully specified.

Various methods can be used to document the design, e.g. narratives, pseudocode, structure charts, and HIPO diagrams.

As the design proceeds, it may become apparent that a higher-level decision has led to awkward or inefficient decomposition at lower levels. The higher-level decision may thus have to be changed, and the system revised accordingly. This is known as back-tracking, and is a fundamental weakness of top-down design (Fairley, 1985). In the extreme case, if the top-down method is interpreted too literally, it seriously delays the detection of feasibility problems at the lowest levels, and the project may have to be extensively reworked or even cancelled after a considerable amount of effort has gone into it (Glass, 1979). As Schach (1988) so aptly put it, top-down development is perfect 'if you know, before you start, exactly what the program is to do, and if you know that this will never change'. To avoid this, a risk analysis should be performed during the earlier phases (Boehm, 1981); or a mixed top-

down, bottom-up method used instead, e.g. the lowest levels designed first (Fairley, 1985), especially if the lowest-level functions are the most complex. Pomberger (1984) believes that top-down design is more suit-able than bottom-up for new systems; while for modifications, a mixture should be used.

The top-down design approach was an im-provement over the previous *ad hoc* methods, but does not provide sufficient guidelines, e.g. on *how* to subdivide a problem – this is left to the experience and judgement of the designer, and so often results in a poor design (Martin and McClure, 1985). The method should therefore only be used for small, simple programs.

The very low number of errors (only 2 per 1000 LOC) discovered while testing the THE multi-programming system, has been credited to top-down design and proof of correctness (Yourdon, 1975; Martin and McClure, 1985). Furthermore, each of the errors was easy to remedy.

Of the organizations in the GUIDE (1979) survey, 47% were using top-down design, another 47% were considering it, and only 6% had rejected it.

Structured design

Structured design (Stevens *et al.*, 1974; Your-don and Constantine, 1979) is an extension of top-down design. Couger *et al.* (1982) classify it as a fourth-generation system development technique. It complements structured analy-sis, so the two should be used together, e.g. structured analysis produces a data flow diagram, which is then used in the structured design. It comprises (Bell *et al.*, 1987):

- data flow design (a procedure for system-atically modularizing large programs or systems);
- coupling and cohesion (criteria for assess-ing and choosing between alternative designs);
- notations (data flow diagrams and program structure charts).

It therefore includes steps for developing, documenting, evaluating, and improving the design, and each step is supported by a set of design strategies, guidelines, and documentation techniques (Martin and McClure, 1985).

The designer must identify the data flow through the system, and the transformation that the input data undergoes in the process of becoming output (Peters and Tripp, 1977).

A structure chart is produced from the data flow diagram, showing the procedural components of the program or system, their hierarchical arrangement, and the data connecting them.

A number of criticisms have been made against this method, for example, it is not suitable for purely computational problems; the terminology is confusing; the structure chart does not contain enough information to measure coupling and cohesion; and the method does not include data design (Bell *et al.*, 1987; Martin and McClure, 1985). On the whole, therefore, Martin and McClure prefer the simpler top-down design. A comparison of this method with SADT and the Litos Method (Schulz, 1982), is contained in Schulz (1982) and Hesse (1981).

Jackson methodologies

Jackson structured programming (JSP) (Jackson, 1975) is a program design method: 'its starting point is a program specification, and it takes the designer through steps that result in a structured design for the program code' (McNeile, 1988). Like structured design, it is also a refinement of the top-down method. It formalizes the design process by providing well-specified steps, graphic diagramming techniques (system network diagram, tree structure diagrams, and pseudocode), and methods to evaluate the correctness of the design (Martin and McClure, 1985).

It aims to make the structure of the program reflect the structure of the problem, which helps produce readily modifiable systems: a small change to the structure of the data should result in a correspondingly small and restricted change to the program (Macro and Buxton, 1987; Bell *et al.*, 1987). It therefore limits the impact of changes.

It is data driven, and is based on the *structure* of the data, not the flow thereof. The program structure is thus derived from the data structure. This aspect is praised by Martin and McClure (1985) as, in most cases, control flow is simple while data structures are complex, and data structure errors are more common than procedural logic errors. However, this also means that it provides only a static, not a dynamic view, and it is weak for logic design. Furthermore, it is limited to second- and third-generation procedural languages, with the input consisting of a sequential stream of records. It is therefore not suitable for on-line systems, nor for database systems (Martin and McClure, 1985). (One might have expected a data structure method to work well with database systems, but Bleazard (1976) agrees that it does not.) It forces a batch-processing view on all design problems, which not only complicates design, but also means that the program does *not* resemble the problem in such cases.

Irrespective of whether the Jackson method is used or not, the structure of the data can have a strong influence on the design (Shneiderman, 1980).

There is a difference of opinion over the range of systems to which this method is applicable. The statement quoted above by Martin and McClure (1985) that it is not suitable for on-line systems is supported by Bell *et al.* (1987), who pointed out that all the literature on the method concentrates on batch processing. However, it is at variance with the claim by Jackson that it is applicable to all types of problem, including on-line systems, process control, and scientific programs (Bell *et al.*, 1987); and with the statement by Bleazard (1976) that it has been found to be applicable to a wide class of commercial applications, including on-line. The unfavorable opinions are more recent, so one is more inclined to believe them.

According to some authorities, JSP is only suitable for designing the structure of simple, individual programs (or modules), and it gives little help in designing the overall structure of a large piece of software which needs to be broken down into programs and modules – a process which introduces the possibility of interface errors (Bell *et al.*, 1987; Martin and McClure, 1985). By contrast, McNeile (1988) and Charette (1986) stated that it is widely used on programs of all sizes, with great success.

Gildersleeve (1978) is critical of the data structure method, because it does not tell us *how* the data is to be structured.

Advantages claimed for the Jackson method include (Martin and McClure, 1985; Bell *et al.*, 1987; Bleazard, 1976; Stephens, 1979):

- it is the most systematic program design method currently available;
- it is more complete than structured design, as it includes logic to read, update, and write a master file;
- it is non-inspirational, i.e. it does not require 'insight, imagination and experience';
- it is consistent, so all programmers produce the same solution to the same problem;
- bugs are designed out.

It is also claimed to produce the *best* design. This is probably true where (but only where) there is a severe structure 'clash', i.e. where the input and output structures are greatly different (Couger *et al.*, 1982; Arthur, 1983).

Martin and McClure (1985) concluded that, because it is more difficult to use than other structured design methodologies, and requires extra effort, it is overkill for simple systems, and is only worthwhile for programs with complex data structures.

The original Jackson methodology, as des-cribed above, applied only to program design, but it is being extended to a full development methodology called Jackson System Development (JSD) (Jackson, 1983), which 'addresses activities in the analysis, design, and programming phases, and is applicable to both data processing and real-time systems', and automatically generates code (McNeile, 1988; Macro and Buxton, 1987). Fairley (1985) stated that more experience with this method was required before its usefulness could be determined, but more recently, Schach (1988) reported that it has had a number of great successes, not just with development but also with maintenance, which is particularly noteworthy as Jackson's book does not mention the latter.

Warnier–Orr

The Warnier–Orr method (Orr, 1977b) is similar to the Jackson method (Couger *et al.*, 1982), and is therefore another refinement of top-down design. It uses functional decomposition to derive a program design (Martin and McClure, 1985). It is a modified version of Warnier's (1974) logical construction of programs (LCP) and uses set theory from mathematics to describe program designs. Couger *et al.* (1982) classify it as a fourth-generation system development technique.

The program structure is derived from the structure of the *output* data, i.e. this is a *backward* (and therefore *unnatural*) design approach (Martin and McClure, 1985). The output is therefore the most important part of the system. However, many requirements are not immediately obvious from an examination of the system output, and the method offers little assistance 'other than to keep looking'. This can also lead to underestimates of the amount of work and the degree of difficulty. (Treating the output as the most important part of the system is consistent with the viewpoint expressed by Cho (1987), that the product of a software development process – the product desired by the software user – is *not* the software itself, but the *output* of the software. The software is merely the means to an end. The software processes data, so an analogy may be drawn with a factory manufacturing say automobiles. What the user wants is the output of the factory, namely the automobiles, and not the factory itself. This point of view is a valuable one, but the analogy with a factory could cause confusion, as the term 'software factory' is generally used to refer to the DP department, which is logical, as it manufactures software (Matsumoto, 1989).)

The objective of the methodology is to design reliable, adaptable systems, and this is achieved by improved communications among users, analysts, and programmers, because of the Warnier–Orr diagrams, which are easy to understand. They are the central design tool, and show the hierarchical structure and process flow of activities, functions, and data. However, the method can only handle hierarchical data structures, and so cannot handle network databases (Martin and McClure, 1985). In fact, it does not address the design of database systems, or the role of data dictionaries. (Though relational data files can be designed with logical construction of systems (LCS), which is an extension of LCP (Warnier, 1981; Parikh, 1984; Schach, 1990).) It provides no guidelines for control logic design, and no checking to ensure the logic is correct, and the design complete. Martin and McClure therefore concluded that it was suitable only for small, report-oriented design problems, and for them it is too tedious.

Higher-order software (HOS)

Martin and McClure (1985) and Zachmann (1981) attribute this methodology to Hamilton and Zeldin (1976), though Charette (1986) claims a mid-sixties origin. It covers all functions from requirements through specifications, high-level design, detailed design, and coding. It has a high graphics component, and its objective is to produce provably correct software. It is based on mathematical axioms, graphical representations, and an automated language (Charette, 1986). A set of rules is provided governing the function and interfacing of modules (Peters and Tripp, 1977).

(Chorafas (1986) also uses the term 'higher-order software', but he appears to be using it in a more general sense, to refer to any fourth- or fifth-generation software, with natural language capabilities and expert systems. Zachmann (1981) uses the term 'higher-level software' in a similar context, presumably to distinguish it from higher-order software. Similarly, Martin (1983b) refers to 'high-order software', which includes the provably correct, bug-free aspects of higher-order software, and also takes advantage of advanced machine architectures, particularly the Japanese fifth-generation project.)

Benefits claimed for this technique are (Martin and McClure, 1985; Zachmann, 1981; Enos and Van Tilburg, 1979; Charette, 1986):

- it uses one language throughout the lifecycle, instead of a different (and probably incompatible) language for each function;
- the graphical representations are computerized, and so are easily changed;
- it is the most rigorous of any structured technique;
- it is based on mathematical axioms, which guarantees that the resulting design is logically complete and correct;
- the decomposition process follows precise rules which ensure mathematically correct decomposition;
- it incorporates computerized verification and cross-checking – at each stage, an analyser automatically checks that the axioms have not been violated, thereby ensuring there are no errors, omissions, or inconsistencies;
- not only are the modules internally correct,

but the interfaces between subsystems are also rigorous and provably correct;

- it enhances structured design methodology by providing additional criteria for evaluating design constructs;
- the verification catches not only errors etc. in the design, but also reveals most inconsistencies and errors in the specifications;
- because errors are caught early, they are cheap to correct;
- design may be either top-down or bottom-up;
- it permits a strict separation between the specification and the implementation;
- it is machine independent, and allows the specification to be independent of hardware/software interface boundaries;
- executable program code is generated automatically from the design, so coding time is eliminated;
- these programs are bug-free;
- it reduces the testing effort (because it eliminates the need for most dynamic program testing and most debugging);
- development is speeded up, so more time is made available to avoid specification errors;
- it can be used for any application, including very complex systems with complex logic;
- there is less maintenance, because the original system was thoroughly specified;
- the areas affected by each change are revealed automatically, and the system ensures that all consequential adjustments are made;
- when any change is made, its consequences are automatically shown on the screen and can be quickly adjusted;
- maintenance is therefore easier and faster.

The net effect is that productivity is greatly improved, and the number of errors is greatly reduced – it was estimated that 87% of the preflight software errors in NASA's moonshot, Project Apollo, would have been caught had higher-order software been used (Hamil-

ton and Zeldin, 1976; Martin and McClure, 1985).

The methodology therefore sounds very impressive, but has received relatively little attention in the literature, and is not widely used for functional decomposition (Radice and Phillips, 1988). There are a number of possible reasons for this:

- it is *different*, an 'alien' methodology, so staff are likely to resist it (Martin and McClure, 1985);
- training is required, and it takes time to become skilled in it;
- it is not 'user friendly' (though it can be coupled to existing front ends);
- Martin and McClure (1985) imply that it is not needed in less complex commercial DP applications;
- Charette (1986) seems to imply that further development work is required ('long way to go') – perhaps he is referring to the fact that it is not yet linked to commonly used commercial software such as DBMSs;
- similarly, Martin and McClure (1985) stated that 'much embellishment is needed to make the technique easy to use and powerful'.

Another possibility is that it is not as good as its enthusiasts claim; recall the general warning by Macro and Buxton (1987) quoted in the introduction to this section: 'be careful of claims made by their authors (and other enthusiasts) for these methodologies'.

Zachman (1981) concluded that methodologies such as higher-order software should become available in usable form over the next few years.

Conclusion

Peters and Tripp (1977) concluded that none of the five methods they studied (stepwise refinement, structured design, higher-order software, etc.) was ideal for every type of problem.

Fairley (1985) gave a table showing what

each method was suitable for: stepwise refinement and structured design were recommended for scientific applications and utility programs, and are useful for data processing applications, but not for operating systems and real-time systems; JSP was recommended for data processing applications, and is useful for scientific applications; and so on.

Pomberger (1984) stated that techniques like JSP, LCP (logical construction of programs), and the Litos method, usually emphasize only certain facets of design, and are tailored to particular task types. As stated earlier, he believes that task oriented stepwise refinement is the best method. However, he did not discuss higher-order software, which would surely be the top choice of Martin and McClure (1985).

Magnitude of effect on.productivity

Walston and Felix (1977) found that, where top-down development was used to produce more than 66% of the code, development productivity was 1.6 times higher than where it was used for 33% or less. However, this figure may include the effect of other, correlated factors, specifically other modern programming practices, as they were usually used together (Boehm, 1981). Holton (1977) found that top-down design and implementation were moderately effective in improving the productivity of both development and maintenance.

By contrast, one organization which uses the bottom-up approach reported very high productivity (over 100 LOC per day compared to the more usual 15–50), including high maintenance productivity, though this may be because of their policy of subdividing their systems into many small, simple programs, rather than into a few large, complex, generalized ones (Orkins and Weiss, 1975). They had not had compatibility problems between the many programs and associated files, probably because they devote considerable effort to the design of their files. This

approach is particularly suitable in an environment where the user's needs are constantly changing: by the time a large integrated system had been developed, the information it provided would no longer be needed.

The benefits of structured design are hard to quantify. Gane and Sarson (1979) claimed that systems designed using this method are seven times easier and cheaper to change than those designed by conventional methods. Independent confirmation of this figure would be appreciated as it is too reminiscent of the early claims made for structured programming, which subsequent experience indicates were too optimistic. Their figure was apparently obtained from a project by Inmon (1976) which used several techniques besides structured design, such as CPTs and structured walkthroughs, so the contribution from structured design alone was probably much less than 7:1.

The JAD (joint application design) concept includes a structured design methodology. It has been claimed to improve productivity by 20:1 (JAD earns hurrahs in Canada, *IBM Inform*, Aug. 1983, p. vii), but as stated earlier, this seems very high, even though it is the combined effect of two factors. The other factor is user participation. Walston and Felix (1977) found that productivity was 2.4 times higher where there was much user participation than where there was none. This implies that structured design achieves a (20/2.4 =) 8.3:1 improvement in productivity, which agrees with the Gane and Sarson estimate. However, the 2.4:1 may include the effect of other, correlated factors (Boehm, 1981), and so may itself be too high, in which case the contribution from structured design is even higher than 8.3:1. However, if the productivity improvement from JAD is only 40% (Wood and Silver, 1989), then both structured design and user participation have much smaller influences on productivity than even the 2.4:1, let alone the 8.3:1.

With HOS, although more care has to go

into the specification stage, specification and design costs are nevertheless halved because of improved communications, the speed of using the graphics editor, and the automatic detection of errors (Martin and McClure, 1985). In addition, the programming costs disappear, and the costs of testing largely disappear; there is less maintenance, and maintenance is much easier and faster to perform. The overall effect from these and other benefits is a 10:1 improvement in productivity.

Martin (1981) stated that the data structure method, when used well, gave a higher productivity than other forms of structured programming, but did not put a figure on it. Figures given by Parikh (1984) suggest that the Warnier–Orr method can give savings of around 10% p.a. in maintenance programming costs.

According to Hall (1987), structured design methodologies produce software that is twice as easy to maintain.

Representation

There is an old saying that a picture is worth a thousand words. Variations on this are given below.

- 'Clear diagrams do help in creating programs and also in debugging them' (Martin and McClure, 1985).
- 'The structure of program systems and algorithms can best be illustrated through graphic notation' (Pomberger, 1984).
- 'It is easy to get tongue-tied when describing an involved procedure or set of rules' (Parkin, 1980).
- 'Perceptual psychologists have amply demonstrated the advantage of imagery over words or numbers for certain applications. Error rates and time can be reduced substantially when a proper graphic representation can be found' (Shneiderman, 1980).
- Data flow diagrams 'provide a graphic

technique to reduce the wordiness of specifications' (Dunn and Ullman, 1982).

It is therefore helpful to use graphical methods. (Parikh (1984) put it more strongly. Drawing an analogy with Roman and Arabic numerals – it is far easier to multiply say 23 times 15 than XXIII times XV – he argued that improved tools, such as the Warnier–Orr diagram, are essential for advances in software technologies.) By contrast, Casner (1991) found that graphics are not invariably superior to tables, text, etc., but rather that *particular* graphics are superior for *particular* tasks, i.e. the graphics must be designed to directly support a specific task. For example, line graphs are supportive of some tasks that manipulate continuous data, but are detrimental to the performance of others.

Designs can be represented in many ways: flowcharts, decision tables, etc. Some of the better-known methods are described below. (These are not necessarily the best methods, but it is nevertheless valuable to point out weaknesses in widely-used methods.) A more comprehensive discussion (of over a dozen methods) can be found in Martin and McClure (1985). These representations also aid the design process, and form part of the system documentation as well. System-level representations form part of the specifications. Because of their graphical nature, representations aid communication with users Law and Longworth, 1987; Davis, 1983c), but they may require special, graphics skills – people 'who can draw and letter neatly' – unless computer-aided design systems are in use (Dunn and Ullman, 1982). Representations of complex projects can become large and unwieldy. From a cost viewpoint, there is generally little to choose between alternative representations (Glass, 1979).

Because of the large number of methods, descriptions of them or explanations of how to use them are not included – that can be found in many books. Instead, their advantages and disadvantages, which are not as well covered, and which are in any case more directly relevant to a discussion of productivity, are considered in detail.

Structure charts

Structure charts give a visual picture of the overall architecture of a program (Mittra, 1988). Modules, which are the basic building blocks of a program, are arranged in a hierarchical manner, with modules performing high-level tasks placed at the upper levels of the hierarchy, and modules performing lower-level (i.e. more detailed) tasks placed at successively lower levels (Martin and McClure, 1985). At execution time, modules at one level are called by the modules at the preceding (higher) level. Various rules are given by McClure (1978), e.g. if module A calls module B, then module B cannot call module A; and a module cannot call itself. These rules avoid loops, and thus help preserve program clarity.

Structure charts are a strong communication and documentation aid (Couger *et al.*, 1982). They are small enough to be worked on all at once by the designers. This prevents some parts of the program being optimized at the expense of the rest of the program. They have an advantage over flowcharts, as they show the invoking relationships between modules, which are hard to determine from flowcharts, and they also show the calling parameters (Stevens *et al.*, 1974). Also, flowcharts show when (in what order and under what conditions) blocks are executed, and so unnecessarily complicate the general program design phase. With structure charts, such details can be deferred until detailed module design.

However, structure charts have disadvantages. They can become cluttered with large amounts of information. They do not show structured programming control constructs: pseudocode is usually used to show detailed internals of the modules (Martin and McClure, 1985). They show data flow but not data structure (Couger *et al.*, 1982).

Computerized tools are available for drawing and updating structure charts. Examples are STRADIS/DRAW (McAuto, McDonnell Douglas Automation Co., St Louis), and Excelerator (InTech, 5 Cambridge Center, Cambridge MA 02142). The latter runs on PCs, and is linked to a dictionary (Martin and McClure, 1985).

Along with data flow diagrams, structure charts are the most commonly used structured design methodology (Martin and McClure, 1985).

Hierarchy charts

Hierarchy charts are one component of HIPO diagrams (the 'H' in 'HIPO') (Mittra, 1988). (The other, main, components are discussed below.) They show the top-down structure of a program by decomposing it into modules (based on functions), and are therefore very similar to structure charts. A hierarchy chart is also known as a VTOC (visual table of contents). Mittra prefers hierarchy charts to structure charts for very complex programs, because they are less cluttered. In general, Martin and McClure (1985) prefer structure charts, as they show how the components of the program are interrelated via data.

Gildersleeve (1978) describes hierarchy charts as a fine tool for emphasizing those aspects of system structure that have the most impact on effective system design, but states they are inferior to decision tables, at least as a documentation tool. They encourage abbreviation, and so are usually incomprehensible. Each box should therefore be backed up by a decision table or, 'as a very poor minimum', by a narrative description of the processing represented by the box.

HIPO diagrams

Hierarchical input processing output diagrams were developed by IBM, and form part of that organization's IPT (improved programming technologies) (IBM, 1974). They were an attempt to overcome the disadvantages of flowcharts (Dunn and Ullman, 1982). They are a graphic technique, used to show both functions and data flow at the system overview level, but have been used for detail representation as well (Glass, 1979). There are, in fact, three types of diagram: the hierarchy chart (discussed above), and overview and detail diagrams. The latter two diagrams each consist of three sections: input, processing, and output – and are therefore known as IPOs.

HIPO diagrams are well-covered in the literature, and many books describe their advantages and disadvantages – it seems that every author knows of different advantages and disadvantages. The problem is compounded by the fact that there are a number of variations on HIPO diagrams, as well as basic and extended versions, making it difficult to generalize. Space considerations prevent reproduction of all this information here, but instead just a selection of the pros and cons is given.

According to Lucas (1985), HIPO facilitates the top-down design process, and produces documentation as a by-product. By contrast, Couger *et al.* (1982) stated that it is primarily a documentation package, supporting design more than directing it, though many organizations have successfully adopted it as a design methodology, because it encourages its users to consider a wide range of issues in order to satisfy its information requirements.

The diagrams make use of symbols, and a special template. Bleazard (1976) is critical of this, as it multiplies the number with which the programmer must be familiar. He also says the symbols are unnecessarily cumbersome and time-consuming.

Couger *et al.* (1982) also have some criticisms of the method. It does not analyse the 'goodness' of the design – that must be done by the designer (Davis, 1983c). Data structure is only weakly handled. Control structure is not formally considered, so the diagrams need to be supplemented by, for example, flowcharts, to show control flow (Lucas, 1985). However, Couger adds that they strongly support physical design and the construction process, and clearly define the physical system. They can also be used to define the structure and detail of existing systems, and can therefore be used during maintenance (Davis, 1983c).

According to Canning (1979), they encourage the analyst to focus on one process at a time, rather than several processes and the interactions among them.

Parikh (1984) quoted opinions of them ranging from 'the most effective form of documentation that is currently available and the one most likely to be around ten years from now', to 'belongs to the past'.

Some attempts have been made to automate HIPO diagrams, such as Univac's PROVAC system (Mortison, 1976), and IBM's HIPODRAW and PANEL (Parikh, 1984).

The cost of HIPO is not significantly more than that of alternative techniques (Glass, 1979).

Only 7% of the operational systems in the Lientz *et al.* (1978) survey used HIPO. By contrast, 31% of the organizations in the GUIDE (1979) survey were using HIPO diagrams, another 46% were considering using them, and only 23% had rejected them.

Warnier–Orr diagrams

Warnier–Orr diagrams (Orr, 1977a, 1977b) are an alternative to HIPO diagrams and structure charts. Like these two techniques, they aid the design of well-structured programs, and they are easy to learn and to use – though they can become large and difficult to read when used at a low level (Martin and McClure, 1985). They show the hierarchical structure of a program, system, or data structure. They can thus be used for both procedure and data-structure design, and so are more powerful than a structure chart.

They can also be used for both high-level and detail design. However, control logic (conditions being tested) is not shown in the body of the diagrams, but in footnotes, which detracts from their readability.

Warnier–Orr diagrams have been used extensively to design new systems and to document existing systems. According to Martin and McClure (1985), studies have shown that data-structure documentation is more useful to overall program understanding than procedural documentation. The ability of Warnier–Orr diagrams to provide good data-structure documentation is therefore a major benefit.

Orr described them as 'the flowchart of the future' (Parikh, 1984). According to Orr (1977b), by subdividing each piece into simpler pieces, and by providing a simple means for dealing with order and logic, they provide a major benefit over other structured documentation tools, such as HIPO diagrams and pseudocode. They help to express a systems problem simply, completely, and logically. They allow us to concentrate on the logical requirements of a problem instead of on the physical ones. They state problems in a fashion understandable to a user, which 'helps significantly to overcome many of the serious communications problems that always have kept us away from the problem'. They therefore serve as a communication tool with users, though they seem to require a higher degree of user education than Jackson diagrams (Couger *et al.*, 1982). They handle sequential files and hierarchical databases, and can also describe complex data structures (Orr, 1977b).

Parikh (1984) claims they are a powerful tool, equally effective for designing major modifications, and says they are clearly superior to HIPO diagrams. Other benefits he claims are that they provide a compact, pictorial format; they provide a formal method of hierarchical decomposition; they lead to faster design; they stress design over coding; they help develop programs that are logically correct; programs run correctly, usually on the first effective test; they lead to faster coding; they include the basic structured programing constructs; and they do not require intermediate steps such as pseudocode. He also claims they can be used to design teleprocessing, distributed data processing, process control, communications, real-time, and on-line systems, and non-computer procedures as well.

In contrast with these favorable comments, Gildersleeve (1978) stated that, while they are good for structuring programs after the data has been structured, they are of little use when part of the problem is *how* the data is to be structured, as is the case during system design. They are also a poor procedure description tool – 'when he wants to show procedure, Warnier falls back on flowcharts' – and they encourage abbreviation.

Martin and McClure (1985), like Parikh (1984), prefer Warnier–Orr diagrams to HIPO diagrams, except for their lack of a capability to relate data to processing steps. Other major disadvantages are that they are not database oriented, and they can only represent hierarchical data structures. They are better suited to small problems, especially output-oriented ones with simple file structures. (This conflicts with the statements quoted above by Orr (1977b).)

Automated tools, such as Ken Orr and Associates' Structure(s) and DocumentOrr, are available (Parikh, 1984; Simpson, 1987). These products provide on-line support, automated diagramming, validation of entity diagrams, or generation of COBOL code.

Jackson diagrams

There are three types of Jackson diagram: data structure, program structure, and system network. A form of pseudocode can also be used, bringing the number of types of representation up to four. Jackson diagrams can therefore be used to represent both data and program structure.

The data structure diagram is tree-structured. It can be used for any data structure: file, record, character string, or print line (Bleazard, 1976). It looks very different to a Warnier–Orr diagram, but its content is very similar.

The program structure diagram is also tree-structured, and is similar to the data structure diagram. In fact, because the methodology makes the structure of the program reflect the structure of the data, it may be possible to convert the data structure diagram into the program structure diagram by merely writing 'process' in every box (Bleazard, 1976; Bell *et al.*, 1987). Because it consists of rectangles arranged in levels and connected by lines, it is similar in appearance to structure charts. It does not show the data passed between the components, but this could be added (Martin and McClure, 1985; Couger *et al.*, 1982). It shows structured programming constructs such as selection and repetition, but does not show how the choice is made, nor what controls the repetition.

The system network diagram is an overview diagram. It shows both programs and data streams. It contains similar information to a data flow diagram, which could be used instead (Martin and McClure, 1985).

Martin and McClure (1985) stated that Jackson diagrams, by mapping input data structures to output data structures, are an aid to clear thinking in program design. For straightforward data processing, this methodology is claimed to lead to code with fewer problems than other commonly-used structuring methods. However, they also have some criticisms: the method does not help with complex program logic, and it treats database systems as though they were essentially the same as file systems.

Decision tables

As its name implies, a decision table is a tabular representation. It describes a problem and the means of its solution by setting out all the combinations of conditions and the consequent actions in tabular form (Law and Longworth, 1987). Decision tables are used to show detailed program logic, and are seldom used for high-level program structure (Martin and McClure, 1985). They were, in fact, intended as a supplement to flowcharts, and should be used to supplement other tools such as structure charts and data flow diagrams. They are more compact than flowcharts. However, decision tables have also been used as both a systems analysis and a systems design tool.

Automated aids are available, either by means of a preprocessor or built into a compiler, to produce code (e.g. COBOL) from the table (Lee, 1978). This avoids the introduction of errors at the coding stage. Examples of automated aids are DETAB/GT from SOWACO (Software Consulting), and DETAB/65 from the Los Angeles Chapter of the Association for Computing Machinery (SOWACO, 1976; Couger *et al.*, 1982).

Decision tables are a second-generation design methodology, with decision table processors (i.e. the automated aids) being third-generation (Couger *et al.*, 1982).

The cost of decision tables is equivalent to that of alternative, applicable techniques (Glass, 1979). For simple situations, alternative methods such as action diagrams are probably better, and relate more directly to the program structure; but for complex combinations of conditions, a decision table is a major help in clear thinking (Martin and McClure, 1985). It causes the systems analyst and the program designer to look at every possible combination of conditions, ensuring none is glossed over – as happens so easily with narrative descriptions (Gildersleeve, 1978). Decision tables simplify data validation provided they are supported by sufficiently powerful decision table processors, e.g. ones which allow all the errors in an input record to be determined at the same time (Kessel, 1975). They also simplify documentation, and making changes is simple and controllable, i.e. they are quick to draw and redraw, which is an important advantage, as the complex problems for which they are used result in their being redrawn many times (Martin and McClure, 1985). They facilitate communication among users and analysts, and can even be drawn by users (Lucas, 1985). Their net effect is to speed up the total development process, and facilitate system modifications (Couger *et al.*, 1982). In fact, the standardized method made possible through the use of decision tables has resulted in programs being developed and tested in half the time taken with flowcharts, while DETAB/GT has been claimed to reduce testing time by up to 50% (Kessel, 1975; SOWACO, 1976).

Gildersleeve (1978) provides methodical procedures for eliminating duplications and redundancies, and identifying contradictions within the table. (An example of an error is two columns (rules) with the same conditions but different actions.) The size of tables should be limited to prevent errors (Parkin, 1980). Size guidelines are given by Gildersleeve (1978) – a table should fit on one page – and by Lee (1978) – a maximum of 4 conditions, giving 16 rules. Larger tables should be subdivided, leading to a hierarchy of tables.

Gildersleeve (1978) has a strong preference for decision tables, whereas Glass (1979) stated that they are only applicable to a limited range of problems. He also stated that because of this, and because staff lacked knowledge of the concept, the technique was not widely used. As Martin and McClure (1985) put it, decision tables have been 'surprisingly neglected'. However, 46% of the operational systems in the Lientz *et al.* (1978) survey used them, making them the most widely used of the aids surveyed; and according to Kessel (1975), decision table processors have been used extensively for data validation programs, so presumably even more people and programs use the technique without an automated aid. Furthermore, the statement by Couger *et al.* (1982) that 'it took so long

for industry to adopt the decision table approach', implies that they may now be widely used. Perhaps Glass and Martin and McClure were referring to the fact that early decision table processsors were not widely used – they were initially too slow (Couger *et al.*, 1982); or perhaps those systems which used the method did not make extensive use of it, because decision tables are only applicable to some types of program.

Flowcharts

Flowcharts are a long established tradition, and were by far the most commonly used method of documenting the design of a program (Glass, 1979; Dunn and Ullman, 1982). They can be used as either a design aid, or as documentation. They are unambiguous, and maintenance staff seemed to like them (Pomberger, 1984; Dunn and Ullman, 1982). However, they are currently in disfavor for a variety of reasons, e.g. they are time-consuming to update; they focus on process rather than structure; encourage abbreviation, which reduces their communication value; and provide no mechanical check against incompleteness, contradiction and redundancy (Gildersleeve, 1978). They have also been accused of encouraging GOTOs (Martin and McClure, 1985), but this is disputed by Macro and Buxton (1987), who describe them as 'entirely neutral', i.e. it is the *designer* who is to blame, and not the tool. They have been dismissed as 'oversold, a curse, obsolete'; of no value 'not even as a design aid'; and it was recommended that the US Department of Defense *not* procure them with delivered software (Brooks, 1975; Glass, 1979; Gildersleeve, 1978). According to Glass, the attacks were mostly directed at the documentation usage of flowcharts: as a design aid, they were still acknowledged as a reasonable alternative.

Experimental results quoted by Shneiderman (1980) and Conte *et al.* (1986) are mixed, with one experiment favoring flowcharts

(Kammann, 1975); and others showing mixed benefits, e.g. flowchart users made fewer mistakes initially but forgot the information sooner (Wright and Reid, 1973), or flowcharts assisted in program composition, but may hinder learning and comprehension (Mayer, 1975). To complicate the situation still further, the experiments by Shneiderman, Mayer *et al.*, McKay and Heller (Shneiderman, 1977) (and a repeat of them by Brooke and Duncan (1980)) are generally interpreted to show no advantage to flowcharts (Conte *et al.*, 1986; Shneiderman, 1980), but they may instead just show that practice is required in their use: the group which had apparently not been trained in their use performed better without them; but the group which had been trained generally performed better with them (though only by small margins).

However, these experiments apparently referred mainly to *detailed* flowcharts. Detailed flowcharts have been likened to studying a book in English, and a translation of the book in French (Conte *et al.*, 1986). The translation simply repeats what is in the original, and so is of no help to someone who cannot understand the original. Therefore, even if detailed flowcharts provide no signifi-cant advantage, e.g. because they are so spread out and merely duplicate the code, *summary* flowcharts of large programs, where each box represents about one page of code, should help show the relationships between the modules. Shneiderman (1980) speculated that right-brained (visually oriented) people prefer flowcharts, while left-brained (verbally oriented) people prefer source code. If up to 95% of computer professionals are left-brain dominant (Ruete, 1991), then the great major-ity of them should prefer source code, and perform better with code than with flow-charts, but the evidence quoted above is not as clear-cut as this. Furthermore, some of the disadvantages, such as being difficult to update, apply to alternative methods as well, and are alleviated by computerized graphics tools.

Nassi–Shneiderman diagrams

Nassi–Shneiderman diagrams (Nassi and Shneiderman, 1973) arose from the desire to develop a flowchart that restricted logic to the valid structured programming constructs (Gildersleeve, 1978). They are intended for use with top-down, stepwise refinement methods (Martin and McClure, 1985). They are used for detailed design and documen-tation, and are not suitable for showing the high-level control structure of a program. Unlike traditional flowcharts, Nassi–Shnei-derman diagrams can easily show nesting. They are also easier to read than traditional flowcharts, pseudocode, and detailed HIPO diagrams; and can be converted into program code more easily.

However, the diagrams do not show the interfaces between the components; they can only be used to design procedures, not data structures; they are not always easy to draw – in fact, they can take three or four times longer to draw than to write the equivalent pseudocode; and they are not database oriented, and do not link to a data model or a data dictionary (Martin and McClure, 1985). Furthermore, according to Macro and Buxton (1987), they 'lack all reference to time, con-currency, etc.,' and are suitable only for simple, small to medium applications; and according to Gildersleeve (1978), they are useless as a practical logic documentation tool, and the minimum addition required to make them useful is Yourdon's 'cycle struc-ture' (a single connector at the entrance to each module).

Data flow diagrams

Data flow diagrams (DFDs) are also known as 'bubble charts'. They are part of the struc-tured design methodology of the Yourdon group (Yourdon and Constantine, 1979), but are used with variations (mostly in the graphics standards) across other methodologies (Couger *et al.*, 1982). (An example is the Gane and Sarson (1979) version.) They are primarily a systems analysis tool, and are used to specify software requirements (Martin and McClure, 1985; Dunn and Ullman, 1982). They are a tool for top-down analysis, and can provide both high-level and detailed views of a system or program (Martin and McClure, 1985). They are a way of documenting systems, but can also serve as a design aid (Dunn and Ullman, 1982; Macro and Buxton, 1987). (Davis (1983c) described them as a good *starting* point for design.) They resemble flowcharts, but define the flow of data rather than the flow of program control. Put another way, they show *what* happens in the program or system, *not how* it happens. One therefore cannot determine from the diagram *which* path will be taken – it merely shows which paths *can* be taken (Dunn and Ullman, 1982).

As is the case with HIPO diagrams, data flow diagrams are well-covered in the literature, and many books give different advantages and disadvantages of them. Because of space considerations, no attempt is made to reproduce all this information here, but instead just a selection of the pros and cons, is given.

The Yourdon and Constantine version has four components:

- **data flow** through the system;
- **process** or transformation converting that data from input to output (represented by a circle or 'bubble');
- **data store**; and
- **terminator**, an external data source or destination. (The destination is also known as a 'sink'.)

Four is the minimum number required to model a commercial system (Couger *et al.*, 1982). The Gane and Sarson version has additional components and shows additional information, making it more powerful. Martin and McClure (1985) also imply that it is more suitable for computerized graphics.

Data flow diagrams can be drawn in three ways (Bell *et al.*, 1987):

- hierarchical decomposition (start with a single large 'bubble', and break it down into smaller 'bubbles');
- work backwards from the output; or
- work forwards from the input.

With hierarchical decomposition, process boxes are successively expanded to create more detailed diagrams (Martin and McClure, 1985). This is known as 'levelling'. The highest level represents the total system, while successive levels show more and more detail. For small, simple systems, only one or two levels are necessary; three levels should be adequate for most systems (Mittra, 1988). Each level should contain about seven processes – another example of the magical number seven, plus or minus two (Miller, 1956).

Couger *et al.* (1982) cited several weaknesses of the method. The creation of the hierarchical structure chart from the data flow diagram is poorly defined, causing the design to be poorly coupled to the results of the analysis. The method does not formally provide for an extensive documentation package – function description, processing logic detail, and output formats must all be added. It shows global structure, but local structure is at the option of the user. It does not show data structure.

Because the method is concise, shows a logical model of the system (i.e. independent of hardware, data structure, etc.), and is graphical, it is easily understandable by users, and so is an excellent communications tool between them and developers (Law and Longworth, 1987; Davis, 1983c). End users can be quickly taught to read, check, and sometimes even to draw the diagrams (Martin and McClure, 1985).

Martin and McClure (1985) also criticized the lack of documentation. To rectify this, a process specification for each box in the lowest level diagram is required. So also is a data dictionary containing definitions of all data. (This is not the same as a DBMS data dictionary.) The dictionary can include physical information as well, such as the data storage devices and data access methods. Other criticisms are that diagrams for complex projects become large and unwieldy, and are also difficult to update without a computerized graphics tool; and the technique is often used badly, both in production environments, and in textbooks and on courses. An example of poor use is when changes are made to low-level diagrams, and the developer does not go back to the higher-level diagrams and update them accordingly, resulting in inconsistencies. (Martin and McClure pointed out that not all computerized tools do this either.) Data flow diagrams are not good for drawing program architectures, and have been overused and misused in this area. Because of their inadequacies, they must be used in conjunction with other tools, and must preferably be linked to them, otherwise bad specifications, with inconsistencies, omissions, and ambiguities, often result. Improvements are required, to show synchronization among separate events, and data layering. However, Martin and McClure also have much praise for them. For example, they are an essential and valuable tool for understanding and charting the flow of documents and data in complex systems, and are an excellent overview tool.

Dunn and Ullman (1982) also had mixed comments. The diagrams make it easier to determine impossible operations (instructions that can never be executed), and data transformations that are incorrect, but for medium to large systems they can cover a great deal of paper.

Arthur (1988) described how the diagrams can help determine the cause of bugs.

Macro and Buxton (1987) praise them, as the notation is intuitively simple and relatively informal.

Bell *et al.* (1987) pointed out that the technique gives no guidance on how to design the insides of each module, so another technique, such as Jackson, should be used as well.

Automated tools are available. Data flow diagrams can be produced, for example, by Teamwork/SA (Chapter 6). The functions in this product are integrated, and include an editor for easy drawing and re-drawing of the diagrams, and an automated consistency checker (Charette, 1986). They can also be produced by 'Data Flow Diagrammer', which is one of the capabilities included in KnowledgeWare Incorporated's Information Engineering Workbench/Workstation (IEW/WS) (Simpson, 1987), and by Excelerator and STRADIS/DRAW (Martin and McClure, 1985). Excelerator links the diagramming technique to a data dictionary. Benefits claimed for STRADIS/DRAW are: significant time and cost savings, especially when changes are made; elimination of the potential for introducing errors when diagrams are updated (and therefore elimination of the need for proofreading); and it can produce very large diagrams.

Data flow diagrams have been widely used for many years in straightforward data processing (Macro and Buxton, 1987). In fact, along with structure charts, they are the most commonly used structured design methodology (Martin and McClure, 1985).

Entity-relationship diagrams

An 'entity' is a place, thing, person, event, idea, etc. (Simpson, 1987). Entities can either be real objects, such as people, books, machinery, or suppliers; or conceptual or abstract objects, such as orders and accounts (Law and Longworth, 1987). Each entity in an entity-relationship diagram should correspond to a data store in a data flow diagram, and vice versa (Mittra, 1988). The choice of entities depends on what is meaningful to the application. Poor initial choice can be corrected subsequently, so there is no need to delay making the decisions (Parkin, 1980).

Entities have *attributes*, e.g. color, value, name, place, or time. These correspond to fields in a record or columns in a table. Entity-relationships tend towards profuse documents which are not easy to follow without extensive experience with the technique (Macro and Buxton, 1987). Large diagrams, with more than a dozen or so entities, are difficult to draw, and very difficult to maintain, without computer graphics (Martin and McClure, 1985). This discourages changes, which is a serious disadvantage, especially on complex projects, as the more interaction, discussion, and modification at the planning and design stages, the better. Large diagrams may be impressive, but they are impractical. With computer graphics, subset diagrams can be made, and these are much more useful.

Comments

Some general advice is given by Arthur (1983).

- Most diagramming methods are manual. The diagrams are therefore not easily maintained, and so become out of date. They should therefore only be used at a high level.
- Organizations should select a standard, and stick to it: providing a programmer with IPO diagrams one day, and Nassi–Shneiderman diagrams the next, is not the way to improve productivity.
- The tools selected should not overlap: 'consider the redundancy in IPOs and pseudocode, or among data flow diagrams and structure charts'.

Similar advice is given by Martin and McClure (1985) and Couger *et al.* (1982). The detailed information they give – such as tables showing what each method can draw (none of the methods can draw everything that is needed); how easy each type of diagram is to draw, read, and modify; and whether executable code can be generated

automatically – is invaluable in setting up a policy.

Couger rated each tool according to how strongly it supported structure (system and program), control (system and program), data flow, data structure, communication, and documentation. If his individual ratings are added up (without applying any weightings), then it produces the following composite ranking, in descending order of power:

- Jackson charts
- HIPO (IPO Chart)
- Warnier–Orr diagrams
- Structure charts (Yourdon)
- HIPO (VTOC)
- Data flow diagrams
- Pseudocode
- Chapin charts
- Function descriptions

Martin and McClure's preferences are as follows.

- Processes
  - Strategic overview of corporate functions: action diagram
  - Logical relationship among processes: action diagram, HOS chart, or DFD
  - Overall program structure: action diagram or HOS chart
  - Detailed program logic: action diagram, decision table, or HOS chart
- Data
  - Strategic overview of corporate data: entity-relationship diagram
  - Detailed logical data model: entity-relationship diagram or data model
  - Program-level view of data: data model or data navigation diagram
  - Program usage of data: data navigation diagram, action diagram, or HOS chart.

('Data model' is a general term. It refers specifically to a detailed expansion of the entity-relationship diagram, and more generally to the different DBMS models – hierarchical, relational, etc. Martin and McClure (1985) define it as a map showing how the different data-item types in a database are associated with each other.)

The difference between the two lists of preferences – the lack of overlap – is striking. The second list is three year's later than the first (1985 compared to 1982), but this seems insufficient to account for such a large difference. It is probably attributable instead to differing emphasis and goals of the authors. Couger was probably concentrating on methods which were widely used; and Martin and McClure on methods which were newer and better, but which were not yet widely used. Zvegintzov (1989) stated that Arthur (1988) is 'much closer to reality' than Martin and McClure (1983). (These are both books about software maintenance.) Martin and McClure (1985) does set a very high standard, and hence Couger *et al.* (1982) might be rated as 'much closer to reality'.

Most of the top methods were discussed above. The most notable exceptions are: action diagrams and data navigation diagrams.

Action diagrams

Action diagrams look like a program design language with brackets added. They therefore combine graphics and narrative, but with the emphasis on narrative – 'it doesn't look much like my idea of a diagram' (Avison and Fitzgerald, 1988). They must not be confused with the activity diagrams from SADT (structured analysis and design technique) (Fairley, 1985). Action diagrams cover all levels from high-level overview to detailed program logic, which permits the design 'to move naturally between the high levels and the low levels' (Martin and McClure, 1985). By contrast, other techniques cover only part of the requirements, e.g. high-level only or low-level only, so a combination of incompatible methods has to be used. Action diagrams are claimed to be easy to construct and use, by both analysts and users (Avison and Fitzgerald, 1988). They are one of the capabi-

lities included in KnowledgeWare Incorporated's Information Engineering Workbench/ Workstation (IEW/WS), which is 'based largely on the design concepts and philosophies of James Martin' (Simpson, 1987). It incorporates consistency checking and an encyclopedia.

Data navigation diagrams

These show the sequence in which records in a database are accessed, superimposed on the data model. They lead to procedure design and, in turn, to structured program code. They highlight the transaction-driven nature of good database usage, which is beneficial, as many analysts find the design of such systems difficult to grasp, because they learned techniques that (like many structured techniques) are batch oriented (Martin and McClure, 1985).

These two methods are new, and are based on the work of James Martin. There is, as yet, a lack of corroborating evidence in the literature. It is therefore worth repeating the general advice given by Macro and Buxton (1987): 'be careful of claims made by their authors (and other enthusiasts)'.

8.4.4 CODING

The coding function has received much attention, perhaps because of its close relationship with structured programming – which is both a design and a coding philosophy (Dunn and Ullman, 1982) – or because improvements are more visible and measurable. The coding process is speeded up by the use of:

- high-level languages;
- technological aids such as pre-compilers and decision table processors;
- pre-written common modules (re-used code).

The GUIDE (1979) survey found that modern programming practices improved code quality.

Programs should be written so they are easy to understand. This can be achieved in several ways, some cosmetic and some more fundamental (related to program design).

Cosmetic readability can be achieved by following maxims such as (Van Tassel, 1978; Martin and McClure, 1985; Arthur, 1988; Boehm, 1981):

- use prologue comments;
- incorrect comments are worse than no comments at all;
- comments should explain what the code does not show clearly;
- use blank spaces to improve readability;
- use good mnemonics for paragraph and data names;
- use a prefix or suffix on file names;
- one statement per line is enough;
- parentheses are cheaper than errors;
- use indentation to show logic structure;
- use indentation to show data structure.

(A mnemonic is a name which is designed to aid the memory.)

Comments should include the objectives, assumptions, and constraints, i.e. not just *what* is being done, but also *why* (Boehm, 1981).

More fundamental rules include (Yourdon, 1975; Weinberg, 1971):

- do not use program switches;
- restrict the size of modules;
- do not use the COBOL ALTER verb;
- limit the sharing of variables;
- do not misuse language instructions.

The ALTER verb can change the execution of a program while it is running, making it very difficult to determine the action of a program simply by looking at its source coding (Verity, 1986c). The REDEFINES clause in COBOL has been accused of clouding the logic of programs (Verity, 1986c). Arthur (1988) described NOT logic (e.g. IF A NOT = B) as 'particularly nasty'. It 'omits more than it tells, which is why programmers have such a hard time understanding them', especially when they are coupled with ANDs and ORs. He gave examples of restructured code in which the NOT logic had been reversed. In most cases, this required the addition of an ELSE clause to the IF statement. However, this is beneficial, as one of the most frequent logic errors is *missing* logic, and expanding the logic in this way minimizes the risk of any of it being overlooked and omitted.

Apart from the misuse of language instructions, the above rules are not limitations imposed by compilers, but are rather standards set by each installation and so vary from one installation to another.

Adhering to these rules will not necessarily speed up coding – it may even be slowed down – but it should speed up maintenance and debugging, because readable programs are easier to understand and so can be modified quickly and without introducing errors.

There is, however, a difference of opinion over some of the above maxims.

Source code comments

While most authorities advocate the use of comments in program source code – 'there is nothing in the programming field more despicable than an uncommented program' – in practice, the comments may be redundant, obsolete, incorrect, vague, incomplete, or indecipherable by anyone other than the original programmer (Yourdon, 1975). They are dangerous, and interfere with debugging by misleading the programmer, if not updated when the program is changed. They are particularly misleading when the code is incorrect, but the comment is correct (Weinberg, 1971). In addition, some people argue that they obscure the code; disrupt visual scanning; and introduce more page turns because they lengthen the program (Shneiderman, 1980). For these reasons, many experienced programmers cover all the comments when scrutinizing the source code for errors. Weinberg stated that, for certain unspecified types of code, programs can be understood faster and more reliably without comments. Experimental evidence is inconsistent.

- According to Yourdon (1975), some unnamed experiments have shown it is faster and easier to fix bugs in someone else's program by first removing all the comments.
- An experiment by Okimoto (1970) found that uncommented programs could be understood more quickly.
- One by Newsted found no difference (Schneiderman, 1980).
- While ones by Woodfield *et al.* (1981a), Weissman (1974a, 1974b), Yasukawa, and Shneiderman (Shneiderman, 1980), produced results which were generally favorable to the use of comments, with an advantage of up to 20% (e.g. in recall, or in finding and fixing bugs) – heavily commented programs proved superior to lightly commented ones; and a block of comments at the beginning of a subroutine proved superior to individual comments spread throughout the subroutine (though possibly only because the block in this experiment consisted of a high-level functional description, whereas the individual comments were low-level ones which merely repeated what the statement did).

Mnemonics

Intuitively, it would seem desirable to use meaningful variable and procedure names, but experimental results are inconsistent.

- Experiments by Weissman (1974a, 1974b) and McKay (Shneiderman, 1980) showed an advantage of up to 40% in comprehension scores and debugging for the use of mnemonics.
- An experiment by Dunsmore (1985) showed an advantage of nearly 2:1 in recall or look-up time, and of nearly 6:1 in accuracy.
- An experiment by Newsted surprisingly

found that programs with non-mnemonic names were easier to understand (Shneiderman, 1980).

The value of some of these experiments must, however, be questioned, as Newsted's test programs contained comments, and in one of McKay's experiments the programmers were familiar with the algorithm, which would have reduced or negated any advantage of mnemonics.

Experiments have also been conducted to determine the optimum name length. The experiment by Dunsmore found that names of 9–12 characters in length resulted in 50% more errors, and took about 20% longer to recall or look up, than names of 5–8 characters; and an experiment by Conte *et al.* found that names of 10–30 characters resulted in about 20% fewer correct answers than names of 5–9 characters. Short names may be so abbreviated that many are similar, resulting in errors when trying to recall them; but long names inevitably mean more to remember (and take longer to enter at a keyboard), and so have greater scope for error.

Van Tassel (1978) recommended that standard abbreviations be used, otherwise three different programmers might, for example, use MSTR, MAST, and MST, as abbreviations for MASTER, making it more difficult for them to understand each other's programs, or at least slowing down reading and understanding. Jackson (1967) gave a set of rules for abbreviating, e.g.:

- a maximum of three words in the abbreviation;
- initial letters must always be present;
- delete vowels rather than consonants.

A simple guideline therefore, is to delete vowels from right to left.

Weinberg (1971) gave examples of misleading names, e.g. PEND might be short for 'pending', or for 'end of part P'. He also quoted a case where a symbol named FIVE contained the value 4 which, not surprisingly, led to confusion and wasted time. (It originally contained the value 5, but the program was modified, and the programmer did not have enough time to change all the references to it, so he kept the original name.) Mnemonics, like source code comments, should therefore be updated.

Indentation

Intuitively, it would seem desirable to indent source coding. This is widely recommended, programmers prefer it (Shneiderman, 1980), and there are tools available to do it, e.g. dAnalyst for dBASE III programs, and RECODER for COBOL programs (TranSec, 1986; Language Technology, 1987b), but once again, experimental results are inconsistent, with most showing no significant advantage (particularly if the programs are commented), and others showing only a small advantage (20% at most) (Love, 1977; Weissman, 1974a, 1974b; Shneiderman and McKay, 1976). Indentation apparently disrupts visual program scanning (Shneiderman, 1980). Furthermore, the coding in deeply nested programs is shifted to the right, effectively shortening the lines, and thereby forcing some to be split. Shneiderman therefore suggested using blank lines instead, to separate functional units.

8.4.5 TESTING AND DEBUGGING

Testing

Testing is the primary verification and validation technique, but is nevertheless merely an *ad hoc* process, based on heuristic rules – though these are well thought-out (Martin and McClure, 1985). Less seems to be known about testing than any other aspect of software development, and there is a sparsity of literature on the topic (Myers, 1979). Andriole (1986), de Millo *et al.* (1987), Hetzel (1987), Myers (1979) and Perry (1983) are among the few books devoted largely or exclusively to the subject.

Traditionally, a test is viewed as successful if no errors are revealed. This results in such statements as 'the system has passed all its tests', which can lead to misplaced complacency, as large programs are rarely, if ever, bug-free (Sommerville, 1989). The failure of the test suite to detect errors therefore does not necessarily mean that the program does not contain errors, but rather that the tests chosen have not exercised the system in such a way that the errors are revealed. To overcome this attitude, testing is defined by Myers (1979) as: 'the process of executing a program with the intent of finding errors'. A test is therefore successful if it finds an error, and unsuccessful if it does not. This is the opposite way round from the customary viewpoint. By changing the goal of testing in this way, its effectiveness is improved.

Testing is inherently an extremely difficult and mentally taxing task (Myers, 1979), particularly in the case of interactive systems (Shneiderman, 1980). It requires 'unorthodox thinking patterns, a willingness to explore unusual circumstances, and the capacity to break away from mainline behavior' (Shneiderman, 1980). It therefore demands great creativity. Test personnel are responsible for preventing unreliable software from reaching the user (Cho, 1987). They can help save users millions of dollars, and even prevent loss of human lives. The best personnel must therefore be assigned to design, implement and analyse test data and test results. In spite of this, testing has been considered a less prestigious activity than design. It is looked on as a tedious, uninteresting task. Too often, inexperienced and junior people are assigned to this important activity, resulting in the unreliability of many software products.

Testing has other disadvantages: it is performed late in the development process, and is invariably inefficient and usually expensive as well (Martin and McClure, 1985; Jones, 1986b). The inefficiency, however, may be due to the factors identified above.

Methods

Testing should be performed in a systematic or 'structured' manner (Walsh, 1977). It can be performed in a top-down or a bottom-up fashion, or in a mixture of the two so as to derive the advantages of each method. Top-down tests the top modules first, using stubs for the remaining modules (Martin and McClure, 1985). This method has a number of advantages, e.g. the high-level modules (which represent the overall structure of the program) are tested more often, and errors in them are detected sooner; and it supports incremental delivery of systems (Arthur, 1988). (With incremental delivery, the system is built and delivered to the user in stages, instead of all at once (Gilb, 1988).) However, top-down testing can be carried to extremes: the entire system may be used as a test driver for program modules as they are developed, which results in elaborate runs with correspondingly long turnaround (Boehm, 1981). Bottom-up tests the lowest-level modules first. This method tests the lowest-level modules more often, which is valuable if the lowest-level functions are the most complex, or when execution speed is critical; but it postpones testing of the highest-level logic, which can result in extensive rework of the system – every module may have to be changed – if there are design errors at the higher levels (Arthur, 1988; Yourdon and Constantine, 1979). It also necessitates the construction of test drivers or harnesses – temporary programs that call the module being tested in a way that simulates its eventual role in the complete system (Martin and McClure, 1985; Bell *et al.*, 1987).

In practice, there is little to choose between the top-down and bottom-up strategies (Macro and Buxton, 1987). Most small- and medium-sized systems seem to be tested on a bottom-up basis; while many large and very large systems seem to be tested on a top-down or quasi top-down basis. The relative costs of the two approaches are similar.

Macro and Buxton recommend a careful, incremental approach: 'build a bit, test a bit; build a bit more, test a bit more'.

Testing can be either 'black-box' (functional) or 'white-box' (structural) (Van Tassel, 1978; Myers, 1979; Martin and McClure, 1985). In 'black-box' testing, test cases are designed from the program specifications alone, so no knowledge of the internals of the program is required. In 'white-box' testing, test cases are designed by considering the internal structure of the program. (This is why it is also known as 'glass-box', which is a more meaningful description (Bell *et al.*, 1987)). The two types of testing are therefore likely to find different types of error, so both should be used. This is known as 'gray-box' testing (Arthur, 1988). According to Fairley (1985), black-box testing and a programmer's intuition together achieve a 60–70% statement coverage. White-box testing considers the number of paths in the program. Structured programming reduces the number of paths, thereby simplifying testing (Martin and McClure, 1985).

Another method of testing – though it 'is more talked about than actually practised' (Jones, 1986b) – is intentional failure or 'bebugging' (Glass, 1979; Van Tassel, 1978). Bugs are deliberately inserted ('seeded') into the program by a second party. The success with which the original programmer finds the inserted bugs provides an indication of how many genuine bugs remain, and the time taken can be used to estimate how much more time should be allowed. This technique requires that someone other than the original programmer know the program, which could add 20% to the testing cost (Glass, 1979). Other disadvantages are that it is difficult to design good bugs, and there is no guarantee that the inserted bugs will be representative of the actual errors (Glass, 1979; Weinberg, 1971), though collecting statistics by error type from real programs can help (Gilb, 1977). However, this method can motivate the error seeker to find the errors: 'if he didn't find them, other people would know about it' (Weinberg, 1971).

A number of maxims are given by Myers (1979), Martin and McClure (1985), McClure (1981), Cho (1987) and Van Tassel (1978), including:

- start testing early;
- schedule adequate time for testing;
- assign the best personnel to the task;
- keep the software static during testing;
- hand test the design first;
- try out a simple first version to test the basic design;
- calculate the expected output before the test is executed;
- document test cases and test results;
- test the simplest cases first;
- test valid input data before exception conditions;
- examining a program to see if it does not do what it is supposed to do is only half the battle – the other half is seeing whether the program does what it is not supposed to do;
- keep in mind the difference between correctness and usability;
- a good test case is one that has a high probability of detecting an as-yet undiscovered error;
- test the normal, extreme, and exception cases – over half the errors in the Thayer *et al.* (1976) study occurred when the software was handling data singularities and extreme points;
- retest after every change (regression testing).

A programmer should avoid testing his own program, as author's tend to be 'blind' to their errors, and an error may be incorporated into the test in exactly the same way as it occurs in the code (Macro and Buxton, 1987). Worse, programmers do not want to see evidence that their creations are imperfect, so consciously or subconsciously, program tests will be selected which fail to find an error (Sommerville, 1989). Macro and Buxton

therefore describe testing by the authors as 'benevolent'. By contrast, the existence of an independent testing group has been cited as the key to the quality ethic (Joyce, 1989). On the other hand, the original programmers' detailed knowledge of the structure of a program can be extremely useful in identifying appropriate test cases (Sommerville, 1989).

If many errors are discovered in a program during testing, then it may be advisable to rewrite it. (The average rate of 40 errors per 1000 LOC in Table 8.42, can be used as a basis for deciding if the number of errors is excessive.)

Amount of testing

In most cases, exhaustive testing is impossible because of the virtually infinite number of possible test cases (Myers, 1979; Boehm, 1973) – Van Tassel (1978) gives an example of a very small and simple program which could nevertheless take 50 *billion* years of machine time to test, if all the 2^{64} possible input values were tested! A carefully selected subset of the test cases must therefore be made, to provide a range of different tests which is representative and comprehensive, but manageable in size. However, even carefully selected test cases may overlook some conditions, so there is an advantage in using completely random data as well. The best approximation to random input has come from real-time and time-sharing production systems (Boehm, 1981).

Because of the impossibility of exhaustive testing, it is not cost-effective to test for 100% defect-free software. Arthur (1988) and Dunn and Ullman (1982) therefore gave guidelines for deciding when to stop testing, e.g. when the rate of error detection decreases to below a pre-determined limit, or when a certain number of error-free tests have been performed. The amount of testing necessary depends on the type of program (e.g. batch programs need less than real-time) and the consequences of an error (e.g. if human life would be endangered), and therefore varies from one system to another.

Some programmers, having lived with the same program for weeks, are impatient to go on to new things, and so tend to be hasty with testing; while others are afraid of being recalled to the program if it fails in the future, and so are very thorough (Dunn and Ullman, 1982).

A small system would probably be subjected to only two stages of testing: testing of each program individually, and testing of the system as a whole. Larger systems would undergo additional stages, e.g. testing of individual modules, integration testing, acceptance testing, installation testing, alpha and beta testing, and field testing (Van Tassel, 1978; Glass, 1979; Myers, 1979; Lee, 1978). Included in these tests might be: boundary tests, parallel running, volume testing, performance testing, recovery testing, stress (overload) testing, and so on. Lists of definitions can be found, for example, in Van Tassel (1978), but different authorities define these terms differently. For example, Gilb (1988) defines alpha testing variously as module or unit testing and author testing, and beta testing as system testing; while Macro and Buxton (1987) define alpha testing as exhaustive testing of the whole system by the author or other team members, and beta testing as independent second-party testing; alternatively alpha testing is by the organization which developed the software, and beta testing is by selected customers voluntarily acting as guinea pigs. Therefore no attempt at precise definitions of these terms is made here. Suffice to say that the cost of all this testing can be high.

Tools

Technological aids, such as interactive programming, test drivers, test coverage analysers, environment simulators, test data generators and file comparators, assist the

Table 8.65

Type of testing	Typical efficiency
Unit testing (single modules)	25%
Function testing (related modules)	35%
Integration testing (complete system)	45%
Field testing (live data)	50%

Source: Jones (1986b)

testing process (Chapter 6). Static analysers (Chapter 10) can also help, by pointing out which modules are complex and therefore error-prone, and so will require additional testing, or should even be re-written. However, the various tools are expensive to acquire and use, and a different tool may be needed for each capability, so a combination of tools must be used, yet they are not integrated: 'test-support environments that include an integrated package of powerful tools are yet to be developed' (Martin and McClure, 1985). 4GLs reduce the amount of testing required, and can even eliminate some testing, particularly white-box testing (Chapter 6).

Effectiveness

According to Gilb (1988), testing is a maximum of 50–55% effective at defect identification and removal for a single test process.

Jones (1986b) gave the observed defect removal efficiencies given in Table 8.65.

Myers (1979) described three experiments to determine which method of testing is the most effective.

1. The first experiment found black-box testing and white-box testing to be equally effective. They were more effective than individual code reading, but only about half the errors were found (Hetzel, 1976).
2. In the first part of the second experiment, black-box testing, a combination of black- and white-box testing, and three-person code inspections were found to be equally

effective in detecting errors, but the code inspections used more time (Myers, 1978). In the second part of the experiment, two pairs of people independently tested the program, and their time and results were pooled. They found different errors, so a greater total number of errors was found, but more time was consumed, giving the same time per error ratio as the basic methods. Although all the subjects in the experiment were highly experienced – 7–20 years experience, though some were not currently practising programmers (Lucas, 1985) – there were large variations in their performance.

Only a little more than one-third of the errors were found.

(Because the subjects in this experiment were so experienced, the results are very disappointing. However, Boehm (1981) pointed out that some of the errors were much more subtle than normal, so it is risky to try to generalize from them.)

3. The third experiment showed no difference in effectiveness between testing by the original programmer, and testing by a second party (Musa, 1976).

Schach (1990) quoted two experiments comparing black-box testing, glass-box testing, and code inspection by one person, which produced the following results.

1. In the first experiment (Hwang, 1981) found all three methods equally effective.
2. In the second experiment, Basili and Selby (1987) tested 3 groups:
   - 32 professional programmers – code reading detected more faults than the other two methods, and the fault detection rate was faster;
   - Group 1 of 42 advanced students – no significant difference between the three methods; and
   - Group 2 of the students – code reading and black-box testing were equally good, and both outperformed glass-box testing.

The rates at which the students detected faults were the same for all methods.

Overall, code reading led to the detection of more interface faults than did the two testing methods, while black-box testing was most successful at finding control faults.

The main conclusion that can be drawn is that one-person code inspection is at least as successful at detecting faults as glass-box and black-box testing.

Boehm (1981) reported the results of several studies of the effectiveness of unit testing (Table 8.66). The Jones (1977) figures refer to code which had previously been inspected. There were thus fewer errors to be found by testing, and this also permitted a faster testing rate.

On average, therefore, and excluding Jones, unit testing proceeded at the rate of 14 delivered source instructions per man-hour, and found 58% of the errors. Comparing these figures with those given in Table 10.13 for code inspections, implies that unit testing requires three times as much effort as code inspections (only 14 statements per hour compared to 40), but only finds about as many errors (58% compared to 60%).

Taken together, these results suggest that each type of test typically finds less than 50% of the errors, but a *combination* of several types is much more effective.

The figures in Table 8.66 indicate that, where fewer delivered source instructions were tested per man-hour – in other words, where more effort was expended – more errors were detected. In fact, where 10 or fewer delivered source instructions were tested per man-hour, the effectiveness was nearly twice as high as when the rate was 20 or more: an average of about 70% compared to an average of under 40% (even if the Jones figures are excluded). A testing rate of 20 or more statements per man-hour therefore

Table 8.66 Unit testing – effort and effectiveness (Boehm, 1981)

Source	Effort (delivered LOC/ man-hour)	Error removal
Jones (1977)	18–40	20% (after inspection)
Myers (1978)	24	36
Project A	20	40
"	10	68
"	5	89
Crossman (1979b)	10	50–60
Average (approximate)	16	50
Excluding Jones	14	58

finds just under 40% of the errors if the code has not previously been inspected, compared to 20% if it has.

Installation

The installation of a system may be viewed as the final part of the testing function, but can also be viewed as a separate function. The extra attention resulting from the latter approach caters better for systems installed at multiple sites: more problems are likely in such cases. It has another benefit. Installation tends to be neglected, and this can have serious and expensive consequences, e.g. errors might go undetected, or operational difficulties might go unresolved, prejudicing users against the system, or even making the system impractical to run.

Lucas (1985) gave an example of an airline reservations system, where a spotlight shone on the CRTs, making them difficult to read. Furthermore, the terminals were positioned in such a way that the operators (who were not typists), had to bend slightly to use them. The net result was that the computerized system was several times *slower* than the old, manual system. He also gave an example of a pilot test at which the entire computer staff were present in the small user department to answer questions. However, they were not present when the full-scale system was intro-duced into the whole manufacturing plant, with the result that it was a total disaster.

These examples emphasize the importance of including all aspects, and not just programming aspects, in testing, and of making the test situation as realistic and representative of actual operations as possible.

User involvement

User involvement is a two-way process. On the one hand, feedback from the user leads to improvements to the system. In particular, users may get lost in the technicalities of the system specifications, but they normally understand the data being processed, and so can say if the test cases being developed are realistic, and the test results correct, and can even develop test data themselves (Gildersleeve, 1978). On the other hand, the user learns how to run the system. If the user was closely involved with the project throughout its development, e.g. if a prototype was set up or a pilot study done, then much of this interchange of knowledge will already have occurred; if not, then it must be done at installation time, and it must not be rushed (Lucas, 1985). User involvement with testing, and DP involvement with installation, should continue past initial learning and other problems (Shneiderman, 1980). Training of users should include a training manual; a phased step-by-step training programme; and even a training mode built into the system, so new users can run it without the danger of corrupting live data.

The future

Martin and McClure (1985) paint a gloomy picture. Not only was there no solid theoretical foundation for testing, no mathematical rigor, but research was likely to lead to a dead end. Nevertheless, if the advice given above was followed, e.g. if there were more books on the subject, if the best personnel were assigned to testing, if testing was more organized and comprehensive – and if people were *taught* how to do testing – then its effectiveness would be greatly improved.

Debugging

Millions of dollars are spent on this activity, yet it has received far less attention than it deserves (Cho, 1987). It is a mini software life-cycle, directed toward developing a program part to replace a wrong program part, and comprises requirements definition, design, coding, and (re)testing.

Debugging is a two-part process (Van Tassel, 1978):

- determining the exact nature and location of an error whose existence has been established; and
- fixing the error.

Locating the error consumes 95% of the debugging time (Myers, 1979).

Debugging is a difficult task (Cho, 1987). In fact, according to Myers (1979), it is the most mentally taxing of all software development activities, and it is usually performed under pressure. Worse, although programmers are often trained in programming, they are seldom trained in debugging (Van Tassel, 1978), so they do not know where to look for errors, and often waste a great deal of effort looking in the wrong place – e.g. they concentrate on normal processing at the

expense of special processing situations and invalid input (Myers, 1978). They then find it difficult to look elsewhere, because their thinking becomes locked on one possible cause, blinding them to other possibilities (Weinberg, 1971). They do not know what errors are most likely to occur, nor do they know when they have isolated all aspects of an error, nor how to track its total effect through the program (Martin and McClure, 1985). Programmers are therefore not very successful at finding errors.

It is best to get the program right the first time and thereby avoid bugs, because debugging is so expensive (Van Tassel, 1978).

Thayer *et al.* (1976) showed that a managerial directive to fix all problems quickly leads to minor, simple errors being fixed quickly. A better directive would therefore be to fix the serious problems first.

Curtis *et al.* (1979b) showed that Halstead's effort metric is well correlated with the observed effort to debug small programs.

Defensive programming

Traditionally, data is validated when it enters a computer system, and thereafter it is assumed to be correct (Bell *et al.*, 1987). This assumes that the error-filtering process is water-tight, and that no errors are introduced subsequently (e.g. by software bugs). By contrast, 'defensive programming' assumes that errors will occur, e.g. that bad data will be passed to a subroutine, that table subscripts will overflow and overwrite other parts of the program, that there will be blanks in numeric fields, that attempts will be made to divide by zero, that update programs will delete records which should not be deleted, and so on (Van Tassel, 1978; Arthur, 1983).

Defensive programming aims to simplify the debugging task, e.g. by checking data at strategic points in a system, or by having control totals in update programs to balance input and output record counts, and by putting out error messages which are meaningful, relevant, comprehensive, and constructive (Chorafas, 1986). This entails an overhead for both compile time and run time.

These checks may be at compile time or at run time. A debugging (checkout) compiler checks more thoroughly for syntax errors by examining the interaction of instructions as well as the correctness of each single instruction. It checks, for example, for undeclared variables and data type inconsistencies at compile time; and it performs checks such as out-of-range subscripts and uninitialized variables during program execution (Van Tassel, 1978; Martin and McClure, 1985). Debugging compilers are therefore a form of defensive programming.

Compile time checking can *prevent* a program from crashing, is very cheap, and need only be done once (Bell *et al.*, 1987). (In practice, of course, most programs are compiled more than once; but nevertheless, they are run much more often than they are compiled.) By comparison, run time checking is like an aircraft 'black-box' flight recorder, which is powerless to prevent an aircraft from crashing, but can be used in diagnosis to ascertain what happened, after the event. Run time checking is also a continual overhead, slowing down the program. As a result, such checks are usually switched off when development is complete. This has been likened to testing a ship with the lifeboats on board, but then discarding them when the ship starts to carry passengers (Bell *et al.*, 1987). (In fairness though, many jobs, particularly batch jobs, can easily be rerun, with the extra checks re-activated.)

Compile time checking is therefore superior to run time checking, but it cannot check everything, so run time checking is vital (Bell *et al.*, 1987).

Error detection code adds complexity, so it is possible to introduce more errors than the code will detect (Arthur, 1983).

Fault tolerance

'Fault-tolerant' software takes defensive programming one step further. It aims to minimize the harmful effects of an error, e.g. by permitting the program to continue running wherever possible: an operating system, for example, should not abort. This, however, is difficult. As Glass (1979) put it: 'How do you anticipate an error when, if you knew it existed, you would obviously seek to eliminate it? And how does a software system adjust itself to overcome the problem?' He listed four techniques to provide a fault-tolerant capability:

- confinement of the error to the portion of the program where it occurred;
- error detection procedures (extra code to test for errors);
- error recovery procedures (to resume correct processing after the error, or even to replace bad data with valid values);
- dual programming (e.g. two different teams develop the same system, and when the computer detects an error in one version, it switches to the other).

(Replacing bad data with valid values might seem impossible, but Weinberg (1971) gave examples, e.g. when a compiler detects an error, it can attempt to correct it, and ask the programmer to confirm its choice: 'This is the way we interpret your statements. If any are incorrect, please retype the statement correctly' (Klerer and May, 1965). (In this example, the source code of one program is the input data to another program, the compiler.))

Dual programming, as might be expected, can nearly double development costs (Glass, 1979). Error confinement, detection, and recovery can increase total costs by at least 35%.

Various hardware and DBMS features, such as disk mirroring, concurrent update, logical unit of work (LUW), before and after images, and dual logging (Chapters 5 and 6) also provide fault tolerance, to hardware as well as program failures (Mittra, 1988).

Tools

Some technological aids assist debugging, e.g. debugging compilers, source language debug, interactive debug, and assertion checkers (Chapter 6).

Methods

There are several basic methods of debugging (Myers, 1979; Fairley, 1985):

- **brute force**, which requires little thought but is inefficient;
- **induction**, which uses the symptoms of the error as its starting point;
- **deduction**, which works by a process of elimination;
- **backtracking**, which works backwards from where the error was observed;
- **testing**, which varies test cases to pinpoint the error.

Debugging by testing is used with the induction and deduction methods.

General problem-solving guidelines are given below (Fairley, 1985; Arthur, 1988; Myers, 1979):

1. Collect all the available information.
2. Define the problem (e.g. look for clues, such as a pattern in incorrect results).
3. Develop hypotheses about the cause (use your experience, checklists, and the most common causes of errors).
4. Select the most likely ones.
5. Select a strategy for proving or disproving these hypotheses.
6. Compare each hypothesis in turn against the available evidence.
7. When a hypothesis is found which fits all the evidence, implement the appropriate corrections (either to a back-up copy of the code, or after having made a back-up).

8. Verify that the corrections fix the observed symptoms (and that they have not introduced any other problems).

(These guidelines are based on the induction method, but guidelines based on the deduction method would be similar.)

Arthur (1988) described several different strategies:

- **top-down** – start from the (high-level) structure chart, and identify in which module the error is most likely to be;
- **bottom-up** – start from the field in error, and work backwards;
- **fan-out** – start from the field in error, and use the compiler cross-reference listing to find every statement that modifies it;
- **fan-in** – start from where the data enters or leaves the program, and work inwards into the software.

Traditional debugging methods include (Arthur, 1988; Van Tassel, 1978; Fairley, 1985):

- putting traces into the program: this might consist, for example, of just displaying paragraph names to show control flow, or it might mean inserting statements to display the contents of selected variables;
- examining the input data, as the garbage output may simply be a reflection of garbage input;
- printing a memory dump, to give a 'snapshot' of the program at the time the error occurred.

More modern techniques include the interactive debugging capabilities (Chapter 6), assertion-driven debugging, and execution histories (Fairley, 1985). An example of an assertion is comparing the value contained in a variable against a constant, or against the value in another variable, e.g. IF $I < 10$, or IF $A = B$. With assertion-driven debugging, certain assertions are inserted into the program. If an assertion is violated, then the program will take certain specified action, such as passing control to the user's terminal. An execution history 'is a record of execution events collected from an executing program'. It is stored typically in a database, and is examined after the program has terminated, e.g. you can trace backwards to see how a computation was influenced by previous events.

Debugging may be performed by the original programmer, or by another programmer. The latter is known as foreign debug, or second-party debugging (Glass, 1979; Myers, 1979). As with bebugging, foreign debug requires that someone other than the original programmer know the program, which could add 20% to the testing cost (Glass, 1979), but it can motivate the original programmer to write better programs: if he knows that someone else will be reading his program, seeing his poor techniques, and finding his mistakes, he may be more careful (Van Tassel, 1978). Debugging by a second party is effective because it avoids the blind spot or 'psychological set' of the original programmer (Aron, 1974; Weinberg, 1971) – in fact, according to Knight (1978), computer-based debugging by the original programmer appears to be one of the least efficient debugging methods. However, second-party debugging may prevent the original programmer learning from his mistakes. Furthermore, when it is their own error, 'they become much more interested in discussing how to prevent it. They are much more likely to suggest meaningful ideas because they understand the error more thoroughly' (Jones, 1985). There are subtle reasons for making some errors, and the apparent cause may not be remotely related to the real cause. Another danger is that programmers who are rushed, or who do not take a pride in their work, may become even more careless, knowing that someone else will have to clean up the mess. (The Big Eight accounting firms in the USA 'do nice clean jobs when they're going to have to certify the results a few months later' (Hodges, 1987a).)

Myers (1979), Arthur (1988), and Yourdon (1975) give several maxims, including:

- use debugging tools only as a second resort;
- see if the error is repeatable and consistent;
- isolate one error at a time;
- be thorough, methodical, and logical;
- investigate the simplest clues first;
- investigate the most likely cause first;
- don't take anything for granted;
- if you reach an impasse, sleep on it;
- if you reach an impasse, describe the problem to someone else;
- fix the error, not just a symptom of it.

Having found the error, the programmer should look for similar errors in the rest of the program (or JCL), as most programmers make the same errors repeatedly (Martin and McClure, 1985). Weinberg (1971) related the story of the 'mad bomber', who had made the same mistake in each of the three steps in his job. The programmer should also look for other errors in the same portion of the program (or JCL), as 'bugs tend to cluster' (Arthur, 1988) – the probability of more errors in a section of a program is proportional to the number of errors already found in that section (Myers, 1979). As Davisson so graphically put it: 'Where you see one cockroach, you know there are hundreds you do not see' (Verity, 1986c). In one extensive study, T.C. Jones found that the average module was compiled 30–50 times during development, but that those modules that later turned out to be defect-prone (more than 100 defects per thousand lines of executable code), had had to be compiled more than twice as often (De-Marco, 1982).

Myers (1979) places his emphasis on *thinking*, whereas Van Tassel (1978) places more emphasis on debugging *aids*. However, Van Tassel does quote (unnamed) studies in which the people who used the computer were no faster at debugging than those who merely read the program listing; and Myers quotes experiments in which those people who used aids (such as the expected versus the actual output) were no more successful (Gould, 1975; Gould and Drongowski, 1974), which is surprising, but they may have used them as a *substitute* for thinking. As Wirth (1987) put it, people rely on tools and think less carefully. Nevertheless, it seems reasonable to suppose that the *intelligent* use of aids increases effectiveness.

Much can be learned by analysing every error (Myers, 1979):

- When was it made?
- Who made it?
- What caused it?
- How could it have been prevented?
- Why was it not detected earlier?
- How could it have been detected earlier?
- How was it found?
- What methods were used to find it?
- What were the finder's thought processes?

The knowledge thus gained can be invaluable, both in preventing repetitions of the same types of error, and in recognizing the cause of an error from its symptoms should it recur, which will decrease debugging time (Yourdon, 1975; Myers, 1979; Van Tassel, 1978).

A good system contains software monitoring probes which tabulate errors (Shneiderman, 1980).

The above techniques, coupled with general problem-solving techniques, would change debugging from an art into a structured methodology (Yourdon, 1975).

Effectiveness

Despite the large amount of time spent debugging, very little research has been conducted into the subject. Myers (1979) quoted only three experiments:

- the experiments which showed that aids, such as expected versus actual output, did not increase debugging effectiveness (Gould, 1975; Gould and Drongowski, 1974); and
- an experiment which showed that the

original programmer and a second party were equally effective in debugging (Musa, 1976).

Martin and McClure (1985) quoted several studies and opinions:

- Myers found that the most cost-effective method for finding errors was to employ two programmers who work independently of one another, and later pool their results (Shneiderman, 1980).
- Fagan found that group walkthroughs and inspections were a more effective debugging method (in terms of programmer time and computer time) than when the original programmers debugged their own code individually (Shneiderman, 1980).
- Experiments by Gilb (1977) showed that simple source code reading is more effective than use of test data in finding errors.
- Similarly, Shneiderman (1980) claimed that the source listing is the most important debugging aid.
- Van Tassel (1978) believes that desk-checking a source listing can be as effective as studying program dumps.
- Weinberg (1971) suggested that automatically generated flow diagrams can be used to supplement code reading.

Shneiderman (1980) quoted several additional experiments, but confined his comments largely to error statistics rather than debugging methods. However, he did point out that giving the programmer the line number of the error (as generally happens with say a zero divide), halved debug time (Gould and Drongowski, 1974); that an interactive debug system which was available in one experiment was rarely used, even though the participants were familiar with it (Gould, 1975); and that experienced programmers were more competent at removing bugs (Youngs, 1974).

Conclusion

Martin and McClure (1985) recommended the following composite method. Two second-party programmers should work independently, using a combination of desk checking and computerized debugging tools, and then pool their results. Using more than one method, and more than one debugger, may seem extravagant, but it is cost-effective because more errors are found sooner, and it provides mutual support and education: 'a better program and better programmers will result'.

8.4.6 DOCUMENTATION

General information about documentation is given below. Specific types of documentation were discussed under the function they are most closely associated with, e.g. specifications under requirements/specifications, flowcharts under design, and source program comments under coding.

Documentation must, of course, be accurate, current, and thorough (Dunn and Ullman, 1982).

Some organizations have found that documentation is improved by having professional documenters: their work is uniform and of high quality, reflecting a pride in their job, and skill gained from experience (Shneiderman, 1980). Also, software engineers do not like doing documentation (Macro and Buxton, 1987); Yourdon (1975) quoted one program, written by a super-programmer, which contained just *one* comment!

Documentation is an integral part of software development, not an add-on. This makes it even more important that it be quality-assured – most is not – and that the high standard be maintained throughout its life, i.e. throughout the maintenance function (Macro and Buxton, 1987).

For the same reason, documentation should be produced in advance (Boehm, 1981), and milestones should be set for it. All too often, this is not done. Flowcharts, for example, are often only drawn after the program has been tested (a practice which is encouraged by tools which automatically

draw the flowchart from the source code). Similarly, programmers may exclaim: 'I'm too busy coding to write down the requirements' (Charette, 1986). Some documentation (the design, code listing, and test history) is highly volatile during development, so it is understandable and justifiable that deliverable (cosmetic) versions should be left until the end of the job, except that it is then done poorly, or not at all (Macro and Buxton, 1987).

The opposite approach should therefore be adopted. For example, an early version of the users' manual should be given to the users, so they can see how the system will affect them, and negotiate changes before they become too expensive (Boehm, 1981). Similarly, the operating instructions should be produced before testing begins, and testing run from them, to ensure that any errors or omissions in them are found and corrected before the system goes live.

With electronic means now widely available for entering and updating documentation, there is less excuse for not doing it, and not doing it well.

A small amount of good documentation takes longer to produce than a large amount of poor documentation (Boehm, 1981).

Walston and Felix (1977) found that productivity was related to the amount of documentation. Where less than 33 pages of documentation per 1000 LOC were produced, productivity was 1.6 times higher than where more than 88 pages were produced. This seems rather a large difference to be accounted for solely by the time spent producing the documentation, and this figure may include the effect of other, correlated factors. In particular, systems which are complex and so have a low productivity, probably also require more documentation.

However, documentation usually only forms a major portion of the total effort in large systems (and generally therefore for larger organizations), commercially marketed systems, contractually-produced software, and civilian government and military systems, and therefore only has a significant effect on productivity in these situations (Jones, 1986b). The cost of documentation can be reduced by using skeletons of standard documents, word processing equipment, touch-typing, graphics/text workstations, and presumably also by a close relationship with users, and inspections and reviews, which reduce the number of changes and corrections.

Alan Perlis (1981) suggested there must be something wrong if saying (documenting) what a line of code does is much more time-consuming than writing the code itself. According to Capers Jones, most companies do *too much* paperwork: 'it's to convince management that we really know what we're doing rather than because we really need it'. In a large system, cutting down on paperwork is cost-effective, and does not diminish the coding speed.

8.4.7 MAINTENANCE

Maintenance is similar to development – so much so that it has been described as just a continuation of testing (Yourdon, 1975). However, maintenance does not consist solely of correcting errors: in fact, as can be seen from the breakdown of maintenance activities given earlier, much of it is enhancements, so it is really development in disguise (Glass, 1979). (Because of this, authorities like Arthur (1988) and Charette (1986) prefer the term 'evolution': software must *evolve* to meet the changing needs of users.) For these reasons, the techniques used in the previous functions apply to maintenance as well. In fact, some modifications require *all* the development functions ('maintenance is a microcosm of development, and its activities span the entire spectrum of software engineering'), and are done by development rather than maintenance staff (Fairley, 1985; Dunn and Ullman, 1982). Various differences between development and maintenance are discussed below but, as will become apparent, these are not differences in kind, but are rather differences in emphasis and degree.

Differences between maintenance and development

The major difference between maintenance and development probably lies in the documentation area. While it may be true that no form of documentation is unique to maintenance (Dunn and Ullmann, 1982), nevertheless comments in source listings, and cross-reference listings, are of greater benefit during maintenance, e.g. they help perform an impact analysis (Glass, 1979; Yourdon, 1975). An impact analysis should take into account not only which programs will need to be changed, but also which documentation, and the effect the changes will have on the people who use the system. Every document that is affected should have the change incorporated: 'the cost of redoing the documentation alone is staggering' (Charette, 1986). Even a small change in the source code often requires extensive changes to the test data and the supporting documents (Fairley, 1985). Cross-reference directories should therefore not only show which programs are affected, but also which documents.

There is also a greater need during maintenance for a formal procedure for reporting errors, and for handling (analysing, implementing, and tracking) requests for changes (Glass, 1979). This should be automated, e.g. the information should be stored on the computer. This also helps ensure there is only one master copy, which is up to date, and is not easily lost – unlike a piece of paper (Arthur, 1988). (This is part of configuration management, which is discussed in Chapter 11.)

In addition, regression testing is more important here. However, the test data may already exist, and debugging is easier because errors are in the new or modified code (Arthur, 1988).

According to Lientz *et al.* (1978) and Warnier (1978), managerial issues are more
important than technical ones during maintenance.

User involvement

Maintenance staff have a significant amount
of contact with users, and so must be
responsive to their needs (Lucas, 1985).
Proposed changes should be discussed, to
ensure they are clearly understood. The
maintenance staff should inform the user
precisely what will be done, how long it will
take, and what the cost will be; and they (the
maintenance staff) should themselves suggest changes which would make the system
more useful.

Efficiency

'Perfective' maintenance includes changes to
improve the efficiency of a program (Arthur,
1988). Efficiency may be improved by restructuring the code (though a contrary opinion
is quoted later). However, Arthur warns
against attempting to improve efficiency
unless the program has a high usage, and has
a reasonable remaining life span (at least a
year). Operating system logs can highlight
which programs use the most computer
resources, and this data can be used to select
programs for efficiency improvements. Similarly, software monitoring probes (execution
monitors) can be built into a system, to
provide statistics about performance, which
can then be used to improve the system
(Chapter 5).

Maintenance might degrade performance,
so this aspect should be monitored after each
change (Gilb, 1988).

Maintainability

Maintainability refers primarily to the clarity
and modularity of a program, and the quality
of its internal and supporting documentation
(Fairley, 1985). Factors affecting maintenance

productivity – and therefore maintainability –
were given in Chapter 2. They included the
size of the program, the decision and GOTO
densities, and so on.

Perfective maintenance includes changes
to improve the maintainability of a program
(Arthur, 1988). However, facts are required
to pinpoint the problems. Complexity measures (discussed earlier) highlight programs or
modules which are complex, and so will be
difficult to maintain. Records should be kept,
to provide statistics about errors, which can
then be used to improve the system. Similarly, a record should be kept of all changes,
to see for example which portions of the
system are the most volatile, and might
benefit from a re-write (possibly in a higher
level language) to make them more flexible or
easier to modify. The statistics can also
highlight where additional training is
required (e.g. the most common types of
mistakes), and can be used to schedule
manpower and other resources (e.g. by
assuming that past patterns of errors and
enhancements will continue).

In the experiment by Weinberg and Schulman (1974), the team which was required to
produce the clearest program – and therefore
the easiest to modify – took longer than most
of the other development teams. It is therefore understandable that software is generally not developed for ease of maintenance
(Conte *et al.*, 1986). However, as maintenance
is generally believed to consume more time
than development, correspondingly more
weight must be given to it: maintainability
should thus be made a primary development
goal. It must therefore be built into the
software, not added on afterwards (Fairley,
1985). It is not sufficient, though, for maintainability to be a goal only during development: it should also be a goal during
maintenance: 'It is not unusual for a well
designed, properly implemented, and adequately documented initial version of a software product to become unmaintainable due
to inadequate maintenance' (Fairley, 1985).

As Brooks (1975) so graphically put it: 'maintenance is an entropy-increasing process, and even its most skilful execution only delays the subsidence of the system into unfixable obsolescence'. Eventually, therefore, the stage is reached where it becomes easier and cheaper to rewrite a program than to modify it.

Improving a program's maintainability therefore has the additional benefit of extending its life: 'it delays the day of unfixable obsolescence' (Arthur, 1988). (Software life, and the benefits of extending it, are discussed in Chapter 13. Arthur (1988), for example, implies that replacement costs are up to 40 times higher than maintenance costs.)

Arthur (1988) recommends a complete redesign and rewrite if more than 20% of the program must be changed, but warns of the danger of overlooking, and so omitting, functions in the rewrite. Where the changes are less extensive but are frequent, a rewrite might also be advisable. Where they are less extensive and are infrequent, but the program is difficult to maintain, a less drastic step which may be sufficient, is to restructure the code – either the whole program or just the portions being modified. This is similar to the advice: 'don't patch bad code – rewrite it' (Kernighan and Plauger, 1974). Restructuring can be done manually, or with the help of a tool for indenting code, etc. (Chapter 6). This technique can also be employed to improve flexibility, portability, etc. The rewritten or restructured code will provide the usual benefits attributed to structured programming, such as programs which contain fewer errors and are easier to understand; quicker implementation of corrections and enhancements, leading in turn to increased job satisfaction for maintenance staff through achieving more and better work; and so on. Arthur (1988) provided a checklist for restructuring (e.g. are decisions commented? are inputs range tested?), but it could be used for development as well. He also provided guidelines for restructuring, e.g. do it one

step at a time: first remove the NOTs, then the GOTOs, and so on, retesting after each step. (This is because, when programmers try to do two things at once, they make mistakes and miss things.)

There is another benefit of restructuring code. According to Arthur (1985), modules containing more than 100 lines of executable code often contain as much as 30% redundant (duplicate) code. One change may therefore have to be implemented several times, once for each occurrence of the duplicate code. This is both time-consuming and error-prone. Maintenance costs will therefore be reduced if the module is restructured to eliminate the duplication, i.e. by having one subroutine, which is called several times, from different places in the program. If, for example, the total number of lines of code is halved, then maintenance costs will also be halved (Arthur, 1988). (Arthur admits that such a large reduction may seem unlikely for real-life programs, but he has personally achieved it more than once.)

What is required is a quantitative measure of maintainability, like the complexity measures discussed earlier (possibly an extended version of these complexity measures). For example, Curtis *et al.* (1979b) showed that Halstead's effort metric is well correlated with the observed effort to modify small programs. Alternatively, bebugging could be used, with the time taken to fix the inserted errors serving as the maintainability measure (Fairley, 1985). (This would be much more time-consuming than an automated measure.) Whichever method was used, the measures would be applied to a program after it had been written, and after maintenance changes. They would indicate how long, on average, it would take to implement subsequent fixes (or enhancements) to the program (the mean time to repair, MTTR); how long it would take to recover from the effects of a bug; and what the probability was that errors would be introduced during maintenance (Gilb, 1988). However, this is an ambitious goal, and no work had yet been done to produce such a model (Dunn and Ullman, 1982).

Activities

Hall (1987) divided maintenance into three broad activities: the programmer must understand the requested change and the software that is to be changed; the change must be made, and the associated documentation updated accordingly; and the software must be revalidated. Parikh (1984) subdivided these into no fewer than 17 activities. These are just the programming activities: there are other activities as well, e.g. the modified version may then have to be distributed to user sites.

According to Arthur (1988), editing forms up to 70% of a maintainer's effort. This can be done more efficiently on a PC, so each programmer should be supplied with one for this purpose. The PC should, however, be linked to the mainframe, and the compiling and testing done on that.

Difficulties

Maintenance can be difficult. For example, as Hall (1987) so graphically expressed it, 'It's next to impossible to revalidate the software if you can't figure out what it was supposed to do in the first place'. In fact, maintenance programmers can spend over 50% of their time just attempting to understand the logic and documentation of the program, and its data – they have to thumb through listings or page through display screens, and talk to colleagues, users, or operations staff (Hall, 1987; Parikh, 1988). This large amount of time may be the result of poor documentation, or clever rather than straightforward programming techniques (Dunn and Ullman, 1982). The problem is aggravated (especially for emergency fixes) by the fact that maintenance is generally not performed by the original programmers, and even they are likely to

have difficulty with such programs as little as six months after writing them.

The defects that can be introduced into code that is not understood can be out of proportion to the benefits of the modification (Dunn and Ullman, 1982). These defects are not necessarily limited to the function which has been changed. If a program has not been properly modularized, then a change to one function may affect other functions as well. As Macro and Buxton (1987) put it, the software might be unmodifiable and intrinsically unreliable in the sense that the slightest disturbance of it, such as via an error, modification, or hardware failure, 'may cause propagated effects up to the level of a substantial failure'. Even if poor (or unusual) structure is well documented, the maintenance programmer might – quite understandably – not notice the warnings.

Another difficulty is that new functions must be designed to fit the current structure of the program (which is especially difficult if the program consists of spaghetti code), and should change as little of the current system as possible (Arthur, 1988). The programming style (e.g. for naming and indenting) should also be kept consistent, as a mixture of styles retards reading and understanding (Fairley, 1985).

Programmer attitudes

Maintenance is unpopular (Glass, 1979; Yourdon, 1975) – in fact, according to Couger and Colter (1985), it has only 50–66% of the motivating potential of other programming work. There is a stigma attached to it (Fairley, 1985). For a variety of reasons, programmers regard it as unfair (Hall, 1987; Charette, 1986).

- They feel they are in a no-win situation, as the user comes back again and again with more changes (it is rather like running on the spot, or like a housewife, whose work is never done).

- The programs they have to maintain are of low quality.
- Information they need to do the job is missing, e.g. because the documentation is incomplete or out of date, or does not explain *why* the product works the way it does, and they cannot obtain the missing information from the original developers, as they have left the organization. (Macro and Buxton (1987) pointedly observed that software engineers do not like doing documentation, but are the first to complain when encountering badly documented software not of their making.)

Because of all these difficulties, maintenance can be a humbling, ego-crushing, and depressing experience (Parikh, 1988). Through no fault of his own, the programmer may be unable to make a 'simple' change quickly and correctly – or may be unable to do it at all. Worse, his manager may, understandably but wrongly, conclude that he is incompetent.

However, attitudes can be changed. Maintenance is demanding, but programmers *want* a challenge (Zvegintzov, 1981). Furthermore, maintenance has been a neglected area, so little is known about it: 'the literature is nearly vacuous' (Glass, 1979). Parikh, 1988; Martin and McClure, 1983; Couger and Colter, 1985; Glass and Noiseux, 1981; Lehman and Belady, 1985; Arthur, 1988; Higgins, 1987 are amongst the few books devoted to the subject. Worse still, there is a lack of training: 'colleges don't teach maintenance because nobody knows enough about it yet', 'Most programmers spend half their careers in, or in the management of, maintenance, yet few are ever trained for this task' (Lientz *et al.*, 1978; Zvegintzov, 1981; Glass, 1979; Parikh, 1984; Hall, 1987). (Parikh (1984) further warns that teachers must have good practical experience in the logical construction of systems and programs.) Maintenance is therefore still 'a frontier in software engineering'

(Zvegintzov, 1981), which should further excite programmers.

The high turnover amongst maintenance staff can be reduced in a number of ways, e.g. (Hall, 1987; Fairley, 1985; Arthur, 1988):

- they can be trained in the technology that is being used to develop new systems, so that they will be able to maintain those systems once they are put into production;
- they can be rotated between maintenance and development (this is discussed later); and
- they can be allowed to participate in scheduling and decision making.

Another suggestion made by Arthur (1988) is that maintenance programmers be granted 'ownership' of programs and tasks like testing. This is an interesting suggestion, as it runs counter to the principles of 'ego-less' programming (Chapter 10), which he supports (Arthur, 1983).

Organizational structure

Maintenance may be performed by either the developers or by a separate group. Using the original staff has the advantages discussed earlier: they are thoroughly familiar with the system, and so can maintain it quickly and safely – they will introduce fewer errors due to ignorance (Dunn and Ullman, 1982). Furthermore, knowing that they will have to maintain it themselves will encourage them to produce a higher-quality product (Fairley, 1985). The disadvantages are firstly that they may skimp on the documentation; and secondly that they will have begun to develop another system, and will have to divide their time between the two systems, so the new project may suffer slippage as a result.

Using a separate group has the opposite advantages and disadvantages. It has the added disadvantage that maintenance is unpopular, so few programmers would willingly work in a group doing only maintenance. This can be resolved by rotating staff between the two functions, which brings added benefits, e.g. (Arthur, 1988; Fairley, 1985):

- it shows development staff the effects of poor techniques and inadequate documentation: 'strictly development programmers rarely know how to build easy-to-maintain software';
- it provides both groups with an appreciation of the skills required for the other function;
- it increases staff flexibility; and
- it broadens and improves their experience.

As a result of the difficulties in understanding the program etc. outlined earlier, 80% of the Fortune 500 corporations have applications supported by specialists, as only they understand the application's logic (Hall, 1987). It is not clear, however, if this means staff who specialize in maintenance of particular systems, or staff who specialize in particular systems, i.e. both develop and maintain those systems. In the former case, the developers can give presentations of the new systems to the maintenance staff; or, better, the maintenance staff can participate in walkthroughs and inspections of the systems as they are developed. These methods can also be employed by organizations which do not have application specialists.

At least two people should maintain each product (Fairley, 1985). They can then discuss ideas with each other, and inspect each other's work, and the organization is not dependent on a single person, who might be taken ill or leave.

Management

Glass (1979) claims that maintenance has been neglected largely because managers are happy with maintenance productivity, but in view of the large amount of time devoted to maintenance and the long backlog of work, this is surprising. The managers may merely believe that productivity is as high as can be expected under prevailing circumstances, or perhaps they are not aware that the productivity can be improved (Lientz et al., 1978). Hall (1987) implies that managers receive more praise for new systems than for maintenance of old systems, and as a result, spend only 1% of their time on maintenance, and 30% on new applications. He also stated that management had only recently realized that software is not an expense, but is a corporate asset. It is valued at between $5 and $50 per line of source code (this is roughly the development cost – see Table 13.3), and maintenance of it can be essential to preserving profits. Maintenance can also delay expensive – and risky – redevelopment, as pointed out earlier. Charette (1986) offers yet another explanation. Management is not interested in maintenance, 'as it seems an admission of guilt that the product didn't work correctly originally', which may or may not be the case. (An example of this reasoning can be found in Macro and Buxton (1987).)

Maintenance reduction and productivity improvement

According to Peters and Austin (1985), the key to maintenance productivity is to do most things a little better or faster. According to Arthur (1988), the best maintenance staff are at least an order of magnitude better than the worst, due to differences in their level of knowledge and skill. Providing staff with the latest knowledge, skills and techniques will therefore reap significant productivity and quality improvements.

A number of the specific recommendations made elsewhere will reduce the amount of maintenance and thus increase maintenance productivity, e.g. improved QA, improved documentation, coding standards, source code comments, prototyping, modularization, structured programming, project milestones (including for documentation), and the use of fourth-generation languages, on-line programming and debugging, application packages, DBMSs, and data dictionaries. Other methods for reducing maintenance (Parikh, 1981; Glass, 1979; Lindhorst, 1973; Yourdon, 1980; Arthur, 1988; Fairley, 1985; Gilb, 1988; Hall, 1987; Schneider, 1983) are given below.

- Use portable languages, tools, DBMSs, and operating systems.
- Pay special attention to human factors aspects such as screen layouts when systems are designed, as this is one source of frequent changes.
- Store constants in tables, rather than having them scattered (and duplicated) throughout the program.
- Encourage the interchange of knowledge between maintenance programmers, and the documentation of their methods.
- Use standard methodologies, so that everyone within the organization is familiar with the thought processes used to create the system, and with the documentation formats.
- Employ preventative maintenance techniques, such as selecting limits for tables that are larger than are likely to be needed.
- Separate the functions which are most likely to be changed from those which are inherently more stable.
- Identify likely enhancements, and design the software so that they can easily be incorporated.
- Introduce scheduled maintenance (i.e. on certain dates only, with no changes allowed in between). This forces users to think more about the changes they are requesting (both the details thereof and their priority); aids planning (scheduling and allocation of resources); and, by grouping changes, permits more thorough problem analysis, allows time to design changes to fit in with the existing design, reduces testing time, and improves productivity by eliminating repeated learning and understanding.

- Introduce structured maintenance, which includes techniques for documenting existing systems, guidelines for reading programs, and so on.

Scheduled maintenance is recommended; at the opposite extreme are emergency repairs. As the name implies, they are usually performed within short time frames, as a result of which little regard is paid to careful design and integration of the changes (Arthur, 1988). Furthermore, attention focuses on the obvious symptoms, in one program, yet the problem may have wider implications, and may affect other programs and even other systems. In addition, the modifications may introduce unexpected side-effects. It is important therefore that they be thoroughly examined afterwards. Because of the dangers of emergency repairs, as few changes as possible should be treated in this way. Arthur gives guidelines for deciding which defects are serious and urgent enough to warrant such treatment, e.g. if human life is endangered, or if they cause a significant number of people to be unproductive.

Most of the respondents in the GUIDE (1979) survey believed that modern programming practices improved maintenance time or cost.

Conclusion

Historically, very little attention has been paid to preparation for this major activity (Simpson, 1987). However, because maintenance consumes so much time, more attention should be devoted to finding ways of reducing it. There may, however, be a price to pay, a trade-off against increased development costs, as shown by the Weinberg and Schulman (1974) experiment.

8.4.8 PHASEOUT (RETIREMENT)

Sooner or later, every system will cease to be used. It will either be replaced by another system, or its functions will no longer be required. True retirement is a 'somewhat rare' event that occurs when a product has outgrown its usefulness (Schach, 1990). A system is replaced because a stage is reached where any further maintenance would not be cost-effective, e.g. because a drastic and therefore expensive change to the design as a whole is required; because many previous changes have introduced complex inter-dependencies that could easily be inadver-tently upset by even a minor change; or because the documentation is seriously and dangerously out of date.

If a system is being replaced, then there must be a smooth transition to the new system (Boehm, 1981). This is similar to a conversion or upgrade. Even if there is no successor system, the data and documen-tation from the system should be stored in case they are needed. These activities should also be documented.

8.5 PROTOTYPING

System development is a learning process for systems analysts and end users alike (Cer-veny *et al.*, 1987). The analyst must learn the user's job, and the user must learn computer methods and jargon. The analyst cannot produce correct and complete specifications unless he fully comprehends the user's requirements; and the user cannot confirm that the specifications are correct and com-plete unless he fully understands them, including any subtle nuances and unwritten assumptions (Kuekes, 1987; Lott, 1987). Worse, the user may himself not be sure what he really needs.

With conventional system development, the entire system is developed, at great cost, before the user can see what it gives him. Then follows a protracted and expensive iterative process as the user requests one change after another until the system has been tuned to his satisfaction. The resulting programs are therefore heavily modified (even though they are new), and so are likely to be of low quality, which is not a good start to their production life.

This iterative process can be short-circuited, thereby saving a considerable amount of effort, by building a 'prototype'. A prototype is an *initial* and *partial* version of a system. Prototyping is therefore a form of incremental development, and of the 'build-it-twice' approach, and in fact Peters and Austin (1985) advocate that the prototype be delivered to selected users so they can experiment with it. A prototype can differ from the final, production version in several ways. It may contain only certain, critical portions of the final system. It may contain non-critical portions, but not low-priority functions. It may contain all the desired functions, but exclude 'user friendly' features (such as help messages), validation checks on input data, error handling and fault-tolerance capabilities, or back-up and recovery. Or it may contain all of this, but be slow because little attention was paid to efficiency con-siderations. Because the prototype is only part of the required system, it can be deve-loped much more quickly, and at far lower cost. The process is further speeded up by appropriate technological aids, e.g. a rela-tional DBMS with an active, integrated data dictionary, a powerful *ad hoc* query language, a non-procedural data manipulation lan-guage, and screen and report generators (Klingler, 1986; Jones, 1986b); specific pro-ducts such as Dan Bricklin's Demo Program (for PCs) (Pournelle, 1986); or even a simple first version in APL or BASIC (Van Tassel, 1978) – though these are the lowest level languages Jones (1986b) would recommend.

8.5.1 BENEFITS

The prototype enables the user's needs to be established quickly, easily, accurately, and at minimal cost. In one case, a system which was estimated to take one year was com-pleted in two months, a productivity impro-vement of 6:1 (Schach, 1987). In another case, using prototyping and fourth-generation facilities, 10 major high-volume applications were written in only two years, giving a 13:1 gain over COBOL (Guimaraes, 1987). Peters and Austin (1985) estimated that the development time can be cut by 50% or more. Prototyping has therefore been acclaimed as the answer to the development backlog (Klingler, 1986). Other estimates, however, are more conservative. A 10-week study by Boehm *et al.* (1984), using 7 teams each of which contained 2 or 3 graduate students, found that prototyped projects averaged 45% less development effort (and 40% less code) than conventionally specified software; while Jones (1986b) gives a figure of only 13%.

One would expect subsequent maintenance of systems to be considerably reduced, but Jones (1986b) gives a figure of only 17%. He is probably treating the initial 'tuning' of the system as development, but nevertheless, this figure is (17/13=) 30% higher than his estimate of the saving in development effort. No maintenance was performed in the Boehm *et al.* (1984) study.

Because the required system is better known, the development effort can be estimated more accurately (Weisman, 1987).

Prototyping is also a useful tool for defect prevention and removal (Jones, 1986b). According to him, formal code inspections (Chapter 10), and modelling or prototyping the final code, provide the highest efficiencies in code defect removal, at more or less moderate costs. Only these two methods appear to consistently rise above 60% in overall defect removal efficiency.

Another benefit is that it helps ensure user involvement (Klingler, 1986). The user and the systems analyst may sit down before the terminal, and together define the user's needs and develop the prototype.

The prototyped versions in the Boehm *et al.* (1984) study were rated higher on ease of use and ease of learning.

To sum up, prototypes are valuable because users do not know what they need until they can see it and 'experience' it (Hopkinson, 1986; Martin, 1982b) – 'hands-on experience by system users is the most effective known way of eliminating requirements ambiguities and external design problems' (Jones, 1986b). Prototyping shows them what the proposed system will do for them, and so is a powerful technique in ascertaining their needs (Klingler, 1986). It incorporates their experience of the system much more cheaply than if the whole product had been built.

8.5.2   TYPES OF PROTOTYPE

Traditional prototyping focuses on system externals such as screens and reports, and generally defining the user interface; functional prototyping models the internal decision logic, and may incorporate AI techniques and expert system shells (Guimaraes, 1987; Weisman, 1987). Functional prototyping is valuable where the internal logic is complex, such as exception processing and complicated validation. It is particularly valuable in high-risk situations, e.g. where new and untried techniques are being attempted, or where the required functions are complex or may require heavy machine resources. The high-risk portions of the system can be prototyped, and this tells us quickly if they work, and if they consume excessive resources.

There are two views of prototypes. One view is that they are a 'quick-and-dirty' throwaway development aid. The prototype is developed, and then rewritten (normally using a lower-level language for more efficient use of machine resources), as the production system. In other words, the *coding* from the prototype is thrown away, but the *lessons* learned from it are incorporated into the rewrite. The other view of prototypes is that they are kept, and become, or are incorporated into, the production system (Cerveny *et al.*, 1987; Klingler, 1986). The latter viewpoint has gained popularity, probably because even a prototype can consume a large amount of effort, and it is wasteful to discard this. Guimaraes (1987) quoted a case in which users spent an average of 250 hours per prototype, and the systems development group spent between 75 and 225 hours repeating what had already been done in the prototype, so 30–90% of the original effort was redundant. There is, however, the danger that prototypes which were intended to be thrown away will be retained. These will not have been subjected to the normal high standards for system development, e.g. they will not be adequately documented, will contain no validation, and will have little provision for backup and recovery. Prototyping should therefore be incorporated into the life-cycle model. This is more obvious where the prototype is to be kept, but Klingler (1986) presents a life-cycle model for throwaway prototypes as well: 'Without a model, prototyping is just uncontrolled development that often leads to failure'. The iterative nature of prototyping must be incorporated into the model.

Cerveny *et al.* (1987) divided systems into three basic categories:

- **Transaction processing** The primary function of these systems is to add, delete, or change records. Examples are inventory tracking, payroll, and automatic teller systems. The requirements are relatively well known and structured, so prototyping concentrates more on the user interface (using text editors and screen generators), and on efficiency considerations (using mathematical modelling and discrete event simulation languages). Prototypes of these systems would usually be thrown away, and the system rewritten in a lower-level language.
- **Reporting and control** The purpose of these systems is to track, allocate and control the use of organizational resources. Examples are reports on variances from budget, and slow-moving inventory items.

The requirements are less well known, so the purpose of the prototype is to establish them (using relational DBMSs and 4GLs), in addition to modelling the user interface. The prototype may or may not have to be rewritten using a third-generation language.

- **Decision support** This is typically where the user wants to ask 'what if' questions. Examples are determining the impact of wage negotiations, and predicting inventory demand for a new product line. The requirements have a high degree of uncertainty (e.g. because there is little experience in the problem area), so the objective of the prototype is to define them. Tools used are relational DBMSs, 4GLs, spreadsheets and high-level modelling languages. The prototype is often retained as the final system.

All systems are a combination of the three categories, but by determining which category gives the best match with the proposed system, the analyst can establish the type and degree of prototyping which is necessary.

8.5.3 DISADVANTAGES

Prototyping has a number of potential problems. Some have already been referred to, either explicitly (such as lack of documentation), or implicitly (such as the heavy resources consumed by prototypes, making them unsuitable for production use in some circumstances, particularly high-volume applications). They are also not suitable for all systems. As a general rule, all systems that will have significant interactions with end users, and which are larger than about 5000 source statements, are good candidates for prototyping (Jones, 1986b). Boehm (1981) was more specific. Bearing in mind the limitations of current tools, prototyping was suitable for small business applications, inventory control, and some scientific applications; but was not yet suitable for most real-time distributed processing systems, command and control systems, and large, integrated, corporate information systems.

There is also the danger of concentrating on near-term user needs, and neglecting foreseeable longer-term needs (Boehm, 1981). In the Boehm *et al.* (1984) study, the prototyped versions rated lower on functionality and robustness, and specifying produced more coherent designs and software that was easier to integrate. In addition, management support is necessary for the concept to be successful. Training is necessary, but little formal training is available, except in the use of the tools (Klingler, 1986). Users may like the prototype so much that they insist on it becoming the production system, not realizing that important components such as validation checks are absent. Many of the prototyping tools are so powerful and easy to use, that users might try to develop their own production systems. This can result in duplicated and inconsistent versions of otherwise elaborately controlled corporate data, and can rapidly consume all the available disk space and machine time. The powerful tools also enable users to make mistakes faster.

8.5.4   CONCLUSION

Prototyping is a powerful aid in establishing users' requirements, in ensuring user involvement, in avoiding feasibility problems, in providing quality systems, and in improving the productivity of both development and maintenance. In fact, it 'is turning out to be one of the most effective technologies to emerge since the computing industry began' (Jones, 1986b). There are dangers involved, and the concept cannot be used in every case, but on balance it is a valuable tool which should be used more widely: 'As of 1985, high-speed prototyping is starting to enter the mainstream' (Jones, 1986b).

8.6   STRUCTURED PROGRAMMING

Structured programming is one of the few productivity-related topics which have been extensively covered in the literature. Many entire books have been written on the subject (McClure, 1978; Lim, 1980; Ashley, 1980; Linger *et al.*, 1979; Yourdon *et al.*, 1979a, etc.). Conte *et al.* (1986) counted no fewer than 40 recent textbooks on the subject, and the Addison–Wesley Computing Catalogue for 1988 has five books on structured FORTRAN 77 alone (Addison–Wesley, 1988).

8.6.1   DESCRIPTION

History

The origin of structured programming is generally traced back to the mid-1960s, and is credited to Bohm and Jacopini (1966) and Dijkstra (1965, 1968a), though some authorities claim earlier dates and different authorships (Gruenberger, 1974; Butterworth, 1974; Bleazard, 1976). Structured programming is therefore not new, and some portions of the DP industry have been deriving whatever benefits it provides for many years.

Objectives

The objectives of structured programming are variously given as:

- to decompose programs into small, discrete units (Yourdon, 1975; Mittra, 1988);
- to make programs more readable (Lim, 1980), and therefore more understandable (Glass, 1979; Linger *et al.*, 1979);
- to restrict complexity – 'the use of structured programming constructs has the effect of reducing the complexity of a program to a level approximately linearly proportional to its overall size' (Bleazard, 1976; Macro and Buxton, 1987);
- to reduce the number of errors, i.e. to make programs more reliable, thus reducing costly downtime (McClure, 1978; Arthur, 1988);
- to facilitate proof of correctness (Anderson, 1979; Bell *et al.*, 1987);
- to improve maintainability (Lim, 1980; Bleazard, 1976);

- to reduce the cost of programming, by allowing programmers to control larger amounts of code, and by increasing programmer productivity (Martin and McClure, 1985);
- to provide a discipline for programming, by forcing programmers to think, by systematizing the programming process, and by enforcing system integrity (Martin and McClure, 1985).

Although not identical, these objectives do overlap, and their ultimate aim is to improve quality and productivity. It is easier, for example, to maintain a readable program, and it is easier to produce a rigorous proof of the correctness of a program if the program is simple (Dunn and Ullman, 1982) – as Macro and Buxton (1987) put it, 'the maintenance of gratuitously complex programs is a particular trial in software engineering, and comprises a major cost of software'.

Definition

There is no general agreement on terminology, nor even on what is meant by structured programming – 'structured programming has yet to be precisely defined' (McClure, 1978; Lucas, 1978). The term structured programming is generally used to embrace both detailed design and coding (Dunn and Ullman, 1982). Martin and McClure (1985) give both a narrow definition – it comprises only structured coding – and a broad definition – it is a collection of methodologies that encompass the entire programming process. Van Tassel (1978) defines it as comprising top-down design, modular programming and structured coding. A narrower definition is given by Baker (1972) and Holton (1977), namely that structured programming consists of the coding constructs listed below, and the coding conventions listed earlier (section 8.4.4). Van Tassel calls this combination 'structured coding'. Glass (1979) groups coding constructs, coding conventions, restrictions on module length, etc., under the heading 'programming standards'.

Wider considerations

It is not enough, though, for the software alone to be structured: the entire software development and maintenance process must also be structured (Infotech, 1979; Dunn and Ullman, 1982), and so must the training of staff. Accordingly, structured methodologies have been developed for other functions, thus we have structured systems analysis, structured English (for specifications), structured design, structured maintenance, structured walkthroughs (for QA in all functions), and so on – in fact, this has become something of a bandwagon, with the description 'structured' being tagged onto everything: 'The word "structured" is now so widely used that it has lost a rigorous definition, and has become a kind of stock phrase' (Jones, 1986b). Jones defines it as a general concept. It means that activities are carried out in a rational and predetermined manner. It is like a stage play where the actors follow a written script, instead of improvising as they go along.

Dunn and Ullman (1982) even include data structure – variables, tables, files, data typing (integer, real, Boolean, character, etc.) – in their discussion of structured programming, and they liken the use of pointers to the use of GOTOs (Hoare, 1975). Bell *et al.* (1987) discuss another aspect of data, namely the weakening effect that global data has on abstraction. Briefly, with structured programming, all the coding for a particular function is combined into one module (loose coupling and high cohesion). Each module is therefore self-contained. To understand a particular function, you need only look at the corresponding module. Global data runs counter to this, as each module containing global data is affected by what happens to that data in other modules. Program flags (switches or control variables) have the same effect.

Although the various structured techniques can be used independently, they complement each other, so it is logical to use them together. It is easier, for example, to have a walkthrough of a well-structured program (Yourdon, 1979b). An improvement in productivity therefore results when a *combination* of these techniques is used. One particular combination of techniques is the CPT (chief programmer team) concept, of which structured programming is a component. It is also a component of IBM's 'Improved Programming Technologies' (Bleazard, 1976).

Structured programming can be used with any department structure, but it may be more common in CPTs because it is a component of the concept.

Technical aspects of structured programming are examined below.

Design

People are sequential processors (Van Tassel, 1978). Structured programming produces sequential programs, i.e. ones which are read and executed from top to bottom (Lucas, 1985; Harrison, 1987), as opposed to the switching backwards and forwards which happens in conventionally-designed programs. The structure of the program therefore matches the capability of the programmer. As Bell *et al.* (1987) put it: 'In the Western world we are used to reading left to right and top to bottom. To have to begin by reading forwards and then to have to go backwards in the text is rather unnatural; it is simpler if we can always continue onwards'.

In reality, though, even structured programs contain backwards and forwards switching, due to loops and called procedures. This is true not only of the generated machine code where it is less important (Thompson, 1987; Whetton, 1987), but also of the source code. Martin and McClure (1985) state that sequential organization is *not* an effective means of controlling program complexity as programs grow in size, so a structured program is *not* sequentially ordered: it is always *hierarchically* ordered in accordance with the following scheme:

- the first level of the hierarchy contains only one module, the root module, which contains a high level summary of the program's functions;
- the second level consists of modules that contain more detailed descriptions of the functions in the root module;
- similarly, each succeeding level consists of modules that contain more detailed descriptions of the functions of the modules in the preceding level.

Bell *et al.* (1987) drew an analogy with a plate of lasagne. We can peel off layers of the lasagne, one by one, uncovering the interesting detail of successive layers, and understanding each separately from the others. By contrast, to understand a plate of spaghetti, we have to understand it all.

Coding constructs

Coding constructs are closely related to program design – they can be classified as detail-level design. Three basic coding constructs are permitted (Lim, 1980; Bleazard, 1976):

1. process block or box – also known as 'linear', 'sequence' or 'concatenation';
2. IF–THEN–ELSE – also known as 'selection', 'binary decision', 'condition', or 'choice';
3. DO–WHILE/UNTIL – also known as 'iteration', 'loop', or 'repetition'.

These constructs conform to the rule for modules (or blocks of code) of having only one entry and one exit (Bell *et al.*, 1987; Dunn and Ullman, 1982). They are also hierarchical or nested: if a diagram is drawn of the constructs, then each box in the diagram may contain a (lower-level) construct of any of these three types (Macro and Buxton, 1987).

Every program could be written using just

these constructs (Bohm and Jacopini, 1966), but they are 'too minimal to allow an uncontorted description of procedure' (Gildersleeve, 1978), so there are additional permissible constructs (Lim, 1980; Van Tassel, 1978; Yourdon, 1975; Martin and McClure, 1985; Bleazard, 1976):

- CASE (GO TO DEPENDING ON) – this is an extended IF–THEN–ELSE;
- CALL or PERFORM;
- decision tables;
- escape or exit (e.g. after an error).

Modular programming

Modules are used extensively in structured programming. In traditional modular programming, the modules may be large and interdependent (Bleazard, 1976) – programmers sometimes say their programs are modular when in fact they are not: 'I simply write my program without any regard to the 500-statement maximum rule; then, if the final result turns out to be 3000 statements long, I simply go chop! chop! chop! – and I have six modules!' (Yourdon, 1975). Structured programming, by virtue of the nested boxes described above, and its adherence to the more general concepts of coupling and cohesion, and the hierarchical modular scheme described earlier, helps prevent this (Lim, 1980; Yourdon, 1975).

McClure (1978) criticized structured programming on the grounds that it does not tell us how to select the best way to modularize a program. By contrast, Gildersleeve (1975) stated that structured programming shows you how to organize and localize code in a methodical way.

Coding conventions

One of the aims of structured programming is improved readability. This can be achieved by following certain coding conventions, so these rules are usually included under the general heading of structured programming. Examples are:

- indent to show logic and data structures;
- use descriptive paragraph and data names;
- have only one statement per line;
- use comments.

This was discussed earlier (section 8.4.4).

Top-down coding

The previous paragraphs discussed *how* a program should be coded. The following paragraphs discuss *when* it should be coded.

Generally, coding does not begin until the entire program has been designed. In the extreme form of top-down coding, however, this is not the case. As each level of a program is designed (top-down design is presupposed), so it is coded, i.e. each level is coded *before* the next level is *designed* (Yourdon, 1975).

This method facilitates top-down testing and can result in earlier detection of design errors (Linger *et al.*, 1979), but it does mean that, when changes are made to the design (as happens frequently, as design is an iterative, trial-and-error process), some completed code may have to be changed.

Aron (1974) claimed that top-down implementation may take only half as long as bottom-up. This is consistent with Holton's (1977) finding that top-down design and implementation are 'moderately effective' in improving the productivity of both development and maintenance.

Language suitability

Structured programming principles can be implemented no matter which programming language is being used, but it is easier to do so in some languages than in others.

Those having a block structure, such as PL/1, PASCAL and ALGOL, lend themselves more readily to structured programming than do COBOL and BASIC (Yourdon, 1975; Van Tassel, 1978). It can be implemented in FORTRAN, though use of a preprocessor may make it easier to do so (Tenny, 1974). It can even be implemented in ASSEMBLER, by using macros (McGowan and Kelly, 1975). Structured programming principles are embedded in RPG syntax: 'it is not possible to branch from detailed calculations to total' (Garber, 1976). Furthermore, improvements can be made to the languages. For example, Microsoft's new version of BASIC, Quick-BASIC, is more structured than the older BASICA (Microsoft, 1986a); the newer version of FORTRAN, FORTRAN 77, is structured (Conte *et al.*, 1986); and the latest version of COBOL, COBOL 85, includes 'desperately needed' structured programming features (Chapter 6).

The GOTO instruction (section 8.6.2), which is not permitted in structured programming, is part of a language's design. Avoiding the GOTO is more difficult in languages such as FORTRAN and COBOL (particularly in older versions of these languages). Some languages, such as MODULA-2 and the systems implementation language BLISS, have been designed *without* a GOTO instruction. BLISS has a LEAVE verb, which can be used in some circumstances where a GOTO might have been used, but is safer (Yourdon, 1975).

Technological aids

There are various tools that indent coding, or even restructure it to comply with structured programming rules. In fact, this is likely to be a high-growth activity throughout the 1990s (Jones, 1986b). Examples are NEATER2 for PL/1 (Conrow and Smith, 1970), dAnalyst for dBASE III programs (TranSec, 1986), and RECODER for COBOL programs (Arthur, 1988; Language Technology, 1987b). However, these tools cannot redesign programs, correct fundamental logic flaws, eliminate duplicate code, separate functions into modules, or use better algorithms, and the restructured programs have to be retested and relearned. For example, 'if you pass an unstructured, unmodular mess through one of these restructuring systems, you end up with at best, a structured, unmodular mess' (Wendel, 1986). However, they do make programs more readable, so that logic flaws and other errors become readily apparent, the maintenance effort and costs are reduced, and program life is extended (Parikh, 1984; Arthur, 1988; Jones, 1986b; Language Technology, 1987b). Parikh quoted two productivity claims for tools of this nature. One organization obtained a productivity improvement of more than 2:1; while one authority claimed an improvement of 5% in development productivity, and 10–50% in maintenance productivity.

When provided as a service, the restructuring fees range up to perhaps $2 per source code statement (Jones, 1986b). The restructured programs are typically about 10–15% larger than the original versions. Performance is typically 10–20% slower, but total machine usage is sometimes lower than the original versions because of fewer errors and fewer reruns.

Static analysers (Chapter 6) can indicate if a program is well-structured.

8.6.2 THE GOTO CONTROVERSY

The aspect of structured programming which has probably caused the most controversy is the abolition of the GOTO statement. (The verb used differs between languages. It is typically GO TO.) This question aroused controversy when structured programming was first introduced over 20 years ago, and the dispute is still raging, as witnessed by the many letters which appeared in *Communication of the ACM* in 1987. The arguments for and against the GOTO are discussed briefly below. They are very similar to the arguments for and against structured programming as a whole.

Quality

According to Van Tassel (1978), the quality of a program is often inversely proportional to the number of GOTO statements in it. According to Dijkstra (1965, 1968a), the quality of a programmer is a decreasing function of the density of GOTO statements in his programs. Shneiderman's version is that the number of bugs in a program is proportional to the square of the number of GOTOs (Shneiderman, 1980). (Schnebly (1987) understood Dijkstra (1968a) to be saying that the proportion of GOTOs was related to the number of times the software had been modified. This is a very different interpretation, and the difference is fundamental. Instead of the errors being the *result* of the GOTOs, they may even be the *cause*, i.e. the GOTOs may have been introduced in the modifications to correct the errors. Furthermore, the modifications, in turn, probably introduced more errors, because modifications introduce errors, irrespective of the GOTO question. However, no-one else seems to subscribe to this interpretation.)

Understandability

Most authorities believe that a large number of GOTOs, especially backward transfers of control, make a program difficult to understand, and therefore difficult to debug and maintain. A contrary opinion, however, is expressed by Rubin (1987a): to avoid using GOTOs, 'programmers must devise elaborate workarounds, use extra flags, nest statements excessively, or use gratuitous subroutines. The result is that GOTO-less programs are harder and costlier to create, test, and modify'. In support of his view, he pointed out that an error in the GOTO-less version of his test program was only noticed by one person: 'The fact that so many people responded to my letter, but did not see this error, supports my view that GOTO-less programming is not inherently clearer or easier to debug' (Rubin, 1987c). He also argued that it is easier to spot the target of a GOTO than to match each DO with its END, and each IF with its ELSE (if any): the target is

usually nearby and is outdented from the text, and there can only be one statement with a given label, whereas there can be numerous ENDs and ELSEs before you find the matching one – and 'once you have found the label, it stays found, but one END looks like any other, so you find yourself searching over and over for the same pairs' (Rubin, 1987b).

As mentioned above, avoiding GOTOs may lead to complex nested IF statements. These are difficult to understand, so a maximum of three levels is recommended (McClure, 1978). Modular design helps avoid this pitfall.

Wendel (1986) believes that modularity is more important than structured code: 'I have an easier time dealing with programs with a bunch of GOTOs than one with its control logic spread out over the entire program'.

Avoiding GOTOs may also lead to extra flags (switches or control variables). Whetton (1987) argues that a program containing a proliferation of flags whose functions are far from obvious is hard to understand. By contrast, Gintowt (1987) argues that flags can add meaning rather than complexity.

Avoiding GOTOs may also lead to hand-coded counters (accumulators) (Moore, 1987). These can easily be misused, and should be avoided wherever possible.

The removal of GOTO statements sometimes results in an exponential increase in module interface complexity (Cho, 1987).

On the other hand, solutions using GOTOs contain more labels than would otherwise be necessary (Logan, 1987). This is a serious disadvantage: 'when we look backwards, we are defeated as soon as we reach a label, because we have no way of knowing how we reached it' (Bell *et al.*, 1987).

Moore (1987) argues that the GOTO statement is easily misused. Bell argues that it is too primitive a construct. It can be used for a variety of different purposes: to perform repetition, to exit from the middle of a loop, to avoid a piece of code which is to be executed in different circumstances, and so on. When you see a GOTO, it is therefore not immediately obvious which purpose it is being used for. However, each different use corresponds to one of the permissible structured programming constructs. Put another way, the GOTO statement is irrelevant, as any program can be written without it, by using the permissible constructs instead (Bohm and Jacopini, 1966). So, by using these instead, more information is conveyed to the reader. (Whetton (1987) suggested replacements for the GOTO, such as SKIP and BREAK, which would achieve a similar effect.) As Martin and McClure (1985) put it, higher-level control structures (such as DO–WHILE and CASE) appear to be easier to comprehend, easier to modify, and less error-prone, because they have a higher semantic level and avoid machine-related issues, and programmers prefer them because they improve program readability and reduce the number of instructions that must be coded.

Avoiding the GOTO instruction is, however, more difficult in older languages such as FORTRAN and COBOL, as they do not have adequate coding constructs, such as an escape or exit, which can lead to the use of extra flags. (Though newer versions of these languages do include improvements.) Even relatively new languages like PASCAL have limitations (Moore, 1987). Worse, tools such as spreadsheets and database languages which are intended for end users, suffer from the same limitations and consequent dangers: 'If professional programmers can introduce subtle errors into program code, how much greater is the risk when end users do what comes naturally – and let their code jump all over the place?' (Foster, 1987).

Reducing the number of GOTO statements, however, is not an end in itself – it is the *result* of good design (Dieperink, 1977). A program must be designed so that its structure matches the structure of the problem (Gillings, 1987; Thompson, 1987). This will automatically result in simpler programs –

not only can GOTOs be eliminated, but so also can deeply nested code (Cashing, 1987).

In the experiment by Rubin (1987a) (section 8.6.5), the programs which used GOTO statements were shorter, had fewer operands, and fewer tokens, and were therefore less complex. (Tokens are basic syntactic units distinguishable by a compiler, and can be subdivided into operators and operands (Conte *et al.*, 1986) (Chapter 2).) However, Wu (1987) argues that these measures are only *syntactic*, whereas GOTOs are especially harmful to the *semantics* of programs; and Dijkstra (1968a) and Cashing (1987) argue that GOTO statements interfere with the static/dynamic structure correspondence. Static structure is the line-by-line text, and dynamic structure is the order in which statements are executed. Programs are easier to understand if the two structures are in harmony, i.e. if successive statements in the program text also correspond to successive actions in time (Bell *et al.*, 1987; Conte *et al.*, 1986).

To sum up, where use of a GOTO produces coding which is easier to understand – and thus easier to debug and maintain – then a GOTO should be used (Bleazard, 1976). Otherwise, it should not be used.

Productivity

Gillings (1987) acknowledges that GOTO-less programs take longer to design and longer to code, but believes that this time is more than recovered later during debugging and maintenance. This is probably the majority opinion (Wu, 1987; Cashing, 1987), but it is not shared by Rubin (1987b) for reasons already given. Experimental results are given later.

Hardware cost

GOTOs can make a program more efficient (Dunn and Ullman, 1982; Bell *et al.*, 1987).

However, that is less important than maintainability (Cashing, 1987), and in any case, it is more difficult for a compiler to optimize code containing many GOTOs (Gillings, 1987; Wu, 1987).

Conclusion

There are strong differences of opinion about the GOTO. Macro and Buxton (1987) stated that it 'is not regarded with the rooted antipathy of former years', but the letters in *Communications of the ACM* in 1987 seem to show otherwise. Experimental results are generally unfavorable to GOTOs, but they are mixed, so more evidence is needed. Nevertheless, it is safe to say that both extremes – the excessive, undisciplined use of GOTOs, and contortions to avoid their use – should be avoided. This can be achieved by careful program design. GOTOs should be used when necessary, but only when necessary. As Knuth (1974) put it: 'Certain GO TO statements which arise in connection with well understood transformations are acceptable, provided that the program documentation explains what the transformation was. The use of four letter words like GOTO can occasionally be justified even in the best of company'. Languages need to be improved to reduce or eliminate the need for GOTOs. Guidelines for the limited use of GOTOs are given by Yourdon (1975), Bleazard (1976), Van Tassel (1978), McClure (1978), Lim (1980), Knuth (1974) etc.

8.6.3 ADVANTAGES

The objectives, and therefore the intended benefits, of structured programming – improved readability, maintainability, etc., and the resultant improvement in productivity and quality – have already been stated. Additional benefits claimed for structured programming are (Crossman, 1980; Smith, 1981; Glass, 1979; Linger *et al.*, 1979; Arthur, 1983; van Wyk, 1978; Lucas, 1985; etc.):

- it *prevents* defects, so there are fewer testing problems;
- it promotes modularity;
- programs are easier to code;
- programs are easier to debug – i.e. it assists in correcting errors;
- the improved readability helps programmers learn by studying other peoples' programs;
- because programs are quicker and easier to maintain, there is more time for development;
- it increases job satisfaction, as programmers are able to accomplish more and better work;
- it extends the life of programs, which is equivalent to a further increase in productivity.

The last benefit may need explaining. As was discussed earlier (section 8.4.7), after repeated modifications, programs become increasingly difficult to modify further, so eventually they must be rewritten. Rewriting is necessary sooner for programs which were badly designed or badly written. Short life is equivalent to low productivity, as there is less time for the development costs to be recouped, and the system is rewritten sooner (Chapter 13).

8.6.4 DISADVANTAGES

Despite its advantages, structured programming has been criticized on several grounds:

- The rules are restrictive – they limit creativity, and programmers have a need to be creative (Yourdon, 1975).
- Structured programming is 'the centerpiece of management efforts to de-skill programmers' (Kraft, 1977).
- It removes a tool (the GOTO), so the skill in using the tool is no longer required, and the programmer is left with a narrower choice of tools from which to make a discriminating selection (Bell *et al.*, 1987).

- It is awkward in certain circumstances, e.g. at EOF (End of File) in COBOL (Yourdon, 1975; Gildersleeve, 1975).
- GOTO-less programming may result in deeply-nested programs, extra flags, and hand-coded counters.
- Experienced programmers often have difficulty in adjusting to it (Yourdon, 1975; Holton, 1977; Arthur, 1983).
- It did not improve programmer morale in Holton's (1977) survey of 40 organizations.
- The programmers in the Lucas and Kaplan (1976) experiment found the unstructured programs more enjoyable, though that may be because they had not been taught how to avoid GOTOs.
- It requires much more documentation – data flow diagrams, HIPO diagrams, etc. (Arthur, 1983).
- It has little effect on current maintenance, i.e. on the maintenance of old, unstructured programs: 'They were unstructured when written and will probably remain so until they are retired. Trying to patch them up and turn them into structured programs will be more time-consuming than rewriting them' (Arthur, 1983).
- The simplest method is not necessarily the best: 'I wonder whether intellectual history offers any other example in which the practitioners of a science were exhorted to limit themselves to the most simple and primitive methods at their disposal, the limitations being touted as a great advance' (Fletcher, 1974).
- Similarly, Bentley (1987) argues that one should use all the features of a programming language, including ones which are not amenable to formal proofs of correctness.
- It is not a cure-all: it is possible to write 'murky' programs even if only the permissible constructs are used (Anderson, 1979; Bell *et al.*, 1987).
- It may increase the hardware cost: programs may be bigger and execute more slowly (Patrick, 1980a; Aron, 1974) –

figures of up to 15–20% are given by Jones (1986b) for restructured programs.

Because of these disadvantages, there is resistance to the use of structured programming – 'the GOTO becomes so thoroughly ingrained in programmers that it may take a priest to exorcise it' (Arthur, 1983) – and they may pay just lip service to it. However, some of these disadvantages have been disputed. According to Lucas (1985), for example, it takes *more* skill and planning to write GOTO-less code; and Boehm (1981) argues that the extent of use of structured programming disproves the 'restrictive, de-skilling' arguments. It is only partly true that structured programming limits the programmer to the simplest and most primitive methods, as the DO–WHILE is a higher-level construct than the GOTO. Furthermore, the evidence on hardware cost is inconsistent (Weiland, 1975; Kraft and Weinberg, 1975; McClure, 1978), and in any case (Patrick, 1980a; Yourdon, 1975; Kraft and Weinberg, 1975; Lucas and Kaplan, 1976; Van Tassel, 1978):

- because there are fewer bugs, and bugs are easier to find, less testing and debugging are required, and therefore less machine time for testing and debugging;
- similarly, long-term costs (including hardware costs) are lower, because of less and easier maintenance;
- structured programming can improve execution speed by reducing paging in machines with virtual memory;
- many programs are inefficiently written anyway;
- hardware costs have decreased considerably;
- operating systems have a high machine overhead; and
- structured programming aids optimizing compilers.

8.6.5 EXPERIMENTAL RESULTS

There have been a number of experiments to test the value of structured programming in general, and the GOTO statement in particular.

Shneiderman (1980) quoted several experiments:

1. In the Sime *et al.* (1973) experiment, nested IF–THEN–ELSE constructs were easier to use than IF–GOTOs (more problems solved the first time).

2. In Sime's subsequent experiment, by contrast, although nested IF–THEN–ELSE constructs gave fewer semantic errors per problem than IF–GOTOs, they gave more syntactic errors, longer error lifetimes, and fewer error-free problems per subject (Sime *et al.*, 1977). However, this experiment also showed that a proposed enhanced version of the IF–THEN–ELSE (in which additional information is shown on NOT and END clauses, to unambiguously pair them with the matching IF statements) was superior to both the unenhanced version and the IF–GOTO in nearly all these respects.

   (Shneiderman therefore speculated that nested IFs may be better when the tested items are unrelated, and when forward comprehension questions are asked.)

3. In an experiment by Lucas and Kaplan (1976), using 32 graduate students, the unstructured programs took 20% less time to write, and required 10% less machine time for development, but the structured programs were superior in these respects for maintenance (30% less programmer time and 30% less machine time). However, the group that worked with structured programs had not been taught how to avoid GOTOs, and initially struggled to do so, so the results of the experiment are misleading.

   (One aspect of concern is that the unstructured programs were rated more enjoyable not only for development, but even for modification.)

4. Studies by Weissman of a 50-line and a 100-line program, using 24 undergraduate and graduate subjects, showed a significant difference (of about 100%) favoring structured constructs in self-evaluations, and a much smaller difference (of about 25%) favoring them in quizzes, but no difference in modification performance.

5. In a study by Love (1977), the structured versions of 15- to 25-line FORTRAN programs were significantly easier to memorize and recall.

6. Experiments reported by Sheppard *et al.* (1979), using 36 experienced programmers and 36- to 57-statement FORTRAN programs, showed improved memorization/reconstruction and modification when structured control flow was used.

Conte *et al.* (1986) also quoted several experiments:

1. Elshoff (1977) compared 120 programs written by professional programmers before they were taught structured programming, with 34 programs they wrote afterwards. The proportion of GOTO statements decreased by a factor of four (from 12% to 3%); the proportion of DO–WHILE statements increased by a factor of 14 (from 1.3% to 18%); and the proportion of IF statements with ELSE clauses doubled (from 17% to 36%). Also, the average program size decreased by 30% (from 853 statements to 593).

2. In an experiment by Sheppard *et al.* (1978), 36 professional programmers attempted to understand programs written in both structured and unstructured FORTRAN. The mean comprehension score for the structured programs was 33% higher (56% compared to 42%).

3. Conte gave more details of the Sime *et al.* (1973) experiment quoted above. Nine subjects were given five programs to write using a structured language, and another nine subjects were given five programs to write using an unstructured language. All of the subjects who used the structured language solved all the problems assigned

to them, and only four had difficulty with any program. By contrast, only four of the subjects using the unstructured language were able to complete all the assigned problems, and eight of them had difficulties. In addition, the structured programs were completed quicker.

In the second week, the subjects wrote the same programs again, but this time using the *opposite* language. Having already written the programs once, both groups should have been faster the second time. Instead, while those who used the structured language in the second week were faster, those who used the unstructured language were slower.

4. In another experiment, which appears to be similar to the Sime *et al.* (1977) experiment (it also used an enhanced IF-NOT-END), programmers took 6% less time to figure out the conditions to make a program perform a designated action (Green, 1977).

In an experiment by Rubin (1987a), the programmers who used GOTO statements completed the test program faster than those who did not. Also, their programs were shorter (only half as many statements), had 30% fewer operands, and 40% fewer tokens.

In most cases, therefore, structured programming proved superior, though in two cases – Sime *et al.* (1977) and Green (1977) – language enhancements contributed to the improvement.

8.6.6 PRODUCTIVITY GAINS

It is generally believed that structured programming improves productivity, but the gains are difficult to quantify, and 'there are more claims than facts' (Stephens, 1979; McClure, 1978).

Program development

The productivity rates quoted in Chapter 2 indicate productivity gains of about 3 or 4:1 (Brooks, 1981; Yourdon, 1975; Boehm, 1973).

Structured programming is one of the components of the CPT concept, which is claimed to improve productivity by perhaps as much as 6:1 (though some claims are much lower – see Chapter 3), so it is logical to conclude that the productivity gains obtainable from it alone are lower than those obtainable from the CPT concept as a whole. (On the other hand, there are factors which restrict the wider use of CPTs – such as the shortage of suitable chief programmers – so structured programming is more widely usable than CPTs, and thus has a potentially greater effect on the productivity of the industry as a whole.)

Walston and Felix (1977) found that productivity was 1.8 times higher where structured programming was used for more than 66% of the code than where it was used for 33% or less. On the one hand, the ratio for 100% structured programming compared to 0% would be (much?) higher than 1.8:1. On the other hand, the 1.8:1 may include the effect of other modern programming practices, as they were usually used together (Boehm, 1981), in which case the gain from structured programming alone is (much?) less than 1.8:1.

Brooks (1981) analysed the Walston and Felix data to exclude correlated effects, and concluded that structured programming improved productivity by 1.3:1 for small programs, and by 3:1 for large programs. According to Conte *et al.* (1986), this study 'rules out other possible explanations for the increased productivity observed in structured programs. In particular, neither differences in personnel capability nor code explosion could account for the observed differences'.

Martin (1981), quoting an IBM survey (Jones, 1979), claims an even lower improvement – an average of only 10%, or 1.1:1. He later gave the slightly higher figure of 25% (Martin and McClure, 1985), but that may have been from all structured techniques combined, and not just structured programming.

Holton (1977) found that structured programming was effective in speeding up testing and debugging, but was not very effective in lowering overall development costs, or in achieving faster implementation.

Yourdon (1975) believes the gains may be higher when developing 'real-time' systems such as operating systems, presumably because they are so complex and the current very low productivity on them leaves more room for improvement.

The intermediate version of the COCOMO cost-estimation model uses a productivity improvement of 1.5:1 for the combined effect of various modern programming practices, including structured programming (Boehm, 1981). The contribution from structured programming alone is therefore somewhat less than 1.5:1. For modern programming practices (section 8.7) a typical value of the productivity gains claimed is 1.5:1.

According to Arthur (1983), structured programming evolved as a means of directing programmers to the 'right' solution despite their differing abilities. This implies that it reduces the productivity gap between low- and high-ability programmers. The productivity *gain* for low-ability programmers is therefore higher than that for high-ability programmers. Brooks (1981) goes further. His findings apparently indicate that the productivity of programmers of low ability is the same as that of programmers of high ability, provided they use structured programming – a surprising result.

Arthur (1983) also stated that the productivity gains from structured programming are negated by the large amount of documentation required, especially as the documentation is graphical and requires 'excessive' time to draw and update: 'The burdens these methods carried often consumed the productivity benefits they were supposed to provide'. However, he is referring to data flow diagrams, HIPO diagrams, etc., which are not part of the narrow coding construct definition of structured programming; and in any case, extra documentation is often advisable for non-structured programs as well.

Infotech International, in a study of 1000 users of structured programming techniques, found 50% cuts in project times (Parikh, 1984).

In the experiment by Rubin (1987a), the programmers who used GOTO statements completed the test program faster than those who did not. He did not give a figure, but there was a reduction of about 40% in the number of LOC, operands, and tokens. As these factors are related to productivity, this could be used to surmise a productivity gain of around (100/(100−40)=) 1.7:1 for *unstructured* programming (and therefore a productivity loss for GOTO-less programming of around 0.6:1). Rubin's general experience is that use of GOTOs reduces the number of LOC by around 20–25%, and therefore probably increases productivity by about 1.3:1. (Put the other way around, this is equivalent to a productivity loss for GOTO-less programming of about 0.8:1.) (The effect which structured programming has on the number of LOC was discussed in Chapter 2. There is a lack of consensus as to whether it increases or decreases the size.)

Shneiderman (1980) quoted several experiments favoring structured programming, but gave productivity figures for only one of them (Lucas and Kaplan, 1976). In this experiment, the programmers who wrote structured programs took 25% *longer* than those who wrote unstructured ones (giving a structured/unstructured productivity ratio of 0.8:1). However, this figure is not very valuable, as they had not been taught how to avoid GOTOs.

Conte *et al.* (1986), when quoting several experiments favoring structured programming, did not give quantitative productivity figures for any of them, but some of his figures could be used to surmise productivity gains:

- The Elshoff (1977) study suggested that structured programs had 30% fewer source

Table 8.67 Development productivity gain from structured programming

Source	Ratio	Comment
McClure (1978)	5 or 6:1	Includes other factors
NYT (see Chapter 3)	1.1 to 6:1	Includes other factors
Inmon (1976)	same as NYT	Includes other factors
Yourdon (1975)	4:1	
Boehm (1973)	3 or 4:1	Predicted
Brooks (1981)	3:1	Large programs
Infotech (Parikh, 1984)	2:1	
Walston and Felix (1977)	1.8:1	May include other effects
COCOMO (Boehm, 1981)	1.5:1	Includes other factors
Conte *et al.* (1986)	1.3:1	Includes other factors
Brooks (1981)	1.3:1	Small programs
Martin and McClure (1985)	1.3:1	Maximum 1.8:1
Jones (1986b)	1.2:1	
Martin (1981)	1.1:1	
Arthur (1983)	small	
Holton (1977)	small	
Rubin (1987a): general	0.8:1	
Lucas and Kaplan (1976)	0.8:1	No training
Rubin (1987a): experiment	0.6:1	

statements. As productivity is related to the number of LOC, this suggests a corresponding productivity improvement for structured programming.

- The Sheppard *et al.* (1978) study showed an improvement in comprehension of 33% for structured programs.
- In the Green (1977) study, programmers took 6% less time with the enhanced language to figure out the conditions to make a program perform a designated action.

The three figures quoted above are mostly small (an average of under 30%). Worse, the evidence from the first study is weak because it refers to *different* programs, which might have been 30% shorter than the previous programs anyway, even without structured programming (Chapter 2). Worse still, the last experiment included language enhancements, which probably contributed to the improvement.

Figures given by Jones (1986b) imply a reduction in effort due to structured coding of only 13%. (This includes all development functions – programming, systems analysis, management, and documentation. If only the programming functions are taken into account – which is probably the case for some of the other claims quoted above – then the gain would be higher, but would probably still be under 20%.)

These, and other figures (from Chapter 3), are summarized in Table 8.67.

The average of the ratios in Table 8.67 is about 2:1, but one cannot have much confidence in this figure as the ratios differ so widely. The reason there are large discrepancies between them is that the highest ratios include the effects of other factors such as structured walkthroughs and CPTs; and some of the highest ratios also refer to individual projects and so may be atypical, especially as the team members were probably of above-average ability and experience, and highly motivated. The figures given by, for example, Brooks (1981), Boehm (1981) and Martin (1981), should be the most reliable, as they are comprehensive, were obtained from more typical (prosaic) circumstances, and mostly do not include other factors, but still there is a large discrepancy between them.

The following comments may help to explain the discrepancies.

- 'Structured programming *does* represent an improvement over our currently chaotic way of doing things' (Yourdon, 1975).
- 'Program design has, historically, followed any arbitrary route the wanderings of the programmer's mind might select. It was utterly without structure save for that which, without formal awareness of the process, the programmer gave it here and there' (Dunn and Ullman, 1982).
- 'The early days of American programming were characterized by an unstructured and often brute-force approach. A programmer would look at a problem, write out lines of code, and try running it. If it didn't work the first time (and it rarely did), the programmer would tinker with the coding until it finally ran. There was often little rhyme or reason to the order in which the code was written' (Baron, 1988).

There *were* standard methods before the introduction of structured programming (e.g. modular programming, the 'balanced line' algorithm for update programs (Lim, 1980), and standard design models, were used before the term structured programming was coined), so the chaos was not universal. Yourdon's, Dunn and Ullman's, and Baron's comments suggest therefore that some of the claimed productivity gains were obtained by comparison against untutored programmers, i.e. ones not using the standard methods. Martin's low figure, by contrast, may represent the productivity gain over the previous standard methods, while Walston and Felix's intermediate figure may be the gain over a mixture of untutored programmers and various standard methods. Bleazard (1976) throws some light on the question. He stated that 'A great deal of the publicity and enthusiasm for structured programming emanates from the USA, and there is strong evidence that the

concepts of modularity and simplification of execution structure of programs emerged somewhat more slowly in the USA than in the UK. It follows that an installation unaware of these concepts, and perhaps using a monolithic approach, would quite naturally tend to react enthusiastically to structured programming ideas'. Anyone who learned programming in the UK at that time may be somewhat skeptical of the enthusiasm.

It is interesting to note that a study by Kapur (1980) found that 60% of the designs of simple master file update programs contained errors, probably because only 8% of the programmers copied a standard design model. Arthur (1983) estimated that, once generic (skeleton) designs become widely used, productivity will increase by 50 to 80%. It may be significant that this figure is within the range of productivity gain claimed for structured programming.

It is also interesting to compare the two figures given by Boehm (1973 and 1981). The later one is lower, indicating that structured programming did not live up to the original high expectations for it. In fact, an examination of the tabulated values shows that the earlier (1970s) claims are, on average, about double the later (1980s) ones – about 3.3:1 compared to about 1.4:1 – which implies an initial general over-optimism.

Maintenance

Shneiderman (1980) quoted several experiments indicating that structured programming should prove superior for maintenance, but gave quantitative figures for only two of them. In the Lucas and Kaplan (1976) experiment, unstructured programs took 40% longer to modify than structured ones. By contrast, in the experiment by Weissman, there was no difference, which is surprising, as this experiment showed advantages favoring structured constructs of about 25% in quizzes, and about 100% in self-evaluations.

Figures given by Jones (1986b) imply that it

Table 8.68 Maintenance productivity gain from structured programming

Source	Ratio	
Holton (1977)	2:1 to 20:1	
Infotech (Parikh, 1984)	5:1	
COCOMO (Boehm, 1981)	1.5 to 2:1	Includes other factors
Lucas and Kaplan (1976)	1.4:1	
Jones (1986b)	1.1:1	
Weissman (Shneiderman, 1980)	–	

takes 13% less effort to maintain structured code.

Infotech International, in a study of 1000 users of structured programming techniques, found an 80% reduction in program maintenance (Parikh, 1984).

Holton (1977) found that structured programming resulted in a 50–95% improvement in maintenance productivity, although his figure of 95% seems very high.

The intermediate version of the COCOMO cost-estimation model uses a productivity improvement of 1.5:1 for the combined effect of various modern programming practices (including structured programming) in the case of small programs (2K LOC), and 2:1 for very large programs (512K) (Boehm, 1981). The contribution from structured programming alone is therefore somewhat less than these values. For modern programming practices (section 8.7) the productivity gains claimed are mostly much higher than 1.5 to 2:1, so the contribution from structured programming alone may be correspondingly higher.

In the Rubin (1987a) experiment, unstructured programs were developed quicker, but the quality of the unstructured programs was criticized. Gillings (1987) showed the code to eight colleagues: 'All remarked that the structure was unclear and the code was of very poor quality', and some of them were unable to identify the function of the code. This would affect maintenance productivity. However, perhaps their response would have been the same had they been shown the structured version of the code instead. Also, what would the response have been had either the structured or the unstructured code been shown to a group of programmers who normally used GOTOs?

These figures are summarized in Table 8.68, in which the average of the ratios is about 3:1, but one cannot have much confidence in this figure as the ratios differ so widely and there are so few of them. Nevertheless, these figures do indicate that structured programming produces better quality programs (and so also extends their life), and that it has a greater impact on maintenance productivity than on development productivity (3:1 compared to only 2:1 or less).

Error rate

McClure (1978) credited structured programming with reducing the number of errors discovered in production programs by a factor of 15. However, as discussed under CPTs (Chapter 3), this translates into an overall productivity improvement, for development and maintenance combined, of only about 10%.

Because it reduces the number of errors made, structured programming is likely to give greater productivity gains in a batch environment than it can with interactive programming, as errors can be fixed more quickly with the latter.

8.6.7 EXTENT OF USE

Structured programming 'has gained immense popularity' (McClure, 1978), so one would expect a large proportion of programmers to be using it, but the evidence on this point is inconsistent.

Only 8% of the 40 organizations in the Holton (1977) survey were using it, although another 28% were evaluating it.

The Lientz *et al.* (1978) survey, of 69 organizations, yielded a higher figure – 25%.

Of the 800 organizations in the GUIDE (1979) survey, 51% were using it, and another 44% were considering it. Only 5% had rejected it.

Of the 20 organizations in the van der Poel (1982) survey, 85% were using it, but most of the organizations (55%) were using a modified form – only 30% were using a strict form.

In apparent contrast, according to Dunn and Ullman (1982), 'the use of structured programming in the design phase is still far from universal'. According to Bell *et al.* (1987), 'there are still many places where structured programming is not practiced'.

If it was widely taught to new entrants to the profession – and according to Martin and McClure (1985), by the end of the 1970s, large numbers of programmers and analysts were fed through mass-produced courses on structured techniques – why did Gordon *et al.* (1977) find that students used four times as many GOTOs as programmers with three years' experience. As recently as 1986, one

organization, L.L. Bean, found that graduates of both computer science and other training programs had had 'no introduction to structured techniques at all' (Dight, 1986).

This information is summarized in Table 8.69 in chronological order. The various survey figures appear to show a rapid and consistent increase in the use of structured programming, so usage of it should be virtually 100% by now, but the picture they paint is strongly at variance with the non-quantitative claims.

If, at the one extreme, only 8% of organizations are using structured programming, then there is considerable scope for productivity improvement from this factor; but if, at the other extreme, 85% of organizations are already using it, then clearly there is very little scope left for further productivity improvement, at least for development. However, if the modified versions used by 55% of the respondents in van der Poel's survey are inferior, perhaps watered-down to minimize staff resistance, and if this is generally true, then there would still be considerable scope for further productivity improvement.

The preceding discussion refers to the use of structured programming for development. Older programs, developed using non-structured methods, must still be maintained. According to Martin (1985), about 75% of mainframe COBOL programs were

Table 8.69 Extent of use of structured programming (percentages)

Source	Using	Evaluating	Rejected
Holton (1977)	8%	28%	
Gordon *et al.* (1977)	students use GOTOs		
McClure (1978)	immensely popular		
Lientz *et al.* (1978)	25%		
GUIDE (1979)	52%	44%	5%
van der Poel (1982)	85%		
Dunn and Ullman (1982)	far from universal		
L.L. Bean (Dight, 1986)	no graduates taught		
Bell *et al.* (1987)	many don't practice		

unstructured. Structured programming techniques can be used during maintenance of them, for additional coding or when changing bad coding, but nevertheless structured programming is probably used much less for maintenance work than for development. The position will change as existing operational programs are phased out or replaced by new, structured ones.

8.6.8 SUMMARY AND CONCLUSIONS

Structured programming improves productivity, though not by as much as often claimed, and the gain compared to previous standard methods may be very small.

Language limitations prevent the full benefits of structured programming from being realized.

Structured programming is widely used, though not as widely as might be expected, and it might be used mostly in modified forms.

There is resistance to it from programmers accustomed to other methods – they may never be persuaded to use it – but they form an increasingly smaller proportion of the total. However, there is doubt over whether the large numbers of new entrants are routinely being taught structured programming.

In view of all the above facts, it is possible (though unlikely) that most of the benefits which can be obtained from structured programming are already being obtained, at least for development.

Structured programming probably gives a much higher productivity gain for maintenance than for development, but only for maintenance of structured programs: it has little effect on the maintenance of unstructured programs, and these probably comprise the great bulk of maintenance work. Maintenance productivity as a whole will therefore only gradually improve, as systems developed using structured methods form an increasing proportion of the total being maintained. The improvement in maintenance

productivity thus lags behind that in development productivity.

As a bonus, structured programming extends the life of programs, which is equivalent to a further increase in productivity.

Structured programming probably increases the hardware cost, as programs may be bigger and execute more slowly.

8.7 MODERN PROGRAMMING PRACTICES

Various methods are commonly grouped together under such titles as MPP (modern programming practices) and IPT (improved programming technologies). Different authorities include different methods under these titles, but typically, different combinations of the following methods are included (Boehm, 1981; Bleazard, 1976; Parikh, 1984):

- top-down requirements analysis, design, and implementation;
- structured design notation;
- HIPO diagrams;
- top-down incremental development;
- design and code walkthroughs or inspections;
- structured coding;
- chief programmer teams (CPTs);
- project librarians; and
- the program production or development support library

(Contrary to the word 'programming' in the MPP and IPT titles, these methods are not limited to the strictly programming functions, but cover the entire software development and maintenance process.) The effect of these factors as a group is discussed below.

8.7.1 DEVELOPMENT PRODUCTIVITY GAIN

In 1975, an IBM systems engineer stated that many companies report that IPTs improve programmer effectiveness by up to 400% (Parikh, 1984). However, figures Parikh himself gave imply a much lower improvement. If a methodology saves 20% on maintenance,

Table 8.70 Productivity gains/losses

	Unstruc- tured	Structured	Ratio
Development	33	36	0.9:1
Maintenance	67	54	1.2:1
Total	100	90	1.1:1

Source: Parikh (1984)

and 10% on total life-cycle costs, then a 1:2 development:maintenance ratio implies a *loss* of 10% on development productivity – 'you may spend more on the front-end development cycle' – (Table 8.70).

Figures given by Jones (1986b) imply that structured requirements, structured design, and structured coding, together reduce the development effort by (62/45=) 1.4:1, though this includes the effect of a slightly more powerful language: PASCAL instead of COBOL. (This includes all development functions – programming, systems analysis, management, and documentation. However, if only the programming functions are taken into account, then there would apparently be little or no change to this figure.)

Albrecht (1979) reported a productivity gain of about 3:1 over a period of five years, and cited structured programming, high-level languages, on-line development, and use of a programming development library as the chief causes.

Gilb (1988) believes that some methods – such as inspection, evolutionary delivery, and even formal specification of objectives – give 'impressive' gains in productivity, much higher than the gains provided by tools such as programming languages, software support environments, database support systems, and operating systems.

By contrast, Curtis *et al.* (1988) stated that several studies (Walston and Felix, 1977; Boehm, 1981, 1987; McGarry, 1982; Vosburgh *et al.*, 1984) demonstrated that methods had a relatively small effect on software produc-

tivity, and that one study (Card *et al.* 1987) found that they had no effect at all.

The methodology taught at IBM's Software Engineering Institute – modularity, stepwise refinement, structured programming, defect prevention, etc. – was expected to decrease development costs by 10% or more, once the people were over the learning curve (Carpenter and Hallman, 1985). (It may seem that 10% is a small improvement, but after only a two-week course it represents a high return on investment.)

Similarly, Yourdon (1989) stated that structured techniques – structured analysis, design, and programming (and he was possibly including software metrics, proofs of program correctness, and software quality assurance as well) – have had only a modest impact, typically just 10–20%, on the productivity of systems development professionals.

The Aetna Life Insurance Co. introduced a comprehensive system development methodology as well as new tools (including a programmer/analyst workbench), education, and end-user involvement, including JAD (joint application design), and expected to achieve an overall productivity improvement of 50% over three years (Bradley, 1989).

According to the intermediate version of the COCOMO cost-estimation model, productivity is 1.5 times higher where modern programming practices are routinely used, than where they are not used (Boehm, 1981). (The MPPs included here are: top-down requirements analysis and design, structured design notation, top-down incremental development, design and code walkthroughs or inspections, structured code, and program librarian.) The effect of MPPs is small in the initial functions – a productivity gain of only 1.1:1 for the requirements function – but steadily increases, reaching 2.3:1 for integration and test. This reflects both the fact that the earlier errors are discovered, the less they cost to fix, and that MPPs take this one step further by *avoiding* errors.

The GUIDE (1979) survey found that about

Table 8.71   Development productivity gain from MPPs

Source	Productivity gain
McAuto 73 (Boehm *et al.*, 1975b): 3K LOC	0.7:1
Parikh (1984)	0.9:1
Card *et al.* (1987)	none
Curtis *et al.* (1988)	small
GUIDE (1979): 23% of installations	1.0–1.1:1 additional
IBM (Carpenter and Hallman, 1985)	1.1:1
Yourdon (1989)	1.1–1.2:1
GUIDE (1979): 40% of installations	1.1–1.25:1 additional
GUIDE (1979): 12% of installations	1.25–1.5:1 additional
McAuto 74 (Boehm *et al.*, 1975b): 6K LOC	1.3:1
Bank of Montreal (Comper, 1979)	1.4:1
Jones (1986b)	1.4:1
SNETCo (Pitchell, 1979)	1.5:1
Aetna (Bradley, 1989)	1.5:1 (includes other factors)
COCOMO (Boehm, 1981)	1.5:1
Galinier (1978)	1.6:1
IBM (Boehm *et al.*, 1975b): 2K–500K LOC	1.7:1
Hughes (Boehm *et al.*, 1975b): 10K LOC	2:1
Boeing (Black *et al.*, 1977)	3:1 (range 1.1–6:1)
Albrecht (1979)	about 3:1 (includes tools)
per IBM, in 1975 (Parikh, 1984)	up to 4:1
IBM (Walston and Felix, 1977)	8:1 (correlated effects)
Gilb (1988)	impressive

40% of the more than 600 installations could realize an *additional* 10–25% productivity gain, over and above what they were already getting from MPPs, if they used their current MPPs as extensively as practical; and about 12% could realize an additional 25–50%; while 23% could realize an additional gain of less than 10%.

These figures, and the corresponding figures from other authorities, are shown in Table 8.71.

Comments

The figures in Table 8.71 refer to different (combinations of) methods, so differences in the productivity gains are only to be expected.

In two of these cases, development productivity actually went *down*, which is surprising. The Parikh figure has already been explained: it is the price to be paid for lower maintenance, and lower total, effort. The McAuto figure was due to the staff not being sufficiently familiar with the techniques, so they did not use them correctly – similar to an example discussed under structured programming. Adequate training must therefore be given, and the techniques must be introduced at a pace the staff can absorb.

Boehm (1981) believes that the high gains reported by Black *et al.* (1977) may be due to deficiencies in the cost-estimation model he used.

The IBM value quoted by Parikh (1984) gives no indication of the average value, which may have been considerably lower than the quoted upper limit of 4:1.

The four MPPs included in the Walston and Felix (1977) figure – structured programming (1.8:1), design and code inspections (1.5:1), top-down development (1.6:1), and CPTs (1.9:1) – together imply a productivity gain of 8:1, but the four methodologies were usually used together, so each of the apparently individual ratios really contains the combined effect of all the factors (which explains why they are so similar in magnitude) (Boehm, 1981). The actual productivity gain from the four MPPs combined was probably therefore about 2:1, which is in good agreement with the other tabulated values.

A study by Brooks (1980) found that the productivity gain from MPPs is higher for larger projects (a finding which is consistent with the admittedly scanty tabulated figures). This is plausible, as there is greater scope for improvement because of the lower productivity on larger projects. Brooks also found that MPPs reduced the negative effects of other factors such as complexity and hardware constraints.

Conclusion

The average of the values in Table 8.71 is around 2:1. If the three highest values are omitted (because they can be challenged), then the average is only about 1.3:1. In the study of some individual MPPs, e.g. structured programming and CPTs, the conclusion was that many of the claims made for them were over-optimistic, and that the impressive gains attributed to them were mostly due to the use of better people, higher motivation, etc. Even so, an improvement of only 2:1 (or less) from all the practices combined is surprisingly low. In the light of the preceding figures, the apology given in the opening paragraph of section 8.4 about devoting relatively little space to the topic proves to have been unnecessary.

8.7.2   MAINTENANCE PRODUCTIVITY GAIN

In 1975, an IBM systems engineer stated that many companies report improvements of up to 1600% when maintaining programs produced using IPTs (Parikh, 1984).

Yourdon (1989) stated that systems developed using structured techniques – structured analysis, design, and programming (and he was possibly including software metrics, proofs of program correctness, and software quality assurance as well) – generally have substantially lower maintenance costs and substantially higher reliability, often by as much as a factor of 10 or more.

Yale University estimated that new functions could be added to existing programs between 200 and 1000% faster, depending on complexity, a productivity increase of 2:1 to 10:1 (Parikh, 1984).

Parikh himself gave a figure of 20% (Parikh, 1984), which presumably means he believes that typical gains are much lower than the upper limits given by the authorities he quoted.

The intermediate version of the COCOMO cost-estimation model uses a productivity improvement of 1.5:1 for the combined effect of various modern programming practices in the case of small products (2K LOC), and 2:1 for very large ones (512K) (Boehm, 1981).

Figures given by Jones (1986b) imply that it takes only one-quarter as much time to maintain code produced using structured requirements, structured design, and structured coding (though this includes the effect of a slightly more powerful language: PASCAL instead of COBOL).

The methodology taught at IBM's Software Engineering Institute enabled one group to complete the design and coding phases for adding a component to an existing operating system in only *one-sixth* the time of a sister project (Carpenter and Hallman, 1985). Also, new programmers became productive very quickly.

These figures are given in Table 8.72. The average of the ratios is about 5:1, but they differ so widely and there are so few of them, that one cannot draw confident conclusions. Nevertheless these figures are much more impressive than the development gains, and indicate that maintenance is where the real benefit of improved methods lies.

8.7.3   OVERALL PRODUCTIVITY GAIN

What is the productivity gain from MPPs for development and maintenance combined?

Table 8.72 Maintenance productivity gain from MPPs

Source	Productivity gain
Parikh (1984)	1.2:1
COCOMO (Boehm, 1981)	1.5:1 to 2:1
Yale University (Parikh, 1984)	2:1 to 10:1
Jones (1986b)	4.3:1
IBM (Carpenter and Hallman, 1985)	6:1
Yourdon (1989)	often 10:1 or more
per IBM (Parikh, 1984)	up to 16:1

Table 8.73 Productivity gains for development and maintenance combined

Source	Unstructured effort	Structured effort	Ratio
Jones (1986b) – original data			
Development	62	45	1.4:1
Maintenance	30	7	4.3:1
Total	92	52	1.8:1
Adjustment (×5) for all maintenance			
Development	62	45	1.4:1
All maintenance	150	35	4.3:1
Total	212	80	2.7:1
Adjustment for 1:2 time split			
Development	33	24	1.4:1
All maintenance	67	16	4.3:1
Total	100	40	2.5:1

Parikh (1984) gave a figure of 'at least 10%' by using the right methodology.

Jones (1986b) gave a figure of 1.8:1 from structured methodologies (Table 8.73). However, his figures for maintenance effort apparently include only the effort required to implement fixes, not enhancements, and therefore they understate the impact of structured methodologies on overall productivity. If we multiply his figures for maintenance effort by five (figures earlier in this chapter indicate that fixes comprise only about 20% of the total maintenance effort), then his ratio for the impact of structured methodologies on overall productivity becomes 2.7:1. An alternative method is to apply the individual productivity improvement ratios for development and maintenance to the amount of time typically consumed by each of these activities. If we assume that maintenance consumes twice as much time as development, then we arrive at the combined ratio of 2.5:1, which is almost the same answer as that obtained by the other method.

If we similarly use the 1:2 development: maintenance split method on the COCOMO ratios in Tables 8.71 and 8.72, and on the 1975 IBM figures which Parikh quoted (also in the same tables), and on the averages of the values in those two tables, then we obtain combined ratios for with and without MPPs as shown in Table 8.74.

The figures for individual authorities are then summarized in Table 8.75. The average of those individual authorities who gave both a development and a maintenance productivity

Table 8.74 Analysis of overall productivity gains from MPPs

	COCOMO			IBM (Parikh)			Tabulated averages		
	Without	With	Ratio	Without	With	Ratio	Without	With	Ratio
Development	33	22	1.5:1	33	>8	<4:1	33	17	2:1
Maintenance	67	22–34	1.5–2:1	67	>4	<16:1	67	13	5:1
Total	100	44–56	1.8–2.3:1	100	>12	<8:1	100	30	3:1

Table 8.75 Overall productivity gain from MPPs

Source	Productivity gain
Parikh (1984)	1.1:1
Jones (1986b)	2.7:1
COCOMO (Boehm, 1981)	1.8–2.3:1
per IBM, in 1975 (Parikh, 1984)	up to 8:1
Average (approximate)	3:1

gain therefore agrees with the value calculated from the averages of all authorities for development and for maintenance (Table 8.74).

8.7.4 OTHER BENEFITS

A number of other benefits have been claimed for MPPs.

- Marathon Oil found that, with structured design and programming, together with HIPOs, people think in terms of functions, and their thinking becomes easier to follow and to implement (Parikh, 1984).
- Hartford Insurance found that, when IPTs were used, the finished product was of excellent quality, and was concluded ahead of schedule, using fewer resources than projected (Parikh, 1984).
- About 600 members of IBM's user group, GUIDE (1979), evaluated MPPs, with results as shown in Table 8.76, i.e. 11% of the respondents thought that MPPs greatly improved project estimating or control; 51% thought they resulted in some improvement; and so on.

There is therefore wide agreement that MPPs

have a beneficial effect on many aspects of software development and maintenance, but this agreement is not universal: the Thayer *et al.* (1980) survey found that methodologies such as structured programming, analysis and design, 'contribute meagerly' to developing good quality and cost-effective software (Cho, 1987). This survey identified 20 problems in software engineering management (such as poor project planning), none of which conventional software methodologies have been able to solve, the implication being that management should supplement or even replace these methodologies with new ones that would help solve these problems. In particular, Cho claims that statistical quality control offers solutions to some of these 20 problems.

8.7.5 IMPLEMENTATION

To ensure the successful introduction of MPPs, Boehm (1981) made a number of suggestions.

1. Ensure management commitment.
2. Ensure that the first people to use the methods are enthusiastic – 'champions of the cause' (Gilb, 1988).
3. Embed MPPs within an overall productivity-improvement program.
4. Ensure that management and staff agree on objectives and performance criteria.
5. Phase in MPPs:
   - 'Implement *slowly*, preferably one technique at a time' (Parikh, 1984);
   - 'Go after the easy stuff first' – 'the best way to overcome resistance to change

Table 8.76 GUIDE (1979) evaluation of MPPs

Factor	Improvement?			
	Yes		No	
	Large	Small	None	Negative
Project estimating or control	11%	51%	36%	1%
Communication with users	16	40	44	1
Organizational stability	8	35	55	2
Accuracy of design	29	52	19	1
Code quality	35	49	16	<1
Early error detection	37	48	15	1
Programmer productivity	27	58	13	1
Maintenance time or cost	31	48	19	2
Programmer or analyst morale	19	50	28	3
Average	24	48	27	1

is in taking tiny steps' (Peters and Austin, 1985).

6. Allow enough time for training.
7. Ensure that the techniques are being used.
8. Allow deviations from the rules where justified.
9. Do not be afraid of mistakes.
10. Do not expect instant results – there may even be a temporary drop in productivity initially.
11. Establish an ongoing monitoring and feedback mechanism.

Arthur (1988) recommended that only 30–50 people at a time should be introduced to a new tool or method, and warned that the phasing in process could, in total, take five years.

Further advice on the implementation of new technology can be found in Bouldin (1989) and Buckley (1989).

Because MPPs involve a change in people's work methods, there is likely to be resistance (witness the GOTO controversy), making it all the more important to follow the above suggestions. (Resistance to change is discussed in general terms in Chapter 9.)

The average usage of the four MPPs (CPTs, structured programming, structured walkthroughs and HIPO), in the Lientz *et al.* (1978) survey of 69 organizations, was only 20%.

Couger (1982) predicted that, based on past experience, it would be another decade before the majority of firms implemented fourth-generation system development techniques (structured analysis, structured design, etc.).

There is a tendency to concentrate on technology and neglect people. However, DP is a labor-intensive industry (Chapter 1), so a large amount of attention should be devoted to people; Boehm (1981) rates personnel factors as having the greatest single impact on productivity. Some aspects have already been discussed – people-structures (Chapter 3) and ergonomics (Chapter 4) in particular. Motivation of staff is discussed in Chapter 11, while psychological aspects are discussed at various points throughout this study. Additional aspects – the shortage of staff, high staff turnover, training, experience, ability, and resistance to change – are discussed in this chapter.

The behavior of people is not completely predictable, and different people behave differently, but more information is becoming available which helps us understand what makes people more productive (Boehm, 1981). However, a word of caution is necessary. Software engineers are not machines, so measurement of their performance must be tempered with sensitivity: it is demotivating, for example, to tell a programming team that it is only 15th-percentile material.

9.1 SHORTAGE

9.1.1 MAGNITUDE

Some commentators believe that the industry is undermanaged rather than undermanned (van Niekerk, 1980; Cooper, 1975) – as Davies (1988) put it, 'there is no skills shortage, only skills wastage; many MIS divisions are stifled by bureaucracies, many of their own making'. There *is* reason to believe that the

quality of management needs improving (Chapter 11), but nevertheless it is generally agreed that there has been a serious shortage of staff (Martin, 1982a; Couger and Zawacki, 1980). The slow response to user requests, and the accompanying large backlog of work (Chapter 8), could be cured if sufficient extra staff were available, so it is a major problem.

Estimates of the magnitude of the shortage vary widely. Apart from the 1% reported in Japan – 470 000 software engineers and a shortage of only 4000 – (Matsumoto, 1989; Japanese MITI, 1987), they range from a little under 15% to more than double that figure (Westcott, 1988; McKenzie, 1988; Urwick, 1975; Cockburn, 1988; Steyn, 1980). Worse, some authorities believe that the published figures are underestimates (Pienaar, 1980). More recently, though, US-based statistics show the number of job openings in the IT industry were down by nearly 40% from the previous year (Ramsey, 1992).

Most estimates give just the size of the present shortage, but some look ahead, and predict that a large intake will be required every year to match the expected growth of the industry (Chapter 12).

Opinions about trends vary from 'improving only marginally, at best', and 'only keeping up with the growth', to 'growing problems' and 'there will always be a shortage' (Neill, 1980a; Steyn, 1980; Hyman, 1982). Figures from Adams (1981) show periodic fluctuations in the shortage superimposed on a slow worsening.

The number of staff is reportedly growing: see Table 9.1, in which the claims are listed in chronological order, to reveal any trends and to highlight any discrepancies between the

Table 9.1 Growth in the number of staff

Source	% p.a.
Dolotta *et al.* (1976)	3–4
Morrisey and Wu (1979)	3–4
Phister (1979)	13–14
Gilchrist *et al.* (1983)	7
National (1983)	7
Productivity Software (1988)	3
Davis (1989b)	5
Average (approximate)	6

figures. The figures appear to show a fluctuating increase, while the obvious discrepancy is the 10% difference between the two sets of figures for 1979.

More detailed figures are given in Table 9.2, which confirms that there was a much higher increase during the middle of the period shown. They therefore confirm the high increase claimed by Phister (1979), while the much lower Morrisey and Wu (1979) figures, obtained from Boehm (1981) are probably for 1977.

The Brandon figures, for both number of staff (Chapter 8) and rate of increase, are higher than the others, and so should be viewed with caution, but nevertheless they do show the same trends, namely an increase in growth around 1979/80, and a higher growth for analysts than programmers.

Most authorities believe that the demand for programmers will be severely reduced by the increasing use of technological aids – they 'will become obsolete' (Coetzer, 1983a) – and there is evidence that the slowdown has begun from Edwards (1983a) and the Hodges (1987b) figures in Table 9.2. However, other authorities – perhaps because they have been proved wrong in the past (Woodland, 1977) – are more cautious. Steyn (1983) even predicted that 'there is always going to be a demand for programmers in our lifetime'.

One commentator stated that there were severe shortages 'at all staff levels', while others believed that the shortage was of 'trained' and 'experienced' people, and still others said that it was of 'good' and 'suitable' people (Neill, 1980a; Eberhard, 1976; Gray, 1980a; Tebbs, 1980a).

The evidence indicates that the shortage was of *experienced* staff, as it was greatest in those job categories for which the most experience is needed: the shortage of analysts (33%) in the Adams (1981) survey, was greater than that of analyst/programmers (27%), which in turn was greater than that of programmers (21%). This is consistent with the finding of the Cooper (1975) survey that the average coder had only two years' software experience. Furthermore, most authorities believe there is no shortage of applicants – in fact, there are more than the industry can absorb (Neill, 1980a; Dight, 1986). One training

Table 9.2 Rate of staff increase (percent per annum, compound)

	Programmers	Analysts	Operators/ technicians	Total
Hodges (1987b)				
1972/77	4	12	4	5
1977/82	14	13	10	11
1982/87	5	11	4	6
1972/87	8	12	6	7
Brandon (1978)				
1975/77				10
1977/80				22
1975/80	8	24		17

course had five to ten qualified applicants for each place; when another organization advertised a pilot training program for its staff, almost one hundred staff members, from all over the organization, applied for the six places; and another organization received over 5000 applications a year, of whom only 50 were hired (Dight, 1986). Many trainees have therefore entered the industry, and it will take the newcomers years to gain the necessary experience (Gray, 1980a; Neill, 1980a).

Apart from the shortage of overall experience, there are also shortages of specific types of experience. One authority, for example, predicted a jump in demand for telecommunications specialists and database professionals, whereas programmers who work in second- or third-generation languages are becoming abundant: 'their areas of expertise will become overcrowded' (What are you worth in '88? *Datamation*, 1 Oct. 1988, pp. 53–66).

In addition, there is a shortage of qualifications.

- One academic complained that 'people are going into programming with no background – it's pretty horrifying' (US battle looming over regulation for software, *Computing S.A.*, 14 Mar. 1988, pp. 22 and 39).
- The proportion of entrants with degrees dropped from 33% in the 1960s to 13% in the 1970s, according to one survey (Coetzer, 1983b) – though one consultant stated that some of the best and most creative programmers he knew did not have college degrees yet (*Computing S.A* article cited above).
- The proportion of programmers with degrees in this survey was about the same in 1980 as it had been in 1971, i.e. about 16%, but coupled with the growth of the industry, this means that the number of non-degreed staff increased.
- The pass rate in one entry-level COBOL

examination averaged only 43% (Maudlin, 1983a).
- The pass rate in the corresponding examination for computer operators (who are one source of supply of new programmers), was even lower: it averaged only 24%.

The evidence therefore indicates that many DP staff lack skills, and may even be of low caliber (Aron, 1974; Kraft and Weinberg, 1975). The shortage of skills is, however, not restricted to DP: there is a *general* shortage of skilled people (Big business for mini computers, *Computronics*, 13 Feb. 1980, p. 8).

9.1.2 CAUSES

The shortage of staff has been attributed to a wide variety of causes: low productivity, lack of training, recruitment, economic recessions, poor deployment of staff, people leaving the industry, high turnover, and the growth of the DP industry. Each is now considered in turn.

Low productivity

The lower the productivity of existing staff, the more additional staff are needed.

Lack of training

New recruits

Few organizations are prepared to take on inexperienced staff, because:

- they want people with proven track records (Jones, 1986b);
- they are afraid that their staff, having been trained at great expense, will be poached by other organizations: 'you are training people for your competitors – after a trainee has graduated from your class, gained a year or two of experience, and gotten over being grateful for the chance to get into programming, he may walk across the street and get a $10 000 raise' (Dight, 1986);

- several authorities claim that DPMs in the past had to persuade users to ask for work, so they could not be sure they could use any extra people taken on (Gray, 1980a; Zimner, 1978a; van der Veer, 1976; Doepel, 1977);

but mainly because of the time, costs and bother involved (Aspro for headaches, *Dataweek*, 11 Jan. 1980, p. 7; What are you worth in '88? *Datamation*, 1 Oct. 1988, pp. 53–66).

Existing staff

Organizations are unwilling to train existing staff for the same reasons they are unwilling to take on trainees, and also to avoid short-term disruptions (Kapur and Associates, 1979). Training is seen as less urgent than, say, inventory control or budgeting for salaries, so organizations cannot spare employees from everyday work (Hawkridge *et al.*, 1988; Institution of Production Engineers, 1986). This restricts the productivity of existing staff, thereby aggravating the shortage.

Training Facilities

The lack of good training facilities limits both the number of new entrants, and the amount of training of existing staff (During, 1978).

Recruitment

There has been an emphasis on mathematics as a requirement for trainee programmers, and this may have discouraged suitable candidates from entering the profession (Neill, 1980a; Weinberg, 1971). Similarly, the emphasis at universities on Computer Science, FORTRAN and PASCAL, rather than on Business Data Processing and COBOL, may also have discouraged entrants, and may have led to the acceptance of candidates not suited to commercial computing: 'many Computer Science graduates would rather design a compiler than write the application code you need' (Dight, 1986). However, more

attention is being paid now to commercial computing (Crossman, 1982; During, 1978).

The shortage may cause organizations to lower their selection standards, resulting in unsuitable candidates being accepted (Adams, 1981).

Career guidance counsellors and employment agencies may not be fully aware of the opportunities available in DP (Eberhard, 1976; During, 1978).

Economic recessions

Recessions have opposing effects:

- organizations cut down on training, so productivity suffers, which has the same effect as a shortage;
- financial restrictions make productivity improvement an even more urgent necessity;
- there is a reduction in the amount of work requested by users, so fewer staff are required – but once the recession is over, they ask for all the work they had been holding back.

Poor deployment of staff

This is caused by bad management – many DP managers 'are not aware of true people management', resulting in potential lying unused (Gray, 1980a; Dickmann, 1971; IBM, 1979; Johnston, 1980; Aspro for headaches, *Dataweek*, 11 Jan. 1980, p. 7; Weinberg, 1971):

- failure to retrain staff in areas to which they are more suited, e.g. not training operators who have the aptitude, as programmers;
- staff with insufficient work;
- waiting time between jobs – McKenzie (1982) estimated that 20 days (=8%) per annum are lost for each employee through this factor alone;
- highly-qualified staff doing clerical work, running errands, etc. (Chapter 4);
- over-qualified staff – this may be done deliberately
  - so that the organization will be ready for future expansion;

– because highly-qualified staff can do a job better than someone who just meets the requirements; or
– to handle occasional crises.
- staff may be pushed by their managers, by social or career pressures, or the desire for more money, into promotion, yet they may be less suited to the new type of work, or may not have the skills for the new position, so they are less valuable than before and may even be ineffective (Weinberg, 1971), e.g. if a good programmer is promoted to systems analyst, but does not have the aptitude or is not retrained, the organization loses a good programmer and gains a poor analyst.

This last point is an example of the Peter Principle: in a hierarchy, every employee tends to rise to his level of incompetence (Peter and Hull, 1969).

Singer (1982) uses an analogy: the data processing organization usually hands an employee a new office key and says 'Congratulations, you are now a manager', but the medical profession does not hand a hospital orderly a scalpel and say 'Congratulations, you are now a brain surgeon!'

Also, staff may be reluctant to move to jobs more suited to their skills, e.g. because many of the jobs offered are in small organizations, where opportunities for subsequent promotion are limited.

People leaving the industry

This may be due to (Ramsey, 1980; Doepel, 1977; Gray, 1980d):

- unsuitability;
- dismissals;
- dislike of irregular hours;
- disillusionment with DP in general;
- DPMs promoted to top management;
- family responsibilities, especially in the case of mothers*;

* This factor may be disputed, but only half the women in a Gallup survey (1990) said they would keep their job if they had children.

- retirement;
- serious illness, disablement, or death.

High turnover

Staff turnover is discussed later, but it should be pointed out here that some components of turnover – such as emigration and staff becoming freelancers (independent contractors) – while they may not affect the *total* number of staff in the industry, can result in *localized* shortages, e.g. in a particular organization or country. People leaving the industry are actually another component of turnover.

The adverse effects of turnover, and specifically the temporary decrease in productivity, aggravate the shortage. It has been calculated that, if the turnover could be reduced to 6.25% p.a., the staff shortage would be cured (Aspro for headaches, *Dataweek*, 11 Jan. 1980, p. 7).

The growth of the DP industry, especially the many small organizations computerizing for the first time

Users want more information, and this is now made possible by the hardware price reductions and price/performance improvements (Chapter 5).

This could be by far the main cause of the staff shortage (Gray, 1980a; During, 1978; Neill, 1980a). (See also Chapter 1.)

9.1.3 CURES

Solutions are mostly obvious from the causes, e.g. increase productivity and reduce turnover (these measures will not reduce the shortage, but will have the same *effect* as a reduction in the shortage); or permit staff with family responsibilities to work half-days or at home (Singer, 1982), rather than lose their services altogether (this will directly reduce the shortage).

Two other suggestions are worth singling out (Eberhard, 1976):

- organizations which sponsor university training should extend their sponsorship to suitable DP-oriented courses;
- organizations should make their DP facilities available to non-DP staff who want to learn, and then be transferred to, DP.

Some of the causes are outside the control of individual organizations, e.g. the economic climate.

There will be resistance to some of the solutions, e.g. there are valid reasons for the reluctance of organizations to take on trainees.

9.1.4 CONCLUSION

There has been a serious shortage of staff, and it was worst among experienced staff.

There is evidence that the shortage was growing worse, but even if this is still the case, with the large number of applicants, it need not remain so.

There are many reasons for the shortage, but the main ones are the rapid growth of the industry, and the reluctance of employers to spend the necessary time and money training new recruits.

There are also many ways to alleviate the shortage, e.g. by increasing productivity, improving deployment of staff, and devoting more resources to training.

9.2 TURNOVER

Some turnover of staff is inevitable and is even beneficial. It can, for example, assist the interchange of knowledge; it is also the consequence of getting rid of misfits; and one industry executive even advised young managers to 'Do a lot of job hopping. Never stay in one place more than two years. Find out what environment matches your personality by working for several different com-

panies' (Aspro for headaches, *Dataweek*, 11 Jan. 1980, p. 7; Boehm, 1981; Davis and Flynn, 1987). However, most commentators agree that turnover is too high – 'the software profession has been one of the most volatile occupations in world history' (Jones, 1986b) – and has damaging effects, including loss of productivity. Personnel continuity, however, is only taken into account in one of the nine cost-estimation models surveyed in Boehm (1981). This may be because so many projects have about the same level of staff turnover, making it more difficult – and less important, at least from a cost-estimation point of view – to estimate the magnitude of the effect.

Turnover usually means a move from one organization to another, possibly on promotion, but it can also include internal promotions, internal transfers, emigration, dismissals, staff becoming freelancers (independent contractors), and people leaving the industry. Internal transfers are people moved from one project team or department to another, within the same organization. This could be foreseen, e.g. specialists who only work for a limited time on each project (Boehm, 1981), or unforeseen, e.g. because a particular project is behind schedule, and extra staff are added to it.

There is some overlap between this topic and the previous one: emigration, for example, can result in local staff shortages.

9.2.1 MAGNITUDE

An informal survey some years ago reported a turnover of 70% p.a. among programmers in the USA (Yourdon, 1975), and Jones (1986b) knows individual organizations with a rate of 65%. At the US Department of Defense, programmers stayed, on average, only two years (Baron, 1988). In general, though, it has been about 25–35% p.a. (Aspro for headaches, *Dataweek*, 11 Jan. 1980, p. 7; McLaughlin, 1979; Hyman, 1982). This means that DP personnel stay, on average, only three or four years in their jobs. However, subsequent figures give a value of about 12% (US Bureau of Industrial Economics, 1984), and only 9% in 1986, and 7% in 1987 (What are you worth in '88, *Datamation*, 1 Oct. 1988, pp. 53–66). This is in accordance with a prediction by Davis (1983b) that turnover would decrease.

There are differences between job categories. Hodges (1987c) reported that, in large companies in New York, the turnover in operations was 14%, while in systems it was 21%. In the Hyman (1982) survey, the turnover for managers, at 30%, was the lowest in the survey, while that for operators, at 40%, was the highest. The Hyman figures, but apparently not the Hodges figures, illustrate a phenomenon not limited to DP: there is less 'job hopping' at senior levels. This has been ascribed to fewer vacancies and greater maturity at the senior levels (Deyzel, 1978).

There are also differences between different sectors of industry, e.g. the turnover for the financial sector, at 15%, was double the all-industry average of 7% in a survey of over 400 organizations (*Datamation* 1988, article cited above). However, these differences are not constant: the turnover in the banking sector, for example, was 15% in 1988, but only 8% in 1987.

There are also regional and national differences (Steyn, 1980). For example, the turnover in 1986 was only 1.3% in Seattle, but nearly 16% in New York (Hodges, 1987c). Turnover rates are lower in areas where employees are anxious about job availability. Once again, however, these differences are not constant: for example, the expected turnover in Philadelphia was less than 5% in 1986, but nearly 15% in 1987.

Some individual organizations report much lower (almost zero) turnovers (Jones, 1986b; Ramsey, 1980). Yet again, however, these figures are not constant. For example, one organization had a zero turnover in 1986, but expected a 20% turnover in 1987, due to an increase in staff and a change of vendor

(Hodges, 1987c). By contrast, another organization had a 20% turnover in 1986, but expected only a 5% turnover in 1987, due to their moving away from an area where housing costs were high and there was a shortage of staff.

Five years after one programmer training school had opened, only 5% of the more than 600 graduates had left their first jobs (Neill, 1980a). This may just be because the school avoids placing its graduates in firms with high turnovers (Pritchard, 1980b), but it is consistent with the statement by Jones (1986b) that organizations with entry-level recruiting tend to have long-term, fairly loyal employees, with attrition rates often being less than 5%, whereas the rate in one large, multi-national corporation which practices senior-level recruiting was over 20%.

Jones (1986b) also reported that turnover at IBM was related to appraisal scores: the higher the score, the higher the turnover, e.g. the turnover of those staff rated 'excellent' might be 30%, compared to only 20% for those rated 'not satisfactory'. This is plausible as the best people 'are the most salable', but Jones nevertheless doubts if it is generally true.

The accuracy of turnover figures in general has also been questioned: they may, for example, have been understated by the respondents in the surveys to show the DPMs in a better light; or conversely, they may have been inflated to allow for the effects of turnover (Coetzer, 1983b; Aspro for headaches, *Dataweek*, 11 Jan. 1980, p. 7).

9.2.2 EFFECTS

In moderation, staff turnover may be beneficial, but it also causes damage: short-term effects, a chain effect and other consequences.

Short-term effects

There are several short-term effects (Biebuyck, 1980; Moraitis, 1980; Ramsey, 1980;

Singer, 1982; Aspro for headaches, *Dataweek*, 11 Jan. 1980, p. 7).

- Organizations with a high turnover cannot function at peak efficiency and will seldom meet organizational objectives.
- The person who left may take all the expertise with him – which is the usual final end result of the Inverse Peter Principle: people rise to an organizational position in which they become irreplaceable, and get stuck there forever (Boehm, 1981).
- He may be a security risk.
- The project he was working on is disrupted, and may have to be rescheduled.
- There is a handover period.
- There are recruitment costs, e.g. advertising and personnel agency fees – which alone can be over $10 000 (Jones, 1986b) – transport costs associated with the interviews, and the relocation costs of the successful applicant.
- A higher salary must be offered to attract a replacement, and to outbid the competition – the difference between the 'going' and the 'buying' rates – 'we're forced to bring in new people at a higher salary than we pay our old people' (Dight, 1986).
- The organization's managerial and technical staff must participate in the interviews and other aspects of the selection process, which can take two weeks of staff time per vacancy (Jones, 1986b).
- The induction and familiarization time and costs, for the new employee to learn about the organization, its policies, and the projects he was hired for.
- It takes time for the new employee to become productive: this has been variously estimated at from 6 to 18 months (Adams, 1981; McLaughlin, 1979), but these figures seem rather high.
- Experience has shown that it frequently takes as long as six months for professionals changing job assignments (within the same organization?) to become com-

fortable and respected in their new jobs, while with computer science graduates entering industry for the first time, this can take as long as two years because of the terminology gap between industry and educational institutions, and the burden of learning a new vocabulary (Carpenter and Hallman, 1985).

- The time and therefore also the costs of the 'on-board' staff in bringing the newcomer up to speed.
- The replacement might not fit into the job, and so might soon leave.

Adding these factors together, the equivalent of one man-year of work is lost for each resignation (Aspro for headaches, *Dataweek*, 11 Jan. 1980, p. 7). Now the true cost of staff, taking into account paid vacations, medical coverage, life insurance, disability insurance, working space, furniture, stationery supplies, clerical support, etc., is about double their salary, i.e. there is an overhead of about 100% (A computer person costs twice his salary *CPL Comment*, Aug. 1979, p. 4; Gray, 1980c; Gildersleeve, 1974a; Phister, 1979). Thus tens of thousands of dollars are lost for each resignation – it can be as much as $100 000 for a senior position (Jones, 1986b) – though little of this amount appears in the organization's accounts books (Aspro for headaches, *Dataweek*, 11 Jan. 1980, p. 7; Westcott *et al.*, 1981). If DPMs realized the true cost of turnover, they would realize that the alternatives are bargains.

The disruptive effects can be softened if:

- the organization has a popular model of computer, or a popular operating system, programming language, or DBMS;
- it uses a high-level language;
- its systems are simple, are easy to understand and modify, and are easy to use (e.g. have a 'HELP' feature).

These factors reduce the learning time of new

staff. It also helps if other members of staff are familiar with the systems (e.g. by having structured walkthroughs), thereby reducing dependence on specific individuals (Wingfield, 1976).

Chain effect

One resignation leads to an advertisement, which leads to another resignation, and so on. A vicious circle is thus formed: the shortage of staff leads to higher salaries and more poaching, i.e. turnover increases, which in turn results in lower productivity, and therefore the shortage is effectively worsened (Aspro for headaches, *Dataweek*, 11 Jan. 1980, p. 7; What are you worth in '88, *Datamation*, 1 Oct. 1988, pp. 53–66).

Other consequences

Some staff move about so much that they never become productive, never do a job properly, and never gain good experience (Weinberg, 1971).

The merry-go-round image destroys the users' confidence (Steyn, 1980).

An attitude of mind is created – employees do not develop a loyalty toward their organization, and managers expect and accept the high turnover – which worsens the situation (Adams, 1981).

If, as some evidence presented earlier suggests, it is generally true that turnover is highest amongst the best staff, then the average level of skill in an organization may decline to hazardous levels unless equally skilled replacements are found (Jones, 1986b). Worse, once such a trend starts, it may be difficult to reverse, as the organization will acquire a bad reputation, making it difficult for it to attract good staff.

9.2.3 CAUSES

Turnover is caused and affected by many factors:

1. Shortage of staff and skills (as discussed in the previous section).
2. Lack of promotion possibilities and a clearly-defined career path, especially in one-man DP departments (Wingfield, 1976).
3. Conversely, some people do not like working for a large organization, and so leave. (This could explain the observation that turnover in large organizations, at 10%, was double that in small organizations (5%) in the 1988 survey What are you worth in '88, *Datamation*, 1 Oct. 1988, pp. 53–66. High turnover has also been ascribed to a high growth rate of an organization: 'Faster turnover is just one unfortunate product of dynamic expansion'.)
4. The 'elephantine slowness' of large personnel departments, which causes a 'brain drain' to smaller, hungrier organizations (Mallinick, 1977).
5. Changes in an organization (What are you worth in '88, *Datamation*, 1 Oct. 1988, pp. 53–66).
6. Staff pushed by their managers, by social or career pressures, or the desire for more money, into promotion (Aspro for headaches, *Dataweek*, 11 Jan. 1980, p. 7; Weinberg, 1971). They may not want the change of duties, may be less suited to the new work, or may not have the skills for the new position, so they leave.
7. The desire for personal growth, e.g. to study further and improve one's qualifications, or to gain wider experience – programmers are intelligent, and want a challenge (Tebbs, 1980a; Ramsey, 1980; Biebuyck, 1980; Hyman 1982; Ballantine and Moore, 1983). In particular, they want to work with state-of-the-art technology. For example, those Government departments which have high technology or supercomputers, such as the National Aeronautics and Space Administration (NASA), 'have little or no staffing problems' (Kirchner, 1986).

8. Emigration, which is mainly from less-developed to more-developed countries, and has been ascribed to tax rates, political factors, and the desire for higher salaries and wider experience (Tebbs, 1980a; Deyzel, 1978; Hyman, 1982). People therefore leave a country for much the same reasons they leave an organization.

9. Staff becoming freelancers (independent contractors). They, however, can then provide specialized knowledge, handle peaks or special projects, or fill in when people are on vacation, thereby enabling organizations to have a lower number of permanent staff, and thus ensuring no unused capacity (Ramsey, 1980).

10. Staff who are unsuitable or inefficient, e.g. DPMs lacking the ability to communicate, and who are therefore dismissed – in one two-year period, nearly half the DPMs in the US 'were sidelined or lost their jobs' (Mitchell, 1979; Biebuyck, 1980).

11. Poor matching of job applicants and employers – 70–80% of placements reportedly leave within a year, mainly because of dissatisfaction (Moraitis, 1980).

12. Over 80% of job placements are reported to fail due to personality conflict (Buchalter, 1989). People tend to be employed for their technical abilities only, and are lost for behavioral reasons (Battle, 1988a). Most organizations want the people to fit the system, instead of the system fitting the people.

13. Too many people, often the least competent, are nevertheless able to change jobs easily (National Productivity Institute, 1983): organizations are so short of staff that they are willing to accept mediocre applicants.

14. Programmers are often more loyal to their profession than to their employer. In particular, senior-level people brought in from outside have no special invest-ment in their new organization's policies or history (Jones, 1986b).

According to Stevens (1988), staff fall into two categories. Some need security and stability, and prefer to work in a comfortable, familiar environment. They are loyal to both their employer and to familiar technology, and form a stable work-force, but they may lack drive, and they frequently avoid additional responsibility and more sophisticated technology. By contrast, other staff continually seek new challenges and knowledge, even at the expense of stability, security and familiarity. They are loyal to themselves and their continuing education in the latest technology, so their technical expertise is often extremely valuable, but they can be unstable employees and may cause a negative atmosphere within their organization. Organizations should employ a blend of the two types.

15. Staff who are unhappy at their work, because of (Steyn, 1983; Mann, 1984; Ballantine and Moore, 1983; Johnston, 1980; Biebuyck, 1980; Big, 1980; Tebbs, 1980a; etc.):

- low salaries e.g. entry-level positions in Government departments (Kirchner, 1986);
- poor or dangerous location, or because their employer wants to transfer them to a different location, one which they do not like;
- a combination of low pay and location – the salaries in some regions are half that in other regions – one organization, by moving to a location only 75 miles away, will be operating where DP salaries average 18% lower (What are you worth in '88, *Datamation*, 1 Oct. 1988, pp. 53–66);
- poor working conditions, e.g. office lighting which causes eye-strain among VDU users, or the hot, noisy, overcrowded programming bullpen (Chapter 4);

- irregular hours or a large amount of overtime;
- pressures, e.g. on bureau staff;
- frustration, which may result from various factors, e.g. high growth need, or restrictions such as those imposed by structured programming as DP staff have a need to be creative, while one worker at the Xerox Palo Alto Research Center (PARC) 'watched them develop technological marvels, none of which the company seemed interested in marketing. Finally, he couldn't stand it any longer, and went out to start his own company' (Pournelle, 1986);
- lack of consultation and autonomy;
- lack of feedback;
- too much maintenance, especially simple routine maintenance, e.g. after systems have settled down, because no new work is being done due to an economic recession, or because the organization makes extensive use of application packages – Boehm (1981) described this as 'binding a programmer in perpetuity to a boring maintenance job in much the same way that the medieval serf was bound to a feudal estate'.

(Some of these factors may be disputed, e.g. Boehm (1981) does not accept the criticisms of structured programming, while some programmers generally *prefer* maintenance to development, and the figures in the 1988 survey (*Datamation* article cited above) indicate that junior programmers in the employ of the Government (not counting Education) are not particularly badly paid. Furthermore, some of these factors can operate in reverse, e.g. staff may remain in a job they do not like to *avoid* re-location, while outside the major metropolitan areas, there are fewer organizations they can move to if they want to continue working close to home.)

16. The economic situation, e.g. a recession (or a localized depression) has opposing effects:
    - it may bring to a halt all new development work, causing staff to spend all their time on unpopular maintenance, leading to their resignations;
    - during budget-cutting, there is insufficient money to provide staff with state-of-the-art equipment, which again leads to resignations;
    - on the other hand, during a recession, people are reluctant to change jobs, so turnover tends to decrease.

    Other factors can have the same effect as a recession, e.g. a drop in military expenditure adversely affects organizations which rely on the military for work (What are you worth in '88, *Datamation*, 1 Oct. 1988, pp. 53–66).

17. Mergers and takeovers, which can treble turnover in the affected organizations – not just because of redundancies, but also because of differences in organizational culture and management style (Hamlyn and Minto, 1988). Recessions may increase the number of mergers and takeovers.

18. Turnover is aggravated by the activities of employment agencies, e.g. headhunting, bounty payments, and the high salaries advertised, though this is disputed by the agencies (McLaughlin, 1979; van Niekerk, 1980).

Many of the factors which lead to high turnover can be attributed to inept management (Jones, 1986b; Cashmore, 1985).

An investigation of nearly 300 people found that people left their jobs for the following reasons (Cashmore, 1985):

- More experience   24%
- Better prospects   20
- Mobility of job   13
- Retrenchment   12
- Better remuneration   11
- Management failings   8
- Entering computer field 7

- Personality clashes   5
- Working conditions   3

9.2.4 CURES

As the high turnover is so widespread and is not restricted to the DP industry, it may not be possible to cure. Nevertheless, the low turnover at some organizations suggests that significant improvements are possible. Many solutions are obvious from the causes, e.g. recruitment, training, career development, and job satisfaction.

Recruitment

There is a need for better career guidance, and for better matching – on experience, ability, debugging skills, personality, communications skills, customer relations skills, specialized knowledge of the tools and application area, etc. – of potential employees with specific employers and specific jobs (Arvey and Hoyle, 1973). As Boehm (1981) put it, 'Analyst and programmer capability are highly multidimensional attributes, and ratings must be made with respect to the particular combination of skills needed for the job'. For example, applicants who had difficulty relating to people during their interviews and in their college lives may not be suitable for a position that requires constant user interaction (Singer, 1982). Conversely, an extremely gregarious, talkative, and people-oriented applicant may not be suitable for a position that involves individual effort with limited interaction with other people. Cost-estimation models such as COCOMO (Boehm, 1981) can help to quantify some of these factors.

Job advertisements could specify that a stable background is required, but one survey showed that this was not a good guide to future stability (Coetzer, 1983b), so employers should rather look at the *reasons* why the applicant left his previous employment.

One study reported that females 'seem more stable' (An international refrain, *Dataweek*, 11 Jan. 1980, p. 6), implying that preference should be given to them, but another survey reported the opposite to be the case: the turnover among women 'was significantly higher' – 25% left within the first 8 months, and 50% within the first 15 months (Coetzer, 1983b).

The much higher turnover among senior-level recruits quoted earlier, indicates that senior-level recruiting is not a successful long-term strategy, and should only be used for critical projects (Jones, 1986b).

Newcomers can be made fully productive more quickly by having well-documented systems, and a comprehensive procedures manual containing, for example, the procedures for authorizing source library changes and for documenting problems (Singer, 1982).

Training

Training leads to a stable staff who identify with the organization – there is a 'psychological contract' between the employee and the organization (Coetzer, 1981; Dight, 1986; Lutz, 1980). (Many Government employees have a similar dedication to public service (Kirchner, 1986).) Singer (1982) even argues that organizations should not accuse trainees of being ungrateful if they leave after a year. The actual problem lies in the organization's training program: 'Too often, there just isn't any'. With inadequate training, staff cannot do as good as job as they would like, and may even feel overwhelmed. A good training program reduces turnover by giving the staff more opportunities for success, thereby improving their morale.

If the initial training of recruits is provided by a variety of staff members, including some from user departments, each in his own area of expertise, then the newcomers obtain a wider range of knowledge of the organization, and are also introduced to more people who can be of assistance to them in the future. This method also gives them a better *understanding* of the organization, which helps them identify with it, and so tends to improve their loyalty and motivation.

Career development

Job hoppers should realize that career development is more important than short-term money advantage (Ramsey, 1980). However, this is a two-edged sword: many people *further* their careers by changing jobs.

Kraft (1977) argues that, for supervisory positions, there is a natural career path, e.g. a senior supervisor is in charge of more people than a supervisor, but that a similar path does not exist for technical staff – you are 'either an engineer or something else which is not an engineer' – so all management can do is create a series of job titles, such as 'programmer' and 'senior programmer', with appropriate salary differences, to give the *appearance* of a career structure. An alternative view is that larger and more complex programs can be reserved for senior programmers, and so can more complex tasks such as operating system interfaces; they can provide technical advice, solve junior programmers' problems, teach the juniors, participate in decision making, and substitute for the project leader in his absence (Singer, 1982).

Job satisfaction

The most effective way to reduce turnover is to ensure that staff are happy: 'good people in good jobs stay in them' (Sivers, 1976). This can be done by establishing where the staff are on Maslow's 'hierarchy of needs', and adjusting their 'rewards' accordingly. In descending order of importance, the needs are physiological, safety, social, esteem, and self-fulfilment (Maslow, 1954). For example, people who are starving – a physiological need – will not be concerned about improving their

computer skills – a self-fulfilment need (Couger and Zawacki, 1980). Furthermore, once a need has been met, it ceases to provide motivation (Chapter 11).

There are specific ways of keeping staff happy (Couger and Zawacki, 1980; Aspro for headaches, *Dataweek*, 11 Jan. 1980, p. 7; Barclays talks business sense, *Computronics*, 28 May 1980 p. 5; McLaughlin, 1979; Ramsey, 1980; Tuval, 1980; van Rijswijck, 1983; Shone, 1975; Jones, 1986b; Boehm, 1981; Singer, 1982; etc.).

- Make the job more interesting. Changing job titles will not help, but changing functions might, and so will projects which are interesting and are perceived as being useful, i.e. the job must 'turn them on' (Zawacki, 1989).
- Recognize the worth of the individual, value his work, and make him feel special.
- Reward and honor people according to the value of their contribution, not their job title.
- Stretch and grow your staff to the limit of their capabilities, so that they can contribute fully to the organization.
- Have a career development system tailored to the unique requirements and abilities of each individual.
- Permit good technical staff to remain in technical capacities, instead of promoting them to management. The CPT is the obvious example of this solution, but the non-supervisory positions such as 'lead programmer/analyst', as suggested by Singer (1982), and the Schach (1988) version of the CPT, in which much of the managerial role is removed from the CP (Chapter 3), may be even better.
- Promote from within the organization. This leads to a feeling of shared goals and aspirations at all levels.
- Train your staff.
- Find out how people feel about their jobs – e.g. by opinion surveys, an 'open door' policy, or regular discussions – to eliminate

ill-feeling and misunderstanding, to define their problems, and to draw out their ideas.

- Do not take reprisals against those who express negative views.
- Allow greater participation, and give staff freedom and autonomy to organize their own work (Chapter 11).
- Have flexible work hours to enable employees to modify their schedule to handle outside and family responsibilities.
- Encourage loyalty toward the organization. This can be achieved by involving DP staff more in the work of the organization, e.g. by appropriate organizational structures such as the application organization, steering committees, or information centers with fourth-generation software.

Good management is therefore the key. However, managers should not only be capable, but should also be *perceived* as such (Jones, 1986b).

If an employee is unhappy, he should discuss the reasons with his manager (who may already have plans for him); this can eliminate the cause of the dissatisfaction, and so prevent him from leaving.

It has been said that an employee begins 'leaving' on the day he is hired (McLaughlin, 1979). People review their situation continually, so managers should never take their staff for granted (Coetzer, 1983b). The time to worry about keeping employees is therefore when they are first hired, not when they suddenly show up in three-piece suits and ask to take two-hour lunch breaks (Singer, 1982).

9.2.5 CONCLUSION

Turnover has been too high in the past, but has decreased.

Some turnover is beneficial, but high turnover causes a variety of serious problems, e.g. it is very disruptive and very expensive.

People change jobs for many reasons, e.g. for a higher salary, promotion, or personal growth, or because of pressure of work, frustration, etc. in their current job.

There are many steps which can be taken to reduce turnover, e.g. staff training (which promotes loyalty), a career-development system, allowing greater participation and autonomy, regular discussions with their managers, better matching of recruits with employers, and so on.

9.3 TRAINING

9.3.1 EFFECTS

Benefits

Without adequate training, most people cannot do their job properly, let alone prepare for more demanding assignments, higher responsibilities, promotion to a different type of work (e.g. supervision), or give advice on the use of new technology (Singer, 1982; Metzger, 1981; Parikh, 1984). They may get the job done, but it will not be done efficiently, or be of high quality. Training leads to fewer mistakes and omissions, more accurate time and cost estimates, higher productivity, better quality products, and better service to customers, thereby improving the image of the organization, and resulting in turn in increased sales (Winfield, 1986; Hawkridge et al., 1988). Thus the US Bureau of Labor Statistics (1982) predicted that industries that do much training would grow faster; while one study found that, among private sector organizations in Britain, high business performance was strongly associated with a high level of training on every single measure (Manpower Services Commission, 1985). Put the other way round, organizations which fail to train lose their competitive edge, unless they can poach trained staff from other organizations.

Lutz (1980, 1984) reports that organizations which provide 10–15 days training per year tend to have higher productivity than those which provide no training at all, and suggests there is a correlation between staff technical training and software productivity. According to Jones (1986b), those organizations which encourage education and professional activities appear to be among the leading-edge organizations in terms of economic productivity. ('Economic productivity' is defined as goods or services produced per unit of labor or expense, i.e. it is a general definition which is not tied to any particular unit of measure, and therefore avoids the mathematical paradoxes caused by using LOC as the unit of measure (Chapter 2).) Various authorities have quantified the effect of training on productivity. Training can improve the productivity of keyboard operators by typically 25%, and by over 100% in exceptional cases (Chapter 4). According to Meakin (1979), advanced training can improve the productivity of programmers by 20–50%. In an example in Boehm (1981), two man-months of training per person in modern programming practices was expected to raise productivity by 20%, and would therefore pay for itself within a year. The productivity of one group improved by 10% after attending the two-week Software Engineering Workshop at IBM's Software Engineering Institute, while another group completed the design and coding phases for adding a component to an existing operating system in only *one-sixth* the expected time (Chapter 8).

Training helps employees to 'move up the corporate ladder' (What are you worth in '88, *Datamation*, 1 Oct. 1988, pp. 53–66), but it can also avoid the consequent danger of the Paul Principle: people rise to an organizational position in which their technical skills become obsolete in five years (Armer, 1966). Similarly, because of the rapid evolution of the computer field, it is important for organizations to provide opportunities for their staff to grow with the field. Failure to do so can lead to major disasters when the skills are required 'as several organizations attempting to implement large real-time distributed data

processing systems with armies of second-generation, tape-oriented COBOL programmers have found' (Boehm, 1981). (The importance of this point is brought home by a study by Rajan (1985), which found that, in only five years, there had been significant technical changes in about 80% of the nearly 2000 organizations surveyed.)

Training should therefore be treated not as an added cost or overhead – as is done by many organizations (Dorsman and Griffith, 1986) – but as an investment producing a measurable return, or as a capital expenditure which creates an asset bringing benefit to the organization over a long period, just like research and development expenditure (Burnett, 1987).

When training is thought of as an overhead, it is one of the first expenses to be cut during difficult economic times, as it is considered to be a luxury (Metzger, 1981).

It is false economy to spend thousands on equipment, and then balk at spending hundreds on training that would make the users of the equipment – and therefore the equipment as well – fully productive (Yeomans, 1988).

Dangers

Excessive training can be detrimental – it can, for example, lead to boredom – and even moderate amounts may result in the newly-trained staff being poached, or acquiring enough knowledge to be a security risk (Edmonds, 1983).

On completion of a training course, too much may be expected too soon of the returning student. On the other hand, he may find that his colleagues do not share his enthusiasm for his newly-learnt ideas, or – if the training was provided long before it was needed – the opportunity to use the skills may not arise, so it may have to be repeated later (Barclays talk business sense, *Computing S. A.*, 13 May 1983, p. 4; Mann, 1984; Tebbs, 1980a). Either way, the new knowledge would not be used, and the student may be so frustrated that he resigns. (Training *should* be provided before the knowledge is required, but *not* long before.)

If some categories of staff receive less training than others – e.g. computer operators less than programmers – they may become resentful. However, different categories *need* different amounts, so inequalities are unavoidable. Such resentment can, however, be minimized or even eliminated, if the *reasons* for the inequalities are made known, and all categories of staff receive as much training as they need.

9.3.2   AMOUNT

Amount of training

In terms of student days, the private, in-house training programs of major US corporations probably approach the combined Computer Science departments of US academic institutions (Jones, 1986b).

The Arthur Andersen DP consulting firm gets its staff by hiring MBAs and sending them to an 8-week programming school, after which they spend one year programming (Hodges, 1987a).

Trainees at the Hartford Insurance Group also start with an 8-week classroom course, after which they have 9 months of structured on-the-job training, including 50–60 more days of classroom work (Dight, 1986).

L. L. Bean originally had a 4-month course, but were able to cut this to one month when they began taking on people with some DP background instead of raw beginners (Dight, 1986).

According to Mitchell (1981), programmers receive ten days training a year. This is in good agreement with the 1988 survey (*Datamation* article cited above), which found that the average IS employee was given 64 hours training in 1987. Jones (1986b) expands on this. Bell Labs and IBM provide 10–15 days training per employee per year; many organ-

izations provide less than a week; and *thousands* provide *no* internal training at all. In fact, according to DeMarco (1982), more than *half* of all programmers in the US have *never* taken a training course!

One can therefore become a programmer after, perhaps, only a three-month course, and thereafter receive perhaps only ten days training a year, and frequently none at all. In the light of these figures – and the evidence (Chapter 3) that many programmers read very few books, etc. on programming, never attend a technical meeting, and so on – it is difficult to see how programming can be classified as a profession. Training is expensive, but lack of training is even more expensive (Mitchell, 1981).

Mitchell (1981) stated that the amount of training provided had increased, and Eurich (1985) predicted that training needs will continue to expand rapidly.

Hawkridge *et al*. (1988) predicted that, with the increased use of computer-based training, there would be less emphasis on initial training in the future, and more on 'learning-as-you-go'.

Amount spent on training

Some surveys have shown that organizations spend less than 1% of their DP budget on training (IBM, 1980). Other surveys have produced higher figures: 2% for the average installation, and 4% for small ones (Urwick, 1975; Douglas, 1979). The higher figure for small organizations is probably just a reflection of the fact that training costs are relatively higher for them (Hawkridge *et al*., 1988). In fact, one study found that most small manufacturing companies had no training policy at all, and provided the minimum training (Institution of Production Engineers, 1986); and some authorities claim that small organizations are less committed to training than large ones – they are the 'greatest culprits' in not sending staff on training courses – whereas large organizations have better training facilities, and planning of training is better organized (Maree, 1981; Steyn, 1983). Furthermore, the education budgets of the Fortune 500 companies (i.e. the largest organizations) in the US, probably exceed those of the 500 largest universities and colleges in that country (Jones, 1986b): IBM, for example, is reputed to spend $1 billion a year on training, worldwide, and AT&T is said to spend the same amount in the US alone (Hawkridge *et al.*, 1988).

Organizations should analyse their training needs, and should conduct a feasibility study before spending money. For example, Hawkridge *et al.* (1988) quoted one organization which was using videotape, and which then looked at mainframe-based CBT (computer-based training), but decided it was unlikely to be effective for them, and chose interactive videodisks instead. Similarly, another organization he quoted decided that PC-based CBT would not be as cost effective as their existing use of videocassettes. Hawkridge did not find any organizations which had conducted a feasibility study that covered all possible aspects, but did quote one organization which spent two years on an initial needs assessment.

When an organization is investigating the purchase of a 4GL or a DBMS, etc., the training costs of the competing products should be taken into account, as some are easier to learn than others (Singer, 1982). Organizations should have a policy review body, e.g. consisting of the training manager and several heads of user departments. The body would, for example, monitor the implementation of new training methods (Hawkridge *et al.*, 1988).

Organizations are not fully aware of how much they are spending on training (Eurich, 1985). Training costs include (Heaford, 1983; Craig and Evers, 1981):

- the salaries (including fringe benefits) of trainers, trainees and administrative staff;
- the cost of travel, accommodation and subsistence, for all these categories of staff, if training is held away from the normal place of work;
- the cost of the travel time (salary equivalent), if the travelling is done during business hours;
- the 'lost opportunity' cost, i.e. the cost of having the people do training rather than some other job for the organization, such as selling, which makes a direct profit;
- administrative expenses;
- the cost of acquiring or developing training materials, including any software such as authoring tools (the languages used to write the courseware);
- the cost of the training facilities, including the equipment costs; and
- a proportion of the organization's overheads.

The largest single hidden item is the salaries of employees while being trained (Hawkridge *et al.*, 1988).

Arthur Andersen & Co. spend $5000 per employee for training in the first year (Hodges, 1987a).

Morgan Stanley & Co. hire only the very best college graduates. They are paid a high starting salary, but much of their first six months is spent in operations, i.e. in a productive capacity, so in effect they pay for their training (Dight, 1986).

The 64 hours training of the average IS employee in 1987 cost an estimated $2800 (What are you worth in '88, *Datamation*, 1 Oct. 1988, pp. 53–66).

9.3.3 TRAINERS

The number of educational personnel in the Fortune 500 companies in the US approximates the total faculty size of all US universities – IBM and ITT, for example, both have internal faculties of more than 1000 instructors (Jones, 1986b). Nevertheless, there is a serious shortage of well-trained trainers (Mitchell, 1981; Hawkridge, 1988).

Large organizations have full-time trainers;

small ones do not. In fact, small and medium-sized organizations, if they have training officers at all, probably have comparatively untrained ones (Institution of Production Engineers, 1986). By comparison, IBM uses people with an average of ten years experience to teach a two-week course on software engineering, and in spite of their long experience, they must first undergo nine months full-time training in how to teach this course (Pietrasanta, 1989). Because of the importance of training, and because it is seen as less urgent than production work, the training responsibility should be formally assigned to a specific individual, otherwise it will not get done (Singer, 1982). Few organizations are prepared to use their best staff as trainers: they would prefer to use their weaker staff as they would not be missed as much, but this tendency should be resisted because of the importance of training (Pritchard, 1980a). However, organizations should not go to the other extreme and blindly select their best DP staff as trainers. Teaching and doing are two different skills, and it is difficult to find someone who is good at both (Dight, 1986). The people selected as trainers should therefore be whichever members of staff would make the best trainers.

Trainers themselves need to be trained. They must keep up to date with developments, otherwise their departments stagnate, and they also need continual practical experience so as not to lose touch – so, after two years, it's 'back to the real world' (Johnson, 1980b).

The trainers do not only have to train other DP staff: they must also provide appropriate training for end users.

Trainers never have enough resources, and have to deploy the insufficient resources as best they can (Sokol and Bulyk, 1986).

Computers can assist trainers, e.g. the trainers can use word processing packages to prepare course material, and spreadsheets or databases for keeping student records (Hut-inger, 1986). At a more sophisticated level, with computer-based training (CBT) systems such as the Tandberg Educational Computer System, the students have their own terminals or PCs, and the teacher has a master console which controls all audio, video and data functions (Tandberg, 1986). Students' workstations are linked to the master console to allow the teacher to monitor all learning activities, and assist where necessary. The teacher maintains full control of the class without having to leave the master console, thereby avoiding distractions caused by people moving about the room.

CBT can therefore reduce the number of trainers required (Rothwell, 1983; Steele, 1989; Hawkridge *et al.*, 1988). In fact, Fassl (1986) stated that, in some cases, interactive video instruction (IVI), which is an enhanced form of CBT, can *eliminate* a trainer. However, CBT is not seen as a way of doing away with human tutors: trainees complain if they do not have someone to turn to for help, and some packages are designed to be used with a supervisor on call. Furthermore, preparing CBT takes much longer than for conventional training, so increases in the number of design staff may outweigh savings in the number of presentation training staff.

9.3.4 TRAINEES

There are various tests, some of which are commercially-available, for screening applicants for ability, interest, and motivation. Examples are the Berger Aptitude for Programming Test, the SRA (Science Research Associates, Inc.) Computer Programmer Aptitude Battery, the Wolfe–Spence Programming Aptitude Test, the IBM Programmer Aptitude Test (PAT), the Test on Sequential Instructions (TSI), and the Strong Vocational Interest Blank (SVIB) (Dight, 1986; Weinberg, 1971). However, such tests have produced, at best, only very weak correlations with programmer capability (Boehm, 1981), and even a wider-ranging study, in which factors such as past high school achievement and age were considered, found little correlation with computer proficiency (Evans and Simkin, 1989).

Apart from the poor examination results referred to earlier, there is evidence that many trainee programmers are of low quality: many of the students at some private training establishments 'have spent a few years failing at university or college prior to taking the course' (During, 1978); and graduates of some of these training schools often fail recognized aptitude tests (Neil, 1980b). On the other hand, those who have been trained at their own expense are fairly highly motivated (Dight, 1986), which may compensate for other deficiencies. Also, the knowledge they have acquired means they may only need another two weeks training, to teach them the programming standards of the organization which employs them, and instill in them the organizational culture.

Selection of applicants for entry-level training courses should be done by the education staff and not DP managers, as they have generally had more experience in interviewing people with little or no work experience (Dight, 1986).

While programming ability is the most important consideration when selecting applicants for entry-level programmer training, managerial potential and the potential to become systems analysts should also be taken into account, as these are the traditional career paths of programmers (Dight, 1986).

Of Morgan Stanley's recruits, 90% are not Computer Science majors, but rather have a background similar to that of their end users: 'they look, talk, and act like our end users', which gives the DP staff greater credibility with the users (Dight, 1986).

Trainees who have had work experience make better students than someone just out of college: 'they have a better idea of what the business world is all about' (Dight, 1986).

Adults will only learn what they perceive is useful on the job: 'If they don't understand what is expected of them, or if they don't know how to apply learning outcomes, it's unlikely they will learn at all' (Applied Learning Corp., 1988).

People with negative attitudes, e.g. who are afraid of failure or are scared they might destroy data, learn more slowly and make more errors (Walther and O'Neil, 1974; Shneiderman, 1980).

Trainees are frequently not provided with the tools and physical resources they need in order to learn (Dight, 1986). They need computer time during the day while the class is in session, with ample access to terminals or PCs and printers. They also need adequate classroom space, blackboards, training manuals, and even a place to go during class breaks.

Computers can assist trainees in various ways, e.g. by providing hands-on experience and by computer-based training. In addition, trainees can use word processing packages to write assignments (Hutinger, 1986). One study found that students who used a PC to write their papers achieved higher grades than those who used typewriters (an average of B+ compared to B−), and none of them failed (Rider, 1987). Computer-aided papers appear cleaner and have far fewer spelling errors, as most word processing programs can check spelling. Also, because it is easier to make changes, the computer-aided papers are often much better organized.

Education is a life-long process.

9.3.5 TRAINING ORGANIZATIONS

Computer training is provided by a variety of different types of organization:

- computer manufacturers;
- software vendors;
- universities;
- commercial programming schools;
- correspondence colleges;
- adult education schools;
- user organizations;

- organizations which market training packages, e.g. ASI and Deltak;

and now even schools.

Much of this section refers to the training of entry-level programmers, but other types of training are also important. For example, it is in their own interest for software vendors to provide training in their products. Even if this contributes little directly to their revenue, it benefits them in other ways. They will have fewer queries to answer – 35% of the telephone hot-line enquiries of one supplier, and 90% of the after-sales queries of another, were due to computer illiteracy – while the purchasers will make better use of the products, so they will be happier and will buy more products from the same vendors, or at least will be willing to serve as reference sites (Diversifying for growth, *Computer Mail*, 27 Feb. 1987, pp. 46–55; Coetzer, 1989).

ASI (Advanced Systems, Inc.) and Deltak together apparently have more than 8000 courses, containing over 20 000 hours of study material (Auerbach, 1988a).

University training is an education for an entire working life, rather than immediate training for a specific job. Subjects are studied for their own sake or as intellectual training (Dick, 1980). By learning 'why' rather than 'how', students are better able to adjust to subsequent changes in technology (Crossman, 1982). University instruction in the past was oriented toward Computer Science rather than Business Data Processing, but the emphasis has changed, and good commercially-oriented courses are now available (During, 1978). Carpenter and Hallman (1985) reported that recent graduates from schools with good computer science curricula appear to be better prepared technically than ever before, and they sometimes have better understanding and technical know-how than those who have been in the profession for many years.

There was a debate a few years ago in *Datamation* on the merits of various university curricula. One writer argued that 'Most CS students haven't the foggiest idea of how a business is run, and most MBA students know little more than where the on/off button is on their terminals' (Milosevich, 1986); while another writer said that the two MIS courses he took for his MBA were more than adequate for what is, after all, a general degree (Dufner, 1986). An MBA graduate is not required to have the detailed knowledge to solve a problem: he merely needs to know whom to see to obtain the answer, and how to direct and guide the solution.

Many training courses for entry-level programmers have taught coding rather than the design of programs, i.e. syntax rather than problem solving (Klein, 1981). These courses do not nomally provide a business background either (Dight, 1986), but that is less surprising.

Some of the clients of one training organization had their own in-house training facilities, but they used this outside organization for specialized training (Diversifying for growth, *Computer Mail*, 27 Feb. 1987, pp. 46–55). Organizations which provide in-house training include the Hartford Insurance Group, which runs four programmer trainee classes simultaneously, each with 20–30 students (Dight, 1986).

In-house training can range from assigning one staff member to spend a relatively small amount of time teaching a few hires how to program, to mass production of programmers using a separate faculty and elaborate training facilities (Dight, 1986).

In-house training has several advantages, e.g. it saves on travelling costs, and it can be better tailored to the organization's specific needs (both as regards the timing of the course and its content). Also, key staff members remain accessible to solve any work-related problems which might arise, but this is a mixed blessing, as interruptions are not conducive to progress on the training course. Another disadvantage, particularly in small organizations, is that trainers spend time attending to technical aspects of the equipment (e.g. setting it up) when they should be using it to teach (Arvanitis, 1989).

Organizations which train their own programmers can train them in their own standards, and inculcate in them their own organizational culture (Dight, 1986). They can also ensure that good habits are learned from the start, as bad habits can form very quickly and are difficult to correct: 'old habits die hard' (Winfield, 1986).

9.3.6 SUBJECTS

Most attention has focused on entry-level programmers, with little attention being paid to other staff such as senior programmers, analyst/programmers and project leaders (van Niekerk, 1980), but other instruction is both needed and available:

- keyboard training;
- operator training;
- advanced programming;
- systems analysis;
- project leadership;
- management;
- DP knowledge for non-DP staff;
- business knowledge for DP staff.

Some organizations, such as universities and computer manufacturers, cover several of the above fields. The computer-based courses described in Hawkridge *et al.* (1988) also cover several of the above fields, as well as word processing, spreadsheets, telephone techniques, verbal communications skills, telephone diagnosis of customer problems, and topics such as 'In Case of Fire', 'Writing for Results', and teaching managers how to conduct performance appraisals, in addition to topics such as the training of aircraft pilots, which are not relevant to this study.

Training courses for entry-level programmers typically include basic DP concepts, COBOL, JCL, programming techniques such as structured coding, and work on programming problems (Dight, 1986). Other courses such as database tools, problem solving, mathematics and logic, may also be given. Wirth (1987) advocates teaching the predicate calculus, for use in proving programs and algorithms correct. Denning *et al.* (1989) and Gibbs (1989) provide more details of the content of Computer Science curricula.

Many training courses try to do too much at once (Dight, 1986). They isolate students in a classroom for 15 weeks, and try to teach them everything there is to know about programming. By the 15th week, the students often cannot remember what they were taught in the third week. Instead, there should be a phased approach, with formal training alternating with practical on-the-job experience, so that the students get the opportunity to use their newly-acquired knowledge, and thereby complement and reinforce it. Frank Fella, the owner of a DP training consulting firm, recommends that the first formal course should last six weeks and consist of programming fundamentals, and subsequent formal periods should be of one week each and teach more advanced material (Dight, 1986).

A study of the errors people make often reveals training deficiencies (Winfield, 1986). Program debuggers, for example, can record the causes of the errors they correct. This information can then be analysed by the trainers, to show them which topics require more attention.

9.3.7 METHODS

Learning methods include:

- on-the-job;
- reading manuals;
- correspondence courses;
- lectures;
- programmed instruction texts;
- audio and audio-visual;
- computer-based training, e.g. PLATO and PHOENIX;
- hands-on;
- role play and behavior modelling;
- emulating others;
- workshops;
- discussion groups;

- conferences and seminars;
- structured walkthroughs and inspections.

About 60% of training in the US is in-house, on- or off-the-job (Carnevale and Goldstein, 1983). One US study estimated that informal training amounts to 80–90% of all job-related training (Lusterman, 1985).

Conventional methods

Role play is an effective method for acquiring some skills, e.g. interviewing techniques. The role play situations can be recorded on videotape and played back to the participants, thereby increasing the effectiveness of the method.

Discussion groups include computer users' groups, workshops, conferences, seminars, and structured walkthroughs and inspections. Exchange of information, i.e. learning, takes place during discussions (Henneberry–Muratore 1986.) In fact, some of the best teachers at a conference are not those at the front of the class, and some of the best lessons are learned visiting outside the classroom (Forest, 1985).

On-the-job

On-the-job training is time-consuming (Mitchell, 1981). For example, Singer (1982) believes that a graduate of an in-house DP training program can become productive in *one-tenth* the time it would take through on-the-job training; and one training organization stated that it only takes about one month for a user to become fully proficient in the Lotus 1–2–3 spreadsheet package after he has attended a course, compared to about *six* months if he learns through a manual alone (Diversifying for growth, *Computer Mail*, 27 Feb. 1987, pp. 46–55). On-the-job training also requires guidance time from experienced personnel in a master/apprentice relationship (Kraft, 1977). On-the-job training is therefore costly and inefficient, and so cannot produce as many people as are needed (Hawkridge *et al.* 1988).

This does not, however, contradict the support for family teams (Chapter 3). The two methods complement each other, and so should be used together. Trainees should first be put through a formal training program, and should then be placed in a work situation where expert help is close at hand. Furthermore, Hawkridge *et al.* (1988) predicted that, with the increased use of computer-based training, there would be a merging of training and information acquisition at work, e.g. through the provision of HELP facilities in the software being used. Products such as Morgan Computing's Advanced Trace86 interactive debugger, and the ITC syntax editor for Modula-2, described later, are other examples along these lines. There will therefore be less emphasis on initial training, and more on 'learning-as-you-go'.

Classroom

According to Hawkridge *et al.* (1988), low-technology, instructor-led or 'stand-up' training still accounts for more than 80% of training time. However, it is notoriously unstandardized, varying with the trainer and the training center. It is also pitched at the level of the average student, who makes up about 65% of the total (Brown, 1986). More advanced students are bored, and less advanced ones are anxious, so the remaining 35% of the students are unhappy. This problem can be avoided by having more uniform groups. However, this would probably mean smaller groups. As Shneiderman (1980) pointed out, some research suggests that small groups encourage individuals to perform better, as they feel that group members will recognize good work and criticize poor performance; but on the other hand, learning is hindered by small groups, since anxiety and fear of failure are heightened. An alternative solution is to first put the students through a CBT course, to bring them up to the same level (Meiring, 1988). A study of American classrooms showed that, on average, a teacher waited only three seconds between asking a question and either providing the answer or moving to another child (Lewis, 1987). This is particularly damaging for that group of students classified as 'intellectual thinkers' (who comprise one-quarter of the students), who need time for reflection before they can answer.

Training is always likely to be seen as more effective if it is accessible and timely, i.e. is available where and when needed. Classroom training is not always timely: you might, for example, have a long wait for a place on a course. It is also centralized, especially if only a few training facilities are available, and centralized training is expensive and difficult to organize, particularly in organizations with far-flung branches (Hawkridge *et al.*, 1988). Alternative training methods, such as the multi-media and computer-based methods described below, suffer less from these disadvantages, i.e. they are decentralized and timely.

Nevertheless, classroom training does provide individual help, for which there is a need (PC users equipped – but undertrained, *Bank Systems & Equipment*, Jan. 1986, p. 62). Not only can students ask questions at the time the problem arises, but they can also learn from the questions other students ask (Theron, 1988). They also make worthwhile contacts and friendships among other students.

Hands-on experience should be included in classroom training (*Bank systems & Equipment*, article cited above).

Austin Rover found that 15 hours of effort was required to produce one hour of conventional training (Perryman and Freshwater, 1987), but Hawkridge *et al.* (1988) feel that this figure is too high.

Programmed instruction texts

Programmed instruction texts are good for teaching facts, they provide a consistent message, and can be used virtually anywhere and at any time, though it is preferable if a teacher is on hand to solve any difficulties, and they are otherwise limited, e.g. they are general ('generic') and so may not meet the organization's specific needs (What does the future hold? *Computer Systems in S.A.*, June 1982, pp. 19–27; Parikh, 1984). Their modern counterparts, the audio-visual (multi-media) methods, have similar advantages and disadvantages.

Audio-visual

Videotape courses used to be regarded as a plaything, but they are cost-effective, provide motivation, are 'an excellent way' to learn new skills, and can provide a degree of privacy which is welcomed by senior staff who do not want to be embarrassed in front of their juniors (Video communication beats the paper war and confusion, *Rydge's*, Dec. 1985, pp. 90–2; Hoard, 1981). (Some of the other methods, such as programmed instruction texts and CBT, also provide this advantage.) Consequently, videotape courses are now widely used: most of the top companies in Australia, for example, use video teaching techniques to train staff in the use of computer software (Video communication beats the paper and confusion, *Rydge's*, Dec. 1985, pp. 90–2). The disadvantages are that videotape is 'linear', i.e. it consists of a predetermined sequence of pictures and sound, which the trainees watch passively, apart from the occasional interruption for group discussion (Hawkridge *et al.*, 1988).

An example of a video course is Pavlovian from Typing Technology, which teaches touch typing in 10 hours (Interactive video training, *Business Systems and Equipment*, Mar. 1986, p. 56).

Photographic slides are an alternative to video. They are cheaper and provide higher quality images, and multi-image slide programs can provide 'an extravagant range of visual effects', but are otherwise less impressive and less powerful, though they can be combined with audio tape to give synchronized sound with the pictures (Sutherland, 1986; Hawkridge *et al.*, 1988).

In general, students like a variety of media in their courses (Hawkridge *et al.*, 1988). Furthermore, a wide range of media should be used, to suit the subject and the audience.

According to Mitchell (1981), multi-media methods halve training time compared to ordinary classroom teaching. One organization found that the version of a course using programmed texts and audiotape took 20 hours, compared to two weeks for the face-to-face version, i.e. only about a third as long (Hawkridge *et al.*, 1988). Video (images and sound) should be superior to audio only, as research has shown that people retain only about 25% of what they hear, but 45% of what they see and hear (Smith, 1988). However, unless they are properly supervised, multi-media methods require self-discipline by the students.

Computer-based methods

Dictionaries differentiate between computer-based training (CBT), computer-aided instruction (CAI), computer-assisted learning (CAL), and so on, but here no attempt is made to do so; we will use only the term computer-based training.

Computer-based training involves interaction with the computer, which motivates the student. It should therefore be a better method than multi-media, particularly for students lacking self-discipline.

Waldhauser (1991) pointed out that, nowadays, people are used to being entertained, or at least kept interested, and they learn more in those circumstances. Computers are better able to provide this stimulus than some teachers.

PLATO (programmed learning for automated teaching operations) is a proprietary CBT product, and has a central software 'bank' of 10 000 hours worth of instruction (Hawkridge *et al.*, 1988). It has been claimed

to reduce learning time by 40% (Education, *Computing at Escom '84*, Mar. 1984, pp. 26–7). PHOENIX is another proprietary CBT product, and was claimed to be the leading mainframe system, with over 3000 users in 1600 locations (Hawkridge *et al.*, 1988). Both of these systems maintain records which enable trainers to monitor each trainee's progress, and thereby specify what material each trainee should study next.

PC conferencing can be used for training purposes. One authority argued that electronic distance teaching is not only more cost-effective than campus-based contact teaching, but is also of higher quality and relevance (Steele, 1989).

Hands-on

Hands-on methods are also computer-based, and can therefore be classified under the general heading of CBT. They are interactive, so they also provide motivation. They are very effective for acquiring some types of skill (Hartley, 1984), e.g. how to use a word processing package. Similarly, a programming language is more effectively learnt if the student actually writes a program and debugs it as part of his training. Hands-on methods are effective because people retain only about 25% of that they hear, and only 45% of what they see and hear, but 70% of that they see, hear and do (Smith, 1988).

Morgan Computing's Advanced Trace86 interactive debugger, with its screen-oriented, full-information approach, has been described as 'an excellent tool' for learning assembler language, as the programmer can see the effect of each program statement as it executes (Webster, 1986).

According to Bridger (1986), the ITC syntax editor for Modula-2 makes it easier to learn the language.

Interactive video instruction (IVI)

Interactive video instruction (IVI) is an enhanced form of computer-based training. It combines a laser disk player with a PC, enabling the PC to display high resolution visual images and voice. An interactive video disk system is self-paced, and can allow the user to interrupt a recorded presentation to review information, answer questions, or go back to a specific frame (Ferralli and Ferralli, 1986). The standard 12-inch laser disk it uses is durable, and can store up to 54 000 still frames.

When used well, this method can really bring a subject to life. However, it has also been criticized on the score that 'desk top machines make very poor viewing machines' – they are far less impressive than viewing the same image on a projection screen (Sehr, 1986) – though PCs can be linked to projection systems. Also, according to Philippe Kahn of Borland, some people find illustrations distracting. Training courses using this method should therefore not merely display text on the screen, but should make full use of the capabilities of the equipment: graphics, sound, simulations, animation, storylines, vignettes, realistic sequences of action and reaction, and even games (Hawkridge *et al.*, 1988). (Waller (1986) commented: Reading text on a computer screen is rather like reading a scroll, and scrolls went out of regular use in the fourth century AD. Bound books offer information in much more accessible form than electronic text. They present developed arguments in a linear and coherent fashion, and provide for skimming, scanning and browsing.)

According to Fassl (1986), research has shown that people retain 15% more through using this method. Other figures suggest a higher value. According to Smith (1988), research has shown that people retain only about 45% of what they see and hear, but 70% of what they see, hear and do, i.e. (70 – 45=) 25% more; and according to Bates (1989), some organizations achieve as much as 80% better retention with IVI than with classroom instruction.

Studies have shown that the ASI (Advanced Systems, Inc.) IVI system raises training efficiency by up to 300% (ASI, 1986). Their system uses touch-sensitive screens, and comprises over one hundred modules covering operating systems, DBMSs, personal computing, etc.

Artificial intelligence

Shaw (1986) found that some topics could be better taught through an expert system than through conventional CBT. The expert system helped trainees more, by offering advice, explaining its reasons, prescribing alternatives and when to use them, offering opportunities to explore the problem, and explaining the consequences of wrong decisions.

'Logica Tutor' is a prototype CBT system with built-in intelligence. It builds up a model of the trainee based on the level of skill the trainee is displaying, and then chooses an appropriate teaching strategy comprising topics and level of instruction (Ford, 1986). Similarly, the education software supplied by Degem Systems includes an expert system which tracks the student's work, suggests help in solving the problem, analyses the solution path chosen, continuously collects data on the student's performance, and evaluates the performance (Cox, 1989b).

Options

The hardware used for the various computer-based methods may be dedicated solely to training purposes, or it may be the hardware used by the staff for their daily production work. The latter is known as **embedded CBT**, and is very convenient. Computer users, while doing their normal work, can have instant access to initial training, refresher courses (particularly valuable for infrequently practised procedures), or HELP, just by pressing a particular function key – in fact, the CBT used for initial training can remain available afterwards as an on-line job-aid (Hawkridge *et al.*, 1988). Furthermore, the students remain at their workplace and can easily be called away from training to attend to urgent other business. However, as pointed out earlier, this is a mixed blessing, as interruptions are not conducive to progress on the training course. In addition, embedded CBT places an extra work-load on the production computer, and there can also be the danger of production data being corrupted by trainees.

The hardware used may be a mainframe (or mini) or a PC. Mainframes are more expensive and cannot accommodate complex graphics or video, while PCs cannot handle the memory-intensive record-keeping dealt with by the mainframe (Hawkridge *et al.*, 1988). The trend is away from mainframes and towards PCs.

The software used may be custom-built or off-the-shelf. The latter is called 'generic', because it provides training in skills needed in many organizations. It is equivalent to application packages (Chapter 7), and shares the cost and immediate availability advantages of packages, but like packages, may not be precisely matched to the needs of each user organization.

Classroom training and CBT are not mutually exclusive. CBT programs can be used by themselves, or can complement or even be integrated into classroom training (Seaver, 1987; Baxter, 1988a). Surveys indicate that many users want the interaction of classroom training as well as being able to learn on their own from CBT (Hawkridge *et al.*, 1988).

Some of the courses described in Hawkridge use workbooks or training guides. In one case at least this was because the instructors felt it was crucial that students have some hard copy to take away at the end of the course.

Extent of use

Only 5% of the organizations in one survey were using CBT methods; only 16% of all US

organizations with 50 or more employees used interactive video to deliver job-related training in 1986; another study found that small and medium-sized organizations knew very little about the new technology; and many organizations even used classroom training for a spreadsheet program like Lotus 1–2–3 rather than the CBT tutorials provided (Hawkridge *et al.*, 1988; Stevens, 1989; Dorsman and Griffith, 1986). However, other surveys showed that 36% of all organizations with over 10 000 employees used interactive video, and 66% of large organizations were using CBT (Annual Industry Report, *Training Magazine*, Minneapolis, 1986; Hirschbuhl, 1986); and other evidence produced by Hawkridge (surveys, a prediction, and expansion plans of individual organizations) indicates that usage of CBT will continue to increase.

Advantages and disadvantages

Many advantages have been claimed for the various forms of CBT. It should be pointed out, though, that many of these advantages can also apply to other methods such as printed training materials, and not all the advantages can be realized in every CBT installation – in fact, CBT is not suitable for all training tasks (Hawkridge *et al.*, 1988). Some advantages have already been mentioned, e.g. the reduction in the number of trainers, and the fact that CBT is self-paced, decentralized, timely, and provides motivation. The advantages and disadvantages are discussed in detail in Hawkridge *et al.* (1988) and in articles such as Auerbach (1988b, 1988c); Bates (1989); Meiring (1988). The advantages are listed here.

- The trainees must be *active* (Kearsley, 1983), i.e. not just see and hear, but also *do*.
- Training is standardized and of a consistent quality.
- It reduces the time required for training. Over 20 cases are described in Hawkridge *et al.* (1988), with savings ranging from

15% to nearly 90%, most of which were in the 30–50% range. Other figures, e.g. the 50% reduction in Smith (1988), and the 30–50% in Bates (1989), confirm this range. A much larger saving is implied by Stevens (1989). For example, 20 hours with an intelligent tutoring system gave the equivalent of four years of on-the-job training (Lesgold, 1989). However, as the saving was measured against on-the-job training, it is more difficult to quantify and compare it, e.g. on-the-job training is part-time, and is very specific to the job needs.

- The reduction in training time means that employees spend less time away from their jobs.
- Trainees finish IVI courses more often than they do other courses (Seaver, 1987).
- Once the courseware has been developed, it can be used to train large numbers of students – in fact, CBT thrives on large numbers which strain traditional methods. CBT can therefore meet sudden large-scale training needs, such as increases in staff numbers due to rapid expansion of the organization, and retraining of all the staff due to the introduction of new technology. It also excels where staff turnover is high, and new employees must be trained quickly.
- CBT is convenient and flexible. It provides training where and when it is needed, even 24 hours a day – 'CBT can be delivered at any time and any place' (Hawkridge et al., 1988). (Though Parikh (1984) argues that, for optimum benefits, a regular time should be scheduled, to allow each topic sufficient time for digestion without disrupting normal work-loads.) Trainees do not have to wait for a place on a course. They also do not have to travel to a distant training center – in fact, they may not even have to leave their desks. There is therefore minimal disruption to normal work commitments. Trainees can also apply immediately what they have learned (Griffiths, 1986).

- Trainees like it (Rothwell, 1983; Seaver, 1987): they feel well-trained, with a better understanding of the task, giving them more confidence (Thirkettle, 1986).
- Trainers also like it, and in addition, obtain job satisfaction from developing the courses (Hawkridge et al., 1988; Thirkettle, 1986).
- Students can train in private, making it less threatening for them than a classroom. It is also non-threatening in the sense that incorrect responses are not dangerous, e.g. they will not corrupt production data. (Though this may not always be true for embedded training.) They therefore feel freer to experiment and make mistakes than in a classroom situation (Auerbach, 1988b).
- It is trainee-centred. Students work at their own pace, making it suitable where a group of students have widely varying knowledge or learn at widely varying speeds – the more able ones, for example, do not get bored. In addition, students can omit topics they already know well, or can repeat sections if they wish, until they achieve mastery – in fact, CBT is very effective where repetitive drill and practice is necessary. Furthermore, the computer provides immediate feedback, informing the student whether his responses were correct or not, and providing advice.
- CBT can keep detailed records of trainees' progress, even to the extent of recording the number of incorrect responses, and the time taken to correct the fault (Beech, 1983). Slow trainees with problems can therefore be identified early on, and helped. However, just as managers should not be present at walkthroughs (Chapter 10), so it might not be advisable to pass test scores or other potentially sensitive information back to the trainees' managers: performance on the job is what really counts. (This is the confidentiality which is practised at IBM's Software Engineering Institute (Car-

penter and Hallman, 1985).) Such a policy further aids the non-threatening aspect of CBT.

- Improved job performance. This is the real measure of success of a training program, not the number of hours spent in the training sessions, or the professionalism of the slide presentations (Singer, 1982). Hawkridge *et al.* (1988) quote several cases of improved productivity, reduced wastage and delays, and less tangible benefits of greater customer satisfaction, e.g. in one case, keyboard productivity increased by 50% (from 6000 to 9000 depressions per hour), and in another case, delays (in the de-icing of aircraft) were reduced by 85% (Open University, 1985; Beech, 1983; Thirkettle, 1986). Van Greunen (1988) quotes a case in which errors (by insurance sales and support staff) dropped by 4%. Kimberlin (1982) describes an army study in which three groups of students took a course on missile electronic troubleshooting. One group took a lecture course, one a CBT, and one an IVI. After the courses, the students were given actual faults to troubleshoot. The lecture group solved only 25% of the faults, whereas both the other two groups found 100%. The lecture and CBT groups took about the same amount of time to find the faults, whereas the IVI group took only half as much time.

However, CBT also has some disadvantages:

- It is time-consuming and expensive to develop. In fact, Apple Computer concluded that, for product training, good CBT takes so long to develop, that by the time it is completed, the product or need has changed and the training is obsolete (Hawkridge *et al.*, 1988). According to Brauer (1987), it takes between 45 and 200 hours to author a one-hour CBT course. Raymond Neff gives a figure of 1000 hours (A month after the launch, NeXT is still the talk of the US industry, *Computing S.A.*, 21 Nov. 1988, pp. 32–3). Figures given by Hawkridge, e.g. from Perryman and Freshwater (1987), range from 50 to 200 hours. Other cases he quoted, e.g. Treadgold (1987), contained insufficient quantitative information, but they appear to show development-to-delivery ratios ranging from perhaps 15:1 to 300:1. (The wide range is doubtless due to factors such as differences in the complexity of different subjects, and differences in power of the various authoring tools used (the languages used to write the courseware).)

- CBT requires more rigorous design than conventional training. British Telecom found that preparing CBT takes at least four times longer than for conventional training (Hawkridge *et al.*, 1988). Austin Rover use a similar but higher ratio of 7:1 (Perryman and Freshwater, 1987), while Brauer (1987) gives a range of 2 to 10:1. By comparison, Hawkridge believes that the front-end cost for developing CBT may be a *hundred* times as much as for conventional training.

- It requires experts to develop it, or at least people who have been given proper training: when conventionally-trained trainers are simply told to 'try their hand', the risk of failure is increased. Furthermore, this training must be provided before any employee training with the new technology can take place.

- Developing and managing CBT requires a combination of skills, e.g. both training and video production personnel should make up an IVI development team.

- It is inflexible: CBT systems ask all the questions, allow only a limited range of answers, and cannot handle spelling errors in the answers (Dean and Whitlock, 1982; Ayre and Ayre, 1991). Equivalent and possibly better answers might therefore be rejected. As Melmed (1987) put it, most current CBT systems are relatively unsophisticated in their capacity to analyse trainee responses, and can do little more than carry out a rough matching of the responses against a range of 'valid' responses defined by the developer of the system.

- Special hardware may be required, and the programs can only be used on the hardware they were written for.
- The hardware can be expensive. Capital costs (central processor, VDUs, and disk drives), network costs, depreciation, operating costs and maintenance costs, must all be included (Rothwell, 1983; Beech, 1983).
- CBT is more demanding on buildings than most other forms of training. It requires sufficient space to house the hardware and store the software. The space should be clean, as dust damages the equipment. The electricity supply must be dependable. Special office furniture, ergonomically suited to training, may be needed. All these costs must be included, e.g. as an annual overhead. (In the case of software engineers, these requirements will mostly already be met.)
- CBT is not as easy to use or transport as the printed word.
- Without managerial support, innovation such as CBT is always difficult, and the chances of failure are high. Furthermore, without on-going managerial support, the changes will not last. A successful pilot project is a powerful way to convince management that wider implementation would be in the organization's interest.
- Trainers may also resist CBT, as the new technology requires them to learn new skills, and may also destroy their existing work patterns. Without their support, implementation is also likely to fail.
- Conversely, training departments often *want* the technology as it adds to their prestige, but they may not be able to program it, and are even less likely to be able to repair and maintain it.
- There may be inter-departmental rivalry, e.g. the training department and the DP department may both want control over the equipment. This problem can be addressed by establishing a team containing members of all the affected departments.

Another criticism is that CBT is too impersonal. It is an *isolating* experience: can it build teams? does it allow people to bounce ideas off one another? (Hawkridge *et al.*, 1988). As one trainer put it, the best training results from the personal inspiration of a good trainer, from his ability to communicate with the trainee and whet the appetite for further knowledge and ways to use that knowledge (Manpower Services Commission, 1986). Perhaps a good trainer who developed a CBT program should be able to build at least some of this inspiration into the program? Furthermore, CBT does provide a one-to-one relationship between the student and the instructor (Smith, 1988), even if the instructor is a computer.

Some of the opinions and evidence presented by Hawkridge *et al.* (1988) indicate that CBT provides a higher standard of training (Johnson, 1986; Rothwell, 1983), but other opinions and evidence he presented indicate that the standard is not improved. He did not, however, present any evidence of a *drop* in standards.

There is also a lack of agreement over the question of updating CBT materials. The materials are held centrally, making it easier to correct them and keep them up to date. However, they cannot be modified as quickly and easily as for face-to-face training – in fact, updating can be a lengthy and costly process. CBT is therefore less suitable for courses where the contents change frequently. One way to moderate this problem is to supplement the courses with printed text containing the updates, rather than to update the CBT materials themselves every time.

A reduction in training costs (including travel and administrative costs) is also given as an advantage of CBT (Hawkridge *et al.*, 1988; Rothwell, 1983; Stevens, 1989). For example, one organization found that running costs were about half those for conventional training (Perryman and Freshwater,

1987); while other studies which included grading of students and follow-up tutoring, have shown IVI to be three to five times less expensive than conventional classroom training (Ketner, 1982; Reeves and King, 1986). However, another organization quoted by Hawkridge found that the average cost per student was much the same as for conventional training, while yet another found, after a pilot study, that IVI was unlikely to be cost-effective for them. A reduction in running costs is to be expected, because of the reduction in training time, but CBT is expensive to develop, and the initial costs will only be recovered if they are spread over a sufficiently large number of students, and this will vary from one organization to another, and even from one course to another within the same organization. One organization calculated that the breakeven point for one electronics course was 113 trainees (Perryman and Freshwater, 1987), but another organization calculated that usage of its videotex system would have to rise to well above 50 000 trainee-hours a year before it became cheaper than face-to-face training (Mortimer, 1983). Nevertheless, several organizations calculated that their initial costs were recovered in anything from 4 years down to only 6 months (Mace, 1986; Treadgold, 1987; Beech, 1983; Rothwell, 1983). Furthermore, three organizations quoted by Hawkridge *et al.* (1988) found that CBT cost them less than $10 per trainee per program (these were apparently all generic programs), while a fourth organization found that it cost them less than $20 per student hour (this was apparently a custom-built program).

9.3.8 SUMMARY AND CONCLUSIONS

Training can improve productivity significantly.

Generally, too few resources are allocated to training, but on the other hand, training can be overdone, and it must be well timed.

New entrants to the profession should be carefully selected, e.g. the selection should be done by the education staff, and factors such as work experience and even managerial potential should be taken into account.

There have been deficiencies in initial training, e.g. entry-level courses have taught coding rather than design, and universities have concentrated on academic rather than commercially-oriented subjects, but this has improved.

Attention often concentrates on entry-level programmer training, but other types of training, e.g. advanced programming techniques, are also important.

Computers can help trainers and trainees alike. This help can take a variety of forms, from word processing and spreadsheets to CBT and IVI.

There are a variety of training methods, each with its own advantages and disadvantages. CBT and IVI are the most modern and most powerful, and significant benefits have been attributed to them – e.g. greater convenience and a reduction in training time – but they are expensive to develop and there is still a need for personal help.

9.4 EXPERIENCE

A person's ability to perform a given task depends on his innate ability (or potential) and on his knowledge (gained through training and experience). In practice, these factors are closely linked, and it may be difficult to separate the effects due to each. To complicate the issue, Sackman *et al.* (1968) claim that increased experience tends to override differences in intrinsic ability, while Jones (1986b) describes the productivity variations observed by Sackman as being the result of individual 'experiences', whereas other authorities attribute the variations to differences in ability. Jones, in fact, does not discuss ability. Presumably it is incorporated into his discussion of experience (and therefore his productivity ratios for experience include the effect of ability). Despite these difficulties, the two subjects will be dealt with separately, with experience being discussed here, and innate ability in section 9.5.

9.4.1 EFFECT ON PRODUCTIVITY

It has often been demonstrated that productivity improves as familiarity increases: the learning curve (Teichroew, 1964; Ullmann, 1976). This is in line with Baker (1972), who stated that a low level of experience leads to less than optimum programming, and with McClure's statement that the success of well-publicized projects such as the NYT (New York Times) may have been due to a higher level of experience (McClure, 1978). Weinberg (1971) takes an extreme example to illustrate this point: certain programming work cannot be done by a team of trainees, no matter how large the team. Jones (1986b) uses a similar argument based on amateurs instead of trainees.

The effect was quantified by Aron (1974), who gave the following weighting factors:

- Senior Programmer   0.5
- Programmer   1.0
- Apprentice Programmer   1.5
- Trainee Programmer   3.0

i.e. a senior programmer is, on average, (3/0.5 =) 6 times more productive than a trainee, all other things being equal. However, as a senior programmer is more likely to already have a detailed knowledge of a particular job, giving him an added advantage, the ratio obtained in practice is more likely to be 8:1. (By comparison, senior programmers are only paid twice as much, on average, as juniors (What are you worth in '88, *Datamation*, 1 Oct. 1988, pp. 53–66; Gray, 1980b), and are therefore not paid what they are worth. There is thus a very obvious – though limited and short-sighted – way to reduce costs: use only senior staff. (Kraft (1977) gives a salary ratio of around 4:1 instead of 2:1, for 1975, but this apparently includes the effect of organization size, i.e. senior programmers from large organizations were apparently compared against junior programmers from small organizations. Perhaps, while junior programmers in different sized organizations may get similar salaries, the highest paid senior programmers in large organizations would generally get higher salaries than those in small ones).)

Aron cautioned that his figures are arbitrary – some people use factors which are twice as large, others use ones which are much smaller. They are in good agreement with the 5:1 improvement which was obtained in writing three successive FORTRAN compilers (McClure, 1969), and even with general figures based on the learning curve of 3 to 6:1 (Teichroew, 1964; Ullmann, 1976), but other values quoted later are lower.

Aron also stated that improvements in program execution speed of up to 9:1 are possible in PL/1 by making full use of the software features available. It is not unreasonable to speculate that the level of knowledge which can achieve this should also be able to produce similarly large reductions in development times.

A study by Takahashi and Kamayachi (1989), using data from 30 projects, found that programmer skill (defined as the average number of years of programming experience), was one of the three factors with the greatest influence on error rates.

Shneiderman (1980) quoted a number of experimental results.

1. Chrysler (1978a, 1978b) found that experienced programmers used fewer statements in the data division of COBOL programs. (As programmers can only code a certain number of statements per day, more compact code – whether due to superior techniques or a higher level language – implies a higher productivity (Chapter 2).)
2. Gordon *et al.* (1977), also in a study of COBOL programs, found that students required nearly seven times as many runs,

and had nearly three times as many diagnostics, as programmers with three years' experience. It was also found that the students' programs were longer (by 30% in the one case, and 4% in the other), and that the students used four times as many GOTOs (which would have an impact on maintenance productivity – see Chapter 8). (Once again, the smaller number of statements implies a higher productivity. In this study, the improvement was perhaps 1.2:1 for the two cases combined.)

3. Youngs (1974) in an experiment comprising a variety of high-level languages, found that professional programmers had just as many errors on the first run of a program as did novices, but the novices had 30% more errors in total, i.e. the professionals were more competent at removing bugs.
4. A study of text editors by Walther and O'Neil (1974) found that people who were experienced in the use of on-line systems worked faster with the flexible version of an editor (which permitted abbreviations, default values, etc.), whereas inexperienced users were overwhelmed by its many features. (This indicates that productivity is improved if full use is made of the available features.)

These details, however, are of limited use here, as the information directly related to productivity was not quantified.

Walston and Felix (1977) found a productivity range of 3.1:1 for high 'overall personnel experience and qualifications' compared to low, but their figures may include the effect of other, correlated factors (Boehm, 1981). (This specific figure probably includes the effect of ability.)

The COCOMO cost-estimation model uses a value of 2.5:1 for the combined effect of the three components of experience included in the model (Boehm, 1981).

Jones (1986b) gives productivity ranges due to differences in experience of 2.5:1 for

development, and 2.2:1 for maintenance. This represents the difference between 'high' and 'low' experience, i.e. between reasonably competent programming and simple inexperience not catastrophic incompetence. He adds that the difference between 'the great programming talents of the world' and 'the greenest amateurs' would be perhaps 20:1. This figure presumably includes the effect of ability. On the other hand, Jones draws a distinction between novelty and experience, and gives separate productivity ranges for the two. Novelty can be viewed as an extreme case of lack of experience. It refers to types of applications that are entirely new, in areas that have never before been automated: it is like a jump into the dark. Users are uncertain of their requirements, so redirections and recoding are necessary as requirements change, and much higher maintenance is required. Brooks (1975) even argues that you should plan on throwing away the first attempt. Computerization of novel systems, in areas such as psychology and linguistics, has even revealed flaws and fallacies in existing methods. It may even be unclear how to test the system. Because of all this uncertainty, the difficulty is often underestimated, and there is a higher failure rate.

Novelty can therefore have a profound impact, but it is far more exciting and challenging than programming applications such as payrolls that not merely cover known ground, but ground that has been covered thousands of times before.

According to Jones (1986b), between 1944 and 1964, 75% of applications were novel, but this has steadily decreased, so that by 1990, fewer than 10% would be.

The productivity ranges Jones gives for novelty are 2.1:1 for development, and 4.5:1 for maintenance, but these figures are misleading as the base system he is comparing against was a rewrite, so there was, for example, very little requirements analysis necessary. One can expect, therefore, that novelty has a smaller impact on productivity

Table 9.3 Effect of experience on productivity

Source	Ratio	
Gordon *et al.* (1977)	1.2:1	
Conte *et al.* (1986)	2–4:1	
Jones (1986b)	2.1:1	Development; novelty
Jones (1986b)	2.2:1	Maintenance; high vs low experience
Jones (1986b)	2.5:1	Development; high vs low experience
Boehm (1981)	2.5:1	
Walston and Felix (1977)	3.1:1	May include other factors
Teichroew (1964); Ullmann (1976)	3 to 6:1	
Beware* (1979)	3:1 to > 10:1	Includes motivation
Jones (1986b)	4.5:1	Maintenance; novelty
McClure (1969)	5:1	
Aron (1974): general	8:1	
Aron (1974): PL/1	up to 9:1	
Average (approximate)	4:1	

* Beware of the future, *Systems Stelsels*, Jan 1979, p. 11.

than these figures would suggest. On the other hand, the programmer of the novel system in his example was knowledgeable in the application area, which would not always be the case, so novelty may have a *greater* impact on productivity than these figures would suggest.

These and other figures are given in Table 9.3.

9.4.2 CAUTIONS

According to Jones (1986b), there was currently no real consensus on whether experience develops with time, through breadth of assignments, or is 'an intangible factor that varies with uncontrollable human responses'. Perhaps it is a mixture of all three.

Length of experience

Greater experience, by itself, is not a guarantee of higher productivity.

- Weinberg (1971) gives an example of a programmer with two years' experience, whose work was inferior to that of some trainees.
- On one of the problems in the experiment by Grant and Sackman (1966), the two

most experienced programmers (11 years each) produced, respectively, the best and the worst performances.

- Kapur and Associates (1979) found that veteran programmers took just as long to write a test program as did the least experienced programmer tested.

Kapur attributed his findings to a lack of subsequent training received by the veterans, and blamed this on their employers: they were too frightened to provide the training, as it would equip the programmers with the credentials to apply for another job.

Furthermore, Knuth (1971) found that the complexity distribution of statements in programs written by experienced programmers, was similar to that in students' programs, which indicates that the experienced programmers were not making greater use of more advanced features in the language.

There is therefore a difference between ten years' experience, and one year's experience repeated ten times (Linger *et al.*, 1979).

Relevance of experience

Experience must be relevant to the task in hand – as Boehm (1981) put it: 'three years of

Table 9.4 Effect of specialized knowledge on productivity (Aron, 1974)

	Specialized knowledge required?				
	No		*Yes, but not available*		
Time taken by:	*Factor*	*Time*	*Extra time*	*Total time*	*% increase*
Trainee	(× 3.0)	300	100	400	33
Programmer	(base)	100	100	200	100
Senior programmer	(× 0.5)	50	100	150	200

batch business programming on an IBM OS/VS system does not help much if the next job involves the detailed use of OS/VS teleprocessing and networking features'. One must be familiar with the tools and techniques to be used, as well as with the application, and a general knowledge of related subjects also helps. In other words, one should have a wide range of knowledge, without any gaps. Aron (1974) gives weighting factors for relevant knowledge. These are applied in the same way as the ones he gives for amount of experience (quoted in section 9.4.1), but they are probably less easy to understand.

Consider the example, based on a total 'weighting' of 100, illustrated in Table 9.4. (The '% increase' compares the total time where specialized knowledge is required to the time where it is not, and therefore represents the penalty for not having the requisite knowledge.)

Lack of specialized knowledge therefore has a proportionately greater impact on the productivity of a senior programmer than a trainee.

The figures in Table 9.4 represent the extreme case, where much specialized knowledge is required but none is available. Generally, only some specialized knowledge is required, and some is available, so a job will take, as a global average, 25% longer.

The Walston and Felix (1977) survey (Table 9.5) is not directly comparable, but their findings are in broad agreement with Aron's figures. They do not give a global average which could be checked against Aron's 25%, but the ratios they give for individual factors (i.e. specialized knowledge) range from 0.6:1 to 3.2:1, i.e. up to 220%. These ratios refer to 'much' or 'extensive' experience, compared to 'none' or 'minimal', e.g. productivity was 3.2 times higher where the programmers had extensive experience with the programming languages than where they had minimal experience.

It is not clear why, in the one case (customer experience with the application area), greater experience was accompanied by *lower* productivity. It could indicate that, where the customers knew what the

Table 9.5 Effect of type of experience on productivity

Type of experience	*Ratio*
Customer experience with the application area	0.6:1
Previous experience with operational computer	2.1:1
Previous experience with size and complexity	2.8:1
Previous experience with programming languages	3.2:1

Source: Walston and Felix (1977)

Table 9.6 Effect of type of experience on productivity (Boehm, 1981)

Type of experience	*Ratio*
Applications experience (>12 years versus <4 months)	1.6:1
Virtual machine experience (>3 years versus <1 month)	1.3:1
Programming language experience (>3 years versus <1 month)	1.2:1

computer could do for them, they did not restrict themselves to simple requirements, but instead asked for much more. Alternatively, Conte *et al.* (1986) suggested that there may have been too few projects in some categories for the average to be meaningful, and pointed out that the ITT (International Telephone and Telegraph Corporation) study (Vosburgh *et al.*, 1984), which examined 100 variables in 44 projects, arrived at the opposite conclusion to Walston and Felix.

It is also not clear why the ratio for 'overall personnel experience and qualifications' (3.1:1, quoted earlier), is lower than one of the individual ratios (the 3.2:1 for 'previous experience with programming languages'), i.e. the sum of the parts is greater than the whole. However, this is presumably just due to the averaging-out of extreme values.

In view of the large impact which size and complexity have on productivity (Chapter 8), it is interesting to note that productivity also depends on the amount of experience with programs of similar size and complexity. Programmers working on their first large or complex program can therefore be expected to have an exceptionally low productivity.

The COCOMO model (Boehm, 1981) also has productivity ratios for individual components of experience (Table 9.6). Here, virtual machine experience refers to experience with the operational computer's hardware and system software – operating system, DBMS, etc.

It would appear that, except for application experience, where the Walston and Felix figure is anomalously low, Boehm's figures are noticeably the lower of the two sets. This could be ascribed to the effect of other, correlated factors in the Walston and Felix figures (Boehm, 1981). However, there are differences between Walston and Felix's and Boehm's definitions, i.e. they are not measuring exactly the same things. In particular, in the case of application experience, Walston and Felix's ratio refers to the effect which *customer* experience had on DP productivity, whereas Boehm's ratio refers to the effect of *DP staff* experience. Caution must therefore be observed when comparing their ratios.

Jones (1986b) does not give separate ratios for language and virtual machine experience, and he includes the effect of techniques experience in his combined ratio for these factors. He therefore uses only two factors: application experience, and tools and techniques experience. He also gives different ratios for each of these two factors, depending on whether the experience level for the other factor is high or low: a high level of experience in one factor moderates the impact of the other factor on productivity. If the level of application experience is high, then experience with the tools and techniques affects productivity by up to 1.25:1 for development, and up to 1.1:1 for maintenance. However, if the level of application experience is low, then experience with the tools and techniques affects productivity by up to 1.7:1 for development, and up to 1.6:1 for maintenance. Similarly, if the level of experience with the tools and techniques is high, then experience in the application area affects productivity by up to 1.5:1 for development, and up to 1.4:1 for maintenance. However, if the level of experience with the tools and techniques is low, then experience in the application area affects productivity by

Table 9.7 Effect of type of experience on productivity

Source	Application	Virtual machine	Language	Tools/ techniques
		Type of experience		
GTE (Daly, 1979)	1.2:1			
Jones (1986b): maintenance	1.4–2:1			1.1–1.6:1
TRW (Wolverton, 1974)	1.5–1.7:1			
Jones (1986b): development	1.5–2:1			1.25–1.7:1
COCOMO (Boehm, 1981)	1.6:1	1.3:1	1.2:1	
RCA (Freiman and Park, 1979)	1.7:1	1.2:1	1.2:1	
Doty (Herd *et al.*, 1977)		1.9:1		
Boeing (Black *et al.*, 1977)	2.0:1			
IBM (Walston and Felix, 1977)	2.8:1	2.1:1	3.2:1	
NARDAC (Williamson, 1979)	3.0:1			
Average (unweighted)	1.9:1	1.6:1	1.9:1	1.4:1

up to 2:1 for both development and maintenance.

These, and other figures given in Boehm (1981), are presented in Table 9.7. The Doty value shown under 'virtual machine experience' refers to 'first software developed on CPU', which implies extreme lack of experience with the virtual machine. It is the highest of all the factors in that model (Boehm, 1981), which is consistent with the statement by Frangos (1980) that 50% of the software written for new mainframe installations has to be rewritten within six months (Chapter 13).

The most anomalous of the tabulated values is Walston and Felix's 3.2:1 for language experience, which is much higher than the corresponding values given by other authorities. This figure has already been queried, as it is higher than Walston and Felix's own ratio for overall experience and qualifications.

If Jones had given separate figures for virtual machine experience and language experience (and techniques experience), then these would probably have been lower than any of the corresponding tabulated values. (If each factor had the same impact on productivity, then the impact of each would have been the cube root of the combined impact, i.e. under 1.2:1 for both development and maintenance.) However, his figures for application experience are amongst the lowest tabulated, so his low ratios for tools and techniques experience probably have no additional significance.

In addition to the above figures, a Delphi survey by Scott and Simmons (1974) rated 'programmer experience in functional area' as having one of the highest correlations with programmer productivity. By contrast, a study by Jeffery and Lawrence (1979) found very little correlation between experience and productivity.

A study by Chrysler (1978a) showed a close correlation between applications experience, language experience, and total programming experience, implying that the majority of programmers in the organization studied had spent most of their careers writing only business applications in COBOL. The same is probably true of many other programmers in many other organizations. In many cases, therefore, it is not necessary to distinguish between the different types of experience: a composite productivity ratio will suffice (Boehm, 1981).

Hardware experience is taken into account in seven of the nine cost-estimation models surveyed by Boehm (1981); applications experience or novelty also in seven; and language experience in only five of the nine models.

Too much experience

Knowledge and experience also have *disadvantages*, e.g. the staff may be exposed to *too much* new knowledge, i.e. at a faster rate than they can absorb, so they would not derive the full benefit from their experience; or they may become over-qualified for their jobs, resulting in boredom and causing them to resign (Tebbs, 1980a; Johnston, 1980).

Too much time can be spent acquiring knowledge. Much of the emphasis in this section is on the interchange of knowledge through meetings and discussions. This is particularly necessary because, as pointed out in Chapter 3, many DP personnel are insular and preoccupied with their own immediate tasks, and so are ignorant of developments outside their own immediate world; they possess or read very few books, journals, or articles on programming; they never discuss techniques with a colleague; and never attend a technical meeting. Worse, in many organizations, programmers are discouraged from talking, and discussion or sharing of ideas is frowned upon (Bell *et al.*, 1987). However, meetings and discussions should preferably be regular, official ones, else the low social needs of programmers (Couger and Zawacki, 1980) may result in the meetings falling into disuse; and unless they are properly controlled, they could be inefficiently run and last too long. (Guidelines for meetings were given in Chapter 3.) Furthermore, some staff might become preoccupied with new techniques and recent advances, at the expense of productive work (Yourdon, 1975).

9.4.3 USING EXPERIENCE

Staff with more experience are generally more productive. How can this fact be used to advantage? It might appear to be of academic interest only, as each organization has a certain complement of staff, each of whom has a certain level of experience which only increases with the passage of time. However, closer examination shows that it *is* of practical value:

- firstly, the organization can ensure that it uses to the full the experience available, by
  - having an optimal organizational structure;
  - ensuring interchange of knowledge; and
  - optimal allocation of work; and
- secondly, the increase in experience can be accelerated by
  - selective recruitment;
  - appropriate training;
  - interchange of knowledge; and
  - carefully planned allocation of work to maximize the rate of learning.

(Selective recruitment means recruiting experienced staff, particularly those possessing specialized skills which the organization lacks. The recruits then transfer their knowledge to the existing staff.)

It can thus be seen that there are two points of view which must be considered:

- the *short-term* view considers the *existing* experience and how it can best be used to achieve maximum productivity on *current* work; while
- the *long-term* view considers the *increase* in experience, and how this can be *accelerated* to achieve maximum productivity on *future* work.

Put another way, there are *dual goals* to be met: production and training (Weinberg, 1971). While short-term actions such as training which advance people's long-range career objectives also enhance an organization's long-term software productivity (Boehm, 1981), nevertheless there can be conflict between short-term and long-term goals. For example, the inexperienced members of a team lower its productivity (and therefore delay completion of the project), but the experience they gain increases their productivity on subsequent projects. Thus a lower short-term productivity is traded against a higher long-term productivity.

It seems reasonable to assume that long-term effects will outweigh short-term effects. (Cost-estimation models such as COCOMO provide a basis for estimating such trade-offs, and therefore for detailed project personnel planning to arrive at an optimal solution, but the effect on morale and job satisfaction must also be taken into account.) Therefore, while in exceptional circumstances – if the project is particularly urgent, complex or large, or if the senior staff dislike working with juniors – it is justifiable to staff a project with only the most experienced people, generally, each team should contain a mixture of experienced and inexperienced staff (Van Tassel, 1978; Mumford and Henshall, 1979). On the other hand, if the inexperienced programmers are still trainees, then grouping them together allows training facilities to be concentrated. Having staff with qualifications in education readily available may well result in higher productivity than in mixed teams.

Even if only short-term effects are taken into account, a trade-off situation still exists. Putting the most experienced people on one project maximizes productivity on that project, but deprives the remaining projects of experienced people, so productivity on them suffers, and the productivity loss on the remaining projects may more than offset the gain on the first project. (Once again, cost-estimation models provide a basis for estimating such trade-offs.) Furthermore, bearing in mind Weinberg's belief that some work cannot be done by a team of trainees, no matter how large the team (Weinberg, 1971), there is likely to be a lower limit of experience, below which performance becomes unacceptably poor.

Recruitment

Because of the shortage of staff, particularly experienced staff, recruitment is not a generally viable option – though it might be necessary in extreme cases, or if the organization lacked expertise in some specialized fields (Ramsey, 1980). However, by recruiting staff from other departments in the organization and training them in DP, the DP department gets staff who already have experience in the specific applications, which helps (Grindley, 1980).

Learning

Training, particularly formal courses, is a subject in its own right and has already been discussed, so it will suffice to mention firstly, that there are integrated training schemes, in which the training is individually selected to fill gaps between each employee's existing skills and the skills required for his job (Tuval, 1980); and secondly, that the learning process can be accelerated in several ways besides formal courses:

- by having inexperienced people working together with experienced staff;
- by senior staff checking the work of juniors;
- by walkthroughs or inspections;
- by regular meetings at which problems are discussed, and newly acquired knowledge is interchanged – 'What so often results from a bull session is either a new technical idea or a pitfall to avoid' (Metzger, 1981);
- by job rotation;
- by doing maintenance, which exposes juniors to the wealth of experience contained in the programs, and also shows them the consequences of bad technique (Baker, 1972; Van Tassel, 1978).

One word of caution is necessary about the

last suggestion. It is dangerous for juniors to do maintenance, as inept maintenance can destroy all the good work done during development. They should therefore work under supervision, and should not be used for urgent maintenance (Glass, 1979; Gildersleeve, 1974a).

Metzger (1981) advocates job rotation, arguing that programmers who complain about the computer room operations can both learn much and contribute much just by becoming computer operators for a few days; operators will become better operators by taking some basic programming courses; and typists who take a basic course in DP will do a better job of transcribing 'all those scribbles'. Job rotation between maintenance and development was discussed in Chapter 8.

Although each of the listed measures can be implemented with any of the possible structures of the DP department discussed in Chapter 3, some structures may lend themselves more to one measure than another. For example, walkthroughs fit more naturally into the matrix structure because of its democratic nature, and are less likely to be used in a rigid, bureaucratic organization.

Program size

Where the programs are small enough to be developed by one person, it is likely that the senior staff already reserve the more complex programs for themselves, but they would probably do the whole of each program – it is unlikely that they would do only the more complex parts, leaving the simpler parts to juniors. Thus senior staff would spend part of their time doing simple work, so there would be some room for productivity improvement. However, splitting programs up to avoid this disadvantage requires extra effort, and increases the amount of non-productive communication, which offsets the productivity gains. Furthermore, such splitting of work leads to job impoverishment – the junior programmers, for example, might

be largely reduced to coders – which could have a detrimental effect on job satisfaction and therefore on productivity.

However, programs which were too big to be written by one programmer, and which therefore had to be split anyway, could be split between experienced and inexperienced people without incurring any additional overhead or communications penalty.

Where programs are small enough to be written by one person working alone, the interchange of knowledge is likely to be limited.

Department size

Where the number of staff is small, options for accelerating the acquisition of experience through allocation of work are limited, so there is little room for productivity improvement through this method. On the other hand, staff in small departments may well handle a greater variety of work than those in large departments, where greater specialization is possible.

Small departments may have an informal atmosphere with many discussions, resulting in a high degree of interchange of knowledge. On the other hand, the programs they develop are likely to be small and simple – ones which are written by one person working alone, which would tend to restrict the interchange of knowledge, as mentioned above.

Supervision

In traditional programming teams (those not practicing 'ego-less programming'), the leader of the team is likely to check the work of the juniors, but not that of the experienced members. Although the juniors are the people most in need of the senior's experience, the evidence presented earlier shows that many experienced staff can also benefit, so there is room for productivity improvement. This can be achieved by using the methods for increasing interchange of know-ledge listed earlier (walkthroughts, discussions, etc.), or by the senior checking their work as well.

There are disadvantages incurred by having experienced programmers in supervisory positions, e.g. they have to divide their time between administrative duties and programming.

Where the supervisors spend all their time on administrative and supervisory duties (as happens in the hardware/software split Type 4 DP structure), there is less of the central technical control that characterized the successful CPT projects. There is, therefore, the danger of a lowering of quality. On the other hand, conflict may arise, and confusion regarding division of responsibility, if a CP-like person, subordinate to the supervisor, were incorporated into this structure. (The position of lead programmer in a project team, as described by Long (1979), corresponds to the situation being discussed here.)

Despite the above reservations, because the supervisor is freed from technical responsibilities, he can concentrate on managing. He would thus be more aware of the importance of ensuring that the distribution of work is optimal, and that there is interchange of knowledge. Furthermore, ensuring that these functions were carried out would occupy a higher priority among his duties.

If the supervisor is an ex-systems analyst, he may ensure optimal allocation of work and interchange of knowledge at the system level, but be less able and less enthusiastic about doing the same at the programming level, with consequent adverse effect on programming productivity.

Blurring of functions

It is not clear what the effect is of the blurring of functional separation between systems analysts and programmers (as happens in the hardware/software split Type 4 DP structure). On the one hand, it tends to counteract

the problems caused by having ex-systems analysts as the supervisors – they may have had considerable recent programming experience as well – and the staff are more flexible regarding what work they can do. On the other hand, they need a wider range of knowledge – programming and analysis, instead of just one or the other – so their knowledge may lack depth, causing a lower productivity both short-term and long-term.

Project team DP structure (type 5)

Some of the factors discussed above are relevant to this structure:

- the project leader may only be a part-time supervisor;
- he may be the most experienced member of the team, and will normally be a systems analyst (Appendix D);
- some programs would be large enough to split between experienced and inexperienced programmers; and
- there may be a blurring of functional separation between systems analysts and programmers.

There is, however, a fundamental difference between this and the Type 1 to 4 department structures. In them, the group of programmers includes all the programmers in the department, and the group of systems analysts all the analysts. There is thus considerable flexibility regarding allocation of work: each task, no matter which project it is part of, can be given to whichever member of the department can do it best or would benefit most from it. Under the project team structure, the staff are divided into teams, and each project is allocated to a specific team. Each task would normally only be given to a member of the team working on the project, even if there was someone on another team who could perform the task better or benefit more from it.

The project team structure therefore introduces a degree of rigidity which tends to lower productivity. This effect will be more pronounced for permanent teams, but will occur even when teams are set up solely for the duration of a project. Suppose, for example, a project contains enough advanced work for 1.75 experienced programmers. (Cost-estimation models such as COCOMO produce fractional answers like this (Boehm, 1981).) Probably, two senior programmers would be allocated to the team, resulting in some work being done by programmers who were overqualified for it. The importance of this factor should, however, not be exaggerated. As the figures in the example indicate, it is small in magnitude: the bulk of the difficult work is done by senior staff, and of the easy work by junior staff, irrespective of the department structure. In any event, it is doubtful if many organizations try to be as accurate as this, especially as a measure of prediction is involved, and forecasting the degree of difficulty of an unwritten program is not yet an exact science (Aron, 1974; Schach, 1990).

The project team structure is also likely to affect the interchange of knowledge. On the one hand, the interchange might tend to be confined within each team, thereby limiting the spread of knowledge; but on the other hand, there may be an *increase* in the interchange *within* each team, for a variety of reasons:

- because the members of the team work on related tasks – and simply because they are on the same team – they may be more interested in (and better understand) their colleagues' problems;
- the group is smaller and more manageable;
- its smaller size may result in a less formal and friendlier atmosphere.

Permanent teams have additional benefits, such as more knowledgeable allocation of work to aid career development (Chapter 3).

Matrix DP structure (type 6)

This structure also consists of project teams, so most of the considerations applicable to the previous structure apply here as well. However, the matrix structure is less formal, which may encourage interchange of knowledge, e.g. walkthroughs may be commonly used. On the other hand, there is the danger that the 'loose, amorphous' nature of authority (Bebbington, 1980), coupled with the informal reporting, may allow the 'innovative thinkers' who comprise the teams to degenerate into anarchy, with each using his own standards and techniques – methods with which no-one else was familiar. Even if these methods were good, their benefits would have to be weighed against the disadvantages. Either additional training would have to be provided, or additional discussion encouraged, so that all members of staff were familiar with each other's methods, or a low productivity would have to be accepted during the maintenance phase as the maintenance staff struggled to understand the unique techniques which had been used (Weinberg, 1971).

The matrix structure is flexible – in fact, it is the most fluid of all the structures (Bebbington, 1980) – so it does not suffer from the rigidity problems of the project team structure regarding allocation of work. Further, because of the overlap of the teams, interchange of knowledge is less likely to be confined within each team. However, the overlap may also lead to a division of interest and loyalty, and a lessening of the benefits of project teams, particularly those of permanent teams, such as consistent methods (Chapter 3).

Chief programmer teams (CPT)

The CPT is a particular form of project team, one where experience is emphasized. In fact, this is the first topic discussed by Baker (1972) in his account of the NYT project. Furthermore, he classifies a programmer with a few years' experience as 'relatively junior'. By contrast, some job advertisements for senior programmers specify as little as two or three years' experience required; the job descriptions used in the annual *Datamation* salary surveys specify only three years' experience for the 'senior' classifications (What are you worth in '88, *Datamation*, 1 Oct. 1988, pp. 53–66); and Boehm (1981) classifies three years' programming language or virtual machine experience as 'high' (though six years' applications experience are needed to meet his 'high' classification for that). By comparison, the average coder in the Cooper (1975) survey had two years' software experience.

The CPT ensures a 'rubbing off' of experience. The chief programmer scrutinizes the code generated by everyone else in the team, not just that generated by the juniors. As this is officially one of his duties, it would normally be done, thereby spreading his experience to all other members of the team. In turn, the code he writes is public property, and parts of it are read and used by others. So, although it is not one of the duties of the juniors to check and approve it (as would be the case in a walkthrough), there is some public scrutiny leading to a sharing of knowledge.

Experience, however, plays an even more important and central role than this in a CPT. The whole project is organized around a very experienced person, the chief programmer – he is the pivot (Baker, 1972). He also does critical parts of the programming. One of the aims of the concept was to counteract the situation where so many senior programmers become managers, and it should also reduce the flow of programmers into systems analysis. Instead, experienced programmers stay with what they do best: programming (van Wyk and Kamfer, 1976). The CPT therefore goes further than just splitting work between experienced and inexperienced staff, so this structure might make the best possible use of experience.

A CPT should only contain one or two less-experienced programmers, otherwise quality and productivity suffer (Baker, 1972; Macro and Buxton, 1987). In fact, Macro and Buxton state that the first trainee on a team should be assumed to have *zero* productivity, and each additional trainee should be assumed to have a serious *negative* impact on productivity, because of the supervision and team-interaction time required. Little training is therefore done in CPTs, so alternative methods of training must be considered, such as maintenance work, or specialist training sections for junior staff. The trainees in a CPT could perform the librarian and testing roles. As in the case of maintenance, this helps to make them aware of good software engineering practice. They could also be supervised by specialist training staff, who might not themselves be members of the teams, and who would be responsible for the training of all juniors, irrespective of which team the juniors were in. All in all, past experience has shown that trainees must be carefully assimilated into the teams.

In sharp contrast to the above views, Fairley (1985) believes that the only situation where CPTs are effective is where they are composed largely of juniors. This situation may occur either where the programs are simple enough to be written by relatively unskilled programmers (under the supervision of the chief programmer), or where the juniors are being trained in an apprenticeship setting, as happens in family teams (Chapter 3). In other words, instead of the training section being separate from the CPTs as suggested above, the CPTs would *be* the training section.

9.4.4   SUMMARY AND CONCLUSIONS

The evidence presented shows that many experienced staff have gained little knowledge from their experience.

Most authorities – e.g. Yourdon (1975) and Van Tassel (1978) – advocate simplicity, and most of the evidence does show that low productivity accompanies complexity (Chapter 8). However, some of the evidence in this chapter indicates that substantial productivity improvements are possible by making full use of the software features available, and by using advanced techniques, for which greater knowledge and experience are required, i.e. it is *unnecessary* complexity which should be avoided – greater knowledge and experience would help determine what complexity was necessary and what was unnecessary. A higher level of training would however have to be provided, and a higher quality of staff may be required.

Innovation can also increase productivity, but there are dangers involved – e.g. the innovative techniques might be incomprehensible to others – so adventure must be tempered with caution.

Improved allocation of work, to take account of both short-term and long-term needs, and greater interchange of knowledge (e.g. by discussions or job rotation), are also necessary to take full advantage of experience, and to accelerate its acquisition.

If these suggestions are acted upon, and provided the precautions are observed, this factor can produce a substantial improvement in the productivity of the software industry.

9.5 INNATE ABILITY

In the previous section, the importance of experience was discussed. In this section, the closely-related subject (from the viewpoint of observed results) of innate ability will be examined.

9.5.1 RANGE OF PROGRAMMER ABILITY

There is a widely-held belief that people differ in innate ability, and there is ample evidence to support this belief. For example, the top 20% of authors, football players, inventors, policemen, and fighter pilots, produce about 50% of the output, while the bottom 50% of them only produce about 20% (Augustine, 1979).

Authorities in the computer field share this belief (Table 9.8). The Sackman (1969) ratio was the ability range for a group of students; the Grant and Sackman (1966) ratio was the ability range for experienced programmers; and so on.

Gunther's figure is one of the more conservative, probably because he excluded extreme values at either end. (In both the

Table 9.8 Range of programmer ability

Source	Ratio
Brooks (1977)	100:1
Weinberg (1971)	30:1
Van Tassel (1978)	25:1
Jones (1986b)	20:1 (great talent vs green amateur)
Sackman (1969)	16:1 (students)
Sackman *et al.* (1968)	16:1 to 28:1
Grant and Sackman (1966)	18:1 to 28:1 (experienced programmers)
Boehm (Gunther, 1978)	13:1 (10th–90th percentile)
Arthur (1988)	> 10:1 (maintenance)
Yourdon (1975)	> 10:1 (in typical programming group)
Martin (1985)	10:1
Shneiderman (1980)	5:1 to 100:1
Wang (1984)	3:1 (graduate students)
Gilb (1977)	2:1 to 10:1 (bebugging)
Average (approximate)	20:1

Grant and Sackman (1966) and the Sackman (1969) studies, for example, the wide productivity ranges were due to a small number of extreme performances (Boehm, 1981).) Gunther's ratio is therefore of more practical use as a working figure.

Conversely, Jones's 20:1 is the ratio by which 'true experts' – 'the great programming talents of the world' – outperform the greenest amateurs, but he also gives a second ratio, of only 2.5:1 (just one-eighth as much), for competent programming compared to simple inexperience. However, both these figures include the effect of experience. Once again, the lower ratio is of more practical use.

Additional evidence of differences in ability is provided by the high productivity rates achieved on the super-programmer, NYT and other projects, but factors other than ability may have contributed to their success – as is generally the case in real-world situations: there are so many factors involved, that it is difficult to isolate the effect of any one factor.

It was pointed out earlier that senior programmers are only paid twice as much, on average, as juniors. The salary differential for other categories of staff, such as systems analysts, is similar (What are you worth in '88, *Datamation*, 1 Oct. 1988, pp. 53–66). The most capable staff would rapidly be promoted to senior positions, while the least capable ones would remain in more junior positions. In general, therefore, the staff with high ability are only paid twice as much on average as those with low ability, and so are not paid what they are worth. There is thus a very obvious way to reduce costs: use only the best staff. This is in accordance with the 'principle of top talent' – use better and fewer people – but the small number of superstars limits the general applicability of this solution (Boehm, 1981).

In the light of all the above evidence, it is surprising that ability is taken into account in only three of the nine cost-estimation models surveyed in Boehm (1981).

9.5.2   MAXIMIZING BENEFITS OF ABILITY

Staff with greater innate ability should have a higher productivity. How can this be used to advantage? It might appear to be of academic interest only – even more so than for experience, as experience at least increases with time whereas innate ability does not (Weinberg, 1971). However, closer examination shows that, even if innate ability cannot be increased, *better use* can be made of it. This can be done by ensuring the following:

1. That people work at the maximum of their ability – for example, that they are not held back by lack of knowledge or motivation.
2. That their ability is used where it can produce maximum benefit. This can be achieved by suitable allocation of work. Although, in practice, this is already being done to at least some extent – it would be unusual, for example, to allocate the most difficult work to the least able person (Boehm, 1981) – there should still be scope for productivity improvement from this factor.

When staffing project teams, a trade-off situation exists: putting the most able people on one project maximizes productivity on that project, but adversely affects productivity on the remaining projects. As in the case of personnel experience, cost-estimation models provide a basis for estimating such trade-offs, and therefore for detailed project personnel planning to arrive at an optimal solution.

Although the innate ability of individuals cannot be increased, the pool of DP staff in an organization is not fixed, so the average ability in the organization can be increased. This can be done in several ways.

1. Recruiting high-ability staff from outside the organization.

As the best staff are relatively under-paid, it should be cost-effective for organizations to offer higher salaries to attract quality recruits. However, in view of the shortage of staff, and the consequent difficulty in recruiting staff of average ability let alone of high ability, this is not a generally applicable solution. In any case, although it would solve the problem for some organizations, it would only worsen the situation in others, namely the ones from which the staff had been recruited.

2. Recruiting high-ability staff from other departments within the organization.

   Although similar to the previous option, this solution has the advantage that it increases the number of staff in the DP industry. Also, the detrimental effects of the 'poaching' are likely to be less serious, as all the departments concerned come under the same top management, who would not condone the transfers unless the organization as a whole benefitted from them.

3. Retaining high-ability staff within the organization.

   Strictly speaking, this is just the converse of the first point, but it is worth having it as a separate item, to emphasize how poor management can cause an organization to lose its best staff. IBM, for example, reportedly lost one of its top salesmen, Ross Perot, because of a regulation limiting his maximum income (Heller, 1981), though this story has been disputed (Church, 1992).

4. Retaining high-ability staff within the DP Department in productive capacities.

   One of the objectives of the CPT structure is to keep senior programmers in a productive (as opposed to a managerial) capacity. This ensures that the most able programmers continue doing the type of work they are best at, but without preventing those who would be outstanding managers from becoming managers.

9.5.3 FACTORS LIMITING BENEFITS

Greater innate ability is not always accompanied by higher productivity, i.e. there is a difference between potential and achievement. There are several reasons for this.

Lack of knowledge

It should be obvious that someone who lacks knowledge, whether due to inadequate training or lack of experience, will not perform at the maximum of his potential. Sackman *et al.* (1968) goes further than this, implying that knowledge overrides differences in innate ability. This is plausible, as knowing how to perform a task removes a difficult (and therefore time-consuming) part of the task. Carrying out the task is therefore reduced almost to a mechanical process – though even here a more able person might still outperform his less-gifted colleagues, though perhaps by not as much. Weinberg (1971), in agreement with Sackman, states emphatically that good programmers are made, not born, and points out that learning can even increase scores in IQ and programmer aptitude tests.

If Weinberg and Sackman are correct, then most of our energy should be devoted to creating good programmers (and other categories of staff?) by training them, rather than to selecting them. However, the reported differences in ability are so large that it would be unwise to accept this conclusion uncritically. Furthermore, even if better training of less-gifted programmers enables them to perform at the levels currently being achieved by the best programmers, better training of the latter might enable them to reopen the gap. Other actions – for example, different allocation of work – might have the same effect, i.e. the best programmers may be spending part of their time on easy programs, yet they may not perform much better than weak programmers on easy programs. Put the other way round, it is probably only on difficult programs that the variations in ability really make a difference. (This is analogous to the claim by Weinberg quoted earlier, that certain programming work cannot be done by a team of trainees, no matter how large the team.) In other words, existing circumstances may be limiting the performance of the most able staff. (This is reminiscent of the Youngs (1974) experiment which found that professional programmers made just as many errors as novices, but were more competent at removing them.)

Are Weinberg and Sackman correct? Few DP personnel seem to agree with them. The majority apparently believe that programming requires a 'knack', and if you do not have the aptitude, then neither motivation nor training can compensate (Hoard, 1981; Dight, 1986; Pritchard, 1984). According to Turton (1985), who is a personnel consultant, only 5% of the population have the ability to become programmers. Interestingly, Martin (1982a) stated that the best 4GL programmers were often not very productive with conventional programming.

Mental attitude

Stress can interfere with the ability to come up with creative solutions to programming and management problems (Fialkoff, 1981). It is therefore only to be expected that people who are anxious or worried, who are rushing to meet a deadline, or who have negative attitudes, will perform badly and make more mistakes (Walther and O'Neil, 1974; Shneiderman, 1980).

Motivation is a topic in its own right, covered in Chapter 11, so it will suffice to mention here that lack of motivation results in people achieving below their potential in the work situation, the training situation, and in experiments: 'programmers can have all of the ability in the world and will not produce to their potential if they're not motivated' (Zawacki, 1989).

Undesirable characteristics

The average coder in the Cooper (1975) survey was generally sloppy, inflexible, and introverted. Cockcroft (1988) also believes that systems development staff tend to be introverted, and in addition, states that they are generally loners, short on communication skills. Couger and Zawacki (1980) found that programmers and analysts 'have a startlingly low proclivity to social interaction', and can therefore be expected to interact less with subordinates, and communication skill may not come naturally for them. I suspect that undesirable characteristics such as these are present in intensified form in programmers of outstandingly high ability.

- Some super-programmers write programs which are undocumented or impossible to understand (Yourdon, 1975), and so are impossible to maintain. Furthermore, in an experiment conducted by TRW, a program written by an ordinary programmer in a straightforward way was estimated as being 96% reliable, whereas a version of the same program with clever loops and tricks, written by a super-programmer, scored only 89% (Gilb, 1977). Unmodifiable programs have to be rewritten, thereby negating the high original productivity. Worse, most programs are not rewritten because they are intrinsically bad, but because the maintenance programmer simply cannot understand and adapt to the design philosophy of the program (Glass, 1979). In view of the large proportion of time spent on maintenance, and the fact that the average production program is maintained by ten people during its lifetime (Chapter 8), this is a serious problem.
- Other super-programmers are unsociable (Martin, 1981; Yourdon, 1975).
- Others are eccentric and unreliable in their

behavior or in their dress. They may have attitudes such as: 'great DP systems are written by guys in sandals – nobody in a gray flannel suit ever wrote great code' (Yourdon, 1975; Hodges, 1987a).

Many organizations consider such characteristics less desirable than efficient programming: 'eccentricity is not acceptable' (Hodges, 1987a; Yourdon, 1975). They would prefer to employ a less-able programmer who did not exhibit these traits. This is not as illogical as it may seem (Yourdon, 1975).

- These factors *do* have a detrimental effect on productivity. Programmers who are unreliable in their behavior can cause hasty, last-minute and less-than-optimum rescheduling and rearrangement of work. Also, people are unlikely to give of their best if they do not get on well with their colleagues. Furthermore, according to Van Tassel (1978) an entire project can be a disaster if, in a CPT, the chief programmer and the back-up programmer are incompatible. Because of the large amount of interaction between programmers (Weinberg, 1971), it is insufficient for them to merely not be bad at social interaction: they should be *good* at it. They should therefore have good communication ability, and should also be motivated toward group rather than individual achievement (Boehm, 1981).
- Productivity is not the only consideration: few people, for example, would choose to work with someone they did not like, no matter how productive that person might be.
- The current state of knowledge makes it impossible to know quantitatively just how good a programmer really is, at least not with any degree of precision or certainty, or how serious an impact his behavior has on others. It is therefore not possible to state authoritatively that organizations have their priorities wrong, or are making a mistake in any particular case.

It is possible that many programmers – whether super-programmers or not – are more interested in systems programming, or work in a 'software house', developing technological aids and fourth-generation products, than in working with users (Martin, 1981; Big business for mini computers, *Computronics*, 13 Feb. 1980, p. 8). Such work preferences are an advantage where the programmer is correctly matched to the type of work he prefers, but are a disadvantage where he is not, especially if the supply of each type of programmer is out of balance with the demand, e.g. applications programmers who would have preferred to do systems programming.

There may be a link between work preferences and the undesirable characteristics. Those programmers who prefer systems programming or working in a software house, may also be the ones who are unsociable and eccentric in their dress – as one authority put it, operating systems specialists seem to be anti-social types who cannot be easily integrated into the corporate culture (What are you worth in '88, *Datamation*, 1 Oct. 1988, pp. 53–66). (This provides a striking contrast with the great majority of Morgan Stanley's entry-level MIS recruits, who 'look, talk, and act' like their end users (Dight, 1986).) If this is the case, then such characteristics will be less of a problem, as these programmers will be correctly matched not only with the type of work they prefer, but also with the type of department or organization which is less upset by such behavior (Yourdon, 1975; Martin, 1981). (Though unreliable behavior and unmodifiable programs would still be frowned on.)

These undesirable characteristics may be difficult (and therefore time-consuming) to eradicate. In fact, where they are deeply-ingrained personality traits, eradication may prove impossible. (Corrective methods include reviews of work and the program production library, which ensure that standards are being observed and procedures such as backups are being followed.) Even where these characteristics are not present, constant vigilance may be required to ensure they do not creep in, or return where they were eradicated. Either way, productivity is adversely affected.

Different types of ability

Software engineering incorporates a multitude of different types of work, such as design, coding, testing and documentation, and these types can be further subdivided (see, for example, the AFIPS Programmer Job Description Survey (AFIPS, 1973)). Different types of work require different types of ability, e.g. (Weinberg, 1971; Boehm, 1981; Aron, 1974):

- we need someone with an analytical mind to find an error, but someone with a synthetic mind to fix it;
- finding an error may require considerable persistence;
- documentation requires the ability to write plain English;
- working in a team requires good communication ability, and the ability to get on with and cooperate with others;
- some problems require 'painstaking attention to detail', while others require the ability to 'sit back and take the broad view of things';
- managers need largely the broad view, while their subordinates need to pay more attention to detail.

People differ (DeMarco, 1982). Some people, for example, are inherently more meticulous than others, and some have better memories (Weinberg, 1971). Furthermore, those who are good at one type of work are not necessarily good at another (Yourdon, 1979b). In fact, DeMarco stated that people who rank highest in some skills rank lowest in others. (As Sackman *et al.* (1968) put it, 'when a programmer is good, he is very, very good, but when he is bad, he is horrid'.) Left-brain-dominant thinkers – verbal people – who reportedly form the majority of DP staff, tend to study the trees but miss the forests (Ruete, 1991; Lewis, 1987). Therefore, while we may find differences in ability of 30:1 on each type of work – as can be seen in small, selective laboratory experiments – the observed differences in real-life are mostly much smaller, as each person's tasks include a variety of different types of work, some of which he is good at, others not. This leads to an *averaging-out* of his overall performance which, according to Weinberg, reduces the observed differences between individuals to ratios of 2 or 3:1.

This claimed reduction seems rather large to me, and the evidence produced by Weinberg to substantiate it is inadequate, but it does give fairly good agreement with the productivity differences claimed by other authorities (Table 9.9), and with the actual productivity differences between the Super-Programmer and NYT Projects, and ordinary projects, of (much?) less than 6:1 (Chapter 3). If it is accurate, it confirms the claims quoted above that those people who are very good at some things, are very bad at others. It also therefore means that extra care must be taken when staffing a project team, to ensure that the abilities of the team members complement each other.

To complicate the issue, Weinberg stated that even the remaining differences of 2 or 3:1 may often be due to external factors. Another complication is that most authorities do not explicitly specify whether their figures are averaged-out or not, so a deduction had to be made from the wording and context, into which category the figures fell. For example, the COCOMO value includes 'ability, efficiency and thoroughness, and the ability to communicate and cooperate' (Boehm, 1981). It therefore includes several types of ability, so it was logical to treat it as the averaged-out ability range. This value actually introduces a further complication. As it includes communication and cooperation,

Table 9.9 Averaged-out differences in ability

Source	Ratio
Weinberg (1971)	–
COCOMO (Boehm, 1981)	2:1 (15th to 90th percentile)
Weinberg (1971)	2 or 3:1 (may include other factors)
Conte *et al.* (1986)	2–4:1 (large team projects)
Yourdon (1975)	3 or 4:1
Super-programmer, NYT (about 1970)	up to 6:1 (Chapter 3)
Air Force (1974)	5:1
Sweet (1986)	5:1
Average (approximate)	3:1

it evaluates programmers as members of a team rather than as individuals.

Conte *et al.* (1986) also commented on the large reduction in the observed variations in productivity (from as high as 26:1 on small one-person programming jobs down to perhaps only 2–4:1 on large team projects), but attributed this to the need for greater communication among team members, and to the averaging effect of differing individual productivity rates. This implies that the best staff are slowed down by communication – and by their less capable colleagues? – but he is probably comparing variations in *team* productivity rather than in individual productivity.

These and other figures are given in Table 9.9. The COCOMO figure for programmers is 2.0:1. The corresponding figure for analysts is almost identical: 2.1:1 (Boehm, 1981). These figures are amongst the lowest listed, probably because they exclude extreme values at either end.

The Yourdon ratio was derived from his productivity rates quoted in Chapter 2. It is the approximate difference between the range for super-programmers (50–200) and that for structured programs (35–65).

The Air Force figure is the effect due to 'personnel', and may therefore include both analyst and programmer ability, and the effect of experience.

In addition to the tabulated figures, the Walston and Felix (1977) ratio of 3.1:1 for

'overall personnel experience and qualifications' probably includes the effect of ability.

Some aspects of the different types of ability are discussed in more detail below.

Specialization

If some specialization is present, the averaging-out effect will be less severe. The observed productivity differences will therefore lie between the minimum value of say 2–3 times (where no specialization is present), and the maximum value of say 20–30 times (where full specialization is present). In other words, some programmers are anything from 2 to 30 times more productive than others, depending on the degree of specialization.

Specialization is discussed further in Appendix F, so it will suffice to mention here that it introduces a degree of rigidity. The programmers only do certain types of work, and so might experience idle time, e.g. while waiting for work of the type in which they specialize. In practice, therefore, one would expect the observed productivity differences to be lower than the theoretical maximum.

Intelligence

There is another ability which is important to programming success: intelligence (Weinberg, 1971). In fact, this is probably the *first* ability most people would think of, hence the widespread use of intelligence-type tests in selecting would-be programmers. Although these tests have been criticized, the criticism is generally aimed more at the limited scope of the tests, rather than at denying the importance of intelligence. Such criticism is justified, as there are at least 61 separate intellectual talents, yet IQ tests measure, at most, only about eight of them (Lewis, 1987). Furthermore, because of the large number and wide variety of abilities which contribute to programming success, the performance of individuals is often not related to their IQs (Wingfield, 1976). However, care should be taken not to over-react to deficiencies in the tests, as it is unlikely that a person of low intelligence could become a successful programmer, even if he possessed all the other necessary attributes. Therefore, support exists for the view expressed by Shneiderman (1980), that intelligence tests are 'useful guides'.

People can only hold a few pieces of information in their minds at once, i.e. they have a limited 'span of attention' (Malik, 1985; Aron, 1974). These pieces of information are stored in their working memories (Shneiderman, 1980). Intelligent people may have a higher-capacity working memory, and therefore have a greater span of attention, and so may be able to manipulate more items in their heads at the same time before losing control. If so, the difference in performance between a more-intelligent and a less-intelligent programmer will grow as the size of the program increases – which could explain Weinberg's observation that some programmers are successful on small programs but not on large ones (Weinberg, 1971). This would be aggravated by the claimed rapid increase in complexity with increasing size (Aron, 1974). Programs become so complex that they exceed the capability of the people who have to develop and maintain them: they get 'beyond intellectual control' (Laws of programming, *Dataweek*, 30 Nov. 1979, p. 3). As a result, productivity is seriously degraded, as can be seen from the very low productivity rates for large and complex programs.

A distinction can be drawn between intelligence and intelligent *behavior* (Weinberg, 1971). Prevention is better than cure. Someone who *avoids* problems is likely to be more productive – and certainly less disruptive – than someone whose actions lead to many problems which he then proceeds to solve brilliantly. Other examples of intelligent behavior are:

- using one's strengths and avoiding one's weaknesses;
- realizing one's limitations; and
- being flexible and adapting to changed circumstances.

Super-programmers

Why are some programmers super-programmers?

- Do they generate better code?
- Or, do they merely generate ordinary code at a faster pace?
- Or, both?

If their code is better:

- is it because they invent superior techniques themselves, or
- is it merely because they use superior existing techniques?

If they code faster, is it because they are more intelligent?

Weinberg (1971) quotes an example in which a super-programmer devised a more imaginative technique. (This was in a diagnostics program for a peripheral.) Yourdon (1975) implies that their programs are both better and completed faster. This is plausible, as:

- a more intelligent person should be able to program faster, as he can solve problems more quickly;
- he should also have mastered a wider range of time-saving techniques;

- even if the tools or techniques to be used are unfamiliar to him, he should be able to master them more quickly (Boehm, 1981); and
- even if he is not inherently more creative, he may have more confidence to experiment with his ideas – greater speed would be a help here as well, especially if the ideas proved impractical and he had to do the job again using conventional techniques.

On the other hand, a less intelligent person, realizing his limitations, may resort to intelligent behavior to compensate for his lack of intellectual ability. Thus he may:

- design and desk-check his programs more carefully before he starts coding, thereby saving on time-consuming restarts and debugging; or
- he may make a point of learning many time-saving techniques.

The super-programmers I have known generally exhibited a reluctance to work on other people's programs, which could show a lack of flexibility; and their programs frequently worked the first or second time, possibly because of more thorough desk-checking.

A more detailed study of super-programmers should be made, to determine why they are so fast, as the knowledge thus gained may enable ordinary programmers to improve their speed.

9.5.4 SUPER-ANALYSTS, SUPER-MANAGERS, ETC.

Much of the above discussion refers specifically to programmers. It seems reasonable, however, to suppose that 'super' performers exist among other categories of DP staff. Thus, although the preceding text mentions only super-programmers, it assumes that super-programmer/analysts also exist, as chief programmers are programmer/analysts not just programmers.

Data capturers

The definition of a super-data-capturer would probably be one who types rapidly and accurately. This helps the software staff by providing a faster turn-around on their coding sheets, with fewer mistakes. Furthermore, when keying-in data, super-data-capturers would be able to resolve more problems by themselves, and so would need to ask fewer questions of the systems analysts. Similarly, when keying-in programs, they would need to ask fewer questions of the programmers.

However, with a wider definition, super-data-capturers would be ones capable of correcting syntax errors in the programs they keyed in (though control would have to be exercised). They would also be able to relieve part of the programmers' work-load by writing and maintaining their own data-entry programs. They would be using user-oriented data-entry languages, such as on specialized programmable data-entry machines such as Sperry's old UTS (Universal Terminal System) range (van Olst, 1977; Pellerano, 1978): COBOL programs would probably be beyond them, as the ability to type rapidly and accurately is not necessarily accompanied by the ability to write COBOL programs – and if they could write COBOL programs, they would probably become full-time programmers. (Sperry's UTS must not be confused with Amdahl's UTS (Universal Timesharing System), which is their mainframe version of UNIX.)

Computer operators

Super-operators can also relieve the programmers' burden:

- by performing some functions which are usually carried out by programmers, such as simple tuning of systems (Dolphin, 1978), though once again control would have to be exercised;
- by providing them with a faster turnaround

on testing jobs run in batch mode – long delays result in memory lapses, with consequent increase in the number of errors and lowering of productivity (Weinberg, 1971); and

- simply by needing less assistance from the programmers because they are so good at their jobs.

Programming is one career path for computer operators. Super-operators are likely to take this step, and thereby help to relieve the programmer shortage.

Clerks

Super-clerks would probably not be satisfied with clerical duties for long, and would move on to more intellectually demanding tasks: the position of program secretary or librarian on a CPT would be one way to give them entry to such work, and these positions have the added advantage of relieving part of the normal programmers' work-load. Their knowledge of the user applications might make systems analysis a more appropriate career path for them than programming. However, super-clerks can help the software staff even if they remain clerks:

- by checking the output of test runs (as they would the output of production runs); and
- simply by needing less assistance from the software staff because they are so good at their jobs.

A super-clerk in a user department should be able to generate his own reports, and may even be able to develop simple systems, using appropriate user-oriented fourth-generation languages and application generators.

Systems analysts

Good analysts work more efficiently, and spend less time resolving interface and communications problems, and in false starts and error correction (Boehm, 1981), i.e. they not only work faster, but also make fewer mistakes, which in turn further speeds them up. According to the COCOMO cost-estimation model, a project takes twice as long if the analysts are of very low capability (15th percentile) than if they are of very high capability (90th percentile) (Boehm, 1981). It is not just the analytical tasks which are affected: the programming tasks (detailed design, code and unit test) also take nearly twice as long, because of more requirements and system design reworks, and less effective response to programmers' questions. Other conclusions which may be drawn from the COCOMO model are that good analysts can compensate for poor programmers, and vice versa; but when both analysts and programmers are very poor (15th percentile), productivity is only one-quarter of what it is when both are very good (90th percentile).

The relative abilities of programmers and analysts is particularly relevant to CPTs. Friction can arise if the systems analyst is more intelligent than his supervisor, the chief programmer. How common is this? The average analyst probably has more intellectual ability than the average programmer, for the following reasons.

- Systems analysis is generally considered a promotion, and a poor programmer is unlikely to be promoted.
- The analyst needs the 'big picture' – he must keep and manipulate in his mind an entire system at a time, whereas the programmer needs to do this with only one program at a time. While some individual programs are very large – bigger than many complete systems – a program is only a component of a system, so the average system is much bigger than the average program and needs a correspondingly better mind to manipulate it.
- A systems design error can have much more serious consequences than a program design error – it might, for example, result

in many programs being modified, and not just one.

- Many lower-quality recruits have entered the programming profession (as evidenced, for example, by the poor examination results quoted earlier), and they will probably never make the grade as analysts.
- The proportion of systems analysts with university degrees in one survey was higher (albeit only marginally) than that of programmers (18% compared to 16%) (Adams, 1981), and the average coder in another survey had only two years' college-level education (Cooper, 1975).

On the other hand, there are probably more super-programmers than super-analysts, because:

- the technical (machine-oriented) side of programming has a fascination which attracts brilliant people – the 'bit-twiddlers' (Martin, 1981); and
- simply because there are more programmers than analysts (Chapter 8).

However, even if there are more super-programmers than super-analysts, they may not be uniformly distributed, e.g. the super-programmers may be concentrated in systems programming departments, at computer manufacturers, in universities, or in software houses (Martin, 1981). There may thus be local imbalances, resulting in many CPTs having a chief programmer who was less able than the analyst on the team, with consequent personnel problems.

Managers

A manager may be in a first-level managerial position (e.g. project leader or chief programmer), or in a higher-level position (e.g. project manager, DPM or above). Managerial skills are an essential part of a project leader's make-up (Van Tassel, 1978; Baker, 1972), and one who excelled in this area would probably

achieve rapid promotion. The productivity of the DP department can be markedly affected by management decisions in many and varied areas (Martin, 1981; Weinberg, 1971; Dolphin, 1978):

- in the choice of structure for the DP department;
- in the choice of hardware, software, and techniques;
- in the choice of office equipment;
- in personnel management; and
- simply in the ordinary day to day running of the department.

Boehm (1973) stated that the main productivity problems on medium and large projects are management problems. Boehm (1981) listed six factors – assigning the wrong (combination of) people to project jobs; creating task overlaps and underlaps through poor organization, delegation, and task monitoring; etc. – each of which has often been responsible for *doubling* software costs. Furthermore, bad decisions by top management in other areas, such as finance and marketing, can even bankrupt an organization (Heller, 1981), so the software engineers' hard work would be discarded.

Management is a topic in its own right, covered in Chapter 11.

9.5.5 SUMMARY AND CONCLUSIONS

The evidence presented shows that there are large differences in ability between people. One way to take advantage of these differences, provided better ways of measuring ability can be devised, is to be more selective in recruiting entrants to the profession. It might be thought that this solution was of limited value: in an industry which is short of staff, it is better to have average staff than too few. However, there is actually an abundance of would-be programmers, but even if there were not, changed circumstances in the future (lower demand for software, or higher productivity, resulting in fewer staff being required), would permit more selectivity.

The evidence presented also shows that ability is very narrow. Therefore, to take full advantage of the differences in ability, staff would have to specialize more. Provided this were not carried so far as to seriously impoverish their jobs (Appendix F), substantial gains in productivity could be expected. Furthermore, provided better selection techniques could be devised, organizations could be more selective in recruiting. Applicants would be selected not only on overall ability, but also on *specialized* ability. The selected staff would thus be better matched to the specific vacancies, and so would be more productive.

High ability might be accompanied by innovation, which can increase productivity, but there are dangers – for example, imaginative techniques might be incomprehensible to others – so care has to be exercised.

High ability might also be accompanied by undesirable characteristics, such as unsociable or unreliable behavior, which can adversely affect productivity (of both the able person and his colleagues). Corrective measures include reviews of work, and better matching of staff with specific types of organization and types of work.

Super-programmers are probably more intelligent and more imaginative, but they may also be less flexible. A more detailed study should be made of them, as the knowledge thus gained may enable ordinary programmers to improve their speed.

Evidence was also presented of high ability among systems analysts, and in fact, the average analyst probably has more intellectual ability than the average programmer.

Poor management can seriously affect the productivity of the software staff.

Other categories of staff – data capturers, computer operators and clerks – may also exhibit high ability, and this can be used to help the software staff, e.g. data capturers can write their own data-entry programs, and clerks can check the output of test runs.

9.6 RESISTANCE TO CHANGE

This study lists many ways of improving the current, inadequate productivity. These recommendations may meet with opposition from management and workers alike, for a variety of reasons, e.g. (Argyris, 1976; Glass, 1979; Martin, 1982b; Reese, 1978; Doepel, 1977; Van Zijl and Evans, 1978; Nies, 1983):

- skepticism of the claimed benefits;
- the cost of implementation;
- inertia;
- dislike of change;
- a natural desire to keep things as they are – 'old methods die hard';
- fear of the new situation;
- features of the new situation which genuinely irritate;
- fear of loss of employment or status;
- disruption to social groups;
- inability to do the changed jobs;
- control and regimentation imposed by the change;
- having to learn new methods;
- the knowledge that 'pioneers often get killed';
- resistance to the methods used to institute change;
- DP personnel look on computers as a tool for users not for themselves;
- technical people are often very conservative.

In addition, traditional software engineers are totally immersed in, and often blinded by, their current methods (Martin and McClure, 1985).

Shneiderman (1980) believes that inertia is often a more powerful force than survival of the fittest. Grace Hopper said that 'Human beings seem to be pretty much allergic to change. You've got to show that guy why it is in his interest to accept a new way. Challenging a mind-set is the toughest job there is'

(Leopold, 1986). McKee (1986) believes that 'DP people are probably the most inflexible of all'. He thinks this may be due to the high initial effort required to master their field, and the perpetual battle to renew their skills.

If the changes are not successfully 'sold' to the people affected, they will not succeed. Even if they are installed, they will be avoided and sabotaged in a myriad of ways, and so will fail (Dickson and Simmons, 1976).

DP staff, particularly systems analysts, should be well versed in selling change, as they are themselves agents of change (Feeney and Sladek, 1977; Lee, 1978). Part of their ordinary duties is to persuade users to accept new methods. Instruction on persuasion techniques can therefore be found in books on systems analysis. Persuasion is also part of a manager's duties: he must persuade his subordinates to carry out his directives.

Resistance to some specific changes, such as the introduction of CPTs, is discussed at the appropriate points in this study. Similarly, suggestions to overcome some specific resistance, e.g. to the introduction of MPPs, are also given at the appropriate points. More general advice is given below.

To be successful, persuasion requires (Stephens, 1979; Dickson and Simmons, 1976; Martin, 1982c; Carnegie, 1913):

- facts and education, so that the people affected will fully understand the change, and be convinced that it will benefit them and meet their needs – without facts, they are being asked to make an act of faith;
- emphasis on the new challenges;
- skill in human relations, and mastery of motivational technique;
- a knowledge of how people react;
- a concern for the people affected – for what frightens them, motivates, excites and interests them – and a recognition of their dignity as individuals;
- participation – the people affected should feel they are instigating the changes them-

selves, and should see the decisions as being their own;
- clear lines of communication, so that grievances can be aired – emotional problems will not disappear if not faced, but will remain to obstruct successful implementation of the change;
- an atmosphere of mutual trust;
- strong and on-going management support.

A definite plan of action should be (jointly) drawn up. Initial resistance will gradually break down as the benefits become apparent – the new methods will start to sell themselves (Stephens, 1979).

One effective way of introducing change is the 3-step process (Couger and Zawacki, 1980):

> unfreeze : change : refreeze

The first step is for the person to conclude that there is a need for change, so he 'unfreezes' his existing behavior pattern. In the second step, he makes the change in his behavior. The final step is for him to conclude that the change was justified, causing him to maintain – i.e. 'freeze' – his new behavior pattern.

Couger and Zawacki quote an example of this technique. During the Korean war, the Communists used stooges to convince a captive priest that he was a bother to other people, and not a help to them as he had thought. Thus convinced, the priest resolved to change his beliefs, and more stooges were used to assist this process, by helping him establish a new set of beliefs, and welcoming the change (Schein, 1961). (The technique failed in this case. During the refreezing step, the priest heard children outside his prison window singing a song he had taught them, and this awoke his old attitudes.)

Conclusion

People often resist change, and for a multitude of reasons. Sometimes they have good cause to resist, e.g. the change may benefit their employer but not themselves, or because of the high initial effort required, but they sometimes even resist change which is to their benefit, e.g. out of fear of the unknown, or even inertia.

Change must therefore be introduced with tact. The people affected must not only be persuaded that the change is in their interest, but should participate in the decisons, so that they themselves instigate the change.

Quality and Quality Assurance (QA) affect software engineering productivity: the time spent on testing, etc. lowers productivity initially, but the higher initial quality improves longer-term productivity. The productivity of end users is also affected, and software engineers are themselves the end users of many software systems. Also, quality is important to end users (Jones, 1986b). An organization that can produce higher-quality goods using fewer resources than other organizations will have the competitive edge (Cho, 1987). Costs are also incurred, both in building a high-quality product and due to any remaining defects in the product when it is used. This money could otherwise have been spent on, say, improved tools for the programmers.

Arthur (1983) believes that, if you take care of software quality, then 'the productivity problems will take care of themselves'. According to Opperman (1988), quality in information systems development is a key success factor in increasing productivity, and in fact, QA has the potential of becoming the most effective productivity tool in the 1990s. Similarly, statistical quality control, rather than modern technology such as computers and lasers, has been called the third industrial revolution, and has been claimed to result in a jump in productivity of thousands of percent (Cho, 1987). According to Jones (1986b), defect removal costs (such as testing and debugging) are always among the top three expense items for software products; and correcting software defects accounts for more than $7.5 billion per year in the US alone (DeMarco, 1982). One of the most direct and effective methods for improving productivity therefore, is to utilize better defect prevention and removal technologies.

A study of productivity would therefore not be complete without an investigation of quality.

Quality and QA overlap with many of the other topics discussed in this study, e.g.:

- software produced by CPTs should have integrity of design, because all the design is done by one person (Chapter 3);
- poor quality can have expensive consequences, e.g. direct losses to the user organization caused by bugs in production programs (Chapters 3 and 5);
- data dictionaries ensure quality and integrity of data by helping to validate it, and by controlling access to it (Chapter 6);
- programs written in high-level languages generally contain fewer errors than those written in low-level languages (Chapter 6);
- application generators generate bug-free code (Chapter 6);
- when people are anxious or nervous, they make more mistakes (Chapter 6);
- prototyping improves quality (Chapter 8);
- testing is a major method for ensuring that programs produce correct results (Chapter 8);
- software developed using structured methodologies is usually well organized, and more readily understandable and easier to maintain (though deeply-nested IF statements are difficult to understand) (Chapter 8);
- MPPs improve communication with users and accuracy of design, assist early error detection, reduce maintenance time, and generally result in better quality products (Chapter 8);

- hasty work results in low quality, and constant modifications degrade the quality of a software product (Chapters 8 and 11);
- people who are well trained should produce higher-quality work (Chapter 9);
- high quality is a consequence of professionalism, and so can be a motivating factor (Chapters 1 and 11).

In addition, quality is a management responsibility (Cho, 1987). (Management is discussed in Chapter 11.) Macro and Buxton (1987) emphasize that quality must be a 'strongly managed' issue: it is not enough to leave it to the 'technical wizards'. Managers must ensure, for example, that the various defect prevention and detection procedures are carried out, and they also perform some of the quality-related activities themselves, such as personnel appraisals (which assess the quality of staff), and setting standards. Management must also ensure a climate free of fear, so that software engineers – and users – will admit to mistakes or delays, and corrective action can be taken before unnecessary harm is caused (Cho, 1987; Weinberg, 1971). The QA staff should report directly to management above the project manager level (Sommerville, 1989).

Software reliability, which is an important aspect of quality, has been neglected (Glass, 1979). Few software projects make use of concepts such as 'cost of quality' (Jones, 1986b). Fewer than 14% of the respondents in one survey measured software quality or defect removal (Jones, 1986b); and at a conference on measurement, when the speaker asked how many people in the audience of 50 worked in an environment where defects were counted, not one raised a hand (DeMarco, 1982). In fact, according to DeMarco, many companies, particularly in the US, studiously *avoid* collecting defect data! According to Siegel (1989), software quality engineering is still in its relative infancy, and even lacks standard terminology. Quality is discussed in many books on software engineering, but not at length: Glass (1979), Dunn and Ullman (1982), Deutsch and Willis (1988), Vincent *et al.* (1988) and Cho (1987) are amongst the few books which specialize in the subject, though there are also some books which specialize in testing (Chapter 8). Jones (1986b) stated that the measurement of the key factors affecting quality was 'surprisingly under-reported' in the literature. There were, for example, no thorough or exhaustive studies that covered the costs, efficiencies, and general applicability of the various defect removal methods, and few controlled studies to back up the claims and assertions that are common in the literature. Conte *et al.* (1986) concluded that continued research on software quality was a pressing priority.

It is not surprising, therefore, that there are often many errors in production programs (Chapter 8). A study by the Food and Drug Administration (FDA) concluded that manufacturers should place increased emphasis on thoroughly validating software prior to its release (Battle, 1988b). According to one software safety expert, many people are unaware of the scope of the problem, and in most industries, the attitude toward software reliability is 'cavalier'; while according to another such expert, software for personal computers routinely contains numerous bugs, but is nevertheless knowingly sold, sometimes without a warning or the promise of a corrected version. In fact, most microcomputer software is notable for the fact that it clearly states that there are no guarantees, either explicit or implied (Jones, 1986b; Cho, 1987).

Fortunately, most flawed software programs are not life-critical, and therefore inflict no real harm when they malfunction (Battle, 1988b), and many errors are in portions of the programs that are not used very often (this is discussed later). Also, there is some evidence (Chapter 8) that programs nowadays contain fewer errors than in the past, implying that more attention is now being paid to quality; and designers of computer-controlled equipment in particular *are* stepping up efforts to prevent disasters caused by bugs in critical software.

10.1   DEFINITION

The word 'quality' has many definitions and many ambiguities associated with it (Jones, 1986b). As Siegel (1989) put it, software quality engineering even lacks standard terminology: what some refer to as 'quality assurance', others refer to as 'testing'. Sommerville (1989) draws a distinction between QA on the one hand, and verification and validation on the other, but acknowledges that in some organizations, no distinction is made between these activities. Many people, if asked to define quality, would equate it to reliability, i.e. to errors or the absence thereof (Conte *et al.*, 1986). This, however, is only one aspect of the question. As Conte put it, most users do not consider error-free code that is difficult to understand, use, and modify, to be of high quality. Jones (1986b) effectively gives two definitions: a fundamental one and an extended one. The fundamental definition is that a high-quality programming system can be considered one without defects that would cause the system to stop completely or produce unacceptable results; the extended definition adds extensibility, maintainability, and so on. A software product must also do what the user wants. (This is known as the 'correctness' of a program, and is defined as the degree to which it satisfies the user's functional specifications (Arthur, 1983; Pomberger, 1984).) This, in fact, is a fundamental or even the primary requirement of any software product (Glass, 1979; Pomberger, 1984), yet many end products do not meet it (Garnham, 1988). It may be better, though, to require that the software 'be able to produce usable output for its intended users' (Cho, 1987), because what users *ask* for is not necessarily what

they *need* (Schach, 1988), and may not even be practical.

In addition to the above, a software product must also (Boehm, 1981; Fairley, 1985; Arthur, 1983; Pomberger, 1984; Gildersleeve, 1974a, 1978; Cho, 1987):

- be completed on time and within budget;
- be cost-effective;
- reduce costs;
- be efficient in its use of all resources, including memory, CPU time, input/output channels, and peripheral devices, e.g. be economical on disk storage;
- be faster than the previous method, if any;
- be tunable;
- comply with the installation's standards for documentation, structure, coding, etc.;
- be self-documenting;
- be easy to learn;
- be easy to test;
- be flexible;
- be fault-tolerant, i.e. the effects of hardware, software, and user errors, should be minimized;
- permit rapid recovery in the event of failure;
- have good security;
- be hard to misuse;
- be auditable;
- be portable;
- interface easily with other systems;
- enrich the user's job;
- and so on.

There are additional requirements for an interactive program (Shneiderman, 1980; Martin, 1985; Winfield, 1986; Cho, 1987):

- response should be consistent, and neither too fast nor too slow;
- it should give warnings about delays;
- it should permit short-cuts, e.g. abbreviations, for knowledgeable users;
- it should not display too many options at once;
- inexperienced users should only have to make one decision per step;
- commands should be self-explanatory;

- it should reduce the possibility of errors by making inputs seem natural and consistent, and the design should be changed if necessary, to eliminate common user errors;
- it should encourage experiment;
- it should be helpful when users get into difficulties, e.g.:
  - it should be forgiving of errors;
  - it should allow a command to be corrected, instead of it having to be retyped in its entirety;
  - messages should be courteous, non-threatening, meaningful, constructive, and indicate corrective action, but should also be brief;
  - it should allow users to find out what they have done, and what options are open;
  - it should protect against costly mistakes, e.g. erasing a file;
  - actions should be reversible, and in particular, it should allow escape from danger, and should assist return to the correct dialog;
  - it should provide different levels of help, e.g. a brief reminder as the first level, followed by an optional more detailed explanation;
- the users must be convinced that they are in control of the system ('in the driver's seat'), and not the system in control of them.

It is these factors which distinguish a high quality product, so they can be used as a detailed definition of quality. A shorter, more general definition is that quality is to get people to do the right things in the right way, to do it right the first time, at the right cost, more efficiently and within the set time limits. A narrower definition, of the reliability aspect only, is that reliability is the probability that the software will perform its intended functions satisfactorily over its next run, or its next quantum of execution time (Boehm, 1981).

Garnham (1988) drew a contrast between the old and new attitudes towards quality. It used to be thought of as having the right standards, procedures, audits, and checks in place, but is now viewed as being all about saving money and delivering what the customer wants on time and within budget.

One might have thought that the main requirement of any software product is that it must do what the user wants (the 'correctness' requirement). However, Sommerville (1989) believes that reliability is the most important product attribute (i.e. the product must *reliably* do what the user wants), because of the increasing use of software systems in life-critical applications and the consequent danger of loss of life, and also because unreliable systems are discarded or never brought into use. The development effort is therefore wasted. The primary task of the QA process is thus to assure product reliability. Cho (1987) identified four goals of software engineering, and rated them in the following order of importance: reliability, efficiency, understandability, and modifiability. As he so pointedly remarked, if a piece of software is efficient but does not work right all the time, 'then it would damage its user – efficiently'.

Some of the above criteria (specifically correctness and reliability, but even modifiability) are *mandatory* (the system must comply with the criteria, and must continue doing so even after modifications); while others (such as efficiency and portability) are *optional* for a given system (Macro and Buxton, 1987). In fact, some may be irrelevant for a particular product, e.g. it may be *possible* to transfer a system from a microcomputer to a large mainframe (the portability requirement), but this is often a nonsensical thing to do (Sommerville, 1989). Some of the criteria (such as modifiability) are *objectives*; while others (such as structuredness and understandability) are the *means* to achieve them. Ideally, we would like to maximize the presence of each of these characteristics, but some of them are potentially contradictory, e.g. improvements in portability and understandability usually result in decreased efficiency (Conte *et al.*, 1986), as evidenced by the Weinberg and Schulman (1974) experiment discussed in Chapter 2. The software quality plans for a particular project should therefore explicitly identify those quality attributes which are most significant for that project, and should state quantitatively the standard that must be met for each attribute, e.g. that the system must be available for 99% of the time (Sommerville, 1989). (Measurement of quality is a difficult issue, discussed in section 10.4.)

Quality therefore has many facets. It applies to people as well as to the software products the people produce, and to the accompanying documentation; it applies to the data processed by the software products, and to the equipment and tools the people use. However, most of the following discussion refers to the quality of software products.

10.2 CONSEQUENCES OF LOW QUALITY

Low quality has many damaging consequences. The extended definition of quality given above draws attention to the consequences, e.g. software products which are difficult to understand, learn, debug and maintain, and which therefore lower software engineering productivity. In addition, low-quality products have more errors, yet it is extremely important to deliver defect-free software to customers (Conte *et al.*, 1986). Low quality software may also be inefficient, difficult to use, and not do what the user needs, and therefore adversely affect the productivity of end users as well as that of software engineers. In the extreme case, the product has to be extensively redesigned and rewritten. According to Opperman (1988), many organizations are wasting up to 50% of their systems development resources through lack of attention to quality, as a result of the effort expended on reworking, post-implementation debugging, incorrect specifications, and systems that do not meet user requirements. This figure agrees with the reduction of about 45% in maintenance costs experienced by IBM when they rewrote the error-prone modules in their IMS DBMS (Jones, 1986b) – and as stated earlier, defect removal costs are always among the top three expense items for software products. Programmers in particular may have to work overtime to meet their deadlines, and may be called out at night to resolve problems in production programs.

One of the major complaints noted by Jones (1986b) in a study of software and hardware reviews was the failure of examples to actually work: 'Few things are more frustrating to a user seeking to learn a new program than to copy an example keystroke for keystroke, only to have it fail'. All examples in the documentation should therefore be tried out, and should work exactly as stated.

Worse, software errors, like hardware failures, can lead to heavy financial losses, and even loss of life (Chapters 3 and 5). For example, it was a software bug that was blamed for causing a linear accelerator radiation machine to administer extreme overdoses, as a result of which two patients died (Joyce, 1987). An American unmanned space vehicle to Venus went off course and was never seen again, because of a period instead of a comma in a DO statement (Bell *et al.*, 1987). In 1979, an error was found in the program that had been used to design the cooling systems of nuclear reactors, so five plants were shut down because their safety became questionable.

Low quality systems are also more susceptible to fraud and other computer crimes. If, for example, run controls and audit trails are insufficient or non-existent, security breaches may go undetected, resulting in stolen profits and pilfered information. Arthur (1983) quoted an average loss of $500 000 from 400 cases of computer crime; it is doubtful that any organization can afford to lose so much money. An example – one which emphasizes the importance of QA during the system installation phase – is the multi-million dollar theft from one chain of jewellers (Ostroff, 1983). After the initial loading of data, a shortage of about one million dollars was discovered. Furthermore, three out of sixteen inter-branch transfers were not being displayed on the screen, so some persons thought the computer had dropped the items, and that if they took them, nobody would be the wiser! If these problems had been resolved at the time, before the system was used in production, the theft would probably not have occurred.

Failure to meet contractual obligations (e.g. to complete a project by a certain date), can add non-performance penalties or litigation expenses to the overall cost of the project (Jones, 1986b). Programs that deal with sensitive financial or personal information are subject to various legal sanctions. Anyone who knowingly allows problems such as cheating on financial statements and income tax, or hiding of payments to foreign governments, to enter or remain in their software, is in violation of the law (Arthur, 1983). In future, there may be money-back guarantees, or legal liability for negligence or culpability for consequential damages due to errors in the software.

The above consequences are multiplied in the case of defects in commercially-marketed packages, or even in reused code, so additional QA is necessary for them (Jones, 1986b). According to Jones, the market success of commercially-marketed software is more heavily affected by customer-perceived quality than by any other factor. In some cases, error-prone modules were almost responsible for withdrawing the products from usage. Fixing the defects in these modules often costs more than the development expenses by an order of magnitude for products with many customers and with delivery support and field maintenance.

10.3 CAUSES OF LOW QUALITY

Low quality in a software product can be ascribed to a number of causes, e.g.:

- too short a schedule (Chapter 11);
- shortcutting prototyping or design in order to start coding, shortcutting reviews in order to start testing, or shortcutting testing in order to go live (Chapter 11);
- similarly, it is not uncommon to find developers conducting feasibility studies, preparing preliminary design documents, estimating project budgets and schedules, and sometimes even proceeding with design and coding, without fully knowing the nature or extent of the data the software must handle, the user's detailed output requirements, or the level of performance the user will demand as a criterion of acceptability (Cho, 1987);
- haste caused by the desire to keep an interactive dialog going (Shneiderman, 1980), too fast a machine response, too slow a machine response during peak loading periods, or pressure of work (Chapters 5 and 6);
- omitting the three life-cycle steps of product (i.e. output) concept formulation, product quality characteristics specification, and product design, without which it is difficult to apply statistical quality control (Cho, 1987);
- lack of user and management participation (Chapters 8 and 11);
- lack of long-term management commitment (Battle, 1988b);
- failure to learn from experience (Chapter 9);
- the psychological state of the software engineers – anxiety, lack of motivation, negative attitudes, fear of failure – which is affected by (Hackman *et al.*, 1975):
  – the meaningfulness of their work;

- their degree of autonomy and responsibility;
- the amount of feedback they get;
- the amount of recognition they get for good work;
- too short a schedule;
- and so on.
- personality, i.e. some people finish a job quickly, even at the expense of quality, if they are told to work as quickly as possible, or if they are impatient to go on to new things (Shneiderman, 1980; Dunn and Ullman, 1982);
- divided attention, e.g. working on two jobs at once (as can happen with the matrix structure – see Chapter 3); or, with interactive programming (Chapter 6), watching the screen for a response instead of concentrating on the problem (Shneiderman, 1980);
- conflicting goals (as illustrated by the Weinberg and Schulman (1974) experiment discussed in Chapter 2);
- design defects can be caused by poor understanding of requirements or specifications (possibly because they are unclear) (Conte *et al.*, 1986);
- coding defects can be caused by poor understanding of the design, poor choices of data structures or algorithms, or by errors in logic or syntax (Conte *et al.*, 1986);
- failure to use MPPs, or lack of training in the methods (Chapter 8);
- modules which are too large (Chapter 8);
- deficiencies in equipment, e.g. keyboards which do not give an audible confirmation when a key is depressed (Chapter 4);
- failure to use tools such as test coverage analysers, mathematical checkers, assertion checkers, and file comparators, and also 4GLs, CASE tools, etc. (Chapter 6);
- tools which the programmer is not familiar with, or which are too complicated (Chapter 6);
- lack of training in the application area (Jones, 1986b);
- lack of a manufacturing background, and

lack of familiarity with statistical quality control (Cho, 1987);
- use of programmers to model the software, yet programmers lack the requisite knowledge of systems, applications, users' needs, constraints, and so forth (Cho, 1987);
- assignment of programmers to projects that exceed their current abilities (Jones, 1986b);
- lack of ability – poor performers are responsible for an order of magnitude more defects than are the best performers, and lower-average performers for twice as many as upper-average (DeMarco, 1982);
- lack of knowledge, both as to what constitutes good quality, and as to how to achieve it, e.g. they may not have been taught how to find errors (Chapter 8);
- ignorance of its importance, i.e. of the consequences of low quality;
- inadequate testing, e.g. inappropriate test data (Conte *et al.* 1986);
- lack of follow-up, i.e. not monitoring the performance of a system and user satisfaction with it, or not rectifying any problems unearthed;
- reluctance on the part of a software user to admit he has accepted poor-quality software (Cho, 1987).

Lack of standards, or failure to enforce them, can be added to this list. For example, even if individual programmers write high-quality programs, if they use different methods, their colleagues will have difficulty understanding their work, and loss of time, misunderstandings and errors will result (Arthur, 1983). Without a common way of working, it is difficult to hold walkthroughs, inspections, and quality audits. The presence of standards also prevents walkthroughs etc. deteriorating into opinionated battles over what quality is and what it is not. The existence of standards (for development methodologies, requirements specifications, generic program designs, and testing) by itself encourages adherence. Standards thus ensure uniformity, and therefore reduce the learning effort when starting new work (Sommerville, 1989). In fact, lack of standards often 'marries' the programmer to the program: no one else can understand it, so the original programmer has to do all the maintenance. Standards encapsulate the best, or most appropriate, practice. This knowledge is often only acquired after a great deal of trial and error, and building it into a standard avoids the repetition of past mistakes.

Another cause of low quality is complexity (Chapter 8); it is one of the factors having the greatest effect on productivity, so it is worth repeating here that the more complex a program is, the more difficult it is to understand, and therefore debug and modify; the more errors it contains; and the more difficult it is to prove the program correct. Complexity may be inescapable, e.g. complicated but essential functions to meet the user's needs; or it may be unnecessary, being merely the result of poor software engineering.

According to Jones (1986b), some 30 different factors have been identified as causing error-prone modules, of which 3 account for more than 90% of all cases observed: individual human errors due to lack of training and ability; modules too large; and lack of testing. In fact, one of the commonest reasons for error-prone modules is that the modules were never tested because the test personnel did not know they existed! This was often due to requirements and design changes late in the development cycle, as a result of which there were no written designs or specifications for these modules. Better configuration management (Chapter 11) would have prevented this.

Some of the above causes, such as personality deficiencies, are *primary*, i.e. poor quality is built into the product; others, such as inadequate testing, are *secondary*, i.e. the built-in poor quality was not detected and corrected.

10.4   MEASUREMENT OF QUALITY

Measurement of defect rates and costs raises workers' consciousness of the problem, and that by itself helps to reduce the number of defects (DeMarco, 1982).

Quality measures identify products that are of low quality, badly written, error-prone, or will be difficult to test or maintain. Appropriate action – such as additional testing or inspections, elimination of marginally-useful features to reduce size and complexity, a rewrite, or training of the programmer to prevent a recurrence – can then be taken.

Ideally, we would like to define metrics for each component of quality, and then combine them in some way to produce a single 'figure of merit' for each particular software product (Conte *et al.*, 1986), or check that all of the components of quality which are most important for this product, meet the minimum requirements. However, quality is difficult to measure, and quality measurement is still in its infancy (Myers, 1979; Shneiderman, 1980; Cho, 1987). The difficulty is compounded by the fact that some aspects of quality may be irrelevant for a particular product, and some are potentially contradictory. Furthermore, the programmers may resent quality measurement, as it reveals defect-prone workers, and has 'a vague scent of corporate fascism' (DeMarco, 1982), and they may even distort the measures to their advantage, just as can happen with productivity measurement (Chapter 2).

10.4.1   SUBJECTIVE MEASURES

Programs can be manually graded. This is difficult, but is done regularly by instructors (Shneiderman, 1980). Grading must be performed against a written set of standards, with fixed points being allocated to different portions and aspects of the program, and their total provides a quantitative measure of a program's quality. More than one person should be used to do the grading, and their scores compared.

Peer ratings are a similar technique, but the grading is done by the programmer's peers (Myers, 1979). Programmers anonymously evaluate each other's work, assigning subjective ratings to factors such as how easy the program was to understand, and how easy they think it would be to maintain. Shneiderman (1980) quoted studies which showed that there is close agreement between different raters, i.e. different raters usually award similar scores to the same program. Most of the participants in these studies said they had learnt from the experience, and they thought that peer ratings could be effective in improving the standard of programming.

Gilb (1977) developed the multi-element component comparison and analysis (MECCA) method for comparing alternatives, such as for hardware and software selection, and alternative software designs. This is a formal method for allocating points to alternatives. They are evaluated against a list of factors, such as contract guarantees, with subjective point scores being awarded to each competing alternative for each factor, and the one scoring the highest total should be the best.

Cho (1987) defines software 'understandability' as the number of instructions that can be understood per unit of time. Quantification of understandability might appear to be objective rather than subjective, but it depends not only on the quality of the software and its documentation, but also on many other factors such as one's background, programming proficiency, familiarity with the software application area, and so on.

10.4.2 OBJECTIVE MEASURES

There are two types of model that assess defects: *static* models use software metrics to estimate the number of defects in the software, while *dynamic* models use the past defect discovery rate to estimate this rate for the future (Conte *et al.*, 1986).

Gilb (1977) presented a set of basic software

metrics which cover both static and dynamic measures. He included metrics for reliability, maintainability, flexibility, portability, performance, availability, structural simplicity, etc. Structural simplicity, for example, is the ratio of the number of module linkages to the number of modules. However, these metrics were not yet of much practical use, as they are difficult to obtain and are not independent (Shneiderman, 1980).

Dynamic models

Probably the most obvious measure of the quality of a software product is the total number of defects it contains. This figure is made up of two components: the number of known defects which have not yet been corrected, and the number of unknown defects. The former is easy to determine; the latter, consisting as it does of defects which have not yet been detected, can only be estimated. The total number of defects encountered to date can be used to estimate the figure. Many of these defects will, of course, already have been corrected – in fact, most would have been corrected during development – but they must be included in the calculation, as the probability of the existence of more faults is proportional to the number of faults already found (Chapter 8). Static analysis methods, such as the various complexity metrics, and even just the size of the program, can also be used to estimate the number of remaining defects.

Most software reliability models are based on the hypothesis that the error detection rate is proportional to the number of errors remaining in the program (Misra, 1983), yet Littlewood (1977) stated that he had never seen a program where this assumption was valid. Reasons for this are given below.

The MTBF (mean time between failures), or MTTF (mean time to failure), is another way of looking at the error detection rate. It provides an indication of the likely number of remaining (as yet undetected) defects in a product, but like the error detection rate itself, is not always reliable for a number of reasons. The product may not be used very often, thereby giving a misleadingly high MTBF: the small number of defects detected is not a true indication of the number remaining in the product. For example, when a software package is first released, it has few users, so few errors are discovered (Shneiderman, 1980). On the other hand, the most probable faults are likely to be discovered early (Sommerville, 1989), and in fact the maintenance effort 'hump' due to omitted requirements covers only the first 15% of the system's productive life (DeMarco, 1982), so there may well be a large number of faults discovered quickly, resulting in a misleadingly *low* MTBF initially. Only certain input values cause erroneous behavior, and many of these are unlikely. In other words, most of the remaining errors in the product may be in the coding to handle unusual conditions, and this coding, by definition, is not used very often. In fact, most programs only abort when they encounter unanticipated and exceptional conditions. Similarly, different users and environments are likely to exercise the product in different ways. Some of these ways may not be used very often, and the errors may be in these parts of the system. This highlights an important practical consideration: software faults in parts of the system which are unlikely to be used make little difference to the *perceived* reliability (Sommerville, 1989). In fact, in a study of errors in IBM software products, Adams (1984) noted that many of the errors were only likely to occur after hundreds or thousands of months of usage. Similarly, experience at the Toshiba Fuchu Software Factory in Japan led Matsumoto (1989) to believe that two-thirds of the faults in their production programs do not cause errors during the first ten years of operation. The work of Mills *et al.* (1987) suggested that, for the products studied, removing 60% of the defects would only lead to a 3% improvement in reliability.

An alternative measure is the number of errors discovered per thousand delivered source instructions per year (Boehm, 1981). For a system of 50 000 lines of code (this is a typical system size, according to Table 8.3), there is typically about one abnormal ending per month due to all causes (Chapter 8). Boehm (1973) quoted one large real-time system containing 2 700 000 instructions, in which one error per day was discovered. This is equivalent to about one error per two months in a 50 000 instruction system (30*50 000/2 700 000), and is therefore in good agreement with the typical rate quoted above. However, this measure suffers from the same unreliability disadvantages as the MTBF.

(If there is typically about one abnormal ending per month as stated above; if these are the only errors detected (as stated in Chapter 8, it probably excludes minor errors, which are probably more numerous); if this rate remains constant (another dubious assumption: it is more likely to decrease as the more common errors are detected and eliminated – or it may increase if the system was not used very much initially); if the average production program contains 8 errors per thousand lines of code (Table 8.41); and if a typical system contains 50 000 lines of code (Table 8.3); then a typical system contains (8/1000* 50 000 =) 400 errors initially, and it will take 400 months or *33 years* for all the errors to be removed. This is consistent with the statement by Adams (1984) quoted above, that many errors are only likely to occur after hundreds or thousands of months of usage.)

Instead, therefore, of measuring failures against calendar time, it is more accurate to measure them against the amount of machine time consumed, or – in the case of say a bank auto-teller system – against the number of transactions processed (Sommerville, 1989). AT&T, for example, measure the number of failures per job steps executed (The quest for zero defect software, *Computer Week*, 13 Feb.

1989, p.21). Furthermore, the lack of user documentation is a major defect in a product, but it does not directly affect the MTBF (Gilb, 1988). Gilb therefore proposed the alternative measure 'Likely user error reports avoided (LUERA)'. Similarly, Conte *et al.* (1986) suggested counting the number of customer complaints.

Corrections to a product, and other maintenance changes, alter the product, and may introduce new errors, so previous reliability figures for it, using any of these methods, are at least partly invalidated (Sommerville, 1989). This is illustrated by an example given by Conte, of the number of defects detected against date detected, for three versions of a popular commercial compiler, quoted in Chapter 8.

The MTTR (mean time to repair) and cost of repair provide an indication of how easy the product is to modify (which indicates how readable and understandable it is). This could be weighted by the severity of the error (Chapter 8), as QA methods should concentrate on avoiding or detecting the most serious or high-cost errors (Shneiderman, 1980). The costs of any downtime, and of repairing the *results* of the failure, and recovering to the pre-failure state (Chapter 5), should be included in the severity weighting. The European Space Agency, for example, uses a 'normalized error time' metric. Each software failure is rated according to the duration of the failure and its severity, e.g. failures affecting all space-craft have a severity weighting of 10 000; while trivial failures such as a typographic error, carry a weighting of only 1 (Formica, 1978).

The *availability* of the application software takes into account both the repair and the recovery time. It is computed by dividing the time the system *was* available, by the time it *should* have been available (Gilb, 1977) (excluding preventive maintenance time or computer downtime (Boehm, 1981)). This measure is most appropriate for systems like telecommunications systems, where the repair or restart time is significant, and the loss of service during that time is important (Sommerville, 1989).

MTBF and MTTR were derived by analogy with hardware. However, various authors such as Macro and Buxton (1987) disapprove of their use for software, because large sample-size failure statistics are not available. Unlike with hardware, standard components are lacking. Hardware wears out (physical deterioration and wear and tear) and breaks, whereas software 'wears in' (progressive detection and correction of errors, leading to increasing intervals between software failures, at least in high-quality software). Hardware component failure tends to be permanent, in that the component stops working until repaired, but software component failures are transient, in that they are only exhibited for some (often unusual) inputs, so the system can continue in operation (Sommerville, 1989). Also, software component failures, once corrected, remain corrected, whereas the replaced or repaired hardware components will eventuallly wear out or break again (Dunn and Ullman, 1982). MTBF and MTTR mean much more when used in the context of a system rather than a single program or module (Yourdon, 1975). (This is presumably because users typically use entire systems rather than just individual components thereof. Also, the larger number (of components) provides a better approximation to the hardware analogy.)

Various technological aids (Chapter 6) such as test coverage analysers, mathematical checkers, assertion checkers and file comparators, do not measure the quality of a program as such, but nevertheless do reveal low-quality programs. It was claimed that a simple test coverage analyser could help find 25% of program errors; a sophisticated one, which would check all sequences of segments (not yet technologically feasible because of the astronomical number of possible combinations), 65%.

Static models

Halstead's Software Science

Halstead's Software Science includes a number of metrics – e.g. for program size, programming effort, program level, number of bugs, and language level – which are related, directly or indirectly, to quality. There is good agreement between his metrics and actual development effort (Chapter 2) but (Chapter 1) his methods have been questioned, and the supporting evidence has been challenged.

The number of unique operands may be useful in identifying *at an early stage* those modules most likely to contain errors (Conte *et al.*, 1986). It may therefore be used to target certain modules for early or additional testing, in order to increase the efficiency of the defect removal process.

Halstead also defines 'impurities', such as ambiguous operands (using the same name for different things), and synonymous operands (using different names for the same thing). Programs written by novices often have many impurities; published programs, almost none (Shneiderman, 1980). Generally, an impurity is coding which is not as compact as it could be. An example of the 'complementary operation' impurity is (Vincent *et al.*, 1988; Christensen, 1980):

$$A = (B * C) / (D * C)$$

which is better written as

$$A = B / D$$

and of the 'unnecessary assignment' impurity:

$$A = B * C$$
$$D = A * A$$

which is better written as

$$D = (B * C) ** 2$$

Arthur (1985) estimated that, in programs that had undergone maintenance for several years, removal of impurities and GOTO statements could reduce their difficulty by as much as 50–75%, and could also reduce the number of lines of executable code by 10–30%. However, impurities, and specifically 'unnecessary assignment' impurities, are not invariably bad. A large, complicated mathematical formula may be simplified by assigning a unique name to part of it, and then using that name only once (Shneiderman, 1980). In particular, if part of the equation is a recognizable mathematical formula, then use of such a name can *enhance* clarity. Any complexity metric which did not take such aspects into account would give misleading answers, with damaging consequences (Chapter 8).

Halstead's metrics also help determine if a program has been optimally modularized (Shneiderman, 1980).

Complexity measures

Complexity measures – McCabe's 'cyclomatic' complexity measure, TRW's reliability metric, and McClure's measures (Chapter 8) – are related to quality. For example, McCabe's method for measuring the complexity of a program also provides a guide to its quality, and identifies modules that will be difficult to maintain. McClure's measures indicate if a program was subdivided into too many modules, making it difficult to understand.

Other measures

Loose coupling and high cohesion (Chapter 8) should suggest adaptability, but it is not possible to measure either directly (Sommerville, 1989). Nevertheless, the number of data items shared by modules is one measure of how loosely coupled they are (Shneiderman, 1980; Bell *et al.*, 1987).

Tools

Some of these metrics can be easily mechanized, and some cannot (Arthur, 1983).

Because of the enormous amount of source code in organizations, manual analysis is impractical.

Compilers and static analysers (Chapter 6), or suitably extended versions of such programs, can be used to automatically measure the quality or complexity of a program, by counting the number of errors or violations of the installation's coding standards, or by applying the various complexity measures (Chapter 8), thereby making the metrics much more useful (Shneiderman, 1980). In particular, compilers should calculate and print the various metrics, so that programmers have immediate feedback on the quality of their work. McCabe's complexity measure is the basis for the software tool, Inspector, which analyses IBM mainframe COBOL programs, and produces reports indicating the quality of the program (Language Technology, 1987a).

These tools quickly identify the potential problem programs, so QA can concentrate its attention on them, and any problems are fixed early, before they can cause further harm and costs (Arthur, 1983).

Word processing packages which permit spelling checks, grammar checks, etc., or measure the 'fog index' (Chapter 6), perform static analysis on documents. Arthur (1983) believes that it is too expensive to evaluate document quality manually.

10.4.3 CAUTIONS

Caution must be observed when using metrics. Some aspects of quality are optional or even irrelevant for a given system, and some are potentially contradictory. For example, for some programs, efficiency is of paramount importance, so other factors, even program clarity and therefore maintainability, must be sacrificed to achieve this (Sommerville, 1989). Worse, although there is evidence confirming the validity of the various measures, there has also been criticism of them, and some of the evidence has

been challenged (Chapter 8). For example, McCabe's complexity measure denies that size affects complexity, and does not take into account the ordering of the statements. The erratic performance of the various metrics – including Gilb's metrics, Halstead's Software Science, reliability models based on bug counting, and McCabe's metrics – indicates that there are other variables which must be taken into account (Shneiderman, 1980). Many of the important characteristics of quality are difficult, if not impossible, to quantify, and some of them are subjective and difficult to assess (Conte *et al.*, 1986; Sommerville, 1989; Macro and Buxton, 1987).

No software metrics have been unequivocally demonstrated to be generally useful as quality predictors (Sommerville, 1989). Reliability models such as the one by Thayer *et al.* (1978), are still in the research domain, and 'we are left with no real metric', and the same is true of other aspects of quality, such as modifiability, testability, and structuredness (Macro and Buxton, 1987). It is therefore not surprising that there are currently no well-established software quality metrics – for example, neither Halstead's nor McCabe's metrics seem to have gained widespread acceptance – and it is also thus not possible to guarantee the reliability of software in most cases.

Individual organizations must therefore systematically evaluate the metrics, and assess the validity of particular metrics to their own products and software process (Sommerville, 1989). This involves collecting data, which is best done during product development. It should not be done subsequently, as this means either relying on the (imperfect) recollection of past events, or performing a post-release analysis of products, the cost of which is often very high. Data collection should be automated, and should be integrated into the development process, otherwise it is unlikely to be successful. A sufficiently large quantity of data is necessary, and this must be promptly analysed and archived as an organizational resource.

10.5   COST AND BENEFITS

Quality provides benefits, but also incurs costs, and the two are interrelated. These aspects are discussed here in general terms. Costs and benefits relating to specific QA methods are discussed under those methods.

10.5.1   BENEFITS

The consequences of low quality listed earlier, such as errors in production programs and programmer overtime, in themselves imply what the benefits of high quality are. For example, if programming and documentation are of a higher standard, and if requirements- and design-based defects can be eliminated prior to integration and testing, then the usual rash of overtime and around-the-clock defect repairs that often occur are eliminated also (Jones, 1986b; Arthur, 1983).

Higher quality has multiple benefits, including:

- fewer errors will be made, so there will be fewer to correct during checkout, as well as during production;
- errors will be detected earlier, and the sooner an error is detected, the cheaper it is to fix (Chapter 8);
- modifications, whether to correct an error or to comply with changed user requirements, will be easier, quicker and cheaper to implement;
- there will be fewer modifications because the user's needs will be more accurately established initially, and the systems will be more general.

AT&T's focus on quality and defect-free software has yielded a number of benefits, including greater end-user productivity, customer satisfaction, lower development costs, lower operational costs, faster product delivery, lower maintenance costs, and heightened self-esteem of the IS personnel (The

quest for zero defect software, *Computer Week*, 13 Feb. 1989, p. 21).

Jones (1986b) quotes an example in which the system with the higher required reliability (a commercially-marketed system with 9 defect removal steps, compared to an internal system with only 5), had only one-third as many defects at delivery, the MTTF was five times as long, and it took only half as many months to stabilize, i.e. achieve a stable and trouble-free operational system.

Figures given by Dunn and Ullman (1982) quoted in Chapter 8 indicate that a QA program halves the number of defects in production programs.

At the end of two-and-a-half years of quality effort, British Rail had reduced project (development?) costs by between 26 and 40%, and time-scales by 16% (Garnham, 1988).

Hitachi reduced 'spoilage' from 1.48% of the project cost in 1976, to only 0.08% in 1979, a reduction of nearly 20 times in just three years (DeMarco, 1982). ('Spoilage' here includes only the post-delivery defect cost, and probably does not include the effects of specification errors.)

An analysis of IBM's delivered software systems found that those systems with the lowest defect rates in field use were also the systems with the lowest incidences of slipped schedules and delayed deliveries, and they also had somewhat higher productivity (Jones, 1986b). Contrary to what one might expect, projects that aim from the beginning at achieving the highest possible levels of quality and reliability tend to have the best schedule adherence records, the highest productivity, and even the best marketplace success.

Johnson (1980b) claimed that QA can improve productivity by possibly 10–25%. One consultant claimed that, in over 50 quality evaluations, his firm consistently identified savings on (development?) costs and time of between 15 and 40% as a result of a quality management program (Garnham, 1988). These figures are in broad agreement with the Opperman (1988) claim, that many organizations are wasting up to 50% of their systems development resources through lack of attention to quality, and with the estimate (Chapter 8) that debugging typically consumes about 20% of the development effort, while testing and debugging can consume more than 50% of the total software development time and budget on large projects.

One might expect the figure for maintenance to be at least as high, but according to Table 3.2, even the total prevention of errors in production programs would only increase maintenance productivity by under 25% ($50/(0.7 + 40.0)$). However, this discrepancy is removed – or even reversed – if we include the reduction in 'other' maintenance (such as enhancements), which is not shown in Table 3.2, and the estimate by DeMarco (1982) that as much as half of the lifetime maintenance cost of a typical system is due to requirements that were missed during requirements analysis (Chapter 8).

Two of the benefits deserve more detailed discussion: earlier detection of errors (section 10.5.4) and the reduction in the time spent on maintenance (section 10.5.5).

10.5.2 COSTS

QA measures take time, which must be set against the above savings. The tools used (such as test coverage analysers and static analysers), also incur a cost. However, direct comparisons between cost reduction and the cost of the QA function may be impossible (Arthur, 1983). It is not surprising, therefore, that quality programs are often seen as little more than expensive overheads (Garnham, 1988), and management may be reluctant to budget and staff such a function.

The figures in Chapter 8 indicate that testing and debugging typically consume about 30% of the total development effort, while some of the estimates were over 50%. One organization which manufactures linear accelerators costing about $1 million, spent more than $500 000 on a series of exhaustive reviews, including hiring an outside consultant to read every line of code in the massive set of programs directing its new radiation machine (Battle, 1988b). Worse, every time the software is revised, the new code must be subjected to the same rigorous review. This requires long-term management commitment. In large corporations with formal QA organizations, the resources devoted to this activity range from less than 1% to the high of approximately 10% which IBM applies to marketed commercial systems (Jones, 1986b).

Jones (1986b) quoted an example of a commercially-marketed system compared to an internal system: the former took 25% more effort to develop. According to Macro and Buxton (1987), the cost of quality is normally 30–35% of the whole development cost of the system. However, if loss of human life is a possible consequence of failure, then it may be 60–150%. (As they so pointedly remarked, where only a marginal amount is spent on quality, 'the results have been known to show it'.) Similarly, according to the COCOMO cost-estimation model, a very high required reliability (where human life is at stake) can almost double the overall development effort, because extra effort pervades all aspects of system development (Boehm, 1981). Stress testing is required, plus verification and validation by an independent organization, mathematical verification, and so on, which would not be necessary, or cost-justifiable, for a low reliability requirement system. The consequences of malfunction must therefore be detailed early in the life-cycle, and this will determine if any special means and methods of QA are necessary (Macro and Buxton, 1987). The COCOMO figures give good agreement with the projects making up Boehm's database, provided the effect of other factors, such as ability, experience, and MPPs, is eliminated. According to Conte *et al.* (1986), the cost of producing highly reliable code may be several times that for low reliability code; and some experimentation by Boehm (1981) with the RCA model (Freiman and Park, 1979), also yielded a much higher figure, of 6 or 9 times the overall project effort (compared to COCOMO's doubling in effort), though that includes the effect of other factors. It is surprising, therefore, that required reliability is used in only two of the nine cost-estimation models Boehm (1981) surveyed.

The high cost of QA is not surprising, as some software projects that are released to commercial customers experience as many as *13* defect removal stages (requirements review, top-level design review, etc., through to customer acceptance testing) (Jones, 1986b).

10.5.3   TRADE-OFFS

Because of the cost incurred, a product must not be made more reliable than necessary. For example, although aircraft flight software must be very reliable, the postflight data reduction software does not require the same level of reliability (Boehm, 1981). The required reliability should therefore be specified individually for each system or subsystem (Sommerville, 1989). Gilb (1988) gave a good example: Bell Laboratories took *eight years* to raise the availability of their computerized telephone switching system from 99.9 to 99.98%, an improvement of *only 0.08%*. Gilb added that the British Ministry of Defence was reputed to require 99.9999999% availability, and pointedly asked: 'When do you estimate their projects will pass acceptance tests?'.

On the other hand, caution must be observed when relaxing the reliability requirement. Quality costs money, but the price of poor quality may be far higher (Macro and Buxton, 1987). Low initial quality ensures low productivity throughout the life of the system (van Wyk, 1978). There are additional errors in production programs. The system may be difficult to use. Mainten-

ance effort is increased. This is vividly illustrated by a table in Pomberger (1984) showing the effect of ten different aspects of quality (such as correctness and readability). Nearly all of these aspects result in higher development time and cost, but nearly all result also in lower operating and maintenance costs, and in lower total (lifetime) effort as well. According to the COCOMO model, relaxing the reliability requirement by one step on its five-step rating scale decreases development effort (and therefore increases development productivity) by about 15%, but results in an increase of about 15% in annual maintenance costs (Boehm, 1981). (The maximum impact that required reliability has on maintenance productivity (between 'high' and 'very low' required reliability) is 40%, or 1.4:1, according to this model.) For a software product with a long life, life-cycle maintenance costs will eventually exceed development costs (as they generally do for large projects), making it more expensive in the long run to decrease the required reliability during development (Chapter 8).

Similarly, Jones (1986b) quoted an example of a commercially-marketed (and therefore high required reliability) system compared to an internal system (with average required reliability). The former took 25% more effort to develop, but only one-third as much effort to maintain (if delivery support and field service are excluded, so as not to obscure the essential comparison), so total life-cycle costs over five years were 12% lower. (Jones was probably including only defect repair time in his maintenance effort, but this is of more relevance to the current topic than other forms of maintenance.) In addition, although the development schedule of the system with the higher required reliability was slightly longer (by 4%), if the time for the systems to stabilize is taken into account, i.e. if we measure from project startup to stable run mode, then it was actually completed *sooner*. One can therefore argue that the system with the higher required reliability actually had the shorter *true* development schedule (by 12%).

The relative costs (on a 10-point scale), covering both acquisition and usage, of some three dozen software reliability tools and methods are given by Glass (1979). His list also includes the relative values (also on a 10-point scale) of most of these tools and methods. This list should be of considerable relevance, but it is not reproduced here because Glass warned that no attempt should be made to quantify or compare these value/cost numbers, as they were assigned merely for ordering purposes, and so are not in proportion to the actual values and costs – and they also contain subjective as well as objective judgements.

10.5.4 EARLIER ERROR DETECTION

An error detected after a program has gone into production may cost more than ten times as much to correct as it would have cost had it been detected earlier in the software life-cycle, because of the additional effort required (Chapter 8). The aim of QA should therefore not be merely to detect errors, but to detect them at the earliest possible stage (Conte *et al.*, 1986). In other words, there should be only a short interval between defect creation and defect discovery (Jones, 1991).

What effect would it have on the total output of the industry if errors were detected earlier?

1. Additional effort would have to be expended in the earlier stages to detect the errors, and this would have to be set against the savings.
2. Probably more important, many errors are already detected early (nearly 40% of the programming errors in the Crossman (1978) study quoted in Chapter 8 (Table 8.60) were discovered before system testing, and 75% before the system went into production), so the overall potential for improvement is much less than a factor of

ten. Using Crossman's figures, if all the errors had been detected immediately after coding, they would have cost only:

> 40 (the total number of errors) * 20 (the average cost to find and correct an error during inspection)

= $800, instead of $3550, to correct, i.e. an improvement of 4.4:1 instead of 10:1.
3. His figures refer to programming only, whereas many errors occur in systems analysis and design. If they were detected there, they would cost even less to fix.

There is not enough data available to be able to apply all these adjustments, but an idea of the magnitude of their effect can be gained by considering the following example.

Supposing a system costs $1000 to develop and maintain for its five year existence, of which say $300 consists of correcting errors detected during both development and main-tenance (including corrections to errors made during maintenance). (This means that debugging is 30% of the total lifetime effort, which is consistent with the (admittedly wide range of) figures given in Chapter 8.) The cost of the system, excluding error correction, is therefore (1000 − 300 =) $700.

If all these errors had been detected soon after they were made, then using only the Crossman adjustment (as calculated above) for simplicity, the cost of error correction would have been only (300/4.4 =) $68, and the total cost of the system (700 + 68 =) $768, which is an improvement in productiv-ity of (1000:768 =) 1.3:1 or 30%.

10.5.5 MAINTENANCE REDUCTION AND ITS IMPACT ON OVERALL PRODUCTIVITY

Maintenance reduction

This topic overlaps with earlier error detec-tion – if errors are detected before a program goes into production, then less maintenance will be required – but the overlap is only partial.

- Most errors (about 80%, according to Tables 8.41 and 8.42) are already detected before the maintenance phase begins, so much of the saving calculated above is outside the scope of maintenance reduction – in fact, almost half ((3550 − 2000)/3550) of it, if we again use Crossman's figures.
- Maintenance does not consist solely of error correction – in fact, about 80% of it is *not* error correction, so major savings are possible which are outside the scope of error correction.

DP departments spend a large portion of their time on maintenance, with most estimates ranging from 40–80% (Chapter 8). This has prompted one authority to declare that the 'single greatest opportunity for improving people productivity is to reduce the effort that is required for maintenance' (Winer, 1978). Improved quality and QA would help towards this end.

- Fewer errors would escape detection during development.
- Fewer modifications would be required, because the user's needs would be more accurately established initially – in fact, many so-called enhancements are requirements that always existed, but were not properly elicited by the initial specification process (DeMarco, 1982) – and the systems would be more general, e.g. not limited by data volumes (Vincent *et al.*, 1988).
- The few changes which were still required would be easier to do, because the systems would be easier to understand and more flexible.

Overall productivity

Consider an installation whose software engineers spent 80% of their time on maintenance. The ultimate limit of maintenance reduction would be to reduce this proportion to nil. The software engineers could therefore spend five times as much time on develop-

ment, so their overall development output would be five times the previous rate – equivalent to an increase of five times in their development productivity.

In practice, however, the potential savings from this factor are much less.

1. Maintenance typically occupies nearer 50% of the software effort than 80%, so often only a doubling in development output/productivity could be expected.
2. No matter how much maintenance was reduced, it would not be simplified or avoided to such an extent that it was eliminated altogether, not even with fourth-generation languages and prototyping.
3. MPPs reduce maintenance effort by about 5:1, according to Table 8.72. As MPPs result in improved quality, this suggests, as a first approximation, that improved quality can raise maintenance productivity by about 5:1. If so, it would raise the overall productivity of the industry by about 70%, even if there were no improvement in development productivity (Table 10.1).
4. However, at the other extreme, improved quality might only raise maintenance productivity by 15% – the lower limit of the range quoted by Garnham (1988). If so, then applying this figure to Table 10.1 implies that improved quality would only be able to raise the overall productivity of the industry by 8%, if there were no improvement in development productivity.

Table 10.1 Effect of quality on productivity

Function	Time spent		
	Low quality	High quality	Ratio
Development	50	50	1:1
Maintenance	50	10	5:1
Total	100	60	1.7:1

Table 10.2   Claims for the impact of quality on productivity

Source	Effect claimed
Reduced effort/cost	
Hitachi (DeMarco, 1982)	1% post-delivery defect cost
Jones (1986b)	12% total life-cycle costs
Johnson (1980b)	10–25%
Garnham (1988)	15–40% development costs and time
COCOMO (Boehm, 1981)	40% or 1.4:1 maintenance
Opperman (1988)	up to 50% development resources
Jones (1986b)	one-third or 3:1 maintenance
Extra effort/cost	
Jones (1986b): formal QA	up to 10% for marketed systems
Jones (1986b)	25% development effort
Macro and Buxton (1987): normal	30–35% of whole development cost
extreme	60–150% "
COCOMO (Boehm, 1981)	almost 2:1 development effort
Conte *et al.* (1986)	several times production cost
RCA (Freiman and Park, 1979)	6 or 9:1 overall project effort (other factors included)

On the other hand, the proportion of maintenance can be expected to increase as more and more new systems are developed and have to be maintained (Chapter 8), so the impact of improved quality on overall productivity can also be expected to increase.

10.5.6   PRODUCTIVITY IMPACT

Various claims for the impact of quality on productivity exist (Table 10.2). Some authorities claim that quality reduces effort (and therefore increases productivity), while others claim that extra effort is required to achieve the higher quality (and therefore productivity is reduced), though it may be recouped by subsequent savings. In particular, high reliability (which is one aspect of quality) can be very expensive to achieve.

In addition, figures in Chapter 8 indicate that testing and debugging typically consume about 30% of the total development effort.

As can readily be seen from the divergent figures of Table 10.2, it is difficult to conclude what effect quality has on productivity. However, higher quality probably reduces overall development effort, and therefore improves development productivity. Few

authorities commented on maintenance productivity, but they agreed that higher quality improves it, and because of this, total life-cycle costs will often also be lower. However, in the extreme case of a high reliability requirement, productivity of both development and maintenance is probably significantly decreased.

10.6   METHODS

Prevention is better than cure. High quality should be the aim throughout the software life-cycle. Training, software tools, methods, organizational structures and standards should be directed towards this goal. Quality should be *built into* the software, not added on afterwards (Van Tassel, 1978; Glass, 1979; Lee, 1978). Quite apart from other considerations, there is the question of cost: self-auditing controls, for example, can be added later only at considerable expense (Arthur, 1983), and the earlier an error is detected, the cheaper it is to fix. Worse, poor quality of the intermediate products (e.g. in the general design) always implies poor quality in the final product (Pomberger, 1984). This is consistent with the claim by DeMarco (1982), based on the finding of the Yourdon 1978–80 Project Survey that more effort is required to test low-quality products, that the major determinants of quality are for the most part already in the software before testing even begins.

This makes it all the more important to build high quality into products, and to detect poor quality early. Methods for building in high quality include structured programming, defensive programming, modularization, etc.; while tools include fourth-generation languages, CASE tools, etc. The list of causes of low quality in itself suggests what preventative action needs to be taken, e.g. schedules should be long enough, adequate training should be provided, and defect-prone staff should be reassigned to work they are better at – probably defect-removal, as 'they get so much practice' at it! (DeMarco, 1982). Jones (1986b) believes that, of all the many variables he discusses, re-usable code and standard (generic) designs have perhaps the largest single impact on quality, because they are certified to very high levels of quality.

These methods are proactive. They are discussed in other chapters. By contrast, QA methods are performed 'after the event'. They can therefore be viewed as less desirable than the proactive methods, but there appear to be no error-free software development techniques in use (or on the horizon), so the testing phase – and presumably other QA methods as well – cannot be eliminated (Conte *et al.*, 1986).

Apart from testing, QA methods are discussed in this chapter. Testing is generally treated as a separate stage in the software life-cycle, and was discussed in Chapter 8. Briefly, it is the primary verification and validation technique, but has disadvantages, e.g. it is only applied to code, it is performed late in the development process, it is inefficient (testing typically finds only about 50% of the errors), and is usually expensive.

Selecting and enforcing standards ensures

high quality is built into the products, and also speeds up QA methods, e.g. it improves the productivity of walkthroughs (Arthur, 1983).

Organizations should analyse every error. By doing so, much can be learned, and the knowledge thus gained can be invaluable, both in preventing repetitions of the same types of error, and in recognizing the cause of an error from its symptoms should it recur, which will decrease debugging time (Chapter 8).

Corrective action is also performed 'after the event'. In most cases, of course, errors are fixed by correcting them: design defects are fixed by changing the design, coding defects by changing the code, and so on. Occasionally, though, coding defects can be 'fixed' by changing the specifications, design or documentation to match the code – 'what you really want is what I have written' (Conte *et al.*, 1986). Sometimes, nothing is done, e.g. poor design may be allowed to remain (Macro and Buxton, 1987), because the cost of improving it outweighs the benefits. At the other extreme is a redesign and rewrite. IBM rewrote the error-prone modules in their IMS DBMS, which led to an overall reduction of about 45% in maintenance costs, and a reduction of an order of magnitude in field-reported defect reports (Jones, 1986b).

There should be a QA step after each phase in the software life-cycle, i.e. the quality of each tangible intermediate product should be demonstrated as far as possible, and the next phase should not commence until this has been done. This minimizes the time interval between defect creation and defect discovery. Not all problems, however, can be picked up. For example, the functional specifications may incorporate infeasibilities, which will only become evident when implemented (Macro and Buxton, 1987). Furthermore, Jones (1986b) has seen no evidence in real life, or citations in the literature, indicating that projects are actually cancelled or re-directed as a result of normal phase reviews:

'Usually it is an audit or some extraordinary management or customer action that triggers the redirection'. This indicates that these reviews are not being given the importance they deserve.

There are many different QA methods. Jones (1986b) lists no fewer than 46 common defect removal methods: 10 for requirements and design (personal editing, management reviews, etc.); 18 for coding (code reading by a peer, group structured walkthroughs, etc.); 12 for user documentation and training material (professional editing, automated dictionary and grammar checkers, etc.); and 6 for supporting and peripheral material (audits of project status, formal document inspections of plans, etc.). However, he lists, for example, code reading by a peer, code reading by a manager, and code reading by a chief programmer, as three separate methods. In a second, similar list, he gives 6 types of business and legal reviews (formal 'make or buy' reviews, project value analysis reviews, etc.); 10 pre-test defect removal methods (prototyping, data structure design review, etc.); 8 testing methods (regression testing, independent testing organization, etc.); and 5 post-release defect removal methods (user satisfaction survey, automated restructuring, etc.); giving a total of 29 methods.

QA methods can be classified in various ways, e.g.:

- they may be static (e.g. code inspections and Halstead's metrics), or dynamic (i.e. testing);
- they may be performed by the originator of the product, or by a second party, e.g. the team leader, independent test groups, outside organizations, auditors, or end users;
- they are performed at different stages in the life-cycle, e.g. a review of the requirements specifications, or checking by control clerks of production reports;
- they may be normal or extraordinary, such as stress testing or proof of correctness, or

even just extra testing or walkthroughs where low quality is suspected, e.g. because a module is very difficult (Jones, 1986b).

Jones (1986b) listed 10 common defect removal methods (personal desk checking, informal reviews, and so on), and their estimated efficiencies. Typical efficiencies ranged from only 25% (for unit testing) to just 65% (for modelling or prototyping), with an average of only 45%. The *cumulative* efficiency, if all 10 methods are used, is over 99%; but the 3-step process of unit testing, function testing and integration testing, would typically find only about 75% of the defects; and less than a 5-step series would not yield a cumulative efficiency high enough for commercially-marketed software.

Glass (1979) listed the relative values of many different software reliability tools and methods. In his opinion, the most valuable ones are modular programming, preventive maintenance, error reporting, regression testing, design reviews, source language debug, desk checking, and peer code review.

Various QA methods are described below. Two methods have received extra attention in the literature, and are claimed to have a large impact on productivity, so they are discussed separately: structured walkthroughs (section 10.7) and inspections (section 10.8).

10.6.1   STATIC METHODS

Static checking of a program refers to the process of finding defects in the program without executing it, e.g. by:

- desk checking by the programmer;
- inspection by the team leader;
- structured walkthroughs or inspections;
- compilers, static analysers and code auditors;
- proof of correctness.

Some of the static methods, such as inspection and walkthroughs, can be applied not just to code, but to specifications, documentation, etc.

Static analysers are programs which examine other programs without executing them, looking for errors, violations of coding standards, and inefficiencies; or which even measure their complexity. They automate the measurement of quality and complexity using various metrics, thereby making the metrics much more useful. Better still, compilers should calculate and print the various metrics, so that programmers have immediate feedback on the quality of their work.

Static methods point to the need for additional testing; or they might show that a program is so complex or badly written that it is virtually untestable or unmodifiable, in which case it would be advisable to reduce its complexity, or even completely rewrite it (McCormick, 1986). Some complexity may be unavoidable, but a program which is badly written is more complex than it need be.

Static methods can also point to the need for training of the programmer; static analysers are particularly valuable in a training environment, as they detect poor technique and permit corrective action, before the bad practices become entrenched.

Sommerville (1989) quoted two studies, one of which found that typically, 60% of the errors in a program can be detected using informal static verification techniques before the program is executed; while the other suggested that more formal static validation techniques using mathematical verification can result in more than 90% being detected before execution. The latter method, combining formal specification and mathematical verification, as well as statistical techniques during testing to assess reliability, reliability growth models to determine when the system has been tested adequately, and incremental development and user feedback, is known as the 'cleanroom' approach, by analogy with the physically clean rooms used to manufacture sensitive electronic devices, where any impurity can cause damage (Mills *et al.*, 1987).

10.6.2 SECOND-PARTY

Second-party testing and debugging were discussed in Chapter 8.

If QA is performed by a separate group (a second-party), then higher quality should result, because this avoids the blind-spot or 'psychological set' of the original developers; because when people know they are being observed, they are more likely to do it right the first time, rather than take short cuts, and in fact they are afraid of having their software found to be defective by someone else; and also because of the additional importance attached to quality – as evidenced by the Weinberg and Schulman (1974) experiment (Chapter 2) and also rather like the Hawthorne motivational effect (Chapter 11) (Arthur, 1983; Weinberg, 1971; Cho, 1987). If the QA group is independent, they are less likely to tolerate poor quality because of friendships with the developers, or miss mistakes because they think the same way as the developers (Vincent *et al.*, 1988); and if they report directly to higher management, they are more likely to have the power to enforce their decisions. There is, however, the disadvantage that someone other than the original programmer must know the program, which could add 20% to the testing cost (Chapter 8). There may also be antagonism between the two groups – there may, for example, be some suspicion amongst the software engineers that an independent QA group is in some way a 'police force' or even an 'espionage service' about their practices – with consequent loss of time and money, and failure to derive the benefits of having a separate group: 'QA and the line function were "at war", and both sides were losing' (Weinberg, 1971; Macro and Buxton, 1987; Methodology for productivity, *Computer Mail*, 31 Oct. 1986, pp. 55–8). Management must therefore encourage the notion of one common objective towards which all parties contribute.

The QA group may be an external organization or an internal team. An external group may encounter problems in being accepted, i.e. they are more likely to meet with resistance than an internal group (Arthur, 1983). If the group is internal, personnel can be rotated through it, as this broadens the technical horizons of software engineers, giving them a better understanding of quality and how to achieve it (Macro and Buxton, 1987). Macro and Buxton recommended that the rotation be on a fairly long-term basis, i.e. staff should spend a few years in the QA group, and this should be part of a positive career development plan. They also recommended that the members of the group be well known, respected, and liked.

According to Jones (1986b), IBM has had 'unusual' success in removing defects in supporting plans and documents by requiring that the QA department sign off on the accuracy and adequacy of the plans before a product can be announced to the external world or delivered to customers.

10.6.3   QUALITY CIRCLES

Quality circles are participative decision-making groups (Crocker *et al.*, 1986). They embody the practical application of industrial-humanist ideas first presented by Douglas McGregor, Abraham Maslow, Frederick Herzberg and David McClelland (Bain, 1982); see Chapter 11.

Quality circles are typically organized within a department to uncover, study, and eliminate problems (Crocker *et al.*, 1986). Staff meet regularly in small groups to develop suggestions for quality and productivity improvements (Arthur, 1983). A quality circle has an average of 8–10 members doing similar work (Crocker *et al.*, 1986; Bain, 1982). Meetings are usually one hour per week. The concept is that ordinary workers, given the opportunity and some basic training in

cause–effect analysis, can provide a powerful QA and productivity boost for their employers (Jones, 1991). The objective is to have quality control built in. Problems of safety and morale may also be addressed, and circles may emphasize team building, or study issues such as absenteeism and child care. Circles decrease accidents, and make the workplace more humane and pleasant: they improve the quality of working life.

By involving both management and workers, vertical communication is vastly improved, and so are labor–management relations (Arthur, 1983; Crocker *et al.*, 1986). There are fewer grievances. There is a commitment to the organization and an interest in working toward organizational goals. Circles also create a sense of teamwork, and solutions reached by consensus enjoy increased and broader-based support than those generated by an individual.

Quality circles allow employees to contribute their education, experience, creativity, and personal interests to the organization: 'they love solving problems' (Arthur, 1983; Crocker *et al.*, 1986). In turn, workers can acquire new skills and knowledge. Circles enrich jobs, which in turn motivates workers. Morale and job satisfaction are improved, and employees gain an increased sense of individual self-worth. Circles re-establish the dignity of employees and the importance of their jobs (Bain, 1982). They must be used as a people-building approach.

Notwithstanding all their benefits, quality circles have disadvantages, and there can be problems as well. They can, for example, become a burden (Crocker *et al.*, 1986). Senior management commitment is needed, because staff must be released from their duties, and resources must be redeployed for many years to come. Time is needed to conduct the required research. Training time is also required, e.g. in basic QC (quality control) techniques (Bain, 1982). Middle managers may resist them, because the circles do work which they believe rightfully belongs to them, and render their positions unnecessary. Patience is required, as it may take two or three years to achieve visible results. Objectives and roles must be clarified. Solutions must be monitored. Feedback to employees is necessary.

Bain (1982) listed eight distinct steps used in the problem-solving process employed within quality circles:

- determine the problem to be attacked and the benefits to be derived by solving it;
- if the problem is of a general nature, select a specific part of it for detailed investigation;
- gather and analyse data to sort out actual causes from possible causes;
- determine a specific course of corrective action;
- develop a plan and timetable for implementing the corrective action;
- implement the plan;
- follow up to determine the effectiveness of the solution;
- communicate to top management, via a presentation, the group's accomplishments.

One of the techniques employed by quality circles is brainstorming (Osborn, 1963), which is based on six rules (Bain, 1982):

- generate a large number of ideas;
- encourage 'free-wheeling': even unsuitable ideas can be thought-provoking;
- the ideas are not criticized until later;
- all members have equal opportunity to participate;
- record all ideas;
- let ideas 'incubate'.

The results of using quality circles are impressive.

Quality circles are used much less extensively in America than in Japan, where 77% of companies with more than 10 000 employees, and as many as one out of every eight employees, giving a total of 6 million workers, participate in some type of small group activities, and there are 600 000 quality circles compared to only 3000–4000 in the US (Crocker *et al.*, 1986; Bain, 1982). The results show it. An American automobile is twice as likely to have a problem as a Japanese one; while American electronic chips are four times as likely to have defects (Arthur, 1983). This has significantly improved the saleability of Japanese products.

The average return on investment found by Ouchi (1981) was 3:1, and it can exceed 8:1. Japan estimates that quality circles have saved over $25 billion since they were set up (Arthur, 1983).

In Japan, the technique has worked well for software (Jones, 1991). In the US, it has not been widely utilized for software, and there is not enough empirical data to judge its effectiveness for US software. Nevertheless, in its first year of using quality circles, Arthur's own project team achieved a productivity twice as high as any of them had expected, apparently through the use of prototyping and reusable code (Arthur, 1983).

10.6.4 USER INVOLVEMENT

User involvement leads to high quality by ensuring that the system meets the user's needs. Their involvement is aided by (Gildersleeve, 1974a; Lee, 1978):

- user confidence and trust in the systems analyst;
- having users on the project teams;
- prototyping;
- joint design groups (e.g. JAD);
- having the user sign off the specifications;
- and so on.

Personal contact with the users can infuse the developers with a greater concern for safety, reliability and efficiency (DeMarco, 1982). If the developers do poor-quality work, then the people who will suffer, and may even lose their lives, will be people they know, and not anonymous, faceless entities. De-

Marco quoted a case where this worked extremely well. An American astronaut, on a visit to the plant which was manufacturing the launch rocket, uttered just the words 'do good work', whereupon the workers started cheering; and then, on their own initiative, had a huge banner made with these words on it, which they displayed in the main work area.

After a system has gone into production, a user satisfaction survey should be conducted, e.g. to evaluate the user interface, and any problems unearthed should be rectified (Sommerville, 1989).

User involvement is discussed elsewhere, particularly in Chapter 8.

10.6.5 QUALITY OF DATA

QA applies not only to software systems, but also to the data processed by the systems.

Edit programs ensure that data accepted by the system is valid, i.e. of good quality – 'garbage in, garbage out' (GIGO) – and validation routines in subsequent programs, e.g. sequence checking of master files, guard against subsequent errors. These aspects were discussed in more detail under 'defensive programming' and 'fault tolerance' in Chapter 8.

QA of data may be more difficult in the case of a database, as the data is shared and can be updated by various users. It is also more difficult where the information is not used for months, as any errors in it could remain undetected for long periods (Lyon, 1976). On the other hand, data dictionaries (Chapter 6) act as a QA tool. Dictionaries are a form of documentation, and so help ensure that documentation is adequate, up to date, and not duplicated (Ross, 1978). Active dictionaries assist with the validation of input data.

Access control helps ensure that data is not corrupted, whether intentionally or unintentionally. The corruption may take place directly, by updating the data itself, or indirectly, by modifying a program which processes the data. Access control helps ensure that programs are not tampered with either. Active dictionaries may assist with controlling access to data.

Control totals such as of amount fields or even just record counts, put out by each program, are a traditional way of ensuring validity of data on files, and that all the data has been processed (Lim, 1980; Parkin, 1980). As Arthur (1983) put it, 'A human cannot be expected to catch the fact that the program processed all but one record out of 20 million'. Update programs should count the records read, added, and deleted, and compare this sum to the number of records written. Control totals are easy to build into programs and to use, and not only indicate that an error has occurred, but also help pinpoint the source, thereby saving valuable time in correcting it. For example, where there is more than one type of transaction (invoices, credit notes, etc.), it is desirable to accumulate control totals of each type, so an error can quickly be traced to a particular type.

10.6.6 CHECKLISTS

The Concise Oxford Dictionary defines a checklist as a list for reference or verification (Sykes, 1977). It may comprise a list of tasks associated with a given activity, or documents to be produced (Lee, 1978). Gilb (1988) describes a checklist as almost a list of standards, rephrased as a series of questions.

The use of checklists therefore aids high quality, e.g. by guarding against omissions in requirements analysis and program design. A programming manager once neglected to include the cost of writing user documentation in the cost estimate for a new project, and this escaped notice until after the bid had been accepted (Jones, 1986b). A checklist could have prevented this. Checklists similarly improve the effectiveness of manual QA methods. For example, a list of common errors such as subscripts out of range and rounding errors, can be used while desk checking or during walkthroughs and inspections (Arthur, 1983). Checklists can be developed for static analysers as well as for walkthroughs and inspections.

Checklists are therefore a powerful aid when thoughtfully constructed (Metzger, 1981).

Checklists are used by everyone, e.g. for grocery lists (Crocker *et al.*, 1986). They can be produced for virtually anything. Gilb (1988) gives a sample checklist for test plans. Lee (1978) gives sample checklists for user manuals, operations manuals, test data files, office accommodation, and so on.

Checklists are also a form of education: they show (i.e. teach) whoever uses them, all that is required in whatever is being checked, and what is required of the person doing the checking (Gilb, 1988).

Checklists are based on experience (Gilb, 1988), and so are added to from time to time as more experience is accumulated. In fact, the checklists themselves often stimulate new ideas (Winfield, 1986).

Gilb (1988) recommended that checklists for inspections should comprise about 25 questions, and should fit on a single page. This is presumably a restriction due to the time limit of inspections, as Parkin (1980) referred to a checklist containing over 90 questions, and Lee (1978) gave several checklists with about 60 items each.

In the simplest case, a checklist consists purely of a list of items. More formal or structured ones also contain a (meaningful) title; a column for the items to be ticked off; and space for such details as the name and department of the person performing the checking, their signature and the date, and the precise document etc. being checked (e.g. which system and program it belongs to); and the items will be grouped together, with sub-headings. More comprehensive ones will also contain (Vincent *et al.*, 1988; Gilb, 1988):

- a column for the relative importance of each item;
- instead of just a simple tick, they will show whether the item is present and correct, present but incorrect, or missing, or they may even have a value column to indicate more precisely how well the item meets the criterion;
- a row for totals; and
- space for comments.

Crocker *et al.* (1986) described an enhanced form of checklist, the checksheet, which specifies what action is to be taken, when it is to be done, by whom, the tools that will be used, and specific instructions.

There is the danger, however, that checklist questions may be too nebulous or general to be of much help, e.g. 'What has been missed?', and 'Does the code do what the design called for?' (Parkin, 1980; Myers, 1979).

10.6.7   DESK CHECKING

Desk checking (carried out at one's desk) is a traditional checkout method – 'one of the earliest forms of software verification' (Glass, 1979). It could be viewed as a one-person inspection or walkthrough (Myers, 1979).

Glass identified three types of desk checking:

- reviewing a program listing;
- doing arithmetic calculations;
- playing computer (manually simulating program execution).

Attention should be concentrated on suspect or problem areas, areas containing not only errors but also inefficiencies. Doing the arithmetic calculations manually is a 'drudgery', but there is no effective substitute. (Glass, 1979) stated that desk checking was sometimes avoided because it lacks stimulation and excitement, but it is cost-effective if used in moderation, and it was still a 'vital' element in software verification. Source language debug and interactive debug are computer-assisted desk checking – the computer itself 'plays computer', but permits the programmer to follow the program flow.

Myers (1979) believes that desk checking is not very effective because it is done by the person who produced the work, and people suffer from blind spots. To avoid this problem, two programmers could swop their work. This is an improvement, but it fails to take advantage of the competitive factor in inspections and walkthroughs when a group of people search for errors together: 'people like to show off by finding errors'. There is therefore a synergistic effect. Another reason desk checking is ineffective is that it is undisciplined, but this can be remedied by working against a checklist, or 'walking' test data through the program ('playing computer').

Van Tassel (1978) recommends that a source code listing be desk checked straight after it has been typed, while it is still fresh in the mind. The justification for desk checking the listing is that a compiler cannot catch all typing errors, only those that cause syntax errors. Even a quick check can eliminate some errors, and thereby reduce compiling and debugging time – 'a few minutes of desk checking can save endless hours of debugging'. Furthermore, the source code listing should not merely be read, but should also be checked against the keypunch sheets and against the flowchart. Desk checking can also be used during debugging. When an error has been isolated to a small area, then that section of the program listing should be read. Van Tassel also recommends that a colleague review everything as well. This should avoid the blind spots Myers (1979) is concerned about, and takes desk checking closer to the formal inspections and walkthroughs.

Jones (1986b) estimated that personal checking of design or documents is typically only 35% efficient in removing defects, and desk checking of code only 40%.

One experiment, using 39 subjects testing three programs, found black-box testing and

Table 10.3 Comparison of desk checking and inspection of code

	Desk checking	Inspections
Line of code (LOC)	3240	11 108
Total hours	14	304
LOC per hour	231	37
Major defects found	0	76
Minor defects found	11	152
Total defects found	11	228
Total defects per thousand LOC	3.4	20.5
Total defects per hour	0.8	0.75

white-box testing to be more effective than individual code reading, but on average the subjects found only about half the errors (Hetzel, 1976).

The comparison between desk checking and inspections in Table 10.3 was obtained from portions of Project Omega (Gilb, 1988). (Comment lines are not included in the lines of code. Rework time has also been excluded. The hours may be man-hours. It is not clear if preparation time and follow-up time are included in the Inspection time.)

Desk checking therefore found far fewer errors, but consumed correspondingly less time.

The figures in Table 10.3 could be used to 'prove', on the one hand, that desk checking does not find major defects, and that it does not find many defects (because it only found (3.4/20.5 =) one-sixth as many defects per thousand LOC as the inspections) (Gilb, 1988). On the other hand, they could be used to 'prove' that desk checking has a higher efficiency than inspections (because defects were detected at a higher rate – 0.8 per hour, compared to only 0.75). However, they could also be interpreted as showing that the more effort spent looking for defects, no matter what method is used, the more defects are found – in colloquial terms, you get what you pay for. An interesting experiment would be to spend much more time on desk checking, to see if the defect detection rate remained high; or if it decreased, and if so, by how much. Because of 'psychological set', and the absence of the competitive factor, probably the efficiency would decrease.

Conclusion

Desk checking is a quick and easy way to find errors. It does not find many errors, but that is probably because relatively little time is spent on it. If more time were spent, then it would prove more effective, but would probably become less cost-effective. However, it does not suffer from the emotional problems to which the alternative method of walk-throughs is subject.

10.6.8 PROOF OF CORRECTNESS

Proof of correctness is the process of using mathematical techniques on a computer program to demonstrate that the program or its design corresponds with its formal specification (Sommerville, 1989; Glass, 1979).

Unlike testing, which can only prove the *presence* of errors, proof of correctness can prove the *absence* of errors (Macro and Buxton, 1987). It makes you aware of assumptions you are making, and forces you to think what the program is all about, and so gives confidence in its correctness (Glass, 1979). Furthermore, because it looks at the program from a different viewpoint, it finds types of error that are missed by testing.

However, the name of the technique is misleading, as you cannot be sure that there is not an error in the proof, and in fact there have been many errors and omissions in published 'proofs' (Gerhart and Yelowitz, 1976; Goodenough and Gerhart, 1975). For example, Schach (1988) quoted a case in which four experts (including Goodenough and Gerhart), over a period of six years, successively discovered a total of seven faults in a published proof (Naur, 1969). Deutsch (1979) quoted a case where a pub-

lished and accepted proof survived for twelve years before it was discovered to be faulty. The proof should therefore be shown to someone else to check if it is correct, though even this is not infallible. Furthermore, this technique does not detect errors or omissions in the specifications – 'it is possible to create a correct program that solves the wrong problem'; 'we can still tell the computer to do things that are stupid' (Martin and McClure, 1985) – nor can it handle errors or peculiarities in the compiler, truncation and rounding errors, or indexes derived from input data, or – in the case of real-time programs – any complex timing dependencies with other elements in the processing environment (Boehm, 1976; Dunn and Ullman, 1982; Deutsch, 1979; Cho, 1987).

In practice, therefore, proof of correctness does *not* prove the absence of errors (Boehm, 1976), and Sommerville (1989) prefers the term 'mathematical program verification'. Furthermore, Jones (1986b) claimed that no hard evidence had yet been published to demonstrate that the operational reliability of programs that used correctness proofs is any better than that of those which did not. Nevertheless, Sommerville (1989) quoted one study which suggested that using mathematical verification can result in more than 90% of the errors in a program being detected before execution, whereas typically only 80% are detected before production using conventional methods (Chapter 8). Figures given by Boehm (1981) also indicate that this technique is highly accurate: perhaps only 1% of the time does it lead to the conclusion that there are no faults, when a fault still exists; and only 2% of the time does it recommend further action and expense (because the situation is too complex to analyse, so the chance of there being an error is high enough), when in fact no fault exists. Miller (1980) confirms this high accuracy – error removal was high, but not 100%. Similarly, according to Wirth (1987), proof of correctness reduces the number of bugs by a factor of ten. The very low number of errors discovered while testing the THE multi-programming system (only 2 per 1000 LOC, compared to the average of around 40 in Table 8.42), has been credited to top-down design and proof of correctness (Dijkstra, 1968b; Yourdon, 1975; Martin and McClure, 1985). Mills *et al.* (1987) reported that, in one case when the 'cleanroom' approach (which includes mathematical verification) was used, only 53 errors were discovered during testing of a 20 000 line language processor. This is only 3 errors per 1000 lines of code, and is therefore less than one-tenth the usual rate of about 40.

Proof of correctness reduces, but does not eliminate, the need for testing (Martin and McClure, 1985; Dunn and Ullman, 1982). For example, four of the seven faults in the Schach (1988) case quoted above could have been detected by testing. As Dunn and Ullman explained, unit testing does not attempt to validate module specifications, but recognition of specification errors is a not infrequent by-product. Sommerville (1989) expanded on this. Part of testing is to check that a program meets its specifications, but testing also reveals whether or not these specifications are correct and appropriate for the user's needs, and if 'non-functional con-straints' – presumably aspects such as memory size and execution speed, or possibly maintain-ability or ease of use (Charette, 1986) – are satisfied by the system. However, there is a difference of opinion over the need for other QA methods. According to Martin and McClure (1985), tools such as static analysers and test coverage analysers are probably not needed, and methods such as structured walkthroughs and inspections can be elimi-nated. However, the proofs could be inspected to eliminate errors in them; Radice and Phillips (1988) argue that the design or code and the corresponding proofs can be read together during the inspection of the design or code to provide a more effective inspection.

There is also a serious disadvantage of this technique: it requires an 'enormous' amount of intellectual effort (Myers, 1979). The proof often consumes several times as much work as the effort required to write the program (Glass, 1979). Goldberg (1973) estimated that one man-month of effort is required to prove 100 LOC. The proof may be several times longer than the program – one 433 statement program required 46 pages of proof (Martin and McClure, 1985). The proof of one 12-statement program required no fewer than 18 lemmas (Hoare, 1971) – a lemma is an assumed or demonstrated proposition used in argument or proof (Sykes, 1977). The proof may therefore contain as many errors as the program being verified (Sommerville, 1989)! The largest program which has been proved correct is variously given as 433 or 2000 LOC (Boehm, 1976; Ragland, 1973; Martin and McClure, 1985; Boehm, 1973). Worse, the work requires expert effort – a 'high level of mathematical sophistication far beyond that of ordinary analysts and programmers' (Goldberg, 1973; Martin and McClure, 1985; Cho, 1987). In addition, a large amount of training and practice are required to use the technique well (Glass, 1979).

The large amount of effort highlights another disadvantage of the technique: it cannot be used in highly volatile situations – a new version of the program must be produced before the original version has been proved correct, so much of the effort in proving the original version correct is wasted (Boehm, 1981).

Structured programming, by simplifying programs, facilitates proof of correctness (Anderson, 1979; Bell *et al.*, 1987); one of Dijkstra's objectives in the development of structured programming was that mechanical proofs might be much easier for a program expressed in some structured form (Yourdon, 1975).

As a result of the large amount of effort required, and the high level of expertise, the cost of this method is very high. According to Glass (1979), it adds 100–500% to the development cost. Miller (1980) found that the cost was $50–500 per delivered source instruction. By comparison, code inspection rates (an average of 40 lines of code per man-hour (Table 10.13)), structured walkthrough rates (about three times as high (Table 10.5)), and testing rates (16 lines of code per man-hour (Chapter 8)), at a salary including overheads of say $6000 per month (Chapter 13); or a rate of about $40 per line of code for development (Table 13.3), of which typically 26% is testing and debugging (Table 8.28); work out at nearer $5 per line of code for the alternative methods.

For these reasons, proof of correctness is not yet of much practical value, and can only be justified where the consequences of an error are serious, such as heavy financial losses, loss of life, or if national security is compromised (Boehm, 1981). (In such extreme cases, it might be difficult to justify *not* using it.) Currently, at least, the technique is of more use in proving that an *algorithm* is correct, rather than an ordinary commercial program (Glass, 1979; Myers, 1979). Glass (1979) estimated that practical use was at least 10 years away. Nevertheless, HOS (higher order software) – (Chapter 8) – incorporates computerized verification. There are also some automated systems which assist verification (Good *et al.*, 1975). However, Anderson (1979) described such tools as 'first attempts' at building mechanical verification systems, and ten years later, Sommerville (1989) stated that completely automated program verifiers had not been developed. Nevertheless, these tools do reduce the amount of effort and the cost of the technique. However, current work is based not on FORTRAN or COBOL, but on languages such as PASCAL, which are more suitable but are not as widely used (Dunn and Ullman, 1982). According to Sommerville (1989), there 'is no reasonable way' to prove a FORTRAN or machine code program correct, because they are too low level.

I presented evidence above that proof of correctness is very expensive. However, this is disputed by Sommerville (1989), who stated that the 'cleanroom' approach, which includes mathematical program verification, is reportedly no more expensive than conventional development and testing. It is difficult to reconcile this with the other evidence. As in the case of other individual projects, especially important or trail-blazing ones such as the NYT (Chapter 3), the exceptionally good results for the 'cleanroom' could be due to the high ability and motivation of the staff on those particular projects. Alternatively, it could be because the 'cleanroom' uses less rigorous, informal correctness arguments. It might be thought that these would be less effective in finding errors, but informal arguments are much shorter than formal proofs (though still lengthy), and so are less likely to themselves contain errors – though Anderson (1979) stated that they are subject to many errors. They therefore require less effort, and are more cost-effective.

10.7 STRUCTURED WALKTHROUGHS

Structured walkthroughs, which are also known as 'team debugging', 'peer code reviews', etc. (Yourdon, 1975; Glass, 1979), are one method of QA which has received much attention. Enthusiastic claims have been made for the effectiveness of the technique, and it is particularly valuable in that it can be used throughout the software life-cycle – as is indicated by the alternative names. For example, Jones (1986b) claimed that the customer review is one of the most widespread and apparently effective methods used for evaluating the supporting plans of commercial software projects. Walkthroughs can in fact be held of virtually anything, e.g.:

- the work assignments and schedules;
- specifications;
- data structure designs;
- program designs;

- documentation, including User manuals;
- code;
- test plans, data, and results;
- maintenance changes.

They can therefore be used in the early stages of software development, such as design and planning, i.e. long before testing can begin; many, perhaps even most, software bugs already exist at these early stages (Chapter 8).

According to Myers (1979), walkthroughs are of equal or even more value in checking modifications to programs, as modifying an existing program is a more error-prone process than writing a new program.

Walkthroughs are similar to Japanese quality circles (Arthur, 1983). They are also similar to inspections (section 10.8), and some people use the terms interchangeably (Metzger, 1981; Yourdon, 1979b; Boehm, 1981) – it is thus not always clear whether a particular authority is referring to walkthroughs or inspections. For example, the widely-published productivity rates obtained by Walston and Felix (1977) include a productivity range for inspections but not one for walkthroughs, yet according to Gilb (1988), about half their projects used inspections, and about half used walkthroughs. The Macro and Buxton (1987) description of walkthroughs stresses formality and management involvement, which are more typically aspects of inspections rather than walkthroughs. Myers (1979) has separate discussions of code inspections and walkthroughs, but also has an 'inspections and walkthroughs' section in which the two are treated together. Fagan (1976, 1977) invented inspections, but his method is referred to – admittedly indirectly – by Pomberger (1984) as walkthroughs. This confusion is not surprising, as even with inspections, one *walks through* the program, and because walkthroughs are a type of inspection – the most simple and least formal type (Vincent *et al.*, 1988). It can therefore be argued that some of the information included here under walk-throughs should actually be under inspections, and vice versa. However, because of the similarity between the two techniques, much of what is true of inspections is also true of walkthroughs, and vice versa.

10.7.1 DESCRIPTION

Different authorities have different opinions over how walkthroughs should be run, and practices vary between different organizations. The description below is quite typical, and some of these variations are highlighted.

Definition

A variety of definitions can be given, e.g. structured walkthroughs are (Yourdon *et al.*, 1979a, Yourdon, 1979b; Van Tassel, 1978; Fairley, 1985):

- a formalization of free discussion;
- a peer group review of any product;
- a review session in which the originator of a product explains it to his colleagues, including the intended function of the product and the reason for the method chosen;
- an in-depth technical review of some aspect of a software system.

Walkthroughs are therefore a static method of QA, i.e. they do not involve execution of a program. They are a variation on the traditional QA methods of desk checking, in which the originator of a product reviews his own work by himself, and inspection by the team leader.

Objective

Walkthroughs are a QA method, so their objective is to ensure high quality, i.e. to find (Yourdon, 1975; Yourdon *et al.*, 1979a; Bell *et al.*, 1987; Fairley, 1985; van Wyk and Kamfer, 1976):

- bugs, misinterpretations, omissions, inconsistencies, ambiguities, and anything that is unclear;
- anything that is complex or difficult to modify;

- deviations from standards (for simplicity, clarity, modularity, structure, documentation, external interfaces, user dialogues, exception conditions and exception handling);
- inefficiencies.

The general opinion is that the objective is to *find* problems not correct them (Tebbs, 1980b; Glass, 1979), because corrections are assumed to be within the province and capabilities of the developer (Metzger, 1981), and because solving a problem is too difficult and time-consuming in a group situation (Bell *et al.*, 1987), and in fact attempts at group design are usually disastrous (Yourdon, 1975; van Wyk and Kamfer, 1976). If necessary, the producer can always seek advice after the meeting from one of the participants. However, Freeman (1975) and Dunn and Ullman (1982) give an opposing viewpoint, and if ideas are flowing, it does seem short-sighted to suppress them. This is especially true if the group is not content to simply identify problems, but also *wants* to solve them. The proposed solutions can be evaluated later, as happens in the case of brainstorming sessions (Gildersleeve, 1978). In particular, solutions could be discussed during a follow-up, 'third hour' meeting held afterwards, as suggested by Gilb (1988) for inspections.

Department structure

Walkthroughs can be used with any of the various alternative structures (Chapter 3) of the DP Department, but fit more naturally into the matrix structure (Type 6) because of its more democratic nature. They are less likely to be used in a rigid, bureaucratic organization. There is a difference of opinion over walkthroughs in relation to CPTs, with some authorities regarding the two concepts as diametrically opposed, and others viewing them as natural partners (Weinberg, 1971; Yourdon, 1975). Similarly, Yourdon (1979b) looks upon family teams as being almost synonymous with ego-less programming, but a family team as described by Thorpe (1976) seems more likely to be patriarchal.

Structured walkthroughs are one aspect of ego-less programming and 'democratic teams' (Yourdon, 1979b; Weinberg, 1971), and are the aspect most likely to be implemented. Many organizations are reluctant to implement the full concept, or failed in their attempts to do so, but will nevertheless implement walkthroughs.

Participants

Different authorities give different recommendations for the optimum number of participants in a walkthrough (Table 10.4). Where the recommendation referred to a specific type of walkthrough – e.g. of project plans, design, or code – this is indicated. Taking the average of these figures, about four people should participate in a walkthrough, with fewer being required at informal reviews than at formal ones. The more people there are, the greater the possibility of timewasting due to differences of opinion (Bell *et al.*, 1987), but the more errors will be uncovered. Reducing the number of participants is discussed later (section 10.7.4).

There are differences of opinion over who should attend walkthroughs, and it also depends on what type of product, e.g. specifications or code, is being walked through. There is general agreement that the author of the product, a maintenance expert, and a member of the QA group should attend (Yourdon, 1979b; Macro and Buxton, 1987). There are both advantages and disadvantages if a manager attends a walkthrough: these are discussed later. Users (or customers) could attend specifications walkthroughs, testing walkthroughs, and possibly design walkthroughs, but not code walkthroughs (Yourdon, 1979b). If users attend walkthroughs, designers may benefit from the increased involvement, but the users may use the walkthroughs to ask for major

Table 10.4 Recommended number of participants in a walkthrough

Source	No. of participants
Patrick (1980a): of project plan	2 (i.e. just one peer present)
Yourdon (1979b): informal reviews	2–3 (early stages of product)
Glass (1979): of code	3–4 (in addition to programmer?)
Yourdon (1979b): formal reviews	3–4 (maximum of 5–6)
Myers (1979): of code	3–5
Bell *et al.* (1987)	3–6
Van Tassell (1978): of design?	4–6
Fairley (1985)	4–6
Metzger (1981)	4–6
Vincent *et al.* (1988): of code, informal	4–8
Vincent *et al.* (1988): of code, formal	up to 10

changes (Fairley, 1985). Other suggested participants include a technical secretary, a highly-experienced programmer, a programming-language expert, a new programmer (to give a fresh, unbiased outlook), someone from a different project, and someone from the same programming team (e.g. the programmer writing the control program, or one writing code which interfaces directly with the code being walked through) (Bell *et al.*, 1987; Myers, 1979; Metzger, 1981).

Frequency of walkthroughs

A walkthrough is normally held of an entire product, or distinct portion thereof, when it is completed, i.e. when something visible is available. For example, as soon as a program or program module has been coded, the code is walked through. However, if the product, or distinct portion thereof, is large, e.g. if it would take six months to do a full functional specification, then it is advisable to have intermediate walkthroughs of the incomplete work. In such cases, Macro and Buxton (1987) recommended that one walkthrough be held per fortnight or per month.

Walkthroughs which discover no errors are too early, and ones which discover a multitude of errors are too late (Bell *et al.*, 1987). Bell was, however, apparently not referring to the amount of material which is walked through. Although the later the walk-through, the more material there is, and the more errors will be discovered, he was apparently referring instead to the fact that a programmer may make the same mistake in other parts of the program or JCL, or that one error can lead to others, rather like one coding error, such as omitting to declare a variable, can cause a compiler to list a multitude of spurious diagnostics (Van Tassel, 1978). Nevertheless, if there is too much material, or if it is riddled with errors, then the walkthrough will be a long and tortuous session, and afterwards the producer will have to spend a great deal of time redoing much of his work.

Time required

Metzger (1981) estimated that, for a one-year project, 3–5 days should be spent on the design review. This amounts to just a few per cent of the total development effort.

Bell *et al.* (1987) stated that the aim should be for a walkthrough to take half an hour, and that it should not be allowed to go on after an hour. Metzger (1981) gave the wider range of from 15 minutes to two hours, and added that, if more time is needed, a second session can be scheduled after an appropriate break the same day, so that continuity is not lost. Myers (1979) stated that a walkthrough should be an uninterrupted meeting of 1–2 hours duration. By contrast, Glass (1979)

Table 10.5 Code walkthrough rates

Source	Source statements/ hour
Bell *et al.* (1987)	50–200
Glass (1979)	100
Yourdon (1979b)	100
Parikh (1984)	at least 250

stated that the concentration of participants wanes after an hour. Yourdon (1979b) expanded on this issue. Walkthroughs are mentally fatiguing, and the reviewers cannot expect to maintain their concentration for more than an hour, or two hours 'at the *very* most'. His advice is therefore to try to keep walkthroughs to 30 minutes if possible, and he added that 'there's nothing wrong with a 15-minute walkthrough'.

Different authorities give different rates at which code walkthroughs can proceed (Table 10.5). Bell's rate was derived from his statements that 50–100 LOC are examined during a walkthrough, and that a walkthrough should last between half an hour and an hour. The Parikh rate is derived from his example in which 500 lines were examined in a review, and the generally accepted maximum duration of two hours for a walkthrough. If he permits longer walkthroughs, or was not differentiating between say one walkthrough of four hours and two walkthroughs of two hours each, then the rate attributed to him may be far too high.

The average of these figures is about 150 source statements per hour, but the Parikh rate seems too high to permit a thorough search for errors, and in any case the derivation of it can be challenged, so a rate of about 100 may be more realistic.

Not all walkthroughs are of source code. The rates suggested by Bell *et al.* (1987) for other material are as follows: 1–3 pages of pseudocode should be reviewed at one meeting, or 5–10 pages of written specifications.

It takes about one hour to prepare for a

one-hour walkthrough (Yourdon, 1979b; Bell *et al.*, 1987; Tebbs, 1980b); this time is spent mainly in studying the material individually, when the problems are discovered, rather than during the walkthrough itself. For the first walkthrough of the product, there will probably also be an overview stage, when the producer presents a brief general description of the material to be reviewed, prior to the step-by-step walkthrough (Yourdon, 1979b; Enos and Van Tilburg, 1979). There are also post-walkthrough activities, but they normally take less time than this:

- the co-ordinator must report the results;
- selected participants may also put in writing their opinions of the project's status, and list the outstanding problems and any suggestions for dealing with them;
- all participants must check that the record/ action list of the walkthrough is correct;
- the producer must inform the reviewers of corrective action taken; and
- the co-ordinator must follow up to ensure that any rework is done and is presented again if necessary

(Metzger, 1981; Bell *et al.*, 1987; Fairley, 1985). A one-hour walkthrough may therefore consume two or three hours of each participant's time, not counting the time taken to correct the faults uncovered.

10.7.2 BENEFITS

Many benefits are claimed for structured walkthroughs, some of which are more tangible than others (Yourdon, 1979b): quality; error detection; readability; testing, debugging and maintenance; staff turnover insurance; training; morale; loyalty and co-operation; better project management; standards; and productivity.

Quality

The Holton (1977) survey of 40 organizations found that walkthroughs produce better quality programs, and Yourdon (1979b) claims that they are one of the most effective ways known, so they can significantly reduce the sometimes heavy losses caused by poor quality, e.g. losses resulting from bugs in production programs. According to Macro and Buxton (1987), there have been many examples of CPTs, the quality of whose work has been very largely attributed, by them, to the saving graces of design review and code reading. According to Metzger (1981), it is very common for a programmer or writer to throw together a 'quick-and-dirty first hack' at a program or document, intending to 'clean it up' later, but often later never comes. Walkthroughs can go a long way toward eliminating such sloppy and dangerous habits, because developers will not knowingly submit sloppy work for such close scrutiny.

Error detection

This is the main objective of walkthroughs (Glass, 1979; Parikh, 1984), and impressive results have been claimed:

- Yourdon (1979b) claims a reduction in the number of errors in production programs of 10 times – and 100 times is 'not uncommon' in systems developed with diligent walkthroughs – and Yourdon (1975) quotes an Australian group which programmed for three months without a single bug;
- walkthroughs find the errors early (Ashley, 1980; Myers, 1979); by exposing a piece of code to 5 or 6 different people, almost all the bugs are eliminated before the program is even run (Bell *et al.*, 1987; Yourdon, 1975) – and the earlier an error is found, the cheaper it is to fix (Chapter 8);
- they find many errors at once (Yourdon *et al.*, 1979a; Myers, 1979), thereby avoiding the time-consuming stop-start one-at-a-time method so often employed by programmers (Chapter 6);

- they are more effective than testing at finding certain types of error (Myers, 1978);
- testing exposes only the symptoms of an error – it may still take a long time to find the cause – whereas walkthroughs expose the actual error (Myers, 1979).

Readability

Fundamental to the concept of walkthroughs is that programs etc. are read by people other than the original producer. Knowing this provides an incentive to produce more readable work; but if any obscure code etc. is written in spite of this incentive, it is quickly picked up (Weinberg 1971; Glass, 1979).

Testing, debugging and maintenance

The improved quality reduces the time needed for these later functions, e.g. (Holton, 1977; Bell *et al.*, 1987; van Wyk, 1978):

- early detection of errors means that fewer errors get through to the later functions;
- improved readability of source code and documentation means that debugging and maintenance changes can be accomplished more quickly;
- testing may also be more effective because of the collective construction of test data.

Staff turnover insurance

Sometimes a member of a project team leaves the team before his work is complete. If his partially-completed work is disorganized and undocumented, it will be very time-consuming for his successor to complete the work. Walkthroughs, by virtue of the high quality they ensure, because of the improved and additional documentation (particularly the *reasons* for decisions), and because staff are familiar with each other's work, minimize such time losses (Yourdon, 1979b; Enos and Van Tilburg, 1979).

Training

Walkthroughs are an effective means of achieving an exchange of knowledge (Bell *et al.*, 1987; Johnson, 1980b), the importance – and necessity – of which was stressed in Chapter 9: many DP personnel are ignorant of developments outside their own immediate world; they read very few books, etc. on programming; never attend a technical meeting; and in many organizations, discussion or sharing of ideas is frowned upon.

Walkthroughs enable juniors to learn from experienced staff, and they also expose the experienced staff to new ideas from the juniors (Yourdon, 1979b); they train people who are new to the project or the organization; and they expose any eccentric or even invalid methods that new people in particular – or disgruntled staff – might have (Metzger, 1981). For example, Weinberg (1971) related how one programmer, unhappy at not having been assigned the task of writing the input–output routines for a system, incorporated his own input–output routines in the section he wrote, which caused a mysterious malfunction four years later after the system was ported to another computer, resulting in a serious delay while the cause was being investigated. This would have been picked up by a walkthrough. With walkthroughs, the staff also get much more rapid feedback on the quality of their work (Yourdon, 1979b).

The general level of expertise in the department can therefore be raised.

Morale

Some authorities have found that walkthroughs improve morale – they make day to day work more fun (Holton, 1977; Yourdon, 1979b). Bell *et al.* (1987) claimed the following morale-related benefits:

- walkthroughs provide personal satisfaction from producing better products more quickly;

- programmers find out what other projects are going on in the organization, and so feel more involved in the total work of the department, rather than being left out in the cold;
- continually learning new techniques by looking at colleagues' work can be interesting;
- it can be really exciting to examine someone else's program and find out how they think or discover a new technique;
- it can be gratifying to find errors in a colleague's program, thus saving him hours of frustration;
- conversely, he can save us hours of time;
- it gives us the opportunity to show off our work of art to our colleagues – they will appreciate its beauty much more than the compiler does;
- walkthroughs extend the opportunities for meeting people, talking, and making friends: this is the social aspect of work, and is part of the satisfaction of going to work.

Where morale is improved, employees become more loyal to the organization, and turnover is reduced (Shneiderman, 1980) (Chapter 9).

Loyalty and co-operation

This point overlaps with the previous one: programmers feel more involved in the total work of the department; there is increased social interaction; morale is improved; and therefore employees become more loyal. Walkthroughs also encourage co-operation rather than competition (Shneiderman, 1980). They get everyone together, and give people a sense of belonging (Metzger, 1981).

Better project management

Walkthroughs assist proactive management, and they can probably help bring the actual time taken much more into line with estimates, so deadlines can be met more easily (Macro and Buxton, 1987; Bell *et al.*, 1987).

- The effort estimates and the schedules should have been walked through, and therefore should be more accurate.
- Walkthroughs make progress, or the lack thereof, visible and comprehensible to management.
- Traditionally, major setbacks arise during the testing stage, especially the integrated system testing, i.e. very late in the software life-cycle. By contrast, when walkthroughs are used, errors are discovered early, when correction effort is low, and there is more time to take corrective action, so catastrophes are rare.
- Specifications, design, etc., are also made public in walkthroughs, so there is less chance of errors in them going unnoticed.

There is therefore better project control, and problems can be anticipated and circumvented.

Standards

Walkthroughs serve as the vehicle for enforcing standards (Arthur, 1983). Adherence to standards, as previously indicated, ensures readability, a high level of quality, and uniformity, which in turn facilitate communication between the group's members, and prevent misunderstandings and errors, and the consequent loss of time. Standards therefore also make it easier to hold a walkthrough, and they help reduce the bickering that can occur during a walkthrough over what quality is. In fact, the opposite of a vicious circle is created: walkthroughs enforce standards, which in turn make walkthroughs easier.

Productivity

Interestingly, productivity is not generally mentioned as a benefit of walkthroughs. Any productivity claims are usually indirect, e.g. walkthroughs contribute to increased team and project productivity as a consequence of error detection (Parikh, 1984). Walkthroughs

are one component of MPPs (Chapter 8). Any productivity benefit from walkthroughs will therefore be less – and possibly much less – than that from all MPPs combined, i.e. less than 2:1 for development, and 5:1 for maintenance (Tables 8.71 and 8.72). The impact on productivity is discussed further later.

Why are walkthroughs effective?

Little research has been done on this question (Myers, 1979), but a number of possibilities may be suggested (Yourdon *et al.*, 1979a; Yourdon, 1979b; Glass, 1979; Myers, 1979; Bell *et al.*, 1987; van Wyk and Kamfer, 1976).

1. 'Two heads are better than one.'
2. People suffer from mental blocks and myopia, and so are poor at finding their own errors: 'what we just cannot see is perfectly obvious to someone else.'
3. Knowing that work will be examined by others, more trouble is taken over it.
4. Describing work to others concentrates the mind.
5. The sessions foster a spirit of competition: 'people like to show off by finding errors'. Walkthroughs therefore increase motivation.
6. Any subsequent problems reflect on all the participants, rather than on just the individual producer, so they are more likely to be careful.

Critical examination of the benefits claimed

A number of benefits claimed for walkthroughs were quoted above – do they stand up to close examination?

Walkthroughs increase social interaction, whereas software staff have low social needs (Couger and Zawacki, 1980). The frequency and duration of walkthroughs should therefore be limited so as not to exceed the staff's tolerance levels.

The claimed improvement in morale is surprising in view of the many psychological problems (section 10.7.4). It seems probable, therefore, that walkthroughs only raise morale in some cases, e.g. with a group of uniformly high ability, and then only if all the rules and recommendations are followed.

Where staff are under considerable pressure of work, as is frequently the case, they may be unenthusiastic about finding out what other projects are going on in the organization, or learning new techniques, or finding errors in a colleague's program.

Although walkthroughs can result in better project management, it can be counterproductive for managers to attend walkthroughs, or even see the results.

If the whole group is responsible for missed problems, then the individual participants may simply leave the work of uncovering problems to their colleagues, and then blame their colleagues afterwards for any that are missed, rather than accepting personal responsibility. (Buchholz and Roth (1987) give several guidelines for encouraging shared responsibility, e.g. reward it when it takes place, and encourage employees to help each other.)

In the preface to his book on walkthroughs, Yourdon (1979b) acknowledged that a book extolling the virtues of walkthroughs should have been written with the aid of walkthroughs, yet he admits that his book was not. If the advocates of walkthroughs do not practice what they preach, are walkthroughs as good as they claim? (On the other hand, he also admitted that the first edition of his book contained 'errors and weaknesses', and it had benefitted from subsequent suggestions and criticisms.)

Dramatic error reduction rates are claimed for walkthroughs; one should be skeptical of the claims for several reasons.

1. I have achieved even more impressive figures – four years programming in one organization, during which time not a single bug was discovered during production in a program I had written – and without the benefit of walkthroughs, simply by thorough desk checking of flowcharts, and comprehensive testing. (Though the programs could admittedly be mostly rated as below average to average in size and complexity.)

   McClure (1978) claims a reduction in errors of 15 times from structured programming alone, so most, if not all, of the Yourdon (1979b) improvement might be due to structured programming, and not to walkthroughs.

2. Producers are effectively encouraged to submit semi-ready products for walkthroughs, because the additional errors motivate the reviewers (Yourdon, 1979b). (However, they will not necessarily succumb to such pressure; developers will not knowingly submit sloppy work for close scrutiny (Metzger, 1981).) It is therefore not surprising if large numbers of errors are found. This policy does have other advantages:
   - less embarrassment to the producer because he has a good excuse for there being so many errors;
   - less ego involvement because less effort has been expended;
   - less work has been done, so there is less to be undone;

   but it also has disadvantages:
   - it may encourage sloppiness;
   - the walkthroughs will take longer;
   - more errors present probably means more errors escape detection;

   so this policy may not be cost-effective.

3. The proponents of walkthroughs use 'worst cases' to back up their arguments. Weinberg (1971) quotes a case in which 20 errors were discovered in only 13 statements. Yourdon (1979b) describes at length one walkthrough in which a large number of errors was discovered, then admits it was highly atypical. He claims as typical, an error rate in production programs of 30–50 bugs per thousand LOC, which is about five times higher than that given by most other author-

ities (Table 8.41): this could account for much of the improvement he claims.

Yourdon claims that programmers *generally* spend days beating their heads against a wall looking for their own bugs, but this is only true of the more difficult or obscure bugs, which are in the minority, and they should in any case ask for help, and ask for it sooner. The milder claim by Bell *et al.* (1987) that most programmers have had the experience of spending hours or even days puzzling over the incomprehensible behavior of a program, is more realistic.

Yourdon's (1975) claim that one week's work on the part of a programmer can be reviewed in only one or two hours, is misleading:

- it omits preparation time for the review;
- the first figure (the one week) is man-hours, whereas the second figure (the one or two hours) is elapse time, and must be multiplied by the number of participants to convert it to the same unit;
- the example given later in Table 10.6 indicates that it might take as much as 16 man-hours, i.e. half a man-week, to prepare for and review one man-week's work.

(The claim by Bell *et al.* (1987) that one or two man-week's work can be reviewed in approximately one man-day, is a truer reflection of the situation. Figures given later for the similar technique of inspection indicate that either over 30 man-hours are required per inspection (Gilb, 1988); or one man-day is required to inspect 100 LOC (Fagan, 1986; Sommerville, 1989). (At 15 fully debugged statements per day, which is a fairly typical rate, 100 LOC would take a little over one man-week's work to develop.))

4. The evidence is not consistent. Experience with walkthroughs and inspections has found them to be effective in finding 30–70% of the logic design and coding errors in typical programs, i.e. sometimes they have only detected 30% of the errors (Myers, 1979). According to Jones (1986b), QA reviews of requirements and design, even if properly staffed, seem to be only 'moderately' successful: informal group design reviews, for example, are typically only 40% effective in removing defects.

5. Most figures quoted for walkthroughs refer only to their effectiveness, and not to the *cost* of achieving it, which may be considerable and so nullify the advantages, except where the consequences of errors are particularly serious. The cost-effectiveness of walkthroughs is examined in section 10.7.4.

   (On the other hand, the figures quoted for walkthroughs also do not refer to the *savings* resulting from the improved effectiveness.)

6. The advantages of walkthroughs are less in an on-line environment (Yourdon, 1979b) – finding only one error at a time is not such a serious handicap if each error can be corrected immediately (though it is still wasteful of machine time).

10.7.3 EXTENT OF USE

Early use

Walkthroughs are not a new idea (Yourdon, 1975, 1979b). Informal design reviews have been used sporadically since the beginning of the computing era, and formal ones since about 1970 (Glass, 1979). Their use was originally largely confined to the government and military, but they have been used increasingly by commercial installations. Code inspections, however, were seldom used in the past.

Subsequent use

The situation has not changed much.

Holton (1977) found that 35% of the 40 organizations he surveyed were using walkthroughs for system planning and general design, and only 5 or 8% for detailed design, coding or documentation.

Only 17% of the operational systems in the Lientz *et al.* (1978) survey of 69 organizations were developed using walkthroughs, but he does not specify what they were used for.

Of over 600 organizations in the GUIDE (1979) survey, 48% were using walkthroughs; 45% were considering using them; and only 8% had rejected them.

Only 10% of the 20 organizations in the van der Poel (1982) survey were using walkthroughs, though a further 15% were using the similar technique of code inspections.

Future use

Authorities are generally pessimistic. They do not foresee a significant spread in the use of walkthroughs (Bleazard, 1976; Yourdon, 1979b).

Weinberg (1971) maintains that, once an organization has implemented walkthroughs, it is 'locked' into them, and he gives examples where ego-less programming continued despite attempts to destroy it. This may be the case where the staff can see they are benefitting from walkthroughs, but I doubt if it is universally true. If the staff:

- are under considerable pressure of work, which is frequently the case; or
- if they dislike walkthroughs – and the psychological factors discussed below indicate that many do; or
- if any of them are incompetent;

then walkthroughs may fall into disuse (Macro and Buxton, 1987; Shneiderman, 1980) – the situation can be characterized as one of 'unstable equilibrium', i.e. it can easily be destroyed, and may be maintained only by management directive and constant enforcement. Shneiderman (1980) describes ego-less programming as a 'quaint 19th-century Utopian vision', and believes it is difficult to maintain the required intense level of co-

operation. By contrast, Macro and Buxton (1987) believe that most software engineers get over their initial anti-walkthrough feelings quite rapidly, though some people never do, which leads to stress at both the personal and team level.

10.7.4 DISADVANTAGES

Why, with their many advantages, are walkthroughs so little used?

In addition to aspects discussed earlier such as possible exaggeration of the benefits, walkthroughs have a number of disadvantages: psychological problems; cost; strain; and debating skills. These are discussed below, together with suggestions for overcoming them. In some cases, the suggestions will make the walkthroughs more acceptable to reluctant staff and reluctant organizations (though possibly less effective), and therefore enable more organizations to use, and benefit from, them. In other cases, the suggestions will make the walkthroughs more cost-effective.

Psychological problems

The first, and probably the most serious, problem is psychological. Walkthroughs, as indicated earlier, can make day-to-day work more interesting, but there are emotional difficulties that must first be overcome. Some programmers are very apprehensive about embarking on a walkthrough (Bell *et al.*, 1987). As Macro and Buxton (1987) put it, very few people, confronted with the prospect for the first time, feel entirely comfortable about having their intellectual creations criticized, however benevolently or constructively. Equally, some people feel acutely embarrassed at being the reviewer. Other authorities use stronger language. In a walkthrough, by its very nature, the stupid errors one has made are exposed to public gaze (Weinberg, 1971). The person whose work is being reviewed is shown to be less than perfect (Myers, 1979). This can be an undignified, humiliating and ego-bruising experience – his pride is wounded (Yourdon, 1979b; Parikh, 1984; Weinberg, 1971). The other participants may have a laugh at his expense. He is at their mercy (Berne, 1964). They may view him as an opponent whom they arrogantly attack and seek to embarrass and destroy.

To the producer, it is a threatening, stressful situation (Yourdon, 1979b). His self-confidence may be destroyed (Yourdon, 1975). He is naturally tempted to argue and defend himself (Yourdon, 1979b; Weinberg, 1971). He may abdicate responsibility.

Bickering and squabbling may break out, perhaps over trivial matters or esoteric features (Yourdon, 1979b). Walkthroughs can degenerate into fierce battles about the definition of quality (Arthur, 1983). Arguments are common; tempers may be lost; noisy brawls can occur. The co-ordinator of the walkthrough may have to order the participants to 'shut their mouths' (Yourdon, 1979b).

The very strength of these epithets – which are the ones used by advocates of walkthroughs – shows how serious the situation can be. Not only can all the benefits of walkthroughs be lost, but they can do far more harm than good. If the walkthrough is organized and methodical, with all participants adhering to an agreed set of rules and procedures, then it is unlikely to degenerate into aimless argument (Yourdon, 1979b), but these measures may not be enough to prevent all the psychological problems, so a number of additional measures may be suggested.

Criticism

Criticism should be tactful and considerate. This has the added benefit that such concern for others can only lead to a better working atmosphere (Bell *et al.*, 1987). Any criticism should be offered in the form of questions or suggestions (Yourdon, 1979b; Gildersleeve, 1974a). Participants should offer positive

comments in addition to the negative ones (Van Tassel, 1978; Aron, 1974; Hayden, 1982). They must remember that it is the *product* which is being evaluated, not the producer (Yourdon, 1979b). Errors should be treated as inevitable due to the complexity of programming and the primitive state of programming methodologies, rather than to weaknesses in the person who committed them (Myers, 1979). The co-ordinator must ensure that these rules are enforced (Yourdon, 1979b).

Weinberg (1971) related an anecdote in which university students (i.e. trainees) willingly and voluntarily discussed their problems with – and therefore exposed their short-comings to – their fellow-students. One could therefore conclude that resistance to walkthroughs would be reduced if staff considered themselves learners for the entire duration of their working lives. However, he also gave contrary evidence. In a study to determine the most commonly made errors in PL/1, he attempted to collect *all* the runs made by a group of 50 beginners. The difficulties in making this collection 'were astounding'. 'Every sort of evasion was used in an attempt to cover up the very existence of errors'. Perhaps they are only open about their errors in front of their peers, and presumably this is because their peers make the same types of mistakes. Alternatively, perhaps people do not mind others *knowing* they make mistakes, but *do* mind them having documentary *proof*.

Although the objective of a walkthrough is to review the product not the producer, this does not alter the fact that it *was* the *producer* who made the mistakes. Walkthroughs *do* expose inferior staff – Yourdon (1979b) and Weinberg (1971) seem quite proud of this – and the more able ones might adopt the view: 'Why should I carry that clod?' (Yourdon, 1979b; Couger and Zawacki, 1980). Possible cures, and their disadvantages, are to (Gildersleeve, 1974a; Glass, 1979; Weinberg, 1971; DeMarco, 1982; Yourdon, 1979b):

- provide additional training for the weaker staff;
- dismiss them, or permit them to resign – with the shortage of staff, this solution is of dubious value;
- restrict participation in each walkthrough to people who are of the same ability. (This solution would reduce the effectiveness of those walkthroughs at which only lower-ability staff were present; and, by minimizing the contact between staff of different ability, might deprive the lower-ability staff of valuable learning experiences.)

Peers

Code walkthroughs are also known as 'peer code reviews', but the term 'peer' is used loosely: senior staff, for example, may have their work reviewed by juniors (Weinberg, 1971; Yourdon, 1979b). This can be a very traumatic experience for the senior staff, especially if they are not accustomed to it. As Schach (1988) put it, a programmer with say 15 years of experience is unlikely to encourage having his code subjected to appraisal by fellow programmers, especially beginners. Possible solutions are to:

- restrict reviews to genuine peers – this solution has the disadvantage that senior staff would not be exposed to new ideas from the juniors;
- provide ongoing training to senior staff, who are usually neglected (Chapter 9), to keep them up to date with new methods (Yourdon, 1979b). Also, experienced staff may not know the theoretical basis for the methods they use, and so may not be able to hold their own in disputes, yet old methods are not necessarily inferior, and may even be more appropriate in some circumstances. Once again, training is the answer.

Conversely, it can also be traumatic for junior staff if a manager is present while their work is being reviewed (Yourdon, 1979b). A manager's presence puts 'a huge damper' on the proceedings, stifling free and frank discussion (Metzger, 1981; Bell *et al.*, 1987). Managers should therefore not attend walkthroughs, unless they are also producers (e.g. chief programmers) and their work is also reviewed, in turn, or if they have far more technical knowledge than their subordinates (Yourdon, 1979b; Glass, 1979; Fairley, 1985; Van Tassel, 1978).

On the other hand, if a manager is present (or even just sees the minutes), he can assess much more clearly the quality of the work and how long it takes the staff to do it. He can therefore appraise them much more fairly than by using other methods of measuring productivity, such as LOC, which are of dubious validity – or worse, using their timekeeping or manner of dress – to determine a pay rise or promotion, or to reassign them to work that makes better use of their abilities (Bell *et al.*, 1987; DeMarco, 1982). Non-DP studies quoted by Shneiderman (1980) show that peer evaluations are more reliable predictors of performance than evaluations by supervisors. If supervisors were present at walkthroughs, then this problem would be at least partly rectified, provided the manager's presence did not stifle free and frank discussion. (Personnel appraisals are discussed in Chapter 11.) Similarly, walkthroughs can assist proactive project management. It is therefore not surprising that Macro and Buxton (1987) believe that the highest level of directly accountable management, such as the overall project or product development manager, should convene and direct walkthroughs.

Privacy

The public nature of walkthroughs contributes to their success: 'people like to show off by finding errors' (Myers, 1979), but it also contributes to the psychological problems.

Possible compromises are to point out the errors in private or in writing, as happens with peer ratings, or to have fewer participants. For example, Bell *et al.* (1987) suggested that reviewers hand to the reviewee at the start of the meeting, lists of any minor typing, spelling, grammatical or syntax errors they have found. These items would not be discussed at the meeting.

These suggestions may significantly reduce the cost of walkthroughs.

Formality

The formal nature of walkthroughs contributes to their success, by ensuring that all the procedures are carried out and by recording all the errors detected, but informal walkthroughs reduce tension, and so are less of an ordeal and are more widely acceptable (Yourdon, 1979b; Glass, 1979). Informality is aided by having fewer and less senior participants. For example, Parikh (1984) recommends an informal 'mini' walkthrough, consisting of just the programmer and one other person.

By contrast, Bell *et al.* (1987) describe egoless programming as a completely informal technique, carried out by colleagues in a friendly manner. It is not a formalized method carried out at fixed times and made into a rigid procedure of the organization. To formalize it would destroy its ethos and therefore its effectiveness. In other words, his vision of walkthroughs is of something which is already informal, and so cannot be made more informal. However, he also stated that they have to be well organized to be effective.

In advance

By presenting *proposed* solutions instead of completed ones, the producer has less ego-investment in them (Yourdon, 1979b). He can 'bounce' ideas off his peers, asking their opinion in advance, especially when he is in doubt (Gunther, 1978). Because less time has been spent in producing the work, it is only to be expected that more errors will be present, so it will be less embarrassing to the producer when they are uncovered. In addition, less work will need to be redone to correct the errors brought to light.

Fewer or shorter walkthroughs

If fewer walkthroughs are held, then the associated problems will be correspondingly less frequent. For example, walkthroughs could be held of difficult or key parts only (Yourdon, 1979b; Glass, 1979; Van Tassel, 1978), or of only those programs which were singled out by static analysers or complexity metrics as being potential problem programs (Arthur, 1983). This should be much more cost-effective, at least from a purely software development point of view, i.e. excluding costs and disruptions caused by errors in production programs. A variation on this idea is for walkthroughs to concentrate on serious or high-cost errors and omissions (Patrick, 1980a; Ashley, 1980) – they will therefore be shorter in duration and should have correspondingly fewer psychological problems. An example is the suggestion by Bell *et al.* (1987) quoted earlier, that reviewers hand to the reviewee at the start of the meeting, lists of any minor errors they have found, and that these items should not be discussed at the meeting.

Cost

The second disadvantage of walkthroughs is their cost. Walkthroughs may be effective, but their cost can be high, or at least exceed the benefits (Glass, 1979; Myers, 1978; Yourdon, 1979b). According to DeMarco (1982), the cost of detecting a missing semicolon in a walkthrough is probably an order of magnitude greater than the cost of letting a compiler detect it. However, not all errors can be detected by compilers, so this is an extreme case. Of more relevance is the statement by Shneiderman (1980) that as much as 10% of a programmer's time may be spent on group reviews. This is in broad agreement with the earlier estimate based on Metzger's (1981) figures, that the time spent on a design review amounts to a few per cent of the total development effort. Metzger did not give a figure for code reviews, but presumably they would consume somewhat more time, because the quantity of code is larger – the design is effectively a summary of the code. (As Gilb (1988) pointed out, source listings are lengthy documents.) Bell *et al.* (1987) estimated an overhead of about 10% of the program development effort for code walk-throughs, though he believes that the time spent by all the participants in preparing for and attending walkthroughs (and presumably following up and finishing off afterwards as well) is more than compensated for by the saving in programmer's time, because the overwhelming proportion of their time is spent clarifying what the program is to do and subsequently in debugging it, and the evidence is that structured walkthroughs can greatly reduce the time spent in both of these activities. (Bell's figure was based on 10 lines of fully-debugged code per programmer per day, six people per walkthrough, one hour preparation per person, 50–100 LOC examined during a walkthrough, and a walkthrough duration of half an hour.) Glass (1979) gives a higher figure than Bell's 10%. According to him, code walkthroughs can add 10–50% to the cost of software implementation. This cost derives from the large amount of time they consume, which directly reduces productivity.

The following example shows that walkthroughs can be relatively costly, and so may not always be cost-effective.

A 200 statement program, at the rate of 50 debugged statements per day, would take four man-days to develop and test. At 6 hours productive work per day (Chapter 2), this is 24 man-hours' work. Walkthroughs of the program source code, at the rate of 100 statements per hour (Table 10.5), would take two hours. Allowing time for preparation by the participants, and following up and finishing off

afterwards, would bring the time up to at least four hours each (section 10.7.1). If there were four participants (Table 10.4), then a total of at least 16 man-hours would be required for the walkthroughs.

To justify the time thus spent, at least 16 hours would have to be saved. The probable savings, using function effort splits based on Table 8.28 (adjusted to exclude non-programming time), and a 50:50 development:maintenance split, are given in Table 10.6.

Instead of saving time, the walkthroughs in this case would have *lost* time – they added (6/48 =) 13% to the total (lifetime) programming effort, or (12/24 =) 50% to the program development effort. These figures are within the 10–50% range given by Glass (1979), and are in good agreement with the 10% of total effort quoted above from Shneiderman (1980), but not with the 10% or so of development effort from Bell *et al.* (1987) and Metzger (1981).

The figures in Table 10.6 do not include design walkthroughs or walkthroughs of maintenance changes. The estimates of a 4-hour (80%) reduction in time spent on debugging, a 1-hour (50%) reduction in time spent on 'corrective' maintenance, and a 5-hour (23%) reduction in time spent on 'other' maintenance, are fairly arbitrary. Both the number of errors and maintenance changes, and the time needed for each error or change, would be reduced, but it is difficult to estimate by how much. The reported development reduction of 2:1 (possibly only 1.3:1) deriving from the use of all MPPs combined (Table 8.71), and the corresponding maintenance reduction of possibly 5:1 (Table 8.72), though this ratio can be challenged, indicates that much larger savings may be possible. The comparison also does not include the cost of a suitable meeting room (which must be air-conditioned and quiet), nor the cost of the presentation media (slides, flip charts, etc.), nor of the appropriate equipment and handouts (Metzger, 1981).

Table 10.6 Effect of code walkthroughs on programmer productivity (1)

Function	Time spent		Saving/loss
	Without walkthroughs	*Using walkthroughs*	
Development			
design/coding	12	12	0
walkthroughs	0	16	16−
testing	2	2	0
debugging	5	1	4
clerical, etc.	5	5	0
Sub-total	24	36	12−
Maintenance			
corrective	2	1	1
other	22	17?	5
Sub-total	24	18	6
Total	48	54	6−

The justification for the walkthroughs in the above example would therefore have to come from a reason other than a direct increase in DP productivity, such as a reduction in costs and disruptions caused by errors in production programs, or an indirect, longer-term increase in DP productivity resulting from the training aspect of walkthroughs. Because the life-cycle time penalty in this example is not large, management would probably decide that it was outweighed by the benefits.

Sensitivity analysis

The values tabulated above were based on typical rates. Table 10.7 assumes the coding rate is twice as high, i.e. 100 debugged statements per day instead of 50, and that the development effort is then halved, i.e. the time penalty for development is proportionately larger and so more difficult to justify.

The time penalty is very much larger: 120% compared to the previous 50%, but this is a simplistic view. If the coding rate is much higher, then the program is probably a simple one, so the walkthrough rate should also be much higher. The maintenance effort

Table 10.7 Effect of code walkthroughs on programmer productivity (2)

Function	Without	With	Penalty
Development excluding			
walkthroughs	12	10	
walkthroughs	0	16	
Sub-total	12	26	14 (= 120%)
Maintenance	12	9	
Total	24	35	11 (= 46%)

is also assumed to be halved (if development proceeds faster, then the program is probably a simple one, so maintenance will probably also proceed faster), giving walkthroughs a total, life-time penalty of nearly 50%, which again is much higher than before. However, development might have proceeded faster because short-cuts were taken, e.g. testing and documentation were economized on. In this case, *more* maintenance would be required, but only for the non-walkthrough option, as walkthroughs should detect and put a stop to such behavior. This would

Table 10.8 Effect of code walkthroughs on programmer productivity (3)

Function	Without	With	Penalty
Development			
excluding			
walkthroughs	24	20	
walkthroughs	0	11	
Sub-total	24	31	7 (= 30%)
Maintenance	24	18	
Total	48	49	1 (= 2%)

Table 10.9 Effect of code walkthroughs on programmer productivity (4)

Function	Without	With	Penalty
Development			
excluding			
walkthroughs	12	10	
walkthroughs	0	11	
Sub-total	12	21	9 (= 75%)
Maintenance	12	9	
Total	24	30	6 (= 25%)

reduce, and possibly even reverse, the time penalty of walkthroughs.

Table 10.8 assumes that the coding rate remains 50, but that the walkthroughs proceed at a faster pace – say 150 statements per hour instead of 100 – then the total time consumed by them would be only 11 man-hours instead of 16 (assuming that correspondingly less preparation and follow-up time are required). The total lifetime effort would therefore be almost the same whether walkthroughs were used or not, though there would still be a time penalty of some 30% for the development phase. The figures in Table 10.8 are much more favorable to walkthroughs.

The first of the above variations increased the coding rate without increasing the walkthrough rate, while the second increased the walkthrough rate without increasing the coding rate. It would be more realistic for *both* to increase: if the program is simple, then both coding and walkthroughs would proceed faster. Table 10.9 assumes a coding rate of 100 debugged statements per day, and a walkthrough rate of 150 statements per hour. The development time with walkthroughs is therefore nearly double that without; while the lifetime effort (development plus maintenance) is 25% higher. The figures in Table 10.9 are much *less* favorable to walkthroughs.

It is therefore not clear how to reconcile the preceding figures with the 1.5:1 improvement in development productivity (and therefore

33% reduction in development effort) found by Walston and Felix (1977): productivity was 1.5 times higher when design and code inspections – and walkthroughs? (Gilb, 1988) – were used for more than 66% of the system than when they were used for 33% or less. Even an inspection rate of 350 statements per hour would not quite equalize the development times (24 hours without walkthroughs, 24.5 hours (12 + (100/350 * 16) + 2 + 1 + 5) with them, which is a penalty of only ((24.5 − 24)/24 =) 2%). Their figures probably refer to much larger programs, where productivity is much lower and where testing and debugging consume proportionately more time (Chapters 2 and 8). Walkthroughs would therefore be of relatively greater benefit, but it seems unlikely that the difference would be enough to account for such a large discrepancy.

For example, Table 10.10 uses a coding rate of only 12 fully debugged statements per day, and a 45% proportion of programming time consumed by testing and debugging, but this only gives walkthroughs about a 10% advantage in total development time.

The Walston and Felix figure (1.5:1) is also difficult to reconcile with the average productivity gain from all MPPs combined of only 2:1, or even only 1.3:1, in Table 8.71. However, their figure may include the effect of other MPPs, as they were usually used together on these projects (Boehm, 1981), and this probably explains the above discrepencies.

Table 10.10 Effect of code walkthroughs on programmer productivity (5)

	Time spent		
Function	*Without walk-throughs*	*Using walk-throughs*	*Saving/loss*
Development			
design/coding	39	39	0
walkthroughs	0	16	16−
testing	13	13	0
debugging	32	6	26
clerical, etc.	16	16	0
Total	100	90	10

It is much easier to reconcile the preceding figures with the 5% improvement in LOC per day output of programming personnel during the implementation phase claimed by Johnson (1980b) for design walkthroughs. This figure was based on the total LOC (all source statements) for a medium-sized project (3–8 managers).

All the preceding figures show that, when maintenance is included, walkthroughs become much easier to justify. In fact, in one of the cases, only a small increase in the impact on maintenance would be enough to reverse the loss on development.

Summary

The various claims for the impact of structured walkthroughs on software effort, and therefore on productivity, are summarized in Table 10.11.

Cost reduction

The cost of walkthroughs can be reduced in a number of ways, e.g. by having fewer participants, conducting them earlier in the software life-cycle, and having fewer walkthroughs.

Fewer participants The cost of a walkthrough is proportional to the number of participants (if we ignore any salary differences, and there is no increase in timewasting due to differences of opinion), but it is unlikely that the same is true of its effectiveness: two heads may be better than one, but are they *twice* as good? Doubling the number of participants should increase the number of errors found, but not by a factor of two, except perhaps when the number is doubled from one to two (Myers, 1978, 1979).

Care should, however, be exercised when economizing in this area, as participants have different outlooks – one, for example, may be a user, and another a maintenance programmer (Walston and Felix, 1977; Yourdon, 1975) – so they find different types of error.

Earlier in the software life-cycle Code walkthroughs are more time-consuming than ones of the program design (as represented, for example, by the flowchart), because the quantity of code is larger – it is effectively an expansion of the design. Furthermore, some of the errors discovered in a code walkthrough are analysis and design errors (Yourdon, 1979b). These could have been fixed much more cheaply had they been discovered at an earlier stage – e.g. by a walkthrough of the design – as it would not have entailed reworking any code – in fact, no code as yet existed. If program design walkthroughs are held, then there may be so few errors after the coding stage, and they may be so easy to fix (mostly syntax and spelling errors), that code walkthroughs would not be cost-justifiable. Metzger (1981) describes the design review as 'probably the most critical of all', because you are about to commit major resources, and once implementation has begun, 'it's exhausting, expensive, and morale-busting to have to stop to do a major overhaul'; and in any case they only add a few per cent to the development effort.

Table 10.11 Summary of claims of impact of structured walkthroughs on software effort

Source/assumptions	% effect
Additional cost	
Metzger (1981): design review	few per cent of total development effort
Shneiderman (1980)	10% of a programmer's time
Bell *et al.* (1987): code walkthroughs	10% of program development effort (recovered)
Glass (1979): code walkthroughs	10–50% of software implementation cost
Stevenson (this text): code walkthroughs only, programming time only	
50 LOC/day; 100 LOC/hour	13% (total effort)
50 LOC/day; 100 LOC/hour	50% (development effort)
100 LOC/day; 100 LOC/hour	46% (total effort)
100 LOC/day; 100 LOC/hour	120% (development effort)
50 LOC/day; 150 LOC/hour	2% (total effort)
50 LOC/day; 150 LOC/hour	30% (development effort)
100 LOC/day; 150 LOC/hour	25% (total effort)
100 LOC/day; 150 LOC/hour	75% (development effort)
50 LOC/day; 350 LOC/hour	2% (development effort)
Saving	
Johnson (1980b): design walkthroughs	5% (implementation phase)
Walston and Felix (1977)	33% (design and code inspections)
Stevenson (this text): code walkthroughs only, programming time only	
12 LOC/day; 100 LOC/hour	10% (development effort)

This will make walkthroughs less costly, and so could reverse the picture painted in Table 10.6.

In practice, most organizations do seem to recognize the economics (van Wyk and Kamfer, 1976; Holton, 1977; Ashley, 1980):

- some organizations have code walk-throughs only of juniors' programs;
- the majority of organizations in Holton's survey of 40 organizations which used walkthroughs, did not use them for code or even for detailed design.

Fewer walkthroughs easy to misuse by over-using: they waste time if no problem exists (Johnson, 1980b). For example, if a programmer is writing his third validation module in a system, there is no need for a formal walkthrough. Walkthroughs should therefore only be held if they are likely to be cost-effective, e.g. hold walkthroughs (Yourdon, 1975, 1979b; Metzger, 1981; Glass, 1979):

- of difficult routines only, i.e. severe design or detailed implementation problems;

- of new or unusual routines;
- of key routines and randomly selected other routines, rather than of entire programs;
- of the interfaces between modules in large programs;
- of program designs rather than of code;
- of juniors' work rather than of every-one's;

and have a follow-up walkthrough only if enough serious problems were exposed in the product (Fairley, 1985).

On the Omega project, only a selected proportion of the documents was inspected, to ensure that the 15% inspection resource for that project was spent in the most effective areas (Gilb, 1988).

Strain

Walkthroughs are hard work; they are a drudgery. They require intense concentration, and so are supertaxing (Glass, 1979; Myers, 1979).

Solutions to this problem include keeping the sessions short.

Debating skills

Discussion is an integral part of walkthroughs, and it may appear to be the perfect method for resolving differences of opinion and arriving at the truth, but it has disadvantage.

- Some people are more articulate than others: they 'can dazzle you with verbal pyrotechnics' (Yourdon, 1979b). The better talker 'always wants to talk things out, because he knows he will win, whether he's in the right or the wrong' (Webber, 1983).
- Debating experience is also relevant. One astronomer, Harlow Shapley, who later became famous, was reluctant to engage in an important debate on the structure of the universe because he suspected that his opponent, Heber Curtis, who was an experienced public speaker, might crush his arguments (Smith, 1983). As a result, although a debate was held, the central issues were largely evaded, and the debate did little to advance scientific knowledge.
- The person with the strongest personality may end up dominating the walkthrough (Yourdon, 1979b).
- Intuition is an important factor for success, and experts react instinctively: they do not make use of rules (Chapter 11). d'Aga-peyeff (1988) believes that no one really works 'by the book' or by logic – they work by 'gut feel'. Many people thus have 'a highly developed intuition', possibly by virtue of long experience, but are unable to prove that their intuition is correct (Yourdon, 1979b). They too would lose an argument even if they were right.
- Group members may be overly influenced by the more glib and assertive members, or by figures of authority or political considerations (Boehm, 1981). Boehm quoted an example where an assertive individual

persuaded his colleagues to use the Parkinsonian estimation method (Chapter 8), yet this method has subsequently been shown to be 'quite inaccurate'.

Discussion is therefore an imperfect way of arriving at the right decision. Training – technical, debating and assertiveness (Dyer, 1978; Schatzki, 1981; Wachs, 1972; Carnegie, 1913) – should go some way towards rectifying this, but the participants in walkthroughs should nevertheless bear these factors in mind. The Delphi technique, with its anonymity, should help.

10.7.5 EGO

Ego-less programming means that all programs are public property, and are reviewed by the programmer's colleagues, so they become effectively joint efforts (Weinberg, 1971; Yourdon, 1975). The basis of ego-less programming, of which concept walkthroughs are a part, is that ego is undesirable and should be suppressed. Schach (1988), for example, believes that if a programmer sees a module as an extension of his ego, he 'is certainly not going to try to find all the errors in "his" code'. This idea is based on the theory of 'cognitive dissonance' (Festinger, 1957).

Parikh (1984) believes that management sometimes wastes millions of dollars because of personal egos. When your ego is hurt, you become upset. When you see someone with superior talents, you may feel jealous, and try to disregard, or even get rid of, him. A gifted programmer may not listen to suggestions from an average one. By contrast, being ego-less leads to self-fulfilment and success in your personal as well as your professional life, and can be beneficial to your well-being and general health. To be ego-less is to be free from preconceptions, to be prepared to look at the new. If you are free of the past, then new thoughts come. You admit you do not know everything, that the other person also has knowledge, so you are prepared to listen to others and take advice from even your subordinates or people of lesser ability than yourself. Without ego, your thinking is clear and free of delusion: you can solve problems better.

Is this anti-ego belief justified? While not denying that problems occur, the above picture may not tell the whole story.

Our goals are high quality and high productivity. Secretiveness and private 'ownership', which characterize traditional programming, are neither right nor wrong of themselves, but should be judged by their results. Private ownership simply means that one person wrote the program, and the identity of the author is common knowledge; public ownership means that the program was a joint effort, and 'belongs' to the team as a whole (Weinberg, 1971; Schach, 1988). If secretive programming and private 'ownership' produce the better results, then that should be the favored method. Conversely, if ego-less programming and public 'ownership' produce the better results, then that should be the favored method. If some people do better using secretive methods, then they should be permitted (and even encouraged) to use those methods; and if others do better using ego-less methods, then they should be encouraged to use those methods. However, any adverse impact on the performance of other members of the team must also be taken into account.

Ego does exist. Rather than expending time and energy fighting it, can it instead be turned to advantage? Weinberg (1971) describes the practice of naming a program after oneself as 'abominable', yet many people name the organizations they establish after themselves, and the multimillionaire Andrew Carnegie increased his fortune considerably by naming enterprises after men with whom he wanted to do business (Carnegie, 1913).

Weinberg argues against programmers 'owning' programs on the grounds that people do not read programs, yet he also argues that people *should* read programs

because it makes them better programmers. In any event, even in a non-ego-less environment, a program has to be read every time it is maintained. The average production program may be maintained by no fewer than *ten* different people before being rewritten or discarded. In most organizations, therefore, nearly every program will eventually be scrutinized by others (Bell *et al.*, 1987). 'Ownership' should therefore be permitted.

To support his views, Weinberg gives a list of explanations commonly used by programmers when a run terminates abnormally. Blaming themselves is not on the list. However, neither do they claim that they were *trying* to achieve an abnormal termination. They are therefore fully aware that something is wrong and has to be corrected. Similarly, jealousy of someone with superior talents implies that one has the honesty to admit – if only to oneself – that the other person *is* superior. Pride of ownership may actually *motivate* them to improve their programs. If they are under severe pressure of time, or if someone else – probably a maintenance programmer – will have to fix any overlooked problems, then they will be more tempted to take short cuts. However, pride of ownership may be an effective counter to such temptations. If they are under severe time pressure, it is in their own longer-term interest to find any problems, and to find them as soon as possible, because, if there are problems, they will surface sooner or later, and the later they are found, the more difficulty they will have in fixing them (Metzger, 1981; Macro and Buxton, 1987); and if someone else will have to fix any overlooked problems, it will be detrimental to their reputations. If, instead, the group 'owns' the program, will the individual programmers take as much pride in their work, and strive as hard for perfection, or will they instead abdicate responsibility? Books advocating ego-less programming have little if anything to say about this issue.

The argument advanced here is reminiscent of a criticism voiced by Shneiderman (1980) of CPTs: the programmers other than the chief programmer 'do not have the satisfaction of having a portion of the project that is wholly their own'. Johnson (1980b) seems to support this view, with his statement that optimal productivity is a result of dedicated, involved *individuals* working on 'their' system. Weinberg himself quotes a survey which found that 'more time to give my work a personal touch of quality' was the joint third most important factor that motivated the programmers surveyed.

Perhaps the poor output of workers in Communist countries, with state ownership, might tell us something about the output of workers in ego-less teams, with joint ownership. Attempts at group design are usually disastrous; there are disadvantages of democratic teams (e.g. their efficiency is more impaired by the presence of an anti-social member – Chapter 3), and we should note that democratic teams and ego-less programming are related concepts. Furthermore, being 'free of the past' might bring the danger of disregarding the *lessons* of the past.

Parikh (1984) speculated that ego cannot be totally eradicated, just as we cannot remove all the bugs from a program.

Macro and Buxton (1987) believe there is no such thing as ego-less behavior, nor is it desirable that there should be. Good software engineering is done by highly capable people doing a very difficult job, often in less than ideal conditions. They therefore have every right to be proud of their achievements. However, they must be willing to subjugate their attachment to their own ideas and creations to the aim of getting the job done as a team.

Bain (1982) stated that ego needs are essentially needs for self-respect. He equated ego to esteem: the need for feeling you are important, that you have made a contribution toward achieving worthwhile goals – and esteem is the fourth of Maslow's 'hierarchy of needs' (Chapter 9).

What is the situation regarding ego in other occupations? A quick scan through the indexes of a number of books failed to reveal any references to ego-less astronomers, biologists, mathematicians, librarians, cooks, accountants, and so on. There are discussions of ego-less management in Arthur (1983), Parikh (1984) and Singer (1982), all of which are computer books. Is software engineering the only occupation where ego is a problem – or is it just the first where it has been *recognized* as a problem? Weinberg (1971) seems to imply that ego, or at least the ownership aspect, *is* a problem in other occupations.

10.7.6 SUMMARY AND CONCLUSIONS

Enthusiastic claims have been made for the effectiveness of walkthroughs, and there are good reasons why these claims should be true, as well as some evidence to back them up. However, doubt can be cast on the evidence, so walkthroughs are probably not as effective as claimed.

There are problems with walkthroughs, particularly psychological problems, which can be serious, though there are steps which can be taken to avoid or reduce the problems.

Walkthroughs may well increase the cost of development, but they probably result in a significant reduction in maintenance effort, so overall lifetime costs are probably reduced.

Walkthroughs have other benefits, such as the interchange of knowledge.

Ego can be harmful, but perhaps it can be beneficial as well.

10.8 INSPECTIONS

Inspections were devised by Michael Fagan in IBM in 1972 (Radice and Phillips, 1988). They are therefore more recent than walkthroughs. They are similar to walkthroughs, but there is evidence that they are more effective (Jones, 1991; Bell *et al.*, 1987). According to Gilb (1988), the method is widely recognized internationally, but it will take years before it is widely used. By contrast, according to Radice and Phillips (1988), inspections are widely used but not universally accepted.

10.8.1 DESCRIPTION

Definition

Glass (1979) defines inspections as the process of examining computer software and related material for correctness, e.g. examining a program to confirm compliance with the specifications. He also defines them as a visual examination for the presence of desired characteristics and the absence of undesired characteristics. They are therefore a kind of proofreading (Gilb, 1988).

Myers (1979) defines a code inspection as a set of procedures and error-detection techniques for group code reading. As Bell *et al.* (1987) put it, a group of people meet to review a piece of work. Inspections differ from code audits, which check just for violations of coding standards, e.g. for comments and labels (Dunn and Ullman, 1982).

Scope

Like walkthroughs, inspections can be used for virtually anything, including specifications and other non-machine processable prose such as documentation, and even non-computer projects, which testing cannot be used on, which is particularly beneficial because 'If you fail to inspect the higher levels of planning and goal-setting, then inspection at the lower levels will only serve to confirm errors made earlier!' (Gilb, 1988). According to some authorities, specification is the area where most errors occur. In addition, it is far cheaper to correct errors at this stage rather than later (Chapter 8). For these reasons, inspections are doubly effective in reducing costs and improving productivity.

As implied above, inspections can be used throughout the software life-cycle, and Gilb (1988) gives a diagram showing a system development life-cycle containing no fewer than 11 inspections. Most attention, however, concentrates on design and code inspections, and Fagan (1976) found that the inspection following unit testing was not cost effective.

According to Myers (1979), inspections are of equal or even more value in checking modifications to programs, as modifying an existing program is a more error-prone process than writing a new program.

Comparison with testing

Inspections replace walkthroughs, but not testing (Gilb, 1988; Dunn and Ullman, 1982). They do, however, reduce dependence on testing, though they might encourage earlier, less formal testing, to 'clean up' a program before it is submitted to an inspection. This contrasts with the earlier statement that producers are effectively encouraged to submit semi-ready products for walkthroughs, because the additional errors motivate the reviewers.

Sommerville (1989) stated that it is impossible to know, in general, whether or not informal verification represents a saving over testing. (He was apparently referring to inspections rather than walkthroughs. They are informal in comparison with mathematical verification.) Testing costs depend on the ability of the testers, how fast the turnaround is, and so on. In some cases, testing will be cheaper, in other cases, the other way round: static verification will result in a lower cost per fault detected. Fagan (1986) suggested that, in most cases, systematic inspection results in a lower cost per defect discovered than testing.

According to Boehm (1981), both inspections and unit tests are good at finding simple programming blunders and logic errors. However, inspections are good at finding developer blind spots, interface errors, missing portions, and specification errors, which unit tests are not good at; whereas unit tests are good at finding numerical approximation errors and program dynamics errors, which inspections are not good at. Jones (1991) adds that inspections are extremely efficient in using the human capacity for inductive reasoning to find subtle errors that testing will miss, but not in finding performance-related problems. Martin and McClure (1985) add that dynamic techniques such as testing often fail to detect data definition errors, incorrectly initialized variables, and unreferenced variables. They also cannot be used to verify the correctness of a requirements or design specification if they are not written in a machine-processable form (though, as previously stated, recognition of specification errors is a not infrequent by-product of testing). Static techniques can be used to determine the appropriateness of the test data used by the dynamic techniques, and can be used at an earlier stage in the software life-cycle than dynamic techniques.

Comparison with structured walkthroughs

Inspections are superficially similar to structured walkthroughs (Bell *et al.*, 1987) – 'the two methods have a lot in common' (Myers, 1979) – but are much more formal and rigorous (Metzger, 1981). In fact, according to Bell, they are intended as a mechanism to provide increased management control, though Myers disapproves of this: 'the use of inspection results by managers can quickly defeat the purpose of the process'.

IBM claim that inspections give markedly greater productivity than structured walkthroughs, and result in fewer errors (Bell *et al.*, 1987). Fagan (1976) listed the advantages of inspections, e.g.

- inspectors have definite roles to play;
- the moderator rather than the reviewee directs the effort;
- an error checklist is used; and

- detailed error feedback is provided to individual programmers.

It is the differences which give inspections the advantage, but at least some of the differences, such as the use of checklists, could profitably be incorporated into walkthroughs. Furthermore, Fairley (1985) stated that inspections do not involve the members of the team which produced the product being inspected, and so do not give the benefits of improved team communications, morale, and education of new members, provided by walkthroughs, though not all authorities would exclude the production team members. Sommerville (1989) stated that the key difference between inspections and reviews is that inspections are solely intended to detect defects. They do not have an explicit educational function, nor are they part of the design process where strategy decisions are made. Nevertheless, the programmer receives feedback on his programming style and choice of algorithms and programming techniques, and his common errors, and the other participants learn from being exposed to another programmer's errors and style (Myers, 1979; Fairley, 1985).

Fairley recommends balanced use of both inspections and walkthroughs.

Formality

The most prominent aspect of inspections is probably the formality. Each member of the team has a definite role. Errors are formally recorded and classified (Bell *et al.*, 1987). Each programmer makes different types of mistake, so these statistics provide valuable individual feedback (Fairley, 1985). They show each programmer's weak areas, thereby highlighting where extra training is required – in fact, the inspections are in themselves a learning experience for all the participants (Gilb, 1988; Myers, 1979). The statistics also identify – and identify early – which modules contain an abnormally high number of errors, and so are error-prone and

Table 10.12   Recommended number of participants at an inspection

Source		No. of participants
Fairley (1985)		1–4
Jones (1991): small projects	minimum	3
Gilb (1988)		3–5
Jones (1991): large projects	maybe	5 or more
Myers (1979)	usually	4
Bell *et al.* (1987)		4
Fagan (1976)		4
Sommerville (1989)	about	4

should be subjected to extra testing. Conversely, if an abnormally large number of errors is found in any module during testing, then that module should be re-inspected (Myers, 1979).

In addition to these individual uses, the statistics provide management with a global picture – a 'software engineering management accounting system' (Gilb, 1988). This can be used to identify a wide range of productivity problems in the software development process, and then to measure and see if the implemented solutions are working as expected. It is like a financial director who analyses accounting data to gain insights into the organization's operational weaknesses. IBM, AT&T, and ICL have regularly used inspections for monitoring and improving their software development processes, in order to improve productivity.

Another aspect of the formality is that inspections make extensive use of checklists. Several authors, such as Dunn and Ullman (1982) and Fairley (1985), give examples of items which could appear on the checklists, and Myers (1979) provides a particularly comprehensive checklist, with 67 questions classified by type of error. According to Gilb (1988), a checklist for a single type of inspection should not contain more than about 25 questions, otherwise it becomes too much to deal with.

A pre-requisite for a code inspection is that the design documentation be thorough, explicit, intelligible, and current (Dunn and

Ullman, 1982). If you do not understand exactly what someone said, you cannot be sure if they are right or wrong: 'often we suspect the writer did not know what he was saying, and hides this fact in obscure language' (Gilb, 1988).

Jones (1986b) rates formal design inspections as being typically 55% efficient in removing defects, compared to only 40% for informal group design reviews.

Because inspections are organized, they can be expected to find more errors than testing (Dunn and Ullman, 1982). However testing should also be well-organized.

The formality of inspections may provoke resistance, but Gilb (1988) warns that the net savings from inspections are directly proportional to the extent to which the rules are observed.

Number of participants

As is the case with walkthroughs, different authorities recommend different numbers of participants (Table 10.12).

More people could attend high-level, 'architectural' inspections, to provide additional points of view (Gilb, 1988).

Participants

Where there are four participants then, depending on what was being inspected, they would normally consist of a moderator (leader or co-ordinator), the designer, the coder, and a test specialist (Myers, 1979; Bell *et al.*, 1987).

In the description given by Myers (1979), the programmer presents his own program. As he is explaining it, he discovers errors in it himself. By contrast, in the description given by Gilb (1988), the originator of the product being inspected is normally not present during the inspection, and can therefore neither explain nor defend it. As he cannot explain the product, there is the possibility that one of the inspectors will misunderstand it, and so record as a defect something which is, in fact, correct, thereby inflating the defect count and so making inspections appear more effective than they really are. Gilb's view is that, if one person misunderstood it, then someone else might also. If, for example, it is the operating instructions which are being inspected, then this could lead to incorrect operation of the system. Any ambiguity or lack of clarity should therefore rightly be recorded as a defect. As the originator is not present to defend the product, acrimonious argument is avoided, and the inspectors can be more frank in expressing their opinions.

A pre-requisite for a code inspection is that all members of the inspection team be fluent in the programming language (Dunn and Ullman, 1982).

There is a difference of opinion over the role played by management. According to Gilb (1988), 'Inspections are carried out by colleagues at *all* levels of seniority, except the big boss'. In fact, in smaller organizations, the moderator may be the project or departmental manager. This is consistent with the emphasis on formality. However, the opposite viewpoint is expressed by Myers (1979): not only should managers *not* attend inspections, but they should also not use (and therefore not even see?) the results. This is consistent with the custom for structured walkthroughs, as evidenced by their alternative name, *peer* reviews (of code, etc.). An intermediate view is expressed by Bell *et al.*

(1987). He stated that management do not usually attend inspections, but are informed of the results.

Alternatively, a metrics group, consisting of measurement professionals who are politically isolated from the project and from the line of command immediately above the project, could collect defect data (DeMarco, 1982). This data would be used only for the benefit of the individual. The metrics group would inform an individual privately that he was defect prone, and the person concerned, motivated by his own self-esteem, would himself ask to be reassigned to a different speciality, in order to maximize his contribution to the effort. Self-esteem is a far stronger motivation than any management could apply. Other, less drastic steps, could also be taken, namely the individual could take more care, or could ask for more training.

Amount of time required

Each inspection session requires about 1.5 hours of preparation (Gilb, 1988). Because it is mentally taxing, sessions should not last more than 90 minutes to 2 hours (Myers, 1979; Gilb, 1988).

During an inspection, participants might think of good solutions to the defects uncovered. However, discussing solutions is not allowed during the inspection session. To prevent these ideas being lost, either this rule should be waived (Freeman, 1975), or a follow-up, 'third hour' meeting, should be held afterwards (Gilb, 1988).

If we include this 'third hour' meeting, and other post-inspection activities, e.g. follow-up to ensure that the problems are fixed, as well as the preparation time, then a 90-minute meeting probably represents over four hours per participant, i.e. about three times the duration of the meeting. This is presumably the basis of the statement by Gilb (1988) that only one-third of the inspection effort is spent on the inspection meeting.

One indication of the large amount of time

required is that 50 pages of documentation may be involved in each session (Gilb, 1988).

Inspection rate

According to Myers (1979), most inspections proceed at a rate of about 150 statements per hour. Sommerville (1989) quotes three rates: about 500 statements per hour during the overview stage; about 125 during individual preparation; and 90–125 during the actual inspection. Fagan (1986) suggests a rate of about 100 LOC/hour. In the Omega project, the average rate was 37 statements per hour, not counting comment lines (Gilb, 1988); see Table 10.3. However, the 'hours' for this project may be man-hours rather than the duration of the inspection, in which case the inspection rate derived is not on the same basis as the other rates quoted here, and two adjustments may be necessary. Firstly, it would have to be multiplied by the number of participants (five?); and secondly, if preparation time and follow-up time are included, and if only one-third of the inspection effort was spent on the inspection meeting, then the figure must be multiplied by three. The figure of 37 is probably therefore much too low, and the true rate may even have been ten or more times as high, but this seems unrealistic: it would then be much higher than any of the others quoted here.

Jones (1991) gives a rate of 75 LOC per hour. He also gives rates of 12 pages per hour for requirements, 15 for functional specifications, 20 for logic specifications, and 20 for user documents. However, he warns that these figures can vary by more than 50% either way due to individual human factors, interruptions, and the number of problems encountered. By comparison, Bell *et al.* (1987) suggested that 5–10 pages of written specifications be reviewed at one meeting. Jones also gives the corresponding inspection rates for the individual preparation stage: these are about twice as high.

Buck (1981) found an optimum figure of 90 source statements per hour at IBM inspection classes using a student problem. He found that there is a rapid drop in the number of errors found if the rate increases only slightly above this value. For example, if the inspection rate is increased by 35%, the number of defects found might drop by one-third or more (Gilb, 1988). Looking at Gilb's histogram, the drop is only half as great as this, but even so, it is important that organizations publicize this phenomenon; that they motivate moderators to maintain the optimum speed; and that they constantly monitor the speed at which inspections are conducted. It is interesting to note that 90 is slightly lower than the rate most authorities recommend for walkthroughs (Table 10.5), and could partly explain the apparent greater effectiveness of inspections. As inspections are more formal than walkthroughs, one might expect them to proceed at a slower pace. At peak effectiveness, errors were found at the rate of 21 per hour. Therefore, 21 errors were found in each 90 statements, i.e. over 200 errors per 1000 LOC, compared to the average of about 40 during development given in Table 8.42. Either the students in this study made many more mistakes than professional programmers in their working environment, or inspections are extremely effective. The former seems the more likely, as the evidence presented in Chapter 8 indicates that typically fewer than 50 errors per 1000 LOC are made during development (because this is the number typically detected during development and production runs combined), unless inspections are so efficient that they detect many errors that are not even detected during production (and evidence presented earlier did show that there are many such undetected errors), or a broader definition of 'error' was used, i.e. including violations of the installation's coding standards and even inefficiencies.

Fagan (1977) observed that the inspection rate is five times faster for application programs than for systems programs: 320–480

Table 10.13 Code inspections – effort and effectiveness (Boehm, 1981)

Source	Inspection rate (delivered LOC/ man-hour)	Effectiveness	Ratio
Myers (1978)	10	38%	4:1
Jones (1977)	10–48	70	1.5:1–7:1
Boehm (1980a)	20	89	4:1
Crossman (1979b)	25	50–60	2:1
Project A	30	64	2:1
Project A	120	41	0.3:1
Average (approximate)	40	60	1.5:1

source statements per hour, compared to only 80.

Boehm (1981) reported the inspection rates and corresponding efficiencies from several studies. Table 10.13 shows these in ascending order of inspection rate (and therefore descending order of time and effort). The ratio is the effectiveness divided by the rate, and is intended purely to simplify comparison. Intuitively, one would expect the effectiveness to decrease as the inspection rate increased. The ratio should therefore decrease accordingly, and should do so rapidly because of the multiplicative effect.

On average, therefore, code inspections proceeded at the rate of 40 delivered source instructions per man-hour, and found 60% of the errors. These figures, like those given above by Buck (1981), show that, in general, the higher the inspection rate, the lower the effectiveness. However these inspection rates are mostly much lower than Buck's, and he found that, at these low rates, effectiveness *in*creased as the inspection rate increased. In all probability, the code being inspected here was more complex than that in Buck's student problem, and the optimum rate is probably lower for complex code.

Inspection rate/time versus preparation rate/time

Jones (1991) gave rates for the individual preparation stage, about twice as high as the corresponding inspection rates, which implies that the preparation time is about half the duration of the inspection. By contrast, the Sommerville (1989) rates show a preparation rate that is only up to (125/90 =) 40% higher; and several authorities state that the preparation time for walkthroughs is about the same as the duration of the walkthrough, which implies that the preparation rate is about the same as the walkthrough rate.

At the other extreme, according to Gilb (1988), only one-third of the inspection effort is spent on the inspection meeting. This might seem to suggest that the preparation time is double the meeting time, and that the preparation rate is therefore half the inspection rate, rather than the other way round. However, as previously discussed, he is probably including post-inspection activities, e.g. follow-up to ensure that the problems are fixed, or the 'third hour' meeting to discuss solutions. His figure therefore indicates that preparation time and rate are probably about the same as the inspection meeting time and rate.

Technological aids

The inspection process is assisted by tools such as static analysers, checkout compilers, and code auditors, i.e. tools which analyse the program, checking it for compliance with coding standards and measuring its complexity (Myers, 1979; Arthur, 1983).

10.8.2 BENEFITS

Benefits claimed for inspections are improved productivity, significantly reduced testing and implementation costs, improved quality, fewer defects, less error repair time, lower maintenance cost, a software engineering management accounting system, motivating people to raise the quality of their work, increased group participation, and training people in the work procedures and content (Arthur, 1983; Gilb, 1988). Inspections ensure that project documentation is clear, self-explanatory, unambiguous, and consistent with all the other project documentation and with the higher level goals of the organization. Inspections reveal weak areas of individual programmers, thereby showing where additional training is necessary. They reveal weak areas in the development process in general, thereby showing where improved methods and tools are necessary. They also measure the value of the inspection process, so it itself can be improved. Because of the higher quality, the finished products are more desirable to the users, or to customers, thereby increasing sales.

Inspections are particularly valuable for real-time systems, because debugging is difficult due to the non-repeatability of error situations (Fairley, 1985).

Various experiments and other studies have quantified the error detection, productivity improvement, and other benefits of inspections. Table 10.13 gave some results, comparing the effectiveness of inspections with the inspection rate; other results are given below.

Uses of code inspections by IBM have shown error-detection efficiencies as high as 80% of all errors found by the end of the testing processes (Perriens, 1977).

According to Jones (1986b), of the common methods for detecting requirements and design errors, evidence indicates that formal group inspections and design simulation or modelling (where users are able to work with running examples of the program's functions), have the highest overall efficiencies, and alone may remove over 65% of the problems – though 55% is more typical for formal design inspections. Similarly, formal code inspections (typically 60% efficient), and modelling or prototyping the final code (typically 65%), provide the highest efficiencies in code defect removal, at more or less moderate costs. Only these two methods appear to consistently rise above 60% in overall defect removal efficiency.

Walston and Felix (1977) found that productivity was 1.5 times higher when design and code inspections were used for more than 66% of the system, compared to if they were used for 33% or less – this represents a 33% reduction in development effort. However, this figure may include the effect of other MPPs, as they were usually used together (Boehm, 1981). Furthermore, Conte *et al.* (1986) pointed out that, according to Walston and Felix's figures, design and code inspections are one of the attributes that appear to have the *smallest* potential impact on productivity.

According to Gilb (1988), about half the Walston and Felix projects used inspections, and about half used walkthroughs, and the average productivity of those which used inspections was about 35% higher than the average productivity of all the projects combined. The productivity advantage of inspections over walkthroughs must therefore be much higher than 35%.

According to Myers (1979), inspections are far more effective than desk checking, because they are performed by a second party. Code inspections and walkthroughs find 30–70% of the logic design and coding errors in typical programs. Furthermore, it is not just the easy errors they find (Shooman and Bolsky, 1975). In one experiment, black-box testing, a combination of black- and white-box testing, and three-person code inspections, were found to be equally effective in detecting errors, but the code inspections used more time and were therefore less cost-effective (Myers, 1978). (As they only found 38% of the errors, it might be more accurate to say that they were equally *in*effective. In fairness, though, Boehm (1981) pointed out that some of the errors in this experiment were much more subtle than normal. It may therefore also be risky to try to generalize from the results of this experiment.) The different methods found different types of error, so a combination of methods should be used, to complement each other. This experiment is valuable because it genuinely compared the effectiveness and cost-effectiveness of inspections against other methods, whereas most claims do not. If, for example, inspections are held prior to the commencement of testing, then one could reasonably *expect* them to reveal more errors than the testing, simply because fewer errors were left for testing to detect. Experiments proving that they do do so therefore do not tell us very much. For example, the Jones (1977) rate in Table 8.66 indicates that testing of code which has previously been inspected finds only about half as many errors as testing of code which has not been inspected, for the same testing effort: only 20% of the errors compared to 40%.

Code inspections, not surprisingly, do not find 'high level' errors such as requirements analysis errors (Myers, 1979), whereas testing, as previously explained, sometimes does.

Based on an inspection rate of about 100 LOC/hour, about an hour's preparation per participant, and four participants, the cost of inspecting 100 LOC is equivalent to roughly the cost of one person working for one day (Fagan, 1986; Sommerville, 1989).

A graph in Boehm (1981) indicates that code inspections find more errors more quickly than unit tests, and in fact the superiority of inspections is quite marked. For example, if error detection activities comprise 10% of the programming effort, then 60% of the errors will have been detected if the 10% was devoted to inspections, but only 20% would have been found if it was spent on testing. However, inspections find at most about 80% of the errors, whereas unit tests can eventually find virtually all the errors, provided sufficient effort is expended, i.e. if the amount of effort spent on testing is about as much as was spent on programming. (By programming, Boehm presumably means detailed design and coding only.) This graph also indicates that maximum cost-effectiveness is achieved if the inspection effort is about 10% of the programming effort.

Other figures quoted by Boehm (1981) are a 58% efficiency for module logic inspections, and 63% for module code inspections (Thayer *et al.*, 1978); and 60–70% for module logic inspections, and 65–75% for module code inspections (Jones, 1978).

Gilb (1988) quoted a number of cases.

1. In the Omega project, 180 staff ported a micro-networking operating system comprising 1.5 million lines of mainly PASCAL code, of which one-third were new or changed, to new hardware. A total of 3787 defects were discovered by 101 inspections of design documents. This averages out at 37 defects per inspection. (Early in the project, errors were being detected at the rate of 56 per inspection, but this decreased to 28 near the end of the project.) Inspections consumed a total of 3097 man-hours, giving a rate of (3787/3097 =) 1 defect per man-hour, and (3097/101 =) 31 man-hours per inspection. Gilb estimated that the inspections were only 30% effective due to inadequate cross-referencing tools and other inadequate support methods, and that there were therefore about 8000 more defects which were missed.

   (Because these figures refer to defects in documents, whereas other rates probably refer predominantly or exclusively to defects in source code, it is risky to compare the above figures with figures from other projects.)

Inspection of test plans resulted in a 57% increase in test coverage due to the addition of further test cases and totally new tests.

Other figures from this project (Table 10.3) were presumably obtained from inspections of part of the code for the project, and not from the inspections of design documents referred to above.

2. In Project Orbit, a networked operating system which contained 500 000 LOC, the system was delivered early, and had about 100 times fewer errors than would normally be expected. This represents a *99%* reduction, and the efficiency was probably so high because *eleven* inspections – of high-level design, low-level design, source code, etc. – were used.

3. At the Standard Chartered Bank, the total error repair cost using inspections (presumably both design and code inspections), was about 30% of the cost when testing was the first effective error-finding process. (If debugging consumes about 20% of the system development effort (Chapter 8), then the error repair cost was reduced to about (30/100 * 20 =) 6% of the development effort, which is a reduction of about (20 − 6 =) 14%.) Of the errors, 80% were found by design and code inspections. Better still, about 98% of the errors were found before the production stage (by inspections and testing combined), compared to the more usual figure of perhaps only 80% (Chapter 8).

4. Other figures from a bank show that, although most errors are found during inspection, they only account for about a third of the total repair costs.

5. ICI in Britain found that 400 inspected programs were 10 times cheaper to maintain than 400 similar non-inspected programs.

6. At a London bank, the very first use of inspections turned up 68 defects in a 30-page sample of design and requirements documentation. One of these defects was 'super-major' – a major sub-system had been entirely forgotten.

Gilb (1988) claims that, based on IBM and other experience, in both large and small environments, all over the world, inspections give the following benefits over alternative methods such as reviews and structured walkthroughs.

- 25–35% earlier delivery but 15–35% for major software projects (Walston and Felix, 1977).
- 25–35% lower development costs.
- 10–30 times lower maintenance effort/costs – a reduction of 90 to 97% (Crossman, 1979b).
- 10–100 times fewer defects – a reduction of 90 to 99%.
- An 85% reduction in testing time and machine time due to better organization of tests, as a result of using inspection to check the quality of test design and planning (Larson, 1975).

If we assume that the testing time referred to above includes debugging, and that testing and debugging together typically consume about 26% of the total development effort (Table 8.28), then an 85% reduction in them is alone equal to about an (85/100 * 26 =) 22% reduction in the total development effort.

Gilb also claims that testing identifies and removes, at most, 50–55% of defects 'for a single test process', whereas inspection is about 80% effective, ranging from 60 to 100%. In addition, he reported high savings in the test planning area (Larson, 1975).

A full inspection program typically comprises 15% of the project time (Gilb, 1988). However, this should be more than recouped by savings later in the development process. Based on a sample of the major errors in the Omega project, Gilb estimated that the cost savings were over 500% on the major defects alone, i.e. five hours saved for every hour invested in inspection. If inspections consumed about 3000 hours, then they must have saved about 15 000 hours (excluding the saving from minor errors); and if full inspections comprise 15% of the development effort, then this portion of the project must have taken about (100/15 * 3000 =) 20 000 hours. Without inspections, therefore, it would have taken about (20 000 + 15 000 =) 35 000 hours, so the saving was about (15 000/35 000 =) 43% (excluding the saving from minor errors). However, these specific figures refer mainly to inspection of documents – 90% of the errors evaluated were in product plans and specifications – so it is risky to attempt to extrapolate from them. In particular, inspections during later phases in the software lifecycle are likely to provide smaller benefits. Furthermore, the project itself was a conversion not an ordinary development.

Fairley (1985) reported the results of two experiments by Fagan. In the first, the inspection team conducted two 2-hour sessions per day, giving a total of 25 hours per person. Of the errors found during development 67% were found by design and code inspections prior to unit testing (Fagan, 1976). During the first 7 months of operation, 38% fewer errors were found than in a similar program for which informal walkthroughs had been used. There was no difference in productivity between the two programming groups, but the inspection time included training, so the comparison is unfair to inspections. In the second experiment, 82% of the errors discovered during development were found during design and code inspections. Programmer productivity rose because less time was spent on module testing, and the consequent savings in programmer resources was 25% of the estimated cost. Fairley also stated that subsequent experiments have reported 70% and greater error removal during design and code inspections (Jones, 1977, 1978).

Dunn and Ullman (1982) reported two experimental results. Firstly, Fagan (1976) found a saving of 94 programmer hours per 1000 non-comment statements for design inspections, and 51 hours for code inspections. (This probably translates into the 25% saving in programmer resources quoted above. At a development rate of 10 debugged LOC/day (a fairly typical value), and 6 hours productive work per day (Chapter 2), 1000 LOC would take 100 days, or 600 hours work. A saving of (94 + 51 =) 145 hours is (145/600 =) 24% of this.) Secondly, an experiment by Gannon (1979) found that inspections unearthed more errors than path testing for five categories of error (input-output, data handling, interface, data definition and database), while the reverse was the case for only two categories (computational and logic). Furthermore, in all seven categories, the average time to find and correct an error was less for inspection than for path testing.

The preceding figures, including those from Table 10.13, are summarized in Tables 10.14 and 10.15. The average efficency for design inspections is about 60%, and the same for code inspections (Table 10.14). If both design and code inspections are used, the efficiency, as might be expected, is higher: an average of about 70%. It is difficult to compare the figures in Tables 10.14 and 10.15. There are wide variations between them – and some of the evidence is contradictory, e.g. some of it indicates that inspections are no more effective than testing, while other evidence indicates that they are much more effective. Nevertheless, the figures in Table 10.15 seem to point to a decrease in development effort of perhaps 30%, and a decrease in maintenance effortof probably over 90%. (With a 50:50 split between development and maintenance, this points to a decrease of ((30/100 * 50) + (90/100 * 50) =) 60% in the total effort, which is equal to an overall productivity increase of (100/(100 − 60) =) 2.5:1.) Inspections can also find over 80% of the errors, but this figure includes errors which would have been found in testing had the code not been inspected first, and in any case, 60% is probably a more typical figure (Table 10.14).

Table 10.14 Efficiency of inspections

Source	Efficiency
Buck (1981)	>200 errors per 1000 LOC code inspections
Project Omega (Gilb, 1988)	21 errors per 1000 LOC code inspections
Project Omega (Gilb, 1988)	(estimated) 30% design document inspections
Myers (1979)	30–70% code inspections
Myers (1978)	38% code inspections
Project A (Boehm, 1981)	41% code inspections
Crossman (1979b)	50–60% code inspections
Jones (1986b)	55% design inspections
Thayer *et al.* (1978)	58% module logic inspections
Jones (1986b)	60% code inspections
Jones (1978)	60–70% module logic inspections
Thayer *et al.* (1978)	63% module code inspections
Project A (Boehm, 1981)	64% code inspections
Jones (1978)	65–75% module code inspections
Fagan (1976)	67% design and code inspections (38% fewer errors in operation)
Jones (1977)	70% code inspections
IBM (Perriens, 1977)	80% code inspections
Standard Chartered Bank (Gilb, 1988)	80% design and code inspections
Gilb (1988)	80% (range 60–100%)
Fagan (1976)	82% design and code inspections
Boehm (1980a)	89% code inspections
Worldwide (Gilb, 1988)	10–100 times fewer errors (a reduction of 90 to 99%)
Project Orbit (Gilb, 1988)	100 times fewer errors (full inspections) (a reduction of 99%)
Average (approximate)	60%

10.8.3 SUMMARY AND CONCLUSIONS

Overall, inspections appear to provide a substantial increase in both development and particularly maintenance productivity, and also find many errors.

Bell *et al.* (1987), however, are critical of inspections. Because management are informed of the results, many programmers feel threatened. They become defensive, and hide their mistakes. How can this improve the discovery of errors, or make programming more enjoyable?

By contrast, Gilb (1988) is an enthusiastic proponent of inspections. He admits that there can be considerable resistance to them, and does quote some criticisms which have been directed at them – time-consuming, disruptive, dubious effectiveness and cost-effectiveness, bureaucratic, unpopular, resented, frustrating, etc. – but dismisses the criticisms without answering them. Presumably, he believes that the good results which have been achieved are sufficient answer. He claims that inspections motivate people to raise the quality of their work, but does not specify if this is due to increased enthusiasm, or to fear of their failings being publicly exposed – although he implies that the latter is the case: 'Inspections make poor practices publicly embarrassing'.

Inspections have similar advantages and disadvantages to structured walkthroughs. Ways to reduce the disadvantages of walkthroughs were discussed (section 10.7.4); similar methods can be used in the case of inspections. Gilb (1988), for example, de-

Table 10.15 Cost and productivity impact of inspections

Source	Effect
Gilb (1988)	consumes 15% of project time
Standard Chartered Bank:	30% of error repair cost
design and code inspections	(=14% reduction in development effort)
Gilb (1988); Larson (1975):	85% reduction in testing time
test design/planning inspections	(=22% reduction in development effort)
Fagan (1976):	
design and code inspections	25% saving in programmer cost
Worldwide (Gilb, 1988)	25–35% reduced development cost
Walston and Felix (1977):	1.5:1 (may include other factors)
design and code inspections	(=33% reduction in development effort)
Walston and Felix, 1977; Gilb (1988)	35% higher productivity than average of walkthroughs and inspections
Project Omega (major defects alone)	>5:1 return on investment
mainly specification inspections	(>43% overall saving)
ICI (Gilb, 1988)	10 times cheaper to maintain (a reduction of 90%)
Gilb (1988); Crossman (1979b)	10–30 times lower maintenance effort/cost (a reduction of 90–97%)
Average (approximate): development	30%
maintenance	>90%

scribed one variation on the concept, with less formality and greater emphasis on discussing solutions. This was devised and requested by the staff in one organization, and the management of the organization agreed to it because the staff were committed to making it work. Another disadvantage mentioned by Gilb is that the inspection process is dependent on the creation and use of less ambiguous design specification languages, but the same is surely true for walkthroughs as well. The increased productivity can enable organizations to pay higher salaries, which should help overcome any resistance – like the Assembler language programmer cited by Woodland (1977), who resisted attempts to persuade him to change to COBOL, until he moved to a higher-paid job. The effects of financial incentives are discussed in Chapters 9 and 11.

10.9 QUALITY IMPROVEMENT PROGRAM

Many ideas have already been given for improving quality, such as rewriting error-prone modules. The list of causes of low quality, and the discussion of QA methods, in themselves suggest what action needs to be taken. However, these should be brought together into a formal, structured, quality improvement program. Chapter 13 contains a formal productivity improvement program, and much of this is applicable to quality as well. Below are some guidelines that apply specifically to a quality improvement program.

Cho (1987) listed the following QC principles: set quality standards; make a plan to attain the quality standards; determine preventive methods to control the manufacturing process; and determine quality of conformance.

One life insurance company has embarked on a process designed to improve substantially the quality of the systems it produces, using a two-pronged attack: changing some fundamentally erroneous beliefs about the concept of quality management; and providing staff with the necessary knowledge, skills and tools to meet the required standards (Opperman, 1988).

Garnham (1988) believes that the main challenge in any quality program is getting people involved. Ways of achieving this include incorporating the staff's opinions in the standards manual, and publishing a QA newsletter, as done by British Rail (see below). He also quoted one consultant who believes that the real challenge in introducing a quality management program lies in persuading people that quality is more about attitudes than manuals. This consultant also stressed the importance of measurement (Chapter 13).

British Rail implemented the following plan. They created a set of standards which were universally agreed and adopted; they incorporated these into a manual; and after the manual had been in use for some time, they revised it to take into account reactions and opinions from their staff – for example, they made the rules more flexible, e.g. the review manager is now allowed to determine how he conducts the review, and meetings are only held if there is a specific reason (Garnham, 1988). People are happy to consult the manual because many of them had a say in its contents, and because experience has shown that the procedures work. A newsletter keeps people informed about QA matters. At the end of two-and-a-half years of quality effort, project (development?) costs had been reduced by between 26 and 40%, and time-scales by 16%.

Arthur (1983) and Sommerville (1989) also advocate standards, but warn that, once developed, they tend to be enshrined in a company standards handbook and difficult to change. They should not be viewed as unalterable commandments. Instead, they should be dynamic, changing with technology, methodology, and the needs of the organization. They should therefore be reviewed and modified periodically to reflect changing circumstances.

One bank developed a QA charter, and an extensive series of supportive standards and QC procedures, which are paramount in the development, delivery, and running of high-quality systems (The quest for zero defect software, *Computer Week*, 13 Feb. 1989, p. 21). A great deal of emphasis is placed on ensuring the involvement of all key players during development, to ensure that application systems meet required standards and are able to provide business solutions and a high level of customer service when they go live.

James Powell, director of information management at AT&T, admitted that it is difficult to get people to change, and ascribed their success to the senior manager's expectations of fault-free systems (The quest for zero defect software, *Computer Week*, 13 Feb. 1989, p. 21). He singled out the following tools and techniques which contribute to defect-free software: structured techniques throughout the analysis, design and programming stages; single-function modules; re-usability; JAD (joint application design); 4GLs; and measurement.

Jones (1986b) recommends a formal QA group with (at least?) one member for every 15 developers.

For operational systems, organizations should record defect statistics per module, and then do a formal code inspection on any module in which more than 10 defects per 1000 source statements were found in the last year or 18 months (Jones, 1986b). If the organization does not record defect statistics in such detail – and evidence was presented earlier that most do not record defects at all – then it should interview the maintenance programmers and get their subjective opinions instead. Similarly, during development, organizations can use the defect counts produced by static analysers, inspections, etc., or ask the designers and programmers which sections of the system are the most difficult, and then give those sections extra inspections and very thorough testing.

Jones (1986b) stated that, in terms of

balancing schedules, costs, and resources against quality, the most successful approach appears to be a combination of formal design inspections for the critical sections of a system; high-speed prototyping or modelling of its major outputs so users can see the results; informal reviews; and standard testing. He warned that any combination which omits design reviews and inspections will suffer from high tail-end costs 'when the undiscovered bugs start showing up during integration and testing'.

The QA function must have the power to prevent poor designs from being programmed, and poor products from being released into production (Arthur, 1983; Macro and Buxton, 1987).

Arthur (1983) warned that an organization which is strictly oriented towards finding fault, offends even the least egotistical programmers. Furthermore, the wholesale introduction of QA into an organization will cause resentment, as well as chaos and confusion, and will therefore be counter-productive. It must instead be introduced gently, and the benefits stressed, such as less overtime, easier maintenance, and higher productivity.

Various quantitative claims for the benefits of a quality improvement plan were quoted earlier: a saving on costs and time of between 15 and 40% (Garnham, 1988); a reduction in project costs of between 26 and 40%, and 16% in time-scales, in less than three years at British Rail (Garnham, 1988); a halving in the number of defects in production programs (Dunn and Ullman, 1982); and a reduction in the post-delivery defect cost (probably not including the effects of specification errors) from 1.48% of the project cost, to only 0.08%, in just three years at Hitachi (DeMarco, 1982).

10.10 SUMMARY AND CONCLUSIONS

Quality has many aspects, and overlaps with topics discussed elsewhere in this study.

QA is necessary throughout the software life-cycle, and high quality in each stage reduces the cost of subsequent stages. In particular, it reduces the large amount of time spent on maintenance, and the losses to the user organization caused by errors in production programs. However, high quality incurs a cost, which must be weighed against the benefits.

There are different ways of measuring quality, but they have been criticized, and should be used with caution.

Low quality has many causes, and there are various methods for ensuring high quality.

It is better to build high quality into the software rather than adding it on afterwards, e.g. it is better to avoid errors than to correct them. This can be done by using appropriate tools (such as 4GLs) and methods (such as modularization).

Two methods of QA – structured walkthroughs and inspections – were discussed in detail. Walkthroughs are an effective way to improve quality, but they are probably much less effective than often claimed, and their main benefit may even be the interchange of knowledge which results. There is doubt over their cost-effectiveness, particularly for development, and they are subject to psychological problems which may be severe. Suggestions were made to make them more cost-effective and to reduce the psychological problems.

Inspections have many similarities to walkthroughs. There seems to be more hard evidence in the literature of their effectiveness, so they appear to be superior, though this might equally just be because collection of statistics is an integral part of the inspection process. There also seems to be less criticism of them. This could mean they are superior, or at least that there is more *evidence* that they are beneficial, but it might just be because they are newer and are probably not as widely used, or perhaps people have just become accustomed to the different way of working.

Evidence was presented that some methods are more effective than others. However, each method has its advantages and disadvantages, and each type of error-removal activity is highly effective against some classes of errors, but much less effective against others (Boehm, 1981). No single method can therefore find all the errors, and in fact, all the methods miss a significant proportion of the errors – as is vividly illustrated by the table in Jones (1986b) which lists the efficiencies of the different methods. For maximum effectiveness, therefore, a combination of methods must be used.

Organizations should implement a formal quality improvement program. Training, measurement, staff involvement, and flexible standards are some of the requirements for such a program.

Poor management has been cited as the major cause of projects failing, or running over budget or time (Weinberg, 1971). Projects may be abandoned, resulting in wasted effort, or their completion may be rushed, resulting in low quality. Either way, productivity is affected, and managerial aspects are therefore relevant to any discussion of software engineering productivity.

Aron (1974) gives an example to illustrate the difference between technical and managerial aspects:

- *designing* a bridge is technical;
- *building* a bridge is managerial.

Management can be subdivided into two related topics: personnel management and project management. Both topics will be considered here.

The topics already discussed are related to management, either directly or indirectly.

- Management chooses the structure of the DP department.
- In small organizations, DP managers interface with the users, and do some of the programming themselves.
- Managers have the final say in the choice of hardware, software, and methods.
- Managers should participate in requirements analysis 'so that surprises may be avoided', e.g. to ensure that the system being developed does not conflict with management's plans for the future.
- Cost-estimation methods provide managers with the information they need to set schedules and determine costs.
- QA is a management responsibility.
- Managers decide how much effort should be devoted to security, reliability, and other aspects of QA.
- Managers are reported to be happy with maintenance productivity.
- Managers decide how much money should be allocated to training.
- It is management which decides whether or not to take on and train raw recruits.
- Managers interview job applicants.
- It is a management responsibility to keep staff satisfied.
- It is a management responsibility to get rid of misfits.

Management is one of the topics discussed in this study which has a much wider application than just DP. It is a large topic in its own right, so the following discussion concentrates on aspects that are of greatest relevance to software productivity. There are numerous books on management, including ones specifically about DP management (Metzger, 1981; Gilb, 1988; Johnson, 1980b; Couger and Zawacki, 1980; Gunther, 1978; Simpson, 1987; Singer, 1982; Gildersleeve, 1974a).

11.1 PERSONNEL MANAGEMENT

11.1.1 MANAGEMENT STYLE

It is generally believed that DP managers are poor people managers and have poor communication skills (Couger and Zawacki, 1980; Gray, 1980a; Singer, 1982). This can be attributed to both their lack of training in these fields, and the fact that they are usually chosen from the ranks of DP staff, who have low social needs.

Insensitive treatment of staff can increase staff turnover, or can lead to staff 'working to rule' – DP staff are 'notoriously bad at being dictated to' (Mann, 1984; Weinberg, 1971). Conversely, sensitive treatment leads to more contented (and therefore, hopefully, more productive) staff, and should also lead to problems being detected earlier, because of a freer and more open atmosphere. For example, they might otherwise be reluctant to admit that they are behind schedule, or that they are having personal problems which are affecting their work. A good manager should therefore be demanding enough to motivate his staff, but sympathetic enough not to alienate and discourage them (Shneiderman, 1980). He must show his appreciation when they do well, but be stern when they falter.

Managers spend a major portion of their time – about 40% – interacting with other people (Westcott *et al.*, 1981; Martin, 1982b; Barclays talks business sense, *Computing S.A.*, 2 Sept. 1983, p. 8), and much of this time is spent trying to influence and lead them. Their leadership style may be either (Hersey and Blanchard, 1976):

- *employee-centered*, i.e. there is an interpersonal relationship between the manager and the subordinate; or
- *job-centered*, i.e. the manager is concerned only with the way the job is done.

McGregor (1960) offers an alternative classification:

- *authoritarian* (theory X); or
- *participative* (theory Y).

Theory X is the traditional and more common style. It assumes that people dislike work, and will avoid it if they can. They must therefore be forced to work, and be threatened with punishment if they fail to work hard enough. It also assumes that the average person prefers to be directed, wishes to avoid responsibility, has relatively little ambition, and wants security – 'the mediocrity of the masses'. Heller (1981) stated that people, by and large, do what they are told: 'discipline is part of the human condition (or conditioning)'. Managers can thus more or less rely on the relative docility of the workers, on their tendency to obey.

Theory Y holds the opposite view, namely that 'man is a wanting animal' – as soon as one of his needs is satisfied, another appears in its place. People thus need to stay active, and work is as natural as play (Bain, 1982). Threat of punishment is therefore not the only way to get people to work. Furthermore, people can learn to accept and even seek responsibility. They can thus grow and develop. This has therefore – most appropriately – been termed the 'agricultural' approach (Townsend, 1984). If they are lazy and uncooperative, for example, then this is the fault of management.

McGregor acknowledges that there is a 'considerable body of evidence' to support theory X, but states that other, readily observable evidence, is not consistent with this view of human nature. Theory X is therefore only partially adequate. He also acknowledges that the assumptions of theory Y had not been finally validated, and they would 'undoubtedly' be refined, elaborated, and modified in the light of further research, but he thought it unlikely that they would be completely contradicted. According to Bain (1982), theory Y managers are consistently able to generate wholehearted support and best effort from employees – they inspire employees to high levels of performance – while theory X managers are less successful – they tend to alienate employees, and are continuously struggling with them in an attempt to achieve results. Similarly, Townsend (1984) attributes his success at Avis Rent-a-Car to theory Y behavior. By contrast, Heller (1981) stated that X management can generate a 'high voltage' which 'drives powerfully' though the organization. He added that there was no evidence that the Y organization is more successful than the X, but that this is currently irrelevant as the X organization has lost the battle for men's minds: 'would anybody even try to set up an X company today? He couldn't get good enough people to work in a Captain Bligh atmosphere, and he could rely on getting terrible publicity'. Heller adds that the only question which counts is: does the style stop people from achieving their potential? He quotes one successful organization, Rank-Xerox in Britain, which was a mixture of X and Y. He concluded that no management style works universally, and suspects that at some time, somewhere, excellent results have been obtained with every conceivable form of organization.

While, on the whole, people need to stay active, they presumably prefer play to work. Some tasks they will enjoy and will do willingly; other tasks they will not enjoy, and will need some nudging: 'where people lack commitment to objectives, external control and authority (theory X) are still necessary' (McGregor, 1960). The secret is therefore for the employee to find a job that contains a high proportion of tasks that he enjoys doing. This theory was confirmed by Couger and Colter (1983), who described ten organizations that have high productivity because they have matched the programmers' needs to jobs.

Theory X and Y styles clash, so managers surround themselves with other managers who share their style. When a new manager of a different style enters an organization, he usually replaces managers of the prevailing style as quickly as he can (Gunther, 1978).

However, the manager's style should not be fixed, but rather he should constantly adjust it according to the situation, and specifically according to the degree of maturity of the subordinate (Hersey and Blanchard, 1976). A subordinate may be 'mature' – responsible, motivated and competent – on some tasks, e.g. designing a program, but 'immature' on others, e.g. he may try to skimp on documentation. Depending on the circumstances therefore, the manager will either:

- *tell* a subordinate what to do and how to do it;
- *sell* a decision which has already been made;
- allow the subordinate to *participate* in making the decision; or
- *delegate* the making of the decision to the subordinate.

Managers should gradually reduce the amount of direction they give their subordinates, giving them increasingly more responsibility and enabling them to grow in maturity. Occasionally though, temporary additional direction is required, e.g. when the subordinate is doing a new and unfamiliar job, such as after a promotion.

Johnson (1980b), however, appears to be skeptical about the wisdom of managers changing their style: 'Nothing is more ludicrous than a pussycat trying to behave like a panzer tank commander, or a malicious, ill-tempered person trying to be Mr Nice-Guy – so be yourself, you won't fool anybody for long anyway' (Kirkley, 1978). Johnson also appears to be skeptical about some of the other concepts discussed in this chapter, namely the Hawthorne effect, and the ideas of Maslow (1970), Herzberg *et al.* (1959), McGregor (1960), and Drucker (1954) – 'folklore straight out of the fifties', 'useless information' – though he may have been thinking of the difficulty in persuading senior management to implement the ideas rather than the intrinsic merits thereof.

Grace Hopper believes that managers should delegate more responsibility, because 'the more you delegate, the more freedom you have to do other things' (Leopold, 1986). Joseph Brophy, head of MIS at Travelers Insurance Company, stated that 'The key is to know how to listen, and to surround yourself with good people' (Carlyle, 1987a). He believes that the most important factor for success is 'a finely developed sense of intuition'. Intuition enables people to know where to get information, whom to trust, and in what way to share. This is consistent with the conclusion by Schach (1988) and Dreyfus and Dreyfus (1986) that experts react instinctively. They are not aware of their skills, and do not make use of rules. Other opinions to this effect were quoted in Chapter 10.

Traditionally (this will not apply in democratic teams), the leader of the team sets, allocates, and co-ordinates the work (Weinberg, 1971). He is the 'father figure' – though the role need not necessarily be filled by a male – and his role is characterized by 'hardness'. His role is complemented by that of the 'team-mother' – not necessarily female – who irons out conflicts and whose role is characterized by 'softness'. The role of team-mother is also a leadership role, so teams having a team-mother have dual leadership, with the team-mother second-in-command. However, because of the different nature of the two roles, and the different personalities of the people filling them, it may be unwise to promote the team-mother to leadership of the team.

Setting standards is part of a manager's job, but example is also an effective method of ensuring that good practices are followed: 'leaders train their successors in their own image' (Thorpe, 1976; Weinberg, 1971).

Democratic and participative methods are claimed to give high productivity. For example, democratic and participative principles are incorporated in the matrix organization (Chapter 3) and in structured walkthroughs (Chapter 10), both of which are claimed to improve productivity, though the evidence is mixed. Bain (1982) goes further, and claims that participative management has the highest productivity potential of any management style, both short- and long-term.

A study by Coch and French (1948), of a change to the manufacturing procedures in a pyjama factory, showed that productivity improvements were directly related to the degree of worker participation in the change.

Furthermore, disruption and turnover decreased with increased participation.

McGregor (1960) claims that participation has been used with considerable success by some people, but warns that it is not a magic formula that will eliminate conflict and disagreement, and come close to solving all of management's problems. The degree of participation can vary, ranging from very little to very much. The amount which is appropriate in any given situation depends on a variety of factors, such as the attitudes and past experience of the subordinates, and the manager's skill. For example, if the subordinates are unaccustomed to having any influence on decisions affecting them, then they should not be presented with a major issue, or be given complete freedom of choice, on the first occasion. One of the major goals of participation is to encourage the growth of subordinates and their ability to accept responsibility, so the degree of participation should be gradually increased. Some managers trick their subordinates into coming up with the answer which they themselves had in mind, but do it so skillfully that their subordinates believe it was their own idea. The managers may call this participation, but it is actually manipulation. Some managers fear that participation will reduce their power and weaken their control. However, according to McGregor, there are many instances of the successful use of participation which have not weakened management's ability to manage. Nevertheless, he believes that such fear can become a self-fulfilling prophecy.

11.1.2   PERSONNEL APPRAISALS

It is part of a manager's job to evaluate his staff. This is normally achieved by means of a staff appraisal system – a formal, systematic method of staff assessment and development, which typically consists of an annual interview between the manager and each member of his staff, individually. Preparation (by both manager and subordinate) is required for the interview, and decisions made at the interview must be followed up afterwards. Records are kept. These are used the following year, and they also help new managers take over more quickly. Particulars of the appraisal scheme should be documented, and copies given to new employees. Staff see their assessments, and can discuss and challenge them. The open, participative nature of this process makes it much better than the management grapevine of whispered innuendo and unsubstantiated criticism (Pratt, 1985).

The manager's own assessment may be supplemented by peer reviews – 'global predictions of performance by peers', i.e. members of a group evaluate each other (Shneiderman, 1980). (Peer reviews must not be confused with peer code reviews, in which individual *products* are examined by peers; these were discussed earlier, under structured walkthroughs in Chapter 10.) Shneiderman quotes (non-DP) studies which show that peer evaluations are more reliable predictors of performance than evaluations by supervisors, possibly because of the closer daily contact of peers, and because people show their best side to their supervisors.

Appraisals should not, however, be limited to this formal, once-a-year process: managers should continue to assess and develop their staff throughout the year. Part of this advice may be redundant; Bain (1982) believes that, whether consciously or subconsciously, regular day to day appraisals are being made in every manager's mind. However, it is not sufficient for the manager to merely frequently *assess* his staff: he must also frequently *comment* to them on their performance. High-performance organizations are characterized by managers who provide their subordinates with constant verbal feedback relating to their performance, based on mutually agreed goals. Such feedback not only improves productivity, but also minimizes security stress, even when the comments are unfavorable. The unknown – in this case, the manager's unspoken thoughts and hidden feelings – generates more security stress than does unfavorable verbal feedback.

A manager's success should be measured by how well he encourages growth, and how fairly he rewards hard work and deals with incompetence. A good manager will not selfishly hide a key employee, but will promote him, even if this means running the risk of losing him to another group, or promoting him to his own managerial level (Metzger, 1981).

Objectives

A number of reasons can be given for having performance appraisals: reviewing the employees' progress over the past year, reviewing their salaries, evaluating their potential, assessing their development needs, planning of training, setting objectives, manpower planning, and motivation of staff. Appraisals provide an opportunity to discuss the work, and how the employees feel about it. For example, the manager's view of staff morale may differ widely from reality. Appraisals therefore provide communication and feedback, which are important (Millman, 1982). Appraisals also help validate the recruitment practices, i.e. confirm that the right people are being selected.

The appraisal process is therefore a rich source of knowledge and information about a whole range of work-related matters, and its ultimate objective is to help each person find a fulfilling job, improve their performance, and thus make the most of scarce resources (Metzger, 1981; Pratt, 1985). People welcome the opportunity to discuss the work, their performance, their problems, and their aspirations, with their manager – they 'attach great importance to this one chance each year to sit down and talk things over on a one-to-one basis' (Pratt, 1985). (Singer (1982) recommends that one-to-one talks be held monthly or even weekly, though without the performance appraisal aspect.) Performance appraisal must be an integral part of any plan designed to improve productivity (Bain, 1982).

Preparation

The appraisers need proper training – in fact, lack of training was the most common problem identified in a survey by Pratt (1985). In addition, suitable documents, describing the purposes of the appraisal interview, and containing a checklist of the topics to be discussed and questions to be answered, should be provided as a refresher to both manager and subordinate, as appraisals are normally only done once a year. As is generally the case with meetings, if staff are to participate constructively in an appraisal interview, they need time to think about things beforehand. Adequate advance notice must therefore be given, yet a survey by Pratt showed that, in many cases, staff receive less than one day's notice.

The manager must review the employee's work over the whole of the period. This should be done in conjunction with the employee's detailed job description, and the objectives set the previous year. If the organization measures employee productivity, then the manager should refer to this data (Parikh, 1984). A broader view of the employee's performance is obtained if other people who have worked with him, including peers and even subordinates, also assess him (Pratt, 1985) – they would normally provide the manager with their assessments beforehand, rather than participate personally in the interview. The manager must prepare points to discuss. Some of the specific questions he can ask himself are: How can I assist the employee? What action can I recommend? What does he like doing? What are the reasons for his short-comings? Have I let him down? What is his assessment of me? The

manager must therefore be prepared for criticism.

The employee may be required to appraise himself beforehand. This helps focus his mind on topics that should be discussed. There is of course the danger that he will overrate himself. However, according to Pratt (1985), recent research has shown that most people are able to make a realistic assessment of their performance, though they may not necessarily be *willing* to do so. If he wishes, the employee can give his self-assessment to his manager, to help him in his preparation, though there is the danger that a lax manager will just use this as the basis for his own assessment (Singer, 1982). The manager should therefore complete his assessment before being given the employee's self-assessment. Even if the employee does not formally appraise himself, he should nevertheless review his own performance. He should make a list of the assignments he completed during the evaluation period (Parikh, 1984). He should list also the training courses he completed, the professional books he read, and the conferences or seminars he attended. He should note in particular his accomplishments, and any examples of innovation or suggestions for improvements to his environment. If the organization does not measure employee productivity, then he should collect his own productivity data. He should write down his own goals. He should prepare details of work that he did not enjoy, skills not being utilized, difficulties he had in carrying out his work, and any help or training he might need. By highlighting problems which are not his fault, he can provide information about the effect and weaknesses of management policies and working methods. However, he must also be prepared to face up to his own weaknesses. He should decide whether, in order to achieve his goals, he wants to build on his strengths or correct his weaknesses.

The interview

Most interviews last between 15 minutes and an hour (Pratt, 1985). Some last less than 15 minutes, but it is difficult to see how a person's work, problems, and development, can be adequately covered in such a short time.

The manager should be as objective as possible. He should remember that it is the employee's *work* that is being evaluated, not the employee himself (Parikh, 1984). He should therefore try not to be swayed by personal dislike, or a recent argument. The interviewing techniques commonly taught to systems analysts are of use during the appraisal interview (Shone, 1975). Interviewing techniques include the methods discussed under structured walkthroughs, such as asking questions instead of criticizing, so that the person can discover his own mistakes. Criticism should be constructive. How can the weaknesses be corrected? What can be done so that the mistakes will not be repeated? How can the performance be improved?

The interview provides an opportunity to discuss the work. The employee's successes and failures should be identified – not in isolation, as people do not work in isolation, but in the light of organizational pressures, problems, and constraints. Appraisal and criticism should therefore be a two-way process. Instead of the manager doing all the appraising and criticizing, the employee should also voice any criticism of the organization, including his manager (Pratt, 1985). The employee should therefore be encouraged to speak out. He should be pleasant and diplomatic, but if he thinks he is right, he should be forceful and persistent, and should not allow himself to be intimidated (Parikh, 1984). Disagreements should be discussed, and agreement reached. The participants must therefore be prepared to modify their views, not for the sake of reaching agreement, but where a change is necessitated by the explanations advanced.

The manager should discuss his subordinate's successes as well as his failures (Aron, 1974). When the manager is satisfied, he must *say* so, as people need praise (Metzger, 1981). According to Bain (1982), repeated surveys of many organizations have shown that 'full appreciation for work done' is the most important factor in employee job satisfaction. The manager should therefore focus on the employee's strengths and accomplishments, rather than his weaknesses and failures. After all, everyone who works makes mistakes, especially if he tries new techniques. This turns a potentially unpleasant experience into a positive one. Appraisals can become motivators rather than threats.

The employee should state his ambitions, though these should be tempered with realism. What does he really want to do? Does he feel a sense of accomplishment? He can then be put in touch with the relevant people – typically senior managers – who can assess his aspirations in a practical and realistic manner. Requests for training must also be realistic. By the same token, the manager must not make rash promises.

Problem areas

A number of problems or potential problems may be identified, some of which have already been mentioned. For example, it is not sufficient to discuss just the job *content*: the *context* must also be discussed. Employees do not work in isolation, and their performance is affected by external, organizational factors, such as the attitudes of the work group, the policies of the organization, the prevailing management style, frequent interruptions, inadequate testing time, and repeated changes to the program specifications (Pratt, 1985; Singer, 1982).

Other problems are discussed below:

amount of effort, accuracy of assessement, sensitive issues, continuity and timeliness.

Amount of effort

The appraisal process is time-consuming, and requires careful planning, commitment, and constant attention, otherwise the benefits will 'evaporate in the heat of work pressures and new developments' (Pratt, 1985).

If all the appraisals are concentrated within a short period, say one month, then this imposes a heavy workload. There is therefore a temptation to spread them over the entire year, e.g. appraise each employee on the anniversary of his joining the organization. However, this should be resisted, as it makes it more difficult to compare staff consistently (Johnson, 1980b).

Accuracy of assessments

Because of the difficulty in measuring programmer productivity, it is difficult to evaluate programmers properly (Singer, 1982), and it may be even more difficult to evaluate other categories of software engineers. The manager must therefore be knowledgeable about the jobs assigned, and understand their difficulty (Johnson, 1980b). He must be able to detect and differentiate between those who *claim* they are achievers and the *real* achievers, i.e. between people who constantly try to impress others with their knowledge and success, and who may even take credit for work done by others, and those who are unable to present a professional image, but who actually get the job done. According to Singer, there have been many instances in which supervisors misread an employee's job performance, did not understand his work environment, or indirectly *caused* poor job performance by their own mismanagement. Singer adds that it is difficult to rectify such situations without destroying the supervisor's credibility. He recommends that all poor reviews be dis-

cussed between the supervisor and his manager; higher managers should question all poor reviews; and supervisors who seldom give good reviews should be carefully reviewed themselves.

The factors evaluated should be relevant to the job, and should not include vague generalities or subjective personality criteria such as 'versatility', 'perseverance', 'co-operation' and 'resourcefulness'. Instead, the evaluation should be restricted to traits which are capable of assessment, and then only where corrective action can be taken (Pratt, 1985).

Boehm (1981) recommends that managers should not use detailed project planning and control figures as a performance-appraisal device. He describes this as 'personnel management by the numbers', and warns that it can lead to people 'gaming' the system in ways 'which de-emphasize team co-operation and emphasize a minimal interpretation of project responsibilities'. Hence the recommendation that trainees' test scores should not be seen by their managers (Chapter 9), and the warning that, where LOC is used as the unit of productivity measurement, programmers might 'pad' their programs with additional, non-essential lines, in order to appear more productive (Chapter 2). Boehm, however, does approve the use of such numbers as part of an overall, primarily subjective, performance appraisal method, i.e. they can be used as a rough guide, and provided they are used in conjunction with other factors.

The manager's ratings might be biased, and this can take a number of forms. He may dislike certain members of staff, or be friends with others. Some managers rate all their staff highly, while others are universally harsh. Sometimes such ratings are justified, e.g. perhaps all his staff *are* above average. Other managers avoid allocating high or low ratings, and instead rate everyone as average – this is known as 'central tendency'. They may do so because they are indecisive, because it is the easy way out, or because they are being diplomatic and just want a quiet life. Most of these problems can be counteracted by supplying the managers with a distribution chart showing the proportion of the organization's staff graded at each level in the previous appraisal, e.g. 2% of the total staff may have been rated outstanding, 10% excellent, and so on, down to say 3% unacceptable (Pratt, 1985). This profile shows the manager how many of his staff should probably be placed in each category.

Sensitive issues

Some people find it embarrassing to point out someone else's faults or discuss their personality traits, and will avoid doing so until forced to (Pratt, 1985; Metzger, 1981). If handled badly, it demotivates. The interview may also provoke a clash of personalities, which would otherwise not have occurred.

The information is confidential. Performance ratings must therefore not be shown on the front page of the form. Also, if the information is stored on a computer, then care must be taken not to violate any legal requirements for personal data. However, if the information is used for staff development rather than for assessing comparative performance, then computerization may be unnecessary (Pratt, 1985).

If the employee's salary increase is announced at the interview, he will be preoccupied with this, and so will not be fully attentive to the other, important topics being discussed. However, announcing a predetermined increase is at variance with the open, participative nature of appraisals. The formal appraisal process should form part of the procedure to determine any increase, so the amount can only be announced some time after the interview.

The issue of promotion may be difficult. It can be demotivating to tell someone that he is not suitable for promotion. Apparently, people can accept criticism for poor performance much better than being told they lack poten-

tial (Pratt, 1985). However, poor performance in his present job does not necessarily mean that the employee is unsuitable for promotion – it may instead merely indicate that the job does not provide a challenge, or utilize his skills. Conversely, good performance does not necessarily mean that he is suitable for promotion. The qualities required in the senior position may be different from those required in the current position, making performance in the current job an unreliable indicator. The decision should therefore be based on how well he meets the requirements for the senior position, though that may be difficult to determine. Johnson (1980b) describes a procedure, using a variation of the screening matrix (Chapter 8), for selecting the best candidate for promotion; he also lists some criteria for promoting someone to a first-level manager, e.g. he should have good communication ability, be respected by his peers, and be able to plan, organize and direct. Perhaps the best way to inform someone that he is not suitable for promotion, is to tell him – truthfully – that he is ideally suited to his present duties, so promotion would be inappropriate, and the organization cannot afford to lose his present services.

The opposite situation can also occur. Some people *are* suitable for promotion, and the organization *wants* to promote them, but they do not want to be promoted. McGregor (1960) quotes a district manager who was ideally qualified for promotion to a policy-level position at headquarters, but who did not want the job because he enjoyed the direct contact with field staff which his current job afforded, and the life-style in a small city. The organization pressured him into accepting the promotion, but he was thoroughly unhappy in his new position.

Continuity

There may be a lack of continuity from one appraisal to the next, e.g. the employee may have a different manager in successive years, or there may be changes in the appraisal scheme from one year to the next.

Timeliness

When people go off course, their manager must put them back on course, and must not postpone doing so (Metzger, 1981). He must therefore not wait for the next performance appraisal. People do learn and change as a result of feedback, but the most effective feedback occurs immediately after the behavior (McGregor, 1960). People can learn a great deal from a mistake provided it is analysed while all the evidence is immediately at hand. It is unlikely that they would learn much from an experience if it is only analysed several months later at the annual appraisal.

Follow up

The decisions made at the interview need to be implemented. A whole chain of events may be necessary – for example, if the employee asks for more training, the manager must make a note of the request then forward it to the training manager, who must confirm that appropriate courses as well as the necessary funds are available, and so on – and the chain can break down. To avoid this happening, the manager must make diary entries to remind him to check on progress and to keep the staff informed. Spot checks by management should also be carried out. However, in the final analysis, it is the employee himself who stands to gain the most, so he must bear the ultimate responsibility for ensuring that his requirements are not forgotten or ignored (Pratt, 1985).

Conclusion

There can be problems with performance appraisals, but they can also provide recognition and encouragement, and so have the power to motivate staff. In addition, they provide communication and feedback, bring organizational problems to light, and help to develop staff and raise their productivity.

11.1.3   MOTIVATION

It is part of a manager's job to motivate his staff (Drucker, 1954). Highly motivated people can accomplish remarkable tasks, so the manager who can improve morale and motivation can propel his staff to complete projects on time (Shneiderman, 1980). No manager can ask for more than the enthusiasm of a dedicated staff. As Jones (1986b) put it, 'There is no question that experienced, skilled personnel are perhaps the most valuable assets that enterprises have. If they are well treated and properly rewarded, then they tend to do their best for the enterprise'. Couger and Zawacki (1980) found that DP professionals have a higher motivation potential than most other categories of staff. There is, however, no good rating scale on which to evaluate motivation level.

The studies at the Hawthorne Works of the Western Electric Company in the 1920s showed that motivation increases productivity (Mayo, 1945). The International Data Corporation (1981) survey of large-system productivity concluded that morale ranked among the most significant factors in affecting productivity. According to Gellerman (1963), most productivity studies have found that motivation has a stronger influence on productivity than any other factor.

Magnitude of effect

Some authorities claim that the effect of motivation on productivity could be as high as a factor of ten (Beware of the future, *Systems Stelsels*, Jan. 1979, p. 11), but the following points argue against these claims.

- The claims of a ten times improvement were not supported by any evidence.
- They were isolated claims: most of the literature did not give any figure at all. For

example, even though the studies at the Hawthorne Works were described in many more recent references (Weinberg, 1971; Starr, 1972; Albers, 1965; Shneiderman, 1980; Conte *et al.*, 1986; Boehm, 1981), not one of them gave the *magnitude* of the increase in productivity. The literature also implied that the increase was temporary: 'people respond positively to any form of unusual attention, but the response never lasts' (Heller, 1981). In fact, the overall increase was around 30%, and the increases were maintained during the study's five-year duration (Mayo, 1945).

- Those figures contained in the literature which were supported by evidence were much lower (Table 11.1).
- Weinberg (1971) claims the opposite, namely that programmers are *over*-motivated – so much so that additional pressure can *lower* productivity rather than raise it. This view is consistent with the finding of Wynne and Dickson (1976) that poorer performance was connected with a relatively high need-achievement. There is thus an *optimum* level of motivation (Massimo, 1982).
- A number of DP staff I have known lacked motivation – the ones who spend much time talking, who read magazines surreptitiously on their laps, who do crossword puzzles hidden under their program listings, and even managers who are fond of reading newspapers during office hours – but most staff work hard. Boehm (1981) stated that programmers have a very high achievement motivation – they 'will generally work very hard to give you what you asked for'. He was thinking of the Weinberg and Schulman (1974) experiment, in which nearly every team performed best on the goal it was set (Chapter 2). Boehm also appears to argue that some short-sighted, heavy-handed managers exploit this, by setting unrealistically short deadlines, knowing that their staff will work extra hard to meet the objectives. However, they will not be able to maintain the pace for long, and will resent such unfair treatment.

Furthermore, Weinberg (1971) pointed out that sometimes when staff *appear* to be socializing, they are in fact *working*. Access control and telephone management systems limit the amount of time spent socializing, but staff are likely to resent such restrictions and react negatively to them, and people must have a break 'to recharge their batteries' (Chapter 4).

How big an increase in productivity can higher motivation therefore produce? Couger and Zawacki (1980) quote several studies.

- Weed (1971) reports a 4:1 productivity increase among navigation equipment assemblers at Texas Instruments, together with a reduction in absenteeism, turnover, complaints, and trips to the medical centre, resulting from a work redesign program in which they were divided into small groups, and asked to help management set production goals. Part of these improvements can be attributed to higher motivation. Texas Instruments also implemented a job enrichment program for janitors. Better equipment, selection and training of staff, increased communication and feedback, and improved wages and fringe benefits, resulted in a 20% increase in cleanliness ratings, a 40% decrease in number of staff (equivalent to a (100/(100 − 40) =) 67% (or nearly 1.7:1) increase in productivity), and a 91% decrease in quarterly turnover. Once again, part of the improvements can be attributed to higher motivation.
- A job enrichment program for keypunch operators at Travelers Insurance Co. – they were given responsibility for their own accounts, and interfaced directly with their clients – produced a 40% increase in productivity, a 40% reduction in the number of staff, a 35% reduction in the error rate, a 17% improvement in job satisfaction, and a 24% reduction in absenteeism (Hackman *et al.*, 1975).
- Of the workers in a Gallup survey of the

US work force, 40% stated that they could increase productivity by as much as 30%, and 60% stated that they could increase productivity by as much as 20%.

Drucker (1954) describes a work redesign program for the handling of customer letters at a mail-order plant. Nearly all customers letters are answered by printed form letters. However, whereas previously each clerk handled only one type of motion – complaint, enquiry, installment credit, etc. – subsequently, each clerk handled the entire range of 39 motions. Even though the work was just as predetermined and almost as repetitive as before, productivity nevertheless rose by almost 30%, and turnover dropped by two-thirds.

Short (1977) describes how the average production of keypunch operators at a country-wide service bureau rose from under 850 000 key depressions a month, to more than 1300 000, an improvement of 1.5:1, after the introduction of piece-work. However, this increase apparently includes the effect of the 'natural weeding-out process' which resulted: ineffective people dropped out, and quality staff were attracted to the organization. In other words, the output of individual operators may not have increased very much, and most of the improvement may have been due to higher quality staff rather than higher motivation. Contrary to

what might have been expected from the higher speed, the error rate did not increase – in fact, it apparently *dropped* significantly, but this was due to making full use of the power and self-checking features of the key-to-disk equipment. Another benefit from the introduction of piece-work was that absenteeism dropped from 25% in the worst areas, to under 5%.

At least half the 6000 analysts and programmers studied by Couger and Colter (1983) were bored with their work – they found their tasks unchallenging and boring. The less routine maintenance work they did, the more programmers were motivated. Computer staff working on projects that motivated them increased their productivity by up to 40%.

McGregor (1960) stated that a good individual incentive plan can increase productivity by perhaps 15%.

A summary of these findings and other studies are given in Table 11.1.

Jones's figures are for a high-morale environment compared to a low-morale environment. He assumes that the best analysts and programmers in organizations with low morale and low salaries for technical staff have either moved into management or have left. The project teams are therefore staffed by a majority of new employees, with

Table 11.1 Effect of motivation on productivity

Source	Effect*
Texas Instruments (Weed, 1971)	4:1 equipment assemblers
Boehm (1981)	2:1 software development
Texas Instruments (Weed, 1971)	1.7:1 janitors
Short (1977)	1.5:1 keypunch operators
Travelers Insurance Co. (Hackman *et al.*, 1975)	1.4:1 keypunch operators
Couger and Colter (1983)	up to 1.4:1 programmers, analysts
Drucker (1954)	1.3:1 unskilled clerks
Jones (1986b)	1.3:1 software development
Gallup (Couger and Zawacki, 1980)	up to 1.3:1 workers in general
Jones (1986b)	1.2:1 software maintenance
McGregor (1960)	1.15:1 individual incentives

*May include other factors

a small number of long-term but average analysts and programmers. His figures therefore include the effect of low ability and experience, but are nevertheless amongst the lowest tabulated, which implies that, in his opinion, motivation has very little *direct* effect on productivity.

The tabulated values indicate that improved motivation can increase productivity by perhaps 30%. It is probable however, that some of this increase – perhaps as much as half – can be attributed to lower turnover and absenteeism, so it may be more accurate to describe it as an *apparent* increase in productivity, or as an increase in *output*.

Motivation of maintenance personnel might be more difficult, given the unpopularity of maintenance work (Chapter 8). This was confirmed by Couger and Colter (1985). According to them, maintenance has only 50–66% of the motivating potential of other programming work. By contrast, nearly 40% of the respondents in the Lientz *et al.* (1978) survey of 69 organizations stated that motivation of maintenance personnel was not a problem, and only 10% believed it to be more than a minor problem. The Jones (1986b) figures in Table 11.1 can be interpreted either way. They could imply that maintenance personnel are more highly motivated than development personnel, so there is less scope for improvement, but they could also mean that it is not possible to motivate maintenance personnel to the same high level as development personnel. Quantitatively, his figures indicate that maintenance has only (20%/30% =) 67% of the motivating potential of development, which is in good agreement with the Couger and Colter (1985) range.

Some words of caution are necessary. Firstly, motivation by itself is not enough; aptitude and knowledge must accompany it (Hoard, 1981). Secondly, although the objective of this study is to determine how to improve productivity, an over-concern with productivity can take the fun out of programming, e.g. by eliminating both technical

challenges and stimulating research (Boehm, 1981).

This can adversely affect motivation, and therefore be counter-productive from a productivity point of view, especially in the long term. Both extremes should therefore be avoided, and a balance found, e.g. research can be included in a project, but in moderation and not on the critical path (see PERT charts, section 11.2.1). If a project depends on the development of new techniques, then there is the danger of it being seriously delayed.

Factors that motivate people

Insight into factors that motivate people is provided by Maslow's hierarchy of needs (Chapter 9). In descending order of importance, the needs are physiological, safety, social, esteem, and self-fulfilment. For example, people who are starving – a physiological need – will not be concerned about improving their computer skills – a self-fulfilment need. Furthermore, once a need has been met, it ceases to provide motivation.

Further insight is provided by Herzberg *et al.* (1959), who draw a distinction between motivating factors, which *stimulate* performance, and 'hygiene' factors, which *prevent loss* of performance. Dissatisfaction and satisfaction are not the endpoints of a continuous line, but are instead two separate scales. Without certain things (work conditions, job security, pay, etc.), workers will be dissatisfied; but if only these 'maintenance' needs are met, the workers will *not* be satisfied – they will only be *not dissatisfied* (Couger and Zawacki, 1980). For example, when employees perceive their pay to be inequitable, they are *very* unhappy; but when they perceive it as equitable, they are only *slightly* happy. To be satisfied or happy, workers need jobs that have motivational characteristics or satisfiers (such as recognition, advancement, and the work itself).

These are general considerations. There

have been studies specifically of DP staff. In a survey by Weinberg (1971) at one large shop, the most important factors that motivated programmers were found to be a salary increase and/or bonus; personal involvement in planning of their tasks; promotion (because of the extra money); and more time to give their work a personal touch of quality. The least important were assistance in documentation, copying, etc.; placement in a prestige position; relaxation of target dates; tightening of target dates; and lessening the scope of their work. Relaxation of target dates may only have been given a low rating because the deadline of the project the respondents were working on was some distance in the future. This highlights a general danger of surveys: caution must be observed when trying to generalize from them. A survey by Couger and Zawacki (1980) found that DP people are more highly motivated by growth needs than by social needs. Fitz-Enz (1978) also found this – his survey showed that the most important motivational factors for programmer analysts were achievement, possibility for growth, the work itself, personal life, technical supervision, advancement, and interpersonal relations with peers; while the least important were job security, company policy and administration, working conditions, and status. Fitz-Enz also showed that programmers and analysts are more strongly motivated than their supervisors by opportunities for technical supervision, by peer relations, and by personal life; and are less strongly motivated by recognition, responsibility, and status.

In view of their high growth needs, it is important that programmers' creative instincts should not be dulled as a means of ensuring uniform and understandable programs (Boehm, 1981). This does not, however, mean that unintelligible programs – which can result from creative individualism – should be encouraged. Fortunately, we are not necessarily in an either–or situation. According to Lucas (1985), for example, it takes *more* skill and planning to write GOTO-less code (Chapter 8).

The Fitz-Enz survey, and possibly the Couger and Zawacki survey as well, indicates that pay is not one of the prime motivators of programmers and analysts. This is not surprising, as software engineering is a highly-paid occupation (Weinberg, 1971; What are you worth in '88, *Datamation*, 1 Oct. 1988, pp. 53–66), i.e. this need has already been met, and therefore, in accordance with Maslow's 'hierarchy of needs', ceases to provide motivation. Conversely, the high rating for 'personal life' may be a reflection of the disruption caused by problems in production programs at night and weekends (Singer, 1982). The pay situation is aggravated by income tax. As McGregor (1960) put it, 'Within the present income tax structure, what is the real significance, motivationally speaking, of a 5 or even a 10 per cent salary increase to an individual making $15 000 or $20 000 a year?'. However, by contrast, the International Data Corporation (1981) survey of large-system productivity concluded that the reward structures ranked among the most significant factors affecting productivity. This is consistent with the statement by Weinberg (1971) that there is no real justification for believing that programmers as a group are any less concerned with money than any other group at a comparable pay scale. It is also consistent with the statement by Jones (1986b) that organizations with fairly high overall software productivity, such as IBM, tend to have dual compensation plans, under which technical staff can achieve salary levels equal to those of third-line managers, or even higher; whereas organizations with fairly low productivity often have compensation plans for technical staff which stop at about the level of first-line management, thus forcing technical employees to either get into management or leave the organization in order to achieve economic parity: 'enterprises that do not treat their technical workers well or reward them properly tend to lose their best workers in relatively large numbers, thus lowering the average skill levels of the enterprise and lowering net productivity as well'.

How can we reconcile the opposing evidence? Perhaps higher pay motivates software engineers sufficiently to change jobs, but not sufficiently to work harder. Or perhaps what people *say* (in response to surveys), and what they *do*, are sometimes two different things (Weinberg, 1971). Higher pay also provides higher status, and is additionally a symbol of the value that is placed on their work, but these are also not prime motivators of software engineers, so they cannot explain the discrepancy either. However, even if factors such as salary, status, and recognition are not the prime motivating factors for software engineers, this does not mean that they provide no motivation at all, let alone that they have a negative effect.

Conclusion

The factors that primarily motivate programmers and analysts are thus often significantly different from those that primarily motivate their managers. Managers should therefore realize that their subordinates are different from themselves, and so should not expect them to be motivated by the same factors (Boehm, 1981).

This is the basis of Boehm's 'modified golden rule'. The Golden Rule is 'do unto others as you would have others do unto you' (Luke 6,31). The modified golden rule is 'do unto others as you would have others do unto you – *if you were like them*'. If we manage by doing unto our programmers as we would have them do unto us – e.g. by offering rewards in terms of increased status – we will often be very disappointed by the results.

Methods

A number of methods can be used to increase motivation, and therefore productivity:

- bonus payments
- other rewards
- by example
- by seeing results
- by understanding the purpose
- management by objectives
- job satisfaction
- training
- feeling valued
- participation
- MPPs

However, Townsend (1984) warns that you cannot motivate people: 'That door is locked from the inside'. You can only create a climate in which the people motivate themselves to help the organization achieve its goals. If people perceive that their personal goals are in harmony with the organization's goals, they will contribute more to the organization's goals (Koontz and O'Donnell, 1972; Boehm, 1981). This 'principle of harmony of objectives' is facilitated if the people's goals are incorporated into the organization's goals, which in turn requires that we understand what software people's goals are. Put the other way round, the organization will suffer if it ignores personal needs and goals, and it must prove to its employees that their goals coincide with those of the organization (McGregor, 1960). However, it is not always possible to satisfy both the organization's and the employee's goals.

The methods listed above are now considered in more detail.

Bonus payments

A Japanese firm might award an employee $600 for a patentable idea, whereas General Motors offers employees up to $10 000 per usable suggestion (Bain, 1982). The European Space Agency has a scheme for awarding incentive payments to software maintainers which has proved effective (Formica, 1978), while the 1986 Peat Marwick Cost Performance study showed that banks with higher productivity had incentive pay schemes

(Stone, 1986). The virtually error-free soft-ware produced for the Space Shuttle may be at least partly attributable to the financial incentives for the developers and testers (Joyce, 1989).

Bonus payments can increase motivation (Thorpe, 1976; Short, 1977), but unequal payments to members of the same team can harm the team spirit (Yourdon, 1979b; Weinberg, 1971). Managers must therefore encourage a balance between competition and co-operation (Shneiderman, 1980). Furthermore, Bain (1982) warns that monetary incentives usually fail, for a variety of reasons: the incentive programs are often poorly designed and include faulty measurement; there may be doubts about the fairness of the programs; they are viewed by some managers as a substitute for supervision; and the payments must be at least 15% of the employee's total salary to generate enough interest. Worse, where the amounts are perceived to be unfair (even though this may be due to difficulty in accurately determining rewards), incentive programs can even become a *de*motivator rather than a motivator.

McGregor (1960) adds a number of other warnings. For example, although people want money and will work harder to get more of it, most people also want the approval of their fellow workers, and if necessary, will forgo increased pay to obtain this approval; they will not believe managerial assurances that incentive rates will remain inviolate regardless of how much they produce; and the average worker is sufficiently ingenious to outwit any system of controls devised by management, i.e. they will 'game' the system to obtain higher rewards. McGregor believes that even a good individual incentive plan may only increase productivity by perhaps 15%, and this is often more than offset by the cost of administering the plan, including the cost of measures to counteract gaming. All in all, therefore, he concludes that the typical incentive plan is of limited effectiveness in moti-

vating people to direct their efforts toward organizational objectives.

Other rewards

McGregor (1960) made the telling point that most of the rewards employers customarily offer their employees – salary, vacation, pension, etc. – cannot be enjoyed on the job: 'you've got to leave work, get sick, or retire first – no wonder people aren't having fun on the job' (Townsend, 1984). However, this need not necessarily remain the case. Employees who do consistently well can be rewarded with improved office space or working conditions, or an office with a view; by allowing them choice of their tasks; by providing them with further education or allowing them to attend conferences; by thanking or praising them in the in-house newspaper; by awarding them certificates of merit; or (in Japan) by presenting them with a company button or a ball-point pen; as well as by salary increases or promotion (Shneiderman, 1980; Bain, 1982). Once again, though, the team spirit may be harmed.

Example

If the supervisor works hard, it is more likely that his subordinates will also. The reverse can also occur: hard workers may shame a lazy supervisor into exerting more effort, though there is the danger that he will instead take advantage of the situation, and rely on them to 'carry' him.

Similarly, if the manager views certain tasks as unpleasant, he may unconsciously and unintentionally communicate his negative feelings to his subordinates (Singer, 1982).

Seeing results

Being able to see preliminary results, as happens with prototyping, serves as an incentive (Wetherbe and Berrisford, 1979).

Understanding the purpose

If a person understands the purpose of his assignment – for example, if a programmer sees how the output of his program will be used, how it will benefit the organization – he performs better and more willingly (Aron, 1974; Singer, 1982). This understanding is assisted by direct contact between DP staff and users, as happens with some DP department structures (e.g. the application organization), with joint design (e.g. JAD), and with prototyping.

Management by objectives (MBO)

MBO is a technique devised by Drucker (1954) used in conjunction with performance appraisals. Objectives or targets, together with priorities, are set jointly by the employee and his manager, and his performance is judged by how well he meets his targets (Gunther, 1978; Couger and Zawacki, 1980; Mallinick, 1976). Results are measured at pre-established intervals. The targets may consist of completing certain tasks within specified schedules, or improving productivity or reducing errors by specified percentages (Johnson, 1980b). The targets provide motivation, and the technique is well suited to highly-skilled programming staff (Maslow, 1970), though it may be difficult to set realistic objectives (Ingham, 1976) – in fact, it may be difficult to think of a range of substantive objectives for some levels of staff (Pratt, 1985). Another disadvantage of MBO is that it is time-consuming. However, it concentrates on results rather than personality, and so helps avoid bias by the manager, and may also avoid personality clashes during the interviews.

The GOALS (goal-oriented approach to life-cycle software) method (Boehm, 1981) is a form of MBO. It establishes explicit personal commitment to product and process goals, provides a framework for checking the completeness of the goals, establishes a sequence of sub-goals required to achieve the goals, provides early warning if any sub-goals are not being achieved, and provides checkpoints for reconciling quantitative and qualitative goals. It is described in more detail later.

Bain (1982) describes MBO as an attitude or philosophy, rather than a system. It is an internalized concept embraced by high-performance managers who are aware that human needs must be fulfilled if performance is to improve. However, it is not a magic wand that will improve the performance of the organization regardless of the operating climate.

According to Pratt (1985), the technique was declining in use (at least as a management technique). Heller (1981) criticizes it as being too rigid: it does not fit the errors and omissions in plans, and the need for people to improvise and adjust. He quotes a management consultant, who places it at the top of 'has-been' management concepts, and another authority who stated that it is not suitable for government departments, as power in them is so diffuse. Bain (1982) described it as a dismal failure, even though it was well accepted and widely used. He argues that the concept should be extended. As described above, it is only concerned with each person's individual tasks. However people perform best when they have an overview of the total work situation, and a feeling that what they are doing is important and worthwhile to the total effort. People will strive to achieve the organization's goals if they know what those goals are, understand them, and can derive some need satisfaction from contributing to their achievement. Management must therefore accept all employees as important to the achievement of its goals, and so must recognize that all employees are worthy of being given the 'big picture'.

Job satisfaction

According to Bain (1982), a recent study indicated that 85% of both managerial and non-managerial work groups in the USA were dissatisfied with their work situation: 'That means that most people spend 30 to 40 years working at something from which they receive little personal satisfaction. What a waste, not only in terms of human needs unfulfilled but also in terms of the unrealized productivity potential which is bound to result'. Staff who are happy, e.g. because they have the right amount of autonomy, participation and feedback; because they receive recognition for their efforts; because their tasks are interesting, and provide a challenge and a sense of achievement; because they are working with state-of-the-art technology; because they are not bound to a boring maintenance job; or because they have adequate working space, privacy and quiet; are more highly motivated (Chapters 4, 8 and 9). People who have tasks that appeal to them and are within their capabilities can tolerate many bad things (Metzger, 1981).

Training

Multi-image slide programs (Chapter 9) are claimed to 'inspire personnel to higher levels of achievement' (Sutherland, 1986). Interactive training methods, such as CBT, also provide motivation. In addition, the mere fact of receiving training is in itself good for morale.

Feeling valued

The Hawthorne experiments show that the workers' morale is raised if they believe that management is showing an interest in them.

Participation

If staff participate in a decision, then they will be more committed to ensuring its success. For example, if programmers participate in estimating the effort and schedules for the programs they write, then they will strive harder to meet the deadlines (Chapter 8).

This also allows them to plan their own jobs, and gives them more control over their destinies (McGregor, 1960). Siegler (1987) however, warns that developers do not always have the tools and data they need to calculate schedules. By contrast, Metzger (1981) quotes one authority, from IBM, who believes that technical people are generally very good at estimating, but not at *defending* their decisions.

Modern programming practices (MPPs)

Almost 70% of nearly 600 respondents in the GUIDE (1979) survey believed that MPPs improve programmer or analyst morale. (Though it may be significant that most of the responses were prepared or reviewed by managers (Boehm, 1981), who may not have been aware of – or may not have wanted to admit to – any adverse effects such as deskilling.)

Comments

If we compare these methods with the factors that primarily motivate programmers and analysts – such as growth, technical supervision, peer relations and personal life – we find little overlap. This is partly because many of the methods were not included in the surveys. One wonders how they would have been rated if they had been included; but without prejudging the issue, it does seem that researchers are not surveying some potentially effective motivational methods. The limited overlap also suggests that organizations may not be taking advantage of all the factors that motivate staff.

11.2 PROJECT MANAGEMENT

There is strong evidence that the standard of management of DP projects is low. Only 30% of the projects in one survey were completed in the allocated time, and only 10% within the budgeted cost (Dickson and Powers,

1973). Conte *et al.* (1986) even claimed that schedule slippage is the rule rather than the exception. Devenny (1976) quotes a project, a US Air Force command-and-control project, which was estimated at $400 000, but which eventually cost $3 700 000. Kirchner (1986) quotes a $35 million life-cycle cost overrun by the US IRS. Boehm (1973) quotes two large airline command-and-control systems (Univac/United and Burroughs/TWA) which had to be 67% and 95% rewritten after delivery because they did not match the user's requirements. Boehm (1981) quotes two multi-million dollar projects (the Univac-United Airlines reservation system, and the Advanced Logistics System), which lacked appropriate requirements and early feasibility analyses, and which were cancelled when they were found to be infeasible. He also quotes a system, for urban school attendance, which would have been a failure even if the time and budget targets for its development had been met, because it did not meet the organization's *human* goals: the savings produced by the system would have been achieved by making disadvantaged working mothers redundant. Similarly, Metzger (1981) classifies management of a project as a failure if the project meets its schedule, but at the expense of excessive overtime, as this deprives the development staff of a pleasant experience, and severely affects their private lives.

Jones (1986b) quotes a system which was contracted for 18 months, but which eventually took *five years* because, when system testing began, it was found to be unworkable as a system, even though some components had been successfully tested alone. He also claims that, within major corporations, perhaps 10–15% of really catastrophic failures are at least partly caused by personal human dislikes, and political or territorial disputes. As an example, he quotes a cost-estimating project which, after three years and the expenditure of $500 000, still had no predictive capabilities, only accounting features, because of personal antagonism between the

manager handling the accounting portion and the manager developing the predictive portion.

According to Jones (1986b), a high percentage of projects in large organizations are never finished or delivered to end users – in two large corporations, between 20% and 30% of all projects larger than 100 000 source statements were not completed, and were cancelled before delivery. Projects may be cancelled because of enormous cost or schedule overruns, because of customer cancellation, or because the organization has a deliberate policy of letting two or more competing projects get started, and then selecting the best for final delivery. (This can be compared to prototyping.) In the large-system divisions of IBM, the cancellation rate from the last factor alone has been about 25%.

The US government conducted 151 management audits of problems in the acquisition and use of computer systems, which showed that deficiencies in management planning (50%) and control (34%) caused significantly more problems than technology factors (only 15%) (General Accounting Office, 1977). Similarly, one project of the US IRS was criticized for having no genuine program management, no contingency plans, no system acceptability testing, no parallel simulation, and inadequate training, and it was delivered to users who had raised 'a cacophony of protest' (Kirchner, 1986). These are *management* not technical deficiencies. This is consistent with Metzger's experience. He gives a long list of problems – ill-defined contract, unstable problem definition, inexperienced management, political pressures, ineffective change control, unrealistic deadlines, and particularly poor planning (or no plan at all) – all of which are *management* deficiencies (Metzger, 1981). Conspicuous by its absence from his list is technical difficulty. Many jobs are technically difficult, but few are beyond the 'state-of-the-art'.

However, Humphrey (1985) reported that

the skills of programming managers – he was presumably referring specifically to those working on large systems at IBM – have continued to improve. They have grown in their appreciation of business and marketing issues. The typical programming manager has a technical education and often an advanced degree. They now have an understanding of programmers and their jobs, have extensive management training, know the products, and have a technical as well as an intuitive sense of the programming process and how to improve it.

Consequences of overruns

When a project overruns its schedule or budget, there follows 'a great deal of painful and frustrating human drama which everybody involved in wishes they had never gotten themselves into' (Boehm, 1981).

- Users have made plans to phase out their existing operations, cut off old supplies, reassign personnel, order new equipment, etc. All these plans will have to be reworked.
- Project team members are urged to work harder, and longer hours, to compensate for problems they did not create.
- Other projects which depend on staff from the delayed project will be postponed or cancelled, i.e. a domino effect is created. Their benefits will therefore also be postponed or cancelled.
- The additional costs may be met out of the budget for other projects, so either some other projects are cancelled or postponed, or their budgets are cut, making it difficult for the other teams to keep within their new budgets.
- Research and training budgets may be cut, which will detrimentally affect morale and long-term productivity.

Contractual obligations (e.g. to complete a project by a certain date) can have a major impact on costs and productivity, and in extreme cases can add non-performance penalties or litigation expenses to the overall cost of the project (Jones, 1986b). In future, money-back guarantees and consequential damages may also be added. Jones was apparently thinking not only of schedule overruns, but also of factors such as the large amount of documentation required, especially for government and military systems; the number of bugs in the system; legal requirements for sensitive financial and personal data; and the execution speed and response time provided by the system. However, these other factors can be responsible for overruns, e.g. the additional time required to produce the extra documentation, or the additional QA to reduce the number of bugs. In particular, documentation activities are often on the critical path, yet there is an almost universal lack of integrated text/graphics support, and there can be bottlenecks in the reproduction and distribution of documentation. Contractual constraints probably affected only about 5% of the programs in existence in 1985, but this will increase. (The preceding factors should, of course, be allowed for in the estimates, but they can be overlooked or under-estimated, especially where the amount of documentation, quality standard, etc. are much higher than the estimator is accustomed to.)

Causes of overruns

Some reasons for overruns have already been mentioned, e.g. products which did not meet the user's requirements and therefore had to be revised; products which were found to be unworkable or infeasible during testing; and personal antagonism between the members of the project team. Other reasons are discussed below.

Some overruns are caused by disasters, such as a fire destroying the organization's building and all its contents, including the programs being developed, the supporting documentation, and all backup copies (Metzger, 1981).

Metzger (1981) claims that half the horror stories about programming involved either bad contracts or no contract at all. He also stated that many projects have foundered because individual programmers independently designed files, and later found that other programmers had had different file designs in mind, and had written their programs accordingly, resulting in incompatibility.

According to Johnson (1980b), 80% of project lateness involved task definition and man-day assignments (presumably incomplete, ambiguous, unclear, or changed specifications or responsibilities, and optimistic effort estimates). The remaining 20% were caused by not executing a step successfully because of poorly defined milestones, a missing PERT chart, burdensome control procedures, or poor programming techniques.

Yourdon (1975) attributed many overruns to unrealistic schedules: 'I am continually amazed at the number of projects that are developed with a schedule that the programmers consider totally unrealistic'. Bell *et al.* (1987) claim that managers consistently underestimate the time required, typically by a factor of two. Jones (1986b) claims that the biggest single cause of major catastrophes is making schedule and cost commitments that cannot be achieved, and which are known to be impossible by the technical personnel.

Jones (1986b) also gives several other reasons for overruns. He attributes massive overruns, and even outright project failures, to the use of unstructured programming methods. Overruns may also be caused by 'redirections' during a project: changes to the customer's requirements, or change of hardware, software tools or techniques, leading to partial redesign and redevelopment. (Such changes are normal, but the project's costs and schedule should be extended accordingly.) Furthermore, several projects have notably overrun their budgets because of serious errors in support materials: in one case, the programming manager failed to include the cost of writing user documentation in the cost estimate, and this escaped notice until after the bid had been accepted. Overruns are also influenced by the organizational structure. About 5 out of every 10 matrix managed projects having more than 50 000 lines of source code run into schedule delays and cost overruns, compared to only about 3 out of every 10 hierarchically managed projects of the same size. Jones also claims that, contrary to what one might expect, projects that aim from the beginning at achieving the highest possible levels of quality and reliability tend to have the best schedule adherence records, whereas projects that aim at achieving the shortest possible schedules regardless of quality tend to have fairly frequent schedule and cost overruns. In particular, one of the classic causes of late delivery is short-cutting reviews or prototyping in order to start testing early, 'and then finding that the program doesn't work and can't be made to work without extensive redesign'.

This is one example of bad management, which is probably the main cause of overruns. However, no matter how well a project is managed, it will rarely be completed on time and in budget if the schedule and budget are unrealistically low. Overruns may therefore be the result of underestimates.

Underestimates

There are a variety of reasons for underestimates:

- Poor estimation methods. Good methods were not available in the past, but better methods are now available (Chapter 8). The worst methods are Parkinsonian and 'price-to-win'. Commitments are made as a result of orders from management, or because the organization's sales department has already signed a contract with the customer, before all the requirements were known or a proper estimate made (Jones, 1986b). Management may insist that the promised completion date be met with insufficient staff. This may be done to ensure that there is no unnecessary expansion of work to fill the time allotted to it (Parkinson's Law), thereby ensuring that the organization is kept at peak efficiency. Alternatively, the contract may call for 'something like an 18-month delivery schedule for projects of such scope and magnitude that no similar systems have ever been developed in less than 36 months' (Jones, 1986b). This is typically done to secure a contract against competitive bids.

- The person who made the estimate may have no real knowledge of the amount of effort required to develop a system (Jones, 1986b).
- There may be an error in the estimate (e.g. an arithmetical error).
- Estimation involves an element of the unknown.
- The estimation model may have been calibrated for a different environment, e.g. a different type of application. (This can be rectified by using any standard adjustments which may be available for the model, or by recording how people spend their time during each project in your environment, and tuning the model accordingly.)
- Failing to allow for the impact of geographical separation (in large organizations, particularly multinational corporations, or small organizations working as subcontractors). Systems which are developed at multiple sites can take 20% more calendar time, even if there are good communications facilities (such as teleconferencing) linking them, and 40% more if there are not (Jones, 1986b).
- Failing to allow for the impact of legal involvement. Jones (1986b) quotes a case in which the legal reviews took twice as long as developing the product, and the

attorneys' fees were greater than the software development costs!
- Failing to allow for the impact of restricted access to classified data needed for testing, e.g. on military projects (Metzger, 1981).
- Failing to allow for any of the other cost drivers/effort multipliers, such as inexperienced staff or inadequate tools.
- Failing to allow for 'non-productive' time, such as progress reporting, training and vacations (Johnson, 1980b).
- The use of constant values (e.g. not taking inflation into account) for salaries, overheads, and supplies – this is particularly serious on long-duration projects (Boehm, 1981).
- Much of the code is unobtrusive and is therefore overlooked. Boehm (1981) quotes a case in which only 2 or 3% of the code was directly related to the obvious (mission-oriented) goal of the product, the rest consisting of overheads such as help messages, error processing, etc. Non-delivered support software (test drivers, etc.) also comes under this 'easily overlooked' category, and on a very large project it could amount to as much as *four* times the delivered (operational) code (Chapter 2).
- Similarly, support materials are also easily overlooked (cf. the case of a programming manager who failed to include the cost of writing user documentation in the cost estimate).
- The scope of the system may have been expanded during its development. In a set of 64 IBM cost estimates, the average size of the software when delivered was 44% larger than the initial estimate (Jones, 1986b). This was not the result of poor or over-optimistic estimating, as 35% of the delivered functions were not in the initial requirements, but were added later as afterthoughts by the clients. Yet, in spite of the expanded scope of the work, the development staff were urged to meet the initial schedules.

- Personality-related issues, such as optimism, or a desire to avoid confrontations.

In addition, the earlier an estimate is made, the less accurate it is. According to Boehm (1981), once a software product has been designed, the effort required to develop it can be estimated to within a factor of 1.25; and when an estimate is within a factor of 1.25 of the 'ideal', a good project manager can turn it into a self-fulfilling prophecy. If the estimate is too high, Parkinson's Law ensures that the excess time which has been made available will be consumed. If it is too low, the 'deadline effect' ensures that the deadline will nevertheless be met. People work harder as a deadline approaches. They put more energy into the time spent on the project, and they spend more time on it, either by working overtime, or by postponing other activities (work on other projects and 'non-productive' activities such as training and vacations) until after the deadline (Boehm, 1980a, 1981) – the shortfall in output can often be made up by the last factor alone, as 'non-productive' activities typically consume about 30% of the staff's time (Chapter 2). Deadlines set after a software product has been designed can therefore usually be met (provided, of course, a good cost-estimation method was used).

Gildersleeve (1974a), however, believed that, even with the primitive estimating techniques then available, poor estimating was seldom the cause of severe overrun – poor management was a much more likely cause.

11.2.1 GUIDELINES

A number of guidelines should be followed if a project is to be successfully managed, and time and budget overruns avoided (Boehm, 1973, 1981; Glass, 1979; Gildersleeve, 1974a; Weinberg, 1971; Golding, 1978; Gunther, 1978; Lee, 1978; Weinwurm, 1970; Patrick, 1980a; Siegler, 1987; Baroni and Hotka, 1986;

Metzger, 1981; Johnson, 1980b; Singer, 1982; Rossman, 1986).

- Become knowledgeable about the proposed system.
- Break the project into components to make it simpler, and so that the real size of it can be grasped.
- Do not attempt too much at once.
- Pinpoint the goals of the proposed system, and work towards them.
- Communicate the goals to the team members.
- Identify your user (e.g. who is paying for the system?): there are often many users (including less obvious ones such as auditors), all of whose needs must be satisfied, but where their needs conflict, someone must officially have the authority to make a choice in favor of one user over another.
- Gain user support.
- Have a formal written statement (a contract) clearly showing what the customer (user) wants and what you agree to provide, 'even if the customer happens to be your buddy down the hall and you both work for the same organization' (Metzger, 1981).
- If the user wants to change the requirements, negotiate a new price and schedule – frequently, when faced with higher costs and a longer schedule, the user will decide that the changes are not so important after all.
- Have clear and complete specifications, otherwise when the user wants a change, he will deny that it is a change: 'This is only something I expected to get for my money in the first place' (Metzger, 1981).
- Have precise interface specifications.
- Use checklists to ensure that nothing important, e.g. high volumes, is overlooked.
- Use a good cost-estimation method.
- Remember that almost anything will take twice the time and money you expect, so build in buffers.

- Provide for adequate testing time.
- Allow for the effect of month-end production processing on testing response or turnaround time.
- Allow for 'non-productive' time, such as progress reporting, training and vacations.
- Allow time for other projects, and especially urgent maintenance.
- Have a detailed project plan, including manpower and machine requirements.
- Allow for task precedences and dependencies – one task cannot be started until another has been completed.
- Draw up test plans.
- Do not make foolish promises.
- Keep your commitments.
- Have good contingency plans, for sickness, hardware failure, errors in specifications, etc.
- Remember that men and months (effort and schedule) are not interchangeable (Brooks' Law).
- Plan ahead: experienced programmers think 7–14 days ahead, capable analysts plan their work 14–21 days in advance, and good managers should look 30 days into the future (Sweet, 1986).
- Have realistic and measurable milestones computed according to the effort required to accomplish the task, monitor progress against them, and take prompt corrective action if they are not met.
- Monitor the activities on the critical path particularly closely.
- Slipping a schedule by two weeks a month before the promised delivery date is better than moving it by one week the day before (Sweet, 1986).
- Subdivide the job sufficiently so that missing a milestone is a warning not a catastrophe, but not so much that there is a milestone – and therefore a potential crisis – every week.
- Ensure that all parties understand what is expected of them.
- The project leader must not do too much detail-level work.

- Hold regular project status meetings – though one DP director stated that he probably gets more done through informal conversations than in an entire formal status meeting (Winkler, 1986).
- Hold oral reviews. These give a break from routine; they provide a forum for uncovering problems and broaching better solutions; they give people an opportunity to be heard; they help give the staff a sense of belonging; they help them understand the part their work plays in the total job; and they counteract the manager's image as an unapproachable recluse.
- If a project management scheme is too complex or requires too much work, then it will be abandoned.
- Maintain a history of important project data and events (manpower and machine usage estimates and actuals, missed milestones, contract changes, etc.), for use in estimating later phases of the project, or entirely new projects.
- On completion of each project, ask yourself what you would do differently if you were to repeat the job.

In addition, Gildersleeve (1974a) recommends that, at the end of each function in the software life-cycle, a 'go/no go' decision be made whether or not to proceed with the next function (Chapter 10), i.e. you always commit yourself to only the next function, not the entire remainder of the project, so potential losses are similarly contained, and the successive decisions are based on increasingly more accurate estimates of costs and benefits. Johnson (1980b), however, claims that this method requires extra, unnecessary documentation. Worse, it is not management, but a 'cop-out', and promotes indecision. The net result is that resources are wasted and productivity is low. As the risk of heavy losses is reduced, there is a danger perhaps that managers will get careless and not do a thorough feasibility study or cost-benefit analysis at the beginning of the project, but nevertheless the technique has some value.

As stated already, bad management is probably the main cause of overruns. Many overruns could therefore be avoided by following the guidelines given here. However, Boehm (1973) pointed out that, although the importance of such factors had been known for years, they were still not being adhered to. Alternatively, organizations should – as an interim measure – assume that poor management will occur, and plan accordingly, i.e. appropriate contingency allowances or buffers should be built into estimates. Boehm (1981) believes it is bad management practice to 'reward' poor managers by giving them more resources to do a job than a good manager would be given. To me, that is like saying that a poor programmer should not be allowed more time than a good programmer. Some staff are weaker than others, and will therefore take longer. While an organization must try to raise the performance of the weaker staff, until such time as this has been achieved, it has to face reality and allocate more resources to them, otherwise they will not be able to complete their tasks, at least not without working a significant amount of overtime, and the organization could be left with a string of unfinished projects – or rushed poor-quality systems – and very unhappy users. Nevertheless, notwithstanding his above comments, Boehm does include a management reserve to take care of contingencies, in his COCOMO effort-estimation model.

Good project management is important for maintenance as well as for development (Lientz *et al.*, 1978).

Good project management is more important for large projects than for small ones (Boehm, 1973). Failure is more expensive on large projects. Project management activities grow much more rapidly than low-level design, coding and unit testing, as project size increases (Jones, 1986b). In addition, on small projects, there is generally enough personal contact for the manager to discover problems directly, without the assistance of complex monitoring and reporting aids; but on large projects, the manager cannot keep in close personal touch with each detailed activity (Boehm, 1981). Metzger (1981), however, warns that managers of small projects can become overconfident. They produce neither a project plan, nor the requirements specifications, nor most of the other documentation. When a small project goes wrong it is doubly embarrassing, as 'it's expected that a competent manager can run the little job without bankrupting the company'.

Personal qualities

Managers should, of course, be able to plan, organize, and direct (Johnson, 1980b). They should also be resilient, be able to take knocks easily, and have very thick skins (Winfield, 1986). The best managers tend to be level-headed, and possess an even, stable disposition (Singer, 1982). An excitable, highly strung person is not suited to handling job pressures or touchy interpersonal conflicts which involve other highly excitable people. Such managers are responsible for frequent outbursts and sarcastic remarks. They therefore cause problems and help trigger a high staff turnover.

Managers should have good communication ability, both oral and written, but if they are poor at oral communication, then they should write things down (Metzger, 1981). They should be good listeners. Too often, managers do all the talking – they conduct a monologue instead of a dialogue – but if they do not listen to the ideas and suggestions of their staff, then they miss valuable information and limit their range of choices (Singer, 1982).

Managers require conceptual breadth rather than meticulous handling of details (Aron, 1974). In fact, they do not require detailed knowledge (Chandor, 1976). They should rise above the immediate situational demands, and take a long-term view (Win field, 1986). They should direct innovation, not be led by it. Solid managerial experience is more important to data processing managers than outstanding technical ability. Similarly, a project leader need not be the greatest analyst, designer, or programmer that ever lived, but he must keep himself current in these areas, otherwise how can he understand the team members when they explain their problems to him (Gildersleeve, 1974a)? Technical knowledge also gives him credibility in the eyes of his subordinates (Davis and Flynn, 1987). He can maintain his skill in these areas if he periodically assigns himself a detailed task. However, as the co-ordinator of the project, the tasks he assigns himself should be ones which keep him oriented to the overall system, rather than making him an expert on some relatively small part of it. Suitable tasks are therefore writing the user manual and developing the system test. These tasks, however, have the disadvantage of only providing a limited range of technical involvement, so a small amount of time should also be spent pro-gramming part of the system. The CPT concept (Chapter 3) caters for these conflict-ing requirements.

Metzger (1981) analyses the question in more detail. First-level managers are nor-mally directly involved in the technical work, and so must be technically knowledgeable. Second-level managers spend more time on financial matters, proposals, planning, person-nel matters, and the like. Higher-level managers spend successively less time on technical matters. However, upper-level man-agers should still have a 'feel' for technical developments. They can acquire the requisite knowledge by reading specifications, attending briefings by their subordinates, or returning periodically to technical work (job rotation): 'it can do wonders for your technical com-petence and greatly enhance your confidence in being able to manage the next job'. However, this should not be carried too far. Metzger quotes one project whose manager

'couldn't resist the urge to get into the programmers' code. While he was messing with bits, his project fell apart and was eventually cancelled'.

Aids

Project management can be assisted in a variety of ways, ranging from traditional exception reports to automated graphical tools.

An ongoing record should be kept of the time spent on each project, and the expenses incurred. Reports should then be produced periodically to show actuals to date versus budgeted, for expenditure, schedule, and personnel levels. In particular, exception reports should be produced at each project milestone, to show serious over- or under-discrepancies, but especially to provide an early warning of any schedule slippages or cost overruns. The figures should then be extrapolated (e.g. by rerunning the cost-estimation model with updated estimates of program sizes and cost drivers) to obtain revised costs and completion date for the project, which in turn should be compared against the budget and schedule. Where necessary and possible, corrective action should be taken, to bring the project back within the agreed costs and schedule (e.g. by allocating more staff to the project or pur-chasing more development tools), or the user's approval should be obtained to extend the deadline or pay a higher price. However, the exceptions should first be investigated. Apart from the possibility of errors in them – i.e., they may not be exceptions after all – they may reveal deviations from the project plan rather than overruns. For example, the project may have been staffed with more people than planned, in which case the costs to date will be higher than budgeted for, but the project will be completed sooner.

Most of the respondents in the GUIDE (1979) survey believed that MPPs improve project estimating or control. Jones (1986b) believes that structured methods do much to lower the risks of massive overruns and even outright project failures. Metzger (1981) pointed out that many methodologies, such as structured programming and code inspections, are both technical tools and management tools: they help both the technical staff and management do their respective jobs. In particular, they help managers understand what the programmers are doing.

Configuration management

Configuration management is the art of co-ordinating software development and maintenance to minimize problems such as debugging a program using an out-of-date source code listing; one programmer overwriting another's changes; two programmers independently fixing the same bug; the same bug in two versions of a program and only one version being fixed; commencing system testing while unaware that one of the modules has not been unit tested; and releasing a program that is not yet ready (Arthur, 1983; Babich, 1986). Metzger (1981) describes configuration management as follows: define a program to be produced, control all changes to that original definition, and show that the final product is completely consistent with the original definition as modified by the accepted changes. Configuration management is like an inventory control system for all the programs and documentation comprising a software product (including, for example, the budget and staffing plan). A definitive version of any software product, or completed (baselined) portions thereof, can therefore always be produced.

Configuration management ensures that the status of the project is always visible (like the program production library concept in CPTs). It is particularly useful for vendors of products such as application packages and technological aids, which have multiple releases, and may also have different adaptations for different operating environments.

A multiplicity of different versions is therefore in simultaneous use by different customers, each version of the package may have different versions of the same program modules, and customers running old versions still expect to receive fixes. Chaos can easily result. Configuration management addresses this problem. Metzger (1981), however, warns that configuration management, at least as stipulated in many US government contracts, means such a mass of manuals, regulations, specifications, and so on, that it 'scares people to death'.

Charts

PERT charts are network diagrams which show the activities comprising a project, their duration, dependencies between them (i.e. they are shown in sequence), and possibly when they are scheduled to start and finish (Boehm, 1981; Metzger, 1981). The **critical path** is the longest path through the network, i.e. the path with the highest total duration. This is how long the project will take. This is therefore the path which one should try to shorten, e.g. by reallocating staff, rearranging activities, or providing extra tools such as integrated text/graphics support, so that the project will be completed sooner. Conversely, any slippage in the activities on this path will delay completion of the project. Slack time can be determined from the charts, and the relevant activities adjusted accordingly if necessary, e.g. a particular activity can be started later, to meet a personnel constraint. Activities on the critical path, by definition, do not have any slack.

Johnson (1980b) recommends that a maximum of about 50 activities be shown on a PERT chart, as people cannot realistically work with more than that. If the project contains more than 50 activities, then a hierarchy of charts should be drawn, i.e. any of the 50 activities on the chart can be expanded into its own PERT chart on a separate page; any of the activities on that chart can in turn be similarly expanded; and so on.

PERT charts are most valuable during the design and integration test activities, when management attention is directed towards fitting things together (Metzger, 1981). They are less useful in between these functions, when individual program modules are being written and tested, because the focus is then on individual pieces of the system more than on their interactions. The usefulness of these charts therefore falls off after the design is completed, so they are often abandoned at that time, which may explain why they have had 'only spotty success' in programming. Metzger warns that a significant amount of effort is required to keep them up to date as the project progresses, and this diverts managers from supervising individual tasks. It is therefore not uncommon for a chart to fall behind during the programming phase. Once this happens, it should be abandoned. Automated tools help minimize this problem, but Johnson (1980b) disapproves of their use. While agreeing that PERT charts are time-consuming, he believes that this is not a disadvantage. Manually drawing a PERT chart provides the planners with a more thorough understanding of the relationships. The greatest value of a PERT chart is the planning and thinking required to prepare it. Furthermore, in most cases, modifications do not require redrawing the chart. He also warns of the time and expense of automated systems: the time to learn the package, input data, update the data, and interpret the results; and the expense to obtain and run the package. He believes that the time penalty for automated PERT charts is so great that significant benefits are only possible in 0.5% of all the projects in the world. However, with the subsequent proliferation of PC packages, the cost-benefits have probably changed significantly.

Gantt charts – also known as bar charts – devised by Henry L. Gantt, are a scheduling technique which shows the project activities (the tasks and the people performing them) superimposed on a calendar. They show at a glance how the project is progressing against the milestones on the pre-determined plan. Unlike PERT charts, they do not show dependency relationships, and therefore do not show if any slippage is on the critical path, but by the same token, they are easier to develop and update. They are therefore more suitable for simple projects, in which the dependencies are intuitively clear, with PERT charts being more suitable for complex ones (Boehm, 1981).

A project organization chart (a more detailed version of the DP organization charts shown in Chapter 3) shows how the project manager has delegated authority and responsibility for project functions to the people identified in the chart (Boehm, 1981). It is a valuable asset in clarifying project responsibilities, and in complying with principles of good project management. Cost-estimation methods can help when creating these charts, as they determine how much effort – and therefore how many people – will be needed to perform each function.

Automated aids

Some people believe that large projects are too complex to be managed by manual techniques (Johnson, 1980b). However, although Johnson himself appears to disagree, at least in the case of PERT charts, there is reason to believe that project management can be assisted by technological aids. In fact, project management software is a growth area. Many products have become available, including ones which support project managers with planning, estimating and control features, and ones which can produce PERT charts and Gantt charts (Chapter 6; Simpson, 1987). However, few of these products are suitable for the management of software projects (McCusker, 1989), and Frank (1990) recommends using MRP-II (manufacturing resource planning) software packages instead. However, one concept explicitly for this purpose was discussed in Chapter 6. Test plans, dependent relationships between tasks, etc. can be held in a database, which is then updated by each software tool as it is used. The database therefore always contains up to date project management information.

Goals

To ensure that the economic and human goals of a system are met, and not just the narrow programming-type goals, Boehm (1981) proposed the GOALS (goal-oriented approach to life-cycle software) method. Separate solutions are developed for each goal, and are then examined to ensure that the solution to one goal does not violate any of the other goals. If it does, then a new solution is developed. This method divides the goals into product goals and process goals, each of which is further subdivided into quantitative and qualitative goals. Examples of product goals are a reduction in costs (quantitative), and an improvement in the jobs of users (qualitative). Examples of process goals are a completion deadline (quantitative), and career development of the members of the project team (qualitative).

After the goals have been set and checked, the means for achieving them are defined: who is responsible for achieving each goal; how, when, and where they will be achieved; and what assumptions must be valid for them to be achieved. Then follows an iterative process in which the goals are worked towards, reviewed, adjusted if necessary, and achieved successively. Side by side with, and independent of this process, progress is periodically reviewed against the entire goal structure.

Successful software engineering therefore requires a continuous process of identifying goals, reconciling and making decisions with respect to conflicting goals, and managing with respect to several simultaneous goals. It

is rare to have only one goal to be met, and dangerous to act as if there were only one.

11.2.2 EFFECT ON PRODUCTIVITY

Gilb (1988) and Remus (1980b) believe that most of the techniques that can produce really big improvements in productivity are managerial in nature, not technical. This is plausible since most problems are caused by managerial not technical deficiencies (General Accounting Office, 1977; Kirchner, 1986; Metzger, 1981). Motivation and organization increase human productivity in 'relevant' directions, whereas technical devices may increase it in the wrong direction (Peters and Austin, 1985). For example, a higher-level language may just help us produce the wrong product faster. (With prototyping and CASE tools, this is surely becoming less of a danger.)

According to Boehm (1981), it is difficult to estimate the effect that management has on productivity. Poorly-managed projects rarely gather much data on their experiences. Had they gathered more data, they would probably have been better managed. Nevertheless, he claims that *each* of the following areas has often been responsible for doubling software development costs:

1. assigning the wrong people to the job;
2. creating task overlaps and underlaps through poor organization, poor delegation, and poor task monitoring;
3. demotivating people by unnecessarily poor working conditions and failing to reward good performance;
4. bringing large numbers of people onto the project before there is a clear understanding of their responsibilities;
5. failing to prepare needed resources, such as computer time, terminals, test data, and support software;
6. failing to validate software requirements and design specifications, and to identify and resolve high-risk elements early.

Boehm adds that, if managers do not genuinely want higher productivity, they will not get it, and they must continue to *show* that they want it, by investing in better tools, by recognizing and rewarding outstanding performances, and by enforcing standard practices, e.g. they must resist pressure to take short-cuts – such as skimping on documentation or testing – that would produce rapid results, but would degrade long-term productivity – 'run now, crawl later'.

Optimum deployment of staff is necessary for successful project management and high productivity. If all 'distraction and confusion' are eliminated, i.e. if (McDonough, 1981; Brooks, 1975; Weinberg, 1971):

- data or information required from other sources is available when it is needed;
- waiting time for testing can be minimized;
- staff do not have to work on other jobs at the same time;
- waiting time in between jobs can be eliminated;
- interruptions can be prevented;

– in short, if the manager can create a well-ordered environment and 'eliminate his people's excuses for failure' (Townsend, 1984), then productivity can be increased by 10–25% according to McKenzie (1982), Johnson (1980b) and McDonough (1981), and by a factor of two according to Boehm (1981). McDonough claims that this is the quickest and cheapest way to improve productivity.

Metzger (1981) expands on the effects of interruptions. If a programmer is interrupted in the middle of a complex piece of code, he must later backtrack to pick up the threads of what he was doing. Worse, he may easily forget part of what he had in mind, with the result that a bug is introduced into the code, with all the consequences that has for wasted man and machine time, and the effect of erroneous output if it is not corrected before the program is released into production. Furthermore, the frustration caused by frequent interruptions may cause him to give inadequate attention to the cause of the

interruption, e.g. if he was asked a question he might give an incorrect answer, thereby causing further harm.

According to Jones (1986b), cancelled projects, temporary code, etc. can have a dramatic impact on an organization's overall productivity (measured by dividing the total annual output by the total number of staff). The organization may have a productivity of more than 15 LOC per employee per day for delivered code, but its productivity may drop to only 1 LOC per day when the time spent on the remaining code is taken into account. This is worrying enough, but what is worse is that Jones claims that these figures 'are not uncommon'. However the 20–30% cancellation rate in some organizations, and the 4:1 maximum ratio (for very large projects) of non-delivered to delivered code (Chapter 2), suggest that in most organizations the two factors combined have a much smaller impact than 15:1.

11.2.3   RUN NOW, CRAWL LATER

One source of problems is worth singling out. There is intense pressure for rapid completion of projects and this pressure is difficult to resist. Spectacular short-term results are at a premium (Parkin, 1980; Van Tassel, 1978). Sometimes, the benefits from a system are so great that the pressure is readily understandable. For instance, Weinberg (1971) quotes the example of a linear program for an oil refinery, which could save a million dollars a month – 'even one month's delay in schedule would result in a loss that could not be recovered if the program were run free of charge for ten years' – and Kirchner (1986) reports that widespread computer systems problems cost the US Government millions in interest owed to taxpayers whose refunds could not be mailed on schedule. However, for most systems, the benefits are much smaller than this, and are greatly outweighed by the consequences of giving in to the pressure.

Consequences

The consequences of giving in to the pressure are frequently multiple.

- More errors are made, but inspections, walkthroughs and testing are nevertheless hasty, casual, or cut short (Jones, 1986b). As a result, the discovery of many errors is postponed to the later stages of testing, and partially debugged programs may be released into production – and if an error is discovered late in the software life-cycle, it may cost ten times (and perhaps even a hundred times) more to fix than if it had been discovered earlier (Chapter 8).
- The errors may be so numerous or serious that major repairs or even redesign are necessary, or the code may have been patched so often that it is difficult to maintain any further (Jones, 1986b).
- The haste is likely to result in poorly structured – and therefore complex – programs (Chapter 8), and in higher data complexity as well (Jones, 1986b). Jones claims that haste is possibly the commonest cause of unnecessary complexity.
- Haste therefore results in lower quality products, and low initial quality ensures low productivity throughout the life of the system (Chapter 10). For example, Boehm (1981) uses his COCOMO effort multipliers to show how initial savings through low reliability requirements can be offset by higher maintenance costs: 'the lower the required reliability, the more effort is required to fix latent faults in the software, and to update a software product having inaccurate documentation and code'. This is of particular concern in the case of large products with long lives. It is thus with justification that programmers complain: 'Why do we never have enough time to do it right the first time, but always have plenty of time to fix it later?' (Van Tassel, 1978).
- Similarly, the quantity and quality of documentation may suffer, and more effort is required to update a software product having incomplete, incorrect, or out of date documentation.
- Projects that aim at achieving the shortest possible schedule tend to have fairly frequent schedule and cost overruns (Jones, 1986b). For example, Brooks (1975) describes how an attempt to save three months on the design of one large system, IBM's OS/360 operating system, resulted only in the addition of one year to the debugging time.
- Some features which the user has requested may be postponed, to get the system operational sooner. Their benefits will therefore also be postponed. (In general, incremental delivery may be a good thing, but not if it is hasty and unplanned.)
- Requirements which are often left unstated, such as ease of use or enriching the user's job, may be omitted. As a result, the system may achieve its stated, 'mission-oriented' goals, such as processing the payroll, but be disliked by its users, which will adversely affect the organization's profits in the long term.
- The user's requirements may not be properly defined or may be misunderstood, resulting in the wrong product being developed. The job therefore has to be done again.
- One common method of achieving earlier completion is to work overtime, but Metzger (1981) describes excessive overtime as 'sloppy management'. Worse, 25% more hours a week does not necessarily mean that 25% more work will get done: it can easily produce 10% *less* work, or at least *less usable* work, instead. Faced with more hours to work each day for an extended period, most people unconsciously slow their efforts to fill the scheduled time, and morale suffers as well.
- If the schedule is tight, but achievable, the staff may work together as a happy,

cohesive team – they feel 'a kind of excitement that comes from overcoming shared challenges' (Jones, 1986b). A feeling of teamwork develops that is actually enjoyable. However, if the schedule is totally unrealistic, and no amount of over-time can allow it to be met, the team members become angry and frustrated. Management is (justifiably) viewed as incompetent and insensitive, and morale drops to rock bottom. The best staff leave, and their replacements must be brought up to speed, and the net impact is so great that the project may be cancelled.

Over-designing

There is a danger of requirements being omitted (as a result of haste), but there is also the opposite danger of 'gold-plating', i.e. over-specifying or over-designing a program or system (Weinberg, 1971; Boehm, 1981). This may consist of additional features to meet the user's wants (as distinct from his needs), or because the development staff find them interesting and challenging. The additional features may therefore only be marginally useful or seldom used. Alternatively, the gold-plating may consist of additional internal sophistication, e.g. to make a program more efficient, yet fast execution may not be necessary. Either way, the additional work consumes extra development time, thereby delaying project completion. The additional features or internal sophistication may also make the system more complicated, thereby further slowing down development, and making maintenance more difficult as well. These problems can be detected or even avoided by more thorough requirements analysis or walkthroughs or inspections, so this is a good example of that old adage: 'the more haste, the less speed'. Paradoxically, therefore, haste can result in both too few and too many features.

Importance of deadlines

Deadlines can sometimes be very important, such as in the oil refinery and tax refunds examples quoted above; to obtain a competitive advantage; or where a contract has been signed, with penalty clauses for late delivery. However, in other cases, less attention can be paid to due dates. Jones (1986b) argues that, while project managers usually worry about delivery dates, achieving a stable and trouble-free operational system is in many ways a more significant milestone, and the market success of a product is more heavily affected by customer-perceived quality than by any other factor. As Sweet (1986) put it, 'just as customers will pay a steep price for a good product, they will wait patiently for that product if they trust the delivery date'. These opinions are consistent with a survey at the Michigan National Bank, which showed that, given a choice between on-time installation of a product that did not fully meet requirements, and a late installation that met all requirements, 70% of users preferred the latter, whereas DP managers thought that the due date was more important (Siegler, 1987). One conclusion which may be drawn from this is that incremental delivery may be unnecessary for many systems.

Effect on productivity

Some of the above factors are quantified by Boehm (1981). According to him, *each* of the following customer-related actions has often been responsible for doubling software costs:

1. Imposition of impossibly short schedules, which force large personnel commitments before the job is understood. (Schedule compression was discussed in Chapter 3, where it was stated that a 25% compression is the maximum practical or even possible.)
2. Reluctance to define software requirements early, or growth of customer-developer misunderstandings which cause the wrong product to be developed.

3. Frequent redirection of project effort by stipulating changes in requirements, interfaces, facilities, or personnel. (Requirements volatility was discussed in Chapter 8.)

Reasons for succumbing to the pressure

It is understandable that users should press for rapid results, but DP and particularly DP management should realize how unwise it is to give in to such pressure. Their failure to do so may be attributed to a variety of causes.

- Some people are easily intimidated – 'He found it impossible to look a Vice-President in the eye and say no' (Metzger, 1981).
- A desire to please the users or management (Conte *et al.*, 1986).
- Higher estimated costs, or longer estimated schedules, might result in confrontations, which people prefer to avoid (Boehm, 1981) – by telling users (or your manager) what they want to hear, you 'buy time': the confrontation is postponed, and subsequent events might prove your estimate was too high, in which case the confrontation would have been unnecessary.
- A feeling of insecurity and a need to prove themselves.
- Their own personalities – managers tend to dislike detail, they make rapid decisions, and are quick to act (Aron, 1974).
- People are basically optimistic (Boehm, 1981; Conte *et al.*, 1986). A study by Augustine (1979) found a 'fantasy factor' of 1.33 in schedule estimates, i.e. jobs typically took 1.33 times longer than estimated – though Boehm also quoted another study which, by contrast, showed that managers would rather miss a business opportunity than risk making a loss, i.e. they were pessimistic (Canada, 1971).
- Other people, by virtue of their job role, benefit by being optimistic, e.g. a salesman or manager may be rewarded for winning a

contract, and he is more likely to win it if his estimate is optimistic.
- Estimators and managers often assume that all the members of the project team have a level of capability as high as their own (Conte *et al.*, 1986; Yourdon, 1979b).
- People, particularly managers who no longer write programs, make false comparisons with their own past performances, e.g. the programs they developed took them much longer than they remember: 'everyone would prefer to forget about those "fuzzy" periods of systems analysis and the tedium of testing, and remember instead the brilliant few days of coding'; they forget the amount of time they spent coding overheads such as support software and the user-interface; and in addition, users expected less in the past, and more documentation is required nowadays (Yourdon, 1979b; Boehm, 1981).
- Conversely, managers who do not have programming experience, and therefore do not understand that you must design before you code, may demand to know why coding has not yet begun: this is known as the WISC (why isn't Sammy coding?) syndrome (Metzger, 1981; Johnson, 1980b). By contrast, after the first year on the two-year, high-productivity NYT project, only the file maintenance system had been written (12 000 LOC out of 83 000), and most code was only written in the last six months (Schach, 1988).

It may therefore be difficult to rectify the situation. Accurate and reliable software cost-estimation methods (Chapter 8) are probably the best remedy. They not only produce an estimate, but also enable the estimator to defend his position with hard facts that are difficult to argue against.

11.3 SUMMARY AND CONCLUSIONS

The standard of DP management is often – and perhaps generally – low. This adversely affects productivity, and causes many projects to be completed late and over budget. The extremely low productivity on very large projects may be mainly due to poor management. Better management may well be the quickest and cheapest way to improve productivity, and may even give the biggest improvement.

Managers should continually adjust their management style to fit different circumstances, e.g. they should reduce the amount of direction they give their subordinates as the latter become more mature.

Participation and performance appraisals are two methods management can use to improve productivity.

People must be highly motivated to give of their best. To a large extent, people – and software engineers in particular – are already self-motivated, e.g. they will voluntarily keep themselves active, but outside pressure is also needed at times.

There are many ways to motivate people, e.g. by bonus payments, providing them with challenging assignments, explaining to them the purpose of their assignments, training, and so on.

There are also many guidelines which should be followed for successful project management, e.g. gain user support, have realistic milestones, monitor progress, etc.

Project management can be assisted by aids such as PERT charts and automated tools.

Haste has an adverse effect on productivity. It is typically caused by pressure from users or management. The best way to avoid unrealistically short schedules is probably to use a good cost-estimation method.

PART THREE

CONCLUSION

WILL THESE FACTORS BE EFFECTIVE ENOUGH? 12

In Part Two, a large number of factors affecting productivity were examined, and the conclusion was reached that many of them can significantly improve productivity, though their potential is not as great as often claimed. However, evidence for many of the factors was lacking, or varied widely. Furthermore, resistance to their use further restricts the gains that are actually achieved. There is thus uncertainty as to how big an increase in productivity can be expected. There is also uncertainty over how big an increase is required.

One can take an optimistic or a pessimistic view. The *optimistic* view is to believe the claims of a 100:1 improvement from fourth-generation languages, a 30:1 improvement by specializing, and so on; and to believe that only a 20% increase in productivity is required. The *pessimistic* view would hold that a 100:1 improvement in productivity is required, but that only a doubling can be achieved. What is a *realistic* view? This chapter attempts to answer that question.

12.1 HOW EFFECTIVE ARE THESE FACTORS?

12.1.1 OTHER PEOPLE'S PREDICTIONS

Hopkins (1972) and Gruenberger (1974) pointed out that various ideas were put forward in the past for solving '*the* computer problem' – comprehensive operating systems, higher-level languages, project management techniques, time-sharing, virtual memory, programmer education, appli-

cation packages, modular programming, flowcharting, etc. For example, 'defining the life cycle was considered the ultimate weapon in achieving productivity and quality' (Jones, 1986b). All these ideas helped, but none provided the complete answer: 'They told us the solution was to use structured programming, writing re-usable program modules and combining them, and also to set up an information center to assist our users in writing programs in end-user languages, but these solutions were not enough' (Tamaki, 1987). The same may be true of the other factors examined. Schach (1988, 1990) stated that *nothing* can solve the intrinsic difficulties of software development – it is an 'impenetrable barrier', like the speed of light, or the non-zero width of an atom.

Table 12.1 lists some predictions of the productivity gain which can be expected from the combined effect of many factors. Abbott predicts a doubling in productivity if a comprehensive combination of tools and techniques is used. Similarly, Patrick gives a long list of factors affecting productivity, but warns that few organizations can expect even a doubling in their productivity. However, he concentrated on managerial and personnel aspects rather than technological aids, so his figure should be adjusted upwards.

Both Conte predictions cover a period of ten years. The lower prediction includes only the effect of controlling and improving the most significant factors affecting productivity, and it is limited to the gains achievable with conventional ('evolutionary') methods, i.e. it excludes 'revolutionary' methods that

Table 12.1 Predicted productivity increase

Source	Productivity increase
Abbott (1983a)	2:1
Patrick (1980b)	2:1
Conte *et al.* (1986)	2:1–4:1 significant conventional methods
Conte *et al.* (1986)	2:1–10:1 controllable factors
Yourdon (1989)	2:1 (10:1 in special cases)
Jones (1986b)	2.2:1 development
Smith (1981)	up to 2.4:1
Boehm (1973)	2.4:1 in ten years
van der Poel (1982)	3:1
Albrecht (1979)	3:1
Druffel (1982)	4.3:1 in ten years
Jones (1986b)	4.3:1 maintenance
Butler Cox (1983b)	5:1 in eight years
Boehm (1981)	5:1 most organizations
Boehm (1981)	8:1 some organizations
Martin (1982a)	10:1
Average (approximate)	4:1

attempt to bypass the coding process altogether, such as automatic program generators, ultra-high-level languages, and re-usable program parts. These methods promise much greater productivity improvements, but are far from perfected. The question of which factors are the most significant – and how many there are – was left open: only 'customer interface requirements' and 'personnel qualifications' – both of which are people-oriented – were subsequently singled out. The higher prediction is the improvement that can be achieved by better managing those factors that are controllable, including MPPs, tool availability, improved programming environments, personnel capability and experience, use of higher-level languages, and reduced requirements volatility.

Yourdon believes that each of the approaches he discussed – hiring more talented programmers and systems analysts and giving them superior working conditions, letting users develop their own systems, better programming languages, attacking the maintenance problem, software engineering disciplines, and automated tools

for systems development – might individually lead to only a 10–15% improvement in productivity, but taken together, they can easily double the productivity of the organization, and in special cases, perhaps even improve productivity by a factor of ten.

The Jones figures are the differences between organizations which are at the leading-edge in terms of tools, methods, and skill levels, and those which are at the trailing-edge (Chapter 2). Jones believes that the many claims in the commercial software press of 10:1 increases are based on either very small projects, or on coding only, i.e. they do not include requirements, planning, etc. However, he himself claims that leading-edge organizations are capable of delivering almost 10 times the functionality per unit of labor as industry averages of a few years earlier.

The 2.4:1 ratio attributed to Smith was derived from his predicted 50% reduction in development cost, his 75% reduction in maintenance cost, and his 40% development, 50% maintenance, 5% operations and 5% evaluation split. His predicted reduction is based on a comprehensive combination of factors affecting productivity, such as structured programming, non-procedural languages, database management systems, data dictionaries, programmers' workbench, automated system design methodology, incremental development, application packages, CPTs, project management planning and control systems, etc.

The 2.4:1 prediction attributed to Boehm (1973) was derived from his predicted 9% p.a. increase in the number of machine instructions per man-month, and covers a period of ten years. Ten years was chosen partly to bring it into line with some of the other predictions, and partly because this is a reasonable time-scale for new tools and techniques to filter through: 'it took the DP profession ten years to swing from assembly language as the main form of programming to widespread use of COBOL and PL/1' (Martin, 1982a).

The 3:1 ratio attributed to van der Poel is the improvement which would have been achieved if all the projects in his survey had had the same efficiency as the best project; see his efficiency rates in Chapter 2 (Table 2.14). It therefore only provides a rough guide as to the productivity increase which may be expected. For example, the variations observed might not have been due to differences in efficiency as such, but to uncontrollable differences in the products, e.g. problem complexity, in which case the potential productivity gain might be much less than 3:1. On the other hand, if there had been say more support from top management, greater use of structured walkthroughs, greater use of non-procedural languages, and so on, then the efficiency of *all* the organizations might have been much higher, in which case the potential productivity gain is much *more* than 3:1.

The 3:1 ratio attributed to Albrecht is the improvement he observed in a study of 22 projects completed over a 5-year period, during which the development technologies and programming languages were improved.

This increase was attributed mainly to the use of structured programming, high-level languages, on-line development, and a programming development library.

Druffel based his estimate on the cost drivers in the COCOMO cost-estimation model (Boehm, 1981). It reflects the productivity increase which is anticipated in the space of ten years if management attempts to control ten selected factors affecting productivity – use of software tools, MPPs, software re-use, etc. (If no such attempts are made, then he gives the much lower prediction of 30% in seven years, which extrapolates to under 1.5:1 in ten years, i.e. only one-third as much.) He anticipates that productivity increases of about 10% each are possible from most of the selected factors. This is much lower than the COCOMO figures. Druffel apparently based his increases on *nominal* values for the cost drivers (i.e. he used *typical* productivity rates as his starting point), rather than giving *maximum* values (corresponding to the difference between maximum and minimum productivity rates). Conte *et al.* (1986) nevertheless warned that it is difficult to assess the extent to which these gains are achievable, especially when they are applied to the entire software industry. (This warning could probably be applied to some of the other predictions as well.)

The Butler Cox prediction applies to both development and maintenance. They believe that most DP departments can double their productivity in 3–4 years, and raise it by a further 400% in 6–8 years. The tabulated value of 5:1 assumes that the 400% and the 6–8 years are measured from the initial productivity and date. If instead they are based on the situation after the initial 3–4 years, then the prediction becomes a 10:1 improvement in total, in 9–12 years.

Boehm (1981) predicts a 2:1 increase in 3–4 years, and a 5:1 increase in 6–8 years, for most organizations; and a 3:1 increase in 4 years, and an 8:1 increase in 9 years, for some organizations. (The latter group presumably consists of those organizations which currently have a low productivity. These organizations may experience a more rapid initial increase in productivity – though Conte *et al.* (1986) warned that it is difficult to improve poor productivity – but in the long term the rate will slow down, and their productivity will approach that of the other organizations.) The predictions apply to both development and maintenance. They assume an integrated, long-range productivity improvement program, with a good deal of planning and investment. On the other hand, they do not include the effect of factors such as motivation, management, experience, and re-used code, and they underestimate the maintenance benefits of MPPs, so much higher increases are possible for both development and (especially) maintenance.

It is interesting to note the similarity between the Butler Cox (1983b) and Boehm (1981) predictions.

Martin (1982a) claims that productivity improvements of over 1000% are not uncommon with database user languages, report generators, graphics packages, and application generators. He concedes that these tools often only replace small application programs, but points out that these comprise 70% of all applications. (As Jones (1986b) put it, 'industrial and commercial software is characterized by very large volumes of very small applications'.) Furthermore, almost all the pressure from end users is for applications which can be developed using these tools. (These are also some of the tools which end users can use to develop their own applications, and end-user development is currently limited to small applications – see Chapter 3. Therefore end users can now, to an increasing extent, develop their own urgent applications.)

(Parikh (1984) referred to claimed gains of up to 1000%, but added that such high gains will only be achieved if the 'methodology' – he was including tools such as database languages in his definition – fits your work. If it does not, then the gains might only be 10%.)

In addition to the tabulated figures, Nies (1983) stated that James Martin advertises that 1000-fold increases in programmer productivity are feasible. However, this figure is so much higher than any of the others that it must be viewed with caution. I suspect that it is a misprint, or a mistaken reference to the 1000 *per cent* improvement quoted by Martin (1982a), which is 'only' a 10:1 increase in productivity.

Conclusion

The figures in Table 12.1 cover a wide range, but that is only to be expected as they include different factors. The average of the figures is about 4:1 (equivalent to an increase of 15% p.a., compound, for 10 years), but most of them are between 2 and 3:1 (equivalent to about 10% p.a.), which is more consistent with the doubling of productivity in ten years which was achieved at the Liquor Control Board of Ontario (Liquor Control Board moves to relational DBMS with DLI TRANSPARENCY, *ADRWARE News*, 1986, **3**(2), pp. 12–14), and with the 1.6 times improvement in eight years (measured in equivalent assembler source lines) at the Toshiba Fuchu Software Factory in Japan (Matsumoto, 1989).

It is interesting to compare these figures with the actual increase in productivity of only about 5% p.a. (and possibly decreasing) which has been achieved in the past (Chapter 2). At that rate, productivity would only increase by 1.6:1 in 10 years. This suggests that the above predictions are optimistic, or at least that more attention must be paid to productivity in order to achieve the improvements which are possible.

The tabulated predictions do not show any obvious trend, but even if they did, it might be due to psychological reasons, e.g. an increased optimism not founded on facts.

12.1.2 MY PREDICTION

There are so many factors affecting productivity that it is reasonable to conclude that significant gains are possible. This optimism would seem to be borne out by the much higher productivity – perhaps 5:1 – which is achieved by some organizations than others (Chapter 2), and by the high productivity achieved on some projects – perhaps also as much as 5:1 on the NYT (Baker, 1972) and Inmon (1976) projects, where combinations of improved techniques were used (Chapter 3). The predictions of most other authorities therefore seem too cautious, and in any case do not include all possible factors, so **as a ballpark figure, I predict that the productivity of the software industry can be increased by a factor of ten with existing technology and know-how.**

Some qualifications are necessary.

- Synergism should result in a higher increase than would be expected from the individual factors – Yourdon (1979b) believes that synergism can *double* productivity.
- Past predictions and expectations have proved over-optimistic, and the same might be true of mine.
- Resistance to the factors will restrict their use and therefore the benefits derived. The surveys by Holton (1977) and Lientz *et al.* (1978), for example, showed that little use was being made of the available tools and techniques, while Zelkowitz (1985) found that software engineering practices of US companies were 'marginal'. Parikh (1984) claims that most managers and programmers are not familiar with the tools that are available. Martin and McClure (1985) state that automated tools and non-procedural languages were mostly created by pragmatic craftsmen–programmers with no knowledge of computer science theory, and most computer scientists have taken no interest in the new tools, and do not even know their names. Conversely, the new, structured languages were designed by academics and do not reflect real commercial problems (Goodwin, 1986). All of this could explain why some tools have

been unprofitable, causing vendors to discontinue marketing them. A double prediction is therefore necessary.

- How much difference *can* the factors make?
- How much difference *will* they make?

However, resistance tends to die down as the benefits become apparent, so if we take a sufficiently long time-scale, this factor can be ignored.

These factors will, to some extent, cancel each other out, so I will stick to my prediction that a 10:1 productivity gain is possible.

I did not specify whether the 10:1 applied to development, maintenance, or overall productivity. I anticipate that a gain of 10:1 is possible for development, and that the gain for maintenance will be much higher than that for development, with the overall gain being in between. However, to be on the cautious side, I will predict only that overall productivity can be increased by 10:1.

I also did not specify the time-scale that would be required. The predictions in Table 12.1 are mostly for a period of 10 years or less, and the predicted increases are mostly much less than 10:1. It is therefore logical to conclude that it will take much longer than 10 years – and possibly more than 20 years – to achieve a 10:1 increase.

12.1.3 COMPARISON WITH SURVEYS

A number of surveys have investigated the relationship between various factors and productivity. Surveys like those of Holton (1977) and Walston and Felix (1977) found that many factors have a significant effect on productivity, and their findings have been incorporated into this study. However, two surveys – those by Nelson (1966) and van der Poel (1982, 1983) – failed to show the expected correlations. Even factors such as fourth-generation languages, experience, CPTs, structured walkthroughs and structured programming appeared to have no significant effect, which is surprising. It is in agreement with the pessimistic views of Hopkins (1972) and Gruenberger (1974) quoted above, and also with the very low development productivity gain (perhaps only 1.3:1) from all MPPs combined (Chapter 8), but if true, it means that my prediction is much too optimistic.

Although there are wide variations in the evidence presented earlier, with some evidence indicating that certain factors have a major impact on productivity and other evidence indicating that the same factors have little impact, it is nevertheless surprising to find surveys showing that *no* factors have a significant impact.

However, these surveys can be faulted. The van der Poel (1982, 1983) survey covered only a small (20 organizations) and uniform sample. For example, all the programmers in it were rated as high ability, so it is only to be expected that differences in their performance would be correspondingly small and difficult to observe. Similarly, all the staff were highly motivated, nearly all used some form of structured programming, hardly any used structured walkthroughs, and all the teams were small.

The Nelson (1966) survey is more difficult to explain. He examined over 100 factors (candidate cost drivers) in 169 projects – in fact, Boehm (1973, 1981) stated that this was the most exhaustive quantitative analysis ever conducted. In spite of this, Nelson found no correlation between productivity and, for example, the average experience of analysts and programmers, whereas Walston and Felix (1977) and Boehm (1981) found that this influenced productivity by perhaps 3:1 (Chapter 9), making it one of the factors with the greatest influence. However, some of his factors are of limited relevance. For example, the percentage of mathematical instructions is probably not significant in the majority of commercial programs, and commercial programs comprise the majority of all programs (Chapter 1); and the same is probably true of

the number of personnel trips, as the great majority of programming systems developed in the world are produced at a single location (Jones, 1986b). Also, his survey was conducted a long time ago, before the introduction of CPTs, fourth-generation languages and personal computers, the widespread use of interactive programming, and so on.

In addition, Boehm (1981) warned that the SDC effort-estimation model, which was derived from Nelson's survey, is counter-intuitive. A project with all zero ratings (not an abnormal situation) is estimated at *minus* 33 man-months; and changing from a high-level language to assembler adds 7 man-months, irrespective of project size. Conte *et al.* (1986) also warned about major shortcomings in the model. Firstly, even when applied to its own database, it produced quite large discrepancies between projected and actual effort. (This is probably because the model is linear, and linear models have not proven satisfactory for effort estimation: there are too many non-linear aspects of software development for a linear cost-estimation model to work very well. If effort is highly non-linear, e.g. if it increases exponentially, then a linear model cannot adequately capture the non-linearity, and discrepancies must be expected.) Secondly, the model takes size into account only indirectly (through the number of subprograms), not directly, whereas size is used in eight of the nine cost-estimation models surveyed by Boehm (1981), and in fact almost all other models assume that effort increases with program size. (One of these eight models is actually the Nelson model which, in apparent contradiction to Conte, and even to the Nelson effort-estimation formula reproduced by Boehm himself, is shown as including size directly, through the number of object instructions.)

The discrepancies between these two surveys and the remaining evidence may also be due to apparently subtle differences in the factors surveyed. For example, both surveys examined *experience*, whereas it appears to be *knowledge* which makes the difference (Chapter 9). Although these terms are commonly treated as synonymous, in fact they are not. If, therefore, the surveys had examined knowledge, they might well have found a noticeable difference. Another possible explanation is that sometimes people *say* they are using a particular method when in fact they are not (Yourdon, 1975). They would therefore not be getting any benefits from the method.

Both surveys did, however, show a correlation (albeit a poor one), between *groups* of factors and productivity.

- The successful CPT concept is a combination of several factors (Chapter 3).
- It is difficult to hold a walkthrough of a badly structured program (Chapter 8).
- There is a ripple effect which an improvement in one factor can produce (Chapter 3).

Taking all aspects into account, it would be premature, on the basis of these two pessimistic surveys, to dismiss my prediction.

12.2   HOW BIG AN INCREASE IS NEEDED?

An investigation into productivity would not be complete without discussing how large an improvement is required. The increased productivity may be needed to cover a shortage of staff, the increase in demand for staff, an increase in gross domestic product, an increase in maintenance or an increase in hardware capacity.

Shortage of staff

The obvious answer to the question is that the productivity increase required corresponds to the shortage of staff, i.e. if there is a 20% shortage, then a 20% rise in the productivity of existing staff would cure it – and an increase of more than 20% would permit a reduction in the existing number of staff.

However, there are problems with this approach. Firstly, the published figures for the staff shortage might not be reliable – they may, for example, be based on the size of the backlog of work, and as there is an 'invisible' backlog (Chapter 8) which may be even larger than the documented one, the true shortage of staff may be 40% not 20%, and therefore a 40% increase in productivity is necessary. Secondly, these figures refer to the magnitude of the *present* shortage. The demand for staff can be expected to grow – and an increase in the shortage *was* predicted in Chapter 9 – so the *longer-term* shortage – the increase in the demand for staff – must also be taken into account.

Increase in demand for staff

Ohno (1989) reported that the information-processing industry was growing by a factor of 4 every 10 years (= 15% p.a., compound), compared to a factor of only 2.4 (9% p.a.) in programmer productivity. An article in *Business Week* (Missing computer software, 1 Sept. 1980, pp. 46–53) predicted that the need for programmers would increase by a factor of 3, from under 500 000 in 1980, to 1.5 million by 1990, an increase of 12% p.a. (500 000 is much higher than the other estimates for that time tabulated in Chapter 8, but for the present purpose we are only interested in rates of increase, not absolute numbers.) Charette (1986), Martin (1983a), and Boehm and Standish (1983) (military needs) all estimated that the demand for computing specialists was growing at a rate of 12% per year. According to one software supplier, the demand for application development staff was increasing by 20% p.a., and the supply of trained personnel by only 3% (Productivity Software, 1988). If, for example, the demand is increasing by 20% p.a., then an increase in productivity of 20% p.a. would eliminate the need for employing more staff. (Because of people leaving the industry, the increase in productivity would actually have to be a little higher than 20% p.a. to maintain current staff levels.)

Increase in gross domestic product (GDP)

The increase in the GDP can be used as an indication of the increase in the demand for software, and therefore the increase in demand for staff or the corresponding productivity increase required. Based on the increase in the Japanese GDP, Matsumoto (1989) reported that domestic demands for software were expected to increase by 6% every year in monetary value (Japanese Ministry of International Trade and Industry, 1987). The average productivity of system engineers would therefore have to be improved by 5% every year in monetary value of the products, while that of programmers would have to be improved by 8% every year. The expected increase in the teaching capability at schools was taken into account in this estimate. If this improvement is not attained, then the shortage of software engineers in Japan could increase from only 4000 in 1985 (out of 470 000), to as much as 970 000 in the year 2000, i.e. the shortage could be double the number of software engineers. However, this method can be challenged, as it does not allow, for example, for the backlog in demand for software.

Increase in maintenance

After a system has been developed, it must be maintained: 'Each new development project adds to the maintenance burden' (Arthur, 1988). Staff would therefore have to be transferred from development to maintenance, thereby seriously restricting the amount of new development. However, a mathematical model by Capers Jones showed that an increase of more than 15% a year in the total number of programming staff would prevent this happening (Jones, 1986b). (An increase in quality would also counteract it, by reducing the amount of maintenance. This

is a superior solution, and is equivalent to an increase in productivity.)

Increase in hardware capacity

The increase in capacity of installed hardware (Chapter 5) provides an indirect method of determining the increase in demand for software, and therefore the increase in demand for staff or the corresponding productivity increase required.

Boehm (1981) argued that the reported 24% p.a. increase in the total number of computers (Phister, 1979) suggests a proportionally high annual growth rate in the demand for new software. Carl Reynolds of the Hughes Aircraft Co. stated that equipment output increased 100 million times in the previous 30 years, compared to an increase of only about five times in programmer output (Pantages, 1987). Martin (1981) took this argument one step further. Based on the expansion of the market (the number of computers used for scientific or commercial applications was expected to continue growing by at least 25% p.a.), and their increasing power (he predicted they would increase in speed by a factor of at least 10 in the next 10 years), he calculated that the productivity increase needed by 1990 was no less than 93.1 times (= 57% p.a., compound). In other words, if there was no increase in productivity, then nearly 100 times as many programmers would have been needed in the space of 10 years. The number of programmers in the US would therefore have had to increase from 300 000 in 1981, to 28 million in 1990. This is a much higher figure than obtained from other sources – e.g. it is an order of magnitude higher than the prediction in *Business Week* mentioned earlier, and also contrasts with the estimate by Charette (1986) that there would be a million person shortfall in trained personnel by 1990 – and for a number of reasons, this method is simplistic.

1. The demand for hardware is driven by the

demand for DP applications, i.e. the need for software is the *cause*, and the sales of hardware are only the *effect*. The number of programmers required therefore depends ultimately not on the output of the hardware manufacturing plants, but on the needs of the users. If, in the extreme case, organizations ran out of new applications to be computerized, then hardware sales would suffer a drastic decline. This is unlikely, because there is 'a very strong underlying growth in the need for information' (Huskisson, 1977), but nevertheless it seems implausible that the demand for software will grow indefinitely: just as most households need only one telephone, so most organizations need only one payroll system. This opinion is supported, for example, by the claims that both the corporate PC software market and the high-end DBMS market are showing signs of saturation (Chapters 5 and 6).

Martin (1981) did give a figure which is more closely related to the demand for software. He quoted an unnamed IBM survey which found that the number of applications in data processing centers was growing by 45% p.a., and added that this growth was likely to continue. (Seven years later he repeated this claim (Martin, 1988), so presumably he believes that this high rate of growth *has* continued.) Using this figure results in a halving of his estimate: 'only' 41.1 times as many programmers would be required in 10 years, not 93.1.

Furthermore, figures given in Chapter 2 from other authorities suggest that the number of installed applications is increasing by *less* than 45% p.a.: Jones (1986b) gives a figure of 26% p.a. for the total lines of installed code worldwide from 1950 through to 2000 (41% p.a. between 1960 and 1980, but decreasing to only 13% p.a. between 1980 and 1990, and just 4% p.a. between 1990 and 2000); while Charette

(1986) gives a figure of 32% p.a. for the number of deployed systems at the Department of Defense between 1960 and 1978. Perhaps, therefore, 'only' 30 times as many programmers – or even just twice as many – will be needed in the space of 10 years.

However, this approach also has its problems. The number of applications would be increasing by more than 45% p.a. were it not for the shortage of staff. Worse, Martin (1981) predicted that the number of data processing centers would grow by perhaps a factor of 10 in the next 10 years, because of the rapidly dropping cost of computers. (The proliferation of PCs has vindicated his prediction.) This presumably implies that *411* times as many programmers would be required in 10 years, not 41.1 times, but this figure seems too high to be realistic. In any case, many PCs run only one application, such as word processing or a spreadsheet. (According to Diagnostic Research, MS-DOS users regularly use an average of 3.7 software packages on their machines, while Macintosh users average 5.8 (Dvorak, 1989). However, Dvorak himself, and apparently McMahon (1989) as well, believe that these figures are too high: 'the average MS-DOS machine is used for as few as 1.7 applications'.)

2. The prediction does not allow for *changes* in trends. New application areas such as computer graphics and OA (office automation) have accelerated the demand for software, and so in particular has the proliferation of microcomputers. On the other hand, software packages are also proliferating (not just application packages but especially word processing packages, spreadsheets, etc.). Furthermore, Martin (1981) assumed that hardware prices would continue to drop, whereas evidence (Chapter 5) indicates that they have already levelled off. Although the price/performance ratio is still improving,

this may not have as much effect on sales as price alone, and it too may level off causing sales to slow – and the evidence in Chapter 5 indicates that this may already be happening, as hardware improvements are becoming more difficult to achieve, and sales *have* slowed down. In any case, the total cost per program instruction doubled in 24 years despite the drastic reduction in hardware costs (Wright, 1978). (Figures given by Jones (1986b) also show a doubling in 20 years, but this was largely due to the 'mathematical paradox' associated with the change from Assembler to COBOL. It is not clear if the same explanation applies to Wright's figures. Nevertheless, even if we avoid this pitfall, the figures given by Jones show only a 33% drop in the cost of developing a system.)

The wider use of fourth-generation software has a dual impact. It increases both the productivity of programmers, and the number of people who do programming, by enabling end users to write and maintain their own programs (Chapter 3).

3. There are large differences in speed and capacity between different computers, so the number of machines should be weighted by these factors, especially as the majority of machines are small and slow. While Martin apparently did make an allowance for this – his figure for the growth in the number of computers (25% p.a. in 1981) appears to exclude the smallest computers (Chapter 5) – the situation since then, particularly the proliferation of personal computers for commercial use, may necessitate an adjustment to his figures.

4. Operating systems are more sophisticated, so computers spend more and more time performing 'housekeeping' tasks at the expense of the users' tasks. For example, provision of a virtual machine costs both storage and speed of execution (Lemmons, 1986), while up to 40% of the raw

power of IBM's 3090 series computers may be consumed by their MVS/XA operating system 'in looking after itself', and the corresponding figure for the latest DEC computers was 20% (The King is dead; long live the King, *Computer Mail*, 27 Feb. 1987, pp. 21–31). According to Marjoribanks (1983), usage of memory by the operating system, and usage of disk by the system software, utilities and application code, increased by a factor of 10 in a few years. (Boehm (1981) gave an example, of a large multi-processor system, which forcefully illustrates this effect. Each processor in the system contributed some overhead, so that, with nine processors, the overhead was so high there was virtually no throughput at all. Another extreme example is 'thrashing'. The CPU spends all its time paging (moving pages of data between main memory and backing storage), to the exclusion of any processing (Chandor *et al.*, 1985; Collin, 1989). It is caused by a design deficiency in virtual storage systems.)

Similarly, languages are at an increasingly higher level, i.e. they do more of the work thereby improving programmer productivity, but to do so they 'soak up' the improvements in hardware speed and capacity: 'ease of use requires computer memory' (Huskisson, 1977; Shneiderman, 1980).

5. The size of programming problems increases to fill the machine storage available (Chapter 5). (The previous point provides examples of this.)

6. The average computer is not being fully utilized – for example, one study showed that central computers were only being utilized at 23% of their efficiency; one survey showed that PCs were only used for 5.1 hours a day; and some workstations are just status symbols (Chapters 4 and 5). Using PCs instead of mainframes and minicomputers usually also results in under-utilized hardware. When the user

of a PC is idle, the PC is generally also idle, as it is not normally available to other people; but when any individual user of a mainframe or mini is idle, the mainframe or mini is generally *not* idle – it is still being used by other people. Where resources are shared, a lower total capacity is required.

7. Similarly, with interactive programming and interactive application systems, the processor is idle for much of the time (Chapter 6). This is true during office hours, when programmers and end users are working interactively, but is especially true outside office hours. Previously, batch jobs kept computers running to capacity 24 hours a day, but these old batch systems are being replaced by interactive systems (Chapter 8), and few people work overnight. Part of the computer workload is therefore transferred from night-time to daytime, so additional capacity is required during the day to handle it, but it stands idle at night. The 5.1 hours a day usage of PCs quoted above is also an example of this effect.

8. Hardware power is sometimes consciously traded against people-time, e.g. inefficient programs are accepted as the price to pay for faster programming, and trial and error tests are run to speed up debugging (Chapters 5 and 6).

Adjustments for all the above factors should be calculated.

Conclusion

The above estimates cover a wide range, from a one-time increase of 20% (based on the shortage of staff), up to 57% p.a. (based on the increase in hardware capacity). However, sizeable adjustments must be applied to both these extreme estimates, and the adjustments will bring them closer to the remaining estimates. The remaining estimates cover the much narrower range of 5% p.a. to 20% p.a., and it seems likely that the required increase in productivity lies within this range.

12.3 HOW BIG AN INCREASE IN OUTPUT IS BEING ACHIEVED?

Martin's (1981) prediction, based on the increasing number of computers and their increasing speed, that nearly 100 times as many programmers would be required in 10 years, seems unnecessarily alarmist, as he himself reports – and in the same reference – a 45% p.a. increase in the number of applications. This figure seems very high, but must be considered plausible as the additional hardware is being bought, i.e. the software industry and end users *are* finding a use for it. In particular, Martin and McClure (1985) quoted a prediction that there would soon be one computer for every 10 employees in the US, and the claimed 40 million MS-DOS installations (Chapter 6) implies that this stage has already been reached, but there is not one professional programmer for every 10 employees. (The figures in Chapter 8 indicate that there are currently probably less than one million professional programmers in the USA.) Somehow or other, therefore, the output of the industry is increasing rapidly. It is not clear how this is being achieved:

• by a rapid expansion in the number of software engineers?
• by a rapid increase in productivity?
• by a rapid increase in end-user programming?
• by the large number of packages run on smaller machines?
• are systems smaller or simpler than in the past?
• is the hardware just being used less efficiently?

The number of software staff is only increasing by about 6% p.a. (Chapter 9); productivity has only been increasing by about 5% p.a. (Chapter 2); and the evidence indicates that, apart perhaps from the movement to microcomputers, systems are getting bigger, not smaller (by perhaps 20% p.a.), and are increasing in complexity (probably by about the same amount) (Chapter 8). (The increase in size and complexity of applications makes the claimed 45% p.a. increase in the number of applications even more surprising.)

The increase in size and complexity can be expected to cancel the increases in productivity and number of programmers. It is therefore likely that either there has been a significant improvement in indirect ('invisible') productivity, e.g. by the wider use of application packages, or that end users are creating a significant number of systems themselves. This view is supported, for example, by the claimed 20–30% p.a. rate of growth of packages (Chapter 7); by the survey which showed that in 31% of installations, users did more than three-quarters of the systems development work (though other evidence indicates that end-user development is still rare – see Chapter 3); and by the fact that there are at least six computers to every programmer (Chapter 7). Coupled with the less efficient use of the hardware (because of more sophisticated software, interactive systems, the increased use of PCs, etc.), it seems likely that the software industry and its users will continue to absorb the output of the hardware manufacturing plants for the immediate future – and the foreseeable future? – without any special additional measures.

12.4 CONCLUSION

Earlier, I predicted that the *productivity* of the software industry could be increased by a factor of 10 with existing technology and know-how. I also concluded that the *output* of the industry was already rising rapidly, largely due to an increase in 'invisible' productivity, e.g. through the use of application packages, and end-user programming. However, an even larger increase in both productivity and output is necessary, and it must be sustained for at least the next few years, in order to clear the backlog of work and provide faster response to user requirements. Nevertheless, the potential productivity increase is so large that it may be concluded not only that significant gains will be achieved, but also that these will be sufficient to meet reasonable user demands. However, some qualifications to this statement are necessary.

1. The gains will not be achieved through one measure alone (or even a composite measure such as MPPs, which itself consists of multiple different measures), but through many, and will require a long, sustained effort: 'The payoffs are large, but they require a long-range commitment. There are no easy, instant panaceas' (Boehm, 1981; Conte *et al.*, 1986).

2. Even if the gains achieved are lower than I have predicted, they will nevertheless be large enough to be visible. The users will *see* that their needs are being met far more promptly, and so will be much happier than they are at present: they will regard DP personnel as 'heroes' (Dean, 1983; Martin, 1982a). The software industry will therefore gain a breathing-space in which to make further improvements.

3. Parkinson's Law (Parkinson, 1957) applies here: no matter how great an improvement is achieved, users will always find more work for the DP department. The current backlog, while admittedly too long, performs a valuable service as a sieve to ensure that only those applications which are really needed, which have a high payoff, or which are most cost-effective, are developed (Chapter 8).

4. Generally, instant satisfaction of the user's needs is not necessary. Organizations are in competition with each other, and the competitors have similar problems. If an organization falls behind its competitors, it will suffer, but provided it can keep abreast of them, it will survive, and it need only remain slightly ahead to prosper (Jones, 1986b).

5. From a cost point of view, what is important to the user is the *total* cost of meeting his needs. As long as this is decreasing, he will be happy. He is not interested in how much of the total is due to hardware and how much to software. In the past, hardware was the more expensive component, the 'weakest link in the chain': 'We're paying this computer six hundred dollars an hour, and we're paying you two dollars an hour' (Boehm, 1981); but this has now changed: 'As late as the mid-1950s, 90% of application costs were devoted to hardware, but now 90% of the costs are for software' (Shneiderman, 1980). Lower hardware prices, higher programmer salaries, and the additional effort to make systems easier to use, have made software the more expensive component – it has become the weakest link – so attention is now focused on it (Yourdon *et al.*, 1979a). Improvements can therefore be expected, of which fourth-generation software is the forerunner. (As Lu (1986) put it, first hardware overtakes software, then software catches up and overtakes hardware.) Larger computer memories and higher processing speeds have made such improvements a practical possibility.

From a narrow software industry point of view, the improvement in software productivity need only be large enough to make hardware once again the weakest link, as that will turn attention back to hardware. An IBM survey showed that, for over 90% of application programs, software development and maintenance costs exceeded the total lifetime execution costs by a factor of 10 (Kendall, 1978). If software costs are lowered by a factor of 10 due to improved productivity as predicted above, and hardware costs are increased (as part of the price of the improvement in productivity), then hardware will again become the more expensive component.

The following chapter – the final one – summarizes the conclusions, and discusses some associated topics.

The main findings of this study are summarized in this chapter, but some associated topics are also discussed. Are the predicted gains in productivity accurate? What action must be taken to realize the predicted gains? What action can be taken to supplement the gains?

13.1 AREAS FOR FURTHER RESEARCH

In Part 2, many factors affecting productivity were examined. Some of these factors can apparently raise productivity significantly. However, although I quoted a considerable body of supporting evidence, some of it can be challenged. For example, what is true for a group of computer science students in a small-scale experiment, is not necessarily also true for a team of professional programmers working on a large-scale production system (Chapter 1). There is thus a lack of rigorous scientific proof to support all the claimed improvements, and therefore uncertainty as to how big an increase in productivity can be expected. To remedy this, I have drawn up the outline of a research program which would provide additional evidence, and fill some of the gaps in our knowledge. Software development is not yet a true science, but it is moving in that direction (Jones, 1986b), and my proposed research program will help it along the way. Furthermore, like Shneiderman (1980) in the preface to his book *Software Psychology*, I hope that my book will encourage further experimentation. Shneiderman ends nearly every chapter in his book with a 'researcher's agenda', giving ideas for further research. Similarly, several of the chapters in

Boehm (1981) end with a section 'topics for further research'.

Many of the topics discussed in this study can be classified as areas requiring further research, so I have given only a few selected suggestions: projects which appeal to me. The ideas are not fundamentally new, so the projects are intended rather to confirm some of the evidence already presented, provide more up to date information, or explore the topics in greater depth. Confirmatory studies carry less prestige in the research world than original research, but nevertheless frequently reveal new underlying relationships, and lead to new hypotheses (Conte *et al.*, 1986).

Survey

In Chapter 2, evidence was presented that some organizations are five times more productive than others. The purpose of the proposed survey is to confirm this, and to determine the reason. Relatively little information is required to provide the confirmation – basically just the total number of DP staff (programmers, analysts, managers, secretaries, etc.), plus their combined rate of output (as measured by the total number of lines of code, function points, etc., per day, month, or year), for each of the organizations surveyed. However, far more information is required to determine the *reasons* for any differences found. In fact, detailed information like the 104 candidate cost drivers in the 169 projects surveyed by Nelson (1966) is necessary. The proposed survey will therefore record, for each organization, information such as the organizational structure, the quantity of training provided, the qualifications of the staff, the programming languages used, the design methods, and so on.

The information should be recorded on a form designed for the purpose. For example, Boehm (1981) designed a set of forms for recording software cost-estimating information in a standard, consistent way. The forms are based on his COCOMO cost-estimation model. One of the forms therefore has a column for each of the cost drivers in that model. It has additional columns for calculations, as well as space for identifying information such as the name of the project, the name of the analyst, and so on. Similarly, Jones (1986b) designed a form for recording information for his SPQR (software productivity, quality, and reliability) model. It is very comprehensive, containing over 200 questions, with many of the questions having five or more alternative answers. For example:

> Maintenance funding?
> 1) Maintenance is funded from overhead or enterprise funds.
> 2) Maintenance is covered by informal contract or agreement.
> 3) Hybrid: partial overhead and partial charge-out funding.
> 4) Maintenance is charged out to users.
> 5) Maintenance funding is currently undefined.

Boehm (1981) warned about the problems in gathering data. For example, detailed data will probably not be available for completed projects; where data was obtained from different sources, some of it might include support software, while the remainder does not (Chapter 2); or the time spent by chief programmers on managerial duties might have been counted twice – once under programming (because the work was done by a programmer), and once under managerial (because it is managerial work). Expert help and spot checks may be necessary to guard against such problems.

Many (most?) surveys are restricted to the development stage, and they overlook quality considerations. Systems analysts often build into their systems only the user's immediate requirements (Expertise within the IMS environment, *Corporate Computing Today*, Oct. 1989, pp. 9–10). (This happens, though in a pre-planned way, with incremental delivery.) Their systems therefore are initially small and simple with a correspondingly high development productivity, but have a high level of subsequent maintenance as the remaining requirements are added. Worse, figures by Jones (1986b) indicate that, depending on the quality of the base code and how well documented it is, and on how scattered the changes are, enhancements take 20–60% longer than developing the equivalent amount of code for a new program, because of the need to understand and test the base code, and integrate the new code with it; while according to DeMarco (1982), enhancement productivity is one or two orders of magnitude lower than development productivity. Jones's figures also indicate that up to 40% more time is required to maintain an enhanced program, presumably because of errors introduced by the enhancements, and the increased entropy of programs after they have been modified (Chapter 8). A survey which looked at only the development stage would therefore record misleadingly high productivity rates.

Similarly, some programs are 'completed' quickly (with a correspondingly high apparent productivity) due to minimal time spent planning and testing, but then require many modifications to fix all the defects. Once again, conventional surveys do not adequately reflect the situation. In both cases, organizational policy – a stress on rapid results – leads to, or aggravates, such behavior ('run now, crawl later' – Chapter 11). Cancelled projects and re-used code are also not adequately catered for in conventional surveys.

The proposed survey takes a step towards rectifying these inadequacies. Instead of just recording and comparing figures for the development stage of individual programs, it will also compare the *total* time expended by each organization's DP staff with the *fruit* of that effort as measured by, for example, the number of systems, programs, function points, or lines of code, including re-used code and application packages, which had been used in production. Jones (1986b) calls this a 'sanity check' on the organization's productivity. An organization which spent much time reworking the same code over and over again as described above, trying to get it right, or even just successively adding omitted functions as these came to light, would have less to show for its efforts, and the same is true of organizations which experience a high project cancellation rate. Conversely, organizations which make extensive use of re-used code or application packages will obtain a more accurate picture of the benefits they are receiving (which could be used to justify any additional costs of these methods). This technique also permits measurement of the productivity of organizations which do not keep detailed records of the time spent on individual programs.

Super-programmers

Just as some organizations apparently have a much higher productivity than others, so some programmers are super-programmers (Chapter 9). Why? Ability? Greater knowledge? Better methods? Use of clever loops and tricks? Careful study is needed to determine what they do that is different from ordinary programmers (Arthur, 1988).

The proposed investigation will select, and then make a detailed comparison of, a number of super-programmers and ordinary programmers, to identify the differences between them. It will then attempt to establish which of these differences cause the large discrepancies in productivity, e.g. the differences might be factors which are known to have a large impact on productivity.

Complexity distribution

This research project was motivated by Knuth's (1971) finding (Chapter 9) that the complexity distribution of statements in programs written by experienced programmers was similar to that in students' programs, which indicates that the experienced programmers in his study were not making greater use of more advanced features in the language. Has the situation changed since then? Is it generally true? Does it adversely affect productivity? How can his finding be reconciled with those of Chrysler (1978a, 1978b) and Gordon *et al.* (1977) that experienced programmers used fewer statements, and fewer GOTOs, than novices?

The proposed research project will examine many programs. For each program, it will record the following.

- The complexity distribution of the statements in the program, e.g. for COBOL (McClure, 1978):
  - a simple statement is: MOVE ZERO TO A
  - a more complex one is: PERFORM LOOP VARYING COUNTER FROM 1 BY 1 UNTIL COUNTER > LOOP-END

  In Knuth's study, of FORTRAN programs, 86% of the assignment statements involved no more than one arithmetic operator, 95% of DO loops used the default increment of 1, and 87% of the variables had no more than one subscript.
- The knowledge level of the programmer (measured e.g. by the amount of training he had received, and the variety and relevance of his experience, and not just his length of experience).

Also to be recorded are the usual data needed to measure productivity, such as the amount of time it took to develop the program, the size of the program, the language used, and so on.

It would be interesting to compare also the programmers' styles, e.g. as shown by the proportion of GOTOs, or by patterns in the graphs generated by the FLOW tool when FORTRAN source code is fed into it for analysis (McCabe, 1976; Shneiderman, 1980).

The objective is to determine if there is any relation between these factors, and quantify it.

- Do knowledgeable programmers use more powerful commands?
- Are programs with a large proportion of powerful commands completed more quickly?

A large proportion of powerful commands might also indicate that the job the program is doing is particularly complex, or even that the programmer has overdone the use of powerful commands. Furthermore, if the programmer is not fluent in the commands, e.g. if he does not use them often, or has only just returned from an advanced programming course, then his productivity is likely to be low.

Suitably adapted static analyser programs or even compilers could be used to determine the complexity distributions (Chapter 10).

As a by-product, this investigation will show if training, particularly advanced training, correlates with the use of more complex techniques, or with high productivity, and will quantify the relationships (productivity improvement figures given in section 9.3.1 ranged from only 10% to over 80%). Another by-product will be to confirm and quantify the evidence presented in Chapter 6 that less powerful versions or sub-sets of languages give lower productivity than the full languages. (The programs examined would, of course, have to include ones which had been written in different versions of the same language.)

An interesting extension to this project would be to implement some maintenance changes to programs with low and high proportions of complex statements, to see what effect this had on the ease, speed, and accuracy of maintenance.

One consideration is that structured programs contain a lower proportion of GOTO statements (a simple construct), and a higher proportion of DO-WHILE statements and IF statements with ELSE clauses (which are more complex constructs) – see Chapter 8. Therefore experiments which compare structured programming with unstructured programming overlap with the research project proposed here. For example, experiments which show that structured programs are easier to maintain suggest also that programs with a high proportion of complex statements may be easier to maintain. The proposed research project will investigate these aspects in more detail.

Which function should be given the most attention?

A disproportionate amount of attention in the literature has paid to one particular function in the software life-cycle: the writing of programs (Appendix C). The objective of the research project proposed here is to determine how much attention *should* be devoted to each function, i.e. which function has the highest payoff potential for cost reduction or productivity improvement? It will take into account:

- how much time is currently spent on each function (Chapter 8);
- the salary of the person (job category) who performs the function (e.g. systems analysts are generally paid about 20% more than programmers – see Chapter 8);
- the cost of the machine time (if any) used in that function (e.g. the function split percentages for testing would be about 20% higher if machine costs were included – see Chapter 8);
- the cost of any software, clerical support, etc. currently used in that function;
- the cost of errors made in that function (in particular, errors made early in the life-cycle are expensive to correct if they are not detected quickly – see Chapter 8);
- the potential for productivity improvement of that function (e.g. if much attention has

already been devoted to it, there may be little scope left for further improvement);

- the difficulty in improving the productivity of that function (e.g. if much attention has already been devoted to it, with little success, subsequent attempts may be equally unsuccessful).

The proposed research project will also take into account the *disadvantages* of attempts to improve productivity, such as the cost of extra technological aids, additional machine time, the likely increase in the number of errors if less time is spent on the function, and possible resistance to the measures.

For greater accuracy, maintenance will not be treated as a single function, but will be subdivided into its components (requirements, design, etc.), as is customarily done for development.

Team size and project duration

The evidence presented in Chapter 3 indicates that the large numbers of people who work together on big projects spend a considerable amount of time communicating with each other, and a considerable amount of time is spent co-ordinating their efforts, and this is equivalent to a large productivity loss. Intuitively, therefore, there should be major productivity gains by making teams smaller (though this would generally make project schedules longer), and Walston and Felix (1977), for example, did find that productivity was almost doubled. However, some of the other evidence (Chapter 3) indicates that there is little, if any, improvement. The purpose of the proposed research program is therefore to establish which of the conflicting evidence is correct.

The research program will therefore gather data on team size, project duration, and productivity rate, as well as on the usual other factors affecting productivity, such as system and program size, and tools and methods used. It will also attempt to take into

account the disadvantages of delaying project completion, such as changes in the users' requirements during the extended development period, and the delay in receiving the benefits provided by the system (Chapter 3). The disadvantages would, however, vary greatly from one system to another.

How good are fourth-generation languages?

Claims for productivity improvements derived from fourth-generation languages range from under 1.3:1 to over 100:1 (Chapter 6). Even allowing for differences in power between various 4GLs, this is a very large discrepancy. Facts must therefore be gathered to establish the true figure.

To answer the question, another question must first be answered: how do you compare fourth-generation languages – both against each other and against conventional languages? LOC, the traditional unit of measure, does not work well with different language levels (Chapter 2); and the improved cost-estimation methods which are now available (Chapter 8) are also of limited help, as they are largely based on LOC.

The first part of this research will therefore be to choose or find a usable standard of comparison. Some suggestions have already been made in Chapter 2: use the number of systems, the number of programs, the number of operators and operands in the programs, the number of characters in the source code, the number of inputs and outputs, or the number of function points. (Function points are probably currently the most popular and accurate alternative. The number of characters method was suggested specifically for 4GLs.) One way to determine the best unit of measure is to record the number of lines of code, the number of function points, and a variety of alternative measures, for a large number of projects. It can then be established which is the most accurate and reliable, and under which circumstances (e.g. for which type of program) each measure is reliable. This will also enable the various measures to be calibrated against each other (Jones, 1986b), e.g. it will confirm and refine the conversion table between function points and lines of code for various languages presented in Chapter 2. The chosen unit of measure will then be applied to many systems, some of which had been developed using a 4GL, and others using a conventional language, and the results compared.

A more direct, but more expensive method of determining how good fourth-generation languages are is to develop several complete systems twice, once using a fourth-generation language, and once using conventional methods, and then implement some maintenance changes to both versions. (In some of the examples given by Martin (1982a), the systems *were* developed twice.) (Maintenance must be part of the comparison as it forms a large proportion of the total software time, and there is always the danger that a language which provides easy development may not provide easy maintenance – see Chapter 6.) The test systems would have to be carefully chosen so as to provide a representative cross-section of software engineering activities, otherwise the experiment might just confirm that 4GLs give a high productivity on some types of program (e.g. *ad hoc* enquiries), and not tell us how good they are on other types.

Conclusion

The proposed research program will identify the factors affecting productivity (or confirm that they were correctly identified in this study), and will quantify the magnitude of their effect. The next step will be to persuade those organizations and staff with low productivity to institute appropriate changes wherever possible. If a large improvement in productivity ensues, it will confirm that the factors affecting productivity, the factors responsible for the large differences in productivity between various organizations and

various people, have been correctly identified.

13.2 PRODUCTIVITY IMPROVEMENT PROGRAM

This study investigated various factors thought to affect productivity, and attempted to determine the magnitude of their effect. However, it is not sufficient to merely know which factors affect productivity, or even by how much: we must also know how this information can be put to practical use to improve productivity, and then we must put it to use. Furthermore, evaluating the potential productivity gains in any individual organization requires a sound assessment of that organization's current practices.

13.2.1   PLAN OF ACTION

Just as most books on programming and software engineering have little to say about productivity, so most books on productivity do not provide a formal plan for improving it. Boehm (1981) outlined the following program to improve software productivity. It has certain basic similarities with software development projects, and with the guidelines in Chapter 8 for introducing MPPs. Perhaps that is why other authorities pay little attention to the subject.

Obtain top management commitment

If management does not genuinely want improved productivity, then the organization will not get improved productivity (Chapter 11). Some measures require authorization from top management. Examples are approving high salaries for top performers, phasing out misfits, enforcing disciplined practices, holding the line with customers on unrealistic schedule demands or requirements changes, and stimulating a higher proportion of 'not invented here' software.

Make somebody – the software productivity agent – specifically responsible for improving productivity

This role would be filled by the development centre (Chapter 3) in organizations which have one. The functions of the productivity agent are to identify ways in which productivity can potentially be improved; evaluate alternative proposals and external aids; collect and analyse software productivity data; and serve as a 'corporate memory' and consultant on productivity-related issues. The agent should have a good knowledge of software and the organization; quantitative analysis skills (measurement is discussed later); and a strong desire to help people improve their productivity.

Arrange broad-based participation

Improving productivity involves making changes which affect many people. Participation in defining and planning the changes helps stimulate their enthusiasm rather than their resistance (Chapters 9 and 11). Furthermore, involving more people ensures a more accurate and complete assessment of the environment.

Identify objectives, alternatives, and constraints

The broad *objectives* might be to produce the same functionality at a reduced cost, with no loss of quality, and with an improved career path for staff. An additional objective might be to improve productivity on large projects in particular. The *alternatives* are the factors which can (to a greater or lesser extent) be controlled, such as the work environment; use of packages; choice of programming language; use of program generators and software tools; execution time and main storage constraints; testing turnaround time; virtual machine and requirements volatility; product size; schedule constraint; use of modern programming practices; selection and promotion of staff; motivation; and

management. In addition, although required reliability, product complexity, performance requirements, and database size are generally not under management control, sometimes these contraints are 'gold-plating' or are arbitrary, and are therefore negotiable. The organization's *constraints* may include personnel ceilings, investment in existing hardware and software, office space limitations, government regulations, etc.

Evaluate the alternatives

A cost-estimation model is useful here. It can be applied to the current situation in a specific organization, taking into account, for example, the extent of use of software tools, to estimate the likely productivity impact of various possible courses of action. Subjective factors, such as the likely effect of the alternative courses of action on the staff's motivation and career goals, must also be taken into account.

Choose the best combination of alternatives

Maximum productivity gains will not be achieved through one measure alone (such as MPPs, management action, or tools), but through many. By using an integrated combination of such measures, you work on the *whole* problem, and also take advantage of synergism. The measures recommended by Jones (1986b) for different sized organizations are given in Table 13.1.

Prepare a phased implementation plan

Concentrate initially on the most likely factors, i.e. the more straightforward, easy to implement, and high payoff items. (The examples given by Boehm were structured code, walkthroughs, stabilizing requirements, and virtual machine support, though these could be challenged, e.g. there may be resistance to the introduction of walkthroughs, and structured code probably only gives a small increase in productivity, at least for development – see Chapters 10 and 8.) The advice in Chapter 8 (for MPPs) was to implement slowly, preferably one technique at a time: 'the best way to overcome resistance to change is in taking tiny steps'. The plan should follow the 'why, what, when, who, where, how, how much' format, and should address all the measures included in the selected combination.

Obtain authority to proceed

This includes authority to commit funds for increased salaries, facilities, tool acquisition, training, and software product acquisition: 'One shouldn't expect threefold or eightfold productivity improvements without the expenditure of some resources'.

Implement the plan

The *whole* plan must be implemented, not just the 'fun' parts. For example, if you do not phase out misfits, then people 'begin to wonder what other parts of the plan are not for real'.

Follow up and iterate the plan

Data collection, e.g. using the forms Boehm designed for recording software cost-estimating information, will determine if the plan is actually being implemented, and if the expected increases in productivity are being realized. Since no long-range plan is perfect, improvements will sometimes be necessary.

Guidelines

Singer (1982) stated that the attitudes of managers toward people, systems, and their own positions help determine both the morale and productivity of the department. They must therefore set a good example. He gave the following productivity-improvement guidelines for first-level managers:

- publicly recognize achievements;
- have weekly sessions with each employee, to discuss all aspects of the work, resolve actual and potential problems, and prevent the employee feeling alienated;
- encourage communication within the group, to prevent co-ordination problems, and to prevent employees feeling isolated;
- promote a team approach, i.e. encourage the staff to share ideas and help each other;
- ensure that the staff realize the importance of their work to the organization, insist that they are treated with courtesy and respect by other managers, and ensure that they are provided with the information they need;
- teach them multi-tasking, e.g. to create the test JCL while they are waiting for the first compile;
- do not re-invent the wheel, e.g. do not redo coding techniques, file layouts, or project planning methods, that have already been used and accepted.

He also gave the following guidelines for higher-level managers:

- always try to choose the path of least risk – an apparent shortcut may prove to be a costly mistake ('run now, crawl later'), and innovation should not be attempted during critical periods;
- define areas of responsibility carefully, e.g. to avoid time-consuming disputes over who will do unpopular tasks;
- insist on written communication for important matters – 'if it hasn't been put on paper, it hasn't been said' – to ensure that the instructions are complete and were thought through, and so that people are sure of what to do;
- do not confine knowledge to the management ranks;
- practice 'ego-less management', i.e. allow the employees to help in decision making, planning, and organization, and let them take the credit: managers not obsessed with their positions can give more time to

managing projects and people, and ensuring the total performance of their section and the job satisfaction of their staff.

Gilb (1988) gave the following guidelines for all levels of management:

- concentrate on determining user requirements;
- note in particular fluctuating or uncertain requirements, which will therefore require a flexible software architecture;
- create an organization which is totally user-result-oriented;
- implement measurement systems which relate all technical work to user benefits and user costs;
- filter user needs through business analysts and systems analysts ('information systems architects'), rather than going directly to the programmers, to ensure that the best possible solution will be chosen – which may mean software tools which are not standard for the organization, a different computer, or even a non-software solution;
- provide users with the means to do as much software development as possible by themselves, e.g. provide them with spreadsheets.

Recommended measures

The measures which Jones (1986b) believes are appropriate for different sized software organizations are given in Table 13.1. This list partly reflects which measures are appropriate for different sizes of project, as small organizations typically undertake only small projects. It also reflects the fact that some measures – such as re-used code – entail high overheads. Therefore, while organizations of all sizes would benefit from them, only large organizations would benefit sufficiently to justify the high costs. Conversely, while organizations of all sizes can benefit from packages, small organizations can generally make relatively greater use of them than large organizations.

Most of the entries in Table 13.1 should be self-explanatory. For example, a 'yes' entry means that the corresponding measure is important, e.g. small organizations should invest more capital in workstations and tools; response times become significant for medium-sized organizations; and so on. Similarly, 'formal' means that large organizations have formal information centers and development centers. Further information is contained in the relevant chapters and appendices, e.g. ways to reduce documentation costs are listed in Chapter 8, and the amount and type of specialization recommended by Jones is described in Appendix F, but some additional explanations are given as footnotes to the Table.

Some of the factors show a clear progression with increasing organization size. Examples are the recommended number of workstations, the degree of specialization, and the use of development centers. Similarly, one would expect that measures such as a DBMS and prototyping, which are recommended for medium-sized organizations, would also be recommended for all larger ones. Perhaps Jones thought this obvious, and therefore considered it unnecessary to repeatedly mention them. In the specific cases of response times, documentation, and defect removal, which 'become significant' or expensive for medium-sized organizations, it is assumed that they are significant or expensive for larger organizations as well.

The list is partly a reflection of current practices in organizations with high productivity (hence the 'exploring' information and development centers entries under medium-sized organizations), the assumption being that it is these practices which are responsible for their high productivity.

Some of the measures – particularly reviews and inspections – are aimed at improving quality rather than productivity, but higher quality can improve productivity in the long run, e.g. fewer bugs means less

Table 13.1 Appropriate measures based on size of software organization (Jones, 1986b)

Measure	Software staff				
	1–10 (small)	10–50 (low-medium)	50–200 (medium)	200–1000 (large)	>1000 (very large)
Organization structure					
Information center			exploring	formal	
Development center		impromptu	exploring	formal	active
Support groups (1)					yes
Specialization		partial	some	yes	full
Hardware					
Workstations: number (2)	yes	yes	adequate	1:1	1:1
Workstations: type (3)			graphics	graphics	yes
Response times			yes	yes	
Software					
Tools (4)	yes	yes			own
Programming language (5)	yes				
Spreadsheet	explore	yes			
DBMS and tools (6)		yes	dict/gen		
Packages	yes	yes			
Methods					
Requirements (7)				rigor	care
User involvement (8)		yes	joint		
Prototyping (9)		very	fairly	very	
Formal design methods (10)			yes	yes	care
Standard designs				yes	yes
Re-used code				yes	yes
Documentation			yes	yes	yes
Reviews/inspections (11)	yes		yes	full	yes
Defect removal (12)			yes	yes	
Training (13)					sizeable
Formal measurement (14)					25%

Source: Jones (1986b).
(1) Internal tool and support groups, to facilitate the work of application developers.
(2) Greater capital expenditure on workstations benefits organizations with up to 50 software employees by reducing schedules. This presumably means that these organizations currently have fewer – *far* fewer? – than one workstation per employee, and so need to buy more. 'Adequate' workstations 'become significant' for medium-sized organizations, which presumably means that they also have less than one to one, and so also need to buy more. Those larger organizations with high productivity generally already have about one workstation for every employee.
(3) 'Graphics' refers to graphics/text workstations, which are required to support formal design methods, but they can also assist documentation.
(4) Greater capital expenditure on tools benefits organizations with up to 50 software employees by reducing schedules. Larger organizations have generally already spent heavily in this area. Very large organizations tend to develop their own tools and many have developed requirements and design tools which are superior to those commercially available.
(5) Choice of programming language can have a significant effect in small organizations, if the staff know more than one or two languages. (Though Dunn and Ullman (1982) point out that the use of a single language is conducive to simpler programming standards, avoids the duplication of utility routines, and obviates the need for hiring or training bilingual programmers.)
(6) Low-medium-sized organizations can often use database products, and if one is selected, other productivity aids associated with the database environment can be used. 'dict/gen' means an active data dictionary, and an application or program generator.
(7) Large organizations concentrate on requirements rigor. Very large organizations take extreme care with requirements.
(8) 'Joint' refers to joint working sessions on requirements and design between users and developers.
(9) Prototyping can be very effective for both productivity and quality improvements in both low-medium-sized and large organizations; and can be fairly effective in improving quality in medium-sized organizations.
(10) Large organizations concentrate on solving design problems, and have adopted good design methods. Very large organizations take extreme care with design.
(11) For very small projects, reviews and inspections sometimes help improve quality, but the skills of the individual staff members tend to outweigh most other factors; for medium-sized organizations, reviews and inspections are fairly effective in improving quality; and for large organizations, they are demonstrably effective for quality as well as productivity.
(12) Larger organizations tackle sizeable programs for which defect removal can be very expensive, with many defects resulting from the original requirements and design. Jones implied that prototyping, formal design methods supported by graphics/text workstations, and close liaison with users during requirements help minimize these costs. Inspections and reviews should also help.
(13) Very large organizations have sizeable internal training programs.
(14) Of very large organizations, 25% have formal productivity and quality measurement groups, to collect, analyse, and report on productivity, compared to less than 10% of smaller organizations.

time spent on debugging and maintenance. In fact, according to Jones, software projects that aim initially at achieving the highest possible levels of quality and reliability tend to have the highest productivity.

Conclusion

Large payoffs are possible, but a long, sustained effort is necessary. Implementation of the productivity improvement plan requires a great deal of organizational will and staying power. Instant results must not be expected. Encouragement and insight are therefore required, and they can be found in the case histories in SHARE-GUIDE (1979) and Paster (1981). These histories include some organizations which have implemented subsets of the above (Boehm, 1981) plan, with highly successful results.

Boehm (1981) recommended that every 'good sized' installation establish a software productivity improvement program. Presumably this does not mean that such programs are ineffective for smaller organizations, but merely that larger ones have more to gain, and can better afford and justify the cost. He added that the best productivity program considers both the life-cycle of the software product and the life-cycle of the software people, i.e. we must avoid common pitfalls such as the Peter Principle (in a hierarchy, every employee tends to rise to his level of incompetence), the Inverse Peter Principle (people rise to an organizational position in which they become irreplaceable, and get stuck there forever), and the Paul Principle (people rise to an organizational position in which their technical skills become obsolete in five years).

Boehm also warned that improved software productivity is a means, not an end. It is a means of helping the users do their jobs better. In other words, we must use non-software solutions where these are superior. Gilb (1988) quoted a computerized personnel records system which cost $1 million to develop, and had an operational cost of $3.60 per document, compared to the old, manual system's 50 cents. The computerized system had no other, redeeming attributes, so it was destroyed and replaced by the old, manual one. Systems analysts are primarily concerned with analysing the function to be automated. Business analysts operate at a higher level, and do not even presume that software is to be written. User needs must therefore first be evaluated by business analysts. Devising non-software solutions will consume time, and will not 'add points to our software productivity scoreboard', but will reveal us to be effective DP professionals.

13.2.2 WHICH FACTORS HAVE THE GREATEST EFFECT ON PRODUCTIVITY?

One of the functions of the software productivity agent is to identify which factors have the greatest potential for productivity improvement in his organization. However, to do so, he needs to know which factors have the greatest effect on productivity, and there is a lack of consensus as to which factors these are.

Boehm

The COCOMO cost-estimation model (Boehm, 1981) rated personnel/team capability (i.e. analyst and programmer capability), as the most important of the 14 effort multipliers in the model (it has a 4:1 effect on development productivity), followed by product complexity (2.4:1), required reliability (1.9:1), timing constraint (1.7:1), applications experience (1.6:1), storage constraint (also 1.6:1), modern programming practices (1.5:1), etc. (Boehm often treated analyst capability and programmer capability as two separate effort multipliers. This gives a total of 15 multipliers instead of 14. The factors having the greatest effect on development productivity then become product complexity (2.4:1), followed by analyst capability (2.1:1), programmer capability (2.0:1), required reliability (1.9:1), etc.) The magnitude of the effect these factors have on maintenance productivity is mostly the same as for development, the exceptions being required reliability (only 1.4:1 instead of 1.9:1), and MPPs (up to 2.1:1 depending on product size, instead of only 1.5:1).

These effort multipliers do not take all possible factors into account. For example, the model assumes that projects are well-managed. Furthermore, it handles re-used code by means of an adjustment factor (in addition to the 14 effort multipliers). This factor can range from 0% to over 100%, a ratio of over 100:1, which is much greater than any of the effort multipliers. The effect of product size is also handled by means of an additional factor, over and above the effort multipliers. According to the COCOMO model (and many others), size has an exponential, and potentially unlimited, effect on productivity. For example, depending on the development mode (organic, semi-detached, or embedded), productivity on a 1000 source statement program is 1.1 to 1.6 times higher than on a 10 000 statement program; 1.3 to 2.5 times higher than on a 100 000 statement program; and so on (Chapter 8).

Boehm singled out the personnel areas of staffing, motivation, and management, as offering the biggest payoffs. (By staffing, presumably he means appointing only the highest-ability people, and avoiding the Peter and other principles listed above.) However, he added that productivity can be improved by a great deal more through the increased use of existing software. (This is presumably a reference to re-used code, but packages – both application and system software – are also 'existing software' used again and again (Radice and Phillips, 1988).) Boehm presumably therefore believes that some factors which are not included in his COCOMO cost-estimation model, or at least are not among the 14 effort multipliers (which are prominently displayed on the front cover of his book), can have a bigger effect than those which are.

A survey by Boehm (1981) showed that managers believed that *project management* actions (better planning, organization, etc.) were the high-leverage items, whereas 'performers' (presumably analysts and programmers) viewed *tools* as the high-leverage items. (This is reminiscent of the statement (Chapter 8) that books on systems analysis and design give high percentages for the proportion of the total time consumed by systems analysis and design; whereas books on reliability give high percentages for testing and debugging.)

Boehm (1981) studied a number of cost-estimation models, including the Walston and Felix (1977) model which is discussed separately later. The other models also provided information which is relevant here, for example: the SDC model, the Doty model and the Boeing model.

SDC model *(Nelson, 1966)*

This model rated concurrent hardware development; stability of design; random access device used; different host, target hardware; developed by military organization; and business application; as having the biggest impact, but with several other factors (percentage math instructions, percentage storage/retrieval instructions, number of subprograms, and number of personnel trips) as having a variable and possibly greater effect in individual cases.

The *Doty model* (Herd et al., 1977)

There are two versions of this model, one for small programs (less than 10 000 source instructions), and the other for larger programs. The version for small programs rated first software developed on CPU (1.9:1), and concurrent development of hardware (1.8:1), as having the greatest impact on effort, followed by CPU memory constraint (1.4:1), developer using computer at another facility (also 1.4:1), development at operational site (also 1.4:1), etc. The version for larger programs is based only on product size, and so does not incorporate these factors. According to this model – using both versions together – product size has an effect on productivity which is similar in magnitude to that predicted by the COCOMO model, e.g. the productivity on programs with 10 000 LOC is 1.2 times higher than on programs with 512K LOC, and the productivity on programs with 1000 LOC is perhaps 3 times higher than on programs with 10 to 512K LOC. (This model exhibits a discontinuity at 10 000 LOC – see Chapter 8.)

*The **Boeing model** (Black et al., 1977)*

This model rated type of application (7:1), hardware timing constraint (3:1 to 7:1), number of programmers (4:1), programming experience with engineering/technical discipline of application (2:1), higher-order language (seasoned compiler) (1.8:1), and re-implementation of existing software (1.4:1), as having the biggest impact on productivity. (Boehm was critical of this model because it grossly over-estimated some projects, and he pointed out that it has fallen out of use, but nevertheless the factors it singled out should provide some insight. The over-estimates may, for example, have been due to the use of MPPs, the very large effort multipliers for many-programmer projects, and the lack of multipliers in the testing phase for higher-level languages, i.e. in other respects, the model may be correct. In any case, many other models have also been criticized, including the Walston and Felix, SDC, and COCOMO models – see, for example, Chapters 8 and 12.)

Walston and Felix

The Walston and Felix (1977) model rated customer interface complexity (4:1), previous experience with programming languages (3:1), and overall personnel experience and qualifications (also 3:1), as having the greatest

effect on productivity, followed by previous experience with application of similar or greater size and complexity (2.8:1), percentage of programmers doing development who participated in design of functional specifications (2.6:1), user participation in the definition of requirements (2.4:1), previous experience with operational computer (2.1:1), complexity of application processing (also 2.1:1), etc. According to this model, product size has an exponential effect on productivity, but the effect is *opposite* to that predicted by most other models, i.e. productivity *increases* with increasing size. For example, the productivity on programs with 10 000 LOC is 1.2 times higher than on programs with 1000 LOC; the productivity on programs with 100 000 LOC is 1.5 times higher than on programs with 1000 LOC; and so on (Chapter 8).

According to Conte *et al.* (1986), three of Walston and Felix's top eight attributes relate to the degree of customer interfacing, while four relate to personnel experience and qualifications. There appear to be some errors in the calculations on which this statement was based, but nevertheless his conclusion is substantially correct. However, the remainder of his conclusion is not correct, as the eighth attribute does not relate to the amount of documentation, but to complexity. Furthermore, his statement that other researchers omit documentation entirely as a significant factor is not completely correct, as it is singled out by Jones (1986b) (see below). (Boehm (1981) omitted it for a variety of reasons: good specifications etc. can lead to *savings*; cross-reference generators, flow-charters, etc. can produce large amounts of documentation with little effort; large amounts of poor documentation can be produced more quickly than smaller amounts of good documentation; and documentation is not an add-on but an integral part of software development.)

A warning worth repeating is that the Walston and Felix figures may include the effects of correlated factors (Boehm, 1981). In addition, Conte warned that, while these productivity ranges are useful indicators, they reflect the projects in one particular environment, and the impact of a particular attribute may be substantially different in another environment. The same warning can presumably be applied to the ranges obtained from the other models.

Conte

Conte *et al.* (1986) singled out people-oriented factors – customer interface requirements and personnel qualifications – which, together with other significant conventional methods, can increase productivity by 2–4:1, but this was not counting 'revolutionary' methods that attempt to bypass the coding process altogether, such as automatic program generators, ultra-high-level languages, and re-usable program parts (Chapter 12). These methods promise much greater productivity improvements, but are far from perfected.

Conte also singled out better managing of those factors that are controllable, including MPPs, tool availability, improved programming environments, personnel capability and experience, use of higher-level languages, and reduced requirements volatility. This can increase productivity by 2–10:1, which is two or three times the productivity gain of the 'significant conventional methods' referred to above.

Conte also examined the findings of various other authorities. Apart from the Walston and Felix and SDC models, which have already been discussed, the most relevant here is the ITT (International Telephone and Telegraph Corporation) study (Vosburgh *et al.*, 1984) which examined 100 variables in 44 projects, and selected 13 having the greatest impact on productivity. The selected variables comprised eight product-related factors (timing constraint, memory utilization constraint, CPU occupancy limitation, number of

resource constraints, program complexity, client participation in requirements specification, client experience with application, and size of product in statements), and five project-related factors (hardware developed concurrently, development computer size in K-bytes of memory, stable requirements specification, MPP usage, and personnel experience). The project-related factors can to some extent be controlled by management, but not the product-related factors (though it was pointed out earlier that sometimes these constraints are 'gold-plating' or are arbitrary, and are sometimes therefore negotiable). One of the conclusions of the study was that management practices can have a substantial impact on improving productivity.

Gilb

Gilb (1988) and Remus (1980b) believe that most of the techniques that can produce really big improvements in productivity are managerial in nature, not technical (Chapter 11). Motivation and organization increase human productivity in 'relevant' directions, whereas technical devices may increase it in the wrong direction, e.g. a higher-level language may just help us produce the wrong product faster. Furthermore, Gilb claims that almost all of the highly-touted productivity tools (programming languages, software support environments, database support systems, and operating systems), have failed to deliver substantial and scientifically proven net improvements in productivity. The claimed gains are based on isolated cases, and so may be due instead to super-programmers on those projects; they do not take into account undesirable side-effects, such as performance destruction or portability reduction; and they are narrow in scope, e.g. they do not address quality, cost, and user benefits. (Gilb's very broad definition of productivity, given in Chapter 2, is evident in these criticisms.) He concluded that he had not yet found any evidence for net productivity benefits which were as impressive as those from inspections, evolutionary delivery, 'and even the simple act of formal specification of objectives'.

A survey by Boehm (1981) showed that managers believed that project management actions were the high-leverage items, whereas 'performers' viewed tools as the high-leverage items. Gilb echoed these sentiments. Technologists seem to believe that productivity is to be had through technical means, such as ever more sophisticated programming languages, or more sophisticated software support, and many of them seem totally ignorant of the existence of the managerial and organizational methods which lead to highly improved human productivity. Both, together, are necessary.

Gilb stated that evolutionary delivery (incremental delivery) is 'the most impressive practical method for ensuring dramatic productivity in software products'. However, he includes completing projects on time and under budget in his definition of productivity, and other factors besides productivity can be responsible for that, particularly accurate effort estimates. He quoted a 50% reduction in development effort from evolutionary delivery. This example was actually a form of prototyping, but evolutionary delivery *is* a form of prototyping. You receive feedback 'from the real world before throwing in all the resources intended for a system', and can correct errors before they become costly live systems. With evolutionary delivery, therefore, you cannot have large failures.

His figures suggest a productivity improvement from inspections of perhaps 2.4:1 for development and maintenance combined (Chapter 10). He also stressed the importance of measurement in improving productivity; the importance of ensuring, frequently and early, that the product does what the user needs, thereby avoiding a rewrite; and the importance of preventing errors: 'early design quality control is at least an order of magnitude more productive than later product testing'. Finally, he stated that the greatest and most dramatic productivity changes result from radical change to the solution architecture, rather than just working harder or more effectively.

Gilb therefore stressed a number of factors, but gave little quantitative information about them, so it is not clear just how valuable he thinks they are, nor how he ranks them in order of impact on productivity.

Parikh

Parikh (1984) stated that a productive programming environment can be created by the effective use of the three Ts: techniques, tools, and training. Tools generally increase staff effectiveness 'dramatically', they are keys to productivity improvement. He also stated that productivity gains of 1000% are sometimes claimed for 'fourth-generation methodologies', but by 'methodologies' he was actually – and this is surely an unusual meaning – referring specifically to tools – database languages, non-procedural languages, and program generators. However, he emphasized that such high gains will only be achieved if the 'methodologies' fit your work. This warning should be borne in mind when evaluating all the other claims presented here (and not just the claimed improvement from tools).

Parikh quoted some impressive claims for improved programming technologies – up to 4:1 for development and up to 16:1 for maintenance, which imply overall gains of up to perhaps 8:1 (Chapter 8). However, he seems to believe that these are extreme cases, as he himself only claimed an increase of 'at least 10%' by using the right methodology, which is surely much lower than the gains typically attained through tools, management, etc. (The other evidence for improved programming technologies presented in Chapter 8 indicates a value in between these two extremes.)

Martin

Martin (1982a) wrote a book advocating the automation of programming, but nevertheless stating that many studies have been done on the productivity of white-collar workers, and arriving at a general conclusion that technology alone is not enough: it is *people* who improve productivity – their work attitudes, their attention to time and efficiency, and above all, their motivation (The challenge of increased productivity, *EDP Analyzer*, April 1981, Canning Publication Inc., Vista, CA; Beaird, 1980). (This is reminiscent of the claim (Chapter 11) that the effect of motivation on productivity could be as high as a factor of 10, but the other evidence presented there indicates that the gain is much lower – probably only 30%.)

Martin and McClure (1985) quoted the Jones (1979) selection given below, and they repeated his emphasis on automation and re-use – e.g. a graphics workstation with computer-aided-design software, a dictionary, a software library, and executable code generated automatically from the design. With database user languages, report generators, graphics packages, and application generators, productivity improvements of 1000% are not uncommon (Martin, 1982a), but some of them can only generate certain well-defined classes of application.

The emphasis of Martin and McClure (1985) on automation seems to contradict the Martin (1982a) emphasis on people quoted above, but this people-emphasis was probably only intended to provide a balance to the automation orientation of the book, i.e. it was included to ensure that readers do not go away with an incomplete and unbalanced view.

Jones

Jones (1979) singled out two general ways to improve productivity by 50–75%. The first is ability (organizations should search out programmers and analysts who have exception-

ally high personal achievement); and the second is program generators, very-high-level languages, development shared by several systems (i.e. re-used code), or various forms of program acquisition in place of program development (i.e. packages). For still greater improvements, he singled out database user languages, report generators, graphics packages, and application generators.

Jones (1986b) believes that claims of a 1000% improvement from a total environment are based on ambiguous data, small projects, or coding only, which comprises only 15–30% of the total effort.

Jones (1986b) gave several lists of factors which have the greatest effect on productivity. Firstly, he singled out technologies which:

- lower defect rates (and therefore minimize the largest cost element of programming);
- minimize paperwork (the second largest cost);
- enhance communication and co-ordination among geographically dispersed sites developing large systems;
- use accurate measurements from past projects for planning and estimating future projects; and
- (especially) technologies which substitute standard designs and re-usable code for unique hand-coded functions.

Secondly, he listed the characteristics which distinguish leading-edge organizations:

- one terminal for each staff member;
- automated estimating and project planning and tracking;
- joint workshops and prototypes to determine users' requirements;
- standard designs, data analysis, and on-line graphics, to help design the products;
- re-usable code library of 200–500 modules;
- automated code library;
- document support tools and standard formats;
- automated screen construction tools;

- prototypes, formal reviews, test specialists, and formal testing, to remove defects.

Thirdly, he stated that, in general, the most productive organizations are, at the one extreme, individual programmers working at home; and at the other extreme, large organizations with more than about 200 programmers in a single location. (The exceptions to this rule include, not surprisingly, those organizations of intermediate size which enjoy the characteristics found in the high-productivity small and large organizations, e.g. because they are subsidiaries of larger organizations and share in corporate policies and resources.) The home programmers are typically senior, experienced professionals, with well-stocked private libraries, having well-equipped PCs (e.g. high-resolution graphics and an 'arsenal' of utility software, together totalling about $20 000), and working on small (under 10 000 LOC) programs. The large organizations with high productivity have usually spent more than $60 000 per programmer/analyst on workstations and support tools, and they also tend to have good research libraries and good supporting services for the professional staff.

Fourthly, he listed characteristics common among high-productivity organizations:

- individual workstations and sufficient office space;
- deliberate policies of encouraging technical and professional growth by means of seminars, internal technical meetings, and external professional associations;
- specialization, e.g. testing specialists, maintenance specialists, professional documentation writers, and data administration specialists;
- active technology exploration, with new tools and products being evaluated and piloted as the need arises;
- an emphasis on requirements and design, with graphics/text terminals, formal specification methods, and prototyping;
- re-usability, in the form of generators,

libraries of standard functions, or database packages;
- measurement of productivity and quality.

This list is approximately a summary of measures which are appropriate for different sized organizations (Table 13.1).

Fifthly, the set of over 50 effort estimates he gave for a variety of situations indicates that spreadsheets (30:1), fourth-generation languages (8:1), and re-used code (5:1), followed by experience (2.5:1), tools (also 2.5:1), third-generation languages (2.4:1), and program generators (also 2.4:1), have the greatest impact on development productivity; while re-used code (7:1), tools (6:1), documentation (5:1), novelty (also 5:1), and defect levels (also 5:1), followed by structured methods (4:1), complexity (also 4:1), program size (also 4:1), and defect removal methods (3:1), have the greatest impact on maintenance productivity. (The ratios for spreadsheets and 3GLs were obtained by comparison against Assembler, and so might be out of date and misleadingly high compared to the other ratios – in particular, the ratio for 4GLs was obtained by comparison against a 3GL. The ratio for program size was questioned in Chapter 8, due to an error and an inconsistency in the figures from which it was derived.)

His figures also show that the number of customers (e.g. for an application package) increases the amount of maintenance considerably. For example, if 10 000 organizations purchase the package then, depending on the number of defects, the vendors might have to spend 90 times as much effort on maintenance as they would for one customer. The number of customers therefore has a much greater impact on effort than any of the other factors. However, this gives the impression that productivity is degraded. A better way is to apportion the effort over the number of customers. In other words, we should view it as not one, but 10 000 systems being maintained, which is effectively how

Table 13.2 Effect of number of customers on productivity (effort in person-months)
(after Jones (1986b))

	Few defects			Many defects		
	Customers			Customers		
	1	10 000	Effort ratio	1	10 000	Effort ratio
Development effort						
total	580	580	1:1	725	725	1:1
per customer	580	0.058	10 000:1	725	0.0725	10 000:1
Maintenance effort						
total	70	6302	1:90	365	7304	1:20
per customer	70	0.6302	111:1	365	0.7304	500:1
Overall effort						
total	650	6882	1:11	1090	8029	1:7
per customer	650	0.6882	944:1	1090	0.8029	1358:1

re-used code is treated. Doing so, using his example figures, produces the result that maintenance effort, per system, is reduced by a factor of up to 500 (Table 13.2). Selling multiple copies therefore *improves* productivity (of development, maintenance, and overall) by much more than any of the other factors.

Jones did not give maintenance figures for programming class (e.g. internal or external program, or developed under private or government contract), because in the specific examples he chose, the customers took over maintenance responsibility. However, programming class probably does affect maintenance productivity; and it is irrelevant who performs the maintenance. Jones defines maintenance as the correction of defects, i.e. he excludes enhancements, whereas they are included here. However, implementing an enhancement is similar to fixing a defect (e.g. both must be coded and tested), and enhancement effort, like correction effort, is affected by the number of existing errors in the software and documentation quality, so it is to be anticipated that, generally, something which reduces correction effort per error by say, 5:1, will reduce the effort per enhancement by a similar amount, though the same may not be true of the *total* error correction and enhancement efforts, as the *number* of

errors and enhancements may be affected to different extents by any given factor.

Jones's figures show that the higher the language level, the lower the development effort. Surely, language level has a similar impact on the maintenance effort, especially as Jones believes that high-level languages reduce the probability of making errors. He also stated that third-generation languages reduce the maintenance effort, as maintenance personnel 'can usually make more sense out of the listings' than they can with Assembler. However, according to most of his figures, language level has no impact at all, and he also stated that the impact of 4GLs on maintenance was ambiguous – see Chapter 6. (He gave three sets of figures which are relevant here. The first set compared Assembler, COBOL, APL, and Spreadsheets, and showed the same amount of maintenance effort for each of the languages. The second set was for program generators, classified here as 4GLs, and these figures *did* show a substantial reduction in maintenance effort through the use of a generator. The third set compared a 4GL against COBOL, and showed no reduction in maintenance effort. Possible reasons why two of the examples showed no reduction in maintenance effort – such as the development orientation in the first example and the short anticipated life in the third – were discussed in Chapter 6.) His example for type of program – batch or real-time – also shows an impact on development effort, but not on maintenance effort. This is particularly surprising in view of the stress he placed on the hardware constraints, which resulted in a program that was less structured than normal in order to achieve higher performance. His example for multi-site development also shows an impact on development effort, but not on maintenance effort. This may be because the emphasis of his example was on development, but it could also mean that maintenance would be centralized as far as possible.

Which factors have the greatest impact on the *total* effort, i.e. on the productivity of development and maintenance combined? We cannot use Jones's effort figures 'as is', as (all?) his figures for the amount of maintenance effort include only the effort to implement fixes, not enhancements, and therefore understate the amount of maintenance by a large amount, probably by a factor of five. (Evidence presented in Chapter 8 indicates that only about 20% of maintenance effort is spent on fixes.) If we therefore multiply the figures he gives for maintenance effort by five, and then combine them with his development effort figures, we arrive at the following ranking. The factor with the greatest impact on total effort is 4GLs (8:1), followed by spreadsheets (6:1), re-used code (also 6:1), APL (4:1), novelty (also 4:1), complexity (also 4:1), documentation (also 4:1), tools (2.8:1), defect levels (2.7:1), and structured methods (also 2.7:1). Various warnings given earlier should be borne in mind when evaluating the combined values, e.g. he did not give maintenance figures for programming class; and the ratios for spreadsheets – and for APL – were obtained by comparison against Assembler, and so might be out of date and misleadingly high compared to the other ratios – in particular, the ratio for 4GLs was obtained by comparison

against a 3GL. APL is sometimes classified as a 4GL. It did not fare as well as the specific category for 4GLs in these figures, because Jones included a maintenance effort for it, but with no reduction due to the power of the language, presumably because APL programs are difficult to understand – see Chapter 6.

Comments

It is difficult to compare Jones' five lists. There appear to be some discrepancies between them, but these can probably be explained. For example, prototyping is included in the second and fourth lists, but not in the others. However, one can – justifiably – argue that it is *implicitly* included in the first list, as it is a 'technology' which both lowers defect rates and minimizes paperwork; one can also argue that the third list is so brief that the exclusion of prototyping from it is not necessarily significant, and in any case, the fourth list is really an extension of the third; and its absence from the fifth list presumably means that it affects quality more than productivity. Similarly, documentation does not appear on the third list, but that is probably only because of that list's brevity. The fifth list was derived from only those 20 major factors for which quantified data exists. It therefore does not include the effect of factors such as training, measurement programs, user participation, etc., some of which appear on his other lists, or were singled out by other authorities. Jones estimated that these factors account for perhaps 30% of the productivity variations that occur. The fifth list in any case is only a partial list: only those factors having the largest impact were selected, and one could argue that the cut-off points were arbitrary, and hence more items should have been included.

Other authorities

Bell *et al.* (1987) stated that 'any differences between the two modes of working [batch and on-line programming] are grossly overwhelmed by the enormous differences between individuals' (Chapter 6).

According to Argyle *et al.* (1958), the introduction of improved methods of working has generally shown increases in productivity ranging from 20 to 200%, while the effect of supervision and group organization may be expected to lead to differences in productivity of only 7–15%. However, if the standard of DP management really is as low as some of the evidence in Chapter 11 suggests, then the impact of improved DP management might be much higher than these general figures.

A study by Kraut *et al.* (1989) of the impact of a computerized record system on the work lives of customer service representatives in a large utility company found that office type (serving business or residential customers) had the largest effect on productivity and job quality, followed by technology, office size, management quality, cut time (the time at which the new system was introduced), age and gender.

Arthur (1983) singled out packages (10–100:1, i.e. 1000–10 000%), 4GLs (compared to 3GLs?) (100–1000%), high-level languages (compared to Assembler) (500%), program and application generators (200%), document and code generators linked to the office automation system with document skeletons (100%), generic designs (80%), and possibly quality circles (3:1 return on investment) and response time (think time increases twice as fast as computer response time).

According to Gellerman (1963), most productivity studies have found that motivation has a stronger influence on productivity than any other factor (Chapter 11).

Johnson (1980b) singled out self-generating code ('high' improvement), application generators (30%), and structured programming (20%).

The Albrecht (1979) study (Chapter 12) found a productivity gain of 3:1, which was attributed mainly to the use of structured

programming, high-level languages, on-line development, and a programming development library.

Yourdon (1989) singled out hiring more talented programmers and systems analysts and giving them superior working conditions, letting users develop their own systems, better programming languages, attacking the maintenance problem, software engineering disciplines, and automated tools for systems development, each of which might lead to a 10–15% improvement in productivity (Chapter 12).

Smith (1981) singled out structured programming, non-procedural languages, database management systems, data dictionaries, programmers' workbench, automated system design methodology, incremental development, application packages, CPTs, project management planning and control systems, etc. (Chapter 12).

Humphrey (1985) attributed the productivity increase of IBM's large-systems programming staff to improved programmer skills, improved methods, and better tools. The skills of their programming managers had also improved.

Conclusion

There appears to be considerable disagreement over which factor has the greatest impact on productivity: type of application? re-used code? number of programmers? staff ability and experience? program generators and ultra-high-level languages? management? Nearly every authority seems to single out something different; some single out so many factors, without quantifying them, that it does not help much; some authorities provide more than one list; some rate highly factors which are rated lowly, or not even evaluated, by others; some factors have a variable impact; and different authorities group the factors differently (i.e. there are definition problems), e.g. should analyst ability and programmer ability be treated separately or together? should tools be treated as one factor or subdivided into ultra-high-level languages, CASE tools, etc.?

Which factors are singled out by this study? Large claims were quoted for some factors, but there was a lack of supporting evidence. Examples are a doubling in productivity from development centers, and a ten times increase from HOS (higher order software). For some other factors, the reverse was true: there were many claims and much evidence, but there were wide discrepancies between the figures. Examples are MPPs (the average of the various claims indicated an overall gain of about 3:1), product size (4:1), and complexity (also 4:1).

My own opinion is that technology, such as ultra-high-level languages and CASE tools – 'revolutionary methods that attempt to bypass the coding process altogether' (Conte *et al.*, 1986) – has the greatest potential for productivity gains. I concede that more powerful tools can just help us produce the wrong product faster, and they can also have undesirable side-effects such as performance destruction or portability reduction, but I believe that on balance they do much more good than harm. In any case, with the wider use of prototyping and CASE tools, it is surely less likely that the wrong product will be produced. As my background is technical more than managerial, I suppose I am open to the charge that this has influenced my conclusion – see the Boehm (1981) survey quoted above, and the similar comments made by Gilb (1988) – though I do not think this is the case. I really do believe that automation is the answer. Software engineering is labor-intensive, and 'real people in real life cannot move a great deal faster than they already do' (Jones, 1979). As Martin and McClure (1985) put it: 'we can teach a swimmer to swim faster by improving his technique, but the increase in speed is small compared with giving him a motorboat'. Large improvements require techniques that *replace* human effort. All telephone calls originally had to be switched manually, and the number of people needed for switching was growing faster than the number of people making calls (Martin, 1982a). It was calculated that eventually almost the entire workforce would be required to switch calls, which was a practical impossibility. The salvation of the telephone industry was automatic telephone switching equipment.

My opinion is consistent with figures given by Jones (1986b), which show that the productivity of the software industry increased by 130% due to the switch from Assembler language to COBOL, compared to only a 30% increase due to the switch from unstructured to structured methods, which does tend to suggest that technology provides greater potential for productivity improvement than methodologies. While it is risky to generalize from just one example, this particular example is a valuable one in that it is not a prediction, or the finding of a small-scale experiment, but an observation of what actually happened in the industry.

Further support is provided by Balzer *et al.* (1983), who believe that orders of magnitude productivity and quality improvements are possible from automated implementation, i.e. tools to implement programs rapidly and reliably from the specifications. Much of the reason for the high anticipated gain is that maintenance, which accounts for perhaps 80% of the total life-cycle effort, would be performed on the specifications instead of on the source code. Source code has been optimized by skilled programmers, i.e. it contains artificially introduced complexities, making it difficult to understand.

Ohno (1989) drew an analogy with the manufacture of material products. High productivity and quality have been achieved through factory automation rather than through human skill. However, he acknowledged that software is different, because it expresses human ideas and has no physical properties, making the analogy inappropriate.

Glass (1979) believes that lack of resources – both human resources and resources to procure adequate support tools – can be the bane of small projects. He also believes that the only answer to the problems of large projects is the development of improved tools. He was referring specifically to the communication problems which plague large projects, but the same may also be true for the problem of very low productivity on these large projects, and anyway, communication is one of the reasons for the low productivity.

Bain (1982), however, cautions that technological advances 'have reached levels where their impact on work processes leaves an unsettling effect'. Furthermore, automation generally requires larger facilities and more modern equipment, and therefore heavy outlays of capital. He was not thinking specifically of the software industry, but his remarks do call to mind the high startup and overhead costs for re-used code, and the much higher productivity of some very large organizations, reported by Jones (1986b).

13.2.3   MEASUREMENT

In theory, it is possible to improve productivity without measuring the results, but in practice 'it seldom happens that way' (Jones, 1986b). This is hardly surprising. Without measurement, you do not have a quantified vision of what productivity and quality mean within the organization; you cannot quantify the benefits of new technology (such as CASE); you do not know where the problem areas are, so you might be directing your efforts in the wrong direction; and even if they are in the correct direction, you do not know if they are proving effective (Carlyle, 1987c). As Lord Kelvin put it, many years ago: 'When you can measure what you are speaking about, and express it in numbers, you know something about it; but when you cannot measure it, when you cannot express it in numbers, your knowledge is of a meager

and unsatisfactory kind' (Conte *et al.*, 1986). Measurement is the basis for setting reasonable expectations for improvement (The quest for zero-defect software, *Computer Week*, 13 Feb. 1989, p. 21.). It tells you how much software costs, how much time is needed to deliver required functions, and especially why variations occur. It enables you to spot, and then 'weed out', bad methods and environments, and nurture good ones. Without measurement, you must 'rely on the faulty memories of old warriors' (Gilb, 1988).

There has been significant progress in the development of metrics and models in recent years, though a great deal of research is still required, both to refine and validate existing models, and to develop new and better ones (Conte *et al.*, 1986). Nevertheless, we now know much more about the primary factors that affect effort, and how much effect each factor can have. We are therefore in a much better position to improve productivity. However, the fact that good metrics and models have been developed is not sufficient by itself to improve productivity – they must be widely used. To encourage this, the US Department of Defense STARS (Software Technology for Adaptable, Reliable Systems) program envisaged the following activities:

- the development of tools that would automatically and unobtrusively collect the required data (this would minimize resistance to the measurement program, and would also ensure consistent data across different organizations and projects);
- the systematic dissemination of information about measurement (e.g. guidelines for data collection, and the availability and usage of tools); and
- the development of training programs and clinics (which would also provide a forum for feedback on problems users experienced in setting up and running a measurement program).

Jones (1986b) gave the following guidelines

for a productivity and quality measurement program.

- Decide whether you want to measure development productivity or delivery productivity – the latter is superior because it reveals, in particular, the considerable benefits that re-used code provides.
- Measure the defect removal efficiencies of reviews, inspections, and testing by comparing the number of defects found by each of these activities with each other, and with the number found during production.
- Measure the distribution of defects, to detect error-prone modules so they can be eliminated.
- Measure the total amount of documentation produced, including on-line documentation, to determine if additional support tools, such as integrated graphics/ text terminals, can be justified.
- Measure productivity using both LOC and function points for the first few years, to calibrate them against each other, and to highlight areas where function points are less effective.
- Measure everything, e.g. all functions in the software life-cycle from early planning onwards; QA time and costs; staff training; travel costs; etc.
- Divide the total number of function points and the total number of LOC delivered to users by the total number of software staff (including secretaries, managers, training personnel, etc.).

The measurement task must be assigned to people who will not merely record the numbers, but will also explore *why* they are what they are. Large organizations often assign an entire team to this task. The team typically consists of a manager, statisticians, analysts, data-entry clerks, and programmers, and generally produces quarterly and annual reports.

Jones warned that measuring productivity and quality is neither easy nor cheap. Organizations typically only start measuring quality at the testing stage, and only measure the productivity of the coding and testing stages, but even a limited program such as this costs from 1.5% to 3% of the software development costs. IBM, which measures productivity and quality throughout the life-cycle, from early design through the lifetime of the product, spends the much higher figure of 5%. Partial measurements are useful, but focus attention on the factors being measured, thereby diverting attention away from those factors which are not being measured, even if some of them are important.

There may be resistance from the people being measured, and they might distort the measurements (Chapter 2).

Effectiveness

One of the highest productivity rates quoted in Chapter 2 was the rate obtained by Kemerer (1987) from a firm which co-operated fully with the research project, and provided good quality data. Most of the managers in five large organizations with permanent software measurement groups thought that the measurement efforts had been worthwhile in eliminating vague and subjective claims, in giving all software projects known targets and common goals, and in helping to understand the problems (Jones, 1986b). These organizations appeared to have higher productivity than seven others which did not have measurements. This suggests that organizations which are sophisticated enough to measure, are also sophisticated enough to solve other problems; and that organizations which are not measuring are not solving their problems, because sometimes they do not know that the problems exist. This provides a justification for the high cost of the measurement program.

13.3 ALTERNATIVES

The conclusion reached in this study is that it is possible to increase productivity sufficiently to satisfy users' reasonable requirements. Supposing, however, that the gains actually achieved are too small (either because the predicted productivity improvements were too optimistic, because there was resistance to implementing the necessary productivity-improvement measures, or because the user's requirements were greater than anticipated). In any event, there will be a delay before significant productivity improvements can be expected. Time will be required to disseminate and 'sell' the recommendations, purchase the hardware and software (where applicable), provide the associated training, and so on – and the backlog of work must also be cleared. For some time to come, therefore, the DP department will continue to provide an inadequate service to its users. Is there anything else organizations can do to alleviate the position, or to supplement the gains? Some possibilities are discussed below.

13.3.1   OBTAINING VALUE FOR MONEY

There are a number of ways organizations can obtain better value for the money they spend on DP. Although these suggestions might not increase software productivity, the financial benefits derived from them could be used to finance methods which do.

Relax the constraints

Performance requirements and budget allocations are often fairly arbitrary. Sometimes, therefore, a small increase in an arbitrarily low budget permits a solution that is much more effective. For example, Boehm (1981) quoted the case of a transaction processing system running on multiple processors, in which spending an extra 10% on the hardware and system software yielded an 80% performance improvement. At other times, a large increase in expenditure produces a solution that is only slightly more effective. (In an example quoted in Chapter 12, also based on this multi-processor system, a further increase in expenditure actually produced a *decrease* in performance, because of higher processing overheads when too many processors were added.) An arbitrarily high performance requirement ('gold-plating') forces an unnecessarily expensive solution. For example, a fast response may only be required for some of the transaction types. A less obvious solution, such as rewriting the operating system to make it more effective, may remove a bottleneck. (In this situation, use of the standard operating system is an assumed constraint.) The moral is to be flexible and creative. Software cost-estimation models can help explore the cost-effectiveness of alternatives.

Technology management

Top management must manage technology correctly, but to do so, they must understand the technology, what it can do for their organization, and what the technological needs of their organization are, and not just what it will cost (van Wyk, 1988). They must therefore regard a technological plan for their organization in the same light as they regard a budget/economic plan, otherwise they cannot hope to harness the exponential benefits that technology can offer them.

High-return systems

One of the recommendations of this study is to have steering committees to ensure that the scarce DP resources are used where they can do the most good, namely on those projects giving the highest return for the smallest outlay. This principle can be extended. Management information systems, statistical techniques, and linear programming – a mathematical optimization technique formulated by Dantzig (1963) – may save organizations large sums of money, but are not widely used, i.e. organizations are overlooking uses of their computers which could provide greater benefits than the systems they are requesting (MacMillan, 1975; Mallinick, 1976): 'Many people are using computers to do what they've always done, but faster. To stand out from the pack, you've got to do new work that's never been done before' (New behaviour needed to learn computer skills, *Bank Systems & Equipment*, Jan. 1986, pp. 66, 78).

One data analyst used SPSS (Statistical Package for the Social Sciences) to analyse economic and consumer trends, as a result of which he proposed a remap of his organization's sales territories, which increased new-customer revenues by 38% in two years (SPSS, 1989). Three years later, he identified current customers likely to need added services, as a result of which average billings increased by more than 20%. Boehm (1981) gave an example in which linear programming was used to enable a software house maximize its profit. (The software house built two types of system, each of which required different numbers of analysts and programmers, and returned different profits. Linear programming showed the organization how many systems of each type it should develop for maximum profit, given the number of available analysts and programmers, and the available computer time.)

Some businesses are therefore now moving beyond traditional DP tasks such as accounting, operations control and forecasting, to direct application of computers and communications to enhance existing products and services, and to serve as foundations for new ones (Simons, 1986). However, deploying information systems as marketing and customer service tools can entail significant risk. Furthermore, many management information systems have failed, primarily because of diseconomies of scale and a lack of understanding of the organization's real

information processing needs (Boehm, 1981; Nel, 1978).

Avoid short-lived systems

Another way to obtain more value for money is to not develop programs which would have only a short life expectancy. The program source statements would not be generated at a faster pace, but each statement would be used for a longer time, and so would provide greater benefit for the original effort. This factor must therefore be taken into account by steering committees when deciding which of the proposed projects will be implemented.

Extend program life

A variation on this idea is to extend the life of programs. This can be done during development by making the programs more general and flexible (though extra initial effort is necessary to achieve this – see Chapter 8). Higher quality achieves the same end: if a program is easy to modify, then the maintenance staff will be less inclined to rewrite it, and more modifications can be applied to it before it will need to be rewritten. Longer program life is one of the benefits claimed for CASE tools (Chapter 6), and for tools that restructure code (Chapter 8). It is generally cheaper to enhance a product than develop a new one, and users accustomed to a program are understandably unwilling to replace it (Dunn and Ullman, 1982).

Arthur (1988) gave some figures which are relevant here. Firstly, he stated that poor design and implementation cause early retirement and replacement of systems at a higher cost: $30/line of code versus $2/line for restructured code; and secondly, that there is as much as a 40:1 difference between replacement and maintenance costs (Pressman, 1982). Presumably the first pair of figures mean that it costs on average $30 to develop each line of code, but only $2 to restructure

Table 13.3 Software cost per LOC ($)

Source	Development	Maintenance	Ratio
Simpson (1987)	2–30		
Johnson (1980b)	5		
Hall (1987)	5–50		
Martin (1981)	10		
Boehm (1981)	19		
Arthur (1988); Pressman (1982)			40:1
Arthur (1988)	30	2	15:1
Martin (1982a): 4GL vs 1-year 3GL			1:1
Wolverton (1974)	38		
Jones (1986b)	46	400	1:9
Conte *et al.* (1986); Jones (1981): Assembler	50		
Gilb (1988)		30–200	
Trainor (1973, 1974): avionics	75	4000	1:53
Conte *et al.* (1986); Jones (1981): high-level lang.	100		
Scott (1981)	100		
Joyce (1989): Space Shuttle	1000		
Median (approximate)	40	1000	1:25

each line, i.e. only one-fifteenth as much. Once restructured, the code can be maintained more easily and cheaply. Presumably, also, the second figures mean that it costs on average up to 40 times as much to rewrite a program as it does to implement a change to it. By contrast, Martin (1982a) stated that the cost of re-creating an existing application in DMS (Development Management System, an application generator from IBM), is often less than the cost of maintaining that application for a year; he also stated that, in some cases, maintaining an application written in a 3GL is more expensive, and takes more time, than creating and maintaining the entire application would have taken with an application generator. Similarly, according to Trainor (1973, 1974), maintaining a line of program code can cost up to 53 times more than its original development cost. Figures given by Gilb (1988) indicate that it costs $30–200 for each line of code changed. Hall (1987) stated that software is a corporate asset, and is valued at $5–50 per line of source code: presumably, the development cost is less than this.

These, and other estimates, are given in Table 13.3. The median ratio was derived by dividing the median development cost by the median maintenance cost. If instead we take the median of the individual ratios, we arrive at a value of 1:1.

The Simpson figures were derived from his estimates that very small projects (under 500 LOC) cost under $1000; and large ones (128–511K LOC) cost $1–15 million.

The Martin (1982a) ratio is based on a combination of his two statements quoted above. It compares a rewrite using a 4GL, with one year's maintenance of a 3GL version of the same program. If the lifetime of the system was less than 1 year, say 6 months, then the ratio would be 1:0.5 (2:1) instead of 1:1. Conversely, if the lifetime was longer than 1 year, say 2 years, then the ratio would be 1:2 instead of 1:1; if it was 5 years, then the ratio would be 1:5; and so on. If the typical life of a system is 5–10 years (Table 13.4), then the ratio would typically be 1:5 to 1:10. However, because it compares a 4GL with a 3GL, it is not comparing like with like, and it is also not a cost per LOC.

The Wolverton figure is the average of a set of 36 rates he gave for six different types of software (control, input/output, etc.) and degree of difficulty (on a 6-point scale). Individual rates varied from about half the average, to double it. For example, the simplest 'algorithm' program cost $15 per LOC, whereas the most complex 'data management' program cost $57, and all 'time critical' programs cost $75 per line.

The Jones (1981) figures were quoted by Conte *et al.* (1986), and apparently by Simpson (1987) as well. It is not clear why they are higher than the Jones (1986b) figures, but they were apparently intended as hypothetical figures, to illustrate a point, whereas the Jones (1986b) figures were intended to be realistic. My conclusion is supported by the fact that the programs in Simpson's version are ten times as large as those in Conte's, but the productivity is the same; and by the fact that Jones (1986b) includes a similar example, with the programs 100 times as large, but the productivity is nevertheless five times *higher*.

The Jones (1986b) figures are the averages of over 50 sets of rates he gave for a variety of situations, depending on some 20 factors, such as the level of language used, the amount of experience of the programmers, the complexity of the program, and so on. For example, it might cost $17 per LOC to develop Assembler programs, whereas equivalent COBOL programs would cost $22, APL programs $36, and spreadsheets $53. Similarly, the cost might be $29 per LOC where the programmers are highly experienced in the programming language, methods, and application area, but $70 for the same program if they have little experience in any of these areas. Jones also gave the cost per function point for some of these situations. The average of those figures is about $3000 per function point.

Jones gave the corresponding maintenance costs for the 50-plus situations, but it is more difficult to calculate cost per LOC from them. His figures indicate that, on average, some 8 man-months is required over 5 years to maintain 1000 LOC. This corresponds to a cost of (8 * $5000 =) $40 000 over the 5 years, or $8000 p.a., which appears to be a rate of $8 per LOC. However, perhaps only 10% of the lines are actually changed every year (Chapter 8), so the $8000 is really the cost of changing only about 100 lines, i.e. the true ratio is about $80 per LOC. This gives a development:maintenance ratio of (46:80 =) 1:1.8, which is reassuringly similar to the 20–60% penalty (1:1.2–1:1.6) he calculated for enhancements compared to development. However, a further complication is that Jones defines 'maintenance' as covering only fixes, not enhancements. It is not clear what the effect of this is, but as only about 20% of maintenance effort is spent on fixes (Chapter 8), it implies that only about 20 of the 100 lines are changed for the cost of $8000, i.e. the rate is actually about (8000/20 =) *$400* per line, which gives a development:maintenance ratio of 46:400, or 1:9.

The Joyce figure reflects the 'enormous expense' of achieving high quality: the error rate in the completed programs was about 100 times lower than the industry average.

Discrepancies

There are large differences between the figures given in Table 13.3. For example, even if we ignore the exceptionally high figure quoted by Joyce, the rates for development range from $2 to $100 per statement, a ratio of 50:1. How can these disparate rates be reconciled? Most authorities do not state what their rates include, making comparison difficult and unreliable. Some may include hardware costs. Johnson (1980b) excludes the cost of test time. Jones (1986b) excludes comment lines, JCL, and temporary code, but includes data definitions, macro expansions (in the case of Assembler), and included code (through the COPY statement in the case of COBOL). The Jones (1986b) and Conte *et al.* (1986)/Jones (1981) figures include the cost of non-programming functions, such as requirements analysis. If these functions were excluded, then the Jones (1986b) development cost, for example, would be reduced from $46 per LOC, to possibly only $30. The Conte/ Jones figures are 'fully supported', which presumably means they include overheads such as paid vacations, but not say clerical support. If these costs were excluded, then their figures would be approximately halved (Chapter 9), which would bring them more into line with the other tabulated values. By contrast, the Jones (1986b) figures cannot be *fully* supported, as they exclude costs such as training, and no mention is made of costs such as paid vacations. Another complication is that the various figures were obtained from different years, so the rates should be increased – by differing amounts – to allow for inflation. An added complication here is that the salary used by Jones (1986b), $5000 per month, is apparently the same as he used five years earlier (Conte *et al.*, 1986; Jones, 1981). (In another example, Jones (1986b) varied the salary to take inflation into account, with rates of $2000 per month in 1964, $3000 in 1974, and $4000 in 1984. This gave costs per LOC of $19 (for Assembler), $37 (for unstructured COBOL), and $38 (for structured COBOL), for 1964, 1974, and 1984, respectively.)

Another reason for the discrepancies in Table 13.3 may be as follows. When maintaining a program, only certain lines of code are changed for any one modification, though each line may be changed several times, in successive modifications. In fact, according to DeMarco (1982), when a (large?) system is retired, less than 5% of it will have been changed – the other 95% did not need to be changed. (Concentration of changes was discussed in Chapter 8.) By contrast, with a rewrite, *all* the lines must be done, even those that would not have to be changed for the current modification, but they only have to be rewritten once. This variety of situations makes it difficult to compare different figures, as they may be referring to different things.

As stated above, the rates for development range from $2 to $100 per statement (exclud-

ing Joyce's exceptionally high rate), a ratio of 50:1. What rate would be arrived at using the figures in this study? A cost of about $5–40 per statement is arrived at if we assume:

- current productivity rates – say 15–50 fully debugged and documented statements per day (Chapter 2);
- 20 days productive work per month, and 210 per year (Chapter 2);
- current salaries – say $2000 to $4000 p.m. (What are you worth in '88, *Datamation*, 1 Oct 1988, pp. 53–66), or $15 (Conte *et al.*, 1986) or $22 (Cost of a cure, *Computing S.A.*, 12 Dec 1988, p. 11) per hour, or $20 000 per year (Bell *et al.*, 1987); and
- overheads – perhaps equal in value to the salary (Chapter 9) – giving a 'fully supported' or 'burdened' salary of $45 per hour (if programmer, hardware, and organizational overheads are included) (Conte *et al.*, 1986), or $5000 (Conte/Jones, 1981) or $6000 (Boehm, 1981) per month, or $50 000 (Mohanty, 1981) or $100 000 per year (Charette, 1986);
- plus inflation.

This is much lower than most of the figures in Table 13.3, which suggests that many of them were obtained from large systems, where productivity is very low and costs are correspondingly high. The presence of an avionics rate among the tabulated figures tends to support this theory.

The maintenance figures in Table 13.3 vary even more wildly, ranging from $2 to $4000 per statement, a ratio of 2000:1. (Wild variations are to be expected in real life, e.g. a small change to a large program can necessitate a large amount of regression testing – see Chapter 8 – resulting in a total cost out of all proportion to the size of the change.) Even if we ignore the $2, which probably refers to an automated restructuring process, we are nevertheless left with the wide range of $30–4000, which is still a ratio of over 100:1. What value will be arrived at using the figures in this study? If one programmer can maintain programs totalling around 10 000–20 000 statements (Chapter 2), and 10% of these are changed every year (Chapter 8), then he changes 1000–2000 statements per year (though some might be changed several times). At the salaries and overheads listed above, this gives a cost of about $25–100 per statement (less if we adjust for statements changed more than once).

The development/maintenance cost ratios in Table 13.3 vary equally wildly, ranging from 40:1 to 1:53, a range of over 2000:1. However, if we leave out the Arthur/Pressman 40:1 – it appears to be the only one tabulated which compares a total rewrite with a single maintenance change, and it is also therefore not a rate per LOC – then the range is reduced to under 800:1. Furthermore, if we also leave out Arthur's $2 per statement maintenance cost as discussed above, then his 15:1 ratio also disappears. If we also leave out Martin's 1:1 – as concluded previously, it is not a rate per LOC – then we are left with the much smaller range of 1:9 to 1:53, a ratio of just 6:1. The calculations in the preceding paragraphs – a cost of about $5–40 per statement for development, and about $25–100 per maintenance – give a range of about 1.6:1 (40:25) to 1:20 (5:100), if we take the extreme values, with an average of about 1:3 ((40 + 5)/2:(25 + 100)/2 = 22.5:62.5), i.e. it typically costs about three times as much to modify a statement as it took to write the statement. This is in good agreement with the conclusion reached in Chapter 8 that about 10% of the coding in a program is changed each year, and this takes about 25% of the original programming time, a ratio of 1:2.5.

The figures in Table 13.3 do not show any obvious trend with time. However, they vary so widely that this is likely to be swamping factors such as the reduction in hardware costs (if included in any of the rates), and the increased power of the software tools, on the one hand; and the increase in programmers' salaries, the cost of the more powerful tools and the more powerful hardware needed to run them (if included in any of the rates), and the increase in system complexity, on the other.

Current software life expectancy

How much scope there is for an increase in software product life depends in part on the current life expectancy, and there is a lack of unanimity as to this figure (Table 13.4).

The value attributed to van Rijswijck (1983) is an estimate based on his statement that 80% of applications have a productive life of less than one year. This seems rather high, but it refers to applications in the 'exception reporting, analysis and query areas', i.e. areas where 4GLs are frequently used, making it more plausible.

The Yourdon (1975) value was derived from his statement that the average computer programmer changed jobs every 1.4 years, and the average lifetime of a computer program is at least twice this. However, he also stated that programs are typically maintained by ten generations of programmers, which implies a life span of 14 years, but this seems very high for a 'typical' life, particularly of a program as opposed to a system. Similarly, Van Tassel (1978) stated that the average production program will be maintained by ten different *people* (Chapter 8) – as opposed to Yourdon's ten *generations* of programmers. As a program might be maintained by more than one programmer from the same generation, Van Tassel's statement translates to a (much?) shorter time span, and therefore seems correspondingly more realistic.

The Fairley figures explicitly exclude the development time of 1–3 years. (Parikh (1984) and Yourdon (1975) also explicitly exclude the development time, and presumably it is excluded from the other tabulated figures as well.) Fairley actually gave two sets of figures. In addition to the figures already quoted, he gave the shorter ranges of 1 or 2 years for development, and 5–10 years for maintenance. This presumably just means

Table 13.4 Software product life expectancy

Source		Life expectancy (years)	
Kendall and Lamb (1977)	programs	1.2	median
Messerschmidt (1982)	programs	1.3	42% <2 months
van Rijswijck (1983)	systems	2	80% <1 year
Yourdon (1975)	programs	>2.8	
Dickson (1987)	systems	5	financial systems
Yourdon (1979b)	systems	5–10	
Fairley (1985)	systems	5–15	software products
Dickson (1987)	systems	8	personnel/payroll
Parikh (1984)	systems	10	range 5–20 years
Wulf (1976)	systems	10	
Blazdell (1988)*	systems	10–15	excludes extremes
Howden (1982)	systems	>10	large projects
Howden (1982)	systems	15–20	medium-size projects
Average (approximate)		5–10	

* Living up to the hype, *Computer Week*, 11 July 1988, pp. 16–17.

that only a few systems take as long as 3 years to develop, or have a productive life as long as 15 years. (Only systems which meet his 'large' classification have a development time of 3 years, though 'extremely large' ones can take up to 10 years.) All his figures refer to 'software products', as distinct from software developed for personal use. It is not clear whether the figures given by the other authorities refer to software products, personal software, or a mixture of the two. Much of the personal software will have a short life span (Grulke, 1983), which could explain the lowest figures in Table 13.4.

The Fairley figures imply that the calendar duration of maintenance is 5 times as long as that of development. Similarly, Charette (1986) stated that a software product currently spent over 80% of its life in maintenance, which implies that maintenance is at least 4 times as long. By contrast, Parikh (1984) stated that 67% of the software lifecycle is maintenance, i.e. only twice as long. However, the context of his statement implies he was not referring to duration as one might have thought, but to costs.

The value attributed to Ray Blazdell (of IBM) is an estimate derived from his state-ment that one-fifth of 5–10-year-old systems come up for redevelopment. Assuming that he means every year, this suggests a maximum life of around 10–15 years, with very few systems surviving beyond that period. However, he does not tell us what happens to systems younger than 5 years or older than 10. In particular, if there are many short-lived systems – and some of the evidence indicates that there are – then they would bring the average down considerably.

In addition to the figures given in Table 13.4, Frangos (1980) stated that 50% of software written for new mainframe installations had to be rewritten within six months, which suggests that software for new mainframe installations has an average life of only one or two years. (Apart from a reference to the number of bugs, he did not give the reason(s) for this, nor is it clear whether it was the mainframe which was new or the installation, i.e. he did not specify if he was referring to a new model of computer or to an organization computerizing for the first time. Presumably, the software was either inefficiently written or heavily patched due to lack of staff familiarity with the new hardware and system software. Virtual machine volatility, which was discussed in Chapter 5, will have a similar effect.)

Also not tabulated is the statement by Dunn and Ullman (1982) that widely-used software has a long life.

Conclusion

The highest figures in Table 13.4 are the life expectancy of systems, while the lowest figures are the life expectancy of individual programs. As systems are typically larger than programs, the trend therefore appears to be that longer life accompanies greater size, which is only to be expected, as the larger the product, the longer its life must be to recover its development cost. By contrast, however, Howden's figures suggest that medium-sized systems have a longer life, on average, than large systems. However, a more fundamental reason for systems having a longer life than programs is that, while individual programs within a system might be replaced, the system itself continues in existence.

Yourdon (1975) stated that it is rare for a program to be used only once or twice. Nevertheless, the values in Table 13.4 indicate that many programs are discarded soon after they have been developed. This would obviously be the case with temporary programs such as test drivers, and with the many small, simple, and frequently one-off programs written using 4GLs. Presumably though, the figures do not include temporary programs. In any event, temporary programs probably only comprise about 5% of the total software effort – though on a very large project, non-delivered code could amount to as much as four times the delivered code (Chapter 2). Strictly speaking, the 4GL programs *should* be included, but it is misleading to do so as they consume far less effort. Perhaps separate life spans should be given for different language levels (just as separate LOC productivity rates should be given for them – see Chapter 2).

Apart from the small, simple programs written using 4GLs, which consume very little development effort, it is questionable whether the cost of developing these short-lived programs is ever recovered. In some cases, it is known beforehand that the program will have only a short life, e.g. a one-off report, though this should not exempt it from the normal cost-benefits selection procedure. In any event, it is doubtful if this is the case for such a large proportion of programs (if the lowest tabulated figures are correct). It therefore seems likely that poor management, and inferior quality work by technical staff, are largely responsible. For example, Weinberg (1971) quoted a project in which insensitive management resulted in the key member of the development team leaving. As a result, the completed system was delivered one year late, and was an inefficient patchwork which was too slow to provide the expected savings, so it was discontinued after only six months.

The average software life expectancy will probably decrease in future because of the many short-lived programs written using fourth-generation languages, and the increasing number of personal systems (Grulke, 1983; Nies, 1983; Chapter 6). This is acceptable provided productivity improves accordingly, and projects are selected on the basis of their costs and benefits. On the other hand, longer life is one of the benefits claimed for CASE tools, and they will also be more widely used in future. This will counteract the shorter life resulting from taking advantage of the greater cost-effectiveness of fourth-generation languages, but it is difficult to predict which factor will have the greater impact.

13.3.2 COST REDUCTION TECHNIQUES

Savings can result from a variety of measures other than those already discussed.

- Factors such as word processors and

planned workflow systems (Chapter 4) benefit users as well as software engineers.

- Effective paper management, e.g. discarding out of date documents, or redesigning and combining two documents into one, saves on filing space and leads to faster retrieval (Been, 1979).
- Intelligent forms design by systems analysts can reduce the number of lines to be printed, resulting in faster printing, and possibly in postponement of a printer upgrade (van Gass, 1979).
- The Univac 1108 computer required $100 000 worth of spares on hand, the newer technology 1100/60 only $300 (Maintenance, *Computronics*, 29 Aug 1979, p. 3).
- In an example in Boehm (1981), purchase of hardware appeared at first glance to be cheaper than rental, but the position was reversed when 'present value' (the effect of interest rates over a period of time) was taken into account: 'deferred payments give us opportunities to do other useful things with our money', even if we only lend it to a bank and collect interest on it (Appendix E).

Brandon (1978) wrote an entire book on how to reduce and control DP costs. It contains numerous ideas, such as centralization (Chapter 3), secretarial support, telephone removal (Chapter 4), meters on photocopying machines, bulk purchases of supplies, re-inking of computer ribbons, etc.

The most effective way to achieve cost reductions (and many other improvements) is to invite suggestions from all employees – they know their jobs better than anyone else – and to reward them accordingly (Barclays talks business sense, *Computing S.A.*, 2 Sept. 1983, p. 8). Bohlin and Hoenig (1989) quoted a major insurance company in which a total of 5000 individual ideas led to $60 million in savings out of an annual budget of $300 million. Suggestions should be obtained through participation, e.g. by holding regular 'ideas sessions', rather than through the traditional suggestion box (Townsend, 1984; McGregor, 1960). Suggestion boxes are impersonal, with remote committees evaluating the ideas in secret. It is better if the person discusses his idea with the committee, in his own worksetting, and participates in evaluating it. Furthermore, many people with good ideas cannot express themselves well on paper, and are afraid of looking stupid. (On the other hand, any people who are not very articulate, are faced with a potentially even more embarrassing situation, as they may look stupid in the presence of the committee.)

Mistakes are not often published, but a manual of 'DO NOTs' based on them could save expensive repeats by others (de Raay, 1975). (The error analysis recommended in the section on debugging (Chapter 8) provides a basis for such a manual.)

13.3.3 RECRUITMENT

Increased recruitment may not improve software productivity, but it would increase the total number of staff in the industry. It would therefore increase the total output of the industry, and thus result in a faster service to users.

The number of software engineers is increasing, and there are many *entrants* to the profession (Chapter 9): the shortage is one of *experienced* staff. Organizations can recruit experienced staff from other organizations, both local and from other countries, but that is merely 'robbing Peter to pay Paul' – it does not increase the total number of staff in the industry, and so does not increase the output of the industry as a whole. (Though perhaps the person would be happier in his new job, or better matched to his new duties, and so would be more productive.) Shortages can also be made up by employing independent contractors or using software houses, but these solutions suffer from the same objection.

One solution which does not suffer from this objection is to encourage women, who left for family reasons, back into the industry, by:

- enabling them to work from their homes, e.g. by providing them with a PC, or a terminal linked into the organization's computer (Olson, 1989; Bailyn, 1989; van den Nieuwenhof, 1983);
- provision of day nurseries at the place of work;
- provision of part-time (e.g. half-day) jobs (Woodland, 1977);
- part-time contract work – they need only work, say, six months of each year, to save on income tax (Gray, 1980a);
- lower income tax rates;
- wives setting up their own companies: they 'can take the risk' (McKenzie, 1982).

Recruitment can also be of people who have *related* experience, e.g. computer operators (many have the aptitude but are not given the opportunity), or staff from other departments in the organization, who are thus familiar with the applications (Chapter 9).

An increasing number of organizations are teaching novices to program, because it is cheaper to train a new programmer than to hire an experienced one; and when they do their own training, they can create the kind of programmers they need, ones who follow their standards, and they can instill in them the organizational culture (Dight, 1986). Organizations which 'grow' their own pro- grammers include the Hartford Insurance Group, and of course computer manufac- turers such as IBM. The Hartford Insurance Group reserves at least five seats on their programmer training classes for their own employees, and have found that internal recruits tend to stay with the organization longer than those from outside. (This is analogous to the organizations with entry- level recruiting tending to have longer-term and more loyal employees than organizations which practice senior-level recruiting – Chapter 9.)

The increasing number of computers in schools should encourage more school leavers to enter the DP profession. Similarly, the increasing number of computers in homes and workplaces means that more non- DP staff now have contact with computers, which could make them want to change their jobs and become programmers. For example, some prominent DP personalities did not begin their working lives in this field: Harlan Mills was a professional mathematician, Ger- ald Cohen (president of Information Builders, Inc.) an operations researcher, and Girish Parikh a civil engineer (Mills, 1988; Myers, 1987; Parikh, 1984). If accepted, these recruits should become productive sooner – unless they first had to unlearn bad habits (Chapter 9)!

13.4 THE FUTURE

It is difficult to see into the future, particu- larly for a fast-moving industry like comput- ing. DP is affected by the economic climate, inflation, labor costs, and political upheavals. Research funding may be reduced. Scientific breakthroughs cannot be predicted.

This study has taken into account not just a static picture of the current situation, but also current trends, such as the improvement in the hardware price–performance ratio, and the consequent proliferation of computers.

To predict the future, two questions must first be answered.

- Will there be any changes to these trends?
- Will there be any breakthroughs or new trends?

James Martin (1980) said that he did not expect any product breakthroughs, as most of the technology we needed was already available. Similarly, a report by British Tele- com and the UK Department of Industry stated that most of the technology that would have the greatest impact on office design over the next 10 years already existed and was in use by leading organizations (Information technology threatens to swamp contemporary offices, *Computer Week*, 9 May 1983, p. 17). In any event, changes are slow to filter through and take effect (Martin, 1982b). Martin pointed out that it took the DP profession 10 years to swing from assembly languages as the main form of programming to widespread use of COBOL and PL/1, and commented: 'It is dismal to reflect that it might take 10 years to swing from COBOL and PL/1 to application generators and other high-level facilities' (Martin, 1982a). Similarly, Couger *et al.* (1982) predicted that, based on past experience, it would be another decade before the majority of firms implemented fourth-generation system development techniques (PSL/PSA II, structured analysis, structured design, etc.). Furthermore, the software industry was talking about analyst and designer workbenches (CASE tools) for 5 years or more, but 'nothing much was done about it', while it was not until the mid-1970s that most MIS organizations accepted that every programmer should have a dumb terminal on his desk, and it took another 5 years for many organizations to actually purchase the terminals and provide a separate mainframe computer for the system development staff (Yourdon, 1989). Current trends can therefore be expected to continue for the immediate future.

I thus predict that:

- increasingly more accurate metrics will be devised for measuring software productivity and quality, and estimating effort;
- more attention will be paid to software productivity and quality;
- capital expenditure on office equipment, e.g. teleconference facilities and desk top publishing, will increase, as a result of which DP staff will be able to work more efficiently, and documentation (program specifications, user manuals, etc.) will be of a higher standard;

- input technologies will improve, e.g. better voice recognition systems;
- hardware improvements – in size, capacity, speed, and price – will continue;
- the hardware price–performance ratio will continue to improve;
- the trend towards standards, such as IBM architecture for large computers, and UNIX as the operating system for intermediate-sized computers, will continue;
- the number of computers sold will remain high, particularly small machines;
- the demand for software will also remain high;
- systems will continue to become larger and more complex;
- software engineers will make greater use of MPPs;
- improved methodologies will be developed;
- organizations will invest more money in hardware and software tools in order to improve productivity, e.g. they will provide each programmer with his own high-technology workstation;
- further improvements in power and ease of use will be made to the software tools, e.g. still higher-level languages, active data dictionaries, and interactive debuggers, as well as the currently popular graphical user interfaces (GUIs), and they will become more widely used;
- CASE tools, which automate systems analysis and design, will improve and become more widely used;
- end users will increasingly employ the new tools themselves, to satisfy their own needs;
- application packages will be used to an even greater extent;
- the output and productivity of the software industry as a whole (i.e. including re-used code, packages, and the work done by end users) will thus continue to rise rapidly, but much of this improvement will be indirect and therefore 'invisible';

- the rate at which code is produced will, however, only rise slowly;
- the 'visible' productivity of DP departments will therefore only rise slowly;
- the rise should be greater than in the past because of the improved tools and our greater understanding of productivity, but will still not be spectacular, because of the increasing size and complexity of the systems being developed, because of reluctance to use the new tools and methods, and because much of the easiest (and therefore highest productivity) work will be done by end users;
- usage of COBOL and other third-generation languages will decline, but they will not die in the foreseeable future;
- the cost of developing the smallest and simplest systems will decrease because of the power of 4GLs;
- however, the cost of developing other systems will continue to rise because of their increasing size and sophistication, because of the higher cost of the new tools and the more powerful hardware needed to run them, and because of inflation and the resultant increase in programmers' salaries, and these increases will outweigh the reduction in hardware costs, and the effect of the more powerful tools and methodologies;
- the cost per LOC will therefore also continue to increase;
- the maintenance millstone will be lightened, but will continue to impede the development of new systems;
- the backlog millstone will also be lightened, but it will not disappear for years to come;
- the average life span of software products will decrease because of the increasing number of personal systems, and the increasing use of powerful and cost-effective 4GLs for one-off programs in particular;
- the number of staff will increase, but not sufficiently to match the increased demand

for software, so the shortage will get worse;
- relatively less time will be spent on programming, and relatively more on systems analysis;
- new recruits to the DP industry will have more DP knowledge than those in the past, gained from exposure to computers at school, work, and home, though many will first have to unlearn bad habits;
- better methods of selecting and appraising staff will be developed, so employees will be better matched to specific jobs;
- many software engineers will specialize more;
- more time and money will be spent on training;
- teaching will improve, e.g. through the wider use of CBT and interactive video;
- software quality will improve, e.g. documentation will be better, and programs released into production will contain fewer bugs;
- the standard of management will improve;
- all in all, the service received by users will improve.

Most of these predictions are supported by evidence presented in this study, but some predictions are wishes or hopes, based on the adage 'necessity is the mother of invention' – it is necessary, therefore it will be made to happen.

It is even more difficult to make longer-term forecasts, but the following developments and changes in current trends, are foreseen:

- a slowdown in the hardware price–performance improvements, though breakthroughs can be expected from time to time;
- a slowdown in the demand for applications to be computerized, though new application areas will stimulate further demand from time to time;
- a reduction in the number of programmers;

- some attention will revert from software back to hardware;
- progress in the use of natural languages for writing programs and interrogating databases;
- progress in the use of AI and expert systems to help software engineers, e.g. by generating a program from the specifications; or by identifying which parts of a system are affected by maintenance changes, and updating them consistently;
- the fifth-generation hardware and software.

When can such developments be expected? Some artificial intelligence type functions have already been successfully used for complex scheduling (Boehm, 1981) and in CBT (Chapter 9). On the other hand, there are dangers and difficulties with natural languages, e.g. ambiguity and lack of power, so it may be years before they can be used (Chapter 6). Conte *et al.* (1986) stated that it was doubtful that expert systems for automatic program generation having a significant impact on productivity would be successfully developed in the near future; and Schach (1988) stated that the current status of the Japanese fifth-generation project was 'silence'.

13.5   GENERAL CONCLUSIONS

The main conclusions of this study are summarized below.

- Insufficient attention is paid to productivity.
- Numerous factors affect productivity.
- There is a lack of rigorous quantitative information on the magnitude of their effect, and on current practices in the industry.
- There is a need for better metrics.
- Measurement is important in improving productivity and quality.
- Large gains in productivity can be achieved.

- Productivity, as measured by the rate at which code is produced, has only been increasing slowly, but large indirect ('invisible') gains have been achieved through the use of packages and re-used code.
- Similarly, use of higher-level languages has enabled greater functionality to be produced for the same amount of code and effort.
- Large increases in total software output have also been achieved, both because of the increase in 'invisible' productivity, and through end-user programming.
- A large increase in productivity is required to meet the increasing demand for software, to provide more sophisticated and user-friendly systems, to clear the backlog of work, and to provide users with one-off reports.
- Many factors have a large effect on productivity, and so provide potential solutions to the problem.
- Authorities disagree as to which factor has the largest effect: some claim it is re-used code, others claim it is management, or type of application, technology (automation), personnel capability, motivation, quality, and so on.
- Better management not only improves productivity, but also spares the DP department the embarrassment of missed deadlines, budget overruns, and bug-ridden production programs.
- Some other factors also have a large effect on productivity, but only in certain circumstances. For example, documentation usually only forms a major portion of the total effort in large systems, commercially marketed systems, contractually-produced software, and civilian government and military systems, and therefore only has a significant effect on productivity in these situations. Similarly, travel and communication costs are usually only significant in systems developed at multiple locations, particularly multiple international locations, so these costs are usually only

significant in large, distributed organizations.

- However, factors which have the greatest *effect* on productivity are not necessarily the ones with the greatest *potential* for productivity improvement, e.g. it is difficult to improve personnel capability.
- My own opinion is that technology, such as ultra-high-level languages and CASE tools, has the greatest potential for productivity improvement.
- One form of technology, fourth-generation software, is of especial benefit to end users, enabling them, in particular, to generate their own one-off enquiries and reports, quickly and easily.
- This solution is also resulting in a slow move away from COBOL as the main programming language for business applications.
- Another solution, application packages, is of especial benefit to small organizations which do not have DP Departments.
- Other software packages, such as spreadsheets and word processing, have even wider use.
- DP departments also benefit from these solutions, both directly and indirectly. Directly, because they can use 4GLs themselves to develop applications, and can use word processing packages to produce system documentation; and indirectly, because the proliferation of application packages and end-user programming means they have fewer systems to develop.

- Solutions proposed in the past have not delivered the expected productivity gains.
- There is often resistance to productivity-improvement measures.
- It will take years before the backlog of work can be cleared, but the backlog acts as a sieve, ensuring that the least profitable jobs are not undertaken.
- The large amount of time devoted to maintenance will be reduced, but maintenance will not disappear as much of it is actually development in disguise.
- Software reliability is improving, at least in those organizations which are attempting to improve quality and reduce the number of defects.
- There are alternative courses of action, such as relaxing arbitrary budget constraints, statistical techniques, and extending program life, which may not improve software productivity, but which do enable organizations to get better value for money from their DP departments.
- Similarly, evolutionary delivery may not improve software productivity, but it does result in a better service to users by providing some of the required functionality quickly.
- Current trends will continue for several years without major changes.

Taking all factors into account, I predict that the present unsatisfactory situation will gradually improve. Software engineering productivity *can* be significantly increased, and if sufficient attention and effort are devoted to it, then it *will* be.

APPENDIX A: ABBREVIATIONS

ACM	Association for Computing Machinery
ADABAS	adaptable data base system
ADDS	Applied Digital Data Systems, Inc.
ADF	application development facility
ADR	Applied Data Research, Inc.
ADS	application development system
AED	automated engineering design
AFIPS	American Federation of Information Processing Societies
AI	artificial intelligence
ALADDIN	assembly language assertion-driven debugging interpreter
ALGOL	algorithmic language
ALL	application language liberator
ANSI	American National Standards Institute
APL	a programming language
APSE	ADA programming support environment
AS	application system
ASCII	American standard code for information interchange
ASI	Advanced Systems, Inc.
AT&T	American Telephone and Telegraph Co.
ATM	automated teller machine
AUT	automated unit test
B & O	Bang & Olufsen
BASIC	beginner's all-purpose symbolic instruction code
BBC	British Broadcasting Corporation
BCS	Boeing Computer Services
BIOS	basic input/output system
BUP	back-up programmer
CA	Computer Associates International, Inc.
CAFS	content addressable file store
CAI	computer-assisted (or aided) instruction
CAL	computer-assisted (or aided) learning
CASE	computer-aided software engineering
CBT	computer-based training
CD-ROM	compact disk, read-only memory
CDC	Control Data Corporation
CEO	chief executive officer
CFT	Cray FORTRAN compiler
CI	Computer Intelligence Corp.
CICS	customer information control system
CIM	computer integrated manufacturing (or manufacture)
CMC	Computer Machinery Company
CMS	conversational monitor system
COBOL	common business-oriented language
COCOMO	constructive cost model
CODASYL	conference on data systems languages
COPMO	co-operative programming model
Corp.	Corporation
CP	chief programmer
CP/M	control program for microcomputers
CPM	critical path method

CPT	chief programmer team
CPU	central processing unit
CRT	cathode ray tube
CSP	cross system product
D & B	The Dun & Bradstreet Corporation
DACC	design assertion consistency checker
DARPA	Defense Advanced Research Projects Agency
DBA	database administrator
DBMS	database management system
DB2	database 2
DDI	Database Design, Inc.
DDP	distributed data processing
DEC	Digital Equipment Corporation
DECA	design expression and confirmation aid
DFD	data flow diagram
dict	active data dictionary
DIN	Deutsche Industrie-Norm
DMS	development management system
DoD	Department of Defense
DOS	disk operating system
DP	data processing; also known as electronic data processing (EDP)
DPM	data processing manager
DSI	delivered source instructions
DSS	decision support system
DTP	desktop publishing
ECSS	extendable computer system simulator
EDLIN	line editor
EDP	electronic data processing
EEC	European Economic Community
ESPRIT	European Program for Research and Development in Information Technology
ESS	electronic spreadsheet
ETH	Swiss Federal Institute of Technology
FACES	FORTRAN automatic code evaluation system
FDA	Food and Drug Adminstration
FORTRAN	formula translation
FSD	Federal Systems Division of IBM
GDDM	graphical data display manager
GDP	gross domestic product
GE	General Electric Corporation
gen	application or program generator
GIGO	garbage in, garbage out
GOALS	goal-oriented approach to life-cycle software
GPSS	general-purpose system simulator
GRC	General Research Corporation
GTE	General Telephone and Electronics Corp.
GUI	graphical user interface
HIHO	humanized input, humanized output
HIPO	hierarchical input processing output
HOS	higher-order software
I/O	input/output
IBM	International Business Machines Corporation
IC	information center (also integrated circuit)
ICI	Imperial Chemical Industries
ICL	International Computers, Limited
ICP	International Computer Programs, Inc.
IDA	Institute for Defense Analyses
IDC	International Data Corporation
IDMS	integrated database management system
IDMS/R	integrated database management system/relational
IEEE	Institute of Electrical and Electronic Engineers
IEW/WS	information engineering workbench/workstation
IFIP	International Federation for Information Processing
IJCS	international job costing system

IMS	information management system
INGRES	interactive graphics and retrieval system
IPO	Input processing output
IPT	improved programming technologies
IQ	intelligence quotient
IRS	Internal Revenue Service
IS	information systems
ISAM	indexed-sequential access method
ISDOS	information system design and optimization system
ISSCO	Integrated Software Systems Corporation
IT	information technology
ITT	International Telephone and Telegraph Corporation
IVI	interactive video instruction
JAD	joint application design
JAVS	JOVIAL language automated verification system
JCL	job control language
JOVIAL	Jules' own version of IAL (or ALGOL)
JSD	Jackson system development
JSP	Jackson structured programming
K	1000 or 1024
KB	1024 bytes
KDSI	thousand delivered source instructions
kHz	kilohertz
K LOC	thousand lines of code
LAN	local area network
lang.	language
LCD	liquid-crystal display
LCP	logical construction of programs
LISP	list processing
LOC	lines of code
LU	logical unit
LUERA	likely user error reports avoided
LUW	logical unit of work
Mac	Apple Macintosh

MAPPER	maintaining, preparing, and processing executive reports
MB	megabytes (1 million bytes (actually 1 048 576))
MBA	Master of Business Administration
MBO	Management by objectives
McAuto	McDonnell Douglas Automation Co.
MECCA	multi-element component comparison and analysis method
MIPS	million instructions per second
MIS	management information system
MIT	Massachusetts Institute of Technology
mm	millimeter
MM	man-month
MMA	Microcomputer Managers Association
MPP	modern programming practices
MRI	magnetic resonance imaging
MRP	materials requirements planning or manufacturing resource planning
MS	Microsoft Corporation
MS-DOS	Microsoft Corporation, disk operating system
MSA	Management Science America, Inc.
MSS	manufacturing software systems
MTBF	mean time between failures
MTTF	mean time to failure
MTTR	mean time to repair
MVS	multiple virtual storage
NASA	National Aeronautics and Space Administration
NCC	National Computing Centre
NCR	National Cash Register Corporation
NIH	National Institutes of Health (or not invented here)
NLOC	non-commentary lines of code
NTIS	National Technical Information Service

NYT	New York Times
O & M	organization and methods
OA	office automation
OCR	optical character reader
OLTP	on-line transaction processing
OS	operating system
OSF	Open Software Foundation
OSI	open systems interconnection
PARC	Palo Alto Research Center
PAT	programmer aptitude test
PC	personal computer; also known as a microcomputer or just a micro
PCF	program checkout facility
PCTE	portable common tools environment
PDL	program design (or definition) language
PERT	project (or program) evaluation and review technique
PET	program evaluator and tester
PL/1	programming language one
PLATO	programmed learning for automated teaching operations
POS	point of sale
POST	power-on self test
PPL	program production library; also known as the development support library
PROFS	professional office system
PS/2	Personal System/2
PSA	problem statement analyser
PSL	problem statement language
PWB	programmers' workbench
QA	quality assurance
QC	quality control (or quality circle)
RACF	resource access control facility
RADC	Rome Air Development Center
RAM	random-access memory
RAMIS	rapid access management information system
RBF	report by form
RCA	Radio Corporation of America
REXX	restructured extended executor language

RFI	radio frequency interference
RISC	reduced instruction set computer
RJE	remote job entry
RM	Ryan McFarland
ROI	return on investment
ROM	read-only memory
RPG	report program generator
SAA	systems application architecture
SADT	structured analysis and design technique
SAGE	semi-automatic ground environment (nationwide air defense system)
SAS	statistical analysis system
SCCS	source code control system
SCRS	software cost reduction specification method
SDC	System Development Corporation
SEI	Software Engineering Institute
SGU	screen generator utility
SIR	scientific information retrieval
SLIM	software life-cycle methodology
SNA	system network architecture
SODU	screen oriented disk utility
SOWACO	Software Consulting
SPQR	software productivity, quality, and reliability model
SPSS	statistical package for the social sciences
SQL	structured query language
SQL/DS	structured query language/data system
SRA	Science Research Associates, Inc.
SREM	software requirements engineering methodology
STARS	software technology for adaptable, reliable systems
SVIB	Strong vocational interest blank
TI	Texas Instruments
TIC	Travelers Insurance Company
TPL	test procedure language

TSI	test on sequential instructions	**VDU**	visual (or video) display unit; also known as a visual display terminal
TSO	time sharing option		
TWA	TransWorld Airlines		
UFO	user files on-line	**VLIW**	very long instruction word
UMI	University Microfilms International		
		VM	virtual machine
UNIS	Univac Industrial System	**VME**	virtual machine environment
UNIVAC	Universal Automatic Computer	**VMS**	virtual memory system
UTS	Universal Terminal System or Universal Timesharing System	**VSAM**	virtual storage access method
		VTOC	visual table of contents
VAX	virtual address extension	**WISC**	why isn't Sammy coding?
VDM	Vienna development method	**XT**	extended technology
VDT	visual (or video) display terminal; also known as a visual display unit	**3GL**	third-generation ('high-level') language
		4GL	fourth-generation language

APPENDIX B: DEFINITIONS

B.1 INDIVIDUAL DEFINITIONS

The reader is assumed to be knowledgeable about data processing, and particularly software engineering, and therefore to be familiar with most of the terms used in this study. Nevertheless, I have gathered together terms which are widely used in the study, are less well known, or which may cause confusion, and they are defined below.

Active data dictionary

See Data dictionary.

Application package

An application package is a *generalized* computer system, and can therefore be used by many organizations. The term has generally been abbreviated here to 'package'. It refers to application software such as general ledger and payroll systems, rather than to system software such as sorts or 4GLs.

Baselining

After a product (such as specifications) has been verified and validated, it is temporarily 'frozen': no changes are permitted to it without the formal agreement of all affected parties. This is known as baselining.

Batch processing

Information (data or programs) is collected into batches, and is then processed by the computer in one run. It allows no interactive processing.

Bebugging

Bebugging (also known as 'intentional failure') is a method of testing. Bugs are deliberately inserted ('seeded') into the program by a second party.

Black-box testing

In black-box testing, the *functions* of the program are tested. Test cases are therefore designed from the program specifications alone, so no knowledge of the internals of the program is required.

Block-structured language

A block-structured language permits individual statements to be grouped together and treated as a compound statement. In some languages, blocks are delimited with explicit words such as BEGIN and END.

Chief programmer

A chief programmer is a programmer/analyst who occupies the position of project leader in a particular form of project team, the CPT. He may, or may not, be a super-programmer.

Chief programmer team (CPT)

A CPT is a combination of a particular form of project team organization and several software methodologies: structured programming, top-down programming, etc.

Code auditor

A code auditor is a program which checks for violations of coding standards, e.g. for comments and labels.

Coding constructs

Coding constructs can be classified as detail-level design. The three basic coding constructs permitted in structured programming are the process block, IF–THEN–ELSE, and DO–WHILE/UNTIL.

Coding conventions

Examples of coding conventions are: indentation, descriptive names, only one statement per line, and use of comments.

Cohesion

Cohesion is the amount of interaction within a module. Cohesion measures how strongly the elements within a module are related to each other – the stronger, the better. Modules performing only one function have high cohesion. Modules should therefore only perform one function each. The degree of cohesion is a criterion for assessing and choosing between alternative designs.

Complexity

Complexity is anything which increases the difficulty, and therefore the effort required, to develop or to maintain software.

Configuration management

Configuration management is the art of co-ordinating software development and maintenance to minimize problems such as debugging a program using an out of date source code listing; one programmer overwriting another's changes; two programmers independently fixing the same bug; the same bug in two versions of a program and only one version being fixed; commencing system testing while unaware that one of the modules has not been unit tested; and releasing a program that is not yet ready.

An alternative definition is: define a program to be produced, control all changes to that original definition, and show that the final product is completely consistent with the original definition as modified by the accepted changes.

Cost driver

A cost driver (or effort multiplier) affects the amount of effort required to develop or maintain software, and therefore affects productivity and costs, e.g. the size and complexity of the software, and the experience and ability of the staff.

Coupling

Coupling is the amount of interaction between modules. Modules with little interaction (loose coupling) are largely self-contained and independent, which avoids complications caused by what is happening in other modules, and restricts damage due to errors. The degree of coupling is therefore a criterion for assessing, and choosing between, alternative designs.

Critical path

The critical path is the sequence of activities which limits the early completion of a project. It is the longest path through a PERT network, i.e. the path with the highest total duration. This is how long the project will take. This is therefore the path which one should try to shorten, e.g. by reallocation of staff or rearranging activities, so that the project will be completed sooner. Conversely, any slippages in the activities on this path will delay completion of the project.

Data dictionary

A data dictionary contains information about the data defined within a system, such as the name of each field, the length of the field, whether it is alpha or numeric, and so on. Dictionaries may be active or passive. Generally, a passive dictionary serves purely as human-readable documentation; while in an active dictionary the information is used by the computer, e.g. as the heading to be used for that field on reports, to assist with the validation of input data, or to control access to the data.

Deadline effect

People work harder as a deadline approaches. They put more energy into the time spent on the project, and they spend more time on it, either by working overtime or by postponing non-productive activities such as training and vacations until after the deadline.

Debugging

Debugging is the process of finding and fixing errors which are already known to exist. In common usage, it is usually treated as part of the testing function.

Decision density

The decision density is the number of decisions (e.g. IF, UNTIL and WHEN statements) per hundred executable LOC.

Decision support system

A decision support system is a management information system designed to assist in the decision-making process.

Delphi technique

Delphi is a technique for obtaining consensus between a group of people, in which the participants remain anonymous to each other.

Democratic teams

Democratic teams are a related concept to the matrix structure (Chapter 3). In democratic teams, there is no fixed leader. Instead, leadership is constantly changing, devolving on whoever is best able to lead the team at the time, e.g. the best debugger might be the leader for the duration of the debugging phase.

Economic productivity

See Productivity.

Efficiency

See Productivity.

Effort multiplier

See Cost driver.

Ego-less programming

Ego-less programming means that programs are written by individuals but then become public property, and are reviewed by the programmer's colleagues, so they are considered to be joint efforts.

Embedded mode

Embedded mode projects are ones where the staff are working in areas unknown to them, reliability is very important, and the project must operate within tight and inflexible constraints of hardware, software, regulations and operational procedures. An example is an air traffic control system – the environment in which it will be run cannot be changed.

Embedded systems

An embedded system is one in which the computer is embedded within a larger mechanical system, such as a robot or a pilotless plane.

End user

An end user is generally a member of another department within the organization, for whom the DP department provides a service. DP write a program, and the end user uses it or its output. The term has generally been abbreviated here to user.

Equivalent lines of code

The equivalent lines of code is obtained by reducing the total line count by a factor which depends, amongst other things, on the number of lines of re-used code in the program. This is done in order to allow for the smaller amount of effort required to re-use code than to write new code.

Ergonomics

Ergonomics is the study of the efficiency of people in their working environment, particularly in relation to the equipment they use.

Evolutionary delivery

See Incremental delivery.

Feasibility study

The objective of a feasibility study is to determine if the proposed system is technically feasible, economically desirable, will fit in with the structure and long-range plans of the organization, if it will be acceptable to the people who will be affected by it, and if key personnel will be available.

Footcandle

A footcandle is the illumination given by a source of one candela at a distance of one foot.

Footprint

The footprint of a PC etc. is the area it takes up on a desk.

Foreign debug

Debugging which is performed by someone other than the original programmer is known as foreign debug, or second-party debugging.

Fourth-generation languages

This study uses a broad definition of the fourth-generation. The term here covers any product (very high-level language, non-procedural language, program generator, etc.) which gives a significant gain in software productivity compared to high-level languages such as COBOL. It includes utilities (e.g. file copies and reformats), and older languages such as EASYTRIEVE and RPG.

The terms fourth-generation software and fourth-generation products have been used interchangeably with fourth-generation languages. Although fourth-generation *languages* is the accepted term, some of the menu-driven, fill-in-the-blanks products bear little resemblance to a conventional programming language.

Function

A function is a task performed by a program, or the group of statements in a program.

Function point

A function point is a weighted sum of delivered functional units – the number of inputs, outputs, enquiries, master files and interfaces. (This definition does not coincide with the more common meaning of the word function, as given above.)

Gantt charts

Gantt charts (also known as bar charts) are a scheduling technique which shows the project activities (the tasks and the people performing them) superimposed on a calendar.

Glass-box testing

This is an alternative and more meaningful name for white-box testing.

Gold-plating

Gold-plating is non-essential requirements, or ones which would only be marginally useful.

Golden rule

The golden rule is do unto others as you would have others do unto you. See also Modified golden rule.

Grey-box testing

This refers to a mixture of black- and white-box testing.

Halstead's Software Science

This includes a number of metrics, e.g. for program size, programming effort, program level, number of bugs, and language level. These are based on various counts, such as the number of distinct operators in the program (e.g. array subscripts, Boolean operators, and COBOL verbs).

Harmony of objectives

See Principle of harmony of objectives.

Hawthorne effect

This is the phenomenon whereby people work harder and produce more if they are highly motivated, particularly if they believe their employer is taking an interest in them.

Heavy-duty software products

Heavy-duty software products are programs or systems which have been more rigorously tested and have a higher standard of documentation than normal. This is necessary for products such as technological aids and application packages, which are used by many organizations remote from and not known to the developers, and which run on a range of hardware configurations and in a range of software environments.

High-level languages

High-level languages are ones like FORTRAN, COBOL, PL/1 and BASIC, which are intermediate in power between Assembler language and fourth-generation languages. They are also known as third-generation languages (3GLs).

HIPO

HIPO (hierarchical input processing output) is a technique for designing and describing systems in terms of the inputs to, and outputs from, systems and programs, and the process that converts the inputs to the outputs.

HIPO diagrams show the structure of systems and programs. There are three types of diagram: the hierarchy chart, and overview and detail diagrams. The latter two diagrams each consist of three sections, input, processing, and output, and are therefore known as IPOs.

Improved programming technologies

See Modern programming practices.

Incremental delivery

With incremental (evolutionary) delivery, a system is phased in. The initial version of the system, as delivered to the user, contains only some of the desired functions. The remaining functions are added gradually. As each function is added, so a new, extended version of the system is delivered to the user.

Incremental development

Incremental development is similar to incremental delivery, but the intermediate products are not delivered to the users.

Inspections

In an inspection a group of people meet to examine computer software and related material for the presence of desired characteristics and the absence of undesired characteristics. It is a formal process, which follows a set of procedures and error-detection techniques.

Interactive processing

The user enters commands or data into the computer, or runs programs, and receives immediate responses. The alternative approach, with no interaction, is batch processing.

Invisible backlog

An invisible backlog is work which users need but have not bothered to ask for because they know they would have to wait so long for it to be done.

Invisible productivity

Invisible productivity is a term coined from the analogy with the invisible backlog. It refers to productivity gains which are indirect and therefore not immediately obvious. It refers particularly to gains achieved by the use of application packages, but it also applies to word processing packages, spreadsheets, etc., and re-used code can also be included in the definition. The increase in total software output due to programming by end users is an analogous situation. They will use 4GLs almost exclusively, so their productivity should be high, but it will not be obvious, nor will it be easy to measure, so it can also be included in the definition.

IPOs

See HIPO.

Jackson structured programming (JSP)

JSP is a program design method based on the structure of the data. It is a refinement of the top-down method, and formalizes the design process by providing well-specified steps, graphic diagramming techniques (system network diagram, tree structure diagrams, and pseudocode), and methods to evaluate the correctness of the design. It aims to make the structure of the program reflect the structure of the problem, which helps produce readily modifiable systems.

Job control language (JCL)

JCL is used by a programmer to tell the operating system how the program should be executed – how much memory it requires, what priority it should have, what names have been given to the physical files, and so on.

Joint application design (JAD)

JAD is a combination of a structured design methodology and an intensive workshop in which users and designers together specify and design the application.

Knowledge worker

A knowledge worker is someone who works with information and makes decisions, such as managers and professionals.

Lead programmer

A lead programmer is a programmer/ supervisor, who does programming himself, and supervises the work of a team of other programmers. He might be a super-programmer, but is not a chief programmer as he has no systems analysis or design duties.

Leading-edge organizations

Leading-edge organizations are those which are at the leading-edge in terms of tools, methods, and skill levels. Trailing-edge organizations are those which are at the trailing-edge in these respects. For example, leading-edge organizations use automated estimating and project planning and tracking, whereas trailing-edge organizations use manual methods; leading-edge organizations use joint workshops and prototypes to determine users' requirements, whereas trailing-edge organizations use text requests and responses; leading-edge organizations use standard designs and re-usable code, whereas trailing-edge organizations hand code nearly all modules; and so on.

Lux

Lux is a measurement of the intensity of light. A lux is one lumen per square meter, where a lumen is the flux per unit solid angle from a uniform source of one candela.

Maintenance

Maintenance is generally defined as any work done on a software system after it becomes operational, but can also be defined as changes which leave the primary functions of the system intact, i.e. more extensive changes are classified as development.

Maslow's hierarchy of needs

This is a classification scheme for the factors that motivate people. In descending order of importance, the needs are physiological, safety, social, esteem, and self-fulfilment. For example, people who are starving – a physiological need – will not be concerned about improving their computer skills – a self-fulfilment need.

Median

The median of a set of numbers arranged in order of magnitude is the middle value, or the arithmetic mean of the two middle values. Half of the numbers are therefore greater than the median, and half are less. The median is also called the 50th percentile.

Metrics

Software metrics is a relatively new area of computer science aimed at assigning quantitative indices of merit to all attributes of a software product, and all stages of the software life-cycle.

Micron

A micron is a millionth of a metre.

Mnemonics

A mnemonic is a name, typically an abbreviation of a word or function, which is designed to aid the memory; used extensively in Assembler.

Mode

The mode of a set of numbers is that value which occurs with the greatest frequency, i.e. the most common value.

Modern programming practices (MPPs)

Different authorities include different methods under this title and under the title improved programming technologies, but typically, different combinations of the following methods are included: top-down requirements analysis, design, and implementation; structured design notation; HIPO diagrams; top-down incremental development; design and code walkthroughs or inspections; structured coding; CPTs; project librarians; and the program production or development support library.

Modified golden rule

The modified golden rule is 'do unto others as you would have others do unto you – *if you were like them*'.

Non-procedural language

A non-procedural language is one where the programmer need specify only *what* is to be done, *not how* to do it. Many 4GLs are non-procedural.

Off-line

See Batch processing.

On-line

See Interactive processing.

On-line databases

see Public on-line databases.

Organic mode

Organic mode projects are ones where the teams are small and the development staff are familiar with the application and the environment (thus minimizing learning and communication); the constraints are flexible (i.e. the specifications can be negotiated to reduce development effort, e.g. 'what you really want is what I have written'); and early completion is not a priority.

Organization

An organization is the whole of a company, firm, corporation, etc. In our context, the organization typically comprises several departments, one of which is a DP department providing a service to the other departments – the end users. The word also means 'structure', but this meaning has been avoided here to prevent confusion.

Package

A package is a *generalized* software product, and can therefore be used by many organizations. There are different types of package.

The technological aids discussed in Chapter 6 are one type, but the term as used in this study refers almost exclusively to another type, the application package.

Passive data dictionary

See Data dictionary.

Peer code review

The source code of a program is examined by the programmer's peers.

Peer review

Members of a group evaluate each other.

Percentile

If a set of data is arranged in order of magnitude, the values which divide it into 100 equal parts are called percentiles. The 15th percentile, for example, means that 15% of the data falls beneath that value. A 15th percentile programmer is therefore one who is better than 15% of all programmers (i.e. very low capability); a 90th percentile programmer is one who is better than 90% of all programmers (i.e. very high capability). The 50th percentile is the median.

Percentile range and ratio

The 15–90 percentile range, for example, is the difference between the 90th and the 15th percentiles for the data. In this study, ratios have been used rather than differences. For example, if the 15–90 percentile ratio is 2:1, then programmers who are better than 90% of all programmers, are twice as good as those who are only better than 15% of all programmers.

Personal computer (PC)

A PC is a small (micro) computer, which is normally used by one person. It is intended mainly for home or light business use.

PERT charts

PERT charts are network diagrams which show each activity comprising a project, the duration of each activity, when each activity is scheduled to start and finish, and dependencies between the activities.

Principle of harmony of objectives

If people perceive that their personal goals are in harmony with the organization's goals, they will contribute more to the organization's goals.

Private ownership

In private ownership the identity of the one person who wrote the program is common knowledge. Public ownership means that the program was a joint effort.

Productivity

In common usage, the terms efficiency and productivity are generally used interchangeably, and refer to the ratio of output to input (effort and cost), but for the purpose of this study, productivity is defined as output achieved with regard for the time taken but not for the cost incurred, whereas efficiency takes the cost into account.

Economic productivity is the goods or services produced per unit of labor or expense, i.e. it corresponds to my general definitions of productivity and efficiency.

These definitions are not tied to any particular unit of measure, and so avoid the mathematical paradoxes caused by using lines of code as the unit of measure.

Productivity improvement

A productivity improvement can be expressed in a number of ways. The one used here is the ratio:

time taken previously:time taken now

Productivity rate

There are many different ways of measuring software engineering productivity. The simplest and commonest measure, and the one mostly employed here, is the number of fully debugged and documented program source statements per person per day. Programming productivity includes all programming time, but only programming time; project productivity includes all time spent on the project whether programming, systems, clerical, or managerial.

Program size

There are many different ways of measuring program and system size. The simplest and commonest measure, and the one mostly employed here, is the number of program source statements.

Programming

The term programming is sometimes used to refer to only the design and writing of programs, but is more commonly used to include testing and debugging, and it is this latter usage which is employed here.

Prototype

A prototype is an *initial* and *partial* version of a system. It is a first working model, which is then tested and adapted to improve it.

Psychological set

Psychological set or mind-set is the blind spot which prevents people seeing something – typically errors they have made – which are obvious to someone else.

Public on-line databases

Public on-line databases consist of information such as airline schedules, news, commercial, credit, financial, marketing, bibliographic, technical, biomedical, and scientific information, which is stored and made available on-line to the public on a bureau basis, with customers being charged according to their connect time.

Public ownership

See Private ownership.

Quality

Quality has many facets. Amongst other things, a software product must be correct; it should comply with the installation's standards for documentation, structure, coding, etc.; it should be flexible and easily maintainable; it should have good security; it should be fault-tolerant; and so on. Interactive systems should also have self-explanatory commands; messages should be meaningful, constructive, and indicate corrective action; response should be consistent, and warnings should be given about delays. Interactive systems should also be forgiving of errors; they should be helpful when users get into difficulties, e.g. they should allow users to find out what they have done and what options are open, should protect against costly mistakes, and allow escape from danger; they should not display too many options at once, should provide different levels of help, should permit short-cuts; and so on.

Re-used code

Re-used code is source code which is used in more than one program. It could refer to code which is copied from one program, and then modified for use in another; to skeleton code (generic designs or standard design models); or to a library of pre-written, pre-tested, generalized subroutines for common functions.

The term could also be applied to pack-

ages, both application and system software packages, as they are also existing source code used again and again, if not in different programs, then at least in different organizations. Application generators also re-use standard modules.

Real-time systems

A real-time system is one that controls or responds to stimuli in the real world, such as a heart-monitoring device that detects heart rate, and sends appropriate signals to a central nursing station in case of dramatic changes.

Redundant data

Redundant data is duplicated data. It can therefore be removed without losing any information. However, the duplication may be done deliberately, e.g. to speed up database systems. It is also a characteristic of traditional file (non-database) systems, where duplicate data may be carried in several files.

Regression testing

Regression testing means that a system or program is retested after it has been changed, to ensure that the changes have not introduced errors. The original, well-defined, test data and test output should have been kept. The data is fed into the changed product, and the output compared with the original output. The data may, however, have to be modified to conform to the changed product. In addition, differences in the output may be due to the changes themselves, rather than to errors in the changes.

Response time

Response time in a real-time system is the elapsed time between the last character entered by the terminal user and the receipt of the first character of the response.

Reverse engineering

Reverse engineering here means analysing existing source code to reconstruct the original source information, design documentation, and specifications, that have long since been lost or forgotten.

Second-party debugging

See Foreign debug.

Semi-detached mode

Semi-detached mode projects are in between the two extremes of organic and embedded mode, e.g. they contain a mixture of experienced and inexperienced people.

Software engineer

A software engineer is someone who practices software engineering. To achieve the goals of software engineering, a software engineer must acquire a broad range of skills, both technical and managerial, and these skills have to be applied to every phase of software production from requirements to maintenance.

Software engineering

Software engineering is a technological and managerial discipline whose aim is the production and maintenance of reliable, cost-effective, quality software, that is delivered and maintained on time and within budget, and satisfies its requirements. It is therefore a collection of techniques concerned with applying an *engineering* approach to the construction of software products, i.e. to managing, costing, planning, modelling, analysing, designing, implementing, testing, and maintaining the products.

Software house

A software house is an organization which specializes in producing software for user organizations. The software may be generalized – technological aids, fourth-generation languages, and application packages – or it may be custom-built systems for individual user organizations.

Software Science

See Halstead's Software Science.

Span of control or span of attention

This refers to the maximum number of workers that a normal supervisor is capable of managing, or the number of pieces of information people can hold in their minds at once.

Static analysers

Static or structural analysers are programs which examine other programs without executing them, looking for errors, violations of the installation's coding standards, or inefficiencies, or which even measure their clarity and complexity.

Stepwise refinement

Stepwise refinement is a design method in which the problem is solved several times, at first in general outline only, and then in successively greater detail. Each solution is a refinement of the preceding solution. Put another way, the primary function of the system is identified first, and then successive sub-functions.

Structured analysis

Structured analysis is a general method for analysing the activities, typically the clerical activities, in an organization.

Structured design

Structured design is an extension of top-down design. It complements structured analysis, and comprises data flow design, coupling and cohesion (criteria for assessing and choosing between alternative designs), and notations (data flow diagrams and program structure charts). It therefore includes steps for developing, documenting, evaluating, and improving the design, and each step is supported by a set of design strategies, guidelines, and documentation techniques.

Structured programming

Structured programming is an organized approach to writing programs according to a specified format or structure. There are many different definitions of it. This study uses a narrow definition, namely that it consists of certain coding constructs (e.g. IF–THEN–ELSE) and coding conventions (e.g. indentation).

Structured walkthrough

See Walkthrough.

Super-programmer

A super-programmer is a programmer of outstanding ability and achievement. He may, or may not, occupy the position of chief programmer or lead programmer.

Synergism

Synergism is where the combined effect of various factors exceeds the sum of their individual effects.

System size

See Program size.

Systems analyst

A systems analyst determines the information needs in an organization, and describes a system to satisfy those needs. The analysis may be of a manual system which is being considered for computerization, or of an existing computer system, to improve or replace it. The term systems analyst is misleading as, in common usage, it means someone who both analyses and designs systems.

Systems programming

Systems programming is programming related to basic system software, particularly operating systems.

Test case

This term may refer to just the test data, i.e. the input, but generally includes the expected output.

Test driver

A test driver or harness is a temporary program that calls the module being tested in a way that simulates the module's eventual role in the complete system.

Testing

Testing is the process of executing a program with the intent of finding errors. It includes the preparation involved, e.g. designing the data most likely to reveal the presence of errors, as well as the subsequent checking of the output. In common usage, the term generally also includes the subsequent activities to correct the errors detected, i.e. 'debugging', but these activities have generally been treated separately in this study.

Third-generation languages

See High-level languages.

Tokens

Tokens are basic syntactic units distinguishable by a compiler, and can be subdivided into operators and operands.

Top-down design

Top-down design is a general, informal strategy for dividing (decomposing) a large or complex problem into its components, i.e. into several smaller problems.

Trailing-edge organizations

See Leading-edge organizations.

User

In most cases, this term is employed as an abbreviation of end user, i.e. a non-DP person who uses a computer system or program written for him by the DP staff, but the user of a fourth-generation language may be either an end user or a full-time member of the DP staff, and the user of an application package generally means the organization as a whole rather than a particular department or person.

User friendly

User friendly means that the product (fourth-generation language, application package, etc.) is easy to learn and easy to use.

Validation

Validation is variously defined as checking if the right product is being built, or establishing that a software product as a whole is suitable for its intended purpose, and is what the user really wants. (A more common meaning, but less relevant to this study, is that validation is the process of checking that data falls within prescribed limits.)

Verification

Verification is variously defined as checking if the product is being built in the right way, or that it conforms to its specifications. (A more common meaning, but less relevant to this study, is that verification is the process of checking the accuracy of transmission of data either into the computer or between two storage devices.)

Virtual Machine

A virtual machine is the operational computer's hardware and any underlying system software (usually the operating system, and sometimes a DBMS as well).

Walkthrough

A walkthrough or structured walkthrough is a review of any product which follows certain rules, e.g. the producer explains it, step by step, to a group of his peers.

Warnier–Orr

Warnier–Orr is a design method which is similar to the Jackson method, and is therefore another refinement of top-down design. It is also based on the structure of the data, but the program structure is derived from the structure of the *output* data.

White-box testing

In white-box testing, the structure of the program is tested. Test cases are therefore designed by considering the internal structure of the program.

Workstation

A workstation is a computer terminal or PC, and does not include the desk on which it is situated, the user's chair, cupboards, etc., or even any printer or modem.

B.2   LISTS OF DEFINITIONS

From time to time, lists of definitions appear in the literature. These are usually glossaries in books (Lee, 1978; Lyon, 1976; Ross, 1977; Simpson, 1987; Kroeber and Watson, 1984; Yourdon *et al.*, 1979a) but many books of definitions have also been published – Vincent *et al.* (1988) list no fewer than ten. Some examples are Chandor *et al.* (1985); Collin (1989); Greenstein (1978); Pfaffenberger (1990); Rosenberg (1984); Samways and Robinson (1988); Sippl (1985a; 1985b); Stokes (1979).

APPENDIX C: LITERATURE COUNTS

C.1 LITERATURE EMPHASIS ON PROGRAM WRITING

The literature has tended to concentrate disproportionately on one function in the software life-cycle, namely the writing (designing and coding) of programs. *The 1979/80 S.A. Computer Guide* (published by Thomson Publications (Pty) Ltd) for example contains nine categories entitled 'Programming' (listing 91 books), and only one category entitled 'Systems Design and Analysis' (listing only 17 books), i.e. programming books outnumbered analysis books by 5:1, whereas the ratio of programming time to analysis time is probably less than half this (Chapter 8).

Furthermore, only nine of the programming books (=10%) mentioned functions other than program writing (testing, debugging and maintenance) in their title or synopsis. This is considerably less than the amount of time actually spent on the other functions (perhaps 90%, if detailed design and coding are only 24% of the development time, and development is only 40% of the total effort – see Chapter 8), and so confirms the existence of this imbalance. The imbalance appears to be carried through to the detail level. Thus only about 10% of some programming books is devoted to testing and maintenance – see, for example, McClure (1978) and Yourdon *et al.* (1979a).

However, the imbalance is not as serious as it appears from these figures. For example, a number of the remaining 82 programming books were about program design (especially structured programming). If a program is well designed, less effort will be needed to test and maintain it, so *indirectly* these books *do* relate to the other functions. It can thus be seen that program design (and therefore program writing) is disproportionately important, and so *deserves* emphasis in the literature. Nevertheless, the emphasis does seem to have been overdone, especially as one can argue that the other functions may *also* be disproportionately important, e.g. they may offer more scope for improvement (because less attention has been paid to them in the past); systems analysts are generally more highly paid than programmers, so more attention should be devoted to the functions they perform; testing and maintenance require computer time, making them more expensive than other functions which do not; and the earlier an error is discovered, the easier and cheaper it is to correct (Chapter 8), making it disproportionately important to improve the quality of the first steps in the development process (especially those done by the systems analyst).

C.2 QUANTITY OF LITERATURE AVAILABLE

A rough estimate of the amount of material available, relevant to this study (based on the number of different magazines and journals, the book catalog referred to above, and the number of American doctoral theses listed by University Microfilms International – and extrapolating these figures to cover other post-graduate theses and the rest of the English-speaking world) was that some 30 000 DP-related magazines, books, journals and theses had been published in the preceding twelve years – and that was not counting organizations' own in-house publications, or fields such as education and management, which are touched on in this study.

C.3 PRODUCTIVITY EMPHASIS OF LITERATURE

The software literature may be graded into three categories.

1. Direct
   Literature whose main purpose is to investigate, or advise on, software engineering productivity.
2. Indirect
   Literature which is not directly concerned with software engineering productivity, but which treats subjects such as structured programming, non-procedural languages, application packages and job satisfaction, which do affect productivity.
3. Weak
   The remainder of the literature: computer architecture, communication networks, security and privacy, legal aspects, users, and so on.

Even 'weak' literature has some effect on productivity:

- more powerful computers give faster response to the people using them, thereby increasing their productivity;
- building security and privacy features into a system lowers, at least initially, the productivity of software engineers; and so on,

but the relationship is weak, and the article was not oriented towards the productivity aspects, and in fact the topics themselves have productivity as, at most, a by-product, whereas the objective of the second category topics is partly, or largely, productivity improvement.

Categorizing the literature in this way gave the following result.

Books

The book catalog referred to earlier was subdivided into 52 subject categories: productivity was not one of them. Of the 366 books listed, only one mentioned productivity directly, and that was in the synopsis not the title. Even when category 2 topics were included, this only brought the number up to 43 (12%).

Magazines

A similar situation exists in the case of magazine articles. Of the 105 feature articles in *Datamation* in one 12-month period (1981), only six (= 6%) came under Category 1, and Categories 1 and 2 combined only contained 14 (= 13%).

In the *Datamation* subject index for a different period (the three months comprising the second quarter of 1986), productivity was not one of the subject headings. Of the 95 titles listed (representing feature articles, news in perspective, etc.), only one (1%) mentioned productivity, while only three (3%) mentioned subjects like application generators and sub-second response times, which are closely related to productivity.

Theses

Productivity is also neglected in postgraduate theses. An inspection of five lists of doctoral dissertations indicated that the emphasis on productivity in them was comparable to that in the rest of the literature, with less than 1% of the theses qualifying for Category 1, and only 12% qualifying for Category 2.

Summary

The preceding figures are summarized in Table C.1. For this summary, the two sets of *Datamation* figures were combined.

Table C.1 Productivity orientation of literature

	Category 1 (direct)	Category 2 (indirect)	Category 3 (weak)
Books	<1%	11%	88%
Magazines	4%	6%	91%
Theses	<1%	12%	88%

It is interesting to note that Sackman *et al.* (1968) commented on the lack of scientific study of programming; and that, in 1971, only 9% of federally-funded computing research projects in the US were directed towards software problems (Davis, 1972), and therefore (considerably?) less than 9% were directed towards software productivity.

APPENDIX D: PROGRAMMING BACKGROUND OF PROJECT LEADERS

D.1 PROGRAMMING VERSUS SYSTEMS ANALYSIS

A small survey of job advertisements, using five issues of each of the weekly newspapers *ComputerWeek* and *Computing S.A.* for 1982, and five issues of each for 1988/89, was conducted to determine what emphasis was placed on programming experience as a requirement for project leaders. These surveys were prompted by the use of programmers as project leaders in CPTs, and the objective was to establish if it was a common requirement. It is more common perhaps for systems analysts to be the project leaders, and Arthur (1983) and Lee (1978) both give organizational structure charts which imply that systems analysts supervise programmers.

Advertisements for leaders of purely programming or purely analytical teams were excluded, as were advertisements for second-level managers. The breakdown of the remaining advertisements is given in Table D.1.

Conclusions

Almost twice as many advertisements mentioned only programming as mentioned only systems analysis (29% to 18%), though only ((29+36)/(18+36) = (65/54) =) 20% more mentioned programming than mentioned systems analysis. These surveys therefore showed a greater emphasis on programming than on systems analysis experience.

Trends

The survey of 1988/9 adverts showed a higher proportion specifying only programming (38% compared to only 12%), but a lower proportion specifying both programming and systems analysis (only 28% compared to 52%). However, at least part of these differences may be due to the small sample sizes, or the brevity of some of the advertisements (they might have omitted some of the requirements), i.e. the trends may be apparent rather than real.

D.2 CURRENT VERSUS PAST

A major inadequacy in the survey was that it did not show whether *current* programming

Table D.1 Programming experience of project leaders

Background mentioned in ad.	1982		1988/9		Total	
	No.	%	No.	%	No.	%
Programming only	7	12	44	38	51	29
Systems analysis only	13	22	19	16	32	18
Both	30	52	33	28	63	36
Neither specified	8	14	20	17	28	16
TOTAL	58		116		174	

Table D.2   Current programming experience of project leaders

Programming experience	1982		1988/9		Total	
	No.	%	No.	%	No.	%
Current	5	9	19	16	24	14
Past	32	55	58	50	90	52
Non specified	21	36	39	34	60	34
TOTAL	58		116		174	

experience was required, i.e. whether the project leaders were still actively writing programs as in the case of CPTs, or whether experience acquired several years earlier would be considered adequate.

Accordingly, the advertisements were re-surveyed. Those which specified 'working knowledge of COBOL', 'strong COBOL background', etc., were assumed to refer to *past* experience. The new breakdown of the advertisements is shown in Table D.2.

The 'none specified' figures contain both the 'neither specified' and the 'systems analysis only' figures from section D.1.

Conclusions

These figures paint a very different picture. Although most project leaders were required to have (perhaps extensive) programming knowledge, only 14% were explicitly stated to require *current* programming experience.

It is therefore evident that few project leaders are actively engaged in programming, so few are likely to be actively and adequately controlling the quality of the programming in the projects they lead. Furthermore, although the proportion required to have current programming experience almost doubled between 1982 and 1988/89, the actual number in this category in 1982 was small, so the difference may not be significant. The apparent increase may also have been due to the brevity of some of the advertisements, combined with a possibly more liberal interpretation. It may be more significant that there were two advertisements for chief programmers in the 1982 data, but none in the 1988/89 data.

APPENDIX E: FINANCIAL BENEFITS OF USING SMALL TEAMS

The following discussion can be described as a sensitivity analysis to determine the effect of team size on the overall cost-effectiveness of software development.

E.1 EQUAL BENEFIT SYSTEMS

Suppose an organization has several systems to be developed. For simplicity, suppose all the systems are the same size and will produce the same financial benefits, $50 000 p.a. each. (These benefits may be tangible or intangible, and may represent increased sales, savings through increased efficiency, improved employee morale, customer goodwill, etc. – see Chapter 8). Suppose further that the systems will take one year each and cost $100 000 each to develop, if produced by one large team, but will take two years each and cost $50 000 each, if small teams are used. (This is equivalent to a communication and co-ordination loss factor of two, which is within the range discussed in Chapter 3.)

Two alternatives will be examined. In the first, one large team will be used. All members of the department will work on each system, thus one new system will be developed each year. In the second, the department will be subdivided into four small teams, with each team working on a different system. Thus four new systems will be developed every two years. Table E.1 shows the comparative cumulative cost/benefits of these alternatives.

At the end of year 1, the large team has finished its first system, while the small teams are only half-way through each of theirs. None of the systems has yet gone into production.

At the end of year 2, the large team has completed its second system, and its first system has been in production for one year. By contrast, the small teams have each just finished their first system, none of which has yet been used in production. The large team, therefore, has a clear financial advantage.

Table E.1 Financial benefits of small teams – equal-benefit systems

	End of year 1	End of year 2	End of year 3	End of year 4	End of year 5	End of year 6	End of year 7
Cost	100 000	200 000	300 000	400 000	500 000	600 000	700 000
Benefit							
Large team	NIL	50 000	150 000	300 000	500 000	750 000	1050 000
Small teams	NIL	NIL	200 000	400 000	800 000	1200 000	1800 000
Net profit							
Large team	100 000–	150 000–	150 000–	100 000–	NIL	150 000	350 000
Small teams	100 000–	200 000–	100 000–	NIL	300 000	600 000	1100 000

At the end of year 3, however, the picture has changed. The large team has just completed its third system, so only the first two have been used in production and have produced financial benefits to the organization. The small teams, on the other hand, have already finished four systems, all of which are in production. They are also halfway through the next four systems. They now have a small, but clear, advantage over the large team, and this advantage grows bigger and bigger as the years pass.

Terminology

The **payback period** is not, as might be supposed from its name, the period during which the cumulative benefits from a system exceed the cumulative costs, i.e. the period during which the system pays for itself. Instead, it is the period *before* it starts to pay for itself, i.e. the period of time required for the investment to pay back the costs and break even (Gildersleeve, 1978). It is also known as the **investment segment** (Boehm, 1981).

The **breakeven point** is that point in time when the cumulative benefits balance the cumulative costs.

The **profitable segment** is the period *after* the breakeven point, i.e. the period during which the cumulative benefits exceed the cumulative costs.

In the above example, the payback period is five years for the large team, and four years for the small teams.

Incremental delivery

It is sometimes possible to phase in a system, gradually adding extra functions and delivering them to the user, and it is desirable to do so for a system having a long development schedule, so that the user can start deriving some of its benefits before the full system has been completed. Gilb (1988) is a strong advocate of this option. The benefits of doing this vary greatly from one system to another. The effect is to increase the net profit throughout the seven years for both the alternatives in the above example, but the increase should be greater for the small teams because of their longer schedules. It therefore gives an added advantage to the small teams in the long-term, and decreases, and may even reverse, their disadvantage in the short-term.

Time value of money

Particularly in an inflationary economy, a dollar spent or received today is worth more than a dollar spent or received a year from now: 'The value of money may be wiped out by a runaway inflation' (Boehm, 1981). (Similarly, the value of goods might be wiped out by oversupply.) In addition, if the money is available now, we have more options for using it: if it is not available now, we may miss a golden opportunity, even if this just means investing it and so earning interest on it (Mittra, 1988). In general, therefore, because of interest rates, the uncertainties of the future (we might not be around to use either the money or the goods), and the effects of inflation, money received now is worth more than money received in the future (Lee, 1978). There is thus a *time* component to the value of money. (In more general terms, people have a time preference for a resource: 'a bird in the hand is worth two in the bush'.) This type of calculation should be part of the feasibility study.

In general, the time value of money alters the position, but it has not been allowed for here as the small teams have such a large advantage that it would not significantly affect the comparison. For example, an inflation rate of 10% p.a. would only reduce the net profit advantage of the small teams by about 6% at the end of year 7, which is 'in the noise level with respect to other considerations' (Boehm, 1981). The net profit advantage in this example is therefore not very sensitive to the inflation rate. In any event, the Consumer Price Index in the USA has been increasing by less than 10% p.a. (It was 113.60 in 1987, compared to 96.50 in 1982, an increase of only 18% in 5 years (Howard and Kunkel, 1988).)

Lost use of money

The costs are the same for both alternatives in this example, so the loss of use of the money financing the system development is also the same for both. For the same reason, interest rates – if the organization is financed by borrowed money – would not affect the position.

The same is not true, however, for the *benefits* from the two alternatives. The benefits represent financial advantages, and the difference in benefits is the advantage of one alternative over the other. This money can, for example, be invested, or be used to finance other projects, thus producing additional, secondary benefits, thereby increasing the benefits and therefore the advantage of one alternative over the other. However, this factor has not been taken into account, as its effect is proportionately smaller. In any event, the definition of 'benefits' could be interpreted to include the secondary benefits.

Maintenance

Computer systems are often subjected to constant change and enhancement. This has been left out of the tabulated values because of another simplifying assumption: equal maintenance costs (in addition to equal development costs and equal benefits). Alternatively, the benefits could be redefined to include the maintenance costs (i.e. *net* benefits). In any event, with maintenance typically costing perhaps only 10% p.a. of the development cost (Mittra, 1988) (though other figures in Chapter 8 are higher), it would not significantly affect the outcome in this example. Maintenance would amount to perhaps only $210 000 in total over the seven years, compared to the $750 000 difference in net profit between the two alternatives, so *differences* in maintenance costs would be dwarfed.

E.2 UNEQUAL-BENEFIT SYSTEMS

Suppose that, instead of equal benefits, one of the systems produces benefits which are considerably higher than those of the others – say $200 000 p.a. instead of $50 000 (Table E.2). This system would obviously be developed first.

It now takes five years, instead of three, for the small teams to overtake the large team. The small teams have a much larger disadvantage in the short-term, so there would be a strong temptation to ignore their long-term advantage, and opt instead for the large team. It would therefore be more important in this case to phase in the systems de-

Table E.2 Financial benefits of small teams – unequal benefit systems

	End of year 1	End of year 2	End of year 3	End of year 4	End of year 5	End of year 6	End of year 7
Cost	100 000	200 000	300 000	400 000	500 000	600 000	700 000
Benefit							
Large team	NIL	200 000	450 000	750 000	1100 000	1500 000	1950 000
Small teams	NIL	NIL	350 000	700 000	1250 000	1800 000	2550 000
Net profit							
Large team	100 000−	NIL	150 000	350 000	600 000	900 000	1250 000
Small teams	100 000−	200 000−	50 000	300 000	750 000	1200 000	1850 000

veloped by the small teams, or at least this one high-benefit system. This would reduce their short-term disadvantage, but would probably not be enough to eliminate or reverse it.

E.3 MIXTURE OF LARGE AND SMALL TEAMS

It might be thought advisable in the preceding example to have the high-return system developed first, by one large team, and then to split the department into four small teams. However, this is not necessarily the case, as is shown in Table E.3. Here, the mixture of large and small teams takes only four years to overtake the large team, compared to the five years taken by the small teams. However, after five years, the small teams have overtaken not only the large team, but also the mixture.

Although the financial benefits obtained by one year extra of running this high-return system more than offset the additional cost of the inefficient method of developing it, the difference is still not large enough with these figures to offset the losses caused by the delay in installing the remaining systems. However, the difference is small, so the organization is likely to opt for the short-term higher-return alternative.

Incremental delivery might influence the decision. If small teams were used throughout, and the high-return system phased in, then the small teams would lose much of their short-term disadvantage. With a smaller disadvantage in the short-term, and a larger advantage in the long-term, the organization might opt to use only small teams.

Because of the small difference between the mixture and the small teams (with these figures), the time value of money, the lost use of money, and differences in maintenance costs would be relatively more important, and could reverse the outcome, making the mixture more profitable after seven years than the small teams.

E.4 CONCLUSION

The higher productivity of small teams gives them a significant advantage over large teams in the long-term. They are at a disadvantage in the short-term, but this disadvantage could sometimes be offset by phasing in the systems. The time value of money would probably have little effect on the relative costs and benefits, and the lost use of money even less.

In general, therefore, organizations would be advised to use small teams. However, where one system has much greater benefits

Table E.3 Financial benefits of small teams – mixture of large and small teams

	End of year 1	End of year 2	End of year 3	End of year 4	End of year 5	End of year 6	End of year 7
Cost	100 000	200 000	300 000	400 000	500 000	600 000	700 000
Benefit							
Large team	NIL	200 000	450 000	750 000	1100 000	1500 000	1950 000
Mixture	NIL	200 000	400 000	800 000	1200 000	1800 000	2400 000
Small teams	NIL	NIL	350 000	700 000	1250 000	1800 000	2550 000
Net profit							
Large team	100 000−	NIL	150 000	350 000	600 000	900 000	1250 000
Mixture	100 000−	NIL	100 000	400 000	700 000	1200 000	1700 000
Small teams	100 000−	200 000−	50 000	300 000	750 000	1200 000	1850 000

than the others, the advantage of small teams is reduced, and might even be reversed in specific cases.

Using a mixture of large and small teams – large teams for systems with very high benefits, and small teams for the remaining systems – produces, as might be expected, results intermediate between those of small teams only and large teams only. Because of the smaller difference in net profit between the mixture and the small teams, the secondary factors, such as the time value of money, are relatively more important, and could reverse the outcome in specific cases.

APPENDIX F: ABILITY AND SPECIALIZATION IN CHIEF PROGRAMMER TEAMS

F.1 ABILITY

The relationship between software engineering ability and one particular department structure, the CPT, is discussed below. This structure was chosen because ability plays an important role in it.

The importance of ability in CPTs

It was pointed out in Chapter 3 that the CPT concept has connotations of skilled people and elite teams, and that there is some justification for this belief. Part of the concept is that the members of the team, or at least the chief programmer, should be of above-average ability, otherwise he would not be able to adequately perform the central, pivotal role required. In addition, the CPT concept is a refinement of the super-programmer project, which was based on the belief that one highly-talented programmer could do the work of a whole group of five or ten ordinary programmers.

Chapter 9 lists several courses of action that DP departments can take to ensure that maximum use is made of ability: recruit high-ability staff from other departments within the organization or from other organizations, retain high-ability staff within the DP department in productive capacities, etc. A case can be made that the CPT combines these courses of action, even recruitment from other organizations, as potential CPs in organizations not having a CPT structure would be drawn

to those which did, to gain greater job satisfaction. However, the most important of the factors is probably work allocation, as the most able person (the CP), personally does the most critical, and usually only the most critical, parts of the work.

The super-programmer and New York Times projects

The CP on the Super-Programmer Project was Harlan D. Mills (McGowan and Kelly, 1975), and on the NYT project, Terry Baker (Schach, 1988). Mills has a PhD in mathematics, is an IBM fellow, is highly skilled in computers, and has a number of publications to his credit (Van Tassel, 1978). Baker also has a number of publications to his credit, as well as being a super-programmer, and a superb manager and leader (Schach, 1988). They thus amply complied with the ability requirements for the position of CP, and the projects may well have been much less successful had different persons been chosen – as Schach put it, Baker's skills, enthusiasm, and personality carried the project. The literature surveyed did not contain any information about the abilities of the remaining team members for either project, other than that some of them were 'experts'. Schach (1988, 1990) put it more strongly: IBM, an organization known for its superb software experts, sent in their very best people. As argued in Chapter 3, it is not surprising they did so.

- IBM developed the NYT system for an external organization, and a newspaper at that, and they might have received much unfavorable publicity had the project not been successful.
- Both projects were also the proving ground for new ideas, and therefore of great interest to management.

With their large pool of top-quality staff to draw on, they could do so without seriously affecting their other projects (Van Tassel, 1978).

The productivity differences due to ability are so great, that this factor alone could account for the success of the two projects, even if the most optimistic claims for them – a productivity gain of 6:1 – are justified. (In fact, differences in ability are so great that, even if super-programmers used poor methods, they should still get above-average results.) Thus we cannot be sure, on this evidence alone, that the CPT concept itself increases productivity.

Cautions

Greater ability is not always accompanied by higher productivity. General reasons for this, such as lack of knowledge, have already been discussed (Chapter 9). Specific aspects relating to CPTs will be discussed here.

Motivation

Motivation and dedication are stressed by Metzger (1981), and they probably played a significant role in the success of the Super-Programmer and NYT projects:

- firstly, the teams were using new methods, or at least a new combination of methods (Baker, 1972), which probably aroused their enthusiasm, inspiring them to work harder; and
- secondly, the mere fact that they had been chosen for these experiments should have motivated the team members – the Hawthorne Effect (Chapter 11).

However, motivation typically raises productivity by less than 50% (Chapter 11), so this factor can only account for part of the observed increase on these projects.

Undesirable characteristics of super-programmers

A CP might possess the undesirable characteristics sometimes exhibited by super-programmers – undocumented programs, eccentric behavior, etc. (Chapter 9).

However, the CPT concept emphasizes documentation and clerical procedures – witness the program secretary and the program production library; and programs are looked upon as public property, and reviews of work take place. These factors should eliminate any tendency to write programs which were undocumented or impossible to understand. There is also a significant amount of direct contact between the CP and users. This should moderate any unsociable, eccentric or unreliable behavior on the part of the CP, as such behavior is likely to go down less well with them than with DP staff who would be more accustomed to it. On the other hand, people possessing such tendencies may not be happy as CPs. This would have a detrimental effect on productivity, and on inter-departmental relations as well, and would limit the general applicability of the CPT concept.

It is unlikely that these undesirable characteristics were present on the NYT project, as the system was revised several times, including major changes after programming was well advanced, yet this did not cause problems (Baker, 1972), which would not have been the case had the programs been undocumented and difficult to understand.

Different types of ability

DP staff need a variety of skills. This is especially true in the case of a CP, as (Van Tassel, 1978; Macro and Buxton, 1987; Baker, 1972):

- he is a programmer, a systems analyst and a project leader;
- he needs managerial skills, as he is responsible for technical, personnel and contract management;
- he must make technical presentations of the project;
- he must be charismatic; and
- he needs creativity and drive;

in addition to having programming skills of the first order.

Most organizations do not have even a super-programmer (Yourdon, 1979b), let alone several of the above paragons: 'there are surely only a few software engineers who actually satisfy these requirements' (Pomberger, 1984). Worse, the backup programmer needs the same high level of skills as the chief programmer (Chapter 3). Organizations are therefore faced with the choice: not use CPTs at all; use CPTs on some projects only; or use CPTs exclusively. These alternatives and their disadvantages are discussed below.

Alternative courses of action if too few suitable chief programmers

Not use CPTs at all

If CPTs are not used at all, then the benefits they can give will not be realized.

Use CPTs on some projects only

Ordinary project teams could be used on those projects comprising only small and simple programs: where the work is easy, and where less co-ordination is required, the productivity improvement attainable by using CPTs may be correspondingly smaller. In fact, in view of the rapid increase in complexity and co-ordination as size increases (Aron, 1974), it is possible that CPTs provide little benefit on small programs, but large benefits on big programs – and these are the

ones most in need of improvement, as productivity on them is so low. (By contrast, some authorities, such as Boehm (1981), believe that complexity does not necessarily increase with size; furthermore, it is not clear if CPTs will work on larger projects (Baker, 1972; Bell *et al.*, 1987).)

Furthermore, the system designers on the ordinary project teams can subdivide the systems into small and simple programs, i.e. ones which can be efficiently produced by the less-gifted programmers in those teams.

However, there are disadvantages to using CPTs on only some projects. If the CPTs are permanent, with the same people remaining in them, they might become elitist groups. While such groups can be very effective – e.g. they are much more productive and reliable than large 'software factories' in completing urgent tasks on time (Pomberger, 1984) – they can also have a detrimental effect on the morale of the remaining members of the department, thereby negating the advantages. They may also run counter to the culture of the organization, or its career structure (Macro and Buxton, 1987). Furthermore, CPs are themselves elite people, so analogous morale problems may be experienced within the team (Fairley, 1985). (Elitism may be one reason why Weinberg (1971) is so strongly opposed to CPTs.)

However, these problems may be moderated if the title chief programmer is an informal one, and different people alternately occupy the position (Gunther, 1978). (Though care would have to be exercised, as productivity would be severely degraded if an inadequate person performed the CP role (Boehm, 1981) – see below.) Morale problems caused by having elitist groups may also be moderated if the groups are temporary structures which are set up only when needed for specific projects, and then disbanded upon their completion. This solution does suffer from the disadvantages relating to temporary teams (inconsistent methods, work allocation not knowledgeable, etc. – see Chapter 9), but these disadvantages are likely to be smaller in the case of elitist teams: e.g. people of high ability need less training.

Another danger is that the members of a successful CPT generally want to stay together for the next job, but the idea of teams electing themselves may be unacceptable to the organization (Macro and Buxton, 1987).

Use CPTs exclusively

If this course of action is chosen, then some people who possessed less than the optimum skills would be CPs. This is not as illogical as it might seem:

- firstly, both the abilities of the available staff and the needs of the various projects cover a range, and they can be matched together so that the least able CPs do the simplest systems, thereby minimizing the harmful affects;

- secondly, those organizations having larger and more complex programs would already have more able staff – they would have actively recruited them, and anyway the best programmers would have gravitated there naturally as being the places most likely to have work which would interest and challenge them – so the gap between the ability required and the ability available in any organization would generally not be too large; and

- thirdly, if CPTs produce large improvements in productivity under ideal conditions, it is likely that conditions would have to be significantly less than ideal to wipe out the productivity advantage completely – in other words, the CPT concept can be expected to give a higher productivity than conventional methods even in circumstances which are not as favorable to it (as Van Tassel (1978) put it, 'past organization methods for large programming projects have done so poorly that it is doubtful that CPTs could lead to worse results').

Nevertheless, there are disadvantages. There is the danger that an inferior CP will do more harm than good: 'with a poor chief programmer, productivity can be very low' (Boehm, 1981). Also, if the CP is not a super-programmer, then the systems analyst reporting to him might be more intelligent. There already exists a 'natural resistance' on the part of systems analysts to CPTs (van Wyk and Kamfer, 1976), as it deprives them of status and their traditional career paths. The systems analyst might accept the situation, albeit reluctantly, if the CP is clearly more intelligent than he, but his resistance is likely to increase if the reverse is the case.

One way to reduce the disadvantages is to remove much of the managerial role from the CP, as suggested in Chapter 3. The CP would therefore not need such a broad range of skills, so there would be more suitable candidates (Schach, 1988).

Conclusion

The chief programmer should be of above-average ability, and should have a variety of skills. Where these conditions are not met, results will be adversely affected. There may even be more harm than good, but this will probably only happen in the more extreme cases.

It is probably best, therefore, to use CPTs on many, but not all, projects.

There are dangers involved in having elitist teams, but there are measures which can be taken to reduce the dangers.

F.2 SPECIALIZATION

Gilb (1988) believes that assigning specialized roles tends to increase team productivity: everyone has their own particular responsibility, 'and nobody else is going to carry it for them'. Weinberg (1971) believes that enormous gains in productivity are possible if programmers specialized more. Instead of performing *all* the functions required to develop a program, each programmer would concentrate on only those functions at which he was best. Conversely, by doing just one type of work, you become very good at it (Bell *et al.*, 1987). Based on typical industry figures, DeMarco (1982) estimated a 4:1 decrease in project lifetime costs can be achieved by reassigning a defect-prone programmer (one who makes many mistakes when writing code), to testing (defect diagnosis and reporting), if he is good at that, which he should be, as he gets so much practice at it! Now specialization in CPTs is stressed by Baker (1972) and Pomberger (1984), and there is truth in this emphasis (Baker, 1972; Yourdon, 1975):

- inherent in the CPT concept is the separation and removal of clerical work from the programmers;
- certain tasks such as complex mathematical routines, or the need for a particular programming language, operating system or file access technique, might require the services of a specialist; and
- on all but the smallest systems, a project manager is used to do the legal, financial, administrative and reporting tasks.

However, this is only part of the picture.

- The programmer who fills the role of *chief programmer* now has analytical and managerial duties which he probably did not have before, so his job has been enriched.
- The same applies to the *backup programmer*. He assumes managerial duties when the CP is away – 'the chief programmer is human, and may get ill, fall under a bus, or change jobs' (Schach, 1988) – and as he and the CP are peers, their roles can be interchanged between projects, so his job is also enriched (Van Tassel, 1978).
- The *secretarial* or *librarian* function, if performed by a programmer, might not change the number of different functions he performs, only the amount of time spent on each, e.g., instead of just maintaining his own program listings, he would

maintain everyone's (Fairley, 1985). However if, as Baker (1972) and Bell *et al.* (1987) advocate, it is performed by a clerk or secretary, it will mean an extension of their duties. In any event, the duties might also include scheduling meetings, recording discussions, configuration control, project status accounting, etc. (Couger *et al.*, 1982). Therefore if, as Macro and Buxton (1987) suggest, the function is performed by a trainee programmer, or is rotated among the programmers, it would even *add* variety to their duties.

- The *specialists'* duties *are* narrow in scope, but more information is required here.
  –Are they unhappy?
  –Do CPTs create *more* specialists, or merely entrench a situation which already exists?
- The *project manager*, as a second-level manager, would probably not be significantly affected by a change to CPTs, though there would be fewer of them if the predicted productivity gains are realized (Yourdon, 1975).
- As far as the *task programmers* go, they stand to lose clerical duties, which would probably please them, but they may also lose program design duties, which they are less likely to be happy about, and they might even be reduced to just coders. To avoid this, senior task programmers could alternate with the BUP on successive projects. However, in Macro and Buxton's (1987) version of the CPT, the team consists of a peer group of practising software engineers, so *all* members do parts of design, coding, testing, etc.; and in the Fairley (1985) version, the programmers write code, debug, document and unit test it; so this problem does not arise.
- The one person whose tasks *are* likely to be significantly reduced in scope is the *systems analyst*. He will lose his system design duties, and any managerial duties (Baker, 1972). To regain these functions, he would not only have to learn, or re-learn,

programming, but would have to change his emphasis to programming as well.

As can be seen from the above discussion, there *is* a degree of specialization inherent in CPTs, but it is of a different order from that described by Weinberg (1971). Furthermore, according to Macro and Buxton (1987), it decreases during the course of the project. All of this means that CPTs benefit only partly from the potential large gains in productivity from specialization, a conclusion which is consistent with the observed gains on CPT projects, which are much lower than the 30:1 or so differences in ability quoted in Chapter 9.

More specialization can be introduced into CPTs while still retaining the central control which is fundamental to the concept – e.g. the CP could do design only and no coding, or a testing specialist could be used – but there would be limits: the CP would probably still be a programmer/analyst and a project leader, and not just a programmer.

Specialization is necessary because software engineering is so complex, and because of the 'large and exploding body of knowledge' (Gilb, 1988; Lucas, 1985). Gilb adds that other professions show that specialization is the norm for large projects. He envisages a number of specialists, including the following:

- a **business analyst**, who is concerned with user productivity, and is therefore also concerned with the non-software aspects of software solutions, or even ensuring that a non-software solution is chosen where this would be better;
- an **information systems architect**, who must choose the best possible solution – which may mean software tools which are not standard for the organization, a different computer, or even a non-software solution;
- a **software architect**, who is responsible for all non-hardware components of the sys-

tem, and co-ordinates the work of specialist software engineers and craftspersons;
- **software engineers**, who translate the requirements into a design;
- **specialist software engineers**, who can find solutions which are ten times better, in some selected attribute, than the non-specialist;
- a **software craftsperson** – coder, test case constructor, documentation writer, quality checker, etc. – who constructs software according to the design of others.

Jones (1986b) advocates specialization for improved productivity, but looks at it from a different angle, namely the amount and type of specialization which is desirable for organizations of different sizes.

- Organizations with 1–10 software staff are too small for specialization.
- Those with 10–50 software staff should have a 'seasoning' of programmers who are expert in selected topics such as networks and database products.
- Those with 50–200 should have some internal specialization, such as testing, design, and database specialists.
- Those with 200–1000 should have permanent test departments with skilled specialists, and permanent maintenance departments with full-time maintenance programmers.
- Those with more than 1000 should have full test departments, formal maintenance and quality assurance departments, data administration groups, etc. Very large organizations allocate skilled personnel to defect removal, quality assurance, database design, network design, and 'several other esoteric domains where ordinary training is not always sufficient'.

However, is a high degree of specialization desirable? Boehm (1981) describes it as 'fragmenting software jobs into small, meaningless pieces', and lists the long-term disadvantages of doing so: people produce uninspired software; they lose interest in both their professional growth and in the organization's objectives; and they lose both their ability to cope with new situations and their self-confidence. Productivity may therefore be increased in the short term, but be adversely affected in the long term.

Couger and Zawacki (1980) also express their disapproval, likening it to the auto assembly line with its boring, repetitive tasks. They argue that jobs should be 'enlarged in scope rather than reduced'. This is in line with Volvo in Sweden, which replaced its auto assembly lines with a structure in which the workers were organized in groups which carried out entire operations. However, not all people welcome having their jobs enriched (Sutermeister, 1976), and some Detroit car workers, after visiting such a factory, decided they preferred the monotonous, repetitive assembly line (Heller, 1981). Heller does not give the reason for their preference. Perhaps they were motivated by money. People are most effective when they are working on one thing at a time, completing small tasks in short periods (Aron, 1974). The assembly line is therefore inherently very efficient, making high salaries possible. It sets a standard of productivity which other methods may not be able to match. However, some authorities believe that job enrichment contributes so much to employee performance, that it offsets the efficiency of the assembly line (Likert, 1961). Perhaps intelligence and education are factors: highly intelligent or highly educated people might prefer greater variety. Evidence of the effect on productivity is inconsistent. Three examples of job enrichment were quoted in Chapter 11, and they produced widely varying increases in productivity, ranging from 4:1 down to only 1.4:1 (Weed, 1971; Hackman *et al.*, 1975), though at least they were in agreement that a productivity *increase* resulted.

Which would software engineers prefer? There are indications that some of them

welcome specialization. One example is the programmer in an anecdote related by Weinberg (1971), who voluntarily spent many months, working late at night, tracking down a bug: such people 'are satisfied – beyond the comprehension of ordinary men – with the work itself', but how typical is he? I, personally, generally prefer maintenance to development. It may also be relevant to mention that, in my own experience, programmers show little interest when systems analysts present overviews of the whole system: they are more interested in just the small portion on which they will be working.

It is not clear if Weinberg himself approves of such a high degree of specialization. In one survey he conducted, lessening the scope of their work was at 'the very bottom of the list' of 19 choices of factors that motivated the programmers surveyed (Chapter 11), which presumably means they would have opposed any such lessening. On the other hand, he points out that specialization is a consequence of ego-less programming, which he advocates. Specialization suffers from the disadvantages he lists in other contexts:

• the difficulty of scheduling work to make maximum use of the expertise available;
• the lack of an alternative type of work if one is having an off day, or in the face of disruptions caused by external problems such as the machine being down;
• the almost universal dislike of some types of work; and
• the friction which exists between testing groups and development groups.

Each of these problems affects productivity, and so limits the amount of specialization which could be allowed.

Bell *et al.* (1987) also has mixed comments. Specialization improves productivity, and therefore improves the organization's profitability, making higher salaries possible, but it removes variety: 'even doing some key-punching makes a change now and again';

and programmers spend longer on the demanding aspects of programming, making them more tired at the end of the day.

Conclusion

Large gains in productivity are possible by specialization, but there are dangers involved, in both the short and the long term, so it should be approached with caution, and should not be carried to extremes.

CPTs provide only partial specialization. More specialization is both possible and desirable in order to increase productivity, but it should be monitored to avoid the dangers.

REFERENCES

Abbey, S. G. (1984) COBOL dumped. *Datamation*, Jan, 108–14.

Abbott, L. (1991) Supercomputers: Big Bang, Big Bucks. *Datamation*, 15 Feb, 73–7.

Abbott, R. (1983a) Doubling productivity not unrealistic target. *IBM Inform*, Aug, VI.

Abbott, R. (1983b) Productivity booster. *IBM Inform*, Aug, VII.

Abdel-Hamid, T. K. (1989) The dynamics of software project staffing: a system dynamics based simulation approach. *IEEE Trans. Software Eng.*, **15**(2), Feb, 109–19.

Acorn (1986) Acorn's Master Compact. *Byte*, Nov, 48F–48H.

Adams, E. N. (1984) Optimizing preventative service of software products. *IBM J. Res. Dev.*, **28**(1), 2–14.

Adams, N. T. (1981) The personnel market. *1981 S.A. Computer Users Handbook*. Johannesburg: Systems Publishers (Pty) Ltd, G1–7.

Addison-Wesley Publishers (1988) *The Complete Computing Catalogue, 1988*. Wokingham, Berkshire: Addison-Wesley Publishers.

AFIPS (1973) *AFIPS Programmer Job Description Survey Booklet*, AFIPS.

Agresti, W. W. (1989) Review of (Kemerer, 1987). *Computing Reviews*, Mar, 153–4.

Air Force (1974) *Proceedings, Government/Industry Software Sizing and Costing Workshop*. US Air Force Electronic Systems Div., Bedford, MA, October.

Akiyama, F. (1971) An example of software system debugging. *Information Processing*, **71**, 353–79.

Albers, H. H. (1965) *Principles of Organization and Management*, 2nd ed, New York: John Wiley & Sons, Inc.

Albrecht, A. J. (1979) Measuring application development productivity. *Proc. Joint Application Dev. Symp.*, SHARE, Inc. and GUIDE International, Oct, 83–92.

Albrecht, A. J. and Gaffney, J., Jr. (1983) Software function, source lines of code, and development effort prediction: A software science validation. *IEEE Trans. Software Eng.*, **9**(6) Nov, 639–48.

Alford, M. W. (1977) A requirements engineering methodology for real-time processing requirements. *IEEE Trans. Software Eng.*, **3**(1).

Amdahl (1988) It's time for UNIX. *Datamation*, 1 Dec, 13.

The Analytic Sciences Corporation (1986) Introducing FASTBOL. *Datamation*, 15 July, 82.

Anderson, A. (1982) Micro sales likely to top R50-m in '83. *ComputerWeek*, 6 Dec, 9–10.

Anderson, R. B. (1979) *Proving Programs Correct*, New York: John Wiley & Sons.

Andriole, S. J. (1986) *Software Validation, Verification, Testing and Documentation*, Petrocelli Books.

Anning, N. (1986) Guarding the network. *Datamation*, 1 Nov, 64-4–64-8.

Appleton, D. S. (1983) Data-driven prototyping. *Datamation*, Nov, 259–68.

Appleton, E., Bunker, T., Moad, J. and Pinella, P. (1991) IBM expects growth of 7 to 10%. *Datamation*, 1 Jan, 39–40.

Applied Data Research (1986) The 4th generation gap just got wider. *Datamation*, 1 Nov, 11.

Applied Learning Corporation (1988) Is your training program working? *ComputerWeek*, 28 Nov, 22.

Appun, F. (1987) Here comes Advanced DOS. *Computer Mail*, 27 Feb, 18–19.

Appun, F. (1988) Lotus/DBMS joins the OS/2 line. *ComputerWeek*, 11 Apr, 4.

Argyle, M., Gardner, G. and Cioffi, F. (1958) Supervisory methods related to productivity, absenteeism, and labor turnover. *Human Relations*, Feb, 24.

Argyris, C. (1976) Resistance to rational management systems. *Readings in Management Information Systems* (eds G. B. Davis and G. C. Everest), McGraw-Hill, Inc.

Armer, P. (1966) *Computer Aspects of Technological Change, Automation, and Economic Progress*. P-3478, The Rand Corp., Nov.

Aron, J. D. (1969) *Estimating Resources for Large Programming Systems*, NATO Science Committee, Rome, Italy, Oct.

Aron, J. D. (1974) *The Program Development Process: Part 1 – The Individual Programmer*, Reading, Massachusetts: Addison-Wesley Publishing Co.

Arthur, L. J. (1983) *Programmer Productivity: Myths, Methods, and Murphy's Law*, New York: John Wiley & Sons, Inc.

Arthur, L. J. (1985) *Measuring Programmer Productivity and Software Quality*, New York: John Wiley & Sons, Inc.

Arthur, L. J. (1988) *Software Evolution: The Software Maintenance Challenge*, New York: John Wiley & Sons, Inc.

Artz, J. M. (1989) Comparative review. *Computing Reviews*, Oct, 510–13.

Arvanitis, T. (1989) Ohio offers total solution with training. *Computing S.A.*, 16 Jan, 19.

Arvey, R. D. and Hoyle, J. C. (1973) Evaluating computing personnel. *Datamation*, July, 69–73.

Ashley, R. (1980) *Structured Cobol*, New York: John Wiley & Sons, Inc.

ASI (1986) Raise training efficiency to new heights with ASI interactive video. *Datamation*, 15 July, 18.

AT&T. (1986) Confessions of a downed computer. *Datamation*, 15 Dec, 46–7.

Atkins, P. (1982) Call for more intelligent approach to systems analysis, design. *ComputerWeek*, 11 Oct, 9.

Atron Corp. (1986) What's the secret debugging weapon used by everybody from Borland to Oracle? *Byte*, Oct, 222.

Auerbach, N. (1988a) Notice to ASI/Deltak clients. *ComputerWeek*, 12 Dec, 9.

Auerbach, N. (1988b) Study shows IVI is preferred instruction method. *ComputerWeek*, 8 Aug, 65.

Auerbach, N. (1988c) Technology must be taught through technology. *Computing S.A.*, 31 Oct, 22.

Augustine, N. R. (1979) Augustine's laws and major system development programs. *Defense Systems Management Review*, 50–76.

Austrian, G. D. (1983) GOALS for the nineteen eighties. *IBM Inform*, Aug, IV, X.

Avison, D. E. and Fitzgerald, G. (1988) *Information Systems Development: Methodologies, Techniques and Tools*, Oxford: Blackwell Scientific Publications.

Ayre, R. and Ayre, S. (1991) 'Master C' tutorial offers solid fundamentals for C programming. *PC Magazine*, 11 June, 67.

Babich, W. A. (1986) *Software Configuration Management: Coordination for Team Productivity*, Reading, Massachusetts: Addison-Wesley Publishing Company.

Babilonia, J. (1988) *Computing Reviews*, Aug, 419–20.

Badgett, T. (1986) A smart data base. *Personal Computing*, June, 211–20.

Bailey, J. W. (1982) Personal correspondence with S. Thebaut, April.

Bailey, J. W. and Basili, V. R. (1981) A meta-model for software development resource expenditures. *Proc. 5th Int. Conf. Software Eng.*, 107–16.

Bailyn, L. (1989) Toward the perfect workplace? *Communications of the ACM*, April, 460–71.

Bain, D. (1982) *The Productivity Prescription*, New York: McGraw-Hill.

Bairdain, E. F. (1964) Research Studies of Programmers and Programming. Unpublished studies, New York, 62, 78, 136.

Baker, A. L. and Zweben, S. H. (1980) A comparison of measures of control flow complexity. *IEEE Trans. Software Eng.*, 6 (6), Nov, 506–12.

Baker, F. T. (1972) Chief programmer team management of production programming. *IBM Systems J.*, **11**, (1) 56–73.

Baker, F. T. and Mills, H. D. (1973) Chief programmer teams. *Datamation*, Dec, 58–61.

Baker, W. F. (1977) *Software Data Collection and Analysis: A Real-Time System Project History*, Final Technical Report. RADC-TR-77–192, Rome Air Development Center, Griffiss Air Force Base, New York, June.

Ballantine, M. and Moore, L. (1983) Changing attitudes of staff in UK. *ComputerWeek*, 18 April, 18.

Balzer, R., Cheatham, T. E. and Green, C. (1983) Software technology in the 1990s: using a new paradigm. *IEEE Computer*, March, 39–45.

Bang & Olufsen (1977) Beomaster 2400. 8.

Barber, R. E. and Lucas, H. C., Jr. (1983) System response time, operator productivity, and job satisfaction. *Communications of the ACM*, Aug, 972–86.

Barna, R. S. (1987) All the wrong choices? *Datamation*, 15 Feb, 3.

Barnett, P. (1985) PC-Touch board with compatibility. *Computing S.A.*, 29 April, 14.

Baron, N. S. (1988) *Computer Languages: A Guide for the Perplexed*, London: Penguin Books.

Baroni, D. L. and Hotka, C. (1986) The keys to automation: plan, commit, follow up. *The Office*, Oct, 12.

Barrington Systems, Inc. (1986) Languages that are causing the biggest programming backlog in history are also eating nice big holes in our pockets. *Byte*, Nov, 25.

Barry, J. (1982) Do you measure up to software perfection? *ComputerWeek*, 19 July, 20.

Barry, T. (1986a) Software and services. *Datamation*, 1 July, 99–100.

Barry, T. (1986b) Software and Services. *Datamation*, 15 Aug, 97–8.

Barry, T. (1986c) Hardware. *Datamation*, 1 Nov, 115–16.

Barry, T. (1987) Real Time. *Datamation*, 15 Feb, 95–6.

Bartimo, J. (1986) Microsoft Windows includes extras. *Personal Computing*, April, 53–5.

Basili, V. R. and Baker, F. T. (1975) *Structured programming tutorial*, Cat. No. 75CH1049-6, IEEE Computer Society, Long Beach, Calif., 216–17.

Basili, V. R. and Perricone, B. T. (1984) Software errors and complexity: an empirical investigation. *Communications of the ACM*, Jan, 42–52.

Basili, V. R. and Reiter, R. W., Jr. (1979) An investigation of human factors in software development. *IEEE Computer*, Dec, 21–38.

Basili, V. R. and Selby, R. W. (1987) Comparing the effectiveness of software testing strategies. *IEEE Trans. Software Eng.*, **13**, Dec, 1278–96.

Bates, T. (1989) Explosive growth of interactive video. *ComputerWeek*, 23 Jan, 11.

Batson, E. P., MD. (1983) Worth noting. *Datamation*, Nov, 28–32.

Batt, R. (1981) Managers urged to talk less, listen more. *Computing S.A.*, 15 April, 20.

Battle, L. (1988a) Industry must align expertise with human resources – Battle. *ComputerWeek*, 17 Oct, 27.

Battle (1988b) Battle against bugs reaches crucial areas. *Computing S.A.*, 7 Nov, 29.

Bauer, F. (1973) Software and Software Engineering. *SIAM Review*, **15**, (2), April, 469–80.

Baxter, J. (1988a) Caltex chooses CIM's Phoenix for its CBT. *Computing S.A.*, 7 Mar, 12.

Baxter, L. (1988b) Expo-Data takes up Dataplan systems. *Computing S.A.*, 22 Aug, 4.

Beaird, R. C. (1980) *Industrial Democracy and Participation Management in Labor Issues of the 1980s*, Corporate Planning Division AT&T, Basking Ridge, NJ.

Bearley, W. L. (1980) Squeezing More From DP. *Datamation*, Jan, 121–4.

Bebbington, B. (1980) Organisational design and the DP function. *Systems for information management*, May, 16–20.

Beech, G. (1983) *Computer-based learning: Practical microcomputer methods*, Sigma Technical Press, Wilmslow.

Been, M. (1979) Tying down the paper tiger. *Computronics*, 25 July, 2.

Belady, L. A. and Lehman, M. M. (1979) The characteristics of large systems. In *Research Directions in Software Technology*, (ed. P. Wegner), Cambridge, MA: MIT Press, 106–38.

Bell, D., Morrey, I. and Pugh, J. (1987) *Software Engineering: a programming approach*, Englewood Cliffs, New Jersey: Prentice-Hall International.

ben-Aaron, D. (1986) Cut-rate PC clones are no bargain for MIS. *InformationWEEK*, 10 Nov, 13.

Benbasat, I., Dexter, A. S. and Todd, P. (1986) An experimental program investigating color-enhanced and graphical information presentation: an integration of the findings. *Communications of the ACM*, Nov, 1094–1105.

Benchmarks (1986). Benchmarks. *Datamation*, 1 Nov, 50.

Bentley, G. D. (1987) GOTO Exit, Already. *Communications of the ACM*, Nov, 908.

Bergen, M. (1989) A CASE for clarification. *Computing S.A.*, 27 Feb, 30.

Berne, E. (1964) *Games People Play*, Ballantine Books.

Biebuyck, P. (1980) What if . . . your DP manager resigns. *Systems Stelsels*, April, 3.

Birkholtz, B. (1983) Screen generator speeds development. *Software Extra*, 31 Jan, II.

Bis Applied Systems (1986) Networking 'heads list of managers problems'. *Communications*, March, 7–16.

Black, A. (1989) Office systems trends in South Africa. *Corporate Computing Today*, Sept, 3–5.

Black, D. and Associates (1979) Speeding up software. *Computronics*, 11 July, 2.

Black, R. K. D., Curnow, R. P., Katz, R. and Gray, M. D. (1977) *BCS Software Production Data*, Final Technical Report, RADC-TR-77-116, Boeing Computer Services, Inc., March. NTIS No. AD-A039852.

Blair, L. (1986) Is it just a VDU scare? *Business Systems and Equipment*, Feb, 45–50.

Blakeney, S. (1983) Mainframes here to stay, says Sperry exec. *Computing S.A.*, 26 Aug, 7.

Blankenhorn, D. (1987) A LAN for the rest of us. *Datamation*, 15 April, 52-3–52-8.

Blankenhorn, D. (1988) Pursuing one peripheral. *Datamation*, 15 Oct, 71–6.

Bleazard, G. B. (1976) *Program Design Methods*, Manchester: NCC Publications.

Blij, G. (1988) Titan systems to take Shoprite into the 1990s. *ComputerWeek*, 8 Aug, 45.

Blum, B. I. (1990) Comment on measure for measure. *Communications of the ACM*, June, 627–8.

Boehm, B. W. (1973) Software and its impact: a quantitative assessment. *Datamation*, May, 48–59.

Boehm, B. W. (1975a) Software design and structuring. *Practical Strategies for Developing Large Software Systems*, Addison-Wesley.

Boehm, B. W. (1976) Software engineering. *IEEE Trans. Computers*, Dec., 1226–41. Reprinted in (Couger *et al.*, 1982).

Boehm, B. W. (1979) Guidelines for verifying and validating software requirements and design specifications. *Proc., EuroIFIP Congress*, Sept, 711–20.

Boehm, B. W. (1980a) Developing small-scale application software products: some experimental results. *Proc., IFIP 8th World Computer Congress*, Oct, 321–6.

Boehm, B. W. (1980b) Software maintenance. *Techniques of Program and System Maintenance*, (ed. G. Parikh), Lincoln, Nebraska: Ethnotech, Inc., 19–22.

Boehm, B. W. (1981) *Software Engineering Economics*, Englewood Cliffs, New Jersey: Prentice-Hall, Inc.

Boehm, B. W. (1987) Improving software productivity. *IEEE Computer*, Sept, 43–57.

Boehm, B. W., Bosch, C. A., Liddle, A. S. and Wolverton, R. W. (1974) *The Impact of New Technologies on Software Configuration Management*, TRW Report to USAF-ESD, Contract F19628-74-C-0154, 10 June.

Boehm, B. W., Gray, T. E. and Seewaldt, T. (1984) Prototyping versus specifying: a multiproject experiment. *IEEE Trans. Software Eng.*, **10**(3), May, 290–303.

Boehm, B. W., Holmes, C. E., Katkus, G. R., Romanos, J. P., McHenry, R. C. and Gordon, E. K. (1975b) Structured programming: a quantitative assessment. *Computer*, June, 38–54.

Boehm, B. W., McClean, R. and Urfrig, D. B. (1975c) Some experience with automated aids to the design of large-scale reliable software. *IEEE Trans. Software Eng.*, **1**, March, 125–33.

Boehm, B. W., Seven, M. J. and Watson, R. A. (1971) Interactive problem-solving – An experimental study of 'lockout' effects. *Proceedings of the Spring Joint Computer Conference*, AFIPS Press, Montvale, New Jersey, 205–10.

Boehm, B. W. and Standish, T. A. (1983) Software technology in the 1990s: using an evolutionary paradigm. *IEEE Computer*, Nov, 30–7.

Boeing Co. (1979) Software cost measuring and reporting. US Air Force – ASD Document D180–22813-1, January.

Bohlin, R. and Hoenig, C. (1989) Wringing value from old systems. *Datamation*, 15 Aug, 57–60.

Bohm, C. and Jacopini, G. (1966) Flow diagrams, Turing machines, and languages with only two formation rules. *Communications of the ACM*, May, 366–71. (This paper was originally published in Italian in 1965 (Yourdon, 1975).)

Boies, S. J. and Gould, J. D. (1974) Syntactic errors in computer programming. *Human Factors*, **16**, 253–7.

Bomberg, H. (1986) Open sesame! *Impact: Office Automation*, Feb, 11–12.

Booz, Allen, and Hamilton, Inc. (1980) *Booz, Allen Study of Managerial/Professional Productivity*, New York: Booz, Allen, and Hamilton.

Borg, A., Blau, W., Graetsch, W., Herrmann, F. and Oberle, W. (1989) Fault tolerance under UNIX. *ACM Trans. Computer Systems*, 7(1), 1–24.

Borland International (1986) Turbo Pascal programming! *Byte*, Oct, 1.

Borland International (1987) Three from Borland. *Datamation*, 1 Jan, 108.

Bouldin, B. M. (1989) *Agents of change: managing the introduction of automated tools*, New York: Yourdon Press.

Bourdon, R. J. (1987) *The PICK Operating System: A Practical Guide*, Wokingham, Berkshire: Addison-Wesley Publishing Company.

Bowen, D. H. (1987) Compatibility forever? *Datamation*, 15 Feb, 112.

Bradley, J. (1989) An educational experience at Aetna. *Datamation*, 1 Apr, 46–7.

Brady, S. E. (1987) Getting a hand on maintenance costs. *Datamation*, 15 Aug, 62–71.

Brandon, R. H. (1978) *Data Processing Cost Reduction and Control*, New York: Van Nostrand Reinhold Company.

Braner, M. (1986) Screaming computers. *Byte*, Oct, 14.

Brauer, B. (1987) One hour of CBT can take 200 hours. *Computing S.A.*, 21 Sept, 10.

Brickman, B. K. (1986) Staying out of the black hole. *Best's Review – Property/Casualty Insurance Edition*, Feb, 86–90.

Bridger, M. (1986) ITC's Modula-2 software development system. *Byte*, Oct, 255–8.

Brooke, J. B. and Duncan, K. D. (1980) An experimental study of flowcharts as an aid to identification of procedural faults. *Ergonomics*, **23**, 387–99.

Brooks, F. P., Jr. (1975) *The Mythical Man-Month*, Reading, Massachusetts: Addison-Wesley Publishing Company.

Brooks, F. P., Jr. (1987) No silver bullet: essence and accidents of software engineering. *IEEE Computer*, April, 10–19.

Brooks, R. (1977) Towards a theory of the cognitive processes in computer programming. *Int. J. Man–Machine Studies*, **9**, 737–51.

Brooks, W. D. (1980) *Software Technology Payoff: Some Statistical Evidence*, IBM-FSD, Bethesda, MD, April, 2–7.

Brooks, W. D. (1981) Software technology payoff – some statistical evidence. *J. Systems Software*, **2**, 3–9.

Brown, H. (1986) Maximise training productivity minimise frustration. *Computing S.A.*, 3 Nov, 7.

Brown, J. R., DeSalvio, A. J., Heine, D. E. and Purdy, J. G. (1973) in *Program Test Methods*, (ed. W. C. Hetzel) Englewood Cliffs, New Jersey: Prentice-Hall, Inc.

Brustman, K. (1978) Software cost estimation: two management perspectives. *Proc., AIAA/TMSA/DPMA Software Management Conference III*, 103–108.

Bryce, M., and Associates, Inc. (1978) Automated systems design methodology. *Systems Stelsels*, Aug, 43.

Brzezinski, R. (1987) When it's time to tear down the info center. *Datamation*, 1 Nov., 73–82.

Buchalter, S. (1989) MBM latest entry in staff arena. *Computing S.A.*, 6 Feb, 13.

Buchholz, S. and Roth, T. (1987) *Creating the High-Performance Team*, New York: John Wiley & Sons, Inc.

Buck, F. (1981) IBM Kingston, New York. Technical Report 21.802, Sept.

Buckley, F. J. (1989) *Implementing Software Engineering Practices*, New York: Wiley Interscience.

Burnett, M. (1987) Accounting for training: a true and fair view? *Training and Development*, **5**(9).

Burnstein, L. (1982) Accuracy and speed assured. *ComputerWeek*, 1 Nov, 7.

Business (1983) Business Systems range gives more for less. *Computer Systems in Southern Africa*, Aug, 47.

Butgereit, L. (1983) Programmers quick to accept Pascal. *SA Software News*, Aug, 10.

Butlein, M. (1985) Online swing causes big rise in idle time. *ComputerWeek*, 20 May, 5. Reprinted from: *Computing U.K.*

Butler Cox Foundation (1983a) Report No. 35. Quoted in: A troubled passage for multifunction equipment. *ComputerWeek*, 11 July, 13.

Butler Cox Foundation (1983b) Report No. 36. Quoted in: DP productivity under review. *ComputerWeek*, 12 Sept, 6.

Butterworth, R. (1974) Restructured programming. *Datamation*, March, 158.

Caine, S. and Gordon, E. K. (1978) PDL – a tool for software design. *Proc. 1975 National Computer Conference*, 44, AFIPS Press, Montvale, New Jersey, 168–73.

Campbell, D. (1978) An outline of computer graphics in civil engineering. *Systems Stelsels*, Nov, 22–3.

Campbell, M. V. (1986) Three packages add value to Lotus spreadsheet. *Wall Street Computer Review*, Nov, 24–30.

Canada, J. R. (1971) *Intermediate Economic Analysis for Management and Engineering*, Englewood Cliffs, New Jersey: Prentice-Hall.

Canning, R. G. (1972) That maintenance iceberg. *EDP Analyzer*, Oct.

Canning, R. (1979) The analysis of user needs. *EDP Analyzer*, Jan.

Carbonell, J. R., Elkind, J. I. and Nickerson, R. S. (1968) On the psychological importance of time in a time-sharing system. *Human Factors*, **10**, 135–42.

Card, D. N., McGarry, F. E. and Page, G. T. (1987) Evaluating software engineering technologies. *IEEE Trans. Software Engineering*, **13**(7), 845–51.

Card, S. K. (1978) *Studies in the psychology of computer text editing*, Xerox Palo Alto Research Center, SSL-78-1, San Jose, California, Aug.

Card, S. K., Moran, T. P. and Newell, A. (1983) *The Psychology of Human–Computer Interaction*, Hillsdale, NJ: Lawrence Erlbaum Associates.

Carlisle, J. H. (1970) Comparing behavior at various computer display consoles in time-shared legal information. Rand Corporation, Santa Monica, CA, Report No. AD712695, Sept.

Carlyle, R. E. (1987a) Color me blue. *Datamation*, 1 Jan, 85–6.

Carlyle, R. E. (1987b) ROI in real time. *Datamation*, 15 Feb, 73–4.

Carlyle, R. E. (1987c) High cost, lack of standards is slowing pace of CASE. *Datamation*, 15 Aug, 23–4.

Carlyle, R. E. (1989a) The selling of IS. *Datamation*, 1 July, 22–6.

Carlyle, R. E. (1989b) IBM's VSE: a victory for the techies? *Datamation*, 15 July, 25–7.

Carlyle, R. E. (1990) Is your data ready for the repository? *Datamation*, 1 Jan, 43–8.

Carlyle, R. E. and Moad, J. (1988) IBM and the control of information. *Datamation*, 1 Jan, 34–44.

Carnegie, D. (1913) *How to Win Friends and Influence People*, Kingswood, Surrey: The World's Work Ltd.

Carnevale, A. P. and Goldstein, H. (1983) *Employee training: its changing role and an analysis of new data*, American Society for Training and Development, Washington DC.

Carpenter, L. C. and Tripp, L. L. (1975) Software design validation tool. *Proc. 1975 Int. Conf. Reliable Software*, April, 395–400.

Carpenter, M. B. and Hallman, H. K. (1985) Quality emphasis at IBM's Software Engineering Institute. *IBM Systems Journal*, **24**(2), 121–33.

Carriere, W. M. and Thibodeau, R. (1979) Development of a logistics software cost estimating technique for foreign military sales, Report CR-3-839, General Research Corp., June.

Cashing, D. L. (1987) '"GOTO considered harmful" considered harmful' considered further. *Communications of the ACM*, June, 477.

Cashman, P. M. and Holt, A. W. (1980) A communications oriented approach to structuring the software maintenance environment. *Soft. Eng. Notes*, **5**(1), Jan, 4–17.

Cashmore, S. (1985) Surprise finding of why DP employees change jobs. *Computing S.A.*, 7 Oct, 9.

Cashmore, S. (1988) World trends in computing as seen by guru James Martin. *Computing S.A.*, 16 May, 22–4.

Casner, S. M. (1991) A task-analytic approach to the automated design of graphic presentations. *ACM Trans. Graphics*, April, 111–51.

Central Computer and Telecommunications Agency (1980) *Stand alone word processors: a report of trials in UK Government typing pools 1979/80*.

Cerveny, R. P., Garrity, E. J., Hunt, R. G., Kirs, P. J., Sanders, G. L. and Sipior, J. C. (1987) Why software prototyping works. *Datamation*, 15 Aug, 97–103.

Chandor, A. (1976) *Choosing and Keeping Computer Staff*, London: Allen & Unwin.

Chandor, A., Graham, J. and Williamson, R. (1985) *The Penguin Dictionary of Computers*, 3rd ed, London: Penguin Books.

Chapin, N. (1974) New formats for flowcharts. *Software Practice and Experience*, **4**, 341–57.

Charette, R. N. (1986) *Software Engineering Environments*, New York: Intertext Publications, Inc.

Cheng, L. L. (1978) *Program Design Languages: An Introduction*, ESD-TR-77-324, prepared by the Mitre Corporation for the USAF AFSC Electronic Systems Division, available as AD-A051672 from National Technical Information Service, US Department of Commerce, Washington.

Cherry, L. and MacDonald, N. H. (1983) The UNIX Writer's Workbench software. *Byte*, **8**(10), 241–52.

Chess, D. M. and Cowlishaw, M. F. (1987) A large-scale computer conferencing system. *IBM Systems J.*, **26**(1), 138–53.

Chiswell, P. (1986) Cobol programs streamlined. *Computing S.A.*, 21 April, 23.

Cho, C-K. (1987) *Quality Programming: Developing and Testing Software with Statistical Quality Control*, New York: John Wiley & Sons, Inc.

Chorafas, D. N. (1985) *Management Workstations for Greater Productivity*, New York: McGraw-Hill Book Company.

Chorafas, D. N. (1986) *Fourth and Fifth Generation Programming Languages*, Vol. 1, New York: McGraw-Hill.

Christensen, K. (1980) *Programming productivity and the development process*, IBM Santa Theresa Laboratory, TR 03.083, Jan.

Chrysler, E. (1978a) Some basic determinants of computer programming productivity. *Communications of the ACM*, June, 472–83.

Chrysler, E. (1978b) The impact of program and programmer characteristics. *Proc. National Computer Conference*, 47, AFIPS Press, Montvale, New Jersey, 581–7.

Church, G. J. (1992) The other side of Perot. *TIME International*, 29 June, 22–9.

Church, R. (1980) Linking the old with the new. *Systems Stelsels*, April, 8–9.

Ciarcia, S. (1986a) Compaq reset switch. *Byte*, Nov, 54.

Ciarcia, S. (1986b) Voice recognition technology in dental research. *Byte*, Nov, 58–61.

Cincom Systems, Inc. (1986) MANTIS 1986. The best just got better. *Datamation*, 15 Aug, 8.

Cincom Systems, Inc. (1987) If you're considering DB2, you better face up to SUPRA. *Datamation*, 15 Feb, 60–1.

Cincom Systems, Inc. (1992) Successful world leaders use SUPRA server from Cincom. *Datamation*, 15 Mar, 66.

Civil Service (1981) Civil Service trial attacks wp costs. *Computer Systems in Southern Africa*, Sept, 21–22.

Clark, C. E. (1989) The facilities and evolution of MVS/ESA. *IBM Systems Journal*, **28**(1), 124–50.

Clark, R. and Oppe, R. (1986) In search of videotext standards. *Telephone Engineer and Management*, 15 Feb, 92–8.

Clemons, E. K. (1991) Evaluation of strategic investments in information technology. *Communications of the ACM*, Jan, 22–36.

Climis, T. (1979) Software cost estimation. Presentation at NSIA Software Workshop, Buena Park, CA, Feb.

Coch, L. and French, J. P. R., Jr. (1948) Overcoming resistance to change. *Human Relations*, **1**, 512–32.

Cockburn, L. (1988) Contracting boom. *Computer-Week*, 18 July, 1–2.

Cockcroft, M. (1988) DP personnel are a breed apart – UK expert. *Argus Computers*, 17 Nov, 4.

Codd, E. F. (1970) A relational model of data for large shared data banks. *Communications of the ACM*, June, 377–87.

Coetzer, J. (1983a) DP management faces uncertain future. *SA Software News*, Aug, 7.

Coetzer, J. (1983b) Staff myths exploded. *ComputerWeek*, 21 Nov, 1–2.

Coetzer, J. (1989) If you haven't got it – please don't get it. *Argus Computers*, 16 Feb, 6.

Coetzer, R. (1981) You need a psychological contract. *CPL Comment*, Feb, 4.

Cohen, S. (1983) Huge slump in DP efficiency. *ComputerWeek*, 9 May, 9.

Cole, H., Eads, W. and Near, C. (1979) *Instruments & Control Systems*, June. Reprinted in: Which For You? *Dataweek*, 4 April 1980, 2.

Collin, S. M. H. (1989) *The Hamlyn Dictionary of Computing*, London: The Hamlyn Publishing Group Limited.

Comcon/FSA (1985) 4GL trend is on an upward growth path. *ComputerWeek*, 21 Oct, 2.

Comper, F. A. (1979) Project Management for System Quality and Development Productivity. Bank of Montreal, Montreal, Quebec, 1979. Also in *Proc. JAD Symp.*, SHARE, Inc. and GUIDE International, Oct, 17–23.

Comptroller General (1979) Contracting For Computer Software Development. General Accounting Office Report, FGMSD-80-4, Washington, DC, 9 Sept.

Computer (1979) A computer person costs twice his salary. *CPL Comment*, Aug, 4.

Computer (1980) Computer Literature. *The 1979/80 S.A. Computer Guide*. Johannesburg: Thomson Publications (Pty) Ltd, 1980, pp. 427–448.

Computer Associates (1988) Computer Associates lifts veil on ADR plan. *Computing S.A.*, 12 Dec, 11.

Computer Innovations, Inc. (1986) Substantiated. *Byte*, Nov, 47.

Computer Sciences (Pty) Ltd. (1978) Do your computer systems give you a head start or a headache? *Systems Stelsels*, Dec, 37.

Computer Services Association (1980a) *Text Processing – future plans for 10 major UK organisations*, quoted in: Fear that wp threatens jobs is discounted. *Systems for information management*, June, 39.

Computer Services Association (1980b) *Text Processing – understanding the possibilities*, quoted in:

Fear that wp threatens jobs is discounted. *Systems for information management*, June, 39.

Connell, C. (1986) Computers that just won't quit. *High Technology*, Dec, 56–7.

Conrow, K. and Smith, R. G. (1970) NEATER2: a PL/1 source statement reformatter. *Communications of the ACM*, Nov, 669–75.

Conte, S. D., Dunsmore, H. E. and Shen, V. Y. (1986) *Software Engineering Metrics and Models*, Menlo Park, California: The Benjamin/Cummings Publishing Company, Inc.

Control Data Corporation (1986) No one outruns Control Data. *Datamation*, 15 Aug, 60-6–60-7.

Cooper, J. D. (1975) Characteristics of the average coder. Personal communication to B. W. Boehm. May.

Corlett, N., Wilson, J. and Manencia, F. (eds.) (1986) *Ergonomics of Working Posture*, New York: Taylor and Francis.

Corley, R. (1991) The apple of his eye. *Datamation*, 1 March, 10.

Couger, J. D. (1973) Evolution of business system analysis techniques. *Computing Surveys*, Sept, 167–98.

Couger, J. D., Colter, M. A. and Knapp, R. W. (1982) *Advanced System Development/Feasibility Techniques*, New York: John Wiley & Sons.

Couger, J. D. and Colter, M. A., (1983) Bored programmers cause huge losses. *ComputerWeek*, 10 Oct, 24. Reprinted from: *Computing UK*.

Couger, J. D. and Colter, M. A. (1985) *Maintenance Programming: Improved Productivity Through Motivation*, Englewood Cliffs, New Jersey: Prentice-Hall.

Couger, J. D. and Zawacki, R. A. (1980) *Motivating and Managing Computer Personnel*, New York: John Wiley & Sons.

Cowpar, E. (1983) System developed in two hours. *IBM Inform*, July, II.

Cox, S. (1989a) Polygon's Sapiens cuts Air Products' workload. *Computing S.A.*, 30 Jan, 6.

Cox, S. (1989b) B & D offers Israeli education software. *Computing S.A.*, 27 Feb, 6.

Crabtree, M. A. (1979) 'White' noise masking systems in offices. *Computronics*, 25 April, 8.

Craig, G. R., Hetrick, W. L., Lipow, M. and Thayer, T. A. (1974) *Software Reliability Study*, Interim Technical Report. RADC-TR-74-250, Rome Air Development Center, Griffiss Air Force Base, New York, Oct.

Craig, R. L. and Evers, C. (1981) Employers as educators: the shadow education system, in

Business and higher education: toward new alliances, (ed. G. Gold) San Francisco: Jossey Bass.

Crawford, D. (1989) Supercomputing: from here to economy. *Communications of the ACM*, Sep, 1048–50.

Crocker, O. L., Charney, C. and Sik Leung Chiu, J. (1986) *Quality Circles: a Guide to Participation and Productivity*, New York: New American Library.

Crossman, T. D. (1978) Programmer productivity measurement. *Systems Stelsels*, March, 19–24.

Crossman, T. D. (1979a) Taking the measure of programmer productivity. *Datamation*, May, 144–7.

Crossman, T. D. (1979b) Some experiences in the use of inspection teams in applications development, in *Proc. JAD Symp.*, SHARE Inc. and GUIDE International, October, 163–8.

Crossman, T. (1980) The use of structured disciplines and an attempt to measure programmer productivity. *Systems for information management*, Oct, 40–7.

Crossman, T. (1982) Wits produces practical people. *ComputerWeek*, 28 June, 15.

Crossman, T. (1983) Prof sees COBOL demise. *Computing S.A.*, 15 July, 1–2.

Crutchfield, R. J. (1986a) Getting down to business. *Datamation*, 1 Oct, 43–8.

Crutchfield, R. J. (1986b) Trimming the fat. *Datamation*, 15 Dec, 37–41.

Cullinet Software, Inc. (1985) IDMS/R – Integrated Database Management System/Relational.

Cullinet Software, Inc. (1986) Access Success. Access Cullinet. *Datamation*, 1 Oct, 16–17.

Cullum, R. (1983) High level languages works only for some. *ComputerWeek*, 31 Jan., 2.

Cunningham, P. (1990) Dell Computer is latest system V.4 convert as UNIX licensees approach 2m. *Computing S.A.*, 3 Dec, 19.

Curtice, R. M. (1986) Getting the database right. *Datamation*, 1 Oct, 99–104.

Curtis, W., Krasner, H., and Iscoe, N. (1988) A field study of the software design process for large systems. *Communications of the ACM*, Nov, 1268–87.

Curtis, W., Sheppard, S. B., and Milliman, P. (1979b) Third time charm: Stronger prediction of programmer performance by software complexity metrics. *Proc., 4th Int. Conf. Software Eng.*, Sept, 356–60.

Curtis, W., Sheppard, S. B., Borst, M. A., Milliman, P., and Love, T. (1978) Some distinctions between the psychological and computational complexity of software. *Proc. US Army/IEEE 2nd Software Life Cycle Management Conf.*, Atlanta, Aug, 166–71

Curtis, W., Sheppard, S. B., Milliman, P., Borst, M. A., and Love, T. (1979a) Measuring the psychological complexity of software maintenance tasks with the Halstead and McCabe metrics. *IEEE Trans. Software Eng.*, March, 96–104.

D & B Computing Services, Inc. (1986) Only NOMAD2 can unleash the power of SQL. *Datamation*, 15 Aug, 84.

D & B Computing Services, Inc. (1987) NOMAD2: A few good names that have helped us build ours. *Datamation*, 15 April, 42–3.

d'Agapeyeff, A. (1969) *Software Engineering* (eds P. Naur and B. Randell) Brussels: NATO Scientific Affairs Division, Jan.

d'Agapeyeff, A. (1988) Discard the myth of ES – d'Agapeyeff. *ComputerWeek*, 18 July, 14.

Dahl, O. J., Dijkstra, E. W. and Hoare, C. A. R. (1972) *Structured Programming*, New York: Academic Press.

Daley, R. F. (1991) Faster than a speeding mouse. *PC Magazine*, 16 April, 369.

Daly, E. B. (1979) Organizing for successful software development. *Datamation*, Dec, 107–20.

Dantzig, G. B. (1963) *Linear Programming and Extensions*, Princeton University Press, Princeton, New Jersey.

Datapro Research Corp. (1986) Oracle Corporation: ORACLE. *Datapro Research Corporation*, SW25-685KA-102, Nov.

Datapro Research Corp. (1987) A Datapro Report on SIR/DBMS. *Datapro 70*, SW25-497QC-101.

Dataproducts International Ltd. (1985) *Dataproducts 8012 & 8022 Matrix Printers*, Egham, UK, P&G/5.85/20 000 (no date, but probably 1985).

Date, C. J. (1977) *An Introduction to Database Systems*, 2nd edn; Reading, Massachusetts: Addison-Wesley Publishing Company.

David, P. A. (1991) Clio and the economics of QWERTY. *Interface*, 3rd Qtr., 30–3.

Davies, A. (1988) MIS divisions wasting resources – Davies. *ComputerWeek*, 24 Oct, 9.

Davis, Dr. R. (1972) Government bureau takes on role of public protector against computer misuse. *Communications of the ACM*, Nov, 1017–18.

Davis, R. (1983a) Gear up to come to grips with 4th generation soon. *ComputerWeek*, 10 Jan., 1–2.

Davis, R. (1983b) 1983: year of the micro. *ComputerWeek*, 17 Jan, 1.

Davis, R., and Blackmarr, B. R. (1983) OA can become a viable reality. *ComputerWeek*, 14 Feb, 1–2.

Davis, C. and Vick, C. (1977) The software development system. *IEEE Trans. Software Eng.*, **3**, Jan, 69–84.

Davis, D. (1989a) US giants run a $50 billion IS tab. *Datamation*, 15 Nov, 42–4.

Davis, G. R. (1986) Tougher copyrights will boost innovation. *Datamation*, 1 Nov, 19.

Davis, L. (1989b) Can education meet IS career demands? *Datamation*, 15 March, 65–72.

Davis, L. (1991a) Inside IBM's System View. *Datamation*, 15 Feb, 62–4.

Davis, L. (1991b) DB2 migration without tears. *Datamation*, 1 May, 67–70.

Davis, S. G. (1987a) FORTRAN at 30: Formula for success. *Datamation*, 1 April, 47–56.

Davis, S. G. (1987b) The superconductive computer in your future. *Datamation*, 15 Aug, 74–8.

Davis, S. G. and Flynn, M. K. (1987) Tomorrow's management generation. *Datamation*, 15 Sept, 126–38.

Davis, W. S. (1983c) *System Analysis and Design: A Structured Approach*, Reading, Massachusetts: Addison-Wesley Publishing Co.

DB2 (1987) DB2 and SQL/DS interfaces announced. *SAS Communications*, 1st Qtr, 5–7.

de Benedetti, C. (1982) Speech in Copenhagen, quoted in: 'Gear up for survival', computer companies told. *ComputerWeek*, 11 Oct, 10.

de Gruchy, W. (1986) PC proliferation can be a corporate headache. *The Office*, Oct, 38.

de Jager, D. (1980) Cost-effective performance when the product is paper. *Systems Stelsels*, March, 41–3.

de Millo, R., McCracken, M., Martin, R. and Passafiume, J. (1987) *Software Testing and Evaluation*, Addison-Wesley.

de Raay, L. (1975) Computers and production applications. *Systems Stelsels*, Nov, 10–12.

Dean, C. (1983) DP suffers for its past. *SA Software News*, Sept, 8.

Dean, C. and Whitlock, Q. (1982) *A handbook of computer based training*. Kogan Page and Nichols, London and New York.

DecisionWare, Inc. (1986) Write right with Right-Writer. *Byte*, Oct, 284.

DeLamarter, R. T. (1986a) *Big Blue: IBM's Use and Abuse of Power*. New York: Dodd, Mead.

DeLamarter, R. T. (1986b) Square pegs, round holes, big bucks. *Datamation*, 1 Oct, 52–60.

Deloitte Haskins & Sells (1986) Fears of the Big Bang, hi-tech crash out. *Banking World*, Oct, 39.

DeMarco, T. (1978) *Structured Analysis and System Specification*, New York: Yourdon, Inc. DeMarco, T. (1981a) *5th Int. Conf. Software Eng.*

DeMarco, T. (1981b) *Yourdon 1978–80 Project Survey Final Report*, New York: Yourdon, Inc., Sept.

DeMarco, T. (1982) *Controlling Software Projects*, Englewood Cliffs, New Jersey: Yourdon Press.

Denning, P. J., Comer, D. E., Gries, D., Mulder, M. C. *et al.* (1989) Computing as a Discipline. *Communications of the ACM*, Jan, 9–23.

DeRose, B. and Nyman, T. (1978) The software life cycle – a management and technological challenge in the Department of Defense. *IEEE Trans. Software Eng.*, 4(4), 309–18.

Deutsch, M. S. (1979) Verification and validation. In *Software Engineering*. (eds R. W. Jensen and C. C. Tonies) Englewood Cliffs, New Jersey: Prentice-Hall, Inc., 329–408.

Deutsch, M. (1981) Software project verification and validation. *Computer*, April, 54–70.

Deutsch, M. S., and Willis, R. R. (1988) *Software quality engineering: a total technical and management approach*, Englewood Cliffs, New Jersey: Prentice-Hall, Inc.

Development (1983) Development time cut. *ComputerWeek*, 10 Jan, 5.

Devenny, T. J. (1976) An exploratory study of software cost estimating at the electronic systems division. Thesis no. GSM/SM/765-4, Air Force Institute of Technology, Dayton, OH, July.

Deyzel, W. (1978) Letter to editor. *Systems Stelsels*, Aug, 34.

Diamond, S. (1986) The laser's edge: electronic publishing. *Modern Office Technology*, Nov, 50–62.

Dick, C. (1980) The big rip-off. *Systems for information management*, July, 45–6.

Dickmann, R. A. (1971) *Personnel implications for business data processing*, New York: John Wiley & Sons.

Dickson, A. (1987) The effective systems for resource management. *GBS Network*, May, VIII.

Dickson, G. W. and Powers, R. F. (1973) MIS project management: myths, opinions and reality, in *Information Systems Administration*. (eds F. W. McFarlan, R. L. Nolan and D. P. Norton) Holt, Rinehart and Winston, Inc., 406.

Dickson, G. W. and Simmons, J. K. (1976) The behaviour side of MIS. *Readings in Management Information Systems*. (eds G. B. Davis and G. C. Everest) McGraw-Hill, Inc.

Dieperink, J. H. (1977) Software, minis and small businesses. *Systems Stelsels*, March, 12–15.

Dight, J. (1986) Grow your own programmers. *Datamation*, 1 July, 75–8.

Dijkstra, E. C. (1965) Programming considered as a human activity. *Proc. IFIP Congress 65*, Washington, D. C.: Spartan Books.

Dijkstra, E. (1968a) GOTO statement considered harmful. *Communications of the ACM*, March, 147–8.

Dijkstra, E. (1968b) The structure of the 'THE' multiprogramming system. *Communications of the ACM*, May, 341–6.

DISPO (1982) The latest in time management by DISPO. Supplement to *Your Family*, Feb.

Dittman, J. T. (1980) *Transferability Factor Manual*, Veterans Administration, Colombia, MO 65201, March.

Doepel, P. S. (1977) There is nothing more difficult . . . than a new order. *Systems Stelsels*, Feb, 8–9.

Doepel, P. (1984) Escom's DP history. *Computing at Escom – '84*, March, 38–9.

Dolotta, T. A., *et al.* (1976) *Data Processing in 1980–85*, New York: John Wiley & Sons.

Dolotta, T. A., Haight, R. C. and Mashey, J. R. (1978) The programmers' workbench. *Bell System Technical Journal*, July–Aug, 2177–2200.

Dolphin, A. T. (1978) Operations status – time for review. *Systems Stelsels*, June, 19–20.

Donaldson, H. (1975) Distributed systems overview. *Data Systems*, Feb, 9.

Dorsman, M. and Griffith, J. (1986) *Small and medium-sized firms, new technology and training: a case for change.* Centre for Educational Development and Training, Manchester Polytechnic, Manchester.

Douglas, H. (1979) Poacher's forecast. *Computronics*, 11 July, 1, 12.

Doyle, L. W. (1986) Understanding misunderstood electronic mail. *Today's Office*, Jan, 35–40.

Drasch, F. J. (1986) LISP library and C programming environment. *Byte*, Nov, 44.

Dreyfus, H. L. and Dreyfus, S. E. (1986) *Mind over Machine*, Blackwell.

Drucker, P. F. (1954) *The Practice of Management*, New York: Harper & Row.

Druffel, L. E. (1982) *Strategy for a DoD Software Initiative*, Washington, DC: CSS DUSD(RAT). Also in (Boehm and Standish, 1983).

Duffy, N. M. (1976) Towards more effective information systems. *Systems Stelsels*, Aug, 35–7.

Duffy, Prof. N. (1983) Wits tests six languages. *Computing S.A.*, 15 April, 2–3.

Dufner, R. F. (1986) MBAs and MIS. *Datamation*, 1 Nov, 15.

Dunn, R. and Ullman, R. (1982) *Quality Assurance for Computer Software*. New York: McGraw-Hill.

Dunsmore, H. E. (1985) The effect of comments, mnemonic names, and modularity: some university experiment results. *Proc. 2nd Symp. Empirical Foundations of Information and Software Sciences*.

Dunsmore, H. E. and Gannon, J. D. (1980) Analysis of the effects of programming factors on programming effort. *J. Systems and Software*, **1** (2), 141–53.

During, P. (1978) The Cinderella of career courses. *Systems Stelsels*, Jan, 2–5.

Dvorak, J. C. (1989) *PC Magazine*, 12 Sept, 73.

Dyer, Dr. W. W. (1978) *Pulling Your Own Strings*. New York: Avon Books.

Easirun International (1988) Who says COBOL is dead? *ComputerWeek*, 12 Sept, 24.

Eberhard, M. H. (1976) Computer Society – Newsletter. *Systems Stelsels*, Oct, 38–40.

Edmonds, M. (1983) Firms must encourage DP training. *ComputerWeek*, 29 Aug, 9.

Education (1984) *Computing at Escom – '84*, March, 26–7.

Edwards, C. (1983a) DPers still get top pay. *Computing S.A.*, 16 Sept, 1, 3.

Edwards, C. (1983b) 4th generation cuts 2-year job to 6 weeks. *Computing S.A.*, 22 July, 4.

Edwards, C. (1984) Visi-On finally on here. *Computing S.A.*, 27 Jan, 5.

Edwards, C. and Loveday, P. (1982) White-collar boost. *Computing S.A.*, 18 June, 16.

Edwards, J. B. (1990) High performance without compromise. *Datamation*, 1 July, 53–8.

Elshoff, J. L. (1977) The influence of structured programming on PL/1 program profiles. *IEEE Trans. Software Eng.*, **3** (5), 364–8.

Elshoff, J. L. (1978) A review of software measurement studies at General Motors Research Laboratories. *Proc. US Army/IEEE 2nd Software Life Cycle Management Conf.*, Atlanta, August, 172–3.

Endres, A. (1975) An analysis of errors and their causes in system programs. *Proc. 1975 Int. Conf. Reliable Software*, April, IEEE Cat. No. 75CH0840-7CSR, 327–36.

Enos, J. C. and Van Tilburg, R. L. (1979) Software design, in *Software Engineering*, (ed. R. W. Jensen and C. C. Tonies) Englewood Cliffs, New Jersey: Prentice-Hall, Inc., 64–220.

Equatorial Communications Co. (1986) Satellite bypass. *Datamation*, 1 July, 100.

Erickson, R. (1982) Small gains only from OA. *Computing S.A.*, 18 June, 4.

Etheridge, J. (1990) A proprietary faith for mid-range users. *Datamation*, 1 May, 102–104.

Etheridge, J., Martin, J., Poe, R. and Tate, P. (1987) From DP dept. to IS Inc. *Datamation*, 1 Nov, 56-2–56-8.

Eurich, N. P. (1985) *Corporate classrooms: the learning business*, The Carnegie Foundation for the Advancement of Teaching, Princeton New Jersey.

Evans, G. E., and Simkin, M. G. (1989) What best predicts computer proficiency? *Communications of the ACM*, Nov, 1322–7.

Ever, J. (1980) Productivity – DP and end user. *Systems Stelsels*, Jan, 12–13.

Fagan, M. E. (1976) Design and code inspections to reduce errors in program development. *IBM Systems Journal*, 15 (3), 182–211.

Fagan, M. E. (1977) Inspecting software design and code. *Datamation*, Oct, 133–44.

Fagan, M. E. (1986) Advances in software inspections. *IEEE Trans. Software Eng.*, 12 (7), 744–51.

Fairley, R. E. (1985) *Software Engineering Concepts*, New York: McGraw-Hill, Inc.

Farquhar, J. A. (1970) A preliminary inquiry into the software estimation process. RM-6271-PR, The Rand Corp., Aug.

Fassl, J. (1986) Interactive video instruction. *Words*, Oct–Nov, 14–16.

Fast, J. (1981) *Body Language*, London: Pan Books Ltd.

Feeney, W. and Sladek, F. (1977) The systems analyst as a change agent. *Datamation*, Nov, 85–8.

Felton, P. (1988) AA adopts Natural 2. *Computing S.A.*, 1 Feb, 5.

Fenton, N. E. (1991) *Software Metrics: A Rigorous Approach*, London: Chapman & Hall.

Ferg, S. (1986) Data independence and the relational DBMS. *Datamation*, 1 Nov, 103–106.

Fernberg, P. M. (1986) Ohio Bureau of Motor Vehicles. *Modern Office Technology*, Nov, 74–80.

Ferralli, A. and Ferralli, K. (1986) Interactive video – a tool for changing times. *Media and Methods*, Jan–Feb, 10–12.

Festinger, L. A. (1957) *A Theory of Cognitive Dissonance*, Evanston, Ill.: Row, Peterson.

Feuer, A. R. and Fowlkes, E. B. (1979) Relating computer program maintainability to software measures. *Proc. 1979 National Computer Conference*. New York: June, 1003–12.

Fialkoff, B. S. (1981) Output problems traced to DPer stress. *Computing S.A.*, 22 April, 21.

Figueroa, G. (1990) PICK & UNIX: Strategic product alliance. *PICK Database News*, Jan, 4, 8.

Finlayson, D. (1979) Increased investment to boost office productivity. *Systems Stelsels*, Nov, 32.

Fisher, E. M. (1986) The dream machine. *Datamation*, 1 Oct, 79–84.

Fitz-Enz, J. (1978) Who is the DP professional? *Datamation*, Sept., 124–9.

Fitzsimmons, A. and Love, T. (1978) A review and evaluation of software science. *Computing Surveys*, 10 (1), 3–18.

Flaherty, M. J. (1985) Programming process productivity measurement system for System/370. *IBM Systems Journal*, 24(2), 168–75.

Fletcher, J. G. (1974) Restructured programming. *Datamation*, March, 29ff.

Folb, L. (1984) Users go it alone. *SA Software News*, March, i ff.

Fong, E. N. (1973) Improving compiler diagnostics. *Datamation*, April, 84–6.

Forage, G. (1986) *4th generation languages and advanced development aids 1984/5*. Inbucon, quoted in: 4GL software gets high UK marks for productivity. *Computing S.A.*, 6 Jan, 20.

Ford, L. (1986) A new intelligent tutoring system. *Interactive Learning International*, 3(4).

Ford, T. (1983) FGS cuts need for DP staff. *SA Software News*, Sept, 5.

Fordham, E. (1988) Voice Mail afloat. *Business Equipment Digest*, April, 33–4.

Forest, W. (1985) Vendor sponsored conferences – are they worth the trip? *AgriComp*, Nov–Dec, 38–9.

Formica, G. (1978) Software management by the European Space Agency: Lessons learned and future plans. *Proc. 3rd Into Software Management Conf.*, AIAA/RAeS, London, Oct, 15–35.

Foster, D. (1987) GOTO, one more time. *Communications of the ACM*, Aug, 659.

Fox Software (1986) FoxBASE wins the dBASE race! *Byte*, Oct, 20.

Frangos, N. (1980) Specialise in growth area is Frangos formula. *Systems for information management*, May, 10.

Frank, D. N. (1990) The software doctor. *Datamation*, 15 Jan, 12.

Frater, G. (1983) Quiet revolution reaches crescendo. *SA Software News*, Sept, 9.

Freeman, R. D. (1975) An experiment in software development. *The Bell System Technical Journal*, Special Safeguard Supplement, S199–S209.

Freiman, F. R. and Park, R. E. (1979) PRICE Software Model – Version 3: An overview. *Proc. IEEE-PINY Workshop on Quantitative Software Models*, IEEE Catalog No. TH0067-9, Oct, 32–41.

Fries, M. J. (1977) Software error data acquisition.

RADC-TR-77-130, Boeing Aerospace Co., Seattle, Wash., (NTIS AD/A-039916).

FTP (1983) Management assessment of user-driven technologies, quoted in: US survey finds corporate micros are white elephants. *Computing S.A.*, 29 July, 7.

Fujitsu (1986) Introducing the new team of Fujitsu business modems. *Datamation*, 1 Nov, 20–1.

Future Computing, Inc. (1985/86) The Personal Computer in large organisations, quoted in *IT News*, Dec 85/Jan 86, 4–5.

Galinier, M. (1978) Personal communication to B. W. Boehm. University of Toulouse.

Gallup (1990) UK women put the family first. *The Argus*, 15 Feb, 11.

Games, P. A., and Klare, G. R. (1967) *Elementary Statistics: Data Analysis for the Behavioral Sciences*, New York: McGraw-Hill Book Company.

Gane, C. (1988) *Computer-aided software engineering: the methodologies, the products, the future*, Rapid System Development, Inc., New York, NY.

Gane, C. and Sarson, T. (1979) *Structured Systems Analysis: Tools and Techniques*, Englewood Cliffs, New Jersey: Prentice-Hall, Inc.

Gannon, C. (1979) Error detection using path testing and static analysis. *Computer*, IEEE Computer Society Magazine, Aug, 26–31.

Gannon, J. D. (1977) An experimental evaluation of data type conventions. *Communications of the ACM*, Aug, 584–95.

Gannon, J. D. and Horning, J. J. (1975) The impact of language design on the production of reliable software. *IEEE Trans. Software Eng.*, 1 (2), 179–91.

Garber, A. (1976) A case for RPG. *Systems Stelsels*, Oct, 28–9.

Garcia-Rose, L. and Fosdick, H. (1990) The maturation of DB2. *Datamation*, 15 March, 75–80.

Garnham, D. (1988) First-class ticket to Quality Street. *ComputerWeek*, 7 Nov, 14–15. Reprinted from: *Computing U.K.*

Gayle, J. B. (1971) Multiple regression techniques for estimating computer programming cost. *J. Systems Mgmt*, Feb, 13–16.

Gehring, P. F., Jr. (1976) A quantitative analysis of estimating accuracy in software development. PhD dissertation, Texas A&M University, Aug.

Gelb, J. P. (1989) System-managed storage. *IBM Systems Journal*, 28 (1), 77–103.

Gell, J. J. (1986) Office publishing opens new windows. *The Office*, Nov, 101–102.

Gellerman, S. W. (1963) *Motivation and Productivity*, American Management Association Executive Books, New York.

General Accounting Office (1977) Problems found with government acquisition and use of computers from November 1965 to December 1976. Report FGMSD-77-14, GAO, Washington, DC, March.

Gerhart, S. L. and Yelowitz, L. (1976) Observations of fallibility in applications of modern programming methodologies. *IEEE Trans. Software Eng.*, 2 (3), 195–207.

Gewald, K., *et al.* (1977) *Software Engineering, Grundlagen und Technik rationeller Programmentwicklung*, Oldenbourg.

Gibbs, N. E. (1989) The SEI Education Program: the challenge of teaching future software engineers. *Communications of the ACM*, May, 594–605.

Gilb, T. (1977) *Software Metrics*, Cambridge, Massachusetts: Winthrop Publishers.

Gilb, T. (1988) *Principles of Software Engineering Management*, Wokingham, Berkshire: Addison-Wesley Publishing Co.

Gilchrist, B., and Weber, R. E. (1972) Employment of trained computer personnel – A quantitative survey. *Proc. 1972 Spring Joint Computer Conf.*, 641–8.

Gilchrist, B. *et al.* (1983) The DP population boom. *Datamation*, Sept, 100–110.

Gildersleeve, T. R. (1974a) *Data Processing Project Management*, New York: Van Nostrand Reinhold Company.

Gildersleeve, T. R. (1974b) Organizing the data processing function. *Datamation*, Nov, 46–50.

Gildersleeve, T. R. (1975) The dark side of structured programming. *Datamation*, Nov, 178–80.

Gildersleeve, T. R. (1978) *Successful Data Processing System Analysis*, Englewood Cliffs, New Jersey: Prentice-Hall, Inc.

Gill, P. J. (1982) Putting 'knowledge workers' on-line. *Computer Systems in Southern Africa*, May, 21–23. Reprinted from: *Information Systems News*.

Gillenson, M. L. (1985) *DATABASE: Step-by-Step*, New York: John Wiley & Sons, Inc.

Gillin, P. (1983) Jungle never same again. *Computing S.A.*, 21 Jan, 11–12.

Gillings, J. L. (1987) If you can take it, more on GOTOs. *Communications of the ACM*, Nov, 980–1.

Gintowt, G. M. (1987) A funny thing happened on the way to the forum. *Communications of the ACM*, July, 633.

Glass, R. L. (1979) *Software Reliability Guidebook*, Englewood Cliffs, New Jersey: Prentice-Hall, Inc.

Glass, R. L., and Noiseux, R. A. (1981) *Software*

Maintenance Guidebook, Englewood Cliffs, New Jersey: Prentice-Hall, Inc.

Goetz, M. A. (1986) Benchmarks show strength of online and batch operations. *ADRWARE News*, **3** (2), 1, 11.

Goldberg, J. (ed.) (1973) *Proc. Symp. High Cost of Software*, Stanford Research Institute, Stanford, CA, Sept, 63.

Golding, D. H. G. (1978) *Project Planning and Control*, Manchester: NCC Publications.

Golding, S. (1986) Illusory speed differences. *Computing S.A.*, 5 May, 8.

Good, D. I., London, R. L. and Bledsoe, W. W. (1975) An interactive program verification system. *IEEE Trans. Software Eng.*, April, 59–67.

Goodenough, J. B. and Gerhart, S. L. (1975) Toward a theory of test data selection. *IEEE Trans. Software Eng.*, **1**(2), June, 156–73.

Goodman, M. (1978) Novel computer shorthand developed in S.A. *Systems Stelsels*, Feb, 33.

Goodman, T. and Spence, R. (1978) The effect of system response time on interactive computer aided problem solving. *ACM SIGGRAPH '78 Conf. Proc.*, 100–104.

Goodwin, C. (1986) Will 'structured' languages work in commercial programming? *Computer-Week*, 15 Sept, 12–13. Reprinted from: *Computing U.K.*

Gordon, J. D., Capstick, C. K. and Salvadori, A. (1977) An empirical study of COBOL programmers. *INFOR*, June, 229–41.

Gordon, R. D. and Halstead, M. H. (1976) An experiment comparing FORTRAN programming times with the software physics hypothesis. *Proc. National Computer Conference*, 45, AFIPS Press, Montvale, New Jersey, 935–7.

Gould, J. D. (1975) Some psychological evidence on how people debug computer programs. *Int. J. Man–Machine Studies*, **7** (2), 151–82.

Gould, J. D. and Drongowski, P. (1974) An exploratory study of computer program debugging. *Human Factors*, **16**, 258–77.

Gould, J. D., Boies, S. J. and Lewis, C. (1991) Making usable, useful, productivity-enhancing computer applications. *Communications of the ACM*, Jan, 74–85.

Grandison, S. (1986) Integration disintegrates. *Micro Decision*, April, 25–6.

Grant, E. and Sackman, H. (1966) An exploratory investigation of programmer performance under on-line and off-line conditions. Report SP-2581, System Development Corp., September.

Graver, C. A., *et al.* (1977) *Cost reporting elements and activity cost trade-offs for defense system software*, General Research Corp., Santa Barbara, CA, March.

Gray, D. (1980a) More training needed – claim consultancies! *Computronics*, 16 April, 8.

Gray, D. (1980b) Salary and wage trends. *The 1979/80 S.A. Computer Guide*, Johannesburg: Thomson Publications (Pty) Ltd, 19–21.

Gray, D. (1980c) How much does your DP professional cost you? *The 1979/80 S.A. Computer Guide*. Johannesburg: Thomson Publications (Pty) Ltd, 26.

Gray, D. (1980d) The Personnel Market 1979/80. *The 1979/80 S.A. Computer Guide*, Johannesburg: Thomson Publications (Pty) Ltd, 22–4.

Green, T. R. G. (1977) Conditional program statements and their comprehensibility to professional programmers. *J. Occupational Psychology*, **50**, 93–109.

Greenstein, C. (1978) *Dictionary of Logical Terms and Symbols*, Van Nostrand Reinhold.

Greyling, B. (1987) Screens help headaches. *The Sunday Star Computing*, 18 Oct, X.

Griffin, E. L. (1980) Real-time estimating. *Datamation*, June, 188–198.

Griffiths, M. (1986) Interactive video at work. *Programmed Learning and Educational Technology*, **23** (3).

Grilz, A. F. (1981) Designing a successful user–computer dialogue. *Computing S.A.*, 1 April, 15–16.

Grindley, K. (1980) Overcoming the programmer shortage. *Computing S.A.*, 13 Aug, 6–9.

Grochow, J. M. (1981). Application generators anticipate requirements. *Computing S.A.*, 22 April, 18.

Grosch, H. (1978) IBM technology goodies coming out of closet. *Systems Stelsels*, Dec, 26.

Grossberg, M., Wiesen, R. A. and Yntema, D. B. (1976) An experiment on problem solving with delayed computer responses. *IEEE Trans. Systems, Man, and Cybernetics*, **6** (3), 219–22.

Grossman, L. (1978) *Fat Paper – Diets for Trimming Paperwork*, McGraw-Hill.

Gruenberger, F. (1974) Structured programming. *Datamation*, Feb, 27–8.

Grulke, W. (1983) The businessman as mass consumer of computing. *IBM Inform*, Aug, VI, VIII.

GUIDE Inc. (1979) GUIDE survey of new programming technologies. *GUIDE Proc.*, Chicago, IL, 306–308.

Guimaraes, T. (1987) Prototyping: Orchestrating for success. *Datamation*, 1 Dec, 101–106.

Gullo, K. (1986) Joining the ranks. *Datamation*, 1 Oct, 24.

Gullo, K. (1987) Steady as she goes. *Datamation*, 15 Jan, 37–40.

Gunning, R. (1962) *Techniques of Clear Writing*, New York: McGraw-Hill.

Gunther, R. C. (1978) *Management Methodology for Software Product Engineering*, New York: John Wiley & Sons.

Gurbaxani, V. and Whang, S. (1991) The impact of information systems on organizations and markets. *Communications of the ACM*, Jan, 59–73.

Guynes, J. L. (1988) Impact of system response time on state anxiety. *Communications of the ACM*, March, 342–7.

Hackman, J. R., Oldham, G. R., Janson, R. and Purdy, K. (1975) A new strategy for job enrichment. *California Management Review*, **17** (4), 57–71.

Haigh, J. (1980) A concern for the future. *Systems for information management*, Nov, 4–5.

Hall, M. F. (1986) The video edge. *Impact: Office Automation*, Feb, 2–4.

Hall, R. P. (1987) Seven ways to cut software maintenance costs. *Datamation*, 15 July, 81–4.

Halstead, M. H. (1977) *Elements of Software Science*, New York: Elsevier North-Holland.

Halstead, M. H. (1978) Software science: A progress report. *Proc. US Army/IEEE 2nd Software Life Cycle Management Conf.*, Atlanta, August, 174–9.

Hamilton, M. and Zeldin, S. (1976) Higher order software: A methodology for defining software. *IEEE Trans. Software Eng.*, **2** (1) March.

Hamlyn, J. and Minto, A. (1988) Acquisitions causing an increase in staff turnover. *Computer-Week*, 5 Dec, 5.

Hammond, C. (1986) The hazards of VDUs. *Practical Computing*, June, 73–5.

Hanata, S. (1989) Management of software production, in *Japanese Perspectives in Software Engineering*, (eds Y. Matsumoto and Y. Ohno). Singapore: Addison-Wesley Publishers Ltd., 279–301.

Hansen, J. V. (1976) Man-machine communication: An experimental analysis of heuristic problem-solving under on-line and batch-processing conditions. *IEEE Trans. Systems, Man and Cybernetics*, **6**, (11), 746–52.

Harding, N. (1986) Products must be perfectly matched. *ComputerWeek FOCUS on IBM Compatibles and the BUNCH*, March, 14.

Harr, J. (1969) Programming experience for the number 1 electronic switching system. *Proc. AFIPS Spring Joint Computer Conf.*

Harris, N. (1983) Free software arrives in SA. *SA Software News*, July, 9.

Harrison, M. J. (1987) A funny thing happened on the way to the forum. *Communications of the ACM*, July, 634.

Hart, M. B. (1986) Status of office systems in 29 Texas companies. *Office Systems Research J.*, Spring, 1–9.

Hartley, I. (1984) Helderberg starts training series. *Computing S.A.*, 23 March, 11.

Hartwick, R. D. (1977) Software verification and validation. *Proc. AIAA Software Management Conf.*, Washington, DC.

Harvey, D. A. (1990) Optical storage primer. *Byte*, IBM Special Edition, Fall, 121–30.

Hawkridge, D., Newton, W. and Hall, C. (1988) *Computers in Company Training*, London: Croom Helm Ltd.

Hayden, T. L. (1982) *One Child*, London: Sphere Books Limited.

Hayes, F. (1992) Exploding desktop myths. *Unix-World*, April, 38–44.

Hayman, A. (1982) Backlogs threaten computer efficiency. *ComputerWeek*, 30 Aug, 16.

Heaford, J. M. (1983) *Myth of the learning machine: the theory and practice of computer based training*, Sigma Technical Press, Wilmslow.

Heath, W. (1986) MEDICL computer system, saving money and lives. *Health Service J.*, 6 Nov, 1458.

Hecht, Sturm, and Trattner (1977) Reliability measurement during software development. *Proc. AIAA Conf. Computers in Aerospace.*

Heller, R. (1981) *The Business of Winning*, Paperback edn, London: Sidgwick & Jackson.

Helmer, O. (1966) *Social Technology*, New York: Basic Books.

Heninger, K. (1980) Specifying software requirements for complex systems: New techniques and their application. *IEEE Trans. Software Eng.*, **6** (1), 2–13.

Henkel, T. (1983) DP centre will die, say researchers. *Computing S.A.*, 13 May, 3.

Henneberry-Muratore, C. (1986) User groups find strength in numbers. *Bank Systems & Equipment*, Nov, 110–13.

Hennecke, H. (1981) The electronic office: One giant leap or gradual exploration? *Computer Systems in Southern Africa*, Oct, 13–16.

Herd, J. R., Postak, J. N., Russell, W. E. and Stewart, K. R. (1977) *Software Cost Estimation*

Study – Study Results, final technical report, RADC-TR-77-220, Vol. 1 (of two), Doty Associates, Inc., Rockville, MD, June.

Herndon, M. A. and Keenan, A. P. (1978) Analysis of error remediation expenditures during validation. *3rd Int. Conf. Software Eng.*, May, 202–206.

Hersey, P. and Blanchard, K. H. (1976) *Situational leadership*, Center for Leadership Studies, San Diego, California.

Herzberg, F., Mausner, B. and Snyderman, B. B. (1959) *The Motivation to Work*, New York: John Wiley & Sons.

Hesse, W. (1981) Methoden und Werkzeuge zur Software-Entwicklung – Ein Marsch durch die Technologie-Landschaft. *Informatik Spektrum*, **4**.

Hester, S. *et al.* (1981) Using documentation as a software design median. *Bell System Technical Journal*, **60**(8).

Hetzel, W. C. (ed.) (1973) *Program Test Methods*, Englewood Cliffs, New Jersey: Prentice-Hall, Inc.

Hetzel, W. C. (1976) *An Experimental Analysis of Program Verification Methods*. PhD dissertation, University of North Carolina at Chapel Hill.

Hetzel, W. (1987) *The Complete Guide to Software Testing*, 2nd edn, Wellesley, MA: QED Information Sciences, Inc.

Higgins, D. (1987) *Data Structured Software Maintenance: The Warnier–Orr Approach*, Dorset House.

Hinomoto, H. (1980) Attitude Study of On-Line Terminal Operators on Work-Station Arrangements. *Information & Management*, **3**, 237–43.

Hirschbuhl, J. J. (1986) The impact of training in enlightened countries. *Interactive Learning International*, **3** (3).

Hoard, B. (1981) Survey shows less than half use DBMS. *Computing S.A.*, 1 April, 12–13.

Hoare, C.A.R. (1971) Proof of a Program: FIND. *Communications of the ACM*, Jan, 39–43.

Hoare, C.A.R. (1975) Data reliability. *Proc. 1975 Int. Conf. Reliable Software*, April, IEEE Cat. No. 75CH0940-7CSR, 528–33.

Hodges, P. (1987a) Do the big eight add up? *Datamation*, 15 Feb, 62–8.

Hodges, P. (1987b) Three decades by the numbers. *Datamation*, 15 Sept, 77–87.

Hodges, P. (1987c) What are you worth? *Datamation*, 1 Oct, 78–92.

Hogan, T. (1986) C versus Assembly – C plus Assembly. *Byte*, Extra edn, 267–84.

Hohmann, M. (1988) PICK installed base shows steady growth. *Computing S.A.*, 25 July, 32.

Holgate, P. (1983) Management to enter new era. *SA Software News*, July, 15.

Holton, J. B. (1977) Are the new programming techniques being used? *Datamation*, July, 97–103.

Holtshousen, R. T., Moore, M. V. E., O'Neill, C. and Tuttelberg, L. R. P. (1979) HIHO – a recipe for better systems. *Systems Stelsels*, March, 24–5.

Holtz, D. H. (1979) A nonprocedural language for on-line applications. *Datamation*, April, 167–76.

Hopkins, M. (1970) *Software Engineering Techniques*, (eds J. N. Buxton and B. Randell) Brussels: NATO Scientific Affairs Division, April.

Hopkins, M. E. (1972) A case for the GOTO. *Proc. 25th ACM Nat. Conf.*, **2**, 787–90.

Hopkins, M. E. (1987) A perspective on the 801/reduced instruction set computer. *IBM Systems Journal*, **26**(1), 107–21.

Hopkinson, J. (1986) Prototyping in computer systems development. *Management Services*, Dec, 18–21.

Hossack, R. (1986) Knowledge workers are the key to better productivity. *Office Equipment and Methods*, Jan–Feb, 83–8.

Howard, B. and Kunkel, G. (1988) More than meets the eye: designing great graphics. *PC Magazine*, 27 Sept, 92–104.

Howard, G. S. (1989) Review of (Modell, 1988). *Computing Reviews*, Sept, 474–5.

Howden, W. E. (1982) Contemporary software development environments. *Communications of the ACM*, May, 318–28.

Huang, A. (1986) Bell Labs develops optical logic device. *Byte*, Oct, 9.

Hughes Aircraft (1989) Hughes latest in US consortium. *Computing S.A.*, 30 Jan, 17.

Hughes, C. T. and Clark, J. D. (1990) The stages of CASE usage. *Datamation*, 1 Feb, 41–4.

Humphrey, W. S. (1985) The IBM large-systems software development process: Objectives and direction. *IBM Systems Journal*, **24** (2), 76–8.

Huskisson, A. I. (1977) Trends in the computer industry. *Systems Stelsels*, Dec, 31–3.

Hutinger, P. C. (1986) Computer hardware. *Media and Methods*, Sept–Oct, 43–6.

Hwang, S.-S. V. (1981) An empirical study in functional testing, structural testing, and code reading inspection. Scholarly Paper 362, Department of Computer Science, University of Maryland, College Park, MD.

Hyman, S. (1982) Personnel. *The 1982 S.A. Computer Users Handbook*, Johannesburg: Systems Publishers (Pty) Ltd, K1–K3.

Hymers, N. (1983) Friendly systems often turn nasty. *SA Software News*, Sept, 11.

Hymers, N. (1987) Only one on the block. *Computer Mail*, 27 Feb, 43–4.

IBM (1974) *HIPO: A Design Aid and Documentation Technique*, GC20-1851. White Plains, NY: IBM Corp.

IBM (1976) IBM's System/32 Leaps Ahead. *Systems Stelsels*, April, 21.

IBM (1979) The best man for the job may already be working for you. *Systems Stelsels*, Sept, 34.

IBM (1980) IBM aims to assist users education. *Dataweek*, 11 Jan, 9.

IBM (1983) IBM enhances application system. *Computer Systems in Southern Africa*, April, 33.

IBM (1985) IBM enhancements for AS. *Computing S.A.*, 15 July, 12.

IBM (1986) IBM ASCII terminals: The case in black and white. *Datamation*, 15 Aug, 48–9.

IBM (1987) *Application System General Information* (Release 5), 3rd edn, GH45-5000-2. IBM Corp., Mechanicsburg, PA, April.

IBM (1988a) IBM's 4GL – planning for tomorrow. *ComputerWeek*, 22 Aug, 31.

IBM (1988b) *SQL/Data System: Application Programming for VM/System Product and VM/Extended Architecture System Product*, Version 2 Release 2, SH09-8019-01. IBM Corp.

IBM (1988c) *Virtual Machine/System Product: Administration*, Release 6., 2nd edn, SH24-5285-01. IBM Corp., July.

IBM (1990a) Announcing AD/Cycle. *Datamation*, 15 Feb, 33.

IBM (1990b) IBM's most popular secret. *Datamation*, 1 Nov, 114.

ICL (1983) ICL package boosts output. *SA Software News*, July, 14.

Ideal Software Ltd (1986) Superchargers for hard disks. *Byte*, Nov, 48H.

Index Technology Corporation (1986) We increased productivity 35% on our first project with Excelerator . . . *Datamation*, 1 Oct, 114.

Index Technology Corporation (1987) Develop better systems using Excelerator – over 8000 systems professionals already do. *Datamation*, 1 Jan, 29.

Information Builders, Inc. (1987) *FOCUS: Product Introduction: TABLETALK*, New York. (no date, but about 1987).

Infotech International (1978) *State of the Art Report: System Reliability and Integrity*, in: *Reliability*.

Infotech International (1979) *State of the Art Report: Structured Software Development*, in: *Systems Stelsels*, June, 26.

Infra-Structures, Inc. (1986) If downtime is a major risk, we suggest a minor adjustment. *Datamation*, 1 Nov, 81.

Ingham, R. (1976) Estimation, planning, and control of programming activities. *Systems Stelsels*, Feb, 4–6.

Inmon, B. (1976) An example of structured design. *Datamation*, March, 82–6.

Installations (1983) *The 1983 S.A. Computer Users Handbook*, Johannesburg: Systems Publishers (Pty) Ltd, 1983, M1–M179.

Institution of Production Engineers (1986) *An investigation into the provision of continuing education and training*. Manpower Services Commission, Sheffield.

International Data Corporation (1980) Computer industry review and forecast 1974–1983. *The S.A. Computer Users Handbook 1980*, Braamfontein: Systems Publishers (Pty) Ltd. I, A9–A14.

International Data Corporation (1981) *Systems Development Productivity*, Waltham, MA: Jan.

Iovacchini, A. (1986) Midlantic enjoys 100% uptime in first 6 months with UPS. *Bank Systems & Equipment*, Feb, 60–1.

Itoh, D. and Izutani, T. (1973) FADEBUG-I, a new tool for program debugging. *Record of the 1973 IEEE Symp. Computer Software Reliability*. New York: IEEE 38–43.

Jackel, L. (1986) 'Neuron' chips emulate brain cells. *Byte*, Nov, 9.

Jackson, M. (1967) Mnemonics. *Datamation*, April.

Jackson, M. A. (1975) *Principles of Program Design*, London: Academic Press.

Jackson, M. A. (1983) *System Development*. New Jersey: Prentice-Hall.

James, S. (1980) Time for industry to police itself. *Systems for information management*, Dec, 8.

Japanese Ministry of International Trade and Industry (1987) *Software Talents in the Year 2000*, Tokyo: Computer-Age Publishing Co.

Jaybe Software (1986) C database management system toolkit. *Byte*, Nov, 44.

Jeffery, D. R. and Lawrence, M. J. (1979) An inter-organizational comparison of programming productivity. *Proc., 4th Int. Conf. Software Eng.*, IEEE Catalog No. 79 CH 1479-5C, Sept., 369–77.

Jensen, K. (1987) Screen to change face of VDUs. *Office Products News*, May, 1.

Jensen, R. W. (1984) A comparison of the Jensen and COCOMO schedule and cost estimation models. *Proc. Int. Soc. Parametric Analysis*, 96–106.

Johnson, D. (1980a) Improve software for greater

productivity. *Systems for information management*, Oct, 23.

Johnson, J. R. (1980b) *Managing For Productivity in Data Processing*, Wellesley, MA: QED Information Sciences, Inc.

Johnson, J. (1986) A CBT field study: productivity gains at Target Stores Inc., USA. *Interactive Learning International*, 1(3).

Johnston, P. (1980) BOREDOM – a growing disease among DP-men. *Systems Stelsels*, March, 33.

Jones, M. (1983a) End user driven computing. *Computer Systems in Southern Africa*, April, 26–8.

Jones, R. (1983b) Assembler outwits the sceptics. *ComputerWeek*, 12 Sept, 12–13.

Jones, R. (1986a) Finding a sixth sense solution. *PC: The Independent Guide to IBM Personal Computers*, March, 88–91.

Jones, T. C. (1977) Program quality and programmer productivity. IBM TR 02.764, 28 Jan.

Jones, T. C. (1978) Measuring programming quality and productivity. *IBM Systems Journal*, 17(1), 39–63.

Jones, T. C. (1979) The limits of productivity. *Proc. Jt SHARE/GUIDE/IBM Symp.*, Oct, 77–82.

Jones, T. C. (ed.) (1981) *Tutorial on Programming Productivity*, IEEE Catalog No. EHO 186-7, Computer Society, Los Angeles, CA.

Jones, T. C. (1983c) Technical and demographic trends in the computing industry. *Proc. the 1983 Data Systems Structured Design Conference*, Ken Orr & Associates, Topeka, KS, October, 3–27.

Jones, T. C. (1983d) Prevention and removal of programming defects. *Electrical Communication – The Technical Journal of ITT*, 57(4) 295–300.

Jones, C. L. (1985) A process-integrated approach to defect prevention. *IBM Systems J.*, 24 (2), 150–67.

Jones, T. C. (1986b) *Programming Productivity*, New York: McGraw-Hill Book Company.

Jones, T. C. (1991) *Applied Software Measurement: Assuring Productivity and Quality*, New York: McGraw-Hill, Inc.

Jones, L. C., and Nelson, D. A. (1976) 'A quantitative assessment of IBM's programming productivity techniques. *Proc., ACM/IEEE 13th Design Automation Conf.*, June.

Joyce, E. (1987) Software bugs: A matter of life and liability. *Datamation*, 15 May, 88–92.

Joyce, E. J. (1989) Is error-free software achievable? *Datamation*, 15 Feb, 53–6.

Judge, P. (1990) UNIX ports in Europe. *Datamation*, 1 Feb, 78–80.

Kammann, R. (1975) The comprehensibility of printed instructions and flowchart alternative. *Human Factors*, 17, 183–91.

Kapur and Associates (1979), in: How literate are SA programmers? *Dataweek*, 30 Nov, 3.

Kapur, G. (1980) Toward software engineering. *Computerworld*, 23 Oct, 1–10.

Kearney, J. K., Sedlmeyer, R. L., Thompson, W. B., Gray, M. A. and Adler, M. A. (1986) Software complexity measurement. *Communications of the ACM*, Nov, 1044–50.

Kearsley, G. (1983) *Computer-based training: a guide to selection and implementation*, Reading, Massachusetts: Addison-Wesley.

Kelly, R. (1988) UNIX market to grow by 135% during 1988. *ComputerWeek*, 8 Aug, 26.

Kelly, J. (1989) Three markets shape one industry. *Datamation*, 15 June, 6–19.

Kelso, T. S. (1987) Astronomical software benchmarks. *Sky & Telescope*, March, 309–10.

Kemerer, C. F. (1987) An empirical validation of software cost estimation models. *Communications of the ACM*, May, 416–29.

Kendall, R. C. (1978) *Management Perspectives on Programs, Programming, and Productivity*, IBM Corp., CHQ Div., White Plains, New York.

Kendall, R. C. and Lamb, E. C. (1977) Program usage studies. *Proc. GUIDE*, May.

Kernighan, B. W., Lesk, M. E. and Ossanna, J. F., Jr. (1978) Document preparation, *Bell System Technical Journal*, 57 (6), 2115–35.

Kernighan, B. W. and Plauger, P. J. (1974) *The Elements of Programming Style*, New York: McGraw-Hill Book Company.

Kernighan, B. W. and Ritchie, D. M. (1978) *The C Programming Language*, Englewood Cliffs, New Jersey: Prentice-Hall.

Kerr, S. (1987) 2 wounded pioneers attempt a comeback. *Datamation*, 1 Jan, 19–20.

Kerr, S. (1989) What's developing in large systems? *Datamation*, 1 June, 18–26.

Kessel, R. (1975) A new approach to system and program development. *Systems Stelsels*, Oct, 15–18.

Kessel, R. (1976) The computer software industry. *Systems Stelsels*, Oct, 31–3.

Kessler, P. (1986) Balanced lighting for the efficient office. *The Office*, Oct, 98–9.

Ketner, W. (1982) Videodisc interactive two dimensional equipment training, in *Proc. 4 Ann. Conf. Video Learning Systems Videodisc for Military Training and Simulation*. Aug 25–27, Arlington, Va. Society for Applied Learning Technology, Warrenton, Va., 18–20.

Kimberlin, D. (1982) US army air defense school distributed instructional system project evaluation, in *Proc. 4 Ann. Conf. Video Learning Systems Videodisc for Military Training and Simulation*. Aug 25–27, Arlington, Va. Society for Applied Learning Technology, Warrenton, Va., 21–3.

Kirchner, J. (1986) Federal computing: the good and the bad. *Datamation*, 15 Aug, 62–72.

Kirkley, J. (1978) Editor's readout. *Datamation*, July, 87.

Klein, Y. (1981) Exams show low training standards. *Computing S.A.*, 11 Dec, 1.

Kleinschrod, W. A. (1986) Thinking about automation in new and larger contexts. *Administrative Management*, March, 58.

Klerer, M. and May, J. (1965) A user-oriented programming language. *Computer Journal*, **8** (2), 103–109.

Klingler, D. E. (1986) Rapid prototyping revisited. *Datamation*, 15 Oct, 131–2.

Knight, B. (1978) On software quality and productivity. *Technical Directions*, IBM FSC, July, 21–7.

Knox, M. (1978) High expectations from management makes a good system. *Systems Stelsels*, Aug, 18–19.

Knuth, D. E. (1971) An empirical study of FORTRAN programs. *Software Practice and Experience*, **1**, April-June, 105–38.

Knuth, D. E. (1974) Structured programming with GOTO statements. *Computing Surveys*, Dec, 261–301.

Knuth, D. E. (1984) *The TeXbook*, Reading, Massachusetts: Addison-Wesley Publishing Co., Inc.

Koffler, R. P. (1986) Using ergonomic logic in designing offices. *The Office*, Oct, 15–18.

Koontz, H. and O'Donnell, C. (1972) *Principles of Management: An Analysis of Managerial Functions*, 5th edn, New York: McGraw-Hill.

Kopetz, H. (1979) *Software Reliability*, MacMillan Press.

Kosy, D. W. (1974) Air Force command and control information processing in the 1980s: Trends in software technology. US Air Force Proj. RAND, RAND Corp., Santa Monica, Calif., June.

Kosy, D. W. (1975) The ECSS II language for simulating computer systems. Rand Corp., rep. R-1895-GSA, Dec.

Kraft, P. (1977) *Programmers and Managers: The Routinization of Computer Programming in the United States*, New York: Springer-Verlag.

Kraft, P. and Weinberg, G. M. (1975) The profes-sionalization of programming. *Datamation*, Oct, 169–72.

Kraut, R., Dumais, S. and Koch, S. (1989) Computerization, productivity, and quality of work-life. *Communications of the ACM*, Feb, 220–38.

Kreitzman, L. (1986) Getting your fax right. *Marketing*, 20 March, 46–7.

Kroeber, D. W. and Watson, H. J. (1984) *Computer-based Information Systems: A Management Approach*, New York: Macmillan Publishing Company.

Kuekes, L. C. (1987) GOTO, one more time. *Communications of the ACM*, Aug, 660.

Kuflik, T. M. (1986) Quality is watchword in magnetic products. *The Office*, Nov, 48.

Lallande, A. (1987) Let the presses roll. *Datamation*, 15 Feb, 48-1–48-6.

Language Technology, Inc. (1987a) COBOL Analyzer. *Datamation*, 1 Jan, 106–108.

Language Technology, Inc. (1987b) If your company doesn't have any problems maintaining its old, unstructured COBOL, cross its name off this list. *Datamation*, 15 Feb, 40–1.

Larson, R. (1975) Test plan and test case inspection. IBM Kingston, New York. Technical Report 21.586, 4 April.

Law, D. and Longworth, G. (1987) *Systems Development: Strategies and Techniques*, Manchester: NCC Publications.

Lawrence, M. J. (1982) An examination of evolution dynamics. *Proc. 6th Int. Conf. Software Eng.*, Sept, 188–96.

Lawrence, P. R. and Lorsch, J. W. (1969) *Organization and Environment*, Homewood, Illinois: Richard D. Irwin, Inc.

le Roux, H. (1976) Minis – the new leaders? *Systems Stelsels*, April, 7.

Leaf, J. J. (1986) Staying in power. *Datamation*, 15 July, 67–72.

Lee, B. (1978) *Introducing Systems Analysis and Design*, 2 vols, Manchester: NCC Publications.

Lee, D. H. (1981) Complexity kills efficiency. *Computing S.A.*, 22 April, 15.

Lee, J. M. and Shneiderman, B. (1978) Personality and programming: Time-sharing vs. batch processing. *Proc. ACM Nat. Conf.*, 561–9.

Lee, M. (1986) Good structure aids efficiency. *ComputerWeek*, 23 June, 8–9.

Leherissey, B. L., O'Neil, H. F., Jr. and Hansen, D. N. (1971) Effects of memory support on state anxiety and performance in computer-assisted learning. *J. Educational Psychology*, May, 413–20.

Lehman, M. M. (1978) Laws and Conservation in

Large-Program Evolution. *Proc. US Army Second Software Life-Cycle Management Workshop*, IEEE Report 78CH-1390-4C, Aug, 140–5.

Lehman, M. M. and Belady, L. A. (1985) *Program evolution: processes of software change*, London: Academic Press.

Leibhammer, B. (1980) Costs go up – but output is down. *Systems for information management*, Nov, 13.

Lemmons, P. (1986) Byte and the 80386. *Byte*, Nov, 6.

Leopold, G. (1986) Beacon for the future. *Datamation*, 1 Oct, 109–10.

Lesgold, A. (1989) A coached practice environment for an electronics troubleshooting job, in *Computer Assisted Instruction and Intelligent Tutoring Systems: Shared Issues and Complimentary Approaches*, (eds J. Larking and R. Chabay) Lawrence Erlbaum, Hillsdale, N. J. To be published. (This work was referenced in (Stevens, 1989).)

Levendel, Y. (1990) Reliability analysis of large software systems: defect data modelling. *IEEE Trans. Software Eng.*, 16 (2), 141–52.

Levine, S. (1988) Yes, indeed! *Computing S.A.*, 21 Nov, 64.

Lewis, D. (1987) *Mind Skills: Giving Your Child a Brighter Future*, Guild Publishing, London.

Lientz, B. P. and Swanson, E. B. (1979) Software Maintenance: A user/management tug-of-war. *Data Management*, April, 26–30.

Lientz, B. P. and Swanson, E. B. (1980) *Software Maintenance Management: A Study of the Maintenance of Computer Application Software in 487 Data Processing Organizations*, Reading, MA: Addison-Wesley.

Lientz, B. P., Swanson, E. B. and Tompkins, G. E. (1978) Characteristics of application software maintenance. *Communications of the ACM*, June, 466–71.

Likert, R. (1961) *New Patterns of Management*, New York: McGraw-Hill.

Lim, P. A. (1980) *A Guide to Structured COBOL with Efficiency Techniques and Special Algorithms*, New York: Van Nostrand Reinhold Company.

Lindhorst, W. M. (1973) Scheduled maintenance of applications software. *Datamation*, May, 64–7.

Linger, R. C., Mills, H. D. and Witt, B. I. (1979) *Structured Programming: Theory and Practice*, Reading, Massachusetts: Addison-Wesley Publishing Company.

Lite, S. (1975) Using a system generator. *Datamation*, June, 44–7.

Littlewood, B. (1977) Software reliability measurements: Some criticisms and suggestions. *Software Phenomenology Working Papers of the Software Lifecycle Management Workshop*, US Army Institute for Research in Management Information and Computer Science, Aug, 473–87.

Lloyd, D. K., and Lipow, M. (1977) *Reliability, Management, Methods and Mathematics*, 2nd edn, published by the authors.

Logan, P. (1987) A beneficial scheme. *Communications of the ACM*, Nov, 982–4.

Logitech, Inc. (1986) LOGITECH MODULA-2/86 Holiday Package. *Byte*, Nov, 243.

Loh, M., and Nelson, R. R. (1989) Reaping CASE harvests. *Datamation*, 1 July, 31–4.

Londeix, B. (1987) *Cost Estimation for Software Development*, Wokingham, Berkshire: Addison-Wesley Publishers Ltd.

Long, L. E. (1979) *Data Processing Documentation and Procedures Manual*, Reston, Virginia: Reston Publishing Company, Inc.

Lott, Steven F. (1987) GOTO exit, already. *Communications of the ACM*, Nov, 907.

Love, T. (1977) Relating individual differences in computer programming performance to human information processing abilities. PhD dissertation, University of Washington.

Lowrie, C. K. (1983) The human connection. *Unisphere*, Jan.

Lu, C. (1986) The year that was (microcomputers). *High Technology*, Dec, 51–3.

Lucas, H. C., Jr. (1976) *Why information systems fail*, New York: McGraw-Hill, Inc.

Lucas, H. C., Jr. (1978) *Information Systems Concepts for Management*, Tokyo: McGraw-Hill Kogakusha, Ltd.

Lucas, H. C., Jr. (1985) *The Analysis, Design, and Implementation of Information Systems*, Singapore: McGraw-Hill Book Co.

Lucas, H. C., and Kaplan, R. B. (1976) A structured programming experiment. *The Computer Journal*, 19 (2), 136–8.

Lusterman, S. (1985) *Trends in corporate education and training*, The Conference Board, New York.

Lutz, T. (1980) *Proc. ITT Technology Planning Conf.*, Bolton, MA, June, 74–79.

Lutz, T. (1984) *Foundation for Growth – Productivity and Quality in Application Development*, Nolan, Norton and Company, Lexington, MA.

Lyne, R. (1980) Point-of-sales terminals promote profits. *Systems Stelsels*, Jan, 15–16.

Lyon, J. K. (1976) *The Database Administrator*, New York: John Wiley & Sons.

Macaskill, F. (1983) APL. *Computer Systems in Southern Africa*, April, 33.

Mace, S. (1986) Syntex calls on micros for training. *Infoworld*, **8**(16).

Macfie, D. (1988) Mantis and Ultra attack the mid-range market. *ComputerWeek*, 21 Nov, 23.

MacMillan, I.C. (1975) Politics and behaviour in organisations. *Systems Stelsels*, June, 12–13.

Macro, A. and Buxton, J. (1987) *The Craft of Software Engineering*, Wokingham: Addison-Wesley.

Maguire, J. N. (1976) Data Base overview. *Systems Stelsels*, Nov, 14–17.

Malik, R. (1985) Mindware? *Intermedia*, **13**(2).

Mallach, E. G. (1990) The RISC payoff. *Datamation*, 15 March, 12.

Mallinick, C. (1976) Mallinick on inflation. *Systems Stelsels*, June, 57.

Mallinick, C. (1977) On lax giants and mighty minis. *Systems Stelsels*, Jan, 8.

Mann, R. (1984) Methodology supersedes all those virtuosi. *ComputerWeek*, 19 March, 14–15.

Manpower Services Commission (1985) *Adult training in Britain*, Manpower Services Commission, Sheffield.

Manpower Services Commission (1986) *A challenge to complacency*, Manpower Services Commission, Sheffield.

Manta (1983). Manta stops phone abuse. *ComputerWeek*, 11 July, 10.

Manuel, R. (1986) COM dramatically increases savings, wards off deadly paper glut. *Bank Systems & Equipment*, Feb, 74–7.

Manx Software Systems (1986) Aztec C . . . The Best C. *Byte*, Oct, 173.

Marais, F. (1980) First there was the word then came electronic text processing. *Systems for information management*, June, 45–6.

Marcus, E. (1986) Outfitting the computer room. *Datamation*, 15 July, 58–62.

Maree, T. (1981) Short-sightedness amongst small businesses. *Systems for information management*, July, 50.

Marion, L. (1992) World IT sales stagger 4.1% to $290 billion. *Datamation*, 15 June, 12–22.

Marjoribanks, A. G. (1983) Cortina analogy is misleading. *ComputerWeek*, 27 June, 2.

Markoff, J. (1986) Computing in groups. *High Technology*, Nov, 56–7.

Marsh, R. E. (1983) Application maintenance: One shop's experience and organization. *AFIPS Conf. Proc., National Computer Conference*, **52**, 145–153.

Marshall, C. (1987) Small beautiful C native language of UNIX. *Computing S.A.*, 2 Nov, 18.

Martin, E. W. (1983a) Strategy for a DoD software initiative. *IEEE Computer*, March, 52–9.

Martin, J. (1978) Martin on the big mess. *Systems Stelsels*, Sept, 5.

Martin, J. (1980) The future according to James Martin. *Computronics*, 21 May, 6.

Martin, J. (1981) DP productivity: The programming dilemma. Lecture presented at the 1981 International Training Conference at Hyatt Regency, Chicago, April 28, published in *Connections*, by Deltak.

Martin, J. (1982a) *Application Development Without Programmers*, Englewood Cliffs, New Jersey: Prentice-Hall, Inc.

Martin, J. (1982b) *James Martin Seminar – Management Day Documentation*, Vol. 1, 3rd edn, 3rd series, Carnforth, Lancashire: Savant Research Studies, 1982.

Martin, J. (1982c) Projections for the future of fourth generation languages. *ComputerWeek*, 4 Oct, 11–13.

Martin, J. (1983b) Manifesto for DP survival. *ComputerWeek*, 25 July, 10–11. Reprinted from: *Computing U.K.*

Martin, J. (1985) *Fourth-Generation Languages, Volume I: Principles*, Englewood Cliffs, New Jersey: Prentice-Hall, Inc.

Martin, J. (1988) A demand for IS change. *Computing S.A.*, 28 March, 22–3.

Martin, J. (1992) James Martin Associates and Applied Learning International. Survey done on mainframes in the UK. *Computing S.A.*, 13 July, 13.

Martin, J. and McClure, C. (1983) *Software Maintenance: The Problem and its Solutions*, Englewood Cliffs, New Jersey: Prentice-Hall, Inc.

Martin, J. and McClure, C. (1985) *Structured Techniques for Computing*, Englewood Cliffs, New Jersey: Prentice-Hall, Inc.

Martin, T. (1979) PEARL at the age of three. *Proc. 4th Int. Conf. Software Eng.*, IEEE, Sept, 100–109.

Maslow, A. (1954) *Motivation and Personality*, New York: Harper & Row.

Maslow, A. H. (1970) The superior person. *American Bureaucracy*, (ed. W. G. Bennis) Aldine, Chicago, 27–37.

Massimo, Dr. J. (1982) The performance connection. *International Gymnast Magazine*, Dec, 42ff.

Matos, V. M. and Jalics, P. J. (1989) An experimental analysis of the performance of fourth generation tools. *Communications of the ACM*, Nov, 1340–51.

Matsumoto, Y. (1989) An overview of Japanese software factories, in *Japanese Perspectives in Software Engineering*, (eds Y. Matsumoto and Y. Ohno) Singapore: Addison-Wesley Publishers Ltd., 303–20.

Matthews, R. (1982) Most word processors badly used. *ComputerWeek*, 25 Oct, 15.

Maudlin, W. (1983a) COBOL pass-rate up. *Computing S.A.*, 21 Oct, 1–2.

Maudlin, W. (1983b) The key is tech merger. *Computing S.A.*, 26 Aug, 9.

Maurer, M. E. (1983) Full-screen testing of interactive applications. *IBM Systems Journal*, **22** (3), 246–61.

Mayer, R. E. (1975) Different problem-solving competencies established in learning computer programming with and without meaningful models. *J. Educational Psychology*, **67**, 725–34.

Mayfield, A. (1986) Truths, half-truths, and statistics. *Datamation*, 15 Aug, 85–6.

Mayo, E. (1945) *The Social Problems of an Industrial Civilization*, Harvard University Press, Cambridge, MA.

Mazor, S. (1982) The heady days are over, says Intel man. *ComputerWeek*, 5 July, 3.

McCabe, T. J. (1976) A complexity measure. *IEEE Trans. Software Eng.*, **2** (6), 308–20.

McCartney, L. (1986) The PC is still not smart enough for executives. *Dun's Business Month*, Sept, 75–6.

McClure, C. L. (1978) *Reducing COBOL Complexity through Structured Programming*, New York: Van Nostrand Reinhold Company.

McClure, C. L. (1981) *Managing Software Development and Maintenance*, New York: Van Nostrand Reinhold Company.

McClure, R. M. (1969) Projection vs performance in software production. *Software Engineering*. (eds P. Naur and B. Randell) Brussels: NATO Scientific Affairs Division, January.

McCormick, J. (1986) Software validation, verification, testing and documentation. *Byte*, Nov, 76–8.

McCormick, M. (1980) Word processing – the future of office systems. *Systems for information management*, July, 66–7.

McCracken, D. D. (1978) The changing face of applications programming. *Datamation*, 15 Nov (Special Report), 24–30.

McCue, G. M. (1978) IBM's Santa Teresa Laboratory – Architectural design for program development. *IBM Systems Journal*, **17** (1), 4–25.

McCusker, T. (1987a) In search of CIM. *Datamation*, 1 Jan, 24–9.

McCusker, T. (1987b) Users seeking precise measure of more complex VM systems. *Datamation*, 1 Aug, 22–4.

McCusker, T. (1989) Project planning made easy. *Datamation*, 15 Oct, 49–50.

McCusker, T. (1991) Classic mainframe software moves to PCs. *Datamation*, 1 Feb, 50–1.

McDonough, C. J. (1981) Supervisor's role seems critical in maximising use of employee time. *Computing S.A.*, 22 April, 18–19.

McGarry, F. E. (1982) What have we learned in the last six years? in *Proc. 7th Ann. Software Eng. Workshop* (Greenbelt, Md., Dec), NASA-GSFC, Greenbelt, Md.

McGonagle, J. D. (1971) *A Study of a Software Development Project*, James P. Anderson & Co., 21 Sept.

McGowan, C. L., and Kelly, J. R. (1975) *Top-Down Structured Programming Techniques*, New York: Petrocelli/Charter.

McGregor, D. (1960) *The Human Side of Enterprise*, New York: McGraw-Hill.

McKee, M. (1986) The IC man cometh. *Computer Mail*, 31 Oct, 72–3.

McKenzie, T. (1982) Swing to part-time DP staff will grow. *ComputerWeek*, 30 Aug, 13.

McKenzie, T. (1988) Contracting – on the up and up. *ComputerWeek*, 18 July, 34.

McLaughlin, R. A. (1979) That old bugaboo, turnover. *Datamation*, Oct, 96–101.

McMahon, D. (1987) Database drive. *Computer Mail*, 27 Feb, 74–6.

McMahon, J. T. (1989) Not quite dead-end user. *PC Magazine*, 28 Nov, 16, 21.

McMullen, J. (1990) Microsoft in the age of networks. *Datamation*, 1 May, 36–9.

McMullen, J. (1991a) CASE tackles software maintenance. *Datamation*, 1 Jan, 65–6.

McMullen, J. (1991b) Flowchart software finds its niche. *Datamation*, 15 May, 43.

McMullen, J. (1991c) Why PC COBOL is gaining ground. *Datamation*, 15 May, 70–2.

McNeile, A. T. (1988) Evolution of a method. *PC Tech Journal*, Dec, 15.

McWilliams, G. (1987a) The mini at middle age: Just a future niche role? *Datamation*, 1 Aug, 41–8.

McWilliams, G. (1987b) Conversions getting easier as number of tool sets grows. *Datamation*, 15 Aug, 26–30.

McWilliams, G. (1987c) DEC moves to protect flank with RISC/UNIX workstation. *Datamation*, 1 Dec, 17–19.

Meakin, T. (1979) 150 attend new course. *CPL Comment*, Aug, 2.

Meeks, B. N. (1986) CP/M hall of fame. *Byte*, Oct, 219–22.

Meiring, N. (1988) SABC's IVI a hit with managers. *Computing S.A.*, 22 Aug, 10.

Melmed, A. (1987) A new educational technology: need and opportunity. Paper read at the conference on Computer Assisted Approaches to Training, Lugano, 25–26 May.

Mendelson, H. (1987) Economies of scale in computing: Grosch's Law revisited. *Communications of the ACM*, Dec, 1066–72.

Mendis, K. S., and Gollis, M. L. (1979) Software Error History and Projection, A Case Study. *Proc. NSIA Software Conf.*, National Security Industrial Association, Feb, 30–7.

Meredith, M. (1986a) Mips measure at RISC? *ComputerWeek*, 17 Feb, 4.

Meredith, S. (1986b) Power play with a friendly face. *Micro Decision*, April, 91–6.

Merrick, P. (1976) Present and future trends in the international computer services industry. *Systems Stelsels*, Dec, 6–9.

Messerschmidt, H. J. (1982) The application development challenge. Lecture presented at the Good Hope Centre, Cape Town, 17 Feb.

Metzger, P. W. (1981) *Managing a Programming Project*, 2nd edn, Englewood Cliffs, New Jersey: Prentice-Hall Inc.

Meyer, M. (1986) Does UNIX matter? *Datamation*, 15 Dec, 73–6.

Micro & Peripheral Distributors. Fujitsu printers: DX2100, DX2200. Sandton, RSA (no date; about 1986).

Microsoft Corp. (1986a) Finally, a language worth leaving BASIC for. *Byte*, Oct, 100–101.

Microsoft Corp. (1986b) We've taken the work out of doing Windows. *Byte*, Nov, 357.

Microsoft Corp. (1986c) The fastest C you've ever seen. *Byte*, Nov, 358–9.

Mill, J. (1986) Database: gap between supply and users' needs. *ComputerWeek*, 20 Oct, 12–13. Reprinted from: *Computing U.K.*

Mill, J. (1987) Relational database helps alleviate London Transport's repair problems. *ComputerWeek*, 6 April, 12–13. Reprinted from: *Computing U.K.*

Miller, D. (1987) System Builder wins coveted international award. *ComputerWeek*, 27 April, 28.

Miller, E. F., Jr. (1975) *Methodology for Comprehensive Software Testing*, Rome Air Development Center, Griffiss Air Force Base, New York.

Miller, E. F., Jr. (1980) Survey of verification and validation technology. *Proc. NRC/IEEE Conf.*

Advanced Electrotechnology Applications to Nuclear Power Plants, IEEE, Jan.

Miller, E. F., Jr., and Wisehart, W. R. (1974) *Automated Tools to Support Software Quality Assurance*, Santa Barbara, Calif., General Research Corp.

Miller, G. A. (1956) The magical number seven, plus or minus two: Some limits on our capability for processing information. *Psychological Review*, March, 81–97.

Miller, L. H. (1977) A study in man–machine interaction. *Proc. Nat. Computer Conf.*, **46**, AFIPS Press, Montvale, New Jersey, 409–21.

Milliman, P. and Curtis, B. (1980) A matched project evaluation of modern programming practices. General Electric Co., RADC-TR-80-6, February.

Millman, D. (1982) How to get your message across. *International Gymnast Magazine*, Dec, 58–9.

Mills, H. D. (1976) Software development. *IEEE Trans. Software Eng.*, **2** (4), 265–73.

Mills, H. D., Dyer, M. and Linger, R. (1987) Cleanroom software engineering. *IEEE Software*, **4**(5), 19–25.

Mills, H. D. (1988) *Software Productivity*, New York: Dorset House Publishing.

Millstein, R. *et al.* (1976) National software works, Status report No. 1. RADC-TR-76-276, US Air Force, Sept.

Milosevich, C. J. F. (1986) MBAs and MIS. *Datamation*, 1 Nov, 15.

Mims, F. M., III (1986) CRT radiation. *Byte*, Nov, 20–4.

Misra, P. N. (1983) Software reliability analysis. *IBM Systems Journal*, **22** (3), 262–70.

Mitchell, P. (1979) JAMES MARTIN Advanced Technology. *Computronics*, 15 Aug, 3.

Mitchell, P. J. (1981) Training now and in the future. *Systems for information management*, July, 17–20.

Mittra, S. S. (1988) *Structured Techniques of System Analysis, Design, and Implementation*, New York: John Wiley & Sons, Inc.

Moad, J. (1986a) All that glitters. *Datamation*, 1 July, 20–4.

Moad, J. (1986b) The child becomes the man. *Datamation*, 1 Nov, 24–8.

Moad, J. (1987) Barking up the wrong tree? *Datamation*, 15 Feb, 22–8.

Moad, J. (1990a) The software revolution. *Datamation*, 15 Feb, 22–30.

Moad, J. (1990b) Maintaining the competitive edge. *Datamation*, 15 Feb, 61–6.

Moad, J. (1990c) Which database for Digital's customers? *Datamation*, 15 Nov, 87–90.

Modell, M. E. (1988) *A professional's guide to systems analysis*, New York: McGraw-Hill, Inc.

Mohanty, S. N. (1981) Software cost estimation: present and future. *Software Practice and Experience*, **11**, 103–21.

Moir, J. (1980) Computer or 5 more employees? *Dataweek*, 25 April, 4.

Montgomery, E. B. (1982) In search of a faster keyboard. *Computing S.A.*, 27 Aug, 25–8. Reprinted from: *Auerbach*.

Moore, D. (1987) '"GOTO considered harmful" considered harmful' considered harmful? *Communications of the ACM*, May 351–2.

Moore, J. (1990) Review of (Wood and Silver, 1989). *Computing Reviews*, June 1990, 291–2.

Moraitis, J. (1980) Better selection methods. *Computronics*, 13 Feb, 11.

Morrisey, J., and Wu, S. Y. (1979) Software Engineering: An Economic Perspective. *Proceedings, Fourth International Conference on Software Engineering*, IEEE Catalog No. 79 Ch 1479-5C, September, 412–22.

Mortensen, E. (1986) Facsimile, its link in the electronic office. *International Business Equipment*, March, 1–6.

Mortimer, R. J. (1983) Viewdata training project: report on Phase II. Internal report (mimeo). Barclays Bank Training Centre Viewdata Unit, Teddington.

Mortison, J. (1976) Tools and techniques for software development process visibility and control. *Proc. ACM Comput. Sci. Conf.*, Feb.

Moskovitz, S. (1987) X25 gateway allows 16 calls per line. *Computer Mail*, 27 Feb, 77.

Motley, R. W. and Brooks, W. D. (1977) Statistical prediction of programming errors. RADC-TR-77-175, Rome Air Development Center, Griffiss Air Force Base, New York, May.

Moulton, P. G. and Muller, M. E. (1967) DITRAN – a compiler emphasizing diagnostics. *Communications of the ACM*, **10**, 45–52.

Mulder, F. (1981) Software and ergonomics combined in processor. *Systems for information management*, Feb, 35.

Mullin, M. A. (1978) Audit retrieval packages – now and in the future. *Systems Stelsels*, Jan, 12–20.

Mumford, E. (1972) *Job Satisfaction: A Study of Computer Specialists*, London: Longmans.

Mumford, E. and Henshall, D. (1979) *A participative approach to computer systems design*, London: Associated Business Press.

Murray, G. (1983) Implementing a fourth generation language. *Systems Stelsels*, April, 32–3.

Musa, J. D. (1976) An exploratory experiment with 'foreign' debugging of programs. *Proc. Symp. Computer Software Eng.*, New York: Polytechnic, 499–511.

Myers, E. (1982) MARK IV for the masses? *Datamation*, May, 88.

Myers, E. (1983) If we could talk to the terminals. *Datamation*, Oct, 181–4.

Myers, E. D. (1986) New lease on life? *Datamation*, 1 July, 30–6.

Myers, E. D. (1987) From operations research to ancient literature. *Datamation*, 15 Aug, 123.

Myers, G. J. (1978) A controlled experiment in program testing and code walkthroughs/inspections. *Communications of the ACM*, Sept, 760–8.

Myers, G. J. (1979) *The Art of Software Testing*, New York: John Wiley & Sons.

Nantucket Corp. (1986) Clipper. *Byte*, Oct, 35.

NASA 1977 Software Specification and Evaluation System, Final Report. Huntsville, Ala.: Science Applications, (NTIS N77-26828).

Nassi, I., and Shneiderman, B., (1973) Flowcharting techniques for structured programming. *ACM SIGPLAN Notices*, Aug, 12–26.

Nastec Corp. (1986) We use DesignAid and LifeCycle Manager to help our clients develop quality software faster and more cost-effectively. *Datamation*, 1 Nov, 8.

National Productivity Institute (1983) *The Manpower Training and Development Needs of the South African Computer Industry*, Jan.

NCC, National Computing Centre (1977) *Data Processing Documentation Standards*, Manchester: NCC Publications.

Naur, P. (1969) Programming by action clusters. *BIT*, **9** (3), 250–8.

Neill, L. (1980a) I want to employ a programmer. *Systems for information management*, May, 22–3.

Neill, L. (1980b) Industry must open doors. *Systems Stelsels*, March, 13.

Neill, L. (1980c) VDU-day in the newsroom. *Systems Stelsels*, April, 41–2.

Nel, A. (1986) Industry has no alternative to UNIX as standard. *ComputerWeek*, 30 June, 5.

Nel, B. M. (1978) Why do management information systems fail or fall into disrepute? *Systems Stelsels*, Nov, 28–9.

Nelson, E. A. (1966) *Management Handbook for the Estimation of Computer Programming Costs*, AD-A648750, Systems Development Corp., 31 Oct.

Nelson, R. (1978) *Software Data Collection and*

Analysis at RADC, Rome Air Development Center, Rome, NY.

Newsted, P. R. (19..) FORTRAN program comprehension as a function of documentation. School of Business Administration, University of Wisconsin, Milwaukee, Wisconsin (no date). (Quoted in Shneiderman, 1980.)

Nielsen, N. R. (1970) ECSS: Extendable computer system simulator. Rand Corp., rep. RM-6132-PR/NASA, Jan.

Nies, T. (1983) DP ignores the computer as a development aid. *Software Extra*, 31 Jan, IX. Reprinted from: *Software News*.

Nixdorf Computer (1987) It's nice to know help is only a phone call away. *Computer Mail*, 27 Feb, 52–3.

Norman, D. R. (1978) The route to enhance business performance for the 80s – tailored software packages. *Systems Stelsels*, Dec, 6–7.

O'Malley, C. (1986) Keyboard shorthand. *Personal Computing*, April, 168.

Oakley, L. C. (1975) The future of minis in the South African market place. *Systems Stelsels*, June, 10–11.

Ohno, Y. (1989) Background and current view of software engineering, in *Japanese Perspectives in Software Engineering*, (eds Y. Matsumoto and Y. Ohno) Singapore: Addison-Wesley Publishers Ltd., 1–18.

Okidata (1987) Funny. It doesn't look like a printer. *Datamation*, 15 Feb, 39.

Okimoto, G. H. (1970) The effectiveness of comments: A pilot study. IBM SDD Technical Report TR 01.1347, (July 27).

Oliver, P. (1979) Handbook for estimating conversion costs of large business programs. ADPESO, US Navy, Washington, DC 20376, Feb.

Oliver, P. (1982) Managing a conversion project. *Computing S. A.*, 22 Oct, 12–15. Reprinted from: *Auerbach*.

Olson, M. H. (1989) Work at home for computer professionals: Current attitudes and future prospects. *ACM Trans. Office Information Systems*, **7** (4), 317–38.

Open University (1985) *PH514: an introduction to computer-based training*, Open University, Milton Keynes.

Opperman, P. (1988) Liberty brings in quality assurance expertise. *ComputerWeek*, 25 July, 5.

Orion Instruments, Inc. (1986) Microprocessor development dreams come true! *Byte*, Oct, 166.

Orkins, M. J., and Weiss, S. F. (1975) Backing into an information system. *Datamation*, Oct, 79–87.

Orr, K. (1977a) Structured systems design: Blue printing the future. *Infosystems*, Feb, 73–6.

Orr, K. (1977b) *Structured Systems Development*, New York: Yourdon Press.

Osborn, A. F. (1963) *Applied Imagination*, New York: Charles Scribner's Sons.

Osborne/McGraw-Hill (1986) X-VIEW 86. *Byte*, Nov, 54.

Ostroff, B. (1983) Kidney ops as Sterns stones removed. *Computing S.A.*, 19 Aug, 1,3.

Ouchi, W. (1981) *Theory Z: How American Business Can Meet the Japanese Challenge*, Reading, Massachusetts: Addison-Wesley.

P-E Corporate Services (1988) COBOL is still 'most known'. *ComputerWeek*, 26 Sept, 9.

P-STAT (1986) Mainframe statistics package on the AT&T UNIX PC. *Byte*, Oct, 46.

Pantages, A. (1987) Today's view from the top. *Datamation*, 15 Sept, 48–52.

Parikh, G. (1981) Three Ts key to maintenance programming. *Computing S.A.*, 22 April, 19.

Parikh, G. (1984) *Programmer Productivity: Achieving An Urgent Priority*, Reston, Virginia: Reston Publishing Co.

Parikh, G. (1988) *Techniques of Program and Systems Maintenance*, 2nd edn, Wellesley, MA: QED Information Sciences, Inc.

Parkin, A. (1980) *Systems Analysis*, London: Edward Arnold.

Parkinson, G. N. (1957) *Parkinson's Law and Other Studies in Administration*, Boston: Houghton-Mifflin.

Parnas, D. L. (1979) Designing software for ease of extension and contraction. *IEEE Trans. Software Eng.*, March, 128–37.

Paster, D. L. (1981) Experience with application of modern software management controls. *Proc. 5th Int. Conf. Software Eng.*, IEEE, March, 18–26.

Patrick, R. L. (1980a) *Application Design Handbook for Distributed Systems*, Boston: CBI Publishing Company, Inc.

Patrick, R. L. (1980b) Probing productivity. *Datamation*, Sept, 207–10.

Pellerano, G. (1978) Growing a decentralised product line. *Systems Stelsels*, May, 36.

Perlis, A. J., Sayward, F. G. and Shaw, M. (eds). (1981) *Software Metrics: An Analysis and Evaluation*, Cambridge, MA: The MIT Press.

Perrella, R. J. (1986) Combining languages. *Byte*, Oct, 22–4.

Perriens, M. P. (1977) An application of formal inspections to top-down structured program development. RADC-TR-77-212, IBM Federal Systems Div., Gaithersburg, Md., (NTIS AD/A-041645).

Perry, W. E. (1983) *A Structured Approach to Systems Testing*, Wellesley, MA: QED Information Sciences, Inc.

Perryman, S., and Freshwater, M. (1987) Industrial dimension of open learning, in *Aspects of educational technology XX: flexible learning systems*, (eds F. Percival, D. Craig, and D. Buglass) London: Kogan Page.

Peter, L. J., and Hull, R. (1969) *The Peter Principle*, New York: William Morrow.

Peters, L. J., and Tripp, L. L. (1977) Comparing software design methodologies. *Datamation*, Nov, 89–94.

Peters, T. J., and Austin, N. (1985) *A Passion for Excellence*, Random House.

Petreley, N. (1988) Relational databases: An in-depth analysis. *InfoWorld*, 18 April, 4 July.

Pfaffenberger, B. (1990) *Que's Computer User's Dictionary*. Carmel, Indiana: Que Corporation.

Philippakis, A. S. (1977) A popularity contest for languages. *Datamation*, Dec, 81–7.

Philips Data Systems (Pty) Ltd. (1982) Modern miracle or expensive scrap? *Cabex 82 Catalogue*, Feb, 45.

Phister, M., Jr. (1979) *Data Processing Technology and Economics*. Bedford, MA: Digital Press.

PICK User Group (1989) Sanctions-proof software creates environment for business success. *Argus Computers*, 16 Feb, 16.

Pienaar, L. (1980) Computerising the files of recruitment consultancies. *Computronics*, 2 April, 10.

Pienaar, M. (1987) *Computer Mail*, 27 Feb, 73–4.

Pietrasanta, A. (1989) Software engineering education in IBM, in *Issues in Software Engineering Education*. (eds R. Fairley and P. Freeman) New York: Springer-Verlag, 5–18.

Pine, B. J., II (1989) Design, test, and validation of the Application System/400 through early user involvement. *IBM Systems Journal*, **28** (3), 376–85.

Pinella, P. (1990a) SAS: architecting an open strategy. *Datamation*, 15 July, 35–7.

Pinella, P. (1990b) Organizational computing arrives. *Datamation*, 15 Nov, 42–8.

Pirow, P. C. (1981) Computers and management information. *Fact and Opinion Paper No. 13*, Graduate School of Business Administration, Witwatersrand University, Jan.

Pitchell, R. (1979) The GUIDE productivity program. *GUIDE Proc.*, GUIDE, Inc., Chicago, IL, 783–94.

Plant, C. R. (1988) Closing the gap in office messaging. *CMA*, April, 66.

Poe, B. (1986) Japan's insecurity complex. *Datamation*, 1 Nov, 64-12–64-14.

Polanyi, M. (1969) *Knowing and Being*, Chicago: University of Chicago Press.

Pomberger, G. (1984) *Software Engineering and Modula-2*, Englewood Cliffs, New Jersey: Prentice-Hall International.

Portman, C. (1975) Personal communication to Frederick P. Brooks. Quoted in (Brooks, 1975).

Potier, D., Albin, J. L., Ferreol, R. and Bilodeau, A. (1982) Experiments with computer software complexity and reliability. *Proc. 6th Int. Conf. Software Eng.*, 94–103.

Pountain, D. (1986a) BASIC to C. *Byte*, Oct, 311–14.

Pountain, D. (1986b) Integration on a new scale. *Byte*, Nov, 351–6.

Pournelle, J. (1986) The show goes on? *Byte*, Oct, 279–91.

Pournelle, J. (1988) Stick shift or automatic? *Byte*, Oct, 101–16.

Pratt, K. J. (1985) *Effective Staff Appraisal: a practical guide*, Wokingham, Berkshire: Van Nostrand Reinhold (UK) Co. Ltd.

Prentiss (1977) Viking software data. RADC-TR-77-168.

Pressman, R.S. (1982) *Software Engineering: A Practitioner's Approach*, New York: McGraw-Hill, Inc.

Price, R. (1987) The on-line trend. *Computer Mail*, 27 Feb, 64–71.

Pritchard, J. (1978) Word processing concepts. *Systems Stelsels*, Feb, 2.

Pritchard, F. (1980a) Getting the right material to train . . . *Systems for information management*, July, 48–9.

Pritchard, F. (1980b) The right material. *Dataweek*, 11 Jan, 8.

Pritchard, F. (1984) DP training system under fire. *ComputerWeek*, 27 Feb, 1–2.

Productivity Software (1988) Getting your decision support into focus. *ComputerWeek*, 19 Sept, 11.

Profile (1983) A profile of the Victor Sirius. *Computer Systems in Southern Africa*, Aug, 48–9.

Prospero Software Ltd. (1986) Now available worldwide: Prospero's professional language compilers for PCs and STs. *Byte*, Oct, 169.

Providing (1986) Providing fast access to database management systems. *Retail & Distribution Management*, Sept–Oct, 20–2.

Pryce-Williams, K. (1988) Mantis now available to ICL VME users. *ComputerWeek*, 22 Feb, 20.

Purvis, G. (1979) Maintenance costs? *Computronics*, 5 Sept, 3.

Puterbaugh, G. (1986) Blind data. *Datamation*, 15 Oct, 19.

Putnam, L. H. (1978) A general empirical solution to the macro software sizing and estimating problem. *IEEE Trans. Software Eng.*, **4**, July, 345–61.

Putnam, L. H., and Fitzsimmons, A. (1979) Estimating software costs. *Datamation*, Sept, 189–98. Continued in Oct, 171–8, and Nov, 137–40.

Quantum Software Systems Ltd. (1986) QNX. Other operating systems may never lift the PC to such heights. *Byte*, Oct, 264.

Quantum Software Systems Ltd. (1989) QNX. The OS for over-achievers. *Byte*, Sept, 69.

Rabinovitz, R. (1986) The Norton Utilities, PC Tools, and Super Utility. *Byte*, Oct, 265–70.

Radice, R. A., and Phillips, R. W. (1988) *Software engineering: an industrial approach*, Vol. 1, Englewood Cliffs, New Jersey: Prentice-Hall, Inc.

Radio Shack (1986) *1987 Radio Shack Software Reference Guide*, Fort Worth, Texas.

Ragland, L. C. (1973) A verified program verifier, PhD dissertation, Univ. of Texas, Austin.

Rajan, A. (1985) *Training and recruitment effects of technical change*, Aldershot: Gower.

Ramsey, S. (1980) Big companies to blame for DP staff shortage. *Computronics*, 2 April, 8.

Ramsey, S. (1992) Over supply of IS people. *Computing S.A.*, 13 July, 18.

RCA PRICE Systems (1978) PRICE Software Model: Supplemental Information. RCA, Cherry Hill, NJ, March.

REALIA (1986) My one-time investment in REALIA COBOL paid for itself in a month. *Datamation*, 1 Nov, 50.

Realtime Computer Services (1989) Elegant software that builds sophisticated applications faster . . . that's PROGRESS. *ComputerWeek*, 13 Feb, 30.

Reaser, J. M., and Carrow, J. C. (1975) Interactive Programming: Summary of an Evaluation and Some Management Considerations. Report USACSC-AT-74-03, US Army Computer Systems Command, March.

Reaser, Priesman and Gill (1974) A production environment evaluation of interactive programming. *US Army Computer Systems Command Technical Documentary Report*, USACSC-AT-74-03.

Redgrave, A. (1986) Space program. *Building*, 7 Nov, 69–71.

Redwine, S. T., Jr., Becker, G. L., Marmor-Squires, A. B., Martin, R. J., Nash, S. H. and Riddle, W. E. (1984) DoD related software technology requirements, practices, and prospects for the future. IDA Paper P-1788, Institute for Defense Analyses, Alexandria, Va., June.

Reed, S. R. (1986) Q & A: Customizing your data base. *Personal Computing*, April, 55, 153.

Reese, J. F. (1978) The evolution of computing in a small consulting firm. *Civil Engineering – ASCE*, June.

Reeves, T., and King, J. (1986) Development, production and programming of an interactive videodisc adult literacy program, in *Proc. 8th Ann. Conf. Interactive Videodisc In Education and Training*, Aug 20–22, Washington, D. C. Society for Applied Learning Technology, Warrenton, Va., 44–9.

Relational Database Systems, Inc. (1986) The problem with most 4GLs is they're finished before you are. *Datamation*, 15 July, 41.

Remus, H. (1980a) Planning and measuring program implementation. *Proc. Symp. Software Eng. Environments*, Lahnstein, Germany (Gesellschaft fuer Mathematick und Datenverarbeitung): North Holland, 267–79.

Remus, H. (1980b) Planning and measuring program implementation. *IBM Technical Report*, TR 03.095, June.

Rickerby, J. G., Mellor, G., and Coan, D. R. A. (1975) *Standards in Operations*, Manchester: NCC Publications.

Rider College (1987) PCs give boost to student grades. *Computing S.A.*, 19 Jan, 11.

Ringo, W. (1980) Plan that office layout for profit. *Office Supplies & Equipment*, Feb, 13.

Ritchie, D. M., Johnson, S. C., Lesk, M. E. and Kernighan, B. W. (1978) The C programming language. *Bell System Technical Journal*, **57**(6), 1991–2020.

Rodney, D. (Ed.) (1986) *What Software To Buy*, Craighall Park, Johannesburg: Systems Publishers (Pty) Ltd, March.

Root Computers Ltd. (1986) Backup utility for UNIX. *Byte*, Nov, 48H.

Rosenberg, J. M. (1984) *Dictionary of Computers, Data Processing and Telecommunications*, New York: John Wiley & Sons.

Rosenthal, S., and Grundy, J. (1980) *Vision and VDUs* Association of Optical Practitioners, UK. Reprinted in Visual display units: Nightmare to the operator? *Dataweek*, 7 March, 6.

Ross, D. T. (1977) Structured analysis (SA): A language for communicating ideas. *IEEE Trans. Software Eng.*, **3**(1).

Ross, R. G. (1978) *Data Base Systems*, New York: AMACOM.

Rossman, R. J., Jr. (1986) Avoiding pitfalls in implementing a system. *The Office*, Oct, 35–6.

Rothwell, J. (Ed) (1983) *CBT case histories*, Manchester: National Computing Centre.

Rubel, M. C. (1986) Four 1/4-inch tape backup units. *Byte*, Oct, 243–7.

Rubey, R. J., *et al.* (1968) Comparative evaluation of PL/1. *US Air Force Report, ESD-TR-68-150*, April.

Rubey, R. J., Dana, J. A. and Biche, P. W. (1975) Quantitative aspects of software validation. *IEEE Trans. Software Eng.*, June, 150–5.

Rubin, F. (1987a) 'GOTO considered harmful' considered harmful. *Communications of the ACM*, March, 195–6.

Rubin, F. (1987b) GOTO, one more time, *Communications of the ACM*, Aug, 661.

Rubin, F. (1987c) Last (gasp!) GOTO. *Communications of the ACM*, Dec, 997, 1085.

Rubin, H. A. (1983) Macroestimation of software development parameters: The Estimacs system, in *SOFTFAIR Conf. Software Development Tools, Techniques and Alternatives*, Arlington, Va., July 25–28, IEEE Press, New York, 109–18.

Rubin, H. A. (1984) *Using ESTIMACS E*, Management and Computer Services, Valley Forge, Pa. Mar.

Rubinstein, A. (1982) Open plan concept is wrongly implemented. *ComputerWeek*, 25 Oct, 13.

Rudkin, R., and Shere, K. D. (1979) Structured decomposition diagram: A new technique for system analysis. *Datamation*, Oct, 130–46.

Rudolph, C. (1979) Programming. *Computronics*, 12 Sept, 2.

Ruete, E. S. (1991) Right minded. *Communications of the ACM*, Jan, 17, 18, 119.

Rushinek, A., and Rushinek, S. F. (1986) What makes users happy? *Communications of the ACM*, July, 594–8.

Russell, V. (1983) Keyboard changes mooted. *Computing S.A.*, 20 May, 11.

Sackman, H., Erickson, W. J. and Grant, E. E. (1968) Exploratory experimental studies comparing online and offline programming performance. *Communications of the ACM*, Jan, 3–11.

Sackman, H. (1969) *Experimental evaluation of time-sharing and batch processing in teaching Computer Science*. System Development Corp., SP-3411, October.

Sackman, H. (1970) *Man-Computer Problem Solving: Experimental Evaluation of Time-Sharing & Batch Processing*. Princeton, N. J.: Auerbach Publishers.

Sakkinen, M. (1989) Why is it difficult to write about programs? *Communications of the ACM*, June, 675.

Samways, B. and Robinson, P. (1988) *Collins Gem: Basic Facts – Computers*, London: Collins.

Sanders, N. (1985) *Computer-aided management*, Cambridge, England: Woodhead-Faulkner Ltd.

Sandler, I. J. (1989) *The PICK Perspective*, TAB Professional and Reference Books, Blue Ridge Summit, PA.

Santa Clara Systems (1986) External RAM Storage for IBM PCs. *Byte*, Nov, 32.

Sayers, D. (1986) 'Bugless' operating system on Series 39. *ComputerWeek*, 21 July, 8. Reprinted from: *Computing U.K.*

Schach, S. (1987) Computer programming. Panel discussion, Holiday Inn, Woodstock, RSA, 16 July.

Schach, S. (1988) Software engineering: Methodologies and management. Course presented at the Mount Nelson Hotel, Cape Town, August.

Schach, S. R. (1990) *Software Engineering*, Boston: Irwin.

Schach, S. (1992) CASE tools and productivity. *Informantics*, June, 8.

Schalkoff, R. J. (1986) muLISP-86. *Byte*, Oct, 249–52.

Schatz, W. (1986a) Fed facts. *Datamation*, 15 Aug, 72.

Schatz, W. (1986b) Clash of cultures. *Datamation*. 1 Nov, 22–4.

Schatz, W. (1987) The gauntlet is thrown: RAMIS challenges Focus. *Datamation*, 15 May, 36, 61, 64.

Schatz, W. (1988) Suffolk law, new studies reinvigorate VDT debate. *Datamation*, 15 Aug, 39–41.

Schatzki, M. (1981) *Negotiation: The Art of Getting What You Want*, New York: New American Library.

Schatzoff, M., Tsao, R. and Wiig, R. (1967) An experimental comparison of time sharing and batch processing. *Communications of the ACM*, May, 261–5.

Schechter, B. (1986) What's hot in software. *Computer Mail*, 31 Oct, 16–20.

Schein, E. H. (1961) Management development as a process of influence. *Industrial Management Review*, **2**, May.

Schindler, P.E., Jr. (1987) CD-ROM technology: its time has come. *InformationWEEK*, 15 June, 17–22.

Schluter, R. G. (1977) Experience in managing the development of large real-time BMD software systems. *Proc. AIAA/NASA/IEEE/ACM Computers in Aerospace Conference*, Los Angeles, October-November, 168–73.

Schnebly, D. A. (1987) GOTO again. *Communications of the ACM*, Nov, 982.

Schneider, G. R. E. (1983) Structured software maintenance. *AFIPS Conf. Proc. Nat. Computer Conf.*, **52**, 137–44.

Schneidewind, N. F., and Hoffman, H.-M. (1979) An experiment in software error data collection and analysis. *IEEE Trans. Software Eng.*, **5** (3), 276–86.

Schroeder, M. T. (1986) What's wrong with DBMS. *Datamation*, 15 Dec, 66–70.

Schulz, A. (1982) *Methoden des Softwareentwurfs und structurierte Programmierung*, Walter de Gruyter.

Schussel, G. (1983) Codasyl is pushed into background by market forces. *Software Extra*, 31 Jan, VII. Reprinted from: *Software News*.

Schussel, G. (1986) Shopping for a fourth generation language. *Datamation*, 1 Nov, 99–100.

Scott, B. (1981) Users must share blame for many 'horror stories'. *Computing S.A.*, 21 Jan, 16–17.

Scott, G. M. (1986) *Principles of Management Information Systems*, New York: McGraw-Hill Book Company.

Scott, R. F. and Simmons, D. B. (1974) Programmer Productivity and the Delphi Technique. *Datamation*, May, 71–3.

Scott-Rodger, I. (1987) Computer firm is dubbed the 'Pick People'. *Argus Computers*, 1 April, 3.

Seaver, D. (1987) Interactive video: yes . . . for technical skills. *Data Training*, March.

Seddon, J. G. (1983) Converting to a package. *Datamation*, Oct, 199–204.

Segal, B. Z. (1975) Effects of method of error interruption on student performance at interactive terminals. University of Illinois Department of Computer Science Technical Report UIUCDCS-R-75-727, (May).

Sehr, B. K. (1986) High noon for CD-ROM. *Datamation*, 1 Nov, 79–88.

Seymour, J. (1991) What's the right PC for today? *PC Magazine*, 12 March, 87–8.

Shafer, L. (1989) Review of (Radice and Phillips, 1988). *Computing Reviews*, March, 126–7.

Shandel, G. (1988) PDC to focus on Pick's growth. *ComputerWeek*, 24 Oct, 28.

Shapiro, E. (1986a) Shareware. *Byte*, Oct, 297–302.

Shapiro E. (1986b) Resident headaches. *Byte*, Nov, 361–8.

SHARE, Inc., and GUIDE International (1979) *Proceedings, Application Development Symposium*, October. Available through either SHARE or GUIDE Secretary, 111 E. Wacker Dr., Chicago IL 60601.

Sharon, W. (1986) A moving experience. *Datamation*, 15 July, 77–8.

Shaw, K. (1986) The application of artificial intelligence principles to teaching and training. *Interactive Learning International*, **3**(4).

Shen, V.Y., Yu, T. J., Thebaut, S. M. and Paulsen, L. R. (1985) Identifying error-prone software – an empirical study. *IEEE Trans. Software Eng.*, **11**(4), 317–24.

Sheppard, S. B., Borst, M. A., Curtis, B. and Love, T. (1978) Predicting programmers' ability to modify software. TR 78-388100-3, General Electric Company, May.

Sheppard, S. B., Curtis, B., Milliman, P., Borst, M. A. and Love, T. (1979) First year results from a research program on human factors in software engineering. *Proc. Nat. Computer Conf.*, **48**, AFIPS Press, Montvale, New Jersey, 73–9.

Shinn, M. (1983) Bosses call the automation tune. *ComputerWeek*, 11 July, 9, 11.

Shneiderman, B. (1980) *Software Psychology*, Cambridge, Massachusetts: Winthrop Publishers, Inc.

Shneiderman, B. and McKay, D. (1976) Experimental investigations of computer program debugging and modification. *Proc. 6th Int. Congr. Int. Ergonomics Assoc.*, July.

Shneiderman, B., Mayer, R., McKay, D. and Heller, P. (1977) Experimental investigations of the utility of detailed flowcharts in programming. *Communications of the ACM*, June, 373–81.

Shone, L. J. (1975) Career development. *Systems Stelsels*, Sept, 13–17.

Shooman, M. L. (1983) *Software Engineering*, New York: McGraw-Hill.

Shooman, M. L. and Bolsky, M. I. (1975) Types, distribution, and test and correction times for programming errors. *Proc. 1975 Int. Conf. Reliable Software*, New York: IEEE, 347–357.

Short, M. (1977) Bureau data capture. *Systems Stelsels*, Aug, 25.

Sieber, J. E., Kameya, L. I. and Paulson, F. L. (1970) Effect of memory support on the problem-solving ability of test-anxious children. *Journal of Educational Psychology*, Feb, 159–68.

Siegel, S. G. (1989) Review of (Deutsch and Willis, 1988). *Computing Reviews*, July, 339–40.

Siegler, T. A. (1987) Sweet talk. *Datamation*, 1 Jan, 115–16.

Sime, M. E., Green, T. R. G. and Guest, D. J. (1973) Psychological evaluation of two conditional constructions used in computer languages. *Int. J. Man–Machine Studies*, **5**(1), 105–13, 123–43.

Sime, M. E., Green, T. R. G. and Guest, D. J. (1977) Scope marking in computer conditionals – a psychological evaluation. *Int. J. Man–Machine Studies*, **9**, 107–18.

Simenon, A. (1986) Microsoft Project. *What Micro*, April, 47.

Simons, D. M. (1986) Implementing corporate videotex. *Videotex World*, March, 5–7.

Simpson, W. D. (1987) *New Techniques in Software Project Management*, New York: John Wiley & Sons, Inc.

Sims, F. (1977) Fire losses increase. *Professional Forum*, 28 April, 5–6.

Singer, L. M. (1982) *The Data Processing Manager's Survival Manual*, New York: John Wiley & Sons, Inc.

Sippl, C. J. (1985a) *Computer Dictionary*, Indianapolis: Howard W. Sams & Co.

Sippl, C. J. (1985b) *MacMillan Dictionary of Data Communications.*, London: MacMillan.

Sivers, G. R. (1976) Room at the top. *Systems Stelsels*, June, 55.

Sivers, G. R. (1978) 'The times they are 'a changing'. *Systems Stelsels*, March, 31.

Sivula, C. (1990) Digital Equipment Corp. *Datamation*, June, 53–4.

Small, H. (1983) Suppliers set the pace in technology. *ComputerWeek*, 10 Oct, 12–13. Reprinted from: *Computing U.K.*

Smith, C. P. (1980) A Software Science analysis of programming size. *Proc. ACM Nat. Computer Conf.*, Oct, 179–85.

Smith, R. A. (1981) Three factors top cost-cutting considerations. *Computing S.A.*, 22 April, 16–17.

Smith, R. W. (1983) The great debate revisited. *Sky & Telescope*, Jan, 28–9.

Smith, S. (1988) DP professionals can now make use of IVI benefits. *ComputerWeek*, 22 Aug, 37.

Sneddon, R. (1986) In search of cheaper transmission. *Byte*, Nov, 18–20.

SoftLogic Solutions, Inc. (1986a) With all these SoftLogic Solutions, you could run out of problems. *Byte*, Oct, 61.

SoftLogic Solutions, Inc. (1986b) Problem: The more experience your hard disk has, the harder it has to work. *Byte*, Nov, 277.

Software (1986) The Software Link, Inc. To over 30 000 installations, MultiLink MultiUser. *Byte*, Nov 1986, 19.

Software (1989) Introducing PC-MOS 3.0. *Byte*, Sept 1989, 76–7.

Software AG (1986a) When success is your only alternative . . . *Datamation*, 15 Oct, 49.

Software AG (1986b) How to cut decades off your application development backlog – in sixty seconds. *Datamation*, 15 Dec, 56–13.

Software AG (1986c) Software AG: An overview. Programming business success. Software AG, MSG 093 1086.

Software AG (1986d) Software AG: ADABAS. Advanced Information Management. Software AG, MSA-017-0886, 10.

Sokol, E. W., and Bulyk, J. C. (1986) Truths of technology training. *Training and Development Journal*, Feb, 43–5.

Soloway, E., and Ehrlich, K. (1984) Empirical studies of programming knowledge. *IEEE Trans. Software Eng.*, **10** (5), 595–608.

Sommerville, I. (1989) *Software Engineering*, 3rd ed, Wokingham, England: Addison-Wesley Publishing Company.

Sorbus (1987) It's OK, you're OK. Thanks to Sorbus. *Datamation*, 15 Feb, 113.

SOWACO (1976) Decision table processor. *Systems Stelsels*, Jan, 14.

Spencer, M. (1982) Data entry – a neglected area. *Computer Systems in Southern Africa*, June, 45–6.

Spiegel, M. R. (1972) *Schaum's Outline of Theory and Problems of Statistics in SI Units*, 1st edn, SI (metric) edn, New York: McGraw-Hill International Book Company.

Sproul, R. (1990) A literate reader responds. *Datamation*, 1 March, 13.

SPSS, Inc. (1989) We'll take your stats and make you the most valuable player in your league. *Byte*, Sept, 287.

St. John Bate, J., and Vadhia, D. B. (1987) *Fourth generation languages under DOS and UNIX*. BSP Professional Books, Oxford.

St. John Bate, J., and Wyatt, M. (1986) *The PICK Operating System*, Collins, London.

Stamps, D. (1990) Finding the right fixes for DB2. *Datamation*, 1 Oct, 89–96.

Starr, M. K. (1972) *Production Management*, 2nd ed, Englewood Cliffs, N.J.: Prentice-Hall, Inc.

Statland, N. (1989) Payoffs down the pike: A CASE study. *Datamation*, 1 April, 32, 33, 52.

STAX (1983) Incompatibility is a major problem area. *ComputerWeek*, 25 April, 5.

Steele, K. (1989) Network may solve teacher shortage. *Computing S.A.*, 27 Feb, 1–2.

Stefanski, M. (1987) Prime deals net ACS R2,5 m. *The Sunday Star Computing*, 6 Dec, I–II.

Stefik, M., Foster, G., Bobrow, D. G., Kahn, K., Lanning, S., and Suchman, L. (1987) Beyond the chalkboard: Computer support for collaboration and problem solving in meetings. *Communications of the ACM*, Jan, 32–47.

Stephens, R. E. (1979) Structured programming at AECI. *Systems Stelsels*, May, 20–24.

Stevens, D. (1988) Staff loyalty and technology. *Computing S.A.*, 14 Nov, 34.

Stevens, S. M. (1989) Intelligent interactive video simulation of a code inspection. *Communications of the ACM*, July, 832–43.

Stevens, W. P., Myers, G. J. and Constantine, L. L. (1974) Structured Design. *IBM Systems Journal*, **13** (2), 115–39.

Stewart, T. (1981) Poorly designed software hinders operators, claims expert. *Systems for information management*, March, 59.

Steyn, P. (1980) Need for responsibility in DP industry. *CPL Comment*, Nov, 1.

Steyn, P. (1982) Bleak year ahead for the micro specialists. *ComputerWeek*, 6 Dec, 11.

Steyn, P. (1983) Programmers pay rise double that of CoL. *Computing S.A.*, 20 May, 3–4.

Stockton, A. (1981) Users should initiate, participate in projects. *Computing S.A.*, 22 April, 12–13.

Stokes, Dr A. V. (1979) *Concise Encyclopaedia of Computer Terminology*, Input Two-Nine Ltd, August.

Stone, H. S. (1978) Final report: Life-cycle cost analysis of instruction set architecture standardization for military computer-based systems. US Army Research Office, Jan.

Stone, H. S. and Coleman, A. (1979) Life-cycle cost analysis of instruction-set architecture standardization for military computer-based systems. *Computer*, April, 35–47.

Stone, J. W. (1986) Staff is 33% of item processing cost. *Bank Systems & Equipment*, Nov, 101–102.

Stratus Software (1990) What do the above have in common? *ComputerWeek*, 18 June, 27.

Summit Software Technology, Inc. (1986) When you need access to full memory, structure, compatibility with GW- & PC-BASICA, or when you need the power and flexibility of C or PASCAL . . . *Byte*, Nov, 377.

Sunohara, T., Takano, A., Uehara, K. and Ohkawa, T. (1981) Program Complexity Measure for Software Development Management. *Proc. 5th. Int. Conf. Software Eng.*, IEEE, March, 100–106.

Sutermeister, R. A. (1976) *People and Productivity*, 3rd edn, New York: McGraw-Hill Book Company.

Sutherland, D. (1986) Presentation creativity on a budget. *Business Marketing*, March, 90–100.

Swain, B. (1986) The electronic options. *Audio Visual*, Nov, 49–53.

Sweet, F. (1986) Milestone management. *Datamation*, 15 Oct, 107–14.

Swidler, G. A. (1986) Pitfalls to avoid in information centre implementation. *Words*, Oct–Nov 18–22.

Sykes, J. B. (ed.) (1977) *The Concise Oxford Dictionary*, 6th edn, Oxford: Oxford University Press.

System Designers Software, Inc. (1986) ADA debugger. *Datamation*, 15 July, 96.

Takahashi, M., and Kamayachi, Y. (1989) An empirical study of a model for program error prediction. *IEEE Trans. Software Eng.*, **15**(1), 82–6.

Tamaki, A. (1987) Audience with Akers. *Datamation*, 1 Jan, 59.

Tanaka, R. I. (1977) International implications of technology trends. *Systems Stelsels*, Dec, 27–9.

Tandberg (1986) System aids slow learners. *Computer Mail*, 31 Oct, 82.

Tandem Computers Inc. (1987) Remote duplicate database. *Datamation*, 15 Feb, 96.

TASS (1979) *Health Hazards of Visual Display Units*, Jan.

Tate, P. (1986) Picking up steam. *Datamation*, 15 Aug, 30.

Tate, P., and Runyan, L. (1986) Desperately seeking database data. *Datamation*, 1 July, 48–56.

Tausworthe, R. C. (1981) Deep space network software cost estimation model. *Publication 81–7*, Jet Propulsion Laboratory, Pasadena, CA.

Tebbs, D. (1980a) Getting the staff we want. *The 1979/80 S.A. Computer Guide*, Johannesburg: Thomson Publications (Pty) Ltd, 28–9.

Tebbs, D. (1980b) Structured programming. *The 1979/80 S.A. Computer Guide*, Johannesburg: Thomson Publications (Pty) Ltd, 111–48.

Teichroew, D. (1964) *An Introduction to Management Science: Deterministic Models*, New York: John Wiley & Sons, Inc.

Teichroew, D. and Hershey, E. A., III (1977) PSL/PSA: A computer-aided technique for structured documentation and analysis of information processing systems. *IEEE Trans. Software Eng.*, 3 (1), 41–8.

Teichroew, D., and Sayani, H. (1971) Automation of system building. *Datamation*, 15 Aug, 25–30.

Tenny, T. (1974) Structured programming in Fortran. *Datamation*, July, 110–15.

Thacker, C. P., McCreight, E. M., Lampson, B. W., Sproull, R. F. and Boggs, D. R. (1979) Alto: A Personal Computer. Xerox Palo Alto Research Center Report CSL-79-11.

Thadhani, A. J. (1981) Interactive user productivity. *IBM Systems Journal*, April, 407–23.

Thadhani, A. J. (1984) Factors affecting programmer productivity during application development. *IBM Systems Journal*, April, 19–35.

Thayer, R. H., Pyster, A. and Wood, R. C. (1980) The challenge of software engineering project management. *IEEE Computer*, **13**, (8), 51–9.

Thayer, T. A., Lipow, M. and Nelson, E. C. (1976) Software reliability study. TRW Systems, Redondo Beach, CA, rep. to RADC, Contract F30602-74-C-0036, March.

Thayer, T. A., Lipow, M. and Nelson, E. C. (1978) *Software Reliability: A Study of Large Project Reality*, New York: North-Holland.

Thebaut, S. M. (1983) *The saturation effect in large-scale software development: its impact and control*, PhD thesis, Department of Computer Science, Purdue University, West Lafayette, IN, May.

Theron, D. (1988) Spartan – avoids 'canned' courses. *ComputerWeek*, 19 Sept, 36.

Theron, J. (1977) Looking for a smooth transition. *Systems Stelsels*, Oct, 3, 7.

Thinking Machines Corp. (1986) Multimicro super. *Datamation*, 1 July, 96.

Thirkettle, N. (1986) Technology-based training versus conventional training. *Interactive Learning International*, 3(3).

This (1982) This editor boosts keyboard productivity by 25% – claim. *Computing S.A.*, 19 Nov, 9.

Thomson, B. (1980) The need for a good dictionary. *Systems for information management*, Dec, 33–6.

Thompson, B. (1982) No need for COBOL to fall into decline. *Software Extra*, 29 Nov, 1.

Thomson, B. (1983) The danger of the fourth generation development aids. *Computer Systems in Southern Africa*, April, 29–31.

Thompson, D. (1987) GOTO exit, already. *Communications of the ACM*, Nov, 907–908.

Thompson, T., and Allen, D. (1986) The Compaq Deskpro 386. *Byte*, Nov, 84–9.

Thorpe, A. J. L. (1976) Family programming teams. *Datamation*, March, 221–4.

Tilley, J. (1986) Facilities management. *Business Equipment Digest*, March, 19–20.

Tireford, H. (1976) Microprocessors. *Systems Stelsels*, Oct, 19–20.

Tjonn, Dr H. and Rycroft, Dr R. (1981) Doctor disputes causes of facial rashes. *Systems for information management*, Feb, 58.

Tottle, E. M. (1986) Not your basic BASIC. *Byte*, Nov, 20.

Touche Ross (1986) Software vendors: a guide for the retailer. *Chain Store Age Executive*, Nov, 95–102.

Townsend, D. F. (1980) Systems analysis: Key to the future. *Datamation*, Oct, 145–8.

Townsend, K. (1986) Graphics for a better business image. *Mind Your Own Business*, March, 47–8.

Townsend, R. (1970) *Up the Organization*, Fawcett Publications, Greenwich, CT.

Townsend, R. (1984) *Further up the Organization*, London: Michael Joseph Ltd.

Tracz, W. (1988) *Software reuse: emerging technology*, IEEE Computer Society, Washington, DC.

Trainor, W. L. (1973) Software – from satan to saviour, in *Proc. NAECON Conf.*, May.

Trainor, W. (1974) Trends in avionics software – problems and solutions. *Proc. Aeronautical Systems Software Workshop*, Air Force Systems Command.

TranSec Systems, Inc. (1986) Convert any dBASE III program to dBASE III Plus . . . *Byte*, Nov, 63.

Trax Softworks, Inc. (1986) *Introducing ESS, the Electronic Spread Sheet.*, Trax Softworks, Inc., Los Angeles, CA.

Treadgold, A. J. (1987) Retraining in the manufacturing sector. Paper read at a conference on Computer Assisted Approaches to Training, Lugano, 25–26 May.

Troy, D. A., and Zweben, S. H. (1981) Measuring the quality of structured designs. *J. Systems and Software*, **2** (June), 113–20.

Truter, R. (1991) Sick building syndrome. *MRC News*, Dec, 7.

Turner, E. (1986) Safer desking marks new direction. *Business Equipment Digest*, March, 65–7.

Turner, J. A. (1984) Computer mediated work: the interplay between technology and structured jobs. *Communications of the ACM*, Dec, 1210–17.

Turner Hall Publishing (1986) Squeeze 10 times as many spreadsheets on a disk. *Byte*, Nov, 363.

Turton, R. (1985) Top consultant urges DP industry to . . . Boost black training. *ComputerWeek*, 9 Dec, 1.

Tuval, Dr Y. (1980) Career development system. *Systems Stelsels*, Jan, 36.

UCCEL (1986) Conversion software without high

support standards is no bargain. *Datamation*, 15 July, 80–1.

Ullmann, J. E. (1976) *Quantitative Methods in Management*, New York: McGraw-Hill Book Company.

Unisys (1988a) If you're not running a Unisys mainframe, chances are you're running a DP department that's 41% overstaffed. *Computing S.A.*, 25 April, 22–3.

Unisys (1988b) Over 3/4 of a million people are using a Unisys 4 GL to solve their business problems. *Computing S.A.*, 27 June, 34–5.

UNIX (1988) The growing UNIX Standard. *UNIX Windows*, **5**, 12. Reprinted from *UNIX Today*, 9 Feb.

Urwick International (Pty) Limited (1975) A Survey of Training in the Computer Industry at December.

US Bureau of Labor Statistics (1982) *Economic Projections to 1990*, The Bureau, Washington DC.

US (1983) US engineers pass a microchip milestone. *ComputerWeek*, 10 Oct, 16.

US (1988) US battle looming over regulation for software. *Computing S.A.*, 14 March, 22 and 39.

US Bureau of Industrial Economics (1984) Department of Commerce, 1984 US Industrial Outlook for 200 Industries with Projections for 1989, US Government Printing Office, Washington, D. C., 550.

Uttal, B. (1980) IBM's battle to look superhuman again. *Fortune*, 19 May, 107.

van den Nieuwenhof, L. (1983) Top women welcome DP career survey. *ComputerWeek*, 1 Aug, 3.

van der Meer, J. (1985) COBOL making way for 4th generation. *Computing S.A.*, 19 Aug, 5.

van der Merwe, Z. (1988) Unidata and the management of change. *ComputerWeek*, 24 Oct, 26.

van der Poel, K. G. (1981) A balanced approach to efficiency in Data Processing System Development. *Systems for information management*, March, 46–52.

van der Poel, K. G. (1982) *Measuring the efficiency of software development in a data processing environment*, MSc thesis, UCT, June.

van der Poel, K. G. (1983) Interview with K. G. van der Poel, Head of Medical Informatics Department, Groote Schuur Hospital, Cape Town, 17 May.

van der Veer, G. D. (1976) In the eye of the hurricane. *Systems Stelsels*, July, 4–5.

van Gass, D. (1979) Watch your printer. *Computronics*, 8 Aug, 4.

van Greunen, M. (1988) Old Mutual opts for video link in staff training. *The Sunday Star Computing*, 20 March, IX.

van Niekerk, J. (1980) Packaged programs. *Computronics*, 26 March, 8–9.

van Olst, R. (1977) Data capture and the minicomputer. *Systems Stelsels*, July, 4–5.

van Rensburg, J. J. (1988) ComputerWeek 10th anniversary. *ComputerWeek*, 5 May, 10.

van Rijswijck, M. (1983) Fourth generation fills breach. *SA Software News*, 12 Sept, 12–13.

Van Tassel, D. (1978) *Program Style, Design, Efficiency, Debugging, and Testing*, 2nd edn, Englewood Cliffs, New Jersey: Prentice-Hall, Inc.

van Tonder, W. (1988) HP and Tetraplan do a deal. *ComputerWeek*, 8 Aug, 54.

van Wyk, R. (1988) Directors must harness the power of technology. *ComputerWeek*, 10 Oct, 2.

van Wyk, W. (1978) Hitting the moving target. *Systems Stelsels*, Aug, 12–14.

van Wyk, W. and Kamfer, L. (1976) Software Development: a new technology. *Systems Stelsels*, Sept, 14–21.

Van Zijl, J. R. and Evans, R. J. (1978) Interactive programme development – is it justified? *Systems Stelsels*, Sept, 13–14.

Varley, H., and Graham, I. (1983) *The Personal Computer Handbook*, London: Pan Books Ltd.

Vaughan, A. (1982) Success will depend on effective DP management. *ComputerWeek*, 1 Nov, 5.

Vaughan, A. (1984) Surveys knock shine off PCs. *ComputerWeek*, 16 April, 4.

Verity, J. W. (1986a) A different viewpoint. *Datamation*, 1 July, 60.

Verity, J. W. (1986b) Minis, micros, and maturity. *Datamation*, 1 Nov, 65–74.

Verity, J. W. (1986c) Suing CES. *Datamation*, 1 Nov, 56.

Verity, J. W. (1987a) A new slant on parallel processing. *Datamation*, 15 Feb, 79–84.

Verity, J. W. (1987b) Round one: IBM 1, AT & T 0. *Datamation*, 15 Feb, 37–46.

Verity, J. W. (1987c) Mainframe users survey: tough times for IBM. *Datamation*, 15 May, 69–82.

Verrijn-Stuart, A. A. (1975) Information algebras and their uses. *Management Datamatics*, **4** (5), 187–97.

Vincent, D. (1983) Response times: is faster better? *Software Extra*, 31 Jan, IX. Reprinted from: *Software News*.

Vincent, J., Waters, A. and Sinclair, J. (1988) *Software Quality Assurance: Volume 1, Practice and*

Implementation, Englewood Cliffs, New Jersey: Prentice-Hall, Inc.

von Oppell, S. (1988) PCs are not always based on OS/2 and MCA. *ComputerWeek*, 19 Sept, 8.

Vosburgh, J., Curtis, B., Wolverton, R., Albert, B., Malec, H., Hoben, S. and Liu, Y. (1984) Productivity factors and programming environments, in *Proc. 7th Int. Conf. Software Eng.*, 143–52.

VRE, Inc. (1986) System improves filing efficiency at Wachovia Services Inc. *Magazine of Bank Administration*, Oct, 90.

Wachs, W. (1972) *How Salesmen Make Things Happen: The Magic Question Technique That Clinches Sales Fast*. New York: Parker Publishing Company, Inc.

Wait, C. G. (1986) How to meet. *Datamation*, 15 July, 105.

Waldhauser, C. (1991) Wanted: Computer teachers. *PC Magazine*, 11 June, 18.

Waller, R. (1979) Applications for microcomputers. Paper given at the British Computer Society Nottingham Winter School, 15th Oct.

Waller, R. (1986) Skimming, scanning and browsing: problems of studying from electronic text. Paper read at a Colloquium on 'Paper versus screen: the human factors issues', organized by the Institution of Electrical Engineers and the Ergonomics Society, 16 Oct 1985 (revised April 1986).

Walsh, D. A. (1977) Structured testing. *Datamation*, July, 111–18.

Walsh, T. J. (1979) A software reliability study using a complexity measure. *Proc. Nat. Computer Conf.*, New York, 761–8.

Walston, C. E. and Felix, C. P. (1977) A method of programming measurement and estimation. *IBM Systems Journal*, 1, 54–73.

Walther, G. H. and O'Neil, H. F., Jr. (1974) On-line user-computer interface: the effects of interface flexibility, terminal type, and experience on performance. *Proc. Nat. Computer Conf.*, 43, AFIPS Press, Montvale, New Jersey.

Wang, A. S. (1984) *The estimation of software size and effort: an approach based on the evolution of software metrics*. PhD thesis, Department of Computer Science, Purdue University, August.

Ward, B. (1983) VDU radiation risk sparks controversy. *ComputerWeek*, 30 May, 6.

Warnier, J. D. (1974) *Logical Construction of Programs*, New York: Van Nostrand Reinhold Company.

Warnier, J. D. (1978) *Program Modification*, Leiden, The Netherlands. Hingham, Mass. Martinus Nijhoff Social Sciences Division.

Warnier, J. D. (1981) *Logical Construction of Systems*, New York: Van Nostrand Reinhold Company.

Webber, Rev. I. T. (1983) Family forum. *Family Radio & TV*, 12–18 Sept, 23.

Webster, B. (1986) Bit by bit, putting it together. *Byte*, Oct, 293–5.

Webster, P. C. (1976) Down to earth experience of a data base user. *Systems Stelsels*, Nov, 10–12.

Weed, E. D. (1971) Job enrichment 'cleans up' at Texas Instruments, in *New Perspectives in Job Enrichment*, (ed. J. R. Mather). New York: Van Nostrand Reinhold.

Weiland, R. J. (1975) Experiments in structured COBOL, in *Structured Programming in COBOL – Future and Present*, (ed. H. Stevenson) New York: ACM Publications.

Weinberg, G. M. (1971) *The Psychology of Computer Programming*, New York: Van Nostrand Reinhold Company.

Weinberg, G. M. and Schulman, E. L. (1974) Goals and performance in computer programming. *Human Factors*, 16(1), 70–7.

Weinwurm, G. F. (ed.) (1970) *On the Management of Computer Programming*, New York: Auerbach.

Weinwurm, G. F. and Zagorski, H. J. (19..) Research into the management of computer programming: a transitional analysis of cost estimation techniques. *SDC Report TM-2712*, Santa Monica, California.

Weisman, R. (1987) Six steps to AI-based functional prototyping. *Datamation*, 1 Aug, 71–2.

Weissman, L. (1974a) A methodology for studying the psychological complexity of computer programs, PhD thesis, University of Toronto.

Weissman, L. (1974b) Psychological complexity of computer programs: An experimental methodology. *ACM SIGPLAN Notices*, June, 25–36.

Wendel, I. (1986) Software tools of the Pleistocene. *Software Maintenance News*, 4 (10), 20.

Westcott, M. (1988) Human resources utilisation. *ComputerWeek*, 10 Oct, 14–15.

Westcott, M., Lindeque, B., Cole, J., Pansegrouw, G., Dawson, P., Ward, J., Ritchie, J., Daniel, R., Pearson, M. and Pace, T. (1981) Human resources utilisation. *Computing S.A.*, 8 April, 8–19.

Wetherbe, J. C. and Berrisford, T. R. (1979) Narrowing the expectations gap. *Systems Stelsels*, Aug, 10–14.

Whetton, C. (1987) Design and analysis of high-reliability and fault-tolerant systems. *Communications of the ACM*, Nov, 981–2.

Whitfield, M. (1989) Waste: Means justified by the end? *Computing S.A.*, 10 April, 13.

Wibier, B. (1980) Computer security to be tighter says DSS. *Computronics*, 4 June, 6.

Wiener, H. (1986) Software: what's hot and what's not. *Datamation*, 1 July, 50–62.

Wilcox, D. (1988) Pick Open Architecture. *Nitpicking*, Jan/Feb, 10–13.

Willett, G. W., *et al.* (1973) *TSO Productivity Study*, American Telephone and Telegraph Long Lines, Kansas City, April.

Williams, C. M. (1973) System response time: a study of users' tolerance. IBM Advanced Systems Development Division Technical Report 17-272, July, 1–28.

Williams, D. A. (1986a) Lack of a command language a limitation. *Business Software*, Feb, 67–9.

Williams, M. (1986b) Mark Williams Co. You are about to be seduced by power and money. *Byte*, Oct, 37.

Williamson, I. M. (1979) NARDAC Model. NRL Technical Memorandum 7503-XXX, 16 July.

Williman, A. O. (1971) Autonetics Programming Cost Data, 1969. Personal communication to Barry W. Boehm, Oct.

Williman, A. O. and O'Donnell, C. (1970) Through the central 'multiprocessor' avionics enters the computer era. *Astronautics and Aeronautics*, July.

Winer, T. (1978) Software tools for increased productivity. *Systems Stelsels*, Sept, 15–16.

Winfield, I. (1986) *Human Resources and Computing*, London: Heinemann.

Wingfield, C. G. (1982) USACSC experience with SLIM. *Report IAWAR 360-5*, US Army Institute for Research in Management Information and Computer Science, Atlanta, GA.

Wingfield, J. M. (1976) Shopping for minicomputers – a bargain basement or a technocratic trauma? *Systems Stelsels*, April, 8–9.

Winkler, C. (1986) Battling for new roles. *Datamation*, 15 Oct, 82–8.

Wirth, N. (1971) Program development by stepwise refinement. *Communications of the ACM*, April, 221–7.

Wirth, N. (1981) Lilith: A personal computer for the software engineer. *Proc. 5th Int. Conf. Software Eng.*, IEEE, March, 2–15.

Wirth, N. (1987) Computer programming. Panel discussion, Holiday Inn, Woodstock, RSA, 16 July.

Withington, F. G. (1969) Data processing's evolving place in the organization. *Datamation*, June, 58–63.

Withington, F. G. (1975) Beyond 1984: A technology forecast. *Datamation*, Jan, 54–73.

Wolverton, R. W. (1974) The cost of developing large-scale software. *IEEE Trans. Computers*, June, 615–36.

Woock, R. (1988) Guru Bill Gates looks into future. *Computing S.A.*, 21 Nov, 12.

Wood, A. (1986) UNIX still has the edge on 'sluggish' PICK, study reveals. *Computing S.A.*, 23 June, 33.

Wood, J. and Silver, D. (1989) *Joint application design: how to design quality systems in 40% less time*, New York: John Wiley & Sons, Inc.

Woodfield, S. N. (1979) An experiment on unit increase in problem complexity. *IEEE Trans. Software Eng.*, 5 (2), 76–8.

Woodfield, S. N., Dunsmore, H. E. and Shen, V. Y. (1981a) The effect of modularization and comments on program comprehension. *Proc. 5th Int. Conf. Software Eng.*, IEEE, March, 215–23.

Woodfield, S. N., Shen, V. Y. and Dunsmore, H. E. (1981b) A study of several metrics for programming effort. *The Journal of Systems and Software*, Dec, 97–103.

Woodland, D. A. (1977) Where have we got to in 21 years. *Systems Stelsels*, Aug, 8–13.

Woodward, M. R., Hennell, M. A. and Hedley, D. (1979) A measure of control flow complexity in program text. *IEEE Trans. Software Eng.*, 5, Jan, 45–50.

Woolcock, K. (1983) Microchips giving way to molecules. *ComputerWeek*, 22 Aug, 6–7. Reprinted from: *Computing U.K.*

Wright, G. (1978) Software and the emerging users. *Systems Stelsels*, May, 2–4.

Wright, J. P. (1979) *On a Clear Day You can See General Motors*, Wright Enterprises.

Wright, M. (1983) Stagnant software hits productivity. *SA Software News*, Sept, 10.

Wright, P. and Reid, F. (1973) Written information: Some alternatives to prose for expressing the outcomes of complex contingencies. *J. Applied Psychology*, 57, 160–6.

Wu, S.-i. (1987) A funny thing happened on the way to the forum. *Communications of the ACM*, July, 632.

Wulf, S. (1975) Data base management systems. *Systems Stelsels*, Dec, 4–6.

Wulf, S. (1976) Data base prerequisites and feasibility. *Systems Stelsels*, Nov, 12–14.

Wybrow, R. (1977) Mohawk solves a productivity snag. *Systems Stelsels*, June, 30.

Wynne, B. E. and Dickson, G. W. (1976) Experienced managers' performance in experimental man–machine decision system simulation. *Academy of Management J.*, 18(1), 25–40.

Yamaha, H. A. (1980) A historical study of typing and typewriter mechanics. *J. Information Processing*, **2**, 175–202.

Yang, F. (1986) IBM's big retail sale. *Datamation*, 15 July, 46–50.

Yeomans, J. (1988) Yeomans to head Sage Training Centres. *ComputerWeek*, 12 Dec, 7.

Youmans, D. M. (1981) User requirements for future office work-stations with emphasis on preferred response times. IBM United Kingdom Laboratories, Report HF058, Hursley Park, England.

Youngs, E. A. (1974) Human errors in programming. *Int. J. Man–Machine Studies*, **6**, 361–76.

Yourdon, E. (1975) *Techniques of Program Structure and Design*, Englewood Cliffs, New Jersey: Prentice-Hall, Inc.

Yourdon, E. (1976) The Emergence of Structured Analysis. *Computer Decisions*, **8**(4).

Yourdon, E. (1979b) *Structured Walkthroughs*, Englewood Cliffs, New Jersey: Prentice-Hall, Inc.

Yourdon, E. (1980) Structured Maintenance. *Techniques of Program and System Maintenance*, (ed. Girish Parikh.) Lincoln, Nebraska: Ethnotech, Inc., 211–13.

Yourdon, E. (1989) *Modern Structured Analysis*, Englewood Cliffs, New Jersey: Prentice-Hall International, Inc.

Yourdon, E. and Constantine, L. L. (1979) *Structured Design*, Englewood Cliffs, New Jersey: Prentice-Hall, Inc.

Yourdon, E., Gane, C., Sarson, T. and Lister, T. R. (1979a) *Learning to Program in Structured COBOL: Parts 1 and 2.*, Englewood Cliffs, New Jersey: Prentice-Hall, Inc.

Yourdon, Inc. (1987) Intelligent CASE Software at an Intelligent Price. *Datamation*, 15 Feb, 5.

Yu, T. J. (1985) The static and dynamic models of software defects and reliability. PhD thesis, Department of Computer Science, Purdue University, West Lafayette, IN, December.

Yulke, D. (1990) Mentor M/ix: The operating system. *PICK Database News*, Feb, 8.

Zachmann, W. F. (1981) Six technologies hold the keys to the future of computing. *Computing S.A.*, 21 Jan, 13–14.

Zawacki, R. A. (1989) The art of motivation. *Datamation*, 1 June, 6.

Zelkowitz, M. V. (1979) *Principles of Software Engineering and Design*. Prentice-Hall.

Zelkowitz, M. (1985) Software engineering practices in the US and Japan. *IEEE Computer*, June.

Zimner, I. (1978a) DP management in a production environment. *Systems Stelsels*, Nov, 8–10.

Zimner, I. (1978b) All data base industrial system. *Systems Stelsels*, Dec, 16–17.

Zolnowski, J. C. and Simmons, D. B. (1981) Taking the measure of program complexity. *Proc. Nat. Computer Conf.*, 329–36.

Zvegintzov, N. (1981) Tips boost maintenance programmer morale. *Computing S.A.*, 22 April, 20–21.

Zvegintzov, N. (1989) Review of (Arthur, 1988). *Computing Reviews*, March, 129–30.

AUTHOR INDEX

SUBJECT INDEX